Paula Smith

ACCOUNTING

5TH EDITION

THE Foundation for Business Success

Lanny M. Solomon
The University of Texas at Arlington

Larry M. Walther
The University of Texas at Arlington

Richard J. Vargo
University of the Pacific

Linda M. Plunkett
University of Charleston, South Carolina

SOUTH-WESTERN College Publishing

An International Thomson Publishing Company

Sponsoring Editor: Elizabeth A. Bowers
Developmental Editor: Sara E. Bates
Production Editor: Peggy A. Williams
Production House: Litten Editing and Production with Benchmark Productions, Inc.
Cover Designer: Michael H. Stratton
Cover Photo: Index Stock Photography Inc.
Internal Designer: Ellen Pettengell Design
Internal Photo Researcher: Feldman & Associates
Chapter Opener Photo Editing: Jennifer Mayhall
Marketing Manager: Sharon C. Oblinger

Copyright © 1996
by South-Western College Publishing
Cincinnati, Ohio

ALL RIGHTS RESERVED
The text of this publication, or any part thereof, may not be reproduced or transmitted in any form or by any means, electronic or mechanical, including photocopying, recording, storage in an information retrieval system, or otherwise, without the prior written permission of the publisher.

ISBN: 0-538-85784-6

1 2 3 4 5 6 7 8 9 D2 3 2 1 0 9 8 7 6 5

Printed in the United States of America

ITP
International Thomson Publishing
South-Western College Publishing is an ITP Company. The ITP trademark is used under license.

Library of Congress Cataloging-in-Publication Data

```
Accounting : the foundation for business success / Lanny M. Solomon
   . . . [et al.].
         p.   cm.
      Includes index.
      ISBN 0-538-85784-6
       1. Accounting.   I. Solomon, Lanny M., 1946-
HF5625.A237      1995
657--dc20                                                       95-37463
                                                                    CIP
```

This book is dedicated to the memory and spirit of

Amanda Welling Dykes
September 3, 1980 – March 3, 1995

Scholar, musician, friend

and beloved daughter of Linda Plunkett

About the Authors

Lanny M. Solomon is currently a professor of accounting at The University of Texas at Arlington. He holds a Ph.D. in accounting and information systems from Case Western Reserve University and is a certified management accountant. Professor Solomon has published articles in *The Accounting Review, Journal of Accountancy, Cost and Management*, and various journals of state CPA societies. In addition, he has presented numerous papers at technical accounting meetings. Professor Solomon is an active member of the American Accounting Association and the Institute of Certified Management Accountants, has public and industrial accounting experience, and has been the recipient of several outstanding teaching awards.

Larry M. Walther is an associate professor of accounting at The University of Texas at Arlington. He received his doctorate in accounting from Oklahoma State University and has experience with an international public accounting firm. Professor Walther is both a certified public accountant and a certified management accountant. Articles by Professor Walther have appeared in *The Accounting Review, Journal of Accountancy, Management Accounting, The Practical Accountant*, and other professional journals. He is a member of the American Accounting Association, Texas Society of Certified Public Accountants, and other professional organizations. Professor Walther has provided consulting services to a number of businesses on accounting and financial reporting matters and serves as a director of a corporation that operates in the Dallas-Fort Worth area.

Richard J. Vargo, currently a professor at the University of the Pacific, received his doctorate in accounting from the University of Washington. He has experience with an international public accounting firm. Articles by Professor Vargo have appeared in the *Journal of Accountancy, CPA Journal*, and other professional publications. He is the author of several other accounting and business books, including one prepared for the American Institute of Certified Public Accountants. Professor Vargo lectures internationally on a variety of financial and managerial topics and has received recognition from the California Society of CPAs for his contributions to the development of accounting education. He has also acted as a consultant to a number of businesses.

Linda M. Plunkett, professor of accounting at the University of Charleston, SC, received her doctorate from Georgia State University. She is a third-generation certified public accountant, with professional experience in both public accounting and private industry. Professor Plunkett has published articles in a variety of publications including *Accounting Horizons, Journal of Accountancy*, and *Accounting Historians Journal*. In addition, she has presented numerous papers at regional and national accounting meetings. She is a member of the American Accounting Association, American Institute of CPAs, Academy of Accounting Historians, and other professional and academic organizations. Professor Plunkett is regarded as being very student-oriented and has won several awards for her teaching and scholarship.

PREFACE

Accounting education has undergone considerable change in recent years. Students have been asked to comprehend a growing number of complex pronouncements; professorial complaints regarding students' reading and analytical abilities have increased; and there is evidence that we are losing our brightest classroom performers to other disciplines on campus. Furthermore, classes often contain a substantial number of students who quickly lose interest in the subject matter, which is often regarded as time consuming and somewhat dry and boring. These are the very problems that prompted us to write the first edition of *Accounting Principles* in 1983.

A primary emphasis on these issues was sufficient for the 1980s and the very early 1990s. Further refinements are needed and have been made, however, in this, the fifth edition. Ethics, the impact of computers, globalization, high-tech manufacturing, interdisciplinary perspectives, the role of information in decision making, financial statement interpretation and use, communication skills, concept application (rather than procedure), and group work are collectively the current focus—key elements required to train the managers of tomorrow (accounting or otherwise). A review of the text's 27 chapters and accompanying package will find numerous revisions that reflect contemporary business practices and the thinking of prominent educators. The book's new title, *Accounting: The Foundation for Business Success*, is indicative of this changing emphasis.

The authors completely agree with a recent statement of the Accounting Education Change Commission, which noted that:

> The knowledge and skills provided by the first course in accounting should facilitate subsequent learning even if the student takes no additional academic work in accounting or directly related disciplines.[1]

We feel that our new edition accomplishes this objective. Discussions of the concepts and rationale that underlie accounting practices are integrated at appropriate points throughout the text. There is an added focus on what is

---

[1] "The First Course in Accounting," *Position Statement No. Two,* Accounting Education Change Commission, *Issues in Accounting Education*, Fall 1992, pp. 249–250.

increasingly becoming known as the "user orientation." Recognizing that there is more to accounting than just calculations, our end-of-chapter problem material asks students to reason, justify, explain, and apply. Combining this approach with a clear, readable, and accurate presentation results in what we believe is an enlightening overview—one that will create a stimulating educational experience for both students *and* faculty.

Additionally, we have monitored readability throughout the text and have strived to make troublesome topics (such as adjusting entries, corporate equity, bonds, and the statement of cash flows) especially understandable to students. To eliminate differences in writing styles, one of the authors has spent countless hours integrating the same tone, approach, and manner of presentation in all 27 chapters. Accounting is a rigorous subject for most individuals. The authors recognize this fact and have worked hard to produce a clear and usable volume. Comments from instructors *and* students indicate that we have, in fact, generated a readable book.

SIGNIFICANT CHANGES IN THE FIFTH EDITION

We have always characterized our approach to accounting subject matter as being balanced and traditional. Recent studies indicate a growing number of instructors who believe that accounting education would be improved if students receive a heavier dose of the "general business side of accounting" and a lighter exposure to journal entries and many of the related procedures. Some books have even gone so far as to eliminate debits and credits from the introductory course.

As authors, we have a duty to monitor market conditions and produce the very best textbook possible. On the basis of user feedback, survey polls, and editorial guidance, we have made a number of changes in the organization and content of our fifth edition. Many of the modifications reflect the shift in thinking just noted; however, the revisions are *not* radical and fit nicely in the confines of this traditional volume. The major changes are summarized in the sections that follow.

CHAPTER/SUBJECT MATTER REORGANIZATION

- We are excited about a new chapter entitled "Understanding and Using Financial Information" (Chapter 7). Positioned early in the text for those instructors who desire to set a financial-statement theme for their courses, this material focuses on how to read and interpret a basic annual report. Key portions of Microsoft's annual report are reproduced to enhance the presentation. The chapter also takes a look at the purpose of financial statement footnotes, the role of auditing, and the financial statements of different entity forms (e.g., banks, utilities, and governmental and not-for-profit organizations).
- Because of a new ruling by the Financial Accounting Standards Board, we have extensively revised the bond chapter (Chapter 18) to better reflect the contemporary topic of financial instruments. The bond discussion has been simplified and includes several new exhibits that better illustrate this complex subject matter for students.
- Ratio material (formerly in the financial statement analysis chapter) is now covered throughout the text. For example, inventory turnover is discussed

with inventories, the current and quick ratios with liquidity, and accounts receivable turnover with receivables. This holistic type of presentation allows for an increased focus on analysis while a topic is still fresh in a student's mind. The ratios are brought together in a summary chart that appears in Appendix B, which also contains a typical investment analyst's report.

SUBJECT MATTER ADDITIONS

A number of new topics have been added to the text. These topics, generally approached from a nonprocedural viewpoint, are relevant for accounting *and* nonaccounting majors. Typical examples (along with the associated chapter reference) include:

- Electronic data interchange (Ch. 5)
- Cash management practices (Ch. 8)
- Asset impairment (Ch. 12)
- Fringe benefits and employee leasing (Ch. 13)
- Revenue recognition practices in different industries (Ch. 14)
- Foreign currency fluctuations (Ch. 14)
- Limited liability partnerships (Ch. 15)
- Reading a stock page (Ch. 16)
- Initial public stock offerings (Ch. 16)
- Bankruptcy/business failure (Ch. 19)
- The value chain (Ch. 20)
- Benchmarking (Ch. 22)
- A focus on speed (Ch. 22)
- Nonfinancial performance measures (Ch. 25)
- Standards in nonmanufacturing firms (Ch. 25)
- Transfer pricing (Ch. 26)
- Capital budgeting in a competitive business climate (Ch. 27).

THE "MORE-IS-NOT-BETTER" PHILOSOPHY

Many accounting textbooks have become mini-encyclopedias, containing more information than can reasonably be covered by even the most efficient and effective instructors. In recent years we have tended to lose sight of the fact that students—more specifically, introductory students—can only absorb so much in the way of subject matter.

In the previous edition of the text we deleted several topics that had either "grown old" or were relatively unimportant in the overall scheme of things. Recognizing that more is not necessarily better, we continued this process in the fifth edition to a somewhat greater degree. The following topics, among others, have been dropped from the text: the adjusting entry method of handling inventory on a merchandising work sheet; voucher systems; discounting of notes receivable; payroll registers; large stock dividends; sinking funds; procedures related to convertible bonds, deferred taxes, and the preparation of consolidated financial statements; horizontal analysis; journal entries for variances; and individual federal income tax regulations. Generally speaking, these changes are consistent with our objective of producing a volume that has an increased user orientation when compared with its predecessor (i.e., addition by subtraction).

BOXED FEATURES

We have modified the boxed features that appear throughout the book.

- Each chapter now begins with an opening vignette that focuses on George Faris and Banner Advertising. The firm, an actual small business based in Texas, has opened its doors to us, allowing students to see various facets of the company's operations and financial activities. The use of one business throughout the book's twenty-seven chapters adds continuity to presentations.
- Boxes labeled "A Further Focus" lend additional insight to discussions by, in many cases, focusing on the experiences of well-known, real-world companies. *The Wall Street Journal*, *Forbes*, and other popular periodicals serve as typical sources for this series of examples.
- Perspective boxes are also new to this edition. Knowing that many accounting topics impact other business disciplines, we secured the services of experts in related fields to discuss the associated interaction(s). Boxes focus on such professions as finance, marketing, human resources, law, economics, health care, music, information systems, and computers.
- Business Briefings (entitled Executive Briefings in the previous edition) look at a topic from a businessperson's perspective and highlight how that topic affects the individual's firm. We have broadened this series to include not only "name brand" corporate giants (General Motors, Wendy's, and AT&T) but much smaller entities as well (San Joaquin Regional Transit District and La Bistro Italian Restaurant). Also, we now feature professionals who occupy vastly different types of positions within an organization (e.g., chief financial officer, plant manager, and a county agricultural extension agent).

END-OF-CHAPTER MATERIALS

Aside from normal revisions, we have made three basic changes to the end-of-chapter assignment material. First, consistent with a user orientation, many of the new exercises focus on business practices and concepts rather than on computations and procedure.

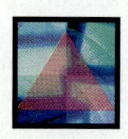

Second, we have reoriented many of our more difficult problems (formerly called Beyond the Basics) into true decision cases (indicated by an icon). The cases are not necessarily more difficult than the regular Series A and Series B problem sets, nor are they just traditional problems with a disproportionate amount of narrative. Instead, these items are introductory cases that focus on a variety of financial and managerial issues and contain a minimal amount of procedure.

Finally, in keeping with contemporary educational processes, we have designed a set of individual and group projects that allow students to expand greatly beyond the material contained in the text. These projects (identified by an icon) include library research, a review of published financial statements, and business interviews. The projects and decision cases, along with our electronic data base problem set (to be discussed shortly), are found under the heading of Expanding Your Horizons.

FOURTH EDITION FEATURES RETAINED

Many features in the fourth edition proved popular with users. Those features, repeated in this edition, include a true managerial section, a heavy use of real-world firms and data, and solid problem material.

A TRUE MANAGERIAL SECTION

The final chapters of an introductory accounting text are normally devoted to cost and managerial accounting topics. The usual approach is to have students calculate this and calculate that, while paying very little attention to the use or impact of the data they are producing. Our approach is to focus on the how and why of planning, control, performance evaluation, and decision making and to present practical applications whenever possible. This balanced presentation should appeal to a wide range of instructors, including those who currently use a separate text for managerial coverage.

HEAVY REAL-WORLD EMPHASIS

Many accounting texts use hypothetical firms in their illustrations and examples. The authors have found that students show an increased interest in the subject matter when exposed to the accounting and financial reporting practices of real businesses. Thus, we include annual report data and "war stories" of over 200 different companies, including McDonald's, American Airlines, Apple Computer, NIKE, and The Coca-Cola Company. We have carefully selected firms from industries with which students themselves have contact. All examples were screened for appropriateness at the introductory level.

SOLID PROBLEM MATERIAL

All problem material contained in this text was carefully designed to reflect current accounting principles and practices. Questions, exercises, and problems range in scope from the simple to the complex; they were written and solved by the authors to assure total coordination with the text presentation. To further ensure accuracy and reliability, we have triple-checked the *Instructor's Solutions Manual*. We are confident the end-of-chapter materials are as trouble-free as repeated multiple checking can make them. These items will provide a solid, well-rounded foundation for accounting students and a varied resource for instructors.

The problem material is divided into Series *A* and Series *B*. Instructors can therefore use one problem for illustration purposes and assign another as homework or use different problem sets in alternating semesters or quarters. Although duplication is important, the authors have not lost sight of the need for variety. Both sets contain an ample variety of material to allow instructors to approach a given topic from varying perspectives.

SUPPLEMENTARY MATERIALS

A complete set of supplementary materials for both student and instructor accompanies this text to help facilitate the learning and teaching of accounting.

FOR THE STUDENT—PRINTWARE

- **Study Guide.** A study guide, available in two volumes, has been written by Larry Walther to reinforce the material presented in the text. The Study Guide contains chapter learning objectives; a detailed chapter synopsis; multiple-choice, two-response, and completion questions; exercises; and answers *with specific explanations*, as well as computer software that provides step-by-step instruction on key accounting topics.
- **Working Papers.** Two volumes of working papers have been prepared: Volume I covers Chapters 1–15 and Appendix A; Volume II covers Chapters 15–27. The inclusion of Chapter 15 (Partnerships) in both volumes recognizes that this topic is covered in the first Principles course at some schools and in the second course at others. Many of the working papers are partially filled in, thereby allowing students to concentrate on accounting concepts as opposed to the pencil pushing associated with problem setup.

FOR THE STUDENT—SOFTWARE

- **Computer-Assisted Accounting Tutorials.** Contained in the Study Guide, these tutorials present essential accounting material on a step-by-step basis. As they proceed through the lesson, students are queried on subject matter presentations through a series of two-response (e.g., yes/no, agree/disagree, logical/illogical), multiple-choice, and computational questions. 
- **Homework Assistant Tutorial (HAT).** This new Windows-based tutorial software, by Ray Meservi of Brigham Young University, visually teaches the relationships between T-accounts, journals, ledgers, and financial statements in solving selected end-of-chapter problems. A built-in tutor function includes numerous hints and help screens. HAT is also ideal as a classroom teaching aid. An icon designates specific assignments for use with HAT. 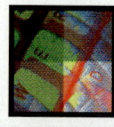
- **Spreadsheet Application Software.** Dozens of exercises and problems can be solved using most standard spreadsheet packages, such as Lotus 1-2-3®, Quattro®, or Excel®. Specific assignments can be easily identified by the icon shown. 
- **Solutions Software.** This best selling educational general ledger software, prepared by Dale H. Klooster and Warren W. Allen of Educational Technical Systems, is tailored specifically to Chapters 2–6 of the text. Related end-of-chapter assignments are identified by the icon shown. This software is available in both Windows and MS-DOS versions. 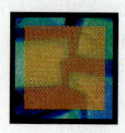
- **Financial Statement Database Software.** Annual report information for over three dozen corporations is provided in easily accessible form for student research.

Additional Items to Assist Students

CONTACCT II. This computer-assisted instruction package consists of tutorials, assignments, and graded homework problems on various topics related to the accounting cycle. These topics include the accounting equation, transaction analysis, journalizing and posting transactions, cash vs. accrual basis accounting, financial statements, and adjusting and closing entries. The assignments and tutorials can be used as a stand-alone course or lab, or with any principles/financial textbook where the instructor desires more procedural coverage. Windows format.

Annual Report Projects and Readings. Written to accommodate either an individual-based or team-based approach, this text helps students make the transition from the classroom to the business world by exposing them to real financial reports. Students request annual reports, proxy statements, and SEC 10-Ks from real companies and analyze financial information using workbook assignments.

Practice Sets. Eleven practice sets tie together various issues discussed in the text.

Larry's Landscape. Appropriate after Chapter 4, this set is available with transactions in narrative form. It provides practice in accounting for a sole proprietorship service business. It may also be solved using the Solutions Software.

Poolside Products. Upon completing Chapter 10 and Appendix A, students will find this set, which is available with business documents, helpful. An optional narrative of transactions may be used. The set provides practice in accounting for a merchandising sole proprietorship that uses a perpetual inventory system and special journals. It may also be solved using the Solutions Software.

Cool Company. This is an interactive, computer-based set that gives immediate feedback as it is being solved. It provides practice in accounting for a merchandising sole proprietorship that uses a perpetual inventory system and a general journal.

Electronic Supply. This is a computerized practice set that covers two months of activity for a merchandising business, spanning Chapters 1–10. A periodic inventory system is featured. Some "what-if" analysis may be employed, and a grading disk is provided for the instructor.

Waterworks. This set is available with business documents. An optional narrative of transactions may be used. The set, for use after Chapter 13, provides practice in accounting (including payroll) for a merchandising sole proprietorship that uses special journals. It may also be solved using the Solutions Software.

First Designs Inc. Appropriate after Chapter 17, this set is available with transactions in narrative form. It provides practice in accounting for a merchandising corporation that operates a departmentalized business and uses a periodic inventory system and special journals. It may also be solved using the Solutions Software.

Compsoft Inc. Students will find this set helpful upon completing Chapter 18. It is available with transactions in narrative form and provides practice in accounting (including corporate debt) for a merchandising corporation that uses a general journal. It may also be solved using the Solutions Software.

SEMO Sporting Goods Supply Inc. This set requires locating errors in recording and posting transactions, preparing correcting entries, and preparing financial statements for a wholesaling corporation.

Ice Inc. This is an interactive, computer-based set that gives immediate feedback as it is being solved. It provides practice in accounting for a merchandising corporation that uses a perpetual inventory system and a general journal. It is appropriate for use with Chapter 19.

Highpoint Solar Inc. For use after Chapter 21, this set is available with transactions in narrative form. It provides practice in accounting for a manufacturing corporation that uses a job order cost system. It may also be solved using the Solutions Software.

Allied Manufacturing. For use with the managerial chapters, this set has students perform some basic transaction processing as well as several spreadsheet applications.

For the Instructor—Printware

- **Instructor's Solutions Manual.** A comprehensive, two-volume manual is available that contains the solutions to all questions, exercises, and problems. In addition, a suggested completion time and difficulty index is provided for each problem along with check figures for distribution to students.
- **Solution Transparencies.** The transparencies contain solutions to all exercises and problems. All are prepared in large, easy-to-read type.
- **Teaching Transparencies.** A set of over 100 teaching transparencies is free to adopters. These helpful color acetates include summaries of key narrative discussions raised in the chapter and various examples, with an emphasis on those that are too time-consuming to present on a chalkboard. A special group of "layered" transparencies is included, allowing the instructor to demonstrate, one step at a time, the completion of a work sheet, the construction of a production cost report, and other troublesome tasks.
- **Test Bank.** A thoroughly revised test bank has been prepared. Each chapter of the text is covered via an ample selection of multiple-choice, true-false, and matching questions, along with a series of multipart exer-

cises and essay questions. The Test Bank is available in printed and microcomputer versions. We have also included various achievement tests that take 40 to 60 minutes to complete and examine a student on approximately three chapters at a given sitting. In addition, there are two comprehensive tests.

FOR THE INSTRUCTOR—SOFTWARE AND OTHER MEDIA

- **Instructor's Resource Manual.** The Instructor's Resource Manual in WordPerfect contains detailed lecture outlines that parallel the text's discussion. These outlines are especially useful for part-time instructors and graduate teaching assistants. The manual also includes suggested homework assignments and a series of short quizzes. A printed copy is available.
- **MicroExam 4.** MicroExam is a microcomputer test-generation package that consists of item banks on disks and the software necessary to create instructor-customized examinations. Random selection of questions is available and, if desired, multiple tests may be generated simultaneously. The software also allows for the import of instructor-created items in ASCII format for more customized testing. MicroExam can be used on the IBM PC and compatible machines.
- **PowerPoint Teaching Transparencies.** These lecture presentation slides are an alternative to the teaching transparencies in acetate form.
- **Video.** A case-study video contains a variety of topics, with each segment featuring the use of accounting information in a service organization.
- **Inspector Disk.**

ADDITIONAL ITEMS TO ASSIST INSTRUCTORS

CONTACCT II. Instructor's Manual and Test Bank Disk.

Annual Report Project and Readings. Instructor's Manual.

Practice Set Keys.

Online with South-Western and Software Technical Support. Instructor resources and software technical support are now available on-line. Check your *Instructor's Resource Manual* for details.

Preferred Accounting Customer (PAC) Hotline. Special benefits and services to assist instructors in course preparation are available through the PAC hotline (800/342-8798).

ACKNOWLEDGMENTS

A project of this nature and magnitude is a team effort, entailing much cooperation, thoughtfulness, and patience. To our team members we owe a tremendous debt of gratitude. Those persons who responded to surveys and reviewed chapters were especially helpful with their comments and suggestions. Therefore, many thanks to the following people:

Sheila Ammons
Austin Community College

Sarah Brown
University of North Alabama

James Del Vacchio
Saint Peter's College

Stephen J. Dempsey
University of Vermont

John Hudson
Lake Superior State University

J. Roland Kelley
Tarrant County Junior College

Charles Miller
Columbia State Community College

Claudio Munoz
University of LaVerne

Beverly J. Piper
Ashland University

James Skidmore
Grand Rapids Community College

Gene R. Sullivan
Liberty University

Joyce Yearley
New Mexico State University

A special thank you goes to Galen Carpenter, Mary Lee Hodge, Glen Jarboe, Padmanabhan Krishnan, Joe Sarkis, Sumit Sircar, and Jeffrey Tsay (The University of Texas at Arlington); Chang Moon, Richard Etlinger, Paul Tatsch, Monroe Hess, James Morgali, and Thomas Brierton (University of the Pacific); Becky Herring (University of Charleston); and Ceil Fewox (Trident Technical College)—all of whom played important roles in the development of the text and supplement components. The assistance from South-Western College Publishing in producing this text was extremely helpful. We especially appreciate the work of Sara Bates, Peggy Williams, Sharon Oblinger, and Malvine Litten. We also owe a special debt of gratitude to Mark Hubble and Elizabeth Bowers, who stuck with us during some very trying times.

And finally, we are deeply appreciative of the support of our families that allowed us to pursue this project. In view of the time commitment and constant deadlines, their patience went above and beyond the call of duty. To Nancy, Scott, and Deborah Solomon; Laurie, Corbett, and Russell Walther; Melinda, Matthew, Blaine, and Mike Vargo; and Ron Plunkett—we love you.

Comments from users are welcomed and appreciated.

Lanny M. Solomon
Larry M. Walther
Richard J. Vargo
Linda M. Plunkett

BRIEF CONTENTS

1. An Introduction to Accounting 1
2. Processing Accounting Information 49
3. Income Measurement and Adjusting Entries 91
4. Completion of the Accounting Cycle 129
5. Accounting/Reporting for Merchandising Operations 173
6. Accounting Systems and Internal Control 217
7. Understanding and Using Financial Information 251
8. Cash and Liquid Investments 287
9. Receivables 323
10. Inventory 357
11. Property, Plant, and Equipment: Acquisition and Depreciation 401
12. Property, Plant, and Equipment/Natural Resources/Intangibles 437
13. Current Liabilities and Employee Compensation 471
14. Financial Accounting and Reporting: U.S. and Global Perspectives 507
15. Partnerships 549
16. Introduction to Corporations 583
17. Corporations: Additional Equity Issues and Income Reporting 619
18. Financial Instruments: An Emphasis on Bonds 661
19. Statement of Cash Flows 711
20. Introduction to Managerial and Cost Accounting 761
21. Job Order Costing Systems 797
22. Process Costing, Activity-Based Costing, and Just-in-Time Production 837
23. Cost-Volume-Profit Analysis 883
24. Budgeting 921
25. Performance Evaluation via Flexible Budgets and Standard Costs 963
26. Decision Making and Contribution Reporting 1007
27. Capital Budgeting 1047

A. Special Journal Systems A–1
B. Assessing a Company's Financial Health B–1
C. Present Value Tables C–1

Index I–1

Contents

1 An Introduction to Accounting   1

What Is Accounting?   3
Users and Uses of Accounting Information   3

Business Briefing   4
Financial and Managerial Orientation   5
Limitations of Accounting Information   6
The Accountant: A Glorified Bookkeeper?   7

The Accounting Profession   7
Public Accounting   7
Private Accounting   9
Governmental/Not-for-Profit Accounting   10

Key Underlying Concepts   11
Entity Assumption   11
Historical-Cost Principle   12
Objectivity Principle   12

A Music Consultant's Perspective   13

Financial Position and the Entity   13
Assets   13
Liabilities   14
Owner's Equity   15

A Further Focus   15

A Closer Look at Owner's Equity   15
Investments by the Owner   16
Withdrawals by the Owner   16
Revenues   16
Expenses   17

A Further Focus   17

The Accounting Equation: An Extended Illustration   17

Financial Statements   21
Income Statement   22
Statement of Owner's Equity   22

Balance Sheet   22
Statement of Cash Flows   22

A FURTHER FOCUS   24

Statement Interrelationships   24

ETHICS AND ACCOUNTING   25

A Changing Environment   25
A Case Study   26
Ethical Challenges for the Accountant   27
A Concluding Comment: The Ethical Individual   27

2 PROCESSING ACCOUNTING INFORMATION   49

THE ACCOUNTING SYSTEM   51

Accounts   52

A FURTHER FOCUS   52

Debits and Credits   54

A FURTHER FOCUS   55

Journals   56
Chart of Accounts   58

POSTING: INTERACTION OF THE BASIC TOOLS   59

Computerized Record Keeping   61

BUSINESS BRIEFING   61

AN EXTENDED ILLUSTRATION   62

TRIAL BALANCE   68

A Helpful (Not Infallible) Report   68
Unequal Totals   69

A BRIEF OVERVIEW   69

3 INCOME MEASUREMENT AND ADJUSTING ENTRIES   91

THE MEANING OF INCOME   92

An Emphasis on Transactions and Events   93
The Accounting Period   93

A FURTHER FOCUS   94

Revenue Recognition   94
Expense Recognition—The Matching Principle   94
Accrual-Basis Accounting   95
Cash-Basis Accounting   96

A HEALTH-CARE CONSULTANT'S PERSPECTIVE   98

ADJUSTING ENTRIES   98

Multiperiod Costs and Revenues   98

A FURTHER FOCUS   101

Unrecorded Expenses and Revenues—Accruals   103
Adjusted Trial Balance   105
Adjustment Errors   107

APPENDIX: AN ALTERNATIVE ACCOUNTING TREATMENT FOR PREPAID EXPENSES AND UNEARNED REVENUES   108

    Accounting for Prepaid Expenses   108
    Accounting for Unearned Revenues   109
    A Comparison of the Two Approaches   110

4 COMPLETION OF THE ACCOUNTING CYCLE   129

WORK SHEET   130

    Work Sheet Construction   131
    Uses of the Work Sheet   132

A LOOK BACK: THE ACCOUNTING CYCLE   139

THE BALANCE SHEET   139

BUSINESS BRIEFING   140

    Limitations of the Balance Sheet   141
    Statement Classification   141
    Notes to the Financial Statements/Full Disclosure   145

A CLOSER LOOK AT LIQUIDITY   146

    Working Capital   146
    Current Ratio   146

A FURTHER FOCUS   147

    Quick Ratio   147

APPENDIX: REVERSING ENTRIES   148

    Case A—No Reversing Entries   148
    Case B—Using Reversing Entries   149
    An Overview   149

5 ACCOUNTING/REPORTING FOR MERCHANDISING OPERATIONS   173

MEASURING MERCHANDISING INCOME   174

    Sales Revenue   175

A MARKETING MANAGER'S PERSPECTIVE   176

    Cost of Goods Sold   179
    Accounting for Merchandise Acquisitions   181

FINANCIAL STATEMENTS OF A MERCHANDISING CONCERN   185

BUSINESS BRIEFING   186

    Income Statement   186
    Statement of Owner's Equity   187
    Balance Sheet   188

A CLOSER LOOK AT INCOME REPORTING   188

    Multiple-Step Income Statements   188
    Single-Step Income Statements   191
    An Evaluation of Income-Statement Data   191

INVENTORY SYSTEMS   193

    Problems With a Periodic System   193

A Further Focus   193

- Perpetual Systems   194
- Inventory and Computers   194
- Taking a Physical Inventory   194

Appendix: Behind the Scenes Work for a Merchandising Business   195

- The Merchandising Work Sheet   195
- Closing Entries   197

6 Accounting Systems and Internal Control   217

Accounting Information Systems   218

- Problems With Contemporary Systems   219
- System Refinements   220

A Further Focus   220

Computerized Accounting Systems   221

- Features of PC-Based System Software   222
- The Concept of Modular Accounting   223
- The Journal Modules   224
- Are Computerized Systems Always the Answer?   226

Internal Control   227

A Lawyer's Perspective   229

- The Internal Control Structure   229

A Further Focus   232

Business Briefing   233

- Fraud in Corporate America   233
- The Impact of the Computer   234

7 Understanding and Using Financial Information   251

Financial Information   253

- Complications to Usefulness   253

A Further Focus   254

Information and the Focus on Income   255

- How Precise Is Income?   255
- The Quality of Earnings   256
- Why Allow Accounting Choice?   256

The Annual Report   257

- Financial Statements   257

A Further Focus   260

- Notes to the Financial Statements   262
- Additional Annual Report Disclosures   263

A Further Focus   264

- Other Information Sources   266

THE ANALYSIS OF FINANCIAL INFORMATION 266
   Comparative Standards 266
REPORTING FOR SPECIALIZED ENTITIES 268
   Utility Companies and Banks 268
   Governmental Units 269
   Not-for-Profit Enterprises 269
THE USER AS A CUSTOMER 270
APPENDIX: AN INTRODUCTION TO CONSOLIDATED FINANCIAL STATEMENTS 270
   Parent and Subsidiary Relationships 271
   Intercompany Transactions 271

8 CASH AND LIQUID INVESTMENTS 287

CASH 289
   Balance Sheet Presentation 289
   Cash Management 289
A FURTHER FOCUS 291
   Cash Control 292
A FURTHER FOCUS 294
   Cash Management and Control in a High-Tech Environment 300
TRADING SECURITIES 301
   Balance Sheet Reporting 301
A FINANCE MANAGER'S PERSPECTIVE 302
   Accounting for Changes in Value 302
   A Parting Thought 304

9 RECEIVABLES 323

CREDIT SALES AND RECEIVABLES 324
A MUSIC CONSULTANT'S PERSPECTIVE 325
   A Cost to the Customer: Bad Credit 325
   Trade and Nontrade Receivables 325
A FURTHER FOCUS 326
ACCOUNTS RECEIVABLE 326
   Direct Write-off Method 327
   Allowance Method 327
   Receivables Insights and Management 332
A FURTHER FOCUS 334
   Credit Card Sales 334
BUSINESS BRIEFING 335
NOTES RECEIVABLE 335
   The Nature of Interest 336

Accounting for Notes and Interest   337
Dishonoring a Note   338

10 INVENTORY   357

WHAT IS INVENTORY?   359
Ownership Problems   359

EFFECTS OF INVENTORY ERRORS ON FINANCIAL STATEMENTS   360
Counterbalancing Errors   361

INVENTORY VALUATION AND INCOME MEASUREMENT   362
Matching: The Key Objective   363
Cost Determination   363
Costing Methods   364
Cost Flow Assumptions   365

A FURTHER FOCUS   366

LOWER OF COST OR MARKET   372
Measuring the Decline in Value   372
Application of the Lower-of-Cost-or-Market Rule   372

BUSINESS BRIEFING   373

INVENTORY ESTIMATES   374
Gross Profit Method   374
Retail Method   375

INVENTORY TURNOVER   376
An Example   376
The Operating Cycle   377

PERPETUAL INVENTORY SYSTEMS AND INVENTORY VALUATION   377
Illustration of a Perpetual System   377
General Ledger Updating   379

APPENDIX: LIFO AND AVERAGE COSTING UNDER A PERPETUAL INVENTORY SYSTEM   379
LIFO   380
Moving Average   381

11 PROPERTY, PLANT, AND EQUIPMENT: ACQUISITION AND DEPRECIATION   401

THE NATURE OF PROPERTY, PLANT, AND EQUIPMENT   403
Determining the Cost of Property, Plant, and Equipment   403
Small Items of Property, Plant, and Equipment   406

DEPRECIATION   406
Determining Service Life   407
Methods of Depreciation   408

BUSINESS BRIEFING 408

A FURTHER FOCUS 409

   Revisions of Depreciation 414
   Depreciation and the Tax Laws 416

LEASES 417

   Operating Leases Versus Capital Leases 417
   Accounting for Capital Leases 418

12 PROPERTY, PLANT, AND EQUIPMENT/NATURAL RESOURCES/INTANGIBLES 437

PLANT AND EQUIPMENT COSTS AFTER ASSET ACQUISITION 438

   Repairs 439
   Additions 439
   Betterments 439

DISPOSALS OF PROPERTY, PLANT, AND EQUIPMENT 440

   Removal of Assets from the Accounts 441
   Sale of Depreciable Assets 442
   Exchanges and Trade-ins of Similar Assets 443
   A Related Issue: Asset Impairment 444

A FURTHER FOCUS 446

NATURAL RESOURCES 446

   Depletion 446
   Depreciable Assets Related to Natural Resources 447

INTANGIBLE ASSETS 448

   Patents 448
   Copyrights 449
   Franchises 449
   Trademarks 449

A FURTHER FOCUS 450

   Goodwill 450

A MARKETING MANAGER'S PERSPECTIVE 452

   Amortization of Intangibles 452

13 CURRENT LIABILITIES AND EMPLOYEE COMPENSATION 471

CURRENT LIABILITIES 473

   Prepayments (Advances) by Customers 473
   Collections for Third Parties 473
   Accrued Liabilities 474
   Current Portion of Long-Term Debt 474
   Notes Payable 475
   Contingent Liabilities 478

A FURTHER FOCUS   480

Balance Sheet Disclosure   481

EMPLOYEE COMPENSATION   481

A HUMAN RESOURCE MANAGER'S PERSPECTIVE   482

Employee Earnings   482
Deductions from Employee Earnings   483
Payroll Recording and Record Keeping   485
Payroll Taxes of the Employer   485
Other Payroll-Related Costs of the Employer   487
Fringe Benefits: The Employer's Perspective   489

BUSINESS BRIEFING   490

14 FINANCIAL ACCOUNTING AND REPORTING: U.S. AND GLOBAL PERSPECTIVES   507

OBJECTIVES OF FINANCIAL REPORTING   509

Characteristics of Financial Information   509

THE FOUNDATION OF ACCOUNTING   512

Generally Accepted Accounting Principles (GAAP)   512

A FURTHER FOCUS   512

Specific Assumptions, Principles, and Modifying Conventions   514

A FURTHER FOCUS   516

INTERNATIONAL ACCOUNTING   523

Uniformity of International Accounting Standards   524
Accounting for Foreign Currency Transactions   525

AN ECONOMIST'S PERSPECTIVE   527

BUSINESS BRIEFING   528

Disclosure of International Financial Affairs   529

15 PARTNERSHIPS   549

CHARACTERISTICS OF A PARTNERSHIP   550

Ease of Formation   550
Mutual Agency   551
Co-ownership of Property and Income   551
Limited Life   551
Unlimited Liability   551

A FURTHER FOCUS   552

Other Factors to Consider   553

PARTNERSHIP ACCOUNTING   553

Partnership Formation and Owner Investments   553

A SMALL BUSINESS CONSULTANT'S PERSPECTIVE   554

Partnership Earnings: Nature and Distribution 555
A FURTHER FOCUS 557

Admission of a New Partner 559
Withdrawal of a Partner 561
Liquidation of a Partnership 563

16 INTRODUCTION TO CORPORATIONS 583

THE NATURE OF CORPORATIONS 585

Corporate Form of Organization: Advantages 585

A FURTHER FOCUS 585

Corporate Form of Organization: Disadvantages 586
Organization of a Corporation 586
Common Stock 588
Preferred Stock: Nature and Characteristics 589
Par-Value Stock 591

A FURTHER FOCUS 593

No-Par Stock 594
Issuing Stock for Assets Other Than Cash 595
Stock Subscriptions 596
Corporate Equity: A Comprehensive Illustration 596

EVALUATIONS BASED ON STOCKHOLDERS' EQUITY 597

Book Value Per Share 597
Return on Common Stockholders' Equity 599

17 CORPORATIONS: ADDITIONAL EQUITY ISSUES AND INCOME REPORTING 619

TREASURY STOCK 621

Acquisitions of Treasury Stock 621
Reissuance of Treasury Stock 622

RETAINED EARNINGS 624

Dividends 624
Other Items That Affect Retained Earnings 628

A FURTHER FOCUS 629

Reporting Changes in Retained Earnings 630

CORPORATE INCOME REPORTING 631

Discontinued Operations 632
Extraordinary Items 632
Changes in Accounting Principle 634

AN INVESTMENT ANALYST'S PERSPECTIVE 635

Net-of-Tax Reporting 635

EARNINGS PER SHARE 637

BUSINESS BRIEFING 637

Weighted-Average Shares Outstanding 638
Earnings Available to Common Stockholders 639
Primary Versus Fully Diluted Earnings Per Share 639
EPS Disclosure 640

18 FINANCIAL INSTRUMENTS: AN EMPHASIS ON BONDS 661

FINANCING A BUSINESS VENTURE 662

Financial Instruments 663

BOND ISSUES 664

Types of Bonds 665
Accounting for Bond Issues: The Basics 666
Factors That Affect Bond Prices 667
Bonds Issued at a Discount 668
Bonds Issued at a Premium 672
Bond Issues and Timing Considerations 675
Bond Retirement 676
An Analysis of Outstanding Debt 677

BUSINESS BRIEFING 678

INVESTING IN FINANCIAL INSTRUMENTS 678

Investments in Bonds 679
Investments in Stock 680

APPENDIX: PRESENT VALUE 683

Compound Interest and Present Value 684
Relationship Between Compound Interest and Present Value 685
Present Value and Annuities 686
Periods of Less Than One Year 687
Present Value and Bond Prices 687

19 STATEMENT OF CASH FLOWS 711

STATEMENT FORMAT AND CLASSIFICATIONS 713

BUSINESS BRIEFING 714

Operating Activities 714
Investing Activities 715
Financing Activities 715
Investing and Financing Transactions That Do Not Affect Cash 715
Cash and Cash Equivalents 716

A CLOSER LOOK AT OPERATING ACTIVITIES 716

A FURTHER FOCUS 717

The Direct Method 717
The Indirect Method 722

Preparation of a Statement of Cash Flows 725

Step 1: Analyze the Cash Account 725
Step 2: Determine Net Cash Flow from Operating Activities 725
Step 3: Analyze Remaining Balance Sheet Items 725
Step 4: Financial Statement Preparation 732

Some Thoughts on Interpretation 734

Business Failure 735

Appendix: Work Sheet for Preparing a Statement of Cash Flows—Indirect Approach 735

20 Introduction to Managerial and Cost Accounting 761

Financial Accounting 762

Managerial Accounting 763

A Cost/Benefit Theme 764
Managerial Accounting Applications 765

Business Briefing 767

Cost Accounting 768

A Changing Face 768

A Further Focus 770

Manufacturing Organizations 771

Manufacturing Costs 771
Financial Statements of a Manufacturer 772

Cost Behavior 777

Variable Costs 777
Fixed Costs 777

21 Job Order Costing Systems 797

Job Order Systems 798

Perpetual Inventories 799

A Further Focus 805

Business Briefing 808

A Closer Look at Overhead 810

Effects of Over- and Underapplied Overhead 811
Today's Manufacturing Environment 812

Job Costing: Service Applications 813

Direct and Indirect Costs 814
An Illustration 814
Client Billings 815

22 Process Costing, Activity-Based Costing, and Just-in-Time Production 837

Process Costing 839

How Process Costing Differs from Job Costing 839

Measuring Production Volume   839
Factors That Affect Equivalent Production   842
Comprehensive Example   844

ACTIVITY-BASED COSTING   847

The Problem of Averaging   849
Extending the Concept to a Business   850
The Nature of ABC   851
The Problems and Benefits of ABC   852

A FURTHER FOCUS   853

JUST-IN-TIME PRODUCTION   853

Characteristics of JIT Production   854
A Focus on Speed   856

BUSINESS BRIEFING   857

APPENDIX: PROCESS COSTING AND THE WEIGHTED-AVERAGE METHOD   858

Features of Weighted-Average Costing   858
An Example   858

23 COST-VOLUME-PROFIT ANALYSIS   883

COST BEHAVIOR   884

Variable Costs   885
Fixed Costs   887
Mixed (Semivariable) Costs   890

COST ANALYSIS   891

Scattergraph   891
Method of Least Squares   892
High-Low Method   893

COST-VOLUME-PROFIT ANALYSIS   894

Equation Approach   894
Contribution Approach   895

A FURTHER FOCUS   896

BUSINESS BRIEFING   897

Target Income   898
Operating Changes   899

A FURTHER FOCUS   901

CVP Analysis for Multiproduct Firms   902

A MARKETING CONSULTANT'S PERSPECTIVE   903

Limiting Assumptions of CVP Analysis   903

24 BUDGETING   921

BENEFITS OF BUDGETING   922

Formalize Planning   923
Serve as a Basis for Performance Evaluation   923
Assist in Communication and Coordination   924

A Product-Line Manager's Perspective 924
Budget Construction 925
Construction Flows 925
Budget Estimation 926
The Budget Period 927
Budget Limitations and Human Relations 928

A Further Focus 929
Comprehensive Budgeting 929
Sales Budget 931
Production Budget 932
Direct Material Purchases Budget 933
Direct Labor Budget 934
Factory Overhead Budget 934
Selling and Administrative Expense Budget 937
Cash Budget 937
Budgeted Income Statement 938
Budgeted Balance Sheet 940

Budgeting and Computers 940
Use of a Spreadsheet 941

25 Performance Evaluation via Flexible Budgets and Standard Costs 963

Responsibility Accounting 965
Responsibility Units 965

A Chief Information Officer's Perspective 966
Reporting System 966
Controllability: The Key to Responsibility Accounting 969

A Further Focus 970
Flexible Budgets 970
Constructing a Flexible Budget 971
Flexible Budgets and Performance Evaluation 971
A Common Misunderstanding 972

Standard Costs 973
Standard Costs and Budgets 973
Setting Standards 974
Levels of Standards 976

Variance Analysis 977
Variance Calculation 977
An Illustration of Direct Material Variances 978
An Illustration of Direct Labor Variances 979

A Further Focus 980
Factory Overhead Variances 980
Variance Investigation 983

A Broader View of Standards and Performance Evaluation 984

Standards in Nonmanufacturing Settings 984

A Further Focus 985

Nonfinancial Performance Measures 985

26 Decision Making and Contribution Reporting 1077

General Approach to Decision Making 1008

Full Project or Incremental Approach? 1009
Decision Making: An Emphasis on the Future 1010
Qualitative Factors 1012
A Summary of the Decision-Making Process 1012

Make or Buy Decisions 1012

Avoidable Fixed Overhead 1013
Opportunity Cost 1014
Qualitative Considerations 1014

A Further Focus 1015

Special Order Pricing 1015

The Pricing Decision 1016

Business Briefing 1016

Contribution Margin in Relation to Capacity 1017

Addition or Deletion of Products or Departments 1018

A Further Focus 1020

Improvements in Performance Reporting 1020

Variable and Absorption Costing 1024

Fixed Manufacturing Overhead: The Key Difference 1024
An Illustration 1024
An Overview of the Two Methods 1027

27 Capital Budgeting 1047

A Further Focus 1049

Capital Budgeting Decisions 1049

Decision Factors to Consider 1049

The Time Value of Money 1051

Compound Interest 1052
Present Value 1052

Capital Budgeting Evaluation Methods 1055

Net Present Value 1055
Internal Rate of Return 1057

A Computer Consultant's Perspective 1059

The Payback Method 1059

A FURTHER FOCUS   1061
Accounting Rate of Return   1061
Capital Investment in a Competitive Business Climate   1062
APPENDIX: CASH FLOWS AND INCOME TAXES   1063
The Aftertax Concept   1063
Depreciation: Why Special Treatment Is Needed   1064

A   SPECIAL JOURNAL SYSTEMS   A–1

B   ASSESSING A COMPANY'S FINANCIAL HEALTH   B–1

C   PRESENT VALUE TABLES   C–1

INDEX   I–1

BANNER ADVERTISING, INC.
OUTDOOR ADVERTISING SPECIALISTS

Dear Accounting Student,

I am pleased to have the opportunity to tell you the story of my business, Banner Advertising, as you study this text. Actually, each chapter opens with a short story that presents some information about my company and shows how the accounting material included in the chapter applies to the firm.

    Not so long ago, I was a business student, just like you. Let's just say I am still well under forty, so it seems like only yesterday that I was struggling through introductory accounting. I got by alright, but really was not that interested in the material. Why? In retrospect, I failed to see its relevance. About the only thing that mattered at the time was doing well enough to complete the course and get on with "my life." What I soon found out was that "my life" would require a day-to-day working knowledge of almost every aspect of accounting—and I am certainly not an accountant.

    My life's story is relatively simple to tell. I graduated with a degree in marketing, made a few "swings" at a pro golf career, then took an entry level management position with a major construction company. The economy almost immediately plummeted (Need I say more?), and I was left scrambling for a way to survive. It quickly became clear to me that the "old ways" of finding a secure job with a big company and looking forward to a generous retirement program were gone. It was also clear that a college degree was no longer a guarantee of anything. In short, I was hungry. I was forced to find a way to survive on my own—I always have to grin when someone refers to this predicament as entrepreneurship!

    At least my brief stint in the construction business afforded me a few business relationships, and I did gain a little useful knowledge about construction. I had become aware of a good location to construct an outdoor advertising sign, and felt like I knew how to get it done. I believed it would generate enough rent to pay for itself and give me a little income. But, I had to convince a banker, a landowner, and a construction crew to have confidence in my plan. Obviously, I had to show them all a few (accounting) numbers. One thing led to another, and, suddenly I found that I was in business for myself—and also beginning to appreciate the accounting knowledge I should have learned better in the first place. The rest of my story is told in the text, but suffice it to say that the past decade has involved a lot of hard work and good fortune.

Clearly, in today's world, the value of your education is found, not in the degree you seek, but in the knowledge you acquire along the way. Your situation, upon graduation, is likely to be much like mine. You are going forth into a world where success and failure are no longer judged by the ability to climb a corporate ladder, but instead by your individual ability to identify opportunity *and* capture it.

In this regard, my advice to you is threefold: starting right now, never underestimate the value of relationships, consistent ethical behavior, and a strong understanding of accounting information. The first two items are hopefully apparent; the third may take some convincing. That is why I have agreed to allow my story to be told in this text. Hopefully, by showing you the relevance of the text's material to a real-world setting, you will better appreciate your authors' presentations and be more motivated in your approach to the course.

Good luck and best wishes,

George Faris

George Faris
President, Banner Advertising, Inc.

1 An Introduction to Accounting

LEARNING OBJECTIVES

After studying this chapter, you should be able to:

1. Identify the users, uses, and limitations of accounting information.
2. Describe the accounting profession and identify accounting-related careers.
3. Explain the use of accounting principles in financial reporting.
4. Define assets, liabilities, and owner's equity, and state the relationship of these components in the accounting equation.
5. Recognize the four factors that cause owner's equity to change: owner investments, owner withdrawals, revenues, and expenses.
6. Describe the impact of various transactions on the accounting equation.
7. Demonstrate a working knowledge of the information revealed by the four basic financial statements.
8. Recognize various ethical issues faced by accountants.

Fifteen years ago, George Faris was a college student enrolled in an introductory accounting course. His major was marketing, but he was not really sure what the future held. In plain and simple terms, he considered accounting as "just another course that I have to take." George now owns a successful company and has agreed to provide a glimpse into the firm's day-to-day activities. This way we can see firsthand how the concepts presented in each chapter are put into action in an actual business setting.

George has agreed to help your authors for one simple reason: "I never intended to be an accountant. To put it mildly, I had no passion for the study of accounting in school. But if the past years have taught me one thing, it's that accounting is essential to good decision making and the successful operation of any business. I only wish I had more fully appreciated this fact while enrolled in the course."

A quick look at George's history is in order. After graduation and a brief stop on the pro golf circuit, George began an outdoor advertising business (i.e., billboards) with virtually no financial backing. Working long hours, he identified several opportunities for advertising signs in saturated markets. George negotiated leases, occasionally purchased land, navigated complex zoning laws, and arranged a variety of financing sources to pay for the costly sign structures. That was only half the battle. He then had to locate clients to lease the signs, provide art support and painting, and attend to numerous other facets of building a business. As you might imagine, the initial years were lean and tough. George struggled to overcome many obstacles, including being an unknown in the eyes of lenders and investors. Over time, though, the firm prospered. Today, Banner Advertising Corporation is growing rapidly, being lifted by its own financial strength and drive. In short, the company is a free enterprise success story.

As you progress through life, you will soon discover that George's experience is not unique. Newly opened enterprises are often full of spirit and short of capital. Through enthusiasm, creativity, proper analysis of alternatives, and hard work by the owners, however, these businesses frequently survive and flourish. Banner is one such example; Sony and Hewlett-Packard (HP) are among the others. Sony was started in a bombed-out department store in Tokyo on $1,600 of personal savings. HP, on the other hand, began with about $500 of capital, trying "anything that would bring in a nickel."[1]

No matter whether you plan to start a company or pursue a career in computer systems, biology, architecture, or law, you will find that a solid understanding of the financial aspects of business activity is highly desirable. This point was succinctly illustrated in a recent article that reported on the value of integrating business training and medical training. Although some might regard the blending of these two disciplines as unusual, such integration can lead to the monitoring and containment of health-care costs. The end result may

---

[1] See "Sometimes a Great Notion," *Inc.*, July 1993, pp. 90–91.

allow more people to have access to our country's health-care system. As *The Wall Street Journal* noted:

> A new type of expert is rapidly gaining power in medical circles: the doctor with the M.B.A. [Master's Degree in Business Administration]. These dual-degree holders can pivot quickly . . . between the world of stethoscopes and the world of spreadsheets. That appeals to hospitals and health plans . . . .[2]

More than likely you are not planning to practice medicine. Nevertheless, you will probably face a number of decisions in the not-too-distant future that require some interpretation of financial information. Consider, for instance, a basic housing decision. Should you rent an apartment or purchase a home? If you are leaning toward the purchase of a residence, the following questions may come to mind:

- Can I afford the extra $250 cash outflow every month?
- Should I finance the purchase by obtaining a fixed rate mortgage or an adjustable-rate mortgage (ARM)?
- What are the income tax benefits associated with the purchase?
- What impact will passage of a school bond issue have on my property taxes?
- How much equity can I accumulate in the home after five years?
- Given that housing prices and my earnings are expected to climb, should I "bite the bullet" and buy a larger residence than I presently need?

These personal decisions, as well as those made by companies, are based on an evaluation of appropriate financial facts. Accounting is the service function within an organization that generates the facts.

WHAT IS ACCOUNTING?

We will define **accounting** as a set of concepts and techniques that collectively measure, summarize, and report financial information about an economic unit. To expand, most disciplines are based on some type of theoretical framework. Accounting is no exception. The foundation for much of what accountants do is a set of underlying principles, assumptions, and practices that have been generally accepted by the accounting profession. These items are used to measure the financial activities of numerous business units ranging from Exxon Corporation to the family-owned corner market and even the local art museum. Once derived, the measurements are processed, summarized, and communicated in the form of financial reports and statistics, allowing users to make decisions about a wide variety of business matters.

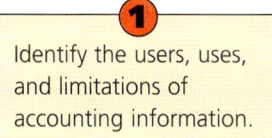

USERS AND USES OF ACCOUNTING INFORMATION

① Identify the users, uses, and limitations of accounting information.

The audience for accounting information is large and diverse. Numerous user groups inside and outside of an enterprise attempt to satisfy their needs by relying on financial disclosures (see Exhibit 1–1). For example:

---

[2] "A New Breed of M.D.s Add M.B.A. to Vitae," *The Wall Street Journal*, September 27, 1994, pp. B1, B11.

BUSINESS BRIEFING

Accounting Knowledge: Helpful in Most Any Career

TRUMAN LAMB
Freestone County Extension Agent
Texas Agricultural Extension Service

My professional training is in agriculture, and my primary mission is to help producers properly manage their farm and ranch lands. Freestone County, Texas is home to many sophisticated cattle-ranching operations, a modest supply of peach orchards, and some forestry activity. As a result, I am often contacted about a variety of agricultural problems—anything from animal husbandry to assessments of timber productivity over a 40-year life cycle.

Given my occupation and background, you may be wondering why the authors asked me to provide commentary for an accounting textbook. The reason is simple. Even though I consult on agricultural issues, much of the consultation typically boils down to dollars and cents. Despite my specific training, I spend a large portion of my time helping people use financial information. For example, I help farmers and ranchers evaluate the profitability of starting a new enterprise, changing land management practices, and investing in new equipment. Most producers are interested in reducing costs, so I also furnish advice that will make their operations more efficient.

The Extension Service offers the public many financial programs such as record keeping, preparing financial reports, and estate planning. If my experience is typical, and I think it is after talking with many friends in different occupations, you will find that a basic knowledge of accounting is indispensable no matter what career path you choose. Life is a series of financial decisions, and accounting is a key tool to understanding and evaluating the information at hand.

EXHIBIT 1–1
Accounting and the Communication Process

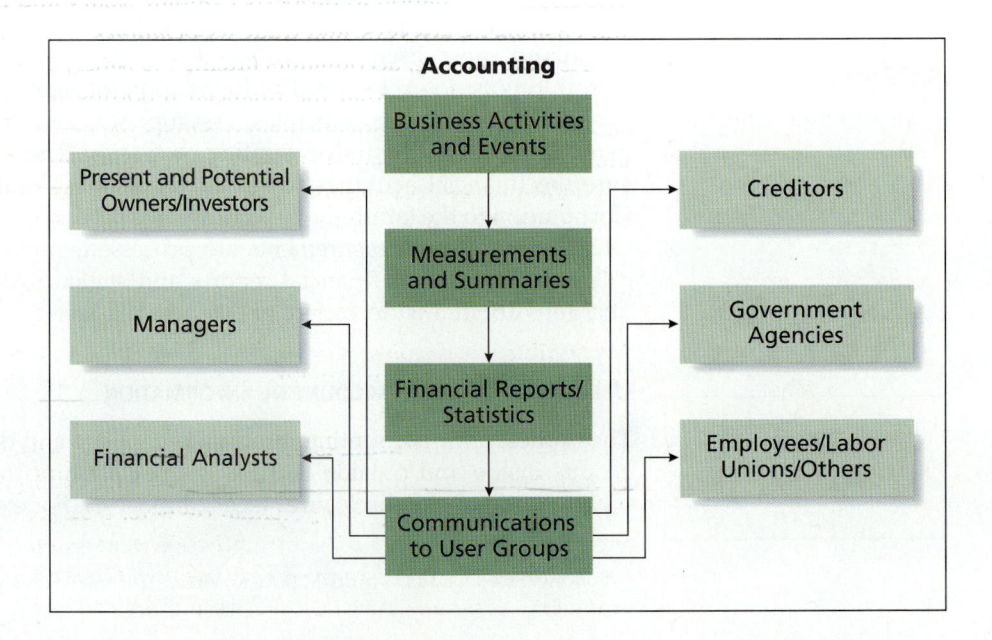

Accounting

Business Activities and Events → Measurements and Summaries → Financial Reports/Statistics → Communications to User Groups

- Present and Potential Owners/Investors
- Managers
- Financial Analysts
- Creditors
- Government Agencies
- Employees/Labor Unions/Others

Owners have invested their precious funds into a business organization. This group requires information concerning investment profitability and whether continuance in an ownership role is economically justified. Potential owners have similar informational needs. These individuals desire insight about a firm's past earnings trends, likelihood for future growth, and cash flow prospects, perhaps in comparison with other businesses in the same industry.

Creditors are those parties who provide a firm with goods, services, and financial resources by either extending credit or making loans. Included in this group are suppliers, banks, loan companies, and other lending institutions. Creditors are interested in knowing whether an organization can settle its obligations (including related interest charges) in a timely manner and on scheduled dates. Thus, an enterprise's existing cash position, outstanding debts, and present and projected earnings are of utmost concern.

Managers are charged with the responsibility of meeting a company's goals and objectives. To achieve this end, managers must select from and implement various projects, evaluate performance, and, if necessary, take corrective action to bring an organization back on target. Depending on the firm involved, information needs will vary and may include product cost data and manufacturing resource requirements.

Government agencies also employ accounting information. Governmental units, along with various programs (such as Social Security and unemployment), are financed from the taxes that are paid by businesses and individuals. These taxes are frequently based on income as defined by numerous tax statutes and rulings. In addition, businesses must often comply with the financial reporting directives of certain regulatory agencies. These agencies are charged with administering a variety of legislative enactments and include the Securities and Exchange Commission (SEC), the Interstate Commerce Commission, and the U.S. Department of Labor, to name just a few.

Finally, other users include *financial analysts*, who advise their clients or employers about various investment alternatives; *employees and labor unions*, who need information to properly evaluate salary and fringe benefit packages; and customers, lawyers, and trade associations.

As you can see, accountants attempt to satisfy many different user groups and needs. Be aware that the financial reporting techniques preferred by one particular group may not adequately satisfy the needs of another. In view of this situation a neutral position is taken, with a company's financial reports having a general-purpose orientation. This orientation means that the information being disclosed is not biased to favor owners, creditors, or any other interested party.

FINANCIAL AND MANAGERIAL ORIENTATION

Accounting encompasses extensive subject matter and consists of many component parts. Two of the field's major segments are financial accounting and managerial accounting.

Financial accounting is primarily concerned with external reporting, that is, communicating the results of economic activities to parties outside the firm. Included in this group are potential owners, creditors, and some government agencies. The financial reporting function centers on a fair presentation of (1) the resources invested in an enterprise and (2) the profitability of operations. Financial accounting is complemented by **managerial accounting,** which involves reporting the results of operating activity to administrators within an organization. Because of its nature and the audience to which it is directed, managerial accounting deals heavily with the areas of planning, control, and decision making.

Although some overlap exists between these two components, there is a significant distinguishing factor with which you should be familiar—regulation. Managerial accounting is characterized by an "anything goes" philosophy. Although there are a number of widely accepted practices, a company can do whatever it pleases when reporting internally to its executives. In contrast, the financial (external) reporting environment is heavily regulated, a situation that is caused, in part, by the wide variety of businesses in our economy. It is essential that financial accounting be standardized somewhat to permit comparative analyses. Imagine the difficulties faced by a potential investor who is attempting to evaluate the economic activities of Ford Motor Company and those of The Gap, Inc. (a much smaller retailer of casual and active wear). If each company were allowed to account for its activities by employing unique, self-prescribed methods, the investor would surely face a formidable task.[3]

The private sector agency that currently oversees external reporting is the **Financial Accounting Standards Board (FASB).** Beginning operation in 1973, the FASB has studied a number of important topics and has issued various pronouncements that detail specific accounting practices. These pronouncements, called *Statements of Financial Accounting Standards*, constitute generally accepted accounting principles and are followed by virtually all large businesses in the United States. The work of the FASB will be cited throughout this text; at this point, simply understand the FASB's existence and basic function.

LIMITATIONS OF ACCOUNTING INFORMATION

Accounting information contains several inherent limitations. Because accounting involves the computation of dollar amounts, many people assume a great degree of precision in financial reports. As you progress through the study of accounting, you will see that numerous estimates, assumptions, and subjective judgments are required in the reporting of business activity. Further, the accountant must frequently select from among various acceptable accounting practices when determining how well an organization has performed over a period of time. Collectively, these factors contribute to a general lack of "exactness" in the financial information disclosed by a company.

Another limitation associated with accounting information is that certain events are not conducive to monetary measurement. For example, the loss of a key manager and low employee morale often have undesirable consequences for a firm; however, placing a dollar value on these items is extremely difficult. How is an organization's profit affected, for instance, if a sales manager suddenly resigns in favor of a new position with a strong competitor? Accountants are unable to express an event such as this in economic terms and therefore use the **monetary unit assumption** when assessing performance. This assumption holds that only events and activities measurable in dollars are entered and recognized in a company's records.

---

[3] Even though standardization is suggested here, businesses are given some leeway in the selection of accounting practices. This fact will become apparent in later chapters.

A further limitation of accounting information is the fact that the measures employed do not necessarily portray true value. As we will see shortly, accounting measures are often based on cost rather than on current worth.

The preceding criticisms should not be interpreted as an indictment of accounting. Logical explanations underlie the need for these restricting factors. In addition, the accounting profession has prescribed certain standards that partially offset the limitations' negative impact. The accountant, for example, often prepares a narrative discussion describing certain nonfinancial events that have a significant bearing on the business organization. Furthermore, the profession is continually reevaluating its position to determine if changes in practices would improve the relevancy and reliability of a firm's information disclosures.

THE ACCOUNTANT: A GLORIFIED BOOKKEEPER?

Many people tend to confuse bookkeeping with accounting. They often express the opinion that these two occupations are identical, or that the accountant is nothing more than a glorified bookkeeper. Both of these notions are incorrect.

Bookkeeping is concerned with record keeping and is composed of numerous mechanical tasks. Accountants may become involved with this type of work at times, but usually their duties are more complex and sophisticated. Accounting focuses primarily on the *use and interpretation* of information as opposed to repetitive data accumulation. In other words, the bookkeeper assists the accountant in generating the figures needed for reporting and analysis.

THE ACCOUNTING PROFESSION

2

Describe the accounting profession and identify accounting-related careers.

The profession of accounting can be traced back many centuries and has had considerable time for growth and development. Accounting and its financial and managerial reporting functions have matured considerably in response to a changing, dynamic business environment.

With this maturity comes an opportunity for well-paid and challenging careers—careers that have blossomed in the last decade for sharp, dedicated individuals. To better understand these career opportunities, a brief overview of the profession's various facets is helpful. (See Exhibit 1–2 for an accompanying pictorial presentation.)

PUBLIC ACCOUNTING

Firms engaged in public accounting provide accounting services for all types of enterprises (e.g., hotels, publishers, equipment manufacturers, and professional sports clubs). In view of the size and multiple locations of many of their clients, several public accounting firms have offices from coast to coast and in foreign countries. Others operate on a much smaller scale and are established on a regional or local basis.

All of these firms, regardless of scope, employ certified public accountants (CPAs). CPAs are individuals who, like physicians, dentists, and lawyers, are licensed to practice their profession. The CPA certificate is granted to those who pass a rigorous multipart examination and meet certain accounting experience and educational requirements.

Using a computer to improve efficiency . . .

Helping a small business with an inventory problem . . .

Attending a professional development class . . .

Learning about the operation of a hospital pharmacy . . .

Advising a client on financial matters . . .

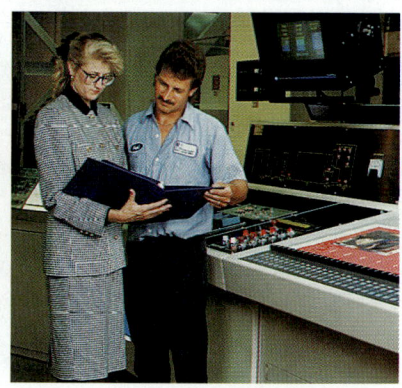

Explaining the features of newly installed, automated machinery . . .

EXHIBIT 1–2
A Day in the Life of an Accountant

Public accounting firms perform numerous services for their clients. Most often their work is in the fields of auditing, income tax, and management advisory services (MAS).

Auditing. Audit work represents the major source of business for most public accounting firms, particularly those organized on the national or international level. Auditing involves the investigation and examination of the transactions that underlie an organization's financial reports. The investigation is conducted by an auditor, who studies the controls that have been built into a client's information-processing system for purposes of error detection and fraud prevention. In addition, the auditor performs statistical tests on accounting data to verify the data's reasonableness.

A major purpose of the audit process is to increase the credibility of the financial statements (reports) prepared by a business. The statements are sent to the owners of the business, to financial analysts, and frequently to government agencies. These parties are very much concerned that the reports result in a neutral and complete presentation of the enterprise's financial activities. The employment of an *external independent* auditor, who performs certain investigative tasks, enhances this process.

Income Tax. Public accounting firms also perform income tax services. These services are somewhat specialized and include much more than the preparation and filing of tax returns. In fact, many of the mechanical procedures associated with tax returns have been computerized, thus eliminating considerable drudgery for the accountant.

Tax accountants must be well-versed in the many and often confusing tax laws. Not only do they determine the amount of taxes owed to federal, state, and local authorities, but tax accountants also ensure compliance with tax laws and plan for the future. They advise clients on various alternatives that might minimize taxes. The suggested courses of action are within the legal boundaries of the tax statutes and therefore center on techniques of tax avoidance, not tax evasion.

Management Advisory Services. Management advisory services (MAS) are the broadest of the services performed by public accounting firms. MAS essentially involve the operation of a management consulting practice for clients. Often the work is only indirectly related to traditional accounting matters, leading some of the larger firms to hire nonaccounting specialists for selected practice areas. Examples include physicians (if a firm has extensive involvement with hospitals), educators (if the firm does considerable work in university administration), computer experts, and engineers.

Listing all the advisory services performed by accountants is an impossible task. However, the following projects seem fairly representative: inventory control, analysis and design of information-processing systems, implementation of production-scheduling systems, cost analysis of lease-versus-buy alternatives, and assistance in product pricing.

PRIVATE ACCOUNTING

Private accounting, sometimes referred to as industrial accounting, is another major branch of the profession. Rather than perform accounting services for many different clients, a private accountant is employed by an individual business to provide services exclusively for that organization. As you can imagine, there is considerable variety within this field. Typical opportunities for employment include jobs with retailers, manufacturers (in such diverse industries as petroleum and filmmaking), and service enterprises (such as airlines, lending institutions, and ski resorts).

There are several other significant distinctions between public and private accounting. For instance, there is no specific licensing procedure for private accountants. (The only accounting "license" is the CPA.) Various programs have been designed, however, to measure competence in the private field. One of the most prominent is the *Certified Management Accountant* (CMA) program, which requires candidates to pass a broad two-day examination. This test covers such disciplines as managerial finance and economics, principles of organizational behavior, business ethics, financial and managerial accounting practices, and quantitative methods. Another program has been designed to measure proficiency in internal auditing. Individuals who pass an examination and meet certain work experience requirements may receive the *Certified Internal Auditor (CIA)* designation.

Much of the work performed in the private field can be subdivided into specialized areas, including the following.

Cost Accounting. Cost accounting, an important component of managerial accounting, deals with the collection, assignment, and interpretation of costs. Cost data are captured by an organization's information system and then assigned to various business segments and activities. Examples of such segments include territories, departments, and products. Activities, on the other hand, may encompass the inspection of manufactured goods, the design of a new advertising campaign, or the operation of a summer recreation program by a city. The purpose of the assignment process is to answer the age-old question, "How much does it cost?" Once cost is determined, management can proceed with an analysis of:

- Anticipated costs for various planning needs.
- Budgeted versus actual costs for control and evaluation.
- Relevant costs of different alternatives for use in decision making.
- Costs of producing goods and services for use in pricing and inventory valuation.

Internal Auditing. Large organizations often have their own personnel to review and monitor established accounting procedures and controls. The review process, which determines whether the procedures and controls are functioning as originally intended, helps to (1) safeguard the company's resources and (2) check the reliability and accuracy of the accounting information being produced. The individuals performing this work are known as internal auditors. Although their duties and responsibilities are similar to those of auditors employed in public accounting (i.e., external auditors), the internal-audit orientation is somewhat different. The internal auditor focuses mainly on controls and procedures. The independent external auditor, while also investigating accounting controls, is concerned primarily with the fairness of the financial statements that are prepared by a business.

Other Activities. Depending on size, many companies engage in accounting activities other than cost accounting and internal auditing. Larger businesses maintain separate *systems departments* to design the methods, procedures, and forms needed to process accounting data. Given our increasingly high-tech world, computers are almost always involved. In addition, many organizations have established *planning departments* that deal heavily with budgeting and forecasting. Finally, large businesses often operate their own *tax departments*. These departments offer in-house advice on various issues and engage in tax planning activities.

GOVERNMENTAL/NOT-FOR-PROFIT ACCOUNTING

The last major segment of the profession is composed of those accountants employed by governmental agencies and other not-for-profit organizations.

Like any business, the government has numerous financial and managerial accounting needs that must be satisfied. Records must be kept, reports prepared, monies accounted for, and operations controlled and reviewed. Governmental accountants assist in all of these tasks—at the local, state, and federal levels. Accountants are employed by the Federal Bureau of Investigation to gather evidence for use in fraud cases; by state regulatory agencies to review rate increase requests of public utility companies; and by the Internal Revenue Service to examine the millions of tax returns that are filed each year. The General Accounting Office (GAO) also employs accountants to assist in its evaluations of governmental programs and agencies. The GAO's work is extremely diverse, with recent efforts including an investigation of NASA's space shuttle program and a look at the effects of competition on airfares.

Not-for-profit enterprises other than the government also have a need for accountants. Hospitals, universities, and charitable organizations require budgets and controls. In addition, selected data must be computed for use in fund raising, and an evaluation must be made to determine whether resources are being used in an efficient and effective manner. The accountant is in an excellent position to perform these tasks and help the not-for-profit organization further its role in society.

KEY UNDERLYING CONCEPTS

3

Explain the use of accounting principles in financial reporting.

Earlier in the text we noted that accounting is supported by a set of underlying principles and concepts. These concepts are presented throughout the text, with an in-depth discussion contained in Chapter 14. At this particular time it is helpful to introduce the entity assumption and the principles of historical cost and objectivity. We will then expand our discussion to focus on an entity's "financial position" and its relevance to the fundamental accounting equation. In short, the following sections provide an introduction to the manner in which accounting measures financial activity.

ENTITY ASSUMPTION

The **entity assumption** holds that an organization must be viewed as a unit that is separate and apart from its owners and from other firms. If this assumption were not made, personal economic activities of the owners (e.g., the purchase of a home, the payment of a spouse's medical bill) would be merged with the transactions of their businesses, thus combining the affairs of two separate and distinct units. The resulting financial statements constructed to report the business's financial health and profitability would therefore not be meaningful.

The entity assumption also notes that a firm should be viewed aside and apart from other firms. Imagine the difficulty of performing a detailed analysis of the computer industry if the operations of IBM could not be distinguished from those of Apple. These are two separate units and their activities must be accounted for accordingly. The entity assumption thus requires segregated accounting systems and individual sets of financial records for each business enterprise.

There are three popular entity forms in this country. The simplest in structure is the **sole proprietorship,** which is a business owned by one individual. A step above the proprietorship is the **partnership**—an organization owned by two or more individuals and managed according to a contractual agreement among them. The third basic form of entity is the **corporation,** in which the owners are its stockholders. Most companies are operated as proprietorships;

accordingly, our initial discussions will focus on this widespread organizational form.

HISTORICAL-COST PRINCIPLE

Accounting is based on the **principle of historical cost.** This principle holds that purchases of goods, services, and other resources are initially entered in the accounting records at acquisition cost. For example, if Stadium Manufacturing pays $200,000 to purchase a parcel of land for use as a future plant site, the land is established in the records at $200,000. Further, if the company had financed the acquisition, not only would the land be set up at this amount, but the accounting records would also reveal a $200,000 bank loan (i.e., mortgage).

The use of historical cost, while beneficial in some respects, creates an interesting accounting problem. Entering a long-term resource in the accounting records at cost at the time of acquisition is satisfactory. Maintaining that resource over its lifetime at cost, however, can result in a severe misstatement of financial condition and profitability. Picture, for instance, what has happened to the real estate market in many parts of the country over the past 10 to 15 years. Prices have risen because of inflation and other factors; yet the historical-cost basis of accounting ignores these increases in valuation. As an example, suppose the land purchased for $200,000 is now worth $350,000. The land, nevertheless, will continue to be carried and reported at $200,000. Because of this treatment, the cost basis is criticized by many users of financial reports as not being in accord with economic reality.

Accountants have taken various steps over the years to compensate for this deficiency, including supplemental publication of selected inflation-adjusted data. Despite the problem with historical cost, it continues to serve as the primary valuation base in accounting. One of the underlying reasons is the objectivity principle.

OBJECTIVITY PRINCIPLE

Accountants strive to produce financial reports that are unbiased, thereby reducing (or eliminating) various user interpretations that may arise. One way of achieving this goal is to follow the **objectivity principle,** which holds that accounting measurements be both definite and verifiable. Although subject to some criticism, historical cost is said to meet these twin criteria.

Consider, for instance, the parcel of land in our earlier example that Stadium Manufacturing acquired for $200,000. The parcel may have cost the seller $110,000 and, at the time of Stadium's acquisition, may have been assessed for property taxes at $150,000. Further, the land may have been appraised by three independent appraisal services at $180,000, $210,000, and $230,000 to determine its "worth" when negotiations were about to occur. Which of these figures is correct? They all are. The cost of $200,000 was entered in Stadium's accounting records, however, because Stadium and the seller negotiated a transaction, agreeing that the land was to be exchanged at a price of $200,000. The use of definite cost figures helps to make accounting reports and information more objective. Conversely, appraisal or market figures can vary and often incorporate personal opinion and bias.

In addition to being definite, historical cost is also verifiable by financial experts. In our discussion of the accounting profession, we noted that auditors examine the financial reports of an enterprise to determine whether the reports result in a fair presentation of economic activity. The use of objective, cost-based information lends itself to this process. Evidence of the cost of goods, services, and resources normally exists in the form of contracts, accounting documents, and canceled checks. Furthermore, objective cost data allow different accountants who may be examining a complex transaction to reach essentially the same conclusions and report the same facts. When subjective market and appraisal values are used, this outcome would probably not occur.

A Music Consultant's Perspective

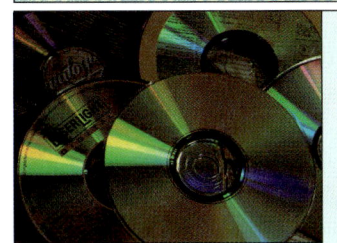

Determining Worth: Determining "worth" in the music business is a very difficult process. The cost of producing a master recording from which all copies are made can range from $100,000 to $1 million. Yet, the recording's actual value to the entity may be much more. Perhaps worth should be computed as some multiple of the tapes and CDs to be sold in the four to six months after release. Or perhaps worth is directly related to what's hot in the music industry and the artist's past history. But wait, past history is not always a good predictor of what the future will bring. Remember that Pearl Jam, Garth Brooks, Celine Dion, and Boyz II Men all had to start somewhere. So what's the true worth of the master recordings that tend to make or break the MCAs, Columbias, and Motowns of the world? Who knows?—it can be likened to the roll of the dice. That's why the historical-cost and objectivity principles make so much sense when preparing the financial statements of these firms and others.

Financial Position and the Entity

④ Define assets, liabilities, and owner's equity, and state the relationship of these components in the accounting equation.

Let us begin our study of the entity (and proprietorships) by focusing on a popular accounting concept called financial position. An entity's financial position reveals the resources owned by the business and the claims on those resources by specified parties at a particular point in time. The specified parties are the firm's creditors and owner, resulting in the relationship shown in Exhibit 1–3.

We will now expand on this relationship, which, in its shortened form, is commonly referred to as the fundamental accounting equation. The shortened form is:

NOTE   Assets = Liabilities + Owner's Equity

Assets

Note   Assets are the economic resources owned by a company that are expected to benefit future time periods. These resources are controlled by the entity and have arisen from past transactions and events.

EXHIBIT 1–3
Financial Position

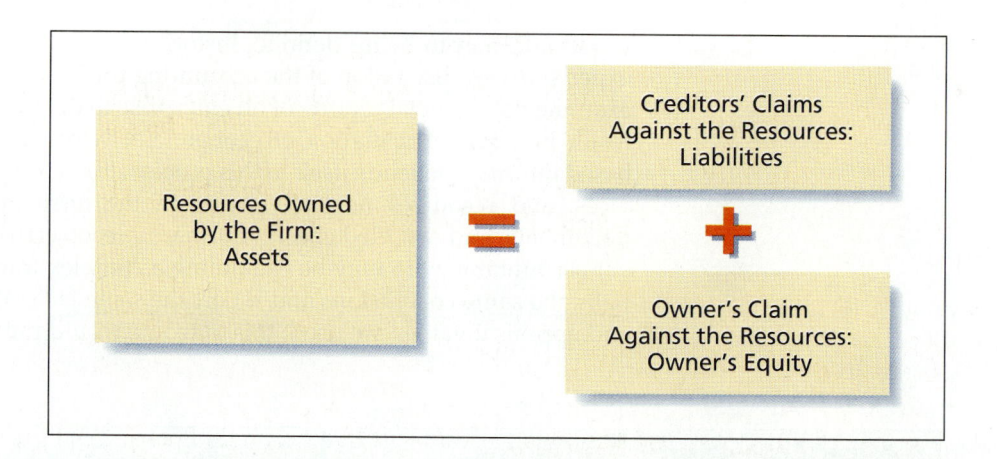

Resources Owned by the Firm: Assets = Creditors' Claims Against the Resources: Liabilities + Owner's Claim Against the Resources: Owner's Equity

An organization can possess many different types of assets. Some assets, such as the cash that a business has on hand and in the bank, inventories of goods maintained for sale, buildings, land, and equipment, have a definite physical existence. In contrast, other business resources lack physical substance but are able to provide benefits because they represent valuable legal rights and/or claims. Two examples are patents and receivables.

A patent, which is granted by the federal government, gives its owner the exclusive right to manufacture, use, and sell a particular product or process. Receivables, on the other hand, are the amounts that a business expects to collect on some future date. The most commonly encountered receivable, *accounts receivable,* represents the amounts due a company from its customers. This asset generally arises from the sale, on credit, of goods and services.

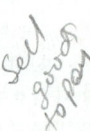

LIABILITIES

The economic obligations of an entity are known as **liabilities.** Such obligations are owed to creditors and, like assets, are created from a variety of past transactions and events. Consider, for instance, that many businesses buy goods and services on credit, with the amounts owed to be paid on a future date. These transactions give rise to a liability known as *accounts payable*. In addition, an entity may borrow funds via a loan (thereby creating a loan payable) and use the funds to acquire equipment, expand a warehouse, or purchase other assets.

Still other liabilities arise when a company has obligated itself to pay certain costs connected with normal business activities. Suppose, for example, that on December 31, the Hernandez Company owes $2,000 of employee salaries, $500 of interest, and $300 for payroll taxes. Assuming that all amounts will be paid on some future date, the company's accounting records at the end of the year would reveal liabilities entitled salaries payable, interest payable, and payroll taxes payable.

Businesses that use credit too liberally sometimes find that a liability's future settlement date approaches more quickly than desired. In other words, the obligation comes due, but the paying firm may be strapped for cash. In such cases the creditors, because they have a legal claim against the firm, can force the sale of business assets to satisfy the amounts due. As shown in the above diagram, it should now be clear that liabilities represent creditor claims against an entity's resources.

Owner's Equity

Owner's equity, or **capital,** represents the owner's stake or "interest" in the assets of a business. It is equal to the company's *net assets* (i.e., assets minus liabilities).

The concept of owner's equity is best explained by resetting the accounting equation in the following format:

NOTE

$$\text{Assets} - \text{Liabilities} = \text{Owner's Equity}$$

Assume for a moment that Colorado Enterprises has assets of $50,000 and liabilities of $30,000, resulting in $20,000 ($50,000 – $30,000) of owner's equity. These figures indicate that the firm has resources that amount to $50,000 and creditor claims against those resources of $30,000. As noted earlier, should Colorado experience financial difficulties and be unable to settle its obligations, the creditors can force the sale of business assets. Law dictates that distributions be made first to the creditors, with any remaining amounts going to the owner. The owner, then, is said to have a $20,000 *residual* interest in the assets of the entity.

A Further Focus

Owner's equity is the mathematical difference between total assets and total liabilities, nothing more, nothing less. Many people are under the impression that equity is equivalent to cash, to be used for future spending and acquisitions. This notion is incorrect; there is *no* direct relationship between this amount and a company's cash balances.

A Closer Look at Owner's Equity

The three components of the accounting equation—assets, liabilities, and owner's equity—change throughout the year in response to various transactions and events. To illustrate, assume the following data apply to Mansfield Builders as of December 31, 19X1:

Assets	$100,000
Liabilities	$ 30,000
Owner's equity	70,000
Total liabilities & owner's equity	$100,000

Suppose that Mansfield desires to purchase a new machine that costs $25,000. Because of insufficient cash balances, the company has arranged to finance the purchase by obtaining a $25,000 loan from the equipment dealer. This transaction results in the following figures.

Assets ($100,000 + $25,000)	$125,000
Liabilities ($30,000 + $25,000)	$ 55,000
Owner's equity	70,000
Total liabilities & owner's equity	$125,000

Assets have increased because of the machine, while liabilities have risen from the loan. Notice, however, that owner's equity has remained at $70,000. We can conclude that any transaction or event that affects both assets *and* liabilities by an equal amount has no impact on owner's equity. Similarly, a transaction that affects *only* assets (such as an acquisition of machinery for a cash payment) or *only* liabilities will leave owner's equity intact. What, then, causes this third component of the accounting equation to rise or fall?

Owner's equity will change during a time period because of four factors:

> **5** Recognize the four factors that cause owner's equity to change: owner investments, owner withdrawals, revenues, and expenses.

FACTOR	IMPACT ON OWNER'S EQUITY
Investments by the owner	Increase
Withdrawals by the owner	Decrease
Revenues	Increase
Expenses	Decrease

INVESTMENTS BY THE OWNER

The owner of an enterprise often takes personal assets and puts (invests) them in a business. Since the investment causes company assets to increase, the owner's net "interest" or equity in these assets will also increase.

WITHDRAWALS BY THE OWNER

A withdrawal is just the opposite of an investment; the owner is removing assets from the business (usually cash) for personal use. Withdrawals therefore decrease the equity of the owner in the firm's assets.

REVENUES

Businesses pursue a variety of activities in an attempt to earn a profit. Such profit-related activities give rise to **revenues,** which are the amounts charged to customers for goods sold or services rendered. These amounts cause owner's equity to increase and, as the following list shows, may take many different forms.

ENTITY	REVENUE FORM
Toys "R" Us, Inc.	Toy sales revenue
Ryder System, Inc.	Vehicle-leasing revenue
Minnesota Vikings Football Club	Ticket revenue
Law firm	Fees earned

EXPENSES

Expenses are the costs of items and services consumed in producing revenue. Examples of expenses include the salaries and wages incurred for employee compensation, utility costs related to the use of natural gas and electricity, advertising, repairs, taxes, and interest costs on loans. Expenses, which cause owner's equity to decline, are logically called the costs of doing business—that is, the costs that arise from attracting and keeping customers.

A careful study of the preceding examples reveals the absence of owner withdrawals. Expenses *must* be related to the revenue-generating process of the firm. Withdrawals, in contrast, arise from a totally different situation (i.e., the personal use of business assets by the owner).

A FURTHER FOCUS

Revenues and expenses should not be equated with the cash inflows and outflows of a firm. Consider, for instance, that a company may receive cash from its owner as an investment or pay cash to acquire land (an asset). Both of these transactions affect cash; in neither case, however, is any revenue or expense involved.

Net Income/Net Loss. The revenues and expenses of a business are periodically compared to measure operating success or failure. Revenues in excess of expenses give rise to **net income**. When an individual states that a company is "making (earning) money," he or she normally means that a net income is being generated.

Companies do not always operate in a profitable manner, perhaps because of a lack of cost control or a depressed economy. Operating in an unprofitable manner means that expenses exceed revenues, creating a **net loss.**

THE ACCOUNTING EQUATION: AN EXTENDED ILLUSTRATION

6

Describe the impact of various transactions on the accounting equation.

To tie together a number of the concepts introduced in this chapter, we will focus on the activities of Vista Transit. Vista, a small proprietorship that provides charter transportation in the town of Oceanside, was founded on January 2 of the current year. The following sections describe the firm's January transactions and show their effect on the accounting equation.

Investment by the Owner—Ted Barto began the operation of Vista Transit on January 2 by investing $40,000 in the firm. As a result of this transaction, the company now has an asset, Cash, of $40,000. In addition, Barto has obtained a $40,000 interest (i.e., owner's equity) in the firm's assets. The items that affect owner's equity are listed individually beneath the column heading for clarity.

	Assets	=	Liabilities	+	Owner's Equity	
					(+) Investments	(+) Revenues
Date	Cash				(−) Withdrawals	(−) Expenses
1/2	+$40,000				+$40,000	

Purchase of Assets for Cash—Vista acquired two used vans for the business at a total cost of $34,000 on January 6. The company paid cash, thereby decreasing its remaining funds to $6,000 ($40,000 − $34,000). Notice, however, that this transaction merely shifts dollar amounts from one asset to another, leaving the total assets intact at $40,000.

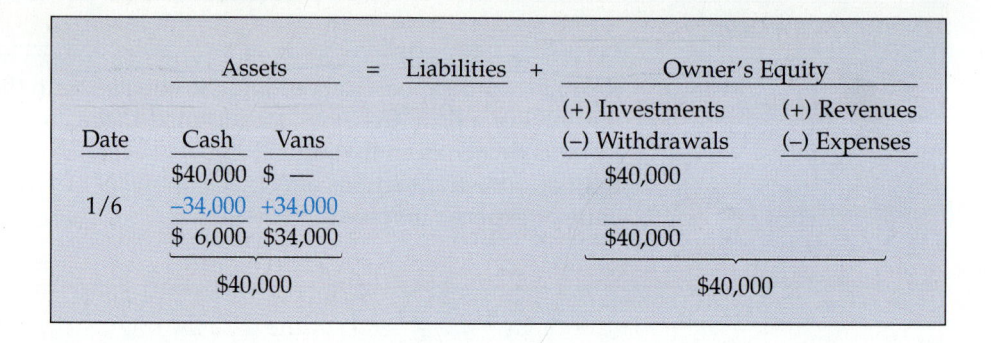

	Assets		=	Liabilities	+	Owner's Equity	
						(+) Investments	(+) Revenues
Date	Cash	Vans				(−) Withdrawals	(−) Expenses
	$40,000	$ —				$40,000	
1/6	−34,000	+34,000					
	$ 6,000	$34,000				$40,000	
	$40,000					$40,000	

Generation of Revenue on Account—The firm completed two charter trips on January 12 and billed clients a total of $1,700. This transaction is representative of Vista's earnings process, causing an increase in total revenue (and owner's equity) for the entity. Furthermore, the clients have been billed and will pay at a later date. An asset, Accounts Receivable, has therefore been created because Vista has a claim against these individuals. This type of transaction is commonly known as a sale of services on account.

	Assets			=	Liabilities	+	Owner's Equity	
		Accounts					(+) Investments	(+) Revenues
Date	Cash	Receivable	Vans				(−) Withdrawals	(−) Expenses
	$6,000	$ —	$34,000				$40,000	$ —
1/12		+1,700						+1,700 (Charter revenue)
	$6,000	$1,700	$34,000				$40,000	$1,700
	$41,700						$41,700	

Note: Assets are normally listed in the following order: cash, near-cash assets (e.g., receivables), and long-term resources (such as the vans). Typically, items that fall in the long-term category are sequenced in descending order of their productive lives—land first, then buildings, equipment, and so forth.

Recognition of Expense on Account—Westside Auto performed miscellaneous repairs on one of the vans on January 16. The repairs amounted to $750; Vista agreed to pay the balance due in 30 days. This transaction involves an increase in Vista's liabilities (Accounts Payable) because of the balance owed to the repair shop. In addition, $750 of expense must be recognized, which reduces owner's equity.

	Assets			=	Liabilities	+	Owner's Equity	
Date	Cash	Accounts Receivable	Vans		Accounts Payable		(+) Investments (−) Withdrawals	(+) Revenues (−) Expenses
	$6,000	$1,700	$34,000		$ — +750		$40,000	$1,700 −750 (Repairs)
1/16	$6,000	$1,700	$34,000		$750		$40,000	$ 950
		$41,700					$41,700	

Collection of Accounts Receivable—A $600 check from a client who was previously billed on January 12 arrived in the mail of January 21. Is this revenue for Vista? The answer is no. Vista performed the service earlier in the month, and revenue was recorded at the time the billing took place. To record the $600 again as revenue would result in a double counting. The client is paying the balance due, requiring a reduction in Accounts Receivable. This type of transaction is frequently referred to as a receipt on account.

	Assets			=	Liabilities	+	Owner's Equity	
Date	Cash	Accounts Receivable	Vans		Accounts Payable		(+) Investments (−) Withdrawals	(+) Revenues (−) Expenses
	$6,000	$1,700	$34,000		$750		$40,000	$950
1/21	+600	−600						
	$6,600	$1,100	$34,000		$750		$40,000	$950
		$41,700					$41,700	

Payment of Accounts Payable—Vista paid $400 to Westside Auto on January 27, partial payment for the repairs performed on January 16. The repairs were initially established as a liability, to be paid on a future date. Because payment is now occurring, the related account payable must be reduced. Transactions of this nature are commonly known as payments on account.

	Assets			=	Liabilities	+		Owner's Equity	
Date	Cash	Accounts Receivable	Vans		Accounts Payable		(+) Investments (−) Withdrawals		(+) Revenues (−) Expenses
	$6,600	$1,100	$34,000		$750		$40,000		$950
1/27	−400				−400				
	$6,200	$1,100	$34,000		$350		$40,000		$950
		$41,300						$41,300	

Payment of Expenses—On January 29, Vista paid $500 to its drivers, subdivided as follows: John Warren, $300; Ben Richards, $200. Each driver earned $200 of wages during the month. Warren received an extra $100 to cover the cost of advertising materials that he designed and distributed to Oceanside residents. The wage and advertising expenditures are expenses for Vista—costs incurred to generate revenue.

	Assets			=	Liabilities	+		Owner's Equity	
Date	Cash	Accounts Receivable	Vans		Accounts Payable		(+) Investments (−) Withdrawals		(+) Revenues (−) Expenses
	$6,200	$1,100	$34,000		$350		$40,000		$950
1/29	−300								−200 (Wages)
									−100 (Advertising)
	−200								−200 (Wages)
	$5,700	$1,100	$34,000		$350		$40,000		$450
		$40,800						$40,800	

Sale of an Asset—Because of the entry of a new competitor in the Oceanside market, Vista decided to sell one of its vans on January 30. The van, acquired on January 6 for $14,000, was sold to a charter client for the same amount. The client paid Vista $10,000 down, with the balance owed to be remitted in two weeks. This transaction affects three different assets, calling for an increase to both Cash and Accounts Receivable and a decrease to Vans.

	Assets			=	Liabilities	+		Owner's Equity	
Date	Cash	Accounts Receivable	Vans		Accounts Payable		(+) Investments (−) Withdrawals		(+) Revenues (−) Expenses
	$ 5,700	$1,100	$34,000		$350		$40,000		$450
1/30	+10,000	+4,000	−14,000						
	$15,700	$5,100	$20,000		$350		$40,000		$450
		$40,800						$40,800	

Withdrawal by the Owner—Ted Barto withdrew $250 from the company on January 31 to meet personal living expenses. This $250 outlay results in a reduction of both Cash and owner's equity.

		Assets		=	Liabilities	+	Owner's Equity	
Date	Cash	Accounts Receivable	Vans		Accounts Payable		(+) Investments (−) Withdrawals	(+) Revenues (−) Expenses
	$15,700	$5,100	$20,000		$350		$40,000	$450
1/31	−250						−250	
	$15,450	$5,100	$20,000		$350		$39,750	$450
		$40,550					$40,550	

One final point is needed before we leave this illustration. As you have seen, business transactions affect the accounting equation in many different ways. Assets, liabilities, and owner's equity can each remain the same or change; there are numerous possibilities. Stated bluntly (and honestly), if your approach to learning this and later material is memorization, you will be fighting a losing battle. *Successful accounting students are those who develop the abilities to reason and analyze, not memorize.*

FINANCIAL STATEMENTS

7

Demonstrate a working knowledge of the information revealed by the four basic financial statements.

Owners, managers, lenders, and analysts use accounting information for a variety of purposes. Much of this information is contained within formal financial reports that are prepared and distributed by companies. These reports are commonly referred to as financial statements.

The financial statements prepared by a business reveal various insights about the entity's operations and financial position, with one of the most important disclosures being net income. Most businesses are organized with a profit objective and strive to generate a return for their owners. Income measurement is a complex task; at this point you should understand that income is probably the single most important barometer of economic success and of utmost interest to financial statement users.

In addition to profit generation, companies seek to maintain a healthy financial position. This means that an entity has the ability to pay its debts when due, along with the potential of generating future positive cash flows. Statement users therefore pay close attention to a firm's cash and near-cash assets in relation to the amounts owed to creditors. Put simply, if a company is unable to meet its maturing obligations, the firm's survival as an ongoing entity could be threatened.

An entity's financial information is disclosed via four financial statements (and accompanying footnotes): the income statement, statement of owner's equity, balance sheet, and statement of cash flows.

INCOME STATEMENT

The **income statement** summarizes the results of operations by disclosing an entity's net income or net loss. This statement, like its counterparts, is divided into two sections: heading and body. The heading reveals the company's name, the name of the statement, and the period of time covered by the statement. The period is usually a month, a quarter, or a year. The statement's body contains detailed accounting information, in this case an itemized listing of revenues and expenses.

The income statement for Vista Transit appears at the top of Exhibit 1–4. Observe how the statement is developed from the right-most column of the extended illustration (pp. 17–21). Because revenues exceeded expenses, the business was profitable during its first month of activity.

STATEMENT OF OWNER'S EQUITY

The **statement of owner's equity** discloses the causes of change in owner's equity during the accounting period. Owner investments, owner withdrawals, and net income/loss—the last item being a "summary" of the entity's revenues and expenses—therefore comprise the heart of this financial report. Vista's statement of owner's equity appears in the middle of Exhibit 1–4. The January 31 balance of $40,200 will carry over to become the beginning owner's equity balance on February 1, 19XX.

BALANCE SHEET

The **balance sheet** focuses on a measure that was introduced earlier in the chapter. By revealing the resources owned by the entity and the claims on those resources by the creditors and owner of the business, the statement's emphasis is on financial position. Appropriately, the balance sheet is sometimes called the statement of financial position.

To be more specific, the balance sheet is a formal listing of the accounting equation's components: assets, liabilities, and owner's equity. This financial report shows that the sum of the individual equity interests, the owner's and creditors', is equal to and in balance with the firm's assets; that is, assets = liabilities + owner's equity. This equality is shown for some particular *point* in time. The statement's heading therefore reflects a single date rather than a time period.

The balance sheet of Vista Transit, which appears at the bottom of Exhibit 1–4, is based on the January 31 final balances of the accounting equation illustration (see p. 21), with one minor exception. So that the information already contained in the income statement and statement of owner's equity is not duplicated, the January 31 (ending) owner's equity balance is reported as a single amount labeled Ted Barto, Capital.

STATEMENT OF CASH FLOWS

As shown in Exhibit 1–5, the **statement of cash flows** summarizes the receipts and payments from a company's income-generating, investing, and financing activities. Being a new business, Vista started the month with a zero cash balance. January's receipts and payments produced a net cash increase and

EXHIBIT 1-4
Income Statement, Statement of Owner's Equity, and Balance Sheet for Vista Transit

VISTA TRANSIT
Income Statement
For the Month Ended January 31, 19XX

Charter revenue		$ 1,700
Less expenses		
Repairs	$ 750	
Wages	400	
Advertising	100	
Total expenses		1,250
Net income		$ 450

VISTA TRANSIT
Statement of Owner's Equity
For the Month Ended January 31, 19XX

Beginning balance, Jan. 1		$ —
Increases		
Owner investments	$40,000	
Net income	450	40,450
		$40,450
Decreases		
Owner withdrawals		250
Ending balance, Jan. 31		$40,200

VISTA TRANSIT
Balance Sheet
January 31, 19XX

ASSETS	
Cash	$15,450
Accounts receivable	5,100
Vans	20,000
Total assets	$40,550
LIABILITIES	
Accounts payable	$ 350
OWNER'S EQUITY	
Ted Barto, capital	40,200
Total liabilities & owner's equity	$40,550

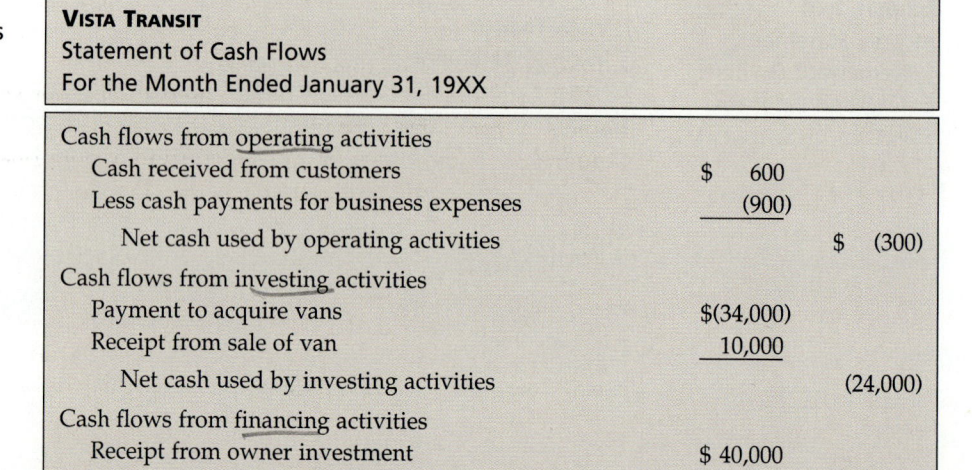

EXHIBIT 1–5
Statement of Cash Flows for Vista Transit

VISTA TRANSIT
Statement of Cash Flows
For the Month Ended January 31, 19XX

Cash flows from operating activities		
Cash received from customers	$ 600	
Less cash payments for business expenses	(900)	
Net cash used by operating activities		$ (300)
Cash flows from investing activities		
Payment to acquire vans	$(34,000)	
Receipt from sale of van	10,000	
Net cash used by investing activities		(24,000)
Cash flows from financing activities		
Receipt from owner investment	$ 40,000	
Payment for owner withdrawal	(250)	
Net cash provided by financing activities		39,750
Net increase (decrease) in cash		$ 15,450
Cash balance, January 1, 19XX		—
Cash balance, January 31, 19XX		$ 15,450

Note: Parentheses denote cash outflows (i.e., decreases).

$15,450 of cash as of January 31. (Notice that this same ending figure is reported on the firm's balance sheet.)

Our discussion here has been intentionally brief, as the statement's underlying details are covered in a later chapter. It is more important to focus on the information revealed and realize that cash flow is the heart of a business. Without cash a company cannot operate. This key report therefore monitors an entity's "pulse" and financial health, allowing users to study the leading sources of funds and the funds' ultimate use.

A FURTHER FOCUS

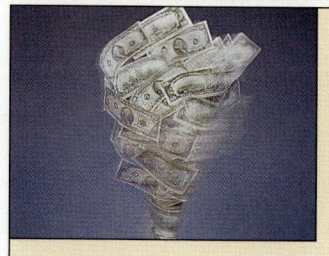

The owner investment was Vista's major source of funding; conversely, investing activities and daily operations consumed cash. Such a pattern of inflows and outflows is typical for a new business, given that significant resources must be acquired and credit customers sometimes take several months to settle their balances due. New ventures are cash-hungry creatures that "must be fed" (i.e., financed) if they are expected to survive.

STATEMENT INTERRELATIONSHIPS

The four statements that we discussed are distinct, with each presenting different types of financial information. Although they do differ, the statements are also interrelated. The income statement furnishes the necessary net income figure for the statement of owner's equity, which, in turn, provides the ending capital amount for the balance sheet.

The statements are also interrelated in another sense. The balance sheet depicts a company's financial position as of a specific date; for example, January 31 in the Vista Transit illustration. Going one step further, the company would subsequently prepare an income statement and a statement of owner's equity for February to disclose monthly activity. To complete the reporting cycle, a new balance sheet would be constructed as of February 28. It is apparent, then, that the income statement and the statement of owner's equity bridge the gap between successive balance sheets when reporting financial information. The same can be said for the statement of cash flows, which presents a detailed look at the change in cash from one balance sheet to the next.

ETHICS AND ACCOUNTING

8
Recognize various ethical issues faced by accountants.

ETHICS ISSUE

Should an accountant accept a financial-reporting assignment that requires skills beyond his or her present level of expertise?

In today's society, it is not uncommon to pick up a newspaper or magazine and be faced with stories that report on a variety of moral issues. Many of these issues deal directly or indirectly with business. Consider, for instance, the 20-year dedicated employee who embezzled $450,000 from a local employer; Sears, which was found guilty of overcharging customers for car repairs; and Jim Bakker, the television evangelist who served prison time for fraud and conspiracy. These examples have a common underlying theme: they all focus on unethical behavior. Ethics is a broad set of moral principles that groups adopt as behavior standards. Such standards are especially important to accountants, given the reliance that investors place on publicly reported financial figures.

Preparation of financial statements (and other reports as well) requires that competent professionals exercise due care. Yet competence and due care are not sufficient to ensure the complete integrity of a company's reporting function. For instance, transactions may be purposely manipulated and records falsified to achieve personal gains—all by qualified, meticulous employees. More is needed, perhaps because of a change in the way that business is conducted.

A CHANGING ENVIRONMENT

The business environment of the 1990s is quite different from that of earlier years. The economy tends to be more volatile, and there is a general decay in cultural values. Many companies are now engaging in global trade, conducted in an international arena where ethical standards sometimes differ from those practiced in America. Also, as one ethics specialist notes:

> Within industry, concentration on short-term results has placed ethical pressures on accountants and businesses to compromise long-term productivity and gain in order to "maximize the bottom line." Managers at all levels seem to be "seeking the quick buck" instead of considering the long-term profitability of their companies.[4]

[4] W. Steve Albrecht, ed., *Ethical Issues in the Practice of Accounting,* South-Western Publishing Co., Cincinnati, 1992, p. v.

Turning to the CPA profession, that same specialist goes on to observe an increasing degree of competitiveness among accounting firms. The dynamics of the environment are accompanied by greater pressures to attract new clients and achieve operating efficiencies. These actions are often realized through the respective implementation of new pricing/promotion strategies and cost containment programs.

Employees frequently need help when operating in pressure-filled conditions, especially if they are trying to satisfy conflicting goals and objectives. Many businesses and professions have therefore adopted an assortment of ethics practices to help guide personnel when making decisions. These practices range from the creation of an ethics "hotline," where an employee can discuss an ethical dilemma in total confidence, to published codes of conduct.

A Case Study

An example of an ethics code is that implemented by General Dynamics, an engineering-based manufacturer that does considerable work for the military and government.[5] The firm's program has three goals: to support individual employees in their daily business conduct; to enhance the administrative performance of the company in basic business relationships; and to build a bond of trust between the company and its customers, suppliers, shareholders, and the communities in which it functions.

General Dynamics has established a series of broad-reaching standards to achieve these goals. Several of the standards follow.

- *Company resources*—Company resources (e.g., patents, buildings, equipment, telephones, computers, cash, and the time and skills of employees) are to be properly used for business purposes. Unauthorized personal use of these resources is not permitted.
- *Gifts, favors, and other items of value to customers*—The company competes solely on the merits of its products and services. Under no circumstances may employees offer or give anything of value to a customer to improperly influence a contract award or other favorable customer action.
- *Information and technology*—Information and technology developed, owned, or entrusted to the company are to be carefully safeguarded against unauthorized disclosure.
- *Inside information*—Individuals who possess significant inside information, which has not been disclosed, must abstain from trading [in the stock of General Dynamics]. A typical example of such information is knowledge about large acquisitions or sales of company assets.
- *Suppliers and consultants*—Source selection, negotiation, determination of awards, and administration of purchasing activities are to be constructed fairly and honestly. Materials, consulting work, and services are to be procured from qualified suppliers based on low cost, high quality, acceptable performance, and the ability to meet schedule.

[5] See *The General Dynamics Ethics Program Update* (1988) and *General Dynamics Standards of Business Ethics and Conduct, Third Edition* (1993). Both of these items are published by General Dynamics Corporation, Falls Church, Virginia.

ETHICAL CHALLENGES FOR THE ACCOUNTANT

Accountants, through certain professional organizations, have developed ethical standards that pertain to financial record keeping and reporting. For example, all accountants should be objective, maintain a high degree of integrity, and not knowingly misrepresent facts to others. In addition, acts should not be committed that reflect poorly on the profession.

As discussed earlier in this chapter, accountants may be employed in such diverse areas as public accounting, industry, and government. Those involved in public practice are faced with the further ethical issue of *independence,* which requires that the accountant be free from the influence of others when performing his or her duties. This standard helps to protect the public interest and must be maintained in both fact and appearance. Certain activities that may impair independence would include an accountant having a financial interest in a company for which he or she provides services; an accountant having a relative in a high-level management position with a client organization; and an accountant serving as trustee of a client organization.

Ethics also affects the managerial accountant, who faces the challenge of balancing a commitment to a particular employer with the ethical rules of the profession. As an employee, the managerial accountant has a direct financial interest in a company as the source of his or her well-being (e.g., salary, fringe benefit plans, and so forth). Consider the difficulty that would arise for the accountant when, in complying with ethical standards of the profession, the financial security of the company is endangered. This situation could occur if the accountant discloses that the employer-firm is in violation of the terms of a major loan agreement (such as the maintenance of certain financial ratios). The loan's due date could be accelerated, forcing the company to settle any outstanding balances immediately. For many businesses this action might lead to bankruptcy (and eventual unemployment for the "whistle-blower").

A CONCLUDING COMMENT: THE ETHICAL INDIVIDUAL

Most individuals are highly ethical. They are honest, loyal, fair, and caring; are responsible citizens; have integrity as well as respect for others; and pursue excellence.[6] Yet when bonuses, promotions, and jobs are at stake, employees will occasionally take desperate actions to improve reported income, financial position, and/or their own well-being.

As you will see throughout the text, accounting is not always black and white. Some variation is present, and employee judgment is needed. Codes of conduct will do little to guide individuals who lack the basic characteristics cited in the preceding paragraph. Stated simply, no set of standards can ensure the ethical behavior of all participants. In the effort to maximize return, companies must therefore pursue upstanding employees—those who can overcome accompanying job pressures to practice their professions in an objective, moral way.

[6] See "The Need for Ethics Education in Accounting" by Michael Josephson in W. Steve Albrecht, ed., *Ethical Issues in the Practice of Accounting,* pp. 1–20.

> **WHO'S THE MOST ETHICAL?**
> A nationwide survey of business people ranked the corporate ethics of various professions or occupations in the following order:
>
> 1. Accountants
> 2. Dentists
> 3. Doctors
> 4. Officers of large corporations
> 5. Public relations practitioners
> 6. Lawyers
> 7. Funeral home operators
> 8. Advertising practitioners
> 9. TV repairmen
> 10. Realtors
> 11. Newspaper reporters
> 12. Stockbrokers
> 13. Union leaders
> 14. Politicians
> 15. TV evangelists
> 16. Used car salesmen
>
> Source: "Ethics Survey Ranks Accountants First," *Journal of Accountancy*, October 1989, p. 110.

END-OF-CHAPTER REVIEW

LEARNING OBJECTIVES: THE KEY POINTS

1. **Identify the users, uses, and limitations of accounting information.** Many groups use accounting information, including owners, creditors, managers, government agencies, financial analysts, employees, and labor unions. These groups study a company's earnings, the ability of an organization to settle its debts on a timely basis, the progress of a business toward meeting stated objectives, and other key issues. The information under review, however, suffers from certain inherent limitations. Accounting, for example, is based on various estimates, assumptions, and subjective judgments. It also lacks the ability to express all events in monetary terms and sometimes fails to portray true value.

2. **Describe the accounting profession and identify accounting-related careers.** The profession and its career options tend to be segmented into public, private, and governmental/not-for-profit accounting. Public accountants render accounting services, such as external auditing, tax planning, and management consulting, to other businesses. In private accounting, an individual provides accounting services for a specific organization, with the work often centering on cost accounting or internal auditing. Finally, individuals employed by not-for-profit organizations typically work for the government, hospitals, universities, and charitable institutions.

3. **Explain the use of accounting principles in financial reporting.** Because of the wide variety of businesses in our economy, some standardization is necessary when reporting to external parties. Financial accounting is therefore governed by a set of accounting principles that includes the monetary unit assumption, the entity assumption, and the principles of historical cost and objectivity. The monetary unit assumption holds that only events and activities measurable in dollars are recognized in a company's accounting records. The entity assumption holds that a business be viewed as a unit that is separate and distinct from its owners and from other businesses. There are three types of business entities: sole proprietorships, partnerships, and corporations. The historical-cost principle requires that goods, services, and other resources be entered in the accounting records at acquisition cost. This

procedure results in an objective valuation amount at the time of acquisition; however, the meaningfulness of cost-based amounts can deteriorate over time, especially in inflationary economies. Historical cost is consistent with the objectivity principle, which holds that accounting valuations be definite and verifiable.

4. **Define assets, liabilities, and owner's equity, and state the relationship of these components in the accounting equation.** Assets are the economic resources of a firm that are expected to benefit future time periods. Typical examples of assets include cash, land, buildings, inventories, and equipment. Certain parties have claims on these resources. Liabilities, for instance, measure the claims on the resources by creditors. In contrast, the owner's equity is the owner's stake or "interest" in the assets of the business. The three components are related, as shown by the accounting equation: assets = liabilities + owner's equity.

5. **Recognize the four factors that cause owner's equity to change: owner investments, owner withdrawals, revenues, and expenses.** An investment by the owner occurs when the owner relinquishes personal assets to the business. Such an event causes the owner's equity of an entity to increase. Conversely, an owner may remove assets from a business for personal use, causing owner's equity to fall. Owner's equity will also change as a result of revenues and expenses. Revenues, which increase owner's equity, are the amounts charged to customers for goods sold or services provided. In contrast, expenses are the costs incurred to produce revenues (e.g., salaries, advertising, utilities, and other similar items) and thus decrease equity. If revenues exceed expenses, a net income is generated; the opposite case creates a net loss.

6. **Describe the impact of various transactions on the accounting equation.** A company's transactions and events affect the accounting equation in many different ways. The purchase of an asset on account, for example, will increase both assets and liabilities. The acquisition of that same asset for cash, however, will leave total assets, liabilities, and owner's equity unchanged. Finally, a withdrawal of cash out of the business will decrease both assets and owner's equity. Memorization of the impact of these transactions and events should not be attempted. Instead, it is best to analyze the ultimate effect on the equation's components.

7. **Demonstrate a working knowledge of the information revealed by the four basic financial statements.** The income statement reveals an entity's revenues and expenses (and associated net income or net loss) for a particular period of time. The statement of owner's equity shows the amount of change in owner's equity during the same time period covered by the income statement. This change is caused by the firm's revenues and expenses, which appear in the summarized form of net income (or loss), owner investments, and owner withdrawals. The balance sheet details a company's assets and liabilities as of a specific date. As its name implies, this financial statement shows that the sum of the assets is equal to and in balance with the individual equity interests, that is, assets = liabilities + owner's equity. Finally, the statement of cash flows reveals the inflows and outflows associated with income-generating, investing, and financing activities.

8. **Recognize various ethical issues faced by accountants.** Many accountants work in businesses that focus on short-term results at the sacrifice of long-run profitability. Under certain conditions these individuals may be faced with situations that compromise their independence, loyalty, and integrity. Such situations may include the use of company assets for personal gain, bribes, access to sensitive information, and falsification of facts when completing a task.

Key Terms and Concepts: A Quick Overview

accounting A set of theories, concepts, and techniques that collectively measure, summarize, and report financial information about an economic unit. (p. 3)

accounting equation A mathematical relationship: Assets = Liabilities + Owner's Equity. (p. 13)

assets The economic resources owned by a company that are expected to benefit future time periods. (p. 13)

auditing The investigation and examination of transactions that underlie an organization's financial statements. (p. 8)

balance sheet A financial statement that presents a firm's assets, liabilities, and owner's equity at a particular point in time. (p. 22)

bookkeeping A discipline heavily involved with record keeping and various mechanical tasks. (p. 7)

certified public accountant (CPA) An individual who is licensed by a state to practice public accounting. (p. 7)

corporation A form of business organization where ownership is in the hands of investors who have acquired shares of the company's stock. (p. 11)

cost accounting An area of accounting that deals with the collection, assignment, control, and evaluation of costs. (p. 10)

entity assumption An assumption that a business is viewed as a unit that is separate and apart from its owners and from other firms. (p. 11)

ethics A broad set of moral practices that groups follow as behavior standards. (p. 25)

expenses The costs incurred in producing revenues. (p. 17)

financial accounting An area of accounting concerned primarily with external reporting—that is, reporting the results of financial activities to parties outside the firm. (p. 5)

Financial Accounting Standards Board (FASB) The private sector organization presently in charge of formulating standards of financial reporting in the United States. (p. 6)

financial position A determination of the resources owned by a company and the claims on those resources at a particular point in time. (p. 13)

financial statements Financial reports that are compiled and distributed by companies. (p. 21)

historical-cost principle The principle of recording goods, resources, and services acquired at cost. (p. 12)

income statement A financial statement that summarizes the results of a company's operation for a given time period by disclosing the revenues earned and the expenses incurred. (p. 22)

internal auditors Individuals in large organizations who review and monitor the organization's accounting procedures and controls. (p. 10)

liabilities Debts that are owed by an enterprise. (p. 14)

management advisory services (MAS) "Consulting" services performed by public accounting firms that are often unrelated to traditional accounting matters. (p. 9)

managerial accounting An area of accounting oriented toward reporting the results of operations to managers and other interested parties within an organization. (p. 5)

monetary unit assumption An assumption whereby only those events and activities measurable in dollars are entered in a company's accounting system. (p. 6)

net income The excess of a company's revenues over expenses for a given time period. (p. 17)

net loss The excess of a company's expenses over revenues for a given time period. (p. 17)

objectivity principle   A principle requiring that accounting information be free from bias and verifiable by an independent party, such as an external auditor. (p. 12)

owner investments   Personal assets put into a business by the owner. The owner is relinquishing asset control and ownership to the enterprise. (p. 16)

owner withdrawals   The removal of assets from the business by the owner for personal use. (p. 16)

owner's equity (capital)   The owner's stake or "interest" in the assets of a business; equal to the company's net assets (assets minus liabilities). (p. 15)

partnership   A company formed by two or more persons and managed according to a contractual agreement among them. (p. 11)

public accounting   A branch of accounting in which an accountant provides services to all types of organizations for fees. (p. 7)

revenues   Amounts charged to customers for goods sold or services rendered. (p. 16)

sole proprietorship   A business owned by one individual. (p. 11)

statement of cash flows   A financial statement that shows the cash inflows and outflows related to a company's income-generating, investing, and financing activities. (p. 22)

statement of owner's equity   A financial statement that discloses the changes in owner's equity during an accounting period. (p. 22)

Chapter Quiz

The five questions that follow relate to several issues raised in the chapter. Test your knowledge of these issues by selecting the best answer. (The answers appear on p. 48.)

1. The principle of historical cost:
   a. holds that acquisitions of goods and services should be entered in the accounting records at acquisition cost.
   b. results in the development of subjective financial statements.
   c. is ideal for use in periods of high inflation.
   d. is not acceptable when constructing general-purpose financial statements.

2. Apex Company had owner's equity of $32,000 on January 1, 19X2. During January, owner investments and withdrawals amounted to $15,000 and $9,000, respectively. In addition, the company generated revenues of $50,000 and expenses of $48,000. The amount of owner's equity on January 31 was:
   a. $8,000.
   b. $36,000.
   c. $40,000.
   d. $58,000.

3. John Davis recently withdrew $1,000 cash from the Davis Repair Shop, a sole proprietorship. This transaction would:
   a. decrease both assets and liabilities.
   b. decrease both assets and owner's equity.
   c. decrease assets and increase owner's equity.
   d. increase both assets and owner's equity.

4. A company's ending accounts receivable balance and the period's advertising expense would be found on which financial statements, respectively?
   a. Balance sheet and statement of owner's equity.
   b. Balance sheet and income statement.
   c. Income statement and balance sheet.
   d. Income statement and statement of owner's equity.

5. X Company had revenues, expenses, owner investments, and owner withdrawals of $45,000, $35,000, $4,000, and $1,000, respectively. The firm's net income was:

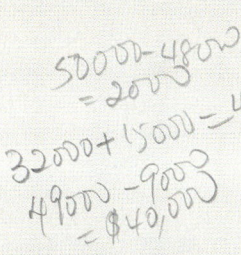

a. $9,000.
b. $10,000.
c. $13,000.
d. $14,000.

SUMMARY PROBLEM

On October 2, 19XX, John Gilbert opened the Gilbert Realty Company. The following transactions occurred during the month:

Oct. 2 Received $25,000 cash from Gilbert as an investment in the business.
6 Received a $3,600 cash commission for services provided on the sale of a home.
10 Paid $400 of transportation expenses. (Gilbert uses his personal auto for business matters and bills the firm for all business expenses.)
14 Sold another home. The commission on this sale was $3,200, but Gilbert will not receive the cash until November.
18 Paid $900 of advertising expenses.
23 Purchased furniture for the office at a cost of $6,500. Made a down payment of $2,000 and agreed to remit the balance owed next month.
24 Paid utility bills of $350 for the month.
27 Returned $600 of office furniture to the supplier. The supplier deducted the return from the amount that Gilbert owes.
29 Paid $1,700 of salaries expense.
30 Processed a $500 cash withdrawal for Gilbert's personal use.

Instructions

a. Analyze the effects of these transactions on the individual elements of the accounting equation.
b. Prepare an income statement for the month ended October 31.
c. Prepare a statement of owner's equity for the month ended October 31.
d. Prepare a balance sheet as of October 31.

Solution

a.

Date	Cash	Accounts Receivable	Office Furniture	=	Accounts Payable	+	(+) Investments (−) Withdrawals	(+) Revenues (−) Expenses
10/2	+$25,000						+$25,000	
10/6	+3,600							+$3,600 (Commissions)
10/10	−400							−400 (Transportation)
10/14		+$3,200						+3,200 (Commissions)
10/18	−900							−900 (Advertising)
10/23	−2,000		+$6,500		+$4,500			
10/24	−350							−350 (Utilities)
10/27			−600		−600			
10/29	−1,700							−1,700 (Salaries)
10/30	−500						−500	
	$22,750	$3,200	$5,900		$3,900		$24,500	$3,450
		$31,850					$31,850	

Assets = Liabilities + Owner's Equity

b.

GILBERT REALTY COMPANY
Income Statement
For the Month Ended October 31, 19XX

Commissions		$6,800
Less expenses		
Transportation	$ 400	
Advertising	900	
Utilities	350	
Salaries	1,700	
Total expenses		3,350
Net income		$3,450

c.

GILBERT REALTY COMPANY
Statement of Owner's Equity
For the Month Ended October 31, 19XX

Beginning balance, Oct. 1		$ —
Increases		
Owner investments	$25,000	
Net income	3,450	28,450
		$28,450
Decreases		
Owner withdrawals		500
Ending balance, Oct. 31		$27,950

d.

GILBERT REALTY COMPANY
Balance Sheet
October 31, 19XX

ASSETS	
Cash	$22,750
Accounts receivable	3,200
Office furniture	5,900
Total assets	$31,850
LIABILITIES	
Accounts payable	$ 3,900
OWNER'S EQUITY	
John Gilbert, capital	27,950
Total liabilities & owner's equity	$31,850

Assignment Material

Questions

Q1–1 Identify typical users of accounting information.

Q1–2 How does financial accounting differ from managerial accounting?

Q1–3 What are several limitations of accounting information?

Q1–4 Paul Martin is contemplating an investment in the Indiana Company. He has secured the firm's audited financial statements, which have been examined by a certified public accountant. How can Martin be satisfied that the statements do not present false and incorrect information to purposely mislead investors?

Q1–5 Explain the entity assumption.

Q1–6 Mr. P, the president of Fairwood Company, recently purchased a new car solely for personal use. He asked Mr. A, Fairwood's accountant, to record the car as a miscellaneous expense of the company's current accounting period. Mr. A refused. Explain the reason behind A's action.

Q1–7 Discuss the use of historical cost in the accounting process. Why is historical cost used, and what is one of its chief limitations?

Q1–8 What is meant by the term "financial position"?

Q1–9 Define the term "owner's equity."

Q1–10 What factors cause owner's equity to change during an accounting period?

Q1–11 The Harter family owns a service station in Vermont. After receiving his first lecture on accounting principles, the youngest of the Harter sons, Teddy, decided to review the accounting records for the year just ended. He noted that net income of $15,800 was generated. At the same time, the balance in the station's checking (i.e., cash) account had decreased by $5,300. Teddy felt that this situation was not possible and that a mistake had been made. Is Teddy correct? Explain and cite several examples to support your answer.

Q1–12 Thomas and Rodriguez are having a heated debate about the order in which certain items should be listed on the balance sheet. Their views are as follows:

Thomas—Cash, Accounts Receivable, Equipment, Rent Expense
Rodriguez—Equipment, Accounts Receivable, Rent Expense, Cash

Who is correct? Why?

Q1–13 Consider the income statement, the statement of owner's equity, and the balance sheet. Which of these statements cover(s) a period of time as opposed to a specific date?

Q1–14 What information is disclosed on a statement of cash flows?

Q1–15 Define the term "ethics."

Q1–16 Briefly discuss the ethical issue of independence as it relates to accountants in public practice.

Exercises

E1–1 Basic concepts (L.O. 4)

Jean's Marine Supply specializes in the sale of boating equipment and accessories. Identify the items that follow as an asset (A), liability (L), revenue (R), or expense (E) from the firm's viewpoint.

a. The inventory of boating supplies owned by the company.
b. Monthly rental charges paid for store space.
c. A loan owed to Citizens Bank.
d. New computer equipment purchased to handle daily record keeping.
e. Daily sales made to customers.
f. Amounts due from customers.
g. Land owned by the company, to be used as a future store site.
h. Weekly salaries paid to salespeople.

E1–2 Basic computations (L.O. 4, 5)

The following selected balances were extracted from the accounting records of Rossi Enterprises on December 31, 19X3:

Accounts payable	$ 3,200	Interest expense	$ 2,500
Accounts receivable	14,800	Land	18,000
Auto expense	1,900	Loan payable	40,000
Building	30,000	Tax expense	3,300
Cash	7,400	Utilities expense	4,100
Fee revenue	56,900	Wage expense	37,500

a. Determine Rossi's total assets as of December 31.
b. Determine the company's total liabilities as of December 31.
c. Compute 19X3 net income or loss.

E1–3 Analysis of transactions (L.O. 6)

Set up the following headings across a piece of paper:

$$\text{Assets} = \text{Liabilities} + \text{Owner's Equity}$$

By using "+" and "–," indicate the effect of each of the following transactions on total assets, liabilities, and owner's equity:

a. Processed a $5,000 cash withdrawal for the owner.
b. Recorded the receipt of May's utility bill, to be paid in June.
c. Provided services to customers on account.
d. Paid the current month's advertising charges.
e. Purchased a $27,000 delivery truck by paying $5,000 down and securing a loan for the remaining balance.
f. Received $11,000 cash from the owner as an investment in the business.
g. Returned a new computer and printer purchased earlier in the month on account. The bill had not as yet been paid.
h. Paid the utility bill recorded previously in (b).

E1–4 Accounting equation; analysis of owner's equity (L.O. 5)

Madison Electric revealed the financial data that follow on January 1 and December 31 of the current year.

	Assets	Liabilities
January 1	$77,000	$51,000
December 31	83,000	58,000

a. Compute the change in owner's equity during the year by using the accounting equation.

b. Assume there were no owner investments or withdrawals during the year. What is the probable cause of the change in owner's equity from part (a)?
c. Assume there were no owner investments during the year. If the owner withdrew $13,000, determine and compute the company's net income or net loss. Be sure to label your answer.

E1–5 Financial statement content (L.O. 7)
You are in the process of reviewing the income statement, statement of owner's equity, and balance sheet of the Weissman Company. On which financial statement(s) would the following information be found?

a. The amount of equipment owned.
b. Withdrawals by the owner.
c. Interest incurred on loan payable.
d. Beginning owner's equity.
e. Ending owner's equity.
f. Amounts owed to creditors.
g. Fees earned for services rendered.
h. Amounts due from customers.

E1–6 Income statement concepts (L.O. 5, 7)
Evaluate the comments that follow as being True or False. If the comment is false, briefly explain why.

a. An income statement reveals the net income or net loss of an entity for a period of time as opposed to a specific date.
b. Withdrawals are properly classified as an expense of doing business.
c. If a company has $50,000 of revenues for March, it stands to reason that cash receipts for March must total $50,000.
d. If expenses exceed revenues, a net loss has been generated.
e. A computer acquired late in the year for use in the business should be disclosed on a firm's income statement.

E1–7 Analysis of income statement versus statement of cash flows (L.O. 7)
Mora Consulting Group has been in business for six years. The practice provides computer services to clients, who take an average of 45 days to settle their balances due. Mora has always been a profitable operation but is sometimes strapped for cash. The following information appeared in the financial statements for the year just ended:

Income statement
    Consulting revenue $245,000
Statement of cash flows
    Cash received from clients $189,000

a. Give two examples of transactions where the amount of revenue earned would not equal the cash received from clients.
b. Which of the two amounts, $245,000 or $189,000, would be more useful to Mora's banker in deciding whether or not to approve a loan for the practice? Briefly discuss.

E1–8 Financial statement relationships (L.O. 7)
The following information appeared on the financial statements of the Altoona Repair Company:

Income statement
Total expenses $ 64,900
Net income 7,200
Statement of owner's equity
Beginning owner's equity balance $113,200
Owner withdrawals 61,300
Ending owner's equity balance 70,800
Balance sheet
Total liabilities $ 97,000

By picturing the content of and the interrelationships among the financial statements, determine:

a. Total revenues for the year.
b. Total owner investments.
c. Total assets.

E1–9 Financial statement presentation (L.O. 3, 5, 7)

The accounting records of Hickory Enterprises revealed the following selected information for the year ended December 31, 19X6:

Cash investments by the owner $ 59,000
Services rendered to customers 86,000
Cash withdrawals by the owner 12,000
Total year-end assets 177,800

Salaries, advertising, and utilities for the year totaled $68,500. The year-end asset total included a parcel of land that had cost the company $45,000. Hickory's accountant used this amount for valuation purposes rather than the land's current market value of $75,000 (as determined by a recent real estate appraisal).

a. Determine the net income to be disclosed on the company's income statement.
b. Compute the increase or decrease in owner's equity during 19X6. On which financial statement would this information appear?
c. Determine and justify the proper valuation for Hickory's year-end assets.

E1–10 An ethical dilemma (L.O. 8)

Pat Holmes maintains the accounting records for Holiday Painting, a sole proprietorship owned by Rex Kemper. Kemper has a hot temper, caused by both his personality and the company's miserable financial performance over the past eleven months.

On December 3, Holiday agreed to paint the exterior of the Nevada Guest Lodge for $3,600. (The price was based on four days of labor and the cost of the necessary paint and supplies.) The job began on December 16 and took less time to complete than anticipated. Additionally, to save money, Rex told his laborers to use left-over paint from another job, even though the color was slightly different than that specified by Nevada.

Nevada's manager, who was out of town from December 15–20, was extremely unhappy when he inspected the finished work. Kemper nevertheless ordered Holmes to bill the lodge for the agreed-upon amount of $3,600.

a. Does Kemper's directive lack integrity? Briefly explain.
b. Discuss the ethical dilemma faced by Holmes.
c. Could this episode have some negative long-term effects for Holiday Painting? Briefly explain.

Problems

Series A

P1–A1 Identification of transactions (L.O. 6)

The following tabulation summarizes several transactions of Ciminelli's, a small restaurant:

	Assets			=	Liabilities	+	Owner's Equity
	Cash	Accounts Receivable	Kitchen Equipment		Accounts Payable		Investments/Withdrawals Revenues/Expenses
Balances	$10,000	$ 3,000	$100,000		$ 7,000		$106,000
(a)			+5,600		+5,600		
(b)	+800	+13,700					+14,500*
(c)	−900				−900		
(d)	−6,000						−6,000
(e)	+4,600	−4,600					
(f)			−500		−500		
(g)	−2,500						−2,500*
	$ 6,000	$12,100	$105,100		$11,200		$112,000

Transactions in the Owner's Equity column designated with an asterisk (*) were caused by the company's income-producing activities. The $6,000 figure is unrelated to such activities.

Instructions

Write a brief explanation of each transaction.

P1–A2 Basic transaction processing (L.O. 6, 7)

On November 1 of the current year, Richard Parker established a sole proprietorship. The following transactions occurred during the month:

1. Received $19,000 from Parker as an investment in the business.
2. Paid $9,000 to acquire a used minivan.
3. Purchased $1,800 of office furniture on account.
4. Provided $2,100 of consulting services on account.
5. Paid $300 of repair expenses.
6. Received $800 from clients who were previously billed in (4).
7. Paid $500 on account to the supplier of office furniture in (3).
8. Received a $150 electric bill, to be paid next month.
9. Processed a $600 withdrawal for Parker.
10. Received $250 from clients for consulting services rendered.
11. Returned a $450 office desk to the supplier. The supplier agreed to reduce the balance due from Parker.

Instructions

a. Arrange the following asset, liability, and owner's equity elements of the accounting equation in a manner similar to that shown on page 18: Cash, Accounts

Receivable, Office Furniture, Van, Accounts Payable, Investments/Withdrawals, and Revenues/Expenses.
b. Record each transaction on a separate line. After all transactions have been recorded, compute the balance in each of the preceding items.
c. Answer the following questions for Parker:
   (1) How much does the company owe to its creditors at month-end? On which financial statement(s) would this information be found?
   (2) Did the company have a "good" month from an accounting viewpoint? Briefly explain.

P1–A3 Statement preparation (L.O. 7)

The following information is taken from the accounting records of Grimball Cardiology at the close of business on December 31, 19X1:

Accounts payable	$ 14,700	Surgery revenue	$175,000
Surgical expenses	80,000	Cash	60,000
Surgical equipment	37,000	Office equipment	118,000
Salaries expense	30,000	Rent expense	15,000
Accounts receivable	135,000	Loan payable	10,300
Utilities expense	5,000		

All equipment was acquired just prior to year-end. Conversations with the practice's bookkeeper revealed the data that follow.

Rose Grimball, capital (January 1, 19X1)	$300,000
19X1 owner investments	2,000
19X1 owner withdrawals	22,000

Instructions

a. Prepare the income statement for Grimball Cardiology in good form.
b. Prepare a statement of owner's equity in good form.
c. Prepare Grimball's balance sheet in good form.

P1–A4 Transaction analysis and statement preparation (L.O. 6, 7)

The transactions that follow relate to Frisco Enterprises for March 19X1, the company's first month of activity.

Mar. 1   Received $20,000 cash from Joanne Burton, the owner, as an investment in the business.
       4   Provided $2,400 of services on account.
       7   Acquired a small parcel of land by paying $6,000 cash.
      12   Received $700 from a client, who was billed previously on March 4.
      15   Paid $800 to the *Journal Herald* for advertising that ran during the first half of the month.
      18   Acquired $9,000 of equipment from Park Central Outfitters by paying $7,000 down and agreeing to remit the balance owed within the next two weeks.
      22   Received $300 from clients for services performed on this date.
      24   Paid $1,500 on account to Park Central Outfitters in partial settlement of the balance due from the transaction on March 18.

Mar. 28 Rented a car from United Car Rental for use on March 28. Total charges amounted to $75, with United billing Frisco for the amount due.
31 Paid $900 for March wages.
31 Processed a $600 cash withdrawal from the business for Joanne Burton.

Instructions

a. Determine the impact of each of the preceding transactions on Frisco's assets, liabilities, and owner's equity. Use the following format:

Assets	=	Liabilities	+	Owner's Equity
Cash	Accounts Receivable	Land	Equipment	Accounts Payable	(+) Investments (−) Withdrawals	(+) Revenues (−) Expenses

Record each transaction on a separate line. Calculate balances only after the last transaction has been recorded.

b. Prepare an income statement, a statement of owner's equity, and a balance sheet in good form.

P1–A5 Financial statement preparation (L.O. 7)

Irene Kurtz opened Decor and More on May 1, 19X9. She started the firm by investing $35,000 of personal savings and obtaining a $22,000 loan from the Small Business Administration. Shortly thereafter, these funds were used to acquire a truck ($19,000) and office equipment ($5,500). In addition, decorator (household) furnishings, treated as assets in the accounting records, were purchased for $17,000. By month-end, the company had written checks that totaled $15,800 for these latter goods.

The following expenses were incurred during May:

Salaries	$9,100	Utilities	$2,300
Advertising	3,800	Postage	1,100
Taxes	900	Interest	200
Miscellaneous	350		

All expenses were paid by May 31 with the exception of $2,900 of salaries. Irene also withdrew $4,200 of cash from the business on May 28.

Decor and More billed customers $21,600 for services provided. Although $4,100 of this amount remains unpaid, collections are not anticipated to be a problem.

Instructions

a. Prepare an income statement for the month ended May 31, 19X9.
b. Prepare a statement of owner's equity for the month ended May 31, 19X9.
c. Prepare a balance sheet as of May 31, 19X9.

P1–A6 Identification of income statement errors (L.O. 7)

The income statement on the following page was prepared by the bookkeeper of the Action Tree Service.

Instructions

Identify and explain the errors in Action's income statement. Tell what should be done to correct the errors. (*Note:* A corrected income statement is not required.)

ACTION TREE SERVICE
Profit and Loss Statement
June 30, 19XX

Revenue			
	Services provided	$34,900	
	Accounts receivable	6,100	$41,000
	Owner investments		16,000
	Total revenue		$57,000
Less:			
	Salaries expense	$15,600	
	Advertising expense	3,400	
	Down payment on truck	1,000	
	Utilities expense	900	
	Rent expense	1,200	
	Tree trimming equipment	1,500	
	Loan payment (includes $600 interest)	1,900	
	Miscellaneous expense	12,000	
	Supplies used	800	
	Owner withdrawals	2,000	
	Total deductions		40,300
Net loss			$16,700

Series B

P1–B1 Identification of transactions (L.O. 6)
The following tabulation summarizes several transactions of the Hartford Company:

	Assets			=	Liabilities	+	Owner's Equity
	Cash	Accounts Receivable	Computers		Accounts Payable		Investments/Withdrawals Revenues/Expenses
Balances	$5,000	$13,000	$29,000		$17,000		$30,000
(a)	–800						–800*
(b)	+1,900	–1,900					
(c)	–2,000						–2,000
(d)	–3,000		+10,000		+7,000		
(e)		+1,500					+1,500*
(f)			+2,500				+2,500
(g)					+900		–900*
	$1,100	$12,600	$41,500		$24,900		$30,300

Transactions in the Owner's Equity column designated with an asterisk (*) were caused by the company's income-producing activities. The $2,000 and $2,500 figures are unrelated to such activities.

Instructions

Write a brief explanation of each transaction.

P1–B2 Basic transaction processing (L.O. 6, 7)

On September 1 of the current year, John McCarthy established a sole proprietorship. The following transactions occurred during the month:

1. Received $25,000 from McCarthy as an investment in the business.
2. Purchased $4,000 of office equipment on account.
3. Provided $1,900 of services on account.
4. Paid $500 of office salaries.
5. Received a $300 electric bill, to be paid next month.
6. Paid $7,000 to acquire a used truck.
7. Processed a $900 withdrawal for McCarthy.
8. Received $650 from clients who were previously billed in (3).
9. Received $200 from clients for services rendered.
10. Paid $450 on account to the supplier of office equipment in (2).
11. Sold $350 of extra office equipment to a neighboring business for $350 cash.

Instructions

a. Arrange the following asset, liability, and owner's equity elements of the accounting equation in a manner similar to that shown on page 18: Cash, Accounts Receivable, Office Equipment, Truck, Accounts Payable, Investments/Withdrawals, and Revenues/Expenses.
b. Record each transaction on a separate line. After all transactions have been recorded, compute the balance in each of the preceding items.
c. Answer the following questions for McCarthy:
   (1) What is the total of the company's assets at month-end? On which financial statement(s) would this information be found?
   (2) What is the owner's equity of the business at month-end? On which financial statement(s) would this information be found?

P1–B3 Statement preparation (L.O. 7)

The following balances are taken from the accounting records of Essex and Associates at the close of its year on December 31, 19XX:

Accounts payable	$ 8,700	Miscellaneous expense	$ 3,800
Accounts receivable	18,350	Postage expense	8,400
Advertising expense	3,850	Repair expense	5,600
Cash	15,000	Salaries expense	34,000
Gloria Essex, capital	26,800*	Service revenue	65,000
Land	9,000	Utilities expense	2,500
Loan payable	5,500	Van	8,000

*This amount represents Essex's capital balance on January 1, 19XX. Owner investments and withdrawals during the year totaled $10,000 and $7,500, respectively.

The van was acquired just before the close of business on December 31.

Instructions

a. Prepare Essex's income statement in good form.
b. Prepare a statement of owner's equity in good form.
c. Prepare Essex's balance sheet in good form.

P1–B4 Transaction analysis and statement preparation (L.O. 6, 7)

Mark Bates, owner of the Bates Company, is a specialist in evaluating and appraising rare works of art. Transactions for June 19X5, the firm's first month of activity, follow.

June 2 Received cash of $95,000 from Mark as an investment in the business.
  3 Purchased $8,000 of land by paying cash. The land will be used as a site for the company's future headquarters.
  4 Occupied temporary facilities and paid one month's rent of $2,500 to the Executive Center Office Park.
  5 Paid $10,000 to BBDO, an advertising agency, for immediate services related to a grand opening "kick-off" campaign.
  8 Provided $7,000 of services on account to Arthur Williams, a client.
  11 Collected $4,500 from Williams for services provided on June 8.
  17 Bought $9,000 of computer equipment at a going-out-of-business sale. Paid one-third down, with the remaining balance due in July.
  18 Received $13,500 cash for services provided to Vanessa Brock.
  20 Given the unexpected early success of the business, decided to pay 60% of the outstanding balance from the transaction on June 17.
  23 Hired Eagle Carpet Cleaning to repair damage that occurred during the grand opening celebration. Eagle charged $225, the amount to be paid during the first week in July.
  28 Processed a $200 cash withdrawal from the company.
  30 Paid office support staff wages of $3,000.

Instructions

a. Determine the impact of each of the preceding transactions on the company's assets, liabilities, and owner's equity. Use the following format:

Assets	=	Liabilities	+	Owner's Equity
Cash Accounts Receivable Land Computer Equipment		Accounts Payable		(+) Investments (−) Withdrawals (+) Revenues (−) Expenses

Record each transaction on a separate line. Calculate balances only after the last transaction has been recorded.

b. Prepare an income statement, a statement of owner's equity, and a balance sheet in good form.

P1–B5 Financial statement preparation (L.O. 7)

On January 1, 19X3, Mike Jeffcote opened the Jeffcote Advertising Agency, a sole proprietorship. Mike was able to begin operations with $90,000 cash, one-third of which was acquired via a bank loan. The remaining amount was obtained from an owner investment. A review of the accounting records for January revealed the following:

- *Asset purchases:* Land, $15,000; building, $40,000; and office equipment, $9,000. These amounts were paid in cash; however, the firm still owes $3,000 for the equipment acquisition.
- *Services performed:* Total billings on account, $29,500. Clients have remitted a total of $8,400 in settlement of their balances due.

- *Expenses incurred:* Salaries, $21,000; utilities, $300; taxes, $150; interest, $800; and miscellaneous, $400. These amounts had been paid by month-end with the exception of $250 of the miscellaneous items.

Further information revealed that Jeffcote withdrew $3,100 of cash from the business on January 31.

Instructions

a. Prepare an income statement for the month ended January 31, 19X3.
b. Prepare a statement of owner's equity for the month ended January 31, 19X3.
c. Prepare a balance sheet as of January 31, 19X3.

P1–B6 Identification of balance sheet errors (L.O. 7)

The following balance sheet was prepared by the bookkeeper of Rapid Cleaning Service, a sole proprietorship owned by Sarah Randolph:

RAPID CLEANING SERVICE
For the Year Ended December 31, 19X4

ASSETS

Amounts due from customers—November	$ 3,000
Amounts due from customers—December	11,000
Cash	5,000
Delivery van*	18,000
Inventory of cleaning supplies	1,000
Investments in the business by owner	22,000
Total assets	$60,000

LIABILITIES & OWNER'S EQUITY

Amounts owed to others	$ 2,000
Business expenses	4,000
Loans from the bank	10,000
Net income	17,000
Sarah Randolph, capital (12/31/X3)	33,000
Total liabilities & owner's equity	$66,000

* Owned by Frank Randolph, Sarah's husband.

Instructions

Identify and briefly explain the errors in the company's balance sheet. *Note:* A corrected balance sheet is not required.

EXPANDING YOUR HORIZONS

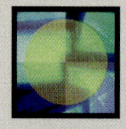

EYH1–1 Starting a new business (L.O. 1)

Individuals who start a new business often begin the venture with little knowledge of how difficult the process really is. The time commitment is normally much greater than one might expect, and the owner may have to sacrifice a regular paycheck for a while. In addition, despite heroic efforts on the part of management, many new businesses fail.

Instructions

Form a team with two other classmates, and locate the owners of three small businesses in your area. Summarize the owners' responses to the following questions:

a. What was the smartest thing that you did in running your business?
b. What has been your biggest mistake to date?
c. If you could give one piece of advice to people who are beginning a new venture, what would that advice be?
d. Do you see any personal benefits from having some (or more) knowledge of accounting and financial matters in managing a small enterprise? Explain.

EYH1–2 Accounting and regulation (L.O. 1)

In addition to the basic financial statements, volumes of other data and reports must flow from a typical accounting system. Many of these reports are required by regulatory authorities.

Instructions

Identify a business type (e.g., a bank, a hospital, a restaurant, or perhaps the place where you or someone in your family works) that might be subject to regulation. Interview a person who is familiar with the regulatory agencies that have jurisdiction over the business. Determine the various reports that must be completed, their frequency of occurrence, and the approximate amount of time each month that the business devotes to regulatory record keeping. Summarize the results of your interview, and be ready to report your findings to the rest of the class.

EYH1–3 A day in the life of an accountant (L.O. 2)

Accountants are professionals who must understand and integrate a wide variety of business topics. For example, accountants employed in a chemical plant will need to have a working knowledge of chemistry and engineering from time to time. Those who work in hospitals will be somewhat proficient in using various medical terms and determining the cost of certain procedures. Working as an accountant often means that a person will gain experience in many different industries or in many separate departments.

Instructions

a. Interview a practicing accountant (public, private, or governmental/not-for-profit) in order to identify what might occur during a typical day. Be sure to ask the accountant to describe several of the most unusual or challenging tasks/events that he or she has experienced. Summarize your findings in a one-page report.
b. Has this interview changed your perception of an accountant? If so, how?

EYH1–4 Unethical behavior in the business world (L.O. 8)

As the text notes, newspapers and periodicals contain many stories that deal with unethical business practices. Fraud, the improper use of sensitive insider information, and a lack of independence are three of the many examples that you may encounter.

Instructions

Go to your local library and perform a literature search to find three dissimilar applications of unethical business practices. (*The Business Periodicals Index* is a good source to use.) Prepare a brief summary of your findings, including the financial implications for the affected company. Also, if disclosed, state what happened to the perpetrator—jail term, job dismissal, reprimand, and so forth. Be prepared to present your findings to the class.

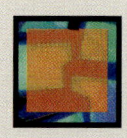

EYH1–5 A look at financial statements: The Promus Companies (L.O. 7)

Promus Companies is a hospitality business, heavily involved in casino gaming and hotels. The firm operates Harrah's Casinos, Embassy Suites, Hampton Inns, and Homewood Suites hotels. Collectively, Promus has over 550 facilities throughout the United States.

Instructions

By using the text's electronic data base, access the balance sheet and income statement of The Promus Companies and answer the questions that follow. Unless otherwise indicated, responses should be based on data for the most recent year presented.

a. What is the total cost of assets owned by the firm? What are the three most significant assets owned?
b. Does the company have enough cash on hand to settle its accounts payable? Briefly explain.
c. Was the firm profitable? Did the company's net earnings increase or decrease from the previous year?
d. How much was the firm's income tax expense (i.e., provision for income taxes)?
e. What type of operation produced the greatest amount of revenue for the company?

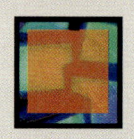

EYH1–6 A look at financial statements (L.O. 7)

This problem is essentially a duplication of Problem EYH1–5. It is based on a company selected by your instructor.

Instructions

By using the text's electronic data base, access the specified company's balance sheet and income statement and focus on data for the most recent year reported. Answer requirements (a)–(d) of Problem EYH1–5 along with the following:

e. Suppose an investor wanted information about the cost of items and services consumed by the company in producing revenue. What financial statement should the investor review? What would he or she find for this business?

EYH1–7 Accounting information: Uses and reporting (L.O. 1, 2, 7)

Frank Bell is an outdoors enthusiast. While employed as a personnel manager at Hansen Engineering in Denver, Frank often helped friends on camping trips and had even built a canoe for river exploration. Luckily, Frank's brother owned a sporting goods store in a neighboring suburb. This was a nice arrangement because it gave Frank access to wholesalers' catalogs, thereby enabling him to acquire specialized equipment at great savings.

Frank's love for camping, coupled with his friends' support, soon led to his resignation from Hansen Engineering and the opening of The Outdoors Store. Frank rented space in a local shopping center and purchased an extensive supply of maps and outdoor equipment. He also acquired some materials and hired a laborer to expand his canoe-building activities. The operation was financed primarily from various investments that Frank had made over the years.

An extensive advertising campaign for the store's opening proved very beneficial, and business was much better than expected. However, as the winter months approached, store traffic slowed. Frank soon realized that his operation faced a problem shared by many other firms—seasonality. In an effort to boost sales during the fall and winter, Frank conducted some market research and decided to add ski equipment and accessories to his product line.

Having resolved that issue, Frank still faced several other problems. An emergency withdrawal had left the store's cash balance at a dangerously low level. Recent canoe-building costs appeared to be skyrocketing, although Frank could not be certain because he did not have a formal costing system. In addition, upon signing the original lease at the shopping center, Frank anticipated conducting business only in the camping field. With a new venture into skiing, however, he rapidly found himself cramped for space. Finally, there was a financing issue. The outlays required for the purchases of ski equipment were more than the store's checking account could bear, creating the need for a bank loan.

In an effort to minimize operating costs, Frank had maintained the financial records for The Outdoors Store himself. Fortunately, he had completed two accounting courses at a local university before being employed by Hansen Engineering. In his own words, however, Frank admitted that "partying came before studying, and I really wasn't a serious student." The bank's loan officer, in a preliminary conversation with Frank, had suggested that the store's financial statements be audited by a CPA.

Instructions
a. How can accounting help Frank in the management of The Outdoors Store?
b. The loan officer had suggested that the store's financial statements be audited by a CPA. Briefly explain the audit process and the rationale behind the banker's request.
c. Assume the role of the loan officer. What information would you like to see before making a decision on a loan for The Outdoors Store?
d. What are the basic financial statements of a business, and what information do these statements report?

COMMUNICATION OF ACCOUNTING INFORMATION

CAI1–1   Audience analysis: Wm. Wrigley Jr. Company (L.O. 2, 4, 5, 7)
Communication Principle: Audience analysis is an important principle of communication. In other words, know your readers (audience) and write to fit their knowledge and interests. Tailoring the presentation to your readers' needs by choosing an appropriate vocabulary and simplified examples will help you deliver the information effectively.

■ ■ ■ ■ ■ ■ ■ ■

The Wm. Wrigley Jr. Company is best known for the manufacture and sale of chewing gum. The firm, headquartered in the historic Wrigley Building in downtown Chicago, is also indirectly involved with various candy products and flavorings. For a recent year, the company's financial statements reported the following information:

> End-of-year total assets: $815 million
> Net income for the period: $175 million

Wrigley has had profitable operations for a number of years.

Instructions
Assume that you are a staff accountant with Wrigley. Management has asked you to prepare lecture materials and speak to a group of sales personnel about the firm's financial statements. All sales personnel have college degrees but have very limited or no accounting knowledge. The average age is 25; attendance at the presentation is required. Management believes that job performance will improve if personnel have

some knowledge of the company's financial situation. The employees may also be motivated by any encouraging data you present and pass on their enthusiasm for the company to colleagues and customers.

For their information, create easy-to-understand lecture notes that answer the questions that follow. In your word choice, examples, and format, be sure to remember the audience. Be as brief as possible, and consider that you will use the notes for an oral presentation. Although the notes should be understandable on a stand-alone basis, assume that you would fill in added details and explanations at the meeting.

a. What are financial statements? Name and briefly describe the content of the financial statements on which total assets and net income would be found.
b. What process was likely performed on the company's financial statements to improve their credibility? Briefly explain.
c. Terminology is very important for proper communication in accounting. The terms "revenue" and "net income" are often confused.
   (1) Briefly distinguish between revenue and net income.
   (2) In all likelihood, is the firm's total revenue greater than $175 million? Why?
d. The terms "asset" and "expense" are often confused.
   (1) Briefly distinguish between asset and expense.
   (2) More than likely, do the amounts owed to creditors exceed $815 million? Why?

Answers to Chapter Quiz

1. a
2. c ($32,000 + $15,000 − $9,000 + $50,000 − $48,000)
3. b
4. b
5. b ($45,000 − $35,000)

2 Processing Accounting Information

Learning Objectives

After studying this chapter, you should be able to:

1. Define accounts, debits and credits, and journals, and explain their interrelationships.
2. Journalize transactions and transfer data to the general ledger.
3. Discuss the purpose of and prepare a trial balance.
4. Determine the impact of errors on the trial balance.

When George Faris of Banner Advertising agreed to share his story with us, we gave him the previous edition of this textbook. As he thumbed through the pages, he grinned when he saw Chapter 2's coverage of basic bookkeeping material. He laughed and said, "Ah, good memories! When first exposed to this material in college, I found it to be boring and mechanical. I never did realize just how prevalent these concepts are in business. Again, let me emphasize that I am not an accountant nor do I perform detailed accounting work for a living."

We asked if computers have lessened the importance of understanding basic bookkeeping techniques. George replied, "Computers have reduced the tedium associated with bookkeeping, lowered costs, and improved accuracy. But both the input to the computer and the resulting output are still framed in a basic 'systems mode.' That is, you really have to understand what goes in, how it is massaged, and the meaning of the resulting screen displays and printouts."

George went on to say that when problems arise in Banner's accounting system, everyone involved sits down and tries to figure out what went wrong. "The real key is knowing how data flow through the system and are processed into useful information. In effect, one could say that all the related tools and terms (such as journals, ledgers, debits and credits) are a unique language. While I found this language to be relatively unexciting, it has provided much more of a knowledge base for my success than I ever would have thought."

Banner Advertising is typical of the many different types of businesses that operate in our economy. Organizations are involved with a multitude of financial events and transactions, such as the sale of goods and services, the payment of creditors and employees, the acquisition of merchandise and equipment, and owner investments and withdrawals. These examples, while not all-inclusive, illustrate the variety of transactions that a company must be capable of handling, recording, and summarizing. Add to this variety the frequency with which these transactions occur, and a genuine record-keeping problem is created.

The Vista Transit example in Chapter 1 showed that a business could process transactions by increasing and decreasing the components of the accounting equation. Although this processing method was satisfactory for illustrative purposes, some modification is necessary in a more realistic environment. It is not uncommon for an enterprise to process thousands of transactions each day. In addition, complex organizations may have dozens of asset, liability, and owner's equity elements that must be updated on a timely basis.

To illustrate the record-keeping problems of real firms, consider Eskimo Pie Corporation and PepsiCo, Inc. Eskimo Pie founded the frozen novelty industry in 1921 with the creation of its famous ice cream bar. The firm currently markets a variety of frozen products under the Eskimo Pie, Welch's, Tootsie Pops, 7UP, and Ghirardelli brand names. The company is certainly not a giant organization by today's standards. Total employees number approximately 175, and total revenues recently amounted to $66.1 million. At first glance, the necessary accounting would not appear much more complex than that required for Vista Transit. However, a closer look at Eskimo Pie's activities discloses the following:

- A 50% ownership interest in a Luxembourg-based frozen novelty business.
- A recent spin-off from the Reynolds Metals Company. Eskimo Pie, a former division of Reynolds Metals, is now an independent, "stand-alone" firm.
- The installation of new machinery to simulate licensee operations, thus reducing the elapsed time from new product design to appearance on the grocery shelf.

Eskimo Pie is also involved with several environmental improvement projects and has two retirement plans that cover virtually all salaried personnel.

PepsiCo, a considerably larger entity, has annual revenues of about $25 billion and conducts activities in three different business segments. PepsiCo's holdings and operations include the following:

BUSINESS SEGMENT	COMPANY
Beverages	Pepsi-Cola Co.
Snack foods	Frito-Lay, Inc.
Restaurants	Pizza Hut, Inc., Taco Bell, KFC

Manufacturing beverages, feeding thousands of people in restaurants, and producing snack foods are only a small part of PepsiCo's daily activities that need summarization in the firm's financial statements. Furthermore, management must have ready and efficient access to operating information for use in planning, control, and decision-making endeavors.

THE ACCOUNTING SYSTEM

Whether large like PepsiCo or small like Vista Transit, all companies need to produce financial statements, generate information for executives, and satisfy numerous governmental reporting requirements. To perform these varied tasks, businesses have found it beneficial to establish formal accounting systems that operate in the following manner:

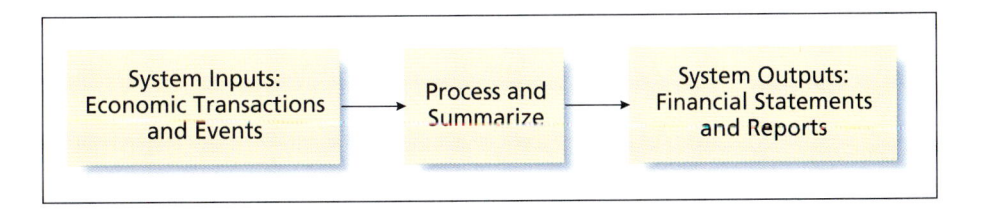

System Inputs: Economic Transactions and Events → Process and Summarize → System Outputs: Financial Statements and Reports

Such accounting systems have long been recognized as a key ingredient to effective management. This fact was stated very succinctly by Franklin Roosevelt, who over 50 years ago noted:

> A good system of accounting, by indicating weaknesses in the structure of the business, may save thousands of dollars to investors and may even save the business itself. The development of natural resources, the exploitation of new fields of commerce, . . . keener competition, higher standards of living and greater complexities of modern business . . . have brought about a condition where an effective accounting system is as essential to the continued life of a business as production and distribution.[1]

A FURTHER FOCUS

Despite Roosevelt's observation, the Federal government itself has been criticized as doing "an abysmal job of rudimentary bookkeeping," having billions of dollars in hidden liabilities. These comments come from a person who should know, the head of the General Accounting Office, approximately one year after the United States hired its first chief financial officer (CFO). The following were among the problems brought to the CFO's immediate attention: $600 million of Medicare overpayments; 79 incompatible accounting systems at the Department of Housing & Urban Development; charges of $35 billion in excess inventory at the Defense Department; and a $1-billion-per-year increase in student loan defaults.

Sources: "Billions Wasted, GAO Says," *The Dallas Morning News*, January 8, 1993, pp. 1A, 10A and "The Accountant as a Diplomat," *Forbes*, February 17, 1992, p. 148.

The accounting systems found in practice today range in scope from the simple to the sophisticated. No matter how complex, virtually all systems employ four basic tools to process transactions into financial information. These tools, which improve efficiency and reduce the cost of the input-to-output conversion, are accounts, debits and credits, journals, and the chart of accounts.

1 Define accounts, debits and credits, and journals, and explain their interrelationships.

ACCOUNTS

As we explained earlier in the text, transactions and events affect the fundamental accounting equation. To accumulate the information needed for financial statement and report construction, a business must keep detailed records of its assets, liabilities, and owner's equity. Assets, for example, should be subdivided into more specific elements such as cash, accounts receivable, and equipment, with individual accountings made for each element.

[1] Letter from Franklin Roosevelt to the president of the American Institute of Accountants, October 12, 1937.

The records that are kept for the individual asset, liability, and owner's equity components are known as accounts. If a company employs manual accounting methods, the record keeping for each account is normally performed on a separate sheet of paper. If electronic data processing is used, the account is located on a storage medium such as a tape or disk. Keep in mind that in both manual and computerized systems, the purpose of the account is the same: to accumulate (record) the increases and decreases that result from transactions. All the accounts taken together comprise a firm's general ledger. Essentially, the general ledger is a book that contains separate listings for each account that appears on an organization's financial statements.

The account may assume several different forms. One form is the T-account, so named because of its shape. A Cash T-account appears as follows:

	CASH		
19XX			
2/1	1,000	2/4	450
2/12	200	2/18	290
2/24	600		740
	1,060 **1,800**		

Observe that the T-account has both a left and a right side. The left side of any account is known as the *debit* side, and the right side is known as the *credit* side. In this particular case, Cash has entries that total $1,800 on the debit side (debits) and $740 on the credit side (credits).[2] The Cash account therefore has a debit balance of $1,060 ($1,800 – $740). If a given account has credits in excess of debits, the account would possess a credit balance.

The T-format presents a concise picture of the various transactions affecting a given account and is useful for understanding how transactions increase or decrease assets, liabilities, and owner's equity. In actual practice, however, the running balance form of account is encountered more frequently. Using the same information that appeared in the preceding example, we can illustrate the running balance form as shown on the following page. Entries on the left side of the T-account are recorded in the debit column; entries on the right side appear in the credit column.

The running balance account form offers the advantage of maintaining an up-to-date balance after each transaction. In addition, an explanation column is provided for descriptive purposes should an unusual entry arise. Normally, however, this column is left blank. The use of the posting reference (Post. Ref.) column will be explained shortly.

---

[2] The small boldface figures are commonly known as *footings*.

CASH					ACCOUNT NO. 101
DATE	EXPLANATION	POST. REF.	DEBIT	CREDIT	BALANCE
19XX Feb. 1			1,000		1,000
4				450	550
12			200		750
18				290	460
24			600		1,060

At this point you should understand the concepts of establishing an account and determining the related balance. However, two important questions have probably occurred to you:

1. Should the dollar amounts be entered as debits or credits?
2. Which amounts in the Cash account represent increases in cash and which are decreases?

The answers to these questions will become clear in the explanation of a second key accounting mechanism, debits and credits.

DEBITS AND CREDITS

Debits and credits are tools used by the accountant to increase and decrease account balances. Certain accounts are debited to record an increase; that is, entries are made on the debit (left) side or in the debit column. These accounts, in turn, are credited when a reduction is needed, with entries being made on the right side (credit) or in the credit column. To keep the accounting equation balanced, other accounts employ the opposite rule; namely, increases are recorded by credits and decreases are recorded by debits. Exhibit 2–1 summarizes the debit/credit rules used in accounting.

To understand the rules, remember that the elements of the accounting equation are assets, liabilities, and owner's equity. In addition, recall that owner's equity changes, in part, from revenues and expenses. We can thus safely identify five basic account types: assets, liabilities, owner's equity, revenues, and expenses.

EXHIBIT 2–1
Debit/Credit Rules

ACCOUNT TYPE	NORMAL BALANCE	TO INCREASE	TO DECREASE
Assets	Debit	Debit	Credit
Liabilities	Credit	Credit	Debit
Owner's equity	Credit	Credit	Debit
Revenues	Credit	Credit	Debit
Expenses	Debit	Debit	Credit

The balance of each account is obtained by offsetting or netting the total debits against the total credits. Certain account types tend to contain more debits than credits and will almost always possess a debit balance. Their **normal balance,** then, is a debit balance. According to Exhibit 2–1, assets and expenses fall in this category. In contrast, liabilities, owner's equity, and revenue accounts generally have more credits than debits and usually possess a credit balance.

A Further Focus

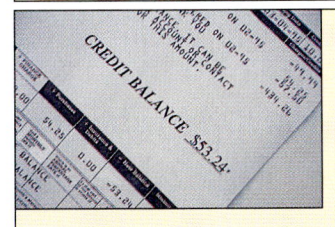

The preceding discussion should not be taken to mean that accounts always contain a normal balance. Certain accounts may, at times, carry opposite balances. For example, Accounts Receivable (an asset) could have a credit balance if a customer overpaid the amount due a business. In other cases, however, an opposite balance generally means that an error has arisen. For instance, a credit balance in Machinery (also an asset) is not possible because a company cannot have "negative" equipment.

The normal balances of accounts correspond to the accounting equation: assets = liabilities + owner's equity. An enterprise's assets (debit balances) are matched against their ownership interests—the creditors' (credit balances) and the owner's (credit balance). Because revenues increase owner's equity, such accounts normally possess a credit balance. Expenses, conversely, have the opposite effect and generally maintain a debit balance. These relationships are shown in Exhibit 2–2.

Exhibit 2–2
Relationship of Normal Balances and the Accounting Equation

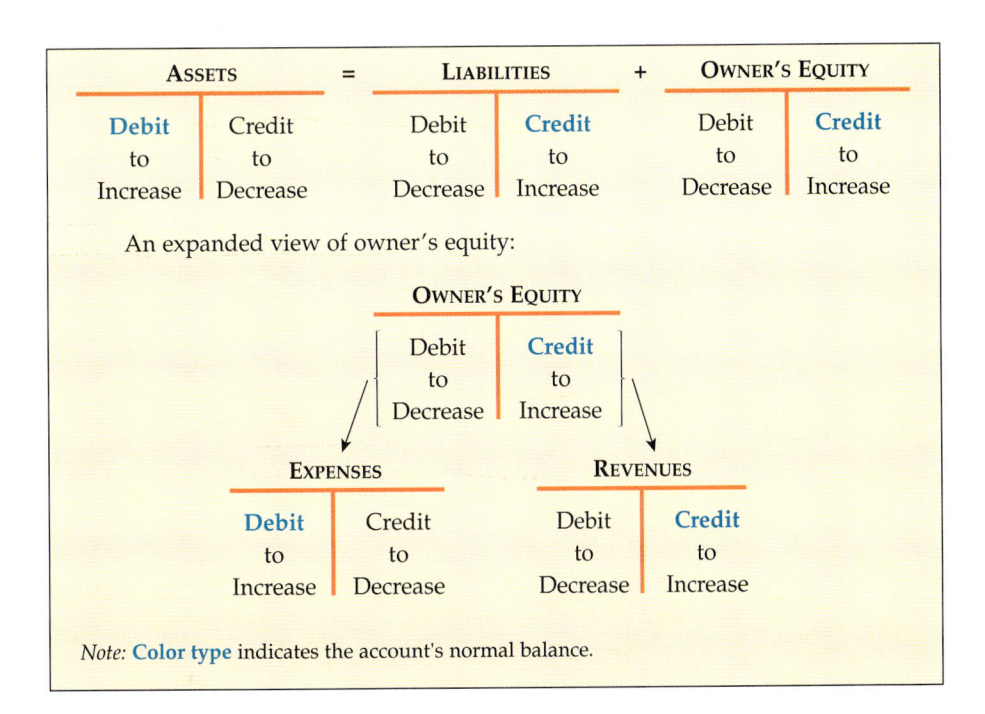

ASSETS	=	LIABILITIES	+	OWNER'S EQUITY
Debit to Increase / Credit to Decrease		Debit to Decrease / **Credit** to Increase		Debit to Decrease / **Credit** to Increase

An expanded view of owner's equity:

OWNER'S EQUITY
Debit to Decrease / **Credit** to Increase

EXPENSES	REVENUES
Debit to Increase / Credit to Decrease	Debit to Decrease / **Credit** to Increase

Note: **Color type** indicates the account's normal balance.

Application of the Rules. A review of Exhibits 2–1 and 2–2 will show that to increase the balance of any asset or expense, the account must be debited. Let us focus for a moment on Six Flags, Inc., which operates a chain of amusement parks. The salaries earned by the firm's employees would be debited to the Salaries Expense account because the company's total salary expense is increasing. In contrast, credits are used to record increases in liabilities, owner's equity, and revenues. Thus, Six Flags would credit an Amusement Revenue account to record the admission fees received from visitors who enter the corporation's various facilities.

The observant accounting student should note that *the procedures to increase any account match perfectly with the account's normal balance.* Therefore, once the normal balance is mastered, all you need remember is to give the account "more of the same" to record an increase. The rules to decrease, of course, would be just the opposite.

Let us return now to the questions raised on page 54 that relate to the Cash account illustration. The answers are as follows:

1. The dollar amounts will be entered as debits or credits depending on whether the amounts increase or decrease the account. Because Cash is an asset, receipts or increases are recorded as debits. Conversely, decreases to Cash are entered on the right side as credits, or in the credit column.
2. This question has really been answered above. Debits of $1,800 ($1,000 + $200 + $600) represent increases to the Cash account; the credits ($450 and $290) are reductions.

Misconceptions About Debits and Credits. There are two common misconceptions about debits and credits. From their experiences with retail stores, many people believe that credits always reduce account balances. When they pay on account or return merchandise, customers are often told that their account will be credited. Because the amounts due from customers are an asset to the retail establishment, these transactions will generate credits to reduce Accounts Receivable. Keep in mind, however, that credits also increase certain balances; specifically, those in liability, owner's equity, and revenue accounts.

A second misconception is that credits are good and debits are bad. This notion is incorrect. Although credits reduce your account on someone else's books ("good"), credits also increase the amounts you owe as shown in your Accounts Payable account ("bad"). Overall, then, it is a matter of perspective. Generally stated, the "good/bad" relationship has no validity and is best forgotten.

At this juncture it would be wise to thoroughly learn (repeat, *thoroughly learn*) the rules presented in Exhibits 2–1 and 2–2. These rules are used throughout the study of accounting, as they form the basis for the proper recording and processing of all business transactions. The sooner that you master the exhibits, the better off you will be.

JOURNALS

The transactions that affect an entity arise from many different sources. Evidence of these transactions is often provided by the receipt or issuance of accounting forms known as **source documents** (e.g., inventory receiving reports, bills from suppliers, customer sales slips, and customer checks). These documents show that a transaction has occurred and thus trigger the recording process. To properly record the account changes caused by a transaction, the source document must be translated into a debit/credit format. This translation takes place in the journal.

The journal, sometimes called the book of original entry, serves as the entry or starting point for transactions into a company's formal accounting system. Many students feel that the journal is a needless repetition of the information contained on the source documents. This is not so. Frequently, transactions are complicated; they affect numerous accounts and are supported by voluminous paperwork that is filed in various places. The journal brings order to the recording process by summarizing a transaction's key financial data in one location. Furthermore, the summarization is done in chronological order.

The Recording Process. To record its many transactions, a business may use different types of journals. For example, sales transactions may be entered in a specialized sales journal, purchases in a purchases journal, cash receipts in a cash receipts journal, and so forth. The journal illustrated in this chapter is commonly referred to as a *two-column general journal*. It has two amount columns (debit and credit) and handles a variety of transactions.

Recording transactions in the journal is a three-step process known as journalizing. The transactions are first analyzed in terms of the accounts that are affected. Next, the appropriate debits and credits are determined. Finally, in their new debit/credit format, the transactions are formally entered in the journal.

To illustrate these procedures, let us examine the following transaction of the Wise Advertising Agency. The agency was founded on May 1 of the current year when Gary Wise invested $9,000 of personal savings into the business. Analyzing the effect of this transaction, we see that the investment increased the agency's cash balance and also owner's equity. Using the format introduced in Chapter 1, the investment would appear as follows:

Assets	=	Liabilities	+	Owner's Equity
Cash				Investments
+$9,000				+$9,000

> ② Journalize transactions and transfer data to the general ledger.

Once the proper accounts are determined, the transaction is next translated into debits and credits. Because Cash is an asset, a $9,000 debit is needed to record the appropriate increase. As we just noted, the investment has also increased owner's equity, namely, the Gary Wise, Capital account. According to the debit/credit rules, increases to owner's equity are recorded by credits. This analysis is summarized in the following general journal entry:

DATE	ACCOUNTS	POST. REF.	DEBIT	CREDIT
19XX				
May 1	Cash		9,000	
	Gary Wise, Capital			9,000
	Owner investment.			

Observe that the debits are recorded first and appear next to the date column. Credits are entered next by using a slight indentation. Finally, a short description is prepared because the general journal will eventually contain a variety of transactions. The explanation notes the purpose of the entry: to record an investment by the owner. The posting reference (Post. Ref.) column is left blank at the time the entry is made.

Upon completion of the recording process, debits of $9,000 equal credits of $9,000, and the entry is said to be in balance. *In any transaction, the total dollar amount of the debits must equal the total dollar amount of the credits*. Naturally, this equality would not be possible if a transaction affected only one account. Accountants, however, prevent this situation from arising by employing a double-entry system of bookkeeping. With such a system, a transaction always affects a minimum of two general ledger components.

To conclude, observe that we are really performing the same operation that was illustrated in Chapter 1—increasing and decreasing the various elements of the accounting equation. Now, though, the increases and decreases are recorded by a system of debits and credits. The overall objective of effecting account balance changes has remained the same; only the method differs.

CHART OF ACCOUNTS

Accounts in the general ledger are usually arranged in the following order: assets, liabilities, owner's equity, revenues, and expenses. Within each grouping the individual accounts are assigned a number according to the **chart of accounts**—a detailed listing of a company's accounts and associated account numbers. For example, the asset portion of a chart of accounts may appear as follows:

Assets (100s)	
Cash	101
Accounts receivable	110
Inventory	120
Land	130
Building	140
Equipment	150

Liabilities might be numbered in the 200s, owner's equity accounts in the 300s, and so on. The determination of a suitable numbering scheme is an issue in systems design work. Sufficient gaps should be left when assigning account numbers for the possible insertion of additional accounts at a later date.

The chart of accounts is a useful tool when recording transactions. To illustrate, suppose Binkert Company paid an electric bill of $1,800 on March 31. The correct analysis should reveal that Binkert's total electrical costs have increased, calling for a debit to an expense account. Also, Cash has decreased. The following entry therefore appears to be needed:[3]

---

[3] This entry is recorded in general journal format. Observe the manner in which the account titles and amounts are staggered, thus duplicating the appearance of the entry in the general journal. It is not necessary to write the words "debit" and "credit" next to the accounts or amounts because this format is well-recognized and understood by accountants.

Mar. 31	Utilities Expense	1,800	
	Cash		1,800
	Paid utilities bill.		

However, a review of the chart of accounts might reveal that Binkert does not use a Utilities Expense account. Rather, in view of the large sums expended for energy costs, the firm has established separate accounts for:

- Electricity expense
- Natural gas expense
- Fuel oil expense
- Telephone expense
- Water and sewer expense

Separate accounts furnish management with more detailed information. The proper entry, then, which could only be made after inspecting the chart of accounts, requires a debit to Electricity Expense.

In addition to assisting with transaction recording, the chart of accounts also reveals how organizations can differ. Although virtually every company has accounts such as Cash, Accounts Receivable, Loans Payable, Sales, and Salaries Expense, businesses often establish accounts that are attuned to their specific area of operation. A review of corporate annual reports revealed the specialized accounts listed in Exhibit 2–3.

POSTING: INTERACTION OF THE BASIC TOOLS

The journal alone is not sufficient to handle the recording process. Many transactions have affected the same account and must be grouped together (i.e., summarized) to allow for the eventual preparation of financial statements. This summarization is achieved through *posting,* a process by which transactions in the journal are transferred to accounts in the ledger. The necessary posting for the entry on May 1 of Wise Advertising appears in Exhibit 2–4. The circled numbers represent the order in which the posting steps are performed.

To explain: ① The transaction recorded in the journal requires a debit to Cash of $9,000. This amount is transferred to the debit column of the Cash account. ② Next, the date of the transaction (May 1) is indicated. ③ J1 is then entered in the posting reference column of the Cash account to signify that

EXHIBIT 2–3
Specialized Business Accounts

FIRM	ACCOUNT	ACCOUNT TYPE
Philip Morris Companies, Inc.	Leaf tobacco inventory	Asset
Southwest Airlines	Deposits on flight equipment purchase contracts	Asset
Kimberly-Clark Corporation	Timberlands	Asset
The New York Times Co.	Unexpired subscriptions	Liability
Chevron Corporation	Exploration costs	Expense

EXHIBIT 2–4

Posting Transactions from the Journal to the Ledger

GENERAL JOURNAL

PAGE 1

DATE	ACCOUNTS	POST. REF.	DEBIT	CREDIT
19XX May 1	Cash	101	9,000	
	Gary Wise, Capital	301		9,000
	Owner investment.			

GENERAL LEDGER

CASH — ACCOUNT NO. 101

DATE	EXPLANATION	POST. REF.	DEBIT	CREDIT	BALANCE
19XX May 1		J1	9,000		9,000

GARY WISE, CAPITAL — ACCOUNT NO. 301

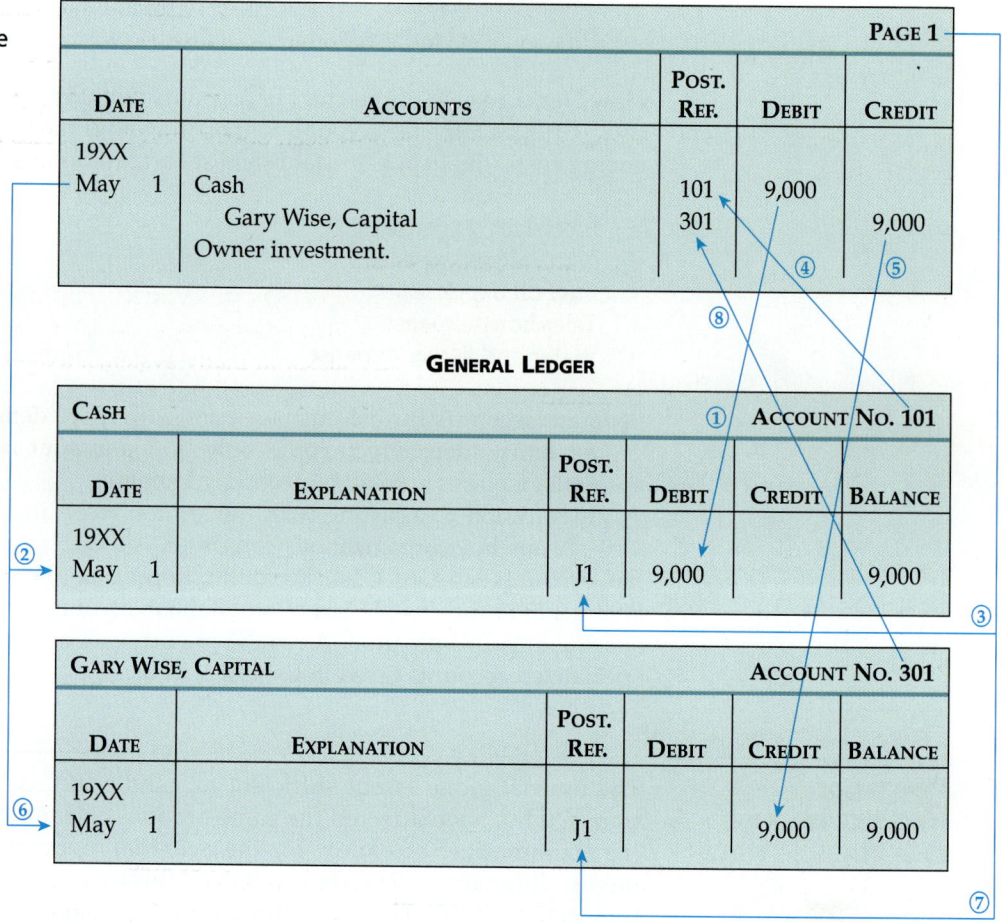

DATE	EXPLANATION	POST. REF.	DEBIT	CREDIT	BALANCE
19XX May 1		J1		9,000	9,000

the debit was transferred from page 1 of the general journal (as opposed to one of the other journals noted earlier). This procedure is performed should the need arise to trace a ledger entry back to its origin. ④ The account number, 101, is next placed in the posting reference column of the journal. This step serves two purposes:

1. The posting reference aids in the tracing process by showing the account to which the debit was actually transferred.
2. The posting reference signifies completion of the posting process. Consequently, a blank in this column is interpreted to mean that an entry has not yet been transferred. This procedure is important; should an interruption occur, the person performing the posting can easily find the proper place to resume his or her work.

The Cash account has now been increased by $9,000. If there were additional debits in the journal entry, they, too, would be posted in this fashion.

Once the debit is posted, the credit is transferred in a similar manner. ⑤ The investment generated a credit to Gary Wise, Capital. Therefore $9,000 is posted from the journal to this account. ⑥ Next, May 1 is transferred to the date column. ⑦ The source of the entry, J1, is then entered in the ledger account. ⑧ Finally, the account to which the credit was transferred (301) is entered in the journal. The credit has now been posted, and the process is complete.

COMPUTERIZED RECORD KEEPING

You have no doubt received the impression that posting (and perhaps transaction processing in general) is very procedural. This impression is correct. For this reason, even the smallest of businesses have acquired computer software to perform the necessary tasks. In many systems, ledger accounts are updated in a matter of seconds by the push of only a single key. The calculation of end-of-period balances and the preparation of financial statements are both automated. Furthermore, data that possess certain characteristics (e.g., an incorrect transaction date) may be rejected by the software and then printed on an exception report for review by a manager.

Suffice it to say that computerized systems have many advantages over the manual systems that once dominated accounting practice. A major portion of Chapter 6 is thus devoted to a study of these electronic timesavers. Realize,

---

BUSINESS BRIEFING

TERRELL B. JONES
President, SABRE
Computer Services
American Airlines, Inc.

The Importance of a Good Transaction Processing System

What does an airline need to fly? Of course, you answered, "airplanes," but you probably didn't answer, "computers." Yet, in today's complex airline environment, computers are just as important as airplanes in making American Airlines fly. With over 600 aircraft, 2,500 daily departures, and 40,000 pilots, mechanics, and flight attendants, there is simply no way we could plan, schedule, and operate our airline without one of the largest transaction processing systems in the world.

American's reservation system (SABRE) today serves 310,000 terminals and printers, handles the reservations of over 30% of the entire industry's travelers annually, and operates at the unmatched speed of up to 4,100 transactions per second. Processing and counting all these transactions is key to our success. It allows us to forecast demand, manage our revenue, and ticket our passengers. Although we have huge batch systems that handle our accounting and billing, it is our transaction processing systems that really make American fly!

And, what started as our in-house computer is now sold as a service as well. We handle the reservations of 360 other airlines and manage the reservations of over 28,000 travel agencies in 72 countries. SABRE not only runs American, it is the core of a huge computing business that makes a fair return on investment. At American, transaction processing is at the heart of our business.

though, that humans must still select the accounts to be debited and credited, and report users should have an understanding of information flows through a system. The computer is a powerful data-processing tool. Its output, however, is highly dependent on the principles and practices shown earlier and on forthcoming pages as well.

An Extended Illustration

The interrelationships among debits and credits, journal entries, and ledger accounts are best viewed by means of an extended illustration. Transactions of the Wise Advertising Agency are now presented, along with the proper journal entries. You should concentrate on each transaction and its analysis prior to viewing the correct entry. Again, follow the process of reasoning, not memorizing.

May 1   Gary Wise invested $9,000 in the business.

Analysis   See page 57.

Entry

PAGE 1

19XX				
May 1	Cash		9,000	
	Gary Wise, Capital			9,000
	Owner investment.			

May 5   Paid $800 of marketing and promotional costs related to the agency's opening.

Analysis   Expenses have increased; thus, Marketing Expense is debited. The Cash account (an asset) has decreased from the payment, requiring a credit.

Entry

5	Marketing Expense		800	
	Cash			800
	Paid promotional costs.			

May 10   Acquired a small parcel of land for $5,500 from Knox Developers. Paid $1,000 down, with the remaining balance due in 10 days.

Analysis   Land is debited to record the appropriate increase. Cash is credited because of the payment. In addition, Accounts Payable is credited for $4,500 ($5,500 − $1,000), as the amount owed to Knox, a liability, has increased.

Entry

	10	Land	5,500	
		Cash		1,000
		Accounts Payable		4,500
		Acquired parcel of land; balance payable in 10 days.		

Note: All necessary debits are recorded first, followed by the required credits. Observe that total debits of $5,500 equal total credits of $5,500.

May 14 Billed clients for services rendered, $1,700.

Analysis The amounts due from clients have increased; thus Accounts Receivable (an asset) is debited. The revenues earned by the agency have also increased, calling for a credit to Agency Revenue.

Entry

	14	Accounts Receivable	1,700	
		Agency Revenue		1,700
		Billed clients.		

May 20 Paid the $4,500 balance due Knox Developers from the transaction on May 10.

Analysis The $4,500 payment has reduced Wise Advertising's cash balance and the amounts owed to creditors. Accounts Payable, a liability, is debited and Cash is credited.

Entry

	20	Accounts Payable	4,500	
		Cash		4,500
		Paid Knox Developers on account.		

May 23 Received $950 from clients on account.

Analysis Two assets are involved in this transaction: Cash and Accounts Receivable. Cash has increased and must be debited. Because the amounts due from clients have decreased, Accounts Receivable is credited.

Entry

	23	Cash		950	
		Accounts Receivable			950
		Received cash from clients on account.			

May 25   Received a $125 electric bill, due in June.

Analysis   Total expenses have increased, requiring a debit to Electricity Expense. Accounts Payable is credited to record the increase in the amounts owed to creditors.

PAGE 2

Entry

19XX					
May 25		Electricity Expense		125	
		Accounts Payable			125
		Received May's electric bill, due in June.			

May 27   Received a call from Kathy Howard, a client, stating that she had not paid her bill of May 14 because of a $100 overcharge. Wise checked the agency's records and found the client was correct.

Analysis   Refer to the entry of May 14. Accounts Receivable and Agency Revenue were each overstated by $100 and must therefore be reduced. The original entry is left intact to improve accountability.

Entry

	27	Agency Revenue		100	
		Accounts Receivable			100
		Corrected error on 5/14 pertaining to Kathy Howard.			

May 28   Paid office salaries of $825.

Analysis   Similar to the transaction of May 5.

Entry

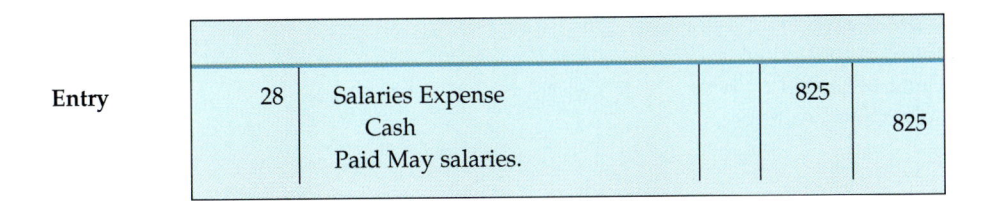

	28	Salaries Expense		825	
		Cash			825
		Paid May salaries.			

May 30 Gary Wise withdrew $200 from the business for personal use.

Analysis Recall that withdrawals decrease owner's equity. Rather than debit Gary Wise, Capital, many companies use a separate **drawing account** to accumulate such amounts. This account, given its "negative" effect on equity, will normally contain a *debit* balance. Wise's journal entry follows.

Entry

	30	Gary Wise, Drawing		200	
		Cash			200
		Owner withdrawal.			

May 31 Billed clients for services rendered, $2,500.

Analysis Similar to the transaction of May 14.

Entry

	31	Accounts Receivable		2,500	
		Agency Revenue			2,500
		Billed clients.			

The linkage between these journal entries and Wise's accounts is shown in Exhibit 2–5 on pages 66–67. Observe that the company's journal now contains posting references, meaning the debits and credits have been transferred to the general ledger. By tracing the transactions from the journal to the ledger, you can see, in part, how information is processed through an accounting system. (Note: We have omitted journal entry explanations to simplify the presentation.)

EXHIBIT 2–5
General Journal and General Ledger of Wise Advertising Agency

GENERAL JOURNAL

PAGE 1

DATE	ACCOUNTS	POST. REF.	DEBIT	CREDIT
19XX				
May 1	Cash	101	9,000	
	Gary Wise, Capital	301		9,000
5	Marketing Expense	520	800	
	Cash	101		800
10	Land	130	5,500	
	Cash	101		1,000
	Accounts Payable	210		4,500
14	Accounts Receivable	120	1,700	
	Agency Revenue	410		1,700
20	Accounts Payable	210	4,500	
	Cash	101		4,500
23	Cash	101	950	
	Accounts Receivable	120		950

PAGE 2

DATE	ACCOUNTS	POST. REF.	DEBIT	CREDIT
19XX				
May 25	Electricity Expense	530	125	
	Accounts Payable	210		125
27	Agency Revenue	410	100	
	Accounts Receivable	120		100
28	Salaries Expense	510	825	
	Cash	101		825
30	Gary Wise, Drawing	320	200	
	Cash	101		200
31	Accounts Receivable	120	2,500	
	Agency Revenue	410		2,500

GENERAL LEDGER

CASH					ACCOUNT NO. 101
DATE		POST. REF.	DEBIT	CREDIT	BALANCE
19XX					
May 1		J1	9,000		9,000
5		J1		800	8,200
10		J1		1,000	7,200
20		J1		4,500	2,700
23		J1	950		3,650
28		J2		825	2,825
30		J2		200	2,625

ACCOUNTS RECEIVABLE					ACCOUNT NO. 120
DATE		POST. REF.	DEBIT	CREDIT	BALANCE
19XX					
May 14		J1	1,700		1,700
23		J1		950	750
27		J2		100	650
31		J2	2,500		3,150

LAND					ACCOUNT NO. 130
DATE		POST. REF.	DEBIT	CREDIT	BALANCE
19XX					
May 10		J1	5,500		5,500

ACCOUNTS PAYABLE					ACCOUNT NO. 210
DATE		POST. REF.	DEBIT	CREDIT	BALANCE
19XX					
May 10		J1		4,500	4,500
20		J1	4,500		—
25		J2		125	125

GARY WISE, CAPITAL					ACCOUNT NO. 301
DATE		POST. REF.	DEBIT	CREDIT	BALANCE
19XX					
May 1		J1		9,000	9,000

GARY WISE, DRAWING					ACCOUNT NO. 320
DATE		POST. REF.	DEBIT	CREDIT	BALANCE
19XX					
May 30		J2	200		200

AGENCY REVENUE					ACCOUNT NO. 410
DATE		POST. REF.	DEBIT	CREDIT	BALANCE
19XX					
May 14		J1		1,700	1,700
27		J2	100		1,600
31		J2		2,500	4,100

SALARIES EXPENSE					ACCOUNT NO. 510
DATE		POST. REF.	DEBIT	CREDIT	BALANCE
19XX					
May 28		J2	825		825

MARKETING EXPENSE					ACCOUNT NO. 520
DATE		POST. REF.	DEBIT	CREDIT	BALANCE
19XX					
May 5		J1	800		800

ELECTRICITY EXPENSE					ACCOUNT NO. 530
DATE		POST. REF.	DEBIT	CREDIT	BALANCE
19XX					
May 25		J2	125		125

TRIAL BALANCE

3 Discuss the purpose of and prepare a trial balance.

Earlier in the chapter we noted that total debits must equal total credits in any given transaction. Because journal entries are transferred (posted) to the ledger, the ledger accounts (taken collectively) should contain equal debit/credit totals as well. To determine whether this equality does in fact exist, the accountant constructs a trial balance. A **trial balance** is a listing of the general ledger accounts, along with the dollar balances contained therein. Unlike the balance sheet, income statement, statement of owner's equity, and statement of cash flows, the trial balance is not a formal financial statement to be distributed outside the firm. Simply stated, its sole use is within an organization to determine whether the accounting records are in balance.

The trial balance of the Wise Advertising Agency appears in Exhibit 2–6. This two-column report lists debit balances in the left amount column and credit balances in the right amount column. The trial balance shows that the required equality is maintained at $13,225.

A Helpful (Not Infallible) Report

4 Determine the impact of errors on the trial balance.

Unfortunately, a trial balance with equal debit/credit totals does not always mean the accounting process was free from error. Several mistakes can occur that have no effect on the required equality. To illustrate, examine the transaction recorded by Wise on May 31:

May 31	Accounts Receivable	2,500	
	Agency Revenue		2,500
	Billed clients.		

Suppose the company had accidentally debited Land rather than Accounts Receivable. There is no way to determine that this error did in fact occur by examining the trial balance. The totals will still be in agreement because $2,500 of debits and credits were entered in the accounting records.

EXHIBIT 2–6
Trial Balance for Wise Advertising Agency

WISE ADVERTISING AGENCY
Trial Balance
May 31, 19XX

Cash	$ 2,625	
Accounts receivable	3,150	
Land	5,500	
Accounts payable		$ 125
Gary Wise, capital		9,000
Gary Wise, drawing	200	
Agency revenue		4,100
Salaries expense	825	
Marketing expense	800	
Electricity expense	125	
	$13,225	$13,225

In general, any type of error in which debits and credits are equal will have no impact on the trial balance's balancing. In addition to using incorrect accounts, other such errors include transaction duplication, transaction omission, the posting of entries to the wrong accounts, and using an incorrect amount within a journal entry (e.g., $3,500 as opposed to $2,500 in the preceding example).

UNEQUAL TOTALS

Several errors do cause the trial balance totals to be unequal. Locating the source of the error is sometimes troublesome, as this report is really a summarization of both the journalizing and posting processes. Mistakes can be made when (1) transactions are placed in the journal, (2) journal entries are posted to the ledger, and (3) the trial balance is prepared. It is generally suggested that one work backward through this sequence when attempting to pinpoint problems.

Aside from basic addition errors, common mistakes that arise include transpositions and the recording of debits as credits, or vice versa. A **transposition** takes place when two digits of a number are accidentally reversed (e.g., the number 560 is listed as 650). Transpositions can be detected by calculating the difference between the debit and credit totals and seeing if the difference is divisible by 9. Turning to the second error, recording a debit as a credit (or vice versa) will cause the trial balance totals to differ by twice the amount of the improperly placed figure. A popular way to catch this error involves computing one-half the difference between the debit/credit totals, and then looking for that amount in the trial balance.

If the problem is still undetected, return to the ledger and examine individual accounts. As a final step it may be necessary to work backward to the journal to inspect individual entries and postings.

> **ETHICS ISSUE**
>
> A trial balance is out of balance by a large amount, and management wants the financial statements NOW. Should an accountant temporarily "fudge" the figures to satisfy management's request?

A BRIEF OVERVIEW

The concepts presented in this chapter have laid the groundwork for comprehending the manner in which accounting information is produced. A transaction (or event) starts the entire process in motion. The transaction triggers the creation of a source document, which is translated into debits and credits and recorded in the journal. The entries in the journal are then transferred to accounts in the ledger by posting. Next, the trial balance is prepared to determine whether the ledger accounts are in balance. This sequence of events can be summarized as shown in Exhibit 2–7.

The trial balance is not the end of the process; it is only an intermediate step in the processing cycle. The next two chapters will illustrate the remaining procedures that must be performed for a transaction to find its way into a company's financial statements.

EXHIBIT 2–7
Basic Sequence in the Accounting Process

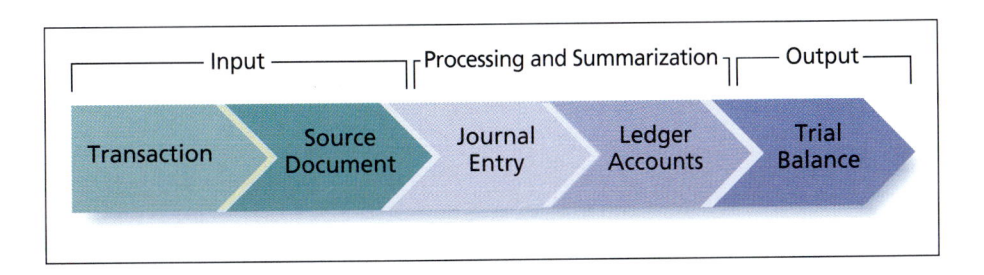

Input: Transaction → Source Document
Processing and Summarization: Journal Entry → Ledger Accounts
Output: Trial Balance

END-OF-CHAPTER REVIEW

LEARNING OBJECTIVES: THE KEY POINTS

1. **Define accounts, debits and credits, and journals, and explain their interrelationships.** The transactions and events that affect a firm trigger the creation of various source documents, such as sales slips and receiving reports. These documents are recorded in the journal by using a debit/credit format. The debits and credits, based on the following rules, are employed to increase and decrease the individual records that are kept for accounts (e.g., Cash, Accounts Payable, Agency Revenue, and so forth).

Account Type	Normal Balance	To Increase	To Decrease
Assets	Debit	Debit	Credit
Liabilities	Credit	Credit	Debit
Owner's equity	Credit	Credit	Debit
Revenues	Credit	Credit	Debit
Expenses	Debit	Debit	Credit

   The entries in the journal are then transferred to the general ledger by the posting process. The possible accounts to use when preparing journal entries are found in a listing called the chart of accounts.

2. **Journalize transactions and transfer data to the general ledger.** The journalizing (recording) process involves an analysis of the accounts that are affected by a transaction. Once this step is performed, the appropriate debits and credits are determined and entered in the journal. The posting process encompasses various procedures that involve the transfer of data contained in the journal to accounts in the general ledger. The major objective of posting is to summarize in one place the many transactions that may affect a given account.

3. **Discuss the purpose of and prepare a trial balance.** A trial balance is a two-column report that is used to check the equality of debits and credits in the general ledger. The procedures for construction involve classifying an account's end-of-period balance as either a debit or a credit. These amounts are then totaled to determine if the required debit/credit equality holds true.

4. **Determine the impact of errors on the trial balance.** Numerous errors can occur when constructing a trial balance. Several of these errors, including transaction omission and transaction duplication, continue to allow total debits to equal total credits. Others, such as transpositions and debit/credit reversals, destroy the required equality. Locating an error involves performing certain tests on the trial balance figures (e.g., determining whether the difference between the debit and credit totals is divisible by 9) and, if needed, on the ledger account data. As a final step, it may be necessary to work backward to the journal to examine individual journal entries.

KEY TERMS AND CONCEPTS: A QUICK OVERVIEW

account A record that is kept for the individual asset, liability, and owner's equity components of an organization. (p. 53)

chart of accounts A detailed listing of a company's accounts and associated account numbers. (p. 58)

credit   A tool used to increase and decrease account balances; also, the right-hand side of a T-account. (p. 54)

debit   A tool used to increase and decrease account balances; also, the left-hand side of a T-account. (p. 54)

drawing account   An account used to accumulate owner withdrawals from a business. (p. 65)

general ledger   A book or computer file that houses an entity's financial statement accounts. (p. 53)

journal   A chronological record that serves as the entry point for transactions into a company's formal accounting system. (p. 57)

journalizing   The process of recording transactions in a journal in the form of debits and credits. (p. 57)

normal balance   The type of balance (debit or credit) usually found in a ledger account. For example, assets usually have debit balances, liabilities normally have credit balances, and so forth. (p. 55)

posting   The process by which the transactions in a journal are transferred to the appropriate ledger accounts. (p. 59)

running balance form of account   An account format that offers the advantage of maintaining an up-to-date balance after each transaction is posted. (p. 53)

source document   A document, such as an inventory receiving report, bill from supplier, or customer sales slip, that provides evidence that a transaction has occurred. (p. 56)

T-account   A form of account named for its shape. The left side is the debit side, and the right side is the credit side. (p. 53)

transposition   An error that occurs when two digits of a given number have been accidentally reversed. (p. 69)

trial balance   An internal report that is used to check the equality of debits and credits in the ledger. (p. 68)

Chapter Quiz

The five questions that follow relate to several issues raised in the chapter. Test your knowledge of the issues by selecting the best answer. (The answers appear on p. 89.)

1. A credit is used in accounting to:
    a. increase an asset account.
    b. decrease a liability account.
    c. increase a revenue account.
    d. increase an expense account.

2. Popcorn, Inc., recently purchased some office equipment on account. The proper entry would involve a:
    a. debit to Office Expense and credit to Accounts Payable.
    b. debit to Office Equipment and credit to Accounts Payable.
    c. debit to Office Equipment and credit to Accounts Receivable.
    d. debit to Accounts Payable and credit to Office Equipment.

3. Which of the following statements is incorrect?
    a. Transactions are initially recorded in the journal and then transferred to the general ledger.

b. A company's accounts are housed in the general ledger.
c. Posting is a process by which accounting data are transferred from one record to another.
d. A source document is initially translated into a debit/credit format in the general ledger.

4. The trial balance:
   a. is prepared at the beginning of an accounting period.
   b. checks the equality of debits and credits contained in the general ledger.
   c. is prepared by extracting information directly from the journal.
   d. is a formal financial statement like the balance sheet.

5. Sofa Company's trial balance will not balance if:
   a. the $2,900 debit balance in the Cash account is entered in the trial balance's credit column.
   b. the bookkeeper accidentally forgets to record a payment of rent in the journal.
   c. a credit to Accounts Receivable is posted as a credit to Accounts Payable.
   d. a $460 purchase of equipment is accidentally entered in the accounting records as $640.

Summary Problem

A chart of accounts and a list of March transactions for the Drake Company follow.

Cash	110	John Drake, drawing	320
Accounts receivable	120	Service revenue	410
Office equipment	130	Salaries expense	510
Accounts payable	210	Utilities expense	520
John Drake, capital	310		

Mar. 1 Received $40,000 cash from John Drake, the owner, as an investment in the business.
18 Services rendered to date: cash, $15,500; on account, $12,200.
20 Paid employees' salaries of $10,500.
24 Purchased $4,000 of office equipment from Peach Equipment Company. Paid $3,200 down and agreed to remit the balance owed in 10 days.
30 Paid the March electric bill of $175.
31 Processed a $1,000 cash withdrawal to John Drake.

Instructions
a. Record the transactions in a general journal.
b. Post the transactions from the journal to the ledger.
c. Prepare a trial balance as of March 31.

Solution

a.

Date	Accounts	Post. Ref.	Debit	Credit
19XX				
Mar. 1	Cash	110	40,000	
	John Drake, Capital	310		40,000
	Owner investment.			
18	Cash	110	15,500	
	Accounts Receivable	120	12,200	
	Service Revenue	410		27,700
	Recorded service revenue from operations.			
20	Salaries Expense	510	10,500	
	Cash	110		10,500
	Paid employees' salaries.			
24	Office Equipment	130	4,000	
	Cash	110		3,200
	Accounts Payable	210		800
	Purchased office equipment; balance due in 10 days.			
30	Utilities Expense	520	175	
	Cash	110		175
	Paid March electric bill.			
31	John Drake, Drawing	320	1,000	
	Cash	110		1,000
	Owner withdrawal.			

b.

Cash   Account No. 110

Date	Explanation	Post. Ref.	Debit	Credit	Balance
19XX					
Mar. 1		J1	40,000		40,000
18		J1	15,500		55,500
20		J1		10,500	45,000
24		J1		3,200	41,800
30		J1		175	41,625
31		J1		1,000	40,625

ACCOUNTS RECEIVABLE					ACCOUNT NO. 120
DATE	EXPLANATION	POST. REF.	DEBIT	CREDIT	BALANCE
19XX Mar. 18		J1	12,200		12,200

OFFICE EQUIPMENT					ACCOUNT NO. 130
DATE	EXPLANATION	POST. REF.	DEBIT	CREDIT	BALANCE
19XX Mar. 24		J1	4,000		4,000

ACCOUNTS PAYABLE					ACCOUNT NO. 210
DATE	EXPLANATION	POST. REF.	DEBIT	CREDIT	BALANCE
19XX Mar. 24		J1		800	800

JOHN DRAKE, CAPITAL					ACCOUNT NO. 310
DATE	EXPLANATION	POST. REF.	DEBIT	CREDIT	BALANCE
19XX Mar. 1		J1		40,000	40,000

JOHN DRAKE, DRAWING					ACCOUNT NO. 320
DATE	EXPLANATION	POST. REF.	DEBIT	CREDIT	BALANCE
19XX Mar. 31		J1	1,000		1,000

SERVICE REVENUE					ACCOUNT NO. 410
DATE	EXPLANATION	POST. REF.	DEBIT	CREDIT	BALANCE
19XX Mar. 18		J1		27,700	27,700

SALARIES EXPENSE					ACCOUNT NO. 510	
DATE	EXPLANATION	POST. REF.	DEBIT	CREDIT	BALANCE	
19XX Mar. 20		J1	10,500		10,500	

UTILITIES EXPENSE					ACCOUNT NO. 520	
DATE	EXPLANATION	POST. REF.	DEBIT	CREDIT	BALANCE	
19XX Mar. 30		J1	175		175	

c.

DRAKE COMPANY
Trial Balance
March 31, 19XX

Cash	$40,625	
Accounts receivable	12,200	
Office equipment	4,000	
Accounts payable		$ 800
John Drake, capital		40,000
John Drake, drawing	1,000	
Service revenue		27,700
Salaries expense	10,500	
Utilities expense	175	
	$68,500	$68,500

ASSIGNMENT MATERIAL

QUESTIONS

Q2–1 Briefly explain how a typical accounting system operates.

Q2–2 In terms of debits and credits, liabilities are decreased by _____, assets are increased by _____, and revenues are increased by _____.

Q2–3 Explain how Accounts Payable could have a debit balance.

Q2–4 Explain the relationship between the accounting equation and normal account balances.

Q2–5 Les Howard accidentally debited an expense account rather than an asset account. As a result of this error, determine whether the following items will be overstated, understated, or unaffected.
a. Total assets.
b. Total expenses.
c. Net income.

Q2–6 What is a source document? How are source documents used in the accounting process?

Q2–7 A student once commented: "I don't understand the purpose of the ledger account. It seems as though the account is an unnecessary duplication of the journal." Is the student correct? Why?

Q2–8 Why is the posting reference column in the journal left blank at the time an entry is recorded?

Q2–9 What is the purpose of a trial balance?

Q2–10 What types of errors will not affect the equality of the trial balance totals?

Q2–11 A $750 debit to Cash was accidentally posted as a credit to Accounts Payable.
a. Will the trial balance be in balance?
b. If your answer to part (a) is "no," what will be the difference between the debit and credit totals?

EXERCISES

E2–1 Recognition of normal balances (L.O. 1)
The following items appeared in the accounting records of Triguero's, a retail music store that also sponsors concerts. Classify each of the items as an asset, liability, revenue, or expense from the company's viewpoint. Also indicate the normal account balance of each item.

a. The tapes and CDs held for sale to customers.
b. A long-term loan owed to Citizens Bank.
c. Promotional costs to publicize a concert.
d. Daily receipts from merchandise sold.
e. Amounts due from customers.
f. Land held as an investment.
g. A new fax machine purchased for office use.
h. Amounts to be paid in 10 days to suppliers.
i. Amounts paid to a mall for rent.

E2–2 Debits and credits, journals, ledgers, the chart of accounts (L.O. 1, 2)
The comments that follow were taken from the test of an accounting principles student. Do you agree with these comments or disagree? For those comments with which you disagree, briefly state the reason behind your position.

a. Debits are used to decrease liability accounts.
b. In general, credits are "good" and debits are "bad."
c. Transactions are normally recorded in the ledger and then posted to the journal.
d. The chart of accounts is a useful device in trying to determine the proper titles of accounts to debit and credit.
e. Failure to credit a revenue account will overstate total revenues on the income statement.

E2–3 General journal and general ledger content (L.O. 1)
St. James Services uses a general journal and general ledger to process transactions. Assume that the volume of transactions has grown in recent months and that all posting procedures have already been performed. A manager has requested that you provide the following data:

a. The total amounts that clients owe the firm as of May 31.
b. The accounts that were increased or decreased by a particular transaction on a specific date.

c. The total cash received during May.
d. The reason for a cash disbursement on May 14.
e. A dated listing of all decreases to the Accounts Payable account during the month.

Evaluate the data requests of the manager independently and determine whether the requests can be answered most efficiently by a review of the company's general journal *or* the company's general ledger.

E2–4 Understanding accounting system components (L.O. 1)

Juan Zermeno, an attorney, is representing a bank in a lawsuit against Mercury Printing Corporation. The suit alleges a gross overstatement of revenue by Mercury on a bank loan application. Zermeno can legally file papers that will force Mercury to disclose key accounting information. If the papers are filed, what accounting records should Zermeno request in order to prove his case?

E2–5 Transaction analysis (L.O. 1)

The T-accounts that follow were taken from the books of Dearborn Data Services on December 31 of the current year. Letters in the accounts reference specific transactions of the firm.

CASH		ACCOUNTS RECEIVABLE		COMPUTER EQUIPMENT
(a) 35,000 | (d) 3,000		(c) 14,000 | (f) 8,000		(b) 26,000
(b) 10,000 | (g) 1,500				(e) 9,000
(f) 8,000 | (h) 800				

ACCOUNTS PAYABLE		LOAN PAYABLE		DEARBORN, CAPITAL
(h) 800 | (e) 9,000		(g) 1,500 | (a) 35,000		| (b) 36,000

FEES EARNED		ADVERTISING EXPENSE		UTILITIES EXPENSE
| (c) 14,000		(d) 2,000		(d) 1,000

Write a brief explanation of each of the transactions (a)–(h).

E2–6 Analysis of journal entries (L.O. 2)

The following journal entries were recorded by the Geary Company:

a. Delivery Equipment   15,000
        Loan Payable   12,000
        Cash   3,000

b. Cash   2,300
        Accounts Receivable   2,300

c. John Geary, Drawing   1,800
        Cash   1,800

d.	Cash	3,700		
	Accounts Receivable	4,400		
	Service Revenue		8,100	
e.	Promotion Expense	1,900		
	Accounts Payable		1,900	
f.	Cash	58		
	Office Supplies		58	

Write a brief explanation of each of the preceding transactions.

E2–7 Basic journal entries (L.O. 2)

Record the following transactions in general journal form. Include explanations.

a. Paid advertising expenses, $600.
b. Provided $280 of services to customers on account.
c. Purchased $2,600 of office equipment on account.
d. Processed a $400 cash withdrawal for Angie McDonald, the company's owner.
e. Received $100 from customers who were previously billed in (b).
f. Purchased land in exchange for $25,000 cash.

E2–8 Basic journal entries (L.O. 2)

The following transactions pertain to Blatt Company:

Nov. 5   Received cash of $50,000 from Mike Blatt as an investment in the business.
      8   Purchased $12,000 of display equipment. Paid $2,000 down and secured a $10,000 bank loan for the remaining balance.
    10   Provided services of $5,400. Customers paid $700 cash and agreed to settle their outstanding balances by December 31.
    15   Paid maintenance costs, $800.
    20   Collected $3,000 from customers for services provided on November 10.
    28   Received the November utilities bill, $460. The bill will be paid in December.

Prepare journal entries (and explanations) to record the preceding transactions and events.

E2–9 Trial balance preparation (L.O. 3)

Brighton Company began operation on March 1 of the current year. The following account balances were extracted from the general ledger on March 31; all accounts have normal balances.

Accounts payable	$12,000	Interest expense	$ 300
Accounts receivable	8,800	Land	?
Advertising expense	5,700	Loan payable	26,000
Bob Brighton, capital	30,000	Salaries expense	11,100
Cash	22,500	Utilities expense	700
Fees earned	18,900		

a. Determine the cost of the company's land by preparing a trial balance.
b. Determine the firm's net income for the period ended March 31.

E2–10 Analysis of accounting data; errors (L.O. 1, 4)

Consider the T-account that follows, which lists selected transactions of Financial Consultants:

ACCOUNTS RECEIVABLE			
3/1	23,654	3/7	18,321
3/5	8,479	3/18	3,210
3/12	5,675	3/22	4,879
3/28	11,111		

a. Determine the account's total debits, total credits, and ending balance.
b. Briefly describe the type of transaction that likely occurred on March 7 and on March 28.
c. A $5,675 check from a client on account was not entered in the accounting records. What is the impact of this error on the true ending accounts receivable balance?
d. The firm's trial balance would not balance, with total credits exceeding total debits by $6,420. Is it possible that the Accounts Receivable account is the cause of the problem? Why?

E2–11 Trial balance errors (L.O. 4)

You are reviewing the month-end trial balance for Schirmer Enterprises and discover various errors (items a–f below). Identify the effect of the errors on the trial balance by using the following codes. Where appropriate, indicate the amount of the error.

1—Debits will exceed credits by $_____.
2—Credits will exceed debits by $_____.
3—Debits will be equal to credits.

a. Failed to record $1,000 of service revenue charged to customers at month-end.
b. Incorrectly understated the balance in the Cash account by $2,500.
c. Recorded the collection of $400 on account as a debit to Cash and a debit to Accounts Receivable.
d. Recorded the $5,000 balance of Equipment in the credit column of the trial balance.
e. Recorded payment of the month's $700 utility bill as a $700 debit to Utilities Expense and a $70 credit to Cash.
f. Recorded a $3,000 payment on account as a debit to Repairs Expense and a credit to Cash.

Series A

PROBLEMS

P2–A1 Accounting system evaluation (L.O. 1, 2)

Mike Scott is a t-shirt/memorabilia street vendor who sells various products just outside the entrance to local rock concerts. He buys the t-shirts for cash from a nearby vendor; all other goods are purchased on account from an importer. Mike receives invoices for these latter items at the end of each month; the due date is approximately 20 days after receipt. The invoices are tossed in a desk drawer until the date of payment.

The vast majority of sales are for cash, although credit is extended to some long-time customers. Mike keeps a record of the amounts due on index cards, notebook paper, or "whatever is available at the time of sale." No receipts are provided to cash customers;

however, noncash customers are asked to initial Mike's records to acknowledge their obligations. All cash receipts (and payments) that pertain to the business are entered in the register that accompanies Mike's personal checkbook.

Instructions

Evaluate Mike's accounting system. What deficiencies do you see with the system? What changes would you make?

P2–A2 T-account and trial balance preparation (L.O. 2, 3)

Consider the following transactions of Delgado Enterprises:

Mar. 3 Received $23,000 cash from Roy Delgado as an investment in the business.
   5 Purchased office furniture for $5,000, paying $2,700 down and agreeing to pay the remaining balance owed by month-end.
   7 Paid advertising costs of $3,000.
   8 Paid office wages of $2,000.
  16 Purchased office supplies on account, $800.
  18 Provided services of $10,000 on account.
  20 Processed a $3,400 cash withdrawal from the business for Roy Delgado.
  22 Returned 20% of the office supplies purchased on March 16.
  27 Paid the remaining balance related to the office furniture acquired on March 5.
  29 Collected $5,800 from customers on account.

Instructions

a. Establish T-accounts for the following: Cash; Accounts Receivable; Office Supplies; Office Furniture; Accounts Payable; Roy Delgado, Capital; Roy Delgado, Drawing; Service Revenue; Wage Expense; and Advertising Expense. Enter the transacations in the T-accounts, and determine the balance of each account.
b. Prepare a trial balance.

P2–A3 Entry and trial balance preparation (L.O. 2, 3)

Lee Adkins is a portrait artist. The following schedule represents Lee's combined chart of accounts and trial balance as of May 31.

110	Cash	$ 2,700	
120	Accounts receivable	12,100	
130	Equipment & supplies	2,800	
140	Studio	45,000	
210	Accounts payable		$ 2,600
310	Lee Adkins, capital		57,400
320	Lee Adkins, drawing	30,000	
410	Professional fees		39,000
510	Advertising expense	2,300	
520	Salaries expense	2,100	
540	Utilities expense	2,000	
		$99,000	$99,000

The general ledger also revealed account no. 530, Legal & Accounting Expense. The following transactions occurred during June:

June 2 Collected $7,500 on account from customers.
      7 Sold 25% of the equipment and supplies to a young artist for $700.
     10 Received a $500 bill from the accountant for preparation of last quarter's financial statements.
     15 Paid $2,100 to creditors on account.
     27 Processed a $1,000 cash withdrawal for personal use.
     30 Billed a customer $3,000 for a portrait painted this month.

Instructions

a. Record the necessary journal entries for June on page 2 of the company's general journal.
b. Open running balance ledger accounts by entering account titles, account numbers, and May 31 balances.
c. Post the journal entries to the ledger.
d. Prepare a trial balance as of June 30.

P2–A4 Journal entries, posting, trial balance preparation (L.O. 2, 3)

Molly's Landscaping Service was founded in January of the current year. The following transactions occurred during the first month of operation:

Jan. 2 Received $25,000 of personal funds from Molly Gregg, the owner, as an investment in the business.
      4 Acquired $21,000 of office equipment from West Office Furniture by paying $6,000 down and agreeing to pay the remaining balance in three monthly installments of $5,000 each, beginning on January 31.
      6 Returned a $3,000 drafting table that was purchased in error. West agreed to reduce the amount of the first installment due; the other installments would remain as originally negotiated.
     10 Designed the landscaping for a new office park; collected $800.
     16 Paid $2,800 to Hurst Office Management for January's rent of $1,000; Molly's portion of the utility bill, $500; and secretarial services of $1,300.
     31 Paid the first installment owed to West.
     31 Billed clients for January consultations and design plans, $13,500.

Molly has established the following chart of accounts for her business:

110 Cash	310 Molly Gregg, capital
120 Accounts receivable	410 Landscaping revenue
130 Office equipment	510 Rent expense
210 Accounts payable	520 Secretarial expense
220 Other liabilities	530 Utilities expense

Instructions

a. Record January's transactions in the general journal.
b. Post the transactions to running balance ledger accounts.
c. Prepare a trial balance.

P2–A5 Journal entry preparation, analysis (L.O. 1, 2)

On January 1 of the current year, MuniServ began operations with $100,000 cash. The cash was obtained from an owner investment by Peter Houston of $70,000 and a $30,000 bank loan. Shortly thereafter, the company acquired selected assets of a bankrupt competitor. The acquisition included land ($15,000), a building ($40,000), and vehicles ($10,000). MuniServ paid $45,000 at the time of the transaction and agreed to remit the remaining balance due of $20,000 (an account payable) by February 15.

During January, the company had additional cash outlays for the following items:

Purchases of store equipment	$4,600
Loan payment, including $100 interest	500
Salaries expense	2,300
Advertising expense	700

The January utilities bill of $200 was received on January 31 and will be paid on February 10.

MuniServ provided services to clients on account amounting to $9,400. All customers have been billed; by month-end, $3,700 had been received in settlement of account balances.

Instructions

a. Present journal entries that reflect MuniServ's January transactions, including the $100,000 raised from the owner investment and loan.
b. Compute the total debits, total credits, and ending balance that would be found in the company's Cash account.
c. Determine the amount that would be shown on the January 31 trial balance for Accounts Payable. Is the balance a debit or a credit?

P2–A6 Preparation of corrected trial balance (L.O. 4)

Nettles Company was founded on January 1, 19X3. The bookkeeper was having difficulty with the December 31, 19X3, trial balance, which follows.

Cash	$ 31,300	
Accounts receivable	26,100	
Building	50,000	
Accounts payable		$ 13,200
Loan payable		55,000
Ralph Nettles, capital		25,600
Ralph Nettles, drawing	6,900	
Service revenue		71,000
Salaries expense		38,900
Utilities expense	4,100	
Advertising expense	7,600	
	$126,000	$203,700

The following facts have been called to his attention:

a. All accounts have normal balances.
b. Receipts of $2,900 from customers on account were debited to Cash and credited to Ralph Nettles, Drawing.
c. Debits in the Accounts Receivable account were incorrectly stated as $5,500 rather than $4,500.

d. The Building account includes the land on which the building is sitting. Correspondence indicates that 80% of the complex's cost is attributed to the building.
e. The December electric bill of $500, due in January, was not recorded.
f. A withdrawal of $1,200 in December was accidentally debited to Ralph Nettles, Capital. The credit was recorded correctly.
g. A $2,900 salary payment was debited to Cash and credited to Salaries Expense.
h. A $3,200 advertising bill was inadvertently recorded and paid as $2,300. The advertising agency agreed to accept the balance due in January 19X4.
i. The Miscellaneous Expense account of $1,900 was accidentally omitted from the trial balance.
j. Credits of $1,000 to the Service Revenue account were overlooked when calculating the account's balance.

Instructions

Prepare a corrected December 31, 19X3, trial balance for Nettles Company.

Series B

P2–B1 Accounting system description and operation (L.O. 1, 2)

Coal Mine Pale Ale, a brew pub/restaurant, recently opened in the downtown area of Seattle. The company uses an accounting system that includes the following components: source documents, general journal, general ledger, accounts, and a chart of accounts. The organization has just hired a brewmaster from Europe who is unfamiliar with how Americans "keep their books."

Instructions

a. Prepare a brief description of the individual components in Coal Mine's accounting system.
b. Prepare a simple diagram that shows how a transaction's financial data flow through the system's components.
c. Would the brewmaster likely have some responsibility or involvement with any of these components? If so, which one(s)?

P2–B2 T-account and trial balance preparation (L.O. 2, 3)

Consider the following transactions of Lopez Service Organization:

May	1	The owner, José Lopez, opened a bank account in the name of the business by depositing $12,500.
	8	Rendered services on account, $4,000.
	16	Paid $1,000 for employee salaries.
	19	Customers, previously billed, paid $2,500 on account.
	24	Purchased $400 of office equipment on account.
	25	Rendered services for cash, $750.
	27	Paid 60% of the amount due for the equipment purchased on May 24.
	28	Purchased land for a future building site. Paid $6,000 down and secured a $14,000 loan for the remaining balance.
	28	Recorded the receipt of the May electric bill of $115. The bill will be paid in June.
	31	Paid $800 for May advertising.

Instructions

a. Show how the transactions would appear in the following T-accounts: Cash; Accounts Receivable; Office Equipment; Land; Accounts Payable; Loan Payable; Lopez, Capital; Service Revenue; Advertising Expense; Salaries Expense; and Utilities Expense. Then determine the balance of each account.
b. Prepare a trial balance.

P2–B3 Entry and trial balance preparation (L.O. 2, 3)

A review of the records of Service City revealed the following trial balance as of October 31, the end of the first month of activity. Account numbers appear in parentheses.

Cash (110)	$31,800	
Accounts receivable (120)	4,600	
Land (130)	28,000	
Accounts payable (210)		$15,700
Roger Gates, capital (310)		42,500
Service revenue (410)		39,900
Wage expense (510)	19,300	
Marketing expense (520)	10,300	
Repairs expense (530)	4,100	
	$98,100	$98,100

The following transactions occurred during November:

Nov. 3 Received $1,800 from customers on account.
7 Paid $900 of wages and $1,200 of marketing expenses.
12 Sold 75% of the land to a client for $21,000 cash.
16 Had $400 of repair work performed; agreed to pay the balance due in early December.
20 Rendered $3,500 of services on account.
28 Paid $3,900 to creditors on account.

Instructions

a. Record the necessary journal entries for November on page 3 of the company's general journal.
b. Open the firm's running balance ledger accounts by entering account titles, account numbers, and October 31 balances.
c. Post the journal entries to the ledger.
d. Prepare a trial balance as of November 30.

P2–B4 Journal entries, posting, trial balance preparation (L.O. 2, 3)

AAA Furniture Leasing was founded on February 1 of the current year to rent furniture and decorative accessories, primarily to apartment residents. The following transactions occurred during the first month of operation:

Feb. 1 James Larkin, the owner, invested $28,000 of personal funds into the business.
4 Acquired $35,000 of rental furniture from Trendsetters, Inc. Paid $10,000 down, with the remaining balance due in five equal monthly installments beginning on February 28.
10 Received $7,000 of additional financing by securing a short-term loan with United Bank & Trust.

Feb. 19 Returned $2,200 of furniture to Trendsetters that was shipped in error. Trendsetters agreed to reduce the amount of the first installment due; the other installments would remain as originally negotiated.

23 Paid operating expenses as follows: salaries, $1,900; utilities, $600; and marketing, $950.

28 Paid the first installment owed to Trendsetters, Inc.

28 Recorded February rental revenues as follows: cash, $2,900; on account, $3,700.

AAA has established the following accounts and account numbers:

Cash	110	James Larkin, capital	300
Accounts receivable	120	Rental revenue	400
Rental furniture	130	Marketing expense	510
Accounts payable	210	Salaries expense	520
Loan payable	220	Utilities expense	530

Instructions

a. Record AAA's transactions in the general journal.
b. Post the transactions to running balance ledger accounts.
c. Prepare a trial balance.

P2–B5 Journal entry preparation, analysis (L.O. 1, 2)

The following amounts were extracted from the May 31, 19X4, trial balance of Cipperly Company:

Cash	$1,235	J. Cipperly, drawing	$1,500
Accounts receivable	2,356	Service revenue	9,630
Land	9,912	Salaries expense	4,888
Loan payable	2,700	Utilities expense	1,711
Accounts payable	2,211	Rent expense	2,439
J. Cipperly, capital	9,500		

Additional data:

1. The company began operations on May 1, 19X4.
2. All accounts have normal balances.
3. The owner made one investment and one withdrawal during May. Both transactions were in cash.
4. All services are provided on account.
5. The land was acquired on May 31 by paying cash of $7,212 and securing a loan for the balance.
6. The first loan payment of $350 will be made on June 30, 19X4. This amount includes $125 of interest.

Instructions

a. Prepare journal entries to record:
   (1) The owner investment and withdrawal.
   (2) Services provided on account.
   (3) Receipts on account from clients.
   (4) Acquisition of the land.
   (5) The first loan payment on June 30, 19X4.

b. The Cash account will contain many individual transactions by the end of any given month. Will the total of the individual credits in the Cash account typically exceed the total of the individual debits? Briefly explain your answer.
c. Were the account balances listed in the problem computed before or after May's transactions were posted to the general ledger? Briefly discuss.

P2–B6 Correction of trial balance errors (L.O. 4)

The bookkeeper of the Bedford Painting Company, a sole proprietorship owned by Richard DiCosola, is having trouble getting the trial balance to balance. The "latest version" showed total debits of $210,500 and total credits of $181,900. The following information is known:

1. All accounts have normal balances.
2. Two accounts were accidentally overlooked when the trial balance was prepared: Advertising Expense ($1,900) and Accounts Payable ($3,700).
3. Accounts Receivable was listed in the debit column as $15,800. A closer look at the account revealed the following:

Beginning balance	$ 18,800
Services provided on account	55,400
Customer receipts on account	(58,600)

4. A $2,200 withdrawal by DiCosola was debited to the Capital account rather than the Drawing account. The credit was recorded correctly.
5. Credits to the Cash account of $600 were overlooked when figuring the account's balance.
6. A quick glance at the trial balance found the following:

    Debit column:
Equipment	$47,900
Loan payable	12,400

    Credit column:
Painting revenue	78,400

7. A $300 payment for truck maintenance was debited to Repairs Expense for $3,000 and credited to Cash for $3,000.
8. The purchase of a $1,200 paint sprayer for cash was debited to Equipment; no credit was ever recorded.

Instructions

a. Determine the correct totals of debits and credits that should appear on the trial balance by starting with the bookkeeper's totals and adjusting for the errors that have been made.
b. Which of the following accounts would be listed in the debit column of Bedford's trial balance?

Advertising expense	Utilities payable
Warehouse	Richard DiCosola, capital
Paint inventory	Van

EXPANDING YOUR HORIZONS

EYH2–1 Source documents for personal transactions (L.O. 1)

Many people fail to obtain source documents (e.g., receipts) for a number of their personal transactions. As a result, information that is useful in explaining and changing one's spending habits may be lost.

Instructions

Obtain a source document for all of your personal transactions over the next week. Be sure to keep a record of transactions where no document is available (e.g., purchases from vending machines). On the basis of these data, prepare a short analysis of your findings, noting anything that was somewhat of a surprise.

EYH2-2   Chart of account variations (L.O. 1)

Charts of accounts vary from one business to the next. These documents reveal both accounts that are unique to the particular business and differences in numbering schemes. Some firms, for example, code transactions by account and also use additional attributes such as the related manufacturing plant and/or product line. The resulting account number may be 10–15 digits in length.

Instructions

Visit two totally dissimilar businesses and ask to see the chart of accounts. (An example may be a retail store and a doctor's office.) Note any accounts that are firm- or industry-specific as well as the coding scheme that is used. Prepare a short write-up of your findings.

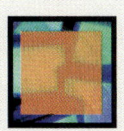

EYH2-3   Comparison of financial statements: Federal Express Corporation and The Home Depot (L.O. 1)

Federal Express Corporation is involved with the delivery of goods and documents throughout the world. The company owns an extensive transportation fleet to perform its service. In contrast, Home Depot is the world's largest home improvement retailer. The firm operates full-service, warehouse-type stores that stock 30,000+ items.

Instructions

By using the text's electronic data base, access the balance sheet and income statement of both firms and answer the questions that follow. Unless otherwise indicated, responses should be based on data for the most recent year presented.

a. Study the operating expenses reported by the two companies.
   (1) Are any of the expenses especially unique to each firm's type of business? Briefly explain.
   (2) Comment on the amount of detail presented by the two companies. Do you see any basic differences in the manner of presentation?
   (3) Compute each firm's operating expenses as a percentage of total revenues.
b. Over the three years reported, which company was more profitable?
c. Consider the nature of businesses in our economy (e.g., service, retail, wholesale, and manufacturing) and study the assets presented on the balance sheet. Do the assets reflect each firm's type of operation? Briefly explain.
d. Each company uses long-term debt to help finance its activities. Are the amounts owed to long-term creditors approximately the same or does one company have substantially more debt than the other?

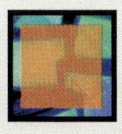

EYH2-4   Comparison of financial statements (L.O. 1)

This problem is a duplication of Problem EYH2-1. It is based on two companies selected by your instructor.

Instructions

By using the text's electronic data base, access the specified companies' balance sheet and income statement and focus on data for the most recent year reported. Answer requirements (a)–(d) of Problem EYH2–1.

EYH2–5 Analysis of accounting system and withdrawal policy (L.O. 1)

Chang Moon has operated a neighborhood bakery since coming to the United States from Korea. He has no accounting training and has not maintained any formal accounting records. All business receipts and payments are entered in a checking account that has been established for the firm.

The bakery acquires all supplies on account and pays vendors in the month following purchase. Amounts owed have increased significantly during the last two quarters because of suppliers' price hikes and the bakery's relatively tight cash position.

Sales volume during this time has been stable. All sales of bakery products to individuals are for cash; in contrast, sales to businesses are on account and amount to about 20% of total volume. Businesses usually pay Chang approximately 30 days after the transaction takes place.

Chang withdraws any monthly increase in the checking account's balance to pay personal living expenses. A summary of cash activities for the past month shows the following:

Receipts		
Cash customers	$20,000	
Business customers	5,000	
Insurance recovery from last year's oven fire	6,000	$31,000
Payments		
Bakery supplies	$12,000	
Employee wages	8,000	
Other business expenses	4,000	24,000
Cash balance increase before withdrawal		$ 7,000
Cash withdrawal by Chang Moon		7,000
Net increase (decrease) in cash		$ 0

Instructions

a. Describe the deficiencies in Chang's accounting system.
b. The bakery's checking account revealed a beginning and ending cash balance for October of $3,000. Given the nature of the bakery's operation, is it possible that Chang may be withdrawing too much cash each month? Briefly discuss.

COMMUNICATION OF ACCOUNTING INFORMATION

CAI2–1 Writing tone: Carnival Corporation (L.O. 1)

Communication Principle: A polite and friendly tone is an important factor in business correspondence. In the situation that follows, you must respond in clear, nontechnical language to a confused and angry stockholder.* Before beginning, consider that any communication from a stockholder is helpful because it indicates interest and gives a firm valuable feedback. Next, consider that your response is actually a "sales" letter—a

---

* A stockholder is an individual who has purchased shares of stock (i.e., ownership) in a corporation.

way of ensuring that the stockholder feels good again about the company. You can also be confident that, unlike most sales letters, this one will be read. You have a captive and highly interested audience—the best kind!

Now, how to make the sale? The best advice is to be polite and warm. Answer the stockholder's question clearly without sounding like a textbook. Don't be too brief or too formal. The stockholder may interpret a very short reply as curt and impolite and a very formal reply as cold and unfriendly. Above all, do not imply by your tone that you think the stockholder is dumb. Treat him as you would a good friend of the family, in a cordial and helpful way.

■ ■ ■ ■ ■ ■ ■ ■

Carnival Corporation sells complete travel packages to people who desire a carefree vacation at sea. The company also generates revenues from hotel, motor coach, and rail operations in Alaska and Canada, although these activities are a small part of its present business.

Carnival's recent financial statements revealed balances for typical accounts such as Cash, Accounts Receivable, Accounts Payable, and so forth. Also disclosed was one "unique" liability account: Customer Cruise Deposits.

This classification is totally correct. The liability was created when customers made advance payments for future trips. The journal entry to record these transactions involved a debit to the Cash account and a credit to Customer Cruise Deposits. The liability indicates that Carnival has a future obligation to either provide a service or refund the money.

You have been assigned to the stockholder relations department of Carnival Corporation. As part of your job, you routinely correspond with stockholders on various matters. The letter that follows was recently received.

> Dear Sir/Madam:
>
> I own 500 shares of your stock and love to travel on your ships. However, I am disappointed with the company's recent financial statements. How can I continue to have confidence in my investment when you obviously cannot prepare a balance sheet correctly?
>
> Please explain why Cruise Deposits appears in the liability section of the balance sheet. Deposits are obviously an asset—I send a check (an asset from my viewpoint) before the cruise departs, and you have the cash in your possession!
>
> I admit that I am not an accountant, but I am not a fool either. Please straighten this out with a prompt reply.
>
> Very truly,
>
> James Allen

Instructions

Draft a response to James Allen.

Answers to Chapter Quiz

1. c
2. b
3. d
4. b
5. a

3 INCOME MEASUREMENT AND ADJUSTING ENTRIES

LEARNING OBJECTIVES

After studying this chapter, you should be able to:

1. Discuss the use of transactions as a basis for measuring net income.
2. Explain the impact of the periodicity assumption on accounting and income measurement.
3. Apply the principle of revenue recognition.
4. Apply the matching principle and record expenses in the proper accounting period.
5. Compare and contrast accrual- and cash-basis accounting.
6. Explain why the adjusting process is needed and recognize which items typically require adjustment.
7. Prepare adjusting entries and show their impact on the financial statements.
8. (Appendix) Describe and use the "income statement approach" of accounting for prepaid expenses and unearned revenues.

Like a number of managers and owners, George Faris of Banner Advertising faces many basic business transactions. For Banner, these include leasing a billboard for a stated period of time, collecting some money, and compensating an artist for painting the sign. Even these relatively simple matters give rise to measurement issues in accounting. For example, consider Banner's cash inflows from leasing activities. Many clients pay monthly; others pay quarterly. Still others will prepay for a full year's worth of services. When should these monies be recognized as revenue—when received or when earned? As George notes, "We've got the cash in hand but the company often has an obligation for an extended future period. It seems as though one could argue the case both ways."

Also think about the cost of painting a billboard face. Banner must pay a trained artist to climb about 50 feet into the sky, stand on a 4' wide catwalk, and paint a picture that is 14' x 48' in size. Should the painting be charged to expense upon completion of the billboard or when the artist is paid? Or perhaps the cost should be spread over the months benefited by the expenditure. George has observed that "over time, under all three approaches, the same total cost will be expensed on the income statement. Yet the proper treatment, whatever 'proper' means, is important, as it will affect monthly net income."

George Faris and Banner Advertising are struggling with two common questions that many firms have raised over the years:

- When is a sale a sale?
- When is an expense an expense?

These issues are significant because they form the basis for assessing the profitability of an enterprise—a key barometer in judging an entity's success or failure. To develop an understanding of the issues just cited, it is perhaps best to begin with a discussion of income from the accountant's perspective.

THE MEANING OF INCOME

1 Discuss the use of transactions as a basis for measuring net income.

Almost all businesses are started with the objective of producing a profit, or "making money." These phrases, when put into accounting terms, mean the generation of net income.

The quest for profits is an integral part of the capitalist system. Profits (or losses) are the result of managers using the economic factors of production—land, labor, and capital—in an efficient (or inefficient) manner. Economists say that we can measure the outcome of this process in terms of being "better off." That is, profit constitutes the amount by which a business is better off at the end of a period compared to the beginning of the period. Profit would therefore represent a comparison of worth or value at two different points in time.

A determination of the degree of "better-offness" normally entails a number of subjective assumptions. For example, assume that an entity's key competitor has just recently gone out of business. Presumably, the surviving entity is "better off"; however, quantifying the event involves obvious difficulties. For instance, will the surviving company attract new customers and increase its market share? Will a new business take advantage of the situation and begin operation? These events will naturally affect the survivor; figuring their impact in dollars, however, is extremely troublesome. Generally stated, the economist's definition of profit is beyond the realm of what the accountant can objectively measure.

AN EMPHASIS ON TRANSACTIONS AND EVENTS

In an effort to overcome this subjectivity problem, accountants have developed a different definition of income (or profit). Accounting income is measured by subtracting an organization's expenses from its revenues. Expenses and revenues arise from *transactions and events*, which are happenings that have economic consequences for a firm and are measurable in dollars. (This latter criterion is consistent with the monetary unit assumption discussed in Chapter 1.)

A company will normally experience many different types of transactions and events. One broad classification, for example, involves exchanges of assets with other entities (e.g., the sale of merchandise to customers and the payment of taxes to a government agency). Another group focuses on measurable *nonexchange* events, such as the financial effects of a flood loss. Overall, recording these exchange/nonexchange happenings allows the accountant to downplay the economic concept of profit. Instead, a more objective transactions approach is used to compute net income.

THE ACCOUNTING PERIOD

② Explain the impact of the periodicity assumption on accounting and income measurement.

The accountant's approach to income measurement is complicated because the transactions and events that affect the financial well-being of an enterprise occur continually over the enterprise's lifetime. An in-depth analysis will find that most economic activities are ongoing; they do not cease and restart at specific times. In view of this situation, how can performance be measured? Owners, creditors, and financial analysts naturally cannot wait until the conclusion of an entity's life to assess whether a firm was successful or unsuccessful in its business endeavors. To address this problem, the accounting profession has adopted a periodicity assumption.

The periodicity assumption holds that for reporting purposes, an organization's life can be divided into discrete accounting periods (e.g., months, quarters, years, and so forth). When measuring annual performance, several different year-ends are available:

TYPE OF YEAR	EXPLANATION
Calendar year	Runs from January 1–December 31.
Fiscal year	Any one-year period other than the above (e.g., July 1–June 30).
Natural business year	Ends at the conclusion of the business cycle (e.g., October 31 for a professional baseball club, which is after the play-offs and World Series). This is generally a slack period, with inventories at reduced levels and virtually all of the year's revenues and income already generated.

> **A FURTHER FOCUS**
>
> Many firms within a given industry employ the same year-end. Food companies that had their start in grain-milling operations often conclude their reporting periods in May or June, around the time of the winter grain harvest. Examples of such firms include Quaker Oats and General Mills. In contrast, many large retailers (e.g., Wal-Mart, May Department Stores, and J. C. Penney) wrap up the reporting cycle at the end of January, just after the close of the busy Christmas season (and related returns).

Although the periodicity assumption seems practical and logical, an allocation problem arises when breaking the life of a company into divisible "chunks." Consider that a business may perform a service in June and collect the accompanying receivable in July. Similarly, a firm may incur an expense in October and settle the related account payable in November. If a given transaction is spread over several reporting periods, to which period does the transaction really belong? To answer this question correctly, one must understand the principles of revenue recognition and matching—the foundation for income measurement.

REVENUE RECOGNITION

3 *Apply the principle of revenue recognition.*

The issue of **revenue recognition** means that the accountant must determine the proper point in time to enter revenue in the accounting records. An obvious solution might be to recognize revenue when it is earned. But exactly when does the earnings process occur? Before deciding for certain, let us explore two examples with which you may be familiar. Bandai America, a toy company, recently faced a situation where demand far outstripped the supply of its popular Mighty Morphin Power Rangers. Nabisco Foods had a similar predicament with Devil's Food Snack Well's, a fat-free, no-cholesterol cookie. Both businesses were basically assured of revenue even before the goods hit the store shelves. In this case, was revenue *earned* when production occurred, or when the firms went through the "routine formality" of sale to the retailers? The correct answer is debatable.

To avoid confusion, the accounting profession has settled on a well-accepted guideline: *revenue is generally recognized at the time services are rendered or when goods are sold and delivered to a customer.* At this particular point, a company has concluded a major part of the economic activity related to the transaction. This point-of-sale recognition rule applies whether the customer pays cash on the spot or promises to pay in the future (or even if the customer has paid in advance).

EXPENSE RECOGNITION—THE MATCHING PRINCIPLE

4 *Apply the matching principle and record expense in the proper accounting period.*

As noted earlier, income is an important figure when analyzing an entity's overall success or failure. Because revenues *and* expenses are significant elements of income, it follows that business expenses be recognized in the same period as the revenues that they helped to produce. This concept is known as the **matching principle**.

INCOME MEASUREMENT AND ADJUSTING ENTRIES   95

The application of the matching principle is usually straightforward when there is a direct *cause and effect* relationship between costs and revenues. An example of such a relationship occurs in a hotel when a customer (guest) occupies a room. The guest uses towels and housekeeping service, and these items are said to help generate revenues for the company. The related costs should therefore be expensed when the occupancy takes place. The fact that the costs might be paid in a later period does not alter the analysis. Put simply, recognition when paid would create a mismatch, with revenues appearing on one period's income statement and the associated expenses on another.

Application of the matching principle can become troublesome when the relationship between costs and revenues is less direct or less strong. Consider, for example, an entity's use of long-term assets such as equipment, machinery, and buildings. These items provide benefits for a number of years. By the end of their lives, the assets are "fully consumed" because of wear and tear, obsolescence, and other factors. Consistent with the matching principle, each period benefited should be charged with an appropriate amount of expense. How much to charge is another matter—it is obviously difficult to figure the exact portion of a long-term asset (e.g., a building) that is used up in, say, one year.

To overcome this computational problem, accountants employ a systematic and rational approach and gradually expense the cost of such assets over an estimated service life. Known as *depreciation,* the mechanics of this process will be introduced shortly. Significantly, this approach is still rooted in a desire to adhere to the matching principle; however, the precision is not as great when compared with those costs that have strong causal relationships with associated revenues.

ACCRUAL-BASIS ACCOUNTING

5 Compare and contrast accrual- and cash-basis accounting.

The revenue and expense recognition principles just presented are fundamental to the accrual basis of accounting. Under the **accrual basis,** revenues are recognized when goods are sold or when services are rendered, and expenses are recognized when incurred. Related expenses are thus matched against revenues, regardless of whether such amounts (i.e., expenses) have been paid. As an example, consider the following data of Denton Enterprises that relate to January of the current year:

- *Services rendered*—The firm rendered $30,000 of services to clients, subdivided as follows: cash, $8,000; on account, $22,000. Customers paid $12,000 of the latter amount prior to month-end.
- *Operating expenses*—Denton incurred $10,000 of operating expenses, of which $7,000 were paid.
- *Rental payment*—At the beginning of January, Denton paid $6,000 for the next three months' rent.
- *Loan*—In the middle of the month, the company secured a $20,000 loan. As of January 31, $100 of interest had been incurred, payable to the bank in February.

Denton's accrual-basis income statement appears in Exhibit 3–1.

Service revenue is $30,000 because the firm provided services and earned $30,000 in January. The expenses incurred in producing this revenue are deducted to determine the month's net income. Note that only $2,000 (⅓ of the rental payment) is deducted as an expense—the remaining portion is applicable

EXHIBIT 3-1
Accrual-Basis Income Statement for Denton Enterprises

DENTON ENTERPRISES
Income Statement—Accrual Basis
For the Month Ended January 31, 19XX

Service revenue		$30,000
Less expenses		
Operating	$10,000	
Rent	2,000	
Interest	100	
Total expenses		12,100
Net income		$17,900

to future periods and will be written off in subsequent months.[1] Finally, interest of $100 is recognized because Denton had use of the loan proceeds to help finance January operations.

CASH-BASIS ACCOUNTING

When measuring income, some companies select another method of accounting known as the cash basis. With the **cash basis,** revenues are recognized in the period of *receipt,* and expenses are recognized in the period of *payment.* Examine Denton's cash-basis income statement, which is shown in Exhibit 3–2.

Note that the statement concentrates on cash flows. Services rendered during the month, for example, total $30,000. Cash receipts from services, however, amount to only $20,000 ($8,000 + $12,000), and this is the amount recorded as revenue. Only $7,000 of the operating expenses are recognized in January; the remaining $3,000 will be recognized in future months when paid. Turning to the rental payment, the entire outflow of $6,000 is treated as January rent expense. The loan, which is a cash receipt, is not considered revenue because it has not been generated by Denton's earnings process. The $100 of interest, applicable to January, can also be ignored, because payment will not take place until February.

EXHIBIT 3-2
Cash-Basis Income Statement for Denton Enterprises

DENTON ENTERPRISES
Income Statement—Cash Basis
For the Month Ended January 31, 19XX

Service revenue		$20,000
Less expenses		
Operating	$7,000	
Rent	6,000	
Total expenses		13,000
Net income		$ 7,000

[1] Accounting for such "prepayments" is explored in more depth in a later section of this chapter.

The cash basis of accounting is often criticized as not being in accord with economic reality. Stated simply, the receipt and disbursement of cash do not adequately measure financial activity within a given time period. This fact is apparent when examining Denton's transactions. Although the company provided services amounting to $30,000, only those services for which cash is received in January are recognized as January revenue. As far as expenses are concerned, the firm incurred and became legally liable for $10,100 of operating and interest expense. Under cash-basis accounting, however, only $7,000 is recognized. Finally, expensing the entire $6,000 rental payment in the current month overstates Denton's "true" rent expense, because $4,000 really relates to February and March.

Additional Problems with Cash-Basis Accounting. Cash-basis accounting can be criticized from two other perspectives. As shown in the preceding illustration, the cash basis does not properly match revenues and expenses. With Denton Enterprises, for example, several expenses that helped to generate January revenues will not be deducted until paid in future months. Furthermore, certain expenses were deducted (e.g., two months' rent) that failed to produce any revenue for the current period.

A second problem arises because cash-basis measurements are affected by the timing of receipts and payments. In the short run, the timing of these items may be manipulated by management. Payment of expenses can often be delayed for a few days or weeks, just long enough for the outlay to occur in the next accounting period. Additionally, collections can frequently be accelerated by inducement or pressure. By following a carefully designed game plan, a company can truly "control" its cash-basis earnings. In contrast, accrual-basis accounting recognizes transactions and events *as they happen* and provides far fewer opportunities for manipulation.

Cash and Accrual Methods in Practice. Because of the possible mismatch of revenues and expenses and the resulting misstatement of financial position, few businesses utilize a strict cash basis of accounting. The cash basis is probably employed most often in the preparation of income tax returns for individual taxpayers. The problem faced by businesses is that many companies have substantial investments in long-term assets such as buildings, machinery, and equipment. Under a strict cash basis these resources would be expensed when paid for, despite the fact that benefits are rendered for a number of years. In light of the amount of dollars involved, the cash basis would severely distort reported income.

Most firms that desire to use the cash basis adopt a **modified cash-basis** system, which is really a combination of both the cash and accrual methods. The cash basis is followed; however, significant expenditures that benefit multiple periods are established as assets in the accounts. As an asset's benefits are consumed, the cost is transferred to the income statement and treated as a business expense. The modified cash basis is often employed by professional practices (e.g., medical and law) and by small service organizations.

In contrast, virtually all large companies use the accrual basis of accounting. Usually, the majority of these firms' purchase, sale, and expense transactions are made on account, creating the likelihood that event occurrence and subsequent payment will take place in different periods. In view of the possible mismatch that can arise, the accrual method is endorsed by the accounting profession and featured throughout this text.

A HEALTH-CARE CONSULTANT'S PERSPECTIVE

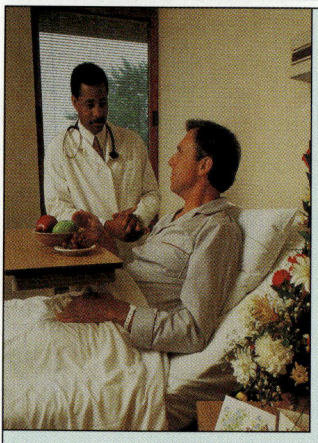

Clinic Net Income: Understanding the difference between accrual, cash, and modified cash-basis systems is extremely important in the field of health-care management. While the accrual basis of accounting provides administrators with excellent information on profitability, this system treats revenues collected in the same manner as revenues that are uncollected. In other words, both amounts increase net income. This is a big problem in health care because government agencies/programs (such as Medicare), insurance companies, and patients may, at any point in time, owe a clinic millions of dollars. These amounts due are a sizable sum for many practices—practices that are subject to heavy cash withdrawals at year-end by the physicians/owners. So that net income more closely reflects the annual receipts, payments, and cash resources of the practice, almost all health-care clinics employ the modified cash basis of accounting.

ADJUSTING ENTRIES

6
Explain why the adjusting process is needed and recognize which items typically require adjustment.

Financial statements that fairly present and measure economic activity cannot be produced by relying solely on information contained in the trial balance. Although the figures listed summarize the daily transactions that have occurred, many accounts need additional updating to reflect their correct status. Because of this situation, a process known as adjusting takes place at the end of the reporting period. In the **adjusting process** the accountant analyzes the various accounts that are maintained by a business. If updating is necessary, adjusting entries (adjustments) are recorded in the journal and posted to the ledger.

Frequently, the adjusting process centers on two specific situations:

1. Previously recorded multiperiod costs and revenues that must be split among two or more accounting periods.
2. Expenses that have been incurred and revenues that have been earned, but not as yet entered in the accounts.

The adjusting process is really an outgrowth of the accrual basis of accounting, with a focus on the revenues *earned* (as opposed to those received) and the expenses *incurred* (as opposed to paid).

MULTIPERIOD COSTS AND REVENUES

Given the continuous nature of business activity, many of the costs and revenues encountered by a company pertain to more than a single accounting period. The three-month rental payment in the Denton Enterprises illustration is one such example. In order to measure financial activity correctly, these items must be split or allocated among the periods affected. The next few pages focus on the related allocation procedures for prepaid expenses, depreciation, and unearned revenues—common types of multiperiod costs and revenues.

INCOME MEASUREMENT AND ADJUSTING ENTRIES   99

> **7**
> Prepare adjusting entries and show their impact on the financial statements.

note

Prepaid Expenses. Prepaid expenses are goods and services purchased for future consumption and paid for in advance. Typical examples include such items as insurance, supplies, and rent. It is important to understand that prepaid expenses are *assets* because the amounts will benefit future accounting periods. As these assets are consumed in the process of producing revenue for a business, a portion of their cost must be written off as expense. This write-off occurs in the adjusting process and ensures a proper match of expense and revenue on the income statement.

To illustrate the required accounting, we will continue (and modify) the Wise Advertising Agency example from Chapter 2. Assume that Wise had transactions during May involving prepaid insurance and supplies.

Prepaid Insurance. On May 1, the agency paid $480 for a two-year insurance policy. The transaction, which creates an asset known as prepaid insurance, is recorded by the following journal entry:

May 1	Prepaid Insurance	480	
	Cash		480
	Purchased two-year policy.		

As each day passes, a portion of the insurance policy expires. Thus, at the end of the period, the Prepaid Insurance account must be updated by an adjusting entry.

The policy acquired provides protection for two years at a cost of $20 per month ($480 ÷ 24 months). By the end of May, $20 of the policy has been consumed; consequently, Wise must credit Prepaid Insurance. This amount represents an expense and, accordingly, total expenses are increased by a debit to Insurance Expense. Here is the necessary adjusting entry:

May 31	Insurance Expense	20	
	Prepaid Insurance		20
	To record expiration of one month's insurance coverage.		

These accounts now appear as follows:

PREPAID INSURANCE		INSURANCE EXPENSE
5/1 480	5/31 Adj. 20	5/31 Adj. 20
460		

The Prepaid Insurance balance of $460 represents the 23 months of insurance that are still prepaid and is disclosed as an asset on the May 31 balance sheet. The Insurance Expense account, which contains the one month of expired insurance at $20, appears on the May income statement.

The transfer of prepaid insurance to expense will continue in later periods. Eventually, by the end of two years, Wise will have a zero balance in the asset account. The cost of the entire policy will have been removed from the balance sheet, indicating that the firm expects no additional benefits from its May 1 payment. The proper accounting for prepaid expenses is shown in a generalized format in Exhibit 3–3.

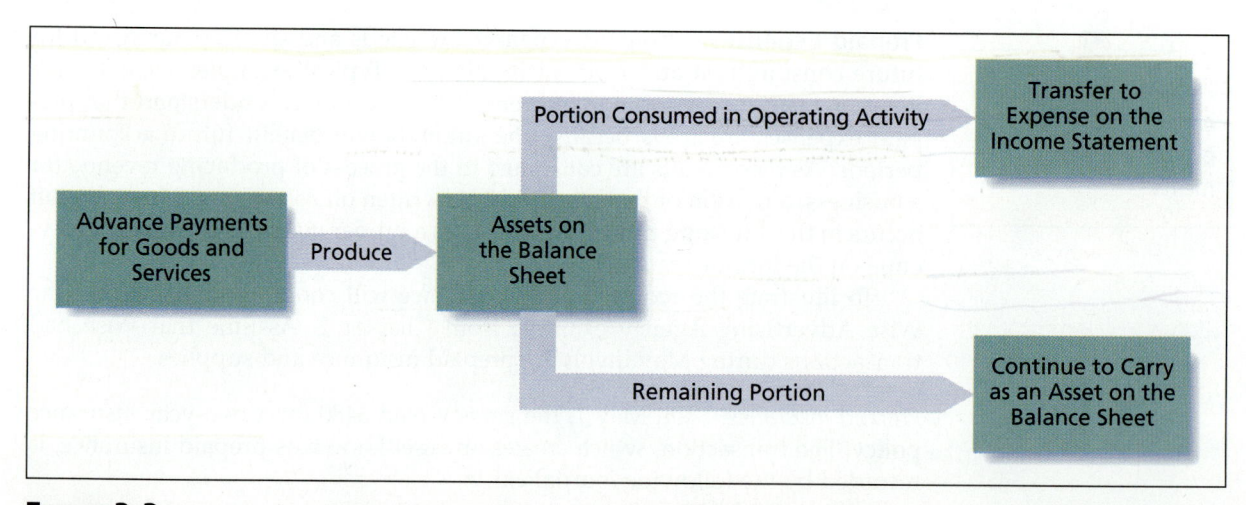

EXHIBIT 3–3
Accounting for Prepaid Expenses

Supplies. On May 4, the agency purchased $340 of supplies for cash. Because these items will be used in future periods, the purchase is recorded in an asset account as follows:

May 4	Supplies	340	
	Cash		340
	Purchased supplies for cash.		

On May 31, Wise determined that various supplies had been consumed in operations and that items costing $260 remained on hand.

An adjusting entry must reduce the asset Supplies from $340 to $260 to reflect the amount owned at the end of the period. Because this account presently has a debit balance of $340, a credit of $80 yields the desired result. The $80 figure, which represents the portion used during May, is an expense and must be debited to Supplies Expense. The necessary adjusting entry follows.

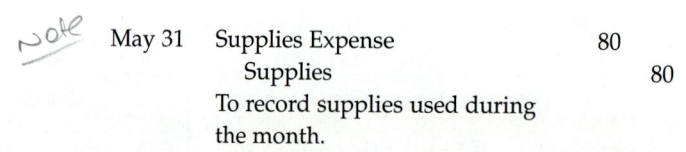

May 31	Supplies Expense	80	
	Supplies		80
	To record supplies used during the month.		

Similar to Wise's insurance transaction, the Supplies Expense balance of $80 would appear on the May income statement. The Supplies account contains $260 ($340 – $80) after adjustment and would be disclosed on the May 31 balance sheet.

Depreciation. Most businesses spend relatively small amounts of money for prepaid expenses. Considerable sums are expended, however, for the acquisition of other assets, such as buildings, machinery, and equipment, that benefit multiple accounting periods. Although these assets normally assist in the revenue-producing process for a longer period of time than the typical prepaid expense, the same basic accounting practice is followed: the asset's balance is written off to expense upon consumption. This expense is called **depreciation.**

Generally speaking, accountants are unable to determine the exact portion of a long-term asset that is consumed in a given period. As a result, it is common

A Further Focus

The proper period of time to write off prepaid items is not always clear. Consider America Online (AOL), a company that offers interactive media services (e.g., games, message boards, and data-base access) to subscribers. The firm incurs significant costs to secure new customers. The typical subscriber stays with AOL for 32 months; yet the company expenses the related outlays over much shorter periods (a maximum of 18 months). In contrast, CompuServe, an AOL competitor, expenses subscriber costs immediately on the grounds that subscribers can cancel at any time. (For an interesting discussion of this issue, see "What Profits?," *Forbes*, October 24, 1994, pp. 74, 78.)

---

practice to systematically expense a fraction of the asset's cost each year the asset is used. One possible approach for doing this, called the *straight-line method*, takes an equal amount of depreciation during each year of service life.

To illustrate, assume that Wise acquired a pre-owned car for cash on May 1 for business use. The car cost $4,500 and was estimated to have a service life of three years. The following entry was made:

May 1	Car	4,500	
	Cash		4,500
	Purchased pre-owned car.		

Annual depreciation will total $1,500 ($4,500 ÷ 3 years). On a monthly basis this amounts to $125 ($1,500 ÷ 12), giving rise to the following adjusting entry on May 31:

May 31	Depreciation Expense	125	
	Accumulated Depreciation: Car		125
	To record one month's depreciation expense.		

Depreciation Expense is debited and increases the agency's total expenses. Notice that the Car account is *not* credited, as accountants prefer to leave the cost of a long-term asset intact in the account where initially recorded. Thus, a separate account is established—Accumulated Depreciation: Car. This account appears as a *reduction* in the asset section of the balance sheet and is appropriately termed a contra asset. As its name implies, the Accumulated Depreciation account keeps a running total of the depreciation taken during the various accounting periods. The car would appear on the May 31 and June 30 balance sheets as follows:

	May 31	June 30
Assets		
⋮		
Car	$4,500	$4,500
Less: Accumulated depreciation	125	250
	$4,375	$4,250

The net figures ($4,375 and $4,250) represent the car's **book value**, or the amount that the car is carried at on the books of the business. Book value is simply the numerical difference between an asset's cost and the depreciation taken to date; it is not the value of the asset in the marketplace.

Unearned Revenues. The last of the multiperiod items to be discussed is unearned revenue. **Unearned revenue** represents future revenue that has been collected but not as yet earned. The earnings process, often called *realization*, will occur when some type of service is performed.

At the time of collection, unearned revenue represents a liability to the recipient, because goods or services are owed in return. Magazine publishers, for example, often establish an Unearned Subscription Revenue account. On receipt of a subscription, the publisher owes the subscriber a specified number of issues. As another example, airlines often report unearned revenue accounts on their balance sheets. Consider USAir Group, Inc., for instance, which owns USAir and several commuter airlines. Recently, the company reported $630 million in a liability account entitled Traffic Balances Payable and Unused Tickets. An explanation of this account was found in the following note that accompanied the financial statements:

> Passenger ticket sales are recognized as revenue when the transportation service is rendered. At the time of sale, a liability is established (Traffic Balances Payable and Unused Tickets) and subsequently eliminated either through carriage of the passenger, through billing from another carrier which renders the service, or by refund to the passenger.

Returning to the Wise Advertising Agency example, assume that the firm received $10,400 on May 16 to design and run a 52-week advertising program for McConnell and Associates. The necessary work on the program began immediately. The following entry records the receipt of cash:

May 16	Cash	10,400	
	Unearned Agency Revenue		10,400
	Receipt for 52-week program.		

Unearned Agency Revenue is a liability account, because Wise owes McConnell a service (advertising work). Observe that the credit increases the agency's obligations to its clients.

By the end of May, two weeks of work had been performed on the contract. Because revenue is earned at the rate of $200 per week ($10,400 ÷ 52), $400 must be recorded as Agency Revenue for inclusion on the May income statement. In addition, the amount of advertising work owed to McConnell has been reduced to $10,000 ($10,400 − $400) and will appear in the liability section of Wise's balance sheet. The proper updating is achieved by the following adjusting entry:

May 31	Unearned Agency Revenue	400	
	Agency Revenue		400
	To record agency revenue earned during the month.		

The impact of the entry is shown by these T-accounts:[2]

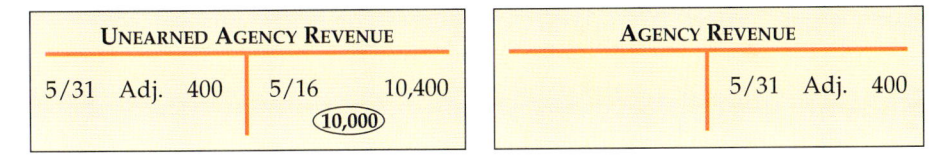

UNEARNED AGENCY REVENUE			
5/31 Adj. 400	5/16		10,400
			10,000

AGENCY REVENUE	
	5/31 Adj. 400

The preceding accounting treatment parallels that shown earlier for prepaid expenses. In this case, an appropriate amount of the liability becomes earned as services are performed, requiring a transfer of dollars from the unearned account to Agency Revenue. This process is illustrated in a generalized format in Exhibit 3-4.

UNRECORDED EXPENSES AND REVENUES—ACCRUALS

Accruals are expenses and revenues that gradually accumulate throughout an accounting period. Unlike the multiperiod costs and revenues just presented, accruals have not as yet been recorded in the accounts. As a result, an adjusting entry is needed so that these items are properly considered when the financial statements are prepared.

Accruals are consistent with the accrual basis of accounting. **Accrued expenses** are expenses that have been incurred but not as yet paid. Examples include the wages incurred by businesses during the last few days of a month and the interest owed to creditors on loans. Both of these expenses gradually accumulate and are likely to be paid in the next reporting period. **Accrued revenues**, on the other hand, have been earned although not as yet received. Common examples of accrued revenues include the interest just mentioned (from the creditors' viewpoint), commissions earned, and unbilled revenues. As you can see, we are focusing on revenues *earned* and expenses *incurred*, and *not* on the related cash receipt or disbursement. These concepts are explored by returning to the Wise Advertising illustration.

EXHIBIT 3–4
Accounting for Unearned Revenues

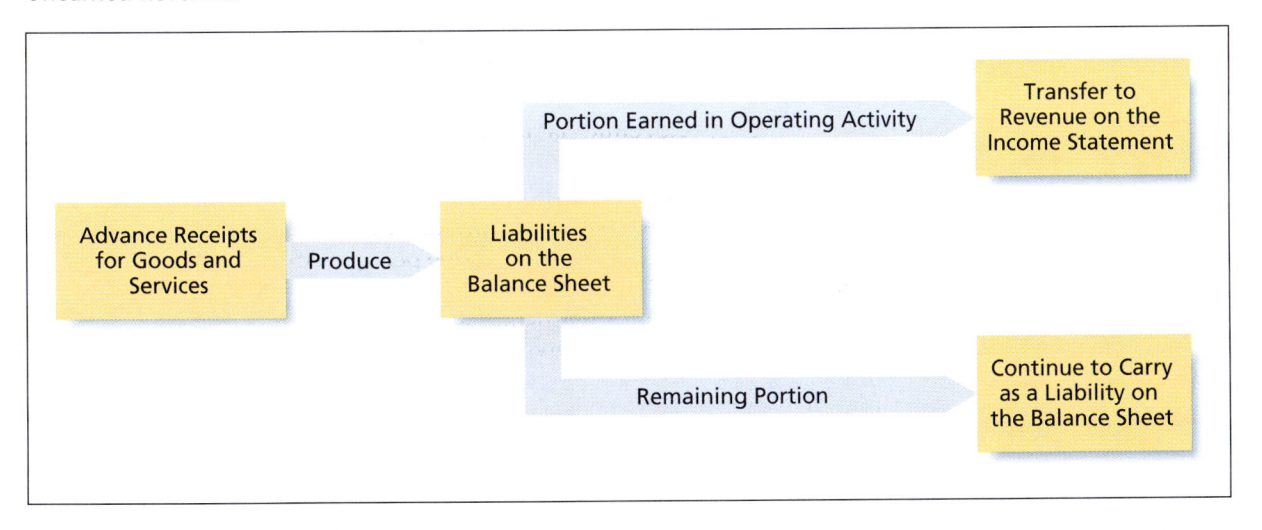

[2] In Chapter 2, the Agency Revenue account was affected by transactions on May 14, 27, and 31. These transactions are omitted here, allowing us to focus solely on the unearned revenue concept.

Accrued Expenses. Suppose that on May 1, the agency obtained a $6,000 loan. Payments are due on the first of each month; interest is computed at the rate of 1% per month on the unpaid balance. The proceeds from the loan are recorded in the following entry:

May 1	Cash	6,000	
	Loan Payable		6,000
	Recorded loan proceeds.		

As of May 31, interest charges have been incurred because Wise had use of the borrowed funds. Although the interest will not be remitted until the first payment date on June 1, the charges arose in May and should appear on May's financial statements. Consequently, an adjusting entry is needed to update the accounts.

Interest is computed at the rate of 1% per month on the unpaid balance of the loan. May's interest thus amounts to $60 ($6,000 × 0.01). This amount represents an increase in Wise's total borrowing costs for the accounting period, requiring a debit to Interest Expense. Further, because payment does not occur until the following month, $60 must also be placed in a liability account to show the firm's obligation as of May 31. Interest Payable is therefore credited, and the adjusting entry follows.

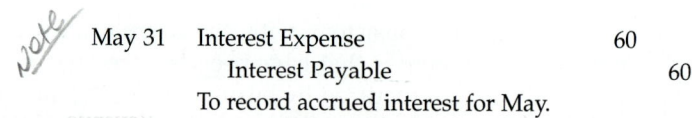

May 31	Interest Expense	60	
	Interest Payable		60
	To record accrued interest for May.		

> **ETHICS ISSUE**
>
> You have been employed to audit the accounting records of X Company, which is having financial difficulties. In an effort to improve reported performance, management strongly desires not to accrue month-end salaries, but to record the expense next month when profitability is expected to rise. As management notes, the same total expense would be reported over the two periods. How would you react?

Accrued Salaries. Focusing on another accrued expense (salaries), assume that Wise's employees work a five-day week. Employees are paid once, on the last Friday of each month, and payday for May occurred on the 28th (see p. 64). As shown in the accompanying diagram, the company has incurred one day of expense (May 31) that will not be paid until the end of June.

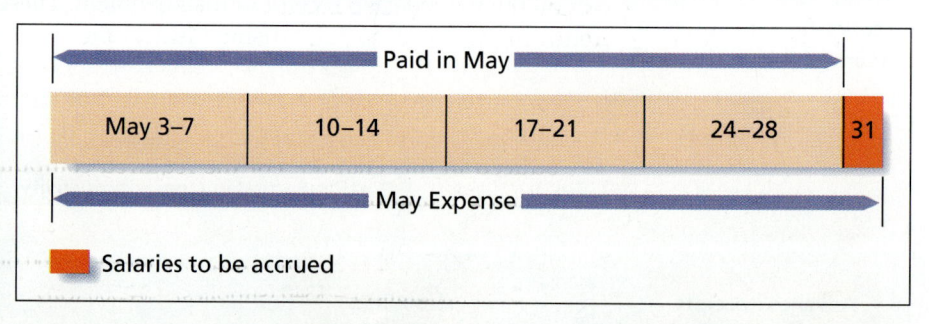

← Paid in May →
May 3–7	10–14	17–21	24–28	31
← May Expense →

■ Salaries to be accrued

This expense properly belongs to May and must be accrued (i.e., recorded) at the end of the month by an adjustment. If salaries for May 31 amount to $50, the necessary adjusting entry is:

May 31	Salaries Expense	50	
	Salaries Payable		50
	To record accrued salaries for May.		

The expense is debited because the agency's total salary cost has increased. Salaries Payable, a liability, is credited to reflect the added obligation of the firm as of month-end.

Accrued Revenues. To illustrate accrued revenue, assume that on May 14, Wise agreed to provide services for Holmes Corporation during the next five months. As of May 31, the agency had rendered services totaling $710. The $710 is properly considered May revenue because the service was provided during May; yet, to date, no entry has been made in the accounting records. The correct adjusting entry is as follows:

May 31	Accounts Receivable	710	
	Agency Revenue		710
	To record accrued revenue for May.		

Accounts Receivable is debited because the amounts due from clients have increased. Also, Agency Revenue is credited to record the increase in the revenue earned from business activity.

An Overview of Accruals. The adjustments required for accruals are an extension of two simple definitions. An accrued expense has been *incurred but not as yet paid,* and an accrued revenue has been *earned though not as yet received.* Given that both of these items must be entered in the accounting records at the end of the period, the adjustments may be pictured as follows:

note

ACCRUED EXPENSE			ACCRUED REVENUE		
Expense	XXX*		Receivable	XXX	
Payable		XXX	Revenue		XXX†

* Amount incurred
† Amount earned

ADJUSTED TRIAL BALANCE

Recall from Chapter 2 that a trial balance is constructed to check the equality of debits and credits in the general ledger. To reflect the account changes that result from the adjusting entries, many companies go one step further and prepare an **adjusted trial balance.** Before we illustrate the necessary procedures, we must update the records of Wise Advertising for the additional transactions introduced in this chapter. For the required computations, study the accounts in Exhibit 2–5 and then review the tabulation that follows.

Cash: $2,625 + $10,400 (unearned revenue) + $6,000 (loan) − $480 (insurance) − $340 (supplies) − $4,500 (car)	$13,705
Prepaid insurance: $0 + $480 (purchase on 5/1)	$480
Supplies: $0 + $340 (purchase on 5/4)	$340
Car: $0 + $4,500 (purchase on 5/1)	$4,500
Unearned agency revenue: $0 + $10,400 (receipt on 5/16)	$10,400
Loan payable: $0 + $6,000 (obtained on 5/1)	$6,000

The double underlined figures (and others) are carried forward to the first two columns of Exhibit 3–5, where preparation is shown. Note that the "regular" trial balance summarizes daily transaction information only; adjusting

EXHIBIT 3-5

Preparation of Adjusted Trial Balance

Account Title	Trial Balance Debit	Trial Balance Credit	Adjustments Debit	Adjustments Credit	Adjusted Trial Balance Debit	Adjusted Trial Balance Credit
Cash	13,705				13,705	
Accounts receivable	3,150		(g) 710		3,860	
Prepaid insurance	480			(a) 20	460	
Supplies	340			(b) 80	260	
Land	5,500				5,500	
Car	4,500				4,500	
Accounts payable		125				125
Unearned agency revenue		10,400	(d) 400			10,000
Loan payable		6,000				6,000
Gary Wise, capital		9,000				9,000
Gary Wise, drawing	200				200	
Agency revenue		4,100		(d) 400 (g) 710		5,210
Salaries expense	825		(f) 50		875	
Marketing expense	800				800	
Electricity expense	125				125	
	29,625	29,625				
Insurance expense			(a) 20		20	
Supplies expense			(b) 80		80	
Depreciation expense			(c) 125		125	
Accumulated depreciation: car				(c) 125		125
Interest expense			(e) 60		60	
Interest payable				(e) 60		60
Salaries payable				(f) 50		50
			1,445	1,445	30,570	30,570

entries are not considered. Columns 3 and 4, on the other hand, reveal the adjustments presented in the preceding discussion.

Observe that both halves of each adjustment (i.e., debit and credit) are keyed or referenced by a letter—the letter (*a*) in the case of insurance. The purpose of this procedure is to facilitate an examination of the adjustments by anyone who so desires. There are no rules regarding the assignment of specific letters to particular accounts.

In several cases an account that is needed in an adjusting entry does not appear in the trial balance. When this situation occurs, the account is simply written on the lines below the trial balance. After all the adjustment information is entered, the columns are totaled to check the equality of debits and credits.

Next, the trial balance data and the adjustments are combined to yield the desired outcome. As an example, the $3,150 balance in Accounts Receivable is combined with a $710 debit (increase) from an adjusting entry, and the result ($3,860) is placed in the debit column of the adjusted trial balance. Similarly, the Prepaid Insurance balance of $480 is credited or reduced by a $20 adjustment. The account's $460 ending balance, a debit, is thus also entered in the debit column. After all extensions have been made, the columns are totaled to verify mathematical accuracy.

Once an adjusted trial balance is prepared, the accountant has an excellent springboard for construction of the financial statements. As you will see in Chapter 4, the data just developed serve as the foundation for a *work sheet*—a columnar form that aids in building the income statement, statement of owner's equity, and balance sheet.

ADJUSTMENT ERRORS

The adjusting process is very important as far as the accountant is concerned. Failure to adjust the books properly at the end of the period will produce errors in the financial statements. To illustrate, assume that Wise's accountant failed to consider the expiration of a prepaid expense. As a result, an expense account was not debited, nor was an asset account credited. The company's expenses were not increased and are therefore understated. Because such amounts are subtracted from revenues on the income statement, the reported net income figure will be too high. Unfortunately, the problem does not stop here, given the manner in which the financial statements are linked together (see Exhibit 3–6).

EXHIBIT 3–6
Prepaid Expense
Adjustment Errors

Entry omitted:
    Expense   XXX
        Prepaid Expense*   XXX
    To record the expiration of a prepaid expense.

*An asset account

INCOME STATEMENT

Revenues	$ OK
Less expenses	Understated
Net income	$ Overstated

STATEMENT OF OWNER'S EQUITY

Beginning balance, Jan. 1		$ OK
Add: Net income	$Overstated	
Deduct: Withdrawals	OK	Overstated
Ending balance, Dec. 31		$Overstated

BALANCE SHEET

Assets	$Overstated
Liabilities	$ OK
Owner's equity	Overstated
Total liabilities & owner's equity	$Overstated

The overstated net income is carried forward to both the statement of owner's equity and the balance sheet. The exhibit reveals, however, that the required equality between assets and the total of liabilities and owner's equity is still maintained because of Wise's failure to credit (reduce) the appropriate asset account.

Should the adjustment error involve an accrual, a similar type of analysis can be performed. Assume, for instance, that Wise's accountant failed to make the $710 adjustment for accrued revenues. The failure to credit Agency Revenue will understate revenues on the income statement. If revenues are understated, net income will be too small. This, in turn, depresses ending owner's equity on both the statement of owner's equity and the balance sheet. The balance sheet will balance, however, because the accountant also failed to debit (increase) Accounts Receivable.

APPENDIX: AN ALTERNATIVE ACCOUNTING TREATMENT FOR PREPAID EXPENSES AND UNEARNED REVENUES

8 Describe and use the "income statement approach" of accounting for prepaid expenses and unearned revenues.

The accounting treatments illustrated in the body of this chapter for prepaid expenses and unearned revenues are used by many businesses. These treatments could be called the "balance sheet approach" because the initial recording of insurance, supplies, and revenues received in advance took place in balance sheet accounts. More specifically, the acquisition of prepaid expenses entailed a debit to an asset account, while the receipt of unearned revenue generated a credit to a liability.

Under an alternative practice followed by some firms (i.e., the "income statement approach"), prepaid expenses and unearned revenues are recorded initially in income statement accounts. Prepaid expenses are immediately charged to expense when acquired, and unearned revenues are credited to revenue accounts upon collection. To illustrate these accounting alternatives, we will continue to use data from the Wise Advertising Agency example.

ACCOUNTING FOR PREPAID EXPENSES

Recall from page 99 that Wise acquired a two-year insurance policy on May 1. The $480 policy cost was recorded in an asset account entitled Prepaid Insurance, indicating use of the balance sheet method. One month of the policy expired during May, requiring a transfer of $20 ($480 ÷ 24 months) from Prepaid Insurance to Insurance Expense via an adjusting entry. These events and the resulting financial statement disclosures are summarized at the top of Exhibit 3–7.

This exhibit also reveals the proper accounting had the agency used the income statement approach. Upon acquisition, the cost of the entire policy is placed in the Insurance Expense account. It is naturally incorrect to show the full policy cost of $480 on May's income statement because the actual expense to the firm is only $20. In view of this situation, an adjusting entry is needed at the end of the month.

To achieve the desired $20 balance in Insurance Expense, this account must be reduced, or credited, by $460 ($480 – $460 = $20). The $460 figure represents the cost of the policy's forthcoming 23 months (i.e., the prepaid portion as of May 31) and is therefore debited to Prepaid Insurance. In effect, the adjustment transfers the *unused* portion of the prepayment from the expense account to an asset. The overall result of this process is one month of cost on the income statement and the remaining 23 months of cost on the balance sheet.

> On May 1, Wise Advertising paid $480 for a two-year insurance policy. The policy expires at the rate of $20 per month ($480 ÷ 24 months).
>
> **BALANCE SHEET APPROACH**
>
> | | | | |
> |---|---|---|---|
> | 5/1 | Prepaid Insurance | 480 | |
> | | Cash | | 480 |
> | | Purchased two-year policy. | | |
> | | | | |
> | 5/31 | Insurance Expense | 20 | |
> | | Prepaid Insurance | | 20 |
> | | To record expiration of one month's insurance coverage. | | |
>
> **PREPAID INSURANCE**
> | 5/1 | 480 | 5/31 Adj. | 20 |
> |---|---|---|---|
> | | 460 | | |
>
> **INSURANCE EXPENSE**
> | 5/31 Adj. | 20 | | |
> |---|---|---|---|
>
> Balance sheet disclosure, May 31:
>   Prepaid insurance, $460
>
> May income statement disclosure:
>   Insurance expense, $20
>
> **INCOME STATEMENT APPROACH**
>
> | | | | |
> |---|---|---|---|
> | 5/1 | Insurance Expense | 480 | |
> | | Cash | | 480 |
> | | Purchased two-year policy. | | |
> | | | | |
> | 5/31 | Prepaid Insurance | 460 | |
> | | Insurance Expense | | 460 |
> | | To record 23 months of future insurance coverage. | | |
>
> **PREPAID INSURANCE**
> | 5/31 Adj. | 460 | | |
> |---|---|---|---|
>
> **INSURANCE EXPENSE**
> | 5/1 | 480 | 5/31 Adj. | 460 |
> |---|---|---|---|
> | | 20 | | |
>
> Balance sheet disclosure, May 31:
>   Prepaid insurance, $460
>
> May income statement disclosure:
>   Insurance expense, $20

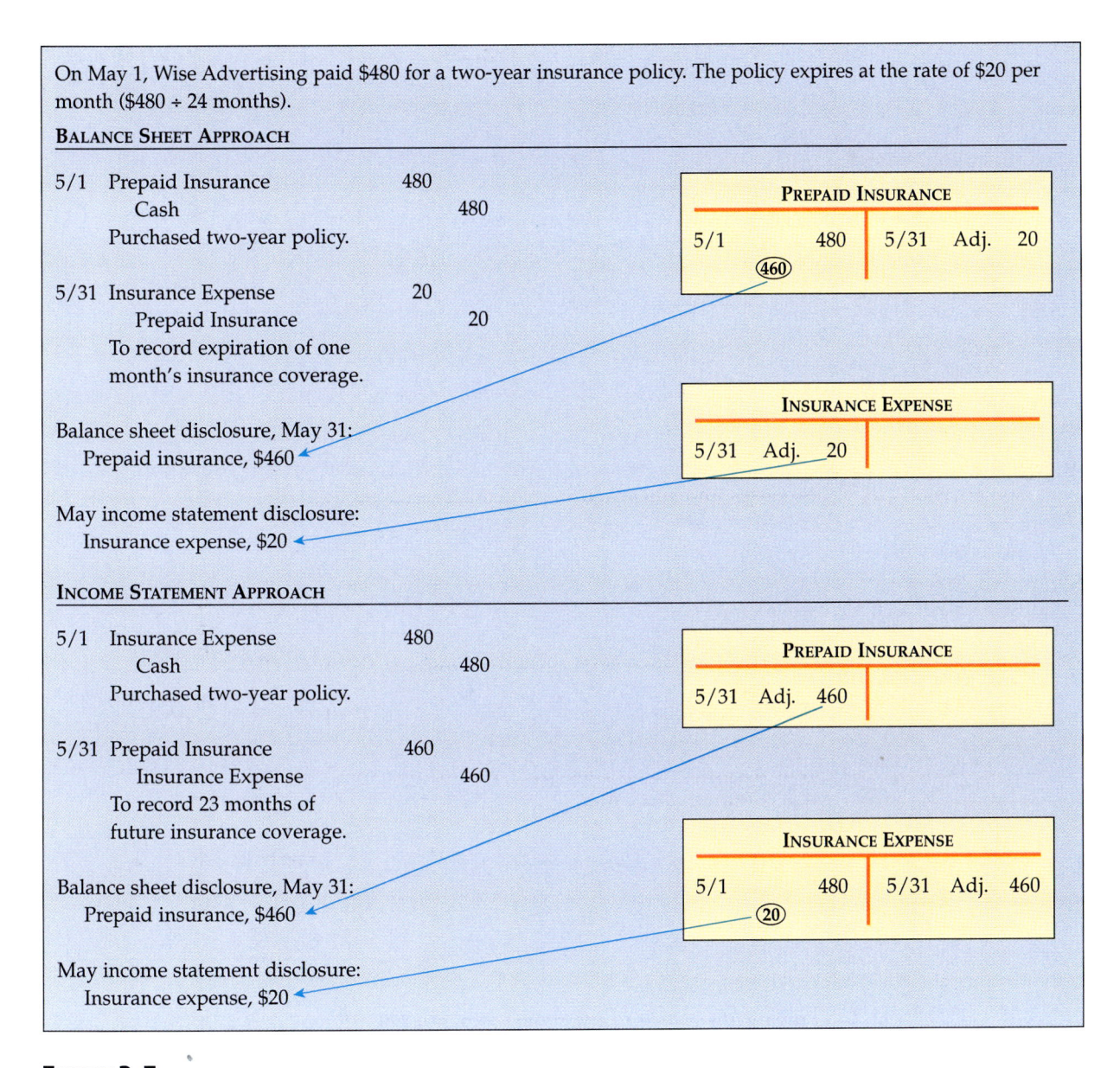

EXHIBIT 3–7
Alternative Accounting Methods for Prepaid Expenses

ACCOUNTING FOR UNEARNED REVENUES

The alternative accounting treatment for unearned revenues is similar to that shown for prepaid expenses. We will once again utilize data from the Wise Advertising example, this time focusing on the May 16 receipt of $10,400 for a 52-week advertising program. The analysis shown earlier in the text on page 102 is summarized at the top of Exhibit 3–8.

Wise originally recorded the receipt by crediting Unearned Agency Revenue, a liability account. Because two weeks of work had been performed by month-end, the adjusting entry transferred $400 from the liability account to Agency Revenue for inclusion on the income statement. The remaining amount of advertising work to be performed ($10,000) is disclosed on the balance sheet.

Had Wise employed the income statement method, the $10,400 collection would have been entered in an income statement account on May 16, namely,

110 CHAPTER 3

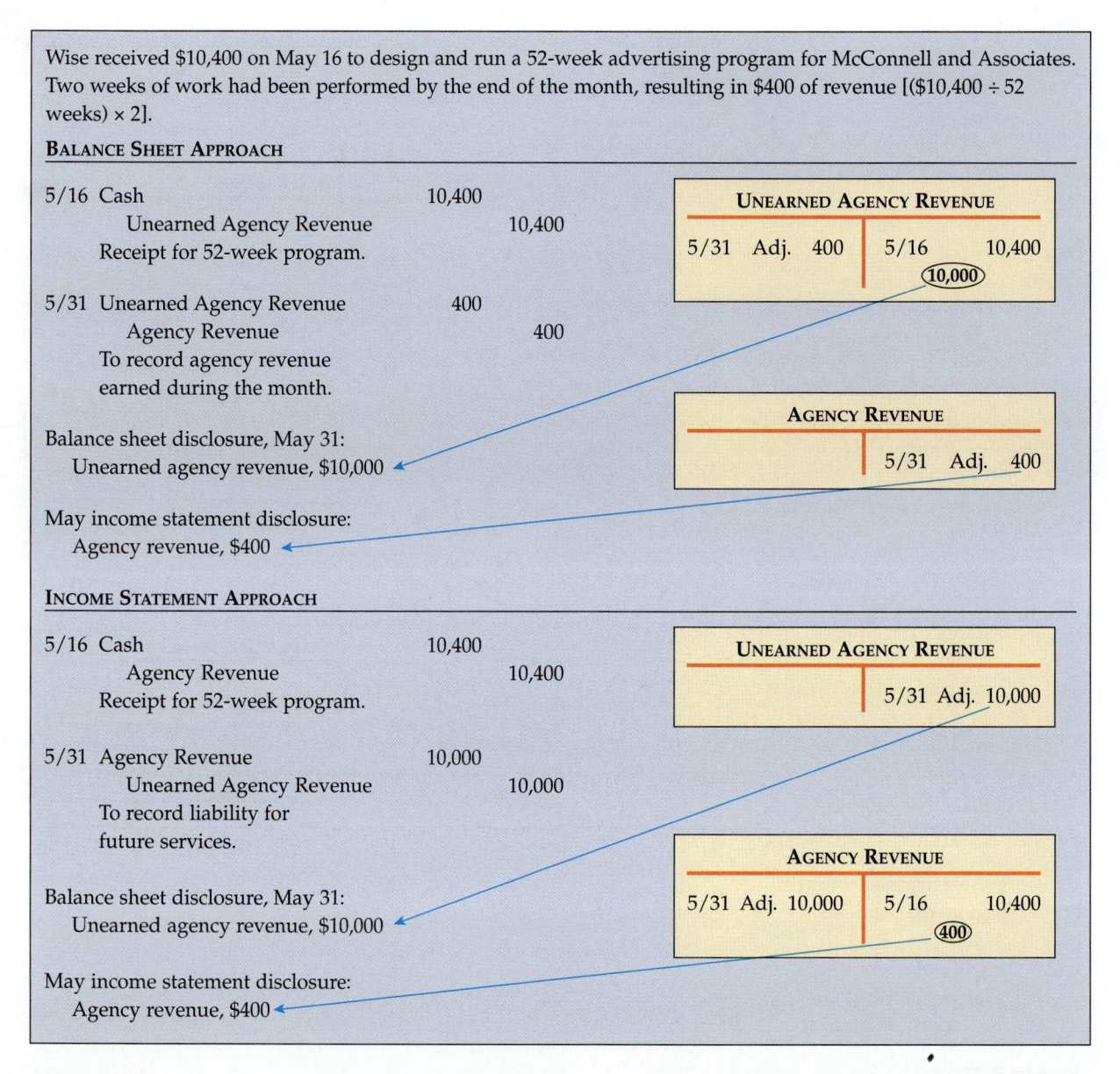

Wise received $10,400 on May 16 to design and run a 52-week advertising program for McConnell and Associates. Two weeks of work had been performed by the end of the month, resulting in $400 of revenue [($10,400 ÷ 52 weeks) × 2].

BALANCE SHEET APPROACH

Date	Account	Debit	Credit
5/16	Cash	10,400	
	Unearned Agency Revenue		10,400
	Receipt for 52-week program.		
5/31	Unearned Agency Revenue	400	
	Agency Revenue		400
	To record agency revenue earned during the month.		

UNEARNED AGENCY REVENUE

5/31 Adj. 400	5/16 10,400
	(10,000)

AGENCY REVENUE

	5/31 Adj. 400

Balance sheet disclosure, May 31:
   Unearned agency revenue, $10,000

May income statement disclosure:
   Agency revenue, $400

INCOME STATEMENT APPROACH

Date	Account	Debit	Credit
5/16	Cash	10,400	
	Agency Revenue		10,400
	Receipt for 52-week program.		
5/31	Agency Revenue	10,000	
	Unearned Agency Revenue		10,000
	To record liability for future services.		

UNEARNED AGENCY REVENUE

	5/31 Adj. 10,000

AGENCY REVENUE

5/31 Adj. 10,000	5/16 10,400
	(400)

Balance sheet disclosure, May 31:
   Unearned agency revenue, $10,000

May income statement disclosure:
   Agency revenue, $400

EXHIBIT 3–8
Alternative Accounting Methods for Unearned Revenues

Agency Revenue. By May 31, the firm had earned a total of $400—the proper amount to disclose on the income statement. An adjusting entry is therefore needed that reduces (debits) the Agency Revenue account by $10,000 ($10,400 − $10,000 = $400). This amount is a liability for Wise because the firm owes $10,000 of future services. Appropriately, then, the adjusting entry removes the amount *yet to be earned* from the Agency Revenue account and places it in Unearned Agency Revenue. The resulting financial statement disclosures reveal the agency's liability and revenue earned at $10,000 and $400, respectively.

A COMPARISON OF THE TWO APPROACHES

Careful study of the balance sheet and income statement approaches shows that the resulting financial statement presentations are identical. Both of these methods are found in practice, with the income statement approach being extremely popular for those items that will be *totally* consumed (or earned) in the accounting period of payment (or receipt). Such items would not require adjusting entries at the end of the period, given the income statement's adjustment focus on the amounts *unused* or *unearned*. The end result is less work at this busy time of the processing cycle.

END-OF-CHAPTER REVIEW

LEARNING OBJECTIVES: THE KEY POINTS

1. **Discuss the use of transactions as a basis for measuring net income.** To evaluate whether a business has improved its overall financial health from operating activities, accountants study the firm's transactions and events. These are a series of exchange and nonexchange happenings that affect the entity's assets, liabilities, and owner's equity. Transactions and events are measurable in dollars and provide a more objective gauge than the economist's concept of "better-offness."

2. **Explain the impact of the periodicity assumption on accounting and income measurement.** The periodicity assumption holds that for reporting purposes, an entity's life is divided into discrete accounting periods. These periods allow feedback to interested parties at specified intervals of time, such as a month, quarter, or a year. Because of the continuous nature of economic activities (e.g., the generation of revenue), the assumption requires that economic activities be allocated or apportioned among the periods affected.

3. **Apply the principle of revenue recognition.** Accountants generally use a point-of-sale rule to determine the proper time to recognize revenue in the accounting records. Revenues are usually entered in the accounts when goods are sold or when services are provided. Both of these situations signify completion of a major part of the economic activity related to the transaction.

4. **Apply the matching principle and record expenses in the proper accounting period.** Expenses are entered in the accounting records in the same period as the revenues that they helped to produce. This concept, known as the matching principle, is relatively straightforward when a strong cause-and-effect relationship exists between revenue and expense. When such a relationship is absent, allocation methods (e.g., depreciation) are needed to charge each period with an appropriate amount of expense.

5. **Compare and contrast accrual- and cash-basis accounting.** With the accrual basis, revenues are recognized in the accounts when goods are sold or when services are provided, and expenses are recognized when incurred. This method of accounting results in a better matching of revenue and expense than the cash basis. Under the cash basis, revenues are recorded in the accounts in the period of receipt, and expenses are recognized when paid. These latter procedures give users the ability to manipulate income.

6. **Explain why the adjusting process is needed and recognize which items typically require adjustment.** The adjusting process is needed because many accounts are not up to date at the end of the accounting period. The items that often need adjustment include previously recorded costs and revenues that must be split among two or more periods (e.g., prepaid expenses, long-term assets, and unearned revenues). Other items that require adjusting entries are accrued revenues and

revenues and expenses that have been earned or incurred in a given period but not as yet entered in the accounts.

7. **Prepare adjusting entries and show their impact on the financial statements.** This chapter introduced the adjustments for prepaid expenses, depreciation, unearned revenues, accrued expenses, and accrued revenues. The proper entries for these items are generalized in the following chart:

	TYPE OF ACCOUNT	
TYPE OF ADJUSTMENT	**DEBITED**	**CREDITED**
Prepaid expense	Expense	Asset
Depreciation	Expense	Contra asset
Unearned revenue	Liability	Revenue
Accrued expense	Expense	Liability
Accrued revenue	Asset	Revenue

The omission of these entries would affect both the balance sheet and the income statement. The failure to debit an expense, for example, would understate expenses, overstate net income, and overstate owner's equity.

8. **(Appendix) Describe and use the "income statement approach" of accounting for prepaid expenses and unearned revenues.** Under the "income statement approach," prepaid expenses are recorded initially in expense accounts, and unearned revenues are entered in revenue accounts. The adjusting process moves the unconsumed part of the prepaid expense from the expense account to an asset account. Similarly, the yet-to-be-earned portion of the unearned revenue is transferred from the revenue account to a liability.

KEY TERMS AND CONCEPTS: A QUICK OVERVIEW

accrual Revenues and expenses that gradually accumulate throughout an accounting period. (p. 103)

accrual basis The accounting basis that recognizes revenues when earned and, for income determination purposes, matches expenses against the revenues generated. (p. 95)

accrued expenses Unpaid expenses that are matched against revenues under the accrual basis of accounting. (p. 103)

accrued revenues Revenues recognized under the accrual basis of accounting as being earned although such amounts have not yet been received. (p. 103)

adjusted trial balance A trial balance prepared after adjusting entries have been made and posted to the ledger accounts. (p. 105)

adjusting process A process performed at the end of the period in which appropriate accounts are analyzed and updated. (p. 98)

book value The amount that an asset is carried at in the accounting records—namely, cost minus accumulated depreciation. (p. 102)

cash basis The basis of accounting that focuses on the cash flows connected with revenues and expenses. Revenues are recognized when received, and expenses are recognized when paid. (p. 96)

contra asset An account used to reduce asset balances in the financial statements. (p. 101)

depreciation   The process used to allocate the cost of long-lived items of plant and equipment to the accounting periods benefited. (p. 100)

fiscal year   Any one-year period other than a calendar year—for example, July 1–June 30. (p. 95)

matching principle   The principle by which expenses associated with the production of revenue are recognized in the same period that the revenue is recognized. (p. 94)

modified cash basis   A method that utilizes features from both the cash and accrual bases of accounting. (p. 97)

natural business year   A year that concludes at the end of the business cycle—for example, October 31 for a professional baseball club, which is after the play-offs and World Series. (p. 95)

periodicity assumption   An assumption stipulating that for reporting purposes, an entity's life can be divided into discrete time periods such as months, quarters, or years. (p. 93)

prepaid expenses   Goods or services purchased for future consumption and paid for in advance. (p. 99)

revenue recognition   The point at which revenue is entered into the accounting records; generally when goods are sold or services provided. (p. 94)

transactions approach   An approach to determining and measuring net income by focusing on business transactions that produce changes in assets, liabilities, and/or owner's equity. (p. 93)

unearned revenue   Future revenue that has been collected but not as yet earned. (p. 102)

CHAPTER QUIZ

The five questions that follow relate to several issues raised in the chapter. Test your knowledge of the issues by selecting the best answer. (The answers appear on p. 128.)

1. The accrual basis of accounting:
   a. is less popular than the cash basis with respect to use by large businesses.
   b. better matches expenses and revenues than does the cash basis of accounting.
   c. recognizes revenues when earned and expenses when paid.
   d. recognizes revenues when received and expenses when paid.

2. Joe Hamilton contacted Denver Painting Contractors in July to paint his office building. The price was agreed on in August, the painting took place in September, and Hamilton paid Denver in October. In which month would Hamilton recognize an expense under the accrual basis of accounting? Under the cash basis of accounting?

	ACCRUAL BASIS	CASH BASIS
a.	July	September
b.	August	September
c.	September	October
d.	August	October

3. The Supplies account of Design Limited contained a $3,200 balance before adjustment on December 31. If $2,400 of supplies remain on hand at year-end, the proper adjusting entry would be:

	Debit	Credit	Amount
a.	Supplies Expense	Supplies	$2,400
b.	Supplies Expense	Supplies	$800
c.	Supplies	Supplies Expense	$2,400
d.	Supplies	Supplies Expense	$800

4. Kip's Appliances sells three-month service contracts to buyers of new appliances. The $32,800 balance in the company's Unearned Service Contract Revenue account is properly classified as:
   a. an expense.
   b. revenue.
   c. an asset.
   d. a liability.

5. As of August 31, Sun Shade Auto Tinting owes $600 of interest (as yet unrecorded) to First Bank and Trust. If payment will take place on September 5, Sun Shade would classify the interest on August 31 as:
   a. a prepaid expense.
   b. an unearned revenue.
   c. an accrued expense.
   d. an accrued revenue.

Summary Problem

Gottom Company began operation on January 1 of the current year. The company's December 31 trial balance follows.

Gottom Company
Trial Balance
December 31, 19XX

Cash	$ 65,000	
Accounts receivable	4,200	
Office supplies	800	
Prepaid insurance	2,000	
Office furniture	16,000	
Accounts payable		$ 10,000
Paul Gottom, capital		30,000
Paul Gottom, drawing	7,400	
Service revenue		85,000
Salaries expense	24,000	
Rent expense	3,000	
Utilities expense	2,000	
Other expense	600	
	$125,000	$125,000

The following adjustment information has come to your attention:
1. Ending office supplies on hand: $300.
2. Prepaid insurance expired during the period: $1,600.
3. Depreciation expense on the furniture: $2,000.
4. Accrued salaries owed to employees: $150.

Instructions

a. Prepare Gottom's required adjusting entries.

b. Is the adjusting process consistent or inconsistent with the accrual basis of accounting? Briefly explain.

Solution

a.

Dec. 31	Office Supplies Expense*		500	
	Office Supplies			500
	To record supplies used during the period.			
31	Insurance Expense		1,600	
	Prepaid Insurance			1,600
	To record expiration of insurance coverage.			
31	Depreciation Expense		2,000	
	Accumulated Depreciation: Office Furniture			2,000
	To record the period's depreciation expense.			
31	Salaries Expense		150	
	Salaries Payable			150
	To record accrued salaries as of year-end.			

* $800 – $300.

b. The adjusting process updates the accounting records at the end of the period. Adjustments are consistent with the accrual basis, given the focus on expenses incurred and revenues earned.

Assignment Material

Questions

Q3–1 Explain the transactions approach to the measurement of a company's net income or net loss.

Q3–2 Present three examples of "exchange-type" transactions.

Q3–3 Differentiate between a fiscal year and a natural business year.

Q3–4 What basic accounting problem arises from dividing the life of a business into discrete periods for reporting purposes?

Q3–5 When is revenue generally recognized in the accounting records?

Q3–6 Explain the matching principle.

Q3–7 Explain when expenses and revenues are recognized under both the accrual basis and the cash basis of accounting.

Q3–8 Explain, by citing several examples, how the cash basis can result in a mismatch of revenues and expenses in a given accounting period.

Q3–9 Explain why virtually all large businesses use the accrual basis of accounting.

Q3–10 Fuller Company uses a calendar year and prepares quarterly reports for its owner. On August 1, the firm prepaid a six-month, $600 insurance premium. What is the proper amount of insurance expense to recognize for the third quarter under (a) the cash basis and (b) the accrual basis?

Q3–11 In reviewing the records of Yager Company, you find that three months' rent of $750 was prepaid to Savage Property Management on November 1. Both companies use the accrual basis of accounting. In view of this transaction,

a. What account and amount would you show on Yager's income statement for the month ended November 30? On Savage's income statement for the month ended November 30?
b. What account and amount would you show on Yager's November 30 balance sheet? On Savage's November 30 balance sheet?

Q3-12 What is meant by the term "depreciation"? What is the purpose of recording depreciation in the accounting records?

Q3-13 A large retailer offers service contracts with the purchase of major appliances by customers. When a contract is sold, the following entry is made:

Cash   XXX
   Unearned Service Contract Revenue   XXX
To record sale of service contract.

On which financial statement and in what section would the Unearned Service Contract Revenue account appear? What is the rationale behind your answer?

Q3-14 How does an accrued expense differ from a prepaid expense?

*__Q3-15__ Modular Products, Inc., recently charged an outlay for prepaid advertising costs to the Advertising Expense account. Describe the adjusting entry that would be required at the end of the period.

EXERCISES

E3-1 Revenue and expense recognition, accrual basis (L.O. 3, 4, 5)
Dave Morris began a law practice several years ago, shortly after graduating from law school. During 19X1, he was approached by Delores Silva, who had recently suffered a back injury in an automobile accident. Morris accepted Silva as a client, and in 19X2 proceeded with a lawsuit against Maddox Motors. The suit alleged that Maddox had knowingly sold Silva an automobile with defective brakes. Late in 19X2, the courts awarded Silva $240,000 in damages. Morris was entitled to 40% of this settlement for his fees. In 19X3, Maddox Motors paid Silva and Morris their respective shares of the judgment.

Morris incurred secretarial and photocopy charges in 19X2 of $12,000—all related to the Silva case. Of this amount, $8,000 was paid in 19X2 and the balance was paid in 19X3.

Assuming that Morris uses the accrual basis of accounting, in what year(s) should the revenue and expense amounts be recognized? Why?

E3-2 Accrual-basis and cash-basis income computations (L.O. 5)
The Continuing Education Department of Southwest Central University conducts various seminars for the general public. The following information relates to the first six months of 19X8:

- *Revenues*—The Department offered 45 seminars, with total fees amounting to $300,000. Of this amount, $50,000 was received prior to the sessions; $240,000 was received at the door, on the days the sessions were held; and $10,000 remains unpaid.
- *Instructional expenses*—Instructors are paid 40% of the gross seminar fees, whether or not the fees are collected. All instructors have been compensated for the seminars they taught.
- *Operating expenses*—Advertising, office expenses, handout materials, and administrative costs amounted to $185,000. All but $25,000 has been paid.

* An asterisk preceding an item indicates that the material is covered in an appendix to this chapter.

a. Compute the department's accrual-basis net income.
b. Compute the department's cash-basis net income.

E3–3 Evaluation of cash- and accrual-basis accounting (L.O. 5)

Engineering Consultants, Inc., a very small company, is about to conclude its 19X4 operations. Net income through the afternoon of December 31 amounted to $21,600, a respectable amount when compared with the figures generated in previous years. The company uses the cash basis of accounting, and the only transaction yet to be processed is a $5,400 payment for December advertising. All employees are on a profit-sharing plan; bonuses are calculated at 40% of net income.

a. Steven Chow, the office manager, has a choice between leaving early to get ready for New Year's or staying an extra 30 minutes to process the payment. Which action would Steven's co-workers likely prefer? Why?
b. Do you see any problems associated with the cash basis of accounting?
c. If Engineering Consultants used the accrual basis of accounting, should Steven process the payment before leaving? Briefly explain.

E3–4 Recognition of concepts (L.O. 6)

Ron Carroll operates a small company that books entertainers for theaters, parties, conventions, and so forth. The company's fiscal year ends on June 30. Consider the items that follow and classify each as either (1) prepaid expense, (2) unearned revenue, (3) accrued expense, (4) accrued revenue, or (5) none of the foregoing.

a. Amounts paid on June 30 for a one-year insurance policy.
b. Professional fees earned but not billed as of June 30.
c. Repairs to the firm's copy machine, incurred and paid in June.
d. An advance payment from a client for a performance next month at a convention.
e. The payment in item (d) from the client's point of view.
f. Interest owed on the company's bank loan, to be paid in early July.
g. The bank loan payable in item (f).
h. Office supplies on hand at year-end.

E3–5 Analysis of prepaid account balance (L.O. 7)

The following information relates to Action Sign Company for 19X2:

Insurance expense	$4,350
Prepaid insurance, December 31, 19X2	1,900
Cash outlays for insurance during 19X2	6,200

Compute the balance in the Prepaid Insurance account on January 1, 19X2.

E3–6 An overview of the adjusting process (L.O. 6, 7)

Evaluate the comments that follow as being True or False. If the comment is false, briefly explain why.

a. Adjusting entries are normally recorded at the end of the accounting period.
b. The balance in an account entitled Prepaid Art Supplies would most likely be disclosed on a company's income statement.
c. If $700 of a $2,900 insurance policy expired during the period, the Prepaid Insurance account should contain a $2,200 balance after adjustment.
d. The Oxnard Aristocrats, a minor league baseball team, records receipts of season ticket revenue in the Unearned Season Ticket Revenue account. The proper

adjusting entry to reflect revenue earned during the period would involve a credit to this account.

e. The adjustment for an accrued expense involves an increase to a liability account.

E3–7 Basic adjusting entries (L.O. 7)

Record the adjusting entries necessary for Gomez Company as of December 31, the end of the current accounting period.

a. Depreciation expense on office equipment, $900.
b. Services provided but not yet billed to clients, $3,000.
c. Accrued interest on loans from Overton Bank, $500.
d. Office supplies used, $320. Earlier in the year, $700 of office supplies were purchased and recorded in the Office Supplies account.
e. Amounts earned from client prepayments, $2,600. The prepayments were initially recorded in the Unearned Service Revenue account.

E3–8 Accounting for prepaid expenses and unearned revenues (L.O. 7)

Hawaii-Blue began business on January 1 of the current year and offers deep sea fishing trips to tourists. Tourists pay $125 in advance for an all-day outing off the coast of Maui. The company collected monies during January for 210 outings, with 30 of the tourists not planning to take their trips until early February.

Hawaii-Blue rents its fishing boat from Pacific Yacht Supply. An agreement was signed at the beginning of the year, and $72,000 was paid for the rights to use the boat for two full years.

a. Prepare journal entries to record (1) the collection of monies from tourists and (2) the revenue generated during January.
b. Calculate Hawaii-Blue's total obligation to tourists at the end of January. On what financial statement and in which section would this amount appear?
c. Prepare journal entries to record (1) the payment to Pacific Yacht Supply and (2) the subsequent adjustment on January 31.
d. On what financial statement would Hawaii-Blue's January boat rental cost appear?

E3–9 Adjustment error (L.O. 7)

The accountant for Village Computer failed to record $900 of accrued salary costs at the end of May. As a result of this error, will the following items be overstated, understated, or unaffected?

a. May revenues will be _____.
b. May expenses will be _____.
c. May net income will be _____.
d. Ending owner's equity as of May 31 will be _____.
e. Assets as of May 31 will be _____.
f. Liabilities as of May 31 will be _____.

*E3–10 Income statement approach, adjusting entries (L.O. 8)

System Consulting had the following transactions on May 1:

- Paid $10,200 for the next six months' rent.
- Received $48,000 to provide consulting services to Midtown Hospital over the next year. The services are to begin immediately.

The company records prepaid expenses and unearned revenues initially in income statement accounts.

a. Record the proper journal entries on May 1.
b. Record the necessary adjusting entries on May 31.

*E3–11   Balance sheet and income statement approaches (L.O. 8)

Wooden & Associates manages the financial affairs of various rock groups. On April 1, 19X3, the firm received $18,000 from Hard Knox to provide services over the next 12 months. A review of Wooden's general ledger revealed accounts entitled Management Revenue and Unearned Management Revenue.

a. Assuming use of the balance sheet approach,
   (1) Prepare Wooden's entries to record the receipt on April 1 and adjust the accounting records on December 31, 19X3.
   (2) Determine the proper presentation of this transaction on the 19X3 income statement and the year-end balance sheet.
b. Repeat part (a), assuming use of the income statement approach.

PROBLEMS

Series A

P3–A1   Accrual and modified cash basis (L.O. 5)

The following information pertains to Beta Company for October:

Services rendered during October to customers on account	$14,380
Cash receipts from	
Owner investment	7,000
Customers on account	5,650
Cash customers for services rendered in October	6,800
Cash payments to	
Creditors for expenses incurred during October	4,400
Creditors for expenses incurred prior to October	2,100
Monroe Equipment for purchase of new machinery on October 1	8,400
Expenses incurred during October, to be paid in future months	3,725

The machinery is expected to have a service life of five years.

Instructions

Calculate Beta's net income for October, using the following methods:

a. Accrual basis of accounting.
b. Modified cash basis of accounting.

P3–A2   Analysis of accrual- and cash-basis data (L.O. 5, 6)

Butch (A.A.) Hallstad is the new general manager of the Tottenham United Soccer Club. After the first five games of the season were played, the club's accountant presented A.A. with the following selected financial data:

	ACCRUAL BASIS	CASH BASIS
Season ticket sales	$ 38,000	$100,000
Individual game tickets	160,000	150,000
Concession sales	70,000	70,000
Player salaries	110,000	335,000
Rent for City Stadium	50,000	—

Tickets are sold both to individual fans and companies.

Instructions

a. Assume the role of the accountant and prepare a brief memo for A.A. that explains the difference between the accrual basis and the cash basis of accounting. In general, which of the two bases is preferred for income measurement? Why?
b. Individually analyze the five items listed, and present a brief explanation as to why the amounts are the same or different between the two bases of accounting.

P3–A3   Adjusting entries and financial statements (L.O. 6, 7)
The information that follows pertains to Fixation Enterprises:

1. The company previously collected $1,500 as an advance payment for services to be provided in the future. By the end of December, one-third of this amount had been earned.
2. Fixation provided $2,500 of services to Artech Corporation; no billing had been made by December 31.
3. Salaries owed to employees at year-end amounted to $1,650.
4. The Supplies account revealed a balance of $8,800; yet only $3,300 of supplies were actually on hand at the end of the period.
5. The company paid $18,000 on October 1 of the current year to Vantage Property Management. The payment was for six months' rent of Fixation's headquarters, beginning on November 1.

Fixation's accounting year ends on December 31.

Instructions

Analyze the five preceding cases individually and determine:

a. The *type* of adjusting entry needed at year-end. (Use the following code: A—adjustment of a prepaid expense; B—adjustment of an unearned revenue; C—adjustment to record an accrued expense; or D—adjustment to record an accrued revenue.)
b. The year-end journal entry to adjust the accounts.
c. The income statement impact of each adjustment (e.g., increases total revenues by $500).

P3–A4   Adjusting entries (L.O. 7)
You have been called in to examine the records of Holiday Company as of November 30, 19X7, the close of the current reporting period. In the course of your examination, you discover the following:

a. Building depreciation totaled $7,500 for the year.
b. Prepaid Advertising has a debit balance of $6,500 on November 30, which represents payment on August 18 for uniform space in 26 issues of a weekly magazine. As of November 30, advertisements had appeared in 12 issues.
c. Salaries earned by employees but unpaid by year-end amounted to $3,900.
d. Holiday agreed that Auto Express could lease some extra space in Holiday's parking lot for $300 per month, effective September 1. Auto Express has yet to pay Holiday, and to date, no entry has been made in the accounting records. (Holiday uses an account entitled Lease Receivable to record such transactions.)
e. The beginning balance in the Office Supplies account on December 1, 19X6, was $2,570. The account was increased during the year for purchases that amounted to $4,420, and a year-end count revealed that supplies costing $4,800 had been consumed by November 30.

f. On March 1, an entry was made in the Unearned Service Revenue account for $24,000. This amount represents a receipt for eight months of services to be rendered beginning on June 1.
g. A review of the Prepaid Insurance account discovered that Holiday had acquired a two-year liability insurance policy for $960 on February 1, 19X7. Another policy that cost $1,320 for six months' coverage of building contents was acquired one month later.

Instructions

The accounts were last adjusted on November 30, 19X6. Present the adjusting entries required on November 30, 19X7, under the accrual basis of accounting.

P3–A5 Preparation of adjusted trial balance (L.O. 7)

The trial balance of the Costello Company as of December 31, 19XX, follows.

COSTELLO COMPANY
Trial Balance
December 31, 19XX

Cash	$ 4,200	
Accounts receivable	35,200	
Office supplies	500	
Vehicles	46,000	
Accumulated depreciation: vehicles		$ 9,200
Accounts payable		11,000
Unearned service revenue		12,000
Bank loan payable		35,400
A. Costello, capital		14,300
A. Costello, drawing	4,000	
Service revenue		23,000
Rent expense	5,000	
Wage expense	8,000	
Telecommunications expense	2,000	
	$104,900	$104,900

The adjustment information below has come to your attention:

1. Services provided but not yet billed, $4,700.
2. Office supplies on hand as of December 31, $100.
3. Depreciation expense on the vehicles, $4,600.
4. Remaining unearned service revenue as of December 31, $3,000.
5. Accrued interest on the bank loan payable, $300.
6. Wages accrued but not yet paid, $750.

Instructions

a. Prepare Costello's required adjusting entries in general journal form.
b. Prepare an adjusted trial balance, using an approach similar to that demonstrated in Exhibit 3–5.
c. Suppose that you were asked to prepare the financial statements of Costello Company. Would the trial balance or the adjusted trial balance be more useful in completing this assignment? Briefly explain.

Series B

P3–B1 Accrual and modified cash basis (L.O. 5)

The following information was gathered from the records of Sinclair Consulting for April:

Beginning cash		$ 9,500
Add: Receipts		
From customers		
For cash services rendered in April	$ 8,000	
For services performed on account	9,600	
From Contemporary Office, Inc.	2,000	19,600
Subtotal		$29,100
Deduct: Payments		
To creditors		
For expenses incurred in April	$ 1,300	
For expenses incurred prior to April	2,800	
Owner withdrawal	5,000	
Purchase of office furniture	14,000	23,100
Ending cash		$ 6,000

During April, the company rendered $14,700 of services to customers on account and incurred $2,500 of expenses to be paid in future months. Finally, on April 1, Sinclair purchased furniture having an estimated service life of five years from Contemporary Office. One day later, Sinclair was given a cash refund upon discovery of a $2,000 billing error.

Instructions

Calculate Sinclair's net income for April, using the following methods:

a. Accrual basis of accounting.
b. Modified cash basis of accounting.

P3–B2 Analysis of accrual- and cash-basis data (L.O. 5, 6)

Pump It Up, the city's newest weight-training club, opened for business on January 1 of the current year. The club's bookkeeper compiled the following selected data for the first quarter by using the cash basis of accounting:

Cash receipts	
Annual memberships	$175,000
Monthly memberships	74,000
Cash payments	
Facility rent	60,000
Salaries	65,000
Utilities	8,000

An analysis of the accounting records disclosed a $1,500 electric bill that will be settled in April. Accrued salaries on March 31 amounted to $3,900, and annual memberships collected but unearned totaled $134,000. Pump It Up had issued a check to Greenville Property Management on January 2 that covered the full year's rent. Finally, $5,800 of monthly memberships had been billed but were not yet collected.

Instructions

a. Analyze each of the five items listed. Determine whether the amount computed under the cash basis would increase or decrease if the club had used the accrual basis of accounting. Present a brief explanation for each of the items.

b. Assume that it is now three years later. Pump It Up has been a success, and management has opened 14 other facilities throughout the western U.S. Would the chain likely use the cash basis or the accrual basis of accounting? Why?

P3–B3 Adjusting entries and financial statements (L.O. 6, 7)

The information that follows pertains to Southlake Enterprises:

1. The Prepaid Insurance account contains a December 31 balance of $5,800. Conversations with the firm's accountant revealed that $4,300 of premiums had expired during the year.
2. Interest owed at year-end on loans payable to Second National Bank amounted to $8,000.
3. Southlake received $10,800 in April for use of a portion of its parking lot by a neighboring business. By December 31, $3,600 of the payment had yet to be earned.
4. Services provided to clients during December not yet billed or collected total $3,700.
5. The Repair Supplies account had a balance on January 1 of the current year of $2,500. Purchases made during the period amounted to $700; supplies costing $1,800 remain on hand at December 31.

Southlake's accounting year ends on December 31.

Instructions

Analyze the five preceding cases individually and determine:

a. The *type* of adjusting entry needed at year-end. (Use the following code: A—adjustment of a prepaid expense; B—adjustment of an unearned revenue; C—adjustment to record an accrued expense; or D—adjustment to record an accrued revenue.)
b. The year-end journal entry to adjust the accounts.
c. The remaining (or resulting) asset or liability after recording the adjustment (e.g., the ending balance in Prepaid Advertising is $900).

P3–B4 Adjusting entries (L.O. 7)

You have been retained to examine the records of Kathy's Day Care Center as of December 31, 19X3, the close of the current reporting period. In the course of your examination, you discover the following:

a. On January 1, 19X3, the Supplies account had a balance of $2,350. During the year, $5,520 of supplies were purchased, and a balance of $1,620 remained unused on December 31.
b. Unrecorded interest owed to the center totaled $275 as of December 31.
c. All clients pay tuition in advance, and their payments are credited to the Unearned Tuition Revenue account. The account was credited for $75,500 on August 31. With the exception of $15,500, which represented prepayments for 10 months' tuition from several well-to-do families, all amounts were for the current semester ending on December 31.
d. Depreciation on the school's van was $3,000 for the year.

e. On August 1, the center began to pay rent in six-month installments of $21,000. Kathy wrote a check to the owner of the building and recorded the check in Prepaid Rent, a new account.
f. Two salaried employees earn $400 each for a five-day week. The employees are paid every Friday, and December 31 falls on a Thursday.
g. Kathy's Day Care paid insurance premiums as follows, each time debiting Prepaid Insurance:

Date Paid	Policy No.	Policy Term	Amount
Feb. 1, 19X2	1033MCM19	1 year	$540
Jan. 1, 19X3	7952789HP	1 year	912
Aug. 1, 19X3	XQ943675ST	2 years	840

Instructions

The center's accounts were last adjusted on December 31, 19X2. Prepare the December 31, 19X3, adjusting entries needed under the accrual basis of accounting.

P3–B5 Preparation of adjusted trial balance (L.O. 6, 7)

The trial balance of the Logo Company as of December 31, 19XX follows.

Logo Company
Trial Balance
December 31, 19XX

Cash	$11,400	
Accounts receivable	7,600	
Prepaid rent	600	
Machinery	13,000	
Accumulated depreciation: machinery		$ 1,500
Accounts payable		1,150
Unearned contract revenue		1,200
Loan payable		7,000
Andrea Logan, capital		13,000
Andrea Logan, drawing	1,850	
Contract revenue		24,400
Wage expense	9,600	
Utilities expense	2,000	
Insurance expense	2,200	
	$48,250	$48,250

The adjustment information below has come to your attention:

1. Rent that expired during the period, $200.
2. Contract services provided but not yet billed, $700.
3. Unearned contract revenues that have been earned during the period, $550.
4. Wages incurred but not yet paid, $725.
5. Accrued interest on the loan payable, $150.
6. Depreciation expense on the machinery, $300.

Instructions

a. Prepare Logo's required adjusting entries in general journal form.
b. Prepare an adjusted trial balance, using an approach similar to that demonstrated in Exhibit 3–5.
c. What is the purpose of the adjusting process at the end of the period? Briefly explain.

EXPANDING YOUR HORIZONS

EYH3–1 Differences in accounting periods (L.O. 2)

Each business entity is permitted to select a 12-month period that best measures its annual operating performance. Some companies use a calendar year, whereas others choose a fiscal year or a natural business year.

Instructions

a. By using information in your library, locate three companies that appear to have selected a natural business year for financial reporting. (Companies and industries should be different from those cited in this chapter.) Prepare a brief write-up of your findings, including a sentence or two on what has determined the "natural year."
b. Interview an accountant to determine if any clients have purposely selected a summer year-end, when activity slows for the accounting firm and clients may be able to negotiate lower billing rates for services performed. Briefly discuss your findings.

EYH3–2 Examples of unearned revenue (L.O. 7)

The concept of unearned revenue is foreign to many introductory accounting students and to many companies as well.

Instructions

By using information in your library, locate five companies that have unearned revenue listed on their balance sheets. Indicate how the unearned revenues arose and how the firms are likely to earn these amounts.

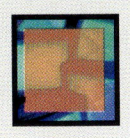

EYH3–3 Reporting periods; items that require adjustment: The Toro Company and The Reader's Digest Association (L.O. 2, 6)

The Toro Company, headquartered in Bloomington, Minnesota, is a leading supplier of lawn maintenance equipment and irrigation products (such as sprinkler systems). In addition to items sold under the Toro brand name, the company also manufactures Lawn-Boy and Wheel Horse products. In contrast, The Reader's Digest Association is perhaps best known for its publishing activities. *Reader's Digest* is the world's most widely read magazine, being published in 17 languages for 100 million readers.

Instructions

By using the text's electronic data base, access the balance sheets of both firms and answer the questions that follow. Unless otherwise indicated, responses should be based on data for the most recent year presented.

a. Determine the year-end for both companies.
b. One of these year-ends is likely based on the firm's natural business year. Identify the company that is using the natural business year for reporting, and explain the rationale behind your selection.
c. Do either of the companies disclose any prepaid expenses? Comment on the amount of prepaid expenses relative to the total assets of the entity.

d. Do either of the companies show relatively large amounts of unearned revenue? If so, what is the likely source of this unearned revenue and how are such amounts eventually earned?
e. Companies often provide purchasers with promises to remedy defects in product quality for a stipulated period of time.
   (1) Do either of the firms provide such a promise, as evidenced by the balance sheet? Explain.
   (2) If you have answered "yes" to part (e1), where are such amounts presented on the balance sheet? What is the logic behind this treatment?

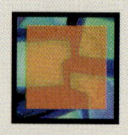

EYH3–4 Reporting periods; items that require adjustment (L.O. 2, 6)

This problem is a duplication of Problem EYH3–3. It is based on two companies selected by your instructor.

Instructions

By using the text's electronic data base, access the specified companies' balance sheets and focus on data for the most recent year reported. Answer requirements (a)–(e) of Problem EYH3–3.

EYH3–5 Accrual- and cash-basis accounting, performance evaluation (L.O. 5)

Beth Regal recently began a swimming pool chlorination service. She visits each of her clients on a weekly basis and applies chlorine gas and other chemicals to their pools. This service is not only convenient for her clientele, but is actually less costly than if the customers performed the process themselves.

Regal started her business on April 1 with a beginning cash investment of $3,000. Through various contacts, she was able to establish an initial client base of 40 customers. Customers are billed when serviced and settle their accounts in the following month. Regal charges each client $30 monthly, thereby generating a 100% markup on the $15 cost of chlorine and other supplies used. Other business expenses (gasoline, telephone, etc.) total $100 monthly and are paid when incurred.

All chemicals and supplies are purchased and paid for at the beginning of each month, the amounts acquired being based on the number of customers to be serviced. On April 1, for instance, purchases totaled $600 (40 customers × $15 each).

Regal's business has grown rapidly, as evidenced by the following data:

Month	Customers Serviced
April	40
May	80
June	160

It has become apparent that the customer base would total 320 for July.

On July 1, Regal approached you about a cash flow problem. She is unable to buy the necessary chemicals and supplies because of a lack of cash. Beth is also quite confused because a friend of hers, an accountant, has prepared monthly accrual-based financial statements that reveal the business is operating at a profit. Beth is now questioning these statements in view of the firm's present cash position.

Instructions

a. Construct Regal's accrual-basis income statements for April, May, and June.
b. Construct Regal's cash-basis income statements for April, May, and June.

c. Compute the end-of-month balances for April, May, and June in the Cash, Accounts Receivable, and Supplies accounts.
d. Using the information generated in parts (a)–(c), explain the pool service's dilemma.

COMMUNICATION OF ACCOUNTING INFORMATION

CAI3–1 Information presentation: Tandy Corporation (L.O. 5, 6, 7)
Communication Principle: The presentation of information is just as critical to communication as the information itself. According to readability principles, writing should be organized and displayed in a way that is easy and fast to comprehend. Readability principles include writing short paragraphs, using ample "white space" (margins and blank space on the page), and setting off important numerical data from text so they are emphasized and easy to follow.

These guidelines will help you produce a professional-looking and readable document:

1. Write short paragraphs (averaging three to four sentences or four to six lines).
2. Use 1½-inch margins and leave some extra space between paragraphs.
3. Leave extra space before and after illustrations (e.g., tabular data) within paragraphs. Be sure to indent illustrations by using a larger left-hand margin than that used with narrative text.

■ ■ ■ ■ ■ ■ ■ ■ ■

Tandy Corporation is one of America's largest specialty electronics retailers, operating over 6,500 Radio Shack and Computer City stores. The company's financial statements report a variety of accrued expenses and unearned revenues. Examples include the following (amounts are in thousands):

Accrued payroll and bonuses	$ 57,600
Accrued interest expense	7,358
Deferred (unearned) service contract revenue	102,223

Instructions

You are presently taking an employment test with Tandy for an entry-level accounting position. Part of this test involves preparation of information (i.e., the answers to the following questions) that will eventually be placed in a management report. Draft sample responses that could be inserted in the report, being sure to use appropriate topic or lead-in sentences with each paragraph. Because involved computations are often hard to understand in the context of a sentence or paragraph, set off any needed calculations in tabular form.

a. Briefly describe the nature of the transaction or event that gave rise to the three dollar amounts presented. Assume the reader of the final report is a relatively unsophisticated user of financial information.
b. Further details are needed concerning the $102,223 year-end deferred contract revenue balance.
   (1) On what financial statement would this amount be reported? What is the rationale behind this treatment?
   (2) Would the Deferred Contract Revenue account be needed under the cash basis of accounting? Why?

(3) Tandy had a beginning balance of $97,044 in the Deferred Contract Revenue account. If, say, $60,000 of contracts were sold during the period, how would the firm's income statement have been affected?

Answers to Chapter Quiz

1. b
2. c
3. b
4. d
5. c

4 COMPLETION OF THE ACCOUNTING CYCLE

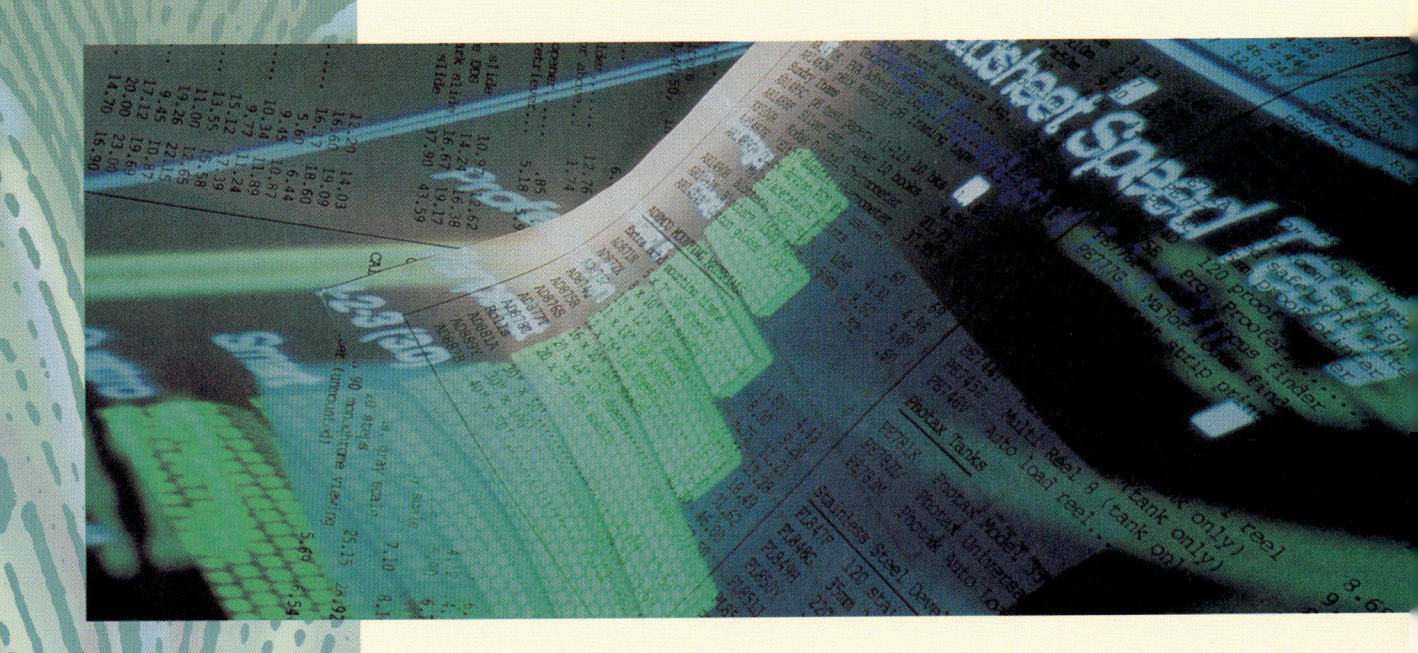

LEARNING OBJECTIVES

After studying this chapter, you should be able to:

1. Prepare a work sheet and the accompanying financial statements.
2. Explain the need for the closing process and close a set of accounting records.
3. Name and describe the various steps in the accounting cycle.
4. Understand the concept of an operating cycle and construct a classified balance sheet.
5. Analyze a company's liquidity.
6. (Appendix) Explain the concept and mechanics of reversing entries.

The successful operation of a company requires the integration of concepts and principles from many different business disciplines. Economics, law, marketing, management, finance, accounting, production, and systems all go hand-in-hand.

George Faris, the owner of Banner Advertising, studied marketing while in college and initially viewed his major as the "center of the business universe." Without good marketing, he reasoned, there would be no money available to worry about the accounting. As he gained work experience, however, George learned quickly just how important accounting really is.

In the early years of his business, George admitted that maintaining up-to-date financial records often took a back seat to other, more pressing tasks. George concedes that he "frequently got behind. My bankers wanted quarterly information along with more detailed financial statements. I really had to struggle to remember the specifics of unrecorded transactions that were several months old. To survive, I had to find a better way."

This chapter takes a look at that "better way," namely, the implementation of certain accounting processes that are performed on a continuous basis. These processes (1) allow for the generation of regular, up-to-date financial statements that adequately disclose a company's affairs and (2) ready the accounting records for the next reporting period. Our presentation concludes with a detailed look at the balance sheet, including the need for added captions within the body of this statement.

Work Sheet

1 Prepare a work sheet and the accompanying financial statements.

Chapter 3 introduced the idea of adjustments—journal entries that are needed to update selected balances before financial statements can be drafted. Most businesses have a large number of accounts in their general ledgers that require adjustment. To help accountants better organize their work for this process, a series of working papers is often prepared. These documents are used for preliminary calculations when deriving financial statement data (e.g., the cost of supplies consumed during the period, a company's depreciation expense, and so forth). Generally speaking, working papers provide evidence of related computations and are useful in supporting the validity of the figures being reported.

There are many different types of working papers, with one of the most popular being the work sheet. The **work sheet** is a large columnar form that assists in the formation of an entity's financial statements. The design of the work sheet not only helps to detect mathematical errors, but it also highlights certain types of discrepancies *before* they are entered in the journal and posted to the ledger. In effect, one could view the work sheet as the accountant's "scratch pad." Proper completion of this document ensures that many end-of-period accounting procedures have been performed correctly.

WORK SHEET CONSTRUCTION

The work sheet and the procedures for preparation will be shown by continuing the Wise Advertising Agency example from the previous chapter. The starting point for preparation is the trial balance and the end-of-period adjusting entries. These data are reproduced in Exhibit 4–1.

EXHIBIT 4–1
Work Sheet of the Wise Advertising Agency

WISE ADVERTISING AGENCY
Work Sheet
For the Month Ended May 31, 19XX

ACCOUNT TITLE	TRIAL BALANCE DEBIT	TRIAL BALANCE CREDIT	ADJUSTMENTS DEBIT	ADJUSTMENTS CREDIT	ADJUSTED TRIAL BALANCE DEBIT	ADJUSTED TRIAL BALANCE CREDIT	INCOME STATEMENT DEBIT	INCOME STATEMENT CREDIT	BALANCE SHEET DEBIT	BALANCE SHEET CREDIT
Cash	13,705				13,705				13,705	
Accounts receivable	3,150		(g) 710		3,860				3,860	
Prepaid insurance	480			(a) 20	460				460	
Supplies	340			(b) 80	260				260	
Land	5,500				5,500				5,500	
Car	4,500				4,500				4,500	
Accounts payable		125				125				125
Unearned agency revenue		10,400	(d) 400			10,000				10,000
Loan payable		6,000				6,000				6,000
Gary Wise, capital		9,000				9,000				9,000
Gary Wise, drawing	200				200				200	
Agency revenue		4,100		(d) 400 (g) 710		5,210		5,210		
Salaries expense	825		(f) 50		875		875			
Marketing expense	800				800		800			
Electricity expense	125				125		125			
	29,625	29,625								
Insurance expense			(a) 20		20		20			
Supplies expense			(b) 80		80		80			
Depreciation expense			(c) 125		125		125			
Accumulated depreciation: car				(c) 125		125				125
Interest expense			(e) 60		60		60			
Interest payable				(e) 60		60				60
Salaries payable				(f) 50		50				50
			1,445	1,445	30,570	30,570	2,085	5,210	28,485	25,360
Net income							3,125			3,125
							5,210	5,210	28,485	28,485

The amounts in the trial balance are combined with the adjustments to produce an adjusted trial balance. Notice, for instance, that the $3,150 debit balance in Accounts Receivable is increased by $710, yielding an ending account balance of $3,860. This procedure should be familiar to you; it is identical to that described in the previous chapter. A review of Exhibit 3–5 and the accompanying discussion that begins on page 105 may be helpful at this time. The review will not only serve as a refresher, but will show that the Chapter 3 illustration coincides precisely with the first six columns of the work sheet. The numbers that appear in colored type (the income statement and balance sheet data) are really the only new elements to master.

Income Statement and Balance Sheet Columns. The data in the adjusted trial balance serve as the "raw material" for a company's financial statements. Thus, each amount listed in the adjusted trial balance is transferred to either the work sheet's income statement section or balance sheet section. This process is performed on a line-by-line basis, starting at the top of the work sheet. *Revenues and expenses go to the income statement. Assets, liabilities, and owner's equity accounts, the last of which includes the drawing account, are extended to the balance sheet.* Although the drawing account does not appear on a formal balance sheet,[1] extension is necessary because withdrawals reduce owner's equity.

Financial Statement Totals. As a final step, after all amounts have been extended, the income statement and balance sheet columns are totaled. Focusing on the income statement, the credit column contains the accounts with credit balances, namely, the revenues. In contrast, the debit column contains the expense accounts. Therefore:

Total revenues (credits)	$5,210
Total expenses (debits)	2,085
Net income	$3,125

The net income figure is placed beneath the debit total and is added to bring both columns into agreement with each other.

Turning to the balance sheet, the firm's net income is entered in the credit column because revenues in excess of expenses raise owner's equity. The income of $3,125 is then combined with the other balance sheet credits, yielding a total of $28,485.

Wise generated net income during May. If the agency had operated at a loss, the procedure for balancing the statements would have been slightly different. With expenses greater than revenues, the loss would be entered in the credit column of the income statement to achieve the desired equality. On the balance sheet the net loss must reduce owner's equity. Appropriately, then, the loss would be listed in the debit column to produce the necessary impact.

USES OF THE WORK SHEET

The work sheet performs several useful functions for the accountant. As is evident from its form, the work sheet lays the groundwork for formal financial statement preparation. In addition, it serves as the basis for completing the

---
[1] Withdrawals appear on the statement of owner's equity.

statement preparation. In addition, it serves as the basis for completing the adjusting process and assists in closing at the end of the accounting period.

Financial Statements. Once the work sheet is completed, the preparation of financial statements is a relatively easy task. Virtually all the information needed for this process is found in the work sheet's income statement and balance sheet sections. The income statement, for example, is simply a formal listing of the income statement debit and credit columns.

The statement of owner's equity cannot be constructed by relying solely on the work sheet. Any investments made by the owner are already buried in the capital account, which appears in the adjusted trial balance. Consequently, it is necessary to return to the general ledger and examine the underlying detail of such transactions (see Gary Wise, Capital, in Exhibit 2–5).

Finally, the balance sheet is prepared by compiling the asset and liability figures that are listed in the balance sheet section. The drawing account of $200 is ignored, because it was used when constructing the statement of owner's equity. As you know, the balance sheet reflects end-of-period amounts. Thus, the ending figure on the statement of owner's equity is carried forward and labeled as Gary Wise, Capital. This procedure was discussed in Chapter 1 and is illustrated in Wise's financial statements, which are shown in Exhibit 4–2.

Adjusting Entries. In the previous chapter, we first introduced the concept of adjustments via formal journal entries (see pp. 99 and 104 as examples). We later used the information contained in these adjustments for purposes of completing the adjusted trial balance and the work sheet. The presentation in Chapter 3 was for illustrative purposes only. In practice, accountants would first prepare the work sheet and then record data from the adjustment columns into the journal. The work sheet, therefore, serves as the basis for the updating process at the end of the period.

Like other journal entries, the adjustments are posted to the general ledger. This procedure achieves consistency with the balances that appear in the agency's financial statements. We will assume that all adjustments presented in the Wise Advertising illustration have already been journalized and posted.

> **2** Explain the need for the closing process and close a set of accounting records.

The Closing Process. Discussion of the closing process should help tie together several loose ends. As we emphasized earlier in the text, four factors cause owner's equity to change during the period: investments, withdrawals, revenues, and expenses. The statement of owner's equity of Wise Advertising (see Exhibit 4–2) reveals an ending balance of $11,925 from these items. Interestingly, however, the capital *account* in the general ledger contains a balance of $9,000. This latter amount reflects only the investment on May 1, which was entered directly in the account. Withdrawals, on the other hand, are located in Gary Wise, Drawing, and revenues and expenses are still housed in the accounts where initially recorded. It is naturally desirable that the ending balance reported on the statement of owner's equity (and the balance sheet) be consistent with the ending balance found in the ledger. This consistency is achieved by placing a set of *closing entries* in the accounting records at the end of the period.

Purpose. The purpose of the closing process is twofold. First, closing corrects the just mentioned lack of agreement between the capital account and the

EXHIBIT 4-2
Financial Statements of the Wise Advertising Agency

WISE ADVERTISING AGENCY
Income Statement
For the Month Ended May 31, 19XX

Agency revenue		$5,210
Less expenses		
Salaries expense	$875	
Marketing expense	800	
Electricity expense	125	
Insurance expense	20	
Supplies expense	80	
Depreciation expense	125	
Interest expense	60	
Total expenses		2,085
Net income		$3,125

WISE ADVERTISING AGENCY
Statement of Owner's Equity
For the Month Ended May 31, 19XX

Beginning balance, May 1		$ —
Increases		
Owner investments	$9,000	
Net income	3,125	12,125
		$12,125
Decreases		
Owner withdrawals		200
Ending balance, May 31		$11,925

---

owner's equity statement. Second, closing reduces the balances in certain accounts to zero. The income statement and the statement of owner's equity each report economic activity for a span of time. On conclusion of a given period, a business must start anew in its accumulation of information for these two financial reports. *Thus, revenue, expense, and drawing accounts must be closed, or reduced to zero, so there is no carryover from one period to the next.* These accounts are appropriately known as **temporary** or **nominal accounts.**

Because the balance sheet reports information at a particular point in time as opposed to a period, *balance sheet components (assets, liabilities, and ending owner's equity) are never closed.* Wise, for example, reported a cash balance of $13,705 on May 31. It would not make any sense to reduce this account to zero so that the firm could start accounting all over again on June 1. The agency has $13,705 of cash to begin June operations, not zero. Accounts whose balances are carried forward from period to period are commonly called **real accounts.**

WISE ADVERTISING AGENCY
Balance Sheet
May 31, 19XX

ASSETS		
Cash		$13,705
Accounts receivable		3,860
Prepaid insurance		460
Supplies		260
Land		5,500
Car	$4,500	
Less: Accumulated depreciation	125	4,375
Total assets		$28,160
LIABILITIES		
Accounts payable		$ 125
Unearned agency revenue		10,000
Loan payable		6,000
Interest payable		60
Salaries payable		50
Total liabilities		$16,235
OWNER'S EQUITY		
Gary Wise, capital		11,925
Total liabilities & owner's equity		$28,160

Technique. Most companies close their books only once a year. For illustrative purposes, however, we will demonstrate the necessary closing process for Wise Advertising on May 31, the conclusion of the agency's first month of activity.

Closing is a four-step process that requires the establishment of a new account entitled **Income Summary.** As its name implies, the Income Summary account is used to summarize the net income or net loss of a business. The four steps to closing are as follows:

1. Close all revenue accounts.
2. Close all expense accounts.
3. Close the Income Summary account.
4. Close the drawing account.

The information needed to perform these steps is obtained from the work sheet.

Closing Revenue Accounts. Revenue accounts normally possess credit balances. To reduce the accounts to zero, the closing entry debits revenue accounts for the amount of their balance and credits Income Summary. This process transfers all revenues earned to the credit side of Income Summary and is shown in Exhibit 4–3.

EXHIBIT 4–3
Closing Revenue Accounts

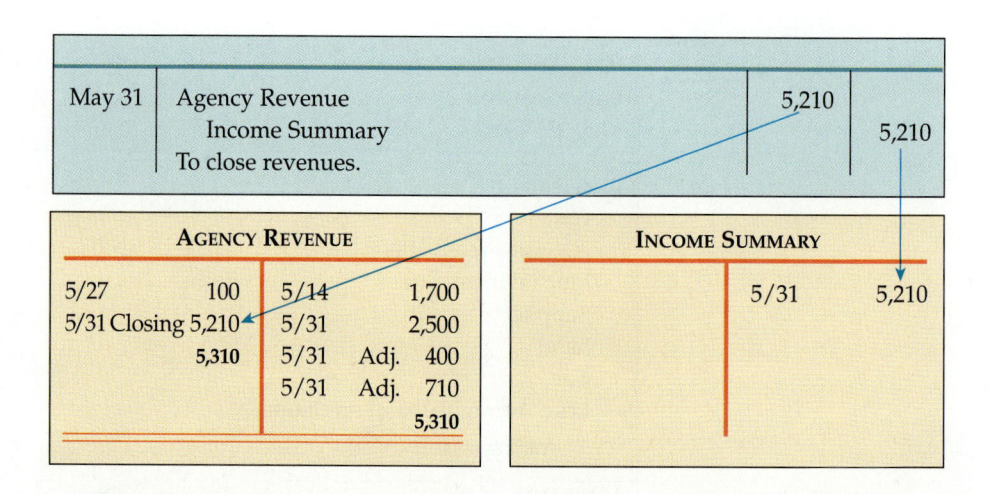

May 31	Agency Revenue		5,210	
	Income Summary			5,210
	To close revenues.			

```
         AGENCY REVENUE                         INCOME SUMMARY
5/27            100  | 5/14        1,700              |  5/31    5,210
5/31 Closing 5,210   | 5/31        2,500              |
              5,310  | 5/31 Adj.    400               |
                     | 5/31 Adj.    710               |
                     |             5,310              |
```

To explain, the Agency Revenue account contains transactions from May 14, 27, and 31 (see Exhibit 2–5) and two adjusting entries (see Exhibit 4–1). The balance *prior* to closing is $5,210 ($5,310 – $100). The closing entry debits Agency Revenue for $5,210, thereby equalizing total debits and credits and reducing the account's balance to zero.

Closing Expense Accounts. The closing of expense accounts is performed in essentially the same manner. Each expense account is credited to eliminate its debit balance. The closing entry's corresponding debit, then, is to Income Summary, which transfers the expenses incurred to the debit side of this account. Rather than close the expense accounts individually, a combined or *compound journal entry* is usually employed to reduce posting. Exhibit 4–4 illustrates the proper entry and the related postings.

Closing the Income Summary Account. The Income Summary account presently contains revenues (credits) of $5,210 and expenses (debits) of $2,085. The resulting credit balance of $3,125 ($5,210 – $2,085) represents Wise's net income for May.

The next step in the closing process is to reduce, or close, the Income Summary account to zero. This is achieved by debiting Income Summary for $3,125. To complete the entry, Gary Wise, Capital, is credited because revenues in excess of expenses (i.e., net income) boost owner's equity. The necessary entry is shown in Exhibit 4–5.

In the case of a net loss, the Income Summary account would possess a debit balance prior to closing. The required closing entry, therefore, is the opposite of that just described.

Closing the Drawing Account. The final step in the closing process is to close the drawing account. From information that is shown in the adjusted trial balance columns of the work sheet, Wise's drawing account contains a $200 debit balance. A credit is therefore needed to reduce the account to zero. Because withdrawals decrease owner's equity, the required entry appears as shown in Exhibit 4–6.

Notice that the drawing account is closed to Gary Wise, Capital, and *not* to Income Summary. The Income Summary account is used to summarize

EXHIBIT 4–4
Closing Expense Accounts

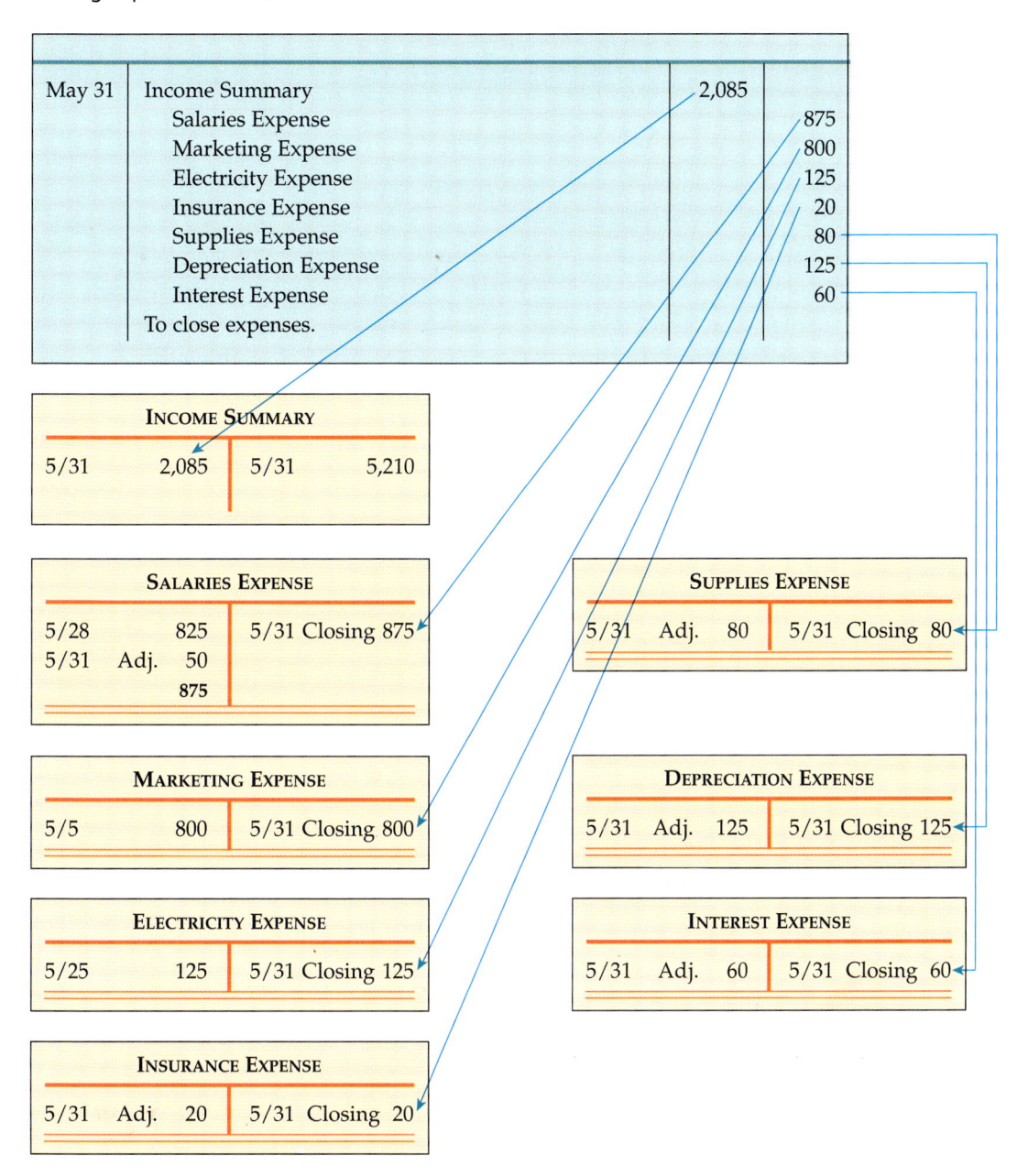

May 31	Income Summary	2,085	
	Salaries Expense		875
	Marketing Expense		800
	Electricity Expense		125
	Insurance Expense		20
	Supplies Expense		80
	Depreciation Expense		125
	Interest Expense		60
	To close expenses.		

INCOME SUMMARY

| 5/31 | 2,085 | 5/31 | 5,210 |

SALARIES EXPENSE

5/28	825	5/31 Closing	875
5/31 Adj.	50		
	875		

MARKETING EXPENSE

| 5/5 | 800 | 5/31 Closing | 800 |

ELECTRICITY EXPENSE

| 5/25 | 125 | 5/31 Closing | 125 |

INSURANCE EXPENSE

| 5/31 Adj. | 20 | 5/31 Closing | 20 |

SUPPLIES EXPENSE

| 5/31 Adj. | 80 | 5/31 Closing | 80 |

DEPRECIATION EXPENSE

| 5/31 Adj. | 125 | 5/31 Closing | 125 |

INTEREST EXPENSE

| 5/31 Adj. | 60 | 5/31 Closing | 60 |

and collect only those elements that affect a company's profitability. Withdrawals of business assets are not expenses and are thus excluded from income computations.

By entering and posting this final journal entry, one completes the closing process. Observe that the revenue, expense, and drawing accounts all contain zero balances and are ready to accumulate June transactions. In addition, note that the $11,925 ending balance in Wise's capital account now agrees with the firm's financial statement disclosures as shown on pages 134 and 135.

EXHIBIT 4–5
Closing the Income Summary Account

May 31	Income Summary	3,125	
	Gary Wise, Capital		3,125
	To close Income Summary.		

INCOME SUMMARY

5/31	2,085	5/31	5,210
5/31 Closing	3,125		
	5,210		

GARY WISE, CAPITAL

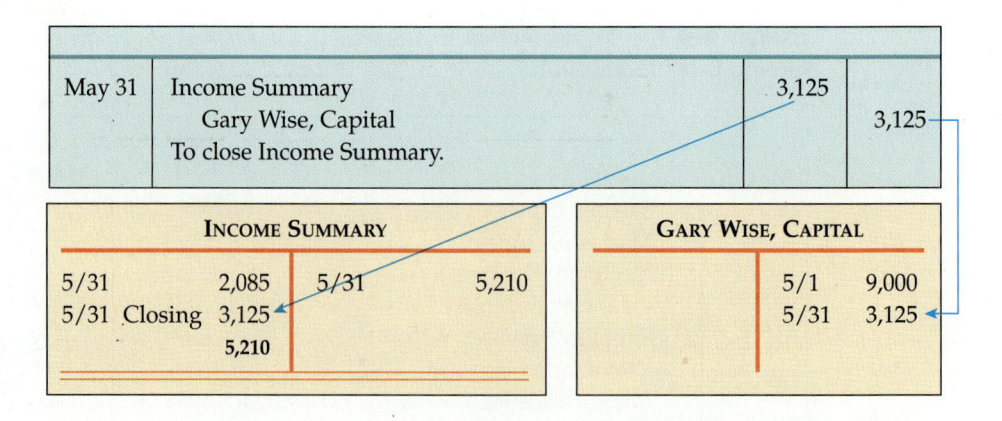

| | | 5/1 | 9,000 |
| | | 5/31 | 3,125 |

EXHIBIT 4–6
Closing the Drawing Account

May 31	Gary Wise, Capital	200	
	Gary Wise, Drawing		200
	To close drawing account.		

GARY WISE, DRAWING

| 5/30 | 200 | 5/31 Closing | 200 |

GARY WISE, CAPITAL

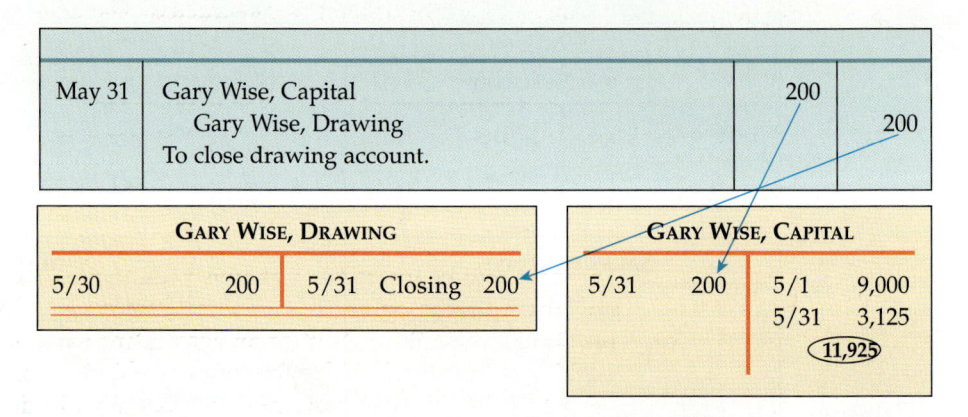

5/31	200	5/1	9,000
		5/31	3,125
			(11,925)

Exhibit 4–7 presents an overview of the preceding discussion. As you can see, closing transfers temporary balances to owner's capital, a permanent (real) element of the accounting equation.

Post-Closing Trial Balance. Errors can occur during the closing process, just as they can in other accounting procedures. To determine whether the accounts are still in balance after the closing entries have been journalized and posted,

EXHIBIT 4–7
An Overview of the Closing Process

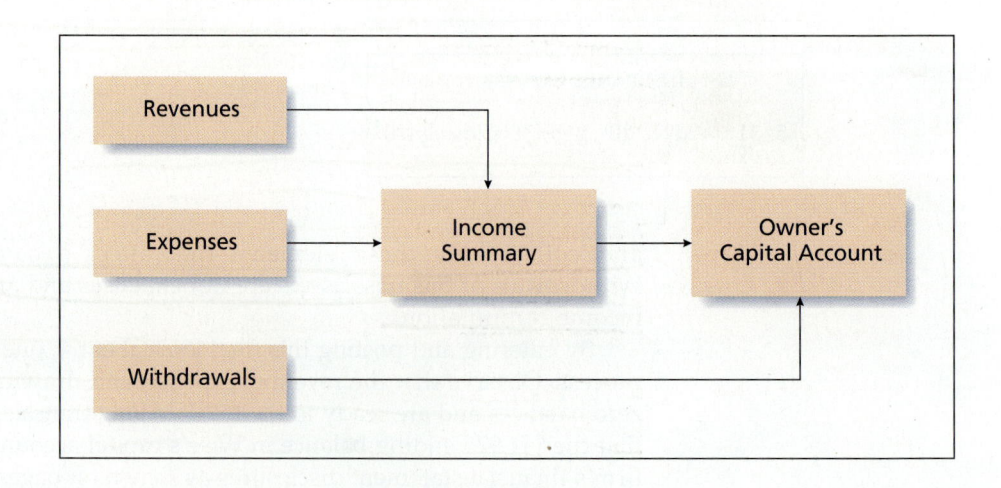

Revenues → Income Summary
Expenses → Income Summary
Income Summary → Owner's Capital Account
Withdrawals → Owner's Capital Account

accountants often prepare a **post-closing trial balance.** The post-closing trial balance examines ledger balances to determine if total debits equal total credits. Because this report is constructed after completion of the closing process, no balances remain in the drawing, revenue, and expense accounts. In addition, the capital account has been updated to reflect these amounts. The post-closing trial balance for Wise Advertising appears in Exhibit 4–8.

A LOOK BACK: THE ACCOUNTING CYCLE

3 Name and describe the various steps in the accounting cycle.

A review of the material presented in this chapter and the previous two chapters reveals that we have been studying the **accounting cycle.** The cycle encompasses the various tasks performed during an accounting period to process transactions. Specifically, (1) transactions are recorded in the journal and then (2) posted to ledger accounts. To determine whether the ledger accounts are in balance, (3) a trial balance is constructed. The trial balance is updated by certain adjustments in the process of (4) preparing a work sheet. From the work sheet (5) formal financial statements are produced, and (6) adjusting entries are recorded in the journal and posted to the ledger. Finally, (7) temporary accounts are closed and (8) a post-closing trial balance is prepared. The entire sequence, which is repeated in the next reporting period, is shown in Exhibit 4–9.

THE BALANCE SHEET

The past few chapters have shown how transactions and events eventually find their way to an entity's financial statements. Recall that financial statements comprise the output of an accounting system and, in fact, are considered by many people to be the primary objective of the accounting function. Because of their importance, we now begin an in-depth probe of the various

EXHIBIT 4–8
Post-Closing Trial Balance of the Wise Advertising Agency

WISE ADVERTISING AGENCY
Post-Closing Trial Balance
May 31, 19XX

Cash	$13,705	
Accounts receivable	3,860	
Prepaid insurance	460	
Supplies	260	
Land	5,500	
Car	4,500	
Accumulated depreciation: car		$ 125
Accounts payable		125
Unearned agency revenue		10,000
Loan payable		6,000
Interest payable		60
Salaries payable		50
Gary Wise, capital		11,925
	$28,285	$28,285

EXHIBIT 4–9
The Accounting Cycle

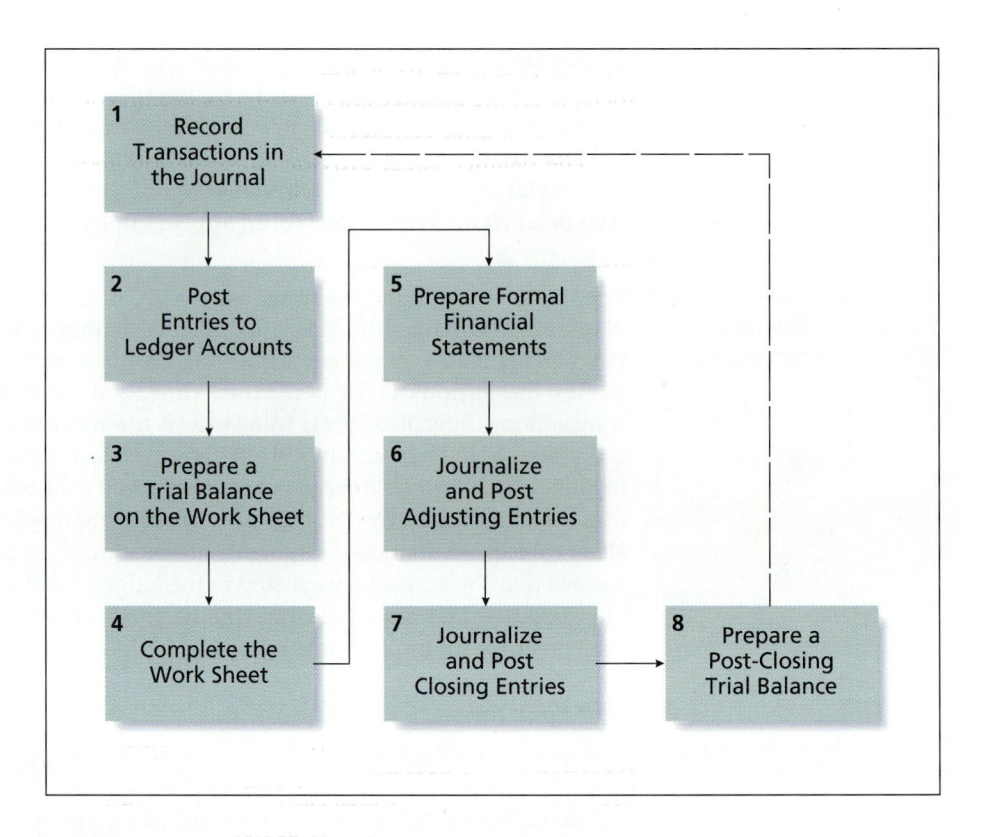

```
1  Record Transactions in the Journal
        ↓
2  Post Entries to Ledger Accounts
        ↓
3  Prepare a Trial Balance on the Work Sheet
        ↓
4  Complete the Work Sheet
        ↓
5  Prepare Formal Financial Statements
        ↓
6  Journalize and Post Adjusting Entries
        ↓
7  Journalize and Post Closing Entries
        →
8  Prepare a Post-Closing Trial Balance
        ⇢ (back to 1)
```

BUSINESS BRIEFING

SHIRLEY CHERAMY
Business Consultant
Jackson Hole, Wyoming

The Year-End Close: It's More Than Just the Journal Entries

The year-end close brings with it a number of opportunities, whether you are a member of a company's financial staff or the independent accountants performing an audit. The opportunities include the time to step back and study the firm's operations for the year—that is, to look at the fundamental business, not at the journal entries that got you there. Are revenues up? Is the increase caused by price increases or by a change in product mix? How do total revenues compare to the budget and to last year? How does the new sales commission and bonus plan affect selling costs? There are lots of *business* (not accounting!) questions to answer.

Closing is also the time to look forward—how the company will do in the future, given operating results of the past year and the firm's current financial position. Such an investigation includes addressing business strategies, the competitive environment, and other nonaccounting issues.

This overview is intended to deliver a message: Take advantage of closing to understand the business. The journal entries and accounting conventions are obviously important, but the entire process involves much more. Talk to operating management; it's more fun and ensures that accounting truly reports on the period's activities.

reports prepared by a business that disclose economic activity. Our initial focus is on the balance sheet, with discussions of the other financial statements to follow in later chapters.

The balance sheet provides information about a company's assets, liabilities, and owner's equity. Such information is useful in many ways to different groups of individuals. For example, the manager of a slumping company can study the level of merchandise inventory at the end of an accounting period to judge the effectiveness of a new ordering policy. Stable inventory levels may prompt the manager to question why the ordering policy has not paralleled significant declines in sales. Creditors review the asset and liability relationships on a balance sheet to determine the adequacy of cash balances for settling a firm's current and upcoming obligations. Creditors also analyze this statement to determine if the owners are investing their own capital in the business or relying on other creditors, such as banks, to finance operations. Lenders, in particular, want the owners to have a sizable stake in the business should financial problems develop.

LIMITATIONS OF THE BALANCE SHEET

Although the balance sheet is extremely useful, it suffers from several limitations. First, current values are seldom employed for asset valuation. As noted earlier in the text, accounting is based on the historical-cost principle. Assets are recorded in the accounts at acquisition cost and, generally, cost remains in the records until disposal (i.e., sale). Consequently, a company that acquired a parcel of land 10 years ago for $50,000 would continue to report a valuation of $50,000 even though the parcel may be currently worth several times that figure.

A second problem is that many of the assets important to the profitability and future existence of a business are not measurable in dollars. These assets, which include a good management, a skilled work force, a prime location, and business contacts and relationships, are therefore omitted from the balance sheet. No one would dispute the value of these items to a firm; yet an objective valuation for accounting purposes is extremely difficult to derive.

STATEMENT CLASSIFICATION

④ Understand the concept of an operating cycle and construct a classified balance sheet.

The balance sheet in Exhibit 4–2 is adequate for an entity such as the Wise Advertising Agency. The business activities of "real-world" firms, however, tend to be more complex and involve numerous and varied accounts. Appropriately, balance sheets (and other financial statements, too) virtually always contain account classification schemes so that important relationships and subtotals can be obtained. Standard classifications improve statement utility because users can better analyze the financial relationships that are relevant and significant to them.

The balance sheet's classifications are discussed on the next few pages.

Assets. *Current Assets.* Current assets consist of cash and those assets that management intends to convert into cash or consume in a relatively short period of time. The time period depends on the operating cycle of the business; that is, how long it takes a company to obtain goods for sale (i.e., inventory), sell the inventory, and ultimately collect the related receivables. Companies selling goods on credit have the operating cycle shown in Exhibit 4–10.

EXHIBIT 4–10
Operating Cycle

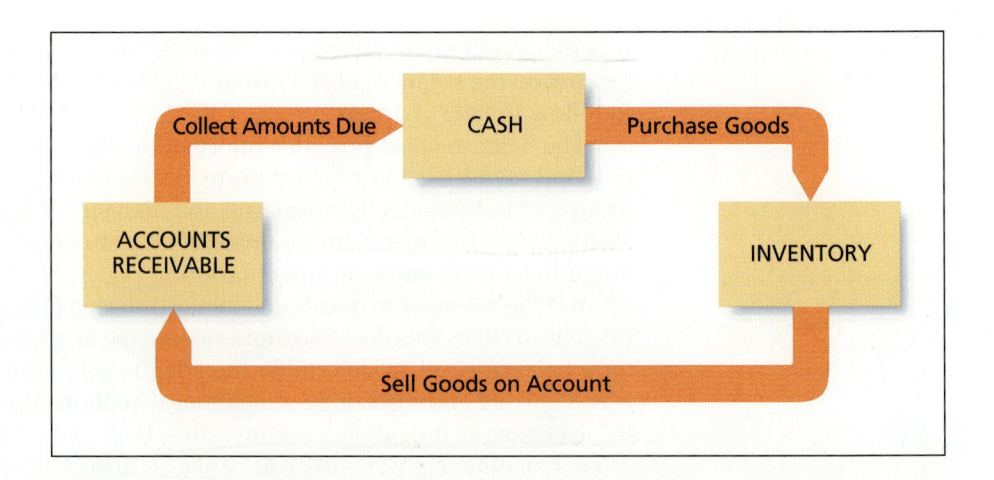

Most businesses have numerous operating cycles within an accounting period and use one year as the minimum time frame for classifying current assets. Be aware, however, that some firms have operating cycles well over one year in length. Examples include tobacco companies, which must cure their tobacco leaf, and liquor producers, which must age their inventory. Thus, the time period for purposes of the current asset definition is *one year or the operating cycle, whichever is longer.*

Current assets include cash, short-term investments and receivables, inventories, and prepaid expenses. These accounts are sequenced on the balance sheet in order of **liquidity,** or how close a current asset is to becoming cash. To illustrate, examine the balance sheet of The Williamsburg Company in Exhibit 4–11. Presented directly after cash is a certificate of deposit. Although the certificate matures six months from the time of origination, it can be converted into cash immediately if necessary. Accounts receivable is listed next and represents claims against customers for inventory already sold or services rendered. The receivables are normally collected in a month or two, depending on the credit and collection practices of the firm. The merchandise inventory has yet to be sold and is presented next. Depending on the type of business involved, several months could elapse before the existing goods are purchased by customers and cash is eventually collected. Prepaid expenses, such as rent, insurance, and supplies, commonly appear as the final current asset. Unlike receivables and inventory, prepaid expenses will not be converted to cash. They will, however, be consumed within a relatively short time.

Long-Term Investments. The next asset classification on the balance sheet is **long-term investments.** These investments are made with the intention of being retained for a prolonged period of time. Examples include land purchased either for speculation or as a future plant site, funds set aside for a company's expansion program, and investments made to acquire other entities.

Property, Plant, and Equipment. **Property, plant, and equipment** consists of assets that are used in the operation of a business and not held for resale to customers. These assets are tangible and have a long-term usefulness to a firm. Examples of property, plant, and equipment include land, buildings, machinery, furniture and fixtures, and vehicles. With the exception of land, the costs of assets in this category are gradually charged to expense via the depreciation process discussed in Chapter 3. Items of property, plant, and equipment are normally listed on the balance sheet in order of the length of their service lives, from the longest to the shortest. A typical presentation is shown in Exhibit 4–11.

EXHIBIT 4–11
Classified Balance Sheet

THE WILLIAMSBURG COMPANY
Balance Sheet
December 31, 19X1

ASSETS			
Current assets			
Cash		$ 181,000	
Certificate of deposit			
(six-month maturity)		50,000	
Accounts receivable		1,389,000	
Merchandise inventory		2,375,000	
Prepaid expenses		36,000	
Total current assets			$ 4,031,000
Long-term investments			
Land (held for future use)			1,000,000
Property, plant, & equipment			
Land		$2,000,000	
Buildings	$3,000,000		
Less: Accumulated depreciation	1,250,000	1,750,000	
Equipment	$1,045,000		
Less: Accumulated depreciation	215,000	830,000	
Total property, plant, & equip.			4,580,000
Intangible assets			
Patents on inventions			40,000
Other assets			
Long-term receivables (due 19X6)			850,000
Total assets			$10,501,000
LIABILITIES & OWNER'S EQUITY			
Current liabilities			
Accounts payable		$3,000,000	
Salaries payable		500,000	
Unearned revenues		400,000	
Current portion of mortgage			
payable		100,000	
Total current liabilities			$ 4,000,000
Long-term liabilities			
Mortgage payable (due 19X9)			1,500,000
Total liabilities			$ 5,500,000
Owner's equity			
Rudy Williams, capital			5,001,000
Total liabilities & owner's equity			$10,501,000

Intangible Assets. **Intangibles** are assets that lack physical existence; at the same time, however, these items represent valuable long-term rights to the business that has acquired or developed them. Examples include franchises, patents, copyrights, trademarks, and product formulas. Each year a portion of an intangible's cost is expensed as the asset's rights are used up or expire. This process and other issues related to intangibles are discussed further in Chapter 12.

Other Assets. Any asset account that cannot be placed in one of the previous classifications is presented in the other assets category. For instance, The Williamsburg Company lists long-term receivables as an other asset.

Liabilities. *Current Liabilities.* Generally stated, liabilities that will be liquidated within one year or the operating cycle, whichever is longer, are called **current liabilities.** Observe the consistency with the current asset definition. Examples of current liabilities include payables to suppliers and utilities, wages payable to employees, taxes payable to governmental units, and interest payable to banks. Another type of current liability is the unearned revenue discussed in Chapter 3. Unearned revenues arise from cash received in advance of goods or services provided. These prepayments are liabilities until the goods or services are given in return, which usually occurs in less than a year's time.

Long-Term Liabilities. Obligations that are expected to be paid after one year or the operating cycle, whichever is longer, are classified as **long-term liabilities.** Examples of such liabilities include certain bank loans and mortgages payable.

Many long-term obligations are paid in annual installments, that is, $X per year. As a result, the portion of a long-term liability that will be paid within one year or the operating cycle is properly disclosed under the heading of "current." To illustrate, notice that Williamsburg owes $1,600,000 from a mortgage due in 19X9. The liability is split according to its payment dates: $100,000 within one year and $1,500,000 after one year.

Owner's Equity. As explained in Chapter 1, owner's equity represents the owner's claim against (or "interest" in) the assets of a business. The owner's equity section of the balance sheet varies with the three forms of business organization: sole proprietorship, partnership, and corporation.

Sole Proprietorship. A **sole proprietorship** is an enterprise owned by one person. From an accounting perspective, owner investments and withdrawals, as well as the company's net income or net loss (i.e., revenues and expenses), are merged into a single account at the end of the period. For The Williamsburg Company, the account is labeled Rudy Williams, Capital. The proprietorship's balance sheet, then, will contain only one owner's equity account: the name of the owner followed by the term "Capital."

Partnership. A **partnership** is a business owned by two or more persons, with a separate capital account established for each partner. Similar to what occurs in the proprietorship, each capital account after closing will contain a partner's investments, withdrawals, and a share of the entity's net income or net loss. Net income or net loss can be divided among the partners in any fashion. Generally, a written agreement stipulates the profit-sharing arrangements; if no written agreement exists, profits and losses are usually divided equally. Accounting problems for partnerships are presented later in the text.

Corporation. A third form of business organization is the corporation. The owners, called *stockholders,* are the investors who have purchased the firm's transferable units of ownership—known as shares of capital stock.

Unlike sole proprietorships and partnerships, corporations do not combine owner investments, net income and net losses, and withdrawals in one capital account. Instead, shareholder investments are recorded in a Capital Stock account, and a separate account called Retained Earnings is used to keep track of the profits generated by management. Just as sole proprietorships and partnerships permit owner withdrawals, corporations follow a similar practice. Corporate withdrawals are termed dividends and represent distributions of income to the stockholders. At any point in time, then, the balance in Retained Earnings represents undistributed profits that are left (retained) in the firm.

A simplified owners' (stockholders') equity section of a corporate balance sheet would appear as follows:

Stockholders' equity	
Capital stock, 10,000 shares authorized and issued	$100,000
Retained earnings	42,500
Total stockholders' equity	$142,500

In practice, accounting for corporate equity can become quite complex. Further discussion of corporations is found in Chapters 16 and 17.

NOTES TO THE FINANCIAL STATEMENTS/FULL DISCLOSURE

The balance sheet classifications just discussed improve a company's presentation of financial information. For most organizations, however, further description is needed. Many business activities are complex and require some explanation—an explanation that goes beyond the numbers shown on the income statement, statement of owner's equity, balance sheet, and statement of cash flows.

In recognition of this fact, the financial statements are normally accompanied by a series of notes that provide an expansion on selected company information. Notes are employed to describe the details of significant accounting policies, major business events that occurred during the period, pending lawsuits, and various other facets of operation. Such information is used extensively by analysts and investors to better understand the figures being reported. Notes are discussed more fully in Chapter 7; examples are presented both there and in numerous illustrations throughout the book.

The use of notes is an example of the accounting principle of full disclosure. Full disclosure means that the financial statements result in a fair presentation of the facts that influence the decisions and judgment of an informed user of financial information. Such facts must be presented in a timely manner and be unbiased and understandable.

A CLOSER LOOK AT LIQUIDITY

5 Analyze a company's liquidity.

The classified balance sheet presented earlier allows a user to investigate various financial relationships. Short-term creditors, managers, and owners have a keen interest in the cash and near-cash position of a firm. These groups are concerned about an entity's overall liquidity, or its ability to settle upcoming bills in a timely manner. The inability to meet these obligations taints a company's reputation, harms its credit rating, and generally means an increase in future borrowing costs.

The study of liquidity may be accomplished by analyzing the relationship between current assets and current liabilities. These items are logically connected, as current liabilities are normally paid or reduced by current assets. Liquidity is frequently analyzed by computing working capital, the current ratio, and the quick ratio.

WORKING CAPITAL

Working capital is the mathematical difference between total current assets and total current liabilities. It is the amount that would remain if all current obligations were paid immediately. Generally speaking, the amount of working capital should be sufficient to meet day-to-day expenses and provide for some expansion.

From the data shown in Exhibit 4–11, we see that The Williamsburg Company's working capital situation is somewhat weak, standing at only $31,000 ($4,031,000 − $4,000,000). Should an unexpected event arise, management may be forced to scramble for cash. Why? Although current assets do exceed current liabilities, observe the current asset composition. Approximately 93.4% of the current asset total is comprised of receivables and inventory, both of which require some time until conversion into cash. Creditors may therefore be reluctant to conduct business with the firm for fear of nonpayment.

CURRENT RATIO

Working capital is often expressed in a format known as the **current ratio.** The related calculation follows.

$$\text{Current Ratio} = \frac{\text{Current Assets}}{\text{Current Liabilities}}$$

Williamsburg's current ratio is 1.01 ($4,031,000 ÷ $4,000,000), again somewhat low. Bankers and other lenders often prefer to see total current assets at least twice as large as total current liabilities. This 2:1 ratio basically means that for every $1 owed and payable in the imminent future, a business has $2 of current assets available or soon available that can be used for payment.[2] Usually, a high current ratio is preferable to a very low one.

The current ratio shares the same problem as the working capital calculation. By relying on *total* current assets and *total* current liabilities, no consideration is given to individual component liquidities. One hundred dollars of cash, for example, is obviously more useful in satisfying existing obligations than $100 of unsold inventory.

---
[2] The exception is prepaid expenses, which will be consumed in operations.

A Further Focus

Current ratios, as well as others, tend to vary by type of business. For instance, consider the following median current ratios from selected industries (so-called *industry norms*):

Local bus charter services	0.8	Cookie and cracker manufacturers	2.5
Petroleum refiners	1.3	Used motor vehicle parts wholesalers	3.2
Housing contractors	1.7	Variety stores	3.8
Travel agencies	2.1	Irrigation services	4.3

These variations are caused by differences in operating practices. Companies in some industries carry high levels of receivables and inventories to service their customers; others rely heavily on accounts payable to finance operations. The general rule of 2 is just as its name implies—general. There are exceptions.

Source: The figures cited here are taken from *Industry Norms & Key Business Ratios*, Dun & Bradstreet, Westport, Conn., 1994.

Quick Ratio

To help overcome the preceding problem, analysts have constructed a more stringent test of debt-paying ability known as the **quick ratio.** The quick ratio excludes inventories and prepaid expenses from the current asset base, leaving only ready or "nearly ready" sources of cash. It is computed as follows:

$$\text{Quick Ratio} = \frac{\text{(Cash + Short-Term Investments + Accounts Receivable)}}{\text{Current Liabilities}}$$

Williamsburg's quick ratio is 0.41 [($181,000 + $50,000 + $1,389,000) ÷ $4,000,000]. Given that many analysts label a ratio of 1.0 as satisfactory (i.e., each dollar of short-term debt is backed by $1 of cash or near-cash assets), the company's situation continues to appear bleak.

Several Cautions About Ratio Analysis. Although widely used in practice, ratios are not a perfect evaluation tool. Be aware that ratios can often be manipulated to enhance financial performance. To illustrate, a business can deliberately improve its current ratio by paying short-term obligations at or near the end of the accounting period. Assume, for instance, that a company has current assets of $100,000 and current liabilities of $50,000 on December 31. If the firm *voluntarily* paid a $10,000 account payable, the year-end current ratio would improve from 2 ($100,000 ÷ $50,000) to 2.25 ($90,000 ÷ $40,000). The practice of intentionally increasing a ratio to improve financial appearance is commonly known as **window dressing.**

Also be aware that ratios are merely a mathematical expression of relationships. In essence, a ratio is like a thermometer, or a gauge of performance. The thermometer can indicate whether one's temperature is elevated; it cannot pinpoint whether an individual has the flu, an infected ear, or mononucleosis. The thermometer simply shows that something is amiss and serves as the starting point for further investigation. Similarly, a ratio presents information

---

Ethics Issue

Ames, Inc., presently has a current ratio of 1.8, which is in violation of the terms of a loan agreement. Management has instructed you to immediately settle several soon-to-be-due payables, an action that will increase the ratio. Although accomplishing the ultimate objective, payment at this time will create a significant strain on cash—possibly causing insufficient funds for the week's payroll. How would you react?

starting point for further investigation. Similarly, a ratio presents information about a single financial relationship; it cannot tell the complete story.

APPENDIX: REVERSING ENTRIES

6

Explain the concept and mechanics of reversing entries.

Our presentation of the accounting cycle concluded with the construction of a post-closing trial balance. Some companies add a further step to the cycle by using reversing entries. To explain, a **reversing entry** is the exact opposite of an adjusting entry. The same accounts are involved, but the debits and credits are reversed. Reversing entries are journalized on the first day of the following accounting period and, it is important to note, are an optional bookkeeping procedure.

To illustrate the concept and purpose of reversals, assume that Houston Enterprises has a $15,000 payroll for a five-day work week. Employees are paid every Friday, giving rise to the following journal entry:

Salaries Expense	15,000	
Cash		15,000
Paid salaries for the week.		

It is now December and the last payroll of the month falls due on Friday, the 26th. The journal entry just shown is recorded once again when cash is disbursed to the employees. By December 31, an additional three working days will have elapsed (Monday, December 29, through Wednesday, December 31). Houston must therefore record the following adjusting entry to properly reflect the salary expense incurred during this period:

Dec. 31	Salaries Expense	9,000	
	Salaries Payable		9,000
	To record accrued salaries.		

The $9,000 adjustment is based on salaries of $3,000 per day ($15,000 ÷ 5 days).

Shortly after the adjusting process is completed, the books would be closed and the balance in the Salaries Expense account reduced to zero. The relevant expense and liability accounts would appear as follows:

SALARIES EXPENSE		SALARIES PAYABLE
12/31 Adj. 9,000 12/31 Closing 9,000		12/31 Adj. 9,000

Note: For illustrative purposes we have omitted the weekly $15,000 debits to Salaries Expense.

CASE A—NO REVERSING ENTRIES

At this point Houston must decide whether it wants to utilize reversing entries. Let us first assume that the firm does *not* use reversals. If this is the case, our example can be completed by focusing on Friday, January 2—the next payday. Houston's $15,000 payroll would be recorded in the following manner:

Jan. 2	Salaries Payable	9,000	
	Salaries Expense	6,000	
	Cash		15,000
	Paid salaries for the week.		

Salaries Payable is debited to eliminate the salaries owed from the previous accounting period. In addition, Salaries Expense is debited to recognize the payroll costs (i.e., an expense) related to the first two days of January ($3,000 × 2 days = $6,000).

CASE B—USING REVERSING ENTRIES

We will now assume that Houston elects to use reversals. On January 1, the first day of the new accounting period, the firm will reverse the December 31 adjustment in the following manner:

Jan. 1	Salaries Payable	9,000	
	Salaries Expense		9,000
	Reversing entry.		

The impact of this entry is best seen by studying the accompanying T-accounts:

SALARIES EXPENSE		SALARIES PAYABLE	
12/31 Adj. 9,000	12/31 Closing 9,000	1/1 Rev. 9,000	12/31 Adj. 9,000
	1/1 Rev. 9,000		

The Salaries Payable account is reduced to zero; Salaries Expense, on the other hand, contains an abnormal credit balance of $9,000. Because of its zero balance, there is no need to debit Salaries Payable when payment takes place on January 2. Instead, the *entire* disbursement is expensed, as follows:

Jan. 2	Salaries Expense	15,000	
	Cash		15,000
	Paid salaries for the week.		

The $15,000 debit, when combined with the account's existing credit balance, leaves $6,000 in Salaries Expense. This amount correctly reflects Houston's salary costs for the first two days of January: $3,000 per day × 2 days = $6,000.

AN OVERVIEW

A comparison of the two approaches reveals identical outcomes. Specifically, the expense is split between the accounting periods affected: $9,000 of expense is recognized in December (3 days) and $6,000 in January (2 days). Further, no balance remains in Salaries Payable, indicating that Houston has completely settled its year-end salary obligation.

As the end result is the same, why would a company use reversing entries? Although an extra journal entry is involved, reversals facilitate the bookkeeping process and reduce the chance for errors. To illustrate, briefly review Case A (no reversing entries). Observe the need to reference the year-end accrual to determine the amount of the January 2 cash disbursement that was expensed in the previous period ($9,000). In contrast, the use of reversals (Case B) allows the bookkeeper to record the normal payroll entry (namely, a debit to Salaries Expense and a credit to Cash). The possibility is therefore eliminated that errors will creep into the accounts on the subsequent payment date from the bookkeeper's failure to consider a previously recorded adjustment.

The basic reversing procedures that were shown for salaries apply to other accrued expenses, with similar procedures available for use with accrued revenues. Generally speaking, reversals are applied to those adjusting items that involve future cash flows. In some cases the reversing process can be employed with prepaid expenses and unearned revenues. These cases are somewhat unusual, however, and will not be discussed here.

END-OF-CHAPTER REVIEW

LEARNING OBJECTIVES: THE KEY POINTS

1. **Prepare a work sheet and the accompanying financial statements.** A work sheet is a columnar form that aids in the construction of financial statements. An entity's trial balance data are combined with appropriate adjustments to yield the adjusted trial balance. Each account in the adjusted trial balance is then extended to one of the work sheet's financial statement sections, with assets, liabilities, and owner's equity accounts going to the balance sheet and revenues and expenses being transferred to the income statement.

2. **Explain the need for the closing process and close a set of accounting records.** The closing process is performed to transfer the balances in temporary accounts (revenues, expenses, and drawing) to the owner's capital account. This procedure allows a company to begin the next period with a "fresh start" in the accumulation of information for the income statement and the statement of owner's equity. The temporary accounts are reduced to zero. More specifically, revenue accounts are debited, with a corresponding credit being made to Income Summary. Next, the individual expenses are credited and the Income Summary is debited. Income Summary, now containing the income or loss of the firm, is closed to the owner's capital account. As a final step, the drawing account is credited and charged against owner's capital.

3. **Name and describe the various steps in the accounting cycle.** The accounting cycle consists of the various tasks performed during a period to process transactions. These tasks include journalizing, posting, construction of a trial balance, and preparation of a work sheet and formal financial statements. Also included are the recording and posting of adjusting entries, the closing process, and preparation of a post-closing trial balance.

4. **Understand the concept of an operating cycle and construct a classified balance sheet.** An operating cycle is the amount of time that it takes a business to buy inventory, sell that inventory to customers, and collect the related receivables. Statement classifications, such as those for current assets; long-term investments; property,

COMPLETION OF THE ACCOUNTING CYCLE 151

plant, and equipment; intangible assets; other assets; current liabilities; long-term liabilities; and owner's equity, help make a balance sheet more useful for purposes of financial analysis.

5. **Analyze a company's liquidity.** Liquidity evaluations are made to assess an entity's ability to meet its short-term obligations. The analyses usually involve calculation of working capital, the current ratio, or the quick ratio. Working capital is the mathematical difference between current assets and current liabilities; the current ratio is current assets ÷ current liabilities. A more stringent test of debt-paying ability, the quick ratio, focuses on cash and near-cash assets by ignoring inventories and prepaid expenses. The quick ratio is computed as: (cash + short-term investments + accounts receivable) ÷ current liabilities.

6. **(Appendix) Explain the concept and mechanics of reversing entries.** Reversing entries are employed to reduce the possibility of errors in an accounting system. These entries are made on the first day of a new accounting period and are the exact opposite of previously recorded adjustments for accrued expenses and accrued revenues. It is important to note that reversals are an optional bookkeeping procedure.

KEY TERMS AND CONCEPTS: A QUICK OVERVIEW

accounting cycle   The various tasks performed to process transactions, including (1) recording transactions in the journal; (2) posting; (3) preparing a trial balance, work sheet, and financial statements; (4) recording adjusting and closing entries; and (5) preparing a post-closing trial balance. (p. 139)

closing process   A process in which the balances in all temporary accounts are transferred to the owner's capital account. (p. 133)

corporation   An entity form whose owners have purchased shares of stock in the enterprise. (p. 145)

current assets   Those assets that management intends to convert into cash or consume in the normal course of business within one year or the operating cycle, whichever is longer. (p. 141)

current liabilities   Debts or obligations that will be paid within one year or the operating cycle, whichever is longer. (p. 144)

current ratio   A measure of liquidity that relates total current assets to total current liabilities. (p. 146)

dividends   Distributions of corporate income to the stockholders. (p. 145)

full disclosure principle   A principle holding that an entity must provide a complete reporting of all facts important enough to influence the judgment of an informed user of financial information. (p. 145)

income summary   An account used in the closing process to summarize the revenues and expenses of a business. (p. 135)

intangible assets   Long-term assets that lack physical existence—for example, patents, copyrights, and trademarks. (p. 144)

liquidity   How close an asset is to becoming cash. Also, the ability of a business to settle its debts in a timely manner. (p. 142).

long-term investments   Investments made with the intent of being held for a long period of time. (p. 142)

long-term liabilities   Obligations expected to be paid after one year or the operating cycle, whichever is longer. (p. 144)

notes to the financial statements   A supplemental, yet integral, part of the financial statements that provides an expansion of the information contained in the body of the reports. (p. 145)

operating cycle   The period of time it takes a firm to buy merchandise inventory, sell the inventory, and collect the related receivables. (p. 141)

partnership   A business owned by two or more persons. (p. 144)

post-closing trial balance   An internal report that examines ledger account balances after the closing process has been completed to determine if total debits equal total credits. (p. 139)

property, plant, and equipment   Assets with long lives acquired for use in business operations and not held for resale to customers. (p. 142)

quick ratio   A liquidity ratio that focuses on cash and near-cash assets; computed as: (cash + short-term investments + accounts receivable) ÷ current liabilities. (p. 147)

real accounts   Accounts whose balances are carried forward from period to period. (p. 134)

retained earnings   The undistributed income that is left in a corporation. (p. 145)

reversing entry   A journal entry made on the first day of the following period that is the exact opposite of an adjustment. (p. 148)

shares of capital stock   A corporation's transferable units of ownership. (p. 145)

sole proprietorship   A business owned by one person. (p. 144)

temporary (nominal) accounts   Accounts that are reduced to zero at the end of the accounting period via the closing process. (p. 134)

window dressing   The practice of intentionally increasing a ratio to improve financial appearance. (p. 147)

work sheet   A columnar form that aids in the construction of the financial statements and assists in the performance of other end-of-period tasks. (p. 130)

working capital   The excess of total current assets over total current liabilities. (p. 146)

Chapter Quiz

The five questions that follow relate to several issues raised in the chapter. Test your knowledge of the issues by selecting the best answer. (The answers appear on p. 170.)

1. When preparing a work sheet, the balance in the Accounts Payable account should be extended from the adjusted trial balance column to the:
   a. income statement debit column.
   b. income statement credit column.
   c. balance sheet debit column.
   d. balance sheet credit column.

2. Which of the following statements about the closing process is correct?
   a. Balances in income statement accounts are reduced to zero.
   b. The owner's capital account is updated to reflect the period's net income and owner withdrawals.
   c. Temporary accounts are given different treatment than real accounts.
   d. All of the above statements are correct.

3. Which of the following is the correct closing entry for Joe Salem's drawing account?
   a. Debit Joe Salem, Drawing; credit Joe Salem, Capital.
   b. Debit Joe Salem, Drawing; credit Income Summary.

c. Debit Joe Salem, Capital; credit Joe Salem, Drawing.
   d. Debit Income Summary; credit Joe Salem, Drawing.
4. The balance sheet's current asset classification:
   a. is normally disclosed after the property, plant, and equipment classification.
   b. includes cash and other assets expected to be realized or consumed within one year of the balance sheet date or the operating cycle, whichever is longer.
   c. includes cash and other assets expected to be realized or consumed within one year of the balance sheet date or the operating cycle, whichever is shorter.
   d. reports the patents and copyrights owned by a firm.
5. Which of the following accounts would be used in a liquidity study of a firm?
   a. Income Summary.
   b. Accounts Receivable.
   c. Machinery.
   d. Ron Owens, Capital.

SUMMARY PROBLEM

Sherry Black operates a tour service for island resorts. The company's December 31, 19X2, adjusted trial balance follows.

SHERRY'S SHORE EXCURSIONS
Adjusted Trial Balance
December 31, 19X2

Cash	$ 5,300	
Accounts receivable	13,650	
Prepaid insurance	1,100	
Building	120,000	
Accumulated depreciation: building		$ 57,650
Equipment	26,000	
Accumulated depreciation: equipment		7,200
Accounts payable		16,500
Salaries payable		7,700
Unearned service revenue		11,900
Sherry Black, capital		40,100
Sherry Black, drawing	8,500	
Service revenue		62,400
Salaries expense	13,400	
Rent expense	6,000	
Insurance expense	1,200	
Depreciation expense	8,300	
	$203,450	$203,450

Instructions

a. Prepare the necessary closing entries for the year ended December 31.
b. Calculate the balance in Black's capital account after closing. *Note:* There were no owner investments during the year.

c. Determine the company's total current assets and total current liabilities as of December 31.
d. Suppose that the company's general ledger contained the following additional accounts: Copyright, Mortgage Payable (due in 19X6), and Land Held for Future Building Site. In what sections of a classified balance sheet would these accounts appear?

Solution

a.

Dec. 31	Service Revenue		62,400	
	Income Summary			62,400
	To close revenues.			
31	Income Summary		28,900	
	Salaries Expense			13,400
	Rent Expense			6,000
	Insurance Expense			1,200
	Depreciation Expense			8,300
	To close expenses.			
31	Income Summary		33,500*	
	Sherry Black, Capital			33,500
	To close Income Summary.			
31	Sherry Black, Capital		8,500	
	Sherry Black, Drawing			8,500
	To close drawing account.			

*$62,400 − $28,900.

b.
Beginning capital, Jan. 1	$40,100
Add: Net income	33,500
	$73,600
Deduct: Owner withdrawals	8,500
Ending capital, Dec. 31	$65,100

c. Current assets
Cash	$ 5,300
Accounts receivable	13,650
Prepaid insurance	1,100
Total	$20,050

Current liabilities
Accounts payable	$16,500
Salaries payable	7,700
Unearned service revenue	11,900
Total	$36,100

d. Copyright—intangible assets; Mortgage Payable—long-term liabilities; Land Held for Future Building Site—long-term investments.

Assignment Material

Questions

Q4–1 What are the key benefits of preparing a work sheet?

Q4–2 Why is the net income amount (as derived from the income statement columns of the work sheet) also entered as a credit in the balance sheet columns?

Q4–3 Why are the adjusting entries that appear on the work sheet also recorded in the general journal?

Q4–4 What are the objectives of the closing process?

Q4–5 Which accounts are closed at the end of the accounting period and which are not?

Q4–6 Is the owner's drawing account closed to the Income Summary account? Why or why not?

Q4–7 What are the basic differences between the adjusted trial balance and the post-closing trial balance?

Q4–8 What is meant by the term "accounting cycle"?

Q4–9 Discuss the limitations of the balance sheet.

Q4–10 Define the operating cycle. Should businesses attempt to shorten the cycle or lengthen it? Why?

Q4–11 How should current assets be organized on the balance sheet?

Q4–12 What is meant by the term "liquidity"?

Q4–13 Are all pertinent facts about a company disclosed directly in the body of a balance sheet and other financial statements? If not, what additional technique is used?

Q4–14 An accountant recently stated that a company's balance sheet lacked adequate disclosure. Explain the accountant's comment.

*Q4–15 What is a reversing entry? Are reversing entries a required or an optional bookkeeping procedure?

Exercises

E4–1 Work sheet extensions (L.O. 1)

The new bookkeeper of Rock Concerts is in the process of completing the company's work sheet for the year just ended. For each of the following items, indicate whether the account should be extended to the income statement section or the balance sheet section. Also determine whether the account should be placed in the debit column or the credit column. Assume that all accounts have normal balances.

		INCOME STATEMENT/ BALANCE SHEET	DEBIT/CREDIT
a.	Accounts payable	_____	_____
b.	Ticket revenue	_____	_____
c.	Advance ticket sales	_____	_____
d.	Speaker equipment	_____	_____
e.	Advertising expense	_____	_____
f.	Tom Buzzini, drawing	_____	_____

* An asterisk preceding an item indicates that the material is covered in an appendix to this chapter.

		INCOME STATEMENT/ BALANCE SHEET	DEBIT/CREDIT
g.	Trademark		
h.	Prepaid insurance		
i.	Tom Buzzini, capital		

E4–2 Preparation of financial statements (L.O. 1)

The adjusted trial balance of Apartment Finders as of December 31, 19XX, appears as follows:

Cash	$16,300	
Accounts receivable	8,900	
Prepaid advertising	2,000	
Equipment	17,500	
Accumulated depreciation: equipment		$ 4,000
Accounts payable		2,500
Commissions payable		5,000
Katie Reubens, capital		18,500
Katie Reubens, drawing	3,000	
Service revenue		37,000
Commissions expense	7,000	
Advertising expense	6,000	
Telephone expense	4,200	
Depreciation expense	2,100	
	$67,000	$67,000

Katie Reubens organized Apartment Finders on January 2, 19XX, with an initial cash investment of $18,500.

Prepare Apartment Finders' income statement and statement of owner's equity for the year ended December 31, 19XX. Also prepare the company's December 31 balance sheet, using a format similar to that shown in Exhibit 4–2.

E4–3 Overview of the closing process (L.O. 2)

Evaluate the comments that follow as being True or False. If the comment is false, briefly explain why.

a. The closing process is performed after adjusting entries have been journalized and posted.
b. Because they both possess a debit balance, Salaries Expense and Susan Franklin, Drawing, are treated in the same manner when accounts are closed at the end of the period.
c. The Equipment account is closed at the end of the period by a debit to Income Summary and a credit to Equipment.
d. If MultiTech incurred a net loss for the period just ended, the Income Summary account would contain a debit balance after the revenue and expense accounts have been closed.
e. If a $4,900 balance is listed in the adjusted trial balance for Dave Miller, Capital, it stands to reason that Miller's capital account in the post-closing trial balance would be listed at $4,900 as well.

E4–4 Closing entries (L.O. 2)

Creative Creations had the following adjusted trial balance on December 31:

Cash	$ 10,650	
Accounts receivable	30,000	
Land held for future use	70,000	
Trademark	5,500	
Accounts payable		$ 35,000
Lynn Harrell, capital		100,150
Lynn Harrell, drawing	28,000	
Consulting revenue		85,000
Wage expense	32,000	
Rent expense	24,000	
Travel expense	20,000	
	$220,150	$220,150

Prepare the closing entries that Creative Creations would record on December 31.

E4–5 Closing entries, errors (L.O. 2)

The closing entries that follow were prepared by a newly hired accountant of Spring Valley, a firm that specializes in real-estate property management. (*Note:* The adjusted trial balance was error-free, and all accounts had normal balances.)

Property Management Fees	235,000	
Lynn Jasper, Capital		235,000
To close revenues.		
Salaries Expense	48,000	
Insurance Expense	12,000	
Depreciation Expense	13,000	
Rent Expense	15,000	
Utilities Expense	8,000	
Supplies Expense	3,000	
Interest Expense	7,000	
Income Summary		106,000
To close expenses.		
Lynn Jasper, Capital	279,000	
Income Summary		279,000
To close capital account.		
Income Summary	18,000	
Lynn Jasper, Drawing		18,000
To close drawing account.		

Review the closing entries prepared by the new accountant and list any errors that you detect. (A corrected set of closing entries is not required.)

E4–6 Report interrelationships (L.O. 1, 2)

The following selected information appeared on reports prepared by the Phantom Company:

	TRIAL BALANCE	ADJUSTED TRIAL BALANCE	POST-CLOSING TRIAL BALANCE
Cash	$15,000	$?	$?
Supplies	2,100	1,400	?
Jones, drawing	?	9,600	?
Jones, capital	?	?	51,700
Accumulated depreciation: equipment	?	31,900	?

All accounts had normal balances, and the company reported $32,700 of net income for the period.

a. Briefly explain the probable reason why the Supplies account decreased by $700 from the trial balance to the adjusted trial balance.
b. What amount would be disclosed for the Cash account on the adjusted trial balance?
c. What amount would be disclosed for the drawing account on the post-closing trial balance?
d. What amount would appear in the Income Summary account just prior to the account being closed?
e. Analyze the balance in the Accumulated Depreciation account and determine whether it would likely be equal to $31,900, greater than $31,900, or less than $31,900 on the:
  (1) Trial balance.
  (2) Post-closing trial balance.

E4–7 Steps in the accounting cycle (L.O. 3)

Vic Dargo, a former employee of Ace Industries, has been charged with sabotaging and destroying some accounting records when his promotion was denied. Tom Gorman, Dargo's attorney, needs to understand the steps in the accounting cycle in order to defend his client.

The following tasks comprise the cycle: (1) formal financial statements are produced; (2) closing entries are journalized and posted; (3) the trial balance is updated by certain adjustments in the process of preparing a work sheet; (4) a trial balance is constructed; (5) a post-closing trial balance is prepared; (6) transactions are posted to appropriate ledger accounts; (7) a work sheet is completed; (8) daily transactions are recorded in the journal; and (9) adjusting entries are entered in the journal and posted to the ledger.

Assist Tom by listing the steps in the correct sequence of occurrence.

E4–8 Balance sheet account classification (L.O. 4)

The balance sheet of Packer Enterprises is similar to that appearing in Exhibit 4–11. Under which classification would each of the following appear?

a. Prepaid advertising
b. Portion of 30-year mortgage due in six months
c. Unearned commission revenue
d. Charles Packer, capital
e. Receivable from Howard Gibson, due in three years
f. Land purchased for speculation
g. Wages payable
h. Delivery vehicles
i. Patents
j. Accounts receivable

E4–9 Current ratio and working capital calculations (L.O. 5)

Selected accounts of McCormick Company, with current balances, are presented in the list that follows:

Accounts payable	$12,500
Accounts receivable	33,000
Accumulated depreciation	24,600
Cash	13,900
Interest payable	6,500
Loan payable, due in two months	10,000
Loan payable, due in three years	45,000
Jason McCormick, capital	36,600
Merchandise inventory	22,600
Prepaid advertising	5,300
Trademark	1,700
Unearned service revenue, to be earned next month	5,000

a. Determine the current ratio.
b. Calculate the company's working capital.
c. If McCormick has a plan to pay off all of its accounts payable, how will working capital be affected?

E4–10 Liquidity ratios (L.O. 5)

Morton, Norton, and Oliver have the following financial information at the close of business on June 4:

	MORTON	NORTON	OLIVER
Cash	$4,000	$2,500	$1,000
Accounts receivable	5,000	5,000	5,000
Inventory	1,000	2,500	4,000
Prepaid expenses	800	800	800
Accounts payable	500	500	500
Notes payable: short-term	3,100	3,100	3,100
Long-term liabilities	3,800	3,800	3,800

a. Compute the current and quick ratios for each of the three companies. (Round calculations to two decimal places.) Which firm is the most liquid? Why?
b. Assuming that all short-term notes payable are due on June 5 at 8:00 a.m., comment on each company's ability to settle its obligation in a timely manner.

*E4–11 Reversing entries (L.O. 6)

Burger Palace, which uses reversing entries, incurred $6,000 of wage and salary expenses during the last few days of 19X1. The company will pay these expenses on January 4, 19X2, as part of the $15,000 weekly payroll.

a. Present the adjusting entry that is needed at the end of 19X1.
b. Assuming a $740,000 balance in the Wage & Salary Expense account prior to the adjustment, present the necessary entry to close this account.
c. Record the company's reversing entry on January 1, 19X2.
d. Present the entry needed on January 4, 19X2.
e. How much of the January 4 payroll is considered expense of 19X2?

*E4–12 Reversing entries (L.O. 6)

Longman and Company uses reversing entries. On December 31, 19X5, the firm's Interest Expense account contained a balance of $57,000 before adjustment. A $3,500 adjusting entry for accrued interest will be made by the company's bookkeeper.

a. Assume the role of Longman's bookkeeper and prepare the adjusting entry for accrued interest on December 31.
b. Prepare an entry to close the Interest Expense account.
c. Prepare the proper reversing entry on January 1, 19X6.
d. The $3,500 will be paid to First State Bank on January 19, 19X6, along with $2,600 of other interest obligations. Prepare the proper journal entry on this date.
e. What is the balance in the Interest Expense account after the entry in part (d)?

PROBLEMS

Series A

P4–A1 Closing entries (L.O. 2)

The accounting records of The Fit Firm, an aerobics studio, revealed the following selected accounts on December 31 of the current year:

Debit balances		Credit balances	
Toni Kramer, drawing	$35,000	Toni Kramer, capital	$15,000
Salaries expense	25,000	Lesson revenue	80,400
Rent expense	6,000		
Utilities expense	2,500		
Insurance expense	3,600		
Depreciation expense	1,800		

Kramer's capital account reflects a $5,000 owner investment made on July 7.

Instructions

a. Prepare the necessary closing entries for the year ended December 31.
b. Compute the December 31, 19XX, balance of Kramer's capital account after the closing process has been performed.

P4–A2 Abbreviated work sheet, financial statements, closing entries (L.O. 1, 2)

Laskin Porter of the Columbia Repertory Theater was in the process of completing some year-end accounting work. The figures that follow properly reflect the adjusting entries made earlier in the day; all accounts have normal balances.

Cash	$23,050
Prepaid insurance	1,350
Office supplies	900
Stage equipment	32,650
Accumulated depreciation:	
stage equipment	7,950
Salaries payable	10,550
Bank loan payable	8,450
L. B. King, capital	31,100
L. B. King, drawing	3,400

Ticket revenue	$36,400
Salaries expense	20,200
Insurance expense	1,150
Travel expense	650
Interest expense	450
Office supplies expense	2,600
Rent expense	5,400
Depreciation expense	2,650

No owner investments in the theater were made during the year.

The theater's owner, L. B. King, desperately needs the financial statements, and Laskin has just started a two-week, out-of-country vacation. As Laskin's assistant, you have been asked to perform the necessary work as soon as possible.

Instructions

a. Complete a work sheet for Columbia for the year ended December 31, 19X6. *Note:* The preceding data should be entered in the adjusted trial balance columns. We have omitted the theater's trial balance and adjustments for the sake of simplicity.
b. Prepare an income statement, statement of owner's equity, and balance sheet. The balance sheet should parallel the format used in Exhibit 4–2.
c. Prepare the theater's closing entries.

P4–A3 Cycle, starting with work sheet (L.O. 1, 2, 3)

Occidental Employment Service has the following trial balance as of December 31, 19XX:

Cash	$ 3,000	
Accounts receivable	6,500	
Prepaid advertising	1,600	
Office supplies	1,200	
Office equipment	17,800	
Accumulated depreciation:		
office equipment		$ 1,400
Accounts payable		2,400
Unearned service revenue		1,800
Loan payable		12,000
Yoko Nishiyama, capital		8,500
Yoko Nishiyama, drawing	10,800	
Service revenue		43,900
Salaries expense	21,100	
Rent expense	4,500	
Utilities expense	1,600	
Interest expense	1,900	
	$70,000	$70,000

Additional accounts maintained by the business include Salaries Payable, Interest Payable, Income Summary, Advertising Expense, Office Supplies Expense, and Depreciation Expense. Occidental's accountant has obtained the following adjustment data:

1. Advertising applicable to future periods: $300.
2. Office supplies used during the period: $800.
3. Depreciation on the equipment: $2,500.
4. Accrued interest on the loan: $1,200.
5. Portion of unearned service revenue that has been earned during the current period: $1,400.
6. Accrued salaries incurred but not yet paid: $1,100.

On May 26, 19XX, Nishiyama invested $5,000 cash in the business. This event is already reflected in the figures reported in the trial balance.

Instructions

a. Complete a work sheet for Occidental Employment Service for the year ended December 31.
b. Prepare an income statement, statement of owner's equity, and balance sheet. The balance sheet should be similar in format to that shown in Exhibit 4–2.
c. Record Occidental's adjusting entries in the journal.
d. Record Occidental's closing entries in the journal.
e. Prepare a post-closing trial balance.

P4–A4 Classified balance sheet (L.O. 4)

Assume that the Wagner Company has the following accounts at the end of 19X1 (listed in alphabetic order):

Accounts payable	$ 6,600
Accounts receivable	33,000
Accumulated depreciation: building	52,000
Accumulated depreciation: office equipment	7,700
Building	430,000
Cash	5,500
Copyright	2,600
Interest payable	3,700
Interest receivable	1,700
Inventory	18,300
Land	50,000
Land held as a future plant site	75,000
Loan payable (due in one month)	12,000
Mortgage payable*	420,000
Office equipment	41,000
Office supplies	1,300
Paul Wagner, capital	146,300
Payable to Emery & Associates (due 19X4)	18,000
Prepaid advertising	1,800
Receivable from employee (due 19X3)	9,500
Salaries payable	2,000
Taxes payable	6,400
Trademark	5,000

* Of this amount, $25,000 is payable within the next year.

Instructions

Prepare a classified balance sheet as of December 31, 19X1, similar in format to that shown in Exhibit 4–11.

P4–A5 Balance sheet errors, liquidity (L.O. 4, 5)

The following classified balance sheet was prepared at the Detroit Company:

DETROIT COMPANY
Balance Sheet
For the Quarter Ended October 31, 19XX

ASSETS

Current assets
Cash	$ 68,500	
Merchandise inventory	27,000	
Accounts receivable	22,000	
Prepaid insurance	8,000	$125,500

Property, plant, & equipment
Buildings & land	$164,000	
Equipment	59,200	
	$223,200	
Less: Accumulated depreciation	45,600	177,600

Intangible assets
Trademark	$ 20,000	
Employee training expenses	27,000	
Increase in value of the company	100,000	147,000
Total assets		$450,100

LIABILITIES & OWNER'S EQUITY

Current liabilities
Accounts payable	$ 70,000	
Unearned service revenue	10,000	
Service revenue	150,000	$230,000

Long-term liabilities
Mortgage payable (payable $10,000 per year for 20 years)		200,000
Total liabilities		$430,000

Owner's equity
Al Choi, capital		43,100
Total liabilities & owner's equity		$473,100

Instructions

a. Indicate the errors in Detroit's balance sheet. *Note*: Do not prepare a corrected financial statement.
b. Calculate Detroit's correct current ratio. Comment on your findings, including an evaluation of the firm's short-term debt-paying ability.

Series B

P4–B1 Closing entries (L.O. 2)

The income statement of Morton's Taxi Service for the year ended December 31, 19XX, follows.

MORTON'S TAXI SERVICE
Income Statement
For the Year Ended December 31, 19XX

Taxi revenue		$144,360
Less expenses		
Salaries expense	$41,640	
Auto rental expense	12,400	
Gasoline expense	14,430	
Maintenance expense	1,500	
License expense	6,200	
Tires expense	970	
Total expenses		77,140
Net income		$ 67,220

Daniel Morton, the service's owner, had a beginning capital balance of $37,300 on January 1, 19XX. During the year, he invested an additional $10,000 into the firm and withdrew $26,000.

Instructions

a. Prepare the necessary closing entries for the year ended December 31.
b. Compute the December 31, 19XX, balance of Morton's capital account.

P4–B2 Abbreviated work sheet, financial statements, closing entries (L.O. 1, 2)

Holly Knight is employed in the accounting department of Expert Systems Company. She was in the process of completing the firm's work sheet for the year ended December 31 and had progressed through the adjusted trial balance columns. A portion of her work is on the following page. Additional information revealed that owner investments in the firm amounted to $7,000 during the year.

Holly was recently called out of town because of a family emergency. You are her assistant and recognize that the various year-end accounting procedures must be performed on a timely basis.

Instructions

a. Complete the work sheet that Holly had begun. *Note:* The preceding data should be entered in the adjusted trial balance columns. We have omitted the company's trial balance and adjustments for the sake of simplicity.
b. Prepare an income statement, statement of owner's equity, and balance sheet. The balance sheet should parallel the format used in Exhibit 4–2.
c. Prepare the firm's closing entries.

	ADJUSTED TRIAL BALANCE	
	DEBIT	CREDIT
Cash	$ 29,200	
Accounts receivable	25,800	
Supplies	2,600	
Prepaid insurance	1,400	
Equipment	42,700	
Accumulated depreciation: equipment		$ 10,400
Accounts payable		18,000
Ray Vogel, capital		65,200
Ray Vogel, drawing	3,900	
Service revenue		56,200
Wages expense	32,100	
Advertising expense	2,400	
Rent expense	5,900	
Miscellaneous expense	1,300	
Supplies expense	800	
Insurance expense	1,100	
Depreciation expense	3,300	
Wages payable		2,700
	$152,500	$152,500

P4–B3 Cycle, starting with work sheet (L.O. 1, 2, 3)
Trimcraft Company has the following trial balance as of December 31, 19XX:

Cash	$ 5,800	
Accounts receivable	8,200	
Prepaid insurance	2,000	
Supplies	2,700	
Equipment	89,800	
Accumulated depreciation: equipment		$ 10,000
Accounts payable		7,250
Loan payable		18,500
Lori Metcalf, capital		56,850
Lori Metcalf, drawing	4,000	
Service revenue		72,000
Salaries expense	30,500	
Rent expense	12,000	
Advertising expense	6,600	
Interest expense	3,000	
	$164,600	$164,600

Additional accounts maintained by the business include Salaries Payable, Interest Payable, Income Summary, Insurance Expense, Supplies Expense, and Depreciation Expense. Trimcraft's accountant has derived the following adjustment data:

1. Supplies on hand: $900.
2. Insurance that expired during the period: $1,300.
3. Depreciation on the equipment: $3,500.
4. Accrued interest on the loan: $400.
5. Accrued salaries incurred but not yet paid: $1,200.
6. Unrecorded service revenue, to be collected in future months: $2,200.

On March 9, 19XX, Metcalf invested $10,000 cash in the business. This event is already reflected in the figures reported in the trial balance.

Instructions

a. Complete a work sheet for Trimcraft Company for the year ended December 31.
b. Prepare an income statement, statement of owner's equity, and balance sheet. The balance sheet should be similar in format to that shown in Exhibit 4–2.
c. Record Trimcraft's adjusting entries in the journal.
d. Record Trimcraft's closing entries in the journal.
e. Prepare a post-closing trial balance.

P4–B4 Classified balance sheet (L.O. 4)

Assume that Kravitz Company has the following balance sheet accounts at the end of 19X1:

Building	$82,000
Accumulated depreciation: office furniture	800
Loan receivable (due May 19X9)	4,200
Cash	5,150
Merchandise inventory	41,570
Loan payable (due 19X8)	74,560*
Office furniture	8,000
Land held for speculation	18,320
Receivable from employee (due 19X5)	25,355
J. Kravitz, capital	40,835
Salaries payable	750
Accounts receivable	31,500
Accounts payable	52,100
Accumulated depreciation: building	19,000
Land	37,500
Payable to finance company (due June 19X2)	71,800
Patents	10,000
Prepaid insurance	900
Office supplies	750
Taxes payable	5,400

* Of this amount, $2,000 is payable within the next 12 months.

Instructions

Prepare a classified balance sheet as of December 31, 19X1, similar in format to that shown in Exhibit 4–11.

P4–B5 Balance sheet errors, liquidity (L.O. 4, 5)

The classified balance sheet on the following page incorporates an alphabetic listing of account titles.

NEW YORK COMPANY
Statement of Financial Health
December 31, 19X3

ASSETS
Intangible assets
    Copyrights $40,000
    Employee receivable (due in 19X5) 35,000
    Patents 60,000
    Service revenue 115,000 $250,000

Current assets
    Accounts receivable $40,500
    Cash 27,000
    Merchandise inventory 122,000
    Prepaid rent 500   190,000

Property, plant, & equipment
    Accumulated depreciation: buildings $(30,000)
    Accumulated depreciation: equipment (5,920)
    Buildings 150,000
    Land 100,000   214,080

    Total assets $654,080

LIABILITIES & OWNER'S EQUITY
Current liabilities
    Accounts payable $70,000
    Salaries payable 45,000
    Taxes payable 20,000
    Unearned service revenue 10,000 $145,000

Long-term liabilities
    Bank loan payable (due in equal
        installments over five years)   218,080

Owner's equity
    R. Maris, capital $341,000
    R. Maris, drawing (50,000)   291,000

    Total liabilities & owner's equity $654,080

Instructions

a. Indicate the errors in New York's balance sheet. *Note*: Do not prepare a corrected financial statement.
b. Calculate New York's correct current and quick ratios. Which of the two ratios is a more severe test of debt-paying ability? Why?

EXPANDING YOUR HORIZONS

EYH4–1   Closing experiences (L.O. 2)
Closing the books at year-end is typically a hectic experience. Almost all practicing accountants have their favorite "closing stories."

Instructions

Make an appointment to visit and interview a local certified public accountant (CPA). Ask the CPA to describe the three most "interesting" closing experiences he or she has ever encountered. Also find out what could (or should) have been done differently. Be prepared to present your findings to the class.

EYH4–2 Unique current assets and current liabilities (L.O. 4)

Our presentation in the text focused on typical current assets and current liabilities. Companies may have a current asset or current liability that is somewhat unique to their operating activities.

Instructions

Using the resources of your library, review the classified balance sheets of several firms and find a unique current asset or current liability. Be prepared to explain to the class what you have found and, specifically, why the item is disclosed in the balance sheet's current section.

EYH4–3 Liquidity differences (L.O. 5)

Each company has a different mix of current assets and current liabilities with which to operate. The mix depends on such factors as the type of business, company profitability, the number of years in operation, management philosophy, and so forth.

Instructions

a. Using the resources of your library, review the classified balance sheets of four companies that operate in distinctly different industries. Compare and contrast the current ratios of the firms, explaining any large differences that you find.
b. Which of the entities is the most liquid? The least liquid?

EYH4–4 Analysis of balance sheet and accompanying notes: NIKE, Inc. (L.O. 4)

NIKE, Inc., designs and markets a wide variety of athletic footwear, apparel, and related items in the United States and throughout the world. These items are sold for use in formal athletic competition and also basic recreational activities.

Instructions

By using the text's electronic data base, access the balance sheet and accompanying notes of NIKE and answer the questions that follow. Unless otherwise indicated, responses should be based on data for the most recent year presented.

a. What are the five largest accounts presented on the balance sheet? Under what classifications do these accounts appear?
b. An analysis of the balance sheet will reveal that the company is organized as a corporation. What section on the balance sheet provides such evidence, and what is the section's total?
c. Did the firm's current ratio improve or deteriorate since last year?
d. Review the summary of significant accounting policies (i.e., the first footnote in the notes that accompany the financial statements).
   (1) What is the basic purpose of this note?
   (2) What method(s) does the company use to depreciate its property and equipment?
e. In general terms, what information is presented by the firm's other note disclosures?
f. By analyzing overseas operations, what was the ratio of revenues generated with unrelated entities in the U.S. vs. foreign lands?

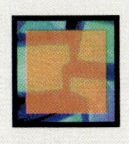

EYH4–5 Analysis of balance sheet and accompanying notes (L.O. 4)

This problem is a duplication of Problem EYH4–4. It is based on a company selected by your instructor.

Instructions

By using the text's electronic data base, access the specified company's balance sheet and accompanying notes and focus on data for the most recent year reported. Answer requirements (a)–(f) of Problem EYH4–4.

EYH4–6 Liquidity, window dressing, ethics (L.O. 5)

Donna Smith, the chief accountant of Apache Plastics, has been asked to do some window dressing for the company's financial statements. The statements are to accompany a loan application that is being prepared for the Bank of Othello.

Apache's executive vice-president, Cliff Jones, has commented: "Sell some delivery trucks—I don't care. And if that doesn't do the trick, arbitrarily increase the ending accounts receivable figure. You be the judge; no one will ever know. If we fail to maintain a current ratio of 1.75 for the bank and they don't renew our loan, you can forget about your job, my job, your new house, and our careers."

Instructions

a. What is meant by the term "window dressing"? How can Donna improve the current ratio by window dressing? Give several examples.
b. How will the examples cited in part (a) affect the quick ratio?
c. What is the basic difference between Cliff's suggestions to sell the delivery trucks and to increase accounts receivable?

COMMUNICATION OF ACCOUNTING INFORMATION

CAI4–1 Writing clear instructions: MCI Communications (L.O. 4)

Communication Principle: Past experience with "easy-to-assemble" products has probably shown each of us that it is difficult to write clear and concise instructions. To provide good instructions, writers must analyze their audience and determine what the reader knows and does not know. Because this knowledge requires time and often trial and error, the writing process may be ongoing. Good instructions are produced by authors who are flexible, ready to answer questions, and patient. The following suggestions will generally be helpful:

1. Begin with a brief overview of the entire process.
2. Review important terms.
3. Arrange steps in a logical order—chronologically or in order of importance.
4. Number the steps.
5. Write in parallel grammatical form. For instance, use short sentences beginning with active verbs (i.e., commands) such as "prepare," "include," "place," or "calculate."
6. Use examples and illustrations.

The steps that follow are editing procedures that should be employed as a writer fine-tunes and works toward the finished product:

1. Check that each activity (step) is roughly equivalent in the amount of effort required.
2. Do not include too many substeps for any one activity. Break long lists of instructions into separate activities.
3. Check that each activity is inclusive, or understandable on a stand-alone basis. Try to avoid directions such as "Refer back to Step 6 and the diagram used with Step 4."
4. Ask an independent party who is unfamiliar with the process being described to follow your instructions. If significant questions arise, some revision is in order.

MCI provides a full range of telecommunications services to businesses and residential customers. The company owns and operates one of the world's largest communications networks, representing a gross investment of more than $10 billion. Selected accounts and balances from a recent set of the firm's financial statements, simplified for purposes of presentation, follow. (*Note:* All amounts are in millions.)

Cash	$ 165
Capital stock	1,928
Long-term debt	2,366
Other assets	2,237
Accounts payable	742
Accounts receivable	2,131
Retained earnings	2,785
Other long-term liabilities	996
Communications system	10,735
Miscellaneous current assets	305
Current portion of long-term debt	215
Accumulated depreciation	4,297
Other current liabilities	2,244

Imagine that MCI has just hired a new computer programmer. The programmer understands the nature of assets, liabilities, and owners' (stockholders') equity, but has no knowledge about how to classify accounts on a balance sheet. You are an accountant for the company and must supervise the new employee while she develops a program to prepare a classified balance sheet.

Instructions

a. Prepare written instructions that will allow the programmer to understand the content and positioning of the specific categories on a classified balance sheet.
b. To give the programmer some guidance in her work, construct the balance sheet that the program should be capable of producing. The balance sheet should be dated December 31, 19X0.

Answers to Chapter Quiz

1. d
2. d
3. c
4. b
5. b

COMPREHENSIVE PROBLEM 1

HAMILTON COMPANY

Hamilton Company, which began operations on May 1, had the following transactions:

May 1 Marc Nichols, the owner, invested $9,000 cash, $12,000 of office equipment, and a building valued at $75,000 in the business. The office equipment has a service life of 5 years, and the building has a service life of 25 years.

1 Paid $240 for a four-month insurance policy.

May 4 Received $660 from a client to render services over the next four weeks.
    6 Purchased $350 of office supplies for cash.
  11 Paid $400 for various computer runs.
  15 Billed clients for services rendered, $6,800.
  21 Received $5,200 from clients on account.
  24 Borrowed $7,000 from the bank.
  25 Received the May electric bill of $100, to be paid on June 4.
  26 Purchased $12,000 of new office equipment; paid $7,000 down and agreed to pay the balance in June. This office equipment will not be depreciated until June.
  29 Paid wages to the office staff, $4,700.
  30 Processed a $2,500 cash withdrawal for the owner.
  31 Recorded $1,000 of miscellaneous expenses that were incurred in May but will be paid during June.

Hamilton's chart of accounts follows.

Cash	110	Unearned service revenue	250
Accounts receivable	120	Loan payable	260
Prepaid insurance	130	Marc Nichols, capital	310
Office supplies	135	Marc Nichols, drawing	320
Office equipment	140	Income summary	330
Accumulated depreciation:		Service revenue	410
office equipment	141	Computer service expense	510
Building	150	Wage expense	520
Accumulated depreciation:		Insurance expense	530
building	151	Office supplies expense	540
Accounts payable	210	Depreciation expense	550
Wages payable	220	Utilities expense	560
Interest payable	230	Interest expense	570
Utilities payable	240	Miscellaneous expense	580

Additional information:

1. As of May 31, accrued interest on the loan amounted to $40, while accrued wages totaled $300.
2. Since the last billing to clients on May 15, the firm had rendered $2,480 of services.
3. Hamilton has earned three weeks of revenue from the prepayment on May 4.
4. Office supplies on hand at month-end amounted to $200.
5. Hamilton must pay $1,000 of the bank loan within the next year.

Instructions

a. Record the transactions of May in the general journal.
b. Post the journal entries to the proper ledger accounts.
c. Complete a work sheet for the month ended May 31. Be certain to analyze *all* data presented to correctly determine Hamilton's adjustments.
d. Prepare an income statement, a statement of owner's equity, and a classified balance sheet. The balance sheet should be similar in format to that shown in Exhibit 4–11.
e. Record Hamilton's adjusting entries in the journal and post to the proper ledger accounts.
f. Record Hamilton's closing entries in the journal and post to the proper ledger accounts.
g. Prepare a post-closing trial balance.

5

ACCOUNTING/REPORTING FOR MERCHANDISING OPERATIONS

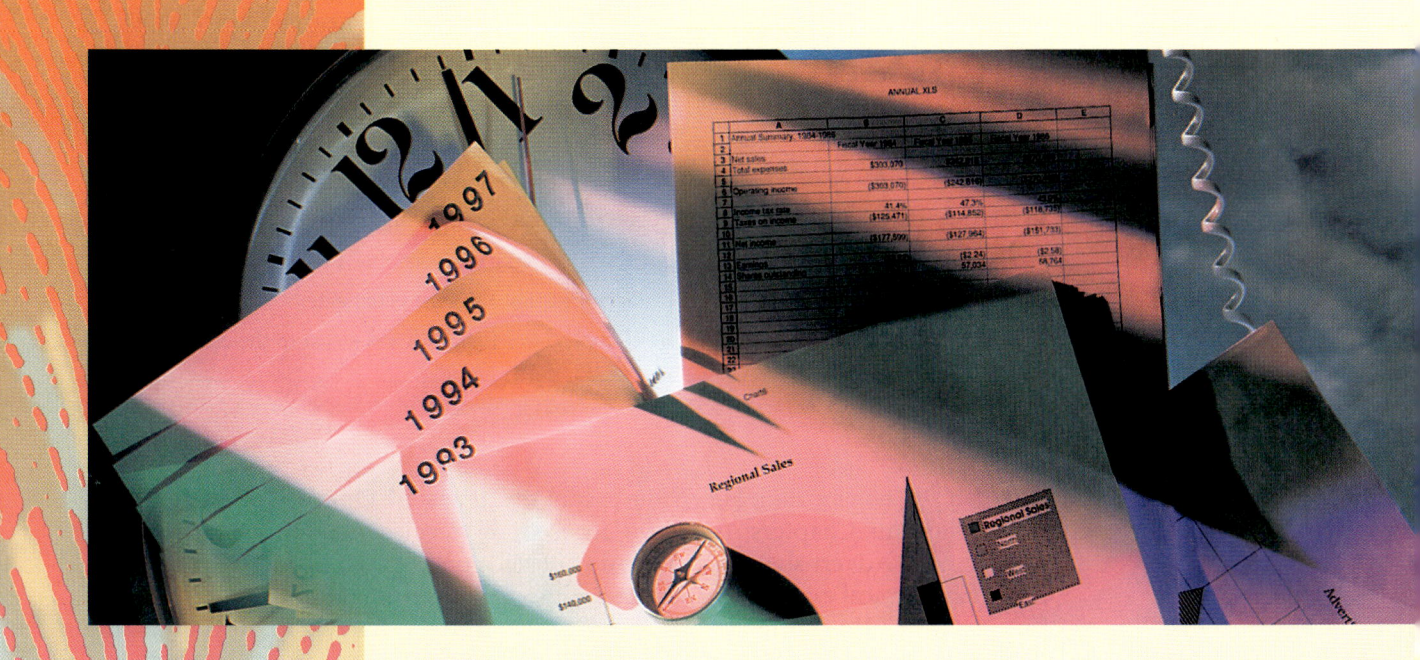

LEARNING OBJECTIVES

After studying this chapter, you should be able to:

1. Account for typical transactions of sellers and buyers of merchandise.
2. Compare and contrast the gross and net methods of accounting for purchases.
3. Compute cost of goods sold and gross profit, and prepare the financial statements for a merchandising concern.
4. Distinguish between multiple- and single-step income statements.
5. Discuss the differences between periodic and perpetual inventory systems.
6. (Appendix) Prepare a work sheet and closing entries for a merchandising business.

Day in and day out, George Faris of Banner Advertising deals with various types of businesses. Many of these firms are similar to Banner and provide a service; others, in contrast, sell some type of product. Clients that fall in this latter category include gasoline and convenience stores, outlet malls, department stores, and fast-food restaurants. When George attempts to sell advertising space to such clients, he notes, "The conversation quickly turns to profit margins. The client is going to compare the cost of advertising against the profit on the additional sales generated by the billboard. It's pretty basic."

Be aware that clients do not compare additional *sales* to the cost of the sign; they look at profit. The generation of sales dollars is not cost-free. Every sale has a cost, especially the cost of the item sold. It is therefore fitting to look at both of these amounts and consider their net difference when making decisions. Put simply, the additional profit that the sign is expected to produce must more than cover the billboard's cost to the client.

The new item here is the cost of the item sold. Our previous discussions in Chapters 1–4 have focused on service enterprises like Banner Advertising. Such firms do not sell a product but instead provide a service. Typical examples of service entities include airlines, theaters, professional sports clubs, and repair shops. Service enterprises charge a fee or commission to clients and are a rapidly growing and significant factor in our economy.

We now turn our attention to a different type of operation: the merchandising business. A merchandising firm acquires goods for resale to others (i.e., **merchandise inventory**) and is exemplified by the retailer and wholesaler. Accounting for retailers and wholesalers is not completely different from accounting for service businesses; thus, most of the material presented earlier is still applicable. The purchase and sale of inventory, however, are accompanied by and create several added complexities for the accountant. These complexities form the basis for this chapter's discussion.

Measuring Merchandising Income

1 Account for typical transactions of sellers and buyers of merchandise.

The success of a business organization is often judged by the size of its "bottom line," or net income. A merchandising entity will be profitable if the amounts charged to customers (i.e., sales revenue) exceed the cost of merchandise sold and the operating expenses of the business. The income statement that appears in Exhibit 5–1, simplified for purposes of illustration, shows that Mid Cities Auto Parts earned 7¢ on every sales dollar ($7,000 ÷ $100,000). Further, by purchasing goods from suppliers and then selling the goods at a higher price to its customers, Mid Cities was able to generate a $52,000 gross profit.

Given this very brief overview of merchandising profitability, let us focus on the details of sales revenue, cost of goods sold, gross profit, and inventory accounting. In so doing, we will study the operations of Peachtree Jeans, an Atlanta-based wholesaler of pants, shirts, and related accessories.

EXHIBIT 5–1
Simplified Income Statement of a Merchandising Firm

MID CITIES AUTO PARTS
Income Statement
For the Year Ended December 31, 19XX

Sales		$100,000
Cost of goods sold		48,000
Gross profit		$ 52,000
Expenses		
Salaries	$30,000	
Rent	12,000	
Utilities	3,000	
Total expenses		45,000
Net income		$ 7,000

SALES REVENUE

The revenues of a merchandising concern are generated from its sales of inventory. The timing and measurement of these revenues are of major importance in accounting; incorrect recognition will result in inaccurate reports of financial position and earnings. An entity should enter revenue in the accounting records when ownership of the goods is transferred from the seller to the buyer. Normally, this transfer occurs at the time of sale. The amount of revenue to be recognized is determined by the transaction price, which is usually the amount of cash received or to be received.

To properly account for its revenues, a business will establish an account entitled Sales. If desired, an entity could utilize separate accounts to determine revenues by product line (e.g., Pants Sales, Shirt Sales, and Accessories Sales). Understand that the Sales account is used *strictly* to record revenues that relate to the sale of merchandise (the sale and/or disposal of other assets are recorded elsewhere). As an example, if Peachtree Jeans sold some extra office supplies for cash, Cash would be debited and Office Supplies would be credited. The Sales account is not affected.

A business must correctly record both cash and credit sales. Although the exact procedures vary, the following description is representative of the practices of many companies. When a cash sale is made, a sales slip or *invoice* is completed by a clerk, who also inputs the transaction into a data-entry terminal (e.g., a cash register). At the end of the day the terminal is closed out, and the following entry is made (amount is assumed):

Apr. 3	Cash	325	
	Sales		325
	Daily cash sales.		

Credit sales are handled in much the same fashion, with either the sales invoices or terminal providing the basis for the necessary journal entry. Computerized data input stations are typically used to capture both cash *and* credit sales and, as transactions occur, are capable of updating merchandise inventory records of units on hand.

ETHICS ISSUE

A new employee in a baseball card shop accidentally marks a rare card with a $12 (rather than $1,200) selling price. He later sells the card to an avid, 13-year-old collector. The shop's owner, realizing the error, finds the customer and requests the extra $1,188. The 13-year-old responds that "a deal is a deal." Who's to blame, and how would you handle this situation?

To illustrate the required accounting for credit sales, assume that Peachtree Jeans sold $700 of merchandise on account to Marty's Outpost on April 7. The following entry would be needed:

Apr. 7	Accounts Receivable	700	
	Sales		700
	Made sale on account to Marty's Outpost.		

A Marketing Manager's Perspective

Sales Price Determination: Company revenues are a function of a very troublesome issue in marketing: calculation of the "correct" selling price. Sales prices that are too high drive away customers and profits disappear; in contrast, prices that are too low fail to cover costs and result in miserable bottom-line performance.

One of the most popular methods of setting a price is to add a fixed markup, say 50%, to the cost of a purchased product. Although a simple approach, a common criticism of this method by marketing managers is that cost should be only one aspect of price determination. Other important factors are convenience, service, supply and demand, and the willingness of a potential customer to pay. You need only look through a newspaper's retail advertising section to see that the cost-plus approach doesn't always work. Words and phrases such as "sale," "up to 40% off," and "extensive markdowns taken" indicate that the sales price decision involves more than just a simple mathematical addition to cost.

Marketing managers feel that the marketplace and customer are other key factors that must be considered. These are factors that accounting doesn't measure, but they have a direct impact on revenue generation and financial performance.

Sales Returns and Allowances. Sales of merchandise often give rise to returns. Customers frequently change their minds, find that merchandise does not fit well once they get it home, or notice defects. If an exchange of goods is neither possible nor desired, most merchandisers will grant a refund or reduce the customer's account balance. Sometimes, particularly in the case of defects or damaged goods, the seller will grant the buyer an *allowance*, that is, a price reduction as incentive to keep the item.

Once a return or allowance is authorized, the seller documents the transaction on a form known as a credit memorandum. For a sale on account, a copy is given to the customer and a copy is forwarded to the accounts receivable department. The credit memo informs the department to credit, or reduce, a particular customer's balance.

The proper accounting treatment for sales returns and allowances is shown by the following example. Suppose that on April 16, Marty's Outpost returned $180 of shirts that it had purchased on April 7. Peachtree Jeans, the seller, would record the transaction as follows:

Apr. 16	Sales Returns & Allowances	180
	Accounts Receivable	180
	Merchandise returned by Marty's Outpost.	

The net amount of the sale is $520 ($700 – $180). Rather than reduce the Sales account by a debit, a separate account entitled Sales Returns & Allowances is established. The use of a separate account is preferable because it allows management and other readers of financial statements to easily compare the amount of returns and allowances with sales volume. This relationship, particularly if returns and allowances are sizable, provides insight into customer satisfaction (or dissatisfaction) with merchandise. In addition, an abnormally high level of returns may reveal the presence of shipping problems, such as merchandise being damaged or mishandled while en route to customers.

The sales on April 3 and 7 and the return on April 16 would appear on an income statement as follows:

Revenues		
Sales	$1,025	
Less: Returns & allowances	180	
Net sales	$ 845	

note   In view of this treatment (i.e., a deduction from Sales), Sales Returns & Allowances is commonly referred to as a **contra revenue** account.

Trade Discounts. Sellers frequently offer discounts to purchasers, more so to businesses than to individual consumers. One type of discount is a **trade discount.** To explain, manufacturers and wholesalers spend considerable time and money to publish catalogs of the merchandise they offer for sale. These publications often show the merchandise at a basic catalog price, or **list price.** Purchasers, however, are normally entitled to a reduction in cost and ultimately pay **invoice price,** that is, list price minus an applicable trade discount.

This procedure may seem somewhat strange. Why not just publish the invoice price in the first place? The use of trade discounts offers several distinct benefits. If a change in market conditions dictates price changes, it is much easier (and cheaper) to quote a different trade discount than to update and reprint an entire catalog. Further, trade discounts can be altered as needed to give customers more incentive to purchase larger quantities (e.g., the larger the quantity purchased, the greater the discount).

Trade discounts are *not* entered in the accounting records, as such amounts are already reflected in the actual selling prices charged by the merchant. To illustrate the proper record keeping, assume that Peachtree stocks a particular style of shirt having a list price of $25. If Peachtree received an order for 600 shirts and granted a 30% trade discount, the purchaser would be charged $10,500, computed as follows:

List price (600 shirts × $25)	$15,000
Less: 30% trade discount	4,500
Invoice price	$10,500

An invoice would be prepared for this amount, and $10,500 would be recorded in the Accounts Receivable and Sales accounts. A separate trade discounts account is not established.

Cash Discounts. When merchandise is sold on account, the seller usually gives the buyer a certain period of time to settle his or her account balance. Often, sales on account are expected to be paid within 30 days of the invoice date. Sellers, however, normally desire to collect the amounts due more rapidly to cover expenses and for purposes of investment. Consequently, to encourage prompt payment, they sometimes offer incentives called *cash discounts.* From the seller's point of view, the cash discount is termed a *sales discount.*

Cash discounts are normally stated on the invoice and expressed in the following format: 2/10, n/30 or perhaps 3/15, n/eom (see Exhibit 5–2). In both examples the first set of numbers indicates the discount rate and the discount period. The second set discloses the invoice due date. The terms of sale are read as follows:

- *2/10, n/30*—A 2% discount from the invoice price is allowed if payment is made within 10 days of the invoice date; otherwise, the total invoice price is due within 30 days.
- *3/15, n/eom*—A 3% discount is allowed if payment is made within 15 days of the invoice date; otherwise, the total invoice price is due by the end of the month (eom).

Several alternatives are available to account for sales discounts. The most popular approach is to record both Accounts Receivable and Sales at the total (gross) invoice price. The underlying rationale is that at the time of sale, the

EXHIBIT 5–2
Example of Invoice

INVOICE
Peachtree Jeans
5130 Meridian Parkway
Atlanta, Georgia 30309

Sold to: Expressway Chic
2200 Madison Blvd.
Birmingham, Alabama 36296

Invoice no.: 6708
Invoice date: 4/10/X7
Your order no.: B-1403
Sales representative: 32

Ship to: Same
Shipped via: Overnight Freight
Shipping terms: F.O.B. Birmingham

Terms of sale: 2/10, n/30

QUANTITY	DESCRIPTION	UNIT PRICE	AMOUNT
40	Jeans—#1630	25.00	$1,000.00
25	Blouse—#5800	20.00	500.00
			$1,500.00

seller has no idea whether the discount will be taken. Later, if the buyer takes advantage of the price reduction, the difference between the cash received and the original amount due is recorded as a discount. In contrast, if the discount is not used, the amount paid by the customer is recorded in the same manner as any other receipt on account.

For instance, assume that Peachtree sold $1,500 of merchandise on account to a customer on April 10, terms 2/10, n/30. The sale and subsequent cash receipt are handled as follows:

Apr. 10	Accounts Receivable	1,500	
	Sales		1,500
	Sale on account; terms 2/10, n/30.		

CASE A: CUSTOMER PAYS ON APRIL 19 AND TAKES THE DISCOUNT

Apr. 19	Cash	1,470	
	Sales Discounts	30	
	Accounts Receivable		1,500
	Collection on account; discount taken.		

CASE B: CUSTOMER PAYS ON APRIL 26 AND FORGOES THE DISCOUNT

Apr. 26	Cash	1,500	
	Accounts Receivable		1,500
	Collection on account; discount missed.		

> **ETHICS ISSUE**
>
> You discover that a customer accidentally paid an invoice twice. What action would you take, assuming the invoice was issued by your firm?

Observe that the sale is recorded at the total invoice price of $1,500. If the customer settles the amount due by April 20, a $30 discount ($1,500 × 0.02) can be taken and the customer will pay $1,470 ($1,500 − $30). Although only $1,470 is received, Accounts Receivable is credited for the full $1,500. This procedure reduces Accounts Receivable to zero, thereby indicating the purchaser has no further obligation to Peachtree. The $30 is debited to Sales Discounts, a contra revenue that is disclosed on the income statement as a reduction from the Sales account.

COST OF GOODS SOLD

Recall from Chapter 3 that accountants use the matching concept when measuring income. To explain, a business incurs various costs and expenses in the process of generating revenue. In an effort to judge profitability, the costs and expenses are matched against (i.e., subtracted from) the revenues that they helped to create (see Exhibit 5–1 as an example).

Keeping this fact in mind, let us now focus on the merchandising enterprise. A merchandising business has many different types of expenditures, perhaps the most significant being the cost of products offered for sale. To achieve a proper match on the income statement, the cost of units sold to customers during the accounting period must be deducted from net sales. This deduction is appropriately termed **cost of goods sold** and is dependent on three underlying items: (1) beginning inventory, (2) net purchases, and (3) ending inventory.

Most entities will begin an accounting period with a certain amount of merchandise held for resale to customers (termed the *beginning inventory*). Subsequently, the stock of inventory on hand is supplemented by purchases from suppliers. Combined, these two amounts represent a "pool" of **goods** *available for sale.* If an entity is in the very fortunate position of being able to sell all of its merchandise, the goods available for sale would correspond to the firm's cost of goods sold. Most companies, however, have some inventory remaining on hand (i.e., unsold) upon conclusion of the reporting period. Known as the *ending inventory*,[1] this amount must be considered in computing the proper dollar figure to match against net sales on the income statement. The following example shows the manner in which this is done.

Assume that Peachtree Jeans had $67,000 of inventory on hand at the start of the current accounting period. Throughout the year the firm acquired $146,000 of goods, meaning that $213,000 ($67,000 + $146,000) of merchandise was available for resale to customers. On conclusion of activity on December 31, accounting personnel checked existing stock levels in the warehouse and determined an ending inventory of $48,000. As shown in Exhibit 5–3, Peachtree has apparently sold inventory that cost the company $165,000.

The concepts presented in this exhibit have important financial statement implications. More specifically, the ending inventory figure will appear on Peachtree's December 31 balance she.et in the current asset section. Cost of goods sold, on the other hand, is deducted from net sales on the income statement. Both of these financial statements will be illustrated later in the chapter.

EXHIBIT 5–3
Determining Cost of Goods Sold

In pictorial terms:

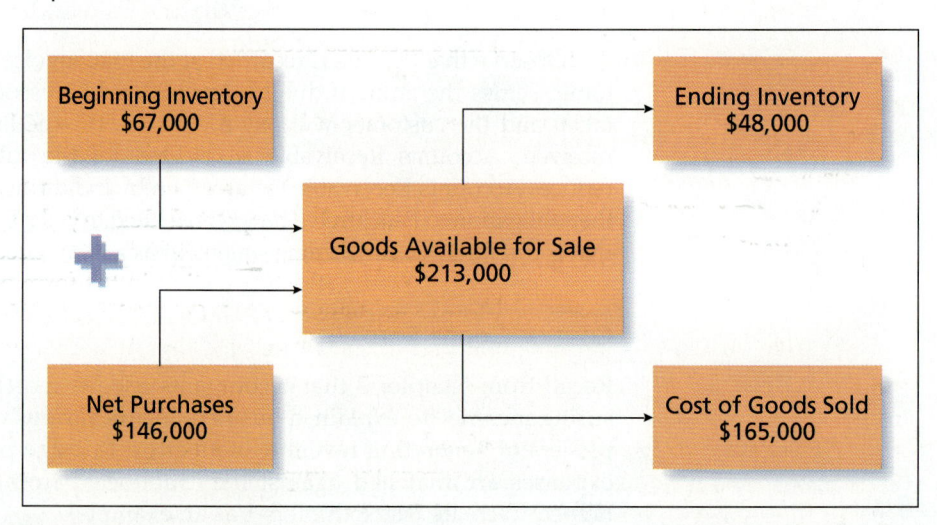

```
Beginning Inventory          →          Ending Inventory
$67,000                                  $48,000

    +        →   Goods Available for Sale
                 $213,000

Net Purchases                →          Cost of Goods Sold
$146,000                                 $165,000
```

In mathematical terms:

Cost of goods sold	
Beginning inventory	$ 67,000
Add: Net purchases	146,000
Goods available for sale	$213,000
Less: Ending inventory	48,000
Cost of goods sold	$165,000

[1] The ending inventory of one accounting period becomes the beginning inventory of the following period.

ACCOUNTING FOR MERCHANDISE ACQUISITIONS

Our study of cost of goods sold introduced the underlying components of beginning inventory, ending inventory, and net purchases. An in-depth discussion of the first two components is more appropriately deferred until Chapter 10. At this point, however, you should begin to understand the financial measurement and reporting problems related to merchandise acquisitions. Such acquisitions are entered in the records in accordance with the historical-cost principle.

To illustrate the necessary accounting, assume that Peachtree Jeans purchased $9,000 of merchandise on account on April 16. The entry would be as follows:

Apr. 16	Purchases	9,000	
	Accounts Payable		9,000
	Purchased merchandise on account.		

The Purchases account normally has a debit balance and appears on the income statement in the cost-of-goods-sold section. The correct manner of disclosure will be shown shortly.

Be aware that Purchases is used *solely* for merchandise. As explained earlier in the text, acquisitions of items that will be used in the business (e.g., equipment and supplies) are recorded in their own respective accounts. The acquisition of supplies, for instance, results in a debit to Supplies and has no impact on the Purchases account.

Purchases Returns and Allowances. As was true for sales, purchase transactions often involve returns and allowances. Returns and allowances are caused by many factors, including the arrival of merchandise (1) in a damaged condition, (2) much later than a requested delivery date, or (3) in error. Before a return or allowance is formally recorded in the accounts, the purchaser prepares documentation of the transaction in the form of either a letter or a debit memorandum. The debit memo informs the seller that its account, an account payable, has been debited (reduced) by the purchaser.

Proper accounting for purchases returns and allowances is shown by continuing the previous example. Suppose that $650 of the goods purchased on April 16 arrived past a requested delivery date. On April 30, Peachtree received authorization from the supplier and returned this merchandise. The following entry would be recorded:

Apr. 30	Accounts Payable	650	
	Purchases Returns & Allowances		650
	Returned merchandise to supplier.		

The net amount of the purchase is $8,350 ($9,000 − $650). Rather than credit the Purchases account for the reduction, it is preferable to establish a separate account for returns and allowances. This procedure allows management to better examine the percentage relationship between returns and allowances and gross purchases, thus providing some insight into the effectiveness of the purchasing department. A large percentage of returns could be caused by sloppy ordering or by dealings with unreliable suppliers.

The purchase and return would appear on Peachtree's income statement as follows:

Cost of goods sold
⋮
Purchases	$9,000
Less: Returns & allowances	650
Net purchases	$8,350
⋮

Purchases Discounts. Recall that sellers frequently offer a cash discount for prompt payment of invoices. From the buyer's perspective this discount is commonly known as a **purchases discount.** If at all possible, buyers should take advantage of this potential reduction in the cost of merchandise acquired. Why? The reason becomes apparent in the example that follows.

Suppose that Peachtree acquired $10,000 of merchandise subject to terms of 2/10, n/30. Management has two options:

1. Pay $9,800 [$10,000 − ($10,000 × 0.02)] within 10 days of the invoice date.
2. Pay $10,000 within 30 days of the invoice date.

If Peachtree forgoes the discount and settles the transaction when due, the firm must pay an additional $200. The $200 outlay allows management to have the use of $9,800 for a period of 20 days (30 − 10) and may be construed as interest. For the 20-day period, then, the effective interest rate is 2.04% ($200 ÷ $9,800). Most interest rates are expressed on an annual basis of 360 days, meaning that the supplier's terms are equivalent to 36.72% (360/20 × 2.04%)! In view of the cost, purchasers should take advantage of cash discounts even if it means borrowing money from the bank. Much cheaper financing is generally available via short-term loans.

Gross Method. A popular approach to accounting for purchases discounts corresponds to the previously illustrated method for sales discounts. Under the **gross method,** both purchases and accounts payable are recorded at the total invoice cost of the merchandise acquired. This technique is logically sound, because at the time of purchase the buyer does not always know whether the discount will be taken.

> **2** Compare and contrast the gross and net methods of accounting for purchases.

Using the gross method, let us assume Peachtree purchased $4,000 of sportswear on account from Wrangler Corporation on April 14, subject to terms of 2/10, n/30. The purchase and subsequent payment would be recorded as follows:

Apr. 14	Purchases	4,000	
	Accounts Payable		4,000
	Purchase on account; terms 2/10, n/30.		

CASE A: PEACHTREE PAYS ON APRIL 23 AND TAKES THE DISCOUNT

Apr. 23	Accounts Payable	4,000	
	Purchases Discounts		80
	Cash		3,920
	Paid on account; discount taken.		

CASE B: PEACHTREE PAYS ON APRIL 27 AND FORGOES THE DISCOUNT

Apr. 27	Accounts Payable	4,000	
	Cash		4,000
	Paid on account; discount missed.		

While Case B is straightforward, Case A needs some explanation. By paying the invoice before the 10-day discount period expires, Peachtree is entitled to an $80 discount ($4,000 × 0.02). Although only $3,920 is remitted to Wrangler, Accounts Payable is debited for the entire $4,000 because the balance is paid in full. The Purchases Discounts account is credited for the reduction in cost and is used later in deriving the net cost of merchandise acquired. It is therefore deducted from the Purchases account in the income statement's cost-of-goods-sold section.

In this particular example the discount was calculated on the basis of the $4,000 invoice cost. If any of the merchandise acquired had been returned to Wrangler prior to payment, the discount would have been figured on the net purchase only. Furthermore, discounts are computed on merchandise cost only; they are never calculated on freight charges incurred by the buyer to acquire goods.

Net Method. Because of the high interest costs associated with missing discounts, many companies follow a policy of taking all discounts offered. In anticipation of securing these reductions in cost, businesses may use an alternative recording procedure for purchases called the **net method.** Under this approach, both purchases and accounts payable are recorded at the net cost of the purchase, that is, total invoice cost minus the anticipated cash discount. If the discount is taken, the liability is removed from the books in similar fashion to other payments on account. Any discounts missed, on the other hand, are entered in an account entitled Purchases Discounts Lost.

To illustrate the net method, we will use the same transaction that appeared in the previous discussion—a $4,000 purchase subject to terms of 2/10, n/30. The April 14 acquisition and subsequent payment on account would be recorded as follows:

Apr. 14	Purchases	3,920	
	Accounts Payable		3,920
	Purchase on account; terms 2/10, n/30.		

CASE A: PEACHTREE PAYS ON APRIL 23 AND TAKES THE DISCOUNT

Apr. 23	Accounts Payable	3,920	
	Cash		3,920
	Paid on account; discount taken.		

CASE B: PEACHTREE PAYS ON APRIL 27 AND FORGOES THE DISCOUNT

Apr. 27	Accounts Payable	3,920	
	Purchases Discounts Lost	80	
	Cash		4,000
	Paid on account; discount missed.		

Under Case A, since the liability is already established at the net figure of $3,920, no additional discount is recorded. With Case B, $4,000 must be paid: $3,920 for the merchandise acquired and an $80 penalty for late payment.

The Purchases Discounts Lost account appears on the income statement as an expense, not as part of cost of goods sold. The presence of a large balance in this account means that a business has missed a considerable number of discounts and often raises questions concerning managerial effectiveness. The discounts may have been lost because of carelessness in paying invoices and allowing discount periods to lapse, or perhaps because of a very tight cash position. Whatever the cause, the firm is incurring extremely high interest costs as a result, and corrective action may be needed.

Freight Charges. The acquisition of merchandise by retailers and wholesalers often gives rise to transportation charges. These charges can be significant, especially when a company deals in bulky or heavy items. Freight costs are borne by either the seller of the goods or the buyer, the exact party being determined by an order's freight terms.

Freight terms are usually expressed as F.O.B. shipping point or F.O.B. destination. F.O.B., or free on board, means the seller will place the merchandise sold on board a freight carrier at no charge. Whether the seller or buyer incurs the transportation costs thereafter is dependent on "shipping point" or "destination." For example, if the terms are F.O.B. shipping point, the seller's responsibility for freight stops when the goods are loaded for shipment. Thus, the buyer incurs all freight charges. In contrast, under F.O.B. destination, the seller's responsibility ceases when the goods arrive at their ultimate destination (e.g., the buyer's warehouse). Consequently, the seller is liable for transportation costs. These points are summarized as follows:

TERMS OF SHIPMENT	WHERE SELLER'S RESPONSIBILITY CEASES	WHO INCURS FREIGHT CHARGES
F.O.B. shipping point	At point of shipment	Buyer
F.O.B. destination	At goods' destination	Seller

The preceding treatment is consistent with the ownership of goods during the in-transit period. With F.O.B. shipping point, for example, title to merchandise legally shifts from the seller to the buyer at the time of shipment. Conversely, under F.O.B. destination, transfer of title occurs at the time of the goods' receipt.

Freight-in and Freight-out. As a logical outgrowth of the historical-cost principle, freight charges incurred on the *acquisition* of merchandise are treated as part of the purchase cost. Rather than bury these charges in Purchases, many firms maintain a separate account entitled Freight-in. Used only for transportation on incoming goods, Freight-in is added to the Purchases account on the income statement (see Exhibit 5–4 on p. 187) to arrive at a net delivered cost of merchandise acquired.

To illustrate accounting for the purchaser under terms of F.O.B. shipping point, assume that Peachtree Jeans purchased $3,000 of footwear on account from Sport Shoe Company on April 22, F.O.B. shipping point. If freight charges amounted to $60, Peachtree would record the following entry:

Apr. 22	Purchases	3,000	
	Freight-in	60	
	Accounts Payable		3,060
	Purchased merchandise; terms		
	F.O.B. shipping point.		

The credit of $3,060 to Accounts Payable shows that Peachtree owes the footwear dealer for the freight. Apparently, as a matter of convenience to the purchaser, Sport Shoe prepaid the transportation costs and expects to be reimbursed. If the costs were not prepaid, Peachtree would disburse $60 to the freight company upon receipt of the goods, requiring a credit to the Cash account.

The preceding treatment applies strictly to freight on incoming merchandise. Transportation charges related to outgoing shipments (i.e., sales) are debited to a different account entitled Freight-out. Generated under terms of F.O.B. destination, such charges bear no connection to an entity's purchases and, hence, are excluded from the cost-of-goods-sold computation. Freight-out is a selling cost and is properly listed among a company's typical business expenses (such as salaries, advertising, utilities, and rent).

Purchasing Activity in a High-Tech Era. The various procedures related to the acquisition of goods have undergone considerable change in recent years, thanks to computers and electronics. Picture the processing of a purchase order and the related invoicing by the seller. These procedures, as well as coordination of delivery dates and even negotiation of prices, are being automated through an increasingly popular practice known as electronic data interchange (EDI). In essence, the computers of one company "talk" to the computers of another, with the result being fewer errors, quicker processing, less paperwork, and lower costs. R.J. Reynolds Tobacco Co., for example, figures orders that formerly cost between $75 and $125 to process now run 93¢. Multiply this by the tens of thousands of purchase orders processed each year, and quite a savings is achieved.[2]

EDI is also used to process the payments for invoices. Chevron, the giant oil refiner, recently reported making more than 5,800 electronic payments per month to suppliers—roughly 14% of the checks it once wrote. Even the federal government has gotten into the act, sending suppliers electronic payments that annually exceed $300 billion.[3]

Purchase-order processing and invoice payments appear to be rather basic applications when compared to a recently announced plan of IBM. To speed up the delivery of software and reduce related shipping costs to retailers and corporate customers, IBM plans to use a satellite system. The system would deliver the software electronically. Customers would select the product they wanted by using a touch-screen computer, and copies would be made from a huge electronic library in a matter of seconds. In addition to the advantages just cited, this system would eliminate a current problem for many software suppliers: a retailer's return of unsold copies of older releases.[4]

FINANCIAL STATEMENTS OF A MERCHANDISING CONCERN

Thus far in the text we have concentrated on three financial statements: the income statement, statement of owner's equity, and the balance sheet. The income statement is prepared first and ties together a number of the concepts discussed in this chapter. It is therefore an appropriate place to begin.

---

[2] "Fire Your Purchasing Managers," *Forbes ASAP*, October 10, 1994, p. 33.
[3] "Electronic Payments Now Supplant Checks at More Large Firms," *The Wall Street Journal*, April 13, 1994, pp. A1, A9.
[4] "IBM To Unveil Plan To Skip Disks, Send Software by Satellite," *The Wall Street Journal*, November 1, 1994, p. A3.

BUSINESS BRIEFING

K. D. SUH
President
K. D. Suh Trading Company

Running a Profitable Merchandising Business: It's More Than Dollars and Cents

To many students, merchandising looks like an easy way to achieve financial success. With their high energy level and intelligence, more than a few young graduates have started merchandising businesses only to see their creations perform below expectations or fail. The missing ingredient is often a thorough understanding of business itself.

Consider our company, a successful California-based exporter of prepared seasonings to Korea and other Asian countries. Like most merchandisers, we have sales and purchases, take advantage of discounts, and worry about shipping costs. But an attractive bottom-line profit in our competitive marketplace depends on more—much more. It's knowledge—knowledge of flavors, regional variations in customer taste, product quality, marketing methods, export and import regulations, and the ability to obtain foreign representation. And it's trust—the ability to establish strong professional relationships and customer loyalty.

From an accounting viewpoint, turning a profit comes one order at a time and is based on price and cost. Getting those orders, however, is the difficult part. A successful merchandiser cannot operate with the attitude of "open the doors and the customer will come." In contrast, the correct formula combines long hours of hard work, thorough product knowledge, and a strong will to service the marketplace and establish a devoted clientele.

---

③ Compute cost of goods sold and gross profit, and prepare the financial statements for a merchandising concern.

INCOME STATEMENT

The income statements of a service business and a merchandising entity differ considerably. While both statements report net income, the introduction of inventory gives rise to several modifications. See Exhibit 5–4, which contains the income statement of Peachtree Jeans. (*Note*: The account balances that appear in Exhibits 5–4 through 5–7 were obtained from Peachtree's general ledger as of December 31, 19XX.)

Consistent with the matching concept, observe that the costs incurred in producing sales are deducted from the sales revenues generated. These costs are operating expenses and cost of goods sold. Operating expenses are expenses that arise from the principal selling and administrative activities of a business and include such items as rent, advertising, wages, utilities, and repairs.

Notice that cost of goods sold is subtracted from net sales to arrive at gross profit (sometimes called gross margin). Gross profit represents the profit that a company produces from the sale of inventory. A review of the figures in Exhibit 5–4 will show that for every dollar of net sales, Peachtree was able to earn $0.45 ($135,000 ÷ $300,000) from merchandise. This amount was used to cover operating expenses and produce net income.[5]

---

[5] In more precise terms, the "average" sales dollar was used as follows:

Sales revenue		$1.00
Recovery of merchandise cost ($165,000 ÷ $300,000)	$0.55	
Operating expenses ($126,000 ÷ $300,000)	0.42	0.97
Net income		$0.03

Finally, you can now see the income statement's expansion to include the various concepts and accounts that we have been discussing. Observe that net sales is derived by subtracting discounts and returns and allowances from the Sales account. Net purchases, a key component of the cost-of-goods-sold calculation, is subdivided into its elements of purchases, freight-in, purchases discounts, and purchases returns and allowances. Furthermore, freight-out, an expense related to the sale of merchandise, is listed among the operating expenses.

STATEMENT OF OWNER'S EQUITY

The statement of owner's equity summarizes changes in the capital account during the reporting period. This financial statement is identical for both a service business and a merchandising concern and is shown in Exhibit 5–5.

EXHIBIT 5–4
Income Statement of a Merchandising Firm

PEACHTREE JEANS
Income Statement
For the Year Ended December 31, 19XX

Revenues				
Sales				$307,000
Less: Sales discounts			$ 5,000	
Sales returns & allowances			2,000	7,000
Net sales				$300,000
Cost of goods sold				
Beginning inventory, Jan. 1			$ 67,000	
Add: Purchases		$148,000		
Freight-in		5,000		
		$153,000		
Less: Purchases discounts	$3,000			
Purchases returns & allowances	4,000	7,000		
Net purchases			146,000	
Goods available for sale			$213,000	
Less: Ending inventory, Dec. 31			48,000	
Cost of goods sold				165,000
Gross profit				$135,000
Operating expenses				
Rent expense			$ 15,000	
Salaries expense			61,000	
Utilities expense			11,000	
Freight-out			7,000	
Advertising expense			13,000	
Depreciation expense			10,000	
Insurance expense			9,000	
Total operating expenses				126,000
Net income				$ 9,000

EXHIBIT 5–5
Statement of Owner's Equity of a Merchandising Firm

PEACHTREE JEANS Statement of Owner's Equity For the Year Ended December 31, 19XX	
Beginning balance, Jan. 1	$147,200
Add: Net income*	9,000
	$156,200
Deduct: Owner withdrawals	6,000
Ending balance, Dec. 31	$150,200
*From Exhibit 5–4.	

BALANCE SHEET

The balance sheets of a service business and a merchandiser are also similar, with the exception of inventory. The inventory of a merchandising firm is an asset and, accordingly, an Inventory account appears in the statement's current asset section. The balance reported in this account represents the amount of merchandise owned upon conclusion of the reporting period ($48,000 in Peachtree's case—see Exhibit 5–3). The company's balance sheet as of December 31, 19XX, is shown in Exhibit 5–6.

A CLOSER LOOK AT INCOME REPORTING

④ Distinguish between multiple- and single-step income statements.

A review of income statements of large U.S. companies will find considerable variation in both formats and disclosures. Some income statements parallel the appearance of the statement shown for Peachtree Jeans in Exhibit 5–4. However, others are more complex whereas still others are more simplistic. In general, companies use either a multiple- or single-step reporting format.

MULTIPLE-STEP INCOME STATEMENTS

With a **multiple-step income statement,** accounts are presented by association so that important relationships can be easily seen by readers. Merchandising firms, for example, deduct cost of goods sold from net sales to arrive at gross profit. In addition, operating expenses, other revenues and expenses, and income taxes are all segregated. Many accountants believe that specific placements and the disclosure of important subtotals (such as gross profit) make the multiple-step format more informative and useful.

The income statement of Peachtree Jeans was multiple-step in format, although somewhat basic. A more realistic example appears in Exhibit 5–7. Note the grouping of accounts by association and the number of steps involved before net income is shown. We will now highlight several new features that relate to Waikiki Trading Company's presentation.

Selling and Administrative Expenses. Observe that operating expenses (i.e., those that relate to normal business activities and operations) are subdivided into selling and general and administrative components. Selling expenses are associated with the sale of merchandise, whereas general and administrative costs are incurred in the management of business affairs. Certain individual

EXHIBIT 5-6
Balance Sheet of a Merchandising Firm

PEACHTREE JEANS
Balance Sheet
December 31, 19XX

	Dr	Cr
ASSETS		
Current assets		
Cash	$ 25,700	
Accounts receivable	19,600	
Inventory	48,000	
Prepaid insurance	4,800	
Total current assets		$ 98,100
Property, plant, & equipment		
Equipment	$124,800	
Less: Accumulated depreciation	34,800	90,000
Total assets		$188,100
LIABILITIES & OWNER'S EQUITY		
Current liabilities		
Accounts payable	$ 36,400	
Salaries payable	1,500	
Total current liabilities		$ 37,900
Owner's equity		
Valerie Bain, capital*		150,200
Total liabilities & owner's equity		$188,100

*From Exhibit 5-5.

expenses may need to be split between the two categories because they relate to both functional areas. An example is depreciation on a building that houses both selling activities and executive offices.

Other Revenues and Expenses. Companies frequently incur expenses (and generate revenues) that are not directly related to normal business operations. For instance, assume that a retail store leased some extra space to a charitable organization for use as an office. The retail store would earn rental revenue and may incur some added expense (such as maintenance) as a result of the lease. On a multiple-step statement, items related to the lease that affect net income would be shown in a separate nonoperating (other) category.

A careful review of Exhibit 5-7 will reveal the disclosure of interest expense in the "other" classification. The rationale for this placement is that interest (be it revenue or expense) is not derived from operating activities, such as selling a product or providing a service. Instead, it arises from a situation of either providing or securing some type of financing and is shown accordingly.

Gains and Losses. Businesses enter into a variety of earnings transactions. Many transactions are routine, such as sales to customers and payments for salaries and supplies; others, however, are not. For instance, a business may only occasionally sell a piece of equipment, a building, or a long-term invest-

EXHIBIT 5–7
Multiple-Step Income Statement

THE WAIKIKI TRADING COMPANY, INC.
Income Statement
For the Year Ended December 31, 19XX

Revenues			
Sales			$510,000
Less: Sales discounts		$ 10,000	
Sales returns & allowances		5,000	15,000
Net sales			$495,000
Cost of goods sold			
Beginning inventory, Jan. 1		$100,000	
Add: Purchases	$120,000		
Freight-in	5,000		
	$125,000		
Less: Purchases discounts	$4,000		
Purchases returns & allowances	1,000	5,000	
Net purchases		120,000	
Goods available for sale		$220,000	
Less: Ending inventory, Dec. 31		50,000	
Cost of goods sold			170,000
Gross profit			$325,000
Operating expenses			
Selling expenses			
Advertising		$ 45,000	
Sales salaries		27,000	
Insurance		13,000	
Depreciation expense: building		10,000	
Depreciation expense: delivery vans		14,000	
Miscellaneous		8,000	
Total selling expenses		$117,000	
General & administrative expenses			
Executive salaries		$ 95,000	
Office salaries		43,000	
Insurance		18,500	
Depreciation expense: building		5,000	
Miscellaneous		12,500	
Total gen. & admin. expenses		174,000	
Total operating expenses			291,000
Income from operations			$ 34,000
Other revenues (expenses)			
Interest expense		$ (7,000)	
Gain on sale of truck		3,000	(4,000)
Income before income taxes			$ 30,000
Income taxes			10,000
Net income			$ 20,000

ment. Market and economic conditions change over time, and management may decide that disposal is the proper course of action to follow.

Transactions that involve the sale of property, plant, and equipment or investments, as well as other events, often give rise to a gain or loss. For example, suppose that a firm purchased a $56,000 parcel of land for use as a future plant site in a companywide expansion program. At some later date the company may sell the land because of a change in plans. If the land is sold for, say, $100,000, there is a gain of $44,000 ($100,000 − $56,000) on the sale.

Gains and losses affect profitability and are therefore disclosed on the income statement. Gains increase net income, and losses cause a reduction. For businesses that use a multiple-step income statement, such gains and losses are usually placed in the other revenue (expense) category.

Income Tax Expense. Corporate entities like The Waikiki Trading Company are subject to federal income taxes; in contrast, sole proprietorships and partnerships are not. Income tax expense is deducted separately from other business expenses when using the multiple-step format. This treatment is justified because the amount of tax is dependent on the calculation of a company's income before tax. In Waikiki's case, the company is subject to a 33⅓% tax rate. Income taxes amounting to $10,000 ($30,000 × 33⅓%) are therefore subtracted to yield a final profit figure of $20,000.

SINGLE-STEP INCOME STATEMENTS

Many business enterprises prepare a *single-step income statement,* which has one section for revenues and another section for costs and expenses.[6] Not only are there fewer "parts," but when compared with the multiple-step approach, most companies usually present less detail.

The single-step format offers the advantage of simplicity. Because many unsophisticated users of financial information may be confused by the various components of earnings, a large number of firms opt for this style of presentation. The single-step income statement of The Waikiki Trading Company, Inc., appears in Exhibit 5–8.

AN EVALUATION OF INCOME-STATEMENT DATA

Regardless of the reporting format used, a close look at the income statement will often reveal significant variations among businesses. These variations typically arise in the areas of gross profit and operating expenses. As evidence, study the bar charts that appear in Exhibit 5–9.

A company's gross profit rate (gross profit ÷ net sales) provides information about the amount of money that a business is making on a particular sale. The rate depends on a number of factors, including the price the consumer is willing to pay, the amount of inventory spoilage, the accepted level of operating expenses, the volume of inventory sold, and management's desire to generate additional sales. A substantial decline in gross profit, caused by either a decrease in selling price or an increase in cost of units sold, can provide massive financial headaches for a firm.

Operating expenses, another area of concern, also require careful monitoring. In times of economic prosperity, organizations tend to spend, spend, spend.

---

[6] If desired, income taxes may be shown as a separate deduction from income.

EXHIBIT 5–8
Single-Step Income Statement

THE WAIKIKI TRADING COMPANY, INC.
Income Statement
For the Year Ended December 31, 19XX

Revenues		
Net sales		$495,000
Gain on sale of truck		3,000
Total revenues		$498,000
Costs & expenses		
Cost of goods sold	$170,000	
Selling expenses	117,000	
General & administrative expenses	174,000	
Interest expense	7,000	
Total expenses		468,000
Income before income taxes		$ 30,000
Income taxes		10,000
Net income		$ 20,000

EXHIBIT 5–9
Gross Profit and Operating Expenses as a Percentage of Net Sales Revenues

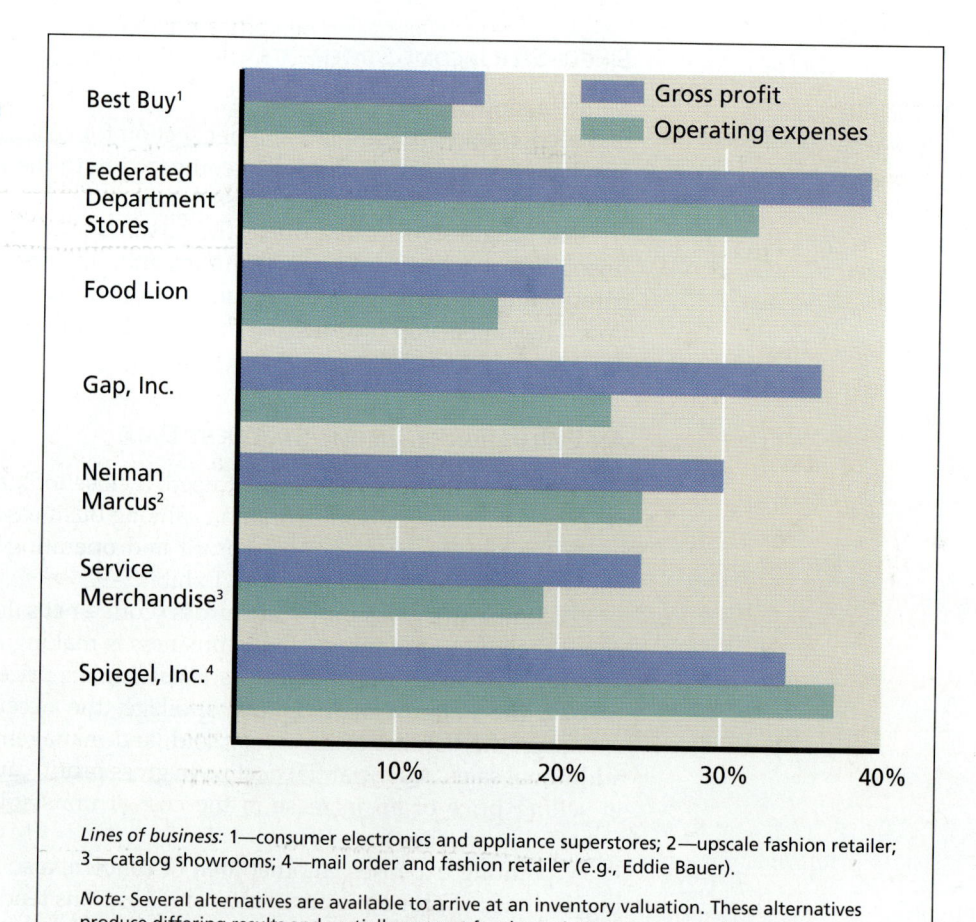

[Bar chart comparing Gross profit and Operating expenses as percentages of net sales for: Best Buy[1], Federated Department Stores, Food Lion, Gap, Inc., Neiman Marcus[2], Service Merchandise[3], Spiegel, Inc.[4]; x-axis from 10% to 40%]

Lines of business: 1—consumer electronics and appliance superstores; 2—upscale fashion retailer; 3—catalog showrooms; 4—mail order and fashion retailer (e.g., Eddie Bauer).

Note: Several alternatives are available to arrive at an inventory valuation. These alternatives produce differing results and partially account for the variations in gross profit rates.

New employees are frequently hired and new levels of management created. The opposite situation arises when times get tough. Layoffs and spending cuts are initiated as businesses try to "trim the fat" and improve profitability.

Bar charts similar to those just shown are helpful in assessing not only gross profit and expense performance, but other relationships as well. If desired, one could easily construct a chart to study various measures *for a given entity* to judge whether the measures are improving or deteriorating over time.

A FURTHER FOCUS

Despite strong demand, many personal computer (PC) manufacturers and retailers have fallen on hard times in recent years because of the so-called PC wars. To be competitive in this dynamic market, firms have been forced time and time again to cut prices. Along with these cuts come shrinking gross profit rates—rates that have fallen much faster than the companies could trim operating expenses. This situation has come back to haunt many businesses in the form of a rapidly disappearing bottom-line (net) income.

INVENTORY SYSTEMS

5 Discuss the differences between periodic and perpetual inventory systems.

Throughout this chapter we have illustrated use of a periodic inventory system. Under this system, merchandise purchases are recorded in the Purchases account and sales are credited to the Sales account. More important, cost of goods sold is calculated periodically (i.e., at the end of the period) when a company determines its inventory of units on hand. The latter figure is derived by physically counting the goods owned by the firm.[7]

The periodic system is employed by companies because of its minimal record-keeping requirements. The system is attractive for businesses that sell slow-moving products and use manual accounting systems.

PROBLEMS WITH A PERIODIC SYSTEM

Two significant problems associated with a periodic system make it undesirable for many organizations. First, a business has no record of the number of units in stock at any given time. Remember, no entries are made to the Inventory account for acquisitions and sales. This lack of information could lead to stockouts and poor customer service.

The second problem lies in the calculation of cost of goods sold. To explain, we present the following computations (the amounts are assumed):

Cost of goods sold	
Beginning inventory	$19,000
Add: Net purchases	47,000
Goods available for sale	$66,000
Less: Ending inventory	24,000
Cost of goods sold	$42,000

By subtracting the $24,000 ending inventory figure, obtained from the physical count, we are *assuming* that $42,000 of goods were sold. This assumption could be erroneous because theft or errors may have occurred. Unfortunately, there is

---

[7] This process is discussed more fully later in the chapter.

no basis for comparison, as the periodic system does not monitor the amount of inventory that *should be* on hand.

Perpetual Systems

The preceding problems are overcome by using a perpetual inventory system. A perpetual system maintains a continuous record of the inflows and outflows of merchandise, resulting in a running count of the goods on hand. More specifically, the Inventory account is directly increased for each purchase and also decreased for every sale.

By keeping records in this manner, a company can readily answer the questions of its salespeople and customers concerning item availability. In addition, a perpetual system leads to improved inventory control. By knowing the number of units that are supposed to be on hand, a business can reorder in sufficient time to avoid (or reduce) stockouts. Furthermore, the extent of any theft or errors can be determined by comparing the inventory records against an actual count of the goods.

Inventory and Computers

Computers have had a dramatic impact on inventories, from both a record-keeping viewpoint and a control viewpoint. Consider, for example, the perpetual inventory system just discussed. An increasing number of businesses are using perpetual systems, primarily because of electronics and state-of-the-art information systems. Computers can monitor inventory levels very easily. With sales transactions, for instance, a customer's order is entered in the system. The computer will check quantities in the warehouse; if a sufficient supply exists, the order is filled and a sales invoice generated. As each sale (or purchase) is made, the number of units in stock is automatically updated.[8]

As many of you have likely noticed, numerous companies are now using bar codes and scanners. These data-entry devices provide cost-effective input to computerized inventory systems. Some bar codes even serve a dual purpose: data input and theft deterrent. The codes that appear on some small disposable tags (e.g., those attached to clothing in a retail store) may actually contain a circuit that is linked to a security system. The circuit is deactivated during the scanning process, allowing the customer to leave the premises with the goods.

Generally speaking, the coupling of inventory systems and electronics has resulted in better management of the business. The outcome is a more profitable, competitive entity.

Taking a Physical Inventory

Regardless of the inventory system used, it is customary practice to count the goods on hand at the end of an accounting period. This process, known as taking a physical inventory, is required under a periodic system so that cost of goods sold can be calculated. It is also recommended with a perpetual inventory system to verify the accuracy of the accounting records. The number of units obtained in the physical count are multiplied by their unit cost. The

---

[8] Although the perpetual system of accounting for *units* is simple, maintaining a running count of *dollar values* creates several unique record-keeping problems. We will address these problems in Chapter 10.

results for individual products are then summed to obtain the total cost of goods on hand.

The inventory count, although costly and time-consuming, strengthens the credibility of the inventory figure reported on the year-end balance sheet. Even so, a physical count of inventory (and its observance by an outside independent auditor) has not always been a required practice. It took a massive fraud case to induce change. The 1937 financial statements of McKesson Corporation (formerly McKesson & Robbins) were found to contain significant amounts of fictitious inventories—all related to a fraud that had been perpetrated by the president and his brothers over a period of 12 years. The fraud was finally uncovered when an accounting executive of the company went to a warehouse to check some reported inventory and found none in existence. As an outcome of this case, generally accepted auditing standards now require the observation of physical inventory counts by audit personnel, as well as other procedures that help to avoid misstatements of assets in the accounting records.

APPENDIX: BEHIND THE SCENES WORK FOR A MERCHANDISING BUSINESS

6 Prepare a work sheet and closing entries for a merchandising business.

The body of this chapter contained the income statement, statement of owner's equity, and balance sheet for Peachtree Jeans. Although our discussion focused on the end product of the reporting process, several procedures are needed that allow a company to get to this point. These procedures include the preparation of a work sheet and a series of related journal entries that ready the accounting records for the next reporting period. This appendix illustrates these concepts by continuing the Peachtree Jeans example.

THE MERCHANDISING WORK SHEET

The work sheet is the underlying foundation for the preparation of financial statements. Recall that trial balance data are combined with the entries in the adjustment columns. These "updated" figures are listed in the adjusted trial balance columns and then extended on a line-by-line basis to the appropriate financial statement section (income statement or balance sheet).

It is important to note that with the exception of Inventory (and Capital), all of the accounts listed in the trial balance reflect transactions that occurred during the period. Remember that the Inventory account under a periodic system is not affected by sales and purchases. As a result of this situation, the account's balance represents the goods on hand at the start of the year—$67,000 for Peachtree Jeans.

Several different approaches may be used when handling the beginning inventory (and also the ending inventory) on a work sheet. We will focus on the *closing entry method,* so named because the Inventory account is updated in the closing process. Please refer to Peachtree's work sheet, which appears in Exhibit 5–10. (*Note:* New accounts presented in this chapter are shown in capital letters.) A careful study of the exhibit will reveal that Peachtree has extended the $67,000 beginning inventory from the adjusted trial balance to the income statement debit column. This procedure is performed because of the inventory's use in the computation of cost of goods sold. A review of the debit column will show that, in effect, the beginning inventory is being added to net purchases to arrive at goods available for sale.

Next, as indicated by the shaded numbers, the $48,000 ending inventory count is inserted in both the income statement credit column and the balance

PEACHTREE JEANS
Work Sheet
For the Year Ended December 31, 19XX

ACCOUNT TITLE	TRIAL BALANCE DEBIT	TRIAL BALANCE CREDIT	ADJUSTMENTS DEBIT	ADJUSTMENTS CREDIT	ADJUSTED TRIAL BALANCE DEBIT	ADJUSTED TRIAL BALANCE CREDIT	INCOME STATEMENT DEBIT	INCOME STATEMENT CREDIT	BALANCE SHEET DEBIT	BALANCE SHEET CREDIT
Cash	25,700				25,700				25,700	
Accounts receivable	19,600				19,600				19,600	
INVENTORY	67,000				67,000		67,000	48,000	48,000	
Prepaid insurance	13,800			(b) 9,000	4,800				4,800	
Equipment	124,800				124,800				124,800	
Accumulated depreciation: equipment		24,800		(a) 10,000		34,800				34,800
Accounts payable		36,400				36,400				36,400
Valerie Bain, capital		147,200				147,200				147,200
Valerie Bain, drawing	6,000				6,000				6,000	
SALES		307,000				307,000		307,000		
SALES DISCOUNTS	5,000				5,000		5,000			
SALES RETURNS & ALLOWANCES	2,000				2,000		2,000			
PURCHASES	148,000				148,000		148,000			
FREIGHT-IN	5,000				5,000		5,000			
PURCHASES DISCOUNTS		3,000				3,000		3,000		
PURCHASES RETURNS & ALLOWANCES		4,000				4,000		4,000		
Rent expense	15,000				15,000		15,000			
Salaries expense	59,500		(c) 1,500		61,000		61,000			
Utilities expense	11,000				11,000		11,000			
FREIGHT-OUT	7,000				7,000		7,000			
Advertising expense	13,000				13,000		13,000			
	522,400	522,400								
Depreciation expense			(a) 10,000		10,000		10,000			
Insurance expense			(b) 9,000		9,000		9,000			
Salaries payable				(c) 1,500		1,500				1,500
			20,500	20,500	533,900	533,900	353,000	362,000	228,900	219,900
Net income							9,000			9,000
							362,000	362,000	228,900	228,900

EXHIBIT 5–10
Work Sheet of a Merchandising Firm

sheet debit column. The credit allows the goods available for sale figure to be reduced by the ending inventory, to yield cost of goods sold. In contrast, the debit is needed so that Peachtree can report the year-end inventory on its balance sheet, along with the other assets owned by the firm.

Adjusting Entries. The work sheet not only assists in the construction of financial statements, but is also useful in the preparation of adjusting entries. When the beginning and ending inventories are treated in the manner just described, the adjusting entries for a merchandising concern parallel those shown earlier in the text for a service business. In Peachtree's case, for instance, the three adjusting entries for depreciation, prepaid insurance, and accrued salaries would be recorded in the journal and posted to the ledger. Please refer to Chapters 3 and 4 should you need a refresher of the proper procedures.

CLOSING ENTRIES

As before, all temporary accounts must be closed at the end of the reporting period. Such accounts would include those listed in the work sheet's income statement section, along with the drawing account. The income statement accounts with debit balances are closed in a combined journal entry by crediting each account and debiting Income Summary. New accounts presented in the chapter's discussion that have debit balances are Sales Discounts, Sales Returns & Allowances, Purchases, Freight-in, and Freight-out. Next, income statement accounts that contain credit balances are debited, with a corresponding credit to Income Summary. New accounts that fall in this category include Sales, Purchases Discounts, and Purchases Returns & Allowances.

Because Inventory is listed in both the income statement debit *and* credit columns, the account is afforded special treatment. Inventory is credited in the first entry for $67,000, a procedure that reduces the balance in the account to zero. It is then debited for $48,000 in the second entry, thereby recording (inserting) the ending balance of goods owned by the firm.

These two closing entries, along with the Inventory and Income Summary accounts, follow. Notice (1) the manner in which the Inventory account has been updated and (2) how the journal entries eventually place the company's $9,000 net income (from Exhibit 5–4) in Income Summary.

Dec. 31	Income Summary	353,000	
	Inventory		67,000
	Sales Discounts		5,000
	Sales Returns & Allowances		2,000
	Purchases		148,000
	Freight-in		5,000
	Rent Expense		15,000
	Salaries Expense		61,000
	Utilities Expense		11,000
	Freight-out		7,000
	Advertising Expense		13,000
	Depreciation Expense		10,000
	Insurance Expense		9,000
	To remove beginning inventory and close income statement accounts having debit balances.		
31	Inventory	48,000	
	Sales	307,000	
	Purchases Discounts	3,000	
	Purchases Returns & Allowances	4,000	
	Income Summary		362,000
	To record ending inventory and close income statement accounts having credit balances.		

INVENTORY			
1/1	67,000	12/31	67,000
12/31	48,000		

INCOME SUMMARY			
12/31	353,000	12/31	362,000
			9,000

To complete the closing process, the Income Summary and drawing accounts are both closed to capital.

Dec. 31	Income Summary	9,000	
	Valerie Bain, Capital		9,000
	To close Income Summary.		
31	Valerie Bain, Capital	6,000	
	Valerie Bain, Drawing		6,000
	To close drawing account.		

END-OF-CHAPTER REVIEW

LEARNING OBJECTIVES: THE KEY POINTS

1. **Account for typical transactions of sellers and buyers of merchandise.** The chapter presents a variety of merchandising transactions, many of which are summarized in the following chart:

	JOURNAL ENTRY	
TYPE OF TRANSACTION	DEBIT	CREDIT
Sale of merchandise on account	Accounts Receivable	Sales
Return on account of previously sold goods	Sales Returns & Allowances	Accounts Receivable
Receipt on account, minus cash discount	Cash, Sales Discounts	Accounts Receivable
Purchase of merchandise on account	Purchases	Accounts Payable
Return on account of previously acquired goods	Accounts Payable	Purchases Returns & Allowances
Payment on account, minus cash discount (gross method)	Accounts Payable	Cash, Purchases Discounts
Purchase of merchandise on account, F.O.B. shipping point, freight prepaid	Purchases, Freight-in	Accounts Payable

Be sure to remember that the Purchases and Sales accounts are used solely for merchandise transactions and not for acquisitions or disposals of other assets.

2. **Compare and contrast the gross and net methods of accounting for purchases.** Under the gross method, the Purchases and Accounts Payable accounts are estab-

lished at the gross invoice price of merchandise acquired. Any discounts taken are credited to Purchases Discounts. With the net method, transactions are recorded at the invoice price minus any discounts that could be taken. If a discount is missed, it is charged to the Purchases Discounts Lost account.

3. **Compute cost of goods sold and gross profit, and prepare the financial statements for a merchandising concern.** Cost of goods sold is calculated as follows: beginning inventory + net purchases − ending inventory. The net purchases figure is derived by adding freight-in to gross purchases and then subtracting any purchases discounts and purchases returns and allowances that occurred during the period. Gross profit, or profit from the sale of merchandise, is computed as net sales minus cost of goods sold. The preceding items all appear on the income statement, with the ending inventory also being disclosed in the current asset section of the balance sheet.

4. **Distinguish between multiple- and single-step income statements.** The multiple-step income statement contains various classifications such as operating expenses and other revenues and expenses, as well as significant subtotals (e.g., gross profit). The multiple-step's format is very informative because of added captions and disclosures. In contrast, the single-step income statement normally presents less detail and places all revenues in one section and all expenses (except perhaps income taxes) in another. This arrangement is said to be easier to understand.

5. **Discuss the differences between periodic and perpetual inventory systems.** Under a periodic system, cost of goods sold is determined at the end of the accounting period. Although this system is easy to use, it suffers from two limitations: the lack of an up-to-date inventory figure and the inability to determine errors and/or theft losses. These two problems are overcome with a perpetual inventory system, which keeps a continuous record of the inflows and outflows of units. The end result is improved inventory control. Perpetual systems are being used by an increasing number of businesses because of the growing popularity of computerized inventory applications.

6. **(Appendix) Prepare a work sheet and closing entries for a merchandising business.** The work sheet for a merchandising business parallels that for a service business, with the only new procedure involving the beginning and ending inventory figures. The beginning inventory is extended from the adjusted trial balance to the income statement debit column. In addition, the ending inventory is inserted in the income statement credit column and the balance sheet debit column.

The accompanying journal entries to update the Inventory account are made during the closing process. All income statement accounts are reduced to zero, and their corresponding balances are transferred to Income Summary.

Key Terms and Concepts: A Quick Overview

cash discount A discount offered to credit customers to encourage prompt payment of invoices. (p. 178)

closing entry method An end-of-period procedure by which the Inventory account is updated through the closing process. (p. 195)

contra revenue An account that is deducted from revenues and used in the computation of net revenues on the income statement. (p. 177)

cost of goods sold The total cost of inventory that a company has sold during an accounting period. (p. 179)

credit memorandum A document prepared by the seller for an allowance or an authorized return of merchandise. (p. 176)

debit memorandum   A document prepared by the purchaser for either an allowance or an authorized return of merchandise. (p. 181)

electronic data interchange (EDI)   A growing practice in merchandise purchasing activities that links together the computers of the buyer and seller. (p. 185)

F.O.B. destination   Freight terms indicating that transportation charges are borne by the seller. (p. 184)

F.O.B. shipping point   Freight terms indicating that transportation charges are borne by the purchaser. (p. 184)

goods available for sale   The beginning balance of inventory plus net purchases. (p. 179)

gross method   A method of accounting for merchandise in which both Purchases and Accounts Payable are recorded at the total invoice cost of the merchandise acquired. (p. 182)

gross profit   Net sales minus cost of goods sold. (p. 186)

invoice price   List price minus applicable trade discounts. (p. 177)

list price   The basic catalog price for merchandise. (p. 177)

merchandise inventory   Goods held by a merchandising business for resale to others. (p. 174)

multiple-step income statement   A type of income statement in which accounts are presented by association, thereby revealing important relationships to readers. (p. 188)

net method   A method of accounting for merchandise in which both Purchases and Accounts Payable are recorded at the net cost of the purchase—that is, total invoice cost minus the anticipated cash discount. (p. 183)

operating expenses   Expenses that relate to the principal selling and administrative activities of a business. (p. 186)

periodic inventory system   A system of accounting in which purchases and sales of inventory are not recorded in the Inventory account. (p. 193)

perpetual inventory system   A system of accounting for inventory in which the Inventory account is respectively increased and decreased for each purchase and sale of inventory made during the period. (p. 194)

purchases discount   A discount secured by the purchaser of merchandise for prompt payment of invoices. (p. 182)

sales discount   A cash discount from the seller's point of view. (p. 178)

single-step income statement   A type of income statement that has one section for revenues and another section for costs and expenses. (p. 191)

taking a physical inventory   The process of counting the goods in a company's possession upon conclusion of an accounting period. (p. 194)

trade discount   A discount frequently offered to customers—specifically, a reduction from the list price of merchandise. (p. 177)

Chapter Quiz

The five questions that follow relate to several issues raised in the chapter. Test your knowledge of the issues by selecting the best answer. (The answers appear on p. 216.)

1. Which of the following statements is incorrect?
   a. Sales Discounts is commonly known as a contra revenue account.
   b. Net sales minus cost of goods sold equals gross profit.
   c. A perpetual inventory system results in better inventory control than a periodic inventory system.
   d. A trade discount is a specialized type of cash discount.

2. Which of the following accounts would not be used if a company employed the net method of recording purchases?
   a. Purchases.
   b. Purchases Discounts.
   c. Purchases Discounts Lost.
   d. Purchases Returns.

3. Harris Company reported the following information for the period just ended: net sales, $5,000; net purchases, $2,900; beginning inventory, $1,700; and ending inventory, $2,000. The company's cost of goods sold is:
   a. $1,800.
   b. $2,400.
   c. $2,600.
   d. $3,200.

4. Hospital Supply, Inc. purchased $8,000 of merchandise on July 9 from Rosen Manufacturing, F.O.B. shipping point, terms 2/10, n/30. Freight charges of $200 were paid by Rosen and appear on the invoice. If Hospital Supply settled the transaction on July 17, the company would pay:
   a. $7,840.
   b. $8,036.
   c. $8,040.
   d. $8,200.

5. Which of the following accounts would most likely appear in the operating expense section of a multiple-step income statement?
   a. Freight-out.
   b. Freight-in.
   c. Sales Discounts.
   d. Interest Expense.

SUMMARY PROBLEM

The Breakfast Bar reported the following information for the period just ended:

Freight-in	$ 8,800
Purchases	349,000
Purchases discounts	6,600
Purchases returns & allowances	3,800
Sales	573,600
Sales discounts	4,000
Sales returns & allowances	11,400

An examination of the firm's Inventory account, which is maintained under a periodic system, revealed a beginning balance on January 1 of $77,200. A hand count revealed that the company owned $95,800 of inventory on December 31.

Instructions

a. Compute the company's (1) net sales, (2) cost of goods sold, and (3) gross profit.
b. Determine the normal balance (debit or credit) of the following accounts: Sales, Purchases Discounts, Freight-in, and Sales Returns & Allowances.
c. When The Breakfast Bar makes a charge to the Freight-in account, would the transaction being recorded involve a purchase with terms of F.O.B. shipping point or F.O.B. destination? Why?

Solution

a. (1)
Sales		$573,600
Less: Sales discounts	$ 4,000	
Sales returns & allowances	11,400	15,400
Net sales		$558,200

(2)
Beginning inventory, Jan. 1			$ 77,200
Add: Purchases		$349,000	
Freight-in		8,800	
		$357,800	
Less: Purchases discounts	$6,600		
Purchases returns & allowances	3,800	10,400	
Net purchases			347,400
Goods available for sale			$424,600
Less: Ending inventory, Dec. 31			95,800
Cost of goods sold			$328,800

(3)
Net sales	$558,200
Cost of goods sold	328,800
Gross profit	$229,400

b. Credit, credit, debit, debit

c. F.O.B. shipping point. The Freight-in account is used for transportation charges incurred by the buyer of merchandise, which occurs under terms of F.O.B. shipping point. With F.O.B. destination, the seller incurs the charges, requiring a debit to Freight-out on the seller's accounting records.

Assignment Material

Questions

Q5–1 Explain the function and use of a credit memorandum.

Q5–2 Rather than publish catalogs that contain invoice prices, many companies follow the practice of printing list prices and then granting a trade discount to purchasers. What advantages are associated with this procedure?

Q5–3 Distinguish between a trade discount and a cash discount.

Q5–4 Explain why a purchaser should normally take advantage of cash discounts, even if it means obtaining a bank loan to do so.

Q5–5 Contrast the gross and net methods of recording purchases. What is an important advantage associated with the latter approach?

Q5–6 The Gomez Company sells an item that has a list price of $1,000. Management is contemplating whether to ship the item F.O.B. shipping point or F.O.B. destination. Compare the trade discounts that would probably be quoted under the two alternatives. Which trade discount would probably be smaller? Why?

Q5–7 A student once commented: "The Freight-in account is very similar to the Purchases Returns account. Both appear in the cost-of-goods-sold section of the income statement as a reduction to determine net purchases." Evaluate the student's comment.

Q5–8 Is the Freight-out account treated differently than the Freight-in account on an income statement? Briefly explain.

Q5–9 Explain the difference between gross profit and net income.

Q5–10 The Ames Company sells its products at approximately 35% above cost; yet, at the end of the current year, a net loss of $15,000 was incurred. Explain how this situation is possible.

Q5–11 Systems, Inc., recently disclosed interest charges in the operating expense section of its multiple-step income statement. Do you agree or disagree with the company's reporting treatment? Why?

Q5–12 Where are gains and losses normally reported on a multiple-step income statement?

Q5–13 Is the use of perpetual inventory systems increasing or decreasing?

Q5–14 Why is a physical count of inventory needed in a perpetual inventory system?

EXERCISES

E5–1 Accounting for sales on account (L.O. 1)

Enchanted Stones, a mail order supplier of fine gems, publishes a catalog showing list prices for its merchandise. Regular customers are entitled to trade discounts from list price; all customers are offered a 2% cash discount for payment within 10 days. Two of the company's transactions follow.

- On January 2, Helen Stephens purchased an emerald necklace having a list price of $8,500. Stephens was not entitled to a trade discount; she paid her account in full on January 8.
- On January 10, Alex Hudson purchased a package of loose diamonds on account. The list price was $12,000, subject to a 20% trade discount. Sixty percent of the diamonds were returned on January 14 because of poor color and clarity. Hudson paid his balance due on January 23.

a. Prepare Enchanted's journal entries to record the preceding transactions. Assume that the customers have correctly followed the firm's cash discount policy.

b. Compute the net sales from these transactions.

E5–2 Gross and net methods of accounting for purchases (L.O. 2)

New Mexico Furniture purchased $40,000 of merchandise on account on May 18, terms 2/10, n/30.

a. Assuming that New Mexico uses the gross method of accounting for purchases, present entries to record the following:
   (1) The purchase on May 18.
   (2) Payment of the invoice if payment was made on May 24.
   (3) Payment of the invoice if payment was made on June 15.

b. Repeat instruction (a), assuming that New Mexico uses the net method of accounting for purchases.

E5–3 Gross and net methods of accounting for purchases: An analysis (L.O. 2)

The Software Shoppe purchased $265,000 of merchandise during the year subject to terms of 2/10, n/30. Returns to suppliers amounted to $12,000; all returns took place prior to any payments on account. An analysis of the company's records revealed a balance in the Purchases Discounts account of $1,050 at year-end. The Software Shoppe uses the gross method of accounting for purchases.

a. Determine the balance in the Purchases Discounts Lost account had The Software Shoppe used the net method of accounting for purchases rather than the gross method.

b. What are some possible causes of lost discounts?

c. Given the company's situation, would use of the net method have been more beneficial? Briefly explain.

E5–4 Purchases discount computations (L.O. 1)

Bullen Plumbing Contractors made the following purchases of merchandise from suppliers A, B, C, and D during a recent month:

	A	B	C	D
F.O.B. terms	Destination	Shipping point	Shipping point	Destination
Discount offered	2/10, n/30	3/10, n/eom	2/10, n/eom	3/10, n/eom
Original purchase	$3,000	$2,500	$1,000	$1,800
Freight charges	700	400	200	350
Purchases returns	—	600	—	100

All purchases returns were made immediately upon receipt of the goods. Freight charges were initially paid by the sellers and, when appropriate, were billed to Bullen.

Determine the amount of cash that Bullen paid to each supplier if the company settled all transactions within the discount period.

E5–5 Journal entries for buyer and seller of merchandise (L.O. 1)

On August 6, Colbert Corporation purchased $64,000 of merchandise from Robinson Wholesale, terms 2/10, n/30, F.O.B. destination. Robinson paid freight charges of $1,800 to Roadway Express one day later. Because of a flaw in several items, Colbert returned $4,000 of merchandise on August 9. The transaction was settled on August 15.

Assuming Colbert uses the gross method of accounting for purchases, prepare journal entries to record the preceding transactions for both companies.

E5–6 Merchandising concepts (L.O. 1)

Evaluate the comments that follow as being True or False. If the comment is false, briefly explain why.

a. Soft Rock Cafe acquired $42,000 of restaurant equipment on account for use in the business. The company should debit Purchases and credit Accounts Payable to correctly record the transaction.
b. The balance in the Freight-out account should be added to the balance in Purchases to arrive at the net delivered cost of merchandise acquired.
c. Cash discounts should be computed on merchandise cost only, excluding any applicable freight charges incurred on the transaction.
d. From an interest rate perspective, it is very costly for a buyer to forgo a 2% purchases discount.
e. Cash discounts and trade discounts are a convenient means of reducing a catalog price to invoice price.

E5–7 Electronic data interchange (L.O. 1)

Route 99, which sells nothing for over 99 cents, has grown from two stores to 175 stores in the past few years. Most of the firm's merchandise consists of surplus goods acquired from 700 suppliers located throughout the country.

In this period of growth, the company has found that its purchasing and accounting departments have expanded in size. Several thousand purchase orders and checks are prepared each month by a large pool of clerical employees. Route 99 is considering electronic data interchange to automate its purchasing and bill-paying processes with a number of its suppliers.

a. Does Route 99 seem like a company that could benefit from electronic data interchange? Why?
b. Briefly explain the benefits that Route 99 would likely experience by using electronic data interchange for purchasing and bill paying.

E5–8 Basic merchandising computations (L.O. 3)

A review of the records of SportsCards, USA found the following information:

Beginning inventory	$50,000	Utilities expense	$ 2,000
Rent expense	3,500	Purchases	64,000
Purchases discounts	900	Freight-in	800
Ending inventory	45,000	Sales	99,000
Sales returns	400	Sales discounts	2,000
Wage expense	11,000	Advertising expense	9,000

Compute cost of goods sold, gross profit, and net income for the company.

E5–9 Merchandising computations: Working backward (L.O. 3)

The following information was obtained from the records of Companies A, B, and C:

	A	B	C
Sales	$90,300	$51,200	$ (g)
Sales discounts	(a)	3,700	2,000
Net sales	88,400	(d)	60,700
Beginning inventory	70,000	39,500	(h)
Net purchases	99,800	(e)	15,600
Ending inventory	(b)	30,000	10,000
Cost of goods sold	62,000	33,200	(i)
Gross profit	26,400	(f)	36,800
Total expenses	(c)	11,200	41,800
Net income (loss)	9,100	3,100	(j)

Compute the amounts that are indicated by the letters (a)–(j).

E5–10 Income statement computations (L.O. 3, 4)

Selected account balances from Marshall Company for the current year include the following:

Sales	$372,000	Sales discounts	$ 1,000
Purchases	206,000	Beginning inventory	98,700
Advertising expense	11,500	Sales salaries	12,600
Administrative salaries	26,300	Insurance expense	4,000
Ending inventory	94,400	Depreciation expense	15,000
Sales returns	2,800		

Forty percent of the insurance and depreciation expense relates to Marshall's sales activities. Calculate the following:

a. Net revenues
b. Cost of goods sold
c. Gross profit
d. Total selling expenses
e. Total general and administrative expenses
f. Net income (loss)

E5–11 Analysis of income data (L.O. 4)

Village Corporation operates a chain of stores that specializes in cellular phones, pagers, fax machines, computers, and other electronic devices. Despite the fact that the company is in a very competitive marketplace, demand for most products is strong because of an aggressive advertising program.

Village has expanded in recent months, adding 12 mid-level managers and two major product lines. Unfortunately, gross profit rates are shrinking and losses are mounting. What actions might Village take to improve overall profitability?

E5–12 Perpetual and periodic inventory systems (L.O. 5)
Jim Charlesworth is about to open a specialized auto parts store that will concentrate on parts for British and Japanese imports. The store will stock approximately 3,000 different items. Jim's accountant has recommended the use of a perpetual inventory system.
a. Briefly describe the operation of a perpetual inventory system.
b. Compare a perpetual system to a periodic system in terms of customer service and inventory control.

*E5–13 Updating the Inventory account; closing entries (L.O. 6)
The following selected balances were extracted from the accounting records of Design Fantastic:

	DEBIT	CREDIT
Karen Jackson, capital		$87,500
Karen Jackson, drawing	$18,000	
Sales		99,300
Sales discounts	2,100	
Purchases	55,400	
Purchases returns		3,000
Wage expense	22,900	
Marketing expense	5,600	
Rent expense	12,000	
Utilities expense	3,700	

The company's Inventory account contains a balance of $21,800, reflecting the cost of the beginning inventory. Goods costing $27,400 remain on hand at the end of the period, December 31, 19XX.

Prepare the journal entries that are needed to update the Inventory account and close the accounting records for the year just ended.

Problems

Series A

P5–A1 Merchandising journal entries (L.O. 1)
The transactions that follow occurred between Poteet Menswear and Catalina Manufacturing.

Nov. 1 Poteet purchased $5,000 of merchandise from Catalina, terms 3/10, n/30.
  5 Catalina issued a $500 credit memorandum to Poteet for the return of defective goods sold on November 1.
  10 Poteet paid the proper amount owed for the merchandise.
  15 Catalina sold Poteet a surplus laser printer and fax machine at cost for $1,600. Terms were n/eom.
  21 Poteet purchased $20,000 of Catalina's spring goods. The transaction is subject to a 40% trade discount and terms of 1/10, n/30, F.O.B. destination. Catalina paid $150 of shipping charges to Hunt Truck Lines.

* An asterisk preceding an item indicates that the material is covered in an appendix to this chapter.

Instructions

a. Prepare the necessary journal entries for Poteet Menswear, assuming the company uses the gross method of accounting for purchases.
b. Prepare the necessary journal entries for Catalina Manufacturing.
c. Suppose that the purchase on November 1 also had $60 of freight charges, which were paid by Catalina, and terms of F.O.B. shipping point.
   (1) Prepare the necessary journal entry for Poteet on November 1.
   (2) Calculate the amount that Poteet would have paid on November 10 to settle the transaction.

P5–A2 Gross versus net purchases method (L.O. 2).

Beth Dotterer runs an athletic footwear store. The store had the following purchasing activity during August:

Date	Supplier	Purchases or (Returns)	Discounts Offered
Aug. 8	Reebok	$6,200	2/10, n/30
11	Reebok	(400)	
13	NIKE	5,500	1/10, n/30

Additional information:

1. The goods returned on August 11 were part of the purchase on August 8.
2. The goods acquired from NIKE were shipped F.O.B. shipping point. Freight charges of $100 were prepaid by NIKE and appear on the invoice.
3. Beth paid Reebok on August 20 and NIKE on August 22.

Instructions

a. Record the five transactions, assuming that Beth uses the gross method of accounting for purchases. All terms of sale are strictly followed.
b. Record the five transactions, assuming that Beth uses the net method of accounting for purchases. All terms of sale are strictly followed.
c. If you were Beth (the owner/manager), which of the two methods would you find most helpful in analyzing purchasing procedures? Briefly explain.

P5–A3 Income statement classification (L.O. 4)

Home Entertainment distributes and sells videotapes to local retailers. The categories below were extracted from the company's multiple-step income statement.

1. Revenue
2. Cost of goods sold
3. Selling expenses
4. General & administrative expenses
5. Other revenue (expense)

The following accounts appear in the general ledger:

a. Marketing expense
b. Sales discounts
c. Warehouse equipment
d. Accounting fees
e. Delivery expense
f. Rental revenue (from a business that leases extra space in the parking lot)
g. Office manager's salary
h. Purchases returns
i. Inventory (beginning)
j. Loss from traffic accident
k. Interest expense
l. Prepaid advertising
m. Travel expense (to visit local retailers)
n. Transportation-in
o. Ray Franklin, drawing
p. Interest earned on investments
q. Sales
r. Purchases
s. Commissions paid

Instructions

Classify Home Entertainment's accounts as to their proper placement on the income statement. If any of the accounts do not appear on the income statement, determine whether they appear on the balance sheet or the statement of owner's equity.

P5–A4 Income statement preparation (L.O. 4)

Presented below is financial information of the Juarez Corporation for 19XX.

Sales	$587,400
Freight-in	10,800
Loan interest expense	5,950
Interest revenue	3,800
Sales returns	4,200
Purchases returns	7,310
Gain on sale of land	18,900
Merchandise inventory (ending)	54,700
Merchandise inventory (beginning)	58,200
Loss on sale of building	24,300
Purchases	226,900
Sales discounts	9,400
Administrative expenses	
Executive salaries	61,800
Depreciation expense: buildings	23,600
Insurance expense	6,300
Miscellaneous expense	3,100
Selling expenses	
Delivery expense	17,900
Sales commissions	31,500
Advertising expense	7,250
Depreciation expense: delivery equipment	10,400
Insurance expense	3,090

The corporation is subject to a 40% income tax rate.

Instructions

a. Prepare a multiple-step income statement for the year ended November 30, 19XX.
b. Explain what you would have done differently if instruction (a) had called for the preparation of a single-step income statement. What benefits does the multiple-step approach offer financial statement users?

P5–A5 Analysis of data, journal entries, inventory systems (L.O. 1, 3, 5)

Westbrook Enterprises, a home improvement retailer, opened for business on January 2, 19X6. The firm's accountant has provided you with the following selected data for the year:

   Credit sales of merchandise: $640,000
   Cash sales of merchandise: 20% of total sales revenues
   Sales discounts: 2%, computed on 70% of credit sales
   Sale of land parcel: $100,000
   Cost of land: $67,000
   Ending inventory count: $325,000

Instructions

a. Calculate the net sales revenues of the company.
b. Prepare journal entries to record the year's cash sales, credit sales, and sales discounts. In preparing the entries, assume that all customers have settled their accounts with the firm.
c. Explain how the land sale would be reported on the company's multiple-step income statement.
d. Westbrook uses a periodic inventory system, and management is fearful that a large inventory theft has occurred. Will the company have some difficulty in trying to pinpoint the cost of any theft? Briefly discuss.

*P5–A6 Work sheet, financial statements, and closing entries (L.O. 3, 4, 6)

The Wheaton Company has the following trial balance as of December 31:

Cash	$ 24,900	
Accounts receivable	36,800	
Merchandise inventory	38,000	
Prepaid advertising	6,400	
Supplies	3,700	
Equipment	72,000	
Accumulated depreciation: equipment		$ 13,400
Accounts payable		30,600
Jerry Wheaton, capital		140,200
Jerry Wheaton, drawing	16,600	
Sales		285,900
Sales returns & allowances	5,700	
Sales discounts	2,000	
Purchases	175,100	
Freight-in	4,400	
Purchases returns & allowances		1,800
Purchases discounts		4,300
Wage expense	58,500	
Insurance expense	2,600	
Rent expense	16,500	
Freight-out	4,300	
Utilities expense	8,700	
	$476,200	$476,200

Additional accounts maintained by the business include Wages Payable, Income Summary, Advertising Expense, Supplies Expense, and Depreciation Expense. Wheaton's accountant has derived the following data:

1. Advertising applicable to future periods: $3,600.
2. Supplies on hand: $1,600.
3. Depreciation on the equipment: $4,800.
4. Accrued wages: $3,100.
5. Ending inventory: $51,600.

Wheaton's capital account includes $4,000 of owner investments made during the year.

Instructions

a. Complete a work sheet for the Wheaton Company for the year ended December 31.

b. Prepare a multiple-step income statement, statement of owner's equity, and a classified balance sheet. The firm's selling activities account for 60% of the wage cost and 40% of insurance, rent, utilities, supplies, and depreciation expense.
c. Record Wheaton's adjusting entries in the journal.
d. Record Wheaton's closing entries in the journal.

Series B

P5–B1 Merchandising journal entries (L.O. 1)
The Patrick Company had the following transactions during April:

Apr. 1 Sold $4,000 of merchandise on account to Campbell Company, terms 2/10, n/30.
3 Purchased $2,500 of merchandise on account from West Enterprises, terms 3/10, n/30. The merchandise was shipped F.O.B. shipping point; freight charges amounted to $80 and were paid by West.
7 Issued a credit memorandum for $200 to the Campbell Company for defective merchandise sold on April 1.
8 Received the proper amount due from Campbell Company.
10 Purchased a computer on account for business use from Bell Resources for $11,400, terms n/eom.
12 Paid the proper amount due to West Enterprises.
18 Received a purchase order from Gibbons Distributing for merchandise having a list price of $6,000. The order was subject to a 40% trade discount and terms of 1/10, n/30. Patrick shipped the merchandise F.O.B. destination and paid $40 of freight charges.
29 Received the proper amount due from Gibbons Distributing.
30 Paid the amount due to Bell Resources.

Instructions
Prepare journal entries for the April transactions, assuming Patrick uses the gross method of accounting for purchases. All terms of sale are strictly followed.

P5–B2 Gross versus net purchases method (L.O. 2)
Beautiful Face operates several small cosmetics stores in shopping malls. During July, store no. 108 had the following purchases transactions:

July 7 Purchased $950 of cosmetics on account from Lovely Lady, terms 2/10, n/30. The goods were shipped F.O.B. shipping point; freight charges of $25 were prepaid by Lovely Lady and appear on the invoice.
12 Purchased $125 of store supplies on account from Atlas Office Supplies.
17 Purchased $1,400 of cosmetics on account from the Charles Norman Company, terms 1/10, n/30.
20 Paid the proper amount due to Lovely Lady.
21 Returned $200 of the cosmetics purchased on July 17 because of a shipping error made by the Charles Norman Company.
26 Paid the proper amount due to the Charles Norman Company.

Instructions
a. Record the preceding transactions, assuming Beautiful Face uses the gross method of accounting for purchases. All terms of sale are strictly followed.

b. Record the preceding transactions, assuming Beautiful Face uses the net method of accounting for purchases. All terms of sale are strictly followed.

P5–B3 Income statement classification (L.O. 4)

Second Time Around, a sole proprietorship, sells its inventory of antiques to tourists. The categories that follow were found on the company's multiple-step income statement: revenue, cost of goods sold, selling expenses, general and administrative expenses, and other revenue (expense).

The following accounts were taken from the adjusted trial balance:

a. Advertising expense
b. Packing supplies expense
c. Freight-in
d. Purchases
e. Sales taxes payable
f. Office rent expense
g. Sales returns and allowances
h. Sales salaries
i. Freight-out
j. Customer entertainment expense
k. Prepaid interest
l. Gain on sale of equipment
m. Interest revenue
n. Ending inventory
o. Purchases discounts
p. Utilities expense
q. Interest expense
r. Accumulated depreciation: warehouse
s. Thomas Quinn, capital

Eighty percent of the utilities expense is related to the company's sales activities.

Instructions

Classify the accounts of Second Time Around as to their proper placement on the income statement. If any of the accounts do not appear on the income statement, determine whether they appear on the balance sheet or the statement of owner's equity.

P5–B4 Income statement preparation (L.O. 4)

The following information was compiled by a newly hired staff accountant of the Hanson Corporation:

Administrative expenses	$ 99,500
Advertising expense	43,500
Beginning inventory	97,100
Depreciation expense: executive offices	31,700
Depreciation expense: sales equipment	15,600
Ending inventory	76,000
Freight-in	14,200
Gain on sale of land	10,000
Insurance expense	27,000
Interest revenue	8,000
Net sales	784,000
Purchases	361,800
Purchases discounts	6,400
Sales discounts	13,600
Sales salaries expense	62,000

Additional information:

1. Administrative expenses consist of executive salaries ($85,000) and interest ($14,500).
2. Insurance expense should be allocated 70% to administration and 30% to sales.

3. Net sales was computed as follows: Sales ($757,900) − sales returns ($8,300) + freight-out ($34,400).
4. Hanson is subject to a 30% income tax rate.

Instructions

a. Prepare a multiple-step income statement for the year ended September 30, 19X4. Be sure to correct any errors made by the staff accountant.
b. If you were a banker considering loaning money to Hanson Corporation, which form of income statement (multiple-step or single-step) would you prefer to examine? Why?

P5–B5 Analysis of data, journal entries, inventory systems (L.O. 1, 3, 5)

Hidden Valley, Inc., a wholesaler of printing equipment, uses a periodic inventory system. During 19X3, the firm purchased $450,000 of merchandise on account and took advantage of a 3% discount on 80% of this amount. Freight-in and freight-out, paid directly to trucking companies in cash, totaled $8,000 and $15,000, respectively. On January 9, Hidden Valley acquired a $42,000 truck by securing a loan payable. Inventory figures were as follows: Beginning inventory: $196,000. Ending inventory: $213,000

Instructions

a. Compute Hidden Valley's cost of goods sold.
b. Present journal entries to record the purchases of merchandise, purchases discounts, freight, and the truck acquisition. In preparing the entries, assume that Hidden Valley has settled all amounts owed to merchandise suppliers.
c. In what section of the company's multiple-step income statement would the Freight-out account appear?
d. Shortly after the ending inventory count of $213,000 was determined, an employee was arrested for theft. Law enforcement officials found $23,000 of stolen merchandise in the employee's garage.
   (1) Compute the true cost of goods sold.
   (2) Generally speaking, would a perpetual inventory system be more useful than a periodic system in monitoring inventory shortages? Why?

*P5–B6 Work sheet, financial statements, and closing entries (L.O. 3, 4, 6)

Phoenix Appliance has the trial balance on page 213 as of December 31. Additional accounts maintained by the business include Salaries Payable, Income Summary, Rent Expense, Store Supplies Expense, and Depreciation Expense. Phoenix's accountant has derived the following data:

1. Rental prepayments expiring during the current period: $4,000.
2. Store supplies used during the period: $1,800.
3. Depreciation on the equipment: $3,700.
4. Accrued salaries: $1,900.
5. Ending inventory: $31,500.

McGarry's capital account includes $15,000 of owner investments made during the year.

Instructions

a. Complete a work sheet for Phoenix Appliance for the year ended December 31.
b. Prepare a multiple-step income statement, statement of owner's equity, and a classified balance sheet. The firm's selling activities account for 70% of the salaries cost and 40% of the insurance, utilities, rent, and depreciation expense.

c. Record Phoenix's adjusting entries in the journal.
d. Record Phoenix's closing entries in the journal.

Cash	$ 37,200	
Accounts receivable	49,300	
Merchandise inventory	41,800	
Prepaid rent	6,400	
Store supplies	3,950	
Equipment	38,500	
Accumulated depreciation: equipment		$ 11,100
Accounts payable		16,820
Mark McGarry, capital		119,850
Mark McGarry, drawing	7,500	
Sales		227,880
Sales returns	1,570	
Sales discounts	4,360	
Purchases	91,720	
Freight-in	1,970	
Purchases returns		970
Purchases discounts		1,750
Salaries expense	51,800	
Marketing expense	11,820	
Insurance expense	10,800	
Utilities expense	3,180	
Delivery expense	16,500	
	$378,370	$378,370

EXPANDING YOUR HORIZONS

EYH5–1 Sales returns (L.O. 1)

On September 26, 1994, *The Wall Street Journal* reported that customer returns have become a nightmare for manufacturers, especially those in the consumer-electronics field. Excessive returns have forced these firms to repack and reship perfectly good merchandise, giving rise to extra costs that reduce income. In some instances the returns are unjustified and could be questioned from an ethical perspective. One such example is the so-called Super Bowl Problem: the purchase of a large-screen television for a Super Bowl party and the set's return on the Monday following the game. Manufacturers place part of the problem on the liberal returns policies of many superstores.

Instructions

Interview three different retail store managers and determine (1) the usual percentage of sales returns relative to gross sales, (2) the managers' most unusual sales return story, and (3) the companies' sales return policy. Inquire whether any changes have been made recently in the sales return policy and whether any changes are being studied. Document your findings in a one-page report.

EYH5–2 Cash discounts (L.O. 1)

Cash discounts are offered to a purchaser as an incentive for rapid account settlement. Sometimes the incentive is effective; on other occasions it is not.

Instructions

Contact the sales and/or credit departments of three different companies that sell goods to other businesses on account. Determine (1) the typical discount terms given to customers, (2) the percentage of customers that take advantage of the discount within the discount period, and (3) the percentage of customers that take the discount even after the discount period has lapsed. With regard to the last issue, inquire about how the company handles the situation. Document your findings in a one-page report.

EYH5-3 Merchandising systems (L.O. 5)

Retailers are using a variety of inventory systems for their respective operations. Some systems are very sophisticated and can gather considerable marketing information that aids in future ordering of goods; other systems are rather basic.

Instructions

Visit three different retail stores (including one large chain store) and interview managers about the type of inventory system used (periodic or perpetual). Determine each system's degree of sophistication along with the system's advantages and disadvantages. Be prepared to report your findings to the class.

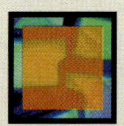

EYH5-4 Merchandising profitability, income reporting: Nordstrom, Inc., and Office Depot Inc. (L.O. 3, 4)

Nordstrom is one of the nation's leading fashion retailers, catering to middle and upper-middle income consumers. The company operates over 50 large specialty stores and four smaller stores, primarily on the West Coast. Office Depot, on the other hand, is the largest chain of office supply superstores in North America. The firm deep discounts everything from pencils to computers and focuses on small and mid-size businesses.

Instructions

By using the text's electronic data base, access the financial statements of both companies and answer the questions that follow. Unless otherwise indicated, responses should be based on data for the most recent year presented.

a. What is the largest current asset on each company's balance sheet? Is this finding somewhat expected, given the nature of the firms? Briefly explain.
b. Determine the cost of goods sold for both firms. Compare each company's presentation with that shown in Exhibit 5-4 and comment on your findings.
c. Determine the gross profit of both firms in dollars and as a percentage of net sales.
   (1) Consider the nature of each company's operation. Comment on what is likely causing the difference in the percentages that you calculated. (*Note:* Assume that both firms use the same methods to value inventory.)
   (2) Are there any differences in the manner of gross profit presentation on each firm's income statement? Discuss.
d. Determine the income statement format (single-step or multiple-step) used by each company. Does the format affect the presentation of gross profit? Briefly explain.

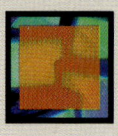

EYH5-5 Merchandising profitability, income reporting (L.O. 3, 4)

This problem is a duplication of Problem EYH5-4. It is based on two companies selected by your instructor.

Instructions

By using the text's electronic data base, access the specified companies' financial statements and focus on data for the most recent year reported. Answer requirements (a)–(d) of Problem EYH5–4.

EYH5–6 Analysis of merchandising data and activity (L.O. 3, 4)

As part of a class project for an accounting course, Paul Davis was asked to evaluate selected income and inventory data of two companies: LaStone and Q-Mart. LaStone operates a chain of jewelry stores in upscale shopping malls throughout the country. Q-Mart, on the other hand, has five discount department stores in California and Oregon. Selected data (in thousands of dollars) from the companies' financial statements follow.

	LaStone	Q-Mart
Net sales	$3,000	$6,400
Net purchases	1,400	3,800
Beginning inventory	400	900
Ending inventory	600	700

Both LaStone and Q-Mart employ a natural business year for reporting purposes, with the year-end occurring at the slowest point in the business cycle.

Davis recently completed a finance course where his instructor talked about gross profit and the ability of a firm to manage its inventories. The instructor noted that some companies sell goods more rapidly than others and are better able to generate cash and avoid inventory financing costs than their competitors.

Instructions

Assume the role of Paul Davis and answer the following:

a. Which of the two firms would probably generate a higher gross profit for each dollar of merchandise sold? Briefly explain the rationale behind your answer.
b. Determine whether your answer in part (a) was correct or incorrect by calculating gross profit for the two companies and then expressing gross profit as a percentage of net sales. Round computations to one decimal place.
c. Picture the movement of goods through the average LaStone and Q-Mart stores. Which of the two entities would probably move merchandise more quickly? Why?
d. Analyze the preceding data and computations. Explain how it is possible for companies that sell high-profit items and those that sell low-profit items to have roughly the same rate of bottom-line income (net income ÷ net sales) for a reporting period.
e. Given these firms' business cycles, would the natural business year most likely end on November 30, December 31, or January 31? Briefly explain.

COMMUNICATION OF ACCOUNTING INFORMATION

CAI5–1 Writing to influence: Woolworth Corporation (L.O. 3, 4)

Communication Principle: As an accounting student, you may think that the purpose for writing most business letters is to convey information. Actually, providing factual information is only one of several objectives. Underlying the obvious informational content may be an attempt to influence.

Most information requires interpretation or comment. With interpretation, the writer guides a reader to make decisions—investment or management decisions, for instance. Most business letters are informative, but they are also persuasive; that is, they persuade us to act or feel in one way or another. Good accounting writers will understand the hidden persuasion behind the numbers they present and will "direct" the reader toward a given outcome.

■ ■ ■ ■ ■ ■ ■ ■

Woolworth Corporation is a large multinational retailer, with over 8,300 stores in 22 countries. In addition to traditional Woolworth and Woolco stores, the firm owns Foot Locker, Kinney Shoes, Kids Mart, Champs Sports, and over 30 other recognizable retail chains. These chains deal primarily in footwear and apparel. A review of the company's income statements for three recent years revealed the following figures (in millions of dollars):

	19X3	19X2	19X1
Sales revenues	$9,626	$9,962	$9,914
Cost of goods sold	6,747	6,683	6,684
Selling & administrative expenses	2,615	2,501	2,575

Assume that you are an employee at Woolworth's corporate headquarters. An inexperienced investment adviser has written the company for selected financial information. (She has a client who is considering investing in Woolworth.) The following information is requested:

- The company's gross profit for each year.
- Yearly gross profit as a percentage of sales revenues, along with a comment on the company's gross profit trend over time.
- The firm's rate of cost incurrence as it relates to selling and administrative costs versus cost of goods sold. That is, examine these amounts as a percentage of sales and comment on your findings. Consider the nature of the retail market in general and Woolworth's operations in particular.

Instructions

Write a letter to the investment adviser that provides the information requested. Understand that the tone and style of your response will influence the advice ultimately given to the client.

Answers to Chapter Quiz

1. d
2. b
3. c ($1,700 + $2,900 − $2,000)
4. c ($8,000 − ($8,000 × 0.02) + $200)
5. a

6 ACCOUNTING SYSTEMS AND INTERNAL CONTROL

LEARNING OBJECTIVES

After studying this chapter, you should be able to:

1. Appreciate the role and importance of a good accounting system.
2. Explain the relationship between control accounts and subsidiary ledgers.
3. Recognize the features of a typical PC-based accounting system.
4. Describe the tasks performed by the general journal module and the processing related to sales and cash receipts as well as purchases and cash payments.
5. Explain the nature of internal control and identify various internal control procedures.
6. Recognize the growing problem of fraud and the need for special controls in a computerized accounting system.

During the first few years of firm operation, George Faris personally maintained most of Banner Advertising's accounting records. Nothing more than a basic manual processing system was needed. Actually, the business was very small and George had a good sense of awareness, allowing him to "mentally manage" the firm's affairs and keep most everything straight. As time progressed and the company grew, he found it necessary to hire a part-time bookkeeper. This solution was satisfactory—at least on a temporary basis.

You can well imagine the large volume (and variety) of transactions that Banner had to process. Each billboard typically required a monthly rental payment to the owner of the land where the board is located. In addition, there were utility bills for lighting, annual tax and permit fees, payments to sign painters and design artists, and commission payments to salespeople or advertising agencies. Banner also had to bill clients, collect receivables, and settle loans related to sign construction.

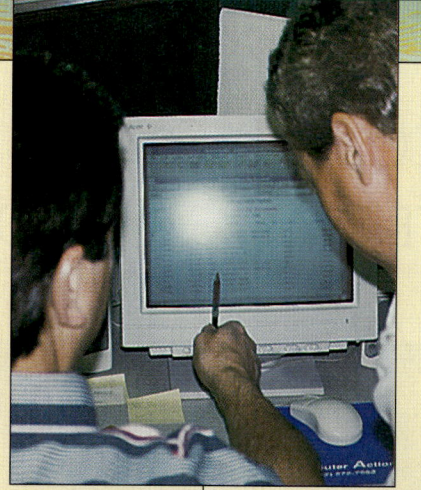

George noted, "I found myself in a rapidly growing business, and it didn't take a rocket scientist to see the benefits from automating our accounting system. The personal computer (PC) was perfectly suited to our needs." As a result, Banner Advertising now relies heavily on a PC-based system. The company uses commercially available software along with other packages that were developed specifically to meet the firm's needs. George observed, "There was a lot of initial grief in getting the system up and running, but I can safely say that our computers have more than paid for themselves. We continually search to automate even more of our mundane and repetitive tasks."

Accounting Information Systems

1 Appreciate the role and importance of a good accounting system.

Banner's experience is very typical. As a company expands, the volume of transactions that must be processed will increase. Furthermore, with more activity taking place, owners become further removed from daily operations and require additional information to manage the entity's financial affairs.

In many situations, overworked systems and personnel begin to be stretched for capacity and time. This is a typical phenomenon that may actually contribute to a slowing or reversal of a firm's growth, as costly accounting errors start to decrease profitability and customer satisfaction. For example:

- Invoices may be paid twice (or cash discounts missed).
- Receivables may go unbilled for extended periods.
- The amount of cash needed to pay bills tomorrow or next week is unknown.
- The availability of items in inventory cannot be readily determined.
- The accounting department may need excessive amounts of overtime to complete seemingly routine tasks on a punctual basis.[1]

[1] See "Computerizing an Accounting System," *DH+S Review,* October 24, 1988, pp. 7–8.

To help prevent these problems from occurring, many companies have made sizable investments in the design of a comprehensive **accounting information system (AIS).** An AIS is the network that processes transactions and ultimately produces financial statements and reports. Such systems generate information from *data* (i.e., a variety of facts, figures, and/or transactions) for use in reporting, planning, controlling, and decision-making activities. In other words, data serve as the raw material for determining the period's income, the ending accounts receivable balance, the total cash inflows related to a proposed investment, and other key measures to evaluate an entity and its associated components (activities, products, and so forth).

PROBLEMS WITH CONTEMPORARY SYSTEMS

Companies are continually striving to improve their accounting information systems, especially in light of sharp business competition and a growing urgency to control costs. Despite the significant progress that has been made in recent years, much work remains to be done. Managers frequently complain that (1) they lack the necessary information to perform their duties properly, and (2) reports arrive too late to be useful. Furthermore, some employees are so overwhelmed with computer printouts that there is not enough time in a day to study all the facts that flow across their desks.

Add to these problems the general "swelling" that has occurred in many companies' accounting departments, and a genuine challenge is created. Although transaction processing can be costly, it has not been subjected to the same streamlining as the manufacturing and marketing of products—the focal point of typical corporate restructuring efforts. As some firms have discovered, sizable savings can result.

To illustrate, Union Carbide recently found that it cost the company $16.22 to process a journal entry—roughly 10 times more than the amount spent by other industrial firms.[2] After performing an analysis of its accounting function, the company was able to eliminate 200 positions and improve profits by $20 million. Johnson & Johnson performed a similar study and made significant changes to its general ledger, accounts payable, and payroll processing systems. Even the manner in which the books were closed was changed. The company shifted from monthly to quarterly closings and reduced the time needed to close from 26 days to 7. All told, Johnson & Johnson has saved $84 million.

The preceding discussion should not be interpreted to mean that accounting systems are, in general, a disaster. This is far from the truth. Systems are light years ahead today in terms of development and capability when compared with the state-of-the-art of, say, fifteen years ago. Most companies have shifted away from manual systems, which are cumbersome, tedious, and inefficient in high-volume operations, to computers. Out of necessity, accountants have designed new methods to better control and streamline the accounting process.

The next few pages will provide you with an introduction to accounting information systems, proceeding from basic issues to the more complex. We will also take a look at various controls that are used to ensure that systems function as originally intended. Let us begin by focusing on system refinement and noting that automation is not mandatory to improve information processing.

[2] This discussion is based on "A Day of Reckoning for Bean Counters," *Business Week,* March 14, 1994, pp. 75–76.

SYSTEM REFINEMENTS

A good processing system does not evolve by accident. Rather, one must carefully consider what information is needed and then design an efficient technique to compile and deliver that information. For example, think about the way in which sales on account were recorded in the previous chapter: a debit to Accounts Receivable and a credit to Sales. The end-of-period receivables balance indicates the total amount due from customers, but how is the balance due from a particular customer to be determined? This is an important question, the answer to which requires a refinement to the processing elements introduced earlier. This refinement is the subsidiary ledger.

Subsidiary Ledgers and Control Accounts. As you already know, the general ledger houses the various accounts that appear on a company's financial statements. Frequently, it is necessary to divide the balances contained in several of these accounts into further detail. Common examples are shown in the table that follows.

> ❷ Explain the relationship between control accounts and subsidiary ledgers.

GENERAL LEDGER ACCOUNT	SUBDIVIDED BY
Accounts Receivable	Customer
Accounts Payable	Creditor/supplier
Merchandise Inventory	Individual inventory items
Sales	Product line and/or territory

A business must keep track of the amounts due from each customer, the balances owed to individual suppliers, and other specific information. Separate accounts are therefore established for each of these subdivisions. These accounts are collectively known as a **subsidiary ledger**—a group of lower level accounts that comprise a general ledger account. The general ledger account that is supported by subsidiary ledger accounts is, in turn, known as a **control account.**

If all accounting procedures are properly followed, the balance in a control account should equal the sum of the individual account balances contained within its subsidiary ledger. Thus, if Woodcraft Company lists $10,000 of accounts receivable on its May 31 balance sheet, the subsidiary ledger should contain customer accounts whose balances total $10,000. The equality between a subsidiary ledger and control account is checked on a periodic basis, often monthly, when a supporting schedule is prepared. The schedule is simply a listing of each account in the subsidiary ledger along with the related balance. Woodcraft's schedule of accounts receivable and the preceding relationships are shown in Exhibit 6–1.

A FURTHER FOCUS

When a credit sale or collection on account occurs, both the control account and the applicable customer account are updated. In many manual systems, for example, individual transactions are posted daily to the subsidiary ledger. The *totals* of these transactions (e.g., monthly credit sales, collections on account) are later posted to the control account, which is housed in the general ledger.

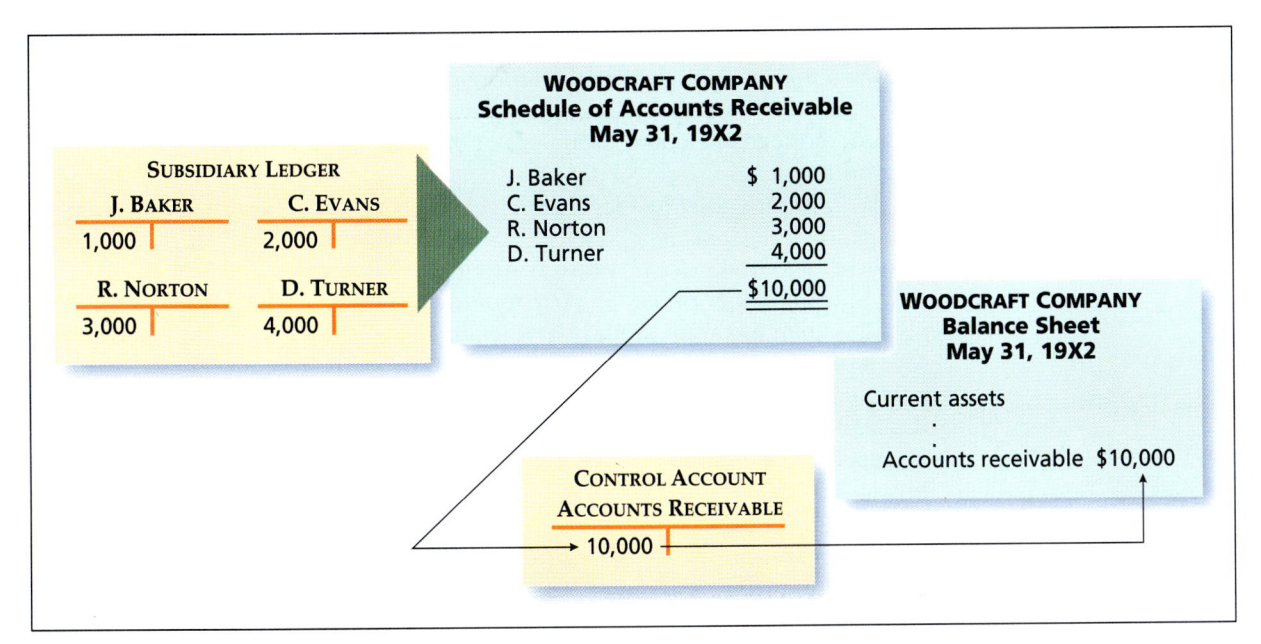

EXHIBIT 6–1
Subsidiary Ledger/Control Account Relationships

Processing Reduction in a Manual System. The use of subsidiary ledgers is but one system refinement. Over time a company is likely to implement a variety of special features that enable the firm to better satisfy its information needs. Unfortunately, as features are added, the system may become more unmanageable. Businesses must address this situation by implementing techniques that reduce the expanded amount of record keeping and detail while still providing the desired information.

A simplified example of such a technique is used by many doctors and dentists. Upon conclusion of a recent trip to a doctor's office, you may have been given a receipt that has a small strip of carbon on its back. It is likely that as the receipt was being prepared, the details of the transaction—date, patient name, amount due, and cash paid—were simultaneously being recorded (via the carbon strip) onto a summary sheet that serves as the practice's journal. Thus, the practice's daily activity in terms of revenues and cash collections can be determined quite readily. It is also highly probable that an individual patient's record, made with "impression paper," is being updated at the same time.

Special Journals. Another way to achieve a meaningful reduction in system procedure is by the use of *special journals*. These journals handle specific types of recurring transactions in ways that significantly decrease recording and posting procedures. Special journals are frequently used for sales of merchandise on account, purchases of merchandise on account, cash receipts, and cash disbursements. Appendix A at the end of the text provides a detailed look at the operation of a manually maintained special journal system.

COMPUTERIZED ACCOUNTING SYSTEMS

Both the carbon strip ("write-it-once") and special journal systems are a major step forward compared to the basic general journal/general ledger system discussed earlier in the book. Nevertheless, these systems are manual in operation and lack the efficiency needed in higher-volume transaction environments. Like Banner Advertising from the chapter's introduction, most companies have found that computers are the answer to a variety of record-keeping problems. Computers can process data more quickly and at a lower error rate than office personnel using manual accounting systems. Stated simply, electrical circuits do not become bored, fatigued, or emotional—real pluses when it comes to productivity.

With improved efficiency from electronics comes a lower cost per transaction processed. Costs have declined in recent years to the extent that even the smallest of companies can afford computers. Hardware and software that provide adequate data processing capability can now be purchased for considerably less than the annual salary and fringe benefit outlays for one bookkeeper. Much of this affordability can be attributed to an increase in the use of small, personal computers (commonly known as *PCs*), which have minimal installation and programming costs. Prewritten, or canned, programs are available for all aspects of a company's accounting activities, including payroll, billing, and inventory control. Thus, a business that uses a PC need not add a data processing specialist to its staff.

A word of caution: Yes, canned programs are readily obtainable and convenient, but no, such packages are not always satisfactory. Most programs that are available over the counter are designed for a broad range of users. Some of these packages can be modified to meet specific individual needs; others are available on an as-is basis. In general, the acquisition of quality accounting software is much like the purchase of a fine suit or dress: a reasonable amount of alteration may be required. This is not to say that functional programs cannot be obtained "off the rack" at very low cost. The comment merely suggests that most businesses are unique to a certain degree, and a customized accounting package may command a relatively high price.

FEATURES OF PC-BASED SYSTEM SOFTWARE

Computerized accounting systems tend to parallel manual accounting systems in terms of function and objective. As an example, both types of systems process transactions by using debits and credits, maintain ledger accounts, and produce financial statements and other reports for management. This is where the similarity ends, however, as the systems' form, organization, and procedures differ greatly. An entity's manual journals and ledgers are replaced by computer files that are kept on a storage medium such as a disk.[3] Posting and report preparation are automated, and the closing process is often performed by pressing a single key on the computer's keyboard. Furthermore, many computerized systems have built-in controls that examine data validity before accepting transactions as input. A transaction that erroneously contains an alphabetic character in a dollar amount field, for instance, would be rejected by the system. Automated systems also include certain maintenance routines that allow the user to add new accounts to the chart of accounts, revise financial statement formats, and perform other similar housekeeping chores.

ETHICS ISSUE

Your company has a very tight cash position and desperately needs an updated computerized accounting system. You can obtain illegal copies of the necessary software from a friend. What would you do?

3 Recognize the features of a typical PC-based accounting system.

---

[3] Accounting data are stored in computers by using records and files. A *record* stores information about one employee, one inventory item, one account, and so forth. A *file*, in contrast, is a group of records. For example, all customer records taken collectively comprise the accounts receivable file.

Most system packages subdivide the accounting tasks to be performed into modules, with each module handling a specific component of the overall accounting process. As you can probably imagine, the various software products on the market treat this division procedure differently. Some packages consist of modules for general ledger activity, accounts receivable activity, and accounts payable activity. Others follow a pattern that more closely parallels a typical manual accounting system, including separate routines for the general journal and each special journal. Modules may also be designed for payroll, cash management, and inventory, and to meet the specialized needs of manufacturers. Whatever the form, these individual units are subsequently integrated and comprise a company's accounting information system.

THE CONCEPT OF MODULAR ACCOUNTING

Processing modules serve to streamline the data entry process. Recording every transaction in general journal entry form is very inefficient, especially if the same type of transaction occurs with a high frequency. Given that each module will handle a specific facet of the work to be performed, it makes sense to provide a standardized format, or template, to input (capture) common data. For example, a module to record sales on account should provide a preformatted computer screen that requests the transaction date, customer name (or number), invoice number, and invoice amount. Also, the software could simplify the procedural steps to be performed by automatically recording certain parts of the transaction. Since a sale on account will always involve a debit to Accounts Receivable for the total invoice amount, the module may be preprogrammed to electronically calculate and input this portion of the entry.

Modules also lead to a division of labor, allowing employees to specialize in handling one part of the overall system (say, cash receipts processing). With specialization comes increased efficiency, as personnel become more familiar with a job and get to know it well.

Another advantage of modules relates to computer operations and parallels the benefit just cited. Generally speaking, transaction processing time and program efficiency are enhanced by breaking the workload into groups of like tasks. When this design approach is followed, software packages run fewer tests and perform less up-front data analysis to determine whether certain routines need to be accessed. In addition, program revision is usually simplified. It is normally much easier to "plug in" a new, self-contained unit than to overhaul an entire multipurpose system.

Accessing the Modules. The modules in a PC-based accounting system are accessed by employing a *menu*—a listing on the computer screen of the various program options available to a user. The options may be displayed by title or perhaps by the use of small pictorial representations called *icons*. A piece of paper may represent a report option, a file cabinet may signify a file routine, and so forth. Once an item is selected, the user is often directed to a submenu of further choices. For instance, if the reports option is selected, a submenu will then be displayed that lists the individual reports that can be produced.

EXHIBIT 6–2
Example of General Journal Module

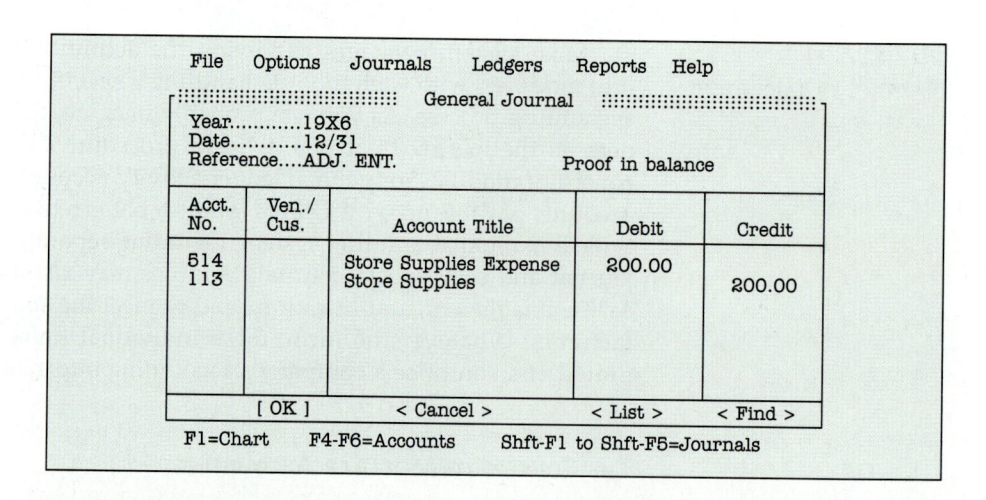

```
File    Options    Journals    Ledgers    Reports    Help
                          General Journal
 Year..........19X6
 Date..........12/31
 Reference....ADJ. ENT.                  Proof in balance

 Acct.    Ven./
 No.      Cus.       Account Title        Debit       Credit

 514                 Store Supplies Expense  200.00
 113                 Store Supplies                      200.00


        [ OK ]       < Cancel >      < List >     < Find >
     F1=Chart     F4-F6=Accounts    Shft-F1 to Shft-F5=Journals
```

> **4**
> Describe the tasks performed by the general journal module and the processing related to sales and cash receipts as well as purchases and cash payments.

THE JOURNAL MODULES

Journal modules are often the most frequently accessed part of an accounting systems package. Exhibit 6–2 contains a **general journal module**, which parallels the general journal introduced earlier in Chapter 2.[4] This module is used to process miscellaneous business transactions.

A close look at the top of the screen display will reveal a "proof" feature. This feature is merely a counter to indicate how much more of a debit or credit is needed to balance a journal entry. A user can thus easily determine the amount of debit or credit needed to complete the recording of a complex transaction.

Another option is shown at the bottom of the screen: F1=Chart. When the F1 button on the keyboard is pressed, the company's chart of accounts will be superimposed on the general journal (see Exhibit 6–3). This feature is desirable because most accounting software processes transactions on the basis of account numbers rather than account titles. Once an acceptable number is input by the system user, the correct title appears automatically, thus saving considerable keystrokes and time. Having fewer manually generated keystrokes also reduces the likelihood of errors.

EXHIBIT 6–3
Example of General Journal Module and Chart of Accounts

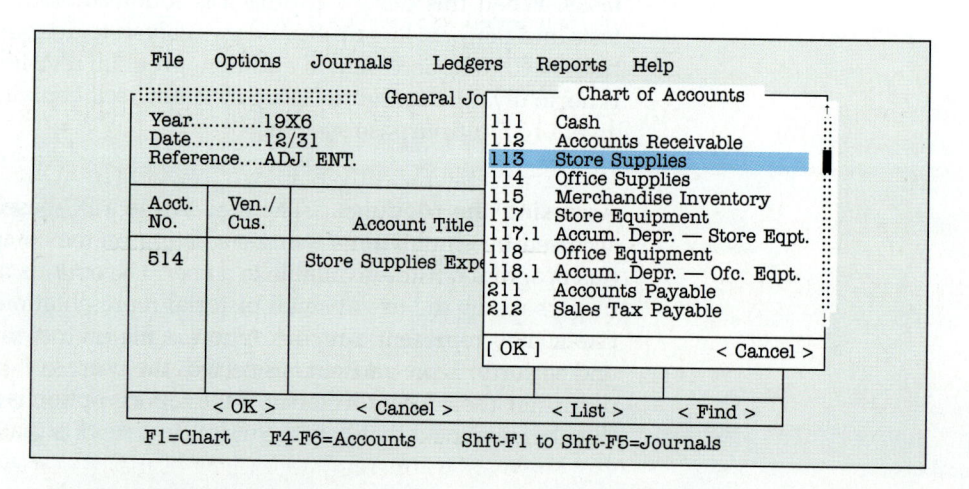

```
File    Options    Journals    Ledgers    Reports    Help
                    General Jo┌──── Chart of Accounts ────┐
 Year..........19X6            │111   Cash                │
 Date..........12/31           │112   Accounts Receivable │
 Reference....ADJ. ENT.        │113   Store Supplies      │
                               │114   Office Supplies     │
                               │115   Merchandise Inventory│
 Acct.    Ven./                │117   Store Equipment     │
 No.      Cus.   Account Title │117.1 Accum. Depr. — Store Eqpt.│
                               │118   Office Equipment    │
 514             Store Supplies Exp│118.1 Accum. Depr. — Ofc. Eqpt.│
                               │211   Accounts Payable    │
                               │212   Sales Tax Payable   │
                               │                          │
                               │ [ OK ]         < Cancel >│
                               └──────────────────────────┘
        < OK >       < Cancel >      < List >     < Find >
     F1=Chart     F4-F6=Accounts    Shft-F1 to Shft-F5=Journals
```

[4] The illustrations that appear on pages 224 and 225 are taken from the software package that accompanies this text.

EXHIBIT 6–4
Example of Sales Journal Module

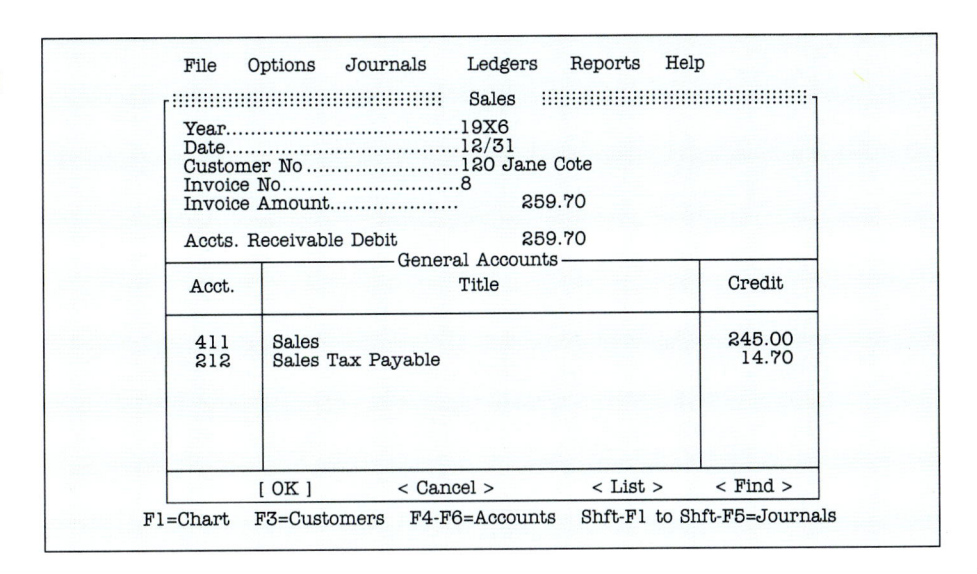

```
File   Options   Journals   Ledgers   Reports   Help
                          Sales
Year..........................19X6
Date..........................12/31
Customer No..................120 Jane Cote
Invoice No....................8
Invoice Amount...............    259.70

Accts. Receivable Debit         259.70
                  ──General Accounts──
  Acct.              Title                      Credit

  411      Sales                                 245.00
  212      Sales Tax Payable                      14.70




        [ OK ]      < Cancel >      < List >      < Find >
    F1=Chart   F3=Customers   F4-F6=Accounts   Shft-F1 to Shft-F5=Journals
```

Processing of Sales and Cash Receipts. Although all transaction recording and posting can be accomplished through the general journal, remember that processing efficiencies are associated with specialization. Exhibit 6–4 reveals the sales journal module, which is used to capture data pertaining to sales on account.

Notice a parallel with the general journal in terms of the basic format and design. The sales journal, though, also captures data relating to the customer and invoice number. (Observe that customer lists are easily accessed by pressing the F3 key.) Further, as shown toward the middle of the computer screen, the necessary debit to Accounts Receivable is automatically generated and recorded. A similar setup known as the cash receipts module is employed to input receipts from customers and other sources.

In more advanced systems, such as that shown in Exhibit 6–5, the software not only provides the basis for account maintenance but also generates various reports and documents. These reports and documents include:

- Sales invoices (see p. 178).
- Reports for management, such as sales subdivided by salesperson, territory, and product line.
- An analysis of receivables that identifies delinquent accounts.

Given that these system components handle both sales and collections, most software packages produce a detailed listing of the accounts receivable subsidiary ledger. The information contained here parallels the monthly billing that is sent to customers in the form of an *account statement* (see Exhibit 6–6).

Processing of Purchases and Cash Payments. The processing of purchases and cash payment transactions is handled in much the same fashion as that for sales and cash receipts. A purchases journal module is used to record purchases on account; the cash payments module is used to enter company disbursements. The operation of these modules is depicted in Exhibit 6–7.

Output from this processing includes numerous reports, such as detailed listings of all purchases on account. Activity sorted by individual suppliers is

226 CHAPTER 6

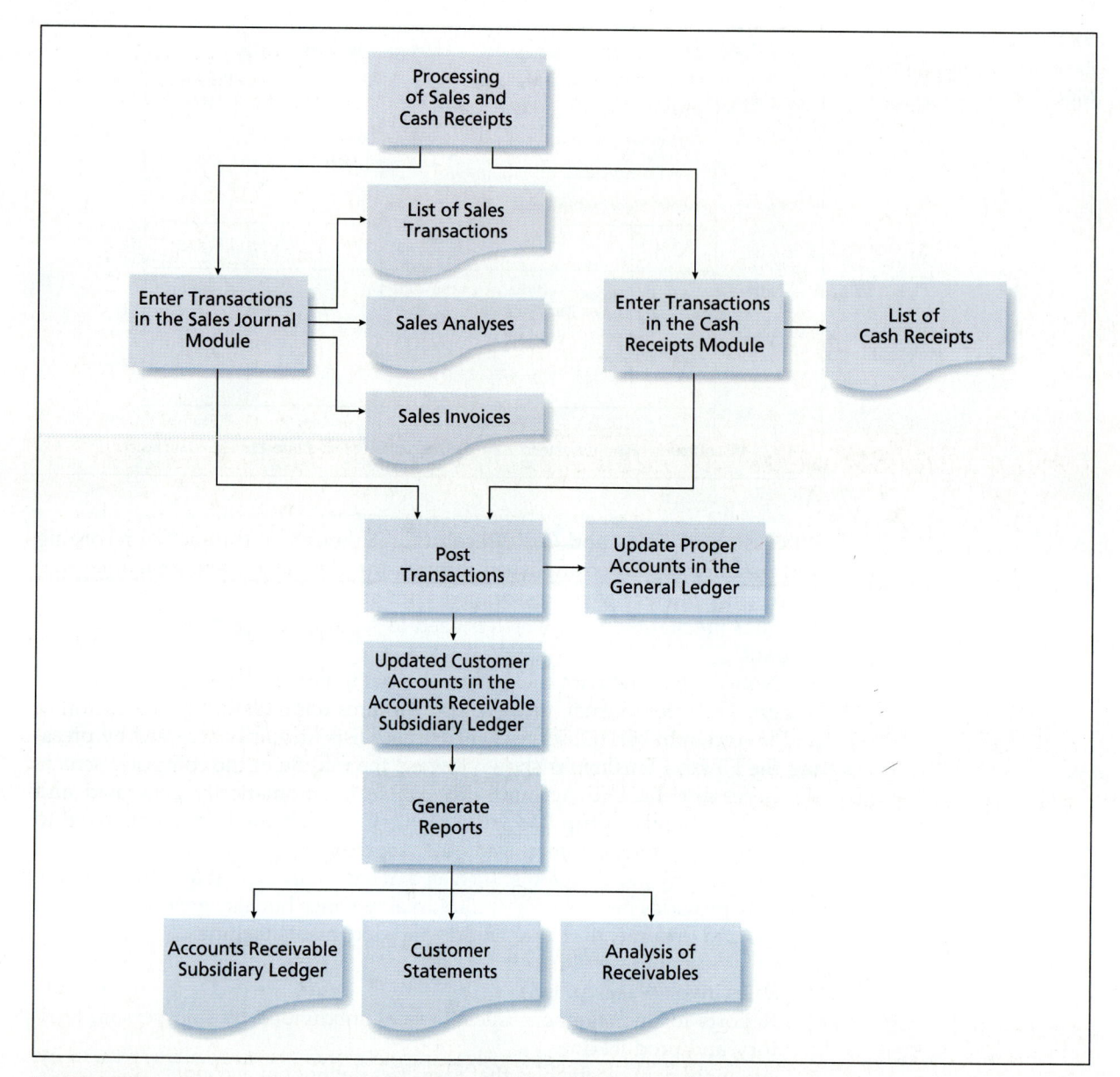

```
                    Processing
                    of Sales and
                    Cash Receipts
                    /          \
                   /            \
        ┌─────────┘              └─────────┐
        │                                   │
        ▼         List of Sales             ▼
  Enter Transactions  Transactions   Enter Transactions
  in the Sales Journal ─────►        in the Cash      ─────► List of
       Module      ─► Sales Analyses  Receipts Module         Cash Receipts
                   ─► Sales Invoices
        │                                   │
        └──────────────┬────────────────────┘
                       ▼
                   Post               Update Proper
                   Transactions ────► Accounts in the
                       │              General Ledger
                       ▼
                Updated Customer
                Accounts in the
                Accounts Receivable
                Subsidiary Ledger
                       │
                       ▼
                   Generate
                   Reports
                  /    │    \
                 /     │     \
     Accounts Receivable  Customer   Analysis of
     Subsidiary Ledger   Statements  Receivables
```

EXHIBIT 6–5
Processing of Sales and Cash Receipts

shown in a subsidiary ledger, which discloses purchases, cash payments, and amounts owed at the end of the period. Many software packages also handle the printing of checks and the attached *remittance advice* (a check stub that indicates the invoice being paid and the discount taken, if any). Such packages frequently contain built-in controls that match the invoices being processed against a list of previously paid invoices. This safeguard helps ensure that the same source document is not paid twice.

ARE COMPUTERIZED SYSTEMS ALWAYS THE ANSWER?

Computerized accounting systems are not a remedy for all business problems. A company should carefully analyze its particular situation to see if in fact the computer will do more to help than to hinder. Earlier in the chapter, for exam-

Statement of Account

WOODCRAFT COMPANY
1809 Highway 26
Colleyville, Texas 76034
(817) 582-2274

STATEMENT OF ACCOUNT

STATEMENT DATE	ACCOUNT NO.
5/31/X2	2943

PAST DUE AFTER THE 20TH.
LATE FEE WILL APPLY.

R. Norton & Associates
2119 Collins Ave.
Arlington, TX 76006

DATE PAID _____ CHECK NO. _____ AMOUNT _____

TRANSACTION DATE	INVOICE NO.	DESCRIPTION	AMOUNT	BALANCE
4/30/X2		BALANCE		126.30
5/03/X2	74632		80.00	206.30
5/10/X2	74719		450.00	656.30
5/17/X2		PAYMENT — THANK YOU!	126.30CR	530.00
5/29/X2	74802		2,470.00	3,000.00

CURRENT	OVER 30 DAYS	OVER 60 DAYS	OVER 90 DAYS	OVER 120 DAYS	TOTAL
3,000.00	0.00	0.00	0.00	0.00	3,000.00

WOODCRAFT COMPANY
1809 Highway 26
Colleyville, Texas 76034

PLEASE RETURN THIS PORTION WITH YOUR PAYMENT.

STATEMENT DATE	ACCOUNT NO.
5/31/X2	2943

AMOUNT REMITTED _____
IF PAYING BY INVOICE, CHECK THE INDIVIDUAL INVOICES PAID.

INVOICE NO.	AMOUNT DUE	✓
74632	80.00	
74719	450.00	
74802	2,470.00	

BALANCE DUE	TOTAL
	3,000.00

Accounts Receivable Subsidiary Ledger
R. Norton & Associates   ACCT. NO. 2943

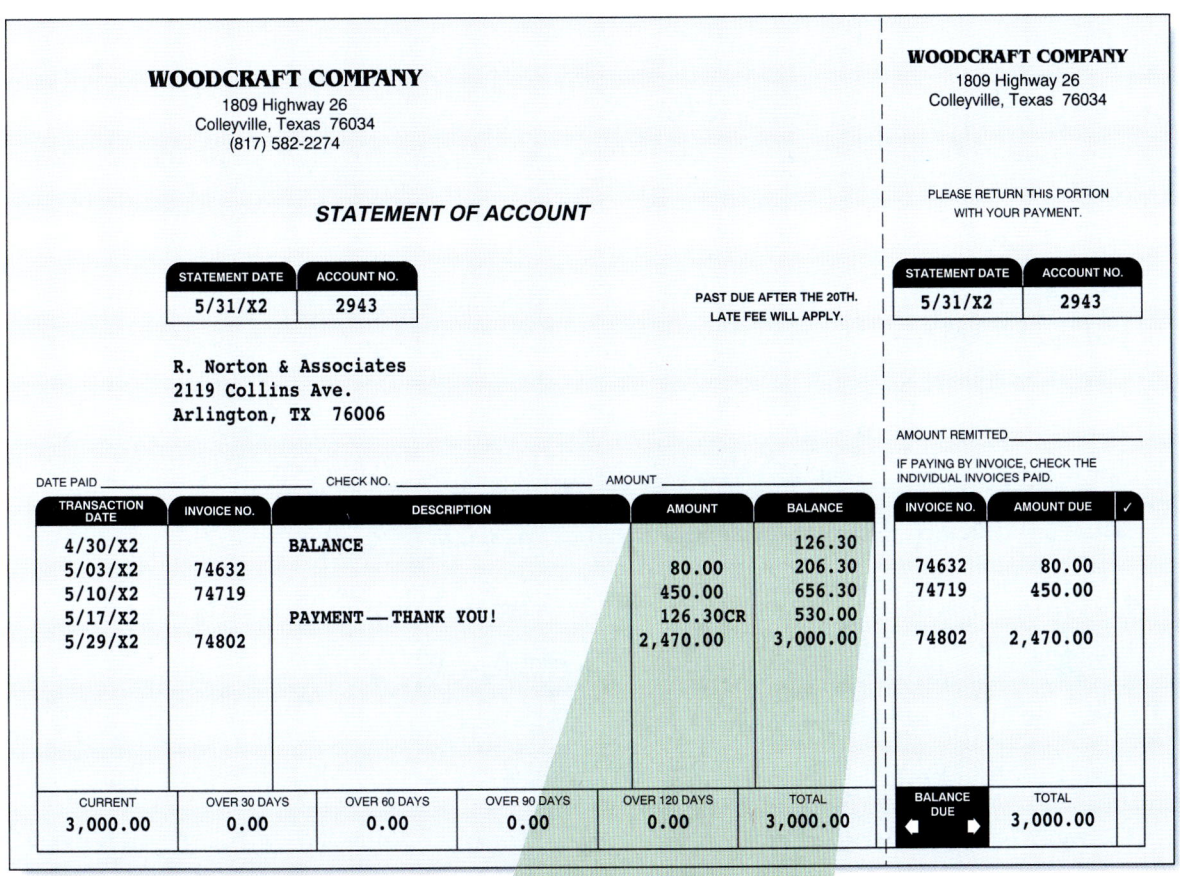

DATE	EXPLANATION	REF	DEBIT	CREDIT	BALANCE
4/30/X2	Balance				126.30
5/03/X2	74632	S29	80.00		206.30
5/10/X2	74719	S29	450.00		656.30
5/17/X2		CR17		126.30	530.00
5/29/X2	74802	S30	2,470.00		3,000.00

EXHIBIT 6–6
Relationship Between Customer Account Statement and Accounts Receivable Subsidiary Ledger

ple, we noted that high-speed processing networks are often accompanied by an endless string of reports and statistics. This mountain of output may not be needed and can potentially obscure important feedback, which gets lost in the shuffle. Also, in many small "mom and pop" businesses, inertia may prevail. Success in the past may lead such companies to adopt an attitude of "Don't fix what isn't broke." For these firms it is probably easier and more efficient to continue using a manual accounting system. As in any business decision, the costs and benefits must be weighed—even for those elements that are not easily quantified. An item that would definitely fall in this latter category is management's attitude toward change.

INTERNAL CONTROL

As noted on several occasions throughout this chapter, selected controls are built into software to prevent and detect the occurrence of errors. Such controls are not used solely with sophisticated computerized systems; they are employed with

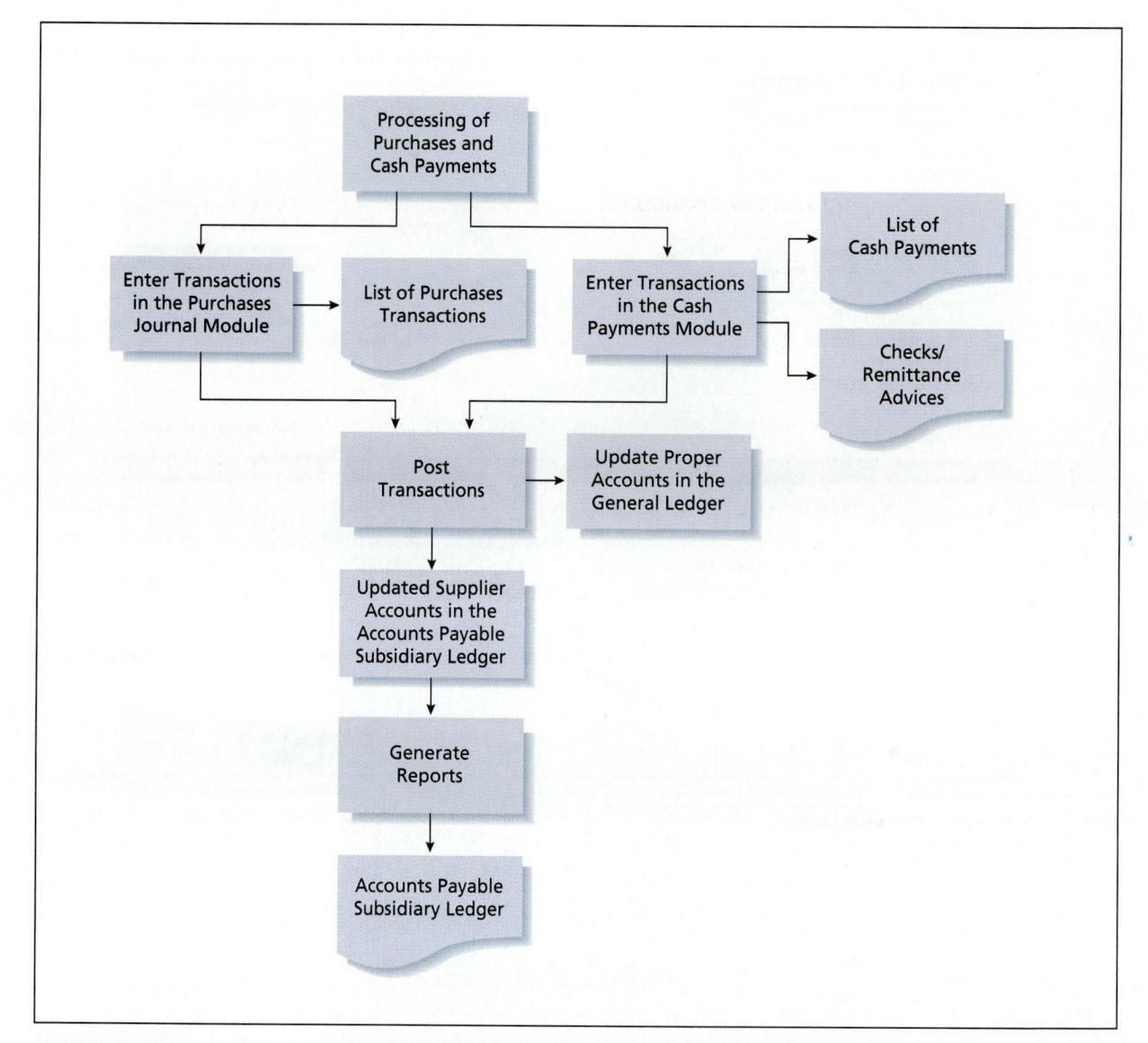

EXHIBIT 6–7
Processing of Purchases and Cash Payments

[Flowchart: Processing of Purchases and Cash Payments → Enter Transactions in the Purchases Journal Module → List of Purchases Transactions; Enter Transactions in the Cash Payments Module → List of Cash Payments, Checks/Remittance Advices; → Post Transactions → Update Proper Accounts in the General Ledger; Post Transactions → Updated Supplier Accounts in the Accounts Payable Subsidiary Ledger → Generate Reports → Accounts Payable Subsidiary Ledger]

basic manual systems as well. Stated simply, virtually all processing networks contain various checks and balances to ensure that data are processed correctly and that other objectives are achieved.

The concept of internal control is actually much broader than our basic examples could possibly convey. Perhaps the best way to start is by citing a 25+ year-old report on the financial health of the Long Island Railroad, a railroad well known to those who live in and around New York City.[5] The report noted that the commuter line was losing revenue and operating in an unproductive manner largely because of a weak accounting system—so weak that the carrier was criticized as being less well managed than the average household. To become more specific:

---

[5] See "Long Island Railroad Is Said to Be Losing Revenue Due to `Weak` Accounting System," *The Wall Street Journal,* February 18, 1971, p. 10.

- Cash balances had not been compared with bank statements for nearly a year, permitting an erroneous statement of cash position.
- Time sheets failed to reflect workers who arrived late and left early.
- Large amounts due the railroad hadn't been billed.
- Approximately 20,000 blank payroll checks were found in an unsecured vault; signed payroll checks were left lying on desks unprotected.
- A study of the number of tickets sold versus the number of passengers riding the trains showed an average of 670,000 free rides a month during a seven-month period.

Although the preceding situation may seem unthinkable and perhaps even laughable, similar occurrences are repeated on a daily basis in many businesses throughout the country.

Accountants recognize that designing a perfect system is an impossibility, as errors and inefficiencies will often occur when transactions are processed. A limited number of accidental errors are expected and tolerated; conversely, intentional errors via employee sabotage, fraud, and/or embezzlement are unacceptable. To minimize the probability of error occurrence and improve the credibility of financial statements and reports, features known as internal controls are designed and used by businesses. We can define **internal control** as the various measures adopted by an organization to safeguard company assets, check the reliability and accuracy of accounting information, ensure compliance with management policies, and evaluate operating performance and efficiency.

> **5** Explain the nature of internal control and identify various internal control procedures.

A LAWYER'S PERSPECTIVE

The Significance of Controls: Large corporations are headed by a group known as the board of directors. This shareholder-elected body is involved with a number of corporate matters, including review of the entity's accounting controls and financial reporting practices. Generally, this work is performed by directors who serve on a separate audit committee.

The audit committee is accountable for the implementation of control procedures that will safeguard resources and ultimately protect the corporation's good name. The group's work has important legal ramifications, since a failure to fulfill these duties may be viewed as a breach of a director's fiduciary responsibility. Consider the outcome of the so-called savings and loan debacle of the 1980s, when many financial institutions failed and investors lost billions of dollars. Weak or nonexistent internal controls were often blamed for this tragedy, as controls failed to detect irregular and sometimes fraudulent activities. The outcome? A number of these institutions and their boards were sued by both investors and banking regulators. This unfortunate situation shows that even straightforward accounting practices (such as internal control) can find their way into the legal system and eventually to the courtroom.

THE INTERNAL CONTROL STRUCTURE

The control structure (i.e., framework) of a business is dependent on several factors, including the accounting system itself, the control environment, and numerous control procedures.[6] Let us focus on the latter two elements for a moment.

A company's control environment represents the combined effect of many factors that relate to the implementation and evaluation of specified firm policies. For example, the environment is influenced by anything from sound personnel practices that enable a business to attract, motivate, and compensate competent personnel, to what may be viewed as the most crucial link in setting the overall control "tone" of the entity: management's philosophy and operating style. Is management prone to take and monitor business risks? What is the company's attitude toward financial reporting? Do executives exercise care in daily operations and in meeting budget and income goals? These issues tend to reflect the overall emphasis and importance of control within a firm, as top management attitudes are often adopted and reflected at lower levels of the organizational structure.

In addition to creating a suitable control environment, a business must also establish various control procedures to ensure that company goals will be achieved. These procedures are integrated into both the control environment and accounting systems and generally include the following.

Limited Access to Assets. The safeguarding of assets is a stated objective of internal control. One way to achieve this objective is by limiting the access to assets to only a few authorized personnel. Limited access may take different forms. For example, customers normally are not permitted in the back of a store to roam freely through the merchandise awaiting sale. This area is reserved for employees only. Furthermore, access to a company's mainframe computer, valuable processing time, and data files is usually gained only after a secret password is entered into a computer terminal. The password is known by a select few. And finally, when many retail establishments close for business at the end of the day, the cash that has been collected is often counted in a locked room. All of these procedures are designed to ensure that assets are adequately protected from theft and unauthorized use.

Separation of Duties. Many different functions (duties) performed within a company pertain to the firm's financial activities. These duties are frequently categorized into the following broad classes:

- Transaction authorization
- Transaction recording
- Asset custody

To explain, someone must first authorize a transaction. Later the transaction must be entered in the accounting records. Finally, because virtually all transactions immediately or eventually affect an asset, an entity must control and closely monitor its valuable resources.

To achieve the stated objectives of internal control, a business must provide for an adequate separation of duties. Incompatible duties, namely, authorization, recording, and custody, must be performed by different employees within

[6] Much of this discussion is based on "Consideration of the Internal Control Structure in a Financial Statement Audit," *Statement on Auditing Standards No. 55*, American Institute of Certified Public Accountants, Inc., Jersey City, New Jersey, 1988.

an organization. Such separation helps to detect errors, since different personnel will be handling different aspects of the same transaction. In effect, then, the employees will be checking each other's work, and the likelihood that an error will proceed through a system from beginning to end is reduced.

Aside from assisting in error detection, separation of authorization, recording, and custody also makes fraud and embezzlement more difficult. As an example, suppose Rhonda Martin and Joe Harrison are both employed at the same firm. Martin physically handles the company's cash receipts, while Harrison maintains the Cash account in the accounting records. An adequate separation of duties is present in this case because physical control over the asset (i.e., custody) is segregated from transaction record keeping. Imagine, however, what could happen if Harrison was laid off and Martin, in addition to her present job, also assumed Joe's duties. If she desired, Martin could steal funds from the company and then adjust the accounting records to conceal the embezzlement. Two incompatible functions have been combined, opening the door for a variety of creative schemes.

Martin would have been less inclined to embezzle in the original situation, because Harrison would be maintaining an independent record of all transactions related to Cash and, in effect, monitoring Rhonda's actions. Of course, even if duties were separated in the appropriate manner, the theft would have still been possible had both employees conspired to defraud the company. Such a conspiracy is called *collusion*.

Accountability Procedures. A business can adopt different measures to achieve financial accountability. These measures, known as **accountability procedures,** may help to pinpoint responsibility within an organization, protect the assets, or detect errors. The measures vary and depend on the size and nature of a firm. Common accountability procedures include duty authorization, prenumbered documents, and verification of records.

Duty Authorization. Pinpointing responsibility is essential in medium and large organizations. In small businesses, the owner/manager handles many of the accounting and financial activities. In larger entities, where the tasks are too numerous for one individual to perform, the accounting duties are divided among the various employees. Each employee is authorized to perform certain functions and, as a result, is held accountable for those functions.

Frequently, the actions taken by personnel result in some form of documentation to provide the necessary basis for accountability. Did you ever observe, for example, that store clerks often initial customer checks, sales invoices, and other similar documents? These procedures assist management in pinpointing responsibility and are especially helpful should a question or problem arise. Management can quickly determine the employee involved and then take any necessary corrective action.

Prenumbered Documents. Important forms such as checks, sales invoices, and purchase orders are usually serially prenumbered and subsequently accounted for. This practice permits the discovery of missing documents by detecting a break in the numbering scheme. An investigation can then commence to locate the source of the problem.

Verification of Records. Another widely used accountability procedure is verification of company records by comparison with company assets. For example:

- At the end of the day, a sales-entry terminal is emptied, and the cash collected is compared against the terminal's tape.
- At the end of the month, a business compares the amount of cash in its checkbook against a statement issued by the bank.
- At the end of the annual reporting period, a firm counts inventory and compares the actual hand count against a perpetual book count.

If the comparisons do not agree, suspicions may be raised regarding errors in the recording process or possible theft.

A Further Focus

A typical example of record verification occurs at the Six Flags Great America theme park in Illinois. To compute the park's official daily attendance, employees compare the number of tickets sold (including visitors who enter on season passes) against turnstile counts. Officials admit, however, that the accuracy of turnstile counts is limited by several factors: malfunctioning meters, wheel-chair and stroller-bound guests who bypass the device, and double-turns by guests. Differences between the ticket and turnstile totals are calculated and are usually insignificant in amount. Any sizable differences are investigated, and after reconciling, the day's attendance is entered in the accounting records.

Source: "Theme Park Accounting: What Do We Really Do All Winter?," *Management Accounting*, February 1994, pp. 48–51.

Independent Review. Personnel changes, the introduction of certain "short-cuts" by employees to improve job efficiency, and other similar occurrences may result in established procedures not being followed. In view of this situation, businesses should continually evaluate their accounting controls to determine if the controls are functioning as originally intended. Such evaluations are commonly made by internal auditors, who are far removed from daily activities to ensure that an independent review may be provided.

Large organizations also have a thorough examination (i.e., an audit) performed by an external CPA firm. Keep in mind that the transactions processed through a system affect an entity's financial statements. Because the external CPA must express an opinion about the fairness of the statements, an evaluation of the internal controls in operation is needed. The results of the CPA's examination are ultimately delivered to management so that appropriate corrective actions may be taken.

Costs and Benefits. Any business can design a system with elaborate controls, but exactly how far should companies go? Should a small firm hire several additional employees just to maintain an adequate separation of duties? Should a company perform a thorough background check and take extra security precautions for an employee who, on a part-time basis, issues cash refunds to customers? For many organizations, these and related questions are difficult to answer.

When designing and installing specific internal controls, the accountant must treat each business individually, because no two entities are alike. The accountant must study the errors that can occur and the probability of occurrence. Once the probability is determined, controls must be selected for which the *benefits of use exceed the costs of implementation and operation*. If this practice is followed, an organization will have a positive and financially beneficial approach to internal control.

BUSINESS BRIEFING

BRUCE HINCKLEY
Vice-President and Controller
Caesars World

Casinos and Internal Control

The internal control procedures over the cash systems in a casino are extensive, similar to those of many financial institutions. In addition to being monitored by both internal and external auditors, procedures relating to cash management, integrity of the games, and credit granting policies are evaluated by state regulators. Violating or failing to comply with proper controls can result in a loss of operating license.

Furthermore, if controls are inadequate or not being followed, theft can occur. As an example, one of our casinos received complaints from patrons that winning football betting tickets, which were being mailed in for redemption, were not being paid. An investigation later found that the tickets *were* being cashed—in the casino's sports book area.

To isolate the problem, an employee placed bets for both teams in selected games and mailed the winning tickets along with instructions as to where the proceeds were to be sent. The automated ticket system was programmed to call security if any of these tickets were redeemed in the sports book area. It turns out that the spouse of a mail room employee was apprehended, as mail room procedures allowed both easy access to winning tickets and the destruction of any accompanying correspondence. Subsequently, additional controls were installed to prevent this irregularity from recurring.

FRAUD IN CORPORATE AMERICA

> **6**
> Recognize the growing problem of fraud and the need for special controls in a computerized accounting system.

KPMG Peat Marwick, a large international public accounting firm, recently took an extensive look at fraud in the United States.[7] America's 2,000 largest companies were surveyed, and 75% of the respondents reported experiencing some type of fraud in the year that preceded the study. In sum, more than 40,000 individual fraudulent acts were committed. The most popular acts were misappropriations of funds, check forgery, credit card fraud, false invoices, and theft. Twenty-three percent of the respondents reported losses of $1 million or more; the median loss was $200,000.

Interestingly, the report's authors concluded that internal controls were both "heroes and villains." Established controls were the most frequently cited reason that frauds were detected; in contrast, poor controls were the most frequently cited reason that frauds took place. The importance of a strong control system cannot be stressed enough, especially given that a majority of respondents anticipate a growth in fraudulent acts in future years.

[7] See *Fraud Survey Results: 1993*, KPMG Peat Marwick, New York, 1994.

THE IMPACT OF THE COMPUTER

The use of computers to process accounting data has added a new dimension to both internal control and fraud. Bear in mind that data are collected, processed, and stored in ways that are not visible to the human eye. This characteristic creates problems with record and file management, hard-copy documentation of system operation, and the possibility of data alteration or destruction. Unique controls must therefore be implemented in an effort to ensure data integrity. Thorough studies of electronic data processing (EDP) systems have gained so much prominence that a new specialty area has emerged in the accounting profession: EDP auditing.

Computer Fraud and Misuse. The chance of fraud is a basic problem associated with EDP systems. **Computer fraud,** which involves the use of computers to aid in and conduct a fraud or embezzlement, seems to be occurring with increased frequency. Schemes have been undertaken to steal anything from credit card numbers to software to cash. The business literature is full of such examples.

Computer fraud is only one of the problems that organizations must face. Sabotage of data files, personal use of a company's computer resources, and thefts of hardware further complicate the picture. Computer crime, be it fraud or otherwise, is big business. It is difficult to assign an exact dollar value to these incidents because of the inability of companies to quantify their losses. Also, for fear of embarrassment and bad publicity, knowledge of computer-related incidents often remains solely within the organization involved.[8] One fact is fairly certain though: computer misuse is often facilitated by inadequate controls in an entity's data processing network.

> **ETHICS ISSUE**
>
> You oversee the payroll system of a huge corporation. To improve security, an employee has suggested hiring as a consultant an ex-computer hacker, who was once the subject of a federal investigation into computer crime. How would you react?

[8] Reporters from *Forbes* magazine assigned a wide-ranging figure to the yearly cost of computer crime: anywhere from a low of $500 million to a high of $5 billion. See "The Playground Bullies Are Learning How to Type," *Forbes*, December 21, 1992, pp. 184–189.

END-OF-CHAPTER REVIEW

LEARNING OBJECTIVES: THE KEY POINTS

1. **Appreciate the role and importance of a good accounting system.** The network that processes transactions and ultimately produces financial statements and other reports is known as an accounting information system. The manual system introduced in earlier chapters is acceptable, but system operation becomes cumbersome as the volume of transactions grows. To avoid costly errors, late reports, and general inefficiencies, companies must adapt and add refinements to their processing methods. These refinements include "write-it-once" systems, special journals, and computer technology.

2. **Explain the relationship between control accounts and subsidiary ledgers.** Control accounts appear on the financial statements and are comprised of various lower level accounts. The "lower level accounts," when taken collectively, make up the subsidiary ledger. As an example, the Accounts Receivable control account on the balance sheet is supported by customer accounts contained in the subsidiary ledger. At the end of a reporting period, the balance in the control account must equal the sum of the balances in the subsidiary ledger.

ACCOUNTING SYSTEMS AND INTERNAL CONTROL

3. **Recognize the features of a typical PC-based accounting system.** Computerized accounting systems tend to parallel manual accounting systems in terms of function and objective. Both types of systems process transactions, maintain ledger accounts, and produce financial statements. However, computerized systems preserve data on storage media such as disks; automate posting, report generation, and closing routines; and have built-in logic tests to judge transaction validity. In addition, most packages divide the accounting process into modules. These modules are integrated to comprise the complete accounting system.

4. **Describe the tasks performed by the general journal module and the processing related to sales and cash receipts as well as purchases and cash payments.** The general journal module is used to process miscellaneous business transactions. Sales and cash receipts processing are handled through the respective use of the sales journal module and the cash receipts module. The latter two components have a direct link with accounts receivable and allow companies to maintain the accounts receivable subsidiary ledger; prepare invoices and customer statements; and generate reports that are used to analyze sales and delinquent accounts. In contrast, purchasing and cash payments processing are handled by the purchases journal module and the cash payments module. Given the tie-in to accounts payable, the related processing results in an updated accounts payable subsidiary ledger, checks and remittance advices, and assorted reports.

5. **Explain the nature of internal control and identify various internal control procedures.** Internal controls are various measures that help to safeguard a company's assets, check the reliability and accuracy of the accounting information produced, ensure compliance with management policies, and evaluate operating performance and efficiency. Such controls may take many different forms, including limiting the access to assets to a few authorized personnel, maintaining an adequate separation of duties, implementing systems of authorization and approval, having prenumbered documents, and performing verifications of company records.

6. **Recognize the growing problem of fraud and the need for special controls in a computerized accounting system.** Fraud is a growing problem in American businesses, one that is expected to get worse in future years. Surveys have indicated that weak internal controls are often a primary contributing factor behind many of the schemes undertaken.

   Special controls are needed in computerized environments to address the issue of data integrity; more specifically, policies and safeguards for file management, system documentation, and data destruction. (Keep in mind that much of the processing takes place in ways that are not visible to the human eye.) Although computers have had a significant impact on business efficiency, they have also created a new problem area for firms: computer fraud and misuse.

KEY TERMS AND CONCEPTS: A QUICK OVERVIEW

accountability procedures Internal control procedures that help to pinpoint responsibility, protect assets, or detect errors. Include duty authorization, prenumbered documents, and verification of records. (p. 231)

accounting information system The network that processes transactions and generates financial statements and other reports. (p. 219)

cash payments module The module in a computerized accounting system that is used to process company disbursements. (p. 225)

cash receipts module The module in a computerized accounting system that is used to input receipts from customers and other sources. (p. 225)

computer fraud   A scheme in which a computer is used to aid and abet in a fraud or embezzlement. (p. 234)

control account   A general ledger account that is composed of various subsidiary ledger accounts. (p. 220)

general journal module   The module of a computerized accounting system that is used to process miscellaneous business transactions. (p. 224)

independent review   An internal control feature that involves the review and evaluation of accounting controls by an independent external auditor. (p. 232)

internal control   The various measures adopted by a company to safeguard assets, check the reliability and accuracy of financial information, ensure compliance with management policies, and evaluate operating performance and efficiency. (p. 229)

menu   A computerized listing that shows the various program options available to a user. (p. 223)

purchases journal module   The module in a computerized accounting system that is used to record purchases on account. (p. 225)

sales journal module   The module of a computerized accounting system that is used to record sales on account. (p. 225)

separation of duties   An internal accounting control that requires separation of transaction authorization, transaction recording, and asset custody. (p. 230)

special journals   Journals that handle specialized (specific) types of transactions (cash receipts, sales, and so forth). (p. 221)

subsidiary ledger   A group of lower level accounts that comprise a general ledger account. (p. 220)

CHAPTER QUIZ

The five questions that follow relate to several issues raised in the chapter. Test your knowledge of the issues by selecting the best answer. (The answers appear on p. 249.)

1. The Accounts Receivable control account:
   a. is found in the subsidiary ledger.
   b. is found in the general ledger.
   c. never appears on the balance sheet.
   d. serves as the basis for preparing the schedule of accounts receivable.

2. A computerized accounting system:
   a. eliminates the need for internal controls.
   b. is appropriate only if a company has a large, mainframe computer.
   c. tends to reduce transaction processing costs in high-volume situations.
   d. focuses on spreadsheets, which are listings of program options available to a user.

3. Which of the following tasks would normally be performed by the general journal module?
   a. Generating sales reports.
   b. Maintaining the accounts receivable subsidiary ledger.
   c. Processing of customer account statements.
   d. Processing of miscellaneous transactions.

4. Which of the following is not consistent with a strong system of internal control?
   a. Transaction record keeping and asset custody are handled by the same employee.
   b. The accounting records are audited at year-end by an external CPA.

c. At the end of the day the cash collected is compared with the tape produced by the sales-entry terminal.
   d. A company's computer facility has a restricted, keycard employee entry system.
5. The implementation of specific internal control procedures should be considered:
   a. only in manual accounting systems.
   b. when the accounting records are in need of verification.
   c. when the benefits of implementation and use exceed the related costs.
   d. regardless of the associated costs.

SUMMARY PROBLEM

Jupiter Company uses a PC-based accounting system, similar to the system described in this chapter.

Instructions

a. Why is a computerized accounting system typically divided into modules?
b. What modules would likely be used to process the vast majority of the firm's customer transactions?
c. Briefly explain the relationship between the Accounts Receivable control account and the Accounts Receivable subsidiary ledger.
d. Assuming that workload is not a problem, comment on the advisability of allowing Jupiter's bookkeeper to work in the firm's mailroom on a part-time basis.

Solution

a. Modules streamline the data-entry process. For example, recurring transactions can be input in a standardized format via a template. Such an approach saves processing time and keystrokes. Modules also facilitate the division of labor, resulting in increased efficiency because of work force specialization. This practice also allows for batch processing of similar transactions, again contributing to a more efficient work environment. Finally, modular systems are easily modified without having to overhaul the complete accounting system.
b. Sales journal module and cash receipts module.
c. The Accounts Receivable control account is housed in the general ledger and contains a "summary" (i.e., total) of the balances due from customers. The account's balance eventually appears on a company's balance sheet. The underlying details of the amounts in the control account are contained in the Accounts Receivable subsidiary ledger. Here, individual accounts for each customer are maintained. If all procedures are properly followed, the period-end balance in the control account should coincide with the sum of the account balances in the subsidiary ledger.
d. This arrangement is not desirable from a control perspective, as it allows the bookkeeper (record-keeping function) to have potential access to incoming receipts from customers (asset custody). The end result is an inadequate separation of duties.

ASSIGNMENT MATERIAL

QUESTIONS

Q6–1 What is a control account and where is it found?

Q6–2 Describe how a system that relies on carbon-backed impression paper can be used to reduce processing tedium.

Q6–3 What are some of the benefits of using a computerized accounting system?

Q6–4 What are some of the similarities and differences between manual accounting systems and computerized accounting systems?

Q6–5 Explain the concept of modular accounting systems. Briefly discuss several benefits associated with the use of modules.

Q6–6 How are modules accessed in a computerized accounting system?

Q6–7 What is a customer statement? What information does the statement disclose?

Q6–8 Briefly explain the meaning of internal control.

Q6–9 In general, which accounting functions should be separated because of a lack of compatibility?

Q6–10 What benefits are provided by an adequate separation of duties?

Q6–11 What is the purpose behind the serial prenumbering of important documents?

Q6–12 List several common procedures that are performed to help ensure that company accounting records are in agreement with company assets.

Q6–13 What is the purpose of the independent review, as performed by an external CPA?

Q6–14 What ultimate guideline should be used to decide the specific controls to build into a system?

Q6–15 Briefly list several of the unique control problems associated with computerized accounting applications.

EXERCISES

E6–1 Control accounts and subsidiary ledgers (L.O. 2)

San Dimas, Inc., maintains a subsidiary ledger for the amounts due from individual customers. A review of the accounting records at the beginning of the year showed customer balances for Carter, $800; Clinton, $400; and Quayle, $750. During January, the company had the following sales on account:

CUSTOMER	AMOUNT
Bush	$700
Cuomo	250
Gore	200
Quayle	600
Wilson	460

By month-end, Clinton and Bush had paid their account balances in full.

a. What is the relationship between control accounts and subsidiary ledgers?
b. Prepare the January 31 schedule of accounts receivable, assuming that all transactions have been properly recorded and posted.
c. Determine the January 31 balance in the Accounts Receivable control account.
d. Is the Accounts Receivable control account found in the general ledger, on the month-end balance sheet, or both?

E6–2 Control accounts and subsidiary ledgers (L.O. 2)

Franklin Manufacturing maintains a subsidiary ledger of the amounts owed to individual suppliers. A review of the accounting records at the end of March revealed the following balances:

Interstate Supply	$5,800
Lincoln Corporation	1,900
Rogers & Hart	2,200

a. Prepare the proper disclosure of this information on the company's March 31 balance sheet.
b. Would the subsidiary ledger ordinarily serve as the source for the answer to part (a)? Explain.
c. What month-end procedure would Franklin probably follow to help ensure that the subsidiary ledger balances are relatively error-free?
d. Suppose that on April 10, Franklin paid Lincoln $1,200 on account. Briefly describe what Franklin must do to keep the accounting records in balance.

E6–3 Overview of computerized accounting systems (L.O. 3)
Dolby Carpet Cleaners uses a manual accounting system. The company has grown over the years, and Dolby is finding that the increase in volume is taxing the capacity of its system and employees. Patricia Green, the firm's CPA, has recommended the acquisition of a personal computer (PC) to ease the record-keeping burden.

What benefits might Dolby experience by using a personal computer and a PC-based accounting system?

E6–4 Analysis of computer output (L.O. 3)
Lucky-K Stores recently installed a computerized accounting software package. The company's banker immediately noticed the computer-generated appearance of the monthly financial statements and asked whether the statements would differ if manual procedures had continued in use.

a. Should the manner in which accounting data are gathered and compiled have any significant effect on the firm's financial statements? Briefly explain.
b. Assume that the monthly financial statements included many additional schedules and reports because of the ease with which the computer generated this information. Do you see any potential problems with this "feature" of computerized accounting systems? Briefly discuss.

E6–5 System modules and their use (L.O. 4)
Epic Superstores uses a computerized accounting system identical to that described in this chapter. The system consists of a general journal module, sales journal module, cash receipts module, purchases journal module, and cash payments module. Identify the module(s) that would be used to record the following transactions or perform the stated tasks:

a. Borrowed $50,000 from Tulsa Federal Bank & Trust.
b. Acquired merchandise on account from Metro Lighting.
c. Generated a report that disclosed revenues earned by each of the company's 28 stores.
d. Recorded the month-end adjusting entries.
e. Produced checks and remittance advices, to be mailed to suppliers.
f. Produced customer account statements.
g. Generated a report that would be used to monitor the company's bank deposits.

E6–6 Overview of systems concepts (L.O. 2, 3, 4)
Evaluate the comments that follow as being True or False. If the comment is false, briefly explain why.

a. A subsidiary ledger is nothing more than a detailed breakdown of a general ledger control account.
b. If all procedures are properly performed, the end-of-period balance in a control account should equal the sum of the individual account balances contained in the subsidiary ledger.
c. The general journal module of a PC-based accounting system is used to process miscellaneous business transactions.
d. To enter a journal entry, most software packages require the user to key in the full and correct account name.
e. Customer account statements are prepared on the basis of information captured by the purchases journal module and the cash payments module.

E6–7 Internal control weaknesses (L.O. 5)

Sarah Stender recently opened a small jewelry store in a major shopping district. Because the business is new, Sarah could afford to hire only one employee. Marci Hopson, an accounting student from the local university, applied and got the job.

When Marci comes to work in the afternoons, Sarah usually leaves the store to run errands and take care of other business. If there are no customers, Marci updates the firm's manual accounting system and also tags jewelry in the back room. Because of this latter procedure, arriving customers may go unnoticed for a minute or two. At the end of each day, Marci verifies that the cash collected matches the amount reported on the store's sales-entry terminal. She then places the receipts in Sarah's desk, and Sarah deposits the receipts at the bank on the next business day.

Comment on any weaknesses in the jewelry store's system.

E6–8 Internal control weaknesses (L.O. 5)

Multiple Charities conducts a large door-to-door fund-raising campaign each year to assist local charitable organizations. Contributions in the form of cash and checks are received by volunteer workers who, in turn, issue an official Multiple Charities' receipt. The fund-raising campaign lasts one week.

This year the officers of Theta Theta Beta fraternity have pledged the services of the entire membership to canvass the homes in Mountain Way, a small college town located approximately 100 miles from the headquarters of Multiple Charities. On Thursday afternoon of the campaign, the brothers of Theta Theta Beta ran out of official Multiple Charities' receipts. Because it was too late to obtain an additional supply, the fraternity's treasurer designed the following form and had it printed on the chapter's copying machine. The form would be given to each contributor.

```
-------------------------------------------------------------
                        Multiple Charities

                                              Date _____

     Contributor _____

     Amount Received _____

                                              Theta Theta Beta

-------------------------------------------------------------
```

After dinner on Thursday, each member grabbed a handful of the forms for use in Friday's collections.

Discuss this system in terms of internal control. Does the system ensure that all contributions collected by Theta Theta Beta will be submitted to Multiple Charities? Why?

E6–9 Separation of duties (L.O. 5)
An important aspect of internal control is separation of duties.
a. Briefly explain what is meant in accounting by "an adequate separation of duties."
b. Determine whether an adequate separation of duties is present in the following cases. If the separation is adequate, label it as such. If it is inadequate, briefly state why.
   (1) The warehouse foreman updates the accounting records for merchandise received.
   (2) An employee who handles customer receipts also proves the equality of the balance in the Cash account with the cash balance as reported by the bank (i.e., prepares a bank reconciliation).
   (3) An employee who approves customer credit also supervises the payment of supplier invoices.

E6–10 Fraud (L.O. 6)
Using a fleet of 400 delivery trucks, Mister V's distributes and sells potato chips in 15 states. The company has roughly 10–15 older, out-of-service trucks at any point in time; the responsibility for these vehicles has been delegated to the director of fleet maintenance.

Little did management realize that the maintenance director was preparing fictitious crash reports on several of these trucks. He later sold the vehicles for cash and pocketed the money. Also, trucks involved in genuine (but minor) accidents were often written off the accounting records as a "total loss" and sold for scrap value to a company owned by the director. The company turned around and sold them at much higher prices. Again, the director benefited.

a. Generally speaking, what is a major contributing factor of fraud in businesses?
b. What procedures could Mister V's install to minimize the likelihood of such frauds?

PROBLEMS

Series A

P6–A1 Subsidiary ledger/control account relationships (L.O. 2)
Haskell Company maintains subsidiary ledger information for both accounts receivable and accounts payable. The general ledger control accounts revealed the following balances as of December 31, 19X2:

Accounts receivable	$19,900
Accounts payable	18,300

Haskell's trial balance was out of balance on this date, with total credits exceeding total debits by $2,500. The individual subsidiary ledgers revealed the following amounts due/owed:

ACCOUNTS RECEIVABLE		ACCOUNTS PAYABLE	
Cato	$6,120	Bluebonnet	$4,000
Green	8,450	Casson	7,500
Honroe	2,500	Jackson	5,200
Jones	4,330	Moore	2,600

Additional facts:

1. A $2,500 sale to Honroe occurred on the last day of the year, and the bookkeeper, in haste, forgot to post the debit to the appropriate control account.
2. Cato's subsidiary ledger account was not updated for a $1,000 sale.
3. A monthly statement received from Casson revealed a balance due of only $6,500.

Instructions

a. Determine the total of the account balances in each of the subsidiary ledgers prior to any corrections.
b. Evaluate the facts concerning the accounts of Cato and Casson. What appears to have happened?
c. Determine the correct balance in the company's Accounts Receivable control account. Also compute the total of the corrected balances in the Accounts Receivable subsidiary ledger.
d. Prepare the proper balance sheet disclosure for Haskell's accounts payable.

P6–A2 Computerized systems; modules (L.O. 3, 4)

Pro Auto Supply has grown rapidly and is considering the implementation of a computerized accounting system. Most sales are on account; merchandise is supplied by a number of vendors, each of whom extends credit for as long as 60 days. Other expenditures are related to purchases of equipment, payment of operating expenses, and miscellaneous costs associated with running a small business. Pro's bookkeeper has a reasonable understanding of accounting concepts and has maintained a manual accounting system for the past several years.

The bookkeeper has reviewed popular accounting software packages and has concluded that none are ideally suited to the company's particular needs. The owner of Pro is willing to hire a computer consultant to develop a specialized program, and conversations with the consultant have recently begun. Thus far, the bookkeeper and consultant have agreed on the function and appearance of the main menu and the general journal module. The appearance and functions of the other modules (sales journal, cash receipts, purchases journal, and cash payments) are not yet decided.

Instructions

a. What may have triggered the company's interest in a computerized accounting system?
b. Consider the design of Pro's system with regard to the processing of sales and cash receipts. Describe the functions performed by these two modules and list the resulting documents and reports.
c. What output results from the interaction of the purchases journal module and the cash payments module?

P6–A3 Using a computerized accounting system (L.O. 4)

Express Boat Repair, formed on January 1, 19X5, had the following transactions during the first month of activity:

Jan. 1 Received $15,000 cash from Keith Price, the owner, as an investment in the business.
   1 Acquired $9,000 of machinery. Paid $4,000 down and financed the remaining balance by a loan that bears interest at the rate of 1% per month. The loan is due in 10 months.
   7 Received $4,200 cash from a client for services rendered.

Jan. 12 Paid $900 for January advertising.
16 Purchased $500 of office supplies for cash.
21 Paid $950 for January rent.
26 Received $650 cash from a client for services rendered.
31 Received the January electric bill of $345, to be paid in February.

The company's accountant noted that adjusting entries were needed for accrued interest ($50), machinery depreciation ($125), and office supplies that remained on hand at month-end ($90). Selected accounts (and account numbers) for Express follow.

Cash	101	Keith Price, drawing	320
Office supplies	120	Service revenue	410
Machinery	130	Office supplies expense	500
Accumulated depreciation	131	Advertising expense	510
Utilities payable	200	Utilities expense	520
Interest payable	210	Rent expense	530
Loan payable	220	Depreciation expense	540
Keith Price, capital	310	Interest expense	550

Instructions

Obtain a copy of the accounting system software that accompanies this text. Using the software's general journal module:

a. Enter Express Boat Repair's transactions and adjusting entries for the month. Post the transactions and adjusting entries to the general ledger.
b. Prepare a printed listing of the journal entries and general ledger, an adjusted trial balance, and the financial statements.

P6–A4 Internal control evaluation (L.O. 5)

Assume that at a recent luncheon meeting, you overheard the following comments made by a group of executives sitting at the next table. From the tone of the conversation you have determined that the executives are directors of the Lucas County Stadium.

a. The staff person who handles the Accounts Payable subsidiary ledger also maintains the record keeping for cash payments.
b. Our recent cost-cutting moves have improved profitability. Patrons now pay the appropriate amounts to the cashier, who grants direct entry into the stadium. The elimination of ticket takers (and tickets) has led to reduced lines and faster admittance.
c. Personally, I don't agree with the county's policy of having Coopers and Young, the local CPA firm, perform an annual review of our accounting procedures. Susan Randolph at the county office has been helping us for years; she thoroughly knows and understands our system and operating problems.
d. Michael Dalby, our treasurer, has just been given new responsibilities. He now handles and deposits cash receipts, issues checks, and maintains all cash payments records.
e. Office employees should continue to initial the important documents and contracts that they have reviewed, prior to submission to the accounting and legal departments.
f. To further consolidate operations, we should combine the positions of supplies receiving clerk and supplies accounting clerk. Greater efficiency will result.

Instructions

Evaluate each of the preceding statements in terms of adequacy and/or understanding of internal control. If internal control is either lacking or misunderstood, briefly tell why.

P6–A5 Internal control weaknesses (L.O. 5)

Trustees of the First Church have asked you to review various internal control procedures. The trustees have read that small nonprofit organizations are susceptible to embezzlement and desire to prevent such incidents from occurring.

A review of the church's procedures finds that cash contributions are accepted during Sunday services. Members are encouraged to use envelopes for their donations and to give checks rather than cash. Shortly after the service concludes, the amounts collected are given to the treasurer, Steve McDowell. Steve updates the accounting records (including members' records) and places the cash and checks received in a locked box that he keeps in a bottom desk drawer. The cash and checks are deposited at a local bank later in the week. In January of each year, members receive a notice of the total amounts contributed. Any errors are later reported to and corrected by the treasurer.

A further study finds that cash collections are occasionally given to program directors to reimburse them for purchases of small items (e.g., sheet music for the choir, miscellaneous office supplies, and so forth). You also find that Steve pays all of the bills and is one of two required signatures on prenumbered checks. The other required signature is that of Mary Hopkins, chair of the trustees. Because of extensive out-of-town travel commitments, Mary signs her name in advance on all checks expected to be written during the month. Finally, the church's accounting records are examined periodically by a retired member of the congregation. The retiree held a series of clerical and bookkeeping positions with Osgood and Sons, a local manufacturer of metal pipe.

Instructions

Identify any control weaknesses in the church's accounting system. Explain why the items cited are weaknesses.

Series B

P6–B1 Subsidiary ledger/control account relationships (L.O. 2)

Bismarck Company's general ledger revealed Accounts Receivable and Accounts Payable balances of $20,800 and $17,400, respectively, at year-end. The following amounts are due from customers on December 31:

Ballot	$ 2,240
Brierton	11,400
Mikowski	5,000
Wagner	4,100

Additional facts:

1. Mikowski's account was not updated to reflect a purchase of $500.
2. A $300 purchase by Wagner occurred on the last day of the year, and the bookkeeper, in haste, forgot to post the debit to the appropriate control account.
3. Bismarck received a telephone call from Ballot noting that the last account statement failed to reflect a $2,140 payment on November 21. An investigation found that Ballot's claim was indeed correct.

Instructions

a. Determine the correct balances in the company's Accounts Receivable and Accounts Payable control accounts at year-end.
b. Prepare a corrected schedule of accounts receivable balances.
c. How would the information contained in a schedule of accounts receivable be disclosed on the year-end balance sheet?

d. Is a monthly account statement more easily generated by using information contained in the subsidiary ledger or the control account? Briefly explain.

P6–B2 Computerized systems; modules (L.O. 3, 4)

Austin Products sells containers that are used in the shipping industry. The company is owned by Henry Lee Harrison, who is 62 years old and close to retirement. Austin has maintained a manual accounting system for many years; however, various transaction processing problems have arisen recently and have started to cut into the firm's profitability. Given this situation and Harrison's desire for more timely, detailed operating information, a new computerized system is being considered. A consultant has recommended the use of modules to integrate flexibility and efficiency into the design, with the initial system consisting of a general journal module, sales journal module, cash receipts module, purchases journal module, and cash payments module.

Instructions

a. What types of transaction processing problems may the firm be experiencing? Briefly describe.
b. Briefly explain how a computerized accounting system speeds up the data-entry process.
c. Focus on Austin's processing of sales and cash receipts. What reports would likely result from computerizing these functions that would help Harrison better manage the business? Briefly describe.
d. Consider Harrison's age, probable computer expertise, and attitude about computers. Would you recommend the installation of a computerized system or would Austin be better off continuing with its manual procedures? Explain.

P6–B3 Using a computerized accounting system (L.O. 4)

Tri Cities Automotive, formed on January 1, 19X3, had the following transactions during the first month of activity:

Jan. 1 Received $25,000 cash from Buddy Hawkins, the owner, as an investment in the business.
      1 Acquired $6,000 of equipment, financed by a loan that bears interest at the rate of 1% per month. This loan is due in nine months.
      9 Purchased $400 of supplies for cash.
     12 Received $3,250 cash from a client for services rendered.
     15 Paid $75 for January insurance.
     23 Paid $250 for January rent.
     26 Received $550 cash from a client for services rendered.
     31 Received the January electric bill of $133, to be paid in February.

The company's accountant noted that adjusting entries were needed for accrued interest ($60), supplies used during the month ($150), and equipment depreciation ($100). Selected accounts (and account numbers) for Tri Cities follow.

Cash	100	Buddy Hawkins, drawing	310
Supplies	110	Service revenue	400
Equipment	120	Supplies expense	500
Accumulated depreciation	121	Insurance expense	510
Utilities payable	200	Rent expense	520
Loan payable	210	Utilities expense	530
Interest payable	220	Depreciation expense	540
Buddy Hawkins, capital	300	Interest expense	550

Instructions

Obtain a copy of the accounting system software that accompanies this text. Using the software's general journal module:

a. Enter Tri Cities' transactions and adjusting entries for the month. Post the transactions and adjusting entries to the general ledger.
b. Prepare a printed listing of the journal entries and general ledger, an adjusted trial balance, and the financial statements.

P6–B4 Internal control evaluation (L.O. 5)

Assume that at a recent luncheon meeting, you overheard the following comments made by a group of executives sitting at the next table:

a. There's no reason why a person who handles cash payments cannot also maintain the record keeping for purchases and the Accounts Payable subsidiary ledger.
b. We have many internal control procedures and can therefore overlook top management's carefree attitude and sometimes irresponsible decision making.
c. The design of a perfect internal control system that detects and prevents all dishonest employee actions is really possible. Top management just won't pay for it.
d. Every week, our store managers compare the cash collected against computer runs from the sales-entry terminal.
e. We save money each year by handling the evaluation of internal control ourselves. The company's internal audit department is efficient and highly competent.
f. Granted, separation of duties does help to make embezzlement more difficult. I don't believe, however, that it reduces the chance for accidental errors when processing data.

Instructions

Evaluate each of the preceding statements in terms of adequacy and/or understanding of internal control. If internal control is either lacking or misunderstood, briefly tell why.

P6–B5 Internal control weaknesses (L.O. 5)

Jimmy's is a small neighborhood restaurant famous for its southern dinners and ice-cold beverages. The restaurant has been open for 45 years, and the present owner, a grandson of the founder, still operates just as his grandfather did.

Patrons come in the front door and seat themselves. Sometimes the single-room restaurant gets quite crowded, and customers stand around chatting by the door while waiting for a table. Waiters usually bring them beverages and refills to make the wait more bearable.

Most of the waiters employed by Jimmy's are local college students with pleasant personalities. The waiters are instructed to be friendly and to treat the customers like family members. To maintain this congenial atmosphere, no order pads are used, and orders are memorized. When patrons are finished with their meals, they wait at the register for their server. The server rings up the order on a cash register (grandfather's original) and makes change. The machine, because of its age, lacks an operator identification key.

Jimmy's does not honor credit cards, but personal checks are accepted without question. The owner pays the waiters from the register at the end of the night and then deposits the remainder of the receipts on his way home.

Instructions

a. Identify the internal control weaknesses in Jimmy's system. Explain why the items cited are weaknesses.
b. Suggest methods to improve the weaknesses that you found.

Expanding Your Horizons

EYH6–1 Accounting software packages (L.O. 3, 4)

Computer stores sell many software packages that handle all or part of a company's accounting and financial reporting needs. Each package has different control and operating features as well as cost.

Instructions

Visit a local computer store. Obtain information about three different accounting system packages by talking to a sales representative and reading the literature (often the box). Use demo disks if they are available. After your brief review, evaluate each package in terms of (1) apparent operating features and ease of use and (2) cost. Summarize your findings in a one-page report.

EYH6–2 Internal control and CPAs (L.O. 5)

The review of a client's system of internal control is an integral part of a CPA's audit. Many operating deficiencies are corrected as a result of this thorough examination.

Instructions

Interview a practicing CPA on the subject of internal controls. Determine how internal controls are evaluated and whether faulty controls have led to any fraud or embezzlement. Also inquire about recent modifications to a client's system to strengthen control. Be prepared to report your findings to the class.

EYH6–3 Computer crime (L.O. 6)

Computer crime is definitely on the rise. The increased use of computers, coupled with advances in telecommunications, have created significant problems for U.S. and foreign companies.

Instructions

Visit your library and find three distinctly different examples of computer crime. At least one example should deal with the theft of cash. In a short report, describe how the crime took place, the estimated amount of loss, and how the crime was detected.

EYH6–4 System outputs (L.O. 1)

Eagle Engineering, a sole proprietorship owned by Felix Wong, is comprised of three departments: Engineering Services, Accounting & Finance, and Marketing. All departments are headed by a manager who reports directly to Felix. Because of recent layoffs and other factors, the managers are working at "120% of capacity." Hours are long and tempers are short. Duties within the firm are subdivided as follows:

	Engineering Services	Accounting & Finance	Marketing
Drafting and design	X		
Field engineering	X		
Construction management	X		
Bookkeeping		X	
Systems design and maintenance		X	

	ENGINEERING SERVICES	ACCOUNTING & FINANCE	MARKETING
Financial reporting		X	
Cost control		X	
Insurance/risk management		X	
Advertising			X
Client development and satisfaction			X
Economic/market trends assessment			X

In addition to the basic financial statements, the company's information system produces the following selected reports and listings:

- Items of equipment owned
- Slow-paying accounts
- Budgeted vs. actual year-to-date expenditures
- Worker's compensation claims
- Construction costs, subdivided by job
- Analysis of fringe benefit costs
- New contracts signed
- Entertainment expenditures
- Unemployment rates and Gross Domestic Product (GDP) data

The nine reports and listings are currently provided to all three departments.

Instructions

a. Ray Jarvis, head of Engineering Services, recently complained that the company's report distribution system is "for the birds" and not accomplishing its intended objective.
   (1) What is the function of an information system?
   (2) Comment on Ray's observation. In all likelihood, what is the cause of his complaint?
b. Create a table similar to that shown in the body of this problem. Leave the department headings as is; replace the 11 duties with the reports produced by the system. Generate a new distribution scheme for the company by noting (with an "X") how the reports are to be distributed to the various departments.

COMMUNICATION OF ACCOUNTING INFORMATION

CAI6–1 A lesson in editing: United Technologies Corporation (L.O. 5)

Communication Principle: Accounting communications often contain long sentences and paragraphs as well as long words and abstract concepts. All of these characteristics make comprehension difficult, especially for readers who are nonaccountants.

How can we edit typical accounting writing so that it is more easily understood? First, break up long sentences and paragraphs into shorter units. Vary sentence length and aim at an average length of 18 words. Next, check your choice of terms for unnecessarily long words or words with endings such as "tion," "ity," and "ance." These suffixes often turn verbs into abstract nouns and make reading more difficult. In general, words with three or more syllables lead to increased problems for readers.

Finally, make the writing parallel natural speaking patterns by adding personal pronouns. For instance, use the personal "we" instead of the impersonal "it" when referring to the organization or company. Before rewriting, read aloud a long, abstract, formal description to see "how it sounds." This effort will help you translate abstractions into concrete, easy-to-understand explanations.

Much of the writing in accounting is complicated because of long sentences, word choice, and an overly formal and impersonal tone. You can make a big difference in reading ease and comprehension by changing the style into something more natural and direct. Your reader will be very appreciative of your labors.

■ ■ ■ ■ ■ ■ ■ ■

United Technologies Corporation (UTC) provides systems, products, and services to customers in the aerospace, defense, building, and automotive industries. The following entities are among the company's holdings: Pratt & Whitney (jet engines), Sikorsky (helicopters), Carrier (air conditioning equipment), and Otis (elevators).

UTC's annual report parallels annual reports of most other companies by containing a "standardized" statement regarding internal control. A portion of that statement follows.

> Management is responsible for the integrity and objectivity of the financial statements, including estimates and judgments reflected in them. It fulfills this responsibility primarily by establishing and maintaining accounting systems and practices adequately supported by internal accounting controls. These controls include the selection and training of management and supervisory personnel; maintenance of an organization structure providing for delegation of authority and establishment of responsibilities; communication of requirements for compliance with approved accounting, control and business practices throughout the organization; business planning and review; and a program of internal audit. Management believes the internal accounting controls in use provide reasonable assurance that the Corporation's assets are safeguarded, that transactions are executed in accordance with management's authorizations, and that the financial records are reliable for the purpose of preparing financial statements.

Instructions

Assume that you have been hired to make UTC's annual report more "user friendly." Redraft the internal control statement to be more understandable to someone with little or no accounting background. (*Note:* Feel free to integrate additional internal control insights based on the text's discussion of the topic.)

Answers to Chapter Quiz

1. b
2. c
3. d
4. a
5. c

7 UNDERSTANDING AND USING FINANCIAL INFORMATION

LEARNING OBJECTIVES

After studying this chapter, you should be able to:

1. Discuss the role of financial reporting in providing useful information for decision making.
2. Recognize that net income is a function of accounting policies and estimates.
3. Use and interpret a basic annual report.
4. Explain the role of notes in providing full and fair disclosure.
5. Discuss the role of auditing in affirming the fairness of the financial statements.
6. Describe the value of comparative standards and segment reporting in the evaluation of financial statements.
7. Recognize that the financial statements of different entity forms have different objectives and appearances.
8. (Appendix) Recognize the meaning of consolidated financial statements and the special treatment needed for intercompany transactions.

In the day-to-day operation of Banner Advertising, George Faris sometimes faces difficult accounting issues. Given that these issues require significant levels of expertise, he has no hesitation about calling his CPA. As George notes, "While I pride myself in understanding basic accounting and tax matters, I don't have the time and knowledge to personally address every problem. My CPA is a trusted professional and can normally provide an immediate answer to most of my questions."

George recently completed a review of invoices from his accountant. He found that for the year just ended, the CPA had provided the following services:

- Preparation of annual and quarterly tax returns.
- Tax consultation related to the potential sale of business assets.
- Preparation of financial statements requested by a local banker.
- Consultation regarding the appropriate service life of certain assets.
- Advice on business succession and family planning issues.
- Guidance on the proper entity form for Banner Advertising.
- Recommendation on rewarding a key employee with shares of the company's capital stock.
- Evaluation of alternative computer systems for data processing work.
- Financial analysis of another firm in which an investment was being considered.

As you can see, a businessperson may find it necessary to confer with a professional regarding diverse matters.

You, too, will discover that accounting involves many complex dimensions and that it is sometimes essential that an expert be consulted. Despite this situation, it is advantageous to have a fundamental understanding of the subject matter to know (1) when consultation may be needed and (2) what types of basic questions to ask. Obtaining this fundamental knowledge, however, is becoming more complicated. For example, a firm that once conducted business solely in a small town now finds itself engaged in international trade. To be competitive, the introduction of new products that formerly took five years from the drawing board to reality must now take place in eighteen months. Communication among firms and employees is commonly being supplemented by videoconferencing, computer networks, E-mail, and electronic data interchange.

In short, business is changing and so is its financial reporting function. Companies and financial institutions have a limited amount of capital to invest and lend. These organizations, as well as individuals like you, seek profitable endeavors that generate a satisfactory return on their outlays. Information (and lots of it) is needed to make the best decisions possible, and financial accounting and reporting are an integral part of this process. As a recent report noted:

> People in every walk of life are affected by business reporting, the cornerstone on which our process of capital allocation is built. An effective allocation process is

critical to a healthy economy that promotes productivity, encourages innovation, and provides an efficient market for the purchase and sale of securities and the obtaining and granting of credit. Whether a *Fortune 500* [Chief Executive Officer], investment professional, or retiree, individuals make important investment decisions every day—or rely on others to make decisions for them—based on the information in business reporting. While the topic may not immediately capture one's imagination, few areas are more central to national economic interest.[1]

FINANCIAL INFORMATION

① Discuss the role of financial reporting in providing useful information for decision making.

Accounting seeks to provide information that helps users make informed economic decisions. For example, an investor may desire to evaluate a speculative new venture in biotechnology. A creditor must determine whether to make or renew a loan and what interest rate to charge. Suppliers must decide whether to extend credit to a business. The decisions of these parties will likely depend on an assessment of the respective entities' financial strength and character, as communicated by the companies' financial reports.

Much thought has been given to the characteristics of information that make it useful. Although we will look closer at these characteristics in Chapter 14, most accountants agree that useful information is both relevant and reliable. Relevancy means that the information influences the actions of a decision maker. Reliability, on the other hand, holds that information is truthful, verifiable, and not biased in favor of any particular user group. As discussed earlier in the text, accounting strives to produce reports that are general purpose in nature.

COMPLICATIONS TO USEFULNESS

There are two basic complications to usefulness: understandability and volume. It seems logical that to make good decisions, the decision maker should have a decent grasp of the information under study. What makes good sense is not always practiced. Earlier we stated that business is more complicated today than it was, say, 15 to 20 years ago. Accompanying this increase in complexity are additional reporting requirements that companies must now follow.

Unfortunately, very few decision makers have the knowledge needed to adequately comprehend a set of financial statements.[2] This situation presents an interesting challenge for the accountant. The profession strives to develop standards and reports that communicate a firm's economic condition and profitability to those who have a limited financial background. Being realistic, however, the communication often takes place with statement users who may comprehend neither the underlying transactions nor the related accounting rules and procedures.

The preceding paragraph should not convey the message that the user be excused from studying financial information. Examining the data will no doubt improve understanding about the situation under review. This examination, though, requires some basic knowledge of the fundamental structure of financial reporting and analysis. Providing you with this structure is one of the goals of this chapter and text.

[1] "Improving Business Reporting—A Customer Focus," The AICPA Special Committee on Financial Reporting, 1994, p. 4.
[2] Keep in mind that the examples presented thus far in the text have been basic—*very basic*.

An Expanded Information Set. The purposes of accounting cannot be fulfilled through the basic financial statements alone. All too often, people tend to look only at the "bottom line" net income or limit their analysis to just the face of the financial statements. This is a mistake. Accounting rules explicitly recognize that the statements by themselves are inadequate when it comes to presenting the complete picture of an entity's economic activities.

Users require additional insights when making investment and credit decisions, insights that may be gained from an item such as a company's annual report. An **annual report** is a corporate publication used to keep stockholders and the general public informed about the firm's business affairs and economic well-being. The typical report includes information about the entity's products and accomplishments, the financial statements, notes to the financial statements, management reports, and an auditor's report. (The last three items are discussed elsewhere in the chapter.)

An informed user will also rely on other sources. As evidence, the following figures are based on surveys that studied where stockholders first turn for financial information when making investment decisions.[3]

	1991	1973
Annual report analysis	26.6%	15.0%
Stockbrokers' advice	20.3	48.8
Financial publications	20.3	18.3
Investment advisers	20.3	17.4
Technical analysis	20.3	10.0
Friends	6.2	4.6

Note: Percentages do not add to 100% because only items ranked first are reported here. Also, some individuals ranked more than one item "first."

It is interesting to note that over time, shareholders seem to be relying more on information provided by annual reports as well as that learned from their own technical analysis. In contrast, there is considerably less dependence on stockbrokers for advice.

A Further Focus

In keeping with our rapidly expanding electronic society, some companies are now releasing annual reports on CD-ROM. Like their paper counterparts, the CD-ROM version typically has many pictures of company operations. What's new, however, is full-motion video and interviews of firm executives and tables of financial data—sometimes with accompanying background music. IBM's version has an extra feature for those readers who wish to "massage" the numbers: the disc's tabular data can be transferred to the reader's own spreadsheet program.

Source: "Showing Sound Financials," *The Dallas Morning News,*" March 30, 1995, pp. 1D–2D.

---

[3] See "Corporate Governance and the Shareholders' Revolt," *Management Accounting*, August 1992, pp. 32–35.

A Tremendous Surge in Volume. One need only visit a major public library to learn of the many information sources available to a financial decision maker. To complicate matters, this information set is growing at an alarming pace, so much so that the average individual can easily become overwhelmed. Not too long ago, for instance, Ernst & Young, a large international public accounting firm, examined a very small part of this glut: the 1972, 1982, and 1992 annual reports issued by 25 well-known companies.[4] The firm found:

- The page count increased an average of 83% (from 35 to 64 pages).
- The average number of pages devoted to notes that accompanied the financial statements increased by 325% (from 4 to 17).

The future may be different on the so-called "information superhighway," as newer, faster technology is developed that has better storage and access capabilities. As one accounting professional has noted, it may be time to limit business disclosures.

> . . . there's no technology to permit us to read at a much faster rate. And there's still only 24 hours in each day to read and understand the growing quantities of information for each company. In financial disclosure we have reached a point where more is not better.[5]

INFORMATION AND THE FOCUS ON INCOME

② Recognize that net income is a function of accounting policies and estimates.

The amount of a company's income is usually of great interest to owners, creditors, employees, and others. This interest is evidenced by reviewing virtually any issue of *The Wall Street Journal* or the business section of most metropolitan newspapers. Many articles are devoted to the income reported by specific companies. If the amount of income includes any surprises, good or bad, the value of corporate stock in the marketplace will often react.

Consider the following examples. America Online shares jumped nearly 5% when the firm reported a profit of $0.33 (per share of stock) for a recent second quarter. This amount, which excluded several special charges, was a vast improvement over the nearly break-even performance of one year earlier.[6] In another case, the shares of CBS fell 2.8% when the company reported significantly lower third-quarter net income as compared with amounts generated in the previous year. Analysts blamed the drop on an absence of sports programming. CBS had lost its contract with the National Football League, and baseball coverage was curtailed because of a players' strike.[7]

HOW PRECISE IS INCOME?

These illustrations are not unique and demonstrate the attention and importance that the investment community gives to reported earnings. In light of this situation, one might believe that the earnings number is a very exact measure

---

[4, 5] "Here's the Annual Report. Got a Few Hours?," *The Wall Street Journal*, August 4, 1994, p. A10.
[6] "Stocks Close Mixed as Investors Brace for New Data on Inflation," *The Wall Street Journal*, February 10, 1995, p. C2.
[7] "Three-Day Rally by Stocks Ends As Cautious Investors Await Data," *The Wall Street Journal*, October 13, 1994, p. C2.

of business performance. As you progress through the study of accounting, you will find that the number is actually somewhat imprecise.

For instance, there are numerous accounting choices that must be made. Alternative methods *can* be used to account for the same transactions and events. Companies employ different approaches to cost inventory, depreciate long-term assets, and account for leases, pensions, and manufacturing operations, to cite just a few topical areas. You will also find the frequent use of estimates in accounting, estimates that involve individual judgment.

Given the related subjectivity, how can reported income be considered reliable? The answer to this question probably has several dimensions. One possibility is that financial statement users may attach more significance to the reported numbers than is really due. More likely, however, the additional disclosures that accompany the income statement are informative and give the user an opportunity to learn (and understand) the methods that a company has employed. In other words, some meaning is given to the figures.

THE QUALITY OF EARNINGS

When evaluating the income of a business, care must be taken to consider the *nature* of earnings. Picture two companies that have identical asset investments and the same net income. Suppose further that both businesses employ straight-line depreciation (see p. 101). If firm A writes its assets off over a 10-year life while firm B uses an 8-year life, we could say that B is employing more conservative accounting practices. That is, B's selection of service life produces greater annual depreciation expense and a bigger impact (i.e., decrease) on income. Other favorable factors must therefore be attributed to firm B, given that total earnings are the same for the two entities.

Additionally, bottom-line income is influenced by both one-time transactions and those that arise from normal business activity. Consider the performance of X Company, which reported $150,000 of income from operations, versus that of Y Company. Assume that Y had $50,000 of income from operations for the period just ended along with a $100,000 gain on the sale of real estate. Although the total earnings figures for the two entities are identical, financial analysts would view X's situation more favorably than Y's. Put simply, income from ongoing activities is typically more attractive than income from a one-time (and possibly irregular) source.

The two preceding examples focus on an organization's **quality of earnings.** In other words, an assessment is made of both the methods used to determine income and the source from which the income arose. "Quality" earnings are said to result from steady, continuous sources and the use of conservative accounting practices.

WHY ALLOW ACCOUNTING CHOICE?

It may seem strange that firms would be permitted flexibility when measuring and reporting income. Perhaps all companies should be bound by the same rules and procedures. On close examination it becomes apparent that *some* choice is needed to recognize the unique features of individual businesses. To illustrate, let us return to the previous "identical asset" example. Assume that firm A has implemented a more extensive maintenance plan than firm B, thereby extending the service life for two additional years. Firm A can thus justify an asset write-off over the longer period of time. Accounting would surely be handicapped if it were based on the premise that all businesses are alike. This premise would, in effect, become reality if underlying rules became too specific and individual judgments were completely eliminated.

Bear in mind that many of the imprecisions associated with short-term earnings are removed by the passage of time. That is, the effects of a given accounting method or estimation are felt more strongly on an annual earnings number than on the income of a longer period. With our asset illustration, for instance, annual earnings would differ between firm A and firm B because of different amounts of depreciation expense. Consider, though, what happens after each of the asset investments is fully "used up" (i.e., consumed). No matter whether the service life was 8 years, 10 years, or some other number, the same total asset cost would have been written off to expense and deducted from each company's revenues. The long-term impact is identical under all approaches.

THE ANNUAL REPORT

3

Use and interpret a basic annual report.

Earlier in the chapter we introduced the annual report as a primary communication link between a company and the general public. We now desire to sharpen your skills in using and interpreting externally available financial information. Our presentation will focus on the major content of an annual report, namely, the financial statements, accompanying notes, management reports, and the auditor's report.

One word of caution is necessary before we proceed. Some of the accompanying exhibits are quite complex and incorporate topics that are reserved for study in advanced accounting courses. You are therefore advised to concentrate on the general issues being presented and *not* the intimate details of the supporting illustrations.

FINANCIAL STATEMENTS

Our discussion of the financial statements contained in an annual report is based on those of Microsoft Corporation, the giant software producer.[8] The firm, perhaps best known for its MS-DOS and Windows operating systems, was recently named the most innovative company in America by a *Fortune* magazine survey of U.S. business executives.

Income Statement. The income statement's purpose is to provide information about business profitability over a stated period of time. Given this fact, it is probably most appropriate to begin by performing an analysis of net income. A comparison of various years' income figures will give a general indication of a company's financial success or failure. Microsoft's comparative income statements, shown in Exhibit 7–1, reveal that earnings have increased greatly over the three-year period. The question that accompanies this behavior is: Why?

A further look is necessary to determine if net income is the result of continuing, ordinary transactions or perhaps one-time items. In Microsoft's case, the only item of note is a $90 million litigation charge in 1994. (Other disclosure in the annual report explained that the amount arose from a jury verdict against

---

[8] The financial data that follow are excerpted from the company's 1994 annual report.

	Year Ended June 30		
	1992	1993	1994
Net revenues	$2,759	$3,753	$4,649
Cost of revenues	467	633	763
Gross profit	2,292	3,120	3,886
Operating expenses:			
Research and development	352	470	610
Sales and marketing	854	1,205	1,384
General and administrative	90	119	166
Total operating expenses	1,296	1,794	2,160
Operating income	996	1,326	1,726
Interest income—net	56	82	102
Litigation charge	—	—	(90)
Other expenses	(11)	(7)	(16)
Income before income taxes	1,041	1,401	1,722
Provision for income taxes	333	448	576
Net income	$ 708	$ 953	$1,146
Earnings per share	$ 1.20	$ 1.57	$ 1.88
Weighted average shares outstanding	588	606	610

See accompanying notes.

EXHIBIT 7–1
Income Statements of Microsoft Corporation (In Millions, Except Earnings Per Share)

the company.) Interestingly, if it were not for this item, reported earnings would have been even higher.

The next step is to review the various types of revenues and expenses, examining trends and watching for anything that appears unusual. The most important revenue form is sales, and there has been a sizable growth since 1992. Cost of revenues (i.e., cost of goods sold) and all operating expenses have increased, but this result is expected in light of the higher sales volume. Percentage studies of these items by the authors actually revealed relatively stable levels of cost incurrence.

Finally, the company's outlays for research and development activities have increased substantially. These amounts, while not necessarily having an immediate payoff, are positioning the firm for a successful future in terms of new product development. In sum, we can conclude that Microsoft has been a prosperous company for the three years reported, having experienced a $438 million (61.9%) rise in net income since 1992.

Balance Sheet. The balance sheet discloses the financial position of an entity on a specific date. This key financial statement provides answers to several basic questions:

- What is the overall financial condition of the enterprise?
- How liquid is the firm?
- What stake do the owners (stockholders) have in the company?

We will answer these questions by reviewing Microsoft's recent balance sheets, as presented in Exhibit 7–2.

A firm's general financial health may be assessed by comparing the relationship between assets and liabilities. Many businesses, like Microsoft, have asset investments that greatly exceed the total amounts owed to creditors. As of

EXHIBIT 7–2
Balance Sheets of Microsoft Corporation (In Millions)

	June 30 1993	June 30 1994
Assets		
Current assets:		
Cash and short-term investments	$2,290	$3,614
Accounts receivable—net of allowances of $76 and $92	338	475
Inventories	127	102
Other	95	121
Total current assets	2,850	4,312
Property, plant, and equipment—net	867	930
Other assets	88	121
Total assets	$3,805	$5,363
Liabilities and stockholders' equity		
Current liabilities:		
Accounts payable	$ 239	$ 324
Accrued compensation	86	96
Income taxes payable	127	305
Other	111	188
Total current liabilities	563	913
Commitments and contingencies		
Stockholders' equity:		
Common stock and paid-in capital—shares authorized 2,000; issued and outstanding 565 and 581	1,086	1,500
Retained earnings	2,156	2,950
Total stockholders' equity	3,242	4,450
Total liabilities and stockholders' equity	$3,805	$5,363

See accompanying notes.

June 30, 1994, for example, the company had total stockholders' equity (i.e., assets minus liabilities) of $4.45 billion—obviously quite a buffer between these two amounts. The firm's economic resources thus far exceed any outstanding obligations. Other businesses may be in a more precarious position.

The second question deals with liquidity, or an entity's ability to settle its short-term obligations when due. Recall from Chapter 4 that a popular measure of liquidity, the *current ratio*, is calculated by dividing total current assets by total current liabilities. At the middle of 1994 this ratio stood at 4.72 ($4,312 ÷ $913), greatly in excess of the general 2:1 rule of thumb. Microsoft's ratio shows that for every dollar owed and payable in the near future, current assets of $4.72 are available or will soon be available for settlement. Also on the positive side, the vast majority of current assets is not tied up in receivables and inventories. Keep in mind that dollars associated with these two assets cannot be used for payment until the goods are sold and cash is collected.

The balance sheet also provides information about the owners' (stockholders') stake in the business relative to that of the creditors. This issue is important because in times of severe financial difficulty, those companies without a sufficient owner investment tend to be the first ones to close their doors. Large levels of debt mean hefty cash outflows for principal and interest at a time when inflows may be few and far between. For Microsoft we can observe a business rarity—the absence of long-term debt as a means of financing asset acquisitions. This situation results in a very high percentage of stockholders' equity to the total of liabilities plus stockholders' equity (83.0% on June 30, 1994).

A Further Focus

To provide additional evidence of Microsoft's healthy position, consider the following equity percentages of other companies. Some of these firms are in the business of computers and high technology; some are not. The range is very eye-opening.

Novell, Inc.	76.5%	Apple Computer, Inc.	39.2%
Tootsie Roll Industries	69.9	Reader's Digest Association	38.6
Intel Corporation	66.1	Maytag Corporation	23.8
The Home Depot	59.9	General Mills, Inc.	22.1
Toys "R" Us, Inc.	51.2	Chrysler Corporation	15.6
Dell Computer Corporation	41.3	Delta Air Lines, Inc.	12.3

Statement of Cash Flows. As we briefly discussed in Chapter 1, this important financial statement reveals the cash flows associated with a company's operating, financing, and investing activities. Microsoft's statement of cash flows is shown in Exhibit 7–3.

For the year ended June 30, 1994, the firm invested heavily ($1.2 billion) in various assets. Most of these investments were short-term in nature as opposed to longer-lived items of property, plant, and equipment. Overall, the cost of Microsoft's investments was more than covered by cash flows from daily operations ($1.59 billion), a very positive situation. Many companies have to rely on considerable outside financing to fund such activities.

	Year Ended June 30		
	1992	1993	1994
Cash flows from operations			
Net income	$ 708	$ 953	$1,146
Depreciation and amortization	112	151	237
Current liabilities	167	177	360
Accounts receivable	(33)	(121)	(146)
Inventories	(40)	(51)	23
Other current assets	(18)	(35)	(27)
Net cash from operations	896	1,074	1,593
Cash flows from financing			
Common stock issued	135	229	280
Common stock repurchased	(135)	(250)	(348)
Stock option income tax benefits	130	207	151
Net cash from financing	130	186	83
Cash flows used for investments			
Additions to property, plant, and equipment	(317)	(236)	(278)
Other assets	(41)	(17)	(64)
Short-term investments	(284)	(723)	(860)
Net cash used for investments	(642)	(976)	(1,202)
Net change in cash and equivalents	384	284	474
Effect of exchange rates	(10)	(62)	(10)
Cash and equivalents, beginning of year	417	791	1,013
Cash and equivalents, end of year	791	1,013	1,477
Short-term investments	554	1,277	2,137
Cash and short-term investments	$1,345	$2,290	$3,614

See accompanying notes.

EXHIBIT 7–3
Cash Flow Statements of Microsoft Corporation
(In Millions)

The entries toward the bottom of the statement show the tremendous growth in cash over the years. Starting with $417 million at the beginning of the 1992 fiscal year, this figure swelled to $1.477 billion by mid 1994. One could say that Microsoft is truly a "cash cow"—a business that generates funds far in excess of amounts needed to support future growth.

Statement of Stockholders' Equity. The statement of stockholders' equity, shown in Exhibit 7–4, is actually the corporate version of the statement of owner's equity. This financial report details the changes in owners' (stockholders') equity that occurred during the year.

	Year Ended June 30		
	1992	1993	1994
Common stock and paid-in capital			
Balance, beginning of year	$ 395	$ 657	$1,086
Common stock issued	135	229	280
Common stock repurchased	(3)	(7)	(17)
Stock option income tax benefits	130	207	151
Balance, end of year	657	1,086	1,500
Retained earnings			
Balance, beginning of year	956	1,536	2,156
Common stock repurchased	(132)	(243)	(331)
Net income	708	953	1,146
Translation adjustment	4	(90)	(21)
Balance, end of year	1,536	2,156	2,950
Total stockholders' equity	$2,193	$3,242	$4,450

See accompanying notes.

EXHIBIT 7-4
Microsoft Corporation's Statements of Stockholders' Equity (In Millions)

In comparison with the statements issued by other corporations, Microsoft's is unusually short and simple. A quick review finds that in each of the three years, the company both issued and repurchased shares of capital stock. Perhaps the most interesting disclosure is the absence of any dividends[9]. This practice is typical of young, rapidly-growing firms, which often reinvest cash back into the business for expansion rather than disburse funds to their owners.

NOTES TO THE FINANCIAL STATEMENTS

④ Explain the role of notes in providing full and fair disclosure.

As explained earlier in the text, companies prepare a series of **notes to the financial statements** to help users better understand the information being reported. The notes are viewed as an integral part of the statements, being essential for a full disclosure of business and economic affairs. Over the past several decades, notes have grown in both number and length to where they now occupy more room in the annual report than the financial statements themselves. There are several reasons for this situation, including added disclosure requirements of the accounting profession, a greater demand for details by statement users, and an increased tendency on the part of U.S. citizens to file lawsuits.

Notes to the financial statements are quite varied, as each company has its own unique set of transactions, contracts, and circumstances. Normally, notes serve one of three basic functions by (1) summarizing significant accounting

---

[9] Recall that dividends are corporate distributions of income, similar to owner withdrawals of a sole proprietorship.

policies, (2) disclosing supplementary information, or (3) providing explanatory information.

Summary of Significant Accounting Policies. Financial statements that appear in annual reports are accompanied by a summary of significant accounting policies. Users need to be aware of the accounting practices employed by a business so that a sound evaluation of the statements can be made.

The summary is typically presented as the first note to the financial statements or in a separate section just before the notes. Within this section companies generally describe those principles and methods that have been selected for use from the available alternatives. In addition, the summary discloses unusual principles and practices that are peculiar to the industry in which the business operates.

Excerpts from Microsoft Corporation's summary appear in Exhibit 7–5. Here we learn, among other things, that sales revenues are recognized when related products are shipped to customers. The company provides for warranties and the return of defective goods, and such costs have been insignificant. Finally, Microsoft uses straight-line depreciation and generally writes off (i.e., expenses) its own computer equipment over a three-year service life.

Supplementary Information. An increasing number of notes are devoted to fulfilling the requirements of regulatory agencies (namely, the Securities and Exchange Commission) and the accounting profession for supplemental (additional) financial information. Two examples of supplemental disclosure involve segment reporting (to be discussed shortly) and interim (quarterly) financial data. The latter data allow users to compare quarterly results and gain insights about the pattern of sales and earnings over the year. Such disclosures are very helpful in the evaluation of seasonal businesses, or those firms that generate the majority of their revenues in a relatively short period of time. Many retail stores fall in this category, with a large percentage of yearly sales taking place in November and December as customers prepare for year-end holidays.

Explanatory Information. Notes may also be used to expand on the information presented in the body of the financial statements. For example, the property, plant, and equipment owned by a firm is often disclosed via a single line-item on the balance sheet. To provide further information, a note may reveal the individual components (land, buildings, equipment) and their related cost. Long-term liabilities are often treated in this manner, with a note used to furnish details on the types and amounts of debt owed by the business.

ADDITIONAL ANNUAL REPORT DISCLOSURES

The notes to the financial statements are not the only things to look at when trying to gain more information about an entity. A review of several management reports as well as the auditor's report is in order to complete the process.

Management Reports. The annual report includes several accounting-related disclosures prepared by management. One, called management's discussion and analysis (MD&A), explains the differences between the current year's financial statements and those of preceding periods. In essence, the discussion

EXHIBIT 7–5
Notes to the Financial Statements

Significant Accounting Policies

Revenue recognition. Revenue from finished goods sales to distributors and resellers is recognized when related products are shipped. Revenue billed upon shipment of finished goods products attributable to both specified and unspecified future product enhancements is deferred and recognized when such enhancements are delivered. Revenue from software maintenance contracts is recognized ratably over the contract period.

The Company warrants products against defects and has policies permitting the return of products under certain circumstances. Provision is made for warranty costs and returns. Such costs generally have not been material.

Revenue from products licensed to original equipment manufacturers is recognized when the licensed products are shipped by the OEM. License fees received prior to product acceptance are recorded as customer deposits.

Provision is made for bad debts. Such costs generally have not been material.

Research and development. Research and development costs are expensed as incurred.

Inventories. Inventories are stated at the lower of cost or market. Cost is determined using the first-in, first-out method.

Property, plant, and equipment. Property, plant, and equipment is stated at cost and depreciated using the straight-line method. Estimated lives are as follows: buildings, 30 years; leasehold improvements, the lease term; computer equipment and other, principally three years.

---

provides an overview, from management's perspective, of what went right and what went wrong during the year. Trends are highlighted, and changes in profitability, financial position, and cash flow are explained.

Most MD&As are quite detailed and lengthy. Further insights about the company's achievements can be gained by reading the **letter to stockholders.** The letter typically appears at the front of the annual report and is written by the company's chief executive officer. This user-friendly communication presents in layman's (not accounting) terms a review of the firm's achievements during the year.

A Further Focus

The letter to stockholders is normally very down-to-earth and open. It may be interesting to read a letter issued by a business that you know from newspaper accounts has had a very bad year. Is the presentation upbeat and optimistic in an attempt to downplay the past or is the mood relatively somber?

> **5**
> Discuss the role of auditing in affirming the fairness of the financial statements.

The Audit Report. The financial statements of a company are the representations and responsibility of management. An audit report, prepared by independent certified public accountants, presents the auditor's opinion concerning whether the statements are free of significant errors and irregularities. The report is the end result of an audit, a process that involves the detailed examination of an entity's transactions, documents, and controls. The audit increases the credibility of a company's financial statements and plays a very critical role in our society. By rendering an objective, unbiased opinion, the auditor helps to instill confidence in management's disclosures.

Microsoft's audit report appears in Exhibit 7–6. Observe that the third paragraph begins with the phrase "in our opinion." The auditor is not guaranteeing the financial statements nor certifying that they are 100% correct. To do so would be impossible, given that estimates are used in the accounting process. Further, an audit is conducted by using statistical sampling techniques and not by checking every transaction that occurred. An opinion, then, merely reflects the auditor's best judgment as to whether the statements are a "fair" representation of a company's economic transactions and events.

EXHIBIT 7–6
Audit Report of Microsoft Corporation

Report of Independent Auditors

To the Board of Directors and Stockholders of Microsoft Corporation:

We have audited the accompanying balance sheets of Microsoft Corporation and subsidiaries as of June 30, 1993 and 1994, and the related statements of income, stockholders' equity, and cash flows for each of the three years in the period ended June 30, 1994, appearing on pages 17, 23, 24, 25, and 28–32. These financial statements are the responsibility of the Company's management. Our responsibility is to express an opinion on these financial statements based on our audits.

We conducted our audits in accordance with generally accepted auditing standards. Those standards require that we plan and perform the audit to obtain reasonable assurance about whether the financial statements are free of material misstatement. An audit includes examining, on a test basis, evidence supporting the amounts and disclosures in the financial statements. An audit also includes assessing the accounting principles used and significant estimates made by management, as well as evaluating the overall financial statement presentation. We believe that our audits provide a reasonable basis for our opinion.

In our opinion, such financial statements present fairly, in all material respects, the financial position of Microsoft Corporation and subsidiaries as of June 30, 1993 and 1994, and the results of their operations and their cash flows for each of the three years in the period ended June 30, 1994 in conformity with generally accepted accounting principles.

Deloitte & Touche

Deloitte & Touche
Seattle, Washington
July 20, 1994

Unqualified and Qualified Opinions. Microsoft's audit report is *unqualified*, indicating that the auditor (Deloitte & Touche) has no significant reservations about the fairness of the statements. If major concerns did arise during the examination process, a *qualified* opinion might be issued. The use of improper accounting principles that produce a sizable impact on the financial statements would typically give rise to such a report.

Be aware that when an opinion is other than unqualified, it may be a "red flag" warning to investors. The opinion could be indicative of serious problems such as a lack of management integrity or the firm's impending financial failure. Often, the relationship among the auditor, management, and investors is strained in these situations. It is not uncommon for attorneys, regulators (the Securities and Exchange Commission), and others to become involved and for the story to be broadcast in the business press.

OTHER INFORMATION SOURCES

> **ETHICS ISSUE**
>
> Ohio, Inc., is seeking investors to fund expansion in a new product line. The company's public relations firm has been instructed to prepare a report about future prospects of this endeavor, relying heavily on information developed by Ohio's marketing and accounting departments. Comment.

An annual report is not the only available information source for evaluating a company. Large corporations are usually the subject of various write-ups prepared by financial analysts and stock brokerage firms. The write-ups will generally include prospective information, that is, how analysts view a company's future prospects with respect to growth, sales, income, and other important variables. Appendix B at the end of the text contains such a report.

Care should be exercised when evaluating analysts' reports since the preparer may not be totally objective. For instance, a brokerage firm may have an interest in the reader acquiring shares of the subject-company's stock because the purchase generates a commission. The preceding comments are precautionary only; they are not meant to suggest a total lack of integrity with information sources other than the annual report. A number of analyst-type publications are highly regarded and readily available at public libraries. Typical examples include Standard & Poor's, Moody's Investment Service, and Value Line.

THE ANALYSIS OF FINANCIAL INFORMATION

6 Describe the value of comparative standards and segment reporting in the evaluation of financial statements.

Acquiring financial information is the first step when trying to gain insights about a company. The second step involves careful analysis. There are many tools that may be used when studying a firm, including one that was introduced earlier in the text (ratio analysis). We now present another popular means to evaluate performance: comparative standards.

COMPARATIVE STANDARDS

Accountants, creditors, and investors continually employ comparative standards when judging an entity's financial relationships. Popular standards include past performance of the business and performance of other entities in the same industry. Relating the current data of a company with data of preceding years helps in determining whether relationships are improving or deteriorating. Unfortunately, single-company analyses do not provide a sufficiently broad basis for evaluation. For example, if a candy manufacturer incurred a net loss of $200,000 in 19X1 and a net loss of only $50,000 in 19X2, the firm has shown considerable improvement. However, if the manufacturer remains the only unprofitable producer in the country, the earnings records of both years can be viewed as being unfavorable.

The use of an external standard (or yardstick) often overcomes the limitation of single-company studies. That is, an entity's performance can be compared with the performance of a similar company or perhaps with averages of several companies in the same industry. The latter measure, known as *industry norms,* was originally introduced on page 147.

Similar-company comparisons, although logical, frequently create problems for the analyst because of size differences and firm diversification. These problems can be overcome by the use of common-size financial statements and segment information, respectively.

Common-Size Financial Statements. With *common-size financial statements,* each figure on a statement is related to a relevant total and expressed as a percentage of that total. This technique allows users to evaluate financial statements in relative terms and not be concerned about differences in absolute size. Consider, for example, recent abbreviated income statements (in millions) of Safeway, Inc., and Albertson's, Inc., two giants in the supermarket industry:

	SAFEWAY, INC.		ALBERTSON'S, INC.	
	$	PERCENT	$	PERCENT
Net sales	$15,214.5	100.0%	$11,283.7	100.0%
Cost of goods sold	11,083.4	72.8	8,492.5	75.3
Gross profit	$ 4,131.1	27.2%	$ 2,791.2	24.7
Expenses & income taxes	4,007.8	26.3	2,394.6*	21.2
Net income	$ 123.3	0.9%	$ 396.6	3.5%

*This figure was adjusted and excludes a nonrecurring $29.9 million charge that arose from a lawsuit.

Safeway's net sales were greater than those of Albertson's, thus producing larger dollar figures for both cost of goods sold and expenses and income taxes. As the data show, Safeway actually did a better job than its competitor in keeping inventory costs as a lower percentage of revenue (72.8% vs. 75.3%). Higher expenses and income taxes (26.3% vs. 21.2%) hurt the firm, however, driving income down to less than 1¢ from every sales dollar. Albertson's had more impressive performance in this respect, earning 3.5% of sales.

Segment Reporting. Many businesses operate in diverse markets with distinctly different product lines. An example is a company that is involved primarily in soft drink bottling but that also engages in the manufacture of small appliances, the operation of movie theaters, and trucking. An analyst studying this organization would definitely err by comparing the firm's financial statements against those of another entity that has only bottling activities. The diversified company's financial statements, of course, would present a combined picture of overall firm endeavors.

To help overcome the problem, companies that are engaged in distinctly different business activities and meet certain criteria must follow a practice known as *segment reporting.* This practice involves the disclosure of selected information to supplement that shown in the financial statements. More specifically, the sales, income, and identifiable assets of the individual segments would be shown as a note to the statements. Segment reporting thus provides an analyst with more detailed information, allowing improved (i.e., "like-for-like") comparisons to be made. Further, the practice makes it more difficult for firms to "hide" segments (winners and losers alike) within the realm of *total* sales, income, and asset figures on the income statement and the balance sheet.

An Example. For an illustration of segment reporting, we will focus on the activities of The Black & Decker Corporation. The company's recent annual report revealed the following segment data (in millions):

Segment	(A) Sales	(B) Operating Income	(C) Identifiable Assets
Consumer & home improvement products	$3,529.6	$215.8	$4,693.9
Commercial & industrial products	591.9	76.5	1,375.5
Information systems & services	760.7	28.9	494.2

The disclosure shows some interesting results. The largest segment, Consumer & Home Improvement Products, generated the greatest amount of operating income. However, when income is considered in relation to sales and the asset investment identified with this segment, Black & Decker's other activities are more "profitable." Commercial & Industrial Products yielded a higher return from each sales dollar, and Information Systems & Services produced the largest profits per dollar invested. These facts become more evident in the chart that follows, which reveals the operating income on sales ratios (B ÷ A) and the return on assets (B ÷ C).[10]

Segment	Operating Income on Sales Ratio Percent	Rank	Return on Assets Percent	Rank
Consumer & home improvement products	6.11%	2	4.60%	3
Commercial & industrial products	12.92%	1	5.56%	2
Information systems & services	3.80%	3	5.85%	1

REPORTING FOR SPECIALIZED ENTITIES

7 Recognize that the financial statements of different entity forms have different objectives and appearances.

Thus far we have discussed how to access and use financial information. It is important to understand that the nature of an enterprise could influence the reporting approach, with specialized industry standards having been implemented where appropriate. A detailed presentation of these standards is well beyond the scope of this text. At the very least, however, you should be aware that not all financial statements look the same.

UTILITY COMPANIES AND BANKS

Utility companies could be criticized as preparing "upside down" balance sheets. In the asset section, plant and equipment is listed first, followed by cur-

---

[10] Return on assets is discussed in more depth in Chapter 16.

rent assets. On the liability side, "capitalization" (i.e., owners' equity and long-term obligations) heads the list and is followed by current liabilities. The rationale for this arrangement is that utilities have substantial investments in plant and equipment, sometimes in the billions of dollars because of nuclear power plants. This investment is normally financed through permanent and long-term capital. Because statement users are particularly interested in these sizable components, evaluations of current assets and current liabilities take a back seat and are positioned accordingly.

Turning to banks, the balance sheets of these financial institutions are void of "current" and "noncurrent" labels. A bank's largest asset is its loans to customers (a receivable). Loans are typically classified by purpose—agricultural, real estate, and so forth. Customer deposits, another key item on the balance sheet, present a special reporting problem. Deposits are a liability to the bank because they are owed to clientele. Given that these amounts are payable on demand by the customer, it becomes difficult, if not impossible, to identify such sums as current or noncurrent.

GOVERNMENTAL UNITS

Governmental units do not operate with a profit objective. Instead, these entities provide services and spend only the amounts that have been approved by appropriate bodies (e.g., a local city council). Given the concern for staying within legally authorized budget limits, the accounting records of a governmental unit are divided into separate funds. For example, a city may have a special sales tax to promote tourism, and the related revenues and expenditures for this activity would be "tracked" out of the Tourism Fund. Similarly, the Capital Projects Fund would be used to account for major asset improvements such as streets and sewers.

A review of a governmental unit's financial reports will find an emphasis on funds. The resulting statements reflect accountability and strive to disclose resource (cash) flows—different objectives than the financial statements presented earlier in the chapter for Microsoft Corporation. These differences give rise to variations in both the statements themselves and presentation formats for the governmental unit.

NOT-FOR-PROFIT ENTERPRISES

Not-for-profit entities include voluntary health and welfare organizations (e.g., the American Cancer Society and the Salvation Army), many hospitals, colleges and universities, and churches. Recently enacted accounting standards stipulate that these organizations' financial statements should be relevant for donors, members, creditors, and other resource providers. In other words, the statements should allow providers to assess:

1. The services furnished and the ability of the not-for-profit entity to continue those services.
2. How well or how poorly the managers and directors have fulfilled their fiscal responsibilities.

A complete set of financial statements includes a **statement of activities** that shows, among other things, the use of resources by specific services and programs. Such information is helpful in judging whether donor contributions are being used for their intended purpose. The statements in general also allow a look at how much is being spent on administrative costs as well as on fund raising activities—frequent areas of scrutiny by contributors.

THE USER AS A CUSTOMER

The accounting profession has been in a constant state of evolution for over fifty years. One group is currently devoting substantial resources to a self-examination and has offered the following observations:

> A lot is right with today's business reporting in the United States. It generally provides users with essential information that heavily influences their decisions. In particular, financial statements are viewed as an excellent framework for capturing and organizing financial information . . . . Yet, many users are strongly critical about certain aspects of reporting.[11]

The profession's system of reporting is not perfect. It has probably gotten too carried away with disclosure, so much so that many investors cannot or will not read the annual reports of companies they own.

The self-examination process should be viewed as a legitimate, honest attempt at improvement. Most important, rather than take the attitude of the past where the profession dictated reporting requirements, the current feeling is that users should be studied (and consulted) to determine their actual information needs. This new attitude is refreshing; the improvements are being driven by a "customer" focus. As a future statement user, you can trust that the profession will seek to provide financial reports that meet your requirements. Even more encouraging, numerous forums exist that give you the opportunity to furnish input to the process.

APPENDIX: AN INTRODUCTION TO CONSOLIDATED FINANCIAL STATEMENTS

8

Recognize the meaning of consolidated financial statements and the special treatment needed for intercompany transactions.

When examining an annual report, it is very common to encounter the term "consolidated financial statements." Many large corporations actually consist of several companies that, in effect, operate as one large economic entity. This type of arrangement occurs for different reasons, including diversification, to attain operating efficiencies, and to ensure a steady source of raw material. As a typical illustration, auto manufacturers often own separate firms that provide financing and other services to customers and dealers.

These separate firms maintain their individual "unit" identity and also keep separate sets of accounting records. Yet their operating and financial performance are reported collectively to investors and other users through a series of consolidated financial statements. **Consolidated financial statements** present a combined picture of the businesses, as if only one organization existed. On a consolidated balance sheet, for example, the Cash account shows the cash owned by all of the firms. Accounts Payable reveals the collective, total amounts owed to suppliers, and so forth.

[11] "Improving Business Reporting—A Customer Focus," p. 8.

PARENT AND SUBSIDIARY RELATIONSHIPS

The companies involved in the consolidation process are known as a parent and its subsidiaries. To explain, businesses frequently acquire a controlling interest in other firms.[12] A controlling interest does not require 100% ownership; however, it does dictate majority ownership. The majority owner is called the parent; the majority-owned companies are termed subsidiaries.

Consolidated financial statements disclose the economic affairs of the total enterprise, namely, the activities that are under the parent's control. Furthermore, the statements provide more insight than could be gained by examining the separate statements of the individual companies.

INTERCOMPANY TRANSACTIONS

Companies within an affiliated group frequently have transactions with one another. Parent firms often purchase materials and supplies from their subsidiaries. In addition, a parent will commonly lend money to a subsidiary to help finance operations or capital improvement programs. Such transactions, referred to as intercompany transactions, present no special accounting problems for the individual entities involved. When consolidated financial statements are prepared, however, it is an entirely different story.

As an example, assume Parent Company owns a controlling interest of Sub Company. Sub is in need of funds and borrows $100,000 from Parent. The transaction would appear on the balance sheets of both enterprises in the following manner:

PARENT COMPANY Balance Sheet	**SUB COMPANY** Balance Sheet

Assets
    Loan receivable $100,000
	Liabilities
	    Loan payable $100,000

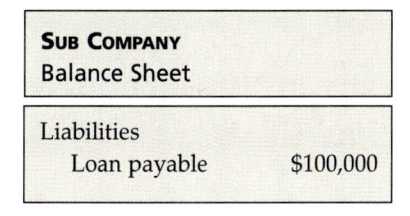

Suppose that a consolidated balance sheet of the two companies is now desired. If the two balance sheets were merely added together to reflect the financial position of the combined entity, the results would be very misleading. Put simply, the combined entity would report that it expects to both receive and pay $100,000 in the near future. Actually, this disclosure is incorrect because the $100,000 represents an expected transfer of cash from Sub to Parent, both of which are in the same economic unit.

Expanding further on our illustration, we emphasize that the combined unit does not have a claim on an outside party, nor does the unit owe an outsider. To properly reflect the impact of this transaction on the Parent/Sub affiliation, neither the loan receivable nor the loan payable should appear on the companies' consolidated balance sheet.

---

[12] Ownership occurs by purchasing shares of stock in the entity. As you will learn in the text, these shares have voting rights attached and thus give the acquirer the ability to control the entity's activities.

Elimination Entries. A set of *elimination entries* is therefore needed for intercompany items contained in the records of the parent and subsidiaries. The required elimination is performed by making an entry on a special work sheet that is used to combine the account balances. The necessary entry debits intercompany credit balances and credits intercompany debit balances. The entry that follows is needed for the $100,000 loan.

Loan Payable (Sub)	100,000	
Loan Receivable (Parent)		100,000
To eliminate intercompany receivable and payable.		

The end result is the absence of the loan on the combined balance sheet.

We stress that eliminations are made *only* on the special work sheet; they are *never* entered in the accounts of the parent or its subsidiaries. Entries into the accounts would formally (and erroneously) cancel transactions between the companies.

The magnitude and ultimate impact of these eliminations can often be seen by studying the segment information in the notes that accompany the financial statements. Here, one can typically examine the total transactions of the individual entities (i.e., segments), the eliminations for intercompany (intersegment) activity, and the resulting consolidated financial statement figures.

END-OF-CHAPTER REVIEW

LEARNING OBJECTIVES: THE KEY POINTS

1. **Discuss the role of financial reporting in providing useful information for decision making.** Accounting strives to furnish information that is useful in making sound economic decisions. This information should be relevant (i.e., important to an individual's decision-making process) and reliable. Reliability means that the information is truthful, verifiable, and not biased in favor of any particular user groups. Usefulness is complicated by the fact that few decision makers have the knowledge to comprehend a complete set of financial statements. Also, the amount of information available to a user is overwhelming in many cases, leaving little or no time for analysis.

2. **Recognize that net income is a function of accounting policies and estimates.** The income reported by companies is somewhat imprecise, being heavily influenced by the accounting policies and estimates employed by the firm. Various alternatives are often available to account for the same transactions and events. These alternatives are needed because no two businesses are identical, and unique attributes should be reflected in the financial statements. The statement reader should assess the reporting company's quality of earnings. Quality earnings are said to result from steady, continuous (as opposed to one-time) sources and from conservative accounting practices.

3. **Use and interpret a basic annual report.** The annual report is a primary communication link between a company and the general public. The report's major content includes the financial statements, notes to the financial statements, management reports, and the auditor's report.

4. **Explain the role of notes in providing full and fair disclosure.** The notes assist a user in better understanding the information being reported in the financial statements. One of the most important notes is the summary of significant accounting policies, which, as its name implies, discloses (1) the principles and methods that have been selected for use and (2) any reporting/accounting methods that are unique to the industry in which the business operates. Other notes are supplemental in nature, providing additional information as specified by regulatory agencies and the accounting profession. Segment and interim financial data fall in this category. Still other notes expand on information presented in the body of the financial statements and, accordingly, provide explanatory information to the user.

    In addition to the financial statement notes, annual reports contain several reports prepared by management. Management's Discussion and Analysis (MD&A) explains changes in the company's financial statements from one year to the next. In contrast, the letter to stockholders presents the firm's accomplishments during the year from a layman's (not accountant's) perspective.

5. **Discuss the role of auditing in affirming the fairness of the financial statements.** An audit involves a detailed examination of a company's transactions, documents, and controls and is performed by independent certified public accountants. The purpose is to determine whether the financial statements are free of significant errors and irregularities.

    The auditors' findings are expressed in an audit report. Most firms are able to secure an unqualified opinion, meaning that the auditor has no significant reservations about the company's statements. If major concerns did arise during the audit (e.g., from the use of improper accounting principles), a qualified opinion would likely be issued.

6. **Describe the value of comparative standards and segment reporting in the evaluation of financial statements.** Comparative standards allow an analyst to gain additional perspectives when evaluating financial information. Comparisons of a company's current data with figures reported in preceding years provide insights about whether relationships are improving or deteriorating. Further evaluations are frequently made with other companies or so-called industry norms to judge how an entity is performing versus other firms in similar lines of business.

    To eliminate differences in size when two or more companies are compared, analysts often turn to common-size financial statements. With this tool, each figure on a financial statement is related to and expressed as a percentage of a key statement total (e.g., net sales).

    Given the diverse nature of many entities, the accounting profession requires that certain firms follow specialized segment reporting practices. The sales, income, and identifiable assets of these companies' business segments are disclosed in the notes that accompany the financial statements, thereby allowing the analyst to make improved comparisons.

7. **Recognize that the financial statements of different entity forms have different objectives and appearances.** The financial statements of certain industries and/or specialized types of "business" units are sometimes governed by unique standards. Utility companies, for instance, list (1) plant and equipment before current assets and (2) stockholders' equity and long-term obligations before current liabilities. This presentation emphasizes the companies' significant investment in plant and equipment, which is normally financed through permanent and long-term capital. Banks, governmental units, and not-for-profit enterprises are also subject to specialized types of financial presentations.

8. **(Appendix) Recognize the meaning of consolidated financial statements and the special treatment needed for intercompany transactions**. Consolidated financial statements merge together the accounts of a parent and its subsidiary companies as if only one massive entity existed. A parent is the majority owner; in contrast, a subsidiary is the majority-owned company.

Because of transactions that occur between the parent and subsidiaries (termed intercompany transactions), special entries are prepared to eliminate the related financial effects from the consolidated statements. (The statements must reflect only transactions with outsiders, not between members of an affiliated group.) These elimination entries are made on a special work sheet and not in the ledger accounts. Placing such entries in the accounts would formally cancel valid transactions between the parties, giving rise to an erroneous set of accounting records.

Key Terms and Concepts: A Quick Overview

annual report A publication prepared by a company for distribution to stockholders and others; contains the firm's financial statements and other information. (p. 254)

audit report A report that presents the auditor's opinion regarding the fairness of the financial statements. (p. 265)

common-size financial statements Statements that reveal account balances in both dollars and percentages, thereby facilitating different types of comparative analyses. (p. 267)

consolidated financial statements A set of financial statements that combines the activities of the parent and controlled subsidiaries as if only one company existed. (p. 270)

elimination entry An entry made on a special work sheet that is used in preparing consolidated financial statements; eliminates intercompany transactions between the parent and its subsidiary companies. (p. 272)

fund The accounting and reporting unit of a governmental entity. (p. 269)

industry norms Averages of several companies in the same industry. (p. 267)

intercompany transaction A transaction between two affiliated companies such as a parent and a subsidiary. (p. 271)

interim financial data Data that are prepared for reporting periods other than a company's year-end. (p. 263)

letter to stockholders A portion of an annual report; explains, in a nontechnical way, the company's accomplishments during the year. (p. 264)

management's discussion and analysis (MD&A) A portion of an annual report; explains the differences between the current year's financial statements and those of preceding periods. (p. 263)

notes to the financial statements A supplemental, yet integral, part of the financial statements that expands on the information contained in the body of the statements. (p. 262)

operating income on sales ratio A ratio, computed as operating income divided by sales, that shows the return generated from each sales dollar. (p. 268)

parent A company that is the majority owner of another company. (p. 271)

quality of earnings An assessment of (1) the methods used to determine income and (2) the sources from which the income arose. (p. 256)

relevancy A characteristic of financial information. Information is deemed relevant if it influences the actions of a decision maker. (p. 253)

reliability A characteristic of financial information. Information is reliable if it is truthful, verifiable, and not biased in favor of any particular user group. (p. 253)

return on assets A ratio, calculated as operating income divided by assets, that shows the profit generated from a given level of investment. (p. 268)

segment reporting The disclosure of selected financial information when a company is involved in several distinct business activities. (p. 267)

statement of activities A financial statement issued by a not-for-profit enterprise that shows, among other things, the use of resources by specific services and programs. (p. 270)

subsidiary A company that has another company as its majority stockholder. (p. 271)

CHAPTER QUIZ

The five questions that follow relate to several issues raised in the chapter. Test your knowledge of the issues by selecting the best answer. (The answers appear on p. 285.)

1. Financial information *should* be:
   a. Reliable.
   b. Useful and reliable.
   c. Useful, reliable, and relevant.
   d. Useful, reliable, relevant, and understandable.

2. Analysts generally look with favor on earnings that result from:
   a. steady, on-going sources and conservative accounting practices.
   b. steady, on-going sources and very aggressive accounting practices.
   c. one-time sources and conservative accounting practices.
   d. one-time sources and very aggressive accounting practices.

3. Annual reports:
   a. are issued to corporate managers but not to stockholders.
   b. contain a corporation's financial statements, accompanying notes, and various other management disclosures.
   c. contain a corporation's financial statements but not the auditor's report.
   d. focus more on marketing the corporation's products than on disclosing financial information.

4. Which of the following would not be found in the notes that accompany the financial statements?
   a. The inventory method used by the company.
   b. Interim (quarterly) financial data, assuming the business is highly seasonal.
   c. A comment by the company's auditors concerning whether the financial statements are free of significant errors.
   d. The underlying details (e.g., interest rates and due dates) of any significant loans that have been obtained by the company.

5. Which of the following would not customarily be reported for a business segment?
   a. Revenues.
   b. Operating income.
   c. Identifiable assets.
   d. Major sources of cash during the period.

SUMMARY PROBLEM

Alicia Bowers recently inherited $35,000 from her grandmother. After purchasing a new car and paying off a college loan, she decided to invest the remaining $7,000 in the stock market. To learn more about business and financial matters, Alicia enrolled in a month-long continuing education course entitled "How to Invest Your Money Wisely."

Paul Harrington, the instructor, quickly made the class aware of various financial information sources. Much of the first session involved discussion of a booklet that focused on how to read and understand annual reports. At the conclusion of the first class, he told each participant to go to the library and study the annual reports of two popular corporations. He also asked that answers be prepared for the following questions:

- What information is typically found in an annual report?
- Do all companies use the same accounting practices to measure income and value assets? Why or why not? Where is information about a company's accounting policies found?
- The annual report contains a nontechnical, easy-to-read source that overviews a company's accomplishments during the year. What is it?
- What is the purpose of an audit? What is the basic difference between an unqualified and qualified audit opinion?
- What is the purpose of segment information? Where is segment information found?

Instructions

Assume the role of Alicia Bowers and prepare answers to the questions assigned by the instructor.

Solution

- An annual report includes information about a company's products and accomplishments, the financial statements, notes to the financial statements, management reports, and the auditor's report. The financial statements consist of an income statement, balance sheet, statement of cash flows, and statement of stockholders' equity. Management reports include management's discussion and analysis (MD&A) and the letter to stockholders.
- Companies do not all use the same accounting practices and reporting methods. The underlying reason is that no two businesses are alike; thus, some reporting diversity is needed to reflect a firm's unique features. Information about a company's policies is found in the notes to the financial statements, specifically, in a separate note entitled summary of significant accounting policies.
- This nontechnical source is the letter to stockholders. The letter is a user-friendly communication that is authored by the company's chief executive officer.
- An audit is a detailed examination of a company's transactions, documents, and controls conducted by independent certified public accountants. The major purpose of the audit is the expression of an opinion about whether the statements are free of major errors and irregularities. Stated differently, the auditors seek assurances that the statements are a "fair" representation of an organization's financial events and transactions. An unqualified opinion indicates that the auditors have no significant reservations about the fairness of the company's financial disclosures. A qualified opinion, on the other hand, signifies that some significant concerns have arisen.
- Segment reporting results in the presentation of selected financial information for highly diversified companies. This information, which is disclosed in the notes to the financial statements, typically includes the sales, income, and identifiable assets of an entity's major business segments. These disclosures help to improve comparative analysis between firms.

Assignment Material

Questions

Q7–1 Have recent years seen an increase or decrease in the volume of information available to financial statement users and analysts?

Q7–2 Right or wrong, many investors and creditors focus on a single accounting measurement to evaluate performance. What is this measure?

Q7–3 An analyst claims that Morton Corporation has a low quality of earnings. Briefly discuss what is meant by this comment.

Q7–4 What is the basic purpose of the notes to the financial statements?

Q7–5 Why are interim data useful to readers of financial statements?

Q7–6 Does a "clean" audit opinion serve to guarantee the correctness of the financial statements? Briefly discuss.

Q7–7 Would a company rather obtain a qualified opinion or an unqualified opinion from its auditors? Why?

Q7–8 Why is financial information of a business often compared with the past performance of the same company and the performance of other companies? What difficulties are sometimes encountered with the latter type of evaluation?

Q7–9 What is one of the basic benefits associated with the use of common-size financial statements?

Q7–10 Do all business enterprises prepare financial statements in the exact same manner? Briefly explain.

Q7–11 Do governmental units and not-for-profit enterprises prepare financial statements that are identical to those of for-profit businesses? Cite several examples to support your answer.

*****Q7–12** Define the term "consolidated financial statements."

*****Q7–13** Would a sale of goods from a parent to a subsidiary appear in the consolidated financial statements? Why or why not?

*****Q7–14** Why are elimination entries needed in the preparation of consolidated financial statements? Where are the eliminations recorded?

Exercises

E7–1 Characteristics of financial information (L.O. 1)
Consider the financial reporting practices of the four companies that follow.
 a. MJP typically reports its first-quarter earnings during the third quarter of the year.
 b. Reliable Storage reports items of property, plant, and equipment at market value as determined by a team of appraisers.
 c. St. John's Lighting does not use a certified public accountant to audit its financial statements. (The statements are prepared by management.)
 d. Lionel, Inc., reports only "bottom-line" net income rather than release a detailed income statement. The company considers sales and cost data to be confidential.

* An asterisk preceding an item indicates that the material is covered in an appendix to this chapter.

These firms are (or may be) violating the financial information characteristics of relevancy and reliability. Determine which characteristic applies in each of the four cases.

E7–2 Net income and accounting alternatives (L.O. 2)

Many people believe that net income is a precise measurement of a company's financial success or failure.

a. Is this belief correct? Briefly explain.
b. Should individual firms be allowed some flexibility in their selection of accounting methods and techniques? Why?

E7–3 Quality of earnings (L.O. 2)

Louisville and Metro are two very similar companies. Both firms are relatively young, engage in the same line of business, and have approximately the same sales. A review of the companies' financial statements found similar levels of operating expense, with the exception of building depreciation. Louisville uses the straight-line method and expenses an equal amount of depreciation each year over an estimated service life of 50 years. In contrast, Metro employs a more aggressive method that expenses a greater portion of the building's cost in the earlier years of asset use. This method is generally accepted by the accounting profession; Metro estimated the building's service life to be 40 years.

a. What is meant by the phrase "quality of earnings"?
b. Which company will likely report a higher net income? Why?
c. Which company appears to have a higher quality of earnings? Explain your answer.

E7–4 Management's discussion, quality of earnings (L.O. 2, 3)

Management's discussion and analysis (MD&A) of Desert Suites, an Arizona-based hotel operator, follows.

> The company is pleased to report a 20% rise in earnings to $180,000 for the year ended December 31, 19X8. This result compares favorably with earnings of $150,000 for the previous year. On a different note, we are obviously concerned and grieved about the August bomb explosion at the Reno facility. The bomb was detonated by a crazed extortionist upon our refusal to meet his demands for a $5,000,000 payment. Because we carry insurance on the replacement cost of assets (as opposed to original acquisition cost), the bombing netted the firm a $50,000 aftertax gain.

a. In general, what is the purpose of management's discussion and analysis?
b. Where is the MD&A found?
c. Evaluate Desert Suites' MD&A with regard to 19X8 earnings and operations.

E7–5 The audit report (L.O. 5)

Please read the audit report of Microsoft Corporation that appears on page 265 and answer the questions that follow.

a. Were the auditors (Deloitte & Touche) responsible for preparation of Microsoft's financial statements? Explain.
b. Were *all* of Microsoft's fiscal-year financial records scrutinized? Briefly discuss.
c. Could Microsoft's financial statements contain some small, immaterial errors?
d. Did Microsoft receive a qualified or unqualified audit opinion?

E7-6 Common-size financial statements (L.O. 6)

Top management of Alpha Resources implemented an extensive cost-cutting program last year in light of increased competition. Dave Fryer, the company's chief executive officer, is concerned that the program is a failure, given that operating expenses and income taxes rose by $178,000 for the year just ended. He has asked you to evaluate the following data (000 omitted):

	This Year	Last Year
Sales	$14,500	$13,200
Cost of goods sold	8,990	8,184
Operating expenses & income taxes	4,930	4,752

a. Prepare common-size income statements that compare this year's results versus those of last year.
b. Is the cost-cutting program a failure? Briefly explain.

E7-7 Segment reporting and analysis (L.O. 6)

Philip Morris is a large, diversified company, perhaps best known for its tobacco, food (Kraft), and brewing (Miller) operations. The firm is also involved in financial services and real estate. A recent annual report revealed the following segment information (in millions):

	Revenues	Operating Income	Identifiable Assets
Tobacco	$25,973	$4,910	$ 9,523
Food	30,372	2,608	33,253
Beer	4,154	215	1,706
Financial services & real estate	402	249	5,659

a. Relate operating income to identifiable assets and determine which segment was the least effective in terms of generating income from each dollar of asset investment.
b. Relate operating income to revenues and determine which segment was most successful in terms of generating income from a given dollar of sales.
c. How do users of financial information benefit from segment reporting?

E7-8 Alternative entity forms (L.O. 7)

The nature of an enterprise and the enterprise's operating objective have a major bearing on the financial statements. With this in mind, explain:

a. Why the balance sheets of public utilities list long-term liabilities before current liabilities.
b. Why governmental entities fail to prepare an income statement.
c. Why donors are often interested in a charitable organization's financial statements, including the statement of affairs.

*E7-9 Intercompany transactions (L.O. 8)

D Company is the parent to Companies A, B, and C. The following sales revenues were generated by the subsidiary firms:

A	$2,000,000
B	800,000
C	400,000
	$3,200,000

A generated $250,000 of sales by selling goods to B. B generated $110,000 of sales by selling goods to C. D's sales amounted to $8.9 million.

a. Are any elimination entries needed in this situation? Why?
b. How much sales revenue should be reported on the consolidated income statement? Briefly justify your answer.

*E7–10 Understanding consolidated statements (L.O. 8)

Payton, Inc., has two subsidiaries: Atlas Manufacturing and Miami Glass Corporation. A recent article in a leading financial publication mentioned a $750,000 loan from Payton to Miami.

a. How would this loan be disclosed on Payton's balance sheet?
b. How would this loan be disclosed on Miami's balance sheet?
c. How would this loan be disclosed on the companies' consolidated balance sheet?
d. Prepare any elimination entries that may be necessary in this situation.

PROBLEMS

Series A

P7–A1 Income information (L.O. 2, 4)

Not too long ago, a headline in the *Akron Gazette's* business section read "Maverick Expects Loss for 1st Quarter." The article noted that Maverick Foods will likely report a first-quarter net loss, which follows a 92% decline in the previous quarter's profit. In response to the news, the restaurant operator's stock fell 18%.

The Ohio company blamed growing competition and the price-consciousness of consumers for the less-than-stellar performance. Maverick also shortened the period over which it expenses sizable pre-opening costs, which are averaging $500,000 per restaurant. The firm now spreads these costs over two years rather than over a five-year period as in the past. The article went on to note that revenue rose 36% to $23.9 million, but revenue from stores open for more than one year fell 7.9%.

Instructions

a. Does this article provide evidence of strong investor reliance on reported income amounts? Briefly explain.
b. The reported earnings drop and net loss are influenced by the accounting methods and estimates used by the company. Where would information on these methods and estimates typically be found in a company's annual report?
c. On the basis of the information presented, has Maverick's quality of earnings improved or deteriorated? Briefly discuss.
d. Explain how revenue could rise 36% when revenues from stores open for more than one year fell 7.9%.

P7–A2 Reading a corporate annual report (L.O. 3)

Jan Clayton was recently asked to analyze the annual report of Microsoft Corporation as part of an accounting class project. Jan's instructor furnished the following list of questions to be answered, all of which pertain to the 1994 fiscal year:

a. What is the company's largest cost or expense?
b. What is the ratio of gross profit to sales?
c. What is the firm's largest current asset?
d. What were the three largest consumers of cash during the year?
e. Was any capital (common) stock issued during the year? If so, how much?
f. What inventory valuation method does Microsoft use?
g. Did Microsoft have a good year?
h. Which accounting firm audited the company's financial statements?
i. Was the accounting firm satisfied with the integrity and fairness of Microsoft's financial statements? Briefly explain.

Instructions

Disclosures from Microsoft's annual report are presented throughout this chapter. Assume the role of Jan Clayton and answer her instructor's questions. Be sure to list the data source (notes to the financial statements, balance sheet, and so forth) for each answer.

P7–A3 Annual report content (L.O. 3, 4, 5, 6)

Two excerpts from an initial rough draft of Garjullo Canning Company's annual report follow.

From the audit report—
We feel strongly that the financial statements of Garjullo Canning Company are 100% correct with respect to the financial position of the firm at December 31, 19X3 and 19X2, and the results of operations and cash flows for each of the three years in the period ended December 31, 19X3.

From the detailed footnotes and supplemental disclosures—
To avoid calling attention to highly-profitable, major components of our diversified business, management has elected not to disclose segment information normally required by the Financial Accounting Standards Board. Such action maintains the integrity of confidential company information and thus helps to preserve the value of shareholder investments.

A review of the letter to stockholders found a detailed lengthy narrative that compared the 19X3 financial statements to those of preceding years.

Instructions

Evaluate the initial draft in terms of sound financial reporting. Include in your evaluation any appropriate suggestions for improvement.

Series B

P7–B1 Income information (L.O. 2, 4)

Libby Co. recently reported lower earnings and a 20% decline in system-wide sales. The restaurant operator blamed two highly-publicized contamination cases that arose from inadequate cooking procedures. Libby also wrote off (as a loss) most of its investment in eight underperforming facilities. These locations were closed and are in the process of being sold.

News wires on April 19 reported quarterly net income of $100,000 as compared to $600,000 for the same period one year earlier. The company's stock closed the day at $6, down $2.

Instructions

a. Why do you think that the price of Libby's stock decreased so much on a single day?
b. Comment on the company's quality of earnings.
c. Is it possible that Libby's action with respect to the underperforming restaurants could signal improved earnings of future periods? Briefly discuss.
d. Would further information on the loss likely be found in the firm's summary of significant accounting policies? Explain.

P7–B2 Reading a corporate annual report (L.O. 3)

Skip Dowdy was recently asked to analyze the annual report of Microsoft Corporation as part of an accounting class project. Skip's instructor furnished the following list of questions to be answered, all of which pertain to the 1994 fiscal year:

a. Did the company declare any dividends during the year?
b. What is Microsoft's largest asset and largest liability?
c. Comment on the firm's trends with respect to sales and net income.
d. What depreciation method does Microsoft use for its long-term assets?
e. How much cash was generated from operating activities and long-term debt issuances, respectively?
f. Which of the company's financial statements were audited by Deloitte & Touche?
g. Did Deloitte & Touche find any significant violations of generally accepted accounting principles by Microsoft? Briefly discuss.
h. Did Microsoft buy back any capital (common) stock during 1994? If so, how much?
i. When does the company recognize revenue from its software maintenance contracts?

Instructions

Disclosures for Microsoft's annual report are presented throughout this chapter. Assume the role of Skip Dowdy and answer his instructor's questions. Be sure to list the data source (notes to the financial statements, balance sheet, and so forth) for each answer.

P7–B3 Annual report content (L.O. 3, 4, 5, 6)

Two excerpts from an initial rough draft of Tacoma Paper Company's annual report follow.

From the detailed footnotes and supplemental disclosures—
To avoid calling attention to certain periods that were extremely profitable, management has elected to omit disclosures of interim financial data. Such data serve only to supplement the figures already shown in the financial statements.

From the audit report (as written by Tacoma's internal audit staff)—
We have thoroughly examined all of our transactions and events. In our opinion, the financial statements present fairly the company's financial position as of December 31, 19X7 and 19X6, and the results of operations and cash flows for each of the three years in the period ended December 31, 19X7, in conformity with generally accepted accounting principles.

A review of the footnotes found a detailed report that depicted changes in Tacoma's stockholders' equity accounts.

Instructions

Evaluate the initial draft in terms of sound financial reporting. Include in your evaluation any appropriate suggestions for improvement.

EXPANDING YOUR HORIZONS

EYH7–1 Earnings announcements (L.O. 2)

Major metropolitan newspapers and *The Wall Street Journal* often contain lengthy articles that discuss corporate earnings announcements. Reported income may be higher or lower than analysts' expectations, perhaps because of on-going changes in operations, one-time activities and events, and even changes in accounting methods.

Instructions

Locate four articles that focus on corporate earnings announcements. Briefly summarize why reported earnings increased or decreased. Also rate the quality of the earnings *change* from your perspective by using a scale of 1 (high quality) to 5 (low quality). Be prepared to report your findings to the class.

EYH7–2 Corporate annual reports; other data sources (L.O. 3)

Obtain an annual report from a large, publicly held corporation and a current copy of a metropolitan newspaper that contains stock price information. (*The Wall Street Journal* may be substituted for the metropolitan newspaper.)

Instructions

After reviewing the annual report and the stock price listings in the newspaper, determine the following:

a. Name of corporation.
b. Key products and/or services.
c. Location of corporate headquarters.
d. Number of members on the board of directors.
e. Most recent calendar or fiscal year reported. *Note:* Items that follow should be answered for the most recent year reported or, if appropriate, the end of that year.
f. Total revenues.
g. Net income.
h. Total assets, liabilities, and stockholders' equity.
i. Current ratio.
j. Retained earnings balance.
k. Largest source of cash from financing activities.
l. Largest use of cash in investing activities.
m. Depreciation method(s) used by the firm.
n. Number of business segments in which the company operates.
o. Name of company's certified public accountants.
p. Type of audit opinion received (qualified or unqualified).
q. Name of stock exchange where the capital stock is traded.
r. Number of capital shares bought and sold during the trading day (see newspaper).
s. The increase or decrease in the capital stock price during the trading day.

EYH7–3 Analysis of letter to stockholders (L.O. 3)

Several years ago, two business reporters advanced an interesting theory (see "The Windbag Theory," *Forbes*, August 3, 1992, pp. 43-44). After performing an analysis of annual reports and the letter to stockholders, the reporters observed a relationship between financial performance and writing style. More specifically, as a company's performance deteriorated over time, the verbosity in the firm's letter to stockholders tended to increase.

Instructions

a. Obtain the annual report of a company whose performance has been marked by wide swings in prosperity over a short period of time. Examples may include retailers, now-bankrupt airlines, failed banks, computer companies, energy-related companies, and so forth. Study the readability of the letter to stockholders in a good year and a bad year. Examine the length of the letter, words per sentence, word length, and overall writing level by using a software program such as Grammatik.
b. Write a brief analysis of your findings. Does your conclusion provide evidence to support or oppose "the windbag theory"?

COMMUNICATION OF ACCOUNTING INFORMATION

CAI7–1 Preparing an oral presentation (L.O. 4, 6)

Communication Principle: Preparing an oral presentation requires imagination and organization. The first challenge is to gain the audience's attention through a dynamic introduction. By using the principles cited in CAI12–1 on page 468, the speaker must focus the audience on the subjects to be discussed. Like the introduction to a report, a presentation's opening introduces and clearly outlines the speaker's main points. In contrast, the conclusion should summarize the major ideas discussed and remind the audience of what they now know or understand.

When preparing a speech, the author should write out the introduction and then the conclusion—word for word. Once these two sections are completed, the remainder of the presentation is developed through a detailed outline. Standard principles of outline organization include the following:

1. Every main point should have two or more subpoints.
2. Main points and subpoints should be of comparable importance and weighted relatively equally in terms of coverage.
3. The organization should be kept as simple as possible. Outlines for oral presentations should contain no more than five main points and preferably only three. Two or three subpoints, including illustrations, are more than enough for an audience to remember.

Above all, be brief. No matter how long the presentation actually is, if you continually tell yourself that the material must be covered in 5 or 10 minutes, you will find it easier to keep the speech to a manageable length. Remember that with a simpler, clearer, and shorter presentation, the audience is sure to be more appreciative.

■ ■ ■ ■ ■ ■ ■ ■

Hillary Lipscomb is the accounting manager of ATP Industries. The local chapter of the Rotary Club has asked that she deliver a 30-minute presentation about "user-friendly" financial reporting. After doing considerable deliberation, she has decided to focus on the following topics:

- Helpful information contained in the notes to the financial statements.
- The concept of segment reporting.
- The usefulness of common-size financial statements.

Instructions

Prepare the speech's introduction, an outline of the major points to be covered, and an appropriate conclusion.

Answers to Chapter Quiz

1. d
2. a
3. b
4. c
5. d

8 CASH AND LIQUID INVESTMENTS

LEARNING OBJECTIVES

After studying this chapter, you should be able to:

1. Describe the composition of cash and explain how cash is presented on a balance sheet.
2. Explain cash management and identify the methods that companies use to accelerate inflows and delay (or eliminate) outflows.
3. Recognize the controls that should be utilized with the processing of cash receipts and cash payments.
4. Reconcile a bank account.
5. Establish and operate a petty cash system.
6. Define and account for trading securities.

Even though it is a very tedious job, George Faris has always paid close attention to Banner Advertising's daily cash receipts and payments. He handles some of the related record keeping himself. "I realize it consumes a great deal of time, but this is cash. Without it I can't pay my bills, and I'd be out of business. Proper cash management is essential for a small firm such as mine."

There are several facets to George's concern. Although he has confidence in his employees, George understands the unique nature of cash and the need to maintain tight control. Because adequate separation of duties is difficult in a small business, he has delegated the task of reviewing cash to hands he can trust—his own.

"Some days I really feel wealthy; then the next day the bills come due, both the expected and the unexpected." George likes to know exactly where he stands at all times. Close monitoring of funds allows him to have ample cash to pay the amounts due. Additionally, he knows when excess cash is available to either reduce costly debt or invest in securities that have a respectable rate of return. By following these practices, George is better able to stay in touch with his business. He understands where the money is going and often asks questions when he thinks that too much is being spent for a particular item.

George could possibly be criticized for consuming excessive hours on monitoring the company's funds. On the other hand, one cannot argue with success. Perhaps there is an important lesson to be learned in observing how successful people oversee the details, especially when those details relate to something as vital as receipts and payments.

Business owners like George are not the only ones who pay close attention to cash (and liquid securities as well). Lenders, creditors, and prospective suppliers often compare the amounts of these assets with current liabilities when judging a firm's debt-paying ability. Investors review the cash and liquid investments of a business to gauge the funds available for dividend distributions as well as for projects that are important to future profitability. Even employees are interested in cash and liquid securities, because salary increases are sometimes tied to the funds available and the balances in these two accounts. It is important, then, that cash and liquid investments be properly accounted for and presented in the financial statements.

CASH

1 Describe the composition of cash and explain how cash is presented on a balance sheet.

The items reported in the Cash account on the balance sheet must be (1) acceptable to a bank for deposit and (2) free from restriction for use in satisfying current debts. Cash therefore includes *coins, currency, funds on deposit with a bank (checking accounts and savings accounts), checks, and money orders*. The following items are not considered to be cash for accounting purposes: postdated checks, IOUs, and travel advances. *Note*

1. *Postdated checks*—Postdated checks are checks that become payable on a date subsequent to the issue date. For example, suppose Buck Company issued a check to Foy Company on April 15. Buck dated the check April 22, because it lacked sufficient funds on the date of issuance. Since Foy cannot cash or deposit the check until the 22nd, the postdated check is not classified as cash. Postdated checks are receivables until the date they can be deposited.
2. *IOUs*—IOUs are written acknowledgments of debts; however, these items are not negotiable and usually cannot be used to pay off liabilities. IOUs are therefore considered to be receivables until the time of collection.
3. *Travel advances*—These amounts have been given to employees to cover out-of-pocket expenses incurred on business trips. The employees must either provide receipts for monies spent or return any unspent funds. As a result, travel advances are normally disclosed as receivables on the balance sheet.

BALANCE SHEET PRESENTATION

The Cash account is listed on the balance sheet in the current asset section. For concise reporting, all cash items are normally combined and presented as a single figure.

As we noted earlier, the amount reported for cash must be available for use in satisfying current debts. Sometimes, businesses establish restricted funds to accumulate cash for specific purposes. As an example, a special fund may be created to repay money borrowed (often termed a *sinking fund*) or to expand a manufacturing plant. These funds should not be classified as current assets on the balance sheet because they are not available to settle current obligations. Likewise, amounts held in foreign banks should not be reported as current assets if governmental regulations restrict the transfer of funds out of the foreign country.

Occasionally, a bank may require that a portion of the amount lent to customers remain on deposit in the bank for the duration of the loan period. These required deposits are termed compensating balances. The existence of compensating balances should be fully disclosed so that financial statement users are made aware of restrictions on the funds availability.

2 Explain cash management and identify the methods that companies use to accelerate inflows and delay (or eliminate) outflows.

CASH MANAGEMENT

Effective cash management is important to the success of any company. Care must be taken to ensure that sufficient cash is available to meet current obligations but that unnecessarily large balances do not remain in checking accounts. Such balances typically earn little or no interest and therefore represent a loss of earnings potential.

Companies use a variety of tools to manage cash. Some of the tools are monitoring devices, allowing a business to study the adequacy of cash balances in meeting normal obligations. The cash budget, for example, is an overall plan that depicts cash inflows and outflows for a stated period of time. This plan is useful in the management of most any organization, because it pinpoints when cash surpluses and shortages are likely to occur. Predicting surpluses and shortages before they take place allows a business to analyze potential high-return investments and locate relatively low-cost sources of funds. Investment and financing decisions are thereby improved.

Other cash management tools focus specifically on receipts and payments. These tools have a goal of accelerating the inflows and postponing (or eliminating) the outflows, thus providing the firm with the optimum cash balances available.

Acceleration of Cash Inflows. Companies have several means to speed up the inflows of cash to the business. Consider the cash discount that was introduced in Chapter 5. By granting terms of, say, 2/10, n/30, a customer has incentive to settle a balance due within 10 days rather than wait the entire 30-day credit period.

A lockbox system is another popular tool that accelerates inflows. You may have noticed that on some credit card invoices (e.g., those issued by certain oil companies), the delivery address is a post office box located in a city different from the company's headquarters. In many of these instances, the firm is employing a lockbox system for the processing of receipts.

Under such a system, a messenger from a regional bank collects the mail and immediately enters customers' checks as a deposit at the bank. Customer payment information is then either wired electronically or mailed to the firm. The end result is that company cash balances at the bank are increased two to three days sooner than would occur under a traditional processing system. (The traditional system is slower because receipts are mailed to the company, which may be thousands of miles away from the customer, processed, and later deposited.)

Postponement/Elimination of Cash Outflows. Accelerating inflows is only one aspect of good cash management. Another key component involves postponing or, where possible, eliminating the outflows. Some relatively simple techniques are available to virtually all businesses (and in some instances, to individuals).

For example, it is common practice to play the float on outgoing checks. The goal is for a business to settle an invoice promptly, but to have the associated check clear the firm's bank account later—much later. Such a procedure increases the amount of funds on hand, thus improving the entity's cash position.

As you may know, float results because checks written by a company are not simultaneously deducted from the company's account at the bank. It may take several days for the check to be processed by the receiving firm and then several more days to be processed through the Federal Reserve's clearing system. To illustrate, assume that Baxter Corporation owes $50,000 to Fidelity Enterprises for purchases of merchandise. The invoice is due on May 14; Baxter is located in Boston, and Fidelity is headquartered in San Francisco. Consider the following chain of events:

> May 9 Baxter writes and mails the check to Fidelity.
> 13 The check is received and processed by Fidelity.
> 15 The check is deposited at Fidelity's bank in San Francisco.
> 18 The check clears Baxter's bank in Boston.

Even if Baxter had a very tight cash position in its checking account on May 9, the firm would have had until May 18 to make a deposit that eased the situation. In so doing, Baxter has successfully played the float and is also in good standing with Fidelity. Of course, cutting things "too tight" could come back to haunt Baxter if, for instance, the check had cleared sooner than expected.[1]

A FURTHER FOCUS

Using a small bank located in a remote location will often lengthen the float time. Check-clearing time may be increased by several days with such a procedure, especially when compared with using a large bank in a metropolitan area. The latter will likely have excellent mail service and be easily accessed by couriers.

Another way to delay outflows is to eliminate the travel advance that was discussed earlier in the chapter. An increased number of companies are now relying on employees to advance the required funds for business trips. The companies, though, are sometimes providing assistance by issuing American Express credit cards. Mobil, the giant oil producer, recently implemented this practice to help cover approximately $50 million in annual domestic travel costs. One of the firm's executives noted that savings under the new system have been substantial, although he wouldn't specify an exact amount. Savings come in the form of avoiding the administrative costs related to issuing, tracking, and collecting the cash; reducing fraudulent reporting by personnel; and eliminating the problems (and expenses) associated with collecting amounts due from former employees.[2]

Finally, there is the age-old barter system, where businesses conserve cash by swapping (instead of purchasing) goods. There are now organized barter exchanges that unite participating companies. Although the barter system is still relatively unknown, it is becoming more popular, particularly with small cash-starved businesses. Two reporters from *The Wall Street Journal* feel that the 1984 Olympic Games helped to improve the overall image of bartering. They noted:

> In one of the larger-scale examples of such trade, the Los Angeles Olympic Organizing Committee swapped the licensing rights of the Olympic logo and mascot, "Sam, the Olympic Eagle," to major corporations. In return, the committee received free transportation from United Airlines, the use of 500 Buick cars from General Motors Corp., and 250,000 rolls of film, plus processing, from Fuji Film.[3]

---

[1] Although it is sometimes practiced, creating negative bank balances by playing the float (i.e., writing checks against undeposited funds) is actually unlawful.

[2] See "To Cut Costs, Companies Are Closing the Cash Drawer," *The Wall Street Journal*, September 29, 1994, p. B1.

[3] "Small Firms, Short on Cash, Turn to Barter," *The Wall Street Journal*, November 26, 1990, pp. B1, B2.

CASH CONTROL

> **3** Recognize the controls that should be utilized with the processing of cash receipts and cash payments.

Cash control systems are the procedures adopted to safeguard an organization's funds. These systems establish adequate internal control over cash. Recall that internal control aids a company in safeguarding its assets, checking the reliability and accuracy of accounting information, promoting operational efficiency, and encouraging adherence to prescribed managerial policies. A strong cash control system is essential, given that employees and others regard cash as a very desirable asset. In addition, cash is difficult to trace because it has no readily identifiable means to establish ownership. Although currency does have serial numbers, companies make no attempt to record these numbers in view of the overwhelming amount of bookkeeping that would be required.

The internal control system for cash is based on the general internal control features discussed in Chapter 6. An organization should limit the access to cash to a few authorized personnel only. Furthermore, incompatible duties such as the authorization of cash transactions, the entry of cash transactions in the accounting records, and the custody of cash should be separated. Finally, the following accountability procedures should be implemented: prenumbered checks, verification of invoices prior to payment, and verification of the cash balance as reported in the general ledger. These general control features become apparent when studying typical accounting procedures for cash receipts and cash disbursements.

Receipts from Cash Sales. The control of cash receipts attempts to ensure that all cash inflows are safeguarded from the time they are received by a company until they are deposited in a bank account. A major source of cash inflows for many firms is cash sales. Control over cash sales is facilitated by the use of an electronic point-of-sale terminal, which requires that a salesperson record each sale in full view of the customer and provide the customer with a receipt. As the clerk enters the transaction information, the sale is simultaneously recorded on a paper tape. At the end of the business day, a store manager compares the cash collected with the total cash sales listed on the tape. The tapes are then forwarded to the accounting department and entered in the company's records. The cash is kept in a vault until deposited in the bank or picked up by an armored car service such as Brink's or Loomis.

Cash sale transactions often give rise to errors. Because of mistakes in giving change, for example, the actual cash on hand may differ slightly from the total indicated sales. If these errors are frequent, significant in amount, or traceable to the same employee, personnel adjustments may be necessary.

The accounting treatment for cash excesses and deficiencies is relatively simple. To illustrate, assume that cash sales for the Eldridge Shop on July 7 amounted to $1,247. However, cash in the terminal's drawer was only $1,237. The following entry is necessary:

Cash	1,237	
Cash Short & Over	10	
Sales		1,247
To record cash sales and cash shortage.		

In contrast to the preceding entry, the Cash Short & Over account would be credited when cash in the terminal exceeds the amount of cash sales recorded.

At the end of a reporting period, the net balance in Cash Short & Over is calculated. A net debit balance would be disclosed on the income statement with other miscellaneous expenses of the business, while a net credit balance is treated as miscellaneous revenue.

Receipts from Customers on Account. Many organizations generate large inflows of cash from customer receipts on account. Assuming use of a traditional processing system, these inflows arrive in the mail and require a careful separation of duties. The following procedures are normally employed:

1. The daily counting of cash receipts is assigned to one person or, in large businesses, to a group of specific personnel. The personnel open the mail, prepare a list of checks received, and forward the list to the accounting department.
2. The checks are forwarded to a cashier, who prepares a deposit slip and deposits all receipts intact on a *daily* basis. Daily deposits prevent bills from being paid out of current receipts; they also minimize the amount of cash left on the premises at the end of the business day, thus reducing the possibility of large losses from theft. A duplicate deposit slip is then sent to the accounting department.
3. The accounting department compares the list of cash receipts with the deposit slip and enters the daily mail-in receipts in the accounting records. Naturally, any discrepancies between the deposit slip and the list of receipts require investigation.

Cash Disbursements. The control over disbursements includes procedures that will allow only authorized payments for actual company expenditures. A cash disbursements system with proper internal control should include the following features:

1. All significant disbursements are made by check so that a record (i.e., written evidence) exists for expenditures.
2. An organization's Cash account in the general ledger is periodically compared with the cash balance reported by the bank.
3. Certain small payments are made by using a *petty cash system*. (The operation of a petty cash system will be explained later in this chapter.)
4. Before a disbursement is made from a company's checking account or petty cash system, the expenditure is verified and approved. Verification may take the form of examining purchase orders, invoices, and receiving reports.

These procedures, like so many others, are aided by a proper separation of duties. For example, the person signing the checks should not be the same individual who prepares the checks. In addition, the comparison of a company's general ledger cash balance with the cash balance reported by the bank (recordkeeping function) should not be performed by an employee who handles cash (custody function). Separation of duties helps in the detection of errors and also makes theft or fraud more difficult.

④ Reconcile a bank account.

Bank Reconciliations. As previously noted, adequate internal control requires the use of checks for significant cash payments. Canceled checks and their endorsements furnish written evidence that payments have been made. In addition, checking accounts provide security and safety for the large cash balances that many businesses must carry.

As you can well imagine, a company will have many cash receipts and disbursements during a given accounting period. Because of the high frequency of transactions and the potential for error, the accuracy of the cash balance in the general ledger (or your checkbook) should be periodically examined. This process, called a **bank reconciliation,** is based on the Cash account and a document called a **bank statement.**

Bank Statements Versus Cash Accounts. Businesses and individuals receive monthly bank statements for every checking account they maintain. An example of a bank statement appears in Exhibit 8–1. Bank statements summarize the activity in a checking account and report the ending monthly balance. It is important to understand that although the Cash account of a depositor (such as Johnson Manufacturing) is an asset, the depositor's account is carried on the bank's records as a *liability.* Consequently, checks and other debits by the bank *reduce* Johnson's account, while deposits and other credits *increase* the account.

A Further Focus

The **electronic debit card,** often called a cash card, is an easy way to remember the effect of a debit on a bank account. These cards are used in conjunction with automated teller machines (ATMs) to process a variety of cash transactions, the vast majority of which are withdrawals (i.e., reductions in cash balances).

Debit cards are also gaining popularity for use in retail sales. Customers can now insert debit cards in point-of-sale terminals that electronically access bank accounts. Once the customer enters the correct personal identification number, the transaction amount is immediately deducted from the purchaser's account and simultaneously recorded as part of the store's receipts.

At the end of a month, the bank statement cash balance and the company's cash records will normally not agree. A major reason for this discrepancy is the timing differences associated with the use of a checking account. Timing differences result in an item being recorded on the depositor's books or the bank's books, but not both, in a given accounting period. As explained earlier in the chapter, some of these differences arise from the operations of the Postal Service and the check-clearing procedures of the Federal Reserve System. Common examples of timing differences include the following:

1. Items reflected on the company's records but not yet reported on the bank statement, such as:
   a. **Deposits in transit**—receipts entered in a firm's accounts but not yet processed by the bank. This situation often occurs when deposits are mailed. Deposits in transit are determined by comparing deposits that appear on the bank statement with deposits as reported in an organization's Cash account.

EXHIBIT 8–1
Bank Statement

FIRST CITY BANK TRUST
101 North James Ave.
Chicago, Illinois 60638

JOHNSON MANUFACTURING CORPORATION
1800 SOUTH MAIN
CHICAGO, ILLINOIS 60634

Account No. 0008564201   Page No. 1

Statement Period
From 7/31/XX   To 8/31/XX

Deposits/Credits		Checks/Debits			Balance	
Date	Amount	No.	Date	Amount	Date	Amount
8/03	3,984.40	606	8/01	1,250.40	8/01	18,257.10
8/05	3,150.43	620	8/02	940.20	8/02	17,316.90
8/06	2,897.04	624	8/05	1,960.85	8/03	21,301.30
8/07	4,925.75	625	8/04	2,640.00	8/04	18,661.30
8/09	5,242.70	626	8/08	375.00	8/05	19,850.88
8/13	4,600.80 NC	627	8/08	675.18	8/06	22,747.92
8/13	75.00 IC	628	8/11	540.20	8/07	27,673.67
8/20	4,167.10	629	8/13	728.40	8/08	26,623.49
8/22	5,145.18	630	8/12	139.50	8/09	31,866.19
8/27	4,752.30	631	8/17	650.53	8/11	31,325.99
8/30	3,237.80	632	8/17	437.29	8/12	31,058.59
		633	8/20	2,147.90	8/13	35,005.99
		634	8/23	989.05	8/17	33,918.17
		635	8/22	12,785.50	8/20	35,937.37
		636	8/27	10,640.90	8/22	28,297.05
		637	8/28	2,470.80	8/23	27,308.00
		639	8/30	740.15	8/27	21,419.40
		DM	8/12	127.90	8/28	18,948.60
		SC	8/31	20.00	8/30	21,446.25
					8/31	21,426.25

Beginning Balance	Deposits/Credits		Checks/Debits		Ending Balance
	No.	Amount	No.	Amount	
19,507.50	11	42,178.50	19	40,259.75	21,426.25

Code Explanation: CM *Credit Memo*   IC *Interest Collection*   SC *Service Charge*
DM *Debit Memo*   NC *Note Collection*

    b. Outstanding checks—checks written by a business but not yet processed by the bank. Outstanding checks are determined by comparing checks reported on the bank statement against checks written on the company's records.
2. Items reported on the bank statement but not yet entered in the company's records, such as:
    a. Nonsufficient funds (NSF) checks—customer checks deposited but returned because of a lack of funds. NSF checks are frequently reported on the bank statement via a debit memo notation, because the bank has reduced the depositor's account.
    b. Bank service charges for account processing.

c. Notes receivable[4] and interest collected by the bank. The collection of a note and interest is sometimes reported with a credit memo notation because of the increase in the depositor's account balance.
d. Interest earned on the account.

In addition to timing differences, errors may cause a discrepancy between the bank statement balance and company accounting records. Errors can be made by either the company or the bank and must be corrected as quickly as possible.

The Reconciliation Process. Several different types of reconciliations can be prepared. The most commonly encountered form results in determining the amount of cash a company has control over and reports on its end-of-period balance sheet. An example appears in Exhibit 8–2.

The exhibit reveals the thrust of a reconciliation. That is, we strive to isolate specific items that cause a difference between the depositor's records and the bank statement balance. The accountant considers these items and adjusts one cash balance or the other to bring both balances into agreement.

If the balances do not agree and the reconciling items are deemed correct, there is an excellent chance that a record-keeping error has been made. Errors must be identified and then added or subtracted on the reconciliation to arrive at the corrected cash balance. For example, if a check written by a firm for $94.50 was incorrectly entered in the accounting records as $49.50, the accounting records will be overstated by $45.00 ($94.50 – $49.50). This amount ($45) should therefore be deducted from the ending cash balance per company records, since the company's books are in error. The bank, of course, will deduct the correct amount of the transaction ($94.50) when the check is received for payment. The reconciliation, then, not only highlights timing differences but also identifies errors made by either the bank or the depositor.

> **ETHICS ISSUE**
>
> The bank reconciliation of Vienna Company reveals a significant bank error in Vienna's favor that will probably go undetected. If an accountant notifies company management and management refuses to contact the bank, what should the accountant do?

EXHIBIT 8–2
Illustrative Bank Reconciliation

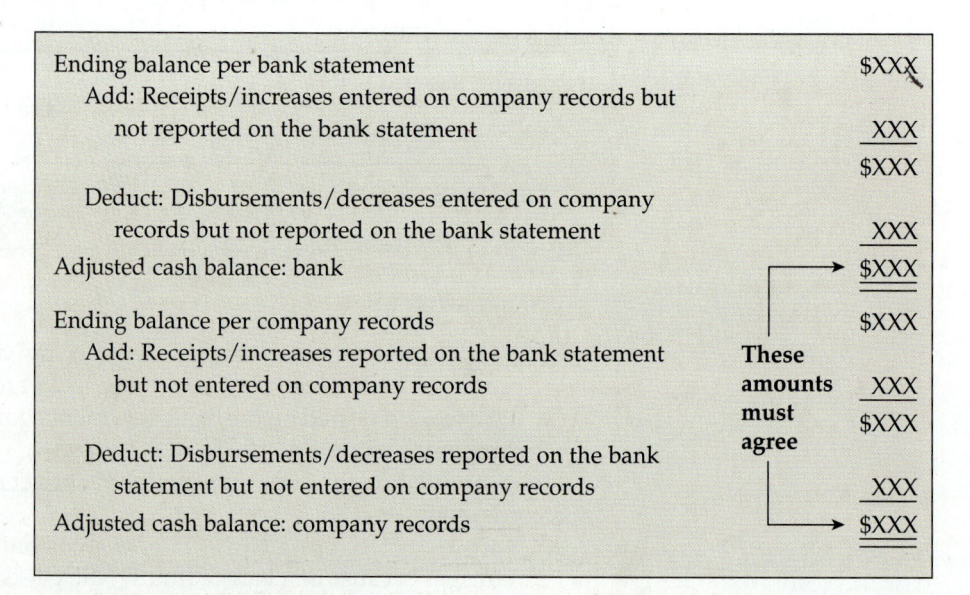

Ending balance per bank statement	$XXX
Add: Receipts/increases entered on company records but not reported on the bank statement	XXX
	$XXX
Deduct: Disbursements/decreases entered on company records but not reported on the bank statement	XXX
Adjusted cash balance: bank	$XXX
Ending balance per company records	$XXX
Add: Receipts/increases reported on the bank statement but not entered on company records	XXX
	$XXX
Deduct: Disbursements/decreases reported on the bank statement but not entered on company records	XXX
Adjusted cash balance: company records	$XXX

These amounts must agree

[4] A note is a written promise by an individual or company to pay a given sum of money on a specific date. Notes will be studied in detail later in the text.

Most bank reconciliations contain adjustments to both the ending cash balance per bank statement and the ending balance per company records. After the reconciliation is completed, *general journal entries must be prepared for adjustments made to company records.* These adjustments are necessary to update the Cash account (and others) for corrections of company errors and information already processed by the bank. It is important to note that no journal entries are needed for adjustments made to the ending bank statement balance. These adjustments reflect items that have already been recorded in a company's accounts; thus, no further updating is necessary.

An Example. Exhibit 8–3 contains summarized data and the bank reconciliation of Johnson Manufacturing Corporation for the month ended August 31, 19XX. It is helpful if you refer back to Johnson's bank statement (see Exhibit 8–1), which serves as the source for much of the information presented.

The reconciliation reveals two increases to the bank statement cash balance: (1) the deposit that was mailed prior to month-end but not reported by the bank and (2) the checks that were recorded by Johnson and are awaiting deposit. Johnson had control over each of these items as of August 31, and they should be included in the ending cash balance. The decrease to the bank statement cash balance was caused by checks Johnson had written that had not yet cleared the bank. The bank will receive these checks shortly, and the funds will then be deducted from the firm's account.

The increase to company records arose from the note receivable and interest, both of which appear on the bank statement. These funds are now on deposit in Johnson's bank account and must therefore be entered in the company's records. The deductions for the NSF check and service charge are also caused by items on the bank statement but not as yet in the firm's ledger. The error in recording check no. 627 was discovered during the reconciliation. Because the bank deducted the correct amount of the check, an adjustment to Johnson's records is required to bring them into agreement with those of First City.

On completion of the reconciliation, journal entries are needed for all items that affect company records. The following entries will be made on August 31:

Cash	4,675.80	
Notes Receivable		4,600.80
Interest Revenue		75.00
Note and interest collected by bank.		
Accounts Receivable	127.90	
Miscellaneous Expense	20.00	
Accounts Payable	18.00	
Cash		165.90
NSF check, bank service charge, and error in recording check no. 627.		

The first entry reflects the increase in cash caused by the collection of the note and interest. The second entry combines the company's three cash reductions. The NSF check is debited to Accounts Receivable because Johnson still has a claim against the customer for $127.90. The bank service charge is recorded as a miscellaneous expense. Finally, the error in recording check no.

EXHIBIT 8–3
Data and Bank Reconciliation of Johnson Manufacturing Corporation

Data
a. August 31 cash balance per bank statement, $21,426.25.
b. August 31 cash balance per company records, $17,473.35.
c. A customer's check for $127.90 was returned because of insufficient funds.
d. A customer's note receivable for $4,600.80 plus $75.00 of interest was collected by the bank and reported on the August bank statement.
e. A deposit for $1,430.00, mailed to the bank on August 30, did not appear on the bank statement.
f. Monthly bank service charge, $20.00.
g. Customers' checks totaling $420.00, already entered in Johnson's records, were on hand awaiting deposit.
h. The following checks written by Johnson were outstanding at the end of the month:

No. 638	$410.00
No. 640	320.00
No. 641	240.00
No. 642	323.00

i. Check no. 627, written for $675.18, was erroneously entered as $657.18 in the company's books. The check involved a payment to a supplier on account.

JOHNSON MANUFACTURING CORPORATION
Bank Reconciliation
August 31, 19XX

Ending balance per bank statement		$21,426.25
Add: Deposit in transit	$1,430.00	
Checks on hand	420.00	1,850.00
		$23,276.25
Deduct: Outstanding checks		
No. 638	$ 410.00	
No. 640	320.00	
No. 641	240.00	
No. 642	323.00	1,293.00
Adjusted cash balance: bank		$21,983.25
Ending balance per company records		$17,473.35
Add: Note receivable collected by bank	$4,600.80	
Interest on note	75.00	4,675.80
		$22,149.15
Deduct: NSF check	$ 127.90	
Monthly service charge	20.00	
Error in recording check no. 627	18.00	165.90
Adjusted cash balance: company records		$21,983.25

627 was found to involve a payment on account; thus, Accounts Payable must be debited. These entries allow Johnson's records to reflect the true amount of cash held by the firm (see the following T-account).

	CASH		
8/31	17,473.35	8/31	165.90
8/31	4,675.80		
(21,983.25)	22,149.15		

Establish and operate a petty cash system.

Petty Cash. Another element in the control of cash is a **petty cash system**. Under this system, a fund is established for use in making small payments, especially those that are impractical or uneconomical to make by check. Examples of such payments include those for minor items like coffee and other miscellaneous office needs.

A petty cash fund is created by cashing a check drawn on the company's regular checking account. The proceeds from the check, sufficient to cover payments for a short period of time (e.g., several weeks), are then placed in a petty cash box that is controlled by an individual known as the fund custodian. The custodian supervises the fund and is held accountable for any discrepancies. Assuming the petty cash fund is established at $200, the necessary journal entry is as follows:

Petty Cash	200	
Cash		200
To establish petty cash fund.		

Making Disbursements from the Fund. As payments are made from the fund, the custodian completes a form known as a petty cash voucher. Each voucher indicates the amount paid, the purpose of the expenditure, the date of the expenditure, and the individual receiving the money. Along with invoices and receipts, petty cash vouchers are used as evidence of disbursements.

The completed voucher is placed in the petty cash box by the custodian. Although a payment has been made, no journal entry is recorded at this time. Preparing a formal journal entry for each disbursement would give rise to considerable bookkeeping work and posting, all for relatively small amounts. At all times the following relationship should be true:

Cash remaining in the fund	$XXX
Plus: Petty cash vouchers	XXX
Original amount of the fund	$ 200

Replenishing the Petty Cash Fund. The petty cash fund is replenished when the amount of cash in the fund becomes low. For instance, assume that a count of the petty cash on hand totaled $32.40. Vouchers revealed that the following expenses had been incurred: postage, $27.50; office supplies, $50.80;

transportation, $73.40; and coffee, $15.90. The journal entry to record replenishment is as follows:

Postage Expense	27.50	
Office Supplies Expense	50.80	
Transportation Expense	73.40	
Miscellaneous Expense	15.90	
Cash		167.60
To replenish petty cash fund.		

Notice that the credit is to the Cash account and not Petty Cash. Although disbursements have been made from the petty cash box, the fund is restocked by writing a check for $167.60 on the company's regular checking account. Thus, payment (and replenishment) is really from Cash.

In addition to being restocked when the fund is low, petty cash is also replenished at the end of each accounting period. This procedure is necessary because no formal journal entries have been recorded for individual fund disbursements. Replenishment requires a journal entry, thereby ensuring that expenditures are charged to the period in which they arose.

Errors in the Petty Cash Fund. Occasionally, the sum of the petty cash vouchers and cash in the fund will not equal the original fund balance. This discrepancy usually occurs because of errors made by the fund custodian, some errors in the company's favor and some against. In such cases, the Cash Short & Over account is employed. Cash Short & Over is debited to record a shortage or credited to recognize an overage at the time the fund is replenished.

CASH MANAGEMENT AND CONTROL IN A HIGH-TECH ENVIRONMENT

The increased reliance on electronics is having a significant effect on the ways that businesses and financial institutions address cash management and control issues. Consider the following:

- *Banking by phone*—Most of you probably have access to information about your checking account by entering an account number and code via a telephone key pad. Experts note that we are just a few years away from being able to pay bills directly and conduct other more complex transactions by the same means.
- *Paperless banking*—Much of the paperwork included with a bank statement consists of canceled checks and deposit tickets. Collecting, sorting, and returning these items is a costly paperwork nightmare for financial institutions. Some of you have likely found this out firsthand. Bank statements are starting to look more like a transactions report (similar to a credit card invoice), without any documents being returned to the customer.
- *Rapid transaction processing*—As cash processing becomes more automated, cash movement becomes almost instantaneous. Deposits will be credited immediately to the proper accounts; conversely, payments will be debited and allowed only when adequate balances exist. The days of NSF checks and playing the float are probably limited.

The preceding changes introduce several unique accounting and control issues. For example, consider the bank reconciliation discussed earlier in the chapter. One will no longer have the source documents to examine but instead will compare the bank's transaction report to the accounting records. This procedure makes it more difficult to identify the nature of some errors and removes the ability to examine returned items for irregularities. Also, transaction controls must be strengthened for money that is moved electronically through a funds transfer system. Controls must ensure that only authorized users have access to the system and that only approved transactions have been processed.

Already, banking regulators have expanded their financial institution audit procedures to include a detailed system review. The regulators are quite concerned that technology not outpace the ability to produce accurate and verifiable account balance information.

TRADING SECURITIES

6 Define and account for trading securities.

Earlier in the chapter we noted that businesses should not accumulate unnecessarily large cash balances in checking accounts. Such action is not prudent and often results in lower earnings than otherwise could have been generated. Effective cash management dictates that balances in excess of planned minimum levels be used to purchase securities that provide a reasonable return to the investor.

Many different types of investments can be acquired. One such type is *trading securities*—investments purchased with the intent of generating profits on near-term sales.[5,6] Examples of securities that may be acquired for trading purposes include the capital stock of other corporations, certain Treasury bills, and bonds. *Treasury bills* are obligations of the U.S. government, whereas *bonds* are issued by corporations and governmental units (e.g., local municipalities) when such entities desire to borrow large sums of money. While being held for ultimate sale, these investments produce a return for the purchaser, as follows:

TYPE OF INVESTMENT	FORM OF RETURN
Capital stock	Dividend revenue
Treasury bills, bonds	Interest revenue

BALANCE SHEET REPORTING

Trading securities are recorded initially at their acquisition price plus any other costs related to the transaction (such as brokerage fees). To illustrate the proper accounting, we will assume that Phillips Corporation purchased 200 shares of Allegro Corporation capital stock at $42 per share (for a total of $8,400). Brokerage fees of $50 were incurred on the purchase. This transaction would be recorded in the manner shown on page 302.

---

[5] The near-term sales intent is very important. Investments acquired for other purposes are classified and accounted for differently, as shown later in the text.
[6] "Accounting for Certain Investments in Debt and Equity Securities," *Statement of Financial Accounting Standards No. 115*, Financial Accounting Standards Board, Norwalk, Conn., 1993.

A Finance Manager's Perspective

Risk and Return: The availability of cash provides the funds needed to pay bills and ensure continuous business operation. Yet these funds also provide no return to a company unless invested in income-producing securities. Different types of securities have different risk levels and rates of return. Generally speaking, firms will place funds in high-risk investments if rewarded with a greater return.

Most money managers follow a conservative game plan when investing excess funds that might later be required to satisfy operating needs. That game plan can be likened to baseball: be satisfied with singles and an occasional double rather than swing for the fence and hit the grand-slam home run. Unfortunately, several recent instances have surfaced of managers becoming a bit too aggressive when investing and "striking out at the plate." Ignoring the risk, the cash manager of a California "Silicon Valley" high-tech firm placed funds in a speculative type of investment, misjudged the market, and lost $9 million—and his job. This also happened in mammoth Orange County, California, just south of Los Angeles, where upwards of $1.7 billion was lost in trying to increase returns by using financial instruments called derivatives. The county, yes, the county, was forced to file for bankruptcy.

```
Trading Securities              8,450
    Cash                                 8,450
Purchased 200 shares of Allegro
Corporation stock.
```

Unlike the values of most other assets, the values of trading securities fluctuate continuously and can be determined on a daily basis. These amounts, influenced by such factors as the economy, investor expectations, and earnings reports, are readily obtainable from *The Wall Street Journal* or the business section of major metropolitan newspapers. Accordingly, the fair market value (i.e., the "true" value) of trading securities is objective, easily verified, and the required valuation base for reporting such investments in the financial statements subsequent to their acquisition.

There is a presumption that trading securities are (1) readily salable and (2) intended to be converted into cash within the operating cycle or one year, whichever is longer. As a result, trading securities are classified as current assets on the balance sheet.

Accounting for Changes in Value

As stated, trading securities are initially recorded at cost. Given that subsequent balance sheet disclosures are at fair market value, end-of-period adjusting entries may be needed to update the accounts. Any decreases in the value of trading securities are accounted for as losses, whereas increases in value are recognized as gains.

To illustrate these concepts, assume that Carr Corporation acquired the following trading securities on June 1, 19X1:

Number of Shares	Corporation	Cost per Share	Total Cost
200 shares	Rolph Corporation	$ 50	$10,000
400 shares	Dana, Inc.	100	40,000
300 shares	Borg Corporation	75	22,500
			$72,500

The following journal entry is made to record the acquisitions:

```
Trading Securities                72,500
    Cash                                     72,500
Purchased Rolph, Dana, and Borg stock.
```

During 19X1, dividends of $4,500 were received. Dividends are revenue to the recipient and are recorded as shown.

```
Cash                              4,500
    Dividend Revenue                         4,500
To record dividends received.
```

Declines in Market Value. On December 31, 19X1, Carr's three securities had the following market values per share: Rolph, $48; Dana, $98; and Borg, $76. The accompanying table summarizes this information.

Security	Cost	Market*
Rolph Corporation (200 shares)	$10,000	$ 9,600
Dana, Inc. (400 shares)	40,000	39,200
Borg Corporation (300 shares)	22,500	22,800
	$72,500	$71,600

* Number of shares multiplied by market value per share.

The table reveals that the total market value of the trading securities is $900 less than cost ($72,500 − $71,600). The entry needed to record this decline in value is as follows:

```
Unrealized Loss on Trading Securities   900
    Trading Securities                           900
To record decline in market value.
```

The loss is labeled "unrealized" because none of the investments were actually sold; instead, they are being held at a loss. This figure would appear on the 19X1 income statement under the other expense classification.

Increases in Market Value. Continuing the previous example, assume it is one year later (19X2) and that dividends of $4,800 were received.[7] The proper entry is:

Cash	4,800	
Dividend Revenue		4,800
To record dividends received.		

Now suppose that on December 31, 19X2, the market values per share were: Rolph, $59; Dana, $99; and Borg, $75. This information is summarized in the accompanying table, along with the market values from the end of the previous year.

SECURITY	MARKET, 12/31/X2*	MARKET, 12/31/X1
Rolph Corporation (200 shares)	$11,800	$ 9,600
Dana, Inc. (400 shares)	39,600	39,200
Borg Corporation (300 shares)	22,500	22,800
	$73,900	$71,600

* Number of shares multiplied by market value per share.

The trading securities would be disclosed on the balance sheet at $73,900, their total market value. Because this amount represents a $2,300 increase in the value reported at the end of 19X1 ($73,900 − $71,600), the following entry is needed:

Trading Securities	2,300	
Unrealized Gain on Trading Securities		2,300
To record increase in market value.		

The preceding events appear in Carr's comparative financial statements for 19X1 and 19X2, as shown in Exhibit 8–4.

A PARTING THOUGHT

Some firms might opt to use a separate account to record changes in market value rather than directly debit or credit Trading Securities. This separate valuation account, perhaps called Market Adjustments, would be added to or subtracted from Trading Securities on the balance sheet. By following this procedure, the firm maintains additional detail about the original cost and related market value changes of its investments. Such detail might prove useful for other measurement issues and accounting tasks (e.g., tax return preparation).

---

[7] This example spans more than one year and may raise questions concerning why the securities are classified as current assets on the balance sheet. Ordinarily, ongoing purchases and sales would have occurred throughout this time period. We have assumed otherwise for the sake of simplicity.

EXHIBIT 8-4
Comparative Financial Statement Disclosures of Carr Corporation

BALANCE SHEET

	19X2	19X1
Current assets		
Trading securities (at market value)	$73,900	$71,600

INCOME STATEMENT

	19X2	19X1
Other revenue (expense)		
Dividend revenue	$4,800	$4,500
Unrealized loss on trading securities		(900)
Unrealized gain on trading securities	2,300	

END-OF-CHAPTER REVIEW

LEARNING OBJECTIVES: THE KEY POINTS

1. **Describe the composition of cash and explain how cash is presented on a balance sheet.** Cash includes those items that are acceptable to a bank for deposit and free from restriction for use in satisfying current debts. Specific items included in cash, which is classified as a current asset, are coins, currency, funds on deposit with a bank in checking and savings accounts, checks, and money orders.

2. **Explain cash management and identify the methods that companies use to accelerate inflows and delay (or eliminate) outflows.** Effective cash management requires that businesses keep sufficient cash balances to meet current obligations and invest any excess funds. Cash management strives to avoid a loss of earnings for the firm, speed up inflows, and delay outflows. Inflows are often accelerated through use of cash discounts and lockbox systems. In contrast, outflows can be delayed or eliminated by playing the float, eliminating travel advances, and participating in barter transactions.

3. **Recognize the controls that should be utilized with the processing of cash receipts and cash payments.** Cash control systems are adopted to safeguard an entity's funds. These systems include such features as using a point-of-sale terminal, making daily deposits, having an adequate separation of duties, making all significant disbursements by check, and preparing a bank reconciliation.

4. **Reconcile a bank account.** A bank reconciliation involves an examination of the accuracy of the cash balance in the general ledger. Items are recognized that cause the depositor's records and the bank statement to differ. Such items, which properly appear on the bank statement but are not as yet on company records, require a journal entry on the depositor's books. The resultant figure from this process is the amount of cash that a company has control over and reports on its balance sheet.

5. **Establish and operate a petty cash system.** A petty cash system for small payments is established by writing a check on a company's regular checking account. As payments are made from the fund, petty cash vouchers are prepared to document each disbursement. When the fund becomes low, it is replenished, and a journal entry is made to record the disbursements that have occurred. The fund is also replenished at the end of the accounting period.

6. **Define and account for trading securities.** Trading securities are investments acquired with the intent of producing a profit on near-term sales. Examples include capital stock, Treasury bills of the U.S. government, and bonds. Trading securities are entered in the accounting records at cost and subsequently adjusted upward or downward to reflect changes in market value. Increases in valuation give rise to unrealized gains, whereas decreases in valuation produce unrealized losses. These gains and losses are disclosed on the income statement in the other revenue (expense) section; the Trading Securities account appears as a current asset on the balance sheet.

Key Terms and Concepts: A Quick Overview

bank reconciliation   A process for determining the amount of cash that a company has control over and reports on its balance sheet. (p. 294)

bank statement   A document that summarizes the activity in a checking account. (p. 294)

cash   Items acceptable to a bank for deposit and free from restriction for use in satisfying current debts. (p. 289)

cash budget   An overall plan of activity that depicts cash inflows and outflows for a stated period of time. (p. 290)

compensating balance   A portion of an amount loaned to a customer that remains on deposit in the bank during the loan period. (p. 289)

deposit in transit   Receipts entered on company records but not yet processed by the bank. (p. 294)

electronic debit card   A "cash card" that is used to process a variety of transactions (mostly withdrawals) in conjunction with automated teller machines. (p. 294)

lockbox system   A means by which deposits are entered more rapidly in a firm's bank account (when compared with procedures that are followed under a traditional receipts processing system). (p. 290)

NSF check (nonsufficient funds)   A customer's check returned by the bank because of a lack of funds. (p. 295)

outstanding checks   Checks written but not yet processed by the bank. (p. 295)

petty cash system   A fund used to make small payments that are impractical or uneconomical to make by check. (p. 299)

play the float   The act of writing a check to satisfy a debt but having the accompanying funds deducted from the issuer's bank account at a later date. (p. 290)

trading securities   Investments made in readily marketable securities with the intention of conversion back to cash within the operating cycle or one year, whichever is longer. (p. 301)

Chapter Quiz

The five questions that follow relate to several issues raised in the chapter. Test your knowledge of the issues by selecting the best answer. (The answers appear on p. 321.)

1. Liberty had a $10,000 balance in its checking account, $15,000 in certificates of deposit, $600 of postdated checks, $200 of employee IOUs, and $900 of cash in the office safe. Further, the company had given out $500 of travel advances. The proper amount of cash to report on Liberty's balance sheet is:
   a. $10,900.
   b. $11,500.
   c. $25,900.
   d. $27,200.

2. Which of the following would not be part of an effective cash planning and control system?
   a. The daily deposit of cash receipts.
   b. The use of a cash budget.
   c. The use of periodic bank reconciliations.
   d. The assignment of cash handling and the related cash record keeping to the same employee.

3. When preparing a bank reconciliation, deposits in transit are:
   a. added to the balance per company records.
   b. subtracted from the balance per company records.
   c. added to the balance per bank.
   d. subtracted from the balance per bank.

4. Soccer, Inc., established a $200 petty cash fund. Five weeks later, the following was found in the petty cash box:

Receipts for coffee and tea	$36
Receipts for office supplies	94
Receipts for postage	?
Coins and currency	58

   If the journal entry to replenish the fund contained a $2 debit to the Cash Short & Over account, the receipts for postage must have amounted to:
   a. $6.
   b. $10.
   c. $14.
   d. none of these.

5. Berry's beginning-of-year portfolio of trading securities had a total cost and market value of $80,000 and $75,800, respectively. The portfolio's market value increased to $84,000 by year-end. For the current reporting period, Berry should disclose:
   a. an unrealized loss of $4,200.
   b. an unrealized gain of $4,000.
   c. an unrealized gain of $8,200.
   d. trading securities carried at $80,000 on the December 31 balance sheet.

SUMMARY PROBLEM

The Donnell Company recently hired Steve Hampton to fill a staff accounting position. On August 1, Hampton established a $400 petty cash fund. The count of petty cash on August 31 indicated that $92.30 remained in the fund. Petty cash vouchers disclosed that the following expenses were incurred during the month:

Postage expense	$137.40
Office supplies expense	102.78
Miscellaneous selling expenses	65.52

Additionally, the following information concerning Donnell's checking account is available:

Balance per bank statement	$1,671.32
Balance per company records	1,419.99
Bank service charge	22.00
Outstanding checks	318.46
Undeposited receipts	208.70
Note and interest collected by the bank but not yet entered in the accounting records (note, $175.00; interest, $7.00)	182.00
NSF check returned by the bank with the bank statement	18.43

Instructions

a. Prepare the August 1 entry to establish the petty cash fund and the August 31 entry for replenishment.
b. Prepare the August bank reconciliation for the firm's checking account. Assume the balance per company records has already been reduced for the petty cash replenishment.
c. Prepare the necessary journal entries related to the bank reconciliation.

Solution

a.

Aug.	1	Petty Cash	400.00	
		Cash		400.00
		To establish petty cash fund.		
	31	Postage Expense	137.40	
		Office Supplies Expense	102.78	
		Miscellaneous Selling Expenses	65.52	
		Cash Short & Over*	2.00	
		Cash		307.70
		To replenish petty cash fund.		

*Original fund			$400.00
Less: Vouchers ($137.40 + $102.78 + $65.52)	$305.70		
Cash in fund	92.30		398.00
Shortage			$ 2.00

b.

DONNELL COMPANY
Bank Reconciliation
August 31, 19XX

Ending balance per bank statement		$1,671.32
Add: Undeposited receipts	$208.70	
Deduct: Outstanding checks	318.46	(109.76)
Adjusted cash balance: bank		$1,561.56
Ending balance per company records		$1,419.99
Add: Note collection	$175.00	
Interest collection	7.00	182.00
		$1,601.99
Deduct: Bank service charge	$ 22.00	
NSF check	18.43	40.43
Adjusted cash balance: company records		$1,561.56

c. All adjustments to company records require journal entries.

Aug. 31	Cash	182.00	
	Notes Receivable		175.00
	Interest Revenue		7.00
	Note and interest collected by the bank.		
31	Miscellaneous Expense	22.00	
	Accounts Receivable	18.43	
	Cash		40.43
	Bank service charge and NSF check.		

Assignment Material

Questions

Q8–1 What items are normally included in the Cash account on the balance sheet?

Q8–2 Briefly discuss the nature of a lockbox system.

Q8–3 What general control features should be built into a cash control system?

Q8–4 How is the Cash Short & Over account classified in the financial statements?

Q8–5 Why should cash receipts be deposited daily?

Q8–6 What is an electronic debit card? How is it most commonly used?

Q8–7 What are the reasons for the discrepancy between the cash balance reported on the bank statement and the cash balance in the accounting records?

Q8–8 Which adjustments on a bank reconciliation require general journal entries in the accounting records?

Q8–9 Briefly discuss the purpose of a petty cash system.

Q8–10 Are journal entries made for individual disbursements from a petty cash system? Explain.

Q8–11 When is a petty cash fund replenished?

Q8–12 Is paperless banking expected to increase or decrease in the future? Why?

Q8–13 What are trading securities? Present several examples.

Q8–14 How are trading securities classified on the balance sheet? What is the reason behind this treatment?

Q8–15 Trading securities fluctuate in value. Are both increases and decreases in valuation recognized in a company's accounts?

Exercises

E8–1 Cash management (L.O. 2)

Morningstar, Inc., a young company involved with the bottling and sale of flavored iced teas, has been growing very quickly. As a consequence, the firm has experienced liquidity problems in recent months. You have been hired by the company to improve its existing cash management program.

a. Explain the basic purpose of a cash management program.
b. Identify and briefly describe several methods that could be used to accelerate cash inflows from customers.
c. Identify and briefly describe several methods that could be used to slow or eliminate cash outflows to suppliers.

E8–2 Internal control: Procedures and weaknesses (L.O. 3)

Mitzi Gifford works in the accounting department of Gaylord Consulting Services. The owner of the firm, Bob Gaylord, has given Mitzi complete authority to make business decisions for the company. Mitzi frequently approves and places purchase orders. She also maintains the general ledger, prepares the financial statements, gets and opens the mail, prepares checks for disbursements, files paid invoices, reconciles the bank account, and maintains the petty cash fund.

Bob Gaylord is the only person authorized to sign checks. After a check is prepared, Mitzi files the related invoice and then places the check in Bob's "in-box" for his signature. All checks and petty cash vouchers are serially prenumbered, and it is Mitzi's responsibility to account for all documents. An exception to this policy occurs with voided checks, which are immediately destroyed.

a. Identify features that are consistent with good internal control procedures over cash disbursements.
b. Identify operating procedures that may create potential control problems for the company.

E8–3 Internal control: Procedures and weaknesses (L.O. 3)

Consider the following independent cases:

a. A cashier stole $150 from a manufacturing business and made the following journal entry in the accounting records:

Miscellaneous Expense	150	
Cash		150

b. Art's Market lost $12,800 (three days' cash receipts) in a robbery early Thursday morning.
c. Disbursements at the alcohol rehabilitation center are made by check. To facilitate payments being made when the director is out of town, five blank, signed checks are kept in the secretary's desk.

For each of the preceding cases, indicate any apparent internal control weakness and suggest procedures that may prevent the irregularity.

E8–4 Items on a bank reconciliation (L.O. 4)

You are preparing the June bank reconciliation for Advanced Systems. Identify the proper placement of items (a)–(f) on the reconciliation by using the following codes:

1— An addition to the balance per bank as of June 30.
2— A deduction from the balance per bank as of June 30.
3— An addition to the balance per company records as of June 30.
4— A deduction from the balance per company records as of June 30.

___ a. Interest earned on the account during June.
___ b. A company deposit taken to the bank at 3:00 P.M. on June 30, but not recorded on the June bank statement.
___ c. A $3,000 deposit, entered in the company records as $300.
___ d. A deposit of Advanced Design Systems, incorrectly credited to Advanced Systems' account.
___ e. A customer's check returned for insufficient funds.
___ f. Check no. 765, which has not yet cleared the bank.

E8–5 Bank reconciliation and entries (L.O. 4)

The following information was taken from the March accounting records of Gorman Company:

Balance per bank	$18,450
Balance per company records	10,740
Note collected by bank	3,100
Interest on note collected by bank	200
Outstanding checks	9,240
Bank service charge	60
Deposits in transit	2,820
NSF check returned by the bank with the bank statement	1,950

a. Prepare Gorman's March bank reconciliation.
b. Prepare any necessary journal entries for Gorman.

E8–6 Accounting for cash (L.O. 1, 3, 4, 5)

Evaluate the comments that follow as being True or False. If the comment is false, briefly explain why.

a. A petty cash fund should be replenished at the conclusion of an accounting period.
b. A journal entry is needed in a company's accounting records to record both a bank service charge and the firm's outstanding checks.
c. As shown on May's bank statement, the Nebraska National Bank incorrectly deducted $200 from the account of Kay's Auto Parts. When preparing its bank reconciliation, Kay's should subtract $200 from the accounting records so the adjusted cash balance (company records) will equal the adjusted cash balance (bank).
d. Customer checks, money orders, and IOUs are properly classified as cash on the balance sheet.
e. To achieve strong internal control, a store cashier should have access to a company's accounting records for cash.

E8–7 Petty cash fund (L.O. 5)

The Chang Company instituted a petty cash system on March 1 to allow for the payment of small expenditures. The information that follows has come to your attention.

Mar. 1   The fund was established at $100.
     31   Cash in the fund had been reduced to $11.72. The petty cash vouchers were sorted into the following expense categories, and the fund was replenished:

Warehouse supplies	$43.11
Postage	25.00
Miscellaneous	20.17
	$88.28

a. Prepare the journal entry necessary to record the establishment of the fund on March 1.
b. Prepare the journal entry necessary to record the replenishment of the fund on March 31.

E8–8 Understanding a petty cash system (L.O. 5)

Bravo Company recently established a $500 petty cash fund and recorded the following journal entry:

Petty Cash	500	
Cash		500

Petty cash vouchers were prepared as disbursements were made during the month. The individual vouchers were then recorded in the books by journal entries similar to those shown.

Supplies Expense	15	
Petty Cash		15
Postage Expense	50	
Petty Cash		50
Etc.		

Cash in the petty cash box at month-end totaled $210, and vouchers written amounted to $280. The fund was replenished for $290, with Bravo recording the following entry:

Petty Cash	280	
Cash Short & Over	10	
Cash		290

a. Identify the errors in Bravo's accounting for petty cash.
b. Despite the errors that have been made, are the ending account balances correct? Briefly explain.
c. From a bookkeeping viewpoint, criticize Bravo's method of entering petty cash vouchers in the accounting records.

E8–9 Trading securities: Acquisition and valuation (L.O. 6)

You have obtained the following information from the records of Matlock Company concerning the firm's trading securities:

		PRICE PER SHARE	
COMPANY	NUMBER OF SHARES	SEPT. 3	DEC. 31
Simpson	300	$20	$25
Cosby	400	30	25

a. Prepare the journal entry to record the acquisition of Matlock's trading securities on September 3.
b. Prepare the journal entry to record the change in market value of the trading securities as of December 31.

E8–10 Valuation and disclosure of trading securities (L.O. 6)

Bonner-Murphy has an established strategy to buy and sell securities in the stock market. The cost and 19X5 year-end market values of the firm's trading securities portfolio are: cost, $1,000,000; market value, $1,260,000.

a. Present the journal entry at the end of 19X5 to properly value the portfolio of trading securities.
b. Show how the portfolio would appear on the December 31, 19X5, balance sheet.

c. Suppose it is now December 31, 19X6. The company is still holding the same securities; however, the market value has fallen to $870,000. Will the firm have an unrealized gain or an unrealized loss for 19X6? How much will the gain or loss be?

Problems

Series A

P8–A1 Cash on the balance sheet (L.O. 1)

John Locatelli, owner of Performance Auto Repair, recently hired his nephew to handle the company's office duties. Since the nephew wanted to make a good first impression, he quickly prepared the following schedule of cash, doing the math in his head:

Cash on hand, including $100 of petty cash	$ 575
Balance in checking account	4,250
Employee IOU	80
Savings account balance	2,000
Employee travel advance, to attend training school	1,400
Customer's postdated check	325
Total	$18,630

Shortly after the schedule was prepared, John found $180 of checking account withdrawal slips that related to various automated teller machine (ATM) transactions.

Instructions

a. Performance Auto Repair currently has $7,800 of bills due from suppliers. Comment on the firm's ability to settle these bills on a timely basis, showing calculation of the total actual cash balance.
b. Describe the balance sheet treatment of items not included in the cash balance computed in part (a).
c. Briefly comment on the quality of the nephew's work.

P8–A2 Bank reconciliation and entries (L.O. 4)

The December 31 bank statement of Eason Company disclosed a balance of $8,400.50. On this same date the Cash account in the general ledger indicated a balance of $4,375.75. The following information has come to your attention:

1. A deposit of $903.88, mailed by Eason on December 28, was entered in the accounting records on December 29 but was not received by the bank until January 3.
2. Outstanding checks on December 31 totaled $1,400.23, computed as follows:

Checks written in November	$ 801.00
Checks written in December	599.23
	$1,400.23

3. A customer's NSF check for $325 was returned with the bank statement.
4. Eason's check no. 888 for a $9,000 machinery acquisition was entered in the accounts as $9,900.
5. Bank service charge, $25.60.
6. A note receivable of $2,950 and interest of $54 were collected by the bank but not as yet recorded in the accounts.
7. A $25 debit memo, representing a check printing charge, appeared on the bank statement.

Instructions

a. Prepare a bank reconciliation for Eason Company.
b. Prepare the journal entries necessary for Eason as of December 31.
c. Determine the cash balance that Eason would disclose on the December 31 balance sheet.

P8–A3 Bank reconciliation from bank statement (L.O. 4)

The Union Company is in the process of reconciling its bank account with Metropolitan Bank and Trust for May. Union's bank statement follows.

METROPOLITAN BANK AND TRUST

UNION COMPANY   **MAY BANK STATEMENT**

| Deposits/Credits || Checks/Debits ||| Balance ||
Date	Amount	No.	Date	Amount	Date	Amount
					5/01	8,440
5/02	400	384	5/02	725	5/02	6,175
5/07	625	406	5/02	1,080	5/05	5,675
5/11	370	407	5/02	860	5/07	5,990
5/16	1,150	408	5/05	500	5/08	5,300
5/19	2,340	409	5/08	690	5/11	5,180
5/27	850 CM	410	5/07	310	5/12	4,750
		412	5/12	430	5/14	4,240
		413	5/11	490	5/16	5,280
		415	5/16	110	5/19	7,620
		416	5/20	665	5/20	6,955
		417	5/24	1,210	5/24	5,745
		421	5/27	800	5/27	5,795
		NSF	5/14	510	5/31	5,785
		SC	5/31	10		

CM Credit Memo   NSF NSF Check   SC Service Charge

The credit memo represents the collection of an $830 note receivable plus $20 interest. Union's cash receipts and disbursements records for May are as follows:

Deposits		Checks Written			
5/6	$ 625	no. 408	$500	no. 417	$1,210
5/10	370	409	690	418	120
5/15	1,150	410	310	419	555
5/18	3,240	411	Void	420	440
5/31	780	412	430	421	800
	$6,165	413	490	422	80
		414	Void	423	90
		415	110	424	100
		416	665	425	200
					$6,790

An examination of the April reconciliation revealed a deposit in transit on April 30 of $400. The following checks were listed as outstanding: No. 384, $725; no. 395, $600; no. 406, $1,080; and no. 407, $860.

Instructions

a. Assuming a cash balance per company records on May 31 of $4,950, prepare Union's bank reconciliation for May. Assume that any errors detected during the reconciliation process are the fault of Union's bookkeeper.
b. Prepare the necessary journal entries for Union as of May 31.

P8–A4 Petty cash fund (L.O. 5)

United Enterprises operates a petty cash fund for small expenditures. The following information relates to August:

Aug. 1 Established the petty cash fund for $150.

12 Replenished the fund. The following items were found in the petty cash box:

Vouchers for postage	$32
Vouchers for supplies	41
Vouchers for miscellaneous expenses	29
Coins and currency	48

22 Replenished the fund. The following items were found in the petty cash box:

Vouchers for postage	$50
Vouchers for supplies	49
Vouchers for miscellaneous expenses	37
Coins and currency	10

31 Replenished the fund. The following items were found in the petty cash box:

Vouchers for postage	$43
Vouchers for supplies	36
Vouchers for miscellaneous expenses	11
Voucher stating: I owe the fund $10.	
Signed: Ronald Hargis (an employee)	
Coins and currency	52

Instructions

a. Record the necessary journal entries on August 1, 12, 22, and 31.
b. Explain the probable reasoning behind the fund replenishment on August 31 despite the presence of $52 cash in the petty cash box.

P8–A5 Trading securities (L.O. 6)

The following schedule shows information about Redford Company's trading securities portfolio, all shares being acquired during 19X7.

	GM	FORD	CHRYSLER	HONDA
Number of shares	200	300	600	500
Cost per share	$44	$27	$47	$35*
Total dividends received	40	75	45	65
Market value per share, Dec. 31	38	25	54	33

* The company paid an additional $300 for brokerage fees.

Instructions

a. Prepare the journal entry that Redford made to record the purchase of Honda on February 28.
b. Prepare a journal entry to record total dividends received during the year.
c. Prepare a journal entry to value the trading securities portfolio on December 31, 19X7.
d. Show how Redford's trading securities would be disclosed on the year-end balance sheet.
e. Suppose that Chrysler's market price at the end of *19X8* was $44 per share and all the other market prices remained the same.
   (1) Prepare the journal entry to properly value the securities at the end of 19X8.
   (2) How would Redford's securities be disclosed on the 19X8 year-end balance sheet?

Series B

P8–B1 Cash on the balance sheet (L.O. 1)
The following information has been gathered from the records of Gateway, Inc.:

Customer's postdated check	$ 900
Reconciled balance in Pacific Bank checking account	8,040
Petty cash fund	350
Money orders on hand	1,960
Savings account balance at Meridian Federal	2,115
Employee IOU	250
Cash on hand	975

Instructions

a. Compute the total cash balance to be reported as a current asset on the December 31 balance sheet.
b. Describe the balance sheet treatment of the items not included in the cash balance computed in part (a).

P8–B2 Bank reconciliation and entries (L.O. 4)
The following selected information appeared on the October 31 bank statement of the Elshazly Company:

Beginning balance, Oct. 1	$6,068
Ending balance, Oct. 31	4,445
Miscellaneous credits	
Note collected ($5,000) and interest ($60)	5,060
Monthly interest earned	50
Miscellaneous debits	
Monthly service charge	70
NSF check from customer	550

The company's Cash account in the general ledger appeared as shown.

CASH			
Balance, 10/1	6,457	Oct. payments	9,432
Oct. receipts	3,000		

Deposits in transit on October 31 are $1,200, and checks outstanding on the same date total $1,310. In the process of determining the outstanding checks, Elshazly discovered an error. Check no. 1213, written for $860 of office supplies, was entered in the company records as $680.

Instructions

a. Prepare the October bank reconciliation for the company.
b. Prepare any necessary journal entries for Elshazly as of October 31.
c. Determine the cash balance that Elshazly would disclose on its October 31 balance sheet.

P8–B3 Bank reconciliation from bank statement (L.O. 4)

The Whitlow Corporation received the accompanying bank statement for September from First City Bank & Trust.

FIRST CITY BANK & TRUST

WHITLOW CORPORATION   SEPTEMBER BANK STATEMENT

Deposits/Credits		Checks/Debits			Balance	
Date	Amount	No.	Date	Amount	Date	Amount
					9/01	10,480
9/02	150	911	9/02	740	9/02	9,890
9/15	2,350	912	9/04	325	9/03	9,490
9/22	1,820	913	9/03	400	9/04	9,165
9/27	740 CM	915	9/06	380	9/06	8,785
9/28	2,570	916	9/08	500	9/08	8,285
		917	9/12	480	9/12	6,965
		918	9/12	200	9/15	9,315
		919	9/12	640	9/18	9,105
		920	9/18	210	9/21	8,320
		921	9/21	370	9/22	8,690
		922	9/22	610	9/25	7,970
		923	9/22	840	9/26	7,670
		924	9/26	300	9/27	8,190
		925	9/27	220	9/28	10,280
		926	9/25	720	9/30	9,750
		927	9/28	480		
		929	9/30	515		
		NSF	9/21	415		
		SC	9/30	15		

CM *Credit Memo*   NSF *NSF Check*   SC *Service Charge*

The credit memo represents the collection of a $700 note receivable plus $40 interest. Whitlow's cash receipts and disbursements records for September disclose the following:

DEPOSITS		CHECKS WRITTEN			
9/14	$2,350	no. 915	$380	no. 924	$ 300
9/20	1,820	916	500	925	220
9/27	2,570	917	480	926	720
9/30	1,580	918	200	928	180
	$8,320	919	640	929	515
		920	210	930	720
		921	370	931	510
		922	610	932	460
		923	840		$7,855

An examination of the August reconciliation revealed a deposit in transit on August 31 of $150. The following checks were listed as outstanding: No. 890, $615; no. 911, $740; no. 912, $325; and no. 913, $400.

Instructions

a. Assuming a cash balance per company records on September 30 of $9,015, prepare Whitlow's bank reconciliation for September. Assume that any errors detected during the reconciliation process are the fault of Whitlow's bookkeeper.
b. Prepare the necessary journal entries for Whitlow as of September 30.

P8–B4 Petty cash fund (L.O. 5)

Dekalb Enterprises established a petty cash fund on July 1 to pay for small expenditures. The following schedule was prepared by Kenneth Ryan, fund custodian, to show activity for the first month:

	JULY 1	JULY 7	JULY 21	JULY 31
Cash placed in petty cash box				
To establish fund	$200	$ —	$ —	$ —
To replenish fund	—	175	180	198
Vouchers found in petty cash box for				
Postage	—	60	70	50
Store supplies	—	110	85	70
Miscellaneous	—	5	20	40

In addition to the vouchers found on July 31, the box also contained a $25 IOU signed by Ryan.

Instructions

a. Record the necessary journal entries on July 1, 7, 21, and 31.
b. On the basis of the preceding information and the journal entries that you prepared, do you have any concerns about Dekalb's petty cash fund in terms of control? Briefly explain.

P8–B5 Trading securities (L.O. 6)

James Company began operations and purchased the following trading securities in 19X7:

	NUMBER OF SHARES	COST PER SHARE	MARKET VALUE PER SHARE, DEC. 31
Mead, Inc.	200	$30	$35
Grace Co.	300	20	10
Russ Corp.	100	60	70

On March 19, 19X8, James purchased 400 shares of Wabash, Inc. for $5 per share, plus $100 of brokerage fees. Total dividends received during 19X8 amounted to $1,670.

Instructions

a. Prepare the journal entry needed on December 31, 19X7, to value the trading securities.
b. Show how James should disclose its trading securities on the December 31, 19X7, balance sheet.
c. Prepare the journal entry needed to record the purchase of the Wabash securities.
d. Prepare the journal entry needed to record the dividends received during 19X8.
e. Assume that by December 31, 19X8, Wabash's market value had increased to $10 per share. All other securities had the same year-end market prices as in 19X7.
   (1) Prepare the journal entry to properly value the securities as of December 31, 19X8.
   (2) Show how the securities would be reported on the company's 19X8 balance sheet.

EXPANDING YOUR HORIZONS

EYH8–1 Personal cash budget (L.O. 2)

College students often seem to be short of cash. Part of the problem may be attributable to an absence of personal financial planning, including the lack of a cash budget.

Instructions

a. Prepare a cash budget for the next semester or quarter. Include as cash inflows the cash that you expect to receive from working, scholarships, loans, parents/guardians, and so forth. Cash outflows should consist of outlays for tuition and fees, books, rent, food, car insurance, clothing, childcare expenses, credit card payments, and social functions.
b. If the budget indicates a shortage or an extremely tight cash position, identify several items that you may want to increase or eliminate.

EYH8–2 Cash embezzlement (L.O. 3)

In many organizations, cash handling procedures are less than satisfactory. This situation is particularly true in small businesses and various not-for-profit entities. Unfortunately, weak cash controls often lead to embezzlements.

Instructions

Go to your library and obtain information on a recent embezzlement of cash. If possible, the theft should relate to a small business or a not-for-profit entity, preferably one within your local area. Prepare a one-page report that specifies both how the embezzlement took place and the internal controls that may have prevented the incident from occurring.

EYH8–3 Reconciling your personal checking account (L.O. 4)

It has come to our attention that too few college students reconcile their personal checking accounts. Understandably, in handling thousands of transactions each day, banks do make errors. Preparing a reconciliation will help to detect these errors along with any bank service charges or interest earned.

Instructions

a. Upon receipt of a monthly bank statement, prepare a reconciliation for your personal checking account. The bank often provides a form for this procedure on the back of the statement.
b. What did you learn as a result of preparing this reconciliation? For example, did you find any errors? Who made the errors? Were you charged any fees that were not previously recorded in your checkbook?
c. By not preparing a reconciliation, do you see any problems with relying on bank personnel or automated teller machines (ATMs) for information on the correct balance of your account? Briefly explain.

EYH8–4 Visiting a stockbroker (L.O. 6)

Much of the trading in the shares of U.S. companies occurs on the New York Stock Exchange (NYSE). The highest priced stock on the NYSE is Berkshire Hathaway, whose price *per share* fluctuated between $15,150 and $19,750 during most of 1994.

Instructions

a. Visit a stockbroker in your area. Using the broker's resources, which are generally available to the public at no charge, determine the price fluctuation for that day in a share of Berkshire Hathaway stock (symbol: BRK).
b. Interview the stockbroker to determine what percentage of clients have a strategy of buying and selling shares in the near term, thereby generating profits (or losses). Inquire about some client success stories as well as some client disasters, and summarize your findings in a one-page report.

EYH8–5 Cash management for a growing company (L.O. 2, 6)

Freeport Foods operates a wholesale food business in a five-state area. The company has grown rapidly in its six years of existence, requiring substantial bank borrowing to support the higher level of sales. Freeport's owner, Scott Porter, desires to secure additional loans to provide more funding. Luis Garcia, a bank officer, thinks that Freeport should generate as much cash as possible from internal sources before it borrows more heavily. As Luis notes, "There's no interest expense on money you can generate internally from more efficient cash management strategies. Further, if you're willing to take a little risk, you might consider acquiring some trading securities."

Instructions

a. If accounts receivable and inventories are at record high levels, what action could the company take to improve its cash position? Hint: Consider the meaning of the "operating cycle" when preparing your answer.
b. What additional means may be available to Freeport to speed up cash inflows and postpone or eliminate cash outflows?
c. What benefits are available from acquiring a portfolio of trading securities? What are the risks that Luis has mentioned?
d. Scott recently requested that an owner withdrawal be processed so that he could settle a personal tax bill from the Internal Revenue Service. Is the withdrawal advisable? Briefly explain.

COMMUNICATION OF ACCOUNTING INFORMATION

CAI8–1 Writing a memo: The Dun & Bradstreet Corporation* (L.O. 2)

Communication Principle: Memos are the most frequent form of written communication used in business. This means of delivering information should be brief and direct, and the tone and style should fit the occasion and the reader. That is, serious subjects require serious and carefully phrased memos; whereas straightforward, informal messages are appropriate for regular business among colleagues.

Memos begin with To, From, Subject, and Date lines. These items allow the communication to be quickly routed and filed. The body of a memo should start with background statements that brief the reader on the context and reason for the memo. Next, using short paragraphs, the memo should explain pertinent details or related information. It should end with forward-looking comments such as "I'd be glad to answer any questions and discuss this further. . . ."

Do not try to include too much information in a single memo or to make the memo multipurpose. Limit what you have to say and maintain a positive, natural, and polite style and tone.

■ ■ ■ ■ ■ ■ ■ ■

Dun & Bradstreet is a huge corporation involved in numerous service businesses. Among the company's activities are publishing (Moody's Investors Service), marketing services (Nielsen ratings), and corporate research. Dun & Bradstreet is also heavily involved with the compilation and sale of credit reports and maintains a data base that includes over 32 million businesses. This data base is useful in helping companies decide whether or not to extend credit to other entities.

Imagine that you work for Dun & Bradstreet in the corporate communications division, and rumors have been circulating about cash flow problems of the company. These rumors began because a newspaper article incorrectly described Dun & Bradstreet as a firm "with cash flow and credit problems" rather than as a company "that provides information about businesses having cash flow and credit problems." The following balance sheet data (in millions) are available:

Cash	$ 650.9
Short-term securities†	17.7
Accounts receivable	1,078.9
Accounts, accrued, & other short-term payables	2,044.1

† These are similar to trading securities.

Instructions

Draft an internal memo for company employees that explains and dispels the rumors. As part of the memo, briefly describe the cash management methods that may be used by Dun & Bradstreet to avoid cash flow problems.

Answers to Chapter Quiz

1. a ($10,000 + $900)
2. d
3. c
4. b ($200 – $36 – $94 – $2 – $58)
5. c ($84,000 – $75,800)

---

* A continuation of this problem is found in Chapter 9 on p. 354.

9 RECEIVABLES

LEARNING OBJECTIVES

After studying this chapter, you should be able to:

1. Identify the costs related to credit sales.
2. Account for uncollectible receivables by using both the direct write-off and the allowance methods.
3. Compare and contrast the income statement and balance sheet approaches of accounting for uncollectibles.
4. Handle account write-offs and subsequent recoveries under the allowance method.
5. Evaluate receivables by using the accounts receivable turnover ratio.
6. Recognize the benefits associated with accepting credit cards.
7. Demonstrate the computations and journal entries for notes receivable and interest, including dishonored obligations.

The sale of goods and services on account is a way of life for most businesses and also for Banner Advertising. Banner's clients that pay for advertising services on a monthly basis are billed each month. This process requires two simple but significant accounting steps: (1) recording the receivable and revenue at the time of invoicing and (2) recording subsequent collection of the balances owed. As George Faris notes, "Accounting for the routine client is no problem. We have a standard billing system, and entering the collection of a receivable is very straightforward. The problems come with past-due accounts."

To stay abreast of receivables, Banner's system produces a report that shows how much time has passed since a customer's last payment. When we talked with George about collections, he observed, "If I can't collect an amount due, it comes right off the bottom line. Not only am I out the revenue, but I also lose because I incurred the costs of designing and painting the billboard. Like any business, I can't afford to let many customers get away without paying. As much as I hate to hound people, I really don't have a choice if I want to survive."

George claims that he retains more clients than he loses by being aggressive. "Over and over I've seen that when clients settle their bills, they will come back and use our services. But if customers get away without paying, we never hear from them again. When we don't collect, we have no chance for future sales."

George admits that Banner has an advantage that many businesses lack. "When a client becomes too delinquent, we just eliminate their ad with a can of white paint. The threat is sufficient to make most reluctant clients pay." Naturally, this situation is not true with most firms because the customer has possession of the product. For these companies, the credit and collection policies are far more difficult to manage.

CREDIT SALES AND RECEIVABLES

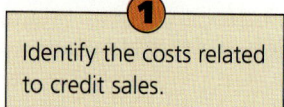

1 Identify the costs related to credit sales.

These observations from George highlight the importance of receivables to a business. Receivables arise from the extension of credit, a significant factor behind economic growth in the United States. The purchase of goods and services on an installment plan, by the use of in-house charge accounts, or through bank cards such as Visa and MasterCard have allowed companies to increase sales and drive up income.

Unfortunately, there is a cost to this process. Credit sales often create the need for a department to investigate customer credit ratings, approve the extension of credit, and attempt to collect delinquent accounts. These activities are expensive in terms of both time and dollars.

Furthermore, companies must wait to receive monies due, and despite the offer of a cash discount, many customers still fail to settle their balances within requested time limits. Thus, businesses must often sell trading securities and secure bank loans to obtain needed operating funds. The former action may result in the loss of future interest or dividends, while the latter may give rise to interest costs.

A Music Consultant's Perspective

Collection of Receivables: At one time, independent record companies distributed records and tapes through music wholesalers. The wholesalers, in turn, sold their products to retailers scattered throughout the country. This method of distribution is currently utilized for thousands of goods; however, it is now history in the music field.

All too often, slow-paying retailers placed a tremendous squeeze on the wholesalers, which resulted in the record companies being paid late. The problem didn't stop here; it continued to work backward through the system. The record companies now suffered because of pressures to pay the artist, the music publisher, and the product manufacturer. In short, the collection of receivables became the curse of the business, with a "hit" record doing the most harm. The companies of today have learned from their mistakes of the past. Major music houses have eliminated the middleman and now distribute directly to retailers, a change that provides more control and speeds up the collection process.

George Faris of Banner Advertising introduced a final cost related to credit sales: customer nonpayments. Firms rarely collect all their accounts receivable because of bankruptcies, layoffs, and so on. This cost, known as *uncollectible accounts expense*, can be especially high for an entity that has tried to increase sales by being very liberal in granting credit. Although some marginal customers may be profitable, the end result is normally increased costs and a lack of collection by the firm.

A Cost to the Customer: Bad Credit

Yes, there are many costs to a business that engages in credit sales. At the same time, there may be a substantial cost to the customer: bad credit. Delinquent payments and bankruptcies frequently affect an individual's credit history and make it difficult for that person to conduct basic transactions (e.g., reserving a hotel room with a credit card). In addition, if a loan can be obtained, a higher interest rate is usually charged because the individual is deemed "high risk."

Several companies in the U.S. do nothing but process reports for businesses that want to check an individual's credit history. Inquiries would typically be made by automobile dealers, loan departments, and even credit card companies that want to run "pre-approved" card campaigns. Delinquent payments and bankruptcies are entered on a person's credit report, and that information will usually stay there for a long period of time. In referring to firms that operate these mammoth data bases, a consumer advocate recently noted: "The American consumer doesn't know how powerful [credit bureaus] are and how much they influence our quality of life."[1]

Trade and Nontrade Receivables

The receivables that so concern business owners are formally defined as claims against customers and others that arise from company operations. Receivables

> **Ethics Issue**
>
> Joe has access to a major bank's computerized data base, which contains records of customer balances and loans outstanding. Joe's father has requested financial information about Susan Turner, a bank customer, for the purpose of increasing her credit limit with his business. If Joe has a close relationship with his father, what should Joe do?

[1] "Credit Conscious," *The Dallas Morning News,* October 1, 1994, pp. 1C, 2C.

A Further Focus

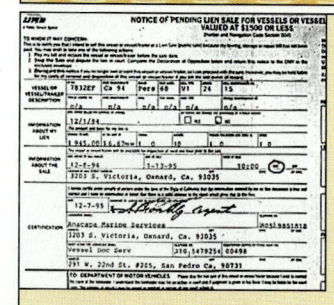

A credit report reveals a wealth of information about an individual. The typical report includes:

- Information about accounts with banks, credit-card companies, stores, and other lenders. Negative information, such as the failure to pay promptly, can remain on a report for seven years.
- Public-record information related to bankruptcies, tax liens, and monetary judgments. Bankruptcies can stay on a report for 10 years.
- A list of companies that have inquired about the individual's credit history.

Source: "What's on a Credit Report?," *The Dallas Morning News,* October 1, 1994, p. 3C.

---

are reported on the balance sheet as either current or noncurrent assets until they are ultimately collected. Those amounts expected to be collected within one year or the operating cycle, whichever is longer, are classified as current assets; all other receivables are classified as noncurrent.

Receivables are subdivided into two categories: trade and nontrade. The majority of receivables are *trade receivables,* which result from the sale of products or services to customers. Trade receivables consist of accounts receivable and notes receivable. In contrast, *nontrade receivables* arise from other transactions and events and include accrued receivables, advances to employees, and deposits with utilities.

In this chapter we will concentrate on the accounting issues associated with current trade receivables. Accounting for other types of receivables is discussed elsewhere in the text.

Accounts Receivable

Accounts receivable represent the amounts due an entity from credit sales of goods and services. As the figures in Exhibit 9–1 indicate, accounts receivable can be a substantial percentage of total assets for many firms.

Given the magnitude of accounts receivable, proper valuation and presentation on the balance sheet are essential. In Chapter 5 we discussed a number of items related to this important asset, including trade discounts, sales dis-

Exhibit 9–1
Accounts Receivable for Various Firms (000 Omitted)

	Compaq Computer	Harley-Davidson	Fieldcrest Cannon	American Greetings
Net accounts receivable	$1,377,000	$ 86,031	$164,419	$ 322,675
Total assets	4,084,000	583,285	740,446	1,565,234
Net accounts receivable as a percentage of total assets	33.7%	14.7%	22.3%	20.6%

Source: Recent annual reports.

counts, and sales returns and allowances. We will now focus on one additional accounting issue: uncollectible accounts.

Despite the use of credit standards, some uncollectible accounts (often called *bad debts*) almost always arise. Uncollectibles have both income statement and balance sheet implications for businesses. On the income statement, for example, an "adequate" amount for bad debts expense should be matched against (deducted from) the sales revenues generated. The objective is to derive a fair measurement of net income. Turning to the balance sheet, the Accounts Receivable account should be reduced to reflect the amounts that a firm has a reasonable expectation of collecting. This latter procedure is an application of conservatism in financial reporting, which permits asset write-downs when related valuations have been diminished or impaired.

There are two methods of accounting for uncollectible accounts: the direct write-off method and the allowance method.

DIRECT WRITE-OFF METHOD

> **2**
>
> Account for uncollectible receivables by using both the direct write-off and the allowance methods.

Under the **direct write-off method,** bad debts are recognized when the actual loss is confirmed. That is, when a specific customer account is deemed uncollectible, the account is written off as an expense of the period. To illustrate, assume that Bill McCracken owes the Warren Company $875. After repeated collection efforts, Warren has just learned that McCracken has filed for bankruptcy. The Warren Company would make the following entry:

Uncollectible Accounts Expense	875	
Accounts Receivable: Bill McCracken		875
To write off uncollectible account.		

The direct write-off method of accounting for uncollectibles is simple and has the advantage of reporting actual losses rather than estimates. This approach presents several problems, however. Frequently, a customer's account is not deemed uncollectible until long after a sale has been made. The direct write-off method could therefore result in the recognition of sales revenue in one period and the expense related to that revenue in a later period. Thus, an improper matching of revenues and expenses would take place. Furthermore, because the write-off may occur in the future, Accounts Receivable is sometimes overstated at the end of the year of sale. Given these problems, the direct write-off approach is typically used by businesses that have relatively low levels of uncollectibles.

ALLOWANCE METHOD

The **allowance method** overcomes the objections to the direct write-off method by associating the revenue and expense in the same reporting period. Correct matching is achieved through the use of *estimates* of uncollectible accounts expense. Reasonable estimates can normally be obtained by studying a firm's past experience with bad accounts and making adjustments for current economic conditions and credit standards.

When the estimate of uncollectibles is determined, a journal entry is recorded at the end of the accounting period in the form of an adjustment. The entry involves a debit to Uncollectible Accounts Expense and a credit to an account entitled Allowance for Uncollectible Accounts.[2] Because credit policy is normally a management decision, Uncollectible Accounts Expense is reported on the income statement as an administrative operating expense. In contrast, the Allowance for Uncollectibles is a contra asset that is offset against Accounts Receivable on the balance sheet, as follows (amounts are assumed):

Current assets
Accounts receivable $19,000
Less: Allowance for uncollectible accounts   2,600 $16,400

Offsetting the Allowance in this manner informs financial statement users of the expected **net realizable value** ($16,400), or the amount of cash expected from the collection of present customer balances. The use of this separate valuation account is required because the specific uncollectible customer accounts are unknown when the financial statements are prepared. As a result, we cannot credit individual subsidiary accounts (and the Accounts Receivable control account) at the time of bad debt estimation.

Uncollectible accounts expense can be estimated by observing historical relationships between the actual bad debts incurred and (1) sales or (2) accounts receivable. These relationships may be summarized as follows:

1. Relationship to sales (income statement approach)
   a. Percentage of sales
   b. Percentage of credit sales
2. Relationship to accounts receivable (balance sheet approach)
   a. Percentage of outstanding accounts receivable
   b. Aging of accounts receivable

> **3**
> Compare and contrast the income statement and balance sheet approaches of accounting for uncollectibles.

Relationship to Sales: Income Statement Approach. Estimating uncollectibles on the basis of sales results in current revenues being matched with the costs incurred in producing those revenues. Stated differently, the sales that ultimately give rise to the bad debts are used as the basis for the period's expense. Because of its matching emphasis, this method is commonly referred to as the **income statement approach.**

The estimate of uncollectible accounts expense may be computed on total sales or credit sales. Generally speaking, most accountants favor estimation of uncollectibles on the basis of credit sales—a more rational approach because bad debts do not arise on cash collections. To illustrate the income statement approach, assume that Lukin Company's sales on account for the current year total $500,000 and that uncollectible accounts have historically amounted to 3% of credit sales. The following adjusting entry for $15,000 ($500,000 × 0.03) would be made:

Uncollectible Accounts Expense   15,000
    Allowance for Uncollectible Accounts   15,000
Adjusting entry

---

[2] The Allowance account is sometimes called the Allowance for Doubtful Accounts or the Allowance for Bad Debts.

Relationship to Accounts Receivable: Balance Sheet Approach. Uncollectibles may also be estimated on the basis of accounts receivable. This method, known as the **balance sheet approach,** focuses on reporting receivables at net realizable value. When using the balance sheet method, *we must therefore consider the previous balance in the Allowance for Uncollectibles account.*

For example, assume Galaxy Electronics has determined that bad accounts normally amount to 3% of the year-end accounts receivable balance. The company's records at the end of the year, prior to the adjustment for uncollectibles, disclose the following information:

Accounts receivable	$600,000
Allowance for uncollectible accounts	2,800 (credit balance)

Collections on receivables are expected to total $582,000 [$600,000 − ($600,000 × 0.03)], thereby requiring an $18,000 balance in the Allowance for Uncollectible Accounts ($600,000 − $582,000). Because $2,800 is presently in the account, an additional $15,200 ($18,000 − $2,800) must be entered to achieve the desired result. The following adjusting entry is needed:

Uncollectible Accounts Expense	15,200	
Allowance for Uncollectible Accounts		15,200
Adjusting entry		

The effect of this entry is shown in the accompanying T-accounts:

UNCOLLECTIBLE ACCOUNTS EXPENSE		ALLOWANCE FOR UNCOLLECTIBLE ACCOUNTS	
Adj. 15,200			Balance 2,800
			Adj. 15,200
			18,000

The resulting balance sheet presentation of Galaxy's accounts receivable appears below.

Current assets		
Accounts receivable	$600,000	
Less: Allowance for uncollectible accounts	18,000	$582,000

Occasionally, the Allowance for Uncollectibles account may possess a debit balance.[3] Suppose, for instance, that Galaxy's Allowance account had a $3,000 *debit* balance prior to the adjustment. As the number scale in Exhibit 9–2 shows, a $21,000 adjusting entry would be necessary. The $21,000 credit to the Allowance, when combined with the $3,000 debit balance, yields the desired $18,000 outcome.

---

[3] The situations that cause a debit balance are discussed later in the chapter.

EXHIBIT 9–2
Allowance for Uncollectibles: Galaxy Electronics

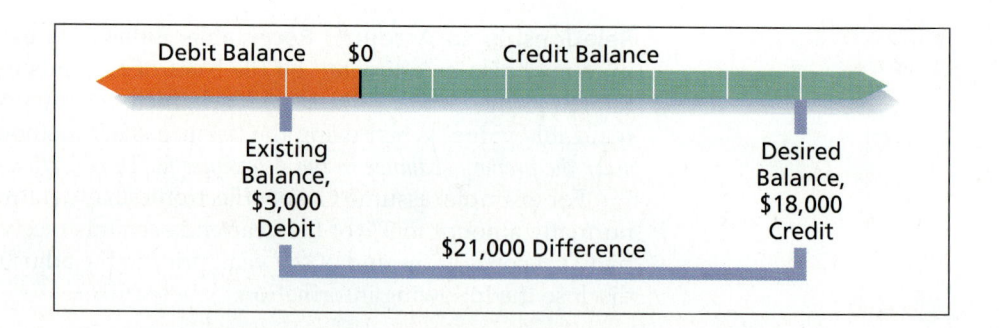

Aging of Accounts Receivable. Estimating bad debts as a flat percentage of outstanding accounts receivable ignores the due date of the many individual accounts that compose the total balance. The length of time a specific account has been outstanding is an important factor when assessing the probability of future collection. That is, a company is more likely to collect an account that is 30 days old than to collect one that is 180 days old. To overcome this problem, accountants have developed a more sophisticated approach to estimate bad debts. This method, termed *aging accounts receivable,* categorizes individual accounts according to the length of time outstanding. A historically developed bad debts percentage is then applied to each age category to determine the estimate.

The aging process not only furnishes information for the bad debt estimate but it also serves as a useful management tool. The analysis of individual accounts provides insight regarding the success or failure of a firm's credit and collection efforts. Furthermore, close monitoring of specific customer activity will determine if any changes in a customer's credit rating are necessary.

To illustrate estimation by the aging process, examine Exhibit 9–3, which contains information from the records of the Livingston Corporation. The aging of individual customer accounts indicates that the Allowance for Uncollectibles must contain a balance of $9,395 on December 31, 19XX.

As before, the previous balance in the Allowance account is considered when formulating the adjusting entry. If a review of Livingston's ledger revealed a credit balance of $2,200, then $7,195 ($9,395 − $2,200) would be needed to bring the Allowance up to the required figure. The following entry is necessary:

Uncollectible Accounts Expense	7,195	
Allowance for Uncollectible Accounts		7,195
Adjusting entry		

4 Handle account write-offs and subsequent recoveries under the allowance method.

Writing Off Uncollectible Accounts. Under the allowance method, individual accounts are written off when they are deemed uncollectible by debiting the Allowance for Uncollectibles and crediting Accounts Receivable. Note that Uncollectible Accounts Expense is not charged at the time of write-off, as such a procedure would result in double counting the bad debt.

In view of this treatment, the write-off of an uncollectible does not affect the net realizable value of the accounts receivable balance. As an example, consider the information below Exhibit 9–3 that appeared on Harvey Company's December 31, 19X1, balance sheet:

EXHIBIT 9–3
Aging Schedule

LIVINGSTON CORPORATION
Aging Schedule of Accounts Receivable
December 31, 19XX

LENGTH OF TIME OUTSTANDING

CUSTOMER	BALANCE, 12/31/XX	UNDER 31 DAYS	31–60 DAYS	61–90 DAYS	91–120 DAYS	OVER 120 DAYS
Clark, Inc.	$ 15,000			$6,000	$5,000	$4,000
Gibbs Manufacturing	36,000	$31,000	$ 5,000			
Madden Co.	19,500	15,000	4,500			
Nunley Co.	18,700	9,000	5,000	3,000	1,700	
Patrick Corporation	27,500	15,500	12,000			
Total	$116,700	$70,500	$26,500	$9,000	$6,700	$4,000

ESTIMATED UNCOLLECTIBLES

AGE	ACCOUNT BALANCES (FROM ABOVE)	× ESTIMATED % UNCOLLECTIBLE	= ESTIMATED AMOUNT OF UNCOLLECTIBLES
Under 31 days	$ 70,500	3%	$2,115
31–60 days	26,500	7	1,855
61–90 days	9,000	12	1,080
91–120 days	6,700	35	2,345
Over 120 days	4,000	50	2,000
	$116,700		$9,395

```
Current assets
    Accounts receivable                          $140,000
    Less: Allowance for uncollectible accounts     6,780    $133,220
```

Assume that on January 18, 19X2, J. Waldrup's $425 balance is judged uncollectible. The entry that follows is made.

```
Allowance for Uncollectible Accounts        425
    Accounts Receivable: J. Waldrup               425
To write off uncollectible account.
```

The write-off will not have any effect on the net accounts receivable balance because the entry reduces both the Allowance and Accounts Receivable by the same amount. This result is shown in the accompanying table.

	BEFORE	WRITE-OFF	AFTER
Accounts receivable	$140,000	–$425	$139,575
Less: Allowance for uncollectibles	6,780	–425	6,355
	$133,220		$133,220

The process of writing off an uncollectible account places debits in the Allowance and may result in a debit balance at the end of the reporting period. This situation usually arises when a firm's estimate of expense (a credit in the Allowance account) is lower than the company's actual write-off experience. The debit balance is easily corrected by increasing the percentages used in the adjustment process.

Collection of an Account Previously Written Off. Occasionally, a customer whose account has been previously written off will pay the amount owed. In such cases the customer's receivable is first reestablished in the accounting records; the payment is then recorded. Continuing the previous example, assume J. Waldrup now pays $225 of his $425 balance. The following journal entries are needed:

Accounts Receivable: J. Waldrup	225	
Allowance for Uncollectible Accounts		225
To reinstate account.		
Cash	225	
Accounts Receivable: J. Waldrup		225
To record collection on account.		

Observe that the reinstatement entry simply reverses the entry that was made for the write-off. If collection of the entire $425 is likely, Waldrup's account would be reestablished for the full amount.

Notice that the net effect on the Accounts Receivable account is zero, because it is debited and credited for the same figure. Yet, this two-entry procedure is preferred over one that results in a single debit to Cash and a credit to the Allowance for Uncollectibles. Why? By going back and reinstating the customer's account on the books, we are showing that an attempt has been made to pay the balance due. This action and information could be useful to management in future credit-granting decisions.

RECEIVABLES INSIGHTS AND MANAGEMENT

A study of bad debt disclosures will reveal various insights about business activities. For instance, the allowance for uncollectible accounts as a percentage of ending accounts receivable varies significantly by company. This variation is caused, in part, by the type of product being sold, customer payment habits, and a firm's credit policy. A review of recent corporate annual reports found, for example, that The Timberland Company has recorded an allowance of about $1 per $100 of accounts receivable, The Coca-Cola Company about $3 per $100 of accounts receivable, and Reebok International about $9 per $100.

As a more extreme case, we cite data of several large U.S. banks. Many of the woes experienced in the past few years by U.S. financial institutions are directly attributable to bad loans that were made by these entities. (Be aware that customer loans are receivables for these firms, to be disclosed as assets on the balance sheet.) As the following figures show ($000 omitted), the amount of uncollectible accounts expense has been staggering in some instances, severely depressing profitability.

FINANCIAL INSTITUTION	UNCOLLECTIBLE ACCOUNTS EXPENSE	NET INCOME (LOSS)
BankAmerica	$ 803,000	$1,954,000
Chase Manhattan	995,000	966,000
Citicorp	2,600,000	2,219,000
First Chicago	270,000	804,500
Wells Fargo & Co.	550,000	612,000

> **5**
> Evaluate receivables by using the accounts receivable turnover ratio.

Accounts Receivable Turnover. A company may have a relatively good record with respect to uncollectible accounts; yet, at the same time, the firm's customers may take an unusually long time to settle their balances due. The longer the collection period, the more funds are tied up in receivables. Abnormally large receivables balances will, in turn, restrict the monies available for investment and other uses.

To provide an indication of the quality of both the receivables and an entity's collection efforts, financial analysts often compute a ratio known as **accounts receivable turnover.** This ratio shows the number of times during the year that a company's receivables turn into cash. Managers and short-term creditors have a keen interest in turnover, as these two groups monitor the funds needed to settle short-term obligations.

Accounts receivable turnover is calculated by dividing net credit sales by the average accounts receivable balance. Average receivables are figured by summing the beginning and ending receivables and dividing by 2. To illustrate the underlying computations, assume that the following data pertain to Handy Corporation:

Net credit sales: $40,000,000
Accounts receivable balance, Jan. 1: $1,500,000
Accounts receivable balance, Dec. 31: $2,000,000

Handy's turnover ratio is 22.86 times:

$$\text{Accounts Receivable Turnover} = \frac{\text{Net Credit Sales}}{\text{Average Accounts Receivable}}$$

$$= \frac{\$40,000,000}{\frac{\$1,500,000 + \$2,000,000}{2}}$$

$$= 22.86 \text{ times}$$

The fact that receivables turned 22.86 times indicates an average collection period of about 16 days (365 days ÷ 22.86 times). To assess whether this result is satisfactory, additional information about Handy's credit terms is needed. If the terms are n/30, then the company is doing an excellent job in granting credit and collecting the resulting accounts. If the terms are n/10, however, questions may surface about receivables management. Perhaps sales have been made to marginal customers, or perhaps the firm's follow-up efforts have been lax.

A FURTHER FOCUS

Like other ratios, receivables turnover and collection periods vary among businesses. This fact becomes apparent when studying the following figures:

TYPE OF BUSINESS	MEDIAN COLLECTION PERIOD (DAYS)
Radio and TV retailers	11
Grocery wholesalers	22
Sports and recreation clubs	34
Knitted outerwear manufacturers	37
Optical goods manufacturers	52

Source: *Industry Norms & Key Business Ratios,* Dun & Bradstreet, Westport, Conn., 1994.

---

6 Recognize the benefits associated with accepting credit cards.

CREDIT CARD SALES

Many retailers and service establishments have found that maintaining credit departments, billing customers, and collecting accounts are costly and time-consuming processes. As a result, a large number of firms have stopped carrying their own accounts in favor of credit cards, such as American Express, Visa, and MasterCard. A merchant's acceptance of these well-known cards usually offers the benefits of increased sales and faster cash inflows. Quicker inflows result because the credit card company pays the merchant very shortly after the sale is made. In addition, the seller assumes little or no risk. If a customer does not pay his or her bill, the credit card issuer suffers the loss.

In exchange for these benefits, a service charge is assessed. This charge is usually a percentage of each sale and, in essence, is a fee for the use of a credit department and customer billing services. The service charge varies and is partially determined by the seller's annual volume of credit card transactions.

Bank Card Sales Versus Nonbank Card Sales. When sales are made on bank cards, the merchant submits the credit card transactions along with daily cash receipts to the bank.[4] The bank increases the seller's account; the service charge is automatically deducted and often appears on the bank statement along with other account charges. In view of this treatment, the credit card sale made on a bank card is really a cash sale.

If the transaction is on a nonbank card, reimbursement is not instantaneous. An account receivable is thus established for the amount of the sale. As an example, assume that Jacobs Jewelry sold $2,000 of merchandise on Charge-It, a nonbank credit card, giving rise to the following entry:

---

[4] In state-of-the-art systems, the transaction is "captured" electronically, and little or no paper changes hands.

Business Briefing

Managing Uncollectible Accounts: The Bottom-Line Impact

When the scorecards are handed out on the new business successes over the last decade, I believe that Discover Card will be judged a clear winner. From a startup at the end of 1985, Discover Card has become the largest single issuer of general purpose credit cards, with over 30 million cardmember accounts, 2 million merchant outlets, $20 billion of cardmember receivables, and—to the surprise of early skeptics—a healthy profit margin.

Once the cardmember and merchant acceptance of Discover Card was assured, one of the biggest risks became exposure to losses from uncollectible accounts. Controlling credit quality is an extensive effort, from establishing credit approval standards that will minimize losses without denying credit to potentially good customers, to implementing rigorous collection efforts on delinquent accounts. Discover Card currently has more than 2,000 employees involved in such activities.

How important is managing uncollectible accounts? Some simple math provides the answer. If you start with an annualized gross yield from interest income and fees on a credit card portfolio of around 16%, from which you deduct representative funding costs of 6% and operating costs of 5%, then the difference between a 3% or a 5% annualized account write-off rate (the normal range for the bank card industry) spells the difference between a good bottom line and no bottom line. We all know the consequence of running a no return business, so at Discover Card we will continue to manage credit quality just as carefully as we know how.

Robert Seass
Senior Vice-President and Controller
Dean Witter, Discover and Co.

Accounts Receivable: Charge-It	2,000	
Sales		2,000
To record credit card sale.		

If the service fee charged by the card company is 5%, Jacobs would update the accounting records in the following manner when the receivable from Charge-It is collected:

Cash	1,900	
Credit Card Expense	100	
Accounts Receivable: Charge-It		2,000
To record collection on account from credit card company.		

Notes Receivable

The financial statements of many entities often reveal an asset entitled notes receivable. **Notes receivable** (sometimes called promissory notes) are written promises from clients or customers to pay a definite amount of money on a specific future date. These instruments are used in extending credit to customers

> **7** Demonstrate the computations and journal entries for notes receivable and interest, including dishonored obligations.

and to lengthen the repayment period of outstanding accounts receivable. Notes are popular in some industries and seldom encountered in others. Exhibit 9–4 illustrates a typical promissory note.

In this particular case Precision Equipment is the **maker** of the note, namely, the person or firm that promises to pay the stipulated amount. Forseth Company is the **payee,** or the party to be paid. The stated amount (face value) of the note, $6,000, is termed the **principal.** Finally, February 9 is the **maturity date**—the date that the note becomes due. The maturity date is computed as follows:

Term of note		60 days
Days outstanding in		
December (31 – 11)	20	
January	31	51
Days outstanding in February until maturity		9

Had the term of the note been two months (as opposed to 60 days), the maturity date would have been February 11, which is two months from the time of issue.

THE NATURE OF INTEREST

Interest is the charge imposed on the borrower of funds. The note in Exhibit 9–4 indicates that Precision Equipment owes Forseth $6,000; however, the amount is not due until February 9, 19X2. In return for this temporary extension of credit, Forseth has become entitled to interest at a rate of 12%. Does this mean that Precision will have to pay the principal plus an additional $720 ($6,000 × 0.12)? The answer is no.

Interest rates are normally quoted on an annual basis. As a result, the term of the note would have to be extended from 60 days to a full year in order for the charge to total $720. To compute interest for a given period, the following formula is needed:

$$\text{Interest} = \text{Principal} \times \text{Rate} \times \text{Time}$$

This formula mathematically expresses the intuitive feeling that interest depends on a financial agreement's rate, amount, and duration.

EXHIBIT 9–4
Promissory Note

$6,000   Boise, Idaho   December 11, 19X1

<u>Sixty days</u> after date   <u>we</u> promise to

pay to the order of   Forseth Company

<u>Six thousand and no/100</u> ------------------ dollars

for value received, with interest of   12%

payable at   First City Bank

Due <u>February 9, 19X2</u>   *Michelle McGregor*
                                        Precision Equipment Company

To fully understand the preceding computation, it is important to know that the definition of principal is expanded somewhat to be more than just the face value of a note. Principal, as used here, is the amount on which interest is figured and may be the balance of an account receivable (in the case of finance charges), the outstanding balance of a loan, or the amount on deposit in a savings account.

Further, the formula's time element can be expressed in either days or months. In our example, for instance, interest would be calculated as follows:

$$\$6{,}000 \times 0.12 \times 60/360 = \$120$$

In many applications and for ease of computation, a year is considered to have 360 days.[5] Because the 12% rate covers an annual time frame, a factor of 60/360 is appropriate.

Had the term of the note been three months, a factor of 3/12 would have been employed, to yield interest charges of $180:

$$\$6{,}000 \times 0.12 \times 3/12 = \$180$$

ACCOUNTING FOR NOTES AND INTEREST

Notes receivable are initially entered in the accounting records at face value, requiring a debit to the Notes Receivable account. Because the note is owned by the payee firm, the associated interest is revenue. Interest revenue is recorded as it is received and as a year-end adjustment if the reporting period ends prior to the maturity date.

To illustrate, we will continue the Forseth Company example. The note in question was received on December 11, 19X1, from Precision Equipment, which desired to extend the repayment period of a previous purchase on account. Forseth would record the note as follows:

Dec. 11	Notes Receivable	6,000	
	Accounts Receivable: Precision Equipment		6,000
	Received note in settlement of account balance.		

Precision has agreed to pay $6,120 on February 9: $6,000 principal plus $120 of interest ($6,000 × 0.12 × 60/360). The amount due on the maturity date, principal plus interest, is commonly referred to as the **maturity value.**

Assume that December 31, 19X1, is the end of Forseth's accounting period. Although no interest has been received as of this date, 20 days' worth has been earned. Therefore, accrued interest revenue of $40 ($6,000 × 0.12 × 20/360) is recorded by the following adjusting entry:

Dec. 31	Interest Receivable	40	
	Interest Revenue		40
	Adjusting entry		

Also on December 31 closing entries would be recorded. The interest T-accounts, after closing, would appear as follows:

---

[5] Federal agencies and a number of lenders use a 365-day year.

INTEREST RECEIVABLE		INTEREST REVENUE	
12/31 40		12/31 Closing 40	12/31 40

On February 9, 19X2, when Precision Equipment pays the note, Forseth will make the entry shown below.

Feb. 9	Cash	6,120	
	Interest Receivable		40
	Interest Revenue		80
	Notes Receivable		6,000
	Collected note and interest from Precision Equipment.		

To explain, the receipt of the maturity value calls for a debit to Cash of $6,120 and a credit to Notes Receivable for the original amount of the obligation ($6,000). One-third of the $120 interest is located in the Interest Receivable account; thus, Interest Receivable must be credited for $40. The remaining $80, which has been earned during 19X2, is revenue. Observe how the adjusting entry effectively splits the interest: $40 of revenue earned in 19X1 (20 days) and $80 of revenue earned in 19X2 (40 days).

DISHONORING A NOTE

Our example assumed that Precision Equipment honored its obligation and paid the proper amount owed to Forseth on February 9. If Precision defaults on its promise, the note is said to be *dishonored.* The following journal entry is needed:

Feb. 9	Accounts Receivable: Precision Equipment	6,120	
	Interest Receivable		40
	Interest Revenue		80
	Notes Receivable		6,000
	To record dishonored note by Precision Equipment.		

Observe that the obligation's face value is transferred out of Notes Receivable and into Accounts Receivable. This procedure leaves only nonmaturing obligations in the Notes Receivable account and generates a record in the Accounts Receivable subsidiary ledger that the company has defaulted. Such information may be useful in future credit-granting decisions.

Furthermore, the entry reveals that any interest that has been earned is (1) recognized as revenue and (2) added to the amount due from the maker. Although this latter procedure may seem bizarre in view of the default, be aware that Forseth has a valid claim against Precision not only for the face value of the note but for $120 of interest as well.

END-OF-CHAPTER REVIEW

LEARNING OBJECTIVES: THE KEY POINTS

1. **Identify the costs related to credit sales.** Credit sales often create the need for a department that investigates customer credit ratings, approves the extension of credit, and attempts to collect delinquent accounts. In addition, credit sales result in cash being tied up in receivables balances. This situation may cause a company to borrow monies to fund activities or possibly sell trading securities. Interest and lost revenues likely result from these actions. Finally, from the company perspective, credit sales give rise to uncollectible accounts. Turning to the customer, delinquent payments associated with credit sales usually culminate in bad credit reports and higher interest rates on loans.

2. **Account for uncollectible receivables by using both the direct write-off and the allowance methods.** Under the direct write-off method, uncollectible accounts are recognized when the actual loss is confirmed. Use of this approach may result in a mismatch of revenue and expense on the income statement and overstated receivables on the balance sheet. With the allowance method, improved matching and receivables valuation are achieved through the use of estimates in the adjusting process. The proper adjusting entry involves a debit to Uncollectible Accounts Expense and a credit to Allowance for Uncollectible Accounts. The latter account is a contra asset that appears on the balance sheet as a deduction from Accounts Receivable.

3. **Compare and contrast the income statement and balance sheet approaches of accounting for uncollectibles.** The income statement approach to estimation involves estimates of uncollectibles that are computed on the basis of sales. This procedure results in matching current revenues with the costs incurred in producing those revenues. Alternatively, under the balance sheet approach, uncollectibles are estimated on the basis of accounts receivable, sometimes by using the aging process. This method focuses on reporting accounts receivable at net realizable value, thereby requiring that the existing balance in the Allowance for Uncollectibles account be considered when constructing the adjusting entry.

4. **Handle account write-offs and subsequent recoveries under the allowance method.** When a customer's account is deemed uncollectible, it is written off against the Allowance account. Should the customer later pay the amount due, the write-off entry is reversed and a second entry is made to record the cash collected.

5. **Evaluate receivables by using the accounts receivable turnover ratio.** The accounts receivable turnover ratio is computed by dividing the average accounts receivable balance into net credit sales. This measure discloses the number of times during the year that a company's receivables turn into cash—an important indication of a firm's ability to settle short-term obligations on a timely basis. The ratio can be divided into 365 days to show how long customers are taking to settle their account balances.

6. **Recognize the benefits associated with accepting credit cards.** The acceptance of credit cards often results in a rise in sales as well as faster cash inflows for the merchant. The latter situation occurs because reimbursements from credit card companies usually happen in less time than the typical customer takes to settle his or her account balance. Finally, with the burden of loss shifted to the credit card company, uncollectible accounts are eliminated (or drastically reduced).

7. **Demonstrate the computations and journal entries for notes receivable and interest, including dishonored obligations.** Notes receivable are written promises from clients or customers to pay a definite amount of money on a specific date. Such obligations are recorded at face value and normally bear interest, a charge for the use of borrowed funds. Interest is computed by using the following formula: interest = principal × rate × time.

Interest is entered in the accounting records as it is received as well as at year-end in the adjusting process. If the maker settles the note when due, the collection is handled in a similar manner to other receipts on account; if the maker defaults, the note is said to be dishonored. The default requires that the obligation's face value and the total interest earned be debited to Accounts Receivable in hopes of future collection.

KEY TERMS AND CONCEPTS: A QUICK OVERVIEW

accounts receivable Amounts that are due an entity from credit sales of goods and services. (p. 326)

accounts receivable turnover A ratio that indicates the number of times during a year that a company's receivables are turned into cash. Computed as: Net credit sales ÷ average accounts receivable. (p. 333)

aging accounts receivable Segregation of individual accounts receivable based on the length of time outstanding; used in the balance sheet approach to estimating uncollectibles. (p. 330)

allowance method of uncollectible accounts A method of accounting that employs a contra asset (Allowance for Uncollectibles) and estimates in the valuation of accounts receivable. (p. 327)

balance sheet approach of accounting for uncollectible accounts A method that employs estimates of uncollectibles based on accounts receivable and focuses on reporting accounts receivable at net realizable value. (p. 329)

direct write-off method of uncollectible accounts A method of accounting under which customer accounts are written off (expensed) when determined to be uncollectible. (p. 327)

dishonoring a note The process of failing to pay a note receivable on the maturity date. (p. 338)

income statement approach of accounting for uncollectible accounts A method that employs estimates of uncollectibles based on total sales or credit sales. (p. 328)

interest A charge made for the use of borrowed funds. (p. 336)

maker The person or firm that promises to pay the stipulated amount of a note. (p. 336)

maturity date The date that a note or obligation becomes due. (p. 336)

maturity value The amount due on the maturity date (principal plus interest). (p. 337)

net realizable value The amount of cash expected from the collection of present customer balances. (p. 328)

nontrade receivables Those receivables that arise from transactions and events not directly related to the sale of goods and services. (p. 326)

notes receivable Written promises owned by a firm that specify the receipt of a definite sum of money on some future date. (p. 335)

payee The party to whom a note is made payable. (p. 336)

principal The amount on which interest is computed. (p. 336)

receivables Amounts that a business expects to collect at some future date from claims against customers and other parties. (p. 325)

trade receivables Receivables that result from the sale of a company's products or services to customers. (p. 326)

CHAPTER QUIZ

The five questions that follow relate to several issues raised in the chapter. Test your knowledge of the issues by selecting the best answer. (The answers appear on p. 355.)

1. The following information is available for Hardy Company:

Credit sales during 19X8	$100,000
Allowance for uncollectibles, 1/1/X8	2,000 (credit)
Accounts written off during 19X8	4,500

    Hardy estimated that uncollectibles would amount to 5% of credit sales. What amount should Hardy record as uncollectible accounts expense for the year ended December 31, 19X8?
    - a. $3,000.
    - b. $4,500.
    - c. $5,000.
    - d. $7,000.

2. An aging schedule indicated that Murphy had $12,500 of bad accounts. Yet, the adjusting entry for uncollectible accounts expense was prepared for only $6,000. This situation arose because:
    - a. there was a $6,500 debit balance in the Allowance for Uncollectibles prior to adjustment.
    - b. there was a $6,500 credit balance in the Allowance for Uncollectibles prior to adjustment.
    - c. Uncollectible Accounts Expense had an existing balance of $6,500.
    - d. $6,500 of bad accounts were written off during the period.

3. The write-off of an uncollectible account by a business that uses the allowance method:
    - a. increases the Allowance for Uncollectibles.
    - b. decreases the net realizable value of Accounts Receivable.
    - c. has no effect on the net realizable value of Accounts Receivable.
    - d. increases Uncollectible Accounts Expense.

4. Accounts receivable turnover:
    - a. is calculated by relying on the ending accounts receivable balance (as opposed to the beginning balance).
    - b. is of interest to short-term creditors.
    - c. is based on both cash sales and credit sales.
    - d. tends to be the same for all businesses.

5. On November 1, 19X6, Trendy Company received a $24,000, 3-month, 10% note receivable. How much interest revenue should be reported in 19X6 from this note, assuming that Trendy closes its books on December 31, 19X6?
    - a. $200.
    - b. $400.
    - c. $600.
    - d. $2,400.

SUMMARY PROBLEM

The Shank Company's balance sheet revealed the following information as of January 1:

Accounts receivable	$75,800	
Less: Allowance for uncollectible accounts	6,500	$69,300

The following transactions took place during the first quarter of the year:

Jan. 2   Received a $4,000, 60-day, 12% note from T. Abernathy in settlement of his account balance.

      18   Wrote off the $1,300 balance owed by Magna Company as uncollectible.

Feb. 17   Received $180 from Pat Young. Young's account had been written off as uncollectible in the previous year.

Mar. 3   Received the proper amount due from T. Abernathy. To date, the company has yet to record any interest on Abernathy's note.

Shank's credit sales for the first quarter totaled $142,000.

Instructions

a. Prepare journal entries for the transactions from January 2 through March 3.
b. Prepare the journal entry on March 31 to adjust the Allowance account, assuming that uncollectible accounts are estimated at 3% of credit sales.

Solution

a. Jan. 2   Notes Receivable   4,000
                   Accounts Receivable: T. Abernathy   4,000
              Received note in settlement of account balance.

        18   Allowance for Uncollectible Accounts   1,300
                   Accounts Receivable: Magna Company   1,300
              To write off uncollectible account.

   Feb. 17   Accounts Receivable: Pat Young   180
                   Allowance for Uncollectible Accounts   180
              To reinstate account.

              Cash   180
                   Accounts Receivable: Pat Young   180
              To record collection on account.

   Mar. 3   Cash   4,080
                   Interest Revenue   80
                   Notes Receivable   4,000
              Collected note and interest from
              T. Abernathy ($4,000 × 0.12 × 60/360 = $80).

b. Mar. 31   Uncollectible Accounts Expense   4,260
                   Allowance for Uncollectible Accounts   4,260
              Adjusting entry ($142,000 × 0.03).

ASSIGNMENT MATERIAL

QUESTIONS

Q9–1 Distinguish between trade and nontrade receivables. Give three examples of the latter.

Q9–2 Explain why uncollectible accounts have both income statement and balance sheet implications for accountants.

Q9–3 Briefly describe the two methods that can be used to record losses from uncollectible accounts.

Q9–4 Discuss some possible deficiencies of the direct write-off method of uncollectible accounts.

Q9–5 Define the term "net realizable value" as it relates to accounts receivable.

Q9–6 Briefly describe the two general approaches that may be used for the estimation of uncollectible accounts.

Q9–7 Discuss the advantages of using aging schedules rather than a flat percentage of accounts receivable for estimates of uncollectible accounts.

Q9–8 Software International uses the allowance method of accounting for uncollectibles. What impact, if any, does the write-off of an uncollectible customer account have on the firm's net income?

Q9–9 In general, would a manager prefer a high or low accounts receivable turnover ratio? Why?

Q9–10 Why do companies accept credit cards such as Visa and American Express?

Q9–11 Distinguish between the principal and maturity value of a note.

Q9–12 What is the interest computation formula? Why must a time factor be included?

Q9–13 Why is Accounts Receivable increased for both the principal and interest earned when a note receivable is dishonored?

EXERCISES

E9–1 Direct write-off method (L.O. 2)

Harrisburg Company, which began business in early 19X7, reported $40,000 of accounts receivable on the December 31, 19X7, balance sheet. Included in this amount was a $550 claim against Tom Mattingly from a sale made in July. On January 4, 19X8, the company learned that Mattingly had filed for personal bankruptcy. Harrisburg uses the direct write-off method to account for uncollectibles.

a. Prepare the journal entry needed to write off Mattingly's account.
b. Comment on the ability of the direct write-off method to value receivables on the year-end balance sheet.

E9–2 Allowance method: Estimation and balance sheet disclosure (L.O. 3)

The following preadjusted information for the Maverick Company is available on December 31:

Accounts receivable	$107,000
Allowance for uncollectible accounts	5,400 (credit balance)
Credit sales	250,000

a. Prepare the journal entries necessary to record Maverick's uncollectible accounts expense under each of the following assumptions:
   (1) Uncollectible accounts are estimated to be 5% of credit sales.
   (2) Uncollectible accounts are estimated to be 14% of accounts receivable.
b. How would Maverick's accounts receivable appear on the December 31 balance sheet under assumption (1) of part (a)?

c. How would Maverick's accounts receivable appear on the December 31 balance sheet under assumption (2) of part (a)?

E9–3 Uncollectible account estimation: Balance sheet approach (L.O. 3)

O'Keefe Company has gathered the following information to estimate bad debts by use of an aging schedule:

Age of Receivable	Amount	Probable Percentage Uncollectible
0–30 days	$520,000	1%
31–60 days	280,000	10
61–120 days	200,000	20
121–240 days	90,000	40
Over 240 days	30,000	70

a. Determine the estimated amount of uncollectible accounts.
b. By how much will O'Keefe's net income be reduced because of this estimate of uncollectible accounts, assuming that the previous balance in the Allowance for Uncollectibles was:
   (1) $13,000 (credit).
   (2) $4,000 (debit).
c. Do the percentages used by O'Keefe parallel those employed by many other companies (i.e., lower percentages applied to fairly recent accounts and larger percentages applied to older accounts)? Briefly explain.

E9–4 Aging of receivables (L.O. 3)

On December 31, 19X2, the Ripley Company had $102,700 of accounts receivable and a $4,200 credit balance in the Allowance for Uncollectibles. An analysis of the firm's records found $81,700 of current receivables, along with the following activity:

	Sales on Account Date	Amount	Receipts on Account Date	Amount
Shawn Butler	Feb. 14	$ 5,300	Apr. 1	$9,000
	Mar. 1	3,700		
	Nov. 8	7,000		
Kevin O'Hara	Sept. 17	$10,000	Oct. 3	$2,000
Suzanne Wilkes	Aug. 15	$ 6,000		

All transactions pertaining to Butler, O'Hara, and Wilkes occurred during 19X2. Ripley anticipates the collection pattern that follows.

Age of Account	Estimated Percentage Uncollectible
Current	3%
31–60 days	10
61–90 days	25
91–120 days	50
Over 120 days	75

a. Prepare an aging schedule and determine the balance that Ripley needs in the Allowance for Uncollectibles at the end of 19X2.
b. Prepare the journal entry needed to record the estimate of uncollectible accounts.

E9–5 Allowance method: Account write-off and collection (L.O. 2, 4)

McKee Company had the following balances at the close of business on April 5:

Accounts receivable	$243,500
Less: Allowance for uncollectible accounts	17,900
	$225,600

On April 6, McKee wrote off a $4,400 receivable from Kinney Limited because the account was judged to be uncollectible. On October 6, McKee unexpectedly received a $1,000 check from Kinney. The check was accompanied by a note explaining that the company was in bankruptcy and no additional payments would be made.

a. Determine the net realizable value of accounts receivable on April 5. Explain in a sentence or two what this amount represents.
b. Prepare the journal entries McKee made to record:
  (1) the write-off of the Kinney account on April 6.
  (2) the payment by Kinney on October 6.
c. Determine the net realizable value of accounts receivable immediately after the Kinney write-off on April 6.

E9–6 Allowance method: Analysis of account write-off (L.O. 4)

The Syracuse Company, which uses the allowance method of accounting for uncollectibles, has just written off the $640 balance of Providence Company. Determine the impact of the write-off (increase, decrease, or no effect) on each of the following:

a. Uncollectible accounts expense
b. Net income
c. Accounts receivable
d. Allowance for uncollectible accounts
e. Net realizable value of accounts receivable

E9–7 Overview of accounts receivable (L.O. 1, 2, 3, 4)

Evaluate the comments that follow as being True or False. If the comment is false, briefly explain why.

a. Accounts receivable is normally classified as a trade receivable.
b. Most large companies use the direct write-off method of accounting for uncollectible accounts.
c. The income statement approach of accounting for uncollectibles focuses on determining the net realizable value of accounts receivable.
d. Aging is an example of the balance sheet approach of accounting for uncollectibles.
e. The recovery of an account receivable previously written off gives rise to two journal entries.

E9–8 Accounts receivable turnover (L.O. 5)

Soldofsky Company imports artwork from the former socialist countries of Eastern Europe. All sales are made on account to art galleries throughout the United States. The firm, which began operation on January 2, 19X5, had the following data for 19X5 and 19X6:

19X5—Sales, $1,000,000; ending receivables, $200,000
19X6—Sales, $2,500,000; ending receivables, $600,000

a. Compute the accounts receivable turnover ratio for both 19X5 and 19X6.
b. Discuss the change in the ratio from 19X5 to 19X6. Be sure to comment on a possible modification of the firm's credit and collection policies.

E9–9 Credit card sales (L.O. 6)

The Little Red School, a private nonprofit school for children under 10 years of age, is considering the acceptance of credit cards to process monthly tuition payments. Up to this point, parents had paid tuition by cash or check.

a. Discuss several benefits of accepting credit cards from the school's point of view.
b. Prepare journal entries to record:
   (1) $3,000 of tuition charged on Charge-All, a nonbank credit card that has a 4% processing fee.
   (2) the subsequent receipt of cash from Charge-All.

E9–10 Notes receivable and interest: Basic computations (L.O. 7)

The following notes receivable were held by Rizzuto, Inc.:

DATE OF NOTE	PRINCIPAL	INTEREST RATE	TERM
April 3	$ 3,000	10%	2 months
June 21	10,000	12	90 days

a. Determine the maturity date for each of the notes.
b. Determine the interest earned on each of the notes if the notes are held until maturity.
c. Assume that Rizzuto's fiscal year ends on June 30. Calculate the amount of accrued interest receivable that the company would disclose on its June 30 balance sheet.

E9–11 Journal entries for notes receivable (L.O. 7)

The Catton Company received a $10,000, 180-day, 12% note from Foote Enterprises on November 16, 19X6. Foote had previously purchased merchandise from Catton and wanted to extend the repayment date of the receivable. Prepare the journal entries required by Catton to record the following:

a. The receipt of the note from Foote.
b. Accrued interest on December 31, 19X6, the end of Catton's accounting year.
c. The payment of the note by Foote on May 15, 19X7.

E9–12 Accrued interest; dishonored notes (L.O. 7)

Sacramento Appliance Company had the following transaction:

Sold Ben's Deli a refrigeration unit for $13,000. Ben's paid $1,000 as a down payment and signed a 120-day, 10% note for the remaining balance.

Prepare Sacramento's journal entries to record:

a. The sale.
b. Accrued interest 90 days after the sale, which coincides with the end of the fiscal year.
c. Ben's failure to pay the note at maturity.

Problems

Series A

P9–A1 Direct write-off and allowance methods; matching (L.O. 2, 3, 4)

The following balances were found in the December 31, 19X5, accounting records of the Hardaway Company: Sales, $247,000; sales discounts, $3,200; sales returns and allowances, $12,000; accounts receivable, $100,000; and allowance for uncollectible accounts, $1,200 (credit).

Instructions

a. Determine the adjusting entry for bad debts under each of the following conditions:
   (1) Uncollectible accounts are estimated at 2% of net sales.
   (2) An aging schedule indicates that $5,000 of accounts receivable will be uncollectible.
b. On March 8, 19X6, Inwood Resources (a customer) declared bankruptcy. Prepare the proper entry to write off Inwood's $2,650 balance if Hardaway Company had used the direct write-off method. Comment on the ability of this method to properly match revenues and expenses.
c. Repeat part (b), assuming use of the allowance method of accounting for uncollectibles.

P9–A2 Allowance method: Income statement and balance sheet approaches (L.O. 3, 4)

Tempe Company reported accounts receivable of $300,000 and an allowance for uncollectible accounts of $31,000 (credit) on the December 31, 19X2, balance sheet. The following data pertain to 19X3 activities and operations:

Sales on account	$2,000,000
Cash collections from credit customers	1,600,000
Sales discounts	50,000
Sales returns & allowances	100,000
Uncollectible accounts written off	29,000
Collections on accounts that were previously written off	2,700

Instructions

a. Prepare journal entries to record the sales- and receivables-related transactions from 19X3.
b. Prepare the December 31, 19X3, adjusting entry for uncollectible accounts, assuming that uncollectibles are estimated to be 2% of net credit sales.
c. Prepare the December 31, 19X3, adjusting entry for uncollectible accounts, assuming that uncollectibles are estimated at 1% of year-end accounts receivable.
d. Compute the amount of the adjusting entry in part (c), assuming that $46,000, rather than $29,000, of accounts were written off in 19X3.

P9–A3 Allowance method; analysis of receivables (L.O. 3)

At a January 19X4 sales meeting, the president of Phone Merchandising complained that the telemarketing staff was not closing enough business. One of the staff noted that the company policy of routing all customer calls to the credit department resulted in good prospects hanging up simply because of "slow service." The president responded that if this occurred, the salesperson should confirm the transaction and write "Code 11" on the order ticket. Code 11 items would then be shipped without credit department approval.

By the end of the year, significant gains in sales had been made, and the president was very pleased. The following data were generated by the accounting department:

	19X4	19X3
Sales	$33,945,000	$6,111,000
Accounts receivable, 12/31	18,946,000	1,127,000
Allowance for uncollectible accounts, 12/31	?	11,000 cr.

The $18,946,000 receivables balance was aged as follows:

Age of Receivable	Amount	Percentage of Accounts Expected to Be Collected*
Under 31 days	$7,875,000	96%
31–60 days	6,590,000	88
61–90 days	3,450,000	72
Over 90 days	1,031,000	60

* Rates based on collection patterns in 19X2 and 19X3.

Phone Merchandising anticipates a 25% rise in uncollectibles in each of the aging categories over the levels experienced in prior years. Assume that no accounts were written off during 19X4.

Instructions

a. Estimate the amount of uncollectible accounts as of December 31, 19X4.
b. What is the company's uncollectible accounts expense for 19X4?
c. Compute the net realizable value of accounts receivable on December 31, 19X4.
d. Calculate year-end accounts receivable as a percentage of sales for both 19X3 and 19X4. (Use gross receivables, not net realizable value.) Do you feel these results are consistent or inconsistent with the company's new Code 11 sales policy? Briefly explain.

P9–A4   Journal entries for accounts and notes receivable (L.O. 3, 4, 7)

Nancy Wagner is the accounts receivable manager for the Kenwood Company. Selected information from the firm's receivables records follows.

	Balance on Sept. 30, 19X4
Customer	
T. Porter	$ 8,700
A. Snodgrass	16,000
G. Yost	7,600
Other	
Allowance for uncollectibles	14,400

The following activity took place during the last quarter of 19X4:

Oct. 2   Received $16,000 from A. Snodgrass in settlement of his account.
      14   Wrote off the balance owed by G. Yost as uncollectible.
Nov. 23   Received a 30-day, 12% note from T. Porter in settlement of her overdue account balance.

Dec. 1 Sold merchandise on account to G. Gordon. Gordon issued a $12,000, 120-day, 15% note in settlement of the amount owed.
23 Porter dishonored her note of November 23 but promised to pay the total amount due within seven days. Because Porter is a valued customer, Wagner has agreed not to charge any additional interest or penalty.
24 Received a $4,000 check from G. Yost in partial settlement of the balance written off in October.
26 Received the proper amount due from Porter, as promised.
31 Recorded the necessary adjusting entries for uncollectible accounts and interest related to the Gordon note.

The year-end accounts receivable balance was $119,400. Of this amount, accounts totaling $17,400 were estimated to be uncollectible.

Instructions

a. Prepare journal entries for the preceding transactions and events.
b. Determine the net realizable value of accounts receivable on December 31, after the adjusting process is completed.
c. Wagner believes that 2% of the company's total credit sales of $980,000 may be uncollectible. Assuming the income statement method of estimation had been used instead of the balance sheet approach, prepare the journal entry to record uncollectible accounts expense.

P9-A5 Notes receivable (L.O. 7)

The following information relates to notes receivable held by Cicero Company:

MAKER	DATE OF NOTE	PRINCIPAL	RATE	NOTE TERM
Fleming Inc.	March 1	$30,000	10%	2 months
Atchley Co.	June 15	20,000	12	120 days
Plovnick Co.	November 15	12,000	9	90 days

Fleming's note was received in settlement of a past-due account balance; the other notes were given to Cicero for sales of merchandise. Cicero's accounting year ends on November 30.

Instructions

a. Prepare journal entries to record:
   (1) The receipt of the notes from Fleming and Atchley.
   (2) Settlement of Fleming's note on the maturity date.
   (3) Atchley's dishonoring of its note on the maturity date.
b. Calculate the maturity value of Plovnick's note.
c. Does the maturity date of Plovnick's note create any special accounting problems for Cicero? Be as specific as possible, and include in your response any journal entries that may be needed.
d. Prepare the proper entry to record settlement of Plovnick's note on the maturity date.

Series B

P9-B1 Direct write-off and allowance methods; matching (L.O. 2, 3, 4)

The December 31, 19X3, year-end trial balance of Yelland Company revealed the account information that follows.

	DEBITS	CREDITS
Accounts receivable	$90,000	
Allowance for uncollectible accounts		$ 2,500
Sales		410,000
Sales returns	10,000	
Sales discounts	8,000	

Instructions

a. Determine the adjusting entry for bad debts under each of the following conditions:
   (1) Uncollectible accounts are estimated at 1% of net sales.
   (2) An aging schedule indicates that $12,050 of accounts receivable will be uncollectible.
b. On January 13, 19X4, Yelland learned that Kaiser Distributors, a customer, had gone bankrupt. Present the proper entry to write off Kaiser's $480 balance.
c. Repeat the requirement in part (b), using the direct write-off method.
d. Compare the allowance and direct write-off methods by:
   (1) Determining the impact on net income of the Kaiser write-off.
   (2) Examining the methods' ability to match revenues and expenses.

P9–B2 Allowance method: Income statement and balance sheet approaches (L.O. 3, 4)

Huffy Company reported accounts receivable of $500,000 and an allowance for uncollectible accounts of $20,000 (credit) on the December 31, 19X4, balance sheet. The data that follow pertain to 19X5 activities and operations.

Sales on account	$7,000,000
Sales returns & allowances	400,000
Sales discounts	210,000
Cash collections from credit customers	6,000,000
Uncollectible accounts written off	19,000
Collections on accounts that were previously written off	2,500

Instructions

a. Prepare journal entries to record the sales- and receivables-related transactions from 19X5.
b. Prepare the December 31, 19X5 adjusting entry for uncollectible accounts, assuming that uncollectibles are estimated to be 1% of net credit sales.
c. Prepare the December 31, 19X5, adjusting entry for uncollectible accounts, assuming that uncollectibles are estimated at 1/2 of 1% of year-end accounts receivable.
d. Compute the amount of the adjusting entry in part (c), assuming that $34,000, rather than $19,000, of accounts were written off in 19X5.

P9–B3 Allowance method; analysis of receivables (L.O. 3)

At a January 19X2 meeting, the president of Sonic Sound directed the sales staff to "move some product this year." The president noted that the credit evaluation department was being disbanded because it had restricted the company's growth. Credit decisions would now be made by the sales staff.

By the end of the year, Sonic had generated significant gains in sales, and the president was very pleased. The following data were provided by the accounting department:

	19X2	19X1
Sales	$23,987,000	$8,423,000
Accounts receivable, 12/31	12,444,000	1,056,000
Allowance for uncollectible accounts, 12/31	?	23,000 cr.

The $12,444,000 receivables balance was aged as follows:

Age of Receivable	Amount	Percentage of Accounts Expected to Be Collected
Under 31 days	$5,321,000	99%
31–60 days	3,890,000	90
61–90 days	1,067,000	80
Over 90 days	2,166,000	60

Assume that no accounts were written off during 19X2.

Instructions

a. Estimate the amount of uncollectible accounts as of December 31, 19X2.
b. What is the company's uncollectible accounts expense for 19X2?
c. Compute the net realizable value of accounts receivable at the end of 19X1 and 19X2.
d. Compute the net realizable value at the end of 19X1 and 19X2 as a percentage of respective year-end receivables balances. Analyze your findings and comment on the president's decision to close the credit evaluation department.

P9–B4 Journal entries for accounts and notes receivable (L.O. 3, 4 ,7)

The following selected transactions and events pertain to the Letterman Company for the last quarter of the year:

Oct. 9   Sold $15,000 of merchandise on account to Dan Owen.
     29   Wrote off the $4,200 balance owed by Worth Company as uncollectible.
Nov. 21   Received a $2,000, 30-day, 12% note from Cindy Raymond in settlement of her past-due account balance.
     28   Received $1,500 in final settlement of Doug Light's $2,400 account balance. Light's account had been written off as uncollectible in the previous year.
Dec. 21   Raymond dishonored her note of November 21 but agreed to pay the proper amount due within five days. Management has agreed not to charge any additional interest.
     26   Raymond paid her account balance in full.
     31   Recorded the necessary adjusting entry for bad debts. On September 30, Letterman reported an $8,200 credit balance in the Allowance for Uncollectibles account.

The Accounts Receivable account contained a balance of $92,100 on December 31. An aging schedule indicates that $8,300 of accounts receivable will be uncollectible.

Instructions

a. Record the quarter's transactions and events in general journal form, assuming that Letterman uses the allowance method of accounting for bad debts.

b. Compute the net realizable value of accounts receivable on December 31.
c. Would an additional adjusting entry have been recorded on December 31 if Cindy Raymond's original note had a 60-day term rather than a 30-day term? Briefly explain.

P9–B5 Notes receivable (L.O. 7)

Smith Trucking Co. received a $6,000 note from Lee Chan in settlement of a past-due account receivable. The note is dated November 11, 19X3, carries an interest rate of 15%, and is due in 90 days. Smith has a December 31 year-end.

Instructions

a. Determine the note's maturity date.
b. Calculate the interest earned in 19X3 and 19X4.
c. Prepare journal entries to record:
   (1) Accrued interest on December 31, 19X3.
   (2) Settlement of Chan's note on the maturity date.
   (3) Dishonoring of Chan's note on the maturity date.
d. Determine the total interest earned by Smith over the note's term if the note is:
   (1) Paid at maturity.
   (2) Dishonored at maturity.

EXPANDING YOUR HORIZONS

EYH9–1 Credit reporting (L.O. 1)

Each of us develops a credit history by purchasing goods and services on account. Many merchants belong to local credit bureaus that have on-line access to these histories—an important source of information in credit-granting decisions.

Instructions

a. Visit a local credit bureau and inquire about how personal credit ratings are maintained and updated. Be prepared to report your findings to the class.
b. If you have purchased goods or services on account, ask how you can get a copy of your own credit history. Read the history thoroughly and check for accuracy. Are there any errors? Such errors can be damaging to you and, as you may find out, very difficult to correct.

EYH9–2 Estimates of uncollectible accounts (L.O. 3)

Companies have different expectations about the collection of receivables. Some businesses expect bad debts of only 1%, whereas other entities anticipate rates of 5% or more.

Instructions

Using reference materials of your library, review the receivables presentations of three large corporations. (The corporations should operate in distinctly different industries.) Determine the percentage relationship between the allowance for uncollectibles and the gross amount of accounts receivable. Write a one-page report that explains (1) the percentage of uncollectibles expected by each company and (2) your thoughts on why these percentages vary or are roughly the same from firm to firm.

EYH9–3 Federal student loan delinquencies (L.O. 3)

Over the last few decades, the federal government has provided billions of dollars in loans to help students pay for their college education. These loans are to be repaid according to prescribed schedules once the students start their careers. Unfortunately, the default rate on these obligations is relatively high.

Instructions

Using reference materials available at your college/university library, find the default rate at five well-known colleges and universities (including your own school). Be prepared to report your findings to the class.

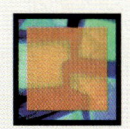

EYH9–4 Analysis of receivables: Ralston Purina and Hershey Foods (L.O. 1, 2)

Ralston Purina manufactures pet foods, animal feeds, a variety of bakery products (Wonder breads and Hostess), and Eveready and Energizer batteries. Hershey, which is known primarily for chocolate products, also manufactures various pasta goods.

Instructions

By using the text's electronic data base, access the financial statements and accompanying footnotes of both companies and answer the questions that follow. Unless otherwise indicated, responses should be based on data for the most recent year presented.

a. Study the balance sheets of both firms and compute net receivables as a percentage of total assets. All other things being equal, if a severe recession hit, which firm would be most affected by slow-paying customers? Why?
b. Did receivables increase or decrease?
   (1) What factors may have caused the increase or decrease?
   (2) Are any of these factors disclosed on the income statements? Briefly explain.
c. Which of the companies provide supplemental information about receivables in the footnotes to the financial statements?
d. Did the balance in the Allowance for Uncollectibles account increase or decrease? What would have caused the increase or decrease?

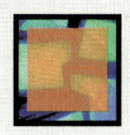

EYH9–5 Analysis of receivables: May Department Stores (L.O. 1, 2)

This problem is a duplication of Problem EYH9–4. It is based on the financial statements of May Department Stores and another company selected by your instructor. May, the largest department store retailer in the country, also owns Payless ShoeSource, a chain of self-service family shoe stores.

Instructions

By using the text's electronic data base, access the two companies' financial statements and accompanying footnotes and focus on data for the most recent year reported. Answer requirements (a)–(d) of Problem EYH9–4.

EYH9–6 Accounts receivable turnover, receivables policy, credit cards (L.O. 5, 6)

Alomar Tire Company is a five-store chain of tire shops located in central Oklahoma. The following information (in thousands) relates to 19X5–19X8:

	19X5	19X6	19X7	19X8
Net credit sales	$4,800	$5,460	$6,400	$6,820
Ending accounts receivable	500	900	700	400
Account write-offs	50	120	42	20

Accounts receivable at the end of 19X4 totaled $300.

Alomar implemented a decentralized credit operation on January 1, 19X5, with each store manager making his or her own credit-granting decisions. Some stores even authorized customer payments over an extended period of time. Beginning in 19X7, the company centralized its decision-making authority and heavily promoted the use of Visa and MasterCard as a way to finance customer purchases.

Instructions

a. Calculate Alomar's accounts receivable turnover ratio for each year.
b. On average, how long were customers taking to settle their accounts in 19X5 and 19X6?
c. Briefly explain the probable reasons behind the reorganization and the promotion of Visa and MasterCard.
d. Do the reorganization and promotion of credit cards appear to be achieving the desired results? Explain and show any appropriate calculations.

COMMUNICATION OF ACCOUNTING INFORMATION

CAI9–1 Communicating via a press release: The Dun & Bradstreet Corporation* (L.O. 1)

Communication Principle: Good public relations is sometimes as important an asset as cash or equipment. Relations with the public and press must be carefully cultivated, and any mistakes must be even more carefully corrected.

In the following situation, the media have made a mistake that has caused confusion both inside and outside the company. A press release is a vehicle that can be used to dispel any rumors that have arisen. Such a release should be written in a thoroughly positive style to explain and correct the situation. Under no circumstances should the media be accused of any intent to harm or of stupidity. Instead, in an objective and constructive way, the release should indicate the difference between what was said and what should have been said.

The press release typically begins with a background statement, referring to the date and misquote. Any mistakes are then corrected. An optimistic overview of the situation is often presented in any brief paragraphs that follow. Overall, then, the release may be used to get some extra press time for the firm. If handled properly, a situation that originally started off badly could turn into a convincing sales appeal.

■ ■ ■ ■ ■ ■ ■ ■ ■

Dun & Bradstreet is a huge corporation involved in numerous service businesses. Among the company's activities are publishing (Moody's Investors Service), marketing services (Nielsen ratings), and corporate research. Dun & Bradstreet is also heavily involved with the compilation and sale of credit reports and maintains a data base that includes over 32 million businesses. This data base is useful in helping companies decide whether or not to extend credit to other entities.

Imagine that you work for Dun & Bradstreet in the corporate communications division, and rumors have been circulating about cash flow problems of the company. These rumors began because a newspaper article incorrectly described Dun & Bradstreet as a firm "with cash flow and credit problems" rather than as a company "that provides information about businesses having cash flow and credit problems." The following balance sheet data (in millions) are available:

---

* This problem is a continuation of CAI8–1; it may be used regardless of whether CAI8–1 was assigned.

Cash	$ 650.9
Short-term securities†	17.7
Accounts receivable	1,078.9
Accounts, notes, accrued, & other short-term payables	2,044.1

† These are similar to trading securities.

Instructions

Draft a press release for newspapers, business periodicals, and wire services that explains and dispels the rumors.

Answers to Chapter Quiz

1. c ($100,000 × 0.05)
2. b ($6,500 credit + $6,000 credit = $12,500)
3. c
4. b
5. b ($24,000 × 0.10 × 2/12)

10 INVENTORY

LEARNING OBJECTIVES

After studying this chapter, you should be able to:

1. Explain the ownership issues related to goods in transit and goods on consignment.

2. Identify the effects of inventory errors on the financial statements.

3. Demonstrate use of the specific identification, FIFO, LIFO, and weighted-average inventory methods.

4. Discuss the factors that are considered when selecting an inventory method and the effects of such a selection on the financial statements.

5. Apply the lower-of-cost-or-market rule of inventory valuation.

6. Explain the importance of inventory estimates and use both the gross profit and retail methods.

7. Recognize the usefulness of the inventory turnover ratio when evaluating a company's inventory management policies.

8. Use a perpetual system to value inventory.

"We don't have a traditional merchandising inventory that is available for sale to customers," notes George Faris of Banner Advertising. "However, we do stock an extensive supply of paints and sign-building materials that must be closely controlled." Outdoor advertising companies require many different colors of paint, some of which (e.g., the bright florescent shades) are extremely expensive. To make matters worse, Banner's painters typically order more paint than is actually needed. George observes that "if we can use these paints on future jobs before they age and spoil, the company can save a lot of money."

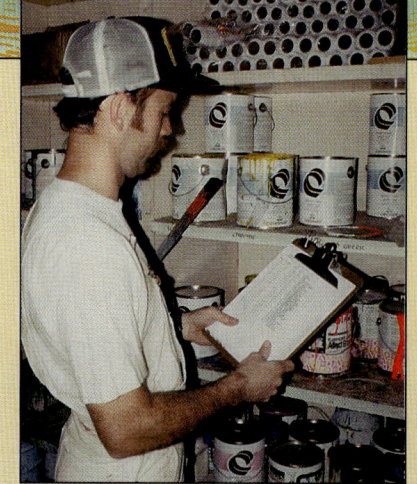

Given the relatively short shelf life, George has developed a special tracking system to monitor the amounts of each color on hand. The system is a micro version of the perpetual inventory system that you learned about earlier in the text. George notes, "Our average paint cost is about $30 per gallon, so every gallon that is spoiled hurts our bottom-line performance. I know that doesn't sound like much, but if we were less careful about managing inventory, the company could easily waste several hundred gallons each year. In a small business like ours, expenditures like these add up and can haunt us very quickly. Paint is no exception."

Inventory, although it affects the income of Banner Advertising, is a relatively minor issue for most service businesses. It is a totally different story for retailers, wholesalers, and manufacturers. Not too long ago, for example, the Commerce Department reported that these groups had collective inventories of $857 billion—a sizable sum to say the least. In view of the dollars involved, these goods typically "catch the attention" of different areas within a business.

A company's finance department, for instance, has the responsibility of securing operating funds and monitoring investments. Inventories, as you can see, represent a significant use of these funds. An entity's marketing function, which is concerned with maintaining a high level of customer service, wants to avoid out-of-stock situations that could result in lost sales and lost customers. The purchasing department negotiates favorable credit terms with suppliers and obtains quantity discounts by proper timing of acquisitions.

The accountant also has a keen interest in inventory. Excessive inventory investments, lost sales, lost customers, credit terms, and discounts all affect net income. Furthermore, for many firms, especially those engaged in retailing and wholesaling activities, inventories represent the largest asset owned by the company. These goods ultimately become a significant element on the income statement in the form of cost of goods sold. The effects of spoilage (such as that experienced by Banner Advertising), changing prices, and other issues merely complicate the picture. This chapter takes a thorough look at inventory accounting and selected facets of inventory management—two key ingredients to successful bottom-line profit performance.

What Is Inventory?

1 Explain the ownership issues related to goods in transit and goods on consignment.

When discussing merchandising businesses, we defined **inventory** as goods acquired for resale to customers. Although this definition is satisfactory for the retailer and wholesaler, it must be expanded for the manufacturer. The manufacturer, of course, does not acquire goods for resale—it makes them. Inventories, therefore, are said to include the following:

1. *Raw materials*—items to be processed into salable products.
2. *Work in process*—goods started but not as yet completed.
3. *Finished goods*—goods completed and awaiting sale.

Since most inventories are used or sold and converted into cash within the operating cycle, they are reported as current assets on the balance sheet. Inventory is usually listed immediately after accounts receivable because, in comparison with amounts due from customers, it is one step further removed from cash in terms of liquidity.

Ownership Problems

In Chapter 1, assets were defined as the economic resources owned by a firm that benefit future time periods. Let us concentrate on ownership for a moment. When the ownership of merchandise transfers to a company, the merchandise should be included as part of that company's inventory and reported on the firm's balance sheet. This principle is followed even though a business may lack physical possession of the units at the end of the reporting period—a situation that often arises with goods in transit and goods on consignment.

Goods in Transit. **Goods in transit** between the buyer and seller belong to the party that holds legal ownership (title) of the goods. Legal ownership, in turn, is dependent on freight terms, namely, F.O.B. shipping point and F.O.B. destination. Recall from Chapter 5 that the F.O.B. point indicates the location where the seller's responsibility for shipping ceases. As a logical extension, the F.O.B. point also indicates where (or when) legal title to the goods is transferred from the seller to the buyer. Under F.O.B. shipping point, for example, title transfers to the purchaser when the goods are shipped. Conversely, under F.O.B. destination, title passes when the goods arrive at their destination (e.g., the buyer's warehouse).

When title passes, the seller should record a sale and the buyer should record a purchase. Accordingly, inventories should be respectively reduced and increased at this time, even though the goods may still be on hand or in transit. To illustrate, suppose a company buys $10,000 of merchandise, F.O.B. shipping point, on December 29. The goods are shipped on December 30 and are in transit at the end of the purchaser's accounting year. Despite this fact, the buyer should enter a purchase in the records and include the goods in the ending inventory count because title has passed.

To simplify bookkeeping *during the year*, many companies operate on a receipt and shipment basis. Specifically, purchases are recorded when received regardless of the F.O.B. point, and sales are recognized upon shipment. If year-end in-transit shipments are significant, firms should examine their records and make account adjustments so that all merchandise owned is properly reflected in the ending inventory balance. Incorrect accounting for sales and purchases

---

Ethics Issue

M, Inc., sells machinery to U.S. customers from a factory in Singapore. The goods are sent on cargo ships; the journey takes two weeks. To raise the current period's sales, M's marketing manager has asked you to alter some invoices to read "F.O.B. shipping point" rather than "F.O.B. destination." The manager claims that the combined sales figures for this period and the next will not be changed by this action. How would you react, knowing it is close to year-end and your bonus depends on company earnings?

will influence inventory and often affect a host of other financial statement components. The effect of such errors will be discussed in a moment.

Goods on Consignment. Some companies transfer merchandise to sales agents (to sell to potential buyers) without transferring ownership. This process is known as **consignment**. If the products on consignment are sold, the agent receives a commission. If the merchandise is not sold, the goods are returned to the supplying company (i.e., the consignor). It is important to note that the consignor retains title to the transferred merchandise even though the goods are held by the sales agent. Consigned goods are therefore reported as part of the consignor's inventory until the time of sale and should not appear in the Inventory account of the agent.

EFFECTS OF INVENTORY ERRORS ON FINANCIAL STATEMENTS

2 Identify the effects of inventory errors on the financial statements.

Many errors are possible when dealing with inventory, especially in the process of taking a physical count. Items may be counted incorrectly, completely omitted in the counting process, or added twice. Furthermore, when computing total inventory cost, mathematical errors can be made when multiplying the number of units owned by the cost per unit. Unfortunately, these errors are carried forward to the financial statements. Incorrect inventory determination can result in incorrect current asset valuation, net income, and owner's equity.

To understand the effect of inventory errors, we will study The Backert Company, which accidentally excluded $2,000 of goods on display in its showroom from the ending physical count. The firm's income statement appears in Exhibit 10–1. The figures on the left are based on the correct ending inventory valuation of $34,000. In contrast, the figures on the right omit the display merchandise and use an ending inventory of $32,000.

EXHIBIT 10–1

THE BACKERT COMPANY
Income Statement
For the Year Ended December 31, 19X1

	CORRECT ENDING INVENTORY OF $34,000		INCORRECT ENDING INVENTORY OF $32,000	
Net sales		$80,000		$80,000
Cost of goods sold				
Beginning inventory	$26,000		$26,000	
Add: Net purchases	59,000		59,000	
Goods available for sale	$85,000		$85,000	
Less: Ending inventory	34,000		32,000	
Cost of goods sold		51,000		53,000
Gross profit		$29,000		$27,000
Operating expenses		20,000		20,000
Net income		$ 9,000		$ 7,000

> **ETHICS ISSUE**
>
> Peggy, an accountant, discovers a sizable error in last year's inventory count, which she originally verified as being correct. If disclosure will embarrass Peggy and negatively affect the firm's profit picture, what action should she take?

Because of the understated ending inventory, Backert is subtracting a number that is too small from goods available for sale. The resulting cost of goods sold is therefore overstated, which depresses net income. Regrettably, the problem does not stop here. Remember that net income is closed to owner's equity. Ending owner's equity, which appears on both the statement of owner's equity and the balance sheet, is thus understated as well. The balance sheet, though, will continue to balance because of a $2,000 inventory understatement in the current assets section. The effects of the display merchandise error are summarized as follows:

INCOME STATEMENT	
Cost of goods sold	Overstated
Gross profit	Understated
Net income	Understated
STATEMENT OF OWNER'S EQUITY	
Ending owner's equity	Understated
BALANCE SHEET	
Ending owner's equity	Understated
Total current assets	Understated

The results of an overstatement of ending inventory are the opposite of those just described. We do not recommend that you memorize this material, as inventory errors can become quite complex. Instead, understand how to trace an error through the system and analyze its impact.

COUNTERBALANCING ERRORS

Inventory errors have counterbalancing effects; that is, errors causing an overstatement of net income in one year create an understatement in the following year and vice versa. This situation arises because the ending inventory from one period becomes the beginning inventory of the next. As an example, assume that the goods on display in Backert's showroom were later sold and that company personnel correctly costed the 19X2 ending inventory at $41,000. Backert's $2,000 inventory error from 19X1 is carried forward as a $2,000 understatement of the 19X2 beginning inventory. The impact on the 19X2 income statement is shown in Exhibit 10–2.

Observe that the understated beginning inventory reduces goods available for sale. The ending inventory is not affected by the earlier error because the $41,000 figure is derived by a separate physical count and valuation. Overall, then, cost of goods sold is understated, which produces an overstated gross profit and net income. The $2,000 depression of net income in 19X1 is therefore counterbalanced by a $2,000 overstatement in 19X2. Although the 19X2 income statement is in error, the ending owner's equity is correct. This outcome is shown at the top of the next page.

	USING CORRECT 19X1 AND 19X2 NET INCOME	USING INCORRECT 19X1 AND 19X2 NET INCOME
Beginning owner's equity, Jan. 1, 19X1 (assumed)	$50,000	$50,000
+ 19X1 net income	9,000	7,000
+ 19X2 net income	11,000	13,000
Ending owner's equity, Dec. 31, 19X2	$70,000	$70,000

INVENTORY VALUATION AND INCOME MEASUREMENT

As we have just shown, inventory affects both the balance sheet and the income statement. Ending inventory valuation and the determination of cost of goods sold are probably the two most significant inventory problems faced by accountants. If a firm purchased all of its merchandise at the same price throughout the year, few difficulties would arise. Ending inventory could be calculated by multiplying the ending quantity of merchandise owned by the unit cost. The resulting amount would then be subtracted from goods available for sale to generate cost of goods sold.

Purchase prices, however, rarely remain constant during an accounting period. To further complicate matters, we are often unable to attach the price paid for an item to the item itself. Picture a concrete company, for instance, whose purchases of sand are all mixed together in huge mounds. If different prices are paid for each ton acquired, the related accounting becomes a problem.

EXHIBIT 10-2

THE BACKERT COMPANY
Income Statement
For the Year Ended December 31, 19X2

	CORRECT BEGINNING INVENTORY OF $34,000	INCORRECT BEGINNING INVENTORY OF $32,000
Net sales	$97,000	$97,000
Cost of goods sold		
Beginning inventory	$ 34,000	$ 32,000
Add: Net purchases	71,000	71,000
Goods available for sale	$105,000	$103,000
Less: Ending inventory (correct)	41,000	41,000
Cost of goods sold	64,000	62,000
Gross profit	$33,000	$35,000
Operating expenses	22,000	22,000
Net income	$11,000	$13,000

MATCHING: THE KEY OBJECTIVE

Throughout a reporting period a business has a "pool" of inventory costs to account for. This "pool" consists of the beginning inventory cost plus the cost of merchandise acquired for resale.[1] In more familiar terms, the pool is equivalent to goods available for sale. By the end of the period, many of the items available for sale have been sold, while others remain on hand. Thus, goods available for sale must be divided between cost of goods sold and ending inventory, as shown in Exhibit 10–3.

We will soon see that several different methods can be used to allocate inventory costs between the income statement and the balance sheet. Often a given method favors one financial statement or the other, but not both. In keeping with the income statement's growth in importance, *a major objective of inventory accounting is to associate or match the costs of the items sold against the sales revenues generated*. Balance sheet valuation, then, may be looked at as a residual. That is, after assignment of costs to the income statement, those costs that remain are carried as inventory on the balance sheet.

COST DETERMINATION

The computation of an inventory item's cost is the starting point for inventory valuation and figuring cost of goods sold. The recorded cost of inventory reflects all expenditures related to acquisition, such as the purchase price of the merchandise (minus any discounts), transportation charges incurred by the purchaser, and insurance costs incurred on the merchandise while in transit.

Once the preceding expenditures are determined, the unit cost of each inventory item can be calculated. The purchase price of inventory is easily associated with specific items, but it is frequently difficult to compute unit amounts for transportation, insurance, and discounts. Keep in mind that transportation and insurance often pertain to shipments that consist of many different goods. Similarly, the purchase discount on a single invoice may relate to numerous products. How, then, should these cost elements be handled?

EXHIBIT 10–3
Allocation of Inventory Cost Between the Income Statement and the Balance Sheet

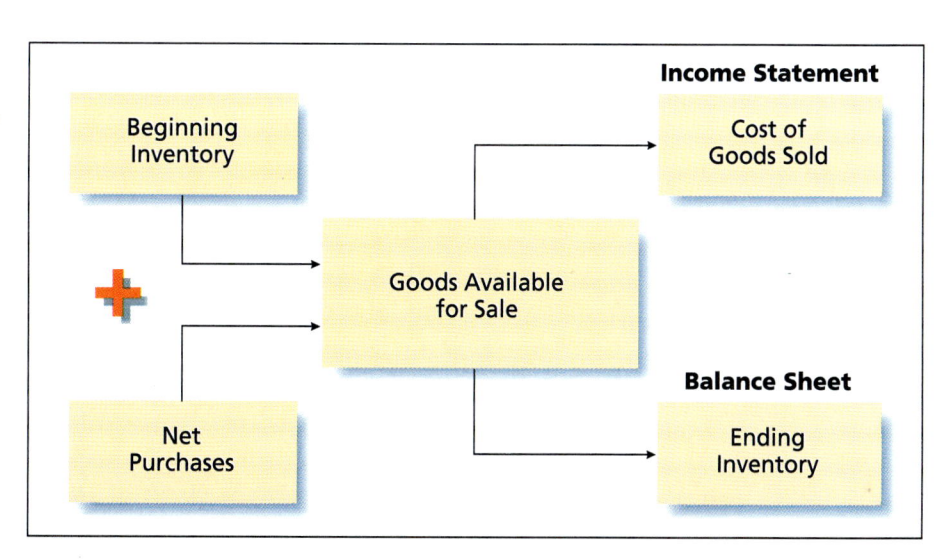

[1] For a manufacturer the cost of merchandise acquired for resale would be replaced by the cost of goods manufactured.

When discounts, transportation, and insurance are traceable to a particular inventory item (i.e., the ideal situation), the cost of that item is computed accordingly. For example, suppose Virginia Company had the following costs for part no. 1088:

Purchase price: 500 units @ $10	$5,000
Add: Transportation charges	350
	$5,350
Less: Purchases discounts	100
Total cost	$5,250

Cost per unit: $5,250 ÷ 500 units = $10.50

It is assumed that (1) these costs relate *strictly* to part no. 1088 and (2) there is no beginning inventory. If 400 units were sold during the year, Virginia's inventory pool would be divided as shown in Exhibit 10–4.

If discounts, transportation, and other acquisition costs are significant in amount and cannot be traced to specific inventory items, some form of equitable proration is necessary between the total ending inventory and cost of goods sold. The lack of such proration could result in a misstatement on both the balance sheet and the income statement. In many cases, however, discounts and transportation charges are fairly small in relation to an item's purchase price. As a matter of expediency, no proration is attempted, and the Purchases Discounts and Freight-in accounts are entered in their entirety on the income statement. This latter approach was illustrated earlier in the text (see Chapter 5).

COSTING METHODS

> **3**
> Demonstrate use of the specific identification, FIFO, LIFO, and weighted-average inventory methods.

Once the unit cost of each inventory item is determined, a firm can begin the necessary assignment to cost of goods sold and ending inventory. The following sections describe four acceptable methods for performing this process.

Specific Identification. The specific identification method requires a business to identify each unit of merchandise with the unit's cost and retain that identification until the inventory is sold. Tags or stickers that reveal a stock number are often

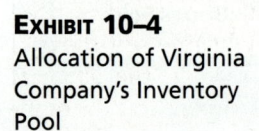

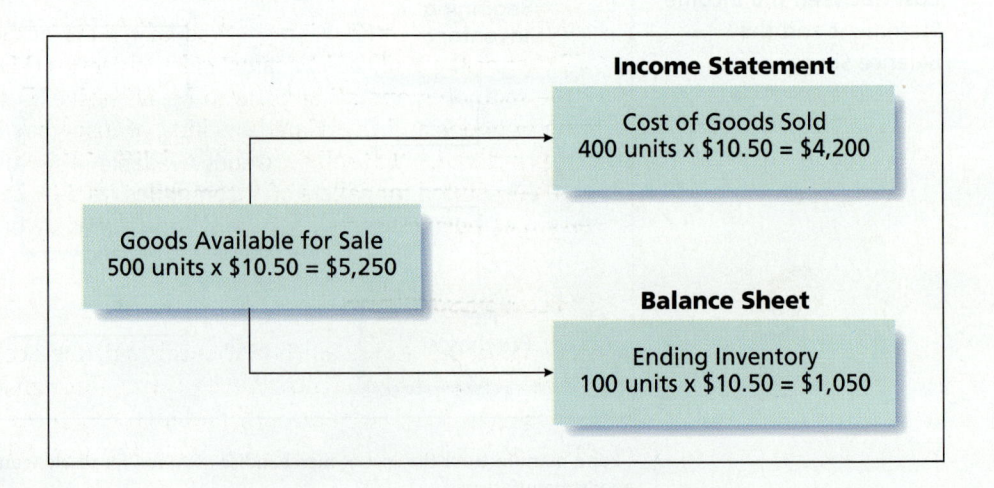

EXHIBIT 10–4
Allocation of Virginia Company's Inventory Pool

Goods Available for Sale
500 units x $10.50 = $5,250

Income Statement
Cost of Goods Sold
400 units x $10.50 = $4,200

Balance Sheet
Ending Inventory
100 units x $10.50 = $1,050

attached to the inventory item; the stock number, in turn, is listed in the accounting records along with the item's cost. You may have noticed, for example, that at many new car dealerships, each car has a number on the windshield or side window. That number references the net invoice cost of the vehicle in the dealer's records.

To illustrate the procedures associated with specific identification, we will focus on the January operations of Unique Creations, a seller of expensive watches and bracelets. Assume the company has the following data:

	STOCK NUMBER	COST
Inventory, Jan. 1		
Watch	4618	$ 6,000
Bracelet	3207	11,000
January purchases		
Watch	4623	7,500
Watch	4624	8,100
Bracelet	3210	14,000
Bracelet	3211	18,000
		$64,600

A physical inventory of the goods on hand on January 31 revealed that three items were still in stock: the watch from the beginning of the year and the two bracelets acquired during the month. The company's ending inventory and cost of goods sold are therefore determined as shown.

Inventory, Jan. 31		
Watch (no. 4618)	$ 6,000	
Bracelet (no. 3210)	14,000	
Bracelet (no. 3211)	18,000	$38,000
Cost of goods sold		
Bracelet (no. 3207)	$11,000	
Watch (no. 4623)	7,500	
Watch (no. 4624)	8,100	26,600
		$64,600

The specific identification method offers the advantage of matching the actual cost of the units sold against sales revenues. Many businesses, though, find the method's operating costs to be excessive. For example, the physical tagging of goods and the related tracking of costs may be impractical for high-volume companies that sell thousands of different items. Specific identification may be best suited for sellers of automobiles, yachts, antiques, and high-priced jewelry (i.e., businesses that handle a limited variety of merchandise).

COST FLOW ASSUMPTIONS

When specific identification is not employed, the accountant must make an assumption regarding the movement of costs through a firm's accounting system. This *cost flow assumption* pertains strictly to the *flow of cost* in the accounts and has no direct relationship to the actual *physical flow of goods*. For

A Further Focus

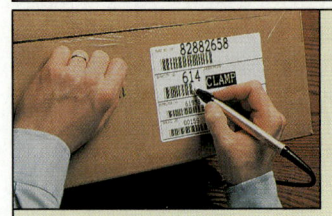

Despite the accuracy associated with specific identification, the method is used rather sparingly because of the difficulties just cited. More than likely, as computerized systems become more sophisticated and additional businesses turn to bar codes and scanners, the method's popularity will increase. Items that have preprinted bar codes by the manufacturer are now very commonplace. This feature, coupled with a system's ability to track cost from an item's acquisition through sale, improves the attractiveness to potential users.

example, picture a company that strives to sell the oldest merchandise first because of a threat of obsolescence or spoilage. It is very possible that this same business will cost these goods at the most recent costs experienced or perhaps even an average cost.

Cost flow assumptions are used to derive computations for cost of goods sold on the income statement and ending inventory valuation on the balance sheet. The selection of an assumption is based on several different factors that will be discussed shortly. At this point, however, we wish to introduce the three most widely used cost flow assumptions in accounting: first-in, first-out (FIFO); last-in, first-out (LIFO); and weighted average.

A General Introduction to FIFO and LIFO. To introduce the FIFO and LIFO cost flow assumptions, it is helpful to visualize a chronological listing of units and their related costs. For example, a company may have an inventory of goods on hand at the beginning of the reporting period. Then, throughout the period, additional goods are acquired by purchases from the firm's suppliers. As depicted in the middle block of Exhibit 10–5, the costs that pertain to a given inventory item can be subdivided into older costs (i.e., the beginning inventory and older purchases) and recent costs (more recent purchases). Collectively, the graphic's vertical height represents goods available for sale.

As discussed earlier in the chapter, a company's goods available for sale figure is allocated between cost of goods sold and ending inventory. This allocation may be performed in several different ways. One such approach, known as first-in, first-out (FIFO), is based on the premise that costs should be matched against revenues in the order that the costs were incurred. In other words, the oldest costs (i.e., those that were "first-in") are matched against revenues first, then the next oldest costs as the firm works forward in time, and so forth. This matching takes place in the form of cost of goods sold on the income statement. The block on the left reveals this process and shows that a company's more current costs wind up in ending inventory on the balance sheet.

The process is reversed under another acceptable approach, the last-in, first-out (LIFO) method. Under this procedure, costs are matched against revenues in the *reverse* order of incurrence. That is, the most recent costs incurred (i.e., the "last-in") are the first to be charged to cost of goods sold, then the next most recent, and so on. By viewing the exhibit's right-hand block, you will see that a user must go backward in time. The recent cost layers are eventually exhausted, meaning that older costs are then allocated to inventory.

EXHIBIT 10–5
A Graphical Overview of FIFO and LIFO

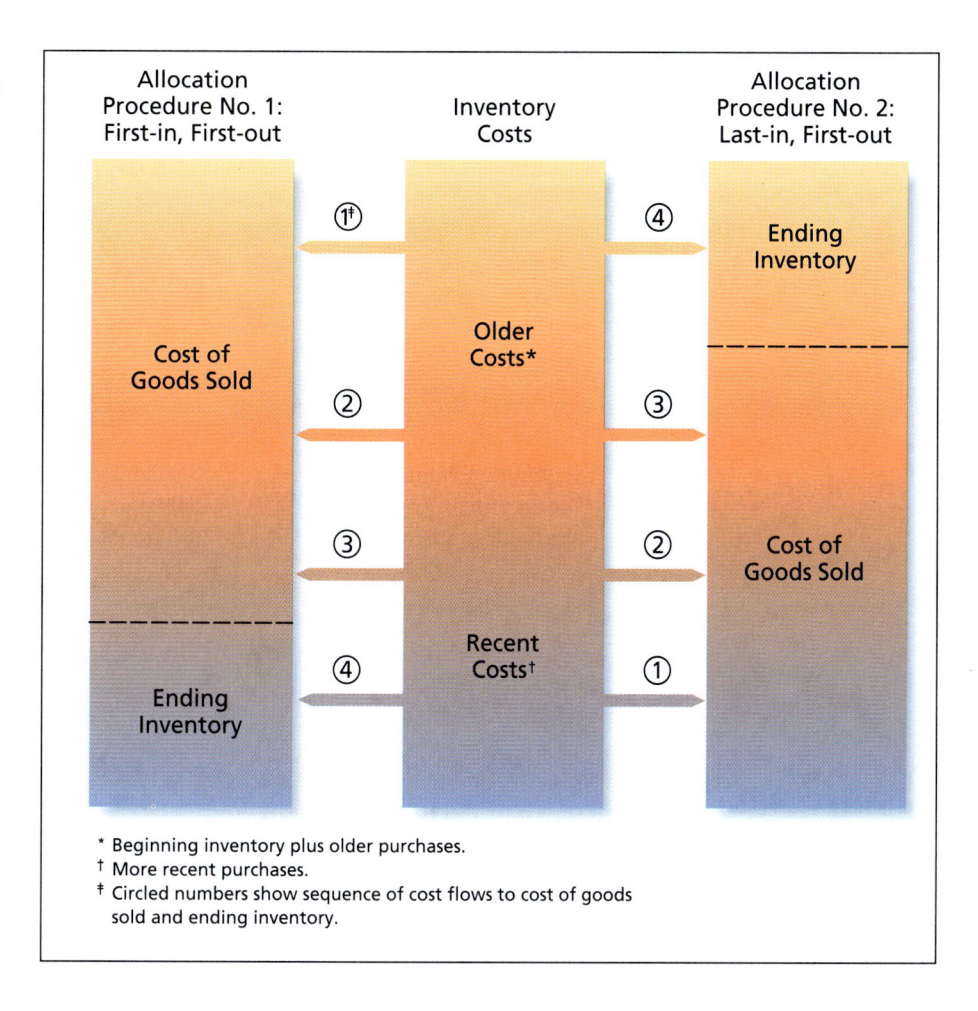

Allocation Procedure No. 1: First-in, First-out — Cost of Goods Sold (older), Ending Inventory (recent)

Inventory Costs — Older Costs*, Recent Costs†

Allocation Procedure No. 2: Last-in, First-out — Ending Inventory (older), Cost of Goods Sold (recent)

* Beginning inventory plus older purchases.
† More recent purchases.
‡ Circled numbers show sequence of cost flows to cost of goods sold and ending inventory.

First-in, First-out Calculations. To illustrate the calculations related to FIFO (and the other cost flow assumptions as well), we introduce the following data of the Tracy Company. The firm uses a periodic system.

	NUMBER OF UNITS	×	COST PER UNIT	=	TOTAL COST
Beginning inventory	3,000		$3.00		$ 9,000
Purchase (Feb. 28)	4,000		3.10		12,400
Purchase (May 15)	5,000		3.23		16,150
Purchase (Aug. 1)	1,000		3.50		3,500
Purchase (Oct. 31)	3,000		3.65		10,950
Goods available for sale	16,000				$52,000

During the year Tracy sold 11,800 units, leaving 4,200 units (16,000 − 11,800) in inventory.

The FIFO computations are most easily understood if we begin with the firm's inventory valuation, which must consist of recent purchases. The 4,200-unit ending inventory is costed in the manner shown on page 368.

Most recent purchase (Oct. 31)	3,000 units × $3.65 =	$10,950
Next most recent purchase (Aug. 1)	1,000 units × $3.50 =	3,500
Next most recent purchase (May 15)	200 units × $3.23 =	646
Ending inventory	4,200 units	$15,096

Observe that only 200 units from the May 15 purchase are needed to complete the accounting [the other 4,800 units acquired in May (5,000 – 200) are no longer on hand].

The cost of the 11,800 units sold may now be calculated by using two different approaches. First, we can focus on the flow of the older (i.e., "first-in") costs to the income statement, as follows:

Beginning inventory	3,000 units × $3.00 =	$ 9,000
Oldest purchase (Feb. 28)	4,000 units × $3.10 =	12,400
Next oldest purchase (May 15)	4,800 units × $3.23 =	15,504
Cost of goods sold	11,800 units	$36,904

Alternatively, the company's ending inventory valuation can be subtracted from goods available for sale:

Goods available for sale (see original data)	$52,000
Less: Ending inventory	15,096
Cost of goods sold	$36,904

Last-in, First-out Calculations. Recall that under this method, the cost of older purchases is assigned to ending inventory. As the figures that follow indicate, the LIFO flow assumption produces a $12,720 inventory valuation for Tracy Company's 4,200 units on hand.

Beginning inventory	3,000 units × $3.00 =	$ 9,000
Oldest purchase (Feb. 28)	1,200 units × $3.10 =	3,720
Ending inventory	4,200 units	$12,720

Although the firm purchased 4,000 units on February 28, the cost of only 1,200 of these units is needed for inclusion in the ending inventory.

The cost of goods sold is $39,280:

Goods available for sale (see original data)	$52,000
Less: Ending inventory	12,720
Cost of goods sold	$39,280

Weighted Average. Another inventory approach, the **weighted-average method,** recognizes that there are both high and low costs during an accounting period. Rather than focus on the time when costs are incurred (i.e., currently or in the past), an average cost is calculated by first weighting (multiplying) the cost per unit with the number of units purchased. Referring to the initial introduction of Tracy's data on page 367, observe that the outcome of this process results in $52,000—the cost of goods available for sale. The weighted-average unit cost can now be computed as shown below.

$$\text{Cost of Goods Available for Sale} \div \text{Units Available for Sale}$$
$$\$52,000 \div 16,000 = \$3.25$$

The unit cost of $3.25 is applied to the ending inventory as follows:

$$4,200 \text{ units} \times \$3.25 = \$13,650$$

Cost of goods sold is computed in the same manner as before, that is:

Goods available for sale	$52,000
Less: Ending inventory	13,650
Cost of goods sold	$38,350

The weighted-average method is, in effect, a compromise between FIFO and LIFO. Those who favor the weighted-average method base their argument on the belief that all goods available for sale in a period should reflect the same unit cost.

Comparison and Evaluation of Alternative Inventory Valuation Methods. The effects of using a particular cost flow assumption are summarized in Exhibit 10–6. The exhibit is based on the assumptions that sales and expenses were $125,000 and $60,000, respectively.

As you can see, each of the three methods results in reporting a different net income and ending inventory valuation. The magnitude of the differences depends on the number of units acquired and sold during the year and the extent of price changes. In light of the historical trend in purchase prices, it is possible that Tracy was experiencing an inflationary economy.

EXHIBIT 10–6
Alternative Inventory Valuation Methods for Tracy Company

	FIFO	LIFO	WEIGHTED AVERAGE
Sales	$125,000	$125,000	$125,000
Cost of goods sold			
Beginning inventory	$ 9,000	$ 9,000	$ 9,000
Add: Purchases*	43,000	43,000	43,000
Goods available for sale	$ 52,000	$ 52,000	$ 52,000
Less: Ending inventory	15,096	12,720	13,650
Cost of goods sold	$ 36,904	$ 39,280	$ 38,350
Gross profit	$ 88,096	$ 85,720	$ 86,650
Expenses	60,000	60,000	60,000
Net income	$ 28,096	$ 25,720	$ 26,650

*Purchases are computed by subtracting Tracy's beginning inventory from the cost of goods available for sale: $52,000 − $9,000 = $43,000.

Because the last-in, first-out method charges recent (higher) costs to cost of goods sold, LIFO will usually report the lowest net income in a period of rising prices. In contrast, FIFO will report a larger net income. The results, of course, are reversed in a period of falling prices. Weighted average normally yields figures somewhere between these two approaches.

All three assumptions are acceptable accounting alternatives, and each is used extensively. A survey of large corporations revealed the data that follow.[2]

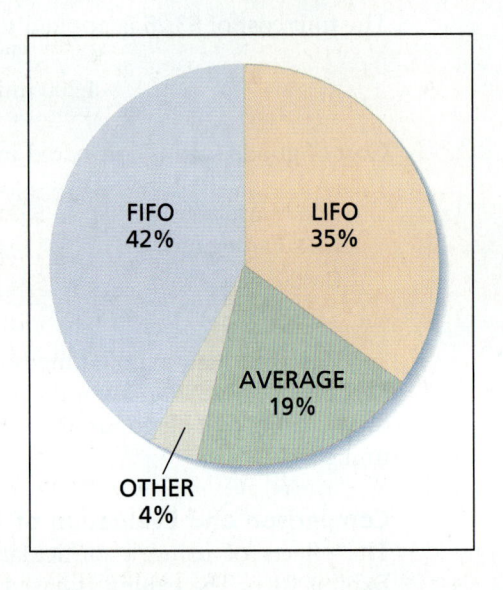

FIFO 42%
LIFO 35%
AVERAGE 19%
OTHER 4%

> **4**
> Discuss the factors that are considered when selecting an inventory method and the effects of such a selection on the financial statements.

Which Method Should Be Selected? It would be nice to generalize and state that, in certain situations, a firm should always use FIFO or LIFO or one of the other inventory valuation methods. Unfortunately, we cannot. No one approach best meets the needs and peculiarities of all businesses. Management considers several factors when selecting an inventory method, including income taxes and their related cash outlays, and financial statement presentation.

Income Taxes. In the past 20 years, LIFO has gained popularity because of overall rising prices in our economy. As just discussed, LIFO will produce lower net incomes and thus lower income tax payments for its users in an inflationary climate.[3] Lower taxes result in more cash available for investment purposes.

The amount of cash is dependent on several variables, such as the rate of inflation and applicable tax rates, and can be especially significant for companies that carry large amounts of inventory. As evidence, study the figures in Exhibit 10–7 that show estimated cash savings from using LIFO (as opposed to FIFO) for valuation of goods.

[2] *Accounting Trends & Techniques: 1994*, American Institute of Certified Public Accountants, Inc., Jersey City, NJ, 1994.
[3] According to current tax regulations, companies that use LIFO for tax purposes must also utilize LIFO for financial reporting.

EXHIBIT 10–7

Estimated Cash Savings from LIFO

CORPORATION	INVENTORY USING LIFO (IN MILLIONS)	INVENTORY USING FIFO (IN MILLIONS)	ESTIMATED CASH SAVINGS (IN MILLIONS)*
Adolph Coors Company	$ 147.2	$ 193.9	$ 16.3
Kimberly-Clark Corporation	775.9	886.1	38.6
La-Z-Boy Chair Co.	67.2	87.9	7.2
Sears, Roebuck & Co.	3,518.0	4,261.7	260.3

* Cash savings are calculated as the difference between FIFO inventory and LIFO inventory, multiplied by the 35% corporate income tax rate in effect at the time of this writing.

Financial Statement Presentation. The resulting financial statements must also be considered when selecting an inventory method. For example, the use of LIFO over long periods of time can generate a somewhat meaningless ending inventory figure on the balance sheet. Since the oldest costs are used as the basis for inventory valuation, units may be carried at costs incurred many years ago. In contrast, FIFO values the ending inventory at an amount close to the cost of replacement.

While producing a reasonable balance sheet valuation, FIFO frequently results in a mismatch of revenue and expense on the income statement. Cost of goods sold is determined by using older costs; revenues, on the other hand, are based on selling prices that were charged to customers during the current accounting period. The use of old costs and fairly current prices generally raises questions about the meaningfulness of the net income figure. The mechanics of LIFO tend to overcome this problem by charging an entity's most recent costs against sales. A better match is produced, leading many accountants to say that LIFO is superior to FIFO from an income measurement viewpoint.

When choosing an inventory valuation method, management must keep in mind that the income statement and balance sheet have somewhat different purposes. On the income statement, cost of goods sold should reflect a fair measure of inventory cost to be matched against revenue. The balance sheet's ending inventory valuation, on the other hand, should be consistent with the definition of a current asset and denote the amount of resources available to meet current obligations. In sum, asset valuation and income determination are not always compatible and often result in compromises to arrive at an acceptable reporting of financial position and profitability.

Consistency in Method Application. The inventory method ultimately selected should be used consistently from one year to the next. Such a practice helps to produce financial statements that can be compared over time and is very useful when assessing trends and performing other types of analysis. Consistency should *not* be interpreted to mean that a business can never change inventory valuation methods. A change can and should be made when it is beneficial in terms of measuring economic activity, for instance, to achieve a better matching of revenues and expenses. If a change is made, the impact should be fully disclosed in the notes that accompany the financial statements.

LOWER OF COST OR MARKET

5 Apply the lower-of-cost-or-market rule of inventory valuation.

Although inventories are generally valued at cost, circumstances sometimes arise where departures from cost are appropriate. As an example, assume that Art Nesbit, a loan officer at the First National Bank, is examining the financial statements of Tuttle Company for purposes of granting a loan. Nesbit's primary concern is Tuttle's ability to meet loan payments as the payments come due. Nesbit is also interested in the value of certain assets that might be pledged as collateral on the loan. The following disclosure appears on Tuttle's balance sheet:

Inventories: at cost $84,000

Nesbit knows that accounting is based on the principle of historical cost and that several cost assignment methods are available for inventory valuation. Because inventory levels and purchase prices have been relatively stable, the assignment method is not an issue. Nesbit's major worry is: Can the bank get $84,000 for the inventory if Tuttle defaults on the loan? Nesbit might have some difficulty with the $84,000 figure if he knew that Tuttle's merchandise had suffered considerable smoke damage from a fire; consisted of numerous perishable goods having a 6-month shelf life that were acquired 10 months ago; and was heavily loaded with fad products that are no longer popular.

Inventories are susceptible to damage, spoilage, and obsolescence. Over time the utility or usefulness of many goods declines, and a business may have to drop its selling price to ensure disposal. To achieve a better valuation of these inventory items, accountants turn to the **lower-of-cost-or-market rule.** The use of lower of cost or market is justified when the market potential for a particular product has been significantly reduced.

MEASURING THE DECLINE IN VALUE

The decline in value of an inventory item is measured by the difference between its cost and market value. Cost is determined by any one of the methods we previously discussed: specific identification, FIFO, LIFO, or weighted average. **Market value** is defined as replacement cost, or the cost that would be incurred to reproduce or repurchase the item. In the case of damaged goods, market value is the amount obtainable from disposal.[4]

To illustrate lower of cost or market, assume Tuttle stocks an electronic component that cost $170 when purchased several months ago. Because of rapidly advancing technology, the component can now be replaced for $155. Tuttle has therefore suffered a $15 decline in value on this inventory item. To value the component at the *lower* of cost or market, we would compare $170 (original cost) with $155 (market value) and choose $155 (the lower).

APPLICATION OF THE LOWER-OF-COST-OR-MARKET RULE

The lower-of-cost-or-market rule may be applied to each individual item in inventory. Suppose, for instance, that Tuttle's inventory consisted of the following:

---

[4] There are exceptions to the replacement cost definition of market value. A detailed discussion of these exceptions is beyond the scope of this text.

Item No.	(1) Quantity	(2) Per Unit Cost	(2) Per Unit Market	(1) × (2) Total Inventory Cost	(1) × (2) Total Inventory Market	Lower of Cost or Market
101	1,000	$12	$10	$12,000	$10,000	$10,000
102	500	20	23	10,000	11,500	10,000
103	3,000	15	16	45,000	48,000	45,000
104	100	170	155	17,000	15,500	15,500
				$84,000	$85,000	$80,500

The proper inventory valuation of $80,500 (right-hand column) is obtained by taking the lower of the cost and market figures for each inventory item. Be aware, however, that other application methods are also acceptable. For example, rather than evaluate each individual item, one can analyze the inventory as a whole. If Tuttle followed the latter approach, the inventory would be valued at $84,000. This figure is obtained by comparing the inventory's total cost ($84,000) with the total market value ($85,000) and selecting the lower amount. Turning to a third method, significant subclasses of inventory can be defined, with the lower-of-cost-or-market rule applied to each subclass. Of the three possibilities, the individual item approach results in the lowest and most conservative inventory valuation.

BUSINESS BRIEFING

Managing Inventories to Avoid Obsolescence

SAMUEL MILLER
Senior Vice-President of Finance and Chief Financial Officer
Liz Claiborne, Inc.

Liz Claiborne is a leading designer and marketer of apparel, selling over 70 million garments annually. The women's sportswear group alone, which accounts for almost 50% of total revenue, has a minimum of 108 separate collections, with each collection having 12 to 25 different styles in various sizes and colors. Because this merchandise is highly seasonal and subject to fashion change, it is considered perishable and must be tightly controlled to avoid excessive markdowns. Such control is exercised through several means.

Since we plan our purchases almost 40 weeks in advance of shipment to retail store customers, we take a conservative approach and anticipate being oversold. That is, sales to individual stores are estimated and then "shaved" to reduce overall supply in the marketplace. We also use sophisticated systems to ensure timely deliveries from our manufacturers in more than 50 countries. If goods arrive late to us, they will likely be marked down earlier than if normal schedules were followed. Finally, even though we plan to oversell production, we typically have some inventory left over at the end of a season. To handle these excess goods, we have opened a chain of factory outlet stores.

Conservative buying, timely deliveries, and control over distribution of excess goods are the tools we use to manage inventories. These tools limit the risk of excessive markdowns and help Liz Claiborne maintain a level of profitability that is one of the best in the industry.

Once the proper valuation is determined, the accounting records must be updated. If Tuttle analyzes its four inventory items individually, a $3,500 reduction in value ($84,000 versus $80,500) is recognized. This reduction in value is a loss and is entered in the accounts as follows:

Loss Due to Decline in Inventory Value	3,500	
Inventory		3,500
To reduce inventory to lower of cost or market.		

The Inventory account now contains the lower-of-cost-or-market valuation of $80,500 and is reported as such on the balance sheet. Furthermore, Tuttle's net income is reduced by the loss.

INVENTORY ESTIMATES

6

Explain the importance of inventory estimates and use both the gross profit and retail methods.

In Chapter 5, we noted that taking a physical inventory is a costly and time-consuming activity. There are several instances in business when an inventory valuation is needed and (1) a count is not possible or (2) management desires to avoid the headaches associated with the counting process. Situations that fall in the first category include disasters like tornadoes and fires, where goods on hand have been destroyed and valuation estimates are needed for insurance claims. Turning to the second category, many companies prepare interim (quarterly) financial statements. Conducting an annual inventory count is troublesome enough; performing the task four times during the year is simply not cost effective.

These situations have prompted accountants to develop several inventory estimation techniques. The techniques not only assist a business as just described, but permit an entity to determine the accuracy of a physical inventory when it is actually taken. A comparison of the estimate with the hand count could reveal the presence of gross errors with respect to counting and valuation. Two widely used estimation techniques are the gross profit method and the retail method.

GROSS PROFIT METHOD

The **gross profit method** estimates inventory on the basis of a company's gross profit rate, that is, gross profit expressed as a percentage of net sales. The rate, which is the key to the entire process, is developed from past transactions and adjusted for any known changes in the entity's recent profit experience. Once the rate is established, gross profit for the period can be determined by applying the rate to the current period's sales. Given this computation, we can then calculate current cost of goods sold and the estimated ending inventory.

To illustrate, assume that Henderson Supply desires to prepare financial statements for August without taking a physical inventory. The information that follows is available for the period ended August 31.

Net sales	$80,000
Beginning inventory, Jan. 1	10,000
Net purchases	40,000
Estimated gross profit percentage	60%

Because gross profit is estimated at 60% of net sales, current gross profit is $48,000 ($80,000 × 0.60). Cost of goods sold for August therefore amounts to $32,000 ($80,000 − $48,000), and the ending inventory is found by the following computation:

Net sales		$80,000
Cost of goods sold		
Beginning inventory	$10,000	
Add: Net purchases	40,000	
Goods available for sale	$50,000	
Less: Ending inventory	?	
Cost of goods sold		32,000
Gross profit		$48,000

The August 31 inventory is estimated at $18,000 ($50,000 − $32,000).

RETAIL METHOD

Both department and discount stores carry a variety of different items that are tagged or marked with retail selling prices. Suppose it is the end of an accounting period and a department store takes a count of the inventory on hand. To determine the "value" of the goods, one need only multiply the quantities found by their readily identifiable retail prices. Unfortunately, the resulting figures cannot be used in the financial statements, which report inventories at cost or at the lower of cost or market, not selling prices. An inventory valued at retail could be converted to cost by inspecting numerous individual paid invoices and other records. This task is a rather formidable one for businesses that carry large product lines. Alternatively, the retail method of inventory valuation can be employed.

The **retail method** is widely used by merchandising firms to value and/or estimate ending inventory. The method first involves determining the ending inventory at retail prices. This amount is then converted to cost on the basis of the percentage relationship between the cost and retail valuations of goods available for sale. As you will now see, the following information must be accumulated in the accounting records to perform the necessary computations:

1. The beginning inventory valued at both cost and retail amounts.
2. Net purchases priced at both cost and retail.
3. Net sales for the period.

To illustrate the retail method, suppose that Boulder Sales Organization desires an inventory estimate as of March 31 in order to compute quarterly income. The required calculations appear at the top of the next page.

Observe that net sales are subtracted from goods available for sale to yield an ending inventory at retail of $180,000.[5] To convert this figure to cost, Boulder has calculated a cost-to-retail ratio of 68%, indicating $0.68 of inventory cost for every $1.00 of retail valuation. As a result, the $180,000 estimated ending inventory is multiplied by the 68% ratio to arrive at the $122,400 cost-based valuation.

[5] Frequently, additional factors (such as markups and markdowns to original selling prices) are considered when computing the ending inventory at retail.

	COST	RETAIL
Beginning inventory, Jan. 1	$ 60,000	$ 88,000
Net purchases, Jan. through Mar.	293,600	432,000
Goods available for sale	$353,600	$520,000
Ratio of cost to retail prices $353,600 ÷ $520,000 = 68%		
Less: Net sales		340,000
Estimated ending inventory at retail		$180,000
Estimated ending inventory at cost ($180,000 × 0.68)		$122,400

In this example the retail method was used to obtain an interim estimate of inventory. This same method can also be employed to study a company's experience with theft and shoplifting. For instance, assume the figures in the Boulder illustration relate to a full calendar year. A physical count on December 31 has revealed an inventory of $171,000 at retail prices. Thus, Boulder has a $9,000 shortage at retail ($180,000 − $171,000), which cost the firm $6,120 ($9,000 × 0.68).

INVENTORY TURNOVER

7

Recognize the usefulness of the inventory turnover ratio when evaluating a company's inventory management policies.

Both the gross profit and retail methods assist a company in determining the dollar amount of inventory on hand on any given day. Just how much inventory, though, should a business carry? Firms that have high inventory levels tie up funds that could probably be invested elsewhere more profitably. Also, high stock levels increase the costs of storage, insurance, obsolescence, and deterioration. In contrast, low inventory levels often lead to stockouts, lost sales, and lost customers. Furthermore, quantity discounts and reduced freight rates may be unavailable because of insufficient purchasing activity.

Insights into the success or failure of a company's inventory management policies can be gained by studying the firm's **inventory turnover ratio.** This ratio shows the number of times each year that the inventory investment is turned into sales. Normally, high turnovers are indicative of sound policies, at least in terms of generating cash for the business.

To explain, turnover is calculated by dividing cost of goods sold by the average inventory. Average inventory, in turn, is computed by adding the beginning and ending inventories and dividing by 2. As the average inventory grows, turnover will decrease unless there is a corresponding increase in sales (and the accompanying cost of goods sold). Thus, a company that stocks a larger-than-normal inventory will have a lower turnover than another business that can generate the same sales with a lower merchandise investment.

AN EXAMPLE

Assume that Handy Corporation recently reported the following data:

Cost of goods sold	$22,000,000
Beginning inventory	4,000,000
Ending inventory	3,900,000

The company's turnover ratio is 5.57 times, computed as follows:

$$\text{Inventory Turnover Ratio} = \frac{\text{Cost of Goods Sold}}{\text{Average Inventory}}$$

$$= \frac{\$22,000,000}{\frac{\$4,000,000 + \$3,900,000}{2}}$$

$$= 5.57 \text{ times}$$

The ratio shows that inventory turned once every 66 days (365 days ÷ 5.57 times). If this result is judged unsatisfactory, management could purchase more conservatively or stimulate sales from existing stock.

THE OPERATING CYCLE

For most businesses, inventory is not converted into cash immediately upon sale. Companies usually generate a large portion of their sales on account, and it is necessary to wait until the receivable is ultimately settled to obtain the funds. The time that it takes for this process can be approximated by using the accounts receivable turnover ratio, as shown on page 333. Handy Corporation, for example, collected its receivables in about 16 days.

In Chapter 4, we presented a concept known as the *operating cycle*—the time needed for a company to purchase and sell goods and eventually collect the related receivable. A large portion of the cycle can be estimated by summing the collection period and the days required to sell inventory. This figure for Handy Corporation amounts to 82 days (16 + 66). Generally speaking, the shorter the operating cycle, the better. A quick cycle indicates that inventory is not spending excessive periods of time in the warehouse or on the shelf and that customers are settling their bills promptly. Such information is of interest to short-term creditors who, themselves, are waiting to be paid with the cash that is collected.

PERPETUAL INVENTORY SYSTEMS AND INVENTORY VALUATION

Earlier in the text we noted that an increasing number of businesses are using perpetual inventory systems. Recall that these systems keep a running count of the goods on hand by monitoring inflows and outflows on a daily (i.e., continuous) basis. The record keeping that accompanies a continuous count of *units* on hand is very straightforward. In contrast, when we turn our attention to the *costs* of these units, the accounting becomes more complex.

8 Use a perpetual system to value inventory.

ILLUSTRATION OF A PERPETUAL SYSTEM

We will illustrate the operation of a perpetual inventory system by focusing on the FIFO cost flow assumption. Assume that the following data were taken from the records of Bankston Company (a supplier of small engine components) and pertain to part no. 1058:

Beginning inventory: 3,000 units @ $5.00

PURCHASES ON ACCOUNT		SALES ON ACCOUNT	
3/10	2,000 units @ $6.25 = $12,500	3/13	2,600 units @ $9 = $23,400
3/19	1,600 units @ $6.50 = 10,400	3/22	2,300 units @ $9 = 20,700
	3,600 $22,900		4,900 $44,100

Because the perpetual system closely monitors inventory levels, subsidiary records are normally established for each item stocked. The subsidiary record for part no. 1058 appears in Exhibit 10–8.

A careful study of this record shows that the purchase on March 10 gives rise to two different cost layers: 3,000 units at $5 and 2,000 units at $6.25. Because the unit costs differ, the layers are maintained separately and listed chronologically. The sale on March 13 reduces the inventory by 2,600 units. Although the units were sold for $9 each, they must be removed from the inventory records at cost. With FIFO, the sale is costed at the oldest purchase price of $5 (i.e., the "first-in"), leaving 400 units from the beginning layer (3,000 − 2,600) plus 2,000 units from the purchase of March 10 on hand. The sale of 2,300 units on March 22 is handled in a similar fashion. The oldest costs (the remaining 400 units from the first layer plus 1,900 units from the second layer) become the cost of goods sold.

The Bankston illustration shows that cost of goods sold is computed when each sale occurs; in contrast, under a periodic system, the calculation is made at the end of the accounting period. Despite the procedural difference, perpetual and periodic systems will yield identical results when FIFO is used. Put simply, no matter when cost of goods sold is determined, this key income state-

EXHIBIT 10–8
Perpetual Inventory Record: FIFO

PERPETUAL INVENTORY RECORD

Part No. __1058__   Reorder Point __3,000 units__

Date	Purchases	Sales	Balance
3/1			3,000 @ $5.00
3/10	2,000 @ $6.25		3,000 @ $5.00 2,000 @ $6.25
3/13		2,600 @ $5.00	400 @ $5.00 2,000 @ $6.25
3/19	1,600 @ $6.50		400 @ $5.00 2,000 @ $6.25 1,600 @ $6.50
3/22		400 @ $5.00 1,900 @ $6.25	100 @ $6.25 1,600 @ $6.50

ment component will always consist of the same (i.e., the earliest) inventory charges.

Our example has focused on the FIFO cost flow assumption. The LIFO and average costing methods may be employed as well. Computations and procedures related to these methods are shown in an appendix to this chapter.

GENERAL LEDGER UPDATING

Recall the control account/subsidiary ledger relationship that was discussed in Chapter 6. Because Bankston has been increasing and decreasing its subsidiary records for part no. 1058, the firm must also enter the purchases and sales in the general ledger control account (Inventory) to preserve the necessary equality. The transactions on March 10 and 13 are recorded as follows:

Mar. 10	Inventory		12,500	
	Accounts Payable			12,500
	Purchased 2,000 units at $6.25.			
13	Cost of Goods Sold		13,000	
	Inventory			13,000
	Sold 2,600 units having a cost of $5 per unit.			
13	Accounts Receivable		23,400	
	Sales			23,400
	Sold 2,600 units at a selling price of $9 per unit.			

Observe that both the purchase and the sale are recorded in the Inventory account. Furthermore, notice that a sale now requires two entries. The first entry on March 13 reduces Inventory and recognizes the cost of the units sold (via a debit to a new account entitled Cost of Goods Sold); the second entry is needed to record the related sales revenue. With the use of entries such as these throughout the period, both Cost of Goods Sold and Inventory are updated continuously. The income on this transaction is derived by subtracting Cost of Goods Sold from Sales and would be disclosed on the income statement in the familiar format of:

Sales	$23,400
Less: Cost of goods sold	13,000
Gross profit	$10,400

APPENDIX: LIFO AND AVERAGE COSTING UNDER A PERPETUAL INVENTORY SYSTEM

The just-concluded Bankston Company example was based on a FIFO cost flow assumption. Perpetual inventory systems may also be used with both LIFO and average costing. These methods will now be shown, with inventory data from Bankston once again serving as the basis for our illustrations. The data are repeated here for your convenience.

Beginning inventory: 3,000 units @ $5.00

PURCHASES ON ACCOUNT		SALES ON ACCOUNT	
3/10 2,000 units @ $6.25 = $12,500		3/13 2,600 units @ $9 = $23,400	
3/19 1,600 units @ $6.50 = 10,400		3/22 2,300 units @ $9 = 20,700	
3,600	$22,900	4,900	$44,100

LIFO

With a LIFO perpetual system, cost of goods sold is figured by using the most recent costs experienced. For instance, in Bankston's case, the company has two layers of goods available for sale after the acquisition on March 10: 3,000 units at $5 and 2,000 units at $6.25 (see Exhibit 10–9). Assume it is now March 13 and the firm employs a LIFO inventory system. The cost of the 2,600-unit sale would be determined by first using the most recent cost layer (i.e., the "last-in"), which is the purchase from three days earlier. As the diagram shows, Bankston must then cut into its older goods to account for the remaining 600 units, leaving 2,400 units (3,000 – 600) at $5 in stock.

After the acquisition on March 19, the company would have two layers of goods: 2,400 units at $5 and 1,600 units at $6.50. The sale on March 22 would again be costed by using the most recent costs, specifically, 1,600 units at $6.50 plus 700 units from the older layer at $5. Bankston's ending inventory is therefore 1,700 units (2,400 – 700) at $5.

Normally, because of the timing of the charges to cost of goods sold, the results obtained with a LIFO perpetual system will differ from those that occur

EXHIBIT 10–9
A LIFO Perpetual Inventory System

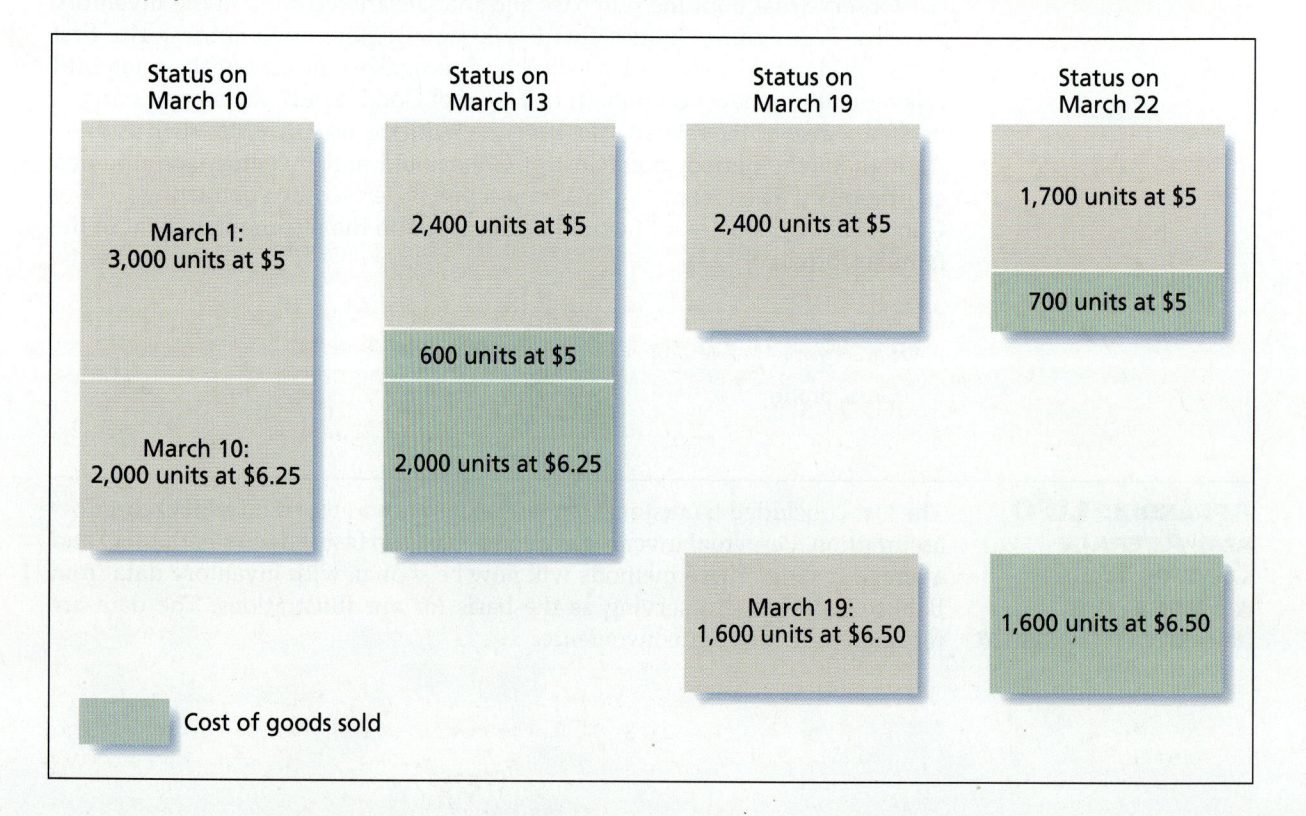

under a periodic system. With the perpetual approach, the most recent costs *at the time of each sale* are evaluated and transferred to the income statement. When a periodic system is employed, the transfer process begins with the most recent costs incurred *during the period*—after all purchases have been made.

MOVING AVERAGE

The average cost approach when used with a perpetual system is often called **moving average.** With this method, a new average unit cost is computed each time that inventory is purchased. This amount is later employed to determine cost of goods sold and ending inventory valuations.

Continuing the Bankston Company example, the firm's acquisition on March 10 will produce the following results:

Inventory on 3/1:	3,000 units at $5.00 = $15,000
Purchase on 3/10:	2,000 units at $6.25 = 12,500
	5,000 $27,500

Average cost per unit: $27,500 ÷ 5,000 units = $5.50

Thus, when 2,600 units are sold on March 13, cost of goods sold will amount to $14,300 (2,600 units × $5.50) and 2,400 units (5,000 − 2,600) will be left in inventory. These latter goods will be assigned a cost of $5.50 as well, yielding an inventory valuation of $13,200 (2,400 units × $5.50).

A new average cost will be calculated on March 19 because of the purchase of 1,600 units:

Inventory on 3/13:	2,400 units at $5.50 = $13,200
Purchase on 3/19:	1,600 units at $6.50 = 10,400
	4,000 $23,600

Average cost per unit: $23,600 ÷ 4,000 units = $5.90

To complete the example, the sale on March 22 would be costed at $13,570 (2,300 units × $5.90), while the month-end inventory of 1,700 units (4,000 − 2,300) would total $10,030 (1,700 units × $5.90).

When using the average costing approach, the difference between the perpetual and periodic systems lies in the frequency of computation. Average unit costs are calculated after each purchase with the perpetual system; in contrast, under the periodic approach, a single average cost is derived upon conclusion of the accounting period. Given the nature of the computation, ending inventory and cost of goods sold will differ between the two methods.

END-OF-CHAPTER REVIEW

LEARNING OBJECTIVES: THE KEY POINTS

1. **Explain the ownership issues related to goods in transit and goods on consignment.** Inventory ownership is dependent on possession of legal title to the goods, which, in turn, is dependent on freight terms. Under F.O.B. shipping point, title

passes to the purchaser when goods are shipped. In contrast, under F.O.B. destination, title passes when merchandise arrives at its destination. With consignment sales, merchandise transferred to sales agents is considered part of the consignor's inventory until sold even though the goods are not in the consignor's possession.

2. **Identify the effects of inventory errors on the financial statements.** An inaccurate inventory figure results in an incorrect income statement, statement of owner's equity, and balance sheet. For example, if the ending inventory is understated, cost of goods sold will be overstated and net income will be understated. This, in turn, produces understated amounts for both ending owner's equity and inventory. Inventory errors are counterbalanced over a two-year period because the ending inventory of one year becomes the beginning inventory of the next.

3. **Demonstrate use of the specific identification, FIFO, LIFO, and weighted-average inventory methods.** With the specific identification method, the cost of the units is associated with the units themselves, often via code numbers and stickers. Because this method has limited applications, most businesses have to adopt a cost flow assumption. With the FIFO (first-in, first-out) assumption, costs are matched against revenues in the order that the costs were incurred. Thus, cost of goods sold is comprised of older costs (i.e., the "first-in"), whereas ending inventory is composed of the most recent purchase prices experienced by the firm. In contrast, the LIFO (last-in, first-out) method results in recent costs being transferred to the income statement for cost-of-goods-sold determination. Older costs therefore remain in inventory. Finally, with the weighted-average method, an average cost is calculated by dividing the cost of goods available for sale by the number of units available for sale. The unit cost is then used to compute both cost of goods sold and ending inventory.

4. **Discuss the factors that are considered when selecting an inventory method and the effects of such a selection on the financial statements.** Income taxes are an important consideration for many businesses. Because LIFO produces lower net income and lower income tax payments than FIFO in periods of inflation, the LIFO method has gained popularity in the past 20 years.

    These flow assumptions also have different effects on the financial statements. For example, FIFO's use of the oldest costs in cost-of-goods-sold calculations produces a poor match of costs and revenues on the income statement. However, the balance sheet valuation is improved because inventories consist of fairly recent costs. The LIFO method would yield results the opposite of those just described.

5. **Apply the lower-of-cost-or-market rule of inventory valuation.** The lower-of-cost-or-market rule requires the write-down of inventories to market if the goods' value has been reduced because of damage, spoilage, or obsolescence. Market is generally defined as replacement cost, or the cost that would be incurred to reproduce or repurchase the item. Write-downs entail the recognition of a loss, which lowers net income, and a reduction in the recorded cost of inventory. This procedure, which produces conservative asset valuations and income figures, can be applied to individual inventory items, to subclasses of similar items, or to the inventory as a whole.

6. **Explain the importance of inventory estimates and use both the gross profit and retail methods.** Inventory estimates facilitate the issuance of interim financial statements and the filing of insurance claims in cases of disaster. Estimates also provide a reasonableness check of actual physical counts. With the gross profit method, inventory is estimated on the basis of a company's gross profit rate. An estimated gross profit figure is derived for use in computing cost of goods sold. Then, cost of goods sold is subtracted from goods available for sale to arrive at the estimate of

inventory. In contrast, with the retail method, ending inventory is first calculated at retail prices. This figure is later converted to cost on the basis of the percentage relationship between the cost and retail valuations of goods available for sale (i.e., the cost-to-retail ratio).

7. **Recognize the usefulness of the inventory turnover ratio when evaluating a company's inventory management policies.** The inventory turnover ratio indicates the number of times each year that a firm's inventory investment is turned into sales. The ratio is computed as follows: Cost of goods sold ÷ average inventory. A relatively high turnover indicates that a company has a lower-than-normal merchandise investment, given the amount of sales generated. This ratio can be converted into days for use in judging the length of a company's operating cycle.

8. **Use a perpetual system to value inventory.** A perpetual inventory system keeps a running count of merchandise inflows and outflows. The Inventory account is increased for acquisitions and decreased for sales. Cost of goods sold is also maintained on a continual basis, being increased when each sale occurs. The perpetual system may be used in conjunction with a FIFO, LIFO, and average cost flow assumption.

Key Terms and Concepts: A Quick Overview

consignment   The process of transferring goods to a sales agent. (p. 360)

cost flow assumption   An assumption regarding the flow of inventory costs through a firm's accounting system. (p. 365)

first-in, first-out (FIFO)   An inventory method based on the premise that costs are matched against revenues in the order of incurrence. (p. 366)

goods in transit   Goods in the process of being transported to the buyer. Ownership is dependent on freight terms. (p. 359)

gross profit method   An inventory estimation method based on a company's gross profit rate—that is, gross profit expressed as a percentage of net sales. (p. 374)

inventory   Goods acquired for resale to customers. Includes the raw materials, work in process, and finished goods of a manufacturer. (p. 359)

inventory turnover ratio   A ratio that indicates the number of times each year that a company's inventory investment turns into sales. Computed as: Cost of goods sold ÷ average inventory. (p. 376)

last-in, first-out (LIFO)   An inventory method based on the premise that costs are matched against revenues in the reverse order of incurrence. (p. 366)

lower-of-cost-or-market rule   A rule whereby inventories are accounted for at acquisition cost or market value, whichever is lower. (p. 372)

market value   The replacement cost of a unit of merchandise. (p. 372)

moving-average method   A perpetual inventory costing system under which a new average cost is computed after each purchase. (p. 381)

perpetual inventory system   A system in which the Inventory account is respectively increased and decreased for each purchase and sale of inventory made during the period. (p. 377)

retail method   An inventory estimation method widely used by retail establishments; derives a cost-to-retail ratio and applies the ratio to the total retail value of inventory. (p. 375)

specific identification method   A method that requires a business to identify each unit of merchandise with the unit's cost and retain that identification until the inventory is sold. (p. 364)

weighted-average method A method of accounting under a periodic inventory system that requires the computation of a weighted-average cost for goods purchased or manufactured. The average is used to value the ending inventory and to determine cost of goods sold. (p. 368)

CHAPTER QUIZ

The five questions that follow relate to several issues raised in the chapter. Test your knowledge of the issues by selecting the best answer. (The answers appear on p. 400.)

1. Because of a mathematical error, the 19X8 ending inventory included goods at a $170 figure that had actually cost $710. As a result of this error:
   a. net income for 19X8 is overstated.
   b. net income for 19X8 is understated.
   c. operating expenses for 19X8 are understated.
   d. total liabilities at the end of 19X8 are overstated.

2. The inventory cost flow assumption in which the oldest costs incurred become part of cost of goods sold when units are sold is:
   a. LIFO.
   b. FIFO.
   c. weighted average.
   d. retail.

3. The LIFO inventory valuation method:
   a. is acceptable only if a company sells its newest goods first.
   b. will result in higher income levels than FIFO in periods of rising prices.
   c. will result in a match of fairly current inventory costs against recent selling prices on the income statement.
   d. cannot be used by major retail establishments.

4. Stanley Company sells two different products. The following information is available at year-end:

INVENTORY ITEM	UNITS	COST PER UNIT	MARKET VALUE PER UNIT
A	100	$4	$6
B	200	5	3

   Applying the lower-of-cost-or-market rule to each item, Stanley's ending inventory balance would be:
   a. $1,000.
   b. $1,200.
   c. $1,400.
   d. some other amount.

5. Which of the following accounting systems maintains a running (continuous) record of merchandising purchases and sales by inventory item?
   a. Perpetual.
   b. Gross profit.
   c. Periodic.
   d. Retail.

SUMMARY PROBLEM

Tiger Company sells a single product and uses a periodic inventory system. The following information was extracted from the accounting records:

	PURCHASES	SALES
Feb.	800 units @ $4.75	1,500 units @ $ 8.50
June	600 units @ $5.50	500 units @ $10.00
Oct.	900 units @ $6.00	

The firm's beginning inventory on January 1 totaled 200 units and cost $800.

Instructions

Compute Tiger's ending inventory, cost of goods sold, and gross profit, using the following inventory valuation methods: (1) FIFO; (2) LIFO; (3) weighted average.

Solution

- Sales

    1,500 units @ $ 8.50 = $12,750
    <u> 500</u> units @ $10.00 = <u> 5,000</u>
    <u>2,000</u> units $17,750

- Goods available for sale

    Beginning inventory   200 units @ $4.00 = $ 800
    Feb. purchase   800 units @ $4.75 =   3,800
    June purchase   600 units @ $5.50 =   3,300
    Oct. purchase   <u>900</u> units @ $6.00 =   <u>5,400</u>
                          <u>2,500</u> units   <u>$13,300</u>

- Ending inventory

    Goods available for sale   2,500 units
    Less: Sales   <u>2,000</u> units
    Ending inventory   <u> 500</u> units

- FIFO ending inventory consists of the most recent costs; therefore:

    500 units @ $6.00 = <u>$3,000</u>

- LIFO ending inventory consists of the oldest costs; therefore:

    200 units @ $4.00 = $ 800
    300 units @ $4.75 = <u> 1,425</u>
                        <u>$2,225</u>

- Weighted-average ending inventory

    $13,300 ÷ 2,500 units = <u>$5.32</u> per unit

    500 units × $5.32 = <u>$2,660</u>

	FIFO	LIFO	WEIGHTED AVERAGE
Sales	$17,750	$17,750	$17,750
Less: Cost of goods sold			
Beginning inventory	$ 800	$ 800	$ 800
Add: Purchases*	12,500	12,500	12,500
Goods available for sale	$13,300	$13,300	$13,300
Less: Ending inventory	3,000	2,225	2,660
Cost of goods sold	$10,300	$11,075	$10,640
Gross profit	$ 7,450	$ 6,675	$ 7,110

* Goods available for sale minus the beginning inventory.

Assignment Material

Questions

Q10–1 What items are reported as inventory for (a) merchandising companies and (b) manufacturing companies?

Q10–2 The Potter Company purchased the following merchandise on December 28:

Supplier	Terms	Amount
Pax Company	F.O.B. destination	$1,800
James Manufacturing	F.O.B. shipping point	2,500

Both purchases were shipped December 30, but neither had been received by December 31. Should the purchases be included in Potter's December 31 ending inventory? Explain.

Q10–3 What are goods on consignment? Who has title to goods on consignment?

Q10–4 The Wood Company made the following mathematical error in determining the cost of its April 30 ending inventory:

Item No.	Quantity	Cost Per Unit	Total Cost
S775	150	$34	$3,100

Determine the effect of the error on the following:
a. Cost of goods sold for the year ended April 30.
b. Operating expenses for the year ended April 30.
c. Net income for the year ended April 30.
d. Owner's equity as of April 30.
e. Total current assets as of April 30.

Q10–5 Why are many inventory errors counterbalanced by the end of two accounting periods?

Q10–6 At the end of an accounting period, goods available for sale is segregated into two different costs. What are these two costs? Explain which of the costs is given primary emphasis by accountants.

Q10–7 Discuss the difference between the physical flow of goods and a cost flow assumption.

Q10–8 Why has LIFO gained popularity in the past 20 years?

Q10–9 Are businesses permitted to arbitrarily change inventory valuation methods from one year to the next? Briefly explain.

Q10–10 What is meant by the term "market" as used in the phrase "lower of cost or market"?

Q10–11 Why do businesses need to estimate their inventory balances?

Q10–12 Briefly explain the inventory turnover ratio to someone with a limited business background.

Q10–13 Why are two journal entries required to record a sale under a perpetual inventory system?

*Q10–14 Will the ending inventory figure computed by using a weighted-average periodic system normally agree with the figure calculated under a moving-average perpetual system? Why?

EXERCISES

E10–1 Inventory errors and income measurement (L.O. 2)

The income statements of Keagle Company for 19X3 and 19X4 follow.

	19X3	19X4
Sales	$100,000	$109,000
Cost of goods sold	62,000	74,000
Gross profit	$ 38,000	$ 35,000
Expenses	26,000	22,000
Net income	$ 12,000	$ 13,000

A recent review of the accounting records discovered that the 19X3 ending inventory had been understated by $4,000.

a. Prepare corrected 19X3 and 19X4 income statements.
b. What is the effect of the error on ending owner's equity for 19X3 and 19X4?

E10–2 Specific identification method (L.O. 3)

Boston Galleries uses the specific identification method for inventory valuation. Inventory information for several oil paintings follows.

		PAINTING	COST
Jan. 2	Beginning inventory	Woods	$11,000
Apr. 19	Purchase	Sunset	21,800
June 7	Purchase	Earth	31,200
Dec. 16	Purchase	Moon	4,000

Woods and Moon were sold during the year for a total of $35,000. Determine the firm's:

a. Cost of goods sold.
b. Gross profit.
c. Ending inventory.

E10–3 Inventory valuation methods: Basic computations (L.O. 3)

The following information is available for the Wheeler Company for the month of May:

May 1	Beginning inventory	800 units @ $4.00
9	Purchase	2,000 units @ $4.30
18	Purchase	1,000 units @ $4.62
27	Purchase	500 units @ $5.00

On May 31, 1,300 units were unsold and remained in inventory. The firm uses a periodic inventory system.

* An asterisk preceding an item indicates that the material is covered in an appendix to this chapter.

Compute the ending inventory balance under each of the following valuation methods:

a. First-in, first-out
b. Last-in, first-out
c. Weighted average

E10–4 Inventory valuation methods: Basic computations (L.O. 3)

The January beginning inventory of the White Company consisted of 300 units costing $40 each. During the first quarter, the company purchased two batches of goods: 700 units at $44 on February 21 and 800 units at $50 on March 28. Sales during the first quarter were 1,400 units at $75 per unit. The White Company uses a periodic inventory system.

Using the White Company data, fill in the chart that follows to compare the results obtained under the FIFO, LIFO, and weighted-average inventory methods.

	FIFO	LIFO	WEIGHTED AVERAGE
Goods available for sale	$	$	$
Ending inventory, Mar. 31			
Cost of goods sold			

E10–5 Analysis of LIFO versus FIFO (L.O. 3, 4)

Indicate whether LIFO or FIFO best describes each of the following:

a. Gives highest profits when prices fall.
b. Yields lowest income taxes when prices rise.
c. Generates an ending inventory valuation that somewhat approximates replacement cost.
d. Matches recent costs against current selling prices on the income statement.
e. Comes closest to approximating the physical flow of goods of a fruit and vegetable dealer.
f. Results in lowest cost of goods sold in inflationary periods.

E10–6 Lower-of-cost-or-market rule (L.O. 5)

The Oberlin Company sells four different products. The following information is available on December 31:

INVENTORY ITEM	UNITS	COST PER UNIT	MARKET VALUE PER UNIT
A4327	200	$8.00	$8.30
B6751	2,000	4.00	3.95
C9085	500	9.10	6.30
D2365	1,000	7.00	7.50

a. Apply the lower-of-cost-or-market rule to each item and determine the company's ending inventory valuation.
b. Briefly explain the purpose of the lower-of-cost-or-market rule.

E10–7 Overview of inventory ownership and costing (L.O. 1, 3, 4, 5)

Evaluate the comments that follow as being True or False. If the comment is false, briefly explain why.

a. Franco purchased goods from Wholesale Supply on December 28. Although the merchandise was still in transit on December 31, Franco should nevertheless report these goods on its year-end balance sheet as an asset if the goods were sent F.O.B. shipping point.
b. If a company sells its oldest goods first, the firm must use the FIFO method of inventory valuation.
c. LIFO normally results in fairly current inventory costs being reported on the income statement as cost of goods sold.
d. Under a weighted-average (periodic) inventory system, all goods sold during a period are costed at the same unit cost.
e. Data on Olympia's inventory follow.

Item	Total Cost	Total Market
A	$15,900	$11,900
B	20,600	24,600

Olympia values its inventory on an item-by-item basis in accordance with rules stipulated by the accounting profession. Because the $4,000 loss suffered on item A is precisely offset by a $4,000 gain on item B, the company need not adjust its Inventory account at the end of the period.

E10–8 Gross profit method and casualty loss (L.O. 6)

Robin Electrical Company had an inventory loss on September 21, 19X9, from a hurricane. Company records kept in a safe revealed that 19X9 sales and net purchases prior to the casualty were $240,000 and $172,600, respectively. The 19X8 financial statements disclosed year-end inventory of $20,000 and a 36% gross profit rate. Management believes that the firm had a similar gross profit experience during 19X9.

Determine the amount of the inventory loss if no goods could be salvaged.

E10–9 Retail inventory method (L.O. 6)

Abercrombie & Pearson sells designer apparel and uses the retail method of inventory valuation. The following information is available on December 31:

	Cost	Retail
Inventory, Jan. 1	$183,500	$320,000
Purchases, Jan.–Dec.	471,700	810,000
Purchases returns & allowances	8,500	15,000
Sales, Jan.–Dec.		890,000
Sales returns & allowances		18,200

Estimate the cost of the store's December 31 ending inventory.

E10–10 Inventory turnover; analysis of operating cycle (L.O. 7)

The following data relate to Fairbanks, Inc.:

	19X8	19X7
Cost of goods sold	$440,000	$350,000
Inventory, Dec. 31	70,000	50,000
Cash, Dec. 31	125,000	110,000
Accounts payable, Dec. 31	115,000	108,000

The company is planning to borrow $300,000 via a 90-day bank loan to cover short-term operating needs. At present, customers settle their outstanding obligations with Fairbanks in 71 days.

a. Compute the inventory turnover ratio for 19X8. Fairbanks rounds all calculations to two decimal places.
b. Estimate the length of the company's operating cycle, and comment on the firm's ability to repay the bank loan on a timely basis.
c. Suppose that the firm's major line of business involves the processing and distribution of fresh fish throughout the United States. Do you have any concerns about the company's inventory turnover ratio? Briefly discuss.

E10–11 Perpetual inventory systems: FIFO (L.O. 8)

Alabama Industries had a beginning inventory on January 1 of 2,000 units that cost $6 each. Purchases and sales throughout the year were as follows:

PURCHASES		SALES	
Apr. 3	3,000 units @ $8.00	Apr. 9	3,500 units @ $10.00
Oct. 4	4,000 units @ $8.85	Dec. 3	3,000 units @ $11.00

The company uses a perpetual inventory system. Calculate the ending inventory valuation by using the FIFO cost flow assumption.

E10–12 Perpetual inventory system; journal entries (L.O. 8)

At the beginning of 19X3, Obasi Company opened for business and installed a computerized perpetual inventory system. The first transactions that occurred during the year follow.

Purchases on account
500 units @ $4 $2,000
Sales on account
300 of the above units   2,550
Returns on account
75 of the above unsold units

a. Obasi's system generates a journal-entry report that summarizes purchases, sales, and returns. Duplicate the entries that would have appeared on that report.
b. Calculate the balance in the firm's Inventory account.

*E10–13 Perpetual inventory systems: LIFO and moving average (L.O. 8)

Refer to the beginning inventory, purchases, and sales data of Alabama Industries in Exercise 10–11. Assuming use of a perpetual inventory system, calculate the company's ending inventory valuation under the following cost flow assumptions:

a. LIFO
b. Moving average

PROBLEMS

Series A

P10–A1 Inventory errors (L.O. 1, 2)

The income statements of Diamond Company for the years ended December 31, 19X1, and 19X2 follow.

	19X1		19X2	
Net sales		$440,000		$483,000
Cost of goods sold				
Beginning inventory	$ 95,000		$109,000	
Add: Net purchases	380,000		404,000	
Goods available for sale	$475,000		$513,000	
Less: Ending inventory	109,000		127,000	
Cost of goods sold		366,000		386,000
Gross profit		$ 74,000		$ 97,000
Operating expenses		58,000		67,000
Net income		$ 16,000		$ 30,000

Diamond uses a periodic inventory system. A detailed review of the accounting records disclosed the following:

1. A review of 19X1 purchase invoices revealed that a clerk had incorrectly recorded a $12,600 purchase as $1,260.
2. A $4,800 purchase was made on December 30, 19X2, terms F.O.B. shipping point. The invoice was not recorded in 19X2 nor were the goods included in the 19X2 ending physical inventory count. Both the goods and invoice were received in early 19X3, with the invoice being recorded at that time.
3. Goods costing $3,000 were accidentally excluded from the 19X1 ending physical inventory count. These goods were sold during 19X2, and all aspects of the sale were properly recorded.

Instructions

a. Prepare corrected income statements for 19X1 and 19X2.
b. Determine the impact of the preceding errors on the December 31, 19X2, owner's equity balance.

P10–A2 Inventory valuation methods: Computations and concepts (L.O. 3, 4)
Alpine Snowboards began business on January 1 of the current year. Purchases of snowboards during the first quarter were: January, 10 boards at $150; February, 20 boards at $155; and March, 55 boards at $160. Two additional purchases were made near year-end:

November	5 boards at $200
December	10 boards at $240

Forty boards remained in inventory on December 31. The company's average selling price throughout the year was $320 per board.

Instructions

a. Alpine uses a periodic inventory system. Calculate ending inventory, cost of goods sold, and gross profit under each of the following inventory valuation methods:
  (1) FIFO
  (2) LIFO
  (3) Weighted average
b. Which of the three methods would be chosen if management's goal is to:
  (1) Produce an "up-to-date" inventory valuation on the balance sheet?

(2) Approximate the physical flow of a sand and gravel dealer?
(3) Report higher profits to a bank for the purpose of securing a larger loan?

P10–A3 FIFO; lower of cost or market (L.O. 3, 5)

On March 2 of the current year, Glen Riley became manager of a newly opened branch store of the Tall Pine Nursery. Riley made the following purchases during the first month of operation:

Spruce trees
    Mar. 2   105 trees @ $30
          16   155 trees @ $40

Elm trees
    Mar. 2   130 trees @ $10
          18   70 trees @ $15
          29   30 trees @ $18

Maple trees
    Mar. 2   40 trees @ $50

An end-of-month physical inventory count revealed that the nursery had 75 spruce trees, 58 elm trees, and 38 maple trees in stock. Total sales for March amounted to $14,500; expenses (excluding cost of goods sold) were $3,100.

The company uses the FIFO inventory valuation method in conjunction with a periodic inventory system.

Instructions

a. Compute the nursery's ending inventory, cost of goods sold, and net income for the first month of operation.
b. Assume that the grower of the elm trees recently announced a price decrease to $14.50. Determine the impact of the announcement on the nursery's ending inventory valuation.
c. Prepare the journal entry necessary to value the company's inventory at the lower of cost or market.

P10–A4 Gross profit method and fire loss (L.O. 6)

On January 28, 19X4, a fire heavily damaged the office and warehouse of Sunset Products. The following information has been obtained:

1. Sunset's condensed income statement for the year ended December 31, 19X3, is as follows:

Sales		$500,000
Cost of goods sold		
Beginning inventory	$195,000	
Add: Net purchases	325,000	
Goods available for sale	$520,000	
Less: Ending inventory	290,000	
Cost of goods sold		230,000
Gross profit		$270,000
Expenses		209,600
Net income		$ 60,400

2. Net sales and net purchases made during the first 28 days of January were $38,000 and $19,900, respectively.
3. Purchases entered in the accounting records but still in transit as of January 28 amounted to $1,700.

Sunset's insurance company agreed to reimburse the firm for the fire loss on the basis of an inventory estimate, derived by using the gross profit method. The gross profit rate will be computed by examining last year's operating results.

Instructions

a. Determine the cost of inventory on hand on January 28.
b. Taking your answer in part (a) into consideration, assume that goods were recovered and sold to a salvage firm for $6,000. Compute Sunset's total fire loss.
c. In addition to computing fire losses, does the gross profit method have other possible uses? Explain.

P10–A5 Retail method and inventory shrinkage (L.O. 6)

Sarah Anne's is a children's store that specializes in novelties and clothing. A review of the store's accounting records disclosed the following information for the year ended December 31:

	CLOTHING		NOVELTIES	
	COST	RETAIL	COST	RETAIL
Beginning inventory	$ 76,000	$146,500	$ 32,000	$ 76,800
Net purchases	496,000	953,500	164,400	414,200
Net sales		980,000		451,000

The company uses the retail inventory method.

Instructions

a. Compute the cost-to-retail ratio of the firm's clothing line.
b. Estimate the cost of the novelty inventory as of December 31.
c. If a physical count of the novelty items on December 31 revealed an ending inventory at retail of $32,000, determine the cost of inventory shrinkage.
d. On the basis of the figures that you calculated, why do you think that retail stores would likely compute cost-to-retail ratios by product line?

P10–A6 Perpetual inventory systems: FIFO (L.O. 8)

The Schaber Company carries parts that are used in emergency medical situations. Given the critical nature of its business, Schaber uses a perpetual inventory system. The following information pertains to a particular heart monitor:

May 1 Beginning inventory: 100 units @ $6,800

PURCHASES		SALES	
May 3	50 units @ $7,100	May 7	30 units @ $11,400
18	75 units @ $7,200	14	70 units @ $11,400
25	40 units @ $7,250	20	55 units @ $11,600
		24	25 units @ $11,600
		29	20 units @ $11,700

Instructions

a. Using a format similar to that of Exhibit 10–8, prepare a perpetual inventory record for the heart monitor. Schaber uses the FIFO method of inventory valuation.
b. Prepare summary journal entries to record total purchases and sales.
c. Assume that Schaber had used a periodic inventory system rather than a perpetual inventory system. Would the company's cost of goods sold and ending inventory differ from the amounts computed in part (a)? Why or why not?

*P10–A7 Perpetual inventory systems: LIFO and moving average (L.O. 8)

Refer to the beginning inventory, purchases, and sales data of the Schaber Company in Problem 10–A6.

Instructions

a. Assuming use of a LIFO cost flow assumption, prepare a perpetual inventory record for the heart monitor by using a format similar to that shown in Exhibit 10–8. (*Note:* Keep in mind that the exhibit illustrates the first-in, first-out method.)
b. Assuming use of the moving-average method, determine the cost of the May 31 ending inventory and also the cost of goods sold during May.

Series B

P10–B1 Inventory errors (L.O. 1, 2)

The income statements of Maxum Company for the years ended December 31, 19X4, and 19X5 follow.

	19X4		19X5	
Net sales		$820,000		$840,000
Cost of goods sold				
Beginning inventory	$245,000		$315,000	
Add: Net purchases	710,000		680,000	
Goods available for sale	$955,000		$995,000	
Less: Ending inventory	315,000		340,000	
Cost of goods sold		640,000		655,000
Gross profit		$180,000		$185,000
Operating expenses		126,000		140,000
Net income		$ 54,000		$ 45,000

Maxum uses a periodic inventory system. A detailed review of the accounting records disclosed the following:

1. Because of a clerical error, 60 units of merchandise in the 19X5 ending inventory count were costed at $540 per unit rather than the correct amount of $54 per unit.
2. A $5,000 merchandise purchase on December 31, 19X4, terms F.O.B. destination, was included in the 19X4 ending physical inventory count even though the goods had not yet been received. An investigation revealed that the invoice was recorded when the goods arrived on January 4, 19X5.
3. An examination of 19X4 purchasing activity revealed that a $26,000 acquisition of land had been incorrectly charged to the Purchases account.

Instructions

a. Prepare corrected income statements for 19X4 and 19X5.
b. Determine the impact of the preceding errors on the December 31, 19X5, owner's equity balance.

P10–B2 Inventory valuation methods: Computations and concepts (L.O. 3, 4)

Roller Blade Company began business on January 1 of the current year. Purchases of skates and roller blades were as follows:

Jan. 5	200 units @ $80	
Apr. 22	60 units @ $90	
June 5	300 units @ $100	
July 8	100 units @ $110	
Nov. 13	40 units @ $120	

Roller Blade sold 440 units at an average price of $175 per unit. The company uses a periodic inventory system.

Instructions

a. Calculate cost of goods sold, ending inventory, and gross profit under each of the following inventory valuation methods:
   (1) First-in, first-out
   (2) Last-in, first-out
   (3) Weighted average
b. Which of the three methods would be chosen if management's goal is to:
   (1) Minimize the amount of income taxes paid to the federal government?
   (2) Match the oldest inventory costs against current revenues on the income statement?
   (3) Use a method that has been generally accepted by accounting practitioners?

P10–B3 FIFO; lower of cost or market (L.O. 3, 5)

Davenport Opticians began business on September 1 of the current year. The following purchases were made during the first few months of operation:

	READING GLASSES	SUNGLASSES	CONTACT LENSES
Sept. 2	1,000 @ $20	450 @ $10	2,500 @ $5
Oct. 15	750 @ $22	200 @ $15	2,000 @ $6
Dec. 6	300 @ $25		1,500 @ $7

The December 31 physical inventory count revealed the following items on hand: 650 reading glasses, 400 sunglasses, and 1,000 contact lenses. Total sales through year-end were $85,000, and operating expenses (excluding cost of goods sold) totaled $17,800. Davenport uses the FIFO inventory valuation method coupled with a periodic inventory system.

Instructions

a. Compute the company's year-end inventory valuation. In addition, calculate cost of goods sold and net income through December 31.

b. Assume that the manufacturer of contact lenses announced a price decrease to $6.50. Determine the impact of the announcement on the firm's ending inventory valuation.
c. Prepare the journal entry necessary to value the inventory at the lower of cost or market.

P10–B4 Gross profit method and insurance from casualties (L.O. 6)

On October 17, 19X9, an earthquake severely damaged the Fresno Home Video Store. The insurance company has agreed to reimburse the owner on the basis of an inventory estimate derived by using the gross profit method. Fresno's rate of earnings has been relatively stable in recent years, with the 19X8 income statement revealing the following:

Net sales	$320,000
Cost of goods sold	192,000
Net income	48,000
Inventory, Dec. 31	35,000

Fresno's accountant has compiled additional information for 19X9:

Net sales through Oct. 17	$265,000
Net purchases recorded through Oct. 17	168,000
Purchases recorded but not received as of Oct. 17	3,000

Instructions

a. Determine the cost of inventory on hand at Fresno Home Video on the date of the earthquake. The gross profit rate is to be based on the company's 19X8 operating experience.
b. Assume that the owner decided not to reopen the store and sold all salvageable videos for $2,000. What would be the amount of the loss claimed for insurance?
c. What would you have done differently in part (a) if, at the beginning of 19X9, the company implemented a $3 across-the-board price hike on all videos sold?

P10–B5 Retail method and inventory shrinkage (L.O. 6)

Pro Stop, a sporting goods store, uses the retail method of inventory valuation. A review of the company's accounting records disclosed the following information for the year ended December 31:

Inventory, Jan. 1		Purchases	
Cost	$ 79,300	Cost	$296,600
Retail	128,900	Retail	498,100
Sales	432,000	Purchases returns	
Sales returns	17,600	Cost	7,200
		Retail	12,500

Instructions

a. Using the retail method, estimate the cost of the company's inventory on December 31.
b. If the firm's physical count on December 31 revealed an ending inventory at retail of $185,500, compute the cost of inventory shrinkage.
c. Pro Stop is located in a fashionable shopping mall. Would you expect that the firm's cost-to-retail ratio is higher or lower than that of a sporting goods department of a locally owned discount store? Briefly explain.

P10–B6 Perpetual inventory systems: FIFO (L.O. 8)

Classrooms, Etc., carries educational materials and supplies for school teachers. The following information pertains to a specialized map of the United States:

Oct.	1	Beginning inventory: 40 maps @ $68.
	3	Purchased 20 maps @ $71.
	9	Sold 16 maps @ $120.
	15	Sold 28 maps @ $122.
	19	Purchased 32 maps @ $72.
	23	Sold 22 maps @ $124.
	26	Sold 10 maps @ $124.
	28	Purchased 16 maps @ $73.
	30	Sold 8 maps @ $125.

Instructions

a. Using a format similar to that of Exhibit 10–8, prepare a perpetual inventory record for the map. Classrooms uses the FIFO method of inventory valuation.
b. Prepare summary journal entries to record total purchases and sales.
c. Briefly explain why the FIFO periodic and perpetual inventory systems produce the same figures for ending inventory and cost of goods sold.

*P10–B7 Perpetual inventory systems: LIFO and moving average (L.O. 8)

Refer to the beginning inventory, purchases, and sales data of Classrooms, Etc., in Problem 10–B6.

Instructions

a. Assuming use of a LIFO cost flow assumption, prepare a perpetual inventory record for the U.S. maps by using a format similar to that shown in Exhibit 10–8. (*Note:* Keep in mind that the exhibit illustrates the first-in, first-out method.)
b. Assuming use of the moving-average method, determine the cost of the October 31 ending inventory and also the cost of goods sold during October.

EXPANDING YOUR HORIZONS

EYH10–1 Inventory methods, annual reports (L.O. 4)

LIFO and FIFO are the most widely used inventory valuation methods in the United States. Use of LIFO in a period of rising prices tends to reduce income taxes.

Instructions

a. Using the resources available at your library, review corporate annual reports and find three companies that use LIFO for inventory valuation. (This information is generally found in the summary of significant accounting policies—footnote no. 1.) Continue to review the notes and determine what the inventory valuation would have been had FIFO been used.
b. Assuming a tax rate of 35%, determine the company's estimated cash savings from using LIFO. Report your findings in a manner similar to that shown in Exhibit 10–7.

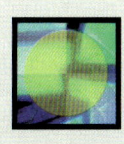

EYH10–2 Lower of cost or market (L.O. 5)

Inventory write-downs of goods that have declined in value are fairly common. Some write-downs are major and may force a company to report a net loss in an otherwise profitable year.

Instructions

Interview the accountants of two different retailers that use the lower-of-cost-or-market rule. Determine if the firms have written down inventory and recognized a loss in value in the accounting records. Try to ascertain (1) what items were written down, (2) the factors that caused the decline in value, and (3) what actions management has taken to reduce the chances of having the same situation again. Summarize your findings in a one-page report.

EYH10–3   Inventory management, turnover (L.O. 7)

Controlling the level of merchandise inventory is a difficult issue that managers must address. Too much inventory increases costs; too little causes disgruntled (and possibly lost) customers.

Instructions

Interview two different retailers and determine what steps they have recently taken to better manage inventories. Inquire about the retailer's inventory turnover and whether this ratio is a concern for the business. Be prepared to report your findings to the class.

EYH10–4   Inventory valuation: The J.M. Smucker Company (L.O. 3, 4, 5)

The J.M. Smucker Company is involved with the manufacturing and marketing of food products. The firm is probably best known for its preserves, jams, jellies, marmalades, and ice cream toppings.

Instructions

By using the text's electronic data base, access the balance sheet and accompanying notes of The Smucker Company and answer the questions that follow. Unless otherwise indicated, responses should be based on data for the most recent year presented.

a. Study the presentation of inventories on the balance sheet.
   (1) Are inventories a sizable portion of the company's total assets? Show calculations to support your answer.
   (2) Does the company disclose different types of inventories? If so, what types are shown?
b. What cost flow assumption is used to value the majority of the firm's inventories? What factors may have been considered in adopting this assumption?
c. Suppose the company had used another popular cost flow assumption.
   (1) Would reported inventory valuations increase or decrease? By how much?
   (2) Would the alternative cost flow assumption result in higher or lower net income for the company?
d. Does the firm make any attempt to record losses related to declines in market values of inventories? Briefly explain.

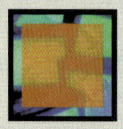

EYH10–5   Inventory valuation (L.O. 3, 4, 5)

This problem is a duplication of Problem EYH10–4. It is based on a company selected by your instructor.

Instructions

By using the text's electronic data base, access the specified company's balance sheet and accompanying notes and focus on data for the most recent year reported. Answer requirements (a)–(d) of Problem EYH10–4.

EYH10–6 An in-depth probe of LIFO (L.O. 3, 4)

The Biscayne Company, a newly organized Florida corporation, is composed of two divisions: Parts Manufacturing and Motor Car Sales. Both divisions currently use the LIFO method of inventory valuation. Because business is slumping, the controller has begun an in-depth review of operations.

The Parts Manufacturing division has experienced skyrocketing raw materials costs and labor difficulties. Two strikes by machinists and assemblers have been especially severe, causing Biscayne to close its plant for the past three months. Fortunately, existing finished goods inventories have been large enough to fill incoming sales orders.

The Motor Car Sales division has been hit with a sharp decline in sales, and the controller is contemplating a change from LIFO to FIFO. The year-end inventory under the LIFO method is anticipated to be $20 million. If FIFO is used, the ending inventory balance would increase to $28 million.

Instructions

a. As the Parts Manufacturing division cuts deeper and deeper into finished goods inventory, which costs (high or low) will be charged to cost of goods sold?
b. Given your answer in part (a), determine the effect of the strike on earnings and the related tax payments.
c. Assuming the Motor Car Sales division is subject to an income tax rate of 40%, determine the effect on net income of the shift from LIFO to FIFO.
d. Present a detailed analysis to Biscayne's president regarding the advantages and disadvantages of making the shift.

COMMUNICATION OF ACCOUNTING INFORMATION

CAI10–1 Communication structure: The Goodyear Tire & Rubber Company (L.O. 3, 5)

Communication Principle: Most business writing and speaking begin with the main point to be communicated (i.e., a purpose statement). This practice aids the reader or listener, who needs to know the context of a discussion to correctly interpret the information that follows. Transition words are often used as pointers to focus on the facts about to be presented. Examples of such pointers include "The major distinction is . . . ," "The most important point is . . . ," and "The basic principles behind this treatment are . . . ."

The purpose statement should be followed by support, such as definitions, comparisons and contrasts, and examples. Typical support phrases are "in contrast," "for instance," "to illustrate," "also," "together with," "in addition to," "therefore," "thus," and "similarly." The support generally closes with conclusion sentences, which help a reader/listener return to and recall the purpose statement. Phrases such as "to rephrase," "in review," "in other words," and "to sum up" help signal that the conclusion is near.

■ ■ ■ ■ ■ ■ ■ ■

The name, Goodyear Tire & Rubber, is certainly familiar. In addition to being one of the world's largest producers of tires and rubber products, the company manufactures and sells various chemicals and plastics as well as other goods and services. As you might imagine, inventory is one of Goodyear's most significant assets, totaling $1.3 billion.

Included in the company's annual report is a note that summarizes significant accounting policies. Within this note is the following description of the firm's inventory valuation methods:

Inventories are stated at the lower of cost or market. Cost is determined using the last-in, first-out (LIFO) method for a significant portion of domestic inventories and the . . . average cost method for other inventories.

The "Summary of Significant Accounting Policies" note is required disclosure. Goodyear's overall summary, like those of many other companies, assumes users are familiar with certain basic accounting concepts. In this case, for instance, some knowledge of cost flow assumptions and declines in valuation is needed.

Instructions

Rewrite Goodyear's note so that a reader with virtually no accounting background could understand the inventory methods used. Be sure to utilize proper organization by providing an introductory (purpose) statement, an explanation, and a conclusion.

Answers to Chapter Quiz

1. b
2. b
3. c
4. a ($400 for A + $600 for B)
5. a

11 Property, Plant, and Equipment: Acquisition and Depreciation

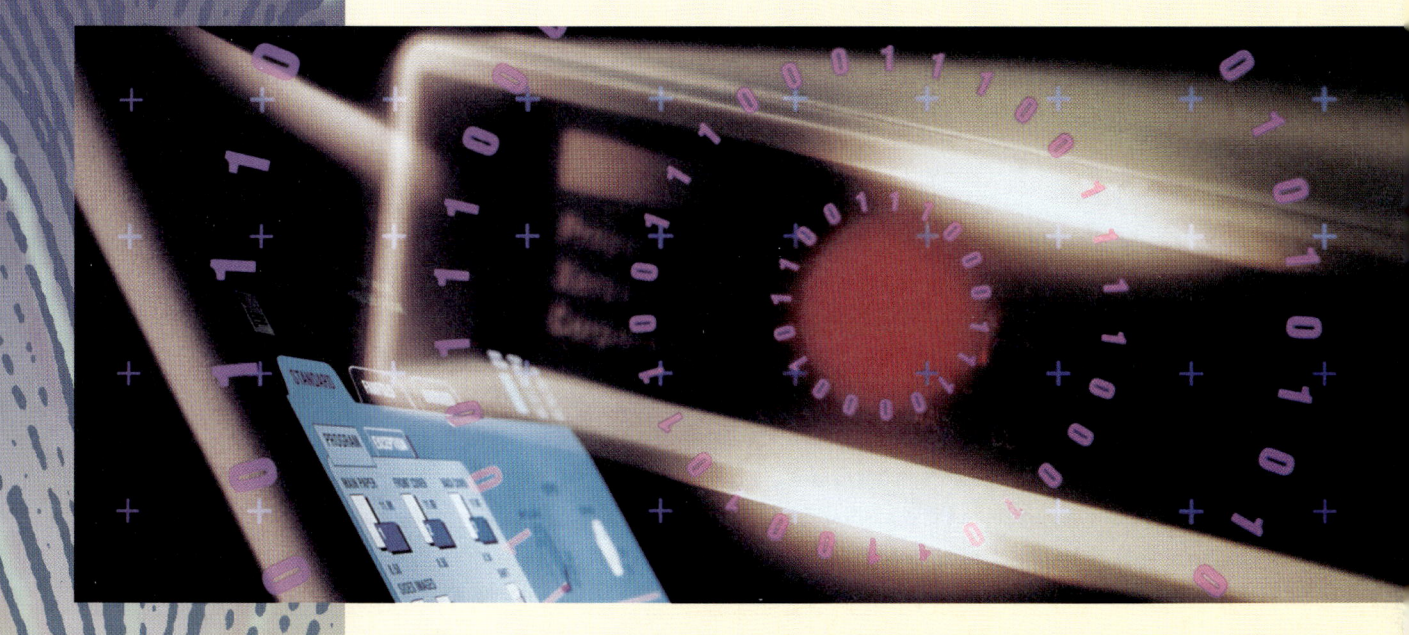

Learning Objectives

After studying this chapter, you should be able to:

1. Discuss the nature of property, plant, and equipment and determine the cost of long-lived assets.

2. Explain the concept of depreciation and recognize the factors that affect asset service life.

3. Compute depreciation by using the straight-line, units-of-output, declining-balance, and sum-of-the-years'-digits methods.

4. Identify the financial reporting issues related to the various depreciation methods.

5. Revise a depreciation rate.

6. Demonstrate a very basic knowledge of depreciation and the tax laws.

7. Recognize the issues related to accounting for leases.

Sitting in his office on a mild spring day, George Faris and your authors recently discussed several accounting problems related to long-lived assets. These problems focused on the proper handling of billboard construction costs and the estimation of a service life for depreciation purposes.

To explain, the construction costs of a billboard are high and varied. In addition to the sign itself, Banner Advertising has outlays for legal and permit fees associated with zoning and construction, site preparation costs, foundation drilling and cementing, and utility line extensions. These costs collectively provide long-term benefits to the firm, and how they are treated for accounting purposes is important.

Technically, a portion of the cost should be written off each year, to be matched against the revenues generated. The cost should really be spread over the billboard's service life. This sounds like an easy process, but deriving an estimate for the life can be troublesome. As George noted, "In the case of a steel billboard, even the calculation of a *rough* estimate presents a challenge. Our engineers predict a physical life for the structure of about 200 years. Maybe, with a little luck and maintenance, we can stretch it to 250. Of course, no one will ever be around this long to know!"

To simplify matters, Banner uses a life estimate that is obtained from publications of the Internal Revenue Service (IRS). While making no attempt to focus on how long the billboard will physically last, the IRS estimate in this case is much closer to the time that the sign will benefit the firm. "We use this estimate for expediency," George says.

The principles of accounting for long-lived assets and the correct way to measure and record depreciation are important issues for Banner Advertising. These issues are also significant for most businesses, especially when one considers the dollars involved. Many organizations invest large amounts of money in assets that are used to manufacture products or provide services. Xerox Corporation, for example, recently reported an investment of over $5 billion, Anheuser-Busch Companies reported $12 billion, and GTE Corporation reported $47 billion. Proper reporting of these sums in the financial statements is essential.

THE NATURE OF PROPERTY, PLANT, AND EQUIPMENT

① Discuss the nature of property, plant, and equipment and determine the cost of long-lived assets.

Assets with long lives acquired for use in business operations are termed **property, plant, and equipment** and include land, buildings, vehicles, office equipment, machinery, store equipment, and furniture and fixtures. This asset category is sometimes referred to as plant and equipment, plant assets, or fixed assets. Property, plant, and equipment is the most descriptive of these titles, however, and has gained the widest acceptance for the presentation of productive and service capacity on the balance sheet.

Assets that appear under the property, plant, and equipment caption may be likened to long-term prepaid expenses, because their acquisition entails an advance payment for years of future service. To explain, a firm that prepays rent for several months into the next accounting period will record a prepaid expense on its balance sheet. If that same firm purchases a building, it has, in essence, prepaid for the future services the building is expected to render.

Like prepaid expenses, items of property, plant, and equipment can provide benefits for only a certain period of time and are said to possess a limited service life. (An exception is land, which provides services indefinitely.) As a result, then, just as prepaid expenses become expenses when consumed, plant and equipment are gradually charged to depreciation as the assets are used in operations.

Our discussion of long-lived assets in this chapter and Chapter 12 will focus on the following key issues, which are depicted in Exhibit 11–1:

1. Measurement of asset cost (Chapter 11).
2. Allocation of asset cost to the accounting periods benefited (Chapter 11).
3. Accounting for expenditures that occur after asset acquisition, such as repairs and improvements (Chapter 12).
4. Recording disposals of plant and equipment in the accounts (Chapter 12).

DETERMINING THE COST OF PROPERTY, PLANT, AND EQUIPMENT

The cost of property, plant, and equipment includes acquisition or construction expenditures (and related amounts) required to ready the assets for business use. For the purchase of equipment, such expenditures include the invoice price of the equipment, freight charges incurred by the buyer, insurance on the equipment while in transit, and installation costs such as special electrical wiring and initial testing. The cost of land includes the purchase price; attorney's fees; commissions to a real estate broker; recording fees with the city or county; surveying costs; costs to clear, drain, and grade the land; and the assumption of any mortgages or delinquent property taxes.

The necessary record keeping for the preceding "add-on" items is relatively straightforward. Suppose, for example, that a company purchased $40,000 of machinery and incurred $7,000 of freight and installation costs. If the firm paid $10,000 down and financed the remaining balance by securing a short-term loan, the following entry would be needed:

Machinery	47,000	
Cash		10,000
Loan Payable		37,000
To record acquisition of machinery.		

EXHIBIT 11–1
Issues Related to Long-Lived Assets

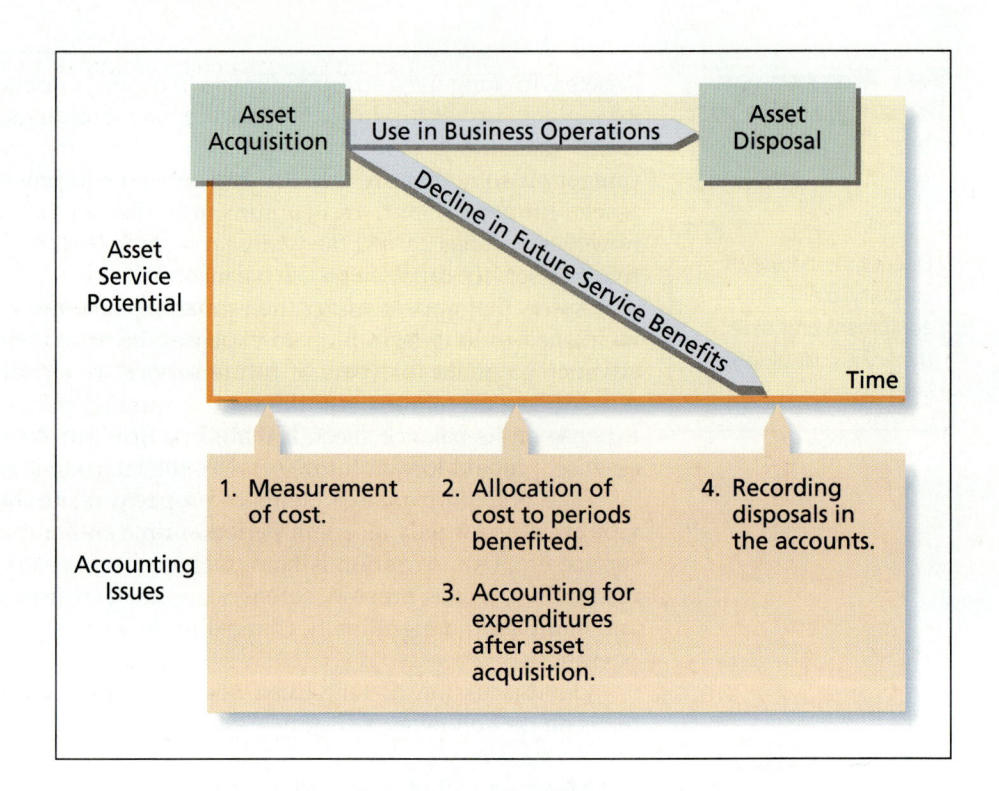

Asset Acquisition → Use in Business Operations → Asset Disposal

Decline in Future Service Benefits

Asset Service Potential / Time

Accounting Issues:
1. Measurement of cost.
2. Allocation of cost to periods benefited.
3. Accounting for expenditures after asset acquisition.
4. Recording disposals in the accounts.

The rationale for the preceding treatment is clear. To charge costs related to asset acquisition as an expense of the acquisition period would result in a mismatch of revenues and expenses. Property, plant, and equipment will serve a business for many years, and incidental expenditures like freight, installation, and broker's fees are necessary for acquisition and subsequent asset use to occur. In effect, then, these items provide long-run benefits and should be shown on the balance sheet as part of an asset's cost.

Expenditures related to asset purchases and preparation that fail to provide future economic benefits are expenses. For example, if a piece of equipment was damaged while being installed, the repair costs would not be added to the cost of the equipment. Instead, the repairs are treated as an expense of the current accounting period. Likewise, if a newly purchased machine was being delivered on the buyer's truck and the truck was involved in an accident, the cost of fixing the truck, any damages paid to other parties, and any fines levied on the driver are not charged to the Machinery account. These outlays are not "ordinary and necessary" to place the machine in a position ready to serve the purchaser and are therefore expensed.

A cost that we failed to cite in the preceding discussion is interest. Stated simply, the proper accounting treatment is dependent on the method of asset acquisition. As a general rule, interest costs incurred to finance the *purchase* of property, plant, and equipment are written off as expense. In contrast, interest charges related to financing the *construction* of plant and equipment for a company's own use are often added to the cost of the asset. These latter charges must be incurred during the construction period and be significant in amount to qualify for this special treatment.[1]

Lump-Sum Purchase. Frequently, a business will purchase a number of assets together for a single amount. For example, the acquisition of developed property will usually include such assets as land, buildings, parking lots, fences, and lawn sprinkler systems. Transactions of this type are termed lump-sum purchases. The cost of a lump-sum purchase must be apportioned among the various assets acquired, for reporting and depreciation purposes. These assets generally benefit a business for different periods of time and therefore require different depreciation rates.

Appraisals are often used to aid in the apportionment. To illustrate, assume that Hartley Development Company purchased a building, land improvements (e.g., parking lots, fences, and lawn sprinkler systems), and land for $40 million cash. The assets' appraisal values along with the necessary cost apportionment follow.

	APPRAISAL VALUE	PERCENTAGE OF TOTAL APPRAISAL VALUE	RECORDED COST
Building	$25,000,000	50%	$20,000,000
Land improvements	5,000,000	10	4,000,000
Land	20,000,000	40	16,000,000
Total	$50,000,000	100%	$40,000,000

The acquisition cost is apportioned on the basis of an individual asset's appraised value relative to the appraised value of the entire purchase. For example, because the building is 50% of the property's total value ($25,000,000 ÷ $50,000,000), the cost of the building is established at $20,000,000 ($40,000,000 × 0.50). The recorded amounts for land improvements and land are determined in the same manner. The journal entry to record the purchase is therefore as follows:

Building	20,000,000	
Land Improvements	4,000,000	
Land	16,000,000	
Cash		40,000,000

To record acquisition of developed property.

Notice that a distinction is made between land and land improvements. It is necessary to establish separate accounts for these assets because a parcel of land has an indefinite life, whereas land improvements do not. As a result, land improvements are depreciated over the number of periods they render benefits or service to a business.

---

[1] "Capitalization of Interest Costs," *Statement of Financial Accounting Standards No. 34,* Financial Accounting Standards Board, Norwalk, Conn., 1979.

SMALL ITEMS OF PROPERTY, PLANT, AND EQUIPMENT

Businesses purchase many long-lived items (e.g., tape dispensers, pencil sharpeners, and office clocks) that technically should be classified as property, plant, and equipment. Because of their insignificant purchase price, however, these items are not established as assets in the accounting records. Instead, such amounts are normally written off as expenses in the period of acquisition. This procedure reduces paperwork costs and avoids depreciating small items over long periods of time. Imagine the record keeping associated with depreciating a $5 wastepaper basket over a 10-year life. Virtually all accountants would agree that the $0.50 annual write-off is hardly worth the effort.

In an attempt to avoid an in-depth analysis of its many expenditures, a business will typically make the accounting-treatment decision by using a preestablished minimum dollar cutoff. If, for example, a firm sets a $100 cutoff, all expenditures of $100 or less would automatically be deemed too small to be recorded as part of property, plant, and equipment. Such amounts would therefore be expensed immediately. On the other hand, outlays that exceed $100 would be considered significant and thus treated as assets, to be written off gradually as benefits are received.[2]

Cost/Benefit and Materiality. Whether an outlay should be expensed or carried as an asset is a matter of professional judgment. When evaluating the two possible treatments, the accountant must assess the magnitude and importance of the outlay in question. The proper decision can be made only after careful consideration of two factors: cost/benefit and materiality. More specifically, the expense of developing exact accounting information must be studied relative to the benefits of added precision. If the cost of a company's efforts exceeds the benefits that financial statement users will receive, the extra precision is deemed wasteful and should not be attempted.

This cost/benefit theme is consistent with the concept of **materiality,** which refers to the significance of a particular item or transaction. If judged to be immaterial, an item or transaction would likely have no influence on the decisions made by informed financial statement users. In such cases, theory would take a back seat to practice, and the accountant would handle the item in the most expedient manner possible. Thus, for items of $100 or less in the preceding example, an immediate write-off is preferred rather than a prolonged allocation to the periods of benefit.

DEPRECIATION

> **2**
> Explain the concept of depreciation and recognize the factors that affect asset service life.

As we previously noted, all items of property, plant, and equipment (except land) have limited lives and render services over several accounting periods. These services often result in the production of revenues for the firm. Proper accounting therefore requires that a portion of the cost of long-lived assets be written off each year to expense, to be matched against revenues on the income statement. Stated differently, because revenues are generated in each year of asset use, it is only correct that each year's income absorb the costs of producing that revenue.

[2] Cutoff limits typically vary from firm to firm and are often dependent on company size. A large expenditure for Joe's Electronics, for instance, could be an insignificant amount to Sony Corporation.

The process used to allocate the cost of long-lived assets to the accounting periods benefited is known as **depreciation.** Although this definition is widely accepted in the business world, be aware that other definitions are sometimes encountered. For example, you may have heard new car owners mention the "depreciation" they have suffered since their purchase. To these people depreciation represents a decrease in value, namely, the difference between the amount paid for the car and the vehicle's present resale value. Accountants make no attempt to integrate information into the accounts about the ever-changing market values of property, plant, and equipment. Instead, assets classified in this category are maintained in the accounting records at cost. For depreciable assets this cost is later allocated as expense to the years receiving service or benefits. In accounting, then, *depreciation is a process of allocation, not valuation.*

DETERMINING SERVICE LIFE

Before an asset's cost is allocated among the periods benefited, a service life must be estimated. **Service life,** sometimes called economic or useful life, is the period of time that depreciable assets provide service to a business. It is important to understand that an asset's service life is frequently different from its physical life. That is, an asset may have physical existence long after the useful life to a business has concluded. Witness, for example, the abandoned equipment behind many manufacturing plants and the numerous railroad tracks that are no longer used by their owners.

When determining an asset's service life, we must consider three factors: physical deterioration, obsolescence, and inadequacy.

Physical Deterioration. The physical deterioration of an asset, sometimes termed "wear and tear," is caused by use in the normal course of business. Repair and maintenance may prolong an asset's service life, but at some point the asset usually requires replacement because it has become worn out. Physical deterioration normally establishes the maximum limit for the estimate of service life.

Obsolescence. Obsolescence is a technological factor relating to being out of date. New technology frequently shortens the service life of assets well before their physical life is over. Businesses that use obsolete machines, for example, cannot compete effectively with companies that use modern, more efficient equipment.

Obsolescence has been a significant factor in shortening the service life of computers. Recent advances in engineering have been dramatic. Businesses that purchased a computer three years ago are finding that faster, more versatile models are now available, making their equipment out of date and less desirable.

Inadequacy. With business growth, the service capabilities of certain items of depreciable property, plant, and equipment may become inadequate. Plants may no longer be able to keep pace with demand, trucks may be too small, and equipment may be too slow. When assets are inadequate to meet the competitive needs of a company, their service lives have ended. Like obsolescence, inadequacy is an economic (as opposed to physical) determinant of service life.

> **ETHICS ISSUE**
>
> The chief accountant, who is paid a bonus based on net income, was notified that the estimated lives of certain machines were too long. The accountant does not agree but is concerned about being accused of overstating income. What should the accountant do?

> **3**
>
> Compute depreciation by using the straight-line, units-of-output, declining-balance, and sum-of-the-years'-digits methods.

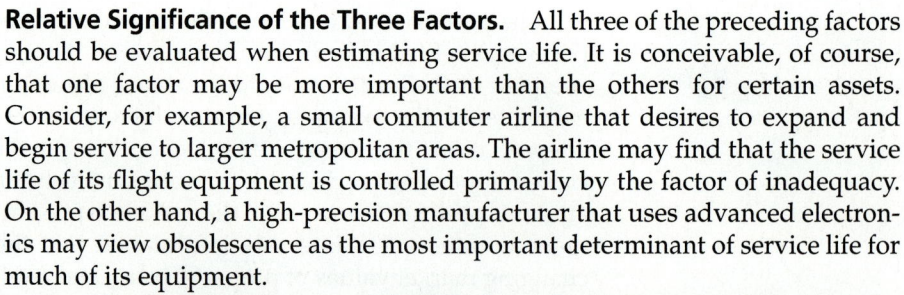

Relative Significance of the Three Factors. All three of the preceding factors should be evaluated when estimating service life. It is conceivable, of course, that one factor may be more important than the others for certain assets. Consider, for example, a small commuter airline that desires to expand and begin service to larger metropolitan areas. The airline may find that the service life of its flight equipment is controlled primarily by the factor of inadequacy. On the other hand, a high-precision manufacturer that uses advanced electronics may view obsolescence as the most important determinant of service life for much of its equipment.

In other business situations, all of the factors may be equally important for a particular depreciable asset. In these cases the estimation of service life becomes more difficult. Companies having no experience with a particular type of asset may seek guidance from their accountants, engineers, trade associations, or the asset's seller.

METHODS OF DEPRECIATION

There are several acceptable methods for computing depreciation. The four methods used most often are straight-line, units-of-output, declining-balance, and sum-of-the-years'-digits. Some of these approaches are so common that they are actually built into electronic spreadsheets. Most spreadsheets, for example, employ function commands, which are a series of preprogrammed

---

BUSINESS BRIEFING

ALEX MANDL
Executive Vice-President and CEO, Communications Services Group
AT&T

High-Tech Depreciable Lives

Estimating the depreciable life for high-tech equipment is not easy. Traditional approaches have relied on historical data for similar equipment or on engineering estimates of how long the equipment can last. These methods just don't work in an environment characterized by ever-shortening life cycles, global competition, and increasingly sophisticated customers.

For example, not too long ago, AT&T had almost $25 billion of equipment invested in its analog long distance network. This network was designed to last until the year 2010. In 1988, two things changed those plans—breakthroughs in digital technology along with the software that makes it work, and accelerating customer demand for services that only digital equipment can provide. Suddenly, the analog network would be economically obsolete by the year 1990—20 years ahead of schedule. Since our traditional equipment life estimates never anticipated this change, AT&T took a writedown of $6.7 billion for the underdepreciated equipment.

The bottom line is that using the engineered life for high-tech equipment will generally give the wrong answer. Instead, the economic service life should be employed. This means looking at market trends, competitor strategies, and what's on the drawing board in the laboratories across the globe, *as well as* identifying the engineered life. It's not easy, but it's the only way to accurately portray the profitability of your business.

A Further Focus

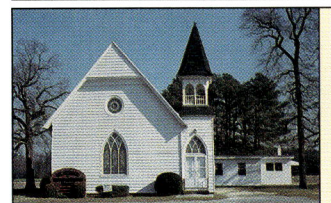

Until very recently, churches were not required to depreciate their houses of worship and monuments. Religious organizations generally argued against recording depreciation on the grounds that cathedrals often last for many centuries. As a retired Treasury Department official noted: "Depreciating churches would be like depreciating the Pyramids and the Sphinx of Egypt, and the Sistine Chapel at the Vatican." Figuring such depreciation would be "the acme of futility." The Financial Accounting Standards Board (FASB) ruled in favor of depreciation, however, with the Board noting that cathedrals are "used up" not only by wear and tear, but also by the continuous destructive effects of pollutants and vibrations. As an FASB spokesman observed, "Church properties can wear out; therefore, they should be depreciated. I can see quibbling about the Pyramids, because their [service] life is so long that the cost per year would be immaterial. But not most churches."

Source: Quotations are taken from "Is Nothing Sacred? Churches Fight Plan to Alter Accounting," *The Wall Street Journal*, April 16, 1987, pp. 1, 20. Reprinted by permission of *The Wall Street Journal*, © Dow Jones & Company, Inc., 1987. All rights reserved worldwide.

---

formulas that accomplish a specific task. To calculate, say, straight-line depreciation, the user need only invoke the proper command and enter basic data such as asset cost and service life. The rest is done automatically.

Straight-Line Method. Partly because of its simplicity, the **straight-line method** is a very popular way to compute depreciation. Under this approach, the cost of a depreciable asset, minus residual value, is allocated equally over the estimated service life. The **residual value** (sometimes called salvage value) is the amount that a business expects to receive upon disposal of an asset at the end of the asset's life. Given the nature of the allocation, the straight-line method is best applied to assets that provide constant, uniform service to an entity.

To illustrate the straight-line method, assume WBBB-TV bought a new hand-held camera for $30,000. The camera has an estimated residual value of $3,000 and an estimated service life of five years. The annual depreciation expense is computed as follows:

$$\frac{\text{Cost} - \text{Residual Value}}{\text{Service Life in Years}} = \text{Annual Depreciation}$$

$$= \frac{\$30,000 - \$3,000}{5 \text{ years}}$$

$$= \$5,400 \text{ annual depreciation}$$

The deduction of the $3,000 residual value from the asset's cost of $30,000 yields a $27,000 **depreciable base**—the total amount that will be written off to depreciation expense over the asset's life.

The following journal entry is used to record depreciation during each year of the camera's life:

Depreciation Expense: Broadcasting Equipment	5,400	
Accumulated Depreciation: Broadcasting Equipment		5,400
To record annual depreciation expense.		

This entry reflects a very common practice: the creation of separate accounts for each major group of depreciable assets (e.g., buildings, office equipment, furniture and fixtures, and so forth). Such breakdowns are helpful for internal management analysis as well as for external financial reporting.

In view of the preceding data, WBBB's income statement would reveal annual depreciation expense of $5,400. The firm's balance sheet would disclose the following:

	YEAR 1	YEAR 2
Property, plant, & equipment		
Broadcasting equipment	$30,000	$30,000
Less: Accumulated depreciation	5,400	10,800
	$24,600	$19,200

These figures show that accumulated depreciation increases by $5,400 during each year of service life. Recall that the cost of an asset, minus accumulated depreciation, is termed **book value.** As the accompanying schedule illustrates, book value decreases each year and equals the residual value ($3,000) at the end of the camera's life. The asset is said to be fully depreciated at this point and no further depreciation is recorded.

YEAR	DEPRECIATION EXPENSE	ACCUMULATED DEPRECIATION	BOOK VALUE
			$30,000
1	$5,400	$ 5,400	24,600
2	5,400	10,800	19,200
3	5,400	16,200	13,800
4	5,400	21,600	8,400
5	5,400	27,000	3,000

Partial Periods. In the preceding example, we assumed that the camera was acquired on January 1. If the purchase was made later in the year, WBBB would record a prorated percentage of the annual depreciation charge. Assuming acquisition on May 1, depreciation for the first year would be $3,600 ($5,400 × 8/12), because the asset provided services for only eight months. The remaining depreciation expense would then be $5,400 for Years 2, 3, 4, and 5 and $1,800 ($5,400 × 4/12) for the first four months of Year 6. As before, depreciation totals $27,000 and is recorded over five years of service.

Units-of-Output Method. The **units-of-output method,** sometimes called the units-of-production or activity method, can be employed when an asset's service life is expressible in terms of output (such as miles, hours, or number of times used). Under this approach the asset's cost, minus residual value, is divided by the total estimated output during the service life. This computation generates the depreciation rate. Annual depreciation expense is then calculated by multiplying the depreciation rate by the yearly output. To illustrate, assume a large corporation purchased a business jet for $4 million that has a residual value of $1.5 million. The service life is estimated to be 10,000 flying hours. The depreciation rate is calculated as follows:

$$\frac{\text{Cost} - \text{Residual Value}}{\text{Service Life in Output}} = \text{Depreciation per Unit of Output}$$

$$= \frac{\$4{,}000{,}000 - \$1{,}500{,}000}{10{,}000 \text{ flying hours}}$$

$$= \$250 \text{ per flying hour}$$

If the jet was used for 500 hours during the year, depreciation expense would total $125,000 ($250 × 500).

The units-of-output method is used when (1) the service capacity of an asset can be reasonably estimated and (2) there is a direct relationship between an asset's use and its decline in service potential. Assets that meet these two criteria include cars, trucks, and machines. In situations where the amount of an asset's output varies considerably from period to period, the units-of-output method achieves a better allocation of cost than do the straight-line or other depreciation approaches. For example, in years of great activity, more of an asset's cost would be depreciated and matched against revenues; in years of low activity, less depreciation expense is recorded. In contrast, the straight-line method produces a constant depreciation charge, regardless of the services provided.

Accelerated Depreciation Methods. The two remaining depreciation methods are declining-balance and sum-of-the-years'-digits. Both approaches speed up the recognition of expense and are appropriately termed *accelerated depreciation methods.* As you will soon see, relatively large amounts of depreciation are generated in the early years of asset use and small amounts in later years.

Businesses may prefer to use an accelerated depreciation method for a variety of reasons. First, companies recognize that the services provided by many assets tend to decline over time. For instance, consider the transportation services provided by a new car versus those of a less dependable older model. Or note the quality of machining obtained from a new high-precision drill press versus that from an older press with less accurate tolerances. If the services provided are actually greater in the earlier years of asset use, a proper matching of revenues and expenses dictates a gradual reduction in depreciation charges over an asset's lifetime.

Another reason for using an accelerated depreciation method is that repair and maintenance costs normally increase as an asset grows older. When combined with a decreasing amount of depreciation from an accelerated method, the total amount of yearly expense is leveled. The end result for assets that furnish uniform service is a better match of expense against revenue than would be possible by the straight-line technique.

Declining-Balance Method. The **declining-balance method** involves applying a fixed depreciation rate to the remaining (i.e., declining) book value of an asset. The rate employed is a multiple of that calculated under the straight-line approach. For instance, if a company is computing depreciation by utilizing the popular **double-declining balance** method, the rate used is twice the straight-line rate. Notice that residual value is ignored in the calculation; however, similar to the other approaches presented, depreciation stops when an asset's book value equals the residual value amount.

Applying the double-declining balance method to the hand-held camera example cited earlier (cost, $30,000; residual value, $3,000; service life, five years), we obtain the accompanying depreciation schedule.

Year	Depreciation Expense	Accumulated Depreciation	Book Value
			$30,000
1	$12,000 ($30,000 × 40%)	$12,000	18,000
2	7,200 ($18,000 × 40%)	19,200	10,800
3	4,320 ($10,800 × 40%)	23,520	6,480
4	2,592 ($6,480 × 40%)	26,112	3,888
5	888 ($3,888 – $3,000)	27,000	3,000

To explain, with the five-year service life, the straight-line depreciation rate is 1/5, or 20%, per year. The double-declining balance rate, therefore, is 40% (2 × 20%). Depreciation expense in the first year is 40% times the $30,000 book value, or $12,000. The journal entry to record depreciation at the end of the year places $12,000 in the Accumulated Depreciation account, thus reducing the camera's book value to $18,000. Depreciation in the second year falls to $7,200, that is, book value of $18,000 × 40%. Similar computations are performed in Years 3 and 4.

The last year of service life is handled differently. If we had continued with the approach just illustrated, depreciation expense in the fifth year would have been $1,555 ($3,888 × 40%). The camera's book value would therefore be reduced to $2,333 ($3,888 – $1,555), which is below the $3,000 estimated residual value. Thus, depreciation expense in Year 5 amounts to only $888 ($3,888 – $3,000).

If the camera had been purchased on September 1, depreciation expense would be computed for only four months in Year 1 and would total $4,000 [($30,000 × 40%) × 4/12]. The necessary procedures for all future periods are similar to those shown in the earlier illustration. For example, because book value at the beginning of Year 2 would be $26,000 ($30,000 – $4,000), depreciation expense for the second year is $10,400 ($26,000 × 40%).

Sum-of-the-Years'-Digits Method. Paralleling the double-declining balance method, the **sum-of-the-years'-digits method** produces more depreciation expense in the early years of asset use. Under this approach, a successively lower depreciation rate is applied each year to a constant depreciable base (cost minus residual value). The rate, which is really a fraction, is derived by setting the numerator equal to the remaining years of life at the beginning of the period. The denominator, in turn, equals the total of the service years. In the case of the hand-held camera, which has a five-year life, the denominator would always equal 15 (5 + 4 + 3 + 2 + 1 = 15). Similarly, for assets having a four-year life, the denominator would be 10 (4 + 3 + 2 + 1 = 10).[3]

Continuing the camera example, the numerator for the first year is 5 because five years of service life remain; then 4 for the second year, and so forth. WBBB's depreciation schedule using the sum-of-the-years'-digits method follows.

YEAR	DEPRECIATION EXPENSE	ACCUMULATED DEPRECIATION	BOOK VALUE
			$30,000
1	$9,000 ($27,000 × 5/15)	$ 9,000	21,000
2	7,200 ($27,000 × 4/15)	16,200	13,800
3	5,400 ($27,000 × 3/15)	21,600	8,400
4	3,600 ($27,000 × 2/15)	25,200	4,800
5	1,800 ($27,000 × 1/15)	27,000	3,000

For assets acquired during the year, the allocation of cost over the service life is more complex. The key to understanding the necessary procedures is to recognize that each fraction (5/15, 4/15, 3/15, and so on) *must be employed for 12 months no matter when the asset is acquired.* For example, if the camera was purchased on April 1 and used for nine months, the 5/15 rate would be applied for the remainder of Year 1, producing depreciation expense of $6,750 [($27,000 × 5/15) × 9/12]. Depreciation expense for the second year totals $7,650 and is computed by using the 5/15 rate for three months and the 4/15 rate for nine months, specifically,

$$\begin{aligned} \$27{,}000 \times 5/15 \times 3/12 &= \$2{,}250 \\ 27{,}000 \times 4/15 \times 9/12 &= \underline{5{,}400} \\ &\ \underline{\$7{,}650} \end{aligned}$$

This process, depicted in the following graphic, is subsequently continued into Year 6.

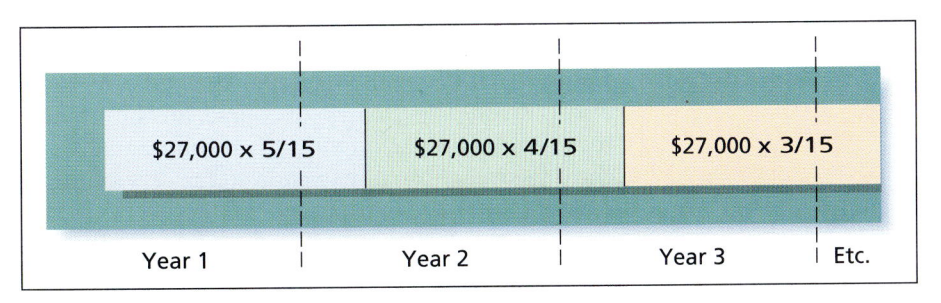

$27,000 × 5/15	$27,000 × 4/15	$27,000 × 3/15
Year 1	Year 2	Year 3	Etc.

[3] The denominator can be easily calculated by the following formula:

$$D = \frac{n(n+1)}{2}$$

where D equals the denominator and n equals the number of service years. For example, the denominator of an asset having a 10-year service life would be computed as

$$D = \frac{10(10+1)}{2} = \frac{110}{2} = 55$$

> **4** Identify the financial-reporting issues related to the various depreciation methods.

Selection of a Depreciation Method. Exhibit 11–2 shows the annual depreciation expense for the three methods used with the camera: straight-line, double-declining balance, and sum-of-the-years'-digits. The units-of-output method is disregarded here because the camera's service capacity in units could not be reasonably estimated.

By summing the annual charges from the preceding schedules, you will see that the same total amount is ultimately written off by all of the methods, namely, cost minus residual value. However, as the exhibit so clearly reveals, the amounts and patterns of the yearly allocations differ markedly. The straight-line approach produces lower depreciation expense in the early years of an asset's life than either of the accelerated methods. The gap between straight-line and the other methods tends to decrease as time passes, with a reversal occurring in Year 3. That is, the $5,400 straight-line expense figure actually exceeds the charges obtained with double-declining balance or sum-of-the-years'-digits in later years of use.

Exhibit 11–2 also reveals the movement of book value over time. Although the book value figures under the various approaches decline at differing rates, the end result is the same: the amount ultimately left on the accounting records is residual value ($3,000).

Which approach, then, should be selected? The answer to this question depends on a number of factors, including usage patterns, the generation of operating efficiencies, obsolescence, and the timing of repair costs. Conceptually, the method chosen should be the one that best parallels the services delivered (or benefits provided) by an asset. Such a selection is consistent with proper matching of revenues and expenses. Because the pattern of service is sometimes difficult to measure, however, practice often differs from theory. Recent surveys of reporting practices have shown the straight-line method to be the most popular approach. Companies that use this method often do so because of the constant nature of the depreciation charge—an element that helps to portray financial stability and smooth earnings over time. Exhibit 11–3 discloses the variation in depreciation policies of several well-known businesses.

> **5** Revise a depreciation rate.

REVISIONS OF DEPRECIATION

The calculation of depreciation depends on two estimates: service life and residual value. Estimates, of course, are subject to change and are often incorrect. As an example, unanticipated suburban growth and new developments on the outskirts of town may shorten the service life of buildings located in older, central-city areas. Equipment may be useful for fewer years due to new technology. Or residual values may need revision because of economic developments that take place after an asset has been placed in service. Such occurrences are commonplace.

When new information alters the estimates used for service life or residual value, the yearly depreciation computation must be changed. This change is achieved by allocating the asset's remaining depreciable base over the remaining service life. Previous years' depreciation amounts are *not* corrected, because the original estimates were based on the best information available at that time.

To illustrate the idea of a depreciation rate revision, suppose that Patriot Company purchased a building 10 years ago for $5 million. At the time of acquisition the building had an estimated $1 million residual value and a 40-year ser-

EXHIBIT 11–2
A Graphical Overview of Depreciation Methods

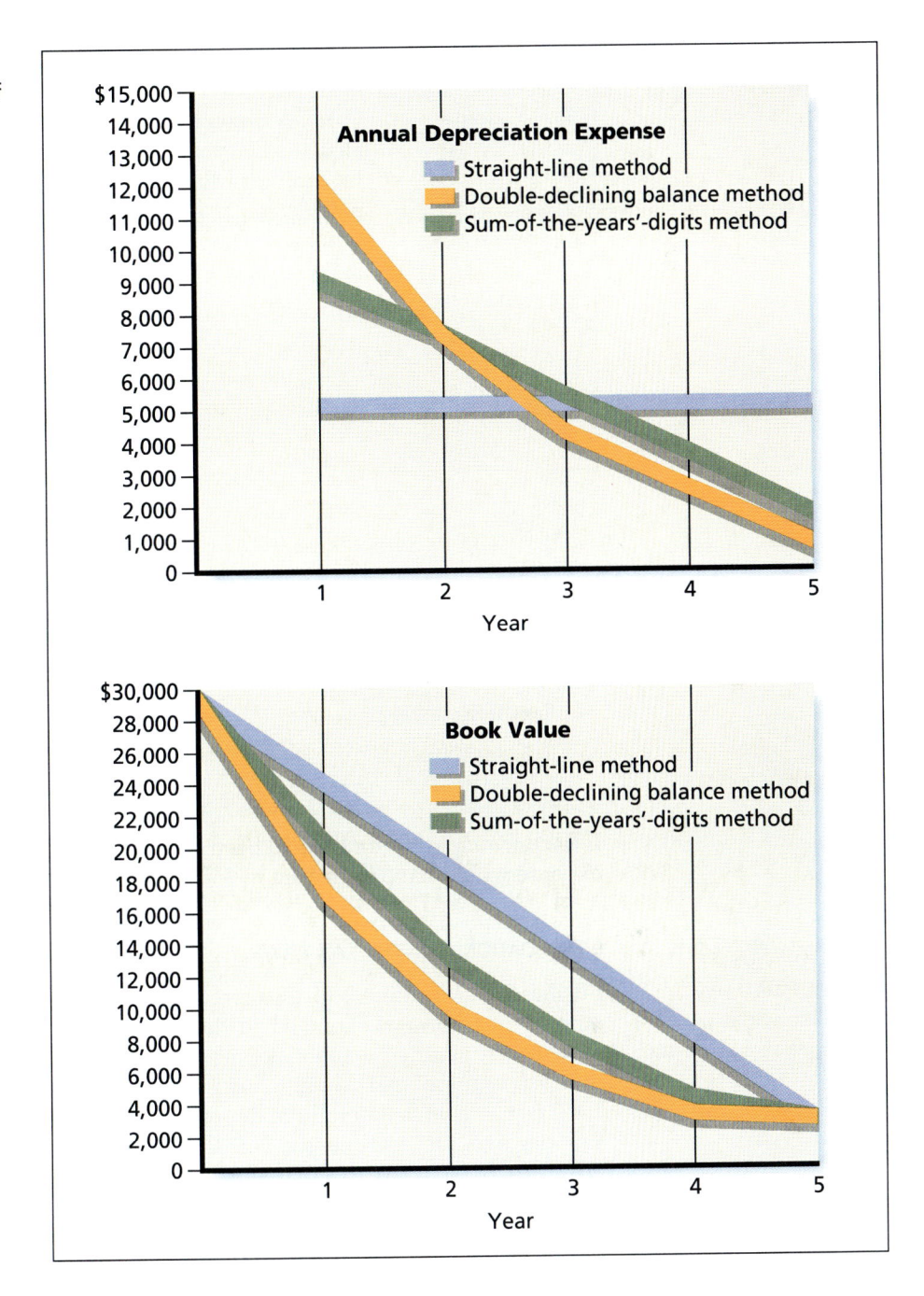

Annual Depreciation Expense
- Straight-line method
- Double-declining balance method
- Sum-of-the-years'-digits method

Book Value
- Straight-line method
- Double-declining balance method
- Sum-of-the-years'-digits method

vice life. Assuming Patriot uses the straight-line depreciation method, depreciation of $100,000 [($5,000,000 − $1,000,000) ÷ 40] has been recorded annually for 10 years. The Accumulated Depreciation account as a result presently totals $1 million. Because of altered traffic patterns, management now anticipates a *remaining* service life of only 20 years. Beginning with the current accounting period, the revised depreciation expense will be $150,000 per year, computed as shown on page 416.

EXHIBIT 11–3
Comparison of Depreciation Policies

COMPANY	DEPRECIATION POLICY
Boise Cascade Corporation	Calculated by the units-of-output method for substantially all of the Company's paper and wood products manufacturing facilities. Other operations use the straight-line method.
Texas Instruments	Computed mainly by either the declining-balance method (primarily 150% declining balance) or by the sum-of-the-years'-digits method.
Zenith Electronics	Straight-line method for additions of plant and equipment with useful lives of eight years or more; accelerated methods for substantially all other plant and equipment items, including high-technology equipment that may be subject to rapid economic obsolescence.

Building cost	$5,000,000
Less: Residual value	1,000,000
Original depreciable base	$4,000,000
Less: Depreciation already taken	1,000,000
Remaining depreciable base	$3,000,000
Remaining life	20 years
Revised depreciation per year	$3,000,000 ÷ 20 = $150,000

If the remaining service life had been extended to 50 years, annual depreciation expense would have decreased to $60,000 ($3,000,000 ÷ 50).

DEPRECIATION AND THE TAX LAWS

6
Demonstrate a very basic knowledge of depreciation and the tax laws.

Businesses are entitled to a depreciation deduction when computing the amount of income taxes owed to the federal government. Such a deduction reduces a company's taxable income and associated income tax payments and thus leaves more cash available for purposes of investment.

The tax laws that pertain to depreciation have changed over the years. Not too long ago, for example, the U.S. Congress enacted a new **Accelerated Cost Recovery System (ACRS)** that allowed for a more rapid write-off of asset cost than was previously possible. The system's provisions were later fine-tuned by the Tax Reform Act of 1986, to become what is known as **Modified ACRS** or **MACRS** (pronounced "makers"). More than likely this legislation will change further as our economy, federal deficit, and trade imbalance come under increased scrutiny in Washington.

The Modified Accelerated Cost Recovery System allows companies to depreciate assets over specified predetermined "recovery periods" when computing taxable income. These recovery periods are 3, 5, 7, or 10 years, among others, and depend on the asset in question. For example, automobiles and light-duty trucks have a five-year recovery period (i.e., are said to be "five-year property"), while most machinery, equipment, and furniture are written off over seven years. In general, the recovery period of an asset is shorter than the service life estimate, thereby permitting a business to reap quicker tax savings. MACRS also speeds up the process of cost recovery by using rates that reflect a specialized accelerated depreciation method, namely, a form of declining balance.

MACRS was designed, in part, to spur taxpayer investment in plant and equipment and makes no attempt to correctly match costs and revenues. As such, it is employed in the preparation of income tax returns and should not be used in a company's financial statements.[4]

LEASES

7 Recognize the issues related to accounting for leases.

Thus far, the chapter's discussion has focused on a situation where a company purchases its assets outright and depreciates them over time. Businesses are faced with several options when acquiring the services of long-term assets, one of which is some form of lease agreement. Recent statistics have shown that leasing has become extremely popular, with a vast majority of large American companies now pursuing this alternative. Items that may be acquired through this means include automobiles, airplanes, office equipment, and machinery.

A lease is an arrangement that allows one party, the *lessee*, to use the assets of another party, the *lessor*, for a stated period of time. Leasing has grown in significance even though in the long run it is usually more expensive than purchasing. From the lessee's viewpoint, leasing offers several advantages:

1. Lease payments are generally 100% tax deductible in the year the amounts are paid.
2. A lease arrangement often permits 100% financing. That is, no down payment may be necessary.
3. The risk of obsolescence on the leased asset rests with the lessor.

OPERATING LEASES VERSUS CAPITAL LEASES

There are two general categories of leases: operating and capital. Under an operating lease, the lessee obtains the right to use leased property for a limited period of time and treats amounts paid under the agreement as expense. The lessor, in turn, recognizes amounts received as revenue and retains the leased asset on its balance sheet. The contract signed by a person who rents a car for a day, a week, or some other short period of time is an example of an operating lease.

In contrast, many lease agreements provide usage rights for nearly the entire service life of the leased asset. Such agreements frequently contain a provision for the lessee to acquire the property at a bargain purchase price upon conclusion of the contract term. Leases that meet these or other specific criteria

---

[4] To achieve consistency between a company's tax return and income statement, many small businesses use MACRS for both tax *and* financial reporting. Although theoretically deficient, this practice is followed when cost recovery amounts are relatively insignificant and do not vary greatly from those computed under conventional depreciation methods.

are known as capital leases.[5] A careful study of a capital lease reveals the lessee is really acquiring an asset through an installment purchase plan. Yet prior to the mid-1970s, long-term lessees were not required to disclose the asset and obligation for future lease payments (a liability) on their balance sheets. This practice gave rise to the term *off balance-sheet financing*. Under current regulations, however, the lessee must now record both the assets leased under a capital lease agreement and the liability to the lessor.

ACCOUNTING FOR CAPITAL LEASES

Although the details of accounting for capital leases are quite complex, you already have a frame of reference to understand the necessary fundamentals. We have indicated that a capital lease is similar to an installment purchase, with the lessee recording the asset leased (i.e., "purchased"), along with the related obligation to the lessor. A typical journal entry would be as follows (the amount is assumed):

Equipment	650,000	
Lease Obligation		650,000
To record long-term capital lease.		

After the initial recording, the lessee will depreciate the asset by using one of the depreciation methods discussed earlier in the chapter.

Turning to the liability, the required accounting is essentially the same as the accounting for a long-term loan. Each lease payment is allocated between principal and interest, and interest is calculated as a percentage of the outstanding balance due the lessor. Payments would be recorded in the following manner (again, the amounts are assumed):

Interest Expense	5,500	
Lease Obligation	4,800	
Cash		10,300
To record monthly lease payment, including interest.		

The following excerpt from a recent annual report of Scott Paper Company provides a representative example of the disclosure that is typically given to capital leases:

> A capital lease transfers substantially all of the benefits and risks of ownership of the leased property to the Company. On the Company's consolidated balance sheet, the following amounts of capitalized leases are included in plant assets and the related obligations are included in debt:
>
> | | (MILLIONS) |
> |---|---|
> | Plant assets under capital leases | $ 58.1 |
> | Accumulated depreciation | (30.2) |
> | Net capital leases | $ 27.9 |

---

[5] See "Accounting for Leases," *Statement of Financial Accounting Standards No. 13*, Financial Accounting Standards Board, Norwalk, Conn., 1976.

Current lease obligations	$ 6.4
Long-term lease obligations	12.9
Capital lease obligations	$19.3

All other leases are accounted for as operating expenses . . . .

END-OF-CHAPTER REVIEW

LEARNING OBJECTIVES: THE KEY POINTS

1. **Discuss the nature of property, plant, and equipment and determine the cost of long-lived assets.** Property, plant, and equipment consist of various assets that are (1) used in a business and (2) benefit several accounting periods. In essence, the assets can be viewed as long-term prepaid expenses.

    Expenditures that benefit future years become part of an asset's cost. Such items include acquisition expenditures and related amounts needed to ready the asset for business use (e.g., freight, insurance while in transit, and installation). In contrast, items that fail to provide future economic benefits are expensed when incurred. A typical example is the cost incurred to repair a damaged asset, assuming the damage occurred during installation.

    Lump-sum purchases involve the acquisition of several assets for a single price. For reporting and depreciation purposes, the amount paid (or to be paid) must be allocated among the various assets acquired. The necessary apportionment is generally made on the basis of an individual asset's appraised value relative to the appraised value of the entire purchase.

2. **Explain the concept of depreciation and recognize the factors that affect service life.** Accountants define depreciation as the allocation of cost of long-lived assets over an estimated service life. Because depreciation makes no attempt to reflect market values in a company's accounting records, it is said to be a process of allocation, not valuation.

    The factors of physical deterioration, obsolescence, and inadequacy must be considered when estimating an asset's service life. Physical deterioration, often called "wear and tear," is caused by asset use and usually sets the maximum limit for the estimate of service life. Obsolescence, a technological factor related to being out of date, often shortens the service life of an asset to be less than the physical life. Finally, inadequacy relates to an asset's inability to meet expected service needs in a competitive environment.

3. **Compute depreciation by using the straight-line, units-of-output, declining-balance, and sum-of-the-years'-digits methods.** With the popular straight-line method, an equal amount of an asset's depreciable base (cost minus residual value) is allocated to each accounting period. In contrast, with the units-of-output method, the depreciation write-off is based on asset use. A depreciation rate is first calculated by dividing the depreciable base by the total estimated output during the service life. The rate is then multiplied by the yearly usage to arrive at depreciation expense.

    The two remaining methods, declining-balance and sum-of-the-years'-digits, are accelerated methods, which generate more depreciation in the early years of an asset's life and less in later years. With declining-balance, a fixed depreciation rate (twice the straight-line rate with double-declining balance) is applied each year to a declining book value. In contrast, the sum-of-the-years'-digits approach uses successively lower rates (fractions) and a constant base (cost minus residual value).

4. **Identify the financial-reporting issues related to the various depreciation methods.** The depreciation method selected affects business income. Conceptually, the method chosen should be the one that best parallels the services delivered or benefits provided by an asset, thereby achieving a proper matching of revenues and expenses. Practically, however, many firms use the straight-line method to help portray financial stability and smooth earnings over time.

5. **Revise a depreciation rate.** Companies often find that original estimates of service life and/or residual value are incorrect and need revision. When this situation occurs, the new estimates are used to determine depreciation expense. Such changes require the remaining depreciable base to be spread over the new estimate of remaining service life, with no corrections being made to prior years' depreciation amounts.

6. **Demonstrate a very basic knowledge of depreciation and the tax laws.** Depreciation is a deductible expense on a company's federal income tax return. Businesses generally employ the Modified Accelerated Cost Recovery System (MACRS) for tax purposes, which gives rise to quicker tax savings from shortened asset recovery periods and a specialized accelerated write-off. Quicker tax savings are attractive to an entity because of available investment opportunities.

7. **Recognize the issues related to accounting for leases.** A lease is an agreement that allows one party, the lessee, to use the assets of another party, the lessor, for a stated period of time. With an operating lease, the lessee obtains the right to use leased property for a limited time and treats the amounts paid to the lessor as an expense. The lessor recognizes the amounts received as revenue and retains the leased asset on its balance sheet. Alternatively, capital leases are structured so that the lessee is, in substance, acquiring an asset through an installment purchase plan. The lessee therefore records the leased asset on its balance sheet, along with the accompanying liability to the lessor.

KEY TERMS AND CONCEPTS: A QUICK OVERVIEW

accelerated depreciation methods   Methods that yield relatively large amounts of depreciation in the early years of asset use and smaller amounts in later years. (p. 411)

book value   The amount that an asset is carried at in the accounting records—namely, cost minus accumulated depreciation. (p. 410)

capital lease   A lease agreement under which the lessee is, in substance, acquiring an asset via an installment purchase plan. (p. 418)

declining-balance method   A method of depreciation by which a fixed depreciation rate is applied to the remaining book value each period. (p. 412)

depreciable base   The cost of an item of plant and equipment minus any residual value. (p. 409)

depreciation   The process used to allocate the cost of long-lived items of plant and equipment to the accounting periods benefited. (p. 407)

double-declining balance depreciation   A method of accelerated depreciation in which the straight-line depreciation rate is doubled and applied against the remaining book value (i.e., a declining balance) each period. (p. 412)

inadequacy   The inability of a depreciable asset to meet the competitive needs of a business. (p. 407)

land improvements   Improvements made to land, such as parking lots and lawn sprinkler systems. (p. 405)

lease An agreement that allows the lessee to use the assets of the lessor for a stated period of time. (p. 417)

lump-sum purchase The purchase of a number of assets together for a single amount. (p. 405)

materiality A concept dictating that an accountant must judge the impact and importance of each transaction (or event) to determine its proper handling in the accounting records. Minor items are treated in the most expedient manner possible. (p. 406)

Modified Accelerated Cost Recovery System (MACRS) A system used to write off (i.e., depreciate) the cost of long-term assets; employed for tax purposes only. (p. 416)

operating lease A lease agreement under which the lessee obtains the right to use leased property for a very limited period of time. (p. 417)

property, plant, and equipment Assets with long lives acquired for use in business operations and not held for resale to customers. (p. 403)

residual value The amount that a business expects to receive upon disposal of an asset at the end of the asset's life. (p. 409)

service life The period of time that depreciable assets provide service to a business; also known as the economic or useful life. (p. 407)

straight-line depreciation A depreciation method by which the cost of a depreciable asset, minus residual value, is allocated equally over the estimated service life. (p. 409)

sum-of-the-years'-digits depreciation An accelerated method of depreciation in which a smaller fraction is applied against an asset's cost, minus residual value, each period. (p. 412)

units-of-output depreciation A depreciation method by which the cost of a depreciable asset, minus residual value, is allocated to the accounting periods benefited based on output (miles, hours, number of times used, and so forth). (p. 410)

Chapter Quiz

The five questions that follow relate to several issues raised in the chapter. Test your knowledge of the issues by selecting the best answer. (The answers appear on p. 435.)

1. A company financed a land purchase by paying $120,000 cash and assuming a $100,000 mortgage payable. County fees to record the transfer of the land to the buyer totaled $150. Costs to clear the land of rocks and trees amounted to $850. The recorded cost of the land is:
   a. $120,000.
   b. $220,000.
   c. $220,850.
   d. $221,000.

2. Depreciation is:
   a. a system of cost allocation, not valuation.
   b. a system of valuation.
   c. recorded in an effort to reduce assets to their fair market value.
   d. based on an asset's cost and residual value, but not service life.

3. A machine that was purchased four years ago for $45,000 has an accumulated depreciation balance of $8,000 and a residual value of $5,000. Assuming use of straight-line depreciation, the machine's estimated service life:
   a. is 4 years.
   b. is 8 years.
   c. is 20 years.
   d. cannot be determined from the above facts.

4. Tiger Lines purchased and began depreciating a new truck on April 1, 19X4. The truck, which cost $60,000, had a five-year service life and a $12,000 residual value. Assuming use of the double-declining balance method, what is the 19X5 depreciation expense?
   a. $13,440.
   b. $14,400.
   c. $16,800.
   d. $18,000.

5. Revising a depreciation rate because of a change in a service life estimate:
   a. requires the correction of prior years' financial statements.
   b. involves allocating the remaining depreciable base over the future years of use.
   c. requires that sufficient cash be available to replace the asset at the end of the new service life.
   d. is permitted only if the service life is shortened.

SUMMARY PROBLEM

On January 1, 19X1, Hardy Company acquired an automatic can labeler for $63,000, which included shipping charges of $1,000. The machine has an estimated service life of five years (or 30,000 hours of operation) and a residual value of $6,000. Insurance on the machine while in transit was $300; insurance against fire and water damage for one year amounted to $500. Finally, installation costs were $2,000 and test runs totaled $700.

During the five years of use (19X1–19X5), the machine was operated for 6,300, 6,000, 5,800, 5,700, and 6,200 hours, respectively.

Instructions

a. Compute the machine's cost.
b. Rounding final calculations to the nearest dollar, compute yearly depreciation expense by using each of the following methods: (1) straight-line; (2) units-of-output; (3) double-declining balance; and (4) sum-of-the-years'-digits.
c. Explain why equipment is depreciated as opposed to being expensed entirely in the year of acquisition.

Solution

a.
Purchase price (including shipping)	$63,000
Insurance in transit	300
Installation	2,000
Test runs	700
Total cost	$66,000

b. (1) Straight-line:

$$\frac{\text{Cost} - \text{Residual Value}}{\text{Service Life in Years}} = \text{Annual Depreciation}$$

$$\frac{\$66,000 - \$6,000}{5 \text{ years}} = \$12,000 \text{ per year}$$

(2) Units-of-output:

$$\frac{\text{Cost} - \text{Residual Value}}{\text{Service Life in Output}} = \text{Depreciation per Unit of Output}$$

$$\frac{\$66,000 - \$6,000}{30,000 \text{ hours}} = \$2.00 \text{ per hour}$$

YEAR	HOURS OF OPERATION	×	DEPRECIATION PER HOUR	=	DEPRECIATION EXPENSE
19X1	6,300		$2.00		$12,600
19X2	6,000		2.00		12,000
19X3	5,800		2.00		11,600
19X4	5,700		2.00		11,400
19X5	6,200		2.00		12,400

(3) Double-declining balance:

5-year life = 1/5 = 20%; 20% × 2 = 40% depreciation rate

YEAR	DEPRECIATION EXPENSE	ACCUMULATED DEPRECIATION	BOOK VALUE
			$66,000
19X1	$26,400 ($66,000 × 40%)	$26,400	39,600
19X2	15,840 ($39,600 × 40%)	42,240	23,760
19X3	9,504 ($23,760 × 40%)	51,744	14,256
19X4	5,702 ($14,256 × 40%)	57,446	8,554
19X5	2,554 ($8,554 − $6,000)*	60,000	6,000

* $8,554 × 40% would reduce the book value below residual value.

(4) Sum-of-the-years'-digits:

YEAR	DEPRECIATION EXPENSE
19X1	$20,000 ($60,000 × 5/15)
19X2	16,000 ($60,000 × 4/15)
19X3	12,000 ($60,000 × 3/15)
19X4	8,000 ($60,000 × 2/15)
19X5	4,000 ($60,000 × 1/15)

c. Equipment has a long life and years of future service potential. Expensing the entire cost when acquired would result in a mismatch of revenues and expenses on the income statement.

ASSIGNMENT MATERIAL

QUESTIONS

Q11–1 Do all items of property, plant, and equipment have a limited life? Explain.

Q11–2 How is the acquisition cost of a machine determined? Which of the following items are included in the cost of an asset: purchase price, freight charges, cost of installation, medical costs of injured installer, special electrical wiring?

Q11–3 Explain the proper treatment of interest costs related to the purchase of a new automobile.

Q11–4 How should the cost of property, plant, and equipment acquired in a lump-sum purchase be apportioned to the individual assets? Why is such a division necessary?

Q11-5 Contrast the accounting treatments for land and land improvements.

Q11-6 How are long-lived, low-cost items (e.g., pencil sharpeners and wastebaskets) normally handled in the accounting records?

Q11-7 Briefly discuss the concept of materiality.

Q11-8 How is the service life of depreciable plant and equipment determined? Discuss the factors of physical deterioration, obsolescence, and inadequacy in the establishment of service lives.

Q11-9 Define the term "depreciable base."

Q11-10 Is the units-of-output method of depreciation more appropriate to use for some items of plant and equipment than for others? Why or why not?

Q11-11 Briefly explain the concept of accelerated depreciation.

Q11-12 How does a change in the estimated remaining service life of a piece of equipment affect past and future depreciation amounts?

Q11-13 What is the Modified Accelerated Cost Recovery System (MACRS)? Can MACRS be used for financial reporting? Briefly discuss.

Q11-14 What is meant by the term "recovery period," as related to the Modified Accelerated Cost Recovery System?

Q11-15 A student once commented, "All leases are fundamentally alike, with amounts paid by the lessee recorded as an expense of the period." Evaluate the student's remark.

EXERCISES

E11-1 Determining acquisition cost (L.O. 1)

Camden Fabricating Company recently purchased a state-of-the-art metal-cutting tool that had an invoice price of $300,000. Other data related to the machine were as follows:

Freight and installation costs	$9,500
Materials used during setup and initial testing	800
Finger guards installed around cutting head	2,500
Property taxes paid for first year of ownership	4,500
Advertising brochure to inform customers of new cutting capabilities	1,500

a. Determine the cost at which the machine should be recorded.
b. Briefly describe and justify the proper treatment of the items that you excluded in part (a).

E11-2 Lump-sum purchase (L.O. 1)

You recently purchased the contents of a barber shop for use in a new location of your hair-cutting franchise, Shear Delight. Prior to negotiations for the purchase, you hired a consultant to appraise the shop's assets. The results of the appraisal are as follows:

Reception area furniture	$ 1,000
Product display racks	—
Plumbing and apparatus	16,000
Barber furniture and fixtures	17,000
Equipment	10,000
Linens and supplies	6,000

On the basis of these figures, you offered and paid $45,000 to acquire the assets.

a. Allocate the purchase price among the various assets.
b. The franchise's chart of accounts revealed the following account titles, among others: Furniture and Fixtures, Plumbing and Apparatus, Other Equipment, and Linens and Supplies. Prepare a journal entry to record the acquisition.

E11–3 Asset acquisition and straight-line depreciation (L.O. 1, 3)

AFCO acquired new equipment on October 1, 19X3, for use in multimedia sales presentations. The invoice cost of the equipment was $32,000. Installation charges were $1,200, freight and insurance costs related to delivery totaled $600, and testing and adjusting by an outside engineering firm cost $2,200. The equipment has a residual value of $12,000, a service life of only four years because of anticipated technological advances, and a physical life of 10 years.

a. Assuming all expenditures were for cash, record the necessary journal entry to enter the equipment in the accounting records.
b. Record the entry for straight-line depreciation at the end of 19X3.
c. How would the equipment and its related depreciation account appear on a balance sheet as of December 31, 19X4? Use proper amounts.

E11–4 Depreciation methods (L.O. 3)

Betsy Ross Enterprises purchased a delivery van for $30,000 on January 1, 19X7. The van was estimated to have a service life of five years and a residual value of $6,000. The company is planning to drive the van 20,000 miles annually.

Compute depreciation expense for 19X8 by using each of the following methods:

a. Units-of-output, assuming 17,000 miles were driven during 19X8
b. Straight-line
c. Sum-of-the-years'-digits
d. Double-declining balance

E11–5 Depreciation computations (L.O. 3)

Alpha Alpha Alpha, a college fraternity, purchased a new heavy-duty washing machine on January 1, 19X3. The machine, which cost $1,000, had an estimated residual value of $100 and an estimated service life of four years (1,800 washing cycles). Calculate the following:

a. The machine's book value on December 31, 19X5, assuming use of the straight-line depreciation method.
b. Depreciation expense for 19X4, assuming use of the units-of-output depreciation method. Actual washing cycles in 19X4 totaled 500.
c. Accumulated depreciation on December 31, 19X5, assuming use of the double-declining balance depreciation method.
d. Depreciation expense in 19X4 and 19X5, assuming use of the sum-of-the-years'-digits depreciation method.

E11–6 Accelerated depreciation; partial periods (L.O. 3)

Hawn Enterprises purchased a special device on June 1, 19X4, that will be depreciated over a service life of four years. The device cost $42,000 and has a $6,000 estimated residual value.

a. Calculate depreciation expense for the year ended December 31, 19X4, by using the sum-of-the-years'-digits and double-declining balance methods.
b. Compute the firm's 19X5 depreciation expense by using the sum-of-the-years'-digits and double-declining balance methods.

E11–7 Depreciation concepts (L.O. 2, 3, 4)
Evaluate the comments that follow as being True or False. If the comment is false, briefly explain why.

a. Depreciation is recorded over the years so that a company's asset valuations are reduced to reflect lower market values.
b. A depreciable asset's cost, minus accumulated depreciation, equals book value.
c. An asset's depreciable base and book value are identical at the end of the asset's service life.
d. A company that uses accelerated depreciation will find that depreciation write-offs speed up, with increased amounts occurring in the later years of an asset's service life.
e. Straight-line depreciation is probably the most popular accelerated depreciation method used by businesses.

E11–8 Selection of a depreciation method (L.O. 4)
At the beginning of the current year, Hyde Construction purchased six pickup trucks for use by job supervisors. Hyde's owner has called your accounting firm to ask how these trucks should be depreciated.

a. List the possible depreciation methods that the company might consider for use in its financial statements.
b. Present several arguments favoring the use of:
   (1) Straight-line depreciation.
   (2) Accelerated depreciation.

E11–9 Revisions of depreciation (L.O. 5)
The Pub bought a $20,000 cooker one year ago, at the beginning of 19X3. At the time of acquisition, the service life and residual value were estimated to be five years and $5,000, respectively. Because of strong product demand, management now anticipates that the cooker will have to be replaced by a larger unit on January 1, 19X6. Residual value at that time is estimated at $8,000.

Calculate the revised 19X4 depreciation expense for the cooker.

E11–10 Leases and lease accounting (L.O. 7)
Henry Company, a small family-owned corporation, is studying the possibility of signing a long-term lease for two new delivery vehicles. Walter Henry, the company's president, is skeptical of leasing and has always believed in the outright purchase of needed property, plant, and equipment.

a. Discuss the advantages of leasing from the firm's viewpoint.
b. Discuss the basic difference between an operating lease and a capital lease.
c. Would Henry's lease probably be accounted for as an operating lease or a capital lease? Why?
d. Discuss the balance sheet impact, if any, of Henry's lease.

E11–11 Lease accounting issues (L.O. 7)
Acer Network Corporation recently entered into two separate lease agreements. One of these agreements was for occupancy of office space at $800 per month; the other was for

use of a copy machine at $200 per month. Acer's accountant evaluated details of the lease agreements and determined that the office space lease should be accounted for as an operating lease. The copy machine agreement, in contrast, was a capital lease, with the following entry being made in the accounting records:

Copy Machine	6,000	
Lease Obligation		6,000

To record long-term capital lease.

a. Prepare Acer's journal entry for the first month's rent of the office space.
b. Given that the copy machine will provide benefits over time, how should the $6,000 asset cost be handled in the accounting records?

PROBLEMS

Series A

P11–A1 Cost treatment (L.O. 1)

Steinberg Company incurred the following costs in connection with its property, plant, and equipment:

1. Cost of sprinkler system for landscaping.
2. Fine for fire code violation in building.
3. Architect's fees for design of new building wing.
4. Freight cost on office equipment while in transit.
5. Damage to office equipment during installation.
6. Cost of parking lot constructed on property.
7. Cost of plastic name tags used to identify building visitors.
8. Cost of three wastepaper baskets purchased for building lobby use.
9. Cost of water sprinklers installed throughout building.
10. Real estate commissions related to land acquisition.
11. Advertising costs to celebrate opening of building addition.
12. Interest incurred to purchase new office equipment on account.
13. Cost to widen building doorway so that office equipment could be installed.

Instructions

Indicate whether the preceding items should be included in the Land account, Land Improvements account, Building account, Office Equipment account, or some other account.

P11–A2 Allocation of costs to asset accounts; lump-sum purchase (L.O. 1)

Cheryl Livingston recently acquired a large Victorian house that she will renovate for use as a bed and breakfast inn. The following transactions occurred during the first five months of the current year:

Jan. 4 Purchased the land, house, and accompanying land improvements for $500,000. The property, which had cost the previous owner $300,000, was appraised recently for $600,000. Forty-five percent of the appraisal value pertained to the land, 40% to the house, and 15% to the improvements.

10 Completed the transaction of January 4; paid $2,800 for legal and title fees. (*Hint:* Allocate this amount among the assets acquired on the basis of appraisal values.)

11 Acquired a one-year fire insurance policy for $3,000 and a policy for miscellaneous liabilities, $2,000.

Feb. 3 Paid a contractor $70,000 for the renovation work.
Mar. 3 Hired an interior designer to plan and order the furnishings for the inn. Paid a $20,000 fee for these services.
    31 Paid $9,500 as follows: $5,000 for an underground sprinkler system and $4,500 for paving a parking area.
Apr. 20 Purchased office equipment for $14,500. Also paid a technician $300 to wire and install the equipment.
    30 Received $180,000 of furniture ordered by the decorator. The trucking company required a $3,000 payment for shipping and handling charges before unloading the goods.
May 25 Paid $1,350 of interest on a bank loan. The loan was used to finance the furniture acquisition.
    31 Purchased $125 of stationery to be placed in guest rooms.

Instructions

Assign appropriate costs to the Land, Land Improvements, Building, and Furniture & Equipment accounts by using the format that follows. Total each column. If a cost is not charged to one of the preceding accounts, indicate how the expenditure should be treated.

DATE	LAND	LAND IMPROVEMENTS	BUILDING	FURNITURE & EQUIPMENT
	$	$	$	$

P11–A3 Depreciation computations; change in estimate (L.O. 1, 3, 5)

Aussie Imports purchased a specialized piece of machinery for $50,000 on January 1, 19X3. At the time of acquisition, the machine was estimated to have a service life of five years (25,000 operating hours) and a residual value of $5,000. During the five years of operation (19X3–19X7), the machine was used for 5,100, 4,800, 3,200, 6,000, and 5,900 hours, respectively.

Instructions

a. Compute depreciation for 19X3–19X7 by using the following methods: straight-line; units-of-output; double-declining balance; and sum-of-the-years'-digits.
b. On January 1, 19X5, management shortened the remaining service life of the machine to 20 months. Assuming use of the straight-line method, compute the company's depreciation expense for 19X5.
c. Briefly describe what you would have done differently in part (a) if Aussie Imports had paid $47,800 for the machinery rather than $50,000. In addition, assume that the company incurred $800 of freight charges, $1,400 for machine setup and testing, and $300 for insurance during the first year of use.

P11–A4 Depreciation calculations, partial periods (L.O. 3)

Executive Lift, an air shuttle service, has three aircraft. Data on the aircraft follow.

	CHEYENNE	FALCON	CESSNA
Date acquired	11/2/X4	10/1/X5	2/1/X6
Service life (years)	16	20	25
Depreciation method	SL	SYD	DDB
Cost	$3,000,000	$5,120,000	$6,300,000
Residual value	600,000	500,000	900,000

Instructions

a. Calculate depreciation expense for the 12-month period ended December 31, 19X7.
b. Compute the December 31, 19X7, accumulated depreciation and book value of each aircraft.

P11–A5 Depreciation methods, partial periods (L.O. 3)

Epson Company purchased a delivery truck for $50,000 on October 1, 19X1. The truck had a residual value of $12,500 and a five-year (200,000-mile) service life. Miles driven during 19X1, 19X2, and the first quarter of 19X3 totaled 9,000, 40,000, and 6,800, respectively. Four different depreciation expense figures for the quarter ended March 31, 19X3, follow.

Method A	$1,275
Method B	2,500
Method C	1,875
Method D	2,700

Instructions

Determine which depreciation method (straight-line, units-of-output, double-declining balance, or sum-of-the-years'-digits) was used to compute each of the preceding expense figures. Epson has a December 31 year-end.

P11–A6 Acquisition cost, errors, depreciation (L.O. 1, 3)

Bubba Clark, a commercial fisherman, bought a used fishing boat for $300,000 at the beginning of 19X1. He estimated that the boat would have a 15-year service life and an $87,000 residual value. Clark made the following additional expenditures before putting the boat in service:

Sales tax	$18,000
Installation of electronic equipment	6,000
Delivery charge	3,000
Annual licenses and registration	2,500
Fuel and supplies	1,500
	$31,000

Clark's business manager has proposed the following disclosure of the boat on the December 31, 19X1, balance sheet:

Boat	$331,000
Less: Depreciation expense	16,267
	$314,733

Depreciation was calculated by using the straight-line method.

Instructions

a. The business manager has made several accounting errors. Identify the errors.
b. Prepare a journal entry to correct the balance in the Boat account at year-end. Assume that all fuel and supplies have been consumed.
c. Present the proper disclosure of the vessel on the December 31, 19X1, balance sheet.

Series B

P11–B1 Cost treatment (L.O. 1)

Consider the following costs of the Jacksonville Company:

1. Cost of three antique works of art for the company's new building.
2. Purchase price of the land and new building.
3. Cost of outside lighting fixtures on the new building's grounds.
4. Cost of initial test runs of new equipment.
5. Interest incurred to purchase equipment on credit.
6. Traffic fines paid by Jacksonville for a driver who was delivering equipment to the new building.
7. Cost of grading land prior to construction.
8. Current property taxes on the land and building.
9. Installation costs of new machinery.
10. Cost of new security fences installed around the parking lot.
11. Cost of delinquent property taxes assumed when purchasing land.
12. The current month's premium for building fire and liability insurance.
13. Significant overhaul costs related to acquisition of used machinery; needed to ready the machinery for its intended use.
14. Attorney's fees related to land acquisition.

Instructions

a. Which of the preceding costs should be charged to asset accounts?
b. For the costs that you identified in part (a), indicate which asset account(s) should be increased.

P11–B2 Allocation of costs to plant asset accounts; lump-sum purchase (L.O. 1)

The following transactions relate to the Sabre Company for 19X5:

Jan. 10	Purchased new machinery for $12,000 cash. Freight charges amounted to $600, special electrical wiring cost $4,000, and test runs totaled $800.
Feb. 19	Purchased developed property from Baxter Company for $1 million. On the date of acquisition, the appraised value of the property totaled $1.5 million and was subdivided as follows: land, $750,000; land improvements, $60,000; and building, $690,000.
Mar. 21	Acquired a 40-year-old apartment building for $1.3 million. The building had cost the seller only $400,000 several years ago.
Apr. 3	Installed $12,000 of security fencing around the apartment.
May 14	Acquired a one-year fire insurance policy on the apartment building for $7,000.
June 16	Paid $50,000 to the Advance Paving Company to construct a parking lot for the apartment tenants.
July 8	Incurred $11,000 of interest on monies borrowed to finance the apartment building acquisition on March 21.
Aug. 9	Acquired a parcel of land by securing a $290,000 mortgage payable and paying $10,000 of delinquent property taxes to Duval County.
Sept. 15	Purchased several smoke detectors for the apartment from a mail-order firm. The detectors cost $64, plus a $6 shipping fee.

Instructions

Assign appropriate costs to the Land, Land Improvements, Building, and Equipment accounts by using the format that follows. Obtain year-end totals. If a cost is not charged to the preceding accounts, indicate how the expenditure should be treated.

Date	Land	Land Improvements	Building	Equipment
	$	$	$	$

P11–B3 Depreciation computations; change in estimate (L.O. 1, 3, 5)

On January 1, 19X2, Furrell Company bought a new $9 million jet plane to transport executives. The jet had an estimated service life of five years (10 million air miles) and an estimated residual value of $900,000. Actual air miles flown during the service life (19X2–19X6) were:

Year	Air Miles
19X2	4,000,000
19X3	2,500,000
19X4	2,000,000
19X5	1,000,000
19X6	500,000

Instructions

a. Compute depreciation for 19X2–19X6 by using the following methods: straight-line; units-of-output; double-declining balance; and sum-of-the-years'-digits.
b. On January 1, 19X5, management extended the remaining service life of the jet to four years. Assuming use of the straight-line method, compute the company's depreciation expense for 19X7.
c. Assume that Furrell's jet was used (rather than new) and required a $475,000 refurbishing before it was placed in service. How should the refurbishing cost be treated in the accounting records?

P11–B4 Depreciation calculations, partial periods (L.O. 3)

Empire Treats, Inc., a food wholesaler, operates three delivery vehicles in central Kansas. Data on the vehicles follow.

Vehicle	Date Acquired	Cost	Residual Value	Service Life (Years)	Depreciation Method
2-ton Chevrolet	8/31/X2	$21,000	$ —	7	Straight-line
2-ton Dodge	5/1/X1	15,000	1,000	5	Double-declining balance
2-ton Ford	1/31/X1	22,000	4,000	4	Sum-of-the-years'-digits

Instructions

a. Calculate depreciation expense for the 12-month period ended December 31, 19X3.
b. Compute the December 31, 19X3, accumulated depreciation and book value of each vehicle.

P11–B5 Depreciation methods, partial periods (L.O. 3)

Sheppard Exports purchased an $8,000 machine on April 1, 19X1. The machine had a residual value of $800 and a four-year (7,500-hour) service life. Hours used during 19X1 and the first nine months of 19X2 totaled 3,000 and 1,600, respectively. Sheppard rounds all final depreciation calculations to the nearest dollar and has a December 31 year-end.

Instructions

Identify which method (straight-line, units-of-output, double-declining balance, or sum-of-the-years'-digits) is appropriate for Sheppard if the company:

a. Desires to use accelerated depreciation and maximize the write-off (i.e., have the largest balance in the Accumulated Depreciation account) as of September 30, 19X2. What will this balance be?
b. Wants to base depreciation on machine usage. How much depreciation expense will be recorded under this method by December 31, 19X1?
c. Desires to use a simple approach that results in the same expense figure from year to year. Calculate the total accumulated depreciation recorded under this method by December 31, 19X2.

P11–B6 Acquisition cost, errors, depreciation (L.O. 1, 3)

On January 1, 19X3, Mike Miller purchased a used combine for his farm. The combine cost $106,000, which includes $6,000 of sales taxes. As part of the purchase, the dealer agreed to recondition the equipment according to Miller's specifications. The following journal entry was made to record the acquisition:

Farm Equipment	106,000	
Reconditioning Expense	3,000	
Cash		19,000
Loan Payable		90,000

The farm's office manager has calculated depreciation by using the straight-line method, a 10-year service life, and a $19,000 residual value. The following presentation of the combine on the December 31, 19X3, balance sheet was proposed:

Farm equipment	$106,000
Plus: Accumulated depreciation	8,700*
	$114,700

* A review of the general ledger found an $8,700 credit balance in the Accumulated Depreciation account.

Instructions

a. Several errors were made when accounting for the combine. Identify the errors.
b. Was the farm's 19X3 net income overstated or understated as a result of these errors? By what amount?
c. Prepare the journal entries needed to correct and update the accounting records as of December 31, 19X3. Assume that the books have not yet been closed.

EXPANDING YOUR HORIZONS

EYH11–1 Variations in service lives (L.O. 2)

Different companies in the same industry often use different service lives for identical plant and equipment. Some financial analysts argue against this practice, maintaining that the same service life should be used.

Instructions

a. Study the annual reports of three companies in the same industry and determine the service lives of similar components of property, plant, and equipment. Such information is often disclosed in the notes that accompany the financial statements. Be prepared to report your findings to the class.
b. Generally speaking, do the differences in service lives have any effect on reported net income? Briefly explain.
c. What might cause some of the differences in service lives?

EYH11–2 Revision of service life (L.O. 5)

Companies often change the service-life estimates of plant and equipment. Not too long ago, for example, Southwest Airlines revised the estimated service lives of its Boeing 737–200 aircraft from 15 years to 15–19 years. This change increased reported earnings for the year.

Instructions

Study several annual reports and review the footnotes that accompany the financial statements. Find a company that recently revised the service life of its plant and equipment and, if disclosed, determine the rationale for the change. Be prepared to report your findings to the class.

EYH11–3 The popularity of leases (L.O. 7)

Leases are a common way to acquire the use of assets. Many different components of property, plant, and equipment can be leased—anything from delivery trucks to airplanes to copy machines.

Instructions

Contact two medium-size businesses and arrange for an interview with an individual knowledgeable about each company's leasing activities. Summarize your interviews in a one-page report and determine:

a. Why the firm has selected leasing rather than an outright purchase of assets.
b. The extent of assets leased by the company.
c. The biggest problem that the business has encountered with leasing.
d. Whether the company accounts for its leases as operating leases, capital leases, or both.

EYH11–4 Analysis of property and equipment investment, depreciation: Rubbermaid Incorporated and The Sherwin-Williams Company (L.O. 1, 3)

Rubbermaid Incorporated manufactures various plastic and rubber goods for consumer and commercial use. The company's products include desk sets, toys, lawn furniture, and a variety of storage containers. In contrast, Sherwin-Williams manufactures coatings and related items. The firm is perhaps best known among consumers for its paint products.

Instructions

By using the text's electronic data base, access the balance sheets and accompanying notes of both firms and answer the questions that follow. Unless otherwise indicated, responses should be based on data for the most recent year presented.

a. Compare the companies' gross dollar investment (before any deduction for accumulated depreciation) to the total assets owned. Which of the two firms has a greater percentage of its assets in the form of property, plant, and equipment?
b. What are the major categories of property, plant, and equipment disclosed by each firm?
c. What method of depreciation is each company using to depreciate its assets?
d. Do either of the companies reveal any information on the service lives that are being used to calculate depreciation? Briefly comment on your findings.
e. Do either of the firms have any "projects" in process with regard to plant and equipment? Briefly discuss and determine which company is currently more active in this area.

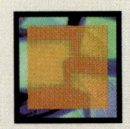

EYH11–5 Analysis of property and equipment investment, depreciation (L.O. 1, 3)

This problem is a duplication of Problem EYH11–4. It is based on two companies selected by your instructor.

Instructions

By using the text's electronic data base, access the specified companies' balance sheets and accompanying notes and focus on data for the most recent year reported. Answer requirements (a)–(e) of Problem EYH11–4.

EYH11–6 The concept of depreciation (L.O. 2)

Chung and Kia Moon, partners in Moon's Dry Cleaners, recently purchased a $30,000 neon sign to increase store traffic. The sign had a service life of 10 years, a physical life of 30 years if properly maintained, and zero residual value.

It is now one year after purchase. The Moons are distressed because the sign's current market value (i.e., "true" worth) is only $2,500. Part of this reduction in value is attributable to the sign's specialized message—one that is totally unique to Moon's Dry Cleaners.

The couple's office manager just reported that after considering sign depreciation of $27,500 ($30,000 – $2,500), the operation lost $8,900 for the year. Chung is concerned because he assured his financial backers that the business would be profitable.

Instructions

a. Should Chung be worried about the store's performance? Briefly explain, showing calculations to support your answer.
b. From an accounting perspective, what is depreciation?
c. After one year of use, the sign's book value and market value differed markedly. Present examples of two other assets where book value and market value would likely differ by a large amount one year after asset purchase.

COMMUNICATION OF ACCOUNTING INFORMATION

CAI11–1 Writing a memo report: General Motors Corporation (L.O. 3, 4)

Communication Principle: A memo report is a short in-house report with limited and specific purposes. In the exercise that follows, you will be writing such a report to your supervisor. Use the memo form and the organizational principle of purpose statements, support, and conclusions (see the communication principles on pp. 321 and 399). The report should be short, consisting of three to four paragraphs that contain all the information requested in the instructions.

Because you are addressing an expert audience, you may use terminology that most experts would know without definition or explanation. However, do not shortcut by eliminating transition words or pointers that tell the reader where you are and where you are going.

■ ■ ■ ■ ■ ■ ■ ■

General Motors (GM), the nation's largest domestic producer of automobiles, includes the following description of depreciation policies in its annual report:

> Depreciation is provided based on estimated useful lives of groups of property generally using accelerated methods, which accumulate depreciation of approximately two-thirds of the depreciable cost during the first half of the estimated useful lives.

Instructions

a. Your supervisor has just completed a reading of GM's annual report and has asked you to analyze the accelerated write-off of a $100,000 asset having no residual value. Determine the percentage of cost written off during the first half of service life by using both the double-declining balance and sum-of-the-years'-digits methods, assuming (1) a 4-year service life and (2) a 10-year service life. Comment on your findings.
b. Briefly explain to your supervisor the rationale that underlies the use of accelerated depreciation methods.

Answers to Chapter Quiz

1. d ($120,000 + $100,000 + $150 + $850)
2. a
3. c [$8,000 ÷ 4 years = $2,000 per year; ($45,000 − $5,000) ÷ $2,000 = 20 years]
4. c [5-year life = 20% per year; 20% × 2 = 40%; $60,000 × 40% × 9/12 = $18,000; ($60,000 − $18,000) × 40% = $16,800]
5. b

12 Property, Plant, and Equipment/Natural Resources/Intangibles

Learning Objectives

After studying this chapter, you should be able to:

1. Explain how plant and equipment costs incurred after asset acquisition are treated in the accounts.
2. Prepare journal entries to record discards and sales of property, plant, and equipment.
3. Account for exchanges of similar assets.
4. Exhibit a basic understanding of the issues related to asset impairment.
5. Calculate natural resource cost and depletion.
6. Recognize the various types of intangible assets and the need for amortization.

Ask any realtor to name three important factors when making a good real estate investment and you'll likely get the following response: location, location, and location. The same factors are essential to the success of an outdoor advertising company. Erecting a billboard in an undesirable location will often result in "Space for Rent" being plastered across the sign's face for a very long period of time. So why not choose only prime sites? When you're a relative newcomer in a crowded field, you've got a problem—a big time problem, as George Faris of Banner Advertising quickly discovered.

There are only so many choice sites. Compounding the situation, billboard construction depends on obtaining a permit from a local governing authority. Given that many municipalities have zoning laws that limit such displays, securing the proper authorization is difficult, if not impossible. George did learn that existing billboards in key areas were "grandfathered" and could remain in use no matter who owned them. Thus, one (and perhaps the only) way to solve the location problem was to acquire competitors' signs.

Banner, though, was a new firm and lacked the capital to purchase these assets outright. An alternative strategy was needed, and that strategy was to trade. Banner had to identify and lock up markets, then proceed to swap selected billboards with other firms. According to George, "It's like collecting a set of trading cards. Everyone wants at least one board at each key location within their geographic operating area. Having that one spot makes it much easier to sell a package deal to large clients that want to dominate their markets."

The exchange-type of transaction—whether it involves billboards, trucks, or office buildings—gives rise to several unique accounting problems. This chapter continues our discussion of property, plant, and equipment by addressing these problems and other related issues as well. We will also examine two other types of assets that provide long-term benefits to their owners: natural resources and intangibles.

PLANT AND EQUIPMENT COSTS AFTER ASSET ACQUISITION

The costs related to fixed assets often do not stop at acquisition. Many expenditures are made after buildings, machines, and various pieces of equipment have started to serve a business. For example, repairs are performed, new features are added to improve efficiency, major overhauls are undertaken, and parts are replaced.

The accountant must determine how to record these items. Whether they are added to the depreciable base of the asset or written off as expenses may have a significant impact on reported profitability for the period. Generally speaking, such amounts are categorized as either capital expenditures or revenue expenditures.

❶ Explain how plant and equipment costs incurred after asset acquisition are treated in the accounts.

Capital expenditures are costs that provide future economic benefits to a business. Future economic benefits are said to occur under the following conditions:

438

1. The service life of an asset is prolonged.
2. The quantity of services expected from an asset has increased.
3. The quality of services provided by an asset has improved.

Given their long-term nature, capital expenditures are debited to property, plant, and equipment accounts. This treatment results in an asset having a larger depreciable base, to be written off gradually in the years to come.

Expenditures that do not fulfill at least one of the three criteria just mentioned are known as revenue expenditures. These amounts benefit the current accounting period only and are thus immediately expensed. We will now explore the capital/revenue distinction with several commonly encountered items.

REPAIRS

Amounts spent to maintain the normal operating condition of an asset are termed repairs. Repairs include regular maintenance, minor parts replacement, painting, cleaning, and inspection. Repairs do not increase the future service potential of an asset; rather, such amounts assist in attaining the original service life estimate and anticipated operating efficiency. As a consequence, repair costs are debited to the Repairs Expense account when incurred.

ADDITIONS

Additions are items that will provide future benefits and be affixed to existing assets. Examples of additions include the installation of air conditioning in a building or vehicle and the construction of a new wing on a building. The cost of an addition is a capital expenditure and is therefore recorded in a property, plant, or equipment account (i.e., capitalized). Normally, the cost is entered in the same account as the original asset to simplify record keeping.

BETTERMENTS

Betterments, sometimes called improvements or extraordinary repairs, are expenditures that improve or increase the future service potential of an asset. Occasionally, a betterment occurs when a major part of an existing asset is replaced with a similar but superior component; for example, the installation of (1) a new, more efficient heating/cooling system in a building or (2) a new engine in a vehicle. In other cases, the betterment may involve an extraordinary repair such as a major overhaul. Extraordinary repairs normally extend the service life of an asset beyond the original estimate.

Often the difference between extraordinary repairs and ordinary repairs and maintenance is not readily evident. The accountant, though, must properly distinguish between these items, because their accounting treatment differs. Ordinary repairs, as we noted earlier, are expenses. In contrast, expenditures that prolong an asset's life are capitalized in the following manner.

An Example. Assume the Simmons Company acquired a freezer on January 1, 19X1, for $20,000. The freezer had an estimated service life of five years, with no residual value. Simmons has depreciated the asset for four years by using the straight-line method, resulting in the following balance sheet disclosure as of December 31, 19X4:

Freezer	$20,000	
Less: Accumulated depreciation	16,000	$4,000

On January 1, 19X5, a new motor costing $1,000 was installed, which extended the freezer's service life by one year. The cost of the new motor is *not* recorded in the Freezer account. Rather $1,000 is debited to Accumulated Depreciation in the manner shown.

Accumulated Depreciation: Freezer	1,000	
Cash		1,000
To record cost of new motor.		

This journal entry reduces the balance in the Accumulated Depreciation account to $15,000 ($16,000 − $1,000). The freezer's new book value of $5,000 ($20,000 − $15,000) will be depreciated over the remaining two years of service life at the rate of $2,500 ($5,000 ÷ 2) per year. Upon conclusion of the six-year life, depreciation expense will total $21,000, which equals the original cost of the freezer plus the $1,000 motor.

Notice that the debit to Accumulated Depreciation increases the asset's book value, as would a debit to the Freezer account. We follow the former approach for expenditures that prolong an asset's life to, in effect, reclaim (reduce) some past depreciation—an appropriate procedure given the service life extension.

The proper treatment of costs incurred after asset acquisition is sometimes confusing. The generalized chart in Exhibit 12–1 may prove helpful when analyzing a transaction and determining its correct handling in the accounting records.

DISPOSALS OF PROPERTY, PLANT, AND EQUIPMENT

Items of property, plant, and equipment are acquired by a firm to render benefits for a number of years. Eventually, these assets will be retired from use by being discarded, sold, or exchanged. When a company disposes of a depreciable asset, depreciation must be taken up to the date of disposal to ensure a proper matching of expenses and revenues.

②

Prepare journal entries to record discards and sales of property, plant, and equipment.

To illustrate, suppose that Bennigan Company acquired a machine on January 1, 19X1, at a cost of $15,000. The machine has a residual value of $1,000 and is being depreciated over a seven-year life by the straight-line method. As of December 31, 19X2, the machine would appear in the accounting records as follows:

MACHINERY		ACCUMULATED DEPRECIATION: MACHINERY	
1/1/X1 15,000			12/31/X1 2,000
			12/31/X2 2,000

EXHIBIT 12–1
Summary of Capital and Revenue Expenditures

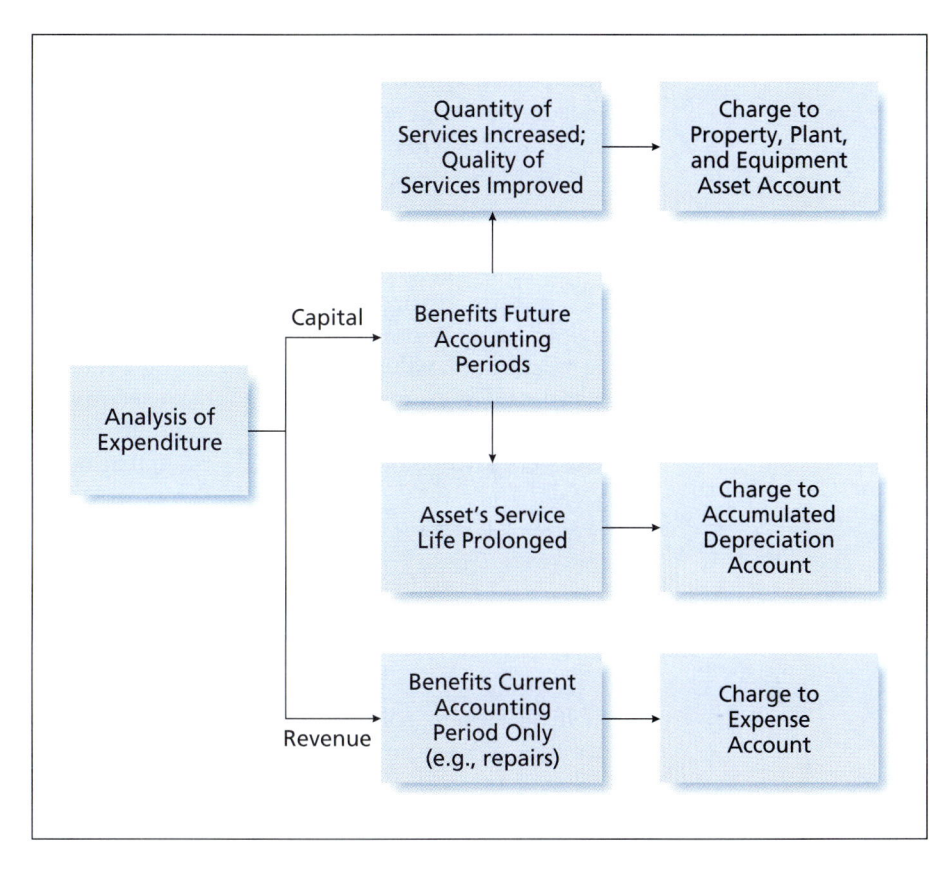

```
                          ┌─ Quantity of           ──▶ Charge to
                          │  Services Increased;       Property, Plant,
                          │  Quality of                and Equipment
                          │  Services Improved         Asset Account
                          │         ▲
                          │         │
                 Capital  │  Benefits Future
              ┌──────────▶│  Accounting
              │           │  Periods
              │           │         │
   Analysis of│           │         ▼
   Expenditure│           │  Asset's Service    ──▶ Charge to
              │           └─ Life Prolonged         Accumulated
              │                                     Depreciation
              │                                     Account
              │
              │  Revenue     Benefits Current   ──▶ Charge to
              └───────────▶  Accounting              Expense
                             Period Only             Account
                             (e.g., repairs)
```

Assume that Bennigan discarded the machine on October 1, 19X3. Because depreciation was last recorded on December 31, 19X2, nine months of additional depreciation must be taken. Thus, $1,500 ($2,000 × 9/12) is entered in the accounts by means of the entry that follows.

Oct. 1	Depreciation Expense: Machinery	1,500	
	Accumulated Depreciation: Machinery		1,500
	To record nine months' depreciation.		

REMOVAL OF ASSETS FROM THE ACCOUNTS

Once depreciation is brought up to date, any account balances associated with the machine must be removed from the books. This step is accomplished by debiting the Accumulated Depreciation account for the total depreciation taken to the date of disposal and then crediting the asset account for the asset's original cost. For Bennigan's machine, the necessary journal entry is as follows:

Oct. 1	Loss on Disposal of Property, Plant, & Equipment	9,500	
	Accumulated Depreciation: Machinery	5,500	
	Machinery		15,000
	To record discarded machine.		

To explain, recall that cost minus accumulated depreciation represents *book value*, which is the "value" of an asset in the accounting records. Because Bennigan received nothing for a machine having a $9,500 book value ($15,000 − $5,500), a $9,500 loss is incurred.

SALE OF DEPRECIABLE ASSETS

In addition to being discarded or abandoned, depreciable assets can also be sold. To properly account for the transaction, the proceeds received upon sale must be compared against book value. If the amount received is greater than the asset's book value, a gain results; if the proceeds are less than book value, a loss arises. For example, assume that an executive desk was acquired for $2,000. Over the years, depreciation in the amount of $1,200 has been recorded. The asset's book value of $800 ($2,000 − $1,200) appears in the accounts as follows:

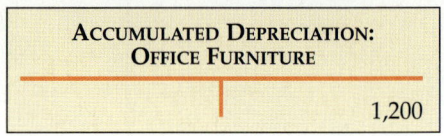

OFFICE FURNITURE		ACCUMULATED DEPRECIATION: OFFICE FURNITURE	
2,000			1,200

If the desk is sold for only $500 because of a low demand for used office furniture, a loss occurs. The entry to record this transaction would be as shown:

Cash	500	
Loss on Disposal of Property, Plant, & Equipment	300	
Accumulated Depreciation: Office Furniture	1,200	
Office Furniture		2,000
To record furniture sold at a price below book value.		

A loss of $300 is generated because the cash received ($500) is less than the book value of the furniture ($800). The loss would have been reduced (and perhaps eliminated) if the selling price had been greater. On the other hand, the loss could have gone as high as $800 if the asset had been discarded with nothing received in return.

Changing the example, if the furniture is sold for $1,500, a gain arises. The proper journal entry is:

Cash	1,500	
Accumulated Depreciation: Office Furniture	1,200	
Gain on Disposal of Property, Plant, & Equipment		700
Office Furniture		2,000
To record furniture sold at a price above book value.		

In this case, a gain of $700 results because the $1,500 sale proceeds exceed the $800 balance sheet valuation.

The preceding examples focused on situations where the amount of cash received differed from the asset's book value. It is possible, of course, that the two amounts could be equal. In such instances, no gain or loss arises. However, a journal entry must still be made to record the sale proceeds and to remove the cost of the asset and any accumulated depreciation from the accounts.

EXCHANGES AND TRADE-INS OF SIMILAR ASSETS

> **3** Account for exchanges of similar assets.

Items of property, plant, and equipment are often exchanged or traded in for newer assets. You may have had some personal experience with trade-ins when purchasing a new car. To acquire the new vehicle, you must surrender the old car, make a cash down payment, and assume an obligation (e.g., a note) for the unpaid balance. The total amount to be paid is dependent on the *trade-in allowance* granted by the dealer for the old vehicle. Sometimes the trade-in allowance is equal to the car's *fair market value* (i.e., the current market price). On other occasions, however, the trade-in allowance varies inversely with the number of cars the dealer has recently sold. If sales are low, trade-in allowances will be high, and vice versa. Because the trade-in allowance can fluctuate for reasons unrelated to the fair value of the asset given or received, it is an unreliable measure to use for accounting purposes.

To properly account for trade-ins, we must attach a value to the old asset. Normally, the asset surrendered is valued at its fair market value, unless the fair value of the asset received is more clearly evident. The fair value of the asset surrendered rarely coincides with the valuation in the accounting records, however, thus giving rise to a gain or loss.

The next few paragraphs focus on the rules related to exchanges of similar or like assets (e.g., the swap of one machine for another). The accounting profession requires that *losses on such transactions be recognized. In contrast, gains are ignored.*[1]

Loss Situation. Assume that Weiss Company has just traded an old delivery truck for a newer model. Data pertaining to the exchange follow.

DELIVERY TRUCK TRADED IN		DELIVERY TRUCK ACQUIRED	
Cost	$10,000	Invoice price	$14,000
Accumulated depreciation	8,500	Fair market value of old delivery truck	300
Book value on date of exchange	$ 1,500	Cash paid	$13,700

Weiss has generated a loss on this transaction because the "true" value of the asset surrendered (fair market value of $300) is far less than the asset's value in the accounting records (book value of $1,500). Stated differently, a $1,200 loss has arisen and is recorded as shown.

Delivery Truck (New)	14,000	
Accumulated Depreciation: Delivery Truck	8,500	
Loss on Exchange of Property, Plant, & Equipment	1,200	
Delivery Truck (Old)		10,000
Cash		13,700
To record acquisition of new delivery truck and trade-in of old delivery truck.		

Notice that the new vehicle is recorded at its invoice price of $14,000.

---

[1] The rules stated here are used in the preparation of a company's financial statements. Different procedures are followed when reporting these transactions in the tax returns that are filed with the Internal Revenue Service. As an example, for tax purposes, neither gains *nor* losses on like-for-like exchanges are recognized.

Gain Situation. When the fair market value exceeds the book value of the asset relinquished, an apparent gain arises. However, the gain is not recognized because an exchange of similar assets does not substantially alter a company's operating capacity or position. In other words, the entity will possess a resource that performs in a manner similar to that surrendered. (One can even think of the transaction as a major refurbishing and upgrade of the original asset.) Any gain recognition at the time of exchange would therefore be premature and not conservative in nature. As a result of this treatment, the cost of the newly acquired asset is the sum of the old asset's book value plus any cash paid or to be paid.

To illustrate, let us assume the same data as in the previous case, with one exception: the fair value of the old delivery truck is now $2,000 rather than $300. The cash paid thus decreases to $12,000 ($14,000 invoice cost − $2,000 fair value), and the following entry becomes necessary:

Delivery Truck (New)	13,500	
Accumulated Depreciation: Delivery Truck	8,500	
Delivery Truck (Old)		10,000
Cash		12,000 |//
To record acquisition of new delivery truck and trade-in of old delivery truck.		

Because the fair market value of the old vehicle ($2,000) exceeds the $1,500 book value, Weiss has generated a $500 gain on the exchange. As the journal entry shows, however, no gain appears in the accounting records. The new truck is therefore carried at $13,500: the book value of the truck relinquished ($1,500) plus the cash paid ($12,000). Future depreciation of the new asset will be based on the recorded cost of $13,500, not the $14,000 invoice price.

The accounting procedures for exchanges of similar assets, as well as for asset discards and sales, are overviewed in Exhibit 12–2.

A Related Issue: Asset Impairment

④ *Exhibit a basic understanding of the issues related to asset impairment.*

The preceding examples dealt with discards, sales, or trades and required the removal of assets from the accounting records. A relatively popular practice seemed to emerge in the mid-1980s and early 1990s, courtesy of a recession and the related economic recovery. The terms "restructuring" and "reengineering" appeared with increasing frequency in the business press, as corporations sought ways to improve profitability. Often the restructuring occurred through layoffs; sometimes it meant the closure of divisions, plants, and/or distribution centers.

A write-down of property, plant, and equipment values typically accompanied this process—even if the assets continued in use. Corporations frequently justified these write-downs on the grounds that changes in plans or market conditions had impaired (damaged) the value of their resources. Unfortunately, accountants had little direction in judging how much of a value reduction was needed or when to record it. These are important issues, especially when one considers that the write-down is accompanied by a loss that reduces income.[2]

---

[2] The write-down procedure parallels that illustrated in Chapter 10 for inventory that is valued at the lower of cost or market.

PROPERTY, PLANT, AND EQUIPMENT/NATURAL RESOURCES/INTANGIBLES   445

EXHIBIT 12–2
Summary of Accounting Rules for Asset Disposals

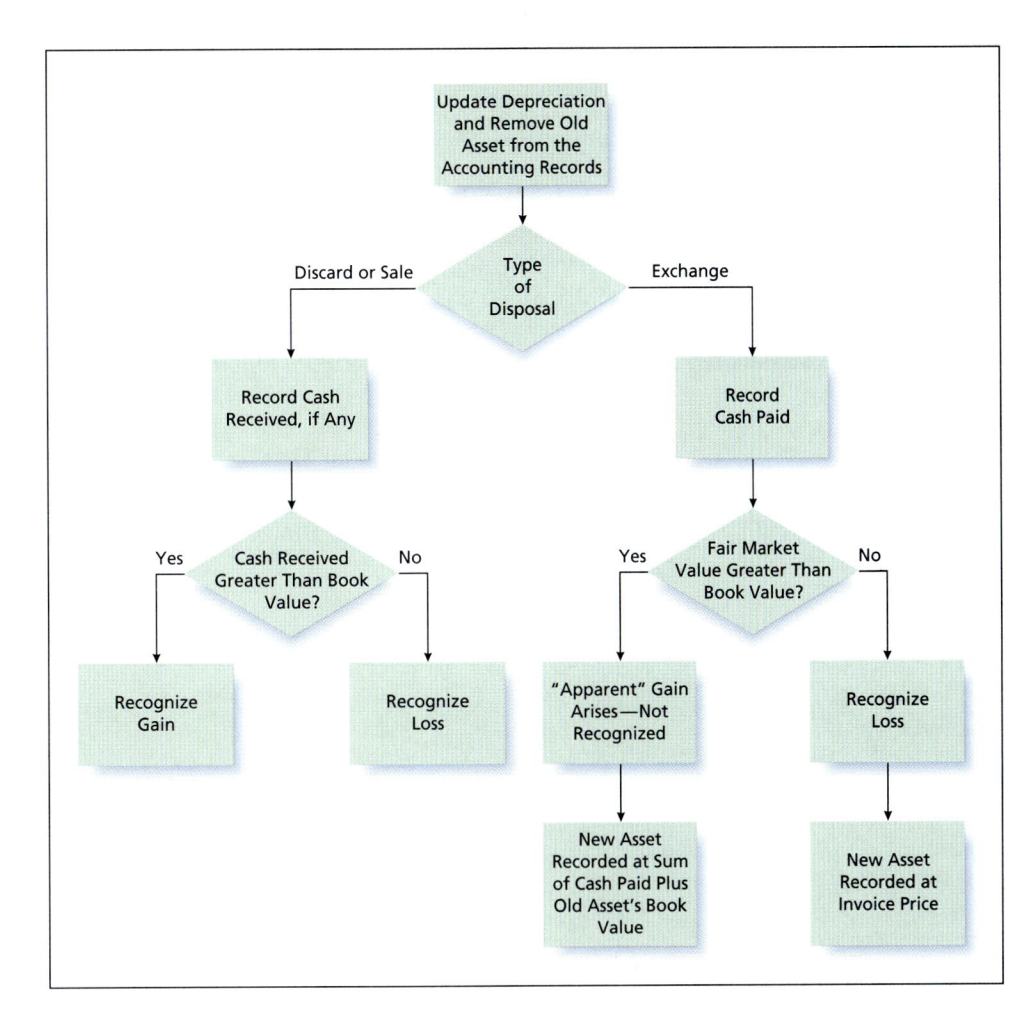

```
                    Update Depreciation
                    and Remove Old
                    Asset from the
                    Accounting Records
                           │
                           ▼
            Discard or Sale    Type    Exchange
          ◄─────────────────   of   ─────────────────►
                             Disposal
                    │                           │
                    ▼                           ▼
              Record Cash                  Record
              Received, if Any             Cash Paid
                    │                           │
                    ▼                           ▼
       Yes    Cash Received    No    Yes   Fair Market      No
     ◄────  Greater Than Book ────► ◄──── Value Greater Than ────►
              Value?                      Book Value?
         │            │                │                  │
         ▼            ▼                ▼                  ▼
      Recognize    Recognize      "Apparent" Gain      Recognize
        Gain         Loss         Arises—Not             Loss
                                  Recognized
                                       │                  │
                                       ▼                  ▼
                                 New Asset           New Asset
                                 Recorded at Sum     Recorded at
                                 of Cash Paid Plus   Invoice Price
                                 Old Asset's Book
                                 Value
```

Just prior to our going to press, the Financial Accounting Standards Board addressed this issue and developed related guidelines, the details of which are beyond the scope of the text. The guidelines are truly needed, as *individual* corporations very often recorded losses that exceeded $100 million through this process. Borden alone took a $642 million restructuring charge not too long ago. Other companies that have recorded sizable losses include Eastman Kodak ($538 million), Sara Lee ($732 million), and Apple Computer ($321 million), to name just a few.

You may be wondering why a firm desires to record huge charges, especially when the magnitude of such a financial beating may not be required. One theory is that bad news is bad news, no matter what the extent. As long as bad news has to be reported, the thinking is to go ahead and "take a big bath." As *The Wall Street Journal* reports, ". . . investors love restructuring because, following a jumbo charge against earnings, a company's profit nearly always improves sharply. That's because lots of companies write off certain expenses all at once that would otherwise be a drag to earnings over a longer period."[3]

[3] "A Restructuring of Write-Offs Is in the Making," *The Wall Street Journal,* November 2, 1994, pp. C1, C2.

A FURTHER FOCUS

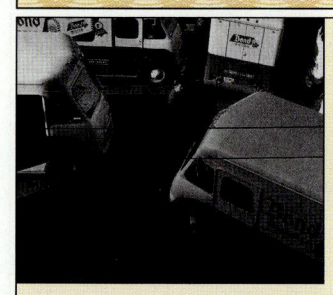

Recognition of losses related to asset write-downs is an important tool for companies that like to "smooth" their income over time. By eliminating peaks and valleys through the careful timing of gains and losses, these businesses are practicing a concept known as *earnings management*. Investors generally prefer income growth from one year to the next. By taking a carefully timed charge and offsetting it against a big gain that may have arisen, a company can prevent income from taking such a huge jump that it can't possibly be bettered in the following period.

A recent article noted that General Electric is an aggressive player of earnings management, netting restructuring charges against gains from asset sales. The following figures (all pretax and in millions) were provided:

Year	Gain From Asset Sale	Restructuring Charge
1983	$ 117	$ 147
1984	617	636
1985	518	447
1986	50	311
1987	858	1,027
1993	1,430	1,011

Source: For an enlightening discussion, see "How General Electric Damps Fluctuations in Its Annual Earnings," *The Wall Street Journal*, November 3, 1994, pp. A1, A11.

NATURAL RESOURCES

5 Calculate natural resource cost and depletion.

Natural resources represent another major group of assets that provide long-term benefits to their owners. Examples of natural resources include oil and gas wells, mineral deposits, and standing timber. These assets are sometimes called *wasting assets* because they are actually consumed (through removal) and do not maintain their physical presence like property, plant, and equipment.

Natural resources are initially entered in the accounting records at cost. This amount includes cost of the properties, legal fees, surveying costs, and sums expended for exploration and development.

DEPLETION

As discussed in Chapters 3 and 11, plant and equipment are depreciated. A similar process, known as depletion, is applied to wasting assets. Depletion is the allocation of natural resource cost to the resources extracted during an accounting period. The depletion computation is virtually identical to the units-of-output depreciation method. That is, the cost of the natural resource, minus any residual value, is divided by the total estimated units (e.g., tons, barrels) in the resource deposit. The result, depletion per unit of output, is then multiplied by the number of units extracted during the period to determine the depletion charge.

To illustrate the necessary calculations, assume Thompson Oil Company purchased the rights to search for oil in Louisiana. The company spent $150,000 for the rights and another $1,850,000 for exploration costs. After estimated oil reserves of two million barrels were discovered, Thompson incurred costs of

$4.2 million to develop a well. The anticipated residual value of the land after the firm's activities have ceased is $200,000. Thompson's depletion charge of $3 per barrel is computed in the following manner:

Cost of project	
Rights	$ 150,000
Exploration	1,850,000
Well development	4,200,000
Total	$6,200,000

(Cost − Residual Value) ÷ Estimated Units in Deposit = Depletion Rate

($6,200,000 − $200,000) ÷ 2,000,000 barrels = $3 per barrel

If 300,000 barrels are extracted and sold in the first year of the well's operation, depletion expense would total $900,000 (300,000 barrels × $3). The year-end journal entry to record depletion follows.

Depletion Expense	900,000	
Accumulated Depletion: Oil Property		900,000
To record depletion expense.		

The Accumulated Depletion account, a contra asset, is deducted from the cost of the natural resource on the balance sheet. Thompson would therefore disclose its oil properties as follows:

Natural resources		
Oil properties	$6,200,000	
Less: Accumulated depletion	900,000	$5,300,000

Companies usually establish separate asset and accumulated depletion accounts for each major category of natural resource owned.

Extracted, Unsold Resources. In the example just presented, the entire $900,000 depletion charge was expensed because all extracted oil was sold. The net result was a proper matching of revenues and expenses. If some of the extracted oil was stored for future sale, a portion of the depletion charge must be allocated to an Oil Inventory account (a current asset). For instance, if only 285,000 barrels were sold, depletion expense would total $855,000 (285,000 × $3). Because 15,000 barrels (300,000 − 285,000) remain on hand, Thompson would inventory $45,000 (15,000 × $3) and add this amount to other oil production costs.

DEPRECIABLE ASSETS RELATED TO NATURAL RESOURCES

To develop a natural resource commercially, a company usually must build facilities and acquire equipment. Often the facilities and equipment cannot be moved after the resource deposits are exhausted. It is therefore common practice to depreciate these assets over their own lives or the life of the deposit, whichever is shorter. Many firms use the units-of-output depreciation method for such properties. These entities logically tie depreciation to the resource removal process by basing the depreciation charge on the number of units (e.g., barrels, tons) extracted during the period.

INTANGIBLE ASSETS

6 Recognize the various types of intangible assets and the need for amortization.

Long-lived assets that lack physical existence and contribute to the earnings capability of a company are termed **intangible assets.** Examples of intangibles include patents, copyrights, franchises, trademarks and brand names, and goodwill. Intangible assets can provide significant advantages to a business and may be instrumental in a firm's financial success. Yet many financial statement users disagree about placing these assets on the balance sheet. Stated simply, in comparison with the benefits received from other resources such as property, plant, and equipment, the benefits of intangibles are less certain and less determinable.

Intangible assets are entered in a firm's accounting records at cost. Cost includes the various expenditures necessary to place the intangible in a service-producing capacity; for example, the purchase price, filing fees, legal fees, and other miscellaneous costs related to acquisition. These expenditures are all capitalized because they help to provide economic usefulness for extended periods of time. Intangibles are normally presented on the balance sheet in a separate section immediately following property, plant, and equipment.

PATENTS

A **patent** provides its owner with the exclusive right to use, manufacture, and sell a product or process for a period of 17 years. The federal government issues patents to inventors as a means of encouraging development of new products and technology. Firms may obtain patents by purchasing existing rights from inventors or by formulating their own products and processes through research and development. Even though the economic usefulness of a purchased patent and an internally developed patent may be the same, their costs are treated differently.

As we noted, the purchase cost of an intangible is carried as an asset. In contrast, *research and development costs related to the creation of a patent are expensed*. Although expensing costs that result in long-term benefits may seem contrary to the accounting treatment noted in this and other chapters, research and development costs are somewhat unique.

Many organizations spend considerable amounts of money for research projects that culminate in a patent. Large sums are also spent on experimental work that is unsuccessful and leads nowhere. It might seem appropriate to expense the costs of unsuccessful research projects and capitalize the costs of those that result in a favorable outcome. Unfortunately, it is often difficult to assign costs to specific patents. Frequently, for example, patents do not result from one project; instead they are the culmination of knowledge that is obtained from many different undertakings. In addition, some research costs are applicable to more than a single endeavor and thus difficult to trace to specific efforts. As a consequence of these practical problems plus the possibility of a "go nowhere" outcome, businesses are required to expense research and development costs when incurred.[4]

COPYRIGHTS

A copyright provides its owners, or their heirs, the exclusive right to produce and sell an artistic, musical, or published work. Like patents, these rights are issued by the federal government and can be sold or assigned to others. A copyright is granted for the life of the creator plus 50 years. Normally, however, the useful life to the owner is a much shorter period.

FRANCHISES

A franchise gives its owner the right to manufacture or sell certain products or to perform certain services. Although most people associate franchises with fast-food restaurants such as Pizza Hut and Burger King, franchises are established for a variety of activities. Cities, for example, often grant franchises to firms for garbage collection, towing services, and taxi services. A franchise may have an indefinite life (perpetual franchise) or a limited life; some must even be renewed yearly.

The cost of acquiring a franchise is carried in a Franchise account. A few franchises involve no acquisition costs; thus, only legal costs and related fees are capitalized. Other franchises are extremely expensive. Consider what an investor would have to pay to acquire a professional sports club (i.e., a franchise) in today's market. A recent study pegged the individual "value" of sixteen such operations at $160 million or more. (The Dallas Cowboys led the list at $238 million, followed by the Miami Dolphins and the San Francisco 49ers.) Factors that were considered in arriving at these numbers included franchise revenues (gate receipts, concessions, parking, and fees from television, radio, and cable broadcasts) and stadium/arena lease agreements (including skybox availability and rentals).[5]

TRADEMARKS

Each day, as consumers, we encounter trademarks, brand names, and symbols. Consider, for example, the golden arches (McDonald's), the peacock (NBC), Oreo (Nabisco Foods), and Tony the Tiger (Kellogg). These intangible assets are very important to the financial well-being of a business, since a unique product name or recognizable symbol is automatically associated with a specific good and/or service.

The cost of a trademark, brand name, or special symbol includes design fees, market research costs, attorney's fees, and registration fees. Focusing on the last item listed, owners can secure exclusive rights to the use of these intangible assets

---

[4] See "Accounting for Research and Development Costs," *Statement of Financial Accounting Standards No. 2,* Financial Accounting Standards Board, Norwalk, Conn., 1974.
[5] For an interesting overview of professional football, baseball, basketball, and hockey franchises, see "Suite Deals: Why New Stadiums Are Shaking Up the Pecking Order of Sports Franchises," *Financial World,* May 9, 1995, pp. 42–43, 46–48, 50, 52, 54, 56.

A Further Focus

Similar in substance to formal franchise agreements, other intangible assets—licenses and rights—give their owners the ability to generate significant amounts of revenue. Consider King World Productions, a leading distributor of television programming. The firm has four principal properties: licenses to distribute *The Oprah Winfrey Show*, *Wheel of Fortune*, *Jeopardy!*, and *Inside Edition*. These intangible assets accounted for nearly 91% of the company's $474 million revenue total in a recent year.

In another example, Twentieth Century Fox and MCA split the distribution rights on Arnold Schwarzenegger's movie, *True Lies*. Fox handled U.S. distribution; MCA handled much of the rest of the world. It was a good deal for both firms, as the movie grossed in excess of $115 million both domestically *and* overseas. Such rights-sharing agreements are growing in popularity, partly caused by skyrocketing production costs of certain blockbuster hits. The agreements allow the financial risk (and cost) to be split between two entities.

Sources: *1993 Annual Report of King World Productions, Inc.*, and "Movie Makers Find That Rights To Films Overseas Often Pay Off," *The Wall Street Journal*, November 22, 1994, pp. B1, B6.

---

by registration with the federal government. Trademarks may be registered for a period of 10 years, with renewals possible if certain conditions are met.

GOODWILL

The term "goodwill" means different things to different people. A business often refers to the customer goodwill that flows from an excellent reputation, superior products, and prime location. A large corporation may claim it is furthering community goodwill by sponsoring a Little League baseball team and a series of concerts open to the public. Do the foregoing types of goodwill have any value to a business? Of course they do. However, placing a dollar amount on these items is very difficult. Considerable personal opinion is involved, and the items cannot be measured objectively. If the owners and managers of a business were permitted to arbitrarily put a value on such goodwill for entry into the accounting records, the resulting financial statements could seriously misrepresent the entity's financial position.

As a result, generally accepted accounting principles allow only the recording of "purchased" goodwill. For example, suppose that Diamond Computers, owner of a chain of computer stores throughout the country, purchased a local retailer (Valley Computer) on October 1 for $500,000 cash. The current values of Valley's assets and liabilities on the date of acquisition were as follows:

Building	$150,000
Store fixtures	30,000
Inventory	300,000
Prepaid expenses	10,000
Bank loan	(90,000)
	$400,000

Why did Diamond pay $500,000 when the individual assets, minus liabilities, were worth only $400,000? In all likelihood, Diamond's management was impressed with the financial history of Valley and anticipated that Valley's earnings record would continue into the future. To an accountant, the $100,000 difference between the purchase price of the business and the current value of the assets and liabilities acquired is an intangible known as goodwill.

The existence of goodwill is normally evidenced by a company's ability to earn a higher rate of income than other organizations in the same field of endeavor. Stated differently, goodwill occurs when the value of the company *as an operating entity* exceeds the value of its individual components *(measurable assets and liabilities)*. The entity's resources, including the special attributes of reputation, favorable location, and skillful management, have all been working together to increase the value of the business in the eyes of the purchaser—an increase that is over and above the current value of the resources acquired and liabilities assumed. Generally, the individual impact of each of the preceding factors is not readily identifiable, and the purchaser is paying a lump sum for their collective benefits.

Accounting for Goodwill. The proper accounting for goodwill is demonstrated by continuing the previous example. It is important to recognize that although Valley developed the goodwill, disclosure by management on Valley's financial statements is not appropriate because of the measurement difficulties cited earlier. Diamond, on the other hand, paid $100,000 for this intangible in a valid business transaction and can record the following journal entry:

Building	150,000	
Store Fixtures	30,000	
Inventory	300,000	
Prepaid Expenses	10,000	
Goodwill	100,000	
Loan Payable		90,000
Cash		500,000
Acquired the assets and liabilities of Valley Computer.		

Observe the manner in which the current value of the assets and liabilities acquired becomes the cost to Diamond. If Valley lacked the ability to achieve above-average net earnings because of a marginal location or other factors, Diamond would have probably paid less than $500,000. If, for instance, the agreed-upon purchase price was $400,000, Diamond would have bought only the separate assets, minus liabilities. Nothing would have been paid for the unique features of the business.

Guidelines for Determining Goodwill. Calculating the amount *paid* for goodwill in the purchase of a business is fairly straightforward, as was observed in the preceding example. Determining how much a purchaser *should be willing to pay* is another matter. Several techniques have been proposed for estimating goodwill. Among these are the following:

A Marketing Manager's Perspective

Goodwill and Brand Equity: Although goodwill has long been an established account on company balance sheets, marketers have only recently begun to give it much attention. This increased attention is courtesy of a concept known as "brand equity." Established brand-name products with reputations for high quality have a great deal of intangible value. Companies and investors recognize that such products command higher prices, generate greater revenues, and pave the way for the introduction of successful new entries into the marketplace. These new entries often have instant name recognition and may be favored by retailers when they allocate a store's scarce shelf space.

After all is said and done, brand equity explains why many consumer goods firms have recently been sold for prices well in excess of net asset values. It is this fundamental Marketing 101 concept that contributes so greatly to the Goodwill account in a company's financial statements.

- Multiply sales during the last 12 months by a stipulated percentage.
- Multiply earnings during the last 12 months by a stipulated percentage.
- Multiply the amount by which earnings exceed an industry norm by a stipulated percentage.

Bear in mind that these techniques are merely estimation tools. The exact amount of goodwill is based on the actual selling price of the business, as decided by the buyer and the seller. The preceding tools are just that—tools—and cannot take the place of sound business logic and intelligent financial negotiation.

AMORTIZATION OF INTANGIBLES

Earlier in the text we discussed the topic of depreciation—a process by which the cost of plant and equipment is allocated to expense over an estimated service life. This same process is applied to intangible assets; the name is changed, however, to **amortization.** The entry to record the periodic amortization of an intangible is a debit to Amortization Expense and a credit to the intangible asset account. This treatment differs slightly from the depreciation entry, where the credit involves the contra asset Accumulated Depreciation. An Accumulated Amortization account is seldom used.

> **ETHICS ISSUE**
>
> In an effort to estimate the service life of a soft drink formula, XYZ's accountant contacted the president of the Soft Drink Trade Association. The president is a close relative of XYZ's chief financial officer. Comment.

Amortization Procedures. The most troublesome issue in amortization is estimating the intangible's service life. Imagine the difficulty of determining when a food trademark, the unique flavor of a soft drink, or an ice cream franchise would have no future economic value to their owners.

Although many intangibles have specified legal lives, the actual service life may be considerably shorter. For example, the inventor of a new electronic device can obtain exclusive manufacturing and sales rights for 17 years through a patent. Yet the patent may be useful for only five years because of intense competition and rapid technological developments in the electronics industry. Accordingly, the patent should be written off over a five-year period. In general, an intangible should be amortized over the shorter of its legal life or service life; however, in no event should the amortization period exceed 40 years.[6] This latter rule is especially applicable to goodwill and other intangibles that provide seemingly unlimited benefits to their owners.

Because it is difficult to measure changes in the yearly benefits provided by intangibles, most companies use the straight-line method of amortization. As in straight-line depreciation, an equal amount of expense is recorded each period.

An Example. To illustrate the amortization of an intangible asset, assume Kelley Corporation purchased a patent from an inventor for $720,000 on July 1, 19X6. The patent was originally granted to the inventor on January 1, 19X1, will provide benefits to Kelley for 8 years, and has no residual value. The entries to record the purchase on July 1 and amortization on December 31, 19X6, follow.

July 1	Patents		720,000	
	Cash			720,000
	To record purchase of patent.			
Dec. 31	Amortization Expense: Patents		45,000	
	Patents			45,000
	To record six months of amortization expense.			

Although the patent has a 17-year legal life, the service life to Kelley is a much shorter period (8 years, or 96 months). Because monthly amortization equals $7,500 ($720,000 ÷ 96), the company will record amortization of $45,000. The Patents account would appear on the firm's December 31, 19X6, balance sheet at $675,000 ($720,000 − $45,000).

END-OF-CHAPTER REVIEW

LEARNING OBJECTIVES: THE KEY POINTS

1. **Explain how plant and equipment costs incurred after asset acquisition are treated in the accounts.** Expenditures incurred after items of plant and equipment are placed in service often prolong an asset's life, increase the quantity of services provided by an asset, or improve service quality. Such expenditures (e.g., additions and betterments) provide future benefits and should be capitalized in the accounts. If an expenditure does not meet at least one of the preceding criteria, it is known as a revenue expenditure and immediately expensed. A typical expense would be ordinary repairs and maintenance, which are incurred to maintain the normal operating condition of the asset.

2. **Prepare journal entries to record discards and sales of property, plant, and equipment.** When an asset is discarded or sold, depreciation must be updated to the date of disposal, and the asset's cost and accompanying accumulated depreciation must be removed from the accounting records. Gains and losses are recognized by comparing the asset's book value with the proceeds received. A gain arises when the proceeds received exceed book value; a loss occurs in the opposite situation.

[6] "Intangible Assets," *Opinions of the Accounting Principles Board No. 17*, American Institute of Certified Public Accountants, Jersey City, N.J., 1970, paragraph 29.

3. **Account for exchanges of similar assets.** When similar assets are exchanged or traded, gains and losses are figured by comparing book value against the old asset's fair market value. In cases where the fair value of the asset given up is less than the old asset's book value, a loss is recognized and the new asset is recorded at the invoice price. When fair value exceeds book value, an apparent gain results. However, the gain is not recognized, and the new asset is recorded at the book value of the old asset plus any cash paid or to be paid.

4. **Exhibit a basic understanding of the issues related to asset impairment.** Asset impairment refers to a situation where a change in plans or market conditions impair (i.e., damage) the value of a company's property, plant, and equipment. Businesses therefore reduce the value of these assets in the accounting records and recognize an accompanying loss. The feeling is that such write-downs allow firms to put bad times behind them and "clear the road" for improved profitability.

5. **Calculate natural resource cost and depletion.** Natural resources, such as oil, gas, and mineral deposits, provide long-term benefits until they are totally consumed through extraction. Such assets are entered in the accounting records at cost, which includes amounts expended for exploration and development. Depletion involves the allocation of this cost to the resources extracted during the period. It is calculated by dividing cost, minus residual value, by the total estimated units in the resource deposit. This computation yields depletion per unit of output, which is multiplied by the number of units extracted to arrive at the depletion charge.

6. **Recognize the various types of intangible assets and the need for amortization.** Long-term assets that lack physical existence and contribute to the earnings capability of a company are called intangibles. Examples of intangibles and accompanying legal lives are patents (17 years), copyrights (life of the creator plus 50 years), franchises, license agreements, trademarks (10 years, with renewals possible), and goodwill. An intangible is gradually expensed via amortization over its legal life or service life, whichever is shorter. In no case may the amortization period exceed 40 years.

Key Terms and Concepts: A Quick Overview

additions   Items that provide future benefits and are affixed to existing plant and equipment. (p. 439)

amortization   The allocation of the cost of intangible assets to the accounting periods benefited. (p. 452)

asset impairment   A reduction in the value of a company's property, plant, and equipment because of a change in plans or market conditions. (p. 444)

betterments   Expenditures that improve or increase the future service potential of an item of plant and equipment. (p. 439)

capital expenditures   Costs that provide future economic benefits to a business. (p. 438)

copyright   An intangible asset that gives its owners or their heirs the exclusive right to produce and sell an artistic, musical, or published work for a stipulated period of time. (p. 449)

depletion   The allocation of natural resource cost to the resources extracted during an accounting period. (p. 446)

fair market value   The current market price of an asset. (p. 443)

franchise An intangible asset representing rights that authorize the manufacture or sale of certain products and/or the performance of certain services. (p. 449)

goodwill The amount paid by the purchaser of a business in excess of the current value of the assets and liabilities acquired. (p. 451)

intangible assets Long-term assets that lack physical existence—for example, patents, copyrights, and trademarks. (p. 448)

patent An exclusive right that permits its owner to use, manufacture, and sell a product or process. (p. 448)

repairs Amounts spent to maintain the normal operating condition of an asset. (p. 439)

revenue expenditures Costs incurred after asset acquisition that are said to benefit only the current accounting period. Such amounts are treated as expenses. (p. 439)

trade-in allowance The amount a buyer is given for an old asset in an exchange-type transaction. (p. 443)

trademark An exclusive right to use specific brand names and symbols for a period of 10 years, with renewals possible if certain conditions are met. (p. 449)

Chapter Quiz

The five questions that follow relate to several issues raised in the chapter. Test your knowledge of the issues by selecting the best answer. (The answers appear on p. 469.)

1. Gamble, Inc., installed a heater in one of its earth-moving vehicles at a cost of $1,200. The vehicle did not previously have a heater. Gamble should account for this cost:
   a. as an intangible asset.
   b. by reducing the Earth-Moving Equipment account.
   c. by reducing the Accumulated Depreciation account associated with the vehicle.
   d. by increasing the book value of the vehicle.

2. Gains and losses on the sale of a depreciable asset are determined by comparing:
   a. book value and the proceeds received.
   b. book value and the asset's cost.
   c. the proceeds received and the asset's cost.
   d. book value and the Accumulated Depreciation account.

3. Solo Company spent $10 million to develop a mine having an estimated four million ounces of silver. During 19X7, 50,000 ounces were mined and processed; 5,000 ounces were sold at $8 per ounce. The 19X7 depletion expense is:
   a. $2.50.
   c. $112,500.
   b. $12,500.
   d. $125,000.

4. On January 1, 19X1, Betty Ross purchased a patent for $102,000. The patent had an original legal life of 17 years at the date of issuance; only six of the 17 years remained when acquired. The expected service life to Ross is two years. The 19X1 amortization expense is:
   a. $6,000.
   c. $51,000.
   b. $17,000.
   d. $102,000.

5. Goodwill:
   a. is an intangible asset that need not be amortized.
   b. is recorded by the seller of a business prior to the sale transaction.
   c. is an intangible asset that must be amortized over a period of 40 years or more.
   d. may be recorded by the buyer of a business when the acquisition is completed.

Summary Problem

Greystone Granite Company operates a granite quarry. The following schedule shows information about selected assets owned by the firm as of January 1, 19X2:

	Original Cost	Cost Written Off in Prior Periods
Building	$ 50,000	$20,000
Office equipment	18,000	7,200
Granite deposits	100,000	40,000

The following activity occurred during 19X2:

1. At the very beginning of January, Greystone paid a contractor to paint, air condition, and reroof the building. The building previously lacked air conditioning, and the roof was expected to extend the structure's life by five years.
2. On October 1, the company traded its old office equipment for new office equipment that had an invoice price of $28,000. Greystone also had to pay $22,000 cash. Management depreciates all equipment by the straight-line method, assuming a five-year life and no residual value.
3. Geologists originally estimated that the quarry contained 100,000 tons of granite. The company extracted 6,000 tons during the year.
4. On December 31, Marble Enterprises extended an offer to buy all the assets (and assume all the liabilities) of Greystone Granite for $270,000. Fair market value and book value figures for Greystone's assets and liabilities on this date were:

	Fair Market Value	Book Value
Assets	$250,000	$185,000
Liabilities	50,000	50,000

Instructions

a. Determine the proper account(s) to debit to record the painting, air conditioning, and reroofing.
b. Present the journal entries needed to record the exchange of office equipment.
c. Compute Greystone's depletion charge for 19X2.
d. Calculate the amount of goodwill that will be recognized if Marble completes its acquisition of Greystone's assets and liabilities. On whose accounting records will the goodwill be recorded?

Solution

a. Painting—Repairs (Painting) Expense
Air conditioning—Building
Reroofing—Accumulated Depreciation: Building

b.
Depreciation Expense: Office Equipment	2,700*	
Accumulated Depreciation: Office Equipment		2,700
Office Equipment (New)	28,000	
Accumulated Depreciation: Office Equipment	9,900†	
Loss on Exchange of Property, Plant, & Equipment	2,100‡	
Office Equipment (Old)		18,000
Cash		22,000

* ($18,000 ÷ 5 years) × 9/12.
† $7,200 + $2,700.
‡ ($18,000 − $9,900) vs. ($28,000 − $22,000).

c. The depletion charge is $6,000 ($100,000 ÷ 100,000 tons = $1 per ton; 6,000 tons × $1 = $6,000).

d.
Amount to be paid	$270,000
Less: Fair market value of assets acquired and liabilities assumed ($250,000 – $50,000)	200,000
Goodwill	$ 70,000

The goodwill will be entered in the accounting records of Marble Enterprises, the acquiring company.

ASSIGNMENT MATERIAL

QUESTIONS

Q12-1 What factors should be considered in determining whether costs incurred after the acquisition of plant and equipment are treated as capital expenditures or as revenue expenditures?

Q12-2 Discuss the accounting treatment normally given to the following:
a. Repairs
b. Additions
c. Betterments

Q12-3 Why is it necessary to update the depreciation accounts when depreciable assets are sold, discarded, or exchanged?

Q12-4 How is a gain or loss on the sale of an asset calculated?

Q12-5 Assume that an asset exchange is about to occur. Should the asset surrendered be valued at fair market value or the trade-in allowance granted by the dealer? Briefly discuss.

Q12-6 How are gains and losses on the exchange of similar items of property, plant, and equipment handled for financial reporting purposes?

Q12-7 What is meant by the term "asset impairment"?

Q12-8 What costs are commonly capitalized in a natural resource account?

Q12-9 Define "depletion."

Q12-10 Explain how a portion of the depletion charge can be included in the current asset section of the balance sheet.

Q12-11 How should a company determine the service life of a company-owned railroad track that is adjacent to a coal mine? Explain which depreciation method may be most appropriate for the railroad track.

Q12-12 Discuss the treatment of research and development costs that are incurred in the development of a patent.

Q12-13 Define "goodwill" and explain how the cost of goodwill is determined.

Q12-14 How is the amortization period of an intangible determined?

EXERCISES

E12-1 Capital and revenue expenditures (L.O. 1)
Consider the following transactions and events:

a. Installed wind deflectors on three trucks to improve fuel efficiency.
b. Replaced the roof on a warehouse.
c. Repainted the interior of a restaurant.
d. Expanded a company's manufacturing plant by 20,000 square feet.
e. Paid a plumber to fix a leak in the hot water heater.
f. Removed asbestos insulation in an old building and installed fiberglass insulation.

Determine whether the transactions and events would give rise to a capital expenditure or a revenue expenditure.

E12–2 Journal entries for costs incurred after asset acquisition (L.O. 1)
Duncan Company had the following transactions:

a. Paid $34,200 for a major overhaul of the firm's overhead conveyor system. The overhaul is expected to extend the system's life by five years.
b. Paid $1,000 to install an extra gasoline tank on a heavy-duty truck.
c. Paid $105 to have a microcomputer repaired.

Prepare the journal entries necessary to record the preceding transactions.

E12–3 Accounting for betterments (L.O. 1)
San Felipe Co., purchased a telephone system for its offices several years ago for $120,000. Straight-line depreciation has been used, assuming a residual value of $20,000 and a service life of 10 years. At the end of the seventh year of use, the system had a book value of $50,000. At the beginning of the eighth year, San Felipe installed new, advanced technology switches at a cost of $30,000. The switches were expected to extend the remaining service life of the system by two years.

a. Compute the balance in the Accumulated Depreciation account at the end of the seventh year.
b. To what account should the switches be debited? Why?
c. Compute the book value of the system after the switches have been recorded.
d. Calculate depreciation expense for the eighth and future years, assuming no change in the estimated residual value.

E12–4 Asset disposals (L.O. 2)
Lincoln Company purchased a truck on January 1, 19X3. The truck cost $90,000, had a service life of eight years, and had an estimated residual value of $30,000. Lincoln uses the straight-line method of depreciation. Consider the following independent cases:

a. If Lincoln sold the truck on April 1, 19X6, for $58,000, compute the gain or loss on the sale.
b. Assume that Lincoln's driver demolished the truck on July 1, 19X8. The company carries no insurance. If depreciation was last recorded on December 31, 19X7, prepare the necessary entries to (1) update depreciation and (2) remove the truck from the accounts.

E12–5 Overview of discards, sales, and exchanges (L.O. 2, 3)
Baubles and Lace purchased four store display units several years ago at a total cost of $35,000. Depreciation to date has amounted to $28,500, and the company has tentatively figured the year's net income at $45,900. Recompute the firm's net income, assuming the occurrence of the following *independent* transactions:

a. The units are donated to a charitable organization, with nothing received in return.
b. The units are sold to another business for $7,100.
c. The units are sold to another business for $3,900.
d. The units are exchanged for new store equipment. The fair market value of the old units is $4,200.
e. The units are exchanged for new store equipment. The fair market value of the old units is $6,800.

E12–6 Accounting for exchanges of similar assets (L.O. 3)

Palmetto Corporation exchanged Machine no. 1678 for a new machine, no. 2451, on May 1, 19X5. The following information is available:

	MACHINE NO. 1678	MACHINE NO. 2451
Date acquired	January 1, 19X2	May 1, 19X5
Invoice cost	$7,200	$12,000
Service life	5 years	10 years
Residual value	None	None

On the date of the exchange, Palmetto received a $3,600 trade-in allowance, which was equal to the old machine's fair market value. The company paid the remaining balance due in cash.

a. Prepare Palmetto's journal entry(ies) to record the exchange. Depreciation was last recorded on December 31, 19X4, by use of the straight-line method.
b. Repeat part (a), assuming the trade-in allowance and fair market value were $2,000 (instead of $3,600).

E12–7 Accounting for disposals and exchanges (L.O. 2, 3)

Evaluate the comments that follow as being True or False. If the comment is false, briefly explain why.

a. Losses on the exchange of similar assets are recognized for financial reporting purposes.
b. When a depreciable asset is sold, a gain results when the cash received exceeds the asset's book value.
c. Both the outright sale of a truck and its exchange for a similar vehicle would give rise to identical treatment of gains and losses in the accounting records.
d. A dealer's trade-in allowance is normally used for financial accounting purposes when valuing an asset surrendered in an exchange transaction.
e. An exchange of similar assets has occurred and must be entered in the accounting records. If the old asset's book value is less than fair market value, the newly acquired asset is recorded at the invoice price.

E12–8 Asset impairment (L.O. 4)

Mocha Magic is a Phoenix-based chain of 100 upscale coffee houses. Several years ago, the company opened three stores in Canada to test new menus, blends, and ideas. The Canadian operation has not met expectations. Higher rental, advertising, and labor costs, coupled with the costs of directing a distant business, have resulted in a "sea of red ink."

a. Should Mocha Magic consider a decrease in valuation of its Canadian assets? Briefly explain.

b. What effect will a write-down have on reported income for the current period?
c. Present several reasons that support a write-down.

E12–9   Depletion (L.O. 5)
Case Company recently incurred the following costs in developing a mine site:

Mine development	$6,400,000
Rights	300,000
Exploration	1,800,000
	$8,500,000

The mine is expected to contain five million tons of ore. Case extracted and sold 410,000 tons during the first year of operation.

a. Present the necessary journal entry to record depletion.
b. Show the proper disclosure of the mining property upon conclusion of the first year of operation.
c. What would you have done differently in part (a) if Case had extracted 410,000 tons but sold only 360,000? Be specific.

E12–10   Amortization of intangibles (L.O. 6)
On October 1, 19X2, Nagato Enterprises paid $97,000 to acquire the following intangible assets from Midland Research Company:

	Amount Paid	Estimated Service Life to Nagato
Patent	$60,000	4 years
Copyrights	10,000	5 years
Trademarks	27,000	9 years

The legal life of the patent expires on September 30, 19X8.

a. Compute Nagato's amortization expense for the year ended September 30, 19X3. Briefly explain your calculation with respect to the patent.
b. Record the proper journal entry for amortization on September 30, 19X3.
c. Assume that in addition to the preceding intangibles, Nagato paid $160,000 to acquire a franchise that has an unlimited service life. Should the franchise be amortized? Briefly explain.

E12–11   Goodwill (L.O. 6)
Dr. Raul Fernandez has agreed to buy a professional soccer team for $28,000. The following information was extracted from the club's most recent balance sheet:

Cash	$ 1,800
Accounts receivable	6,500
Prepaid expenses	4,000
Equipment (net)	5,000
League franchise	20,000
Accounts payable	2,000
Player salaries payable	17,000

The current value of the equipment is $3,000.

a. If Dr. Fernandez assumed the liabilities and purchased the team as planned, how much did he pay for goodwill?
b. Prepare Fernandez's entry to record the purchase. Fernandez paid $23,500 cash and secured a short-term loan for the remaining balance.

E12–12 The nature of goodwill (L.O. 6)

Nick Salvano, owner of Campus Pizza for over 20 years, wants to sell his thriving business and move to a warmer climate. The current value of the restaurant's net assets (assets minus liabilities) is $300,000. In recent years, annual sales and net income have averaged $750,000 and $75,000, respectively. Nick is asking $1 million for Campus Pizza.

a. Discuss the rationale for Nick's asking price.
b. If Nick and a potential buyer agree on a price of $725,000, how much goodwill is created by the transaction?
c. The buyer has argued that goodwill need not be amortized because "the benefits are provided for an indeterminable, indefinite period of time." How would you respond to this comment?

PROBLEMS

Series A

P12–A1 Costs incurred after purchase; disposals (L.O. 1, 2)

The records of Vancouver Equipment Operators revealed the following information about selected assets:

	DATE ACQUIRED	COST	RESIDUAL VALUE	SERVICE LIFE
Warehouse	1/1/X4	$119,800	$25,000	20 years
Machinery	1/1/X2	700,000	40,000	10 years
Forklifts (4)*	10/1/X4	192,000	48,000	8 years

*The cost and residual value figures are for the four forklifts collectively.

The following transactions and events occurred during the year ended December 31, 19X6:

Jan. 1 Sold one forklift to March Manufacturing for $39,500 cash.
     1 Paid $3,690 to add a new loading dock to the warehouse. The new dock will be depreciated over the building's remaining service life and will not affect the facility's estimated residual value.
     1 Paid $90,000 for a major overhaul of the machinery. The overhaul was expected to extend the machinery's remaining service life by three years.
Sept. 3 Paid $250 for miscellaneous repairs to forklift no. 3.

The company uses the straight-line method on all depreciable assets. Depreciation was last recorded on December 31, 19X5.

Instructions

a. Prepare journal entries to record the transactions and events that occurred during 19X6.
b. Determine Vancouver's depreciation expense for the year ended December 31, 19X6.

P12–A2 Journal entries for disposals and exchanges (L.O. 2, 3)

The information that follows relates to printing equipment that was purchased by Beltway Repro on December 1, 19X1:

Acquisition cost	$140,000
Residual value	20,000
Fair market value on:	
January 1, 19X8	45,000
August 1, 19X8	43,000
Estimated service life	8 years

The company depreciates equipment by the straight-line method. Depreciation was last recorded on December 31, 19X7.

Instructions

Prepare all journal entries needed for the following independent situations:

a. The equipment is sold for cash at an amount equal to its fair market value. The sale occurs on:
   (1) January 1, 19X8.
   (2) August 1, 19X8.
b. Assume that the equipment is exchanged for similar equipment having an invoice price of $197,000, with Beltway paying the balance due in cash. The exchange occurs on:
   (1) January 1, 19X8.
   (2) August 1, 19X8.

P12–A3 Disposals and exchanges; analysis (L.O. 2, 3)

Ocean Enterprises, Inc., disposed of five assets during the 19X7 fiscal year. Information pertaining to these assets follows.

Asset	Cost	Accumulated Depreciation	Cash Received (Paid)	Fair Market Value on Date of Disposal
Freezer	$ 5,000	$ 3,600	$ 1,200	$ 1,200
Furniture	4,000	4,000	—	—
Auto	21,000	9,000	(8,200)	8,100
Building	99,000	38,000	77,000	77,000
Machine	75,000	46,600	(36,000)	30,000

A review of the accounting records revealed the following additional information:

- *Freezer*—The freezer was sold to Romar Manufacturing, one of Ocean's customers.
- *Furniture*—The furniture was donated to an American Veterans group.
- *Auto*—The auto was exchanged for a new auto that had an invoice price of $16,300.
- *Building*—The building was destroyed by an earthquake. Insurance proceeds, which were based on market value, amounted to $77,000.
- *Machine*—The company acquired a new machine having an $84,000 invoice price. The machinery dealer took Ocean's old machine in trade along with $36,000 cash and an $18,000 note payable.

The company's accountant is in the process of computing net income for 19X7. He has determined that income before any gains and losses from asset disposals amounts to $70,000.

Instructions

a. Compute Ocean's income after considering gains and losses on the five asset disposals.
b. Suppose (1) the auto's fair market value amounted to $13,000 rather than $8,100 and (2) the invoice price of the new auto was $21,200. In view of this new data, will your answer in part (a) increase or decrease? By how much?

P12–A4   Depletion and natural resources (L.O. 5)

Lockeford Lumber Company recently purchased a large tract of timber in the Northwest. The firm anticipates cutting 500,000 of the tract's five million board feet during the first year of operation. The remaining board feet will be removed equally over the next three years until all timber is harvested. The following information has been gathered from Lockeford's accounting records:

Purchase price	$3,000,000
Land development costs	425,000
Legal/realty fees	175,000
Residual value of land after logging	400,000

Given the tract's remote location, the company will build several dormitories for the workers and field supervisors at a cost of $200,000. These structures have a life of five years, no residual value, and will be abandoned when production ceases. Finally, $100,000 of machinery must be acquired. The machinery, which has a life of 10 years and a residual value of $20,000, will be used at another site after the tract has been totally cut.

Instructions

a. Determine the company's depletion and depreciation expense for each year that logging is anticipated. Lockeford will depreciate the structures by the units-of-output method and the machinery by the straight-line method.
b. Assume that during the first year of operation, 450,000 board feet of timber were cut. If sales were only 380,000 board feet, calculate the year's depletion charge.
c. Consider your answer in part (b). Should Lockeford expense the entire charge during the first year? Explain.

P12–A5   Intangibles: Acquisition cost and amortization (L.O. 6)

The accounting records of Broadway Company revealed the following information:

- *Patents*—Purchased patent no. 158–12412 for $141,000 on June 1, 19X2. The patent had a seven-year legal life at acquisition and was expected to benefit Broadway for five years. The company incurred $6,000 of legal fees in connection with the purchase and governmental registration.

  At the beginning of January 19X3, Broadway registered an internally developed patent, no. 194–27325. Research and development costs related to the patent amounted to $92,735; legal and filing fees totaled $27,200. Management estimated a service life equal to the legal life granted by the government.
- *Franchise*—On April 1, 19X4, Broadway acquired a fast-food franchise by paying an initial fee of $44,000. (Similar franchises sell for $50,000.) The franchise agreement covered a 10-year period.

Instructions

a. Prepare a schedule that shows the acquisition date, cost, service life, and yearly amortization of Broadway's intangibles.

b. Compute the book value of the intangibles as of December 31, 19X5.
c. Prepare a compound (combined) journal entry to amortize the intangibles for *19X6*.

Series B

P12–B1 Costs incurred after purchase; disposals (L.O. 1, 2)
Hollywood Company had the following transactions and events during 19X4:

1. Discarded fully depreciated office furniture on January 1 at the local landfill. Subsidiary records showed that the furniture cost $400 and had accumulated depreciation of $350.
2. On January 1, the company paid $46,000 for a new roof on its building. The new roof will extend the building's service life from an original estimate of 25 years to a total life of 30 years. The building originally cost $800,000, has a residual value of $300,000, and had $200,000 of accumulated depreciation at the beginning of 19X4. Straight-line depreciation is being used.
3. Sold store equipment on January 1 for $4,000 cash. The equipment cost $12,000 and had a book value of $5,000 on this date.
4. Repaired truck no. 10 on March 1 for $75. The accounting records revealed that the truck initially cost $28,000 and had $7,000 of accumulated depreciation at the beginning of 19X4. Depreciation is based on a four-year service life and zero residual value. The straight-line depreciation method has been used.
5. Added a radio unit to truck no. 10 on July 1. The unit cost $600, has no residual value, and will be depreciated by the straight-line method. The radio will provide benefits to the company over the remaining life of the truck.

Instructions

a. Prepare journal entries to record Hollywood's transactions and events. Depreciation was last recorded on December 31, 19X3.
b. Determine depreciation expense for the year ended December 31, 19X4, for the building and truck no. 10.

P12–B2 Journal entries for disposals and exchanges (L.O. 2, 3)
Lansing Regional Transit (LRT) purchased a specialized van on January 1, 19X1, to transport handicapped persons around the city. The van cost $40,000, had an estimated service life of seven years, and had a residual value of $5,000. The company uses the straight-line depreciation method, with depreciation last recorded on December 31, 19X3.

Instructions

a. The van was sold for cash on April 1, 19X4. Prepare the required journal entry to update depreciation and then record the sale, assuming a sales price of:
  (1) $30,700.
  (2) $17,500.
b. Independent of part (a), assume the van was exchanged on January 1, 19X4, for a similar van having a $30,000 invoice price. Prepare the required journal entry to record the exchange if the old van had a fair market value of:
  (1) $26,000 and LRT gave the dealer $4,000 cash.
  (2) $22,000 and LRT gave the dealer $8,000 cash.

P12–B3 Disposals and exchanges; analysis (L.O. 2, 3)
Third Avenue Manufacturing disposed of five assets during the 19X2 fiscal year. Information pertaining to these assets follows.

Asset	Cost	Accumulated Depreciation	Cash Received (Paid)	Fair Market Value on Date of Disposal
Furniture	$ 2,800	$ 2,600	$ —	$ —
Computer	10,400	7,100	3,800	3,800
Truck	15,500	6,800	(7,800)	9,300
Building	86,700	15,400	95,000	95,000
Machine	37,500	22,800	(18,000)	14,000

A review of the accounting records revealed the following additional information:

- *Furniture*—The furniture was discarded at a local landfill.
- *Computer*—The computer was sold to Micromatic Systems, one of Third Avenue's suppliers.
- *Truck*—The truck was exchanged for a new truck that had an invoice price of $17,100.
- *Building*—The building was destroyed by fire. Insurance proceeds, which were based on market value, amounted to $95,000.
- *Machine*—The company acquired a new machine having a $42,000 invoice price. The machinery dealer took Third Avenue's old machine in trade along with $18,000 cash and a $10,000 note payable.

The company's accountant is in the process of computing net income for 19X2. She has determined that income before any gains and losses from asset disposals amounts to $34,800.

Instructions

a. Compute Third Avenue's income after considering gains and losses on the five asset disposals.
b. Suppose (1) the machine's fair market value amounted to $15,100 rather than $14,000 and (2) the invoice price of the new machine was $43,100. In view of these new data, will your answer in part (a) increase or decrease? By how much?

P12–B4 Depletion and natural resources (L.O. 5)

The Bach Mining Company purchased a tract of land, together with mineral rights, for $155,000. After incurring exploration costs of $125,000 and legal fees of $20,000, Bach learned that 140,000 tons of high-grade ore could be extracted from the site. The company estimates that production will be 20,000 tons each year. The mining site is anticipated to have a residual value of $20,000 since the land can be used for farming after all mining operations have ceased.

Bach plans to construct the necessary mining structures (buildings, sheds, and bunkhouses) on the site for $154,000. According to the contractor, the structures will have a life of 20 years, with no residual value; they will be abandoned when production ceases. Finally, machinery and equipment must be acquired that costs $100,000, has a life of 10 years, and has a residual value of $10,000. All equipment will be moved to other company properties after the mine site is closed.

Instructions

a. Determine the company's depletion and depreciation expense for each year the mine is anticipated to operate. Bach will depreciate the structures by the units-of-output method and the machinery and equipment by the straight-line method.
b. Assume that during the first year, 18,000 tons of ore were extracted from the mine. If sales were only 12,000 tons, calculate the total depletion charge and explain how it is treated in the financial statements.

P12–B5 Intangibles: Acquisition cost and amortization (L.O. 6)

The records of Golden State Company revealed the following selected transactions in 19X2:

- *Patent*—Acquired a patent after spending $85,000 for research and development costs and $3,400 for legal and filing fees. The patent is expected to provide benefits for a period equal to the legal life granted by the government.
- *Franchise*—Purchased a franchise to provide cable TV services to the City of Greenville for five years, beginning in 19X3. (Under terms of the agreement, the franchise is renewable if certain conditions are met. Golden State and other cable companies will participate in a competitive bidding process during 19X7; the renewal decision will be made by a vote of the City Council.) Golden State paid $330,000 for the franchise.
- *Copyright*—Paid $3,600 for a copyright. The author died 20 years ago; the company should receive benefits from the copyright for a three-year period.

Instructions

a. Prepare a schedule that shows the cost, service life, and *19X3* amortization of Golden State's intangibles.
b. Prepare a compound (combined) journal entry to amortize the intangibles for 19X3.
c. Comment on the proper handling of items not included as part of the intangibles' cost.

Expanding Your Horizons

EYH12–1 Asset impairment (L.O. 4)

Companies have taken massive write-offs and write-downs of assets in recent years as a part of restructuring programs. Many of these write-offs and write-downs have resulted in a net loss for an otherwise profitable entity.

Instructions

By using the resources of your library, review the income statements, accompanying footnotes, and letter to stockholders of two companies that have reported recent restructuring charges. Prepare a short report that indicates the amount of the charge and a breakdown of the charge into its various components. Were any comments made about the restructuring in the letter to stockholders? If so, what was said?

EYH12–2 Franchising in the United States (L.O. 6)

Many business newspapers (e.g., *The Wall Street Journal*) have sections that deal with the purchase and/or sale of franchises. Apparently, there is always a need for a new type of burger, chicken, pizza, printer, carpet cleaner, and so forth.

Instructions

Review *The Wall Street Journal* or the business section of a major metropolitan newspaper and find a franchise opportunity that interests you. Call the franchisor (an 800 toll-free number is usually provided) and determine (1) the business concept being franchised; (2) the franchise territory, cost, and life; (3) responsibilities of the franchisor; (4) responsibilities of the franchisee; and (5) the company's success record. Prepare a short report of your findings.

EYH12–3 The value of brand names (L.O. 6)

Companies spend vast sums of money each year to maintain the image and "power" of their brand names. After all, it is consumer recognition of names like Coke, Marlboro, and Tide that produce billions of dollars in revenue for their owners.

Instructions

a. Obtain the August 2, 1994 edition of *Financial World* from your library. Briefly describe how the writers assigned a value to individual brand names.

b. According to the article, what are the ten most valuable brand names? What are the ten most valuable apparel brands?

EYH12–4 An overview of intangibles: Duracell International and Campbell Soup (L.O. 6)

Duracell is the world's leading manufacturer and marketer of high-performance alkaline batteries. Campbell Soup, in contrast, is involved with the manufacture of convenience foods and bakery products. Aside from its well-known Campbell's brand, the company also produces foods that are packaged under the following labels: Franco-American, Godiva, Mrs. Paul's, Pepperidge Farm, Swanson, V8, and Vlasic.

Instructions

By using the text's electronic data base, access the balance sheets and accompanying notes of both firms and answer the questions that follow. Unless otherwise indicated, responses should be based on data for the most recent year presented.

a. Both companies disclose property, plant, and equipment and intangibles on their balance sheets. How do the dollar amounts of these two long-term asset categories compare to total assets? Comment on your findings.

b. Define the term "net" as used on the balance sheet when referring to a company's intangible assets.

c. Review the notes that accompany the financial statements.
  (1) What are the major categories of intangibles disclosed by each firm?
  (2) Is goodwill described in unique terminology by either of the companies? Briefly explain.

d. What amortization periods are used by these firms? Does it appear that the firms are following the rules stipulated by the accounting profession? Briefly discuss.

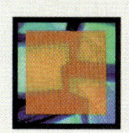

EYH12–5 An overview of intangibles (L.O. 6)

This problem is a duplication of Problem EYH12–4. It is based on two companies selected by your instructor.

Instructions

By using the text's electronic data base, access the specified companies' balance sheets and accompanying notes and focus on data for the most recent year reported. Answer requirements (a)–(d) of Problem EYH12–4.

EYH12–6 Patent accounting; loan decision (L.O. 6)

Dudley Finfrock is the assistant vice-president for commercial lending of the Maplewood National Bank. He has recently been approached by two aggressive companies for business loans. Both companies are engaged in high-technology product development and sales, but each company has used a different approach to achieve its ultimate profit objective.

Linden Electronics is run by two ex-employees of Woodhaven Semiconductor: Judy Brown and Stan Hall. Brown has an orientation toward research; Hall's specialty is sales. With an initial capital of $150,000, the two partners have developed many valuable products. Linden has spent over $80,000 on research and development and has obtained three patents from this effort. (Legal costs and filing fees connected with the patents were negligible because Linden's attorney is a family relative.) Advertising and sales promotion costs have consumed the remaining funds.

Rabway Electronics is also managed by two bright entrepreneurs: Harry Scott and Jack Monroe. Scott and Monroe were finance majors at the local university and possess minimal knowledge of electronics and sales. To establish a viable company, Rabway acquired existing patents from a California firm for $100,000. To generate sales, Scott and Monroe also purchased a franchise for $40,000 to sell a product similar to their own. In this manner the two products could be marketed together. Finally, Rabway spent $10,000 for legal fees related to the patents and franchise.

In the first few years of business, Linden operated at a net loss, while Rabway has generated impressive profits. A comparison of the financial statements and other operating information revealed that sales and production costs of the two companies were virtually identical. In addition, their products were very similar.

Instructions
a. Explain the probable cause behind Linden's net losses and Rabway's profits.
b. If you were in Dudley's position, would you grant a loan to either of the firms? What factors should be considered?

COMMUNICATION OF ACCOUNTING INFORMATION

CAI12–1   Preparing a speech: Bristol-Myers Squibb Company (L.O. 6)
Communication Principle: The most important part of any speech is the introduction. In addition to stating the purpose of the speech, an effective introduction accomplishes these objectives: gains the listeners' attention, relates the subject(s) to the listeners' personal interests, establishes the credibility of the speaker, and creates a friendly, at-ease relationship with the audience.

One or more of the following techniques may be used to get the listeners' attention: recite short, dramatic quotations; tell stories or tasteful jokes; present startling statistics; or use visual aids. Upon completing this step, the speaker should preview the major points to be covered. The points should be numbered, and the list should be short—no more than three or four major issues for a 30-minute presentation. A visual aid is very useful here.

When "show time" arrives, the introduction should not be read. The remarks should be memorized and practiced until they sound spontaneous. By talking directly to the audience, the speaker will establish a friendly, warm, and natural relationship—the equivalent of an inviting style in writing. This approach will dramatically increase the chances of an effective delivery.

■ ■ ■ ■ ■ ■ ■ ■ ■

As explained in the body of this chapter, goodwill means different things to different groups of people. In accounting, though, a specific meaning is attached to the term—one that often appears on the balance sheet itself. Consider the case of Bristol-Myers Squibb, which produces many consumer and health-care products (such as Clairol, NoDoz, and Bufferin). The company uses several descriptive account titles in its financial statements. One of these, Excess of Cost Over Net Tangible Assets Received in Business Acquisitions, is essentially a replacement for goodwill. A related note goes on to say:

> The excess of cost over net tangible assets received in business acquisitions . . . is being amortized on a straight-line basis over periods not exceeding forty years.

Instructions

You are about to prepare a short speech that will be delivered to a group of consumer advocates. The topic is the need for user-friendly annual reports, such as the one published by Bristol-Myers Squibb. (Be sure to cite and thank the company for its efforts.) A small portion of the talk will be devoted to the appropriateness of the firm's amortization policy. Write the introduction to the speech in full and outline the remainder.

Answers to Chapter Quiz

1. d
2. a
3. b ($10 million ÷ 4 million ounces = $2.50 per ounce; 5,000 ounces × $2.50 = $12,500)
4. c ($102,000 ÷ 2 years = $51,000)
5. d

Comprehensive Problem 2

WYATT COMPANY

Wyatt Company's management has always relied on very conservative accounting policies, resulting in the 19X8 year-end balance sheet that appears on page 470. George Wyatt, founder of the company, has been approached by a party desiring to buy the firm at a price equal to 200% of owner's equity. George agreed that the price would be fair if owner's equity were revised to reflect the following:

- *Trading Securities*—The market value of the trading securities was $85,000 on December 31, 19X8. The reported cost of $40,000 was accurate; however, investment values have skyrocketed since acquisition, and this increase has never been recognized. George desires to report the company's holdings at the market value of $85,000.
- *Accounts receivable*—The Allowance account is presently equal to 10% of the outstanding receivables balance. Wyatt believes that the company should estimate uncollectible accounts at 2% of the firm's sales ($400,000). The balance in the Allowance account at the beginning of the year was $3,000, and customer write-offs during 19X8 totaled $7,000.
- *Inventory*—Inventory is valued by using the LIFO method. George reports that income for the last three years would have been $45,500 higher had FIFO been employed. (The company is only three years old.) Wyatt desires to use FIFO when calculating the revised owner's equity figure.
- *Buildings*—The company's three-year-old buildings are being depreciated by the double-declining balance method, based on a 20-year life and $30,000 residual value. George believes the straight-line method would be more appropriate.
- *Equipment*—The equipment, which is two years old and has no residual value, is being written off by the sum-of-the-years'-digits method over a five-year life. Again, George prefers the straight-line method.
- *Patent*—The patent was acquired for $28,000 at the beginning of the current year. George believes that this intangible should not be amortized and desires to report the patent at acquisition cost. The original service life of the intangible should have been estimated at 10 years.

WYATT COMPANY
Balance Sheet
December 31, 19X8

ASSETS

Current assets
Cash		$ 15,000
Trading securities		40,000
Accounts receivable	$ 75,000	
Less: Allowance for uncollectibles	7,500	67,500
Inventory		125,000
Total current assets		$247,500

Property, plant, & equipment
Land		$ 85,000	
Buildings	$289,000		
Less: Accumulated depreciation	78,319	210,681	
Equipment	$ 80,000		
Less: Accumulated depreciation	48,000	32,000	
Total property, plant, & equipment			327,681

Intangibles
Patent	28,000
Total assets	$603,181

LIABILITIES & OWNER'S EQUITY

Current liabilities
Accounts payable	$ 22,000
Salaries payable	7,000
Taxes payable	8,000
Total current liabilities	$ 37,000

Long-term liabilities
Bank loans payable	115,000
Total liabilities	$152,000

Owner's equity
George Wyatt, capital	451,181
Total liabilities & owner's equity	$603,181

Instructions

a. Which of George's preferences violate generally accepted accounting procedures? Briefly explain the reason for the violation.
b. Prepare the balance sheet and compute the purchase price that would result if George's preferences were used. Use generally accepted accounting procedures throughout, especially where George's alternatives are technically incorrect. (*Hint:* All changes in the company's income will be reflected by changes in the owner's capital balance.)
c. Compare your answer in part (b) with the original balance sheet. Why do you think George wants the changes that are detailed in the body of the problem?

13 CURRENT LIABILITIES AND EMPLOYEE COMPENSATION

LEARNING OBJECTIVES

After studying this chapter, you should be able to:

1. Explain the occurrence of and accounting for typical current liabilities of a business.

2. Account for notes payable when interest is included in the face value of a note and when interest is recorded separately.

3. Identify typical contingent liabilities and recognize the guidelines that are used for recording such obligations in the accounts.

4. Calculate and record payroll, including the employer's tax obligation.

5. Recognize other payroll-related costs of the employer: vacation pay, pensions, and postretirement health care.

6. Discuss the problem of rising fringe benefit costs.

George Faris of Banner Advertising dislikes debt. "It's an expensive way to run a business," he observes. "I can live with 30-day obligations that are owed to suppliers, but we try to avoid extended payment periods. Although we have use of our cash for longer periods of time, suppliers and banks hit us with interest. These charges are high and can put a meaningful dent into profits. Payroll obligations also give us fits. Our employees earn wages of $10 per hour, but the company's total cost is in excess of $15."

George's payroll experience is typical and reflects the frustrations of many small business owners. Payroll costs consist of far more than what meets the eye. In addition to wages and salaries, employers also pay Social Security taxes, Medicare taxes, federal and state unemployment taxes, and insurance. These costs are often exorbitant. Banner, for instance, has never had a serious work-related injury. Nevertheless, workers' compensation insurance, which provides compensation to any worker injured on the job, adds another 37% to total payroll. Larger companies have further costs in their efforts to be competitive and attract top managerial talent. It is not uncommon for these entities to offer company cars, physical exams, financial planning services, and club memberships as part of a comprehensive fringe benefit package.

Payroll and benefits are just two of the many obligations that organizations must grapple with in their drive toward profitability. These items and other activities as well give rise to a significant element of the basic accounting equation: liabilities. **Liabilities** are obligations that (1) have arisen from past transactions or events and (2) are payable in cash, other assets, or services.

The measurement and disclosure of liabilities in the financial statements are extremely important because sizable future cash outlays may be involved. Many suppliers, for example, refuse to grant credit to businesses that have high levels of liabilities for fear of nonpayment. Similarly, most investors shy away from companies heavily burdened by debt because of the risk involved. Substantial debt payments are often accompanied by large outlays for interest, which reduce an investor's chance of receiving dividends. Adding to this problem is the fact that the firm's cash position may be extremely weak in periods of a softening economy.

Earlier in the text we noted that liabilities are classified as either current or long term, depending on the due date (or dates). We will discuss current liabilities in this chapter and selected long-term obligations in Chapter 18.

CURRENT LIABILITIES

Explain the occurrence of and accounting for typical current liabilities of a business.

Current liabilities are debts or obligations that will be paid within one year or the operating cycle, whichever is longer. Payment of current liabilities involves the use of current assets (usually cash) or, on occasion, the creation of another current liability. For example, an account payable could be settled by issuing a short-term interest-bearing note to the creditor.

Typical current liabilities include accounts payable and the following:

1. Prepayments (advances) by customers.
2. Amounts collected for and payable to third parties.
3. Accrued liabilities for expenses incurred but not yet paid.
4. The portion of long-term debt due within one year or the operating cycle, whichever is longer.
5. Short-term notes payable to banks and other parties.
6. Contingent liabilities.

PREPAYMENTS (ADVANCES) BY CUSTOMERS

Businesses often receive **prepayments,** or advances, from customers. Insurance companies collect premiums; publishers sell magazine subscriptions; stores issue gift certificates; and transportation firms sell tickets and tokens before their service is delivered. These amounts, frequently termed *unearned revenues* or *deferred revenues*, represent liabilities to the recipient because goods or services are owed in return. You were originally introduced to unearned revenues in Chapter 3 and may find a review of this earlier material helpful.

The balance sheet should report the amount of goods and services owed as of the statement's date. As the obligations are settled, the prepayments are reduced and increased revenues are reported on the income statement. Prepayments for most businesses are relatively modest in amount; however, there are exceptions. In a recent set of financial statements, for example, Allstate Insurance reported unearned premiums in excess of $5 billion!

COLLECTIONS FOR THIRD PARTIES

In the normal course of business, organizations often collect money from customers and employees that is payable to others. Retailers, for instance, accumulate sales tax from customers when goods are sold. Later, the monies collected are remitted to the proper governmental authority. Similarly, companies sometimes become involved in United Way or disaster relief activities, receiving funds that are ultimately disbursed to various social service agencies. And, as shown in another part of this chapter, taxes and other items are customarily deducted from employee wages and forwarded to third parties.

Collections for third parties, such as those just mentioned, are recognized as current liabilities until cash is disbursed to the proper authority. To illustrate the necessary accounting, assume that Yorktown Candle Shoppe sells $1,000 of merchandise on account in a state having a 5% sales tax. The entry to record the sale follows.

Accounts Receivable	1,050	
Sales		1,000
Sales Taxes Payable		50
To record sale and related sales tax.		

A liability of $50 ($1,000 × 0.05) is established for the sales tax, which Yorktown now owes to the state treasury. When the tax is remitted, Sales Taxes Payable will be debited and Cash will be credited. The liability is thus eliminated. Other third-party collections are handled in a similar manner.

ACCRUED LIABILITIES

Accrued liabilities, often called accrued expenses, were also introduced in Chapter 3. Under the accrual basis of accounting, expenses are matched against revenues in the period when incurred. This practice generally results in the recognition of some unpaid expenses and calls for the placement of accrued liabilities on the balance sheet. Examples of accrued liabilities include salaries and wages, income taxes (both federal and state), and interest.

To demonstrate the related procedures, suppose that Rosenthal Company has a five-day workweek and all employees are paid on Friday. Also assume that the end of the annual accounting period, November 30, falls on Thursday. Although employees will not be compensated until December 1, Rosenthal must accrue payroll expense on November 30 for the work performed from Monday through Thursday. In so doing, revenue and expense for the year will be correctly matched, and current liabilities will be properly recorded. If salaries total $10,500 per day, the adjusting entry is as follows:

Salaries Expense	42,000	
Salaries Payable		42,000
To accrue four days of salaries at $10,500 per day.*		

*Payroll taxes should also be accrued at this time.

CURRENT PORTION OF LONG-TERM DEBT

As we noted, long-term liabilities will be discussed at length in another chapter. At this point, however, it is important to understand that the portion of long-term debt due within one year or the normal operating cycle, whichever is longer, is reported as a current liability. For example, suppose that a company borrowed $500,000 via a long-term loan. If $60,000 is payable within the next 12 months, the appropriate balance sheet disclosure would be as follows:

Current liabilities		
Current portion of long-term debt		$ 60,000
Long-term liabilities		
Loan payable	$500,000	
Less: Balance due currently	60,000	440,000

Treatment as a current liability presumes that the short-term portion will be settled by the use of current assets or by the creation of other current liabilities. If not, such amounts remain classified as long-term liabilities until paid or refinanced.

Mortgage Notes. A mortgage note is a common example of an obligation that must be split between the balance sheet's current and long-term classifications. Used to finance the purchase of real estate, these obligations are normally paid in monthly installments over terms that may go 30 years into the future.

Each installment includes a payment for both interest and a small reduction of the note's principal. Although the total monthly payment usually remains constant, the allocation between interest and principal will differ each period. Virtually all mortgage obligations, as well as other long-term loans, require that interest be computed on the basis of the unpaid principal. Thus, each successive monthly payment contains a declining interest charge because of the decreasing note balance.

For example, assume that VoTech secured a 12%, $200,000 mortgage on August 31, 19X5. Based on month-end payments of $3,500, the allocation between interest and principal for September through December would be as follows:

PAYMENT DATE	(A) MONTHLY PAYMENT	(B) MONTHLY INTEREST (1% OF UNPAID NOTE BALANCE)*	(C) REDUCTION IN PRINCIPAL (A – B)	(D) UNPAID NOTE BALANCE (PREVIOUS BALANCE – C)
Issuance date				$200,000
Sept. 30	$3,500	$2,000	$1,500	198,500
Oct. 31	3,500	1,985	1,515	196,985
Nov. 30	3,500	1,970	1,530	195,455
Dec. 31	3,500	1,955	1,545	193,910

* 12% annual rate ÷ 12 one-month interest periods. All figures are rounded to the nearest dollar.

The first payment on September 30 consists of $2,000 of interest expense ($200,000 × 0.01) and a $1,500 reduction in the mortgage's outstanding balance ($3,500 – $2,000). These data are entered in the accounting records by means of formal journal entries. To illustrate, the entry needed on September 30 is:

Sept. 30	Interest Expense	2,000	
	Mortgage Note Payable	1,500	
	Cash		3,500
	To record monthly payment of interest and reduction in principal of note.		

Balance Sheet Presentation. A table such as the one just shown is very helpful for determining VoTech's proper balance sheet presentation. A computer routine would be used to calculate the reduction-in-principal amounts (column C) for *future* payments. The total of these figures for the next twelve months would then be disclosed on the December 31, 19X5, balance sheet as a current liability, reflecting the debt to be settled in the upcoming accounting period.

NOTES PAYABLE

2 Account for notes payable when interest is included in the face value of a note and when interest is recorded separately.

Short-term notes have many uses in the business world. Notes payable are often employed to finance purchases of merchandise, equipment, and other similar assets. In addition, notes can be used to secure short-term borrowings from banks. Polaroid Corporation, for instance, recently reported notes payable to banks of $106.2 million on its year-end balance sheet. Such temporary use of bank credit for periods of less than one year is commonplace and serves as a major source of funds for many businesses.

Notes payable are also issued at the request of creditors when a firm (or individual) is past due in the payment of an account payable. The note is simply substituted for the account payable on the books of the issuing entity. A creditor prefers a note to a delinquent open account: should the issuer fail to pay the debt on schedule, a signed note provides better security if legal remedies are necessary.

Accounting for Notes Payable. To illustrate the proper accounting for notes payable, assume that Corsica Trading Corporation borrowed $80,000 from the Mercantile National Bank on June 3 by signing the obligation shown in Exhibit 13-1. The journal entry to record the receipt of funds and issuance of the note follows.

Cash	80,000	
Notes Payable		80,000
To record note payable to bank;		
180 days at 15%.		

Observe that the face value of the note is equal to the amount borrowed and that no interest expense is recorded on the date of issue. Interest will be incurred on a daily basis over the term of the loan.

Next, assume that Corsica's fiscal year ends on October 31. Because the note was issued on June 3 and does not mature until November 30, total interest expense must be apportioned between two accounting periods. As of October 31, the obligation has been outstanding for 150 days, requiring the following adjusting entry:

Interest Expense	5,000	
Interest Payable		5,000
To accrue interest for 150 days:		
$80,000 \times 0.15 \times 150/360$.		

Corsica's balance sheet disclosure would therefore appear as shown below.

Current liabilities
    ⋮

Notes payable	$80,000	
Interest payable	5,000	$85,000

When the note is paid on November 30, the following entry is necessary:

Notes Payable	80,000	
Interest Payable	5,000	
Interest Expense	1,000	
Cash		86,000
To record payment to bank for		
note payable and interest.		

The additional $1,000 represents the 30 days of interest related to November (1/6 of the loan term).

EXHIBIT 13–1
Example of Note Payable

```
Date June 3, 19XX                          New York, New York  10059

For value received, the undersigned promises to pay the Mercantile National Bank
in  180 days  the sum of  $80,000 , with interest at the rate of  15%  per year.

                                           R. B. Thompson
                                           Corsica Trading Corporation
```

Notes with Interest Included in the Face Value. Many notes, especially those issued to banks and finance companies, do not state interest separately. Instead, interest is included in the obligation's face value. For example, assume that Corsica Trading still needs to raise $80,000. Mercantile National Bank, however, agreed to accept the $86,000 note that appears in Exhibit 13–2.

Corsica's entry to record the proceeds and issue the note follows.

Cash	80,000	
Discount on Notes Payable	6,000	
Notes Payable		86,000
To record note payable to bank;		
180 days until maturity.		

As in the previous case, the obligation is recorded at face value—$86,000 in this instance. Cash received remains at $80,000. The difference between these two figures, $6,000, represents 180 days of future interest, which will be incurred over the term of the note. This amount is entered in an account entitled Discount on Notes Payable, a *contra liability* that is deducted from Notes Payable on the balance sheet. If a balance sheet was prepared immediately after issuance, Corsica would present the following information:

Current liabilities		
Notes payable	$86,000	
Less: Discount on notes payable	6,000	$80,000

The net liability on June 3 is $80,000—the amount borrowed on that day.

Discount Amortization. Assume it is now October 31, the end of Corsica's fiscal year. Because 150 days have passed since the note's issuance, interest expense must be recognized. As we just stated, the discount's $6,000 balance represents 180 days of future interest charges. Thus, $5,000 ($6,000 × 150/180) must be removed from the Discount account and transferred to the income statement. The following adjusting entry is needed:

Interest Expense	5,000	
Discount on Notes Payable		5,000
To accrue interest for 150 days and		
amortize the discount.		

EXHIBIT 13-2
Note Payable with Interest Included in the Face Value

```
Date June 3, 19XX                              New York, New York  10059

For value received, the undersigned promises to pay the Mercantile National Bank
the sum of  $86,000  in  180 days  .

                                          R. B. Thompson
                                          Corsica Trading Corporation
```

The process of reducing the discount by recognizing interest expense is frequently referred to as **discount amortization.**

As a result of the adjustment, the Discount on Notes Payable account will have a $1,000 balance ($6,000 − $5,000) and will appear on the balance sheet as shown.

Current liabilities		
Notes payable	$86,000	
Less: Discount on notes payable	1,000	$85,000

The net liability is now $85,000: $80,000 borrowed plus accrued interest of $5,000. A separate account for interest payable is *not* established because the interest is already part of the note's face value.

To complete the example, the following entry would be necessary when Corsica pays the note on November 30:

Notes Payable	86,000	
Interest Expense	1,000	
Discount on Notes Payable		1,000
Cash		86,000
To record payment of the note and amortize the discount.		

This entry recognizes the remaining $1,000 of interest expense that pertains to November and cancels the balance in the Notes Payable account.

A Brief Overview. A careful observation will reveal that Corsica received $80,000 and ultimately paid $6,000 of interest with *both* notes. Furthermore, both balance sheet presentations at the end of the October 31 fiscal year revealed a total liability of $85,000. To conclude, the notes differed in form only. In the first case, interest was stated separately; in the second case, interest was included in the obligation's face value.

CONTINGENT LIABILITIES

The liabilities presented thus far have been definite and absolute (i.e., there was no uncertainty regarding a company's legal and economic responsibility for the

> **3** Identify typical contingent liabilities and recognize the guidelines that are used for recording such obligations in the accounts.

obligation). Several situations in accounting give rise to a *potential* liability. As a typical example, businesses are frequently the target of litigation, the outcome of which is sometimes unknown at the time of financial statement preparation. To illustrate this situation, consider the following excerpted footnotes from recent annual reports of Johnson & Johnson and Quaker State Corporation:

Johnson & Johnson:
The Company is involved in numerous product liability cases in the United States, many of which concern adverse reactions to drugs and medical devices. The damages claimed are substantial, and while the Company is confident of teh adequacy of the warnings which accompany such products, it is not feasible to predict the ultimate outcome of litigation . . . . [If] any liability results from such cases for injuries occurring on or before December 31, 1985, it will be substantially covered by insurance. Due to the general unavailability of traditional liability insurance, including product liability insurance, the Company is substantially uninsured for injuries occurring on or after January 1, 1986. The Company has a self-insurance program which provides reserves for such injuries based on claims experience . . . .

Quaker State Corporation:
In December 1993, the United States of America commenced a lawsuit against the Company in the U.S. District Court for Northern West Virginia. The complaint alleges the Company violated the federal Resource Conservation and Recovery Act and the federal Clean Air Act at the Congo refinery on various dates starting in 1980 and seeks civil penalties as allowable under federal law not to exceed $25,000 per day for each violation. The Company intends to vigorously defend itself in this lawsuit . . . . In addition, the Company has received notices from the [Environmental Protection Agency] and others that it is a "potentially responsible party" relative to certain waste disposal sites identified by the EPA and may be required to share in the cost of cleanup.

Liabilities of this nature are commonly referred to as contingent liabilities, because their outcome hinges on the future. Future events and happenings will convert the contingency into an absolute liability or eliminate it entirely. In addition to lawsuits, other contingent liabilities include obligations related to product warranties and coupon redemptions.

Accounting Rules for Contingencies. Over the years, the treatment of contingent liabilities has been the subject of much debate. Sometimes, contingent liabilities were recorded in the accounts by a journal entry. On other occasions, disclosure was made in the footnotes that accompany the financial statements. On still other occasions, nothing was done for fear of misleading statement users about a liability that might never materialize.

Because of the wide diversity in treatments, guidelines were eventually issued to "standardize" the related accounting.[1] The guidelines stipulated that contingent liabilities should be recorded in the accounts when (1) it is *probable* that the future event will occur and (2) the amount of the liability can be *reasonably estimated*. Observe the key words in italics. If only one of these criteria is met, no journal entry is made; a footnote to the financial statements is usually deemed appropriate.

---

[1] See "Accounting for Contingencies," *Statement of Financial Accounting Standards No. 5,* Financial Accounting Standards Board, Norwalk, Conn., 1975.

> **ETHICS ISSUE**
>
> S, Inc., is having a bad year financially. To help improve reported performance, management has suggested burying the effects of a significant contingent liability in the notes to the financial statements. A manager was heard saying: ". . . Instead of deriving a reasonable estimate of the financial impact, which we know will be subject to error, simply say that no estimate is possible." Comment.

A Further Focus

Liability estimation may require input from engineers, lawyers, and other professionals. Major airlines, for instance, have frequent flyer programs that offer passengers free trips when certain mileage totals are met. Although not a *contingent* liability, these programs dictate that an estimate be entered in the accounting records to reflect the carrier's obligation to its passengers. The estimate is the cost of fulfilling the award and includes food, beverages, insurance, security, ticketing, and other similar expenditures.

Northwest Airlines disclosed a reliance on engineering formulas to calculate the fuel cost related to its WORLDPERKS program. The carrier first estimates the average fuel cost per pound per hour. Then, the expected average weight of extra luggage and onboard passengers are considered to convert this figure to an amount per passenger per award.

Source: *Prospectus to Issue 20,000,000 Shares of Class A Common Stock,* Northwest Airlines Corporation, March 18, 1994, p. 54.

Warranty Costs. To illustrate accounting for a contingent liability that typically meets both guidelines, we will focus on warranty costs. A **warranty** is a promise made by a seller or manufacturer to remedy defects in product quality and performance. Most appliances, for example, are warranted for one year; the major components of automobiles often have a 50,000-mile warranty.

The cost of warranties can normally be estimated, with reasonable accuracy, on the basis of past experience. Because most warranties help to promote the sale of goods and services, such costs should be matched against revenues in the period of sale. At this same time a contingent liability must be entered in the accounts—to recognize that a firm has a potential exposure to warranty work as some of its products become defective.

For instance, assume that Drake Electronics began to stock a new camera model late in 19X1. The camera has a two-year warranty; 200 units were sold during the year. Drake estimates that 15% of the cameras will require repair work and that the repairs will average $40 per unit. The journal entry on December 31 to record the estimated warranty cost of $1,200 (200 units × 0.15 × $40) and establish the liability is as follows:

Warranty Expense	1,200	
Estimated Liability for Warranties		1,200
To record warranty costs for 19X1.		

As the warranties are honored, Drake will reduce the liability. If 10 cameras are serviced during 19X2, the following journal entry becomes necessary:

Estimated Liability for Warranties	400	
Cash, Salaries Payable, Parts Inventory, and so on		400
To record service cost under warranties: 10 cameras × $40.		

The Estimated Liability for Warranties account would be reported on the December 31, 19X2, balance sheet at $800 ($1,200 − $400). This amount represents the estimated warranty cost in 19X3 of servicing units sold in 19X1.

BALANCE SHEET DISCLOSURE

Current liabilities are normally listed on the balance sheet according to due date (from the earliest to the latest) or maturity value (from the largest to the smallest). Reporting practices vary widely, however. To illustrate a typical disclosure, we present the current liability section from a recent balance sheet of United Technologies, perhaps best known for the manufacture of Pratt & Whitney aircraft engines, Carrier air conditioning systems, Otis elevators, and Sikorsky helicopters (see Exhibit 13–3).

EMPLOYEE COMPENSATION

④ Calculate and record payroll, including the employer's tax obligation.

Employees' wages, salaries, related payroll taxes, and fringe benefits are a significant expense for many businesses, particularly those engaged in providing services. For example, Federal Express recently reported employee compensation and benefits amounting to 48.4% of operating revenues. At H&R Block, salaries and related expenses of $404.4 million constituted over 42% of total operating expenses. Accounting for payroll is important not only because large amounts of money are involved but also because various federal and state regulations must be met. By law, businesses must maintain detailed information on individual employees and aggregate information for the entity as a whole.

For purposes of payroll accounting, an organization must distinguish between employees and independent contractors. The distinction must be made because payroll regulations, whether they pertain to taxes, reporting, or record keeping, apply almost exclusively to an entity's employees. Employees are persons who work for a specific business and are directed and closely supervised by that business. Independent contractors, on the other hand, frequently perform services for many different organizations at the same time or perhaps finish a project for one firm and then move on to service another.

EXHIBIT 13–3
Current Liability Presentation (in millions)

UNITED TECHNOLOGIES	
Current liabilities	
Short-term borrowings	$ 780
Accounts payable	1,815
Accrued salaries, wages, and employee benefits	912
Accrued restructuring costs	245
Other accrued liabilities	2,053
Long-term debt—currently due	240
Income taxes currently payable	314
Advances on sales contracts	561
Total current liabilities	$6,920

Common examples of independent contractors include certified public accountants, attorneys, management consultants, and architects. Observe that an employer/employee relationship does not exist in these situations. Rather, the independent contractor is engaged to provide a service, performs that service without direct supervision from the client, and receives a fee in return.

A Human Resource Manager's Perspective

Employer/Employee Relations: Personnel relationships are changing because of legal considerations. Companies increasingly find themselves being the target of lawsuits filed by former employees—employees who believe that they have been treated unfairly. A fired manager might argue that he or she was guaranteed a lifetime job by a vice-president and was never given an opportunity to correct inappropriate behavior. In one case, an employer lost a suit where an employee was terminated for alleged sexual harassment of a coworker, and the harasser sued the employer for wrongful termination.

According to the Rand Institute, because companies are spending more to prevent lawsuits related to these issues, they are hiring fewer staff. The study suggests that businesses tend to use temporary workers or pay overtime to regular employees before expanding their ranks with additional personnel. In several wrongful termination cases brought by former employees, the courts have awarded the plaintiff as much as $26 million.

Employee Earnings

Wages and salaries earned by employees develop either from a negotiated contract between a company and representatives of its employees or from a direct agreement between the company and individual personnel. The former situation is usually encountered for a firm's labor force; the latter relates most often to management.

The wages and salaries earned are paid after the payroll period has concluded. Accurate record keeping is a must, especially for personnel paid by the hour or on the basis of piecework. Time cards, time clocks, and electronic recording systems are commonly used to ensure that each hourly worker is compensated correctly. For employees who receive wages based on productivity, a daily report must be generated that indicates the output and operations performed.

Proper determination of an employee's hours or output is the first step in the calculation of total, or *gross earnings.* Gross earnings are dependent on many factors, including federal regulations and company policy. According to the Federal Fair Labor Standards Act,[2] for example, businesses engaged in interstate commerce must pay overtime of at least one and one-half times the regular rate for hours worked in excess of 40 per week. In addition, many companies establish their own policies and pay premium rates for work on night shifts, split shifts, holidays, and Sundays.

---

[2] This act is sometimes called the Wages and Hours Law.

To illustrate the calculation of gross earnings, assume that Paula Hite worked 52 hours during a weekly payroll period at Ajax Fabricators. Paula is paid $10 per hour, and the company compensates for overtime at one and one-half times the regular hourly rate. Paula's gross pay for the week would be $580: [(40 hours × $10) + (12 hours × $15)].

DEDUCTIONS FROM EMPLOYEE EARNINGS

As many of you know, an employee's take-home (net) pay is less than his or her gross pay. And normally it is much less! These two amounts differ because of required tax withholdings by the employer and voluntary deductions that have been authorized by the employee. We will now focus on several common deductions.

Social Security/Medicare Taxes (FICA). Retirement, financial, and medical benefits are provided to the aged, disabled, survivors, and orphans under the Federal Insurance Contributions Act (FICA). Employers are required to withhold a portion of each employee's gross earnings to help fund these government programs. Additionally, the employer must match the employee's contributions. As an example, assume that Kathy Durham earns $24,000 and that all of her earnings are subject to FICA taxes. If the proper FICA computation yields, say, $1,800, this amount will be withheld from her paychecks. A total of $3,600 will ultimately be remitted to the government, composed of Durham's contribution and a matching amount from her employer ($1,800 × 2 = $3,600).

Several significant changes in the accounting for FICA taxes have occurred in recent years. First, both the amount of earnings subject to FICA tax (termed the FICA base) and the tax rate have increased dramatically. Upon inception of the Act in 1937, for example, the first $3,000 of earnings was taxed at a rate of 1%, resulting in a maximum employee contribution of $30. At the time of this writing, there is no maximum limit in effect.

Second, more detailed computations and reporting are required. Because of variations in rates and bases, employers must now account for FICA as consisting of two separate components: Social Security and Medicare. Illustrations throughout the remainder of this chapter assume the following taxes:

Social Security: 6.5% on the first $65,000 earned
Medicare: 1.5% on all wages earned

Federal, State, and City Income Taxes. Employers must also withhold a portion of an employee's gross earnings to satisfy federal income tax laws and the laws of many states and local municipalities. These income tax withholdings are later submitted to the appropriate governmental authorities in payment of the employee's tax liability. Given the nature of the system, income taxes are actually remitted on a pay-as-you-go basis.

The amount withheld for federal income taxes is based on employee earnings, the frequency of pay, marital status, and the number of withholding allowances claimed. The allowances are reported to an employer at the time of hire on a Form W-4 (Withholding Allowance Certificate) and depend on various factors, including marital status and number of children.

In an effort to secure operating revenues, many state and local governmental units have enacted laws that tax an employee's gross earnings. The amounts withheld for state and local income taxes vary widely but are often a stipulated percentage of gross pay.

Other Deductions. In addition to required Social Security/Medicare and income tax withholdings, many employees voluntarily authorize other deductions from their paychecks. Common examples of such deductions include payments for insurance programs (life, medical, dental) and U.S. savings bonds, contributions to a pension plan, union dues, and charitable contributions.

Calculation of Take-Home Pay. To illustrate the computation of net or take-home pay, we will focus on Tony Disano, a married employee of Trimble Services who earns a weekly salary of $1,400. The information that follows is available.

1. According to his W-4 form, Disano is claiming three withholding allowances.
2. Ohio, the state of employment, has a 2% income tax (assumed).
3. Social Security/Medicare taxes are as noted on the previous page. Tony's year-to-date earnings before considering the present payroll period amount to $64,400.
4. Disano has authorized a $40 deduction for medical insurance and a $10 contribution to the United Way.

Disano's take-home pay for the current week is calculated as follows:

Gross earnings		$1,400
Less deductions		
Federal income tax	$226	
State income tax ($1,400 × 0.02)	28	
Social Security taxes ($600 × 0.065)	39	
Medicare taxes ($1,400 × 0.015)	21	
Medical insurance	40	
United Way contribution	10	364
Net pay		$1,036

The federal income tax withholding amount is based on tables provided by the government. To determine the appropriate withholding, Disano's employer would refer to the table for married persons who are paid on a weekly basis. Trimble would then locate (or in some cases, figure) the amount that corresponds to three allowances and earnings of $1,400. Assume that this process results in income tax withholdings of $226.

Turning to Social Security, employees are subject to a 6.5% tax computed on a base of $65,000. According to the data presented, Disano has year-to-date earnings of $64,400. Thus, when his current week's salary of $1,400 is considered, the maximum taxable base will be exceeded. For this reason only $600 ($65,000 − $64,400) of the current pay is subject to Social Security taxation, and Trimble will deduct $39 ($600 × 0.065). Conversely, all of Disano's gross pay will be subject to Medicare taxation ($1,400 × 0.015 = $21) because there is no limit on the earnings base.

PAYROLL RECORDING AND RECORD KEEPING

At the end of each payroll period, the gross earnings, deductions, and net pay of all employees are entered in a *payroll register,* a journal-like device used to record a company's salary and wage data. From the information available in the register, a summary journal entry similar to the following can be prepared.

Sales Salaries Expense	1,840	
Office Salaries Expense	1,960	
Employees' Federal Income Taxes Payable		680
Employees' State Income Taxes Payable		76
Social Security Taxes Payable		195
Medicare Taxes Payable		57
Employees' Insurance Program Payable		125
Savings Bonds Payable		15
United Way Contributions Payable		50
Salaries Payable		2,602
To record payroll and withholdings.		

Observe that the employees' gross pay is classified as sales salaries expense or office salaries expense, depending on the type of work performed. In addition, notice that the credit to Salaries Payable represents the net amount that will be disbursed to personnel on payday. (Generally, several days elapse between the end of the payroll period and payday to allow a company ample time to accumulate information and prepare checks.) Finally, the withholdings are current liabilities because the amounts are owed to various authorities (e.g., the federal government, the United Way, and so forth) and must be paid within a relatively short period of time. At the time of settlement, the proper payable is debited and Cash is credited.

Employee Records. Shortly after the conclusion of a calendar year, an employer must furnish an accounting to each employee of the gross wages and salaries earned and the taxes withheld. Individual employee records are therefore a necessity. The employer provides the required information to the employee on a Wage and Tax Statement, more commonly known as a W-2 (see Exhibit 13–4). Upon receipt, an employee can proceed with completion of the various tax forms that are filed with the Internal Revenue Service and state and local taxing authorities.

PAYROLL TAXES OF THE EMPLOYER

Thus far, our discussion of taxes has focused on the employee. Employers are also subject to payroll taxes; specifically, Social Security/Medicare, federal unemployment, and state unemployment.

Social Security/Medicare Tax. The most significant payroll tax levied on the employer is Social Security/Medicare. As we noted earlier, employers must match the contributions of their employees to these programs. Consequently, Social Security and Medicare tax rates on the employee and the employer are identical.

EXHIBIT 13–4
Example of W-2 Form

a Control number				
	OMB No. 1545-0008			
b Employer's identification number 75-1411366		1 Wages, tips, other compensation 65,800.00	2 Federal income tax withheld 10,622.00	
c Employer's name, address, and ZIP code		3 Social security wages 65,000.00	4 Social security tax withheld 4,225.00	
Trimble Services, Inc. 805 Tuck Place Cleveland, Ohio 44108		5 Medicare wages and tips 65,800.00	6 Medicare tax withheld 987.00	
		7 Social security tips	8 Allocated tips	
d Employee's social security number 579-89-1111		9 Advance EIC payment	10 Dependent care benefits	
e Employee's name, address, and ZIP code		11 Nonqualified plans	12 Benefits included in Box 1	
		13 See Instrs. for Box 13	14 Other Insurance: 1,880.00 United Way: 470.00	
Tony Disano 79 Flora Street Cleveland, Ohio 44106				
		15 Statutory employee / Deceased / Pension plan / Legal rep. / 942 emp. / Subtotal / Deferred compensation		
16 State OH	Employer's state I.D. No. 35-11486	17 State wages, tips, etc. 65,800.00	18 State income tax 1,316.00	19 Locality name	20 Local wages, tips, etc.	21 Local income tax

Form **W-2** Wage and Tax Statement **19X4**
Copy B To Be Filed With Employee's FEDERAL Tax Return
Department of the Treasury–Internal Revenue Service
This information is being furnished to the Internal Revenue Service.

Federal Unemployment Tax. The employer is also required to pay tax under the Federal Unemployment Tax Act (FUTA). FUTA is a joint program between the federal government and the various states to financially assist the unemployed. Taxes collected are not distributed directly to those out of work; instead, the funds are used to support the administrative costs of state unemployment programs.

FUTA taxes are levied only on employers. At the time this text was written, the tax was 6.2% of the first $7,000 paid to each employee. Employers, however, can receive a credit of up to 5.4% for amounts remitted to state unemployment funds. Accordingly, many states have set a rate of at least 5.4% for their own programs, resulting in a *net* FUTA cost of 0.8% (6.2% − 5.4%) on a $7,000 earnings base.

State Unemployment Taxes. The various state programs collect state unemployment taxes and then disburse these monies to people out of work. As we just noted, many states have implemented a tax rate of at least 5.4%, also computed on an employee's first $7,000 of gross pay. Normally, however, businesses with good labor records receive a merit reduction. This practice makes sense economically because such firms have a low number of layoffs and terminations, thereby saving the state large amounts of unemployment compensation. Employers receiving merit reductions can still obtain a credit for federal purposes of up to 5.4%.

Recording the Employer's Taxes. The entry to record the payroll taxes levied on an employer is made at the same time payroll is recorded. To illustrate the necessary accounting, we will make the following assumptions:

1. The employer's share of Social Security and Medicare taxes is $195 and $57, respectively. Notice that these amounts are identical to the employees' contributions recorded in the journal entry on page 485.
2. Federal and state unemployment tax rates are 0.8% and 5.4%, respectively, of an employee's first $7,000 of gross earnings. All employees except Pete Roe, a new hire, have earned more than $7,000 for the year. Roe's compensation-to-date totals $500.

The payroll tax obligation, an expense, is recorded as follows:

Payroll Tax Expense	283	
Social Security Taxes Payable		195
Medicare Taxes Payable		57
Federal Unemployment Taxes Payable		4*
State Unemployment Taxes Payable		27*
To record employer's payroll taxes.		

* Unemployment taxes are calculated only on Roe's salary because all other employees are over the limit.
Federal: $500 × 0.008 = $4; state: $500 × 0.054 = $27.

The liabilities will eventually be removed from the accounting records upon remittance to the proper authority.

OTHER PAYROLL-RELATED COSTS OF THE EMPLOYER

> **5**
>
> Recognize other payroll-related costs of the employer: vacation pay, pensions, and postretirement health care.

In addition to the taxes just discussed, employers have numerous other payroll-related costs. These costs include vacation pay, pensions, and postretirement health care.

Vacation Pay. Many businesses provide paid vacations for their employees. By working 50 weeks throughout the year, for instance, a worker may earn two weeks of paid time-off. From the employer's viewpoint, such fringe benefit plans increase the total cost of employee service—in this particular case by 4% of wage cost (2 ÷ 50).

Proper accounting requires that the cost of (and obligation for) paid vacations be spread over the entire year so that each reporting period receives an equal share of expense. Imagine the total compensation expense that many companies would experience in July and August if businesses did not follow this practice. The popularity of summer vacations could very well result in depressed earnings for the third calendar quarter. The end result of this procedure is improved income measurement from matching, because costs are recognized (i.e., accrued) as services are performed.

To illustrate the correct treatment, assume that Prestonwood Company has a two-week paid vacation plan and monthly salaries of $90,000. In view of personnel turnover, the firm estimates that only 60% of the employees will qualify for plan benefits. Prestonwood's monthly vacation pay accrual will amount to $2,160 ($90,000 × 0.04 × 0.60) and is recorded by the following journal entry:

Vacation Pay Expense	2,160	
Estimated Liability for Vacation Pay		2,160
To record estimated vacation pay expense.		

The Estimated Liability for Vacation Pay account is disclosed in the current liability section of the balance sheet and is reduced when actual vacations are taken. For example, assume that Prestonwood now disburses $400 to an employee during her paid time-off. The disbursement is recorded as a debit to the Estimated Liability account and a credit to Cash.

Pension Plans. A **pension plan** is an agreement between a company and its employees that provides for retirement benefits. Once highly discretionary, such plans are now commonplace and are viewed as an important element of virtually all wage and fringe benefit packages. By instituting a pension plan, an entity assumes a very significant (and costly) obligation.

Employers typically finance these plans by making periodic contributions to a separate legal and accounting entity known as a *pension fund*. The fund is responsible for investing firm contributions, administering the plan, and making disbursements to retired personnel or their beneficiaries. Not surprisingly, the contributions of large firms and the earnings thereon have resulted in the accumulation of sizable amounts of pension fund assets. For example, the fair market value of the net assets in the principal pension funds of McDonnell Douglas, the giant defense contractor and aircraft manufacturer, recently totaled $5.3 billion.

The details of pension plan accounting are complex and clearly beyond the scope of this text.[3] What you should gain from this discussion, though, is some understanding of the figures that are shown on a company's (i.e., the employer's) financial statements. Because a pension obligation is created during the term of employment, amounts are charged to expense throughout this period in accord with the matching principle. In all likelihood, during this same period, the employer is also transferring cash to the fund. If the transfers fail to cover the amount of reported expense, a liability is created for the "unfunded" portion.[4] It is important to understand that the liability reported on the employer's balance sheet generally relates to the payment deficiencies and does *not* reflect the actual sum owed to employees. This latter amount is much, much larger and is an obligation of the separate pension entity.

Postretirement Health-Care Benefits. Until just recently, one of the biggest liabilities for many businesses did not appear on the balance sheet. Many full-time employees are covered by health-care plans whose benefits continue after retirement, thereby obligating individual companies to millions (in some cases, billions) of dollars of *future* costs. Under accounting rules in effect as late as 1990, businesses did not have to report these liabilities nor set aside any money for them. (Health insurance benefits were typically expensed when paid.)

The Financial Accounting Standards Board now requires that retiree health-care costs be disclosed on the employer's balance sheet as a liability.[5] Not only does a company have to record obligations for its current retiree population, but postretirement benefits for the present-day work force must be recorded as well.

---

[3] See "Employers' Accounting for Pensions," *Statement of Financial Accounting Standards No. 87,* Financial Accounting Standards Board, Norwalk, Conn., 1985.
[4] Additional liability amounts may need to be reported under certain conditions.
[5] See "Employers' Accounting for Postretirement Benefits Other than Pensions," *Statement of Financial Accounting Standards No. 106,* Financial Accounting Standards Board, Norwalk, Conn., 1990.

FRINGE BENEFITS: THE EMPLOYER'S PERSPECTIVE

> **6** Discuss the problem of rising fringe benefit costs.

Fringe benefits are playing havoc with the bottom line of many businesses. Although employee salaries are on the rise, outlays for fringe benefits are growing much faster. *The Washington Post* reported the following statistics not too long ago:

- Over a recent four-year period, salaries grew 16% but benefits increased more than 27%.
- Benefits now add 41% to the cost of payroll.
- A study by the U.S. Chamber of Commerce found that manufacturing firms provide $15,246 of annual benefits for each worker.
- In certain European countries, because of government mandates, the fringe benefit rate is close to 100% of salary and wage cost.[6]

Small businesses in the United States are particularly hard hit, as these entities often pay 40% more for employee benefits than their larger counterparts. (Small firms are generally viewed as being a greater insurance risk and lack the necessary staff to aggressively manage costs. With respect to workers' compensation, for instance, very few small companies have the time and resources available to implement drug-free workplace policies and safety programs—techniques that can drastically reduce insurance premiums.[7]) Unfortunately, the problem does not stop here. Many organizations bear the expense of operating a separate personnel/human resources department. Additionally, as noted earlier in the chapter, companies are the target of costly employee lawsuits for wrongful dismissals and other charges. Suffice it to say that the well-established policy of having employees on the payroll is very expensive and undergoing change.

Employee Leasing. Employee leasing, a growing trend in this country, is a particularly attractive option for the small business. With this type of arrangement, a professional employer organization (PEO) hires workers, maintains payroll, and provides benefits. The PEO then leases its employees to a client company (e.g., the small business) to perform tasks. In essence, a joint-employment arrangement is formed. The typical arrangement requires that the client pay the PEO a stipulated percentage of gross payroll to provide these services.

There are several advantages of employee leasing. The client organization's record-keeping burden is reduced, as tax and insurance forms and payments are handled by the PEO. Further, the PEO has the ability to negotiate lower insurance rates and provide workers with a greater choice of fringe benefit plans because of its large employee base (i.e., so-called "economies of scale"). The small business also gains from having defined personnel policies and the expertise of an experienced human resources department. The end result of employee leasing is often improved profit performance and added compliance with applicable laws and regulations.[8]

---

[6] See "The Fringe on Top of Paychecks Costs Americans Jobs," *The Washington Post*, December 3, 1993, pp. D1, D9.
[7] Eddie Heinemeier, *Staffing Alternatives Now and In the 21st Century*, Texas Society of Certified Public Accountants' CPE Exposition '94, Arlington, Texas, December 9, 1994.
[8] "Is Employee Leasing for You?," *Small Business: Building America's Future*, U.S. Small Business Administration's Office of Business Initiatives, August 20, 1994.

Business Briefing

Thomas Gallagher
Vice President—
Employee Relations
Chrysler Corporation

Fringe Benefits: The "Hidden" Paycheck

All employees usually understand the direct pay part of their paychecks; however, relatively few understand the total true cost to the company. Fringe benefits are a significant element of the total compensation package. As evidence, consider the following facts based on recent data:

- Thirty-six percent of our salaried employees' compensation is for fringe benefits (time off—9%, profit sharing/holiday bonus—8%, health care—8%, pensions—5%, savings—4%, and life/disability insurance—2%).
- The total cost of fringe benefits for all personnel approximates $3.3 billion annually, adding over $1,900 to the cost of each vehicle produced.
- A typical Chrysler employee starts work at age 27, retires at age 57, and lives to age 75. The estimated total compensation during this worker's lifetime is over $7 million; $3 million of this total relates to pension and health care benefits paid after retirement.

Given today's business environment, it is essential that benefit programs be cost effective and competitive enough to attract and retain outstanding men and women. Moreover, companies must ensure that personnel have an understanding that wages and salaries are just one part of the total compensation package. Fringe benefits, often underestimated and sometimes not appreciated by employees, are the other.

End-of-Chapter Review

Learning Objectives: The Key Points

1. **Explain the occurrence of and accounting for typical current liabilities of a business.** Current liabilities are debts or obligations that will be paid within one year or the operating cycle, whichever is longer. The settlement of current liabilities normally involves the use of current assets (e.g., cash) or the creation of other current liabilities (e.g., a note payable is used to settle an account payable). Examples of current liabilities include accounts payable, accrued liabilities for expenses incurred but not yet paid, the current portion of long-term debt, and short-term notes payable.

2. **Account for notes payable when interest is included in the face value of a note and when interest is recorded separately.** When interest is included in a note's face value, the difference between the note's proceeds and face value is recorded in a contra liability account, Discount on Notes Payable. At the end of each accounting period, this account is amortized (reduced) by the process of recognizing interest expense. In contrast, if interest is stated separately, no Discount account is established. Instead, interest is recorded at the end of the period by a debit to Interest Expense and, if unpaid, a credit to Interest Payable.

3. **Identify typical contingent liabilities and recognize the guidelines that are used for recording such obligations in the accounts.** A contingent liability is a potential liability that may become a definite obligation or be eliminated entirely as the result

of a future event. An example is a lawsuit. Contingencies should be recorded in the accounts when it is probable that the future event will occur and the amount of the liability can be reasonably estimated. If only one of these guidelines is met, a footnote to the financial statements is appropriate.

Warranties typically satisfy both guidelines. Because warranties help to promote the sale of products, an estimated service cost should be matched against sales revenues when the revenues are generated. This procedure, in turn, establishes a liability in the accounting records. The liability is reduced, perhaps several periods later, when the warranties are honored.

4. **Calculate and record payroll, including the employer's tax obligation.** Organizations must maintain detailed payroll records on their employees, keeping track of gross earnings and various payroll deductions (e.g., Social Security/Medicare tax, federal and state income tax withholdings, and medical insurance). The amounts deducted from employee paychecks are liabilities until paid to the appropriate authorities. A firm must also consider and record the following payroll taxes, which are expenses of the employer: Social Security/Medicare, federal unemployment, and state unemployment.

5. **Recognize other payroll-related costs of the employer: vacation pay, pensions, and postretirement health care.** Many employers provide paid vacations to their employees. Proper accounting requires that the cost of these fringe benefits be recorded throughout the year as personnel furnish services to the organization. A pension plan, another fringe benefit, is an agreement between a business and its employees that provides retirement benefits. Because payments to retirees are made from a separate pension fund, the liability that appears on a company's balance sheet reflects the amounts owed to the fund, not to the former employees. Finally, businesses must now disclose a postretirement health care liability for both retirees and the present day work force.

6. **Discuss the problem of rising fringe benefit costs.** Recent surveys have shown that fringe benefits are increasing faster than salaries and wages and constitute a very significant cost to the providing company. Small businesses are being hit particularly hard, primarily because of higher insurance rates for their employees. The rising cost of benefits, the need to maintain human resources departments, and the threat of employee lawsuits have prompted businesses to consider new staffing alternatives. One such alternative involves employee leasing, where a company secures the services of a professional employee organization (PEO). The PEO is responsible for hiring workers, maintaining payroll, and providing benefits—benefits that can usually be obtained at costs lower than those experienced by small businesses.

KEY TERMS AND CONCEPTS: A QUICK OVERVIEW

accrued liability   The amount owed for an accrued expense. (p. 474)

contingent liability   A potential liability whose outcome hinges on the future. (p. 479)

contra liability   An account used to reduce liability balances in the financial statements. (p. 477)

current liabilities   Debts or obligations that will be paid within one year or the operating cycle, whichever is longer. (p. 473)

discount amortization   The process of reducing a discount on notes payable by recognizing interest expense. (p. 478)

discount on notes payable   A contra liability account that represents future interest expense. (p. 477)

employee   A person who works for a specific business and is directly and closely supervised by that business. (p. 481)

Federal Insurance Contributions Act (FICA)   A statute, commonly called Social Security, that requires employers to withhold a portion of each employee's gross earnings and to match the employee's contribution. (p. 483)

Federal Unemployment Tax Act (FUTA)   Federal legislation that requires employers to pay taxes to assist the unemployed. (p. 486)

gross earnings   The total earnings of an employee before any deductions are made. (p. 482)

income tax withholdings   The portion of an employee's gross earnings withheld by the employer to satisfy federal (and sometimes state and local) income tax laws. (p. 483)

independent contractor   A person who frequently performs services for many different organizations at the same time, or perhaps finishes a project for one entity and then moves on to service another. (p. 481)

liabilities   Obligations owed by an organization that have arisen from past transactions or events. (p. 472)

mortgage note   A long-term note issued to finance the purchase of real estate. (p. 474)

notes payable   Written promises to pay a definite amount of money on a specific future date. (p. 475)

pension plan   An agreement between a company and its employees that deals with retirement benefits. (p. 488)

prepayments by customers   Monies collected for future goods and services. (p. 473)

state unemployment taxes   Taxes paid by employers to state governments. The taxes are disbursed to the unemployed through the various state programs. (p. 486)

take-home (net) pay   The amount of cash available to an employee after all appropriate payroll deductions are subtracted from gross pay. (p. 483)

Wage and Tax Statement (W-2)   A statement that an employer must provide each employee showing gross wages and salaries earned and taxes withheld. (p. 485)

warranty   A promise made by a seller or manufacturer to correct defects in product quality and performance. (p. 480)

withholding allowance   A numerical amount used in computing the amount of federal income taxes withheld from an employee's paycheck. (p. 483)

Chapter Quiz

The five questions that follow relate to several issues raised in the chapter. Test your knowledge of the issues by selecting the best answer. (The answers appear on p. 506.)

1. Which of the following comments is false? Current liabilities:
   a. include prepayments (advances) by customers.
   b. will be settled within one year or the operating cycle, whichever is longer.
   c. must be settled by using cash.
   d. arise from past transactions and events.

2. The Discount on Notes Payable account:
   a. usually has a credit balance.
   b. is associated with a note payable when interest is included in the obligation's face value.
   c. represents future interest revenue on the note payable.
   d. is used for notes payable when interest is not included in the obligation's face value.
3. A balance in the Estimated Liability for Warranties account at year-end indicates:
   a. that the accounting records have not been closed.
   b. that the accounting records have not been adjusted.
   c. the amount incurred during the year to service outstanding warranty agreements.
   d. future amounts expected to be incurred when outstanding warranty agreements are honored.
4. Assume that Robert Conrad, a technical engineer, worked 45 hours last week. He is paid $28 per hour, with hours in excess of 40 being compensated at one and one-half times the regular rate. Income tax withholdings amounted to $270; his medical insurance deduction was $30. The Social Security tax rate is 6.5% on the first $65,000 earned per employee; Medicare is 1.5% of total wages. Cumulative gross pay before considering the preceding data totaled $64,170. Conrad's take-home pay is:
   a. $891.70.
   b. $923.60.
   c. $956.10.
   d. some amount other than those listed above.
5. Social Security and Medicare taxes are levied on:
   a. employees only.
   b. employers only.
   c. both employees and employers.
   d. either the employee or the employer depending on the number of withholding allowances claimed by the employee.

Summary Problem

The following transactions took place in July and pertain to Meadowlands Corporation:
1. Two notes were issued during the month to raise needed cash. On July 1, a three-month, 12%, $5,000 note was issued to the First National Bank. The company also executed a 60-day, $3,000 note on July 17 to the Second National Bank. Interest of $80 is included in the face value of the latter obligation.
2. The company recorded its payroll on July 31. Total salaries amounted to $30,000; 80% pertain to the sales staff and 20% to office personnel. Social Security taxes are 6.5% on a base of $65,000 for each employee; Medicare is 1.5% of total wages. All employees are under the Social Security base except for Mike Dixon, who earned his normal monthly salary of $12,000. Additional data follow.

Federal income taxes withheld	$3,850
State income taxes withheld	300
Insurance program withholdings	680

Meadowlands has a fiscal year-end of August 31.

Instructions

a. Prepare entries on July 1 and July 17 to record issuance of the notes.
b. Prepare an entry on July 31 to record the company's payroll.
c. Prepare an entry on July 31 to record the company's payroll taxes. Assume the state and federal unemployment tax rates are 5.4% and 0.8%, respectively. Thirty percent of the gross earnings are subject to unemployment taxes.
d. Prepare the journal entries required on August 31 to accrue interest on each of the two notes.

Solution

a. July 1 Cash   5,000
             Notes Payable   5,000
             To record note payable to bank; three
             months at 12%.

   17 Cash   2,920
       Discount on Notes Payable   80
             Notes Payable   3,000
             To record note payable to bank; 60
             days until maturity.

b. July 31 Sales Salaries Expense   24,000*
            Office Salaries Expense   6,000*
             Social Security Taxes Payable   1,170†
             Medicare Taxes Payable   450‡
             Employees' Federal Income Taxes Payable   3,850
             Employees' State Income Taxes Payable   300
             Employees' Insurance Program Payable   680
             Salaries Payable   23,550
             To record payroll and withholdings.

   * $30,000 × 0.8 = $24,000; $30,000 × 0.2 = $6,000.
   † ($30,000 − $12,000) × 0.065 = $1,170.
   ‡ $30,000 × 0.015 = $450.

c. July 31 Payroll Tax Expense   2,178
             Social Security Taxes Payable   1,170*
             Medicare Taxes Payable   450†
             State Unemployment Taxes Payable   486‡
             Federal Unemployment Taxes Payable   72·
             To record employer's payroll taxes.

   * ($30,000 − $12,000) × 0.065 = $1,170.
   † $30,000 × 0.015 = $450.
   ‡ $30,000 × 0.3 = $9,000; $9,000 × 0.054 = $486.
   · $30,000 × 0.3 = $9,000; $9,000 × 0.008 = $72.

d. Aug. 31 Interest Expense   100
             Interest Payable   100
             To accrue interest for two months:
             $5,000 × 0.12 × 2/12.

   31 Interest Expense   60
             Discount on Notes Payable   60
             To accrue interest for 45 days and amortize
             the discount: $80 × 45/60.

ASSIGNMENT MATERIAL

QUESTIONS

Q13–1 Define the term "current liability."

Q13–2 Why are customer prepayments classified as liabilities?

Q13–3 Present three different situations where a business collects monies from customers and employees and reports such amounts as current liabilities.

Q13–4 Explain how a typical mortgage note payment is allocated between principal and interest.

Q13–5 What does the Discount on Notes Payable account represent?

Q13–6 Does discount amortization increase or decrease a company's reported interest expense for the year?

Q13–7 How does a contingent liability differ from an absolute liability? Present three examples of contingent liabilities.

Q13–8 What guidelines must be met in order for a contingent liability to be recorded in the accounts?

Q13–9 Why is a warranty considered a contingent liability?

Q13–10 Differentiate between "employees" and "independent contractors." Why is this distinction important?

Q13–11 Which payroll taxes are incurred by an employer? How are these taxes treated in the accounting records?

Q13–12 Do most state unemployment programs grant merit reductions to businesses? What is the purpose behind merit reductions?

Q13–13 Does the pension liability reported on a company's balance sheet represent the amounts owed to employees? Briefly explain.

Q13–14 Are fringe benefits a significant or insignificant cost for most businesses?

Q13–15 Briefly explain the concept of employee leasing.

EXERCISES

E13–1 Prepayments by customers (L.O. 1)

Greenland Enterprises began a new magazine in the fourth quarter of 19X2. Annual subscriptions, which cost $18 each, were sold as follows:

	NUMBER OF SUBSCRIPTIONS SOLD
October	400
November	700
December	1,000

If subscriptions begin (and magazines are sent) in the month of sale:

a. Present the necessary journal entry to record the magazine subscriptions sold during the fourth quarter.
b. Determine how much subscription revenue Greenland earned by the end of 19X2.
c. Compute Greenland's liability to subscribers at the end of 19X2.

E13–2 Accrued liability; current portion of long-term debt (L.O. 1)

On July 1, 19X1, Hall Company borrowed $225,000 via a long-term loan. Terms of the loan require that Hall pay interest and $75,000 of principal on July 1, 19X2, 19X3, and 19X4. The unpaid balance of the loan accrues interest at the rate of 10% per year. Hall has a December 31 year-end.

a. Compute Hall's accrued interest as of December 31, 19X1.
b. Present the appropriate balance sheet disclosure for the accrued interest and the current and long-term portion of the outstanding debt as of December 31, 19X1.
c. Repeat parts (a) and (b) using a date of December 31, 19X2, rather than December 31, 19X1. Assume that Hall is in compliance with the terms of the loan agreement.

E13–3 Mortgage notes (L.O. 1)

On July 1, 19X3, Holstrum Company acquired a building complex for $2 million, which included $500,000 of land. Holstrum paid $400,000 down and obtained a long-term mortgage note for the remaining balance. The note carried a 12% interest rate, which is computed on the unpaid balance at the beginning of each month. Holstrum will repay the note in monthly installments of $18,000, with the first installment due on August 1.

a. Prepare the journal entry to record Holstrum's purchase on July 1.
b. Prepare the journal entry to record Holstrum's first payment on August 1.
c. How much interest expense will the company record on September 1?
d. In what section(s) of the December 31, 19X3, balance sheet will the note be disclosed?

E13–4 Notes payable (L.O. 2)

Dyer Galleries remodeled its showroom at a cost of $144,000 and financed the work with a six-month, 10% note payable. The note was signed on November 1, 19X5; Dyer has a December 31 year-end.

a. Prepare the journal entry to record accrued interest on December 31, 19X5. *Hint:* Calculate interest in terms of months, not days.
b. What is the company's total liability related to the remodeling job as of December 31, 19X5? Where would this information be disclosed in the financial statements?
c. Prepare the necessary journal entry to record settlement of the note on May 1, 19X6.

E13–5 Notes payable; discount amortization (L.O. 2)

Morgantown Foods purchased four delivery trucks from Metro Truck Sales on October 1, 19X1, for $240,000. Morgantown signed a nine-month note for $261,000; interest is included in the note's face value. Prepare journal entries for Morgantown Foods to record the following:

a. The purchase of the trucks on October 1, 19X1.
b. Discount amortization for the year ended December 31, 19X1.
c. The note payment and discount amortization on July 1, 19X2.

E13–6 Warranty costs (L.O. 3)

RJV sells sophisticated scientific instruments to fusion research laboratories. All instruments have a two-year warranty. The company estimates that 5% of the 1,200 units sold during 19X8 will require rework or replacement, at an estimated cost of $150 per unit.

a. Is a warranty an example of an absolute liability or a contingent liability? Briefly discuss.

b. Prepare the required journal entry to record warranty costs for 19X8.
c. Present the proper balance sheet disclosure on December 31, 19X9, if 35 instruments were returned for servicing during 19X9. Assume that the actual rework cost per unit conformed to original expectations.

E13–7 Current and contingent liabilities (L.O. 1, 2, 3)
Evaluate the comments that follow as being True or False. If the comment is false, briefly explain why.

a. Collections for third parties normally arise when a business receives prepayments, or advances, from customers.
b. The currently maturing portion of a long-term debt should be disclosed as a current liability, with the remaining portion of the debt being shown as a long-term liability.
c. Discount amortization procedures are employed when accounting for a note that includes interest in the face amount.
d. Because some uncertainty exists, contingent liabilities are never recorded with a journal entry.
e. For financial reporting purposes, warranty obligations should be estimated and recorded in the same period that the related sale is made.

E13–8 Contingent liabilities (L.O. 3)
Consider the following independent cases:

1. On December 15, an explosion occurred at the Vesper Glue Company. Ten people were injured, and five houses located near Vesper's manufacturing facility were severely damaged. The cause of the explosion is currently unknown. Although no lawsuits had been filed by the end of the year, management anticipates future court actions and several out-of-court settlements. The company was not insured for the casualty.
2. Bonanza, Inc., was sued several months ago for discriminatory promotion practices. After thorough review of the facts, Bonanza's lawyers noted that the plaintiffs had a strong case and would likely win the suit. Although the suit was for $8 million, the lawyers felt that it could be settled for $1 million.

a. Discuss the accounting treatment for contingent liabilities.
b. Discuss how each of the cases would be treated in the financial statements. Assume that each company's year ends on December 31.

E13–9 Payroll accounting (L.O. 4)
Assume that the following tax rates and payroll information pertain to Capricorn Publishing:

Social Security taxes: 6.5% on the first $65,000 earned
Medicare taxes: 1.5% of total wages
Federal income taxes withheld from wages: $7,500
State income taxes: 5% of gross earnings
Insurance withholdings: 1% of gross earnings
State unemployment taxes: 5.4% on the first $7,000 earned
Federal unemployment taxes: 0.8% on the first $7,000 earned

The company incurred salary expense of $50,000 during February. All employees had earned less than $5,000 by month-end.

a. Prepare the necessary entry to record Capricorn's February payroll, which will be paid on March 1.
b. Prepare the journal entry to record Capricorn's payroll tax expense.

E13–10 Payroll accounting (L.O. 4)

The following payroll information relates to Simpson Company for the month of July:

Total (gross) employee earnings	$150,000
Earnings in excess of Social Security base earnings	18,000
Earnings in excess of unemployment base earnings	94,000
Federal income taxes withheld	14,500
State income taxes withheld	3,000
Employee deductions for medical insurance	2,200

The Social Security tax rate is 6.5% on the first $65,000 earned per employee; Medicare is 1.5% of total wages. The state and federal unemployment tax rates are 5.4% and 0.8%, respectively, on the first $7,000 earned per employee.

a. Compute the employees' total take-home pay.
b. Compute Simpson's total payroll-related expenses.
c. Assuming a stable work force, is total take-home pay likely to increase, decrease, or remain the same in September? Briefly explain.

E13–11 Accrued vacation pay (L.O. 1)

Don Pedro Mexican Restaurants, Inc., has a two-week paid vacation plan. Monthly salaries and wages average $400,000. Because of high turnover, the firm estimates that only 30% of the employees will qualify for this fringe benefit.

a. Briefly explain the proper accounting treatment for the vacation pay.
b. Prepare the journal entry for March that reflects the proper treatment.
c. Prepare a journal entry to record the disbursement of $7,500 to employees who took their vacations in August.

E13–12 Hiring decision and fringe benefits (L.O. 4, 5, 6)

After years of sluggish sales, new orders for motor homes have American Duralite's plant working at capacity. At present, there are two eight-hour shifts. Management is studying whether a third shift should be added, a shift that requires hiring 60 new employees. The company's chief financial officer feels that rather than hire new personnel, current employees should be asked to work extra hours and be paid an overtime premium.

a. Evaluate both alternatives from the company's perspective.
b. What basis will likely be used to make the final decision?

PROBLEMS

Series A

P13–A1 Current liabilities: Recognition and valuation (L.O. 1, 2, 3)

The transactions and events that follow relate to the 19X2 operations of Quality Products.

1. A customer slipped on a soft drink that he had spilled while walking through a Quality Products store. The customer injured his back and has filed a $50,000 damage suit against the company. Quality's attorneys feel the suit is uncalled for and without merit.

2. Quality purchased merchandise on October 15 for $4,000; terms 5/15, n/60. The company overlooked the discount and intends to pay the supplier in January 19X3.
3. Equipment that cost $12,000 was acquired on November 1 by issuing a three-month, 10%, $12,000 note payable.
4. Office furniture that cost $4,000 was purchased on December 1, with the firm signing a $4,240, 12-month note payable. Interest is included in the note's face value.
5. The company operates in a state where a 6% sales tax has been enacted. Sales of merchandise on account during December amounted to $300,000.
6. On the last day of 19X2, Quality borrowed $1 million from the Monticello Bank. The loan's principal is due in 10 equal annual installments of $100,000 each, with each installment payable on December 31. The loan has a 9% interest rate.

Instructions

Prepare the current liability section of the firm's December 31, 19X2, balance sheet. Indicate how any transactions and events that are not current liabilities would be handled for accounting purposes.

P13–A2 Current liabilities: Entries and disclosure (L.O. 1, 2, 3, 5)

A review of selected financial activities of Long Island Company during 19XX disclosed the following:

Mar.	1	Purchased $6,000 of office furniture on account from the Fenton Company, terms 2/10, n/45.
	7	Bought $18,000 of store equipment; signed an $18,800 note payable due in 120 days.
	10	Established a warranty liability for the Mop-o-Matic, a new product. Sales are expected to total 1,000 units during the month. Past experience with similar products indicates that 3% of the units will require replacement, with warranty costs averaging $8 per unit.
	16	Borrowed $20,000 from the Bank of Long Island by signing a 60-day, 12% note payable. Interest and principal are due at maturity.
	31	Accrued two days of wage expense; daily payroll amounts to $3,700.
	31	Accrued vacation pay amounting to 7% of March's $81,000 wage expense.
	31	Replaced 24 Mop-o-Matics during the month at a total cost of $192.

Instructions

a. Prepare journal entries to record the preceding transactions and events.
b. Determine accrued interest as of March 31, 19XX, and prepare the necessary adjusting entry(ies).
c. Prepare the current liability section of Long Island Company's March 31, 19XX, balance sheet.

P13–A3 Notes payable (L.O. 2)

On October 1, 19X6, D'Angelo Company signed a one-year, 12% note payable to finance a $50,000 purchase of factory equipment from Lafayette Corporation. Shortly thereafter, on November 11, D'Angelo borrowed $80,000 from the First National Bank by signing a 120-day note for $84,800. D'Angelo's year-end is December 31.

Instructions

a. With regard to the Lafayette Corporation note:
   (1) Determine:
      (a) Interest expense for 19X6 and 19X7.
      (b) Interest payable on December 31.
      (c) D'Angelo's total liability as of December 31.
   (2) Prepare journal entries to record:
      (a) Issuance on October 1.
      (b) Accrued interest on December 31.
      (c) Payment on the maturity date.
b. With regard to the First National Bank note:
   (1) Prepare journal entries to record:
      (a) Issuance on November 11.
      (b) Accrued interest and discount amortization on December 31.
      (c) Payment on the maturity date.
   (2) Determine:
      (a) Interest expense for 19X6.
      (b) D'Angelo's total liability as of December 31.

P13–A4 Payroll journal entries (L.O. 4)

The following tax rates and payroll information pertain to the Albany operations of LJP Company for November:

Social Security taxes: 6.5% on the first $65,000 earned
Medicare taxes: 1.5% of total wages
Federal income taxes withheld from wages: $4,400
State income taxes: 6% of gross earnings
Insurance withholdings: 1% of gross earnings
Pension contributions: 2.5% of gross earnings
State unemployment taxes: 5.4% on the first $7,000 earned
Federal unemployment taxes: 0.8% on the first $7,000 earned

Sales staff salaries amounted to $26,000, $3,000 of which is over the unemployment earnings base but subject to all other appropriate taxes. The company's branch manager, Tracy Smith, earned her regular salary of $9,000 during the month. She has been employed by LJP since March 1 and has not missed a single day of work.

Instructions

a. Prepare the journal entry to record the November payroll. Smith's salary is classified as an administrative expense by the company.
b. LJP matches employees' insurance and pension contributions. Prepare a journal entry to record the firm's payroll taxes and other related payroll costs. Assume that these amounts will be remitted to the proper authorities in December.
c. The owner of LJP asked the firm's accountant to reclassify all personnel as independent contractors. The accountant explained that such a reclassification would not be appropriate because, by law, the personnel were considered employees. Briefly comment on the probable reasoning behind the owner's request.

P13–A5 Payroll and fringe benefits (L.O. 4, 5, 6)

StarGlo Cosmetics incurred wages and salaries of $100,000 during July; 75% relates to sales personnel and 25% to administration. Social Security taxes are 6.5% on a base of

$65,000 for each employee; Medicare is 1.5% of total wages. All employees are under the $65,000 base, except for Pat Garza, who has a monthly salary of $10,400. (Pat was hired four years ago.) Additional data follow.

Federal income taxes withheld	$14,470
State income taxes withheld	3,560
City income taxes withheld	1,380

Sixty percent of the gross earnings are subject to unemployment taxes (state, 5.4%; federal, 0.8%).

The company has a generous benefit plan for its employees. With respect to retirement, StarGlo pays 2% of gross earnings at the end of each calendar quarter to a bank trust fund. Medical and dental insurance costs of $12,000 per month are also fully paid by the firm on the same schedule.

Instructions

a. Prepare the journal entry to record the July payroll.
b. Prepare the journal entry to record StarGlo's payroll taxes and benefit plan contributions.
c. Calculate the total of payroll taxes and employee benefit costs as a percentage of gross wages and salaries. Is this percentage likely to remain constant through the remainder of the year? Why?
d. StarGlo is concerned that its total human resource and compensation cost (including benefits) is rather high. Is the company alone in this regard or is this now a fairly common occurrence with American businesses? Briefly explain.

Series B

P13–B1 Current liabilities: Recognition and valuation (L.O. 1, 2, 4)

The transactions and events that follow relate to the 19X7 operations of Advantage Company.

1. During a recent Father's Day promotion, the company sold 400 $25 gift certificates to customers. By December 31, 275 certificates had been redeemed for merchandise.
2. Equipment that cost $40,000 was acquired on May 1 by signing a 12-month, 12% note payable for $40,000.
3. The company introduced a new product on September 1; sales totaled 500,000 units through the remainder of the year. Each unit carries a 12-month warranty. Management estimated that defective units would amount to 2% of sales, with the cost of each unit's replacement averaging $15. No units were replaced during 19X7.
4. A $10,000 computer system was purchased on October 1 by signing a nine-month note payable for $10,900. Interest is included in the note's face value.
5. Accrued salaries payable at year-end total $45,000. This amount was paid on January 3, 19X8.
6. Federal income taxes withheld from employees' paychecks during December totaled $13,000. The withholdings must be remitted to tax authorities by February 1, 19X8.

Instructions

Prepare the current liability section of the firm's December 31, 19X7, balance sheet.

P13–B2 Current liabilities: Entries and disclosure (L.O. 1, 2, 3, 5)

A review of selected financial activities of Visconti's during 19XX disclosed the following:

Dec. 1 Borrowed $20,000 from the First City Bank by signing a three-month, 15% note payable. Interest and principal are due at maturity.

10 Established a warranty liability for the XY-80, a new product. Sales are expected to total 1,000 units during the month. Past experience with similar products indicates that 2% of the units will require repair, with warranty costs averaging $27 per unit.

22 Purchased $16,000 of merchandise on account from Oregon Company, terms 2/10, n/30.

26 Borrowed $5,000 from the First City Bank; signed a $5,120 note payable due in 60 days.

31 Repaired six XY-80s during the month at a total cost of $162.

31 Accrued three days of salaries at a total cost of $1,400.

31 Accrued vacation pay amounting to 6% of December's $36,000 total wage and salary expense.

Instructions

a. Prepare journal entries to record the preceding transactions and events.
b. Determine accrued interest as of December 31, 19XX, and prepare the necessary adjusting entry(ies).
c. Prepare the current liability section of Visconti's December 31, 19XX, balance sheet.

P13–B3 Notes payable (L.O. 2)

The accounting records of Chung, Inc., revealed the following information about notes that had been issued to Hallmark Enterprises and Stateside Marine:

	HALLMARK	STATESIDE
Date of note	May 9	June 27
Face value	$27,000	$18,000
Interest rate	10%	10%
Term of note	120 days	90 days
Maturity date	Sept. 6	Sept. 25
Purpose of note	Purchase of equipment	Settlement of account payable

Chung had also borrowed $32,400 from Union Bank by signing a 120-day note for $33,372. This transaction occurred on May 21.

Instructions

a. Prepare the journal entries that Chung would record on May 9, May 21, June 27, and September 6.
b. The note to Stateside Marine was due on September 25, but Chung lacked sufficient funds for payment. Management authorized issuance of a new 60-day, 12% note for $18,450, the maturity value of the original obligation. Prepare the necessary journal entry for the issuance.
c. Assume now that Chung has a June 30 year-end.
   (1) Prepare the journal entries for accrued interest and discount amortization that would have been necessary on this date.
   (2) Prepare the current liability section of Chung's June 30 balance sheet. The company's Accounts Payable account contains a balance of $45,800.

P13–B4 Payroll journal entries (L.O. 4)

Knight Wholesale incurred wages and salaries of $300,000 during November, 30% of which relate to office personnel and the remainder to sales personnel. Social Security taxes are 6.5% on a base of $65,000 for each employee; Medicare is 1.5% of total wages. All employees are under the $65,000 base except Susan Hatfield, who earned $7,000 during the month. (Hatfield's annual salary is $84,000.) Federal income taxes withheld amounted to $75,900, and state income taxes withheld totaled $9,000. Other deductions from payroll were authorized for pensions (2% of gross earnings), insurance (1% of gross earnings), and United Way contributions (0.5% of gross earnings).

Instructions

a. Prepare the journal entry to record the payroll.
b. Prepare a journal entry to record the company's payroll taxes and other related payroll costs. Assume that state unemployment tax is 4.0% because of a merit reduction, and that federal unemployment tax is 0.8%. Twenty percent of the gross earnings are subject to unemployment taxes. Also, the firm matches employee contributions to the United Way and insurance programs. These amounts will be remitted to the proper authorities on December 15.
c. Compute total payroll expense for November.

P13–B5 Payroll and fringe benefits (L.O. 4, 5, 6)

The following information relates to the November payroll of Deluxe Ceramics:

Gross wages and salaries	$1,000,000
Wages and salaries subject to:	
Social Security taxes (6.5%)	800,000
Medicare taxes (1.5%)	1,000,000
State unemployment taxes (5.4%)	140,000
Federal unemployment taxes (0.8%)	140,000
Withholdings from employee paychecks:	
Federal income taxes	188,000
State income taxes	40,000
Union dues	12,000
Health insurance premiums	20,000
Pension contributions	30,000
United Way contributions	1,000

Sixty percent of the wages relate to sales activities; the remaining 40% are administrative. Deluxe splits health insurance and pension plan costs equally with its employees.

Instructions

a. Prepare a journal entry to record the November payroll.
b. Prepare a journal entry to record payroll taxes and employee benefit plan costs for November. All benefit plan obligations will be paid in December.
c. The company is considering a new paid vacation plan for selected managers. If the managers typically take their vacations during July and August, should Deluxe charge the plan's cost totally to these two months? Briefly explain.
d. Deluxe, a relatively small business, is concerned about skyrocketing fringe benefit costs and its inability to offer a competitive benefit plan to attract new personnel. Is employee leasing an option for the firm? Discuss.

EXPANDING YOUR HORIZONS

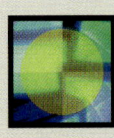

EYH13–1 Contingent liability disclosures (L.O. 3)

The financial statement footnotes of large businesses often contain information about contingent liabilities. Companies are faced with lawsuits, potential liabilities for environmental clean-up, and so forth. In most cases, businesses reveal minimal detail about their contingencies; sometimes, however, considerable information is presented.

Instructions

Using the resources of your library, review the financial statement footnotes of three large companies. One of the firms should be in the tobacco industry and one should be involved with the manufacture of chemical-type products. Prepare a one-page report that summarizes the disclosures that you find.

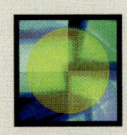

EYH13–2 Postretirement health-care benefits (L.O. 5)

In 1990, the Financial Accounting Standards Board enacted a pronouncement that changed how companies account for postretirement health-care benefits. Amounts spent on retiree health care were formerly expensed when paid, and businesses failed to report a liability for these future outlays. Under the pronouncement, liabilities for the retirees as well as the present-day work force now appear on the balance sheet.

Instructions

a. Perform a search of the business literature from the early 1990s to determine the overall magnitude of these previously unrecorded obligations. Prepare a short report of your findings.
b. Study the balance sheets and accompanying footnotes of two large corporations, including at least one manufacturer. How much has each corporation recorded for its postretirement health-care obligation? In percentage terms, how does this amount compare to the firm's total liabilities?

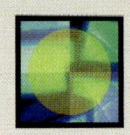

EYH13–3 Fringe benefit costs (L.O. 6)

Fringe benefit plans now comprise a substantial portion of a company's total compensation cost. As noted in the body of the chapter, benefit costs are especially troublesome for the small business.

Instructions

Visit two small businesses in your area that employ 10 or more people. Inquire about the fringe benefit plans offered to employees and the cost of those plans to the company. Has the firm taken any steps to reduce or control the cost of benefits (e.g., the use of employee leasing or temp agencies)? Be prepared to report your findings to the class.

EYH13–4 Current liabilities and contingencies: Sprint and H.J. Heinz Company (L.O. 1, 3)

Kansas City-based Sprint is a diversified telecommunications company that provides voice, data, and videoconferencing services and related products. The firm has a global presence with its long distance, local, and cellular communications network. H.J. Heinz, in contrast, is a worldwide manufacturer of food products and provider of nutritional services. The company is perhaps best known for its Heinz, Weight Watchers, Ore-Ida, StarKist, and 9-Lives brand names.

Instructions

By using the text's electronic data base, access the balance sheets and accompanying notes of both firms and answer the questions that follow. Unless otherwise indicated, responses should be based on data for the most recent year presented.

a. Review the balance sheets and determine:
   (1) The three largest current liabilities disclosed.
   (2) Whether any of the current liabilities are unique to the operations and activities of the company. List the current liabilities that meet this characteristic.
   (3) Whether current assets are sufficient to cover current obligations. Show calculations.
b. Which company has the higher percentage of long-term debt classified as a current liability? Show computations to support your answer.
c. Review the footnotes to the financial statements and focus on sections that describe contingencies and/or litigation and legal matters. Comment on the specifics of each company's disclosure, including associated dollar amounts (if any).

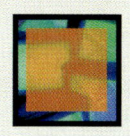

EYH13–5 Current liabilities and contingencies (L.O. 1, 3)

This problem is a duplication of Problem EYH13–4. It is based on two companies selected by your instructor.

Instructions

By using the text's electronic data base, access the specified companies' balance sheets and accompanying notes and focus on data for the most recent year reported. Answer requirements (a)–(c) of Problem EYH13–4.

EYH13–6 Evaluation of staffing alternatives (L.O. 4, 5, 6)

The city of Lawndale owns and operates a municipal golf course. The course, open for nine months during the year, is staffed by 15 employees who each earn an average of $1,500 per month. Total earnings are subject to Social Security/Medicare (8%) and unemployment taxes (6.2%). In addition, vacation pay, health insurance, pension, and postretirement health-care costs total 25% of gross wages. During the off-season, when covered by snow, the course is used for cross country skiing, sledding, and other activities. Staffing in the winter months is reduced to two employees.

A proposal has been received from a private company, U.S. Golf, for maintaining and operating the facility. The city is strongly considering this proposal because personnel turnover is very high and employee processing is consuming a large amount of administrative time. U.S. Golf will charge $260,000 for its services. The company will be responsible for all employee payroll costs as well as the cost of benefit plans. If the proposal is accepted, U.S. Golf will offer the existing city employees 75% of their current wages. Because the contract covers only nine months, the city plans to close the facility during the winter and encourage citizens to use a nearby state park.

Instructions

a. Prepare an analysis that indicates whether the proposal should be accepted.
b. What noncost factors should be considered in the decision to use U.S. Golf?
c. Aside from U.S. Golf's proposal, what other options may be open to the city of Lawndale to staff the course at a reduced cost?

COMMUNICATION OF ACCOUNTING INFORMATION

CAI13–1 Preparing a short report: The Boeing Company (L.O. 3)

Communication Principle: Most reports contain three major sections: introduction, body, and conclusion. The introduction cites some background information and sets forth the major points to be covered. These issues are then discussed one at a time in several paragraphs that constitute the body of the report. Finally, a conclusion reiterates the major points and summarizes the writer's position.

The body of a report should be much longer than the introduction or conclusion and deserves several headings that describe the major issues raised. For instance, if you were writing a report about LIFO and FIFO entitled "A Comparison of LIFO and FIFO," headings that precede several body paragraphs could be "Inventory Valuation and Financial Reporting" and "Income Tax Implications of LIFO." (*Note*: The report's "introduction" and "conclusion" are also labeled.) If properly prepared, a title and body headings should help a reader understand the basic information being presented.

■ ■ ■ ■ ■ ■ ■ ■

The Boeing Company is heavily involved in the development and manufacture of commercial airplanes, aerospace equipment and technology, military equipment, and computer systems and electronics. Much of the company's work is done on a contract basis with the U.S. government.

Exploring new frontiers naturally exposes the firm to a variety of risks and contingencies. A note that accompanies the financial statements includes the following remarks:

> Various legal proceedings, claims and investigations are pending against the Company related to products, contracts and other matters. . . . The Company is subject to several U.S. Government investigations of business and cost classification practices. One investigation involves a grand jury proceeding as to whether or not certain costs were charged to the proper overhead accounts. No charges have been filed in this matter, and based on the facts known to it, the Company believes it would have defenses if any were filed. The investigations could result in civil, criminal or administrative proceedings. Such proceedings, if any, could involve claims by the Government for fines, penalties, compensatory and treble damages, restitution and/or forfeitures. Based upon Government procurement regulations, a contractor, or one or more of its operating divisions or subdivisions, can also be suspended or disbarred from Government contracts if proceedings result from the investigations.

Boeing goes on to say that based on the information available, the outcome of these matters will not have a significant adverse effect on its financial position. (No dollar amount for these items appears on the balance sheet, nor is any dollar amount disclosed in the accompanying notes.)

Instructions

Prepare a short report that addresses the disclosure of contingencies, using Boeing's note as an example. Should Boeing's disclosure raise significant doubts about the company or are such disclosures commonplace? Include as part of the report an argument that businesses should disclose an estimated dollar amount for contingencies, along with several data sources that may be used to derive such estimates.

Answers to Chapter Quiz

1. c
2. b
3. d
4. c [(40 hours × $28) + (5 hours × $42) = $1,330; ($65,000 − $64,170) × 0.065 = $53.95; $1,330 × 0.015 = $19.95; $1,330 − $53.95 − $19.95 − $270 − $30 = $956.10]
5. c

14 Financial Accounting and Reporting: U.S. and Global Perspectives

LEARNING OBJECTIVES

After studying this chapter, you should be able to:

1. Summarize the objectives of financial reporting.

2. Identify and describe the desirable characteristics of accounting information: relevancy, reliability, comparability, and understandability.

3. Explain the need for generally accepted accounting principles and the roles of various groups in the development process.

4. Define the assumptions, principles, and modifying conventions that underlie financial accounting and reporting.

5. Describe the revenue realization principle and apply the percentage-of-completion and installment methods.

6. Identify several of the basic issues related to international accounting.

Banner Advertising is a typical small company, one that basically assists the local business community. Occasionally, the firm might branch out and service other regions, but that is definitely the exception rather than the rule. Several years ago, to the surprise of everyone, George Faris and Banner were approached by a Mexican advertising agency. The agency had several clients that wanted to conduct business in the U.S. marketplace.

Over the course of several meetings, conversations turned to the possibility of Banner constructing billboards in Mexico. George quickly rejected the idea. He recalled, "I didn't have the first clue, and still don't, about how to do business in a foreign country. I have no idea about the laws, taxation, form of government, property rights, transferability of money, and a host of other issues." Did George miss the chance of a lifetime? The uninformed can only guess.

It is quickly becoming apparent that major business opportunities are emerging in global markets, even for the smallest of companies. No doubt many of the pioneers who are trying to seize these opportunities will be successful; others, of course, will fail. But, as George notes, "Chance will favor those who are prepared, and I certainly didn't fit the bill."

One goal of this chapter is to introduce you to global accounting issues, and, perhaps, spark an interest in the study of international business. This way, you will be better equipped if opportunity knocks. The chapter has another objective as well. Consider that many newspapers and business periodicals over the past few years have carried stories about our changing financial times—stories that focused on failed banks, massive fraud cases, and waves of employee layoffs. Some of these difficulties have been caused by a miserable economy and others by poor management. In some cases, though, the primary culprit has been deficient financial reporting and disclosure by the affected organization. Many shareholders, the courts, and Congress are concerned that the financial-reporting system (and the accounting profession) may not be functioning as originally intended.

Previous discussions in this text have focused on specific practices used to record business transactions and disclose financial affairs. In addition to examining various global issues, this chapter presents a broad overview of financial accounting by defining the objectives of financial reporting and the characteristics of accounting information. Our emphasis will be on the assumptions and concepts that serve as the foundation for the balance sheet, income statement, statement of owner's equity, and statement of cash flows, namely, generally accepted accounting principles.

Objectives of Financial Reporting

1 Summarize the objectives of financial reporting.

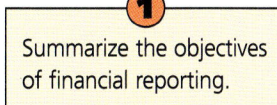

What are the goals of financial accounting and reporting? How can these goals best be attained? Since the mid-1970s, the accounting profession has devoted considerable effort to a conceptual framework project aimed at discovering the answers to these questions. This project has resulted in a series of pronouncements that are expected to provide the necessary structure for the development of improved measurement and disclosure practices.

The first of these pronouncements identified several objectives of financial reporting.[1] The objectives stipulated that the reporting function should generate information that is helpful:

1. To present and potential investors, creditors, and other users in making various types of decisions.
2. In assessing the amounts, timing, and uncertainty of an organization's cash inflows and outflows.
3. In studying an enterprise's resources, the claims to those resources by creditors and owners, and any related changes in either of the foregoing during an accounting period.
4. In examining an enterprise's financial performance, namely, measures of earnings and its components.

These goals relate to the information needs of various groups of financial statement users. Creditors, stockholders, analysts, and others utilize accounting data for a variety of reasons. Creditors, for example, assess an enterprise's debt-paying ability, while stockholders have an obvious concern about corporate earnings and the likelihood of future dividend distributions. In view of this variety, financial statements must maintain a *general-purpose* orientation and satisfy different needs of different parties. Unbiased determination and communication of economic information is therefore of utmost importance.

Characteristics of Financial Information

2 Identify and describe the desirable characteristics of accounting information: relevancy, reliability, comparability, and understandability.

Having established the objectives of financial reporting, the profession then studied desirable characteristics of accounting information.[2] As has been explained throughout the text, firms are often given a choice among various accounting policies. Using specified or unspecified criteria, a business must somehow decide what is the best policy to implement in a specific set of circumstances. Presumably, the selected alternative will be the one that generates the most useful financial information. To judge usefulness, the profession noted that information should possess the following characteristics:

- Relevancy
- Reliability
- Comparability
- Understandability

---

[1] See "Objectives of Financial Reporting by Business Enterprises," *Statement of Financial Accounting Concepts No. 1,* Financial Accounting Standards Board, Norwalk, Conn., November 1978.

[2] See "Qualitative Characteristics of Accounting Information," *Statement of Financial Accounting Concepts No. 2,* Financial Accounting Standards Board, Norwalk, Conn., May 1980.

Sometimes, as we will now see, these characteristics may conflict with one another.

Relevancy. Information is deemed relevant if it influences the actions of a decision maker. On the surface, the concept of relevancy is simple: only produce information that can be actively employed by financial statement users. A closer look, however, reveals several practical problems. As noted earlier, different users have different needs. Obviously, a given set of financial statements cannot satisfy *all* needs of *all* interested parties. Thus, some compromise is necessary. In addition, if the relevancy concept were implemented in the strictest sense, businesses would have to abandon the traditional cost basis of accounting. To illustrate, consider a company that purchased a parcel of land for $40,000 many years ago. Although the land is now worth $500,000, the company's balance sheet continues to reveal a valuation of $40,000. Unfortunately, the latter figure (i.e., cost) is totally irrelevant for a decision maker who is attempting to evaluate the current worth of the entity. This particular problem has prompted accountants to study alternative means of asset valuation and is explored later in this chapter.

Reliability. Financial information must be reliable; specifically, the information must depict the conditions it purports to represent. For net income to be a reliable figure, for instance, it must be a true summary of an enterprise's profit-generating activities. Similarly, the accounts payable figure reported on a balance sheet must depict the trade creditor claims against the entity.

Reliability is influenced by a number of factors, one of which is bias. A measure may represent what it is supposed to, but determination of that measure may be slanted. For example, suppose a company that uses LIFO for valuation of inventory and cost of goods sold is operating in a highly inflationary economy. Assume that management has decided to curtail purchasing activities during the last few months of the accounting period to conserve cash. As a result of this action, inventory levels will decline, and, given the nature of the last-in, first-out system, units that are sold currently will be costed at older (and cheaper) prices. Cost of goods sold will therefore be lower than that computed under the firm's prior (i.e., regular) purchasing program. Overall higher earnings will be reported along with a reliable but possibly biased measure of performance. Cost of goods sold is reliable in that it represents the cost of the units sold. However, the measure may be biased by showing significantly lower costs, caused perhaps by a purposeful manipulation of buying habits and, thus, earnings.

Bias usually benefits certain groups at the expense of others and could erode the public's confidence in financial reporting. Accounting information must be neutral ". . . and report economic activity as faithfully as possible, without coloring the image it communicates for the purpose of influencing behavior in *some particular direction.*"[3] In so doing, accounting and financial reporting are enhanced, thereby increasing their usefulness to parties with widely varying interests.

Comparability. Accounting information is more useful if a company's financial statements are comparable with statements of other enterprises and with those of the same company at different points in time. Comparability among

[3] Ibid., paragraph 100.

entities is difficult because of the variety of accounting methods found in practice—a situation that is not likely to change.

Comparability of a *single firm's* statements through time is achieved by use of the same accounting methods from one period to the next. This practice offers the advantage of better performance evaluation. Imagine the difficulty, for example, of assessing income trends if a company indiscriminately switched depreciation methods during each financial reporting period. Indeed, an analyst would have trouble determining whether variations in net earnings were caused by changes in the entity's activities and efficiency or by changes in its accounting methods. Our discussion here has been intentionally brief; the topic is discussed further in this chapter under the heading of "Consistency Principle."

Understandability. To achieve any degree of usefulness, financial information must be understandable. Often, as is true in many technical disciplines, terminology and jargon can be extremely troublesome. Consider, for instance, the following satirical interaction between Leonard (a stockholder) and President Jones at an annual stockholders' meeting:

> Leonard motioned for the floor and stood up. "You commented previously that total sales increased. Will you comment on our apparent decrease in earnings?"
>
> "Perhaps I should have pointed out," replied President Jones, "that our figures from year to year reflect changes in accounting. For example, we have used LIFO and FIFO. Our depreciation policy is flexible. There is the question of reporting [earnings] per share on the total amount of shares outstanding, the average amount, or the fully converted amount. Our figures also take into account pooling of interest of our latest acquisition. This is a company making a patented banana slicer suitable for any household. Thus it fits nicely into our banana sales. Let me also point out that our final bottom-line figures are reduced by some write-offs. In addition, we have written off some prepaid costs that we know we will incur in coming years. As a result, we had no taxable income this year. We were fortunate in being able to fund some of our short-term borrowings but at an increased interest cost. These and other such adjustments are included in the footnotes to our annual report."[4]

> **ETHICS ISSUE**
>
> A company has had a bad year and is fearful of reporting the results. An accountant has agreed to prepare the financial statements and accompanying notes in an acceptable (although somewhat confusing) manner. Comment.

Many people feel that this parody, written over 25 years ago, accurately reflects the present state of affairs in financial reporting. Economic activities have become so complex that down-to-earth explanations in everyday terms are a near impossibility.

The accounting profession services individuals with varied business and educational backgrounds. Contrary to the impression one may receive when reviewing a firm's financial statements or a company's annual report, accountants do not strive to produce a presentation geared especially for bankers, financial analysts, and other long-term veterans of the business world. Our goal is to produce information that is "comprehensible to those who have a *reasonable* understanding of business and economic activities and are willing to study the information with *reasonable* diligence"[5] (emphasis added).

---

[4] Gerald M. Loeb, "Peter and Leonard Attend an Annual Meeting," *Financial Analysts Journal*, May–June 1971, p. 30. Reprinted with permission of *Financial Analysts Journal*.

[5] "Objectives of Financial Reporting by Business Enterprises," op. cit., paragraph 34.

The Foundation of Accounting

Suppose you are pursuing the study of accounting at a university located in the heart of a major metropolitan area. You are living at home in a nice suburb and must drive 12 miles twice each week to attend class. Assume it is common knowledge that the local police department is lax in its enforcement of driving regulations. Speeding, running red lights, tailgating, and other offenses are common occurrences. Given the goings-on around you, your trip to campus would surely be an "exciting" experience. Different drivers all doing their own thing results in a hectic, if not chaotic, commuting environment.

Much of the same would undoubtedly be said about financial reporting if each company could summarize business activity in its own unique way. Picture the plight of an investor who is attempting to evaluate the performance of two different entities whose profitability is measured by two widely divergent sets of rules. The investor's task would be formidable, to say the least.

Generally Accepted Accounting Principles (GAAP)

3 Explain the need for generally accepted accounting principles and the roles of various groups in the development process.

To bring order to the accounting and reporting process, the accounting profession has developed an underlying foundation for measuring and disclosing the results of business transactions and events. The foundation consists of a set of assumptions, concepts, standards, and procedures collectively known as *generally accepted accounting principles (GAAP)*. The establishment of GAAP does not mean that all organizations report and measure financial activity in the same manner. Witness, for example, the alternatives available for uncollectible account estimates, depreciation computations, and inventory valuation. As noted earlier in the text, each business is unique, and thus a rigid set of measurement and reporting techniques is not feasible. In view of this fact, the accounting profession has formulated a generalized framework within which some diversity is possible.

A Further Focus

The reporting practices of the "good old days" (the early 1900s) truly needed some refinement. To illustrate the goings-on of the era, a review of Royal Baking Powder's corporate annual report found no financial information whatsoever. This is not surprising, as the company failed to publish a balance sheet or a financial statement of any kind for at least 25 years. Amoskeag Manufacturing, then the world's largest cotton mill, produced an income statement that was denominated largely in yards as opposed to dollars. International Business Machines (IBM) combined most of its assets into a single figure. And finally, in an effort to hide management bonuses from financial statement readers, another corporation buried these amounts in cost of goods sold.

Source: For interesting reading on this subject, see "You've Come a Long Way, Shareholder," *Forbes*, July 13, 1987, pp. 282, 285.

The Development of GAAP. For the most part, generally accepted accounting principles are an outgrowth of the profession's efforts over the past 65 years. The accounting profession made very little progress toward the establishment of principles and practices until the late 1920s and early 1930s. As with many developments in this country, a disaster provided the stimulus for change. Both the stock market crash of 1929 and the accompanying depression dictated a need for improvements in financial measurement and reporting. In many cases the financial statements of this period failed to disclose the correct financial position and profitability of an entity. Numerous businesses overstated net income along with their financial well-being. Because of this situation, efforts were made to protect investors and establish a generalized set of accounting principles.

The Securities and Exchange Commission. Given a widespread belief in the 1930s that government should play an increased role in the regulation of business, Congress passed several acts pertaining to the preparation of financial statements for publicly held corporations. The Securities and Exchange Commission (SEC) was given the power to administer these acts and to prescribe accounting principles and reporting practices for companies that issue publicly traded securities. Although the SEC has the ultimate authority for determining what constitutes GAAP, most of the commission's power has been informally delegated to other rule-making bodies of the accounting profession. The SEC has primarily served in an advisory role in the development of proposed accounting standards and has been active in promoting the disclosure of added information for financial statement users.

The Accounting Principles Board. The American Institute of Certified Public Accountants (AICPA) is a national association of licensed CPAs that has been involved with accounting practice for over 50 years. One of the AICPA's major efforts resulted in the formation of the Accounting Principles Board (APB), a policymaking body to advance the development of financial reporting in the United States.

Over the years, the APB studied various problem areas and issued rulings on how to account for selected subjects. These rulings, known as *Opinions*, are considered GAAP by the accounting profession. This designation means that if a company desires to follow practices that are contrary to the *Opinions*, the firm's published financial statements must detail and explain the departure. In view of this situation, most companies use GAAP to avoid negative criticism by creditors and stockholders. (At the same time, these firms reduce the possibility of lawsuits that may arise from misleading, ill-advised reporting methods.)

The APB was the target of considerable criticism in its years of operation, primarily because of two factors. First, members of the Board were part-time, unpaid volunteers. Thus, major policies were being enacted by professionals who could not devote full attention to the issues at hand. Second, given the part-time status, board members maintained relationships with their accounting firms and clients and may have inadvertently compromised positions (and votes).

The AICPA reacted to these concerns by performing a thorough study of the APB's policymaking procedures. In the early 1970s, the APB was replaced by the Financial Accounting Standards Board, a body independent of the AICPA.

Although the APB is no longer in existence, its pronouncements are still in force and considered GAAP unless amended or superseded by newer rulings.

The Financial Accounting Standards Board. Currently, standards of financial reporting in the United States are formulated by the Financial Accounting Standards Board (FASB), a private-sector organization. Rulings of the board are GAAP and are called *Statements of Financial Accounting Standards* as opposed to *Opinions*.

Aside from being independent of the AICPA, the FASB differs from the APB in three major respects. First, members of the FASB serve on a full-time basis and must sever all ties with their previous employers. Member independence is therefore increased since the chance for employer or client influence is reduced (and probably eliminated). Second, FASB members are well paid for their efforts. At the time of this writing, their annual salaries were as follows: chair, $385,000; board members, $313,000. The final difference between the FASB and APB involves representation. Recognizing that accounting has far-reaching effects, the FASB has a broader-based membership, with backgrounds in public accounting as well as industry, government, academia, and the securities markets. This last characteristic enables the board to better serve the public interest.

During its existence the FASB has been relatively active. However, there have been various complaints that the board moves too slowly on certain critical financial-reporting issues, fails to field test its proposals, and overlooks the cost of policy implementation. This criticism has come from the SEC as well as from powerful individuals in the business community.

Other Influential Bodies. In addition to the SEC and the FASB, many other groups influence the establishment of generally accepted accounting principles. Among them are various accounting organizations, such as the *American Accounting Association (AAA)* and the *Institute of Management Accountants (IMA)*. The AAA is comprised primarily of educators; in contrast, most of the IMA's members are employed in business. These organizations play no official role in the development of accounting standards; however, they regularly communicate their position on numerous matters to the profession's policymaking bodies. The *Internal Revenue Service (IRS)*, which administers the tax laws passed by Congress, also has some impact on the development process. Although most tax regulations do not directly affect financial reporting, businesses often simplify matters by using specified tax practices for both the filing of tax returns with the government *and* the preparation of financial statements.

Add to the preceding organizations various professional and trade associations; public accounting and business firms; and bankers, analysts, and other financial statement users. The net result is the formula for how generally accepted accounting principles (standards) are developed in this country. The overall process is depicted in Exhibit 14–1.

SPECIFIC ASSUMPTIONS, PRINCIPLES, AND MODIFYING CONVENTIONS

❹ Define the assumptions, principles, and modifying conventions that underlie financial accounting and reporting.

APB *Opinions* and FASB *Statements* stipulate the proper accounting treatments that are afforded to a number of different topical areas. Throughout the first 13 chapters of this text, you were exposed to the following pronouncements, among others:

Pronouncement	Topic
APB Opinion No. 17	Intangible assets
FASB Statement No. 2	Accounting for research and development costs
FASB Statement No. 5	Accounting for contingencies
FASB Statement No. 34	Capitalization of interest cost
FASB Statement No. 115	Accounting for trading securities

The *Opinions* and *Statements* are detailed technical rules that pertain to accounting practice. Underlying accounting practice is a broad set of assumptions, principles, and modifying conventions (i.e., a collection of general guidelines) that form the basis for much of the FASB's work. These guidelines will be discussed in the following sections.

Entity Assumption. Recall from Chapter 1 that financial reporting is based on the entity assumption, with an entity defined as an economic unit that is organized to pursue business activity. Examples include corporations, individuals, clubs, governmental units, and a host of other organizations. It is important to note that each entity has its own assets, liabilities, revenues, and expenses and must be accounted for accordingly. In effect, the entity is a boundary for reporting.

To correctly assess the outcome of economic activity, each entity must maintain separate accounting records and prepare separate sets of financial statements. That is, a company's business transactions must be segregated from both the owner's personal transactions and those of other independent economic units.

Going-Concern Assumption. A key assumption in accounting is that a business will continue to operate for an indefinite period of time unless there is substantial evidence to the contrary. Stated differently, the business is presumed to be a going concern. Even though all entities do not survive, the going-concern assumption is valid in the majority of cases and forms the basis for many accounting practices. For example, if we expected a business to ter-

EXHIBIT 14–1
The Development of Financial Accounting Standards

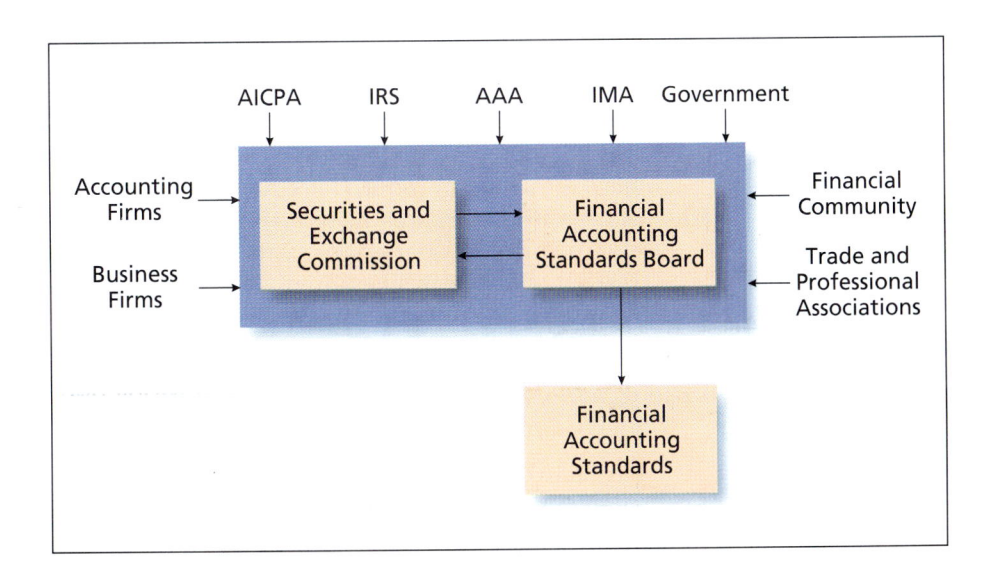

minate in the near future, items such as land and equipment would be expensed upon acquisition because of the low probability of receiving future benefits. These resources, of course, are treated as assets.

The going-concern assumption also provides some justification for the use of an accounting system based on historical cost. Should a company plan to cease operations in the near term, asset valuation on the balance sheet could properly take the form of liquidation (sale) prices in view of the assets' impending disposal.

A Further Focus

It is unusual that a large, well-known company would be the target of a going-concern comment from its auditors. Nevertheless, as USAir Group recently found out, it does happen. In a filing with the Securities and Exchange Commission, KPMG Peat Marwick expressed reservations about USAir's future unless the carrier could negotiate major labor concessions from employees. The auditors noted that the company ". . . has suffered recurring losses from operations and has a net capital deficiency that raises substantial doubt about its ability to continue as a going concern."

The firm, hit with intense competition and losses of $3.13 billion over a recent six-year period, took exception to the assertion by noting implementation of cost-saving measures that total $400 million annually and higher-than-expected cash balances. A USAir spokesperson said, "Nobody argues that this is a pretty picture, but there are plans underway to address . . ." our financial problems.

Authors' note: This issue is unresolved as we go to press. Which point of view (the auditors' or the company's) has more validity will likely be known by the time you read this text.

Source: "Auditors Say USAir's Viability Is in Doubt Without Labor Pacts," *The Wall Street Journal,* April 14, 1995, p. A2

Periodicity Assumption. Although a business is assumed to conduct operations for long periods of time, investors, creditors, governmental authorities, and other financial statement users cannot wait forever to analyze performance. Initially introduced in Chapter 3, the periodicity assumption holds that for reporting purposes, an entity's life can be divided into discrete time periods such as months, quarters, or years. As a result of this assumption, the accountant must assign business transactions to specific reporting periods. In many cases this task presents no special problems. For example, a check written on March 1 in payment of March rent is easily traced to March.

Difficulty arises, however, when dealing with expenditures that span several periods. To illustrate, consider a long-lived machine. If a company wants to furnish a yearly income statement, the machine's cost must be allocated to the period in question via depreciation expense. As you saw in Chapter 11, depreciation can be computed (and cost allocated) by several acceptable methods, each producing different results. Most accountants recognize that cost allocations normally result in arbitrary figures, thus diminishing the usefulness of financial statements. Aside from depreciation, the periodicity assumption also forms the basis for amortization and the adjusting process at the conclusion of an accounting period.

Monetary Unit Assumption. All countries have a unit of exchange. The United States uses the dollar; Mexico, the peso; and Japan, the yen. Business organizations adopt the national currency of their home country to quantify financial activity. Accounting therefore assumes that an entity's transactions can be expressed in terms of a common measuring unit, namely, money. If all organizations in a given country use the same measure, or monetary unit, extensive comparative analysis by financial statement users is possible.

Financial reporting in the United States is based on the premise that the dollar is a stable evaluation unit, thereby permitting dollars of different years to be combined in the financial statements. When computing the balance in a company's Land account, for instance, land transactions of the 1990s are mixed with transactions that occurred in prior years. This calculation is reasonable provided that the dollar is, in fact, stable. Historically, accounting policymakers have generally taken the position that fluctuations in the value of the dollar are small and can be ignored.

Historical-Cost Principle. Accountants have been faced with many problems over the years. One of the most troublesome (and debated) issues has been the financial statement valuation of goods, services, and resources acquired in business transactions. As explained in Chapter 1, accounting is based on the historical-cost principle. That is, acquisitions of the preceding items are recorded in the accounts at cost, with cost defined as the exchange or transaction price.

The use of historical cost has received mixed reviews. In its favor, historical cost is objective and definite. To explain, the use of cost and exchange prices gives rise to objective valuations created by negotiation between two *independent* parties—a buyer and a seller. Also on the favorable end of the spectrum, cost can be verified by inspecting canceled checks, contracts, invoices, and other similar documents.

Critics of historical cost note that employment of the cost basis *subsequent* to asset acquisition produces out-of-date asset valuations and distorted income figures. The latter arise because of cost-based depreciation and amortization computations. Critics therefore contend that fair market values should be integrated in the financial statements. This practice, while having obvious benefits, does have an inherent problem. Assume, for instance, that five accountants are trying to compute the fair market value ("current worth") of an old manufacturing plant. The "current worth" would probably be influenced by a number of factors that are difficult to quantify, such as the plant's physical condition, its location, and the general state of the real-estate market. Even competent appraisal services that specialize in this type of work would have differing ideas, culminating in dissimilar (and subjective) estimates. Subjectivity, of course, would erode the public's confidence in a company's financial statements.[6]

---

[6] Recall that fair market value is used in the year-end valuation of trading securities. An exception to the rule, this amount *is* objective, as it is readily obtainable from *The Wall Street Journal* and various other sources.

Objectivity Principle. The essence of the objectivity principle has been discussed in preceding sections of this chapter. Simply stated, the **objectivity principle** requires that accounting information be free from bias and verifiable by an independent party (such as an external auditor). The resulting financial statements will therefore reflect a fair and neutral view of an organization's business affairs.

Although a high degree of objectivity is desirable, it is difficult to eliminate all personal opinion and judgment from accounting measurement. Consider the accounting procedures related to depreciable assets, for example. Although the cost of a long-lived asset can be determined objectively, estimates are needed when computing service life and residual value, and personal opinion is used when selecting a depreciation method. Naturally, variations in any of the preceding factors will produce different effects on net income and asset valuations. As long as the estimates and related decisions are reasonable, made by a competent party, and verifiable, the objectivity principle is considered to have been implemented to the greatest extent possible.

Revenue Realization Principle. The generation of revenue in our economy takes many different forms. Hospitals earn revenues by providing health-care services; professional sports clubs sell tickets and broadcasting rights; department stores sell merchandise; and construction companies build roads, homes, office complexes, and a host of other facilities. Although our list of revenue-generating activities is far from complete, a question arises as to when these enterprises should recognize revenue in their accounting records. Theoretically, revenue generation is a continuous process for most firms. Practically, however, revenue is said to be *realized* (earned) when both of the following conditions are satisfied:

1. The earnings process is complete or virtually complete.
2. The amount of revenue can be objectively measured.

For most businesses these two tests are met when merchandise is sold or when services are rendered. In either case the transaction and earnings process is complete at this point, and the revenue is measurable on the basis of the exchange price between the buyer and the seller.

Although the time of sale (or rendering of services) is the general rule for recognizing revenue, recognition is sometimes advanced or delayed, as depicted in the time line shown in Exhibit 14–2.

Revenue Recognized During Production. Many companies engage in construction projects that take several years to complete, such as ships, shopping malls, and dams. Because these firms generate revenues over long periods, it may be

---

> **5** Describe the revenue realization principle and apply the percentage-of-completion and installment methods.

EXHIBIT 14–2
Revenue Recognition Time Line

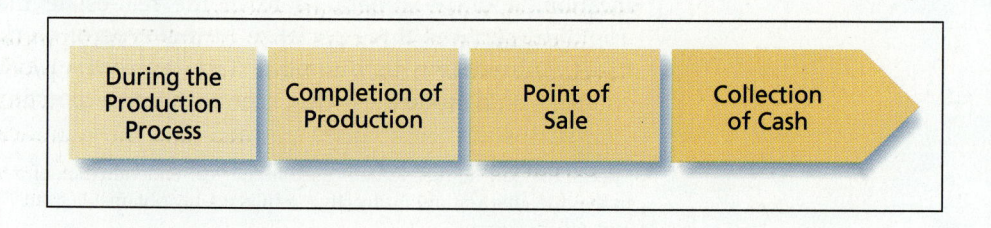

During the Production Process → Completion of Production → Point of Sale → Collection of Cash

more appropriate to enter revenue in the accounting records throughout a project's life instead of waiting until the venture is completed (i.e., the point of sale). Accordingly, a method of revenue recognition termed **percentage of completion (POC)** may be used. Under the POC method, profit is allocated to each accounting period on the basis of progress toward project completion. Completion is usually judged by comparing the current period's construction costs with the total expected costs over the project's life.

As an example, assume that Brennan Construction signed a $44 million contract to build a highway over the next three years. Brennan's accounting department has estimated total construction costs at $40 million, resulting in a $4 million profit for the company. The following schedule shows the actual costs incurred by the firm along with the annual profit recognized:

Year	(A) Actual Costs Incurred	(B) Percentage of Work Completed (A ÷ $40,000,000)	(C) Profit Recognized ($4,000,000 × B)
1	$10,000,000	25%	$1,000,000
2	24,000,000	60	2,400,000
3	6,300,000	Remainder	300,000*
	$40,300,000		$3,700,000

* Remaining amount needed to yield total income of $3.7 million.

For the first two years, the percentage of work completed is derived by dividing the actual costs incurred by the $40 million total project cost. The resulting percentage is then multiplied by the $4 million estimated profit to compute annual income. Year 3, the last year of construction, is handled in a different fashion. Total construction costs amount to $40.3 million, generating an overall contract profit of $3.7 million ($44,000,000 − $40,300,000). Since profit of $3.4 million has already been recognized ($1,000,000 + $2,400,000), Brennan can realize only $300,000 in Year 3.

Because of the objectivity principle, the POC method is used only when a business has the ability to make reasonably dependable estimates of contract revenues, contract costs, and the extent of progress toward completion. In those cases where substantial uncertainty surrounds the estimation process, other procedures are followed.

Revenue Recognized Upon Completion of Production. In some situations revenue is recognized at the end of production. For example, assume that Brennan Construction had great difficulty in determining total contract costs. Because the related percentage calculations would be somewhat questionable, it is more appropriate to recognize the entire profit ($3.7 million) at the time of project completion, when all facts are known.

Recognition also occurs upon completion of production in selected, well-developed markets such as those for certain farm products and precious metals. For instance, farmers may face a situation in which the sale and price of their crops are reasonably assured and no significant delivery costs are involved. Revenue in this case can be recognized upon harvest, as the earnings process is complete and the amount of revenue can be objectively measured.

Revenue Recognized at the Time of Receipt. As we noted in Chapter 3, many professionals (e.g., lawyers, dentists, and architects) use a form of cash-basis accounting for their practices. Under the cash basis, revenue is realized at the time cash is collected from customers and clients. Probably because the method is simple and accepted by the Internal Revenue Service, cash-basis accounting is widely used by individuals and small businesses. The cash basis is not in accord with GAAP, however, because revenue realization is delayed beyond the point where the earnings process is complete.[7] The cash basis is appropriate in those few instances when revenues cannot be correctly determined at the time of sale, specifically, when collectibility of customer accounts is in serious doubt. This situation sometimes arises with installment sales made to individuals who have no (or poor) credit histories.

Installment sales occur in the retail field, especially home furnishings and appliances, where payments are spread over several years. Revenues can be recognized by using a variation of the cash basis called the **installment method**. Sellers that use the installment method allocate a sale's profit to different accounting periods based on the amount of cash received from customers. For example, suppose that on September 1, Beachwood Kitchens sold $1,500 of new appliances to Joyce Chambers, who has no credit history and has been employed for only three weeks. Chambers paid $300 down and agreed to remit the balance owed via 24 end-of-month installments of $50 each.[8] If the appliances cost Beachwood $900, the company has generated a $600 profit, or a 40% return on sales ($600 ÷ $1,500 = 40%). Because each dollar collected from Chambers represents a 40% profit, the company's recognition schedule would appear as follows:

YEAR	CASH COLLECTED		PROFIT PERCENTAGE		PROFIT RECOGNIZED
1	$ 500*	×	40%	=	$200
2	600†	×	40	=	240
3	400‡	×	40	=	160
	$1,500				$600

* $300 down payment + four monthly installments of $50 each.
† Twelve monthly installments of $50 each.
‡ Eight monthly installments of $50 each.

Similar to the cash basis, the installment method does not conform to GAAP unless, as noted earlier, considerable uncertainty surrounds collectibility of the receivable.

Other Methods of Recognition. Some companies use a mixture of recognition methods to properly account for their various revenue sources. Still others follow FASB directives that pertain to specific industries (such as insurance, cable TV, and motion pictures). The following recognition policies were extracted

---

[7] Most professional practices do not issue "published financial statements," or statements to owners (i.e., stockholders) that have been audited by a CPA. "Unpublished" statements need not be prepared in accordance with GAAP.
[8] To simplify matters, we will ignore interest.

from recent annual reports of Blockbuster Entertainment, Carnival Corporation, and The Walt Disney Company:

Blockbuster Entertainment:
Revenue from Company-owned video and music stores is recognized at the time of rental or sale. Revenue from franchise owners is recognized when all material services or conditions required under the Company's franchise agreements have been performed by the Company.

Carnival Corporation:
Customer cruise deposits, which represent unearned revenue, are included in the balance sheet when received. [These amounts] are recognized as cruise revenue upon completion of voyages with durations of 10 days or less and on a pro rata basis [for longer voyages, based on] the number of days completed.... Revenues from tour and related services are recognized at the time the related service is performed.

The Walt Disney Company:
Revenues from the theatrical distribution of motion pictures are recognized when motion pictures are exhibited. Television licensing revenues are generally recorded when the program material is available for telecasting by the licensee and when certain other conditions are met. Revenues from video sales are recognized on the date that video units are made widely available for sale by retailers.

Revenues from participants/sponsors at the theme parks are generally recorded over the period of the applicable agreements commencing with the opening of the attraction.

Matching Principle. Like revenue realization, the matching principle is another important consideration in the calculation of accounting income. Originally discussed in Chapter 3, this principle holds that all costs and expenses associated with the production of revenue should be recognized when the revenue is recognized. Stated differently, expenses should be matched against and deducted from the revenues they helped to create.

The matching principle is the underlying reason behind the adjusting process. Consider, for example, the accounting treatment for depreciable assets. At the end of a reporting period, depreciation expense is recorded in the accounts via an adjustment. Why? Long-term assets such as plant and equipment generate revenues (or benefits) for prolonged periods of time. Thus, a *portion* of the assets' cost (i.e., depreciation expense) is written off each period and matched against the revenues created by the assets' use. Notice that only part of the cost is currently expensed; the remainder will be written off in future periods against the future revenues produced.

Consistency Principle. Financial statements are frequently compared over periods of time to examine trends, assess growth patterns, and so forth. To enhance these studies, accountants have implemented the principle of consistency, which holds that entities employ the same accounting procedures in each reporting period. Picture the difficulties that would result if a company switched back and forth between LIFO and FIFO and other measurement techniques at will. Indeed, such a practice would create havoc for financial statement users who, in many cases, would be forced to compare the noncomparable.

It is important to note that consistency does not prohibit all change. A switch in the methods of recording and reporting business transactions is allowable whenever the end result is a better or more fair presentation of economic activity. When a change occurs, the reason for the change and the impact on net income must be disclosed in the financial statements.

Principle of Full Disclosure. So that investors, creditors, and analysts are not misled, a set of financial statements includes much more than just account balances. An entity must provide a complete reporting (full disclosure) of all facts important enough to influence the judgment of an informed user of financial information. Just what an "informed user" really means is, itself, open to debate. Accountants, however, have agreed that full disclosure should include the following items as a minimum:

1. A summary of the significant accounting policies used in statement preparation.
2. Principles and practices peculiar to the industry in which the entity operates, along with departures from GAAP.
3. Changes in accounting policies and the impact on net income.
4. Impending lawsuits and contingencies.
5. Significant events that occurred after the accounting period being reported but prior to issuance of the financial statements; for example, major casualties such as fires and tornadoes.
6. Significant transactions that took place during the period, such as business acquisitions and mergers.

Full disclosure often takes the form of parenthetical comments within the body of the statements and the separate set of footnotes that accompanies the statements.

Materiality. There are many instances in accounting where theory gives way to expediency, especially when dealing with very small amounts or transactions. To illustrate, suppose a company recently acquired five pencil sharpeners for $75. If the principles and practices introduced on the preceding pages were followed to the letter, the sharpeners would be entered in the accounts as long-term assets and depreciated over their lifetime. To avoid the administrative problems and costs of keeping track of these items over, say, the next 10 years, most companies would expense the entire $75 immediately at the time of acquisition.

This accounting treatment is justified for two reasons. First, the transaction is very small; and second, it will probably have a minimal impact on the yearly financial statements. This example has focused on the concept of materiality. Materiality dictates that the accountant must judge the importance of each transaction (or event) to determine the proper treatment in the accounting records and the resultant impact on the financial statements. In general, an amount is said to be material if knowledge of it would influence the decisions of an informed financial statement user.

As explained in Chapter 11, materiality is a relative concept and is often judged by using comparative analysis. For example, a potential expense item could be compared against some type of dollar limit. If the item exceeds the limit, it is deemed material; if under the limit, the item is considered trivial and would be expensed. There is no guideline stating that 5% is always material or that any expenditure over $500 is always significant. Given the nature of the concept, each item must be evaluated on its own merits.

Conservatism. An accountant is faced with a number of different decisions in attempting to measure and report the financial affairs of an enterprise. Frequently, the "proper" decision is difficult to determine. After exercising sound judgment and considering the objectives of financial reporting, other accounting principles, and industry practices, the accountant often turns to the doctrine of conservatism. Conservatism holds that when alternative valuations and measurements are possible, the alternative selected should be the one least likely to overstate assets and/or net income. A classic example is the lower-of-cost-or-market rule of inventory valuation, which requires write-downs of goods and the recognition of losses on the income statement.

Over the years, conservative financial statements have found favor with statement readers. Conservatism allows users to downplay the impact of overly optimistic company managements who may be inclined to record revenue in the accounts before the revenue is earned, capitalize items that should be expensed, and follow other similar practices, many of which tend to improve reported financial position and profitability. Overly optimistic financial statements could mask impending losses and mislead users.

INTERNATIONAL ACCOUNTING

6 Identify several of the basic issues related to international accounting.

Globalization is a hot subject these days at many companies and business schools. Modern communications systems, transportation technology, and a basic desire to survive have prompted numerous entities to become multinational concerns. Foreign operations are now a key factor in the business plans of most major U.S.-based corporations. These operations make a significant contribution to an entity's total revenues and profit, having a much greater impact than the average "person on the street" may realize. As evidence, we present Exhibit 14–3.

Given the magnitude of world markets, American corporations have a strong desire to develop foreign trade. As these firms are well aware, however, international trade is a two-way street. Witness popular consumer items in this country such as Nestlé chocolate, Mercedes-Benz automobiles, and Seiko watches, all of which are products of companies headquartered in foreign lands.

An increased attention to the accounting aspects of international business is accompanying this globalization of trade. U.S. firms, for example, maintain their records in dollars and settle their transactions in dollars. Companies of other countries, of course, do not. Businesses in the United States produce financial statements that are in accord with generally accepted accounting principles. Foreign entities, in contrast, are often subject to a totally different reporting framework. The last few pages of this chapter address several basic issues related to doing business in foreign markets: uniformity of international accounting standards, accounting for foreign currency transactions, and disclosure of international financial affairs.

EXHIBIT 14-3
Large U.S. Multinational Firms

Rank*	Company	Foreign Revenue as a % of Total Revenue	Foreign Operating Profit as a % of Total Operating Profit
1	Exxon	77.3%	77.0%
2	General Motors	28.0	91.0
3	Mobil	67.5	79.8
10	Procter & Gamble	52.1	65.1
15	Coca-Cola	67.0	67.8
31	Chase Manhattan	48.6	184.8
55	Compaq Computer	49.0	63.6
68	BankAmerica	17.9	27.5
82	Avon Products	61.1	59.9
96	Quaker Oats	35.3	17.8

* Companies are ranked in terms of foreign revenue.
Source: Adapted from "Getting the Welcome Carpet," *Forbes*, July 18, 1994, pp. 276–277, 279.

UNIFORMITY OF INTERNATIONAL ACCOUNTING STANDARDS

As noted several times in this text, a desirable characteristic of financial information is comparability among firms. We have observed that differences in accounting methods sometimes make such comparisons difficult. These difficulties are compounded at the international level because of significant variations in political systems, economic systems, and fundamental principles of measurement. Consider, for instance, the *small* sampling of differences that appears in Exhibit 14–4. (We emphasize the word "small," given the number of variations that actually exist.)[9] In view of this situation, a valid question arises: Can a user rely on and correctly analyze a foreign entity's financial statements when making credit-extension, investment, and other common business decisions?

The International Accounting Standards Committee. As global activities have expanded, the need and demand for uniform international accounting standards have increased. To meet this need, several private-sector and governmental standard-setting organizations have been established. One of the most noteworthy is the International Accounting Standards Committee (IASC).

The IASC membership consists of representatives from professional accounting societies of numerous countries, including the American Institute of Certified Public Accountants from the U.S. The IASC operates in a manner very similar to the Financial Accounting Standards Board (FASB) and issues standards that relate to specific financial reporting topics. Unlike the FASB, how-

---

[9] Some of the more extreme cases involve the state-controlled economies of central Europe, such as Poland and the Czech Republic. The concepts of "profit" and "published financial statements" have only recently begun to surface with the rise of capitalism and the private ownership of companies. As we go to press, several international accounting firms (as well as U.S. universities) are helping to train European business executives, managers, professors, and students in the fundamentals of financial accounting.

Accounting/Reporting Topic	U.S. Practice	Foreign Practice
Inventory costing	LIFO, FIFO, average, other	Australia: LIFO not permitted
Depreciation	Straight-line, units-of-output, declining balance, sum-of-the-years'-digits	Italy: Straight-line
Financial statement disclosure of accounting policies	Full disclosure	Norway: Optional disclosure
Goodwill amortization	Written off over 40 years to expense	Great Britain: Charged to owner's (stockholders') equity, thus boosting income
Effects of inflation	Voluntary disclosure in the notes to the financial statements	Brazil: Impact integrated directly in the financial statements

EXHIBIT 14–4
A Sampling of Differences in Financial Reporting

ever, this group lacks authority to prescribe accounting rules, relying instead on members' attempts to have the standards adopted in their respective countries.

The IASC and other organizations strive to bring a degree of uniformity to international accounting standards and to develop a coordinated worldwide accounting profession. Realistically, achievement of these goals will be a long and difficult process. Keep in mind that the development of generally accepted accounting principles within even a single country (e.g., the United States) usually requires decades of evolution and debate.

ACCOUNTING FOR FOREIGN CURRENCY TRANSACTIONS

International trade is complicated by the various currencies that are used in the world's marketplace. Whenever an entity buys goods from a foreign supplier or sells goods to a foreign customer, the parties involved must agree on the currency to be used in settling the transaction. From the perspective of a U.S. company, if settlement will be made in U.S. dollars, then no unique measurement and reporting problems arise. In contrast, if settlement requires the use of a foreign currency, special accounting considerations are introduced. To appreciate these considerations, it is necessary to have a basic understanding of currency exchange rates.

At any point in time, the currency of one country may be exchanged into the currency of another. The conversion is based on the **spot rate** in effect at the time of exchange. For example, the spot rate might indicate that a U.S. firm could purchase one Swiss franc for $0.70. Spot rates tend to fluctuate throughout a reporting period in response to changes in inflation, interest rates, and political climate. These rates are eventually used to record a host of foreign currency transactions.

Purchase Transactions. To illustrate the necessary accounting for purchases that occur in a foreign currency, assume that Jewelry Import (JI) of New York acquired watches from Alps Exporting of Switzerland. According to terms of the transaction, JI must pay 20,000 Swiss francs to the foreign firm in 60 days. If the spot rate at the time of purchase was $0.70 per franc, how should Jewelry Import enter the transaction in its accounts? Recording the transaction in francs would result in financial records that contain a hodgepodge of different currencies, making data summarization and financial statement preparation impossible. It is therefore necessary to enter the transaction in U.S. dollars even though ultimate settlement will be made in the Swiss currency. The entry needed on the date of purchase is as follows:

Purchases	14,000	
Accounts Payable		14,000
Purchased merchandise on account.		

Notice that the account payable is established at the number of U.S. dollars required to purchase 20,000 francs at $0.70 each. The computation is generalized in the following manner:

$$\text{Transaction Amount in Foreign Currency Units} \times \text{Spot Rate} = \text{Transaction Amount in U.S. Dollars}$$

Sixty days later, Jewelry Import will acquire the francs from a commercial bank at the spot rate in effect on that date. These francs will then be delivered to Alps Exporting in settlement of the transaction. Because exchange rates fluctuate daily, the spot rate will likely differ from the $0.70 rate that existed on the date of purchase. Suppose, for example, that the spot rate has changed and stands at $0.68 on the date of settlement. When Jewelry Import purchases the Swiss currency, the firm will be required to pay only $13,600 (20,000 francs × $0.68). A journal entry to reflect the purchase of francs and the payment to Alps Exporting would be

Accounts Payable	14,000	
Exchange Gain		400
Cash		13,600
Acquired Swiss francs and paid related foreign currency payable.		

This entry indicates that a liability originally established at $14,000 was settled by a cash outlay of only $13,600. The difference constitutes a foreign currency transaction exchange gain. Conversely, Jewelry Import would have suffered an exchange loss had the spot rate risen between the date of purchase and the date of payment.

Sale Transactions. Similar accounting treatment applies to sales on account that will be settled in a foreign currency. Suppose, for example, that American Export sells goods to a British company. The terms of sale require the foreign firm to pay 1,000 British pounds in 90 days. If the spot rate on the date of sale is $1.50 per pound, the transaction would be recorded as follows:

Accounts Receivable	1,500	
Sales		1,500
Sold merchandise on account.		

Ninety days later, assume that the spot rate stands at $1.45 and the purchaser delivers the British currency to American Export. If American Export immediately sells the pounds at a commercial bank for $1,450 (1,000 pounds × $1.45), the appropriate journal entry would be as shown.

Cash	1,450	
Exchange Loss	50	
Accounts Receivable		1,500
Collected British pounds on account and converted to U.S. dollars.		

The exchange loss reflects the fact that American Export agreed to accept 1,000 pounds and that the value of those pounds declined by $0.05 each. If the exchange rate had risen, a gain would have resulted.

An Economist's Perspective

Fluctuating Exchange Rates: Almost all of us have heard a news anchor say that "the dollar fell today" or "the dollar became stronger." In economic terms, what do these phrases mean? Picture Jewelry Import (JI) from your textbook example. In JI's case, the exchange rate fell from $0.70 to $0.68 per Swiss franc—a situation caused by a "strong" dollar relative to the foreign currency.

JI wound up settling its payable for fewer dollars than originally anticipated, thus lowering the cost of goods acquired. If the spot rate for Swiss francs relative to the dollar continues to fall, imported goods from Switzerland become cheaper and may be favored by U.S. consumers—perhaps resulting in a lower overall demand for domestic products. (Of course, the effect on American goods sold in Switzerland would be just the opposite and would have to be considered as well.) The important point here is that currency rate fluctuations have a much broader impact than a simple gain/loss on an importer or exporter's accounting records. The fluctuations can have a significant effect on our overall economy and employment picture.

End-of-Period Adjustments. In each of the preceding illustrations, the exchange gains and losses were recorded upon settlement of the payable or receivable. Because financial statements are often prepared between the date of a transaction and the time of settlement, an end-of-period adjustment is required. Specifically, foreign currency payables and receivables must be adjusted to reflect their U.S. dollar amount as of the financial statement date. For instance, suppose that a U.S. company having a December 31 year-end purchased goods on December 1 and agreed to pay 1 million Japanese yen in 60 days. The spot rate was $0.0095 per yen on December 1, $0.0098 on December 31, and $0.0097 near the end of January when the payable was settled. The entries that follow would be needed.

Dec. 1	Purchases	9,500	
	Accounts Payable		9,500
	Purchased merchandise on account.		
31	Exchange Loss	300	
	Accounts Payable		300
	Adjusted foreign currency payable to reflect spot rate.		
Jan. 30	Accounts Payable	9,800	
	Exchange Gain		100
	Cash		9,700
	Acquired yen and paid related foreign currency payable.		

Notice that on December 31 the payable is adjusted upward by $300 [($0.0098 − $0.0095) × 1,000,000 yen] and the related loss is recorded. On January 30, however, the firm needs only $9,700 to settle its debt. The $100 change from year-end is therefore reported as a gain. This accounting treatment reflects the impact of rate changes on income as the changes occur and also results in proper valuation of foreign currency payables and receivables.

BUSINESS BRIEFING

Doing Business in Foreign Lands

SUSAN QUIGLEY
Director, Finance
Toronto Blue Jays
Baseball Club

More than likely, the mention of "international business" creates a picture of American firms engaged in transactions with Asian, South American, or European entities. We can naturally take an opposite view: a foreign company having significant activities in the United States. That is our situation at the Toronto Blue Jays Baseball Club in Canada.

We receive revenues from several U.S. sources: Major League Baseball's Central Fund (which includes television revenue); corporate licensing royalties and rights fees; and gate receipts from visiting other teams' stadiums. Approximately 20% of our total revenue is in U.S. dollars. In contrast, about 75% of expenses are in U.S. funds. Such expenses include players' salaries, minor league clubs' costs (we have nine such clubs), and scouting and amateur draft outlays.

When our budgets are prepared, Canadian and U.S. currencies are segregated to determine the net requirement in U.S. dollars for the upcoming period. As part of this process, we estimate a spot rate and use techniques that allow us to "lock in" rates, thus removing some of the uncertainty from the foreign exchange process. We are not experts in the foreign exchange game, though: sometimes we win and sometimes we lose. Fortunately, there are companies that specialize in U.S. dollar trading. Considering the escalation in players' salaries in past years, we may soon be using more of their services.

Disclosure of International Financial Affairs

The internationalization of business has led to increased financial statement disclosures, generally in the accompanying notes. Companies that meet certain guidelines must reveal specified information relative to their international operations. Such information is useful to investors and creditors who are sensitive to the unique risks associated with conducting business in foreign lands. For example, if an entity generates a large percentage of its sales and earnings in a country that has a past history of governmental takeovers, a potential (and somewhat pessimistic) investor might shy away from a long-term commitment of funds. Typical corporate disclosures include sales, income, and identifiable assets, all categorized by major geographic area of operation.

End-of-Chapter Review

Learning Objectives: The Key Points

1. **Summarize the objectives of financial reporting.** The financial-reporting function should generate information that is helpful (1) to a wide variety of users who must make various types of decisions, (2) in assessing future cash flows, (3) in studying a firm's financial position and any related changes during the accounting period, and (4) in examining an entity's financial performance (i.e., earnings). Above all, the information conveyed should be general purpose and unbiased in its orientation.

2. **Identify and describe the desirable characteristics of accounting information: relevancy, reliability, comparability, and understandability.** Relevancy relates to the influence of information on the actions of a decision maker. That is, information would be deemed relevant if it influences the actions of an investor, creditor, or other financial statement user. Reliability, on the other hand, refers to the ability of information to accurately depict the conditions it is supposed to represent. To be reliable and to instill public confidence in the information being reported, an entity's disclosures must be free from bias. Comparability refers to making a company's financial statements comparable with the statements of other firms and with those of the same firm at different points in time. Finally, understandability involves making a company's financial statements comprehensible to those who have a reasonable understanding of business activities and are willing to study the information with reasonable diligence.

3. **Explain the need for generally accepted accounting principles and the roles of various groups in the development process.** The foundation that brings order to accounting and reporting is a set of assumptions, concepts, standards, and procedures known as generally accepted accounting principles (GAAP). In the 1930s, the Securities and Exchange Commission was given the power to prescribe accounting principles and practices for publicly held corporations. Since its beginning, however, the SEC has elected to delegate authority to rule-making bodies of the accounting profession. The current private-sector group in charge of formulating GAAP is the Financial Accounting Standards Board. Although other groups influence the development of GAAP, financial reporting is largely the result of FASB and SEC interaction.

4. **Define the assumptions, principles, and modifying conventions that underlie financial accounting and reporting.** Twelve fundamental concepts form the basis for financial accounting. A short description of each follows.

- *Entity assumption*—an assumption that a business is viewed as a unit separate and apart from its owners and other firms.
- *Going-concern assumption*—the belief that a business will continue to operate for an indefinite period of time unless there is substantial evidence to the contrary.
- *Periodicity assumption*—a financial-reporting assumption that an entity's life can be divided into discrete time periods.
- *Monetary unit assumption*—the ideas that (1) an entity's transactions and events can be expressed in terms of a common measuring unit (i.e., the dollar) and (2) the dollar's purchasing power is stable.
- *Historical-cost principle*—the principle of recording goods, resources, and services at cost, with cost defined as the exchange or transaction price.
- *Objectivity principle*—the requirement that accounting information be definite, verifiable, and free from bias.
- *Revenue realization*—the basis that allows companies to enter revenue in the accounting records when earned, which is generally when goods are sold or when services are rendered.
- *Matching principle*—the principle that expenses should be recognized in the same period as the revenues that they helped to produce.
- *Consistency principle*—the idea that businesses should employ the same accounting practices in each reporting period to improve comparability of financial statements.
- *Full disclosure principle*—the requirement that an entity must provide a complete reporting of all facts important enough to influence the judgment of an informed user of financial information.
- *Materiality*—a concept dictating that an accountant should judge the impact and importance of each transaction and event to determine its proper handling in the accounting records. Minor items are treated in the most expedient manner possible.
- *Conservatism*— a doctrine that holds when alternative valuations and measurements are possible, the alternative selected should be the one that is least likely to overstate assets and/or net income.

5. **Describe the revenue realization principle and apply the percentage-of-completion and installment methods.** Revenue is said to be realized when (1) the earnings process is complete or virtually complete and (2) the amount of revenue can be objectively measured. Most revenues are realized when merchandise is sold or services are rendered. However, when the earnings process is spread over several accounting periods, the percentage-of-completion (POC) and installment methods may be used.

    POC is often employed to account for long-term construction contracts. Profit is recognized on the basis of progress toward project completion, which is frequently determined by relating the amount of cost incurred to the total cost to be incurred. Another approach, the installment method, is used in retail environments when collectibility of receivables is in doubt. With this method, profit is allocated to different accounting periods on the basis of cash received from customers.

6. **Identify several of the basic issues related to international accounting.** The text presents three fundamental issues related to the international field. First, because of variations in economic systems and accounting principles, comparability and compatibility of financial information prepared in different countries are impaired.

Several groups, however, are working to bring a degree of uniformity to international accounting standards. Foreign transactions are a second area of concern to accountants, as international trade occurs in various currencies. If settlement is to be made in a foreign currency, a gain or loss must be recorded if the spot rate fluctuates between the transaction date and the date of settlement (or the end of the period). A third issue that must be addressed involves the disclosure of foreign operations. Sales, income, and identifiable assets, all categorized by geographic area of operation, are normally shown in the notes that accompany the financial statements.

Key Terms and Concepts: A Quick Overview

Accounting Principles Board (APB) A former policymaking body of the AICPA charged with the responsibility of developing generally accepted accounting principles. (p. 513)

comparability A characteristic of financial information that allows users to make comparative evaluations among firms and with the same firm at different points in time. (p. 510)

conservatism A concept holding that when different valuations and measurements are possible, the alternative selected should be the one that is least likely to overstate assets and/or net income. (p. 523)

consistency principle A principle stipulating that entities should employ the same accounting practices in each reporting period. (p. 521)

entity assumption An assumption that a company is considered a unit separate from its owner and from other firms. (p. 515)

Financial Accounting Standards Board (FASB) The private-sector organization currently in charge of formulating standards of financial reporting in the United States. (p. 514)

full disclosure principle A principle holding that an entity must provide a complete reporting of the facts important enough to influence the judgment of an informed financial statement user. (p. 522)

generally accepted accounting principles (GAAP) A set of assumptions, concepts, and practices that provides a foundation for measuring and disclosing the results of business transactions and events. (p. 512)

going-concern assumption An assumption that a business will continue to operate for an indefinite time period unless there is substantial evidence to the contrary. (p. 515)

historical-cost principle The principle of recording goods, resources, and services acquired at cost (i.e., the exchange or transaction price). (p. 517)

installment method A method of revenue recognition by which a sale's profit is allocated to different accounting periods. The allocation is based on the amount of cash received from customers. (p. 520)

matching principle The principle that all costs and expenses associated with the production of revenue are recognized when the revenue is recognized. (p. 521)

materiality A concept dictating that an accountant must judge the impact of each transaction (or event) to determine its proper handling in the accounting records. (p. 522)

monetary unit assumption An assumption that an entity's transactions can be expressed in terms of a common measuring unit, such as the U.S. dollar. (p. 517)

objectivity principle A principle requiring that accounting information be free from bias and verifiable by an independent party. (p. 518)

percentage-of-completion method A method of revenue recognition by which profit is allocated to different accounting periods based on the percentage of the total project completed. (p. 519)

periodicity assumption An assumption stipulating that for reporting purposes, an entity's life can be divided into discrete time periods such as months, quarters, or years. (p. 516)

relevancy A characteristic of financial information. Information is deemed relevant if it influences the actions of a decision maker. (p. 510)

reliability A characteristic of financial information. Information is deemed reliable if it accurately depicts the conditions it purports to represent. (p. 510)

revenue realization principle The principle that revenue is earned when (1) the earnings process is complete or virtually complete and (2) the amount of revenue can be objectively measured. (p. 518)

Securities and Exchange Commission (SEC) An agency of the federal government that administers several securities acts and prescribes accounting principles and reporting practices for companies that issue publicly traded securities. (p. 513)

spot rate The rate that is used to convert one currency into another. (p. 525)

understandability A characteristic of financial information. Information is considered understandable if it is comprehensible to those who (1) have a reasonable understanding of economic activities and (2) are willing to study the information with reasonable diligence. (p. 511)

Chapter Quiz

The five questions that follow relate to several issues raised in the chapter. Test your knowledge of the issues by selecting the best answer. (The answers appear on p. 548.)

1. If financial statements are prepared so that creditors benefit at the expense of other user groups, the financial statements are not:
   a. understandable.
   b. reliable.
   c. relevant.
   d. comparable.

2. Generally accepted accounting principles:
   a. vary from state to state.
   b. dictate that all large companies use precisely the same accounting practices.
   c. are currently established by the Accounting Principles Society of America.
   d. are established by the Financial Accounting Standards Board.

3. Which assumption or principle holds that financial statements should be verifiable by an independent party?
   a. Periodicity.
   b. Matching.
   c. Consistency.
   d. Objectivity.

4. Kent signed a $20 million contract to construct a four-mile road over a two-year period. It is estimated that total costs for the road will be $18 million, producing a

$2 million profit. Three miles of the road were completed during Year 1 at a cost of $13.5 million. Kent recognized $1.5 million in profit by following the percentage-of-completion method. If the road was finished in Year 2 at an additional cost of $4.2 million, how much profit should be recognized in Year 2?
- a. $0.
- b. $500,000.
- c. $800,000.
- d. $2,300,000.

5. Tyson (USA) sold merchandise to a Hong Kong company for 100,000 Hong Kong dollars when the spot rate was $0.13 per U.S. dollar. At year-end, the spot rate was $0.15; by the date of settlement, it had risen to $0.16. Tyson would record the sale in its accounting records at:
   - a. $13,000.
   - b. $15,000.
   - c. $16,000.
   - d. some amount other than those above.

Summary Problem

John Lyle and Amy Greenspan are both enrolled in an introductory accounting course at Western University. A recent assignment involved a classroom presentation concerning accounting theory and generally accepted accounting principles. An excerpt from a preliminary draft of Lyle's presentation follows.

> . . . And consistent with the power given to it by Congress, the Securities and Exchange Commission is the major policymaker when it comes to setting present-day accounting standards.
>
> . . . In view of the first part of my presentation, let us now focus on the construction industry as an example. According to the matching concept, revenue should be recognized in the accounting records when the earnings process is complete or virtually complete. This guideline is the sole criterion that companies must follow in this regard. Accordingly, most construction firms use the percentage-of-completion method, which, as its name implies, allows a business to recognize a contract's total profit upon completion of a project.
>
> . . . On a somewhat related issue, these entities are also required to increase long-term asset valuations above cost when the annual inflation rate exceeds 5%. Such a policy is conservative because it makes the accounting records of construction companies consistent with those of other businesses in this country.

John has asked Amy to evaluate his preliminary draft so that any erroneous statements can be corrected before the presentation is given in class.

Instructions

Assume the role of Amy Greenspan and prepare a list of errors, if any, that John Lyle has made.

Solution

John has made a number of errors in his preliminary draft. The errors are detailed as follows:

- a. The Financial Accounting Standards Board is the major policymaker when it comes to setting present-day accounting standards. The SEC serves primarily in an advisory role.
- b. The matching principle is used incorrectly; it focuses on the recognition of expense, not revenue. Revenue realization is the proper principle to cite.

c. Two criteria must be satisfied to recognize revenue in the accounting records, so Lyle is only partly correct. In addition to the earnings process being complete or virtually complete, the amount of revenue must be able to be measured objectively.
d. Under the percentage-of-completion method, profit is recognized during the term of the construction project, not totally upon project completion.
e. Companies are not permitted to increase long-term asset valuations above cost. Such a write-up violates the historical-cost principle.
f. Conservatism means that businesses select accounting practices that are least likely to overstate asset valuations and/or net income. This doctrine has nothing to do with making financial statements comparable with those of other firms. Furthermore, the proposed asset write-up could easily be deemed nonconservative.

Assignment Material

Questions

Q14–1 Financial reporting attempts to generate information that is helpful in assessing the amounts, timing, and uncertainty of an organization's cash inflows and outflows. Briefly discuss why creditors would be interested in this information.

Q14–2 Briefly explain why accountants prepare general-purpose financial statements.

Q14–3 Accountants strive to produce comparable financial statements. Briefly discuss.

Q14–4 Briefly discuss the need for an underlying foundation of financial reporting, namely, generally accepted accounting principles.

Q14–5 Which organization has ultimate authority over the reporting practices of most large corporations? Explain.

Q14–6 Discuss the basic differences between the APB and the FASB.

Q14–7 The going-concern assumption forms the basis for many of the accounting practices illustrated in this text. Define the going-concern assumption and list several of these practices.

Q14–8 Revenue is said to be realized when two tests are met. What are these two tests and when are they met by most businesses?

Q14–9 Present an example of when it is permissible to recognize revenue during the production process.

Q14–10 Present an example of when it is permissible to recognize revenue at the time of receipt.

Q14–11 Metro Delivery was founded in 19X1 and implemented a straight-line depreciation policy for its truck fleet.
a. Should Metro use straight-line depreciation in 19X2 and 19X3? Why? Discuss from the viewpoint of a statement user.
b. *Must* Metro use straight-line depreciation in 19X2 and 19X3? Explain.

Q14–12 Discuss materiality. How is the materiality of a particular item often determined?

Q14–13 Have strides been made toward the uniformity of international accounting standards? Briefly discuss.

Q14–14 How can companies experience gains and losses from foreign currency transactions?

EXERCISES

E14–1 Characteristics of accounting information (L.O. 2)

The accounting profession has identified relevancy, reliability, comparability, and understandability as desirable characteristics of accounting information. Consider the following data concerning buildings that are owned by Company A and Company B:

Company	Cost of Building	Accumulated Depreciation	Fair Market Value
A	$500,000	$200,000	$750,000
B	500,000	150,000	750,000

Company A uses sum-of-the-years'-digits depreciation; Company B uses straight-line.

a. At what figure would Company A's building appear on a balance sheet? Comment on the relevancy of this figure to an investor who is attempting to evaluate the current worth of the entity.
b. By studying the book value of the buildings, comment on a barrier to achieving comparability of the two firms' financial statements.
c. Considering the knowledge level of many potential investors and the use of elaborate accounting methods such as accelerated depreciation, what characteristic of accounting information becomes difficult to satisfy? Briefly explain.

E14–2 Knowledge of GAAP (L.O. 4)

Evaluate the comments that follow as being True or False. If the comment is false, briefly explain why.

a. The entity assumption holds that a business unit may not arbitrarily change its accounting practices from one year to the next.
b. Expenses incurred in the generation of revenue should be recognized in the same accounting period that the revenue is recognized.
c. According to conservatism, small expenditures for assets are expensed as incurred rather than capitalized.
d. The going-concern assumption dictates that financial statements be prepared both quarterly and annually to report financial position and profitability.
e. Increases in the value of equipment assets above cost are ignored in a company's accounting records.

E14–3 Knowledge of GAAP (L.O. 4)

Match the lettered items with the numbered accounting assumptions, principles, and modifying conventions. *Note:* Not all lettered items will be used.

____ 1. Revenue realization
____ 2. Objectivity
____ 3. Consistency
____ 4. Materiality
____ 5. Matching
____ 6. Monetary unit

a. Aids comparability.
b. Rationale for recording yearly depreciation expense.
c. Percentage-of-completion method.
d. An argument in favor of historical-cost valuations for assets.
e. The division of a company's life into discrete reporting periods.
f. Assumes a stable dollar.
g. The basis for footnotes to the financial statements.
h. Justification for the immediate write-off of long-term assets that have a low unit cost.

E14–4 Analysis of GAAP (L.O. 2, 4)

Twenty years ago, the president of Samson Company began a policy of investing excess company funds in classic cars. Total investments over the years have amounted to $102,000. The company is now in need of a bank loan to finance an equipment modernization program. To impress the banker, the president proposed valuing the cars on the company's balance sheet at $157,500—the current fair market value.

a. According to GAAP, at what amount should the cars be valued? Why?
b. Which of the two preceding amounts is consistent with the principle of objectivity and the doctrine of conservatism? Explain.
c. Which of the two amounts is more relevant to the banker? Explain.

E14–5 Revenue realization; percentage of completion (L.O. 5)

In 19X3, DeHaven & Associates signed a contract to build a bridge for $8.9 million. The company anticipates total costs of $8 million and an August 19X5 project completion date. The following schedule shows the costs incurred during each year of construction. Complete the remainder of the schedule, assuming that DeHaven uses the percentage-of-completion method of revenue realization.

	19X3	19X4	19X5
Actual costs incurred	$1,600,000	$4,400,000	$2,150,000
Percentage of work completed during the year	_____	_____	_____
Profit to be recognized	_____	_____	_____

E14–6 Revenue recognition; installment method (L.O. 5)

Lake of the Pines, Inc., sells recreational property. The firm uses the installment method of revenue (and profit) recognition because of the high uncertainty that surrounds customer collections. On October 1, 19X5, Lake of the Pines sold a lot (original cost, $5,000) to Paula and George Benson for $20,000. The Bensons paid $4,000 in 19X5, $10,000 in 19X6, and $6,000 in 19X7. Ignoring interest, calculate the profit that the company should recognize in 19X5, 19X6, and 19X7 from the sale.

E14–7 Revenue realization (L.O. 5)

Consider the following transactions and events, which occurred during 19X3:

1. Eagle Corporation rendered services on account amounting to $34,600. Of this total, clients had paid $27,900 by year-end.
2. Johnson Publishing received $72 on May 5 for a two-year subscription to *The Modern Accountant*, a monthly publication. The subscription began with the magazine's June issue.
3. Crown Construction uses the percentage-of-completion method to recognize revenue. On January 2, the company signed a $70 million long-term contract to build a new manufacturing plant. Total costs were expected to be $64 million. Crown incurred $16 million of construction expenditures during 19X3 related to this project.
4. Ontario Furnishings sold $350,000 of goods on installment contracts at an average gross profit rate of 30%. Outstanding customer balances on these contracts by year-end amounted to $305,000.

All four companies follow generally accepted accounting principles and have a December 31 year-end. In the case of Ontario Furnishings, assume that the installment method is permissible because collectibility of customer receivables is in doubt.

a. Determine the amount of revenue that Eagle Corporation and Johnson Publishing would recognize during 19X3.
b. Determine the amount of profit that Crown Construction and Ontario Furnishings would recognize during 19X3.

E14–8   Revenue recognition (L.O. 5)

Gortronics is a rapidly growing, high-tech company. Unfortunately, with only a few weeks left in the current year, the firm's sales have dramatically slowed. Management has huddled to discuss the problem. "If we don't show higher sales and earnings," notes a vice-president, "the bank will call our loan and we might as well close our doors. Please think about this for a few hours and get me some suggestions on e-mail this afternoon." Three messages were received:

- *Message no. 1*—Let's recognize revenue from Hudson Data Products earlier. We know that Hudson will be placing a large order with us in early January, probably around $175,000 or so. What's a few weeks. We know that we're going to sell the products.
- *Message no. 2*—Several of our assets, like the unused acreage in Los Gatos, have appreciated greatly. Why not increase the value of the land and, at the same time, recognize a gain on the income statement? If we were to sell this property, we could easily get the increased valuation from the buyer.
- *Message no. 3*—Some of our customers owe us favors. Montclair Research Labs, for example, takes forever and a day to pay; we've carried them time and time again. Ship Montclair $250,000 of product and record the sale this year. Ask them to store the goods until early January and then we can process a return. The company is in solid financial shape, and management is very trustworthy.

Discuss how each of the messages should be treated. Assume that Gortronics has a December 31 year-end.

E14–9   Conservatism (L.O. 4)

The following information relates to Trapnell Company, a new business that began operation in 19X7:

1. A $19,200 advertising program was expensed in December 19X7. The program was expected to generate increased sales from December 19X7 through February 19X8.
2. Net income of 19X7 reflected a $13,400 loss related to unsalable inventories. (Trapnell sells high-fashion women's clothing in an outlet mall south of St. Louis.)
3. The company rejected a $70,000 offer for a parcel of land purchased earlier in the year for $52,000. No entry was made in the accounting records to reflect the increased valuation.
4. Straight-line depreciation of $11,000 on newly acquired store fixtures was deducted from revenues when computing 19X7 net income. Management rejected use of the double-declining balance depreciation method.

a. Briefly discuss the doctrine of conservatism as it is used in accounting.
b. Analyze each of the preceding items and determine:
   (1) Whether the company took a conservative approach in its accounting treatment of the item and

(2) Whether the treatment is in accord with generally accepted accounting principles.

E14–10 International accounting (L.O. 6)
Dapore Industries has decided to undertake a significant expansion by doing business with companies located in Hong Kong, Japan, and China. All business will be conducted from Dapore's corporate headquarters in Seattle. Briefly identify the accounting implications of Dapore's decision and the probable impact on the firm's financial statements.

E14–11 International accounting (L.O. 6)
Lubbock Trading Corporation is a U.S. company that engages in numerous transactions involving foreign currencies. Three of the firm's transactions follow.

- *Transaction no. 1*—Purchased merchandise on account from Mizu Company of Japan, agreeing to pay $6,000 in 30 days. On the date of purchase, the spot rate was $0.0093 per Japanese yen. On the settlement date, the spot rate was $0.0089 per yen.
- *Transaction no. 2*—Purchased merchandise on account from Luxar Company of Switzerland, agreeing to pay 30,000 Swiss francs in 60 days. The spot rate was $0.73 per franc on the date of purchase and increased to $0.79 by the settlement date.
- *Transaction no. 3*—Sold merchandise on account to Downing Clothing Corporation of London, agreeing to accept 14,000 British pounds in 90 days. The spot rate was $1.48 per pound at the time of settlement, up from $1.42 on the sale date.

Prepare journal entries for Lubbock Trading Corporation to record each of these transactions and their related settlement. Disregard year-end financial statement adjustments.

E14–12 International accounting (L.O. 6)
On December 1, 19X1, a U.S. company having a December 31 year-end purchased goods on account from a French supplier. Terms of the purchase required the U.S. company to deliver 90,000 French francs to the supplier on January 15, 19X2. The spot rate for a French franc fluctuated as follows:

Date	Spot Rate
Dec. 1, 19X1	$0.18
Dec. 31, 19X1	0.22
Jan. 15, 19X2	0.21

Prepare the three journal entries required by this transaction.

PROBLEMS

Series A

P14–A1 Analysis of GAAP and transactions (L.O. 4, 5)
You are the chief accountant of Atlanta Sound & TV. The owner of the firm, Gene Cummings, having graduated from college several years ago, has decided to update himself in the area of financial reporting. After completing several weeks of accounting at a local university, Cummings became involved in a heated debate with Al Warren, one of your staff members. The following topics were discussed:

a. In reviewing the inventory records, Warren found that LIFO was used to account for CD players and FIFO was used for all other merchandise. Warren maintains that this procedure violates generally accepted accounting principles. Cummings, on the other hand, has no objections to the firm's inventory costing methods.

b. In December 19X1, the company spent $50,000 for 20 vacation tours to Hawaii. The tours will be awarded to employees who produce the highest first quarter sales in 19X2. The following entry was made:

Marketing Expense	50,000	
Cash		50,000

Warren claims the entry is satisfactory. Cummings disagrees, claiming there is no justification for reducing 19X1 income.

c. On May 13, Atlanta sold $3,200 of merchandise on account to Jerry Burns, a valued customer. Warren favors a journal entry on May 13 that reflects $3,200 of sales. In contrast, Cummings feels the sale should be recorded when cash is received by the firm.

d. Atlanta recently completed and occupied a new office building. Following Warren's suggestion, all items of office equipment having a unit cost of less than $100 were expensed. The equipment had an average life of five years and a total cost of $34,000. Cummings is opposed to this accounting treatment for reasons not stated.

e. Two years ago Atlanta acquired a building complex (including land) for $550,000. The current book value is $470,000. A recent appraisal indicated that the land and building are worth $120,000 and $600,000, respectively. Cummings favored the following balance sheet presentation:

Building and land $470,000

The presentation favored by Warren was: Land, $120,000; Building, $600,000.

f. A bid was received to build a loading platform for $4,700. Feeling that the amount was too high, warehouse employees built their own platform for $3,000. Warren feels the platform should be recorded in the accounts at $3,000; Cummings favors the following entry:

Loading Platform	4,700	
Cash, Supplies, and so on		3,000
Construction Gain		1,700

Assume that prior to considering any of these items, Atlanta had tentatively figured 19X1 net income at $234,000.

Instructions

Decide who, if anyone, is correct in each of the disagreements and state the logic for your answer. Cite GAAP when appropriate. In some cases more than one principle may apply.

P14–A2 Analysis of GAAP and transactions; financial statement impact (L.O. 4, 5)

You are reviewing the accounting records of Ballpark Industries for the current year ended December 31. The following information has come to your attention:

1. The company, which uses the accrual basis of accounting, failed to record $8,000 of interest revenue. Collection will take place in the next reporting period.
2. Trading securities purchased by the firm for $22,700 had a year-end market value of $17,600. Feeling that the market would soon rebound, management refused to authorize a December 31 adjustment to properly value the investment.

3. Freight charges of $2,500 relating to the purchase of equipment on December 28 were expensed when incurred.
4. Ballpark paid $22,000 on December 31 to acquire a new car for the vice-president of marketing. Because of a change in plans, the car was given to the vice-president's wife (for her personal use), and the following entry was made in the accounting records:

Miscellaneous Expense	22,000	
Cash		22,000

5. Short-term loans payable of $35,000, recently secured to finance equipment purchases, were accidentally entered in the accounting records at $53,000.
6. The current year's financial statements revealed the following information:

Net income	$ 65,800
Assets	165,000
Liabilities	77,000
Owner's equity	88,000

Instructions

a. Set up a four-column schedule with the following headings: net income, assets, liabilities, and owner's equity. By adjusting Ballpark's reported balances, compute corrected financial statement totals using the information presented in items (1)–(5).
b. For items (1)–(3) only, determine if any generally accepted accounting principles have been violated. Briefly explain your answer.

P14–A3 Understanding revenue recognition (L.O. 4, 5)

I Love Yogurt (ILY) is a franchisor/management company that helps private investors open and operate yogurt shops. The firm provides continuing advice and guidance for a fee. In addition, ILY sells yogurt, cups and spoons, and kitchen equipment, and licenses the use of its name and advertising. The following transactions and events occurred during 19X2, the first year of operation:

- The company received franchise fees of $2 million. Forty percent of the consulting services related to these fees were performed by the end of 19X2 at a cost of $200,000.
- Late in 19X2, ILY ran a regional advertising campaign that cost $280,000. The company plans to bill its franchisees $500,000 in early 19X3 for this service.
- Actual sales of cups, spoons, yogurt, and other products to franchisees totaled $7.2 million. Of this amount, 90% has been billed. Of the amount already billed, 80% has been collected. The cost of products sold totaled $4.1 million.
- ILY sold equipment to new franchisees in the amount of $6 million. By year-end, $2.5 million of the balances due had been collected. This equipment cost ILY $4.2 million; sales will be accounted for by using the installment method.
- Late in 19X2, the company created a construction department to build new stores. By year-end, projects were in progress that had a contract price of $5.8 million and total expected costs of $5 million. Costs incurred to date amounted to $1 million. ILY will use the percentage-of-completion method to account for construction activities.

Instructions

Prepare a schedule that indicates the amount of profit I Love Yogurt earned during 19X2.

P14–A4 Revenue realization: Percentage-of-completion and installment methods (L.O. 5)

Bennett Developers recently signed a long-term contract for the construction of apartments throughout New Mexico for $40 million. Bennett's accounting department has estimated total construction costs of $38 million. The contract stipulated a $900,000 payment to Bennett upon contract signing and periodic payments throughout the project's three-year life. Additional information follows.

	19X1	19X2	19X3
Cash collected	$12,000,000*	$18,000,000	$10,000,000
Actual costs incurred	9,500,000	22,800,000	5,900,000

* Includes the $900,000 payment upon signing.

The project was completed on December 28, 19X3.

In a separate transaction, the company sold a parcel of land to Recreational Housing for $5 million. Bennett originally paid $4.2 million for the parcel. Terms of sale required a 30% down payment on December 1, 19X1, by Recreational Housing and 20 equal monthly payments beginning on January 1, 19X2.

Instructions

a. Calculate the total profit that Bennett has earned on the apartment project.
b. Bennett will use the percentage-of-completion method to account for the apartment project. Prepare a schedule that reveals the profit earned in 19X1, 19X2, and 19X3.
c. Bennett will use the installment method to account for the land sale. Prepare a schedule that reveals the profit earned in 19X1, 19X2, and 19X3.

P14–A5 International accounting (L.O. 6)

Key Manufacturing is a U.S. firm engaged in international trade. The company imports raw materials from several countries in Asia and exports completed products to Europe. The following selected information was obtained from the accounting records:

Imports

- Purchased materials on account from a company in South Korea, agreeing to pay 50 million won in 90 days. The spot rate was $0.0013 per won on the date of the transaction.
- Purchased goods on account from a firm in Thailand. Key agreed to pay 2.4 million baht in 30 days; the spot rate at the time of purchase was $0.039 per baht.

Exports

- Sold completed goods on account to a British firm for 40,000 pounds. Settlement will take place in 40 days; the spot rate on the date of sale was $1.55 per pound.
- Sold finished products on account to a company located in Paris. Key will receive 80,000 francs in 90 days; the spot rate on the transaction date was $0.18 per franc.

The Thai import and British export transactions were settled prior to Key's year-end.

Instructions

a. Prepare journal entries to record the two purchases and the two sales.
b. Prepare Key's journal entries to settle the Thai import and British export transactions, assuming the following spot rates on the date of settlement: Thai baht, $0.041; British pound, $1.58.
c. Prepare the journal entries needed to adjust Key's accounting records at year-end. The year-end spot rates are: South Korean won, $0.0012; French franc, $0.167.

Series B

P14–B1 Analysis of GAAP and transactions (L.O. 4, 5)

You are the chief accountant of Westside Tool & Die, Inc. The president of the firm, Jim Norton, having graduated from college over 20 years ago, has decided to update himself in the area of financial reporting. After completing several weeks of an accounting course at a local university, Norton became involved in a heated debate with Joan Mencer, one of your staff members. The following topics were discussed:

a. Three years ago the company acquired a patent from an inventor for $52,000. The current book value is $40,000 as a result of amortization. A recent appraisal indicated that the patent is worth $115,000. Norton believes that the balance sheet should contain the current valuation of $115,000; Mencer, in contrast, favors $40,000.

b. Westside recently acquired a sophisticated computer system for $240,000. Following Norton's suggestion, all system expenditures costing less than $100 were expensed. Such expenditures totaled $4,000. Mencer felt that these outlays should be capitalized in the Computer Equipment account because they render long-term benefits.

c. Norton had company personnel design and build a security gate for his vacation home. He claimed that no entry is needed on the company's books because the personnel didn't have to work overtime on the project. Mencer believes that the $11,000 cost should be recorded as follows:

Miscellaneous Expense	11,000	
Cash, Supplies, and so on		11,000

d. The company was having an exceptionally poor fourth quarter. Norton instructed the plant's accountant to omit the quarterly adjusting entry for truck depreciation in an effort to boost net income. Mencer was opposed to this treatment for reasons not stated.

e. Westside sold a large machine on the installment basis to the Brazilian Air Force at a profit of $4 million. Norton wants to recognize the profit in the year of sale, even though no cash has yet been received. Mencer prefers to recognize profit as the Air Force settles its obligation, because Brazil has had great difficulty in paying its international debt.

f. The company has been sued for $1 million on a sex discrimination charge by a former secretary. Consultation with Westside's attorney indicates that the secretary has a very strong case. Norton wants to indicate the possibility of a lawsuit in the notes to the financial statements. Mencer claims that a note is unnecessary because the case has not yet been decided.

Assume that prior to considering any of these items, Westside had tentatively figured 19XX net income at $800,000.

Instructions

Decide who, if anyone, is correct in each of the disagreements and state the logic for your answer. Cite GAAP when appropriate. In some cases more than one principle may apply.

P14–B2 Analysis of GAAP and transactions; financial statement impact (L.O. 4, 5)

You are reviewing the accounting records of Reno Enterprises for the current year ended December 31. The information that follows has come to your attention.

1. On December 9, the company determined that a $5,000 uninsured theft of cash had occurred. The accounts have yet to be adjusted for the amount of the theft.
2. The company, which uses the accrual basis of accounting, failed to record $1,400 of wage expense. Payment will take place in the next reporting period.
3. Inventories costing $15,600 had a year-end fair market value of $21,700. Accordingly, Reno's bookkeeper made the following adjustment in the accounting records:

Inventories	6,100	
Income from Appreciation		6,100

4. Import duties of $1,200 relating to the purchase of equipment on December 29 were improperly expensed when incurred.
5. On October 1, Reno purchased $120,000 of equipment at a going-out-of-business sale. The equipment, which normally sold for $150,000, was recorded as follows:

Equipment	150,000	
Cash		120,000
Gain on Bargain Purchase		30,000

Reno expects to use the equipment for 10 years and employs the straight-line method of depreciation.

6. The company's financial statements for the current year revealed the following information:

Net income (loss)	$ (2,000)
Assets	195,000
Liabilities	120,000
Owner's equity	75,000

Instructions

a. Set up a four-column schedule with the following headings: net income (loss), assets, liabilities, and owner's equity. By adjusting the company's reported balances, compute corrected financial statement totals using the information presented in items (1)–(5).
b. For items (2)–(5) only, determine if any generally accepted accounting principles have been violated. Briefly explain your answer.

P14–B3   Understanding revenue recognition (L.O. 4, 5)

Dr. Allison Hardy's introductory accounting class has just completed a study of revenue recognition. One who is innovative and not afraid to try something new, Dr. Hardy gave her class the following assignment: "You always complain that my tests are too hard. Here's your chance—I'd like you to write a short question that deals with revenue recognition. The best questions will be used on the test, and each question's author gets a perfect score on his or her submission." The scenarios that follow were selected.

- Bright Company, which uses the installment method of accounting, sold $600,000 of merchandise on account throughout the year. The goods cost Bright $210,000; customer balances outstanding on December 31 totaled $515,000.
- In November, Davis Corporation published 140,000 copies of its new monthly magazine, *Soaps—Yes!!*, at a cost of $115,500. Sixty percent of the copies were sold to distributors at $1.10 per copy; 38% were mailed to subscribers who had purchased yearly subscriptions for $15; the remaining 2% were unsold and eventually destroyed. Mailing charges totaled $24,200.
- Hamilton Motors trains service technicians for appliance dealers located in the Pacific northwest. Hamilton's training costs totaled $386,000; the company billed the appliance dealers $490,000. Unbilled amounts on December 31 were $39,000; total dealer payments throughout the year were $456,800.
- Montgomery, Inc., uses the percentage-of-completion method to account for long-term construction activities. In 19X5, the company signed a $90 million contract to build a bridge; Montgomery's costs are anticipated to total $80 million for the project. Actual costs incurred in 19X6 totaled $38.4 million.
- Thompson Corporation received $950,000 from State University, partial payment on a $1.4 million invoice for computers sold in October. The computers cost Thompson $1.1 million; the company still owes its supplier $200,000 for this equipment.

Instructions

Show Dr. Hardy that you have an excellent understanding of revenue recognition. Compute the amount of profit that each company would report. *Note:* For Montgomery, Inc., the profit should be calculated for 19X6.

P14–B4   Revenue realization: Percentage-of-completion and installment methods (L.O. 5)

San Diego Shipyards recently won a $35 million bid to build two ships for the Navy. Management anticipates the $32 million total project cost will be incurred over a three-year period (19X2–19X4), and delivery of the ships will occur in late 19X4. The company received $5 million when the contract was signed in January 19X2 and another $10 million at the end of each year. The actual costs were as follows: 19X2, $7,040,000; 19X3, $20,160,000; and 19X4, $4,980,000. San Diego uses the percentage-of-completion method to account for its contracts.

In an unrelated transaction, the firm sold property to a local developer for $2,125,000. (The property had originally cost the company $850,000 when acquired 12 years ago.) San Diego received 30% of the sales price as a down payment in 19X2; the remaining balance will be received in equal amounts during 19X3 and 19X4. Management will use the installment method to account for this transaction.

Instructions

a. For the Navy contract, prepare a schedule that shows the profit to be recognized during 19X2, 19X3, and 19X4.

b. For the property sale, prepare a schedule that shows the profit to be recognized during 19X2, 19X3, and 19X4.

P14–B5 International accounting (L.O. 6)

Topaz Enterprises is a U.S. company engaged in international trade. The following business activity occurred in 19XX:

Jan. 15	Purchased merchandise on account from the Toronto Company of Canada, agreeing to pay 15,000 Canadian dollars in 60 days. The spot rate is currently $0.65 per Canadian dollar.
Feb. 22	Sold merchandise on account to an Israeli company, agreeing to accept 6 million shekels in 60 days. The current spot rate is $0.26 per shekel.
Mar. 16	Settled the purchase of January 15. The spot rate was $0.63 per Canadian dollar.
Apr. 10	Purchased merchandise on account from a Pakistani firm, agreeing to pay 1 million rupees in 90 days. The spot rate on this date stood at $0.026 per rupee.
17	Settled the transaction of February 22. The spot rate was $0.30.
May 1	Sold merchandise on account to Swedish Imports, agreeing to accept 50,000 krona in 50 days. The current spot rate is $0.125 per krona.

Instructions

a. Prepare journal entries to record the preceding transactions.
b. Topaz Enterprises ends its fiscal year on May 31. Prepare any adjusting entries that may be necessary to update the accounting records for exchange gains and losses. The spot rates for foreign currencies on this date are as follows:

Canadian dollar	$0.73
Israeli shekel	0.33
Pakistani rupee	0.035
Swedish krona	0.14

EXPANDING YOUR HORIZONS

EYH14–1 Controversial standards of the FASB (L.O. 3)

Accounting standards in the United States are currently developed by the Financial Accounting Standards Board (FASB). In the process of formulating rules for financial reporting, the FASB follows a lengthy process and invites both written and oral criticism of proposed regulations. The reviews are sometimes so numerous and insightful that the Board rethinks the issue and changes its mind.

Instructions

Using the reference section of your library, locate an article written since January 1990 that is critical of a proposed accounting standard. (*The Wall Street Journal* is often a good source for this material.) Prepare a short summary of the criticism.

EYH14–2 Review of an actual FASB Statement (L.O. 3)

The pronouncements of the Financial Accounting Standards Board are spelled out in publications called *Statements of Financial Accounting Standards* (SFASs). Although quite detailed, the *Statements* provide an overview of the issue at hand, the Board's ruling, and the underlying logic.

Instructions

In your college or university library, locate the accounting pronouncements published by the Financial Accounting Standards Board. These pronouncements may be in the form of individual booklets or perhaps gathered together in a bound volume. Read SFAS No. 2 that relates to research and development costs and answer the following questions:

a. What is the proper treatment of research and development costs?
b. Name five activities that the Board considers to be "research and development."
c. Is quality control during commercial production classified as a research and development activity?
d. In general, what cost elements are associated with research and development activities?
e. How much difficulty did you have comprehending this pronouncement? Briefly explain.

EYH14–3 Revenue recognition (L.O. 5)

Different companies use different methods of revenue recognition. See page 521, for example, which presents the methods utilized by Blockbuster Entertainment, Carnival Corporation, and The Walt Disney Company.

Instructions

Using the resources of your library, review the annual reports of Turner Broadcasting System and four other distinctly different companies to determine how these firms recognize revenue. (Such information is usually presented in the Summary of Significant Accounting Policies.) Be prepared to report your findings to the class.

EYH14–4 Accounting principles; foreign operations: Reebok International Ltd. (L.O. 4, 6)

Reebok International is a designer, marketer, and distributor of sports, fitness, and casual footwear and apparel. The firm's principal operating units include the Reebok Division, Avia Group International, and the Rockport Company.

Instructions

By using the text's electronic data base, access the income statement and accompanying notes of Reebok International Ltd., and answer the questions that follow. Unless otherwise indicated, responses should be based on data for the most recent year presented.

a. Review the summary of significant accounting policies that has been prepared by the company.
  (1) The summary is the result of applying a key principle of accounting. What principle is it?
  (2) What methods does the company use with respect to inventory valuation and depreciation of plant and equipment?
b. Does the income statement reveal that any "unusual" transactions or events occurred during the period? Briefly explain.
c. Do the notes to the financial statements describe any "unusual" transactions or events that occurred during the period? Briefly discuss.
d. The company has operations in other parts of the world.
  (1) What percentage of the firm's sales are made in the United States? Has this percentage changed over, say, the past two years?

(2) Comment on the trend in domestic and foreign operating income over the past few years.

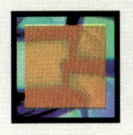

EYH14–5 Accounting principles; foreign operations (L.O. 4, 6)

This problem is a duplication of Problem EYH14–4. It is based on a company selected by your instructor.

Instructions

By using the text's electronic data base, access the specified company's income statement and accompanying notes and focus on data for the most recent year reported. Answer requirements (a)–(d) of Problem EYH14–4.

EYH14–6 Characteristics of accounting information; principles (L.O. 2, 4)

Julia Arens is the president of Arens Real Estate Development Company. She has operated a successful business in the past few years by acquiring real estate from bankruptcy proceedings and other court-ordered liquidations. The company makes needed improvements to the properties and resells the properties for sizable profits. Julia has high expectations for the future of her firm.

Julia understands that the accounting information used in the financial statements should be relevant and reliable. After much consideration, she has decided that the principle of historical cost, presently used by the company, fails the relevancy criterion. She believes that current value (i.e., fair market value) information would be more meaningful to users of the firm's financial statements, given the nature of the business. Julia has come to Sandra McGovern, her accountant, for advice.

Instructions

a. How would Sandra explain the meaning of "relevant" and "reliable" as used in the preparation of financial statements?
b. How would Sandra explain the principle of historical cost and the objectivity principle as used in financial reporting?
c. Does the principle of historical cost fail the relevancy guideline for this type of business? Why or why not?
d. Can Julia use fair market value for presentation of the company's assets on the balance sheet?
e. Given the unique nature of the business, what might Sandra propose to supplement the balance sheet (and help users better understand the company's presentation)? What principle of accounting is being followed here?

COMMUNICATION OF ACCOUNTING INFORMATION

CAI14–1 A checklist for reports: The Black & Decker Corporation (L.O. 4)

Communication Principle: How do we evaluate the success of reports? A report succeeds when it can easily be used to find information or to help make decisions. These qualities help make a report useful:

1. An impartial tone that reassures the reader that the report is a credible, fair, and objective source.
2. A clear organizational scheme reflected in the order of the headings. One such scheme is the movement from general principles to specific illustrations.
3. A traditional format and professional appearance.

In contrast, a report is not effective if it is marked by the following characteristics:

1. The assumption of only one kind of reader—expert or general—and a lapse either into jargon and too many details or into generalities with too few specifics.
2. The lack of a purpose statement that directs the reader and focuses attention.
3. The creation of more questions than answers on the part of the reader. The reader is left with the impression of incompleteness, vagueness, and confusion.

■ ■ ■ ■ ■ ■ ■ ■

Black & Decker is a manufacturer of quality tools/appliances used in and around the home and for commercial applications. Power saws, hedge trimmers, irons, and toaster ovens are just a few of the company's many products.

A review of a recent Black & Decker annual report found the following:

- Sales, operating income, and identifiable assets are subdivided and reported by geographic regions of activity.
- Inventories are reported at the lower of cost or market.
- Property, plant, and equipment are reported at cost. Appropriate assets are being depreciated by use of the straight-line method.
- Individual amounts owed to the company's many suppliers do not appear in the notes that accompany the financial statements.

Instructions

Assume that Karen Sawyer, a Black & Decker employee, was having a bad day. A high-ranking executive heard her say: "Nobody does anything by the book around here." To make the point that the company does do things by the book, the executive has asked Karen to review the firm's financial statements and the accompanying notes. She is to construct a report that (1) discusses the use of generally accepted accounting principles (GAAP) in financial reporting and (2) cites instances where Black & Decker has followed GAAP.

Assume the role of Karen Sawyer and prepare the report, being sure to observe the guidelines set forth in the communication principle. When discussing the use of GAAP at Black & Decker, indicate and briefly explain the specific concept or principle that is being followed.

Answers to Chapter Quiz

1. b
2. d
3. d
4. c ($20.0 million − $13.5 million − $4.2 million = $2.3 million total profit; $2.3 million − $1.5 million = $800,000)
5. a

15 PARTNERSHIPS

LEARNING OBJECTIVES

After studying this chapter, you should be able to:

1. Explain the unique characteristics of a partnership.
2. Account for partnership formation and income distribution, including situations that give rise to an earnings deficiency.
3. Account for partner admissions and withdrawals.
4. Perform the procedures related to partnership liquidations.

When George Faris and your authors met to discuss the opening vignette for this chapter, George just shook his head. "I honestly haven't had much experience with this type of business organization," he explained. "I've seen some recent articles that don't paint a real favorable picture of partnerships, and some of my friends have lost personal assets in partnership deals gone bad. Granted there are a number of them out there, but I'm not really sure what the appeal is."

George summed up his feelings by noting that he probably has a biased view about this organizational form. "It seems to me, and, again, I have limited knowledge, that a partnership is an extremely risky type of endeavor." George has expressed this concern to his attorney on several occasions. In fact, whenever Banner Advertising enters into a joint venture or co-ownership of assets with another firm, George seeks reassurance that the transaction will *not* be viewed as a partnership.

Despite the fact that many businesspeople like George attempt to avoid the partnership type of organization, partnerships are encountered quite frequently. To become a bit more formal, the Uniform Partnership Act, adopted by most states to govern this entity, defines a partnership as "an association of two or more persons to carry on, as co-owners, a business for profit." Partnerships are an attractive organizational form, especially for small emerging companies, which often need more talent, experience, and capital than a proprietorship's single owner can provide.

Most partnerships have fewer than five owners; others, however, are quite large. Arthur Andersen & Co., for example, an international public accounting firm, recently reported having 2,596 partners throughout its worldwide operation in 72 countries. The partnership form of organization is encountered in professional practices such as accounting, law, medicine, and dentistry. Furthermore, it is used by small retail establishments, manufacturers, home builders, and service businesses.

CHARACTERISTICS OF A PARTNERSHIP

Partnerships possess several distinctive features that have important implications for accountants, executives, and entrepreneurs. These features are discussed in the following sections.

1 Explain the unique characteristics of a partnership.

EASE OF FORMATION

A partnership is easily created by a voluntary agreement between two or more people. Although the agreement may be oral and finalized by a handshake, good business practice dictates the creation of a formal written "contract" between the parties involved.

This document is commonly known as the articles of partnership. Generally speaking, the articles detail the rights, responsibilities, and duties of the partners. In addition, specific policies are normally stated with regard to partner investments and withdrawals, the division of net income (and net loss), the admission of new partners, the withdrawal of partners, and procedures to be followed in the event of partner disputes or a partner's death.

MUTUAL AGENCY

Partnerships have mutual agency; that is, each partner acts as an agent of the partnership in business transactions. As a result, the partnership is bound to the commitments and obligations made by any partner on behalf of the firm. For this reason partners must be selected with great care, as irresponsible personnel could create a difficult working environment and spell financial disaster.

CO-OWNERSHIP OF PROPERTY AND INCOME

According to the Uniform Partnership Act, partners are really the co-owners of an enterprise. Thus, a partner who invests a building in the firm retains no personal rights to the building. (The asset becomes jointly owned by all partners.) Similarly, the partnership's net income belongs to all of the partners and can be divided among them in any agreed-upon manner.

LIMITED LIFE

Unless there is an agreement to the contrary, the death, bankruptcy, retirement, incapacity, or withdrawal of a partner ends the partnership. Other events that call for termination of the firm (sometimes known as dissolution) include accomplishment of the firm's objective and the admission of new partners. Dissolution does not necessarily mean that operations cease and the remaining assets are sold. Rather, if the surviving partners agree, a new entity can be formed, and activities can continue uninterrupted.

UNLIMITED LIABILITY

Consistent with the financial reporting principles discussed in the previous chapter, a partnership is viewed as an *accounting entity* that is separate and distinct from its owners. Consequently, the personal economic activities of the partners (e.g., the acquisition of household furniture, the payment of a weekly grocery bill) are not combined with the transactions of the business. In contrast, the partnership is not a separate *legal entity* and as such, has no legal status under common law.

Because of this latter feature, each owner is held personally liable (i.e., has unlimited liability) for the debts of the enterprise. Thus, if a partnership experiences cash flow problems and becomes unable to pay its bills, the partners are required to surrender personal assets to help settle the firm's obligations.

Problems Associated with Unlimited Liability. The unlimited liability feature can present several significant obstacles when trying to conduct business. For example, picture a partnership that is trying to raise substantial amounts of additional capital. Most people who invest in stocks, stamps, art, gold, and other items are willing to absorb an occasional loss. However, because significant personal assets such as a home and lifetime savings may be at stake, many investors tend to shy away from this entity form. The potential exposure is simply too great.

A similar problem surfaces because of our increasingly litigious society, a situation that places personal assets even more at risk. Unprofitable business operations and lawsuits against a partner's firm can harm an individual partner's financial well-being. To illustrate, we cite the case of Laventhol & Horwath, a huge national accounting firm that had to close its doors in 1990. A sizable legal judgment fully consumed the company's assets, forcing partners (and retirees) to contribute approximately $47 million of their own funds to satisfy the claim.[1]

These suits, unfortunately, are becoming more the rule than the exception. To help counter the problem, a number of businesses and the major U.S. accounting firms are turning to a relatively new form of organization called a **limited liability partnership (LLP).** As its name implies, such an arrangement provides partner protection by restricting the amount of loss to the firm's invested capital. The exposure and use of personal assets as a means of satisfying creditor/plaintiff claims is therefore eliminated. We stress that the LLP concept applies strictly to a partner's *personal* situation; suits can still be filed against the firm and damages awarded.

A Further Focus

The problem of lawsuits has created what some call a "financial crisis" in the accounting profession. As an example, figures compiled not too long ago put damage claims against the profession as a whole at $30 billion. A survey of the largest accounting firms (the so-called Big Six) found the following:

- The average liability claim amounted to $85 million.
- The average settlement by a firm was for $2.7 million.
- The average legal cost per claim was $3.5 million.

When one compares the amount of settlement versus the amount of the original claim, the result might indicate that the initial suit had little or no merit.

Because of data such as those just cited, accounting firms and other companies are becoming more willing to settle cases out of court. This procedure avoids the possibility of a much larger award by a hostile jury—a jury that might seek revenge against an organization with "deep pockets." Collectively, this entire situation is forcing accountants to somewhat change their methods of conducting business. There is the LLP arrangement just discussed as well as an attempt by the Big Six firms to avoid high-risk clients and even, in some cases, entire industries.

Source: "Special Report," *Deloitte & Touche Review,* November 2, 1992, pp. 1–8.

---

[1] "Top Accountants To Shield Partners From Lawsuits," *The Wall Street Journal,* July 29, 1994, p. A5.

> **ETHICS ISSUE**
>
> Two of your clients, Big and Small, want to form a partnership. Your independent review of the partnership agreement finds several biases in favor of Big, making Big a much bigger and better client. What would you do?

OTHER FACTORS TO CONSIDER

Although unlimited liability and mutual agency may create problems for partners, the partnership form of organization does offer its users several benefits. Initially, there is the obvious opportunity to combine persons who possess capital and/or specialized skills to start and operate a business. Furthermore, in comparison with corporations, partnerships have greater operating flexibility because of fewer reporting requirements and less governmental regulation. Decisions that require formal, time-consuming actions by stockholders and corporate management can often be settled quickly among the partnership's members.

Income taxes are another factor that should be considered when evaluating this form of business organization. A company that operates as a partnership does not pay income taxes. Instead, the firm's net income (or net loss) is allocated to the partners, and the partners pay income taxes personally on their share. This treatment is in contrast to that afforded corporations. Not only is a corporation a taxable entity, but the shareholders are also taxed on the amount of dividends received.[2] These facts, coupled with differences in corporate and individual tax rates, create a need for effective planning when selecting the entity form for a new business.

PARTNERSHIP ACCOUNTING

[2] Account for partnership formation and income distribution, including situations that give rise to an earnings deficiency.

Partnership accounting does not differ significantly from that described earlier in the text for sole proprietorships. Transactions unique to partnerships arise only in the area of owner's equity and relate to business formation, income distribution, admittance and withdrawal of partners, and liquidation. To handle the necessary record keeping, separate capital and drawing accounts are maintained for each owner.

PARTNERSHIP FORMATION AND OWNER INVESTMENTS

Accounting for a partnership begins when owners (i.e., partners) invest their personal assets into the firm. Investments in a partnership may take the form of cash, noncash assets such as land or buildings, and even an entire operating business. To illustrate the proper record keeping, suppose that Steve Leake and Dotty Mueller, both CPAs, decided to form a partnership on January 2, 19X1. Leake invested $15,000 cash; Mueller invested her existing accounting practice. According to the balance sheet from the preceding year, the practice had the following assets and liabilities:

Assets		
Cash		$ 3,000
Accounts receivable	$4,000	
Less: Allowance for uncollectible accounts	500	3,500
Supplies		1,000
Equipment	$5,000	
Less: Accumulated depreciation	1,200	3,800
Total assets		$11,300
Liabilities		
Accounts payable		$ 2,500

---

[2] Should the shareholders sell their stock, income tax is levied on any gains that arise.

As of January 2, 19X1, the equipment had a fair market value of $6,000. The necessary journal entries to record the partners' investments follow.

Cash	15,000	
Leake, Capital		15,000
To record investment by Leake in the partnership of Leake and Mueller.		
Cash	3,000	
Accounts Receivable	4,000	
Supplies	1,000	
Equipment	6,000	
Allowance for Uncollectible Accounts		500
Accounts Payable		2,500
Mueller, Capital		11,000*
To record investment by Mueller in the partnership of Leake and Mueller.		

* The capital account is credited for the net assets (total assets minus total liabilities) contributed by Mueller.

Observe that the Equipment account is debited for $6,000 and *not* the book value of $3,800. Noncash assets are entered in the new records at fair market value—the actual acquisition cost to the partnership. A failure to use fair market value would improperly ignore prior increases in asset valuation. To explain, suppose the equipment was recorded at its $3,800 book value and immediately sold by the partnership for $6,000. The $2,200 gain would be

---

A Small Business Consultant's Perspective

Partnership Interests: When two people propose to form a partnership, nothing sounds fairer than a 50–50 split of duties and voting rights. Perhaps this is what Steve Leake and Dotty Mueller had in mind. However, many entrepreneurs in a 50–50 arrangement fail to anticipate the problems that arise from a simple difference of opinion. It is very rare that two equal partners see every decision the exact same way, especially over long periods of time. If one partner wants to expand the firm and the other feels differently, operations could come to a halt until the issues are sorted out and the deadlock is broken.

To prevent this problem from occurring, small business consultants often recommend that the two partners find another person to own 1% of the company. Having a 49.5 : 49.5 : 1 arrangement means that an alternative under study must be attractive to two of the three owners. When a consensus is needed and the two major players cannot agree, the 1% partner's role is pivotal. The control given up by the majority owners is often looked at as being an "insurance policy," one that prevents a simple difference of opinion from doing significant harm to the organization.

shared by both partners, which is unfair to Mueller. The increase in valuation occurred while the asset was in her possession; therefore she should receive full and proper credit for her investment. The use of book value in this case would significantly understate Mueller's capital account on the books of the new entity.

PARTNERSHIP EARNINGS: NATURE AND DISTRIBUTION

Paralleling the role of a sole proprietor, partners are considered owners of a firm and *not* employees. Thus, any amounts distributed as remuneration for services rendered are generally treated as withdrawals of capital as opposed to business expenses. Treatment as an expense would destroy net income as a measure of the enterprise's earnings ability, because an owner could set his or her own compensation level and greatly influence the reported profit. Further, unlike sales, office, and administrative personnel, the partner is not just working to earn a weekly paycheck. He or she is striving to improve the overall financial well-being of the business.

In view of this ownership role, partners are "rewarded" at the end of the period by being allocated a share of the company's earnings.[3] Earnings (or losses) can be split in many different ways. Most partnership contracts are quite specific on this matter and are structured to recognize variations in time, talent, and/or money provided. If no provisions are stated, profits and losses are divided equally.

Recognition of Services. A study of many partnerships will often reveal considerable differences among the partners in terms of service. Some partners have been with the business for many years; others are relative newcomers. One partner may have an outstanding reputation for some type of specialty interest, say, open-heart surgery; others, possibly, do not. Variations in these factors, business contacts, and effort devoted to the firm are often recognized in the form of salary differentials. Suppose, for instance, that Leake and Mueller's articles of partnership provide for monthly salary allowances of $1,000 and $1,200, respectively, with any remaining net income to be divided equally. If 19X1 net income amounted to $38,000, the following division would be made:

	LEAKE	MUELLER	TOTAL
Division of net income			
Salary			
Leake ($1,000 × 12 months)	$12,000		$26,400
Mueller ($1,200 × 12 months)		$14,400	
Remainder of $11,600 ($38,000 − $26,400) divided equally	5,800	5,800	11,600
	$17,800	$20,200	$38,000

[3] This procedure is really the same as that illustrated earlier in the text for sole proprietorships. Recall that part of the closing process involves an increase to the owner's capital account for the firm's net income.

Once determined, net income is transferred to the capital accounts by the following closing entry:

Income Summary	38,000	
Leake, Capital		17,800
Mueller, Capital		20,200
To record the division of net income.		

We again stress that partners are owners and *not* employees. Thus, **salary allowances** are not business expenses. Rather, these amounts are considered only in the division of net income.

Partners often withdraw their salaries throughout the year, requiring that entries be made in the drawing accounts. To illustrate the proper accounting, assume that Leake and Mueller have each withdrawn their salary allowances along with an additional $800. End-of-period balances in the partners' drawing accounts will total $12,800 ($12,000 + $800) and $15,200 ($14,400 + $800), respectively. The impact of these events is shown on the firm's statement of partners' (i.e., owners') equity, which appears in Exhibit 15–1.

The statement's bottom line is eventually carried forward to the practice's December 31 balance sheet in the following manner (liability total is assumed):

Total liabilities		$58,500
Partners' equity		
Steve Leake, capital	$20,000	
Dotty Mueller, capital	16,000	36,000
Total liabilities & partners' equity		$94,500

EXHIBIT 15–1
Statement of Partners' Equity

LEAKE AND MUELLER, CPAs
Statement of Partners' Equity
For the Year Ended December 31, 19X1

	LEAKE	MUELLER	TOTAL
Beginning balance, Jan. 1	$ —	$ —	$ —
Increases			
Partner investments	$15,000	$11,000	$26,000
Net income	17,800	20,200	38,000
Subtotal	$32,800	$31,200	$64,000
Decreases			
Drawings: salary	$12,000	$14,400	$26,400
Drawings: other	800	800	1,600
Total	$12,800	$15,200	$28,000
Ending balance, Dec. 31	$20,000	$16,000	$36,000

As a final step, the drawing accounts would be closed to the partners' capital accounts:

Leake, Capital	12,800	
Mueller, Capital	15,200	
Leake, Drawing		12,800
Mueller, Drawing		15,200
To close partners' drawing accounts.		

By tracing through the entries presented, observe that the capital accounts were credited for the initial investment at the time of formation and later for each partner's share of net income. The entry to close the drawing accounts will therefore reduce Leake, Capital, and Mueller, Capital, to the balances reported on the partners' equity statement.

Recognition of Invested Capital. Total invested capital is a major factor in the success of businesses that carry inventory or have substantial equipment needs. Thus, partnership agreements often consider differences in the amount of capital contributed by individual partners. Recognition is particularly prevalent for firms that have "silent" partners, or partners who provide substantial financial support but do not become involved in daily management activities.

Several methods that are commonly employed focus on the amount of a partner's capital contribution. For example, an entity's income (or loss) may be distributed by using a ratio of the beginning-of-period capital balances. If partner A's capital account contains, say, $120,000 on January 1 and B's contains $80,000, the total owners' equity of the firm, $200,000, forms the basis for the proper allocation. In this particular case, any earnings (or losses) generated would be divided in a 60 : 40 ratio (A: $120,000 ÷ $200,000 = 60%; B: $80,000 ÷ $200,000 = 40%).

A Further Focus

A careful study of this procedure could prompt a partner to withdraw vast sums of cash for personal use shortly after the period begins and then to make reinvestments late in the year, just prior to computing the next period's allocation base. Although the partner might personally benefit from this practice, the business could experience a capital shortage. To discourage large withdrawals and at the same time promote capital retention, partnership agreements sometimes call for the ratio to be calculated on the basis of *average* account balances. This latter approach relies on a month-by-month analysis of a partner's invested capital and results in a weighted-average balance for use in the allocation procedure.

The amount of a partner's invested capital can also be recognized by use of an interest allowance, computed on either the beginning or average balance in the capital account. The interest allowance is similar to the salary allowance discussed earlier; it is employed only in the division of net income (or loss) and is not an expense of the partnership.

To illustrate the accounting that accompanies an interest allowance, we will continue the Leake and Mueller example. Assume that the partnership agreement now contains the following provisions:

1. Monthly salaries of $1,000 and $1,200 to Leake and Mueller, respectively.
2. Interest of 15% to both partners, computed on the basis of their beginning capital balances.
3. Any remaining income (or loss) to be divided equally.

It is one year later and 19X2 net income totals $42,000. The proper division between Leake and Mueller follows.

	LEAKE	MUELLER	TOTAL
Division of net income			
Salary			
Leake ($1,000 × 12 months)	$12,000		
Mueller ($1,200 × 12 months)		$14,400	$26,400
Interest*			
Leake ($20,000 × 0.15)	3,000		
Mueller ($16,000 × 0.15)		2,400	5,400
	$15,000	$16,800	$31,800
Remainder of $10,200 ($42,000 − $31,800) divided equally	5,100	5,100	10,200
	$20,100	$21,900	$42,000

* Interest is computed on the January 1, 19X2 (i.e., December 31, 19X1), capital balances. These balances are taken from the statement of partners' equity that appears in Exhibit 15–1.

The journal entry to close the accounting records requires a debit to Income Summary for $42,000 and a credit to Leake, Capital, and Mueller, Capital, for $20,100 and $21,900, respectively.

Earnings Deficiency. In the previous examples, salary and interest allowances were less than the total earnings of the firm. Naturally, it is possible for a partnership to incur a net loss or have insufficient income to cover the allowances. In these cases an *earnings deficiency* arises. Unless provisions are made to the contrary, the partnership agreement is still followed; that is, authorized salary and interest allowances continue to be recognized. Because of insufficient earnings, however, a deficiency is allocated to the partners, normally in the same ratio as that for profits and losses. Leake and Mueller, for example, would share the deficiency equally.

To focus on the related procedures, suppose that Leake and Mueller's partnership agreement continues to stipulate respective monthly salaries of $1,000 and $1,200 and interest allowances of 15%. Now, however, assume that 19X2 net income amounted to only $20,000. The proper allocation follows.

	LEAKE	MUELLER	TOTAL
Division of net income			
Salary	$12,000	$14,400	$ 26,400
Interest	3,000	2,400	5,400
	$15,000	$16,800	$ 31,800
Deficiency of $11,800 ($31,800 − $20,000) divided equally	(5,900)	(5,900)	(11,800)
	$ 9,100	$10,900	$ 20,000

The required closing entry is similar to those shown previously: Income Summary is debited for $20,000, with corresponding credits of $9,100 to Leake, Capital, and $10,900 to Mueller, Capital.

ADMISSION OF A NEW PARTNER

3 Account for partner admissions and withdrawals.

The Leake and Mueller partnership was a new entity formed with investments from both Steve Leake and Dotty Mueller. Observe that Leake did not invest in Mueller's accounting practice; instead, a new business was established. Frequently, individuals are admitted to existing partnerships either by (1) purchasing an interest from one or more of the present partners or (2) making an investment directly in the firm. The method of entry depends on several factors. For example, interests are often purchased when existing partners wish to decrease their involvement in daily activities because of changing goals, illness, or retirement. Investments directly in the business, on the other hand, sometimes occur when firms are growing and have a need for additional capital.

Purchase of an Interest. When an entering partner purchases an interest from a current partner, the assets and liabilities of the firm do not change. To illustrate, assume that Leake and Mueller have capital balances of $20,000 and $16,000, respectively. After lengthy negotiation both partners have agreed to sell 40% of their respective interests in the business to Ann Colby, a CPA. Colby will pay Leake and Mueller $15,000 each. The effect of the transaction, shown pictorially in Exhibit 15–2, gives rise to the journal entry that follows.

Leake, Capital	8,000	
Mueller, Capital	6,400	
Colby, Capital		14,400
To record the transfer of 40% of present capital balances to Colby.		

Notice that the price paid by Colby is in excess of the interest acquired from each partner. This situation arises from the negotiation process and is a personal matter among the parties involved. The cash goes to Leake and Mueller personally, and all that is needed on the firm's records is a transfer of ownership (i.e., capital balances).

Investment in the Firm. In addition to purchasing an interest from existing partners, an incoming partner may invest directly in the business. In this case the new partner makes payment to the firm, and total company assets increase.

EXHIBIT 15–2
Purchase of a Partner's Interest

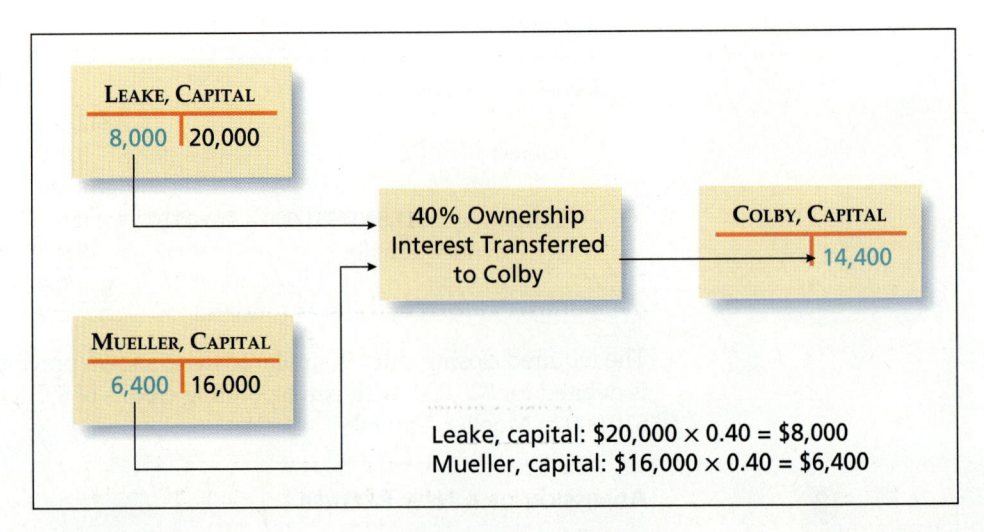

LEAKE, CAPITAL	
8,000	20,000

MUELLER, CAPITAL	
6,400	16,000

40% Ownership Interest Transferred to Colby

COLBY, CAPITAL	
	14,400

Leake, capital: $20,000 × 0.40 = $8,000
Mueller, capital: $16,000 × 0.40 = $6,400

We will first illustrate the most basic situation: when the entering partner's investment is equal to the negotiated percentage of the new entity's total capital. Assume again that Leake and Mueller have respective capital balances of $20,000 and $16,000. Suppose now that both partners have agreed to grant Colby a one-third interest in the business for an $18,000 investment—a transaction that brings total firm capital to $54,000:

Leake, capital	$20,000
Mueller, capital	16,000
Investment by Colby	18,000
Total	$54,000

Observe that the $18,000 investment represents one-third of the owners' equity of the new partnership ($54,000 × 1/3 = $18,000). Colby paid nothing extra to gain a one-third interest; nothing extra was given to her to provide the cash inflow. The necessary journal entry to update the accounting records is as follows:

Cash	18,000	
Colby, Capital		18,000
To record the admission of Colby to the partnership.		

Bonus to Existing Partners. If the prospect of joining a partnership is especially appealing because of past earnings records and other favorable factors, an incoming partner may be required to pay a bonus to the existing owners. Any bonuses paid are allocated to the present partners' capital accounts according to the profit- and loss-sharing ratio in the partnership agreement.

For instance, assume that Colby was required to invest $24,000 for a one-third interest in the firm. The entity's total capital would now amount to $60,000:

Leake, capital	$20,000
Mueller, capital	16,000
Investment by Colby	24,000
Total	$60,000

Colby's interest would therefore be $20,000 ($60,000 × 1/3). Apparently, then, she is paying a $4,000 bonus ($24,000 − $20,000) to Leake and Mueller for admission. If profits and losses are shared equally, the bonus is split 50 : 50 and the required journal entry is as follows:

Cash	24,000	
Leake, Capital		2,000
Mueller, Capital		2,000
Colby, Capital		20,000
To record the investment of Colby and bonus to existing partners.		

Bonus to New Partner. Occasionally, an organization is anxious to attract a new partner who possesses specialized skills, significant capital, or unique managerial ability. In these instances the existing owners may grant the incoming partner a larger business interest than is justified by the amount of the investment. In essence, a bonus is being given to the newcomer.

For example, assume that Colby was required to invest only $9,000 for her one-third interest. As the following figures show, total capital after admission would amount to $45,000:

Leake, capital	$20,000
Mueller, capital	16,000
Investment by Colby	9,000
Total	$45,000

Because a one-third interest has been granted, Colby, Capital, must contain a balance of $15,000 ($45,000 × 1/3) after the transaction. She has therefore received a $6,000 bonus over and above her $9,000 investment—namely, a bonus provided by Leake and Mueller. Given the source of the bonus and the fact that profits and losses are shared equally, $3,000 reductions in each of the existing capital accounts are needed to properly reflect Colby's equity interest:

Cash	9,000	
Leake, Capital	3,000	
Mueller, Capital	3,000	
Colby, Capital		15,000
To record the investment of Colby and bonus to new partner.		

WITHDRAWAL OF A PARTNER

Aside from admission, the composition of a partnership will also change when an owner withdraws or retires from the firm. The exiting owner's business interest may be purchased by the remaining partners or even an outsider (if the other partners approve). In both cases the assets and liabilities of the firm remain unchanged because the exchange of interests is strictly a personal matter among the parties involved. However, a journal entry is needed to eliminate the withdrawing partner's capital balance and to record an increase in the capital account(s) of the purchaser(s). The required entry parallels that shown on page 559 for the admission of a new partner who purchases an interest from a present owner.

Purchase by the Partnership. Rather than sell to other individuals, the withdrawing party may agree to sell his or her interest to the partnership. In this situation, company assets will be used for payment. Quite often, the articles of partnership will specify the procedures to follow and the price to be paid for a withdrawing owner's interest. The price can vary widely and may be equal to, less than, or greater than the partner's capital balance. The first case is the simplest and requires a debit to the appropriate partner's capital account and a credit to Cash. The other situations are more complex and are discussed in the following section.

Payment Less Than or Greater Than the Capital Balance. A partnership may pay less than the capital balance of the exiting owner if past operations have been relatively unsuccessful or if the firm has an extremely weak cash position. In addition, this situation sometimes arises if friction has developed between the partner leaving and those who continue in the business. Because the exiting partner is willing to accept an amount less than that appearing in the accounting records, the remaining owners benefit. A bonus is split among the remaining partners according to the firm's profit- and loss-sharing ratio.

Turning to the opposite case, negotiations between the firm and an exiting partner often result in a settlement price that exceeds the partner's capital balance. Keep in mind that accounting records are based on historical cost; thus, increases in the market values of company assets have been ignored. Historical-cost valuations, coupled with the fact that the partnership may have substantial earnings potential, could produce a somewhat unrealistic (i.e., low) capital balance. If the outcome of negotiation involves a payment that is greater than the withdrawing partner's equity, the capital balances of the ongoing partners are reduced. Stated differently, the remaining partners are "footing the bill" and paying a bonus to the exiting owner.

Death of a Partner. The death of a partnership member automatically ends the legal life of a partnership. At this point, the firm's obligation to the estate of the deceased owner must be determined. It is therefore necessary to compute income (or loss) from the beginning of the current accounting period to the date of death so that a proper share can be included in the deceased partner's capital account.

The articles of partnership typically state the procedures to be followed in the event of an owner's death, including how assets are to be valued and when payment should be made to the estate. Often, insurance policies are carried on all partners, with the firm named as beneficiary. This practice ensures that ade-

LIQUIDATION OF A PARTNERSHIP

Earlier in the chapter we noted that a partnership is dissolved when a new partner is admitted to the firm or an existing partner withdraws from the business. Although dissolution has occurred, the partnership's activities may continue if the remaining partners agree to form a new entity.

If this course of action is undesirable or if the entity has experienced significant financial problems (e.g., sizable losses), it may be in the partners' best interests to cease operations. The process of terminating a partnership and discontinuing business activities is known as *liquidation.* In the usual case, liquidation involves three steps:

1. The noncash assets are sold for cash.
2. The amounts due creditors (i.e., liabilities) are paid.
3. Any cash that remains is distributed to the partners.

These transactions and events normally occur over a period of time and in piecemeal fashion. For simplicity, our illustrative example will assume that all noncash assets are sold for a single, lump-sum amount and all liabilities are settled at the same time. Because liquidations can be complex and are covered in advanced accounting courses, only a basic overview is presented in this text.

Sale of Noncash Assets at a Loss. We begin our discussion by focusing on a situation where the noncash assets are sold at a loss. Assume that the partnership of Leake, Mueller, and Colby has decided to suspend operations. The firm's balance sheet prior to liquidation follows.

Assets		Liabilities & partners' equity	
Cash	$ 60,000	Accounts payable	$ 15,000
Noncash assets	50,000	Leake, capital	43,000
	$110,000	Mueller, capital	40,000
		Colby, capital	12,000
			$110,000

Suppose the noncash assets are sold for $32,000, which results in an $18,000 loss ($50,000 − $32,000) for the firm. The partners absorb such gains and losses in the profit- and loss-sharing ratio as stipulated in the articles of partnership. If the ratio calls for an equal division, the journal entry to record the asset sale would be as follows:

Cash	32,000	
Leake, Capital	6,000	
Mueller, Capital	6,000	
Colby, Capital	6,000	
Noncash Assets		50,000
To record the sale of noncash assets.		

Notice that the loss is charged directly to the owners' capital accounts, resulting in the following balances:[4]

	CASH	+	NONCASH ASSETS	=	ACCOUNTS PAYABLE	+	LEAKE, CAPITAL	+	MUELLER, CAPITAL	+	COLBY, CAPITAL
Prior to asset sale	$60,000		$50,000		$15,000		$43,000		$40,000		$12,000
Asset sale	+32,000		−50,000				−6,000		−6,000		−6,000
	$92,000		$ —		$15,000		$37,000		$34,000		$ 6,000

Once the assets are sold, the liabilities are paid. Any cash that remains is then distributed to Leake, Mueller, and Colby *in an amount equal to their capital balances*. The necessary journal entries are:

Accounts Payable	15,000	
Cash		15,000
To record payment of liabilities.		
Leake, Capital	37,000	
Mueller, Capital	34,000	
Colby, Capital	6,000	
Cash		77,000
To record cash distributions to partners.		

Keep in mind that the profit- and loss-sharing ratio is used in division of liquidation gains and losses, *not* in the allocation of assets among the owners. The ratio's name indicates its purpose. The distribution of assets at liquidation is really the opposite of what occurs when partners invest directly into the firm at the time of business formation. These latter two situations are neither dependent on nor influenced by the income-sharing agreement.

Creation of a Capital Deficiency. In the previous example, each partner's capital account was of sufficient size to absorb the $6,000 share of the loss. Suppose, however, that the noncash assets are sold for only $8,000. In this case a $42,000 loss arises ($50,000 − $8,000), which reduces each of the capital balances by $14,000 ($42,000 ÷ 3). After the liabilities are paid, $53,000 cash remains in the business, and Colby's capital account contains a $2,000 debit balance. These figures are shown in the chart at the top of the following page.

The $2,000 debit balance is commonly referred to as a **capital deficiency**. Just as Leake and Mueller have respective claims against the partnership of $29,000 and $26,000, the partnership has a $2,000 claim against Colby. Notice that until the deficiency is settled, insufficient cash is available for disbursement to the owners who possess credit balances. Colby would therefore be requested to remit $2,000 to the firm.

Removal of a Capital Deficiency. If Colby settles her $2,000 obligation, the deficiency is removed from the accounting records. As a result of this receipt, the

---

[4] An alternative treatment calls for an $18,000 debit to a separate Loss on Sale of Assets account. The Loss account's balance is then allocated equally to the partners, producing the same $6,000 reductions as those just shown.

	Cash	+	Noncash Assets	=	Accounts Payable	+	Leake, Capital	+	Mueller, Capital	+	Colby, Capital
Prior to asset sale	$60,000		$50,000		$15,000		$43,000		$40,000		$12,000
Asset sale	+8,000		−50,000				−14,000		−14,000		−14,000
	$68,000		$ —		$15,000		$29,000		$26,000		$(2,000)
Payment of liabilities	−15,000				−15,000						
	$53,000		$ —		$ —		$29,000		$26,000		$(2,000)

partnership's cash would increase to $55,000 and thus allow a distribution of $29,000 to Leake and $26,000 to Mueller. The required journal entries follow.

Cash	2,000	
Colby, Capital		2,000
To record receipt of cash from Colby to settle deficiency.		
Leake, Capital	29,000	
Mueller, Capital	26,000	
Cash		55,000
To record cash distributions to partners.		

On the other hand, if Colby is unable or unwilling to pay, the $2,000 deficiency is charged against the other partners according to the profit- and loss-sharing ratio. Leake and Mueller would therefore absorb $1,000 each to allow the closing of the partnership's books, producing the balances shown.[5]

	Cash	=	Leake, Capital	+	Mueller, Capital	+	Colby, Capital
After payment of liabilities	$53,000		$29,000		$26,000		$(2,000)
Allocation of Colby deficiency			−1,000		−1,000		+2,000
	$53,000		$28,000		$25,000		$ —

The following entry is needed to record the allocation in the accounts:

Leake, Capital	1,000	
Mueller, Capital	1,000	
Colby, Capital		2,000
To distribute capital deficiency and close Colby's capital account.		

The cash balance of $53,000 would then be distributed, with $28,000 going to Leake and $25,000 to Mueller.

---

[5] In the event of an unequal profit- and loss-sharing ratio, similar procedures would continue to be followed. Suppose, for example, that partners A, B, and C share income in a ratio of 50 : 40 : 10, respectively. If C has an $18,000 capital deficiency, the deficiency would be split between A and B in the following manner: A, 50/90 × $18,000 = $10,000; B, 40/90 × $18,000 = $8,000.

Leake, Capital	28,000	
Mueller, Capital	25,000	
Cash		53,000

To record cash distributions to partners.

Colby's inability to pay the $2,000 capital deficiency does not relieve her liability to Leake and Mueller. If the latter two individuals desire, legal action could be initiated to obtain the amount due. Remember that with unlimited liability, a deficient partner's personal assets can be taken to raise the necessary funds.

Sale of Noncash Assets at a Gain. The focus in our liquidation example has been the sale of assets at a loss, primarily because of the unique accounting problems associated with a capital deficiency. Noncash assets can, of course, be sold at a gain. If, for example, the partnership's noncash assets of $50,000 were sold for $71,000, a $21,000 gain would arise. Assuming that profits and losses continue to be shared equally, Leake, Mueller, and Colby would each pick up $7,000 ($21,000 ÷ 3) of gain. The required journal entry would thus contain credits of $7,000 to each partner's capital account to reflect the increase in equity from the transaction. The remaining journal entries for settlement of liabilities and the partners' cash distributions parallel those shown earlier.

END-OF-CHAPTER REVIEW

LEARNING OBJECTIVES: THE KEY POINTS

1. **Explain the unique characteristics of a partnership.** A partnership is a business owned by two or more persons. This popular organizational form is a separate accounting entity but not a separate legal and tax entity. Partnerships are easy to establish, with any property invested in the business (and subsequent income earned) being jointly owned by the partners. Partners have unlimited liability for the debts of the firm and are bound by the commitments and obligations made by the other owners (i.e., mutual agency). Unless otherwise agreed on, a partnership is dissolved by the withdrawal of a partner or the admission of new partners. As a final note, the growing number of lawsuits in our society has prompted some firms to adopt the limited liability partnership (LLP) form of business organization. Such an arrangement protects the owners' personal assets from the claims of a firm's creditors and plaintiffs.

2. **Account for partnership formation and income distribution, including situations that give rise to an earnings deficiency.** Accounting for partnerships begins when the owners invest their personal assets into the firm. Noncash investments are recorded at fair market value, and both noncash and cash investments are entered in the proper partner's capital account.

    Any net income or net loss of the company's is divided among the partners according to the partnership agreement. If no provisions are stated, profits and losses are shared equally. In the income allocation process, recognition may be given for services provided to the business (via salary allowances) and/or for capital provided (via interest allowances). Such allowances must be considered regardless of the company's earnings. If insufficient income is available to cover the allowances, an earnings deficiency arises, with the deficiency being allocated to the partners in the profit- and loss-sharing ratio.

3. **Account for partner admissions and withdrawals.** When an entering partner purchases an interest from an existing partner, no change in partnership assets occurs. However, the capital accounts must be updated to reflect the transfer of equity interests among the owners. In another type of transaction, an entering partner may make an investment directly in the firm. Company assets increase and the new partner must be given credit in the accounting records for the amount invested (or some multiple thereof). If the amount invested is greater than the capital balance awarded, the existing partners are receiving a bonus. Should the situation be reversed, the current partners are providing a bonus to the incoming owner. Bonuses are divided among the partners according to the firm's profit- and loss-sharing ratio.

    Partner withdrawals are accounted for in a manner similar to that of partner admittances. The withdrawing partner may sell his or her interest to the continuing partners or to the partnership itself. In the latter case, the exiting owner's capital balance is compared against the amount of cash settlement to determine whether any bonuses are involved. Once again, bonuses may be provided either by or to the ongoing partners.

4. **Perform the procedures related to partnership liquidations.** The liquidation of a partnership involves three steps: sale of noncash assets, payment of creditors, and distribution of remaining cash to the partners in the amount of the partners' capital balances. When selling the noncash assets, a gain or loss may arise. Such gains and losses are allocated among the partners according to the profit- and loss-sharing ratio.

    The allocation of losses may cause a capital deficiency (i.e., debit balance) in a partner's capital account. When the deficiency is settled, adequate cash will then be available to pay partners who have credit balances. If the deficiency is not settled, it is allocated among the "nondeficient" partners consistent with the profit- and loss-sharing ratio.

Key Terms and Concepts: A Quick Overview

articles of partnership   The agreement in a partnership that details the rights, responsibilities, and duties of the partners. (p. 551)

capital deficiency   A debit balance in a partner's capital account. (p. 564)

dissolution   The termination of a partnership's life. (p. 551)

earnings deficiency   The condition that exists when a partnership incurs a net loss or has insufficient earnings to cover salary and interest allowances. (p. 558)

interest allowances   A consideration used in the division of net income of many partnerships. The allowances recognize differences in capital provided to the firm by the partners. (p. 557)

limited liability partnership (LLP)   A form of business organization in which a partner's personal assets are not exposed to claims of the firm's creditors and plaintiffs. (p. 552)

liquidation   The process of terminating a partnership and discontinuing operations. (p. 563)

mutual agency   A feature of partnerships whereby each partner acts as an agent of the partnership in business transactions. (p. 551)

partnership   A company formed by two or more persons to carry on, as co-owners, profitable business activity. (p. 550)

salary allowances A consideration used in the division of net income. The allowances recognize differences in seniority, reputation, business contacts, and time devoted to the firm by the partners. (p. 556)

unlimited liability The fact that each partner is held personally liable for the debts of the enterprise. (p. 551)

Chapter Quiz

The five questions that follow relate to several issues raised in the chapter. Test your knowledge of the issues by selecting the best answer. (The answers appear on p. 582.)

1. Which of the following statements about most partnerships is true?
   a. A partnership has an unlimited life.
   b. A partnership pays income taxes on its earnings.
   c. Partners have unlimited liability for the debts of the firm.
   d. Partners who invest assets in a partnership retain sole ownership rights to the assets until it is evident that the business will be successful.

2. Land invested in a partnership by a partner should be recorded in the partnership's accounting records at:
   a. the investing partner's acquisition cost.
   b. the book value on the investing partner's accounting records.
   c. the land's fair market value at the time of investment.
   d. the land's expected selling price on the date of disposal.

3. Rome and Athens formed a partnership by investing $30,000 and $60,000, respectively. The following terms regarding the division of income were agreed on: (1) Rome is to receive a salary allowance of $10,000; (2) both partners are entitled to a 10% interest allowance, computed on the original capital investments. Any remaining amounts are to be split equally. How would net income of $15,000 be divided?
   a. Rome, $6,000; Athens, $9,000.
   b. Rome, $7,500; Athens, $7,500.
   c. Rome, $11,000; Athens, $4,000.
   d. Rome, $13,000; Athens, $6,000.

4. The law firm of Lincoln, Stein, and Dyke is organized as a partnership. The partners' capital balances are $100,000, $200,000, and $150,000, respectively. Lincoln is leaving the firm for health reasons and is being paid $127,000 by the partnership for her interest. As a result of this withdrawal,
   a. Stein and Dyke are paying a bonus to Lincoln.
   b. Lincoln is paying a bonus to Stein and Dyke.
   c. no bonus should be recognized.
   d. company assets are unchanged.

5. The Uncle Otto partnership is being liquidated. The firm's balance sheet follows.

Assets			Partners' equity	
Noncash assets	$108,000		Allen, capital	$ 60,000
			Tyler, capital	41,000
			Flynn, capital	7,000
				$108,000

   If the noncash assets are sold for $38,000 and profits and losses are divided respectively among Allen, Tyler, and Flynn in a 4 : 2 : 1 ratio, how much cash will be distributed to Allen? Assume that any capital deficiencies are not paid by the deficient partner.
   a. $18,000.
   b. $18,500.
   c. $20,000.
   d. $60,000.

Summary Problem

Warren Smithson is a designer of custom jewelry. His firm, organized as a sole proprietorship, has grown over the years and has the following balance sheet data as of December 31, 19X1:

Assets		
Cash		$ 3,500
Accounts receivable	$8,700	
Less: Allowance for uncollectibles	300	8,400
Inventory		19,700
Equipment	$5,000	
Less: Accumulated depreciation	2,100	2,900
Total assets		$34,500
Liabilities		
Accounts payable		$ 6,800

On January 1, 19X2, Smithson and Lisa Anderson formed a partnership known as S & A Associates. Anderson invested $10,000 cash and inventory having a fair market value of $5,800; Smithson relinquished control of the proprietorship's assets and liabilities to the new entity. The proprietorship's inventory and equipment were estimated to have a fair market value of $24,200 and $2,200, respectively, on the date of partnership formation. The partnership agreement called for monthly salaries of $2,000 to Smithson and $1,500 to Anderson, with remaining profits and losses to be shared in a 7 : 3 ratio.

Instructions

a. Prepare the required journal entries on January 1, 19X2, to record formation of the new partnership.
b. If 19X2 partnership income amounted to $48,000, determine the proper allocation of earnings to Smithson and Anderson.
c. If the salary allowances were the only amounts withdrawn during the year, prepare the December 31, 19X2, statement of partners' equity for the firm.
d. Assume that the partnership sells all of its assets and pays all liabilities on January 2, 19X3, as part of a liquidation. If a loss of $50,000 is incurred on the sale of non-cash assets, how much cash would Smithson receive in final settlement of his partnership interest?

Solution

a.
Cash	10,000	
Inventory	5,800	
Anderson, Capital		15,800

To record investment by Anderson in S & A Associates.

Cash	3,500	
Accounts Receivable	8,700	
Inventory	24,200	
Equipment	2,200	
Allowance for Uncollectibles		300
Accounts Payable		6,800
Smithson, Capital		31,500*

To record investment by Smithson in S & A Associates.

* Calculated as the difference between the jewelry firm's total assets and total liabilities.

b.

	SMITHSON	ANDERSON	TOTAL
Division of net income			
Salary			
Smithson ($2,000 × 12 months)	$24,000		$42,000
Anderson ($1,500 × 12 months)		$18,000	
Remainder of $6,000 ($48,000 – $42,000) divided 7 : 3	4,200	1,800	6,000
	$28,200	$19,800	$48,000

c.

S & A ASSOCIATES
Statement of Partners' Equity
For the Year Ended December 31, 19X2

	SMITHSON	ANDERSON	TOTAL
Beginning balance, Jan. 1	$ —	$ —	$ —
Increases			
Partner investments	$31,500	$15,800	$47,300
Net income	28,200	19,800	48,000
Subtotal	$59,700	$35,600	$95,300
Decreases			
Withdrawals	24,000	18,000	42,000
Ending balance, Dec. 31	$35,700	$17,600	$53,300

d.
Smithson's capital balance, Dec. 31, 19X2	$35,700
Less: Share of liquidation loss ($50,000 × 0.70)	35,000
Smithson's cash distribution	$ 700

ASSIGNMENT MATERIAL

QUESTIONS

Q15–1 What are the articles of partnership?

Q15–2 Describe "mutual agency" as related to partnerships. How does this feature influence the selection of partners?

Q15–3 A partnership is said to have a limited life. Does the death of a partner terminate business operations? Explain.

Q15–4 What has prompted the increase in popularity of limited liability partnerships?

Q15–5 Akers and Howard are discussing the formation of a partnership. Howard will invest a computer system that originally cost $24,000. If the system has a $15,000 fair market value at the time of investment, what amount will be recorded in Howard's capital account? Why?

Q15–6 Discuss the accounting treatment of salary allowances that are provided to partners. Are the allowances considered an expense? Why?

Q15–7 What problem could arise if a partnership's earnings are allocated to partners by using a ratio computed on the basis of beginning-of-period capital balances? How can this problem be resolved?

Q15–8 What is an earnings deficiency? How is such a deficiency resolved?

Q15–9 Generally speaking, an incoming partner can acquire an interest in a partnership in two ways. What are these two approaches?

Q15–10 Baker has a $24,000 capital interest in the ABC partnership and is entitled to one-third of all profits and losses. Assume that Baker sells her entire interest to Doane for $60,000.
a. What amount will be recorded in Doane's account on the partnership's books?
b. How much cash will be received by the business?

Q15–11 Briefly distinguish between partnership dissolution and partnership liquidation.

Q15–12 Name the three steps that are performed in a partnership liquidation.

Q15–13 How are liquidation gains and losses divided among a firm's partners? Assuming no capital deficiency, how is any remaining cash divided among the partners?

Q15–14 Capital deficiencies sometimes occur during the liquidation of a partnership. What is a "capital deficiency" and how is it treated for accounting purposes?

EXERCISES

E15–1 Limited liability partnerships (L.O. 1)
Environmental Consultants is a high-profile partnership that conducts land contamination studies for both business and the government. Companies similar to Environmental Consultants have recently been accused of performing faulty work, resulting in substantial out-of-court settlements with clients. The firm is considering changing its organizational form to a limited liability partnership.
a. Briefly explain the difference between a partnership and a limited liability partnership. Why do you think Environmental Consultants is considering the change?
b. Will a switch to a limited liability partnership prevent the firm from being sued and damages being awarded to clients? Why?

E15–2 Partner investments; journal entries (L.O. 2)
The LP partnership was formed on January 1, 19X7, by investments from Bill Levy and Marv Parcells. Levy contributed $30,000 cash and $80,000 of land. Parcells contributed various assets from a business that he had operated over the past five years. A balance sheet from that business disclosed the following:

Accounts receivable	$ 27,000
Allowance for uncollectibles	(3,200)
Equipment	68,000
Accumulated depreciation	(24,000)

The partners confirmed that the allowance for uncollectible accounts should be decreased by $600. In addition, an independent appraisal determined that fair market values of the land and equipment on January 1 were $125,000 and $35,000, respectively.
Prepare the journal entries needed to record the investments of Levy and Parcells.

E15–3 Income distribution: Different arrangements (L.O. 2)

Sanchez, Thomson, and Walters invested $40,000 each and formed a partnership. During the first year of operation, the business generated net income of $63,000. Determine the proper division of income among the partners for the following independent cases:

a. The partnership has no formal agreement on how to split profits and losses.
b. Partners are allowed 10% interest on their investments; the remaining profits and losses are allocated on a 5 : 4 : 1 basis.
c. Sanchez and Walters each receive salary allowances of $36,000 per year; the remaining profits and losses are shared equally.

E15–4 Income distribution among partners (L.O. 2)

The beginning capital balances in the partnership of Kell, Reardon, and Talbot are $20,000, $40,000, and $30,000, respectively. The partnership agreement contains the following provisions for the division of net income:

1. Partners are allowed 10% interest on their beginning capital balances.
2. Reardon and Talbot each have annual salary allowances of $10,000.
3. Remaining profits and losses are shared equally among the three partners.

Determine the appropriate division of net income (or net loss) among the partners for the independent cases that follow.

a. Net income is $47,000.
b. Net income is $14,000.
c. Net loss is $7,000.

E15–5 Statement of partners' equity (L.O. 2)

Mary Schmidt and Frank Latimer are partners in Turnstile Promotions, a company that handles the publicity for sporting events and concerts. Net income for 19X5 was $26,000; other information follows.

	SCHMIDT	LATIMER
Beginning capital balance	$32,000	$40,000
Withdrawals during the year	46,000	38,000
Division of net income:		
Monthly salary allowance	1,000	500
Remaining profits and losses	40%	60%

Prepare a statement of partners' equity for 19X5.

E15–6 Partner admission; journal entries (L.O. 3)

Rhodes and Smith are partners in a toy business and have capital balances of $126,000 and $144,000, respectively. Net income (or net loss) is shared equally. Prepare journal entries to record the admission of a new partner, West, assuming each of the following independent situations:

a. West invests $67,500 and receives a 20% interest in the new partnership.
b. West invests $100,000 in the firm for a 25% interest. Is a bonus being awarded to Rhodes and Smith or to West?
c. West purchases 60% of Smith's interest for $95,000.

E15–7 Partner withdrawal (L.O. 3)

Morgan is retiring from the Adelphi partnership after 25 years of loyal service. He has seen the company grow from a small start-up business into a booming enterprise.

Morgan's present capital balance stands at $258,000; he plans to sell his interest to Newsome, another partner, for $425,000.

a. Present Adelphi's journal entry to record the purchase by Newsome.
b. As a result of this sale, will partnership assets increase, decrease, or remain the same? Why?
c. Suppose that instead of selling to Newsome, Morgan sells his interest directly to the partnership for $425,000. Does any type of bonus arise in this situation? Briefly explain.

E15–8 Partnership liquidation; no capital deficiency (L.O. 4)

Assume that the partnership of Keith Baker and Mary Middleton had the following post-closing trial balance when the partners decided to liquidate:

Cash	$ 2,000	
Noncash assets	78,000	
Liabilities		$15,000
Baker, capital		40,000
Middleton, capital		25,000
	$80,000	$80,000

Profits and losses are divided equally. Consider the following independent situations:

Case 1: The noncash assets are sold for $90,000.
Case 2: The noncash assets are sold for $36,000.

For each of the preceding cases, prepare journal entries to record (a) sale of the noncash assets, (b) payment of the liabilities, and (c) cash distributions to the partners.

E15–9 Partnership liquidation (L.O. 4)

The JKL partnership is about to liquidate. The company's accountant has prepared the following tabulation:

Cash	+	Noncash Assets	=	Accounts Payable	+	Jacobs, Capital	+	Key, Capital	+	Landon, Capital
$60,000		$250,000		$25,000		$80,000		$170,000		$35,000

Assume that the partners share profits and losses equally and if a capital deficiency arises, none of it is paid by the deficient partner. The noncash assets will be sold for $100,000.

a. Determine whether the JKL partnership will experience a gain or a loss on the sale of noncash assets. How much of this gain or loss is allocated to each partner?
b. Does a capital deficiency arise in this situation? Explain.
c. By using the preceding tabulation, show the asset sale, the payment of accounts payable, and the final cash distribution to the partners.

E15–10 Partnership concepts (L.O. 2, 3, 4)

Evaluate the comments that follow as being True or False. If the comment is false, briefly explain why.

a. In the absence of a formal profit- and loss-sharing agreement, all profits and losses are divided equally among the partners.
b. Salary and interest allowances are normal expenses of a partnership.
c. An earnings deficiency is allocated to a firm's partners in accordance with the profit- and loss-sharing agreement.

d. In partnership liquidations, cash is distributed to partners in accordance with the profit- and loss-sharing agreement.
e. Jones invested $50,000 in the Smith/Sampson/Black partnership and was given a $42,000 capital interest in return. As a result of this transaction, the balance in Smith's capital account will increase because a bonus is being given to the existing partners.

PROBLEMS

Series A

P15–A1 Investment by partners; statement of partners' equity (L.O. 2)

Guinn, Horton, and Randall formed a partnership to practice law by combining their respective sole proprietorships. The assets and liabilities contributed to the firm on January 2, 19X4, the date of formation, follow.

	BOOK VALUE	FAIR MARKET VALUE
Guinn		
Land	$40,000	$115,000
Mortgage payable	38,000	38,000
Horton		
Office supplies	42,000	30,000
Office equipment	64,000	48,000
Randall		
Cash	50,000	50,000
Accounts receivable	20,000	18,000
Trading securities	4,000	7,000

Instructions

a. Prepare journal entries to record the investments of Guinn, Horton, and Randall in the new partnership.
b. The partners share profits and losses equally, and the first year's net income was $66,000. Cash withdrawals of $5,000 were made by Guinn, $22,000 by Horton, and $17,000 by Randall. Prepare the December 31, 19X4, statement of partners' equity for the firm.
c. How would the information presented in part (b) appear on the firm's year-end balance sheet?

P15–A2 Income distribution; journal entries (L.O. 2)

Webster, Mullins, and Hardaway invested $20,000 each on January 4, 19X6, and formed a partnership. The articles of partnership indicated that:

1. Partners are granted 12% interest on their beginning investments.
2. Mullins will receive a monthly salary allowance of $5,000.
3. Remaining profits and losses are shared on a 6 : 3 : 1 basis among the partners.

Instructions

a. Complete the table that follows by determining the proper division of 19X6 net income (or net loss) for the three independent cases shown.

Net Income (Loss)	Webster	Mullins	Hardaway
$ 80,000	_____	_____	_____
10,000	_____	_____	_____
(20,000)	_____	_____	_____

b. During 19X6, Webster and Hardaway withdrew their interest allowances plus an additional $6,000 and $10,000, respectively. Mullins withdrew only his stipulated salary allowance. Assuming net income of $80,000, prepare journal entries to record:
   (1) the transfer of net income to the capital accounts.
   (2) the closing of the drawing accounts.
c. Assuming net income of $80,000:
   (1) show how Webster's capital account would appear on the firm's December 31, 19X6, balance sheet.
   (2) determine whether Hardaway's capital account increased or decreased after her initial investment on January 4. Be sure to calculate the amount of the change.

P15–A3 Admission to a partnership (L.O. 3)

Mantle, Maris, and Berra operate a partnership that provides financial planning services. A review of the firm's articles of partnership found no provisions for interest and salary allowances. Further study of this document and the accounting records disclosed the following information:

	Capital Balance, December 31, 19X3	Share of Profits and Losses
Henry Mantle	$90,000	30%
Cheryl Maris	70,000	45
Thomas Berra	40,000	25

Assume that Terri Richardson will be admitted to the partnership on January 1, 19X4, and the partnership agreement will be redrawn.

Instructions

a. Prepare journal entries to record the admittance of Richardson under each of the following independent cases:
   (1) Richardson invests $100,000 in the partnership and receives a one-third interest in the firm.
   (2) Because of increasing friction between Maris and Berra, Maris sells 80% of her interest to Richardson for $30,000.
   (3) Richardson invests $80,000 in the partnership and receives a 40% interest in the firm.
   (4) Mantle gives 20% of his capital interest to Richardson, who is his niece.
   (5) Richardson invests $50,000 in the partnership and receives a 15% interest in the firm.
   (6) Richardson purchases 60% of Berra's interest directly from Berra for $24,000.
b. Focus on part (a3) for a moment. Briefly discuss several possible reasons that might explain why Richardson received a 40% interest in the firm for her $80,000 investment.

P15–A4 Partner withdrawals (L.O. 3)

Pulaski, Smith, and Freeman operate a partnership and had respective capital balances on December 31, 19X6, of $30,000, $22,000, and $48,000. During 19X7, the firm reported sales of $850,000 and expenses of $800,000. In addition, during 19X7, each partner withdrew $15,000 from the business for personal use. At the very beginning of 19X8, Pulaski reported that she is withdrawing from the firm.

Instructions

a. Calculate the partners' capital balances as of January 1, 19X8. Pulaski, Smith, and Freeman share profits (and losses) on a 2 : 3 : 5 basis, respectively.
b. Prepare journal entries to record the withdrawal of Pulaski for the following independent cases:
   (1) Pulaski sells her interest to the partnership for an amount equal to the balance in her capital account.
   (2) Pulaski sells her interest to Freeman for $50,000.
c. Assume that Pulaski sells her interest to the partnership for $17,000. Is a bonus involved in this transaction? If "yes," who is receiving the bonus?
d. Assume that Pulaski sells her interest to the partnership for $41,000. What factors may have been considered in arriving at the $41,000 figure—a figure that differs from the balance in her capital account?

P15–A5 Partnership liquidation (L.O. 4)

Manny, Moe, and Abe operate a delivery business as a partnership and share net income (and net losses) in a 5 : 3 : 2 ratio, respectively. Because the business was not as successful as planned, the partners decided to liquidate. A post-closing trial balance disclosed the following account balances as of December 31, 19X3:

Cash	$ 38,000	
Trading securities	3,000	
Delivery equipment (net)	64,000	
Accounts payable		$ 1,800
Utilities payable		200
Manny, capital		35,000
Moe, capital		60,000
Abe, capital		8,000
	$105,000	$105,000

Instructions

a. Prepare journal entries to record the sale of the noncash assets and payment of the liabilities assuming the noncash assets are sold for:
   (1) $14,000.
   (2) $98,000.
b. Assume that case (1) of part (a) actually occurred.
   (1) Determine the partnership's cash balance after the liabilities are settled.
   (2) Assume that any partner with a capital deficiency is unable to pay the balance due the partnership. Prepare journal entries to allocate the deficiency to the remaining partners and distribute the firm's ending cash balance.
   (3) Assume that any partner with a capital deficiency is able to pay the balance due the partnership. Present journal entries to record the receipt of cash from the deficient partner and distribute the firm's ending cash balance.

Series B

P15–B1 Investment by partners; statement of partners' equity (L.O. 2)

On August 8, 19XX, Parker, Bowen, and Norton formed a partnership to distribute computer supplies. Parker invested cash of $85,000 and a delivery van that originally cost $7,500. The vehicle's fair market value at the time of investment was $5,000. Bowen contributed trading securities consisting of 1,000 shares of U.S. Paper capital stock (cost per share, $40; market value per share, $70). Finally, Norton contributed the following items from his existing business:

	RECORDED VALUE	FAIR MARKET VALUE
Accounts receivable	$32,000	$32,000
Allowance for uncollectibles	(2,000)	(6,000)
Computer supplies inventory	51,000	57,000
Warehouse equipment (net)	0*	7,000
Accounts payable	10,500	10,500

* Fully depreciated.

Instructions

a. Prepare journal entries to record the investments of Parker, Bowen, and Norton in the partnership.
b. Assume that net income of $72,600 was generated through the end of 19XX. Cash withdrawals of $25,000 were made by Parker, $30,000 by Bowen, and $45,000 by Norton. If the partners divide all profits and losses equally, prepare the December 31, 19XX, statement of partners' equity for the firm.
c. How much partners' equity would the firm report on its December 31 balance sheet?

P15–B2 Income distribution; journal entries (L.O. 2)

Jackson, Hudson, and Rice invested $70,000 each at the beginning of 19X2 and formed a partnership to operate a restaurant. The articles of partnership contained the following provisions:

1. Partners are granted 20% interest on their beginning investments.
2. Hudson will receive an annual salary allowance of $10,000; Rice's annual salary allowance is $40,000.
3. Remaining profits and losses are shared on a 4 : 4 : 2 basis among the partners.

Jackson and Rice withdrew their interest allowances during 19X2 along with an additional $12,000 and $20,000, respectively. Hudson had no withdrawals.

Instructions

a. Determine the proper division of net income (or net loss) among Jackson, Hudson, and Rice for the following independent cases:
   (1) Net income of $100,000.
   (2) Net income of $70,000.
   (3) Net loss of $60,000.
b. For part (a1), prepare journal entries to record (1) the transfer of net income to the capital accounts and (2) the closing of the drawing accounts.
c. For part (a1), present the proper disclosure of partners' equity on the firm's December 31, 19X2, balance sheet.

P15–B3 Admission to a partnership (L.O. 3)

Barden, Larkins, and Winter operate a tax practice that is organized as a partnership. The accounting records disclosed the following information at the end of 19X7:

	BARDEN	LARKINS	WINTER
Capital balance	$30,000	$80,000	$40,000
Share of profits and losses	10%	60%	30%

Assume that the existing partnership will be dissolved on January 1, 19X8, when Engle is admitted as a new partner. The options that follow have been considered for Engle's admission:

1. Barden, who is interested in pursuing other opportunities, has offered to give his entire interest to Engle, his niece.
2. Engle agrees to invest $37,500 in the partnership for a 20% interest in the firm.
3. Winter agrees to sell 40% of his interest to Engle for $16,000.
4. Engle is willing to invest $20,000 in the partnership for a 25% interest in the firm.
5. The existing partners agree to give Engle a 10% interest in the firm for an investment of $30,000 in the partnership.
6. Larkins and Winter offer to sell 60% of their interests to Engle for $55,000 and $25,000, respectively.

Instructions

a. Prepare journal entries that the partnership would record for each of the preceding independent situations.
b. Focus on option no. 5 for a moment. Briefly discuss several possible reasons that might explain why Engle was willing to invest $30,000 in exchange for a 10% interest in the firm.

P15–B4 Partner withdrawals (L.O. 4)

Hecht, Livingston, and Martin have operated a business called HLM Outfitters for many years. The capital balances of the partners on December 31, 19X2, were: Hecht, $250,000; Livingston, $300,000; and Martin, $75,000. The first nine months of 19X3 generated very favorable financial results, with the following figures being reported:

Sales	$1,000,000
Cost of goods sold	575,000
Operating expenses	325,000

On October 1, 19X3, Livingston requested an immediate withdrawal from the firm. The request was approved by the other partners.

Instructions

a. Calculate updated capital balances for the partners through September 30, 19X3. Hecht, Livingston, and Martin share profits (and losses) on a 4 : 4 : 2 basis, respectively.
b. What would you have done differently in part (a) if Hecht, Livingston, and Martin had all processed owner withdrawals of cash during March 19X3?
c. Prepare journal entries to record the withdrawal of Livingston for the following independent cases:
   (1) Livingston sells his interest to a new partner, Kennedy, for $740,000.
   (2) Per stipulations in the articles of partnership, Livingston sells his interest to the firm at an amount equal to the balance in his capital account.

d. Assume that Livingston sells his interest to the partnership for $190,000. Identify several possible underlying factors behind the $190,000 figure—a figure that differs from the balance in his capital account.
e. Assume that Livingston sells his interest to the partnership for $460,000. Is a bonus involved in this transaction? If "yes," who is receiving the bonus?

P15–B5 Partnership liquidation (L.O. 4)

Unser, Jenkins, and Paulus operate UJ's Restaurant as a partnership and share net income (and net losses) in a 2 : 3 : 5 ratio, respectively. A national chain has inquired about buying the noncash assets, doing extensive renovation work, and reopening. With the sale of UJ's, the partnership would be liquidated and Unser, Jenkins, and Paulus would go their separate ways. A post-closing trial balance prepared just prior to liquidation follows.

Cash	$ 85,000	
Food supplies	100,000	
Land & building (net)	142,000	
Equipment (net)	58,000	
Accounts payable		$ 70,000
Unser, capital		80,000
Jenkins, capital		200,000
Paulus, capital		35,000
	$385,000	$385,000

Instructions

a. Assume that the national chain paid $550,000 for the noncash assets. Prepare journal entries to record:
   (1) sale of the noncash assets.
   (2) payment of the liabilities.
   (3) cash distributions to the partners.
b. Assume that the chain paid only $180,000 for the noncash assets and that any partner with a capital deficiency is able to pay the amount due the partnership. Prepare all journal entries needed for the liquidation.
c. Assume that the chain paid only $180,000 for the noncash assets and that any partner with a capital deficiency is unable to pay the amount due. Prepare journal entries to:
   (1) allocate the deficiency to the remaining partners.
   (2) distribute the restaurant's ending cash balance.

EXPANDING YOUR HORIZONS

EYH15–1 Family partnerships (L.O. 1)

Many family businesses are organized as partnerships. Some of these firms operate profitably and harmoniously; others are only marginally successful or even a total disaster. A number of universities have recently created Family Business Institutes to study such enterprises.

Instructions

Using the resources of your library, summarize two articles that discuss the trials and tribulations of operating a family business. On the basis of your research, what features should be included in the articles of partnership for these firms?

EYH15–2 Partnership agreements (L.O. 1)

A partnership among friends is occasionally formed on a handshake, and a formal set of "rules" (i.e., articles of partnership) is never prepared. This simple way of doing business often leads to disputes several years later, after oral agreements have long been forgotten.

Instructions

Form a team with other students in your class and interview two local attorneys. The attorneys should be associated with relatively small legal practices and have some experience with partnership clients. Determine (1) the problems they have seen by not having written articles of partnership, (2) the typical provisions in the articles, and (3) the most unusual feature/provision that they have included as part of the formal document. Be prepared to report your findings to the class.

EYH15–3 Limited liability partnerships (L.O. 1)

Limited liability partnerships (LLPs) are being touted as "the wave of the future" for firms that currently use the partnership form of organization.

Instructions

Using the resources of your library, summarize two articles that discuss the advantages and disadvantages associated with LLPs. Also cite several situations where the LLP entity form is neither suitable nor necessary.

EYH15–4 Partnership features (L.O. 1, 2)

Knapp, Shingler, and Smith, three dentists from Indianapolis, recently attended a convention of the National Dental Association. There they heard a speaker who talked about the formation of successful dental partnerships. An excerpt from the speaker's presentation follows.

> Several guidelines should be considered when entering this entity form. First, prospective partners must be compatible; they need the ability to exchange and discuss business and/or professional viewpoints freely. Second, the partnership should provide the anticipated return (i.e., profit) on investment for all parties. Third, prospective partners should be willing to share in the decision making. Finally, all partners must contribute with equal capacity, unless differences are known and accepted in advance. Quite simply, effort and commitment that differ from that originally anticipated are the biggest disrupters of partnerships.

Smith came away impressed and approached Knapp and Shingler about merging their respective practices, forming a partnership, and building suitable professional space.

Knapp is 57 years old, married, with two grown children. Shingler is 33, married, with four young children. Smith is 29, twice divorced, and has no offspring. Knapp and Shingler have conservative life-styles; Smith could be characterized as a "party animal." The three dentists are respected by their patients. Knapp and Shingler are active in community affairs and the local dental society.

Selected data from the three practices during the past 12 months follow.

	KNAPP	SHINGLER	SMITH
Billings for services	$240,000	$180,000	$100,000
Collections	235,000	160,000	75,000
Office expenses	90,000	130,000	50,000
Dental assistants	4	6	1
Hours worked per week	40	50	28

In forming the partnership, each dentist would contribute $50,000. Knapp would write a check for the entire amount, while Shingler would invest $25,000 cash and sign a note for the remaining balance. Smith, on the other hand, is currently strapped for cash and would have to borrow his total contribution from a local bank.

Instructions
a. Analyze the data presented and discuss the possible reasons why Knapp, Shingler, and Smith are considering a partnership.
b. Are the guidelines for a successful partnership present in this proposed merger? Briefly explain.
c. Should written articles of partnership be prepared for the practice? If "yes," list several items to be included in the agreement.
d. Recommend a method to divide the practice's profit (or loss).
e. Briefly assess the likelihood that the proposed partnership will survive on a long-term basis.

COMMUNICATION OF ACCOUNTING INFORMATION

CAI15–1 The follow-up letter: Harrison, O'Brien, and Weinstein (L.O. 2)
Communication Principle: After an important business meeting where a verbal understanding has been reached, a follow-up letter is appropriate. The follow-up letter serves several purposes:

1. The letter documents the agreement, giving everyone involved the opportunity to confirm or deny the stated terms.
2. The written contents serve as an important refresher when memories fade, thus reducing the possibility of future disputes.
3. The letter, once acknowledged by the recipient, may be the only tangible evidence of the agreement and may be useful if arbitration or legal remedies are necessary.
4. Documentation will help ensure that planned actions occur, as it is easier to overlook a verbal commitment than a written one.

The letter should detail the responsibilities of each affected party and clearly identify any financial terms and conditions. If the subject matter is very important, the sender should request that the recipient acknowledge the contents by some specific action. Such actions might include signing and returning a copy of the letter, confirming the agreement with a telephone call, or sending a written reply.

It is important that the letter be written in a concise style so that significant terms are not obscured. Above all, the letter should take a positive tone (e.g., I look forward to a long and prosperous association . . .). The goal is to build a positive future working relationship, not insult, create distrust, or taint the progress that was made in the original meeting.

■ ■ ■ ■ ■ ■ ■ ■ ■

Mary Ann Harrison, senior managing partner in the law firm of Harrison, O'Brien, and Weinstein, has just informed Peter Woodside of his admission into the firm as a junior partner. This is an important day for Peter, who has worked many years for this recognition. His enthusiasm, though, is somewhat tempered by the terms of the offer.

The company's financial performance has declined somewhat in recent years, although Mary Ann believes this situation is temporary. Terms of partnership admittance require that Peter contribute $100,000 to the firm's capital. He will receive a 15% interest allowance, computed on the beginning-of-period balance in his capital account. In addition, a salary allowance will be calculated at $75 per hour, based on hours of work performed that can be billed to clients. (Mary Ann noted that there will be a minimum of 1,000 hours annually.) Finally, the other partners have agreed that both the $75 hourly rate and billable time will double during the next five years. A specified timetable has not yet been agreed to, however.

The firm's income distribution plan is a closely guarded secret, and only senior partners receive written contracts. Although Peter fully trusts Mary Ann, he is uncomfortable with the informal nature of the arrangement. He has agreed to join the firm as a junior partner but wishes to enclose a letter of understanding with his $100,000 capital contribution.

Instructions

Assume the role of Peter Woodside and draft a letter to the firm of Harrison, O'Brien, and Weinstein.

Answers to Chapter Quiz

1. c
2. c
3. c [Rome: $10,000 + ($30,000 × 0.10) = $13,000; Athens: $60,000 × 0.10 = $6,000; deficiency of $4,000 (($13,000 + $6,000) − $15,000) shared equally). Thus, Rome: $13,000 − $2,000 = $11,000; Athens: $6,000 − $2,000 = $4,000.]
4. a
5. a [$108,000 − $38,000 = $70,000 loss; Allen's share: $70,000 × 4/7 = $40,000; Flynn's share: $70,000 × 1/7 = $10,000, causing a $3,000 capital deficiency ($7,000 − $10,000); Allen's share of deficiency: $3,000 × 4/6 = $2,000; cash distribution: $60,000 − $40,000 − $2,000 = $18,000]

16 Introduction to Corporations

Learning Objectives

After studying this chapter, you should be able to:

1. Identify the features, advantages, and disadvantages of a corporate entity.
2. Summarize the distinctions between common and preferred stock.
3. Calculate the dividends associated with preferred stock.
4. Explain the concepts of and demonstrate the accounting treatments for par, no-par, and stated-value stock.
5. Prepare and interpret the stockholders' equity section of a corporate balance sheet.
6. Define, explain, and calculate book value per share.
7. Discuss return on common stockholders' equity, return on assets, and trading on the equity.

Banner Advertising, a relatively small company by today's standards, is organized as a corporation. To hear George Faris speak about this entity form, you would think that he is the marketing director and sales manager of Corporate America. "The corporate form of organization is ideal," he has said time and time again. "It gives me the ability to distribute company ownership to key employees and their families through shares of stock. My personal resources are protected from Banner's creditors, and I have a readily transferable asset in the unlikely event that I ever want to sell the firm." On the downside, "Organizing as a corporation no doubt costs me some in terms of aggravation, extra taxes, and red tape. However, from my perspective, after all things are considered, the benefits far outweigh the costs."

In the next few pages you will learn about the features of corporations and touch on the very same issues that attracted George to this popular organizational form. Further, you will discover a corporation's unique accounting characteristics—characteristics that relate to a typical small enterprise like Banner Advertising and also to the giants of U.S. business and industry.

As we move into Chapter 16, you are probably aware that economic activity in this country is conducted via three basic entity forms: sole proprietorships, partnerships, and corporations. Although the vast majority of companies operate as sole proprietorships, the bulk of private-sector receipts and earnings is generated by corporations. These facts become apparent after studying the data that appear in Exhibit 16–1.

EXHIBIT 16–1
A Comparison of Alternative Forms of Business Organization

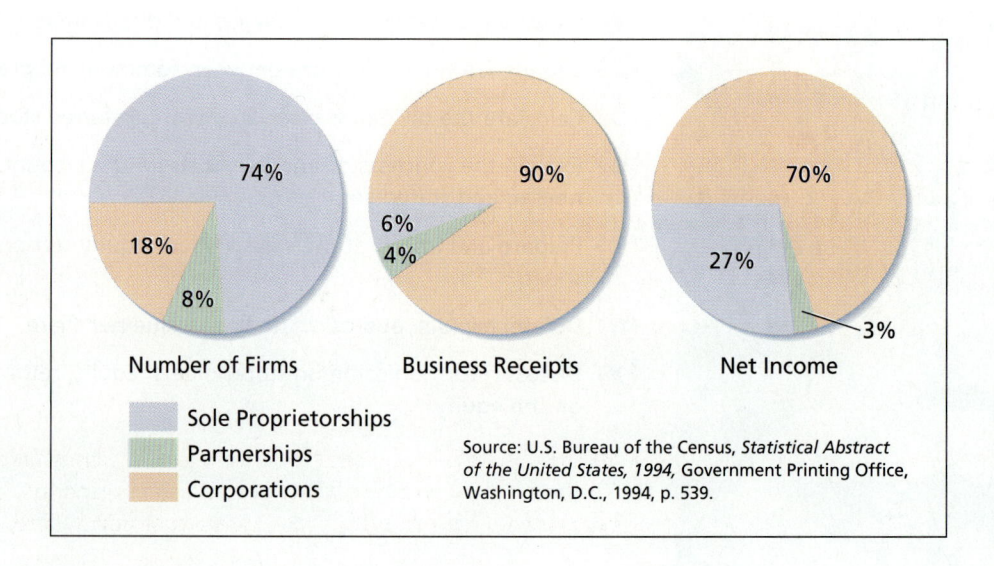

Number of Firms: Sole Proprietorships 74%, Partnerships 8%, Corporations 18%

Business Receipts: Sole Proprietorships 6%, Partnerships 4%, Corporations 90%

Net Income: Sole Proprietorships 27%, Partnerships 3%, Corporations 70%

Source: U.S. Bureau of the Census, *Statistical Abstract of the United States, 1994,* Government Printing Office, Washington, D.C., 1994, p. 539.

Perhaps the most obvious conclusion to be drawn from these figures is that corporations engage in financial activities on a much larger scale than the other entity types. Given that 18% of the firms produce 90% of this country's business receipts, the corporate form of organization clearly dominates our economy in monetary terms.

THE NATURE OF CORPORATIONS

1 Identify the features, advantages, and disadvantages of a corporate entity.

In the early 1800s, Supreme Court Justice Marshall defined a **corporation** as "an artificial being, invisible, intangible, and existing only in contemplation of the law." Consistent with this definition, the corporation is viewed as a legal entity having an existence separate and distinct from its owners. Corporations may therefore buy and sell property in their own names. Additionally, corporations can enter into contracts, defend themselves in court, and transact business in the same manner as a person would.

CORPORATE FORM OF ORGANIZATION: ADVANTAGES

The corporate form of organization is often considered preferable to both a sole proprietorship and a partnership for conducting business affairs. This preference arises for the following reasons.

Transferability of Ownership. Recall from our previous discussions that a corporation is divided into units of ownership called **shares of stock.** These shares are easily passed along from one investor to another without affecting corporate operations. Frequently, the transfer occurs in an organized market such as the New York Stock Exchange, a mechanism where the stocks of roughly 2,000 businesses can be bought or sold. With the possible exception of some family-owned entities or companies owned by a few persons (termed **closely held corporations),** the acquisition and sale of stock are routine matters and do not require the approval of other owners.

A FURTHER FOCUS

Do not liken the closely held corporation to a "mom-and-pop-type" firm. *Forbes* magazine prepares an annual list of the 400 largest private businesses in the United States (i.e., companies that have too few stockholders to be required to file certain reports with the Securities and Exchange Commission or companies whose stock is not available to the general public). The following firms were included in a recent compilation: United Parcel Service, Mars, Montgomery Ward, Levi Strauss, Hallmark Cards, Polo Ralph Lauren, Little Caesar Enterprises, Avis, E&J Gallo Winery, and United Van Lines.

Perpetual Existence. Because a transfer of ownership does not affect business operations, a corporation is said to have a continuous, or perpetual, existence. Contrast this feature with that of a partnership where, unless the partnership agreement states otherwise, a change in ownership terminates the entity's life. Since it is not unusual for larger firms to have more than a million shares traded on a single day, perpetual existence is needed to ensure continuity of financial activities.

Limited Liability of Stockholders.   The owners of a corporation are termed its stockholders. Because of the corporation's separate legal existence, stockholders have *limited liability*; that is, the most they can lose is the amount of their investment. Creditors of the firm have a claim against the entity's assets only; the personal assets of the owners cannot be used to satisfy corporate debts. Recall that this feature does not apply to most partnerships (and sole proprietorships also), where each owner may be held liable for the debts of the business.

Ease of Raising Capital.   Limited liability tends to make the corporation an attractive alternative for investors. This feature, coupled with the fact that ownership is divided into many units, provides a corporation with ready access to additional capital funds. The need for and the ability to raise substantial amounts of capital have prompted virtually all large businesses to adopt the corporate form of organization.

CORPORATE FORM OF ORGANIZATION: DISADVANTAGES

Although the corporation offers many advantages, several disadvantages must be considered.

Double Taxation.   As noted in Chapter 15, partnerships are not taxable entities; instead, an owner is taxed personally on his or her share of the earnings. This same feature also applies to proprietorships. Corporations, on the other hand, are required to pay income taxes. The taxes are heavy and often amount to about 40% of taxable income when both federal and state obligations are considered. In addition, any earnings distributed as dividends are income to the recipient stockholders and are subject to personal income tax. Thus, the same earnings can be taxed twice. The taxing of income to the corporation and the subsequent taxing of dividends to the stockholder is commonly termed double taxation.

Heavy Regulation.   In comparison with sole proprietorships and partnerships, corporations are subject to greater governmental regulation. Most corporations that issue their stock to the general public (termed publicly held corporations) must follow the financial reporting directives of the Securities and Exchange Commission (SEC). Corporate entities are also subject to widely varying state laws. Furthermore, depending on the activities in which it is involved, a corporation may come under the scrutiny of specialized agencies. Examples of such agencies include the Interstate Commerce Commission, the Nuclear Regulatory Commission, and the Federal Deposit Insurance Corporation.

ORGANIZATION OF A CORPORATION

A corporation is created by obtaining a charter from one of the states. The charter is granted after the appropriate state department reviews and approves an application for incorporation. The application spells out, among other things, the firm's business purpose and the organizational structure.

After the entity is created, a stockholders' meeting is usually held to adopt the bylaws that govern the conduct of business activities and also to elect the *board of directors*. The board of directors is entrusted with wide-ranging powers and serves to protect the basic interests of stockholders. In fulfilling its duties and obligations, the board will usually meet several times each year to discuss and evaluate various matters; for example, corporate policy, general business affairs, the declaration of dividends, major contract decisions, and the hiring and remuneration of officers.

Corporate officers manage the company and oversee daily activities. Executives typically included in this select group are a president, several vice-presidents, a secretary, and a treasurer. The president is the chief executive of the company and has final authority (subject to review by the board of directors) for most major decisions. Numerous vice-presidents normally assist the president, often specializing in a functional area such as marketing, finance, production, personnel, and so on. The secretary is charged with maintaining minutes for meetings of the directors and stockholders. The secretary may also become involved in various other legal and contractual matters that affect the corporation.

The treasurer is the custodian of corporate funds and must oversee cash position, monitor cash inflows and outflows, and review major financing activities. Given the nature of their duties, the treasurer and the controller often report to the vice-president of finance. The controller is the chief accounting officer of the firm and is responsible for internal and external reporting. More specifically, the controller oversees the company's internal control system; supplies management with information needed for planning, control, and decision making; and is held accountable for generating financial statements and the various reports that are filed with regulatory agencies (such as the Securities and Exchange Commission). Exhibit 16–2 illustrates the typical upper-level organizational structure of a medium-size corporate entity.

Naturally, in smaller corporations, several of these functions may be combined. For instance, the treasurer and the vice-president of finance may be the same individual. Furthermore, in many family-run businesses, it is not uncommon for a husband/wife team to comprise both top management *and* the board of directors.

Organization Costs. Forming a corporation is more involved and costly than forming a sole proprietorship or partnership. In addition to state incorporation fees, there are legal costs connected with preparing the application for incorporation, expenses incurred by the founders, and numerous other outlays. These one-time expenditures are debited to an account entitled Organization Costs, which is disclosed on the balance sheet as either an intangible asset or an "other asset."

Treatment as an asset is justified because such costs contribute to corporate formation; thus, the benefits derived extend over an indefinite number of years. Most firms amortize organization costs over five years, which is the minimum period allowable under existing income tax regulations. Businesses are permitted to follow this practice because these costs are small in relation

EXHIBIT 16–2
Corporate Organizational Structure

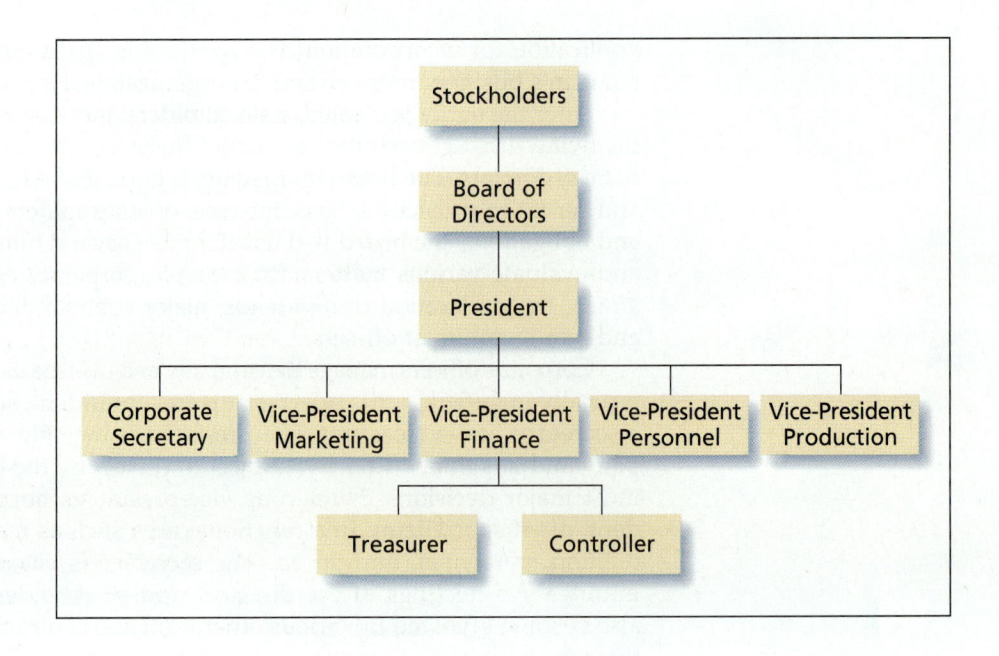

[Organizational chart: Stockholders → Board of Directors → President → (Corporate Secretary, Vice-President Marketing, Vice-President Finance, Vice-President Personnel, Vice-President Production); Vice-President Finance → (Treasurer, Controller)]

to total assets, and the effect of the amortization charge on net income is typically insignificant.

COMMON STOCK

> **2** Summarize the distinctions between common and preferred stock.

The corporate charter specifies the types and number of shares of capital stock that a corporation is permitted to issue. Normally, the charter allows for more shares than are currently needed. This practice saves the time and expense of seeking repeated approvals from stockholders and state authorities for additional issuances at a later date. The number of shares allowed by the charter is termed the **authorized stock.**

Many corporations issue different classes of stock to provide flexibility in raising capital and to appeal to various types of investors. The stock classes usually have distinctive rights and privileges. All corporations issue **common stock**—an ownership interest that controls the board of directors (and thus corporate management) by exercising voting rights. Common stockholders are often rewarded with increased stock values when net income rises and, conversely, penalized with lower values when profitability falls. Overall, then, it is the common stockholder who reaps the benefits of corporate success and pays the price of business failure.

Rights of Common Stockholders. The owners of common stock typically have the following rights:

1. To share in any dividend distributions that may be declared by the board of directors.
2. To subscribe to any additional common stock issued by the corporation (known as the **preemptive right**). Existing stockholders are given the opportunity to maintain their respective interests in a corporate entity by

acquiring additional shares on a pro rata basis. For example, a stockholder who owns 15% of a corporation's common stock is allowed to purchase 15% of any new shares issued before those shares are offered to other investors.

The preemptive right is not a hard-and-fast rule. For instance, stockholders have sometimes waived the preemptive right, thereby permitting large stock issuances for use in acquiring other businesses. In other situations, certain states have allowed the issuance of shares with no preemptive rights attached.

3. To share in the final disposition of assets if the corporation is liquidated. At the end of a corporation's life its assets are sold, and the cash generated is used to settle the claims of creditors. Any remaining cash (or assets) is shared proportionately by the common stockholders on the basis of the number of shares owned.
4. To elect the board of directors and to vote on other important corporate issues. Common stockholders are frequently asked to consider such matters as proposed mergers; the selection of independent auditors; changes in corporate bylaws and management pension programs; and the types and amounts of stock that can be issued.

The preceding rights apply to most common stockholders, not all. Sometimes, different classes of common stock are issued with rights other than those described. The Adolph Coors Company, for instance, perhaps best known for its brewing operation, has Class A and Class B common stock. Class A stock has voting rights and is retained by the Coors family; Class B stock is nonvoting and has been issued to the general public.

PREFERRED STOCK: NATURE AND CHARACTERISTICS

Rather than have multiple classes of common stock, some corporations have achieved differentiation by issuing preferred stock. As its name implies, preferred stock has several preferential rights; in comparison with common stock, however, other rights are given up in return.[1] Normally, preferred stock appeals to investors who want a relatively safe investment with a steady dividend. Why? The reasons become apparent in the upcoming sections where we discuss characteristics of most preferred stocks.

No Voting Rights. Preferred stockholders generally have no vote in corporate affairs. Exceptions are made, however, by special contracts or by state law. In some cases voting privileges are awarded after certain conditions have been met, such as the absence of dividends for a specified period of time.

Dividend Preference. Voting rights are often forfeited in exchange for a preference in dividend distributions. Specifically, preferred stockholders are entitled to receive dividends before any distributions are made to common stockholders. In most instances, though, the owners of preferred shares receive

> **3**
> Calculate the dividends associated with preferred stock.

---

[1] As in the case of common shares, corporations may issue various classes of preferred stock. In what might be an extreme example, Pacific Gas & Electric (a San Francisco-based public utility) has 15 different types of preferred shares, each with its own features and rights.

only a stipulated amount per share regardless of the profitability of the firm. This situation arises because preferred dividends are expressed either on a per-year basis or as a percentage of par value. (Par value refers to the face value of a share of stock and is discussed later in the chapter.) A 10% preferred stock with a $25 par value, for example, has a dividend of $2.50 per year.

Although many businesses take pride in their dividend records, keep in mind that dividend distributions are not mandatory but are subject to the discretion of the board of directors. Consequently, when a company's cash position is weak or when earnings are marginal, dividends may not be disbursed. For this reason most preferred stocks are **cumulative.** That is, the rights to preferred dividends that are omitted in a given year accumulate, with the amounts said to be **in arrears.** Dividends in arrears must be paid before any subsequent dividends can be declared and paid on a corporation's common stock.

An Example. To illustrate these features, suppose Flora, Inc., has 20,000 shares of 10%, $5 par, cumulative preferred stock and 50,000 shares of $1 par common. Dividend distributions for the past four years are listed in the second column of the following table. Because the annual preferred dividend requirement is $10,000 (20,000 shares x $5 x 0.10), the dividends would be divided between preferred and common shareholders as shown.

YEAR	TOTAL DIVIDENDS DISTRIBUTED	ANNUAL PREFERRED REQUIREMENT	DIVIDENDS IN ARREARS	DIVIDENDS DISTRIBUTED PREFERRED	COMMON
1	$27,000	$10,000	$ —	$10,000	$17,000
2	6,000	10,000	4,000	6,000	—
3	3,000	10,000	11,000	3,000	—
4	25,000	10,000	—	21,000	4,000

Observe that distributions in Year 2 amounted to only $6,000. Since preferred stockholders are entitled to receive $10,000, dividends are $4,000 in arrears. All $6,000 thus goes to the preferred stockholders because of their right to receive dividends before any distributions to common. In Year 3, Flora failed to cover the annual preferred requirement by $7,000 ($10,000 − $3,000), raising arrearages to $11,000. Preferred again gets the entire distribution, in this instance $3,000. Finally, the dividends in Year 4 were sufficient to meet not only the arrearage but also the annual requirement. Common stockholders therefore receive the remaining $4,000 ($25,000 − $11,000 − $10,000).

Dividends in arrears are not a liability because they have never been declared by the board of directors. Such amounts are typically disclosed in the notes to the financial statements. Although we have emphasized the cumulative feature, realize that some preferred stock is noncumulative; that is, unpaid dividends do not accumulate and are lost. Because noncumulative preferred stock lacks investor appeal, it is not frequently encountered in practice.

Asset Preference upon Liquidation. Most preferred stock has a preference over common stock in the event of corporate liquidation. After creditor claims are settled, preferred stockholders are entitled to their share of the remaining assets prior to any distributions to the holders of common (i.e., the residual owners).

Callable. Many preferred stocks are callable, which means the issuing corporation retains the right to reacquire (call) the stock at a preset price. The call feature allows a company to raise capital from a stock issuance and later cancel the stock and return the investors' funds. Such actions may be desirable when the cash is no longer needed or the shares become financially burdensome. The latter situation will arise if the preferred stock is issued when interest (and dividend) rates are high. Should the rates drop suddenly, the shares can be called and replaced with cheaper financing.

Convertible. Some preferred stock is convertible into common stock at the option of the stockholder. Conversion normally occurs in a stipulated exchange ratio; for example, one share of preferred may be convertible into five shares of common. Convertible preferred is appealing to both investors and the issuing company. From the investors' viewpoint, there is a strong likelihood of a regular, assured dividend on the preferred stock. Furthermore, should the corporation's common stock rise in value, investors have the privilege of conversion and can thereby increase the worth of their holdings. From the company's point of view, a smaller dividend can usually be paid because investors find the conversion feature attractive.

PAR-VALUE STOCK

> **④** Explain the concepts of and demonstrate the accounting treatments for par, no-par, and stated-value stock.

The common and preferred classifications are based on the rights afforded to the respective groups of stockholders. Stocks can also be categorized as par value or no-par value. Par-value stock has a fixed dollar amount per share specified by the corporate charter. The amount varies among businesses and is sometimes influenced by state laws that tax the par value of shares issued.

The significance of par value is that it represents the legal capital per share of stock. Total legal capital, obtained by multiplying the par value per share times the number of shares issued, denotes the minimum amount of owners' equity that must be maintained for protection of the creditors. To explain, recall that stockholders have limited liability and cannot be held personally liable for corporate obligations. In an effort to provide some protection to the creditors, state laws thus require a minimum permanent investment from the owners to help settle claims on company assets. Dividend declarations that reduce total stockholders' equity below legal capital are therefore not permitted.

Issuing Par-Value Stock. If a corporation is large or is attempting to sell a substantial amount of stock, the services of an investment banking firm will normally be used. Typical investment bankers include Smith Barney Inc., and Merrill Lynch, Pierce, Fenner & Smith Inc. The investment banker, often referred to as an *underwriter,* has the responsibility of selling the stock, at a set price, to the public. Underwriters charge a commission for their services and often advertise stock issuances in newspapers and business periodicals. The sale of stock is typically made on the basis of a prospectus, a document required by the SEC that contains information about the corporation's products, management, and financial affairs.

Issue Price. Stocks may be issued at, above, or below par value, given the arbitrary manner in which par is determined. The latter issuances are seldom encountered and are actually illegal in many states. Why? Although the sale proceeds are less than par, the stock is still considered fully paid. However, the stockholder is held contingently liable to the corporation's creditors for the difference between the sale price and the par amount specified in the firm's charter. Should corporate assets be insufficient to settle creditor claims if operations cease, the original stockholders may be called upon to furnish additional cash. To avoid this situation, virtually all corporations issue stock at or above par.

The issue price for new stock is determined by the corporation along with an underwriter or financial advisers. The following factors are considered: past, present, and future corporate earnings; financial position; expected dividend rates; market position of the company's products and services; current state of the investment market; and recent prices of competitors' stock.

Once stock is issued, its **market price** (the price at which a share can be bought or sold) continually changes. The changes reflect investor evaluation of the corporation's progress and prospects. If growth prospects are evident, the price of the shares should rise; if the future looks bleak, the price should fall. This idea was originally introduced in Chapter 7.

It is important to note that market fluctuations do *not* affect the corporation's financial position. If, for instance, a company issues stock at $50 per share and the market price later plummets to $10 per share, the firm does not suffer directly from the decrease in valuation. The decrease is absorbed by the stockholders. Of course, if more investment capital is needed, the entity may be unable to attract the investors and funds it once did at the original $50 price.

Reading the Stock Pages. *The Wall Street Journal* and virtually all major metropolitan newspapers publish daily stock quotes (i.e., market prices) throughout the year. These publications show that stock prices have their ups and downs, both on a given day and over an extended period of time. As evidence, the following excerpt from *The Wall Street Journal* reveals information about the common stocks of Liz Claiborne and Lockheed Corporation (the giant defense contractor).

52 Weeks					Yld		Vol				Net
Hi	Lo	Stock	Sym	Div	%	PE	100s	Hi	Lo	Close	Chg
26⅝	15⅜	LizClabrn	LIZ	.45	2.8	12	7349	16⅛	15⅝	16	+ ⅜
79½	58¾	Lockheed	LK	2.28	3.1	10	793	73¼	71¾	73⅛	+1½

Liz Claiborne's common stock closed the day at $16 per share, up 3/8 ($0.38) from the previous session's trading. The stock fluctuated in price from a low of $15.63 to a high of $16.13, as 734,900 shares exchanged hands. As you can see, the stock was trading near its low for the year of $15.38. Other data—dividends, yield, and the price/earnings (P/E) ratio—are presented as well. (These concepts are best understood after completion of the next chapter.)

Lockheed Corporation's common stock closed up $1.50 for the day on a lower volume (79,300 shares). Unlike the shares in the preceding example, Lockheed's stock was trading much closer to its 52-week high of $79.50.

Accounting for Par-Value Stock. The issuance of par-value stock may require entries in more than one owners' equity account. Specifically, an amount equal to the par value of the shares issued is placed in a capital stock account, either Common Stock or Preferred Stock. Then, if the stock is issued at a price greater than par, the difference between the issue price and par is recorded in an

A Further Focus

Liz Claiborne and Lockheed are established corporations, and their shares have been actively traded for years. When a new company's shares hit the market for the first time (called an *initial public offering*, or *IPO*), the stock price changes can be significant and volatile. Several factors may account for this behavior. The firm may be an up and coming entity with a novel idea or perhaps many small investors have been drawn into a speculative frenzy. It is even possible that the underwriting firm priced the shares too low (or high).

To illustrate what can happen in a sometimes nonrational stock market, we cite the case of Boston Market (formerly Boston Chicken), whose $20 per share IPO price closed the day at $48.50—a rise of 143% in only a few hours! This restaurant chain's initial offering coincided with the growing popularity among consumers of rotisserie-roasted chicken. Also, several of the key managers were former executives with the enormously successful Blockbuster Entertainment. The IPO left the company with a stock market value of $800 million—not bad for a firm with limited operating history, annual revenues of only $8.3 million, and a net *loss* of $5.9 million.

An IPO for Wilt Chamberlain's Restaurants, Inc. (named after the famous basketball player) behaved in the opposite manner. The company, which had only a single facility in Florida (and plans for expansion), opened for trading at $7 per share but closed one day later at $4.63. The short-term outlook was so bleak that the IPO was withdrawn from the market, a rarity, and investors received their money back.

Sources: "Boston Chicken Soars by 143% on Its IPO Day," *The Wall Street Journal*, November 10, 1993, pp. C1, C2 and "Wilt Shoots an Air Ball With Stock Offer," *The Wall Street Journal*, February 17, 1993, pp. C1, C18.

---

account entitled Paid-in Capital in Excess of Par Value. To state this important allocation differently, the funds received from investors are recorded as legal capital (the par value) and as additional paid-in capital (amounts received in excess of par).

To illustrate the proper accounting, assume McCord Corporation is authorized to issue 50,000 shares of $5 par, 8% cumulative preferred stock and 20,000 shares of $10 par common. Further assume that the corporation has issued 30,000 shares of preferred at par and 10,000 shares of common at $18. The required journal entries follow.

Cash	150,000	
Preferred Stock		150,000
To record issuance of 30,000 shares of $5 par, 8% preferred at $5 per share.		
Cash	180,000	
Common Stock		100,000
Paid-in Capital in Excess of Par Value		80,000
To record issuance of 10,000 shares of $10 par common at $18 per share.		

Observe that in both cases the par value of the issued shares was placed in a capital stock account. In addition, note that the $80,000 paid in excess of par was recorded separately.

Realize that the preceding entries are made *only* at the time of stock issuance. Daily stock transactions of investors (e.g., purchases and sales) normally involve shares that have been previously issued, with no additional cash being received by the corporation. In these instances the corporation does not record a formal journal entry—all that is needed is an updating of the list of stockholders.

> **5**
> Prepare and interpret the stockholders' equity section of a corporate balance sheet.

Balance Sheet Presentation. The owners' (stockholders') equity section of McCord's balance sheet would appear as shown in Exhibit 16–3. Notice how the balance sheet discloses the two major sources of corporate equity: stockholder investments (paid-in capital) and retained earnings. Retained earnings represents capital generated from profitable operations that is kept in the business (and will be discussed in depth in Chapter 17). At this point assume the account's $240,000 balance was obtained from McCord's general ledger.

Exhibit 16–3 reveals several other important points. First, considerable detail is required in terms of disclosure. The features of the various stock issues are described along with the number of shares authorized by the corporate charter, issued by the firm, and held by the stockholders (termed outstanding shares).[2] Second, note that the $80,000 paid by stockholders in excess of par value is considered neither revenue nor profit. It is merely additional invested capital that is shown separately from the capital stock accounts. Finally, as you may have observed, virtually our entire presentation has focused on owners' (in this case, stockholders') equity. The underlying reason is that this balance sheet section is the primary area of difference among the financial statements of sole proprietorships, partnerships, and corporations.

NO-PAR STOCK

In the early days of corporations, the issuance of stock sometimes misled unsophisticated investors. Par value was occasionally equated with the "true" worth of the stock, that is, the market price. This factor, coupled with the contingent liability problem cited earlier (see pp. 591–592), prompted many corporations to consider no-par stock.

Because the par-value concept is absent, the entire proceeds must be credited to a capital stock account. For instance, assume Canton Corporation is authorized to issue 20,000 shares of no-par common stock. If 10,000 shares are issued at $18 per share, the required journal entry would be as follows:

Cash	180,000	
Common Stock		180,000
To record issuance of 10,000 shares of no-par common at $18 per share.		

---

[2] The number of shares issued and the number of shares outstanding can differ. This situation will also be discussed in Chapter 17.

EXHIBIT 16–3
Stockholders' Equity of McCord Corporation

STOCKHOLDERS' EQUITY		
Capital stock		
Cumulative 8% preferred stock, $5 par, 50,000 shares authorized, 30,000 shares issued and outstanding	$150,000	
Common stock, $10 par, 20,000 shares authorized, 10,000 shares issued and outstanding	100,000	$250,000
Paid-in capital in excess of par value: common		80,000
Total paid-in capital		$330,000
Retained earnings		240,000
Total stockholders' equity		$570,000

This illustration has deliberately used the same numbers as the just-completed McCord Corporation example. Notice that both issues of common stock generated identical proceeds: $180,000. With no-par stock, however, total invested capital is recorded in one equity account rather than two.

Stated-Value Stock. Although most states permit the issuance of no-par stock, some states require corporations to set a minimum issue price. This price, known as the stock's *stated value,* allows for protection of the creditors in terms of legal capital. In essence, then, stated value can be likened to par value.

Because of the similarity, accounting for stated-value stock closely parallels that for par-value stock. To illustrate, we will continue the Canton Corporation example. Assume that to comply with state law, Canton's board of directors has assigned a $10 stated value to each share. The issuance of 10,000 shares at $18 per share would now be recorded as follows:

Cash	180,000	
Common Stock		100,000
Paid-in Capital in Excess of Stated Value		80,000
To record issuance of 10,000 shares of no-par common (stated value, $10) at $18 per share.		

The stated value of the issued stock is entered in the Common Stock account. Any added amount is then recorded as Paid-in Capital in Excess of Stated Value, which is similar to additional paid-in capital received on par-value shares.

ISSUING STOCK FOR ASSETS OTHER THAN CASH

Thus far we have concentrated on stock issues that generate cash. The cash, in turn, was used for the purchase of assets, payment of expenses, and other similar purposes. Frequently, corporations issue stock in direct exchange for land, buildings, and even other businesses. In addition, stock is sometimes used to

> **ETHICS ISSUE**
>
> You have the opportunity to audit the financial statements of a cash-poor, publicly held corporation. You would be given a sizable number of common shares for your services. How would you respond, knowing the results of your audit may affect the stock's market price?

settle claims of attorneys and other professionals for services rendered, particularly at the time of corporate formation when cash balances may be low.

The issuance of shares for noncash assets or services creates a valuation problem. Namely, what value should be used to record the transaction? The general rule is that the assets or services acquired are recorded at their fair market value or the fair market value of the stock, whichever is more clearly discernible. If the corporation's shares are actively traded on one of the stock exchanges, determination of the stock's market value is a relatively simple matter. As explained earlier, *The Wall Street Journal* and the financial pages of most metropolitan newspapers will provide the necessary information. When stock is not actively traded, as in a closely held corporation, an appraisal of the asset's (or service's) market value may be more appropriate.

To illustrate the proper accounting treatment, assume Fuqua Industries is a small family-run business located in Wyoming. Fuqua's attorney has agreed to accept 40 shares of $5 par common for $850 of legal work performed in organizing the corporation. The required journal entry follows.

Organization Costs	850	
Common Stock		200
Paid-in Capital in Excess of Par Value		650
To record issuance of common stock in exchange for legal services.		

Because Fuqua's stock is not actively traded, the $850 billing is more clearly determinable as the market value of the transaction.

STOCK SUBSCRIPTIONS

Rather than use the services of an underwriter, small corporations occasionally sell stock directly to investors on a *subscription* basis. Investors agree to purchase the stock at a given price, with payment taking place on a specific future date or via installments. After the subscriber pays in full, the shares of stock are issued.

Issuance of shares in this manner gives rise to two specialized accounts: Stock Subscriptions Receivable and Common Stock Subscribed. Stock Subscriptions Receivable is established to indicate the amounts due from investors and has historically appeared as a current asset on the balance sheet. Common Stock Subscribed, on the other hand, reflects the par value of the shares *to be issued*; it is credited upon receipt of a signed investor contract. Later, when the amounts due are paid and the actual shares are issued, Common Stock Subscribed is debited and Common Stock is credited. Given the manner in which the account is used, any balance in Common Stock Subscribed is disclosed as paid-in capital in the stockholders' equity section.

CORPORATE EQUITY: A COMPREHENSIVE ILLUSTRATION

The stockholders' equity section in Exhibit 16–4 brings together several of the concepts discussed in this chapter. Notice that preferred stock is presented first, followed by common stock. Next, additional paid-in capital is disclosed to

EXHIBIT 16–4
Corporate Equity

STOCKHOLDERS' EQUITY			
Capital stock			
Cumulative 9% preferred stock, $10 par, 30,000 shares authorized, 20,000 shares issued and outstanding			$200,000
Common stock, no-par, $5 stated value, 15,000 shares authorized, 10,000 shares issued and outstanding		$50,000	
Common stock subscribed, no-par, $5 stated value, 2,000 shares		10,000	60,000
Total capital stock			$260,000
Additional paid-in capital			
Paid-in capital in excess of par value: preferred		$120,000	
Paid-in capital in excess of stated value: common		48,000	168,000
Total paid-in capital			$428,000
Retained earnings			150,000
Total stockholders' equity			$578,000

complete total equity contributed by stockholders. The final element is retained earnings. Although variations in terminology and presentation exist in practice, the exhibit is representative and should convey the message that corporate equity is more complex than equity of the other entity forms.

EVALUATIONS BASED ON STOCKHOLDERS' EQUITY

Owners, creditors, and analysts use a variety of measures to assess corporate performance and financial position. Two popular evaluation tools, book value per share and return on common stockholders' equity, are tied closely to the material just discussed.

BOOK VALUE PER SHARE

> **6**
> Define, explain, and calculate book value per share.

Book value per share is the amount of stockholders' equity allocable to an individual share of stock. Looked at from a different perspective, this measure expresses a corporation's net assets (total assets minus total liabilities) on a per-share basis.

The calculation of book value depends on the classes of stock outstanding. If a corporation has only common stock, book value is computed by dividing total stockholders' equity by the number of common shares outstanding at the end of the accounting period. For example, assume Ranger Corporation has $1,000,000 of stockholders' equity, as follows: Common Stock (50,000 shares), $50,000; Paid-in Capital in Excess of Par Value, $350,000; and Retained Earnings, $600,000. The book value per share in this case is $20 ($1,000,000 ÷ 50,000 shares).

An Example with Two Classes of Stock. If a corporation has two classes of stock (e.g., common and preferred), total stockholders' equity must be allocated between the respective ownership interests. The first step in this allocation involves assigning the call value (sometimes referred to as the *redemption* or *liquidating value*) of the preferred stock plus any dividends in arrears[3] as preferred equity. Next, the sum of these two items is subtracted from total stockholders' equity to generate equity attributable to the common shareholders. The book value per common and preferred shares can then be determined by dividing the equity relating to the two stock classes by their respective outstanding shares.

To illustrate the necessary accounting, we will focus on the stockholders' equity section of Orleans, Inc. (see Exhibit 16–5). Further information reveals that dividends on the preferred stock are $4,000 in arrears at year-end. The allocation of Orleans' stockholders' equity follows.

Total stockholders' equity		$870,000
Allocated to preferred stock		
Call value: 400 shares × $110	$44,000	
Dividends in arrears	4,000	48,000
Allocated to common stock		$822,000

Observe that the $5,000 paid-in capital in excess of par on the preferred stock is not allocated to preferred equity. This amount will not be returned to the preferred shareholders should their stock be called.

The book value per share for each class of stock can now be calculated in the following manner:

Preferred stock: $48,000 ÷ 400 shares = $120.00 per share
Common stock: $822,000 ÷ 30,000 shares = $27.40 per share

EXHIBIT 16–5
Stockholders' Equity of Orleans, Inc.

STOCKHOLDERS' EQUITY		
Preferred stock, $100 par value, 5% cumulative, callable at $110, 1,000 shares authorized, 400 shares issued and outstanding		$ 40,000
Common stock, $1 par value, 100,000 shares authorized, 30,000 shares issued and outstanding	30,000	$ 70,000
Additional paid-in capital		
Paid-in capital in excess of par: preferred	$ 5,000	
Paid-in capital in excess of par: common	200,000	205,000
Total paid-in capital		$275,000
Retained earnings		595,000
Total stockholders' equity		$870,000

[3] Dividends in arrears apply solely to cumulative preferred stock.

Meaning of Book Value. Book value is equivalent to a corporation's net assets per share of stock. Some stockholders therefore believe that should the corporation terminate operations and liquidate, they would receive an amount equal to this figure. Rarely, however, does the belief become reality. When an entity liquidates, the assets are usually sold at a price far different from their valuation on a balance sheet. Remember, the balance sheet is cost-based and ignores increases in valuation that arise from inflation. Furthermore, because the corporation is selling out, the amounts received for certain assets may be only a small percentage of their original cost. Added to this is the fact that liabilities are often settled at less than the amount owed. These events alter corporate equity and the amounts disbursed to stockholders upon liquidation.

The importance of book value arises from its inclusion in many legal contracts. In a small corporation, for instance, stockholders may agree to sell their holdings to the other owners at the book value per share existing on specified future dates. Or banks may lend funds to a corporation, subject to the maintenance of a minimum book value. Under no circumstances should book value per share be equated with a stock's market value, as these two measures normally differ. Consider the following recent figures:

CORPORATION	YEAR-END BOOK VALUE PER SHARE	YEAR-END MARKET VALUE PER SHARE
Aetna Life & Casualty	$62.77	$ 60.38
Aluminum Co. of America (Alcoa)	37.90	69.38
Atlantic Richfield	37.89	105.25
Boise Cascade	24.83	23.50
Caterpillar, Inc.	18.12	89.00
Loews Corporation	99.08	93.00

Book value, a measure based on historical cost, is just one of the many factors investors use in studying the appropriateness of a stock's market price.

RETURN ON COMMON STOCKHOLDERS' EQUITY

7 Discuss return on common stockholders' equity, return on assets, and trading on the equity.

Many corporations are heavily financed from investments made by common stockholders. A widely used ratio, called return on common stockholders' equity, measures the profit generated on funds provided by these investors. This ratio is often calculated by dividing net income, minus preferred dividends, by the average common stockholders' equity.[4] By subtracting preferred dividends, we derive the income that belongs to the common shareholders—the true residual owners of a corporation.

To illustrate this concept along with several other important points, we will use selected data of the Riverside Corporation. The following figures were extracted from the company's financial statements:

Net income	$4,900,000
Preferred dividends (10%)	100,000
Interest expense (10%) on long-term loans	600,000

[4] The calculation of common stockholders' equity is similar to the allocation that appears on page 598.

Common stockholders' equity
    January 1 $11,300,000
    December 31   12,700,000
Assets
    January 1   19,400,000
    December 31   20,600,000

Riverside's ratio is computed in the manner shown.

$$\text{Return on Common Stockholders' Equity} = \frac{\text{Net Income} - \text{Preferred Dividends}}{\text{Average Common Stockholders' Equity}}$$

$$= \frac{\$4,900,000 - \$100,000}{\frac{\$11,300,000 + \$12,700,000}{2}}$$

$$= \frac{\$4,800,000}{\$12,000,000}$$

$$= 40\%$$

Recall from earlier chapters that averages are derived by adding the beginning and ending balances and dividing by 2.

Riverside has earned 40¢ for each dollar invested by common shareholders, which is quite impressive. More insight about the company's performance can be gained, however, if we study a related ratio called return on assets.

Return on Assets. The **return on assets,** often termed *return on investment* or *ROI,* measures profitability from a given level of asset investment. This ratio focuses on operations, namely, the effectiveness of resources used in generating profit. Return on investment is typically calculated by dividing net income plus interest expense by the average total assets employed in business activity. The addition of interest expense produces a figure that represents earnings from operations, prior to any financing costs. Stated differently, we focus on how well the asset investment was *used,* not on the related methods and costs of securing those resources. The return on assets for Riverside Corporation follows.

$$\text{Return on Assets} = \frac{\text{Net Income} + \text{Interest Expense}}{\text{Average Assets}}$$

$$= \frac{\$4,900,000 + \$600,000}{\frac{\$19,400,000 + \$20,600,000}{2}}$$

$$= \frac{\$5,500,000}{\$20,000,000}$$

$$= 27.5\%$$

Riverside's rate of return is also quite high. For every $1 of assets employed, the company has generated 27.5¢ of income.

Trading on the Equity. Notice that the return on common stockholders' equity exceeds the return on assets by a substantial amount. This difference is caused by **trading on the equity,** sometimes known as *leverage*. With leverage, a company secures funds at fixed interest and preferred dividend rates and then invests the funds to earn a return greater than their cost. Riverside, for example, is earning 27.5% on its assets. Yet a review of the financial statement data presented earlier will find that the firm is paying only 10% interest for funds obtained via long-term loans and a 10% dividend on preferred stock. The difference between the amounts earned and the amounts paid on such funds benefits the common stockholders and is reflected by the 40% return on their equity.

The company is said to be trading on the equity at a gain; that is, it has positive financial leverage. Naturally, the opposite case is possible. For instance, if Riverside obtained funding at 10% but earned only 7% on investments, the company would be trading on the equity at a loss. Net income suffers along with the payoff to the common stockholders.

END-OF-CHAPTER REVIEW

LEARNING OBJECTIVES: THE KEY POINTS

1. **Identify the features, advantages, and disadvantages of a corporate entity.** The corporate form of organization has several key features, which often make it preferable for conducting business affairs. Shares of ownership are easily transferred, and regardless of any change in ownership, the corporation has a continuous existence. In addition, the stockholders have limited liability, which serves to protect the assets of the owners from being used to satisfy corporate obligations. Finally, because liability is limited and ownership is divided into many shares, capital is more easily raised by corporations than by the other forms of business organization.

    Two disadvantages of corporations are double taxation and heavy regulation. Double taxation is the taxing of income to the corporation and the subsequent taxing of dividends to stockholders.

2. **Summarize the distinctions between common and preferred stock.** Common stock represents an ownership interest that controls the board of directors via the voting process. In addition, common stockholders have the rights to (1) share in dividend distributions, (2) subscribe to any additional common stock that is issued by the company (i.e., the preemptive right), and (3) share in the final disposition of assets in the event of liquidation.

    In contrast, preferred stock is an ownership interest that has certain preferential rights over those associated with common stock. However, to obtain these rights, others (e.g., voting) are given up in return. Preferred stockholders are entitled to receive dividends before any distributions are made to common stockholders. Furthermore, most preferred stock has preference over common stock in asset distributions should corporate liquidation occur.

3. **Calculate the dividends associated with preferred stock.** Preferred stockholders are entitled to receive dividends each period. If the stock is cumulative, any preferred dividends omitted in a given year accumulate and must be paid before future

dividends are declared and paid on common shares. Such accumulated amounts are said to be in arrears and are disclosed in the notes to the financial statements.

4. **Explain the concepts of and demonstrate the accounting treatments for par, no-par, and stated-value stock.** A corporation's stock may be characterized as having a par value or no par value. Par value is an amount specified in the corporate charter; it represents the firm's legal capital (a minimum permanent investment) per share. When par-value stock is sold, an amount equal to the par value of the issuance is placed in a capital stock account. Any receipts in excess of par are recorded in Paid-in Capital in Excess of Par Value. When no-par stock is issued, the entire proceeds are credited to a capital stock account. No-par stock may have a stated value assigned by the board of directors, which, in effect, serves to establish a minimum issue price. Accounting for stated-value stock is similar to that for par-value stock.

5. **Prepare and interpret the stockholders' equity section of a corporate balance sheet.** Stockholders' equity has three sections. The first, called capital stock, discloses the Preferred Stock, Common Stock, and Stock Subscribed accounts. The additional paid-in capital section appears next and contains the accounts for any amounts paid in excess of par or stated value. The final section is for retained earnings.

6. **Define, explain, and calculate book value per share.** Book value per share is the amount of stockholders' equity allocable to an individual share of stock. If a corporation has both preferred and common stock, book value is computed for both classes. To calculate book value for preferred shares, the total of the shares' call (i.e., redemption) value, plus any dividends in arrears if the stock is cumulative, is divided by preferred shares outstanding. The book value of common stock is total stockholders' equity, minus the preferred equity just described, divided by the common shares outstanding. Although book value is not equivalent to the value of stock in the marketplace, it is nonetheless an important element in many legal contracts.

7. **Discuss return on common stockholders' equity, return on assets, and trading on the equity.** The return on common stockholders' equity is a ratio that measures the income generated on funds provided by this important investor group. The ratio's numerator is actually net income minus preferred dividends, allowing the analyst to focus on the income that belongs to the common shareholders. Return on assets, often called ROI, looks at the operating income that is produced from a company's asset investment. The ratio's numerator is calculated as net income plus interest expense, which removes the effects of financing costs and allows a focus on operations.

    Finally, trading on the equity (i.e., leverage) refers to a program by which companies obtain financing at fixed interest and dividend rates and then invest the funds to (hopefully) earn a return greater than the funds' cost. If an organization is successful at this process, the common stockholders benefit by having a return that exceeds the return on assets. Such companies are said to be trading on the equity at a gain and have positive financial leverage.

KEY TERMS AND CONCEPTS: A QUICK OVERVIEW

authorized stock The number of shares of stock a corporation is permitted to issue as specified in its charter. (p. 588)

book value per share The amount of stockholders' equity allocable to an individual share of stock. (p. 597)

callable preferred stock Preferred stock that can be reacquired by the issuing corporation at a preset price. (p. 591)

charter A state-issued document that provides evidence of business incorporation. (p. 586)

closely held corporation A corporation owned by only a few persons. (p. 585)

common stock A corporate ownership interest that controls management by exercising voting rights. (p. 588)

controller The chief accounting officer of a company. (p. 587)

convertible preferred stock Preferred stock that can be converted into common stock at the option of the stockholder. (p. 591)

corporation A form of business organization that is a separate legal entity from its owners. Ownership is in the hands of investors who have acquired shares of the corporation's stock. (p. 585)

cumulative preferred stock Preferred stock where the rights to dividends omitted in a given year accumulate. These dividends must be paid before any subsequent dividends are distributed to common stockholders. (p. 590)

dividends in arrears Dividends that have been omitted on cumulative preferred stock. (p. 590)

double taxation The taxing of income to both a corporation and the corporation's stockholders. (p. 586)

legal capital The minimum amount of owners' equity that must be maintained for the protection of creditors; obtained by multiplying the par value per share times the number of shares issued. (p. 591)

market price The price at which a share of stock can be bought or sold. (p. 592)

no-par stock A share of stock that lacks a par value. (p. 594)

organization costs Costs incurred to organize a corporation, such as state incorporation fees and legal costs. (p. 587)

outstanding shares Shares issued by a firm and held by the stockholders. (p. 594)

paid-in capital The amount of stockholder investments in a corporation. (p. 594)

par-value stock Stock that has an arbitrary fixed amount per share specified in the corporate charter. (p. 591)

preemptive right The right of existing stockholders to maintain their respective interests in a corporation by acquiring additional shares of new stock issues on a pro rata basis. (p. 588)

preferred stock Stock that gives its holders preference over common stockholders in dividend distributions and also asset distributions upon liquidation. (p. 589)

prospectus A document related to new stock issues that is required by the SEC; contains information about the corporation's products, management, and financial affairs. (p. 591)

publicly held corporation A corporation that sells its stock to the general public. (p. 586)

retained earnings The portion of stockholders' equity that has been generated by profitable operations and retained in the business. (p. 594)

return on assets A ratio, computed as follows: (Net Income + Interest Expense) ÷ Average Assets; indicates the effectiveness of resources used in generating profit. (p. 600)

return on common stockholders' equity A ratio, computed as follows: (Net Income − Preferred Dividends) ÷ Average Common Stockholders' Equity; shows the earnings rate on capital provided by the common shareholders. (p. 599)

shares of stock Transferable units of ownership in a corporation. (p. 585)

stated-value stock No-par stock that has a minimum issue price established to allow for protection of the creditors in terms of legal capital. (p. 595)

stock subscriptions Agreements with investors to purchase stock at a given price, with payment taking place on a future date or via installments. (p. 596)

stockholders The owners of a corporation. (p. 586)

stockholders' equity The summation of a corporate entity's capital stock and retained earnings. (p. 594)

trading on the equity The process of securing funds at fixed interest and preferred dividend rates and investing the funds to earn a return greater than their cost; also called leverage. (p. 601)

Chapter Quiz

The five questions that follow relate to several issues raised in the chapter. Test your knowledge of the issues by selecting the best answer. (The answers appear on p. 617.)

1. Which of the following statements is false?
   a. All corporations issue preferred stock.
   b. Stockholders have limited liability.
   c. Corporate earnings are subject to double taxation.
   d. Corporations face heavier governmental regulation than do sole proprietorships.

2. Which of the following rights do not apply to common stockholders?
   a. The right to share in dividends if declared by the board of directors.
   b. The preemptive right.
   c. The right to vote on changes in a corporation's bylaws.
   d. The right to receive dividends that are in arrears.

3. Fenton Corporation is authorized to issue 10,000 shares of $5 par-value common stock. If 60% of these shares are issued at $20, what amount should be credited to the Common Stock account?
   a. $30,000.
   b. $50,000.
   c. $90,000.
   d. $120,000.

4. Equador's balance sheet revealed the following accounts:

Notes payable	$150,000
Preferred stock	100,000
Common stock	200,000
Paid-in capital in excess of par: preferred	10,000
Paid-in capital in excess of par: common	95,000
Retained earnings	400,000

   The total amount invested by stockholders and the total stockholders' equity are:

	INVESTED BY STOCKHOLDERS	TOTAL STOCKHOLDERS' EQUITY
a.	$105,000	$955,000
b.	305,000	805,000
c.	405,000	805,000
d.	555,000	955,000

5. Bright Eyes, Inc., has outstanding 100,000 shares of $5 par-value common stock and 10,000 shares of $100 par-value preferred stock. The preferred stock is cumulative and has a call price of $115 per share. If there are no dividends in arrears and total

stockholders' equity amounts to $4,000,000, what is the book value per share of the common stock?

a. $2.85.
b. $5.00.
c. $28.50.
d. $30.00.

SUMMARY PROBLEM

A review of the accounting records of Paragon Corporation as of December 31, 19X5, found the following information:

Preferred stock, 10% cumulative, $2 par, callable at $9, 60,000 shares authorized, 50,000 shares issued and outstanding	$100,000
Common stock, no-par, $5 stated value, 25,000 shares authorized, 15,000 shares issued and outstanding	75,000
Paid-in capital in excess of par value: preferred	250,000
Paid-in capital in excess of stated value: common	134,000
Retained earnings	380,000

The company has $24,000 of dividends in arrears at year-end.

Instructions

a. Compute Paragon's total legal capital, total paid-in capital, and total stockholders' equity.
b. If all of the preferred stock was sold in a single transaction, what journal entry would have been made? What was the issue price per share?
c. Determine the book value per common share.
d. How would the dividends in arrears be disclosed in Paragon's financial statements?

Solution

a.
Preferred stock, $2 par	$100,000
Common stock, no-par, $5 stated value	75,000
Total legal capital	$175,000

Total legal capital	$175,000
Paid-in capital in excess of par value	250,000
Paid-in capital in excess of stated value	134,000
Total paid-in capital	$559,000

Total paid-in capital	$559,000
Retained earnings	380,000
Total stockholders' equity	$939,000

b.
Cash	350,000	
Preferred Stock		100,000
Paid-in Capital in Excess of Par Value		250,000

To record issuance of 50,000 shares of preferred stock.

The issue price per share of preferred stock was $7 ($350,000 ÷ 50,000 shares).

c.
Total stockholders' equity			$939,000
Allocated to preferred stock			
Call value: 50,000 shares × $9	$450,000		
Dividends in arrears	24,000	474,000	
Allocated to common stock			$465,000

The book value per common share is $31 ($465,000 ÷ 15,000 shares).

d. The dividends in arrears would be disclosed in the notes to the financial statements.

ASSIGNMENT MATERIAL

QUESTIONS

Q16–1 What is a corporation? Discuss the advantages of the corporate form of organization.

Q16–2 Briefly explain the disadvantages of the corporate form of organization.

Q16–3 Discuss the duties and responsibilities of the directors of a corporation. How do directors gain their authority?

Q16–4 Distinguish between authorized stock and outstanding stock.

Q16–5 List the rights typically possessed by common stockholders.

Q16–6 How does cumulative preferred stock differ from noncumulative preferred stock?

Q16–7 What is "callable preferred stock"? Why do corporations issue such stock?

Q16–8 Discuss the meaning of "legal capital."

Q16–9 Why is stock rarely issued below par value?

Q16–10 Discuss the impact of par value in determining the market price of a new stock issue.

Q16–11 Do changes in a stock's market value influence a company's financial position? Briefly discuss.

Q16–12 Discuss the process of selling par-value stock on a subscription basis.

Q16–13 Integrity Machining's common stock has a book value per share of $20. Will the stock's market price be less than, equal to, or greater than $20 per share? Briefly discuss.

Q16–14 If a profitable company is trading on the equity at a loss, will the return on assets be greater than or less than the return on common stockholders' equity?

EXERCISES

E16–1 Stockholders' equity concepts (L.O. 1, 2, 3, 4)
Evaluate the comments that follow as being True or False. If the comment is false, briefly explain why.

a. Corporations are subject to double taxation. Thus, a 40% tax rate on income becomes an effective tax rate of 80% to the corporation.
b. Common stockholders are likely to be rewarded with increases in the market value of their shares as a corporation becomes more profitable.
c. Most preferred stockholders are entitled to receive dividends that are cumulative in nature.
d. Par value virtually always coincides with a stock's original issue price.
e. Par-value stock is generally worth more than no-par stock.

E16–2 Preferred stock dividends (L.O. 3)
Johnson Brothers, Inc., has two classes of stock: $50 par-value, 12% cumulative preferred and $1 par-value common. One thousand shares of preferred and 80,000 shares of common stock have been outstanding since the beginning of 19X3. No dividends were in arrears at the beginning of 19X3.

a. Complete the following table:

Year	Dividends Paid	Dividends in Arrears	Preferred Dividends	Common Dividends
19X3	$4,000	_____	_____	_____
19X4	6,500	_____	_____	_____
19X5	7,500	_____	_____	_____
19X6	9,000	_____	_____	_____

b. Calculate the dividends that would have been paid to the common stockholders in 19X4 and 19X5 if the preferred stock had been noncumulative.

E16–3 Issuance of stock (L.O. 4)

Fresno Company desires to issue 50,000 shares of common stock at $15 per share. Prepare journal entries to record issuances for the three independent cases that follow, assuming that the stock:

a. has a par value of $1 per share.
b. is no-par with a stated value of $10 per share.
c. is no-par and no stated value has been assigned.

E16–4 Issuance of stock; organization costs (L.O. 1, 4)

The Snowbound Corporation was incorporated in July. The firm's charter authorized the sale of 200,000 shares of $10 par-value common stock. The following transactions occurred during the year:

July 1 Sold 45,000 shares of common stock to investors for $18 per share. Cash was collected and the shares were issued.

7 Issued 600 shares to Sharon Dale, attorney-at-law, for services rendered during the corporation's organizational phase. Dale charged $12,600 for her work.

Aug. 11 Sold 20,000 shares to investors for $22 per share. Cash was collected and the shares were issued.

Dec. 14 Issued 30,000 shares to the MJB Company for land valued at $900,000.

Prepare journal entries to record each of the transactions.

E16–5 Reading the stock pages (L.O. 4)

The following information about Norwest Computers was taken from the business pages of a metropolitan newspaper on Wednesday, July 24:

52 Weeks Hi	Lo	Company	Sym	Div	Vol	Hi	Lo	Close	Chg
59	43½	NorwestC	NOC	.20	4463	47	45	46¾	+¾

a. Does the current stock price appear to be somewhat depressed? Briefly explain.
b. What factors might influence a stock's market price?
c. Assume that on July 23, an investor purchased 300 shares of Norwest at the market's closing price. Ignoring broker's commissions, did the investor make money or lose money on July 24? How much?

E16–6 Stock subscriptions (L.O. 4)

Investors subscribed to 8,000 shares of Madden Corporation $2 par-value common stock at $5.50 per share. The firm's year-end balance sheet revealed the following information:

Common stock subscriptions receivable	$10,700
Common stock subscribed	3,000

a. Determine the amount of cash received from subscribers during the year.
b. Have all 8,000 shares been issued? Explain.

E16–7 Analysis of stockholders' equity (L.O. 4, 5)

Star Corporation issued both common and preferred stock during 19X6. The stockholders' equity sections of the company's balance sheets at the end of 19X6 and 19X5 follow.

	19X6	19X5
Preferred stock, $100 par value, 10%	$ 580,000	$ 500,000
Common stock, $10 par value	2,350,000	1,750,000
Paid-in capital in excess of par value		
Preferred	24,000	—
Common	4,620,000	3,600,000
Retained earnings	8,470,000	6,920,000
Total stockholders' equity	$16,044,000	$12,770,000

a. Compute the number of preferred shares that were issued during 19X6.
b. Calculate the average issue price of the common stock sold in 19X6.
c. By what amount did the company's total paid-in capital increase during 19X6?
d. Did Star's total legal capital increase or decrease during 19X6? By what amount?

E16–8 Preparation of stockholders' equity section (L.O. 5)

The following accounts and balances were taken from the adjusted trial balance of Traverse City, Inc.:

Retained earnings	$240,000
Paid-in capital in excess of par value: preferred	40,000
Common stock, $10 par value	500,000
Preferred stock, $100 par value	80,000
Paid-in capital in excess of par value: common	125,000

A review of the corporate charter revealed that the company is authorized to issue 75,000 shares of common stock and 5,000 shares of 12% noncumulative preferred stock.

Prepare the stockholders' equity section of Traverse City, Inc.

E16–9 Preparation of stockholders' equity section (L.O. 4, 5)

The following data relate to Bayview Corporation as of December 31, 19XX, the close of the current accounting period:

- *Preferred stock*—The company has 1,000 shares of $50 par-value cumulative preferred stock authorized. The stock pays a 10% dividend; to date, 400 shares have been issued at $55 per share.
- *Common stock*—A total of 25,000 shares of $1 stated-value common stock is authorized. To date, 10,000 shares have been issued at $10 per share.

Assuming a retained earnings balance of $177,000, prepare the stockholders' equity section of Bayview's December 31, 19XX, balance sheet.

E16–10 Identification of errors (L.O. 1, 4, 5)

Assume that a review of the accounting records of several different corporations disclosed the following:

- *Corporation A*—Expenditures of $34,600 related to corporate start-up and formation were debited to Organization Expense and credited to Cash.
- *Corporation B*—A 1,000-share issuance of $5 par-value preferred stock at $18 per share was recorded in the following manner:

Cash	18,000	
Preferred Stock		5,000
Gain on Stock Issuance		13,000

- *Corporation C*—Cash and Common Stock were respectively debited and credited for the $25,000 proceeds from a 3,000-share issuance of no-par common stock.
- *Corporation D*—The $100,000 proceeds from a 10,000-share issuance of $2 stated-value common stock were recorded as follows:

Cash	100,000	
Stated-Value Stock		100,000

- *Corporation E*—The end-of-period balance sheet had the following captions under stockholders' equity: capital stock, additional paid-in capital, and retained earnings. All three subsections were combined to compute the total paid-in capital for the firm.

Briefly describe any errors that were made by these companies. *Note:* Corrected journal entries and financial statements are not required.

E16–11 Book value per share (L.O. 6)

The Blackford Corporation had the following stockholder's equity for 19X2 and 19X1:

	19X2	19X1
Preferred stock, $100 par, 8% cumulative, callable at $105, 10,000 shares authorized, 3,000 shares outstanding	$ 300,000	$ —
Common stock, $1 par, 1,000,000 shares authorized, 600,000 shares outstanding	600,000	600,000
Additional paid-in capital		
Preferred	30,000	—
Common	14,400,000	14,400,000
Retained earnings	13,809,000	12,000,000
Total stockholders' equity	$29,139,000	$27,000,000

a. Determine Blackford's book value per share for 19X1.
b. Compute Blackford's book value per share of both the preferred and the common stock in 19X2. There are no dividends in arrears.

E16–12 Trading on the equity (L.O. 7)

SensorTech has both preferred and common stock outstanding. The company reported the following information for 19X6:

Interest expense	$ 120,000
Preferred dividends	8,000
Net income	130,000
Average assets	1,100,000
Common stockholders' equity, Jan. 1, 19X6	350,000
Common stockholders' equity, Dec. 31, 19X6	450,000

a. Compute the rates of return on common stockholders' equity and assets, rounding calculations to two decimal places.
b. Does the firm have positive or negative financial leverage? Briefly explain.

PROBLEMS

Series A

P16–A1 Preferred stock dividends (L.O. 2, 3)

Furlow Industries was organized at the beginning of 19X1. Information about the company's stock follows.

Preferred stock
    Class A—$50 par, 8% cumulative, 10,000 shares issued and outstanding
    Class B—$10 par, 10% noncumulative, 6,000 shares issued and outstanding
Common stock—$5 par, 100,000 shares authorized, 80,000 shares issued and outstanding

Class A preferred has preference over class B, and both have preference over common.
    No dividends were distributed in 19X1. Distributions in 19X2, 19X3, and 19X4 amounted to $55,000, $75,000, and $90,000, respectively.

Instructions

a. Would Furlow have any dividends in arrears at the end of 19X1? If "yes," how would such amounts be treated in the financial statements?
b. Determine the dividends distributed in 19X2, 19X3, and 19X4 to class A stockholders, class B stockholders, and common stockholders.
c. Suppose Kenneth Sanchez is considering a purchase of Furlow's stock at the beginning of 19X5, primarily because of the accompanying dividend. What factor(s) should Sanchez consider in deciding whether to acquire class A stock, class B stock, or common stock?

P16–A2 Issuance of stock (L.O. 1, 4, 5)

The bookkeeper of Porter Furniture prepared the stockholders' equity section shown on page 611 for inclusion in the December 31 balance sheet. Both the preferred and common stock issuances occurred on February 2 of the current year and are reflected in the bookkeeper's figures. Unfortunately, two transactions were overlooked:

    Feb. 19   The company issued 500 shares of common stock to its attorney for $7,500 of legal work related to corporate formation.
    Aug. 23   Porter issued 100 shares of preferred stock to the Atlantic Railway in exchange for a parcel of land appraised at $15,000.

Preferred stock, $100 par, 10% cumulative, 2,500 shares authorized, 2,000 shares issued and outstanding	$200,000
Common stock, $5 par, 50,000 shares authorized, 20,000 shares issued and outstanding	100,000
Additional paid-in capital	
Preferred	30,000
Common	160,000
Retained earnings	45,000
Total stockholders' equity	$535,000

Instructions

a. Prepare journal entries to record the transactions of February 2, February 19, and August 23.
b. Prepare the corrected stockholders' equity section of the December 31 balance sheet.
c. Do you see any potential problems for the company if it wishes to have a sizable preferred stock issuance in the not-too-distant future? Briefly explain.

P16–A3 Preparation of stockholders' equity section (L.O. 1, 3, 4, 5)

The following accounts and balances were taken from the accounting records of Rocky Mountain, Inc., as of December 31, 19X6:

Common stock	$1,000,000
Organization costs	35,000
Retained earnings	600,000
Paid-in capital in excess of par value: preferred	50,000
Preferred stock	500,000
Paid-in capital in excess of stated value: common	4,000,000

Additional information:

- The company is authorized to issue 500,000 shares of no-par common stock, which has a $10 stated value assigned by the board of directors. The preferred stock is $100 par value, 8% cumulative, and callable at $112. Fifty thousand shares have been authorized.
- Preferred dividends in arrears on January 1, 19X6, amounted to $20,000. Dividend distributions totaling $45,000 were made throughout the year and are reflected in the preceding figures.
- A recent common stock issuance of 6,000 shares at $45 per share was accidentally omitted from the accounting records.

Instructions

Prepare the company's stockholders' equity section as of December 31, 19X6, along with any appropriate footnotes.

P16–A4 Analysis of stockholders' equity accounts (L.O. 3, 4, 5)

The following selected information relates to the Hastings Corporation at year end:

Preferred stock, ?% cumulative, $7.50 par, 100,000 shares authorized, ? shares issued and outstanding	$ 600,000	
Paid-in capital in excess of par: preferred	?	
Common stock, $? stated value, 700,000 shares authorized, 500,000 shares issued and outstanding	2,500,000	
Paid-in capital in excess of stated value: common	7,500,000	
Loans payable	150,000	
Retained earnings	?	
Total stockholders' equity	12,072,000	
Total legal capital	?	

The preferred stock was issued at an average price per share of $7.90. There were no dividends in arrears on January 1 or December 31. Distributions of $95,000 were made throughout the year, with common stockholders receiving $29,000.

Instructions

Determine the six unknowns of the Hastings Corporation.

P16–A5 Book value per share (L.O. 6)

The stockholders' equity section of Stop and Save, Inc., revealed the following information on January 1, 19X4:

Preferred stock, $100 par value, 9% cumulative, callable at $115	$ 100,000
Common stock, $3 par value	300,000
Paid-in capital in excess of par value: preferred	12,000
Paid-in capital in excess of par value: common	1,200,000
Retained earnings	188,000
Total stockholders' equity	$1,800,000

Dividends in arrears on the preferred stock totaled $18,000 at the beginning of 19X4.

Instructions

a. Calculate the book value per share of both the preferred stock and the common stock on January 1.
b. Calculate the January 1, 19X4, book value per common share assuming that (1) an additional 5,000 preferred shares were issued in a previous year and generated total proceeds of $525,000 and (2) dividends in arrears at the beginning of 19X4 were $72,000.
c. Explain the meaning of book value per share to one of Stop and Save's stockholders. Assume the stockholder has a weak accounting background.

Series B

P16–B1 Preferred stock dividends (L.O. 2, 3)

The information that follows pertains to Hendricks Corporation, which has three types of stock outstanding.

	CLASS A PREFERRED	CLASS B PREFERRED	COMMON
Shares outstanding	5,000	3,000	100,000
Par value	$10	$5	$1
Dividend information			
Fixed rate	4%	10%	
Cumulative?	Yes	No	

Class A preferred has preference over class B, and both have preference over common.

At the end of 19X2, Hendricks had $3,000 of dividends in arrears. Distributions in 19X3, 19X4, and 19X5 totaled $4,300, $3,500, and $5,800, respectively.

Instructions

a. Class A and class B preferred stockholders have a preference over common stockholders in dividend distributions.
   (1) Explain what this comment means.
   (2) Is it possible for common stockholders to receive more dividends than preferred stockholders despite this preference? Briefly explain.
b. Determine the dividends distributed in 19X3, 19X4, and 19X5 to class A stockholders, class B stockholders, and common stockholders.
c. Where would the $3,000 arrearage be disclosed in the 19X2 financial statements?

P16–B2 Issuance of stock (L.O. 1, 4, 5)

Ventures, Inc., was formed on January 1 to invest in artwork. The company is authorized to issue 10,000 shares of $1 par-value common stock and 1,000 shares of 10%, $50 par-value cumulative preferred stock. The following selected transactions occurred during the first quarter of operation:

Jan. 3   Sold 5,000 shares of common stock to the corporation's founders at $30 per share.
     19   Sold 600 shares of preferred stock at $58 per share.
Feb. 4   Issued 100 common shares to an attorney for $3,300 of legal work related to corporate start-up and formation.
     11   Issued 2,000 shares of common stock to Pierre LaTour in exchange for a painting appraised at $75,000.

Instructions

a. Prepare journal entries to record the company's transactions.
b. Prepare the stockholders' equity section of the firm's March 31 balance sheet. The Retained Earnings balance on this date totals $41,000.
c. The president of Ventures believes that organization costs should be expensed immediately. Briefly explain why the president's view is incorrect.

P16–B3 Preparation of stockholders' equity section (L.O. 3, 4, 5)

Treasure City's corporate charter authorized the issuance of 5,000 shares of $100 par, 10% cumulative preferred stock and 100,000 shares of no-par common. The board of directors has assigned a $2-per-share stated value to the common stock. Through December 31 of the current year, the firm has issued 2,000 of the preferred shares, generating $206,000 cash. In addition, common shares were issued as follows:

- Three thousand shares were sold to investors at $30 per share.
- One thousand shares were exchanged for land and buildings having a fair market value of $20,000 and $28,000, respectively.

Dividends on the preferred stock were $22,000 in arrears at the beginning of the current year. Dividend distributions in the past 12 months have amounted to $67,500.

On December 6, Treasure City's finance department learned that one of the initial corporate investors had sold his entire holding of 600 common shares to Vernon Lewis for $54 per share. The investor originally paid $30 per share.

Instructions

Prepare Treasure City's stockholders' equity section as of December 31 of the current year along with any appropriate footnotes. Assume the Retained Earnings balance on this date totals $217,300.

P16–B4   Analysis of stockholders' equity accounts (L.O. 3, 4, 5)

The following accounts appear on the balance sheet of the Graceland Corporation:

Preferred stock, $5 par value	$105,000
Paid-in capital in excess of par value: preferred	189,000
Common stock, $10 par value	270,000
Paid-in capital in excess of par value: common	?
Retained earnings	576,800
Notes payable	59,600

The common stock was issued at an average price of $18 per share. Dividends in arrears on January 1 were distributed to stockholders on March 31.

Instructions

a. How many shares of common stock have been issued?
b. What is the balance in the Paid-in Capital in Excess of Par Value: Common account?
c. What was the average issue price of the preferred stock?
d. Is the preferred stock cumulative or noncumulative? Briefly explain.
e. Compute the total amount of legal capital.
f. Compute the total paid-in capital.
g. Compute the total stockholders' equity.

P16–B5   Book value per share (L.O. 6)

The stockholders' equity section of Travel Resorts, Inc., revealed the following information on January 1, 19XX:

Preferred stock, $100 par value, 10% cumulative, callable at $105	$ 200,000
Common stock, $2 par value	600,000
Paid-in capital in excess of par value: preferred	10,000
Paid-in capital in excess of par value: common	1,400,000
Retained earnings	990,000
Total stockholders' equity	$3,200,000

Dividends in arrears on the preferred stock totaled $20,000 at the beginning of 19XX.

Instructions

a. Calculate the book value per share of both the preferred stock and the common stock on January 1.
b. Calculate the book value per common share assuming that an additional 20,000 shares of common stock were sold to the public at $10.70 per share.
c. Does book value per share indicate the amount that stockholders would receive if a corporation sold its assets, paid its bills, and liquidated? Explain.

EXPANDING YOUR HORIZONS

EYH16–1   Organizing a corporation (L.O. 1)

In the next 10 to 15 years, a number of students in your class will decide to start a business. Many of these ventures will be organized as corporations.

Instructions

Form a team with three other students to investigate the procedures necessary to begin a corporation. Obtain information from your library, an attorney, and your state government.

a. Prepare a flowchart of the steps involved and a budget of the related costs.
b. Briefly describe your team's experiences when interacting with the state government. Could the government be more service-oriented? Explain.

EYH16–2   Stock price movements (L.O. 4)

Many corporations on the New York Stock Exchange (NYSE) have issued common stock and at least one class of preferred stock. Both types of shares are listed in *The Wall Street Journal* when traded, with the preferred shares labeled as "pf."

Instructions

Using a recent issue of *The Wall Street Journal* or other financial newspaper, find five NYSE companies that have both common stock and preferred stock. For each, determine (1) the percentage change from the stock's low price to the stock's high price over the past 52 weeks and (2) which type of stock has greater price movement. Based on a comparison of the current market price to the prices over the past year, assess whether investors in general appear optimistic or pessimistic about the corporation's prospects. Prepare a short report of your findings.

EYH16–3   Initial public offerings (L.O. 4)

The investors in initial public offerings (IPOs) of common stock occasionally see their shares rise rapidly in a very short period of time. It is not unheard of to sell shares within a few days (and sometimes hours) of purchase and make a handsome profit. Other investors in IPOs are not as fortunate, as many end up with sizable losses.

Instructions

Visit a local stockbroker and obtain prospectuses for two companies that had recent initial public offerings. Review the prospectuses and determine the reasons behind the IPOs, what the companies plan to do with the funds received, and the initial prices of the stock. Next, look in a recent issue of *The Wall Street Journal* or other source of stock prices and find the current market price of the shares. Calculate the percentage rise or fall in share prices since the IPO. Be prepared to report your findings to the class.

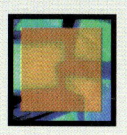

EYH16–4   Understanding corporate equity: MCI Communications Corporation and Capital Cities/ABC, Inc. (L.O. 1, 5)

MCI is a global leader in telecommunications services. Capital Cities, in contrast, is actively involved with broadcasting (through its ABC television and radio networks) and the publishing of newspapers and magazines.

Instructions

By using the text's electronic data base, access the balance sheets and accompanying notes of both firms and answer the questions that follow. Unless otherwise indicated, responses should be based on data for the most recent year presented.

a. Review the balance sheets and determine:
   (1) The total par value of any preferred stock issuances.
   (2) The par value of a share of common stock.
   (3) The number of common shares issued as of the balance sheet date.
b. Locate information in the financial statement notes of Capital Cities relative to ABC issuances of common stock.
   (1) Determine the swing in market value (from low to high) of a share of common stock during the year. What are some general factors that may have caused this swing?
   (2) How many stockholders does the company have?

c. Many corporations have established stock option programs as a fringe benefit for certain personnel. Employees may exercise their options to purchase shares of stock in the firm or the options may lapse (i.e., expire) without being exercised.

Locate each company's disclosure in the financial statement notes, and review the options exercised versus the options lapsed for the three years presented. Have there been any interesting "changes in attitude" over this period for employees of either corporation? If "yes," briefly discuss and include possible reasons for the change.

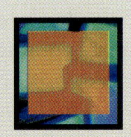

EYH16–5 Understanding corporate equity (L.O. 1, 5)

This problem is a duplication of Problem EYH16–4. It is based on two companies selected by your instructor.

Instructions

By using the text's electronic data base, access the specified companies' balance sheets and accompanying notes and focus on data for the most recent year reported. Answer requirements (a)–(c) of Problem EYH16–4.

EYH16–6 Financing alternatives (L.O. 2, 3)

Jim Seagram is the manager of a local sporting goods store. Recently, during some spare time, he invented a device called SWEAT EQUITY, which allows users to burn off calories very rapidly. Jim has approached Professor Morrales at the local university for assistance in developing a plan to license the device to a large equipment company. Morrales believes that $200,000 of capital will be needed for prototypes, presentation materials, and travel costs. Morrales is excited about the project and is willing to invest $5,000 for a share of the company. Because Seagram can invest only $15,000, considerable outside funding is necessary.

There are three options open to Jim to finance the venture. First, he could incorporate, issue common stock to Morrales and himself, and try to sell the remaining shares to the general public. Second, Jim could incorporate, issue common stock to Morrales and himself, and try to sell 14% cumulative preferred stock to outside investors. Third, he could incorporate, issue common stock to Morrales and himself, and attempt to sell 10% convertible preferred stock to outside investors.

Instructions

a. Discuss several advantages and disadvantages of each of the three alternatives.
b. From a control perspective, which of the three alternatives would Jim find least desirable? Why?
c. If SWEAT EQUITY turned out to be a tremendous success, which alternative would most likely be in Jim's best interests? Explain your answer.

COMMUNICATION OF ACCOUNTING INFORMATION

CAI16–1 Visual aid preparation: American Brands, Inc. (L.O. 2, 3, 4)

Communication Principle: Most modern business presentations include slides or overhead transparencies. These visual aids help gain the listener's attention, provide a sense of organization, and emphasize major points. Further, visual aids accompanied by handouts increase the likelihood that important points will be remembered.

The preparation of visual aids for an oral presentation is a special communication challenge. Every word should count and there should be very few of them. Handouts may simply be copies of the transparencies, unless more detailed written material is needed.

Here are some principles of good visual aids:

1. Keep visuals simple and short. Never crowd a transparency with too much information or too many words. A definition may be put in the form of an equation, for instance. Use phrases instead of sentences, and words instead of phrases wherever possible.
2. Include a list of no more than five major points, all of them brief and about the same length and importance.
3. Use legible, large type—much larger than normal word processing. Do not create transparencies freehand. Nothing looks more unprofessional than sloppy, handmade transparencies.
4. Check spelling and math very carefully. These errors are glaring when enlarged and copied; they are very embarrassing.
5. Use color and different type styles for emphasis.
6. "Show" with exhibits, pictures, graphs, pie charts, and brief tables, instead of trying to "tell" exclusively in words.
7. Use a few good visual aids that support major points instead of many that support every point. Audiences groan when they see a hefty stack of transparencies or a full tray of slides.

■ ■ ■ ■ ■ ■ ■ ■ ■

American Brands, Inc., is a highly diversified corporation, engaged in businesses that range in scope from tobacco production to life insurance. In addition, the company manufactures such recognizable goods as Master locks and Titleist golf balls, among others. The firm's balance sheet is rather involved, including a variety of stockholders' equity components. Among these are redeemable (callable) preferred stock of $17.1 million. The stock is without par value but has been assigned a $30.50 stated value. Further examination of the company's annual report indicates that holders of these shares are entitled to a $2.67 cumulative dividend. In addition, the holders have preference over common stockholders in the event of asset liquidation.

Instructions

You are employed in the company's public relations department. In an effort to address various questions that may arise at an upcoming meeting of the corporation's board of directors, management has asked you to prepare appropriate overhead transparency masters for a presentation. The transparency masters should briefly illustrate the nature of the callable preferred stock issue and disclose the following:

- The reason stock "without par value" has been assigned a stated value.
- The approximate number of shares in the hands of stockholders.
- The nature of a cumulative dividend.
- The preference feature should liquidation occur.

Answers to Chapter Quiz

1. a
2. d
3. a (6,000 shares × $5 per share)
4. c (Invested by stockholders: $100,000 + $200,000 + $10,000 + $95,000 = $405,000; Total stockholders' equity: $405,000 + $400,000 = $805,000)
5. c (10,000 shares × $115 = $1,150,000; $4,000,000 − $1,150,000 = $2,850,000; $2,850,000 ÷ 100,000 shares = $28.50)

17 CORPORATIONS: ADDITIONAL EQUITY ISSUES AND INCOME REPORTING

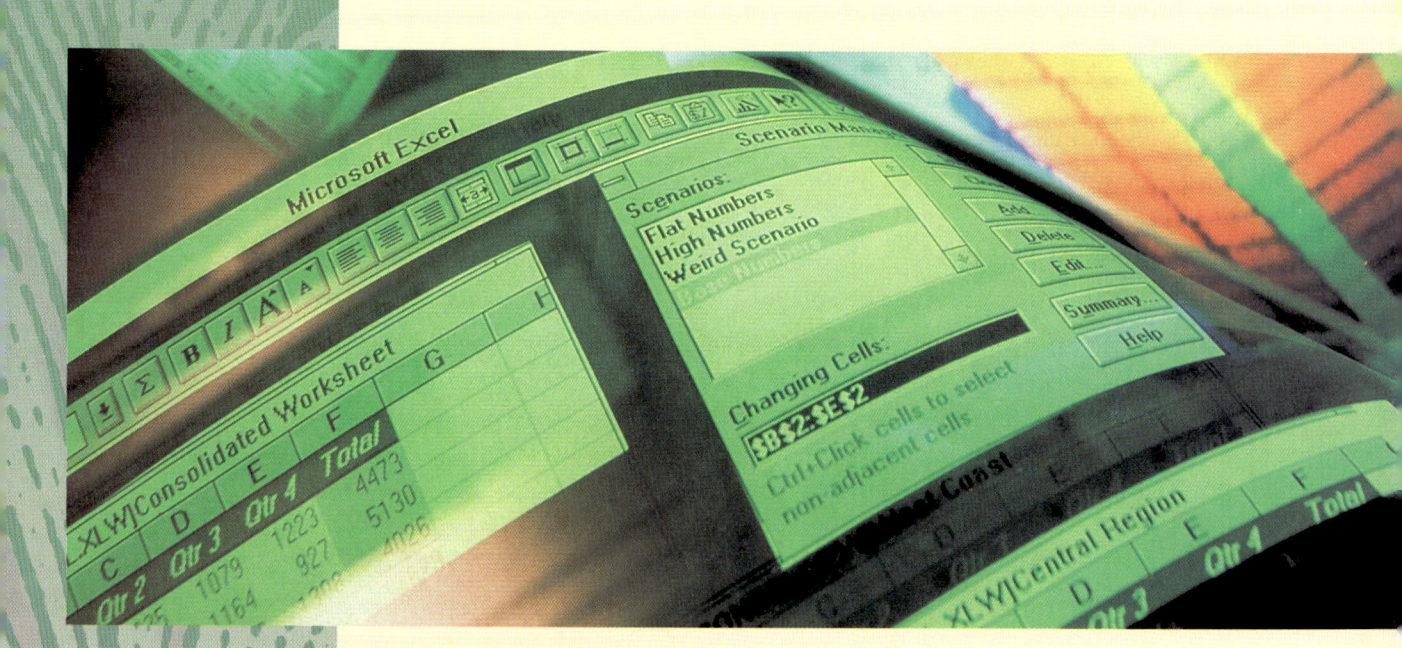

LEARNING OBJECTIVES

After studying this chapter, you should be able to:

1. Define treasury stock and account for its acquisition and reissuance.
2. Account for cash dividends, stock dividends, and stock splits and evaluate a company's dividend policy.
3. Explain the proper treatment of prior period adjustments and restrictions that may be imposed on retained earnings.
4. Apply the disclosure rules for discontinued operations, extraordinary items, accounting changes, and intraperiod tax allocation.
5. Explain the meaning of and compute earnings per share.

George Faris has both time and capital invested in Banner Advertising, Inc. During the company's early years he took only a minimal salary, and dividend distributions were the furthest thing from his mind. The firm's cash position was extremely tight, with the balances on hand being totally consumed by the payment of daily expenses.

The future often brings change, however. Banner matured and has become a very profitable entity. George recalled, "When I first started the business, I was so busy trying to survive that I never gave much thought to what we would do with profits. One day, I just looked up and realized that the company was bringing in enough money to allow distributions." Banner's history is not unlike the story that can be told for many corporations. At first a business struggles and then it grows. During this time the organization will make investments in plant and equipment; later, management will likely retire any related debt. The corporation is eventually able to reward its shareholders with dividends.

Although there are several types of dividends, Banner's distributions have always been in the form of cash. Before authorizing the payouts, George reviews ongoing profitability, relying heavily on the income statement prepared by Banner's accountant. "Unless we can be assured of continued growth, I'm totally in favor of plowing earnings back into the business," he has said time and time again.

This chapter continues our discussion of the corporate form of business organization, including the dividend and income reporting issues alluded to by George Faris. However, the presentation goes much deeper, especially from a practical perspective. Much of the material about to be discussed is particularly important to present and potential investors—some of the key users of financial statements. Newspapers, for example, regularly publish articles with headlines similar to the following:

- General United's Earnings per Share Falls 15%
- Largent Corporation Has 3-for-2 Stock Split
- Garrett, Inc., Declares 10% Stock Dividend

The investing public must have a fundamental understanding of these events to correctly determine the impact on both corporate financial affairs and, more important, investment holdings. Although your present financial position may not permit "wheeling and dealing" in the stock market, your future earnings will likely increase. Our goal is to provide you with an introduction to a variety of topics so that some analysis of corporate equity and profitability is possible.

TREASURY STOCK

> **1**
> Define treasury stock and account for its acquisition and reissuance.

Corporations frequently find it advantageous to reacquire shares of their own stock. These shares, which are commonly reissued at a later date, are termed *treasury stock.* Treasury stock is purchased for a variety of reasons. Some corporations have reacquired their own shares for use in company retirement and employee stock purchase programs. Other firms have purchased treasury stock to rid themselves of a particular stockholder or group of stockholders. For instance, large corporate entities sometimes purchase the interests of very small investors (e.g., those owning 10 shares or less) to save the costs of mailing annual reports, processing minute dividend checks, and so forth.[1] Treasury stock is also acquired for use in future acquisitions of other companies and to guard against hostile takeovers by other firms. Finally, some businesses have secured treasury holdings in an attempt to boost the *earnings per share of common stock*—a measure widely used to judge the operating success of an entity.

Whatever the purpose, the acquisition of treasury stock is commonplace. A review of recent annual reports disclosed the treasury stock holdings that appear in Exhibit 17–1.

Corporate action to purchase treasury stock reduces the number of shares outstanding; however, the number of shares issued is unaffected. Issued shares can be reduced only if they are formally retired and canceled by the corporation. Because treasury stock is no longer outstanding, it is not entitled to voting privileges nor to any cash dividends declared by the board of directors.

ACQUISITIONS OF TREASURY STOCK

The most common treatment for treasury stock acquisitions requires a debit to a Treasury Stock account. Thus, if Hunt Corporation purchased 5,000 shares of its $10 par-value common stock at $70 per share, the journal entry would be as follows:

Treasury Stock	350,000	
Cash		350,000
To record the purchase of 5,000 shares of treasury stock at $70 per share.		

EXHIBIT 17–1
Treasury Stock Holdings

CORPORATION	NUMBER OF TREASURY SHARES	PERCENTAGE OF TOTAL SHARES ISSUED	ACQUISITION COST OF TREASURY SHARES
Alberto Culver	6,526,610	19.1%	$ 49,660,000
Kellogg Company	82,372,409	26.5	1,653,100,000
H.J. Heinz	38,359,744	13.3	1,239,177,000
The Gillette Company	57,697,990	20.7	1,047,100,000
Lotus Development	17,224,000	27.7	248,728,000

Note: All citations refer to common stock only.

---

[1] Kmart extended such an offer not too long ago, using 100 shares as the cutoff point. Approximately 13,200 stockholders took advantage of the proposal, and the discounter was able to buy back 366,285 shares.

Treasury stock is *not* regarded as an asset, since a corporation cannot own part of itself. The acquisition of treasury stock really involves a reduction in stockholders' equity because funds are being returned to the selling stockholders. To illustrate, assume Hunt had authorization to issue 15,000 shares of $10 par-value common stock. Further, assume that all of the shares were issued at $90 per share (for a total of $1,350,000) and that retained earnings amounts to $440,000. After the acquisition of the 5,000 treasury shares, the firm's stockholders' equity section would appear as follows:

STOCKHOLDERS' EQUITY

Common stock, $10 par value, 15,000 shares authorized and issued, 10,000 shares outstanding	$ 150,000
Paid-in capital in excess of par value	1,200,000
Total paid-in capital	$1,350,000
Retained earnings	440,000
	$1,790,000
Deduct: Treasury stock (5,000 shares) at cost	350,000
Total stockholders' equity	$1,440,000

Observe that the Common Stock and Paid-in Capital in Excess of Par Value accounts are not reduced by the treasury stock purchase. However, the cost of the 5,000 shares is deducted later in the stockholders' equity section. Finally, note that the number of shares issued and the number outstanding now differ because of the shares held "in the treasury."

REISSUANCE OF TREASURY STOCK

At the time of reissuance, the Treasury Stock account is credited for the acquisition cost of the reissued shares. If the reissue price exceeds the acquisition cost, the difference is recorded as additional paid-in capital. For example, assume Hunt now sells 1,000 of the treasury shares for $79 per share. The necessary journal entry follows.

Cash	79,000	
Treasury Stock		70,000
Paid-in Capital from Treasury Stock		9,000
To record sale of 1,000 shares of treasury stock at $79 per share.		

The $70,000 credit to the Treasury Stock account is based on Hunt's original $70-per-share outlay. It is important to note that the $9,000 excess over cost is not a gain to be reported on the income statement. As shown throughout the text, gains and losses arise from the sale of goods and services and from other earnings activities. Conversely, transactions that involve the issuance (or reissuance) of capital stock are equity transactions and affect paid-in capital. In

Hunt's case, investors were willing to pay $79,000 for shares that had an original acquisition cost of $70,000; thus, paid-in capital must increase by $9,000. The increase is recorded in a separate account entitled Paid-in Capital from Treasury Stock.

The stockholders' equity section immediately after the reissuance would appear as follows:

STOCKHOLDERS' EQUITY
Capital stock
  Common stock, $10 par value, 15,000 shares
    authorized and issued, 11,000 shares outstanding $ 150,000
Additional paid-in capital
  Paid-in capital in excess of par value $1,200,000
  Paid-in capital from treasury stock   9,000   1,209,000
    Total paid-in capital $1,359,000
Retained earnings   440,000
                                                               $1,799,000
Deduct: Treasury stock (4,000 shares) at cost   280,000
    Total stockholders' equity $1,519,000

Total equity has increased by $79,000 ($1,519,000 versus $1,440,000), reflecting the amount of funds generated from the treasury stock sale.

Reissuance Below Cost. Treasury shares can also be reissued at or below cost. We will now illustrate the latter case because of the complexities involved. Just as reissuance above cost gave rise to additional paid-in capital, reissuance below cost calls for a reduction of paid-in capital. For example, assume Hunt sells an additional 2,000 treasury shares. This time, however, the selling price is only $66 per share. The journal entry to record the sale is:

    Cash   132,000
    Paid-in Capital from Treasury Stock   8,000
      Treasury Stock   140,000
    To record sale of 2,000 shares of treasury stock
    at $66 per share.

As before, Treasury Stock is credited for the cost of the reissued shares, in this case $140,000 (2,000 shares × $70). Because the sale has generated proceeds of only $132,000, paid-in capital must be decreased by $8,000 ($140,000 − $132,000). In effect, the reduction is a cancellation of paid-in capital from earlier treasury stock sales, thereby requiring a debit to the Paid-in Capital from Treasury Stock account for $8,000.

If this account's balance is insufficient to absorb the entire (or any of the) reduction, the remaining debit is entered in the Retained Earnings account. To illustrate, if the 2,000 shares were sold for $128,000, paid-in capital should be reduced by $12,000 ($140,000 − $128,000). As shown in the stockholders' equity section on page 623, however, Paid-in Capital from Treasury Stock has a balance of only $9,000. Consequently, the required journal entry would debit this account for $9,000 and charge the remaining $3,000 against Retained Earnings.

RETAINED EARNINGS

> **2**
> Account for cash dividends, stock dividends, and stock splits and evaluate a company's dividend policy.

We now turn our attention to the last major element of stockholders' equity: retained earnings. As defined in Chapter 16, **retained earnings** represents the portion of stockholders' equity that has been generated by profitable operations and kept in the business. At the conclusion of the reporting period, a corporation's net income is transferred to the Retained Earnings account as part of the closing process. More specifically, the following journal entry is needed (amount is assumed):

Income Summary	150,000	
Retained Earnings		150,000
To close net income to Retained Earnings.		

Because of this treatment, the Retained Earnings account will normally possess a credit balance. On occasion, though, a debit ("negative") balance may arise, which is commonly referred to as a **deficit.** Deficits are usually caused when firms operate at a loss for a number of years or have a sizable loss in one period that wipes out years of profitability.

DIVIDENDS

A number of items affect the retained earnings balance throughout the year, including dividends. **Dividends** represent a distribution of corporate earnings to stockholders and may be in the form of cash, assets other than cash, or additional shares of stock.

Most investors are aware of the the three important dates connected with dividend distributions:

1. **Date of declaration**—All dividends must be declared (approved) by the board of directors. The declaration date is the date when the dividend is formally approved and the corporation becomes legally liable for payment.
2. **Date of record**—The stockholders of a corporate entity change daily as investors buy and sell shares in the marketplace. To determine who will receive a dividend, the corporation establishes a record date. All stockholders as of the date of record are entitled to the declared amount even if they dispose of their holdings prior to the dividend's distribution. As a result, stock sold between the record date and the date of distribution is sold without the current dividend rights attached, that is, *ex-dividend*. The record date follows the date of declaration by a few weeks, thereby allowing any stock transactions that may be in process to be completed.
3. **Date of payment**—As specified in the dividend declaration, the date of payment is the date when the dividend will be issued to the stockholders. Generally, the date of payment is several weeks after the record date.

Cash Dividends. Most dividends are paid in cash. To distribute a cash dividend, companies must satisfy two conditions. First, an entity must have an adequate cash balance. A lack of funds or an extremely tight cash position can force a corporation's board of directors to reduce or omit a payout. Such distribution decisions must be made with great care because dividends are often a key element in an investor's expected return from holding stock. The market price of stock has been known to drop dramatically when a dividend declaration was less than anticipated.

The second condition for a dividend is an adequate balance in the Retained Earnings account. Given that dividends are distributions of earnings, total corporate profits must be sufficient to *support* amounts given to stockholders. Remember, though, that dividends are *paid* not with earnings, but with cash.

To illustrate the necessary accounting for cash dividends, assume Dale Corporation has 100,000 shares of common stock outstanding. On July 15, the board of directors declared a $0.25 quarterly dividend to stockholders of record on August 7. The dividend will be distributed on September 1. The proper journal entries follow.

July 15	Retained Earnings	25,000	
	Dividends Payable		25,000
	To record declaration of cash dividend of $0.25 per share.		
Aug. 7	No entry required		
Sept. 1	Dividends Payable	25,000	
	Cash		25,000
	To record payment of dividend declared on July 15.		

Observe that the cash dividend is based on the number of shares outstanding. If Dale had originally issued 100,000 shares and then reacquired 10,000 as treasury stock, the board of directors would have declared a quarterly dividend of $22,500 (90,000 shares × $0.25). Should a balance sheet be prepared after the date of declaration but prior to the date of payment, Dividends Payable would be disclosed as a current liability.

Stock Dividends. Many corporations distribute additional shares of their own stock as dividends. The distribution, referred to as a stock dividend, most frequently involves the issuance of common shares to existing common stockholders. Additional shares are issued in proportion to stockholders' present ownership in the firm. For example, suppose Ellen Bagley owns 20,000 shares of a cosmetics company that she founded several years ago. Assuming a total of 100,000 shares are outstanding, Bagley has a 20% ownership interest. If the board of directors declares a 10% stock dividend, an additional 10,000 shares (100,000 shares × 0.10) will be issued. Bagley is entitled to 20% of the distribution, which results in the following figures:

	BEFORE STOCK DIVIDEND	10% STOCK DIVIDEND	AFTER STOCK DIVIDEND
Total shares	100,000	10,000	110,000
Ellen Bagley's shares	20,000	2,000	22,000
Ownership interest	20%	20%	20%

As you can see, a stockholder's percentage ownership remains the same. Furthermore, the corporation's assets and liabilities are unaffected because they are not involved in the distribution. Why, then, are stock dividends issued and what is the effect, if any, on corporate equity? The answers to these questions become apparent in the following sections.

Reasons for Issuing Stock Dividends. Several reasons have been advanced for the issuance of stock dividends. First, stock dividends enable a corporation to make a distribution to shareholders while, at the same time, conserving cash. The cash can then be invested in expanding operations, new projects, and other similar undertakings.

Second, stock dividends result in a nontaxable distribution to the stockholder. Cash dividends are taxable when received. Stock dividends, on the other hand, are not income and therefore no taxes are involved. Income taxes are often assessed, however, when and if the shares are sold.

Finally, stock dividends are said to improve a stock's attractiveness. An increased number of shares outstanding will often reduce the per-share market price, making the stock more affordable for the small investor with limited funds.

Accounting for Stock Dividends. The accounting treatment for stock dividends depends on the size of the distribution. Most stock dividends are small, involving issuances of less than 20%–25% of the existing shares outstanding. For small stock dividends the accounting profession recommends a reduction in retained earnings equal to the market value of the additional shares to be issued. Market value is used because stockholders view the dividend's "true worth" as being equivalent to the fair market value of the shares received.

As an example of the proper accounting, assume Mastercraft Corporation had the following stockholders' equity section on June 1:

STOCKHOLDERS' EQUITY	
Common stock, $20 par value, 800,000 shares authorized, 300,000 shares issued and outstanding	$ 6,000,000
Paid-in capital in excess of par value	1,000,000
Retained earnings	12,000,000
Total stockholders' equity	$19,000,000

On June 15, the board of directors declared a 10% stock dividend that will be distributed on July 15. The closing market price of Mastercraft's common stock on June 15 was $33 per share, giving rise to the following journal entry:

June 15	Retained Earnings	990,000	
	Stock Dividend Distributable		600,000
	Paid-in Capital in Excess of Par Value		390,000
	To record declaration of 10% stock dividend.		

The declaration involves the future issuance of 30,000 shares (300,000 shares × 0.10); thus, Retained Earnings must be debited for $990,000 (30,000 shares × $33). Next, an account entitled Stock Dividend Distributable is established for the par value of the dividend (30,000 shares × $20 = $600,000). This account is *not* a liability because Mastercraft has no obligation to distribute cash or any other asset. If a balance sheet is prepared between the declaration date and ultimate distribution of the shares, Stock Dividend Distributable would be presented in the stockholders' equity section as an addition to (i.e., a separate component of) the Common Stock account. Finally, consistent with the material presented in Chapter 16, the difference between the "issue price" ($990,000) and par value ($600,000) is credited to Paid-in Capital in Excess of Par Value.

The following entry is made on July 15 to record issuance of the common shares:

July 15	Stock Dividend Distributable	600,000	
	Common Stock		600,000
	To record issuance of stock dividend of 30,000 shares.		

Stock Dividends and Corporate Equity. The net effect of the stock dividend is to transfer $990,000 of retained earnings to Common Stock and other paid-in capital accounts. The accompanying schedule, constructed from the entries on June 15 and July 15, shows that total stockholders' equity remains unchanged.

ACCOUNT	BEFORE STOCK DIVIDEND	DECLARATION AND ISSUANCE*	AFTER STOCK DIVIDEND
Common stock	$ 6,000,000	$ +600,000 (I)	$ 6,600,000
Paid-in capital in excess of par value	1,000,000	+390,000 (D)	1,390,000
Stock dividend distributable	—	+600,000 (D) −600,000 (I)	—
Retained earnings	12,000,000	−990,000 (D)	11,010,000
	$19,000,000	$ —	$19,000,000

* D = declaration on June 15; I = issuance on July 15.

Overall, a stock dividend is merely a shifting of amounts within the stockholders' equity section. The end result is that (1) $990,000 of retained earnings is no longer available for future dividend distributions and (2) additional shares of common stock are outstanding.

Stock Splits. As noted earlier, stock dividends reduce the market price per share. Given that most stock dividends are fairly small, it is possible that other market influences could obscure (and possibly offset) the impact of the distribution. Corporations that strive for a significant reduction in market price to improve the affordability and marketability of their shares often do so by means of a stock split.

A stock split involves increasing the number of shares outstanding and, at the same time, decreasing the stock's par or stated value. For example, assume that a corporation has 200,000 shares of $10 par-value stock outstanding, and each share is currently selling for $80. The company wants to drop the market price and, accordingly, the board of directors approves a 4-for-1 stock split. This action reduces the par value from $10 to $2.50 ($10 ÷ 4) and raises the number of outstanding shares to 800,000 (200,000 × 4). Total corporate equity thus remains unchanged.

The board's action should proportionately decrease the per-share market price from $80 to $20. Similar to what happened with total corporate equity, this movement has no effect on an existing stockholder's overall financial well-being. An investor who owned, say, 200 shares prior to the split saw the total value of his or her holdings remain at $16,000: (200 shares × $80) versus (800 shares × $20). The investor's position is improved only if the market price of the stock later increases.

Because a stock split does not change the balance in any of the corporation's accounts, no formal journal entry is required. However, a memorandum should be recorded in the journal to note that a stock split has occurred. The memorandum should reveal that (1) the number of shares issued and outstanding has increased and (2) the par or stated value per share has been reduced.

Dividend Policy and Evaluation. Dividend distributions and policies vary significantly from company to company. Many corporations pay no dividends or severely restrict distributions. These firms are often referred to as *growth companies* because they continually reinvest profits in expansionary projects to achieve even greater income levels. Stockholders in these entities expect to realize a return on their investment by, over time, selling their shares at a substantial gain. In contrast, other corporations have sizable distributions. Utilities and companies in stable, mature industries tend to fall in this category.

Investors will typically select a mixture of firms in an effort to maintain a well-balanced stock portfolio. Investments in utilities will provide current cash income, whereas entities engaged in high-tech electronics and scientific research (two rapidly changing fields) often produce attractive long-term rises in share value. It is difficult to find a given stock that will accomplish both of these objectives in an optimum fashion.

To get a better grasp of a corporation's dividend policy, investors often review two ratios. The dividend payout ratio is used to study the percentage of earnings distributed to stockholders. The necessary computations involve dividing the annual cash dividend per share by the earnings per share.[2] A related ratio, the dividend yield, is the annual cash dividend per share divided by the stock's current market price. This measure furnishes insight about the short-term rate of return (from dividends) on invested funds.

OTHER ITEMS THAT AFFECT RETAINED EARNINGS

Although our presentation has concentrated on dividends, other items affect retained earnings as well. We noted earlier in the chapter, for example, that the reissuance of treasury stock at a price below cost may give rise to a reduction in retained earnings. Retained earnings are also influenced by prior period adjustments and restrictions.

---

[2] Earnings per share is discussed later in this chapter.

A FURTHER FOCUS

The dividends distributed to stockholders are dependent on the investment alternatives open to the entity. As noted, growth companies pay no (or few) dividends whereas those firms in mature industries have larger distributions. Recent payout ratios of various corporations appear in the chart that follows.

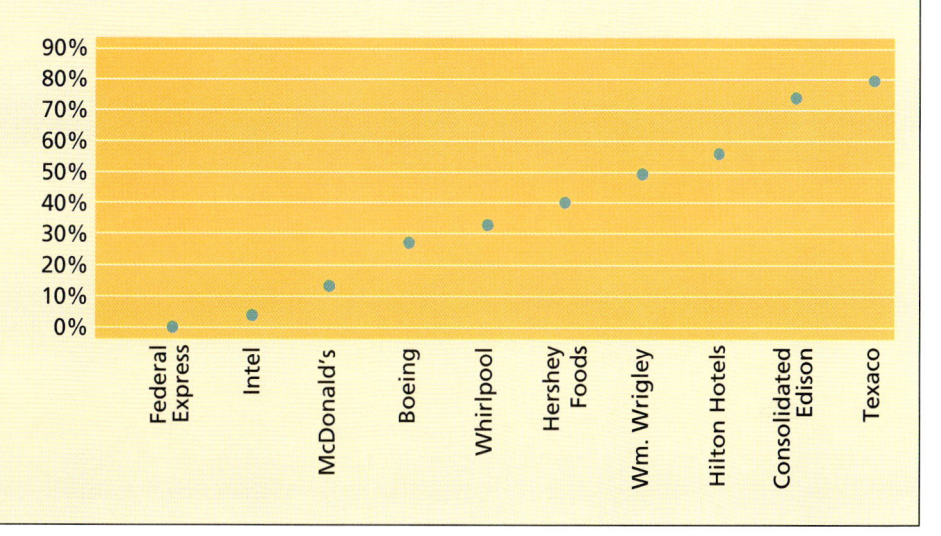

(Chart showing payout ratios: Federal Express ~0%, Intel ~3%, McDonald's ~13%, Boeing ~27%, Whirlpool ~33%, Hershey Foods ~40%, Wm. Wrigley ~50%, Hilton Hotels ~56%, Consolidated Edison ~73%, Texaco ~80%)

---

③ Explain the proper treatment of prior period adjustments and restrictions that may be imposed on retained earnings.

Prior Period Adjustments. Accountants, like other professionals, are not perfect. Even with a strong system of internal control, significant errors sometimes enter the financial records. Most are detected soon after occurrence; some, however, may go unnoticed for several years. Examples of such errors include mathematical mistakes, oversights, and the use of unacceptable principles and methods.

Errors that affect the net income of previous periods are corrected by the use of **prior period adjustments.** To illustrate the proper accounting treatment, assume Mercer Corporation overlooked several pieces of equipment in 19X1 and thereby understated depreciation expense by $10,000. If the error is not discovered until a subsequent reporting period, say, 19X2, the prior period adjustment to correct the records would be as follows:

Retained Earnings	10,000	
Accumulated Depreciation: Equipment		10,000
To correct the 19X1 understatement of depreciation expense.		

Correcting 19X1 depreciation expense directly is not possible because the year's revenue and expense accounts have been closed. The understated expense overstated net income, which in turn overstated the balance in the Retained Earnings account at the end of the period. Retained Earnings is therefore debited to record the necessary reduction.

Prior period adjustments are reported as an adjustment to the beginning retained earnings balance in the year that the correction is made—19X2 in Mercer's case. The adjustment is shown on a net-of-tax basis and is disclosed on the statement of retained earnings. (Both net-of-tax reporting and the appropriate method of disclosure will be discussed shortly.)

Restrictions on Retained Earnings. Corporate business dealings sometimes restrict the amount of retained earnings available for dividend distributions. Some of these restrictions arise from provisions that are contained in debt agreements—provisions that help protect the lender until the debt is settled. In other cases state law may be a factor, as many states require restrictions on retained earnings equal to the cost of any treasury stock held by the entity. Still other restrictions may be self-imposed. For example, the board of directors may change a company's dividend policy because of needed plant expansion or a probable loss of assets from an impending lawsuit.

Although several different methods are available to handle such restrictions, the most popular approach is to use a note to the financial statements. A typical disclosure would appear as follows:

Note 11: Retained earnings restrictions

The Company has a retained earnings balance of $356 million as of December 31, 19X6. Under the most restrictive terms of existing borrowing agreements, amounts free for use in dividend distributions total $125.9 million at the end of the current year.

REPORTING CHANGES IN RETAINED EARNINGS

Changes in the Retained Earnings account are often disclosed on a separate financial report known as the *statement of retained earnings.* A representative example appears in Exhibit 17–2.

Several other options are available to corporations to report this information. For instance, some companies construct a combined statement of income and retained earnings, thereby doing away with a separately prepared income

EXHIBIT 17–2
Statement of Retained Earnings

DONLEY CORPORATION
Statement of Retained Earnings
For the Year Ended December 31, 19X2

Retained earnings, 12/31/X1 (as reported)		$ 80,000
Less: Correction of prior period inventory error (net of $6,000 tax)		9,000
Retained earnings, 12/31/X1 (restated)		$ 71,000
Add: Net income		100,000
		$171,000
Less: Cash dividends on preferred stock	$15,000	
Stock dividends on common stock	45,000	60,000
Retained earnings, 12/31/X2		$111,000

statement. Yet another approach, and one that appears to be gaining in popularity, is the use of a comprehensive statement of stockholders' equity. This report discloses changes that occurred during the period in each of the stockholders' equity components (including retained earnings). The statement reveals beginning balances and summarizes the transactions and events that affected the various accounts. Ending account balances are reported, and these amounts correspond to the amounts presented on the balance sheet.

Exhibit 17–3 contains a statement of stockholders' equity for Donley Corporation. All numbers in this illustration are assumed except for those in the Retained Earnings column. Careful examination of this shaded column will indicate that the data reported are identical to those shown in the "stand-alone" statement in Exhibit 17–2.

CORPORATE INCOME REPORTING

Investors are extremely interested in the periodic net income earned by corporations. Net income provides the basis for dividend distributions and greatly influences the market price of a corporation's common stock. Because of these factors, the income statement must provide adequate disclosure of earnings activities and be constructed in a format that is informative for investors and other users.

To achieve these goals, the accounting profession has stipulated that ordinary business income should be segregated from income caused by unusual and uncommon transactions and events. Why? Imagine the difficulty in evaluating corporate earnings if ordinary business transactions—such as buying and selling merchandise, renting equipment, and paying wages—were mixed together with the results of major catastrophes and other nonrecurring events. A high or

EXHIBIT 17–3
Statement of Stockholders' Equity

DONLEY CORPORATION
Statement of Stockholders' Equity
For the Year Ended December 31, 19X2

	PREFERRED STOCK, $10 PAR VALUE	COMMON STOCK, $5 PAR VALUE	PAID-IN CAPITAL IN EXCESS OF PAR VALUE	RETAINED EARNINGS	TREASURY STOCK	TOTAL
Balance, 12/31/X1	$150,000	$50,000	$110,000	$ 80,000	$(16,000)	$374,000
Prior period adjustment (net of $6,000 tax)				(9,000)		(9,000)
Issued 5,000 shares of common at $30		25,000	125,000			150,000
Purchased 2,000 shares of treasury stock at $22					(44,000)	(44,000)
Net income				100,000		100,000
Cash dividends:						
Preferred				(15,000)		(15,000)
Common				(45,000)		(45,000)
Balance, 12/31/X2	$150,000	$75,000	$235,000	$111,000	$(60,000)	$511,000

low net income figure could be interpreted as being typical, even though it was caused by one-time and unusual happenings.

Current accounting practice dictates separate disclosure for the results of continuing operations (a very useful figure for prediction of future earnings), followed by the results of discontinued operations, extraordinary items, and the financial effects of changes in accounting principle. Because of their unique nature, we will now explore the latter three topical areas.

DISCONTINUED OPERATIONS

> **4** Apply the disclosure rules for discontinued operations, extraordinary items, accounting changes, and intraperiod tax allocation.

Many corporations are involved in diverse types of business activities. Consider Anheuser-Busch Companies, for instance, which is involved with brewing (Budweiser), the manufacture of metal containers, real estate management, entertainment (Sea World, St. Louis Cardinals baseball), bakery products, and snack foods (Eagle). It is apparent that Anheuser-Busch, like many other entities, conducts operations in several distinct business segments. A **segment** is defined as a component of a company whose activities represent a major line of business or class of customer.[3] Normally, the assets and operating results of a given segment are clearly distinguishable from the other assets and operations of the firm.

Occasionally, after an in-depth review of corporate activity and profitability, an entity will decide to dispose of one or more of its segments. A disposal usually results from inadequate earnings or disappointing expectations about the segment's future. Sometimes, however, a segment is sold not because its financial performance has been weak but because the company desires to concentrate in other activities.

> **ETHICS ISSUE**
>
> Your client, a fast-food operator, sold three marginal restaurants and wants to report the transaction under "discontinued operations." You disagree and promptly get fired. If the client then gives you one day to reconsider your position, what would you do?

When a segment is sold, abandoned, or otherwise disposed of, its operations are said to be **discontinued.** The results of discontinued operations are disclosed in a separate category on the income statement immediately after income from continuing operations. Specifically, the operating results of the disposed segment (i.e., revenues minus cost of goods sold and expenses) along with any gain or loss on the disposal must be shown net-of-tax.

To illustrate the proper accounting treatment, we will focus on Quality Products, Inc., a company that produces bakery goods and soft drinks. In addition, the firm operates a chain of movie theaters and golf courses throughout the country. Recently, in a downsizing effort, Quality sold its beverage segment (Hi-Pro Fruit Drinks) and generated a substantial profit on the transaction. A condensed income statement is presented in Exhibit 17–4.

As you can see by analyzing the data, the disposed segment significantly boosted Quality's "bottom-line" earnings. Note also that the bulk of the increase came from the sale of assets and facilities, not from Hi-Pro's daily activities. It should now be apparent that separate disclosure of discontinued operations helps financial statement users better assess the future of an entity's ongoing business affairs.

EXTRAORDINARY ITEMS

Corporate income statements disclose earnings from all types of business endeavors. Occasionally, sizable gains and losses arise from transactions and events that are clearly different from the usual affairs of the firm. Such occurrences, known as **extraordinary items,** are afforded special accounting treatment.

---

[3] "Reporting the Results of Operations," *Opinions of the Accounting Principles Board No. 30,* American Institute of Certified Public Accountants, Jersey City, N.J., 1973, paragraph 13.

EXHIBIT 17–4
Disclosure of Discontinued Operations

QUALITY PRODUCTS, INC.
Income Statement
For the Year Ended December 31, 19X2

Sales		$920,000
Cost of goods sold		640,000
Gross profit		$280,000
Operating expenses		170,000
Income from continuing operations before tax		$110,000
Income tax on continuing operations		35,000
Income from continuing operations		$ 75,000
Discontinued operations		
Income from discontinued operations, net-of-tax	$ 1,500	
Gain on disposal of Hi-Pro Division, net-of-tax	35,500	37,000
Net income		$112,000

To achieve uniformity in reporting, the accounting profession has stipulated that extraordinary items must be *unusual in nature* and *occur infrequently*.[4] Note that *both* criteria must be satisfied. A transaction or event is considered unusual if it has a high degree of abnormality and is unrelated to the ordinary and typical activities of the entity. To judge whether the "unusual" criterion is met, one must consider a company's scope of operation, lines of business, operating policies, geographical location of facilities and activities, and extent of governmental regulation. The second test, that of "infrequency," is satisfied when a transaction or event is not reasonably expected to recur in the foreseeable future.

Applying the Guidelines. Happenings that meet the two criteria (and that give rise to extraordinary gains and losses) are rare. Examples *may* include major casualties such as earthquakes, floods, and hurricanes; a seizure of assets by a foreign government; and newly enacted laws and regulations. From a practical point of view, it is difficult to generalize whether a particular event is always extraordinary. As the following illustration shows, each case must be evaluated on its own merits.

Suppose a business is located in a low-lying area that is prone to flooding once every four or five years. If a heavy rainstorm and its flood waters cause considerable damage to the firm's inventory, the loss is not considered extraordinary because it fails the infrequency-of-occurrence criterion. That is, on the basis of past history, another flood will probably occur in the foreseeable future. Changing the example slightly, suppose the flood loss is caused by a dam that breaks in a nearby valley. The break is highly unusual and, once repaired, is not likely to happen again. Because both tests are met, this flood loss is labeled extraordinary.

[4] Ibid., paragraph 20.

The following specific items are not considered extraordinary by the accounting profession:[5]

1. Write-down or write-off of receivables, inventories, and intangible assets.
2. Gains and losses from the sale or abandonment of property, plant, and equipment used in a business.
3. Effects of a strike, including those against competitors and major suppliers.

Such items, if material, are normally presented among nonoperating (other) revenues and expenses.

Disclosure of Extraordinary Items. Extraordinary items are disclosed in a separate section of the income statement immediately following discontinued operations. If a company has no discontinued operations, extraordinary items are presented after earnings from continuing activities. Again, a net-of-tax amount must be shown.

CHANGES IN ACCOUNTING PRINCIPLE

Recall that accountants follow the consistency principle when preparing financial statements. Consistency requires that the same valuation methods be employed from one period to the next. Occasionally, a company may decide an alternative reporting practice is more appropriate than the method currently in use. For example, in view of changing business conditions, an entity may now find an accelerated depreciation method (e.g., double-declining balance) to be preferable to the straight-line approach, or the weighted-average inventory valuation technique to be more proper than FIFO. The preceding examples illustrate a *change in accounting principle,* namely, a switch from one generally accepted accounting principle to another. To prevent the comparability of financial statements from deteriorating over time, such changes should be made infrequently and only when the newly implemented practice will result in improved financial reporting.

When a company changes its reporting methods and practices, it must compute the cumulative effect of such changes. The *cumulative effect* is the difference between the total net income reported in prior years and the income that would have been reported over the same period had the new practice been in use. For example, assume that Addison Corporation has decided to switch depreciation methods, from straight-line to double-declining balance. A review of the accounting records reveals that total aftertax income would have been $50,000 lower had the accelerated method been employed in earlier years. The $50,000 figure (i.e., the cumulative effect) is reported on the income statement when the change takes place as a reduction in earnings. The reduction is presented at the bottom of the statement, after any discontinued operations and extraordinary items, and is labeled as follows: "Cumulative effect on prior years of a change in accounting principle, net-of-tax."

A corporation's annual report normally includes financial statements from prior periods, thereby allowing the reader to perform various types of comparative studies. These statements typically *are not recast* to reflect the change in principle; however, additional supplemental disclosure is required

---

[5] Ibid., paragraph 23.

to show recomputed amounts for selected items "as if" the new principle had been in use.[6]

An Investment Analyst's Perspective

Reading the Income Statement: The accounting profession has done a credible job in establishing disclosure guidelines for income reporting. Nevertheless, investors and creditors must still exercise extreme caution when interpreting a company's financial statements. Consider a recent example in the airline industry, which I follow very closely. Not too long ago, Delta Air Lines reported a quarterly profit of approximately $7 million. A closer look at the financials revealed a decision to lengthen the depreciable life of aircraft, which boosted earnings by $34 million. Had it not been for this shift in service life estimate, the company would have reported a sizable quarterly loss.

Delta did nothing illegal or immoral; in fact, the firm's accounting practices are now more consistent with those of other carriers. As this example shows, improvements in income from one period to the next are not always the result of additional revenues or cost-cutting moves. The real cause is sometimes learned only after careful study of footnotes and other management disclosures.

NET-OF-TAX REPORTING

Examine the income statement of Bridgeport Corporation, which is presented in Exhibit 17–5. Observe how the statement is consistent with the income reporting categories just discussed and notice the treatment of taxes. The company is following a practice known as intraperiod tax allocation, which relates (i.e., matches) income taxes to the various elements that contribute to a firm's tax bill. These elements include continuing operations, discontinued operations, extraordinary items, changes in accounting principle, and prior period adjustments.[7]

To expand, a careful review of Bridgeport's disclosures will find the company is subject to a 40% income tax rate. Items that raise net income result in a 40% tax expense; items that reduce net income generate a 40% tax savings. From the information presented in Exhibit 17–5, Bridgeport's net tax expense totals $50,000:

Tax on continuing operations	$ 120,000
Tax on Sunrise Division operations	44,000
Tax savings on disposal of Sunrise facilities	(100,000)
Tax savings on flood loss	(24,000)
Tax on change in accounting principle	10,000
Net tax expense	$ 50,000

---

[6] A few accounting changes have been pinpointed by the profession as requiring a restatement of prior period financial statements.

[7] Prior period adjustments and the related tax impact are shown on the statement of retained earnings (or the statement of stockholders' equity). See Exhibits 17–2 and 17–3.

EXHIBIT 17-5
Intraperiod Tax Allocation and Corporate Income Reporting

BRIDGEPORT CORPORATION
Income Statement
For the Year Ended December 31, 19XX

Sales		$2,000,000
Cost of goods sold		1,200,000
Gross profit		$ 800,000
Operating expenses		
Selling	$ 280,000	
Administrative	170,000	450,000
Income from operations		$ 350,000
① Other revenue (expense)		
Loss on sale of machinery		(50,000)
Income from continuing operations before tax		$ 300,000
② Income tax on continuing operations		120,000
Income from continuing operations		$ 180,000
③ Discontinued operations		
Earnings from Sunrise Division operations, less applicable taxes ($110,000 – $44,000)	$ 66,000	
Loss on disposal of Sunrise facilities, less tax savings ($250,000 – $100,000)	(150,000)	(84,000)
Income before extraordinary item		$ 96,000
④ Extraordinary item		
Flood loss, less tax savings ($60,000 – $24,000)		(36,000)
⑤ Cumulative effect on prior years of a change in accounting principle, less applicable taxes ($25,000 – $10,000)		15,000
Net income		$ 75,000

KEY

① *Other revenue (expense):* Before-tax gains, losses, revenues, and expenses that arise from transactions and events not directly related to ordinary business activities (see Chapter 5).

② *Income from continuing operations:* Net-of-tax reporting for the income generated from ongoing activities of the entity.

③ *Discontinued operations:* Net-of-tax reporting for a discontinued segment of the business. The segment's operating results and any gains or losses on the disposal of the segment are disclosed separately.

④ *Extraordinary items:* Net-of-tax reporting for gains/losses that arise from unusual and infrequent transactions and events.

⑤ *Cumulative effect of a change in accounting principle:* Net-of-tax reporting for the impact on prior years' income of a change in reporting practices.

Without intraperiod allocation, the tax expense would appear as a single line item on the income statement, as shown below.

    Income tax expense $50,000

EARNINGS PER SHARE

5 Explain the meaning of and compute earnings per share.

Such a presentation is deficient, especially for the uninformed financial statement user. The presentation fails to show that the company had two significant tax-saving items during the period: the loss on the disposal of Sunrise facilities and the flood loss. Further, the $50,000 expense amount could be construed as being "typical," even though only one of the contributing factors (the continuing operations) is likely to recur in the future. Most accountants agree that intraperiod tax allocation results in improved disclosure, which is less apt to mislead statement readers.

The income statement provides considerable insight into the profitability of corporate activities. Rather than take the time to study all of the statement's intricacies, investors frequently rely on a single computation called **earnings per share (EPS)** of common stock. Earnings per share is similar to the won-loss percentage of a sports club at the end of the season. Specifically, it represents a summary of all items that affect profitability. Earnings-per-share data are

---

BUSINESS BRIEFING

ELIZABETH SANDERS
Business Alliance Partner: Information Systems Process
Lone Star Gas Company

Income Reporting Based on GAAP Is Not Always Acceptable

I work for Lone Star Gas, which distributes natural gas to over one million customers in Texas. Our company uses generally accepted accounting principles (GAAP) when reporting income to shareholders—income that is a function of actual revenues earned and actual expenses incurred.

Being a public utility, the rates that we charge customers (and that determine our revenues) are regulated by a commission established by the State legislature. The commission considers various factors in this process, including gas cost, operating expenses, taxes, and a return on the firm's investment. Interestingly, the items in our financial statements are in accord with GAAP; yet these same items may be adjusted or disallowed in rate-setting cases.

Three examples come to mind. First, similar to other corporate entities, we expense charitable contributions and entertainment costs on our income statement. These amounts are ignored by the commission. Second, like most natural gas companies, we lose gas: at connections, at meters, and so forth. Actual amounts lost are expensed under GAAP; however, in the rate-setting process, the commission limits such losses to 5% of the total gas moved through our system. A third example involves weather normalization. Although our income statement reveals actual revenues earned, these amounts may be adjusted in rate cases to minimize the spikes that occur in gas cost throughout the year. Without this procedure, the firm would generate windfall profits in periods of extreme cold and experience the opposite results in more moderate weather.

The preceding illustrations are only three of the many adjustments to GAAP-based figures that a regulated company such as Lone Star must consider. Sometimes, given the ordeals (and politics) related to the rate-setting process, we truly feel that the first "A" in GAAP is a misnomer.

widely disseminated in the financial press and also are disclosed on the face of the income statement. No other ratio is afforded such prominence.

Earnings per share is often analyzed to assess future prospects for corporate income and dividends. If current earnings are favorable and the financial outlook is bright, investors are usually willing to pay a higher price to acquire shares of the corporation's common stock. Generally speaking, a higher EPS will result in a higher market price.

To study the relationship between market price and earnings per share, investors and financial analysts often use a popular measure called the **price-earnings (P/E) ratio.** The ratio is calculated by dividing a stock's per-share market price by the annual earnings per share. For example, at the time this text is being written, the P/E ratios of Mattel and Service Merchandise are 26 and 7, respectively. By showing a willingness to pay more for each dollar of reported earnings, investors must feel that Mattel's financial future will be more prosperous than that of the popular catalog-showroom retailer.

Two preliminary steps are needed to figure the earnings per share of common stock: (1) determine the weighted-average number of shares outstanding and (2) compute the earnings available to common stockholders.

WEIGHTED-AVERAGE SHARES OUTSTANDING

The computation of earnings per share begins with an assessment of the number of common shares outstanding. In some firms the number of common shares remains constant during the accounting period. For many corporations, however, outstanding shares will change because of new stock issues, the purchase of treasury stock, and other similar transactions. In these situations earnings per share is based on a weighted average. The weighted average is calculated by multiplying the number of common shares outstanding by the fraction of the year the shares are in the hands of stockholders.

To illustrate, assume that Briarwood Manufacturing had 60,000 common shares outstanding at the beginning of the year. On September 1, an additional 15,000 shares were issued. The weighted-average number of shares would be computed as follows:

Outstanding Shares		Fraction of Year Outstanding		Weighted Average
60,000	×	8/12	=	40,000
75,000	×	4/12	=	25,000
				65,000

The weighted average represents the number of equivalent shares that have been outstanding for the entire year. That is, the initial 60,000 shares were outstanding for 12 months. In contrast, the 15,000-share issuance has been outstanding for only 4 months, which is equivalent to 5,000 shares for the entire year (15,000 × 4/12 = 5,000). Thus, Briarwood's weighted-average total is 65,000 (60,000 + 5,000). The weighting procedure is necessary because the capital provided by the new stock has helped generate earnings for only a fraction of the accounting period.

Earnings Available to Common Stockholders

Keep in mind that our goal is to derive the earnings per share of *common stock*. For corporations that have only common shares outstanding, all reported earnings are allocated to the common stockholders. If some preferred stock is outstanding, however, a different procedure is followed. Preferred stock is a *senior security*, so called because of its preferential treatment in dividend distributions and corporate liquidations. As a result, dividend claims of preferred stockholders must be deducted from net income to arrive at the earnings allocable to common shares.

For example, assume that Briarwood had issued 5,000 shares of $100 par-value, 10% preferred stock in addition to the common shares described earlier. If net income for the year amounted to $180,000, the earnings available to common stockholders would total $130,000:

Net income	$180,000
Less: Dividends on preferred stock (5,000 shares × $100 × 0.10)	50,000
Earnings available to common stockholders	$130,000

Earnings per share of common stock can now be computed as follows:

$$\text{Earnings Per Share} = \frac{\text{Earnings Available to Common Stockholders}}{\text{Weighted-Average Common Shares Outstanding}}$$

$$\text{EPS} = \frac{\$130,000}{65,000}$$

$$\text{EPS} = \$2.00$$

Primary Versus Fully Diluted Earnings Per Share

As we noted in the previous chapter, some preferred stocks are convertible into common shares. If these or other types of convertible securities are ultimately exchanged for common stock, the number of common shares will increase and earnings per share will be reduced (i.e., *diluted*). To inform common stockholders of the potential dilution, businesses must disclose additional EPS information. Specifically, corporations with potentially dilutive securities must report both **primary earnings per share** and **fully diluted earnings per share.**

Primary earnings per share is calculated by ignoring the dilutive effect of convertible securities.[8] Fully diluted EPS, on the other hand, is based on the *assumption* that all dilutive securities were converted into common shares during the accounting period. Note that the conversion is merely an assumption. The intention is to show how earnings per share would fall *if* common stock was issued to satisfy all existing dilutive commitments.

---

[8] If convertible securities (and others) meet certain tests, the securities are considered to be equivalent to common stock and enter into primary-earnings-per-share calculations. These tests are beyond the scope of this text and will be ignored.

The discussion here has been deliberately brief, as the underlying calculations are complex and more appropriately reserved for advanced accounting courses. Our goal is to give you a basic familiarity with the primary and fully diluted concepts should you encounter these terms when reviewing an income statement.

EPS DISCLOSURE

The reporting of earnings per share normally parallels the information shown on the income statement. Thus, if a corporation has discontinued operations, extraordinary items, or a cumulative effect from a change in accounting principle, per-share data for these elements are disclosed. Most financial analysts feel that by presenting such disclosures, a clearer picture of performance is made available for evaluation purposes. A sample presentation of per-share data for Midway Corporation, which has 100,000 weighted-average common shares outstanding and no potentially dilutive securities, appears in Exhibit 17–6.

EXHIBIT 17–6
Disclosure of Earnings-Per-Share Data

Income from continuing operations	$100,000
Income from discontinued operations (net-of-tax)	50,000
Income before extraordinary item	$150,000
Extraordinary loss (net-of-tax)	(10,000)
Net income	$140,000
Earnings per share	
Income from continuing operations	$ 1.00
Income from discontinued operations	0.50
Income before extraordinary item	$ 1.50
Extraordinary loss	(0.10)
Net income	$ 1.40

END-OF-CHAPTER REVIEW

LEARNING OBJECTIVES: THE KEY POINTS

1. **Define treasury stock and account for its acquisition and reissuance.** Shares of stock that have been reacquired by the issuing corporation are termed treasury stock. The shares' cost is charged to the Treasury Stock account at the time of acquisition, with the account's balance subsequently disclosed on the balance sheet as a reduction in stockholders' equity. Upon reissuance, the cost of shares sold is removed from the Treasury Stock account. Furthermore, any difference between the cost and proceeds per share is treated as either an addition to or a deduction from Paid-in Capital from Treasury Stock. In some cases, a charge against the Retained Earnings account may be necessary.

2. **Account for cash dividends, stock dividends, and stock splits and evaluate a company's dividend policy.** Dividends represent a distribution by a corporation to its stockholders and may be in the form of cash, noncash assets, or additional shares of stock. Such distributions are declared by the board of directors and issued to stockholders who own shares as of the record date. The ultimate impact of cash and stock dividends is a reduction in the firm's retained earnings balance.

   With stock dividends, Retained Earnings is debited for the market value of the shares to be distributed. The effect of a stock dividend is to shift amounts from Retained Earnings to Capital Stock and Paid-in Capital accounts, thereby producing no increase or decrease in total stockholders' equity.

   A stock split is used to reduce the market value per share. The underlying procedures involve increasing the number of shares outstanding and simultaneously decreasing the par or stated value. Total stockholders' equity remains unchanged, and no formal journal entry is required. A memo notation in the journal is appropriate.

   Finally, corporations have different policies with respect to dividend distributions. Growth companies severely limit distributions, preferring instead to reinvest earnings back in the business. Conversely, corporations in stable, mature industries often have sizable payouts. Two ratios are often used to evaluate an entity's distribution policy: dividend payout (annual cash dividend per share ÷ earnings per share) and dividend yield (annual cash dividend per share ÷ the current market price).

3. **Explain the proper treatment of prior period adjustments and restrictions that may be imposed on retained earnings.** A prior period adjustment (i.e., a journal entry) corrects the Retained Earnings account for errors that affect the net income of previous accounting periods. Such items are reported as an adjustment to the retained earnings balance at the beginning of the year in which the correction is made.

   Restrictions on retained earnings inform statement users that a portion of the retained earnings balance is unavailable for dividend declarations. Such restrictions, which may be voluntary, contractual, or imposed by state law, are generally handled by a note to the financial statements.

4. **Apply the disclosure rules for discontinued operations, extraordinary items, accounting changes, and intraperiod tax allocation.** Financial statement users are extremely interested in the net income generated by corporations. To help users assess future cash flows, the financial results of ordinary business activities are segregated from income that arises because of "unusual" transactions and events. Thus, the results from segments sold, abandoned, or otherwise disposed of during the year are separately disclosed as discontinued operations, after any income from continuing operations. In a similar fashion, gains and losses from occurrences that are both unusual and infrequent are labeled as extraordinary items and disclosed accordingly.

   Another item that requires separate disclosure is a change in accounting principle, such as the change from one depreciation method to another. Such a shift requires presentation of the cumulative effect of the change, which is the difference between total net income of previous years and the income that would have been reported had the new practice been in use.

   By following intraperiod tax allocation procedures, which relate income tax to the items that give rise to the tax, income from continuing operations and the preceding major income statement components, along with prior period adjustments, are shown on a net-of-tax basis.

5. **Explain the meaning of and compute earnings per share.** Earnings per share represents the per-share earnings available to common stockholders. In one of its simplest forms, earnings per share is calculated as net income, minus preferred dividends, divided by the weighted-average common shares outstanding. The calculation of weighted-average shares involves multiplying the number of common shares outstanding by the fraction of the year the shares were in the hands of stockholders. Those corporations that have potentially dilutive securities, such as convertible preferred stock, must disclose two figures: primary earnings per share and fully diluted earnings per share.

Key Terms and Concepts: A Quick Overview

cash dividend   A dividend that involves a distribution of cash and reduces retained earnings. (p. 624)

change in accounting principle   A change from one generally accepted accounting principle to another. (p. 634)

cumulative effect   The difference between the net income reported in prior years and the income that would have been reported by using a new accounting principle. (p. 634)

date of declaration   The date when a dividend is formally declared (approved) by the board of directors. (p. 624)

date of payment   The date when a dividend will be distributed to stockholders. (p. 624)

date of record   The date used to determine the stockholders entitled to receive a declared dividend. (p. 624)

deficit   A debit (negative) balance in the Retained Earnings account. (p. 624)

discontinued operations   A segment of a business that is sold, abandoned, or otherwise disposed of. (p. 632)

dividend payout ratio   A ratio that provides insight about a corporation's dividend distribution policy. Computed as: Annual cash dividend per share divided by earnings per share. (p. 628)

dividend yield   A ratio that indicates an investor's short-term rate of return from dividends. Computed as: Cash dividend per share divided by current market price per share. (p. 628)

dividends   A corporate distribution of income to stockholders. (p. 624)

earnings per share (EPS)   A widely used profitability ratio; computed as earnings available to common stockholders (net income minus any preferred dividend requirements) divided by the weighted-average common shares outstanding. (p. 637)

extraordinary gains and losses   Gains and losses that are both unusual in character and infrequent in occurrence. (p. 632)

fully diluted earnings per share   A calculation of earnings per share based on the assumption that potentially dilutive securities were converted into common shares during the accounting period. (p. 639)

intraperiod tax allocation   The practice of relating income tax expense to the items that give rise to the tax. (p. 635)

price-earnings ratio   A ratio that shows the amount investors are willing to pay for each dollar of corporate earnings. Computed as: Current market price per share divided by earnings per share. (p. 638)

primary earnings per share   A calculation of earnings per share for firms with potential dilution. The calculation ignores the dilutive effect of convertible securities. (p. 639)

prior period adjustments   Corrections of errors that affect the net income of previous accounting periods. (p. 629)

restrictions on retained earnings Restrictions that reduce the amount of retained earnings available for dividend distributions. (p. 630)

retained earnings The portion of stockholders' equity that has been generated by profitable operations and retained in the business. (p. 624)

segment A component of a company whose activities represent a major line of business or class of customer. (p. 632)

statement of retained earnings A financial statement that discloses the changes in the Retained Earnings account during an accounting period. (p. 630)

statement of stockholders' equity A financial statement that discloses the changes in all stockholders' equity accounts maintained by a business. (p. 630)

stock dividend A dividend that involves a distribution of a company's own shares of stock. (p. 625)

stock split An increase in the number of outstanding shares and an accompanying reduction of a stock's par or stated value per share. (p. 628)

treasury stock Shares of stock reacquired by the issuing corporation. (p. 621)

CHAPTER QUIZ

The five questions that follow relate to several issues raised in the chapter. Test your knowledge of the issues by selecting the best answer. (The answers appear on p. 659.)

1. Which of the following statements about treasury stock is false?
    a. The excess of the sales price of treasury stock over the stock's cost is considered paid-in capital.
    b. When treasury stock is reissued at a price in excess of cost, "gains" occur that increase the Retained Earnings account.
    c. When treasury stock is reissued at a price that is less than cost, the transaction may result in a reduction of the Retained Earnings account.
    d. The acquisition of treasury stock causes stockholders' equity to decrease.

2. The declaration of a cash dividend on common stock:
    a. decreases Retained Earnings.
    b. increases Retained Earnings.
    c. decreases total liabilities.
    d. generally occurs shortly after the date of record.

3. Sampson Corporation declared a 4% stock dividend on 20,000 shares of $5 par-value common stock. The stock's market value on the date of declaration was $20 per share. What is the impact of the declaration-date journal entry on total stockholders' equity?
    a. $4,000 increase.
    b. $4,000 decrease.
    c. $16,000 decrease.
    d. No effect.

4. Extraordinary items:
    a. are disclosed on the statement of retained earnings and statement of stockholders' equity.
    b. are disclosed as part of income from continuing operations.
    c. are unusual or infrequent in nature.
    d. are unusual and infrequent in nature.

5. Earnings per share is determined by dividing the weighted-average number of common shares outstanding into:
    a. net income.
    b. net income minus preferred stock dividends.

c. net income minus both preferred and common stock dividends.
d. ending retained earnings.

SUMMARY PROBLEM

Lisbon Corporation began 19X2 with the following stockholders' equity:

STOCKHOLDERS' EQUITY		
Preferred stock, $100 par value, 12% cumulative, 1,000 shares authorized, 500 shares issued and outstanding	$50,000	
Common stock, $2 par value, 10,000 shares authorized, 7,000 shares issued and outstanding	14,000	$ 64,000
Additional paid-in capital		
Paid-in capital in excess of par: common		87,000
Total paid-in capital		$151,000
Retained earnings		99,000
Total stockholders' equity		$250,000

During 19X2, Lisbon had before-tax income from continuing operations of $100,000. A $30,000 uninsured fire loss occurred in March; the loss will be classified as extraordinary. A 40% income tax rate is in effect.

On July 1, the company purchased 2,000 shares of its own common stock at $30 per share. This treasury stock was later reissued on December 31 at $36 per share. No dividends were paid during the year on common shares; however, the preferred stock's regular dividend requirement was satisfied.

In October, Lisbon's accountant discovered that he had incorrectly calculated 19X1 depreciation expense by $7,000. This error resulted in a $4,200 after-tax overstatement of 19X1 net income.

Instructions

a. Prepare the lower portion of Lisbon's 19X2 income statement, beginning with income from continuing operations before tax. Include earnings-per-share data. *Hint:* In performing the EPS calculations, the company reduces income from continuing operations by the preferred dividend requirement.
b. Prepare Lisbon's 19X2 statement of retained earnings.
c. Prepare the stockholders' equity section of Lisbon's December 31, 19X2, balance sheet.

Solution

a.
Income from continuing operations before tax	$100,000	
Income tax on continuing operations, 40%	40,000	
Income from continuing operations		$ 60,000
Deduct: Extraordinary loss (net of $12,000 tax)		18,000
Net income		$ 42,000
Earnings per share*		
Income from continuing operations		$ 9.00
Extraordinary loss		(3.00)
Net income		$ 6.00

* Weighted-average common shares outstanding:
$7,000 \times 6/12 = 3,500$
$5,000 \times 6/12 = \underline{2,500}$
$\underline{6,000}$

Earnings available to the common stockholders:

Income from continuing operations	$60,000
Less: Dividends on preferred stock (500 shares × $100 × 0.12)	6,000
Income from continuing operations available to common stockholders	$54,000

Income from continuing operations per share:

$$\frac{\$54,000}{6,000 \text{ shares}} = \underline{\$9.00} \text{ per share}$$

Extraordinary item per share:

$$\frac{\$18,000}{6,000 \text{ shares}} = \underline{\$3.00} \text{ per share}$$

b.

LISBON CORPORATION
Statement of Retained Earnings
For the Year Ended December 31, 19X2

Retained earnings, 12/31/X1 (as reported)	$ 99,000
Less: Correction of prior period error (net of $2,800 tax*)	4,200
Retained earnings, 12/31/X1 (restated)	$ 94,800
Add: Net income	42,000
	$136,800
Less: Cash dividends on preferred stock	6,000
Retained earnings, 12/31/X2	$130,800

* $7,000 − $4,200.

c.

STOCKHOLDERS' EQUITY

Preferred stock, $100 par value, 12% cumulative, 1,000 shares authorized, 500 shares issued and outstanding		$50,000
Common stock, $2 par value, 10,000 shares authorized, 7,000 shares issued and outstanding		14,000	$ 64,000
Additional paid-in capital		
Paid-in capital in excess of par: common	$87,000	
Paid-in capital from treasury stock	12,000*	99,000
Total paid-in capital		$163,000
Retained earnings		130,800†
Total stockholders' equity		$293,800

* 2,000 shares × ($36 − $30).
† From part (b).

Assignment Material

Questions

Q17–1 What is treasury stock? Why do corporations purchase treasury stock?

Q17–2 Should purchased treasury stock be disclosed as an asset? Why?

Q17–3 Explain how the Retained Earnings account can have a debit balance.

Q17–4 Does a corporation become legally liable for dividend distributions on the date of declaration or the date of record?

Q17–5 What two conditions must be satisfied to declare and distribute a cash dividend?

Q17–6 Discuss the effect of a stock dividend on (1) a stockholder's percentage ownership position and (2) total stockholders' equity of the issuing corporation.

Q17–7 What is the purpose of a restriction on retained earnings? What are some possible causes of restrictions?

Q17–8 Explain the relationship, if any, between the statement of retained earnings and the statement of stockholders' equity.

Q17–9 Why should a corporation segregate ordinary business income from income caused by unusual and infrequent transactions and events?

Q17–10 What two criteria must be satisfied for an event or transaction to be classified as an extraordinary item? Discuss each of the criteria and present three examples of possible extraordinary items.

Q17–11 Briefly discuss the practice of intraperiod tax allocation. Explain what the practice is and why it is used.

Q17–12 Why do stockholders closely monitor an entity's earnings per share?

Q17–13 Is the earnings-per-share calculation based on shares outstanding at the beginning of the year or the end of the year, or on a weighted average of the shares outstanding during the year?

Q17–14 Differentiate between primary and fully diluted earnings per share.

Exercises

E17–1 Treasury stock transactions (L.O. 1)

Stateside Corporation reacquired 20,000 shares of its common stock ($10 par value) on February 2 for $28 per share. These shares were subsequently sold as follows:

Apr. 9   6,000 shares at $35 per share
June 13   4,000 shares at $28 per share
Oct. 18   5,500 shares at $22 per share

Prepare all necessary journal entries for Stateside Corporation.

E17–2 Analysis of operations and retained earnings (L.O. 2)

Serra & Phang (S&P), a promotion and advertising agency, is operating at 60% of capacity because of the loss of several key clients. The company has been approached by the new management of Fast Freddie's Pizza, Inc., to handle marketing needs over the next three years. Annual fees could amount to $200,000.

Prior to signing any contracts, S&P hired a CPA to review Fast Freddie's financial statements. The CPA found no unusual transactions and an absence of dividends in recent years. The company's balance sheet disclosed the following:

Stockholders' equity	
Preferred stock, $100 par value	$ 400,000
Common stock, $0.05 par value	100,000
Retained earnings	(470,000)
Total	$ 30,000

a. What may have caused the $470,000 debit balance in Fast Freddie's Retained Earnings account?
b. Discuss several factors that S&P should consider in deciding whether to work with Fast Freddie.

E17–3 Dividends and stock splits (L.O. 2)

Consider the following transactions and events of Companies X, Y, and Z:

- Company X—Declared a $20,000 cash dividend.
- Company Y—Declared a 10% stock dividend on 50,000 shares of $2 par-value common stock. Market value at the time of declaration was $8 per share.
- Company Z—Authorized a 3-for-1 stock split.

a. Prepare journal entries, if needed, for Companies X, Y, and Z.
b. Set up a chart as follows to show the effects of the transactions and events for the three firms. Use the notation: I = increase, D = decrease, and NE = no effect.

	NUMBER OF SHARES OUTSTANDING	TOTAL PAID-IN CAPITAL	RETAINED EARNINGS	TOTAL STOCKHOLDERS' EQUITY
X				
Y				
Z				

E17–4 Preparation of stockholders' equity section (L.O. 1, 2)

Charlesworth and Son, Inc., had the following equity accounts at the beginning of the year:

Common stock, $1 par value	$100,000
Paid-in capital in excess of par value	200,000
Retained earnings	600,000
Total stockholders' equity	$900,000

The following selected events took place during the current year:

Mar. 18 Declared a $0.50 cash dividend per share.
June 9 Declared and issued a 5% stock dividend; market value at time of declaration was $19 per share.
Aug. 11 Announced a 4-for-1 stock split.
Dec. 14 Reacquired 1,000 treasury shares at a cost of $8 per share.

Assuming net income of $75,900, prepare the year-end stockholders' equity section for Charlesworth and Son, after the accounting records have been closed.

E17–5 Dividend ratios, price-earnings ratio (L.O. 2, 5)

Speed Disc, Inc., and Garden State Utilities are publicly traded corporations. Speed Disc is involved with high-tech computer design and production; Garden State provides electric power by burning waste materials. The following information is available:

	SPEED DISC	GARDEN STATE
Earnings per share	$ 1.20	$ 3.00
Dividends per share	0.18	2.40
Current market price per share	36.00	32.00

a. Calculate the dividend payout and dividend yield ratios for both companies. Provide an explanation as to why the ratios are so different for Speed Disc and Garden State.

b. Compute the price-earnings ratios for the two firms. Which of the two companies seems to have generated more "stockholder enthusiasm"? Briefly discuss.

E17–6 Statement of retained earnings (L.O. 2, 3)

Cary Corporation had an ending retained earnings balance on December 31, 19X2, of $4.8 million. The following information pertains to 19X3:

a. Cash dividends of $300,000 were declared and paid to common stockholders.
b. A 3% stock dividend was declared and distributed on December 31. The stock's fair market value at the time of declaration was $20 per share; 150,000 shares were outstanding.
c. Income was $600,000 before tax.
d. An error was discovered on March 17 that occurred in 19X1 and understated before-tax income of that year by $40,000.
e. Cary is subject to a 40% income tax rate.

Prepare the corporation's 19X3 statement of retained earnings.

E17–7 Statement of stockholders' equity (L.O. 2, 3)

Fischer Corporation, a manufacturer of locks and security devices, began 19X4 with the following stockholders' equity balances:

Preferred stock, $50 par value	$200,000
Common stock, $2 par value	600,000
Paid-in capital in excess of par: common	450,000
Retained earnings	430,000

The following selected transactions and events occurred during the year:

- Issued 5,000 shares of common stock for $70,000.
- Declared and paid $12,000 of preferred dividends and $30,000 of common dividends.
- Generated net income of $47,000.
- Recorded a $24,000 prior period adjustment (net of $16,000 tax) related to an overstatement of 19X2 net income.

Prepare Fischer Corporation's statement of stockholders' equity for the year ended December 31, 19X4.

E17–8 Corporate income reporting (L.O. 3, 4)

Consider the five cases that follow.

1. Patrick's foreign assembly plant was heavily damaged during a violent government takeover in a normally stable country. The company's insurance policy does not cover such losses.
2. United Corporation switched from straight-line depreciation to sum-of-the-years'-digits depreciation for all assets currently in use.
3. AMV, Inc., sold a vacant tract of land next to the firm's warehouse and generated a substantial gain. The company has other tracts of land, some of which may be sold in the future.
4. Commerce, Inc., manufactures recreational and military vehicles. Recently, all military equipment facilities and assets were sold at a large loss.
5. Allstate discovered a mathematical error in 19X7 that related to the computation of 19X6 depreciation expense.

a. Analyze cases (1)–(5) individually and determine the most appropriate reporting classification: other revenue and expense, discontinued operations, change in accounting principle, extraordinary item, or prior period adjustment.
b. Which of the five cases would be disclosed on the income statement?

E17–9 Discontinued operations (L.O. 4)

The following information pertains to Stovall Corporation for the year ended December 31, 19XX:

Sales	$1,000,000
Cost of goods sold	600,000
Selling expenses	150,000
Administrative expenses	200,000

In 19XX, Stovall disposed of its retail division. The retail division generated 20% of the firm's total sales and accounted for 25% and 30% of total cost of goods sold and operating expenses, respectively. The division was sold at a before-tax gain of $25,000. Prepare Stovall's 19XX income statement, assuming a 40% tax rate.

E17–10 Abbreviated income statement (L.O. 2, 3, 4)

LBO, Inc., had income from operations of $180,000 for the year ended December 31, 19X5. A review of the accounting records disclosed the following:

Gain on sale of building	$60,000
Dividends	10,000
Extraordinary loss	40,000
Prior period adjustment from an understatement of advertising expense	25,000

LBO is subject to a 40% income tax rate.

a. Which of the preceding items would not appear on the company's income statement? Where would these items be disclosed?
b. Prepare an abbreviated income statement for LBO, beginning with income from operations. Disregard earnings-per-share data.

E17–11 Equity issues and income reporting (L.O. 1, 2, 3, 4)

Evaluate the comments that follow as being True or False. If the comment is false, briefly explain why.

a. A purchase of treasury stock reduces the stockholders' equity of the acquiring company.

b. A restriction on retained earnings reduces a company's total retained earnings balance.
c. The issuance of a previously declared 3,000-share stock dividend causes a reduction in the Retained Earnings account.
d. If certain criteria are met, extraordinary gains and losses may be disclosed on the statement of retained earnings.
e. Gains and losses from discontinued operations should be disclosed on the income statement on a net-of-tax basis.

E17–12 Earnings-per-share calculation (L.O. 5)

On January 1, 19X5, Forum, Inc., had 80,000 common shares outstanding. The following common stock transactions occurred during the year:

Apr. 1   Sold 28,000 newly issued shares to the public.
Aug. 1   Reacquired 6,000 shares, to be held as treasury stock.
Oct. 1   Reissued all treasury stock holdings.

Forum's financial statements revealed that 20,000 shares of 8%, $5 par-value preferred stock were outstanding throughout 19X5. Net income amounted to $85,000, and all preferred dividend obligations were satisfied.

a. Calculate the weighted-average common shares outstanding.
b. Compute the company's earnings per share.

E17–13 Corporate income reporting (L.O. 5)

The following item appeared under the heading of Business Briefs in a recent edition of the *California Tribune:*

> **SEA BREEZE REPORTS 152% RISE IN EARNINGS PER SHARE**
>
> Los Angeles—David Anthony, chairman and chief executive officer of Sea Breeze, a nationwide retailer of swimwear, today announced a 152% rise in earnings per share. The company reported earnings per share of $2.90 for the year ended September 30, 19X2, which compares favorably with $1.15 per share for 19X1.

Assume that you attended the stockholders' meeting where the announcement was made. The data that follow were distributed to all attendees.

	FISCAL YEAR ENDED	
	9/30/X2	9/30/X1
Earnings per common share		
Continuing retail operations	$ 2.84	$ 2.42
Discontinued operations	0.14	(1.27)
Extraordinary item	(0.08)	—
Net income	$ 2.90	$ 1.15

Evaluate the *Tribune*'s reporting of Sea Breeze's earnings.

PROBLEMS

Series A

P17–A1 Accounting for treasury stock, cash dividends, and stock splits (L.O. 1, 2)

You Fix It, Inc., had the following stockholders' equity on January 1, 19X8:

Common stock, $5 par value, 400,000 shares authorized, 70,000 shares issued and outstanding	$350,000
Paid-in capital in excess of par value	185,000
Retained earnings	360,000
Total stockholders' equity	$895,000

The following transactions and events occurred during the year:

Jan. 11	Approved a 2-for-1 stock split.
Feb. 23	Reacquired 10,000 common shares for $220,000, to be held as treasury stock.
July 6	Declared a cash dividend of $0.80 per share.
13	Sold 3,000 of the treasury shares for $87,000.
Aug. 5	Distributed the dividend that was declared on July 6.
Nov. 22	Declared a cash dividend of $1 per share.
Dec. 15	Sold 6,000 of the treasury shares for $114,000.

Instructions

a. Prepare the journal entries needed to record You Fix It's transactions and events.
b. Prepare the company's stockholders' equity section as of December 31, 19X8. Net income for the year amounted to $112,800.

P17–A2 Equity transactions: Journal entries and stockholders' equity section (L.O. 1, 2)

An examination of the ledger of Goodrich Metals revealed the following accounts on January 1:

Common stock, $1 par, 50,000 shares authorized, 30,000 shares issued, 29,500 shares outstanding	$ 30,000
Paid-in capital in excess of par value	270,000
Retained earnings	370,500*
Treasury stock, 500 shares at cost	6,000

*Goodrich is required by state law to restrict retained earnings at an amount equal to the cost of any treasury shares held by the firm.

The following transactions and events occurred during the year:

Jan. 7	Declared a $0.20 dividend per share to stockholders of record on January 23. The dividend will be distributed on February 8.
Feb. 8	Paid the dividend declared on January 7.
Apr. 15	Sold 300 shares of treasury stock for $4,500.
June 30	Declared a 10% stock dividend on the shares outstanding, to stockholders of record on July 15. The dividend will be distributed on August 15. Fair market value on the date of declaration was $14 per share.
Aug. 15	Issued the stock dividend declared on June 30.
Dec. 31	Net income for the year amounted to $98,000. Closed the Income Summary account to Retained Earnings.

Instructions

a. Prepare journal entries to record Goodrich's transactions and events.
b. Prepare the stockholders' equity section of Goodrich's December 31 balance sheet, along with any appropriate notes to the financial statements.

P17–A3 Statement of retained earnings and stockholders' equity section (L.O. 1, 2, 3)

Roadside Equipment had the following paid-in capital on January 1, 19X2:

Common stock, $5 par, 150,000 shares authorized, 20,000 shares issued and outstanding	$100,000
Paid-in capital in excess of par value	370,000

On December 31, 19X2, prior to the accounting records being closed, the Retained Earnings account contained the following entries:

RETAINED EARNINGS					
2/18	Stock dividend	120,000	1/1	Balance	290,000
5/14	Correction of error	48,000			
12/31	Cash dividend	52,000			

A review of the accounting records disclosed that:

1. A 15% stock dividend was declared on February 18 when the market price was $40 per share. The dividend was distributed one month later.
2. The $48,000 error correction is net of $32,000 of tax and relates to 19X1 sales revenue.
3. Four thousand treasury shares were reacquired beginning in May at a total cost of $140,000. Seventy percent of these shares were later sold for $120,400.
4. 19X2 net income amounted to $110,700.

Instructions

a. Prepare a statement of retained earnings for the year ended December 31, 19X2.
b. Prepare the stockholders' equity section of the company's December 31, 19X2, balance sheet.

P17–A4 Corporate financial reporting (L.O. 4, 5)

Brady Corporation has calculated its 19X4 income from operations at $1,200,000. The following additional items have come to your attention:

1. One of the company's retail centers suffered $100,000 of uninsured damage from a hurricane. Such storms are unusual and infrequent in the area where the center is located.
2. Management authorized the sale of an old warehouse, producing a $35,000 gain on disposal.
3. As the result of a wildcat strike, Brady incurred extra labor costs of $60,000 to fill customer orders on a timely basis.
4. The company sold its Oriental food segment during October, generating a $1.3 million gain on the transaction. The segment had a $600,000 operating loss prior to the disposal decision.
5. Brady has used the straight-line depreciation method since its founding 22 years ago. At the start of 19X4, management decided to change to the double-declining balance method. Prior years' depreciation would have been $180,000 greater had the accelerated method been employed.

Brady is subject to a 40% income tax rate and has 1,000,000 shares of common stock outstanding. All dollar amounts cited in items (1)–(5) are before tax.

Instructions

a. Discuss the proper treatment of the transactions and events described in items (1)–(5).
b. Prepare the lower portion of the company's 19X4 income statement, beginning with income from operations. Include appropriate earnings-per-share information.

P17–A5 Corporate income reporting (L.O. 4, 5)

Astro, Inc., operates a chain of bodybuilding centers and driving schools. The driving schools have been marginally profitable and were discontinued in May 19X3. The data that follow pertain to the 19X3 fiscal year.

	BODYBUILDING CENTERS	DRIVING SCHOOLS
Sales	$5,000,000	$3,400,000
Operating expenses	3,200,000	3,150,000
Loss on disposal of driving school assets		(400,000)
Gain on sale of building	300,000	
Extraordinary flood loss	(100,000)	
Change in accounting principle	70,000	

The change in accounting principle resulted from a switch in depreciation methods for the bodybuilding centers. The cumulative effect of the switch will cause a $70,000 hike in earnings.

Astro had 100,000 shares of no-par common stock outstanding throughout 19X3. Dividends of $20,000 were declared and paid on these shares in October. The company is subject to a 40% income tax rate; all amounts presented in the problem are expressed on a before-tax basis.

Instructions

Prepare Astro's 19X3 income statement for the year ended November 30. Be sure to disclose the company's earnings per share.

Series B

P17–B1 Accounting for treasury stock, cash dividends, and stock splits (L.O. 1, 2)

Bridge Corporation had the following stockholders' equity on January 1, 19X6:

Common stock, $3 par value, 50,000 shares authorized, 12,000 shares issued and outstanding	$ 36,000
Paid-in capital in excess of par value	156,000
Retained earnings	245,000
Total stockholders' equity	$437,000

The following transactions and events occurred during the year:

Jan. 15 Declared a cash dividend of $0.60 per share.
Feb. 15 Issued the dividend that was declared on January 15.
Mar. 21 Authorized a 3-for-1 stock split.
May 9 Acquired 7,000 common shares at $20 per share, to be held as treasury stock.

Aug. 22 Sold 2,000 of the treasury shares for $46,000.
Dec. 12 Declared a cash dividend of $0.70 per share.
     23 Sold 3,700 of the treasury shares for $79,180.

Net income for the year amounted to $66,300.

Instructions

a. Using the format that follows, indicate the stockholders' equity account(s) to be debited or credited as a result of the preceding transactions and events. For example, if the company had issued 5,000 shares of common stock at par, the following notation would be made in the Common Stock column: Credit, $15,000. *Note:* Include the company's net income in the chart and assign a date of December 31. Also, if the Paid-in Capital in Excess of Par: Treasury Stock account is used, place a "T" next to the appropriate dollar amount.

	COMMON STOCK	PAID-IN CAPITAL IN EXCESS OF PAR	RETAINED EARNINGS	TREASURY STOCK
Jan. 15				
Feb. 15				
Etc.				

b. Prepare the stockholders' equity section as of December 31, 19X6.

P17–B2 Equity transactions: Journal entries and stockholders' equity section (L.O. 1, 2)

An examination of the ledger of Home Cooking, Inc., revealed the following accounts on January 1:

Common stock, $10 par, 50,000 shares authorized, 30,000 shares issued, 28,000 shares outstanding	$300,000
Paid-in capital in excess of par value	90,000
Retained earnings	240,000*
Treasury stock, 2,000 shares at cost	25,000

*Home Cooking's board of directors has placed a $70,000 restriction on retained earnings to allow for future equipment acquisitions.

The following transactions and events occurred during the year:

Mar. 14 Declared a 4% stock dividend on the shares outstanding, to stockholders of record on March 28. The dividend will be distributed on April 14. Fair market value on the date of declaration was $15 per share.
Apr. 3 Sold 1,500 shares of treasury stock for $21,000.
     14 Issued the stock dividend declared on March 14.
Oct. 9 Declared a $0.65 dividend per share to stockholders of record on October 23. The dividend will be distributed on November 9.
Nov. 9 Paid the dividend declared on October 9.
Dec. 31 Net income for the year amounted to $105,000. Closed the Income Summary account to Retained Earnings.

Instructions

a. Prepare journal entries to record Home Cooking's transactions and events.
b. Assume that the company's board met on December 30 and increased the restriction for equipment acquisitions by 20% of the original amount. Prepare the stock-

holders' equity section of Home Cooking's December 31 balance sheet, along with any appropriate notes to the financial statements.

P17–B3 Statement of retained earnings and stockholders' equity section (L.O. 1, 2, 3)

Mansfield Merchants, Inc., had the following stockholders' equity on January 1, 19X9:

Common stock, $1 par, 1,000,000 shares authorized, 800,000 shares issued and outstanding	$ 800,000
Paid-in capital in excess of par value	3,200,000
Retained earnings	1,950,000
Total stockholders' equity	$5,950,000

Selected transactions and events from 19X9 follow. The transactions and events occurred in the sequence presented.

Declared (and later issued) a 5% stock dividend. Market value at the time of declaration was $10 per share.	$400,000
Acquired 20,000 treasury shares at $8 per share.	160,000
Declared (and later paid) a cash dividend.	24,600
Sold 12,000 treasury shares at $9 per share.	108,000
Detected an error that took place in 19X8. The company failed to record a $70,000 gain on a land sale, which affected taxes by $21,000.	49,000

Instructions

a. Prepare a statement of retained earnings for the year ended December 31, 19X9. Net income for the year was $736,800.
b. Prepare the stockholders' equity section for the corporation's December 31, 19X9, balance sheet.

P17–B4 Corporate financial reporting (L.O. 4, 5)

Champion, Inc., has requested your advice concerning the proper accounting treatment for each of the following events and transactions, which occurred during 19XX:

1. On October 15, Champion sold stock of Wiser Corporation at a $30,000 loss. The Wiser stock was acquired as an investment several years earlier. Champion regularly engages in such investment activity.
2. The company has utilized the double-declining balance depreciation method on all items of plant and equipment. At the beginning of 19XX, management decided to change to the straight-line approach and calculated that prior years' depreciation expense would have been $150,000 lower had the new method been employed.
3. The company disposed of its oil drilling segment in July. The sale of the division resulted in a $750,000 loss. From January 1, 19XX, through the date of sale, however, the segment had generated $200,000 of income from operations.
4. One of the company's warehouses suffered $300,000 of damage in April when a truck hauling nuclear waste crashed into the structure. Champion's insurance does not cover this type of damage, and the trucking company responsible has filed for bankruptcy.

Champion, Inc., is subject to a 40% income tax rate and had 10,000 shares of common stock outstanding throughout the year. The firm's accountant has correctly computed 19XX income from operations at $880,000. Assume that all dollar amounts cited in items (1)–(4) are before tax.

Instructions

a. Discuss the proper accounting treatment for the transactions and events described in items (1)–(4).
b. Prepare the lower portion of the company's income statement (starting with income from operations of $880,000) for the year ended December 31, 19XX. Include appropriate earnings-per-share information.

P17–B5 Corporate income reporting (L.O. 4, 5)

Far West Importers, Inc., had the following activity during 19X5. (All amounts presented are before consideration of related tax effects.)

Cost of goods sold	$ 7,068,000
Decrease in earnings from cumulative effect of change in accounting principle	20,000
Extraordinary loss from earthquake	36,000
Gain on sale of assets from discontinued segment	240,000
Loss on sale of land	14,000
Net sales	11,400,000
Operating expenses	2,832,000
Operating loss on discontinued segment	50,000

The company is subject to a 30% income tax rate and had 100,000 weighted-average shares of common stock outstanding during 19X5.

Instructions

Prepare the corporation's income statement for the year ended December 31, 19X5. Include any necessary earnings-per-share information.

Expanding Your Horizons

EYH17–1 Stock dividends and stock splits (L.O. 2)

In 1971, a new company called Southwest Airlines began intrastate passenger service between Dallas, Houston, and San Antonio with three Boeing 737 aircraft. Since then, the corporation has been very successful and now flies 180+ planes to over 50 cities.

Instructions

Assume that you were lucky enough to purchase 100 common shares of Southwest Airlines as part of the company's initial public offering. Also assume that you had the wisdom to retain your ownership interest. Using reference materials available at a library or from a stockbroker, determine the cost of the original investment and the number of shares you would have as of December 31, 1995, given the firm's history of stock dividends and stock splits. Be sure to calculate the total current market value of the investment along with the percentage increase over cost. Prepare a short report of your findings.

EYH17–2 The "tone" of income reporting (L.O. 4, 5)

Despite having a bad year, corporations often issue annual reports that "paint a rosy, upbeat picture." While this optimism is perhaps understandable, it reinforces the need for stockholders to thoroughly read the financial statements and accompanying notes to receive a dose of reality.

Instructions

Using the resources of your library, find the annual reports of two corporations that generated a recent net loss or a significant drop in net income. Compare and contrast the tone of the stockholders' letter, as written by the company's chief executive officer or chairman of the board, to the hard facts as presented in the financial statements and notes. Prepare a short report of any inconsistencies that you find.

EYH17-3 Earnings information (L.O. 5)

Corporations report comparative sales, net income, and earnings-per-share information to their stockholders and the financial community. Many astute investors follow this information closely, looking for "surprises" that have not as yet been reflected in the price of the corporation's stock.

Instructions

Review a recent issue of *The Wall Street Journal* for corporate earnings information. Locate five companies that reported very strong growth or drops in earnings per share for the quarter or year. In the same issue, find the change in the market price of the corporation's common stock. (By looking at the paper's index, typically on page B2, determine if this news is reported in a separate, stand-alone article.) Prepare a summary of your findings.

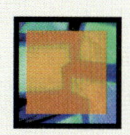

EYH17-4 Corporate equity and income reporting: The Clorox Company and The Home Depot (L.O. 1-5)

The Clorox Company makes a variety of household and food products (e.g., Clorox bleach, Formula 409, Kingsford charcoal briquets, S.O.S. pads, and Hidden Valley salad dressings). The firm's products are sold in more than 90 countries. The Home Depot, in contrast, is America's largest home center retailer. The firm is especially popular with do-it-yourselfers and home remodeling contractors.

Instructions

By using the text's electronic data base, access the financial statements and accompanying notes of both firms and answer the questions that follow. Unless otherwise indicated, responses should be based on data for the most recent year presented.

a. Analyze the financial statements and determine each company's earnings per share and dividends per common share for the three years reported. In general, have changes in earnings per share been reflected in the dividends distributed to stockholders? Briefly comment.

b. Did either of the companies have any discontinued operations? If "yes,"
   (1) How much of an impact did the discontinued operations have on current net income?
   (2) What is the nature of the discontinued operations as described in the notes that accompany the financial statements?

c. By reviewing the statement of stockholders' equity, determine for each firm:
   (1) The nature of any new common stock issuances during the year.
   (2) The nature of any treasury stock transactions during the year.

d. Did either company report a prior period adjustment? If so, briefly describe.

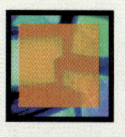

EYH17-5 Corporate equity and income reporting (L.O. 1-5)

This problem is a duplication of Problem EYH17-4. It is based on two companies selected by your instructor.

Instructions

By using the text's electronic data base, access the specified companies' financial statements and accompanying notes and focus on data for the most recent year reported. Answer requirements (a)-(d) of Problem EYH17-4.

EYH17–6 Dividend policy, income reporting (L.O. 2, 4)

Wilderness Herbal Teas, a three-year-old publicly traded corporation, reported the following balance sheet on December 31, 19X7:

Cash	$ 35,000
Other current assets	120,000
Property, plant, & equipment (net)	400,000
Other assets	50,000
Total assets	$605,000
Current liabilities	$ 70,000
Long-term liabilities	270,000
Common stock, $2 par value	200,000
Paid-in capital in excess of par value	20,000
Retained earnings	45,000
Total liabilities & stockholders' equity	$605,000

In its first two years of operation, the company had sizable losses. Wilderness "turned the corner" in 19X7, generating net income of $75,000. This amount includes a $300,000 life insurance payoff to the firm, which resulted from the death of a key vice-president in an air crash.

The board of directors is considering a cash dividend, a stock dividend, or some combination to reward stockholders for their patience during the first two years of corporate start-up. Since the company is facing intense competition and needs funds for marketing programs, any cash dividends are not likely to be repeated for several years.

Instructions

Study all information presented and prepare a short memo to the board about the contemplated distribution. Include your thoughts about (a) having a dividend at this time and (b) the type of distribution to be made, assuming the directors are determined to reward the stockholders. If you propose a cash dividend, be sure to indicate the maximum amount.

COMMUNICATION OF ACCOUNTING INFORMATION

CAI17–1 The personal touch: H & R Block, Inc. (L.O. 4)

Communication Principle: Personalizing a piece of writing for a reader is one way that abstract concepts can be made more comprehensible. Personalizing can be achieved by following several simple procedures:

1. Use personal pronouns such as "you," "I," or "we." In other words, write directly to an individual reader rather than indirectly and generally to just any reader. For instance, the phrase "You can look at the company's continuing operations to see . . ." involves the reader directly, whereas "The company's continuing operations can be seen . . ." does not.
2. Use active voice instead of passive. In an active sentence, "actors" or people come first; in a passive sentence, objects or things come first. To illustrate, "The accountant wrote an excellent report" is active. "An excellent report was written by the accountant" is passive. Experts agree that the more personalized nature of active voice makes writing more effective.
3. Use concrete examples that a reader can understand. In the situation that follows, for instance, examples of discontinued operations may be introduced to help a reader comprehend how such events affect earnings.

4. Write in a style and vocabulary appropriate to the reader's age, educational level, occupation, and culture.

Personalized documents are generally more persuasive than impersonal ones. Because letters are written to one person, they are, by definition, personal. Use this opportunity to communicate information clearly and, at the same time, respond to a client and make a friend.

■ ■ ■ ■ ■ ■ ■ ■

H & R Block, Inc., is a very profitable company, perhaps best known among millions of Americans for its income tax preparation services. The firm also provides information services through CompuServe Incorporated. In two recent successive years, the company reported the following amounts (in thousands of dollars):

	19X4	19X3
Income from continuing operations	$163,995	$171,017
Income after discontinued operations (i.e., net income)	200,528	180,705

Instructions

Assume that a biology professor desires to invest in a company that has reasonable growth in net income and is considering H & R Block on the basis of this criterion. Write a letter that explains, in a nontechnical way, the nature of and reporting for discontinued operations. Be sure to show the amount of gain or loss attributable to discontinued activities for each year. Also include an evaluation of H & R Block's earnings trend as it relates to the professor's investment standard.

Answers to Chapter Quiz

1. b
2. a
3. d [The $16,000 decrease to Retained Earnings (20,000 shares × $20 × .04) is offset by a $4,000 increase to Stock Dividend Distributable (20,000 shares × $5 × .04) and a $12,000 increase to Paid-in Capital in Excess of Par Value ($16,000 − $4,000)].
4. d
5. b

18 FINANCIAL INSTRUMENTS: AN EMPHASIS ON BONDS

LEARNING OBJECTIVES

After studying this chapter, you should be able to:

1. Define financial instruments and identify several of their basic features.
2. Describe the basic differences between bondholders and stockholders and identify the various types of bonds that may be issued.
3. Account for bonds that are issued at, above, or below face value, and distinguish between contract and effective interest rates.
4. Calculate amortization under both the straight-line and effective-interest methods.
5. Account for bonds issued between interest dates and for bond retirements.
6. Analyze the extent of a company's outstanding debt.
7. Account for bond investments.
8. Describe the features of available-for-sale stock investments and the equity method.
9. (Appendix) Use present value techniques to determine the issue price of bonds.

When George Faris and your authors sat down to discuss this chapter's opening vignette, we knew we had a problem. Small companies such as Banner Advertising simply don't use bonds as a means of financing. As luck would have it, bond issuances comprise a sizable portion of the chapter's discussion, with bond investments and stock investments rounding out the presentation.[1] "Wait just a minute," George exclaimed. "Although we have no experience with issuances, I can lend some insight from the investor's perspective. I occasionally purchase bonds as an investment and truly enjoy the dependability of semiannual interest checks."

More often than buying bonds, George dabbles in the stock market—but only after reviewing a firm's annual report and talking with a broker. If he buys a stock, he then follows its price on a regular basis. George subscribes to an on-line computerized data base that can track fast-breaking business news along with changes in the financial markets.

The important point is that George monitors his investments very closely, no matter whether he intends to hold them for six months or five years. Given this readily accessible, electronic means to learn a share's "true" worth, he has never understood the accounting rules that report stock investments at historical cost. George observes, "The relevant value to me (and I assume many others) is market, and it makes sense to use this figure in the financial statements. Who cares that I paid $3,500 for some shares several years ago if today they're worth $8,000?"

After years of relying on a cost-based approach to valuation, the accounting profession recently had a change of heart. In an earlier chapter you learned how fair market value is now used to account for trading securities (a current asset). After studying the next few pages you will be familiar with the latest rules for other types of investments. These rules move the financial statements closer to an approach that makes sense for a typical investor and financial statement user like George Faris. Perhaps more important, you will receive added exposure to the rapidly developing area known as financial instruments.

Financing a Business Venture

As shown earlier in the text, short-term projects and investments in current assets (e.g., inventory buildups) are typically financed by short-term credit such as accounts payable and notes payable. These funding sources, although satisfactory in many applications, are very inadequate for others. Long-term projects such as an expansion of facilities or the addition of a new product line dictate the need for a more permanent source of capital. Imagine the difficulty of financing a new office complex with liabilities that would have to be renewed every three months. Indeed, the prospect of resecuring the necessary credit four times a year for the next 20 or 30 years is unappealing.

[1] Bonds will be defined shortly.

Generally speaking, long-term projects are financed by long-term capital. Long-term capital is obtained from debt sources (bonds, leases, and other multi-year obligations) as well as various equity sources (capital stock and retained earnings[2]). As shown in Exhibit 18–1, the proportions of liabilities, capital stock, and retained earnings as funding sources vary from company to company. Factors that influence these proportions include the age of the firm, past earnings records, interest and dividend costs, industry characteristics, and required investments in property, plant, and equipment.

FINANCIAL INSTRUMENTS

> **1** Define financial instruments and identify several of their basic features.

Most of the long-term funding sources just mentioned fall under the heading of financial instruments, a key element in today's domestic and global economic systems. In the simplest sense, *financial instruments* can be defined as debt and equity tools that are used to fund business transactions.

There are numerous types of financial instruments. Some involve dividend distributions to stockholders; others require periodic interest payments to individuals and lending institutions. Many of these instruments are straightforward and have been used for years; others are relatively new to the marketplace, somewhat risky, and more "exotic" in nature. A review of the business press will find a host of instruments that fall in the last category (e.g., bunny bonds, flip-flop notes, junk bonds, floating-rate notes, strips, and swaps).

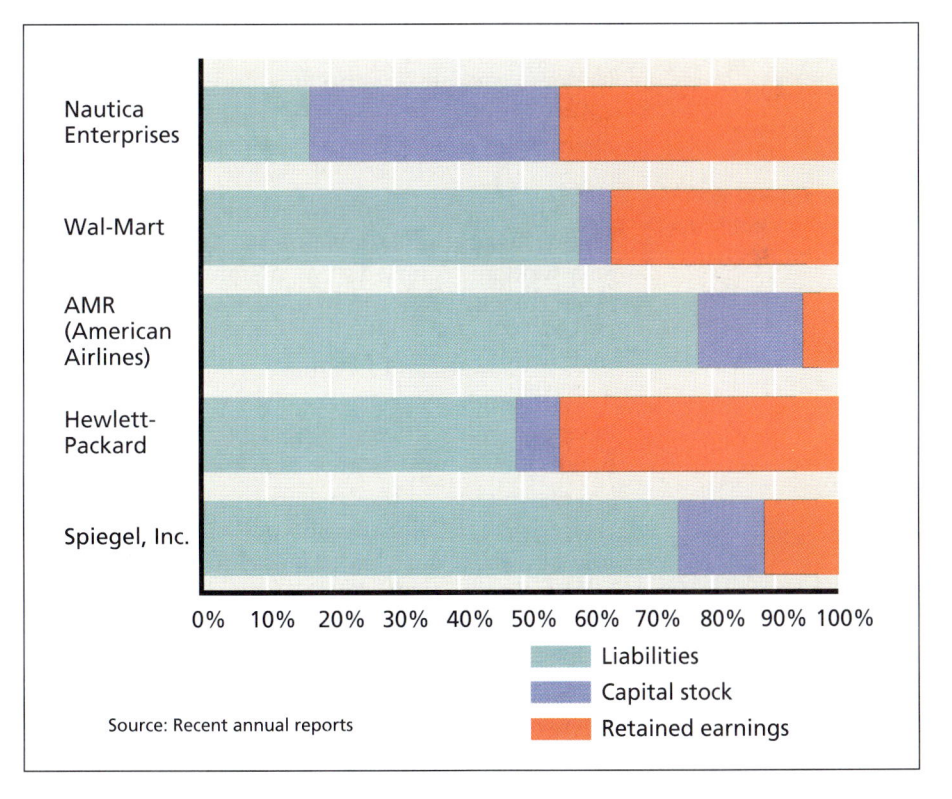

EXHIBIT 18–1
Sources of Financing

[2] Retained earnings as a means of financing dictates that income is reinvested in the business rather than being distributed as dividends. This is a popular practice with young, growing companies, as discussed in Chapter 17.

A number of financial instruments have developed rapidly and do not fit cleanly into the traditional accounting model. As a result, the Financial Accounting Standards Board has been very busy in trying to keep pace with the world's changing financial markets. No doubt a number of the nontraditional instruments will present new and challenging reporting issues over the coming years—issues that go well beyond the scope of an introductory text. Yet it is important that you have some understanding of the ways that entities might "sacrifice" their future. A reliance on the wrong form of funding could produce years of economic adversity for both the company and investor alike.

In Chapter 8, for example, we cited the case of Orange County, California, which had to file for bankruptcy because of massive losses on a financial instrument known as *derivatives*. Derivatives include a number of financial products whose value is based on (derived from) other products and economic measures. Massive losses on derivatives also plagued Odessa College, a junior college in Texas. To pay its bills, the school was forced to borrow $10.5 million on an emergency basis, increase tuition by 20%, and raise real-estate taxes on local property owners by 7.2%. At the same time, administrators slashed the operating budget from $18 million to $16 million.[3] These illustrations make a key point: Unless businesses and governmental units have a fundamental knowledge of financial instruments, innocent stockholders, creditors, and taxpayers may be asked to foot the bill for the mistakes of uninformed decision makers.

BOND ISSUES

②

Describe the basic differences between bondholders and stockholders and identify the various types of bonds that may be issued.

Suppose an automobile manufacturer has decided to build a new plant to produce subcompacts. The plant's construction cost might be more than a single lender is capable of supplying and far exceeds the cash flows generated from daily operating activities. The manufacturer therefore has two basic financing alternatives available: the issuance of additional shares of stock or the issuance of bonds.

Bonds allow a borrower to split a large loan into many small divisible units. Each of these units (known as a bond) is essentially a note payable, that is, a written promise to pay a sum of money on a specified future date. Like capital stock, bonds are issued through an underwriter to the investing public. Once outstanding, such obligations can be bought and sold on organized securities exchanges and are thus easily transferable.

Although stocks and bonds may seem somewhat similar, their holders have distinctly different rights. Stockholders are the owners of a corporation; bondholders, on the other hand, are creditors whose claims are classified as long-term debt on the balance sheet. To protect the bondholders' interests, the issuing firm usually appoints a *trustee*. The trustee, often a large bank, plays the role of a third party to monitor the issuer's adherence to stated terms of the bonds. For example, bond issues frequently permit dividends to be paid to stockholders only if certain working capital levels are maintained. If bond provisions are violated, the trustee may initiate appropriate action, such as lawsuits or perhaps the seizure and foreclosure of any property pledged as collateral on the bond issue. The provisions of a bond issue are normally stipulated in an accompanying document called a **bond indenture.**

---

[3] "How a Texas College Mortgaged Its Future In Derivatives Debacle," *The Wall Street Journal*, September 23, 1994, pp. A1, A5.

Exhibit 18–2 summarizes two further differences between bondholders and stockholders based on the creditor/owner relationship.

TYPES OF BONDS

Bonds are issued by corporations, the federal government, states, school districts, and local municipalities. These entities have varying financial needs, and the bonds they issue appeal to different types of investors. As a result, many types of bonds are used in the fund-raising process.

Secured and Debenture Bonds. Many bonds are secured; that is, assets have been pledged as security for the bondholders should the issuing company fail to meet its obligations under the indenture agreement. Virtually any type of property can be pledged. As an example, mortgage bonds are generally backed by property, plant, and equipment; collateral trust bonds by negotiable securities; and so forth.

In contrast to secured bonds, debenture bonds have no assets pledged as security. The marketability of debenture bonds is therefore based on the general credit of the issuing company. To sell debentures, the issuer must have a long period of substantial earnings as well as favorable prospects for future income and solvency. Many corporations have issued *subordinated* debentures. Should liquidation occur, the holders of subordinated bonds are paid only if sufficient assets remain after settling the claims of other designated creditors (as specified in the indenture agreement).

Registered and Coupon Bonds. Bonds can also be classified by the manner in which the related interest is disbursed. Most of the bonds issued in recent years have been registered bonds; that is, the issuing firm maintains a record of the purchaser's name and address. At the time interest is paid, the disbursing company simply mails a check to the bond's registered owner.

Interest payments on coupon bonds are handled in a different fashion. Coupon bonds have small detachable coupons that correspond to each interest period and are payable to the bearer. The bondholder detaches the coupon as it

EXHIBIT 18–2
Differences Between Bondholders and Stockholders

	BONDHOLDERS (CREDITORS)	**STOCKHOLDERS (OWNERS)**
Claim on income	Bondholders receive interest and have a yearly fixed claim on income. Interest must be paid regardless of the level of earnings.	Stockholders are paid dividends, subject to income levels and the discretion of the corporate directors.
Claim in liquidation	Bondholders have a prior claim on assets in the event of bankruptcy.	Stockholders have a residual claim on business assets. Should bankruptcy occur, the owners receive proceeds from asset liquidation only after the amounts due creditors have been settled.

falls due and deposits it at a bank for collection. By shifting the responsibility for collection to the bondholder and the bank, the issuing company avoids the need to maintain an up-to-date list of bond owners.

Other Bond Classifications. Many bond issues have a single maturity date for the entire issue. With **serial bonds,** however, bondholders are repaid in periodic installments over a number of years. For example, in 19X1 a company could issue $20 million of bonds that begin to mature in 19X6 at the rate of $4 million per year. This staggering of maturity dates allows investors (i.e., lenders) to select bonds that satisfy their cash flow needs.

Companies often create a special fund to repay a bond issue. Cash is set aside each year and invested in income-producing securities. The periodic cash deposits plus the investment income are then used for repayment. Funds of this type are commonly termed **sinking funds** and, appropriately, the bonds are sometimes called **sinking-fund debentures.**

Some bonds are **convertible** into shares of common stock at the option of the bondholder. The conversion feature allows a creditor to exchange a security with fixed interest receipts for one whose increase in value will be substantial should the issuing company enjoy high levels of profitability.

Many bonds are **callable** at the option of the issuing firm. Callable bonds permit the issuer to repay bondholders prior to the specified maturity date, a feature that is often exercised if funds become available at lower interest rates. In return for this feature, the issuer compensates the bondholder by setting a call price that normally exceeds the bonds' face value.

Finally, in the mid-1970s and throughout the 1980s, corporations raised billions of dollars by using so-called **junk bonds.** Such bonds are less than "investment grade" (i.e., somewhat risky) and, thus, speculative in nature. These bonds are sometimes issued by new firms with no track records or by established companies that are in poor financial health.

ACCOUNTING FOR BOND ISSUES: THE BASICS

Accounting for bonds can be quite complex; no doubt you will see why as we proceed through the chapter. For this reason we will start with a very basic illustration, with modifications (and realism) being added along the way. Before doing so, two simple facts regarding bonds must be explained. First, all bonds have a *face value*—a set amount to be repaid on the bond's maturity date. The face value is usually $1,000 or some multiple thereof. Second, bonds can be issued at any price, with the price normally expressed as a percentage of face value. For example, a $1,000 bond issued at 97 will cost the buyer $970.

Given this information, assume that on January 1, Tyler Corporation issued $500,000 of 10-year, 12% bonds at 100. Interest is payable semiannually on January 1 and July 1. The entry to record the issuance follows.

Jan. 1	Cash	500,000	
	Bonds Payable		500,000
	To record issuance of 10-year, 12% bonds.		

The Bonds Payable account is classified in the long-term liability section of the balance sheet until one year prior to the maturity date. At that time the bonds

> **ETHICS ISSUE**
>
> T, Inc., recently experienced a cash shortage and arranged to "borrow" $4 million from a $14 million sinking fund. The fund's trustee is Amy Thomas, an employee of the First National Bank and also the sister of T's president. T returned the monies (with interest) well before the bonds matured. Comment.

> **3**
>
> Account for bonds that are issued at, above, or below face value, and distinguish between contract and effective interest rates.

become a current liability and are disclosed accordingly. An exception to this treatment occurs when bonds will be retired by using a sinking fund, which is a noncurrent asset. Bonds retired by the use of noncurrent assets continue to be classified as long-term liabilities until the date of maturity.

The first semiannual interest date is July 1. Interest of $30,000 ($500,000 × 0.12 × 6/12) will be disbursed to bondholders and is recorded as follows:

July 1	Bond Interest Expense	30,000	
	Cash		30,000
	To record semiannual interest on bonds.		

Upon the bonds' maturity, Tyler must repay the $500,000 it has borrowed. The entry to record the cash outlay and bond retirement is:

(YEAR OF RETIREMENT)

Jan. 1	Bonds Payable	500,000	
	Cash		500,000
	To record retirement of bonds.		

FACTORS THAT AFFECT BOND PRICES

Suppose a large corporation is in the process of issuing bonds that bear a 10% interest rate. In addition to receiving approval from the firm's directors, the corporation must (1) obtain permission from the SEC, (2) have the bond certificates printed, and (3) have the bond issue publicized. All of these procedures take time. Given the dynamic nature of our economy, the original 10% interest rate may or may not be attractive to investors by the time the bonds are actually issued. Investors may therefore be willing to pay more or less than face value to secure a particular holding.

To illustrate, assume the going rate of interest is currently 11%. The corporation attempting to market the 10% bond issue mentioned previously may encounter some difficulty, because investors can obtain higher yields elsewhere. To make the bonds more attractive, the corporation could sell the issue for less than face value. In this manner a bondholder would still receive 10% interest as specified in the indenture (often called the nominal or **contract interest rate**); however, by lending the corporation a smaller amount, the investor's actual yield is increased. For example, if a $1,000 bond is issued at 91, the corporation cited would pay $100 of interest ($1,000 × 0.10) for the use of $910. The actual or **effective interest rate** is therefore greater than 10%. In conclusion, bonds are often issued below face value when their contract interest rate is less than the interest rate prevailing at the time of sale.

Interest rates are but one factor affecting the issue price. Consider, for instance, bond issues of companies with poor earnings records. Suppose that an entity with a history of losses issued 11% bonds at a time when the going rate of interest was 11%. Many investors might possibly be reluctant to purchase these bonds because of the firm's financial difficulties. Bondholders, of course, are concerned about timely interest receipts and the retirement of debt on the scheduled maturity date. As in the previous example, a drop in the issue price may be needed to make the bonds an attractive investment. When bonds are sold at less than face value, the difference between the issue price and face value is commonly referred to as a **discount.**

Naturally, the opposite situation can occur, with issuance at a price in excess of face value. If, for example, a company attempted to sell a 13% bond issue when the prevailing interest rate was 11%, demand could be overwhelming. Investors might be willing to pay more than face value to obtain the 13% receipts, thus depressing the actual, or yield, rate. In this particular case, the difference between the issue price and face value is called a **premium.**

Present Value. The amount an investor is willing to pay for a bond is determined by three items: (1) the cash inflows connected with the bond issue, (2) the timing of the cash inflows, and (3) the rate of return acceptable to the investor. To explain, a bond investment involves two cash inflows: periodic interest receipts and the return of principal on the maturity date. Interest, of course, is a primary consideration. If the receipts are unattractive, the investor will turn elsewhere to find more profitable opportunities.

The timing of these cash flows is also important. After an initial outlay, investors prefer a rapid inflow of funds so that reinvestment and other projects can be pursued. Dollars received soon after an investment is made are therefore regarded more favorably than inflows that occur in later periods. Finally, all investors seek a return on their precious funds. The return they desire is dependent on a number of factors, one of which is risk. Different investments have different risk levels. Consider, for example, the purchase of an insured certificate of deposit at a bank (a safe investment) versus the acquisition of a racehorse, which could produce large profits or large losses. Investors generally require higher rates of return as their exposure to risk increases.

A tool known as **present value** integrates cash flows, their timing, and the rate of return to determine the amount an investor is willing to pay for a bond —or any investment for that matter. An introduction to present value appears in the appendix to this chapter; a more detailed discussion is contained in Chapter 27.

BONDS ISSUED AT A DISCOUNT

To illustrate the necessary accounting for bonds issued at a discount, assume Homestead Corporation sold $200,000 of 4-year, 9% bonds on January 1. The company received only $193,537 because the going rate of interest in the marketplace was in excess of 9%. The entry that follows is needed to record the bond issue.

Jan. 1	Cash	193,537	
	Discount on Bonds Payable	6,463	
	Bonds Payable		200,000
	To record issuance of 4-year, 9% bonds.		

The bonds would appear on Homestead's balance sheet as follows:

Long-term liabilities		
Bonds payable	$200,000	
Less: Discount on bonds payable	6,463	$193,537

By deducting the Discount on Bonds Payable account from the bonds' face value, Homestead's net liability becomes $193,537—the amount borrowed on January 1. Stated differently, the bonds are shown at their *carrying value,* or face value minus the unamortized discount.[4]

Meaning of a Bond Discount. As we discussed in Chapter 13, a discount represents future interest expense. This idea is best understood by examining the cash flows related to the bond issue:

> 4
> Calculate amortization under both the straight-line and effective-interest methods.

Cash to be paid	
Interest payments over 4 years	
($200,000 × 0.09 × 4)	$ 72,000
Face value at maturity	200,000
Total	$272,000
Less: Cash received	193,537
Cost of borrowing	$ 78,463

Although Homestead is required to pay $72,000 of interest per the bond indenture, issuance at a discount has raised the cost of borrowing by $6,463 ($78,463 − $72,000). Not by accident, this increase corresponds with the balance in the Discount account as of January 1.

To reflect the higher borrowing cost, the discount must be periodically transferred to interest expense over the bond issue's life. This process, commonly known as *discount amortization*, is performed by using the straight-line method or the effective-interest method.

Discount Amortization: Straight-Line Method. Under *straight-line amortization,* an equal amount of discount is allocated to each interest period via the following formula:

$$\text{Periodic Straight-Line Amortization} = \frac{\text{Total Discount or Premium}}{\text{Number of Interest Periods}}$$

If we assume Homestead pays interest semiannually on June 30 and December 31, the discount will be amortized over eight installments (4 years × 2 interest periods per year) of $808 each ($6,463 ÷ 8). The following entries are therefore necessary on each interest date:

Bond Interest Expense	9,000	
Cash		9,000
To record semiannual interest payment:		
$200,000 × 0.09 × 6/12		
Bond Interest Expense	808	
Discount on Bonds Payable		808
To record semiannual discount amortization.		

---

[4] Carrying value is defined differently for bonds issued in excess of face value. That definition will be presented shortly.

The two entries show that Homestead's interest expense is determined by the semiannual contractual payment of $9,000 and by amortization of the discount. Interest therefore amounts to $9,808 and grows to $78,464 ($9,808 × 8 periods) over the life of the bond issue. Notice that aside from a $1 rounding error, this figure agrees with the total borrowing cost computed in the preceding discussion.

In addition to affecting Interest Expense, the amortization entry also reduces the Discount account and forces an increase in bond carrying value. For example, Homestead's balance sheet disclosure on June 30 (six months after issuance) would be as follows:

Long-term liabilities
  Bonds payable $200,000
  Less: Discount on bonds payable   5,655* $194,345

* $6,463 − $808.

By the time the maturity date is reached, the balance in Discount on Bonds Payable will be zero, which results in a $200,000 net liability.

A Compound-Entry Approach. Amortization procedures vary somewhat in practice. Many companies record amortization at the end of the accounting period rather than on each interest payment date. Furthermore, rather than have separate journal entries to record discount amortization and the payment of interest, some businesses use a compound (combined) entry. Homestead's entries on June 30, for instance, could have been recorded as follows:

Bond Interest Expense   9,808
  Discount on Bonds Payable   808
  Cash   9,000
To record semiannual interest payment
and discount amortization.

Discount Amortization: Effective-Interest Method. Despite its widespread use and popularity, the straight-line amortization of bond discount has a conceptual flaw. Straight-line amortization recognizes an equal amount of interest expense each period. At the same time, however, the bond carrying value (i.e., the net amount owed) is growing. Many accountants object to the straight-line method because of this apparent inconsistency. That is, if increasing amounts are owed, the amount of interest expense recorded each period should increase throughout the bond issue's life.

The preceding problem can be overcome by using the **effective-interest method** of amortization. Interest expense with this approach is calculated as a constant *percentage* of bond carrying value; thus, increasing carrying values are matched by increasing amounts of expense. Consistent with the method's name, the related computations are derived by using a bond's effective interest rate, not the contract rate. According to a ruling issued by the accounting profession, the effective-interest method must be utilized when it produces results that differ significantly from the straight-line approach.[5] Often, however, the two methods generate similar outcomes within a given reporting period.

[5] See "Interest on Receivables and Payables," *Opinions of the Accounting Principles Board No. 21,* American Institute of Certified Public Accountants, Jersey City, N.J., 1971.

An Example. To illustrate discount amortization with the effective-interest method, we will use the same facts we employed in the previous example. It is necessary, though, to introduce one additional detail: Homestead's bond issue has an effective interest rate of 10%.[6] The semiannual interest cost is therefore 5%—an interest cost that is associated with the firm's balance sheet liability.

Given that Homestead's January 1 outstanding debt is $193,537 (see the financial statement disclosure on p. 668), the interest expense for the first six months is $9,677 ($193,537 × 0.05). Of this amount, $9,000 is paid in cash to the bondholders and $677 is "unpaid" additional expense that arises from the discount. The following journal entries record the interest payment and the related discount amortization:

Bond Interest Expense	9,000	
Cash		9,000
To record semiannual interest payment.		
Bond Interest Expense	677	
Discount on Bonds Payable		677
To record semiannual discount amortization.		

To expand somewhat, examine the diagram that appears in Exhibit 18–3. Observe that the total "debt pool" has a balance of $193,537 at the beginning of the six-month period and a balance of $194,214 at the end. These figures are tied to Homestead's liability disclosures, both before and after the amortization journal entry, as shown on the following page:

EXHIBIT 18–3
Effective-Interest Discount Amortization: A Graphic Overview

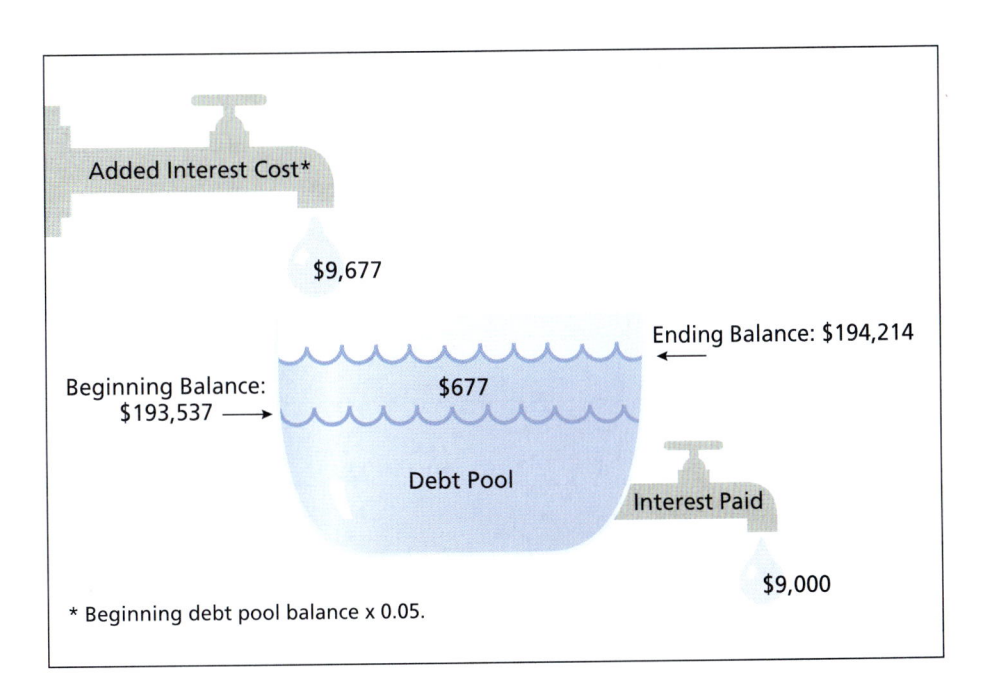

Added Interest Cost*

$9,677

Beginning Balance: $193,537

$677

Debt Pool

Ending Balance: $194,214

Interest Paid

$9,000

* Beginning debt pool balance x 0.05.

---

[6] The 10% rate should be taken as a given. The relationship between bond prices and the effective interest rate becomes apparent after studying the appendix to this chapter.

	JANUARY 1	AMORTIZATION	JUNE 30
Bonds payable	$200,000		$200,000
Less: Discount on bonds payable	6,463	–677	5,786
Net carrying value	$193,537		$194,214

Given that the debt has increased to $194,214, the total interest expense associated with the *second* semiannual period is $9,711 ($194,214 × 0.05): $9,000 in cash and $711 of discount amortization. This process is repeated on each interest date and is documented in the discount amortization schedule shown in Exhibit 18–4. The exhibit reveals that interest expense and discount amortization rise each period, a direct result of applying a constant interest rate against a growing bond carrying value/liability.

BONDS ISSUED AT A PREMIUM

Bonds are sold at a premium when their contract interest rate exceeds the prevailing market rate for bonds of a similar grade. In this particular case, investors are willing to pay more than face value to obtain the higher interest receipts. To illustrate the proper accounting, we will again use the Homestead Corporation example, with one modification. Assume the $200,000, 9% bond issue is now sold for $206,733. The entry to record the bond issue is:

Jan. 1	Cash	206,733	
	Premium on Bonds Payable		6,733
	Bonds Payable		200,000
	To record issuance of 4-year, 9% bonds.		

EXHIBIT 18–4
Discount Amortization Schedule

If Homestead were to prepare a balance sheet on January 1, the bonds would be disclosed as shown on the following page.

SEMIANNUAL INTEREST PERIOD	(A) EFFECTIVE SEMIANNUAL INTEREST EXPENSE (5% × CARRYING VALUE)	(B) SEMIANNUAL INTEREST PAYMENT (4½% × FACE VALUE)	(C) DISCOUNT AMORTIZATION (A – B)	(D) BOND DISCOUNT BALANCE	(E) END-OF-PERIOD BOND CARRYING VALUE (FACE VALUE – D)
Issue date				$6,463	$193,537
1	$ 9,677	$ 9,000	$ 677	5,786	194,214
2	9,711	9,000	711	5,075	194,925
3	9,746	9,000	746	4,329	195,671
4	9,784	9,000	784	3,545	196,455
5	9,823	9,000	823	2,722	197,278
6	9,864	9,000	864	1,858	198,142
7	9,907	9,000	907	951	199,049
8	9,951*	9,000	951	—	200,000
	$78,463	$72,000	$6,463		

*Difference due to rounding.

Long-term liabilities
Bonds payable $200,000
Add: Premium on bonds payable 6,733 $206,733

The bond carrying value of $206,733 is Homestead's net liability and is calculated by adding the premium to the bonds' face value. Since only $200,000 will be repaid at maturity (per the bond indenture), the carrying value must be reduced over the life of the issue. The necessary reduction is achieved through the amortization process discussed earlier.

Meaning of a Bond Premium. The meaning of a bond premium is best explained by examining the cash inflows and outflows related to the company's issue.

Cash to be paid
  Interest payments over 4 years
    ($200,000 × 0.09 × 4) $ 72,000
  Face value at maturity   200,000
  Total $272,000
Less: Cash received   206,733
Cost of borrowing $ 65,267

Notice that Homestead's cash payments for interest amount to $72,000; however, the total cost of borrowing is only $65,267. It is apparent, then, that a premium represents a payment by bondholders that reduces the issuing firm's interest expense, in this instance by $6,733 ($72,000 − $65,267). Observe that the reduction equals the balance in the Premium account on January 1. At this point we can conclude that a premium is the opposite of a discount, given the premium's effect on interest expense and its disclosure on the balance sheet (i.e., an addition to Bonds Payable as opposed to a reduction).

Premium Amortization: Straight-Line Method. A premium can also be amortized by either the straight-line or effective-interest methods. If straight-line amortization is used, $842 of premium ($6,733 ÷ 8) will be written off during each semiannual interest period. The entries that follow are therefore required on June 30 and each subsequent interest date.

Bond Interest Expense   9,000
  Cash   9,000
To record semiannual interest payment:
$200,000 × 0.09 × 6/12

Premium on Bonds Payable   842
  Bond Interest Expense   842
To record semiannual premium amortization.

The amortization entry reduces both the Premium and the Bond Interest Expense accounts, the latter resulting in a six-month borrowing cost of $8,158 ($9,000 − $842). Over the life of the bond issue, total expense will amount to $65,264 ($8,158 × 8 periods), which, except for a small rounding error, agrees with the borrowing cost calculated earlier. Finally, observe that as the premium becomes smaller, the bond carrying value decreases and will eventually become $200,000—the amount Homestead owes as of the maturity date. As partial evidence, compare Homestead's January 1 balance sheet disclosure with that of June 30:

	JANUARY 1	JUNE 30
Long-term liabilities		
Bonds payable	$200,000	$200,000
Add: Premium on bonds payable	6,733	5,891
	$206,733	$205,891*

* $6,733 − $842.

Premium Amortization: Effective-Interest Method. We turn now to the effective-interest method. Assume that the premium arose from an annual effective interest rate of 8%, or 4% if figured semiannually. Exhibit 18–5 shows that the total interest expense for the first six months, $8,269 ($206,733 × 0.04), is less than the $9,000 payment to bondholders. This situation is caused by $731 of premium amortization ($9,000 − $8,269) and gives rise to the following journal entries:

Bond Interest Expense	9,000	
Cash		9,000
To record semiannual interest payment.		
Premium on Bonds Payable	731	
Bond Interest Expense		731
To record semiannual premium amortization.		

EXHIBIT 18–5
Effective-Interest Premium Amortization: A Graphic Overview

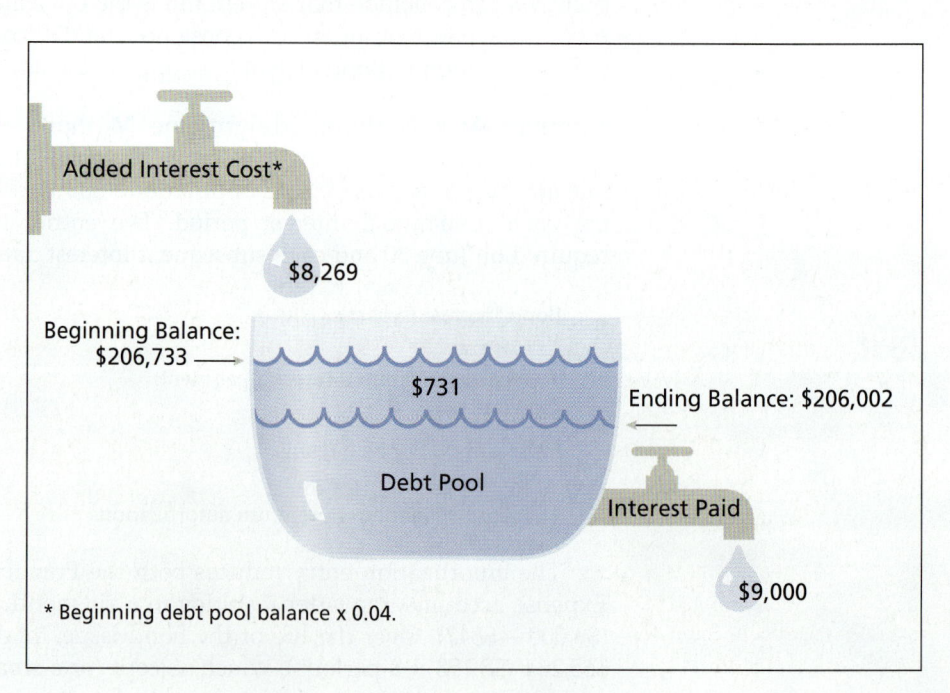

Added Interest Cost*

$8,269

Beginning Balance: $206,733

$731

Debt Pool

Ending Balance: $206,002

Interest Paid

$9,000

* Beginning debt pool balance x 0.04.

The total debt pool is therefore reduced to $206,002 on June 30. Given the decrease in Homestead's liability, interest expense in the next six-month period would fall to $8,240 ($206,002 × 0.04). This mechanical process is repeated throughout the life of the bond issue, as documented in Exhibit 18–6.

BOND ISSUES AND TIMING CONSIDERATIONS

5 Account for bonds issued between interest dates and for bond retirements.

In each of the preceding illustrations, we assumed the bonds were dated and sold on January 1—namely, on one of the interest payment dates. Such is not always the case. Bonds can be issued at any time, and issuance between interest dates occurs quite often. To simplify record keeping, it is common practice to collect from the bond's purchaser any interest that has accumulated since the last interest date. The issuing firm can then pay a full period's interest to the bondholder on the next semiannual disbursement date without having to keep track of the date of sale. As we will now show, the interest that has been collected is eventually returned to the investor.

Assume that Hartford Corporation has a $1 million, 10-year, 12% bond issue that pays interest on January 1 and July 1. If the bonds are issued on May 1, the following journal entry would be needed:

May 1	Cash	1,040,000	
	Bonds Payable		1,000,000
	Bond Interest Payable		40,000
	To record issuance of bonds plus collection of 4 months' accrued interest.		

EXHIBIT 18–6
Premium Amortization Schedule

SEMIANNUAL INTEREST PERIOD	(A) EFFECTIVE SEMIANNUAL INTEREST EXPENSE (4% × CARRYING VALUE)	(B) SEMIANNUAL INTEREST PAYMENT (4½% × FACE VALUE)	(C) PREMIUM AMORTIZATION (B − A)	(D) BOND PREMIUM BALANCE	(E) END-OF-PERIOD BOND CARRYING VALUE (FACE VALUE + D)
Issue date				$6,733	$206,733
1	$ 8,269	$ 9,000	$ 731	6,002	206,002
2	8,240	9,000	760	5,242	205,242
3	8,210	9,000	790	4,452	204,452
4	8,178	9,000	822	3,630	203,630
5	8,145	9,000	855	2,775	202,775
6	8,111	9,000	889	1,886	201,886
7	8,075	9,000	925	961	200,961
8	8,039*	9,000	961	—	200,000
	$65,267	$72,000	$6,733		

*Difference due to rounding.

Hartford has received $1,040,000: the $1,000,000 issue price plus $40,000 of interest, the latter of which has accumulated from January 1 through April 30 ($1,000,000 × 0.12 × 4/12). The interest is recorded as a current liability because it is owed to the bondholders and will be returned on the next interest date.

When semiannual interest is paid two months later on July 1, Hartford will record the following entry:

July 1	Bond Interest Payable	40,000	
	Bond Interest Expense	20,000	
	Cash		60,000
	To record semiannual interest payment.		

Although six months' interest is being paid, remember that the company received four months' accrued interest on May 1. Thus, Hartford's actual expense is for May and June only and amounts to $20,000 ($1,000,000 × 0.12 × 2/12).

Year-End Interest Accruals. In the previous examples we also assumed that one of the semiannual interest dates coincided with the company's year-end. When this situation does not occur, it is necessary to accrue interest from the last payment date until the end of the reporting period. Because premiums and discounts affect interest expense, amortization must be recorded as well.

BOND RETIREMENT

Bonds are sold under the money and credit conditions that prevail at the time of issue. Frequently, in order to raise the necessary funds, the issuing company must incur high effective interest rates and make promises to bondholders that inhibit future financing flexibility. Examples of such promises include restrictions on dividend payments and the maintenance of a certain working capital position (current assets minus current liabilities).

Most companies protect themselves and take advantage of changing market conditions (and possible lower interest rates) by including a call provision on bond issues. Such a provision allows issuers to reacquire the bonds at a stipulated percentage of face value. Bonds may be called and be replaced by an issue that carries a lower interest rate (known as **bond refunding**) or be retired and canceled (known as **bond retirement**). In either case, any difference between the bond carrying value and the call price is treated as a gain or a loss in the year when the call occurs.[7]

To illustrate the proper accounting, assume Troup Manufacturing retired a $400,000, 8% bond issue that had an unamortized premium balance of $16,000. If the bonds were called at 106 on one of the semiannual interest dates,[8] Troup would record the entry that is shown on the following page.

---

[7] Sizable gains and losses that result from the extinguishment of debt are reported on the income statement as an extraordinary item. This special disclosure treatment arose from market conditions that existed in the early 1970s, allowing companies to realize significant gains (sometimes amounting to millions of dollars) on the early retirement of debt.

[8] Prior to recording the retirement, journal entries are needed to update related interest payments and premium (or discount) amortization.

Bonds Payable	400,000	
Premium on Bonds Payable	16,000	
Loss on Bond Retirement	8,000	
Cash		424,000

To record retirement of bond issue at 106.

The retirement calls for the removal of the bonds from the accounting records at their current carrying value ($416,000). Thus, Bonds Payable and Premium on Bonds Payable are both debited. The loss arose because the amount paid was greater than the carrying value; had the opposite situation occurred, a gain would have been generated. Overall, the required accounting treatment is similar to that for the retirement and sale of a depreciable asset. Recall that depreciation expense is first updated. Next, the asset's book value is removed from the records via both the asset and accumulated depreciation accounts. As a final step, a gain or loss on disposal is computed by comparing book value with the sale proceeds.

AN ANALYSIS OF OUTSTANDING DEBT

6 *Analyze the extent of a company's outstanding debt.*

We conclude our study of bond financing by taking a look at Euro Disney, the recently opened European version of Disney World. Monthly operating profit averaged $5.5 million in the park's first year; yet the project lost $920 million. A major cause of the red ink was interest (and lots of it). Euro Disney's total design and construction costs ran about $4 billion, with approximately $2.9 billion of this figure obtained by borrowing, at interest rates as high as 11%.[9]

Although debt is an attractive source of financing, too much debt can severely hamper a business and profitability. Sizable monthly outlays for principal and interest can strain even a healthy company's cash position. Missed payments may eventually cause loans to be called, credit (and bond) ratings to be lowered, and bankruptcy proceedings to begin. These actions will often limit an organization's future financing alternatives and make them more costly. Higher-risk entities are normally subjected to higher interest rates and are forced to maintain certain restrictive ratios, as lenders seek assurances that new debt issuances will be repaid. To assess a company's relative debt position, analysts often compute two ratios: debt to total assets and times interest earned.

Debt to Total Assets. The debt to total assets ratio shows the percentage of total capital provided by a firm's creditors. The ratio is computed as follows: Total Debt ÷ Total Assets. Creditors generally prefer a low ratio, indicating that a large percentage of asset financing is provided by the owners and/or operations. Low debt means affordable monthly outlays for principal and interest and, thus, a reduced risk of nonpayment should sales and earnings fall.

Stockholders, in contrast, sometimes desire a high debt to total assets ratio. As shown in Chapter 16, the presence of debt in the capital structure can give rise to trading on the equity at a gain (i.e., positive leverage), benefiting the common stockholders. Increased debt normally increases leverage. However, too much debt may actually cause the reduction or elimination of common

---

[9] "Mickey N'est Pas Fini," *Forbes*, February 14, 1994, pp. 42–43.

stock dividends, which are subject to the discretion of the board of directors. Generally speaking, debt is acceptable as long as it is used in moderation.

Times Interest Earned. Although a company is heavily financed by debt, earnings may be more than adequate to cover the required interest charges. If, on the other hand, interest coverage is marginal, the creditors' position may be threatened. Insight into the amount of protection that is afforded the long-term creditors is provided by a ratio called *times interest earned.* The ratio is calculated as follows: Income Before Income Taxes and Interest ÷ Interest Expense.

BUSINESS BRIEFING

JAMES PRESTON
Chairman and Chief Executive Officer
Avon Products, Inc.

Debt Can Be Dangerous

Avon found itself with more than $1.1 billion of debt in the late 1980s due to a disastrous diversification effort. That was a monstrous burden for a company with annual sales of just over $3 billion. Interest payments were more than $100 million a year. The company's survival depended on reducing obligations, which meant a total focus on generating cash. Investing in tomorrow was delayed. Research expenses were cut to a minimum. Capital spending for new equipment was limited. Training was virtually eliminated. New market entries were delayed. The banks imposed restrictions to ensure that payment would be forthcoming.

All of these actions would have been bad enough, but Avon's weakened financial position attracted a series of raiders. We were forced to fight a war on two fronts—our competitors in the marketplace and the raiders on Wall Street. In the end, we won both battles. In just two years, we slashed our debt by more than 50%. By year-end 1993 we were virtually debt free, which gave us the flexibility to enter more new markets, to further modernize, and to develop more state-of-the-art beauty products. We're doing a lot of these things again, but with earnings. We borrowed to diversify and almost didn't survive.

INVESTING IN FINANCIAL INSTRUMENTS

The first part of this chapter and much of the content in Chapters 16 and 17 focused on bonds and stock (financial instruments) from the issuer's point of view. We will now introduce the other side of these transactions and look at the investor's accounting records.

The Financial Accounting Standards Board recently changed the way that companies must account for their investments in debt and equity securities.[10] Earlier in the text we introduced the topic of *trading securities*, or investments that were purchased with the objective of generating profits on near-term sales.

---

[10] See "Accounting for Certain Investments in Debt and Equity Securities," *Statement of Financial Accounting Standards No. 115*, Financial Accounting Standards Board, Norwalk, Conn., 1993.

Two other investment classifications were established by the Board in *Statement No. 115:* held-to-maturity securities and available-for-sale securities. Held-to-maturity securities are those investments that a company has the intent and ability to hold until maturity. Available-for-sale securities, in contrast, are investments not otherwise classified as trading securities or held-to-maturity securities. If we picture the three classifications on a continuum, the available-for-sale category falls somewhere between "trading" and "held to maturity."

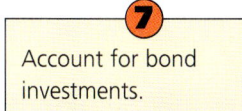

INVESTMENTS IN BONDS

7 Account for bond investments.

Bond investments can be classified as either held-to-maturity or available-for-sale securities. Most bond investments fall in the first category, and we will limit our discussion accordingly. Held-to-maturity securities are reported on the balance sheet at amortized cost, which is the carrying value that results from using effective-interest amortization. As you will now see, accounting for held-to-maturity bond investments is very similar to the accounting practiced for bond issuances.

Recording the Initial Investment and Interest Receipts. Assume that on January 1, 19X1, Foxmire Corporation purchased $300,000 of Harkness Corporation's 8%, 10-year bonds for $262,991. Interest is paid semiannually on June 30 and December 31, and the bonds generated an effective yield to investors of 10%. The journal entry to record the purchase is:

Jan. 1	Investment in Harkness Bonds	262,991	
	Cash		262,991
	To record investment in Harkness bonds.		

Consistent with the proper accounting treatment for all assets, the Investment in Harkness Bonds account is established at cost. Although the bonds were acquired at an amount different from their $300,000 face value, a separate discount (or premium) account is not used. Instead, the discount (or premium) is commingled with the investment and will be amortized over the bond issue's life.

The periodic interest receipts normally represent the primary source of revenue related to a bond investment. Suppose it is now June 30 and Foxmire receives the first semiannual interest check of $12,000 ($300,000 × 0.08 × 6/12). The following entry is necessary:

June 30	Cash	12,000	
	Bond Interest Revenue		12,000
	To record the receipt of semiannual interest.		

Discount Amortization. The $262,991 acquisition cost in this example gives rise to a $37,009 discount ($300,000 − $262,991). Treatment of this discount is very easy to understand if we review Exhibit 18–4 on page 672, which shows the proper accounting for the bond *issuer.* Here we see that the discount increased interest expense to exceed the amounts paid to bondholders. Also observe that through the amortization process, the carrying value eventually increased to coincide with the bonds' face value.

The bond investor follows essentially the same procedures. The increase in interest expense by the issuer is matched by an increase in bond interest revenue by the investor. In addition, the Investment in Harkness Bonds account is increased and, for Foxmire, will reach $300,000 by the time the bonds mature in 10 years. These increases are brought about by effective-interest amortization, which involves the two calculations (steps) that follow.

1. Multiply the bonds' carrying value by the effective interest rate to figure total interest revenue.
2. Compute amortization as the difference between the amount of interest calculated in Step 1 and the cash received for interest.

In our example, the bonds have an initial carrying value of $262,991 and a 10% effective yield. If we focus on June 30, the first semiannual interest date, total interest revenue from Step 1 is $13,150 ($262,991 × 0.10 × 6/12). As described in Step 2, the amortization to be recorded amounts to $1,150 ($13,150 − $12,000), giving rise to the following journal entry:

June 30	Investment in Harkness Bonds	1,150	
	Bond Interest Revenue		1,150
	To record discount amortization.		

The journal entry increases the balances in both accounts, consistent with the desired outcomes cited earlier. The updated carrying value in the Investment account, $264,141 ($262,991 + $1,150), will serve as the basis for the amortization calculation on the next semiannual interest date (December 31).

Premium Amortization. Similar procedures are followed for bonds purchased at a price in excess of face value, that is, at a premium. The premium has the opposite effect of a discount and reduces bond interest revenue over the life of the issue. A premium must therefore be amortized by means of the entry shown:

Bond Interest Revenue	XXX	
Investment in Bonds		XXX
To record premium amortization.		

The debit records the reduction in interest revenue, while the credit lowers the Investment in Bonds account. At the maturity date, the balance in the Investment account will equal the face value of the bonds acquired.

INVESTMENTS IN STOCK

> **8** Describe the features of available-for-sale stock investments and the equity method.

Generally speaking, accounting for stock investments is more complicated than that for bonds. The proper treatment depends on several factors, such as the intent of the investment, the number of shares held, and the ability to influence the company owned (known as the *investee*). We have already explored two types of stock investments: trading securities (Chapter 8) and controlling investments (Chapter 7). The held-to-maturity classification of *FASB Statement No. 115* does not apply here, given that stocks do not come due on a maturity date. By default, stocks purchased without a trading or control intent are categorized as available-for-sale securities. An exception to this classification occurs when a company has the ability to "significantly influence" the corporation whose shares were acquired. The equity method of accounting must be used in the latter situation.

Available-for-Sale Securities. Available-for-sale securities are handled in much the same fashion as trading securities, with investments initially entered in the accounts at cost. These amounts are later adjusted to reflect fair market values at the time of financial statement preparation. In addition, any dividends received from the investment are recorded as revenue.

To illustrate this treatment, assume the following information relates to Savko Company:

- On January 1, Savko purchased 15,000 common shares of Fresno Manufacturing at $30 per share. Fresno has 150,000 shares of common stock outstanding.
- During the year Fresno reported net income of $290,000 and paid $120,000 of dividends.
- On December 31, the close of Savko's accounting period, Fresno's common stock had a market value of $27 per share.

Given that Savko owns 10% of Fresno (15,000 shares ÷ 150,000 shares), the following entries are needed to record these transactions and events:

Investment by Savko
Investment in Fresno Manufacturing	450,000	
Cash		450,000
To record the acquisition of 15,000 shares of Fresno at $30 per share.		

Announcement of Fresno's Earnings of $290,000
No entry required

Receipt of Cash Dividends
Cash	12,000	
Dividend Revenue		12,000
To record the receipt of 10% of Fresno's dividends.		

Valuation at Market Value on December 31
Unrealized Loss on Available-for-Sale Securities*	45,000	
Investment in Fresno Manufacturing†		45,000
To reduce the investment in Fresno to market value: ($30 − $27) × 15,000 shares.		

* This account is given special treatment. It is disclosed as part of stockholders' equity and not considered in the calculation of net income.
† Rather than directly reduce Investment in Fresno Manufacturing, Savko could use an alternative approach and credit a separate Allowance account.

On the basis of these entries, the investment would appear as follows in the long-term investments section of Savko's balance sheet:

Available-for-sale securities
    Investment in Fresno Manufacturing (at market value) $405,000

The Equity Method. When a company acquires a substantial percentage (20% or more) of a corporation's voting shares, the acquiring firm normally gains the ability to significantly influence both the financial and operating policies of the investee. In such instances, unless there is substantial evidence to the contrary, a material economic relationship is formed between the investor and investee, and the *equity method* of accounting must be used.[11]

Under the equity method, long-term investments in common stock are initially recorded at acquisition cost. The Investment account is then increased or decreased to reflect changes in the retained earnings of the investee. Specifically, the Investment account is increased for the investor's share of reported investee net income and decreased for the investor's share of any investee net losses or dividends. The "investor's share" is based on the percentage of voting stock owned; the income, loss, and dividend amounts relate strictly to periods after the stock is acquired. Realize that *the equity method focuses principally on changes in the investee's retained earnings, not changes in the market value of the investee's shares.*

To illustrate the equity method, we will use the same facts as in the previous example. Assume, however, that Savko purchased 45,000 shares of Fresno, resulting in a 30% ownership interest (45,000 shares ÷ 150,000 shares). Savko will make the following entries:

Investment by Savko
Investment in Fresno Manufacturing	1,350,000	
Cash		1,350,000

To record the acquisition of 45,000 shares of Fresno at $30 per share.

Announcement of Fresno's Earnings of $290,000
Investment in Fresno Manufacturing	87,000	
Investment Revenue		87,000

To record 30% share of Fresno's earnings:
$290,000 × 0.30 = $87,000

Receipt of Cash Dividends
Cash	36,000	
Investment in Fresno Manufacturing		36,000

To record the receipt of cash dividends:
$120,000 × 0.30 = $36,000

---

[11] See "The Equity Method of Accounting for Investments in Common Stock," *Opinions of the Accounting Principles Board No. 18,* American Institute of Certified Public Accountants, Jersey City, N.J., 1971. The *Opinion* notes that the ability to exert influence may take forms other than percentage ownership (e.g., representation on the investee's board of directors, interchange of managerial personnel, and technological dependency).

Valuation at Market Value on December 31
  No entry required

On the basis of these entries, Savko's investment would be reported on the year-end balance sheet at $1,401,000 as shown by the following T-account:

INVESTMENT IN FRESNO MANUFACTURING				
Initial investment	1,350,000	Share of dividends		36,000
Share of income	87,000			
1,401,000	1,437,000			

Observe that the $51,000 increase in the investment's carrying value (after the initial acquisition) corresponds to 30% of the increase in Fresno's Retained Earnings account [($290,000 net income − $120,000 dividends) × 0.30 = $51,000]. Also notice that Savko did not recognize any revenue at the time the dividend was received. Although this procedure may seem illogical, bear in mind that (1) dividends represent a distribution of earnings and (2) Savko has already recognized $87,000 of Fresno's net income. If the dividends were recorded as additional revenue, they would be double-counted.

Rationale for the Equity Method. As we have shown on numerous occasions throughout this text, financial statements are used by a number of different parties (e.g., owners, managers, and creditors, to name just a few). To meet the varied needs of these groups, the statements must be objective and neutral. Should bias be present, some users may benefit at the expense of others. For example, if management can manipulate revenue recognition to show higher earnings, creditors and investors may make incorrect decisions regarding the financial health and well-being of the enterprise. It is in this light that the equity method was developed.

Suppose for a moment that a company owned 40% of an investee corporation. Also assume that the investor company was experiencing abnormally low earnings, while the investee was extremely profitable. The investor, with significant influence over operations because of its ownership position, could convince the investee to distribute unusually large amounts of dividends. Had the equity method not been developed, the investor would report the dividends as revenue and thereby manipulate (i.e., control) its own profit. In situations where the ownership interest is 20% or more, the equity method presents a better picture of financial performance because such distributions do not affect investor earnings.

APPENDIX: PRESENT VALUE

As we noted in the body of this chapter, investors use the concept of present value to determine the amount they are willing to pay for a bond issue. To illustrate present value, assume that today is January 1 and you have $1,000 to invest. After studying various alternatives, you have narrowed the field to investments A and B. The investments each promise a $100 cash inflow during the next 12 months. However, as the following schedule shows, the timing differs.

9 Use present value techniques to determine the issue price of bonds.

	A	B
Cash outlay required on Jan. 1	$1,000	$1,000
Forecasted cash inflows		
Mar. 31	$ 25	
June 30	25	
Sept. 30	25	
Dec. 31	25	$ 100
	$ 100	$ 100

Although A and B both yield a 10% rate of return ($100 ÷ $1,000), most people would select investment A for two reasons. First, the future is usually unpredictable and full of uncertainty. Thus, all other things being equal, a more rapid recovery of investment dollars helps to reduce the risk associated with an outlay. The dollars are in hand, and the investor becomes less concerned about events that may stop or inhibit the generation of returns. Investment A is also preferred for another reason. Money has a *time value*; specifically, a dollar today is worth more than a dollar in the future. Dollars received early in the year or in the early years of a long-lived project can be reinvested to produce additional earnings. The inflows associated with investment A can, therefore, be put to work. Nothing, however, can be done with the $100 from investment B until December 31.

Present value recognizes the time value of money and weights cash flows occurring in earlier periods more heavily than those that take place further in the future. Before we proceed, we must first examine a concept with which most of you are familiar—compound interest.

COMPOUND INTEREST AND PRESENT VALUE

Earlier in the text we introduced the computation of simple interest with the following formula:

$$\text{Interest} = \text{Principal} \times \text{Rate} \times \text{Time}$$

Notice that interest is calculated on principal only. In contrast, **compound interest** is figured on principal *and* on previously computed interest as well. To illustrate the related calculations, assume you deposited $100 in a savings account that pays 10% interest. If interest is compounded annually, the deposit will grow to $121 by the end of two years.

	YEAR 1	YEAR 2
Beginning of year	$100	$110
Add: 10% interest	10	11*
End of year	$110	$121

*$110 × 0.10.

The preceding concept is sometimes referred to as *future value,* because it reflects the amount to which an outlay will grow by the end of a designated time period.

Approaching the same example from a slightly different perspective, suppose you are willing to accept a 10% return on your money. If an investment opportunity is available that promises a $110 cash inflow at the end of one year, how much would you be willing to invest today to obtain that inflow? We hope you answered $100. Why? If you invest $100 today at a 10% interest rate, the investment will grow to the $110 you can receive. The $100 is termed the investment's *present value,* or the amount an investor is willing to pay to obtain a specified cash flow ($110) on a future date (one year from now) at a given rate of return (10%).

Observe that the preceding question could have been phrased as follows: Given a 10% rate of return, how much would you be willing to invest today to receive $121 at the end of two years? As before, the answer is $100.

RELATIONSHIP BETWEEN COMPOUND INTEREST AND PRESENT VALUE

By using a factor of $(1 + r)^n$, where r is equal to the interest rate per period and n equals the number of periods, we can illustrate the relationship between present value and compound interest (i.e., future value). For compound interest the calculations are as follows:

ORIGINAL AMOUNT			END OF YEAR 1			END OF YEAR 2
$100	×	$(1.10)^1$ =	$110	×	$(1.10)^1$ =	$121

Alternatively, the same results could have been achieved by the following computation:

$$\$100 \times (1.10)^2 = \$121$$

In either case a present amount is compounded at a 10% interest rate and extended two years into the future.

For present value the situation is reversed—a future amount is *discounted* and brought back to today. This process is diagrammed below.

END OF YEAR 2			END OF YEAR 1			ORIGINAL AMOUNT
$121	×	$\frac{1}{(1.10)^1}$ =	$110	×	$\frac{1}{(1.10)^1}$ =	$100

In a manner similar to compound interest, discounting could have been illustrated as follows:

$$\$121 \times \frac{1}{(1.10)^2} = \$100$$

Fortunately, tables are available to simplify present value calculations. See Table 1 in Appendix C at the end of the text, which is the present value of $1 at various interest rates and for various time periods. The use of the table may be shown with the example just cited. Observe that the 10% column and 2-period row reveal a factor of 0.82645, which is the present value of $1 received in two years at a 10% interest rate. Because we desire to find the present value of $121 and not $1, the following multiplication is necessary:

Cash Flow		Present Value Factor		Present Value
$121	×	0.82645	=	$100

Present Value and Annuities

Most investment opportunities are accompanied by cash flows that occur over a time span of several years. Consider, for instance, the following schedule of discounted cash flows that has been constructed for a planned investment of Westcott Enterprises. The schedule is based on a 10% interest rate.

Year	Cash Flow		Present Value Factor		Present Value
1	$2,000	×	0.90909	=	$1,818
2	2,000	×	0.82645	=	1,653
3	2,000	×	0.75132	=	1,503
4	2,000	×	0.68301	=	1,366
5	2,000	×	0.62092	=	1,242
Total present value					$7,582

Although more cash flows are involved, we continue to multiply monetary amounts by present value factors extracted from Table 1. These factors reveal the time value of money, with the $2,000 inflow that occurs in Year 1 having a greater present value (i.e., "worth") to Westcott than the inflow that occurs in Year 5 ($1,818 versus $1,242). The figures indicate a total present value of $7,582— the maximum amount the firm can afford to pay to acquire this investment and still generate a 10% return on its funds.

As you may have gathered, present value computations can become rather tedious. The Westcott illustration dealt with five cash flows. The calculations would be considerably more burdensome in a longer term, more realistic investment, say 10 years, with different inflows and outflows occurring within a single period. Fortunately, several shortcuts are available to minimize the procedural difficulties.

Notice that in each year the present value factor is multiplied by a $2,000 monetary amount. The calculations would have required less work had the annual cash flow been multiplied by the summation of the individual factors (0.90909 + 0.82645 + 0.75132 + 0.68301 + 0.62092 = 3.79079). As the following figures show, the same result is achieved: $2,000 × 3.79079 = $7,582.

Another possibility is to recognize that this example has focused on the concept of an *annuity*—a series of equal cash receipts or disbursements over a number of years. To further simplify the process, the individual present value factors from Table 1 are often combined to produce an annuity table (see Table 2 in Appendix C). The factor in Table 2 for a $1 annuity to be received over the next five years, discounted at 10%, is 3.79079. Thus, the following calculation becomes appropriate:

Cash Flow		Present Value Factor		Present Value
$2,000	×	3.79079	=	$7,582

A third shortcut involves electronics. Spreadsheets and even the most basic hand-held calculators have built-in present value functions. Users can therefore minimize computational efforts and concentrate instead on an analysis of the underlying numbers.

Periods of Less Than One Year

Virtually all of our illustrations have focused on annual cash flows. Cash flows may occur more frequently; for example, bond interest is often paid on a semi-annual basis, quarterly interest is added to savings accounts, and so forth. The tables included at the end of the text can still be used when this situation arises; however, a slight modification is needed.

The time that elapses between the cash flows under evaluation is termed the *interest period.* It is imperative that *the percentage rate employed correspond with the interest period in question.* For instance, consider a company that desires a 12% return via $50,000 annual cash flows in each of the next ten years. In this particular case, the tables may be used as illustrated in earlier examples, giving rise to a factor from the 12% column and the 10-period row. Suppose, however, that the cash flows will now be $25,000 on a semiannual basis. The semiannual flows occur every six months, giving rise to two interest periods per year and a total of 20 over the project's life. The 12% annual rate must be halved to 6% to become aligned with the six-month period. Thus, the proper factor is found at the intersection of the 6% column and the 20-period row.

The procedures just shown may be used not only with more frequent cash flows but also with more frequent compounding. For instance, if 8% interest is compounded quarterly over the next three years, there would be 12 interest periods (4 periods × 3 years) of 2% each.

Present Value and Bond Prices

The present value concepts discussed in this appendix are often used to determine bond issue prices. The issue price is calculated by figuring the present value of the cash flows related to the bonds, namely, interest payments and the return of principal to investors. As an example, assume Franklin Corporation plans to issue $500,000 of 10-year, 10% bonds. Interest of $25,000 will be payable semiannually on June 30 and December 31 ($500,000 × 0.10 × 6/12 = $25,000). If the going rate of interest in the economy is also 10%, the issuance price would be computed as follows:

Present value of interest payments: $25,000 × 12.46221*	$311,555
Present value of principal payment: $500,000 × 0.37689†	188,445
Total present value (anticipated issue price)	$500,000

* Table 2, 5%, 20 periods.
† Table 1, 5%, 20 periods.

Notice how the present value coincides with the face value of the bonds. The reason is because Franklin's bonds pay interest equal to the prevailing market rate; thus, investors are willing to pay 100% of face value for bond acquisitions.

Modifying the illustration, suppose the annual interest rate for other similar bond issues is now 12%. Franklin's bonds, however, continue to pay 10% (i.e., $25,000 interest for each six-month period). By using factors for the prevailing 12% rate,[12] the present value becomes $442,648:

Present value of interest payments: $25,000 × 11.46992*	$286,748
Present value of principal payment: $500,000 × 0.31180†	155,900
Total present value (anticipated issue price)	$442,648

* Table 2, 6%, 20 periods.
† Table 1, 6%, 20 periods.

The bonds will be issued at a discount because investors can obtain a 12% return elsewhere. By receiving less than face value and still paying the same 10% contract interest, the company has increased the effective yield. Franklin's bonds have now become competitive for the limited funds of the investing public.

[12] The prevailing rate is used in present value calculations because it is the lowest rate of return an investor is willing to accept.

END-OF-CHAPTER REVIEW

LEARNING OBJECTIVES: THE KEY POINTS

1. **Define financial instruments and identify several of their basic features.** Financial instruments consist of various debt and equity tools that are used to fund business transactions. Examples include stocks, bonds, and a host of other financial products. Equity instruments often have related dividend distributions; in contrast, debt instruments usually have mandatory interest payments. Many financial instruments have been around for decades and are popular because of their straightforward nature. Recent years, however, have seen an increase in unusual and high-risk financing methods. A number of these newer entries do not fit the traditional accounting model, prompting considerable study by the Financial Accounting Standards Board.

2. **Describe the basic differences between bondholders and stockholders and identify the various types of bonds that may be issued.** Stockholders are the owners of a corporation. As such, they may receive dividends, subject to the availability of

funds and the discretion of corporate directors. In the event of liquidation, stockholders are entitled to asset proceeds only if monies are available after paying all other claims. Bondholders, on the other hand, are creditors who are entitled to regular interest payments regardless of income levels. Furthermore, creditors have a claim against assets (before stockholders) if a business were to liquidate.

The chart that follows summarizes key characteristics of the bonds discussed in this chapter.

TYPE OF BOND	DISTINGUISHING CHARACTERISTICS
Secured	Has assets pledged as security for the bondholders.
Debenture	Issued on the general credit of the corporation.
Registered	Issuing company maintains a record of bond purchasers and mails interest directly to bond owners.
Coupon	Has small detachable coupons that are used for interest collection.
Serial	Issue has staggered maturity dates.
Sinking-fund debenture	Is repaid by using proceeds from a special fund called a sinking fund.
Convertible	Can be converted into common stock at the option of the bondholder.
Callable	Can be reacquired by the issuing firm prior to maturity.
Junk	Securities that are lower quality and speculative in nature.

3. **Account for bonds that are issued at, above, or below face value, and distinguish between contract and effective interest rates.** The issue price of bonds is influenced by several factors, including the interest rate specified in the bond indenture (the contract interest rate) relative to the going market rate for obligations of a similar nature, as well as the issuer's financial condition. In general, if a bond has a contract rate that is less than the market rate, it will sell below face value (i.e., at a discount). The opposite case will give rise to a premium. The discount or premium causes the actual interest rate, known as the effective rate, to differ from the contract rate. Discounts raise the actual yield rate above the contract rate, and premiums have the opposite impact.

Regardless of the issue price, the Bonds Payable account is credited for the issuance's face value, and separate accounts are established for the related premium or discount. The Premium account is added to the balance in Bonds Payable for disclosure on the balance sheet. Conversely, the Discount account is subtracted. Both the addition and subtraction procedures result in a disclosure that reflects the net amount owed by the corporation on the financial statement date.

4. **Calculate amortization under both the straight-line and effective-interest methods.** Discounts and premiums must be amortized over a bond issue's life to reflect differences between the contract interest cost and the effective interest cost. The straight-line method assigns an equal amount of amortization to each period. In contrast, the theoretically preferred effective-interest method assigns sufficient amortization to each period so that interest expense is a constant percentage of bond carrying value.

5. **Account for bonds issued between interest dates and for bond retirements.** Bonds may be issued at any time. If issuance occurs on a date other than an interest payment date, the purchaser pays the corporation for any interest that has accrued. The first payment by the company will include interest expense from the issue date to the payment date, plus a return of any accrued interest received.

    When bonds are retired, interest and amortization must be updated and the related unamortized premium or discount removed from the accounting records. The difference between the bond carrying value and the amount paid to retire the obligations results in a gain or a loss.

6. **Analyze the extent of a company's outstanding debt.** A high level of outstanding debt can severely restrict a company's operating flexibility because of sizable outlays for interest and principal. Too much debt may cause missed payments, perhaps leading to higher borrowing rates and possible bankruptcy. The debt to total assets ratio is used to assess the level of debt in relation to the funding provided by an entity's stockholders. Another ratio, times interest earned, is employed to study a firm's ability to cover interest payments.

7. **Account for bond investments.** Most bond investments are classified as held-to-maturity securities, which must be accounted for at amortized cost. The bond investment is initially entered in the accounts at acquisition cost; any related discount or premium is then amortized by the effective-interest method. The amortization process affects the Investment in Bonds account, which eventually houses the bonds' face value, and Bond Interest Revenue.

8. **Describe the features of available-for-sale stock investments and the equity method.** Available-for-sale stock securities consist of investments made for purposes other than trading or control. These securities usually produce dividend revenue and are disclosed at fair market value in the financial statements. Any unrealized gain or loss that arises in this valuation process is disclosed as a component of stockholders' equity.

    An exception occurs when the investor has the ability to exercise significant influence (typically 20% or more ownership). In this case the equity method is used, and the Investment account is increased for the investor's share of investee net income and decreased for any dividends received and net losses incurred. The Investment account therefore parallels changes in the retained earnings of the investee corporation.

9. **Use present value techniques to determine the issue price of bonds.** Present value represents the amount an investor is willing to pay to secure a stream of future cash flows at a given rate of return. The cash flows related to a bond issue are the periodic interest receipts and the return of principal. These amounts are multiplied by the appropriate factors, which are available in table form and based on the number of periods and the effective interest rate, to derive the issue price. The periodic receipts of interest often represent an annuity, or a series of equal cash flows.

KEY TERMS AND CONCEPTS: A QUICK OVERVIEW

annuity   A series of equal cash flows over a number of years. (p. 686)

available-for-sale securities   Investments not otherwise classified as trading securities or held-to-maturity securities. (p. 679)

bond   A formal written document that provides evidence of long-term indebtedness. (p. 664)

bond discount The difference between the face value of bonds and the issue price, when issuance occurs below face value. (p. 668)

bond indenture A document that stipulates the provisions of a bond issue. (p. 664)

bond premium The difference between the face value of bonds and the issue price, when issuance occurs above face value. (p. 668)

bond refunding The replacement of a bond issue with other bonds that carry a lower interest rate. (p. 676)

bond retirement The cancellation of bonds that have been called. (p. 676)

callable bond A bond that can be reacquired by the issuing firm prior to the maturity date. (p. 666)

carrying value of a bond Face value of a bond minus the unamortized bond discount (or plus the unamortized bond premium). (p. 669)

compound interest Interest that is calculated on both principal and previously accumulated interest. (p. 684)

contract interest rate The interest rate that is used to calculate interest payments to bondholders; specified in the indenture agreement. (p. 667)

convertible bond A bond that can be converted into common stock at the option of the bondholder. (p. 666)

coupon bonds Bonds having small detachable coupons that correspond to each interest period and are payable to the bearer. (p. 665)

debenture bond A bond that has no assets pledged as security and is issued on the general credit of the corporation. (p. 665)

debt to total assets ratio A ratio that shows the percentage of total capital provided by a firm's creditors. Computed as: Total debt ÷ total assets. (p. 677)

effective-interest amortization A method of bond discount and premium amortization by which interest expense is calculated as a constant percentage of bond carrying value. (p. 670)

effective interest rate The actual interest rate (i.e., yield) on a bond, which may be different from the contract interest rate. (p. 667)

equity method A method of accounting for long-term stock investments; used when an investor has significant influence over the investee company. (p. 682)

financial instruments Debt and equity tools that are used to fund business transactions. (p. 663)

future value The amount an original sum will increase to, given an interest rate and a designated time period. (p. 685)

held-to-maturity securities Investments that a company has the intent and ability to hold until maturity. (p. 679)

interest period The time that elapses between cash flows in future value and present value computations. (p. 687)

investee A company whose shares have been acquired by an investor. (p. 680)

junk bonds Bonds that are less than investment grade and speculative in nature. (p. 666)

present value The amount an investor is willing to pay to secure a specified cash flow on a future date at a given rate of return. (pp. 668, 685)

registered bond A bond for which the issuing company maintains a record of the purchaser's name and address and mails interest to the registered bond owner. (p. 665)

secured bond A bond for which assets are pledged as security for the bondholders. (p. 665)

serial bond A bond issue in which bonds mature at different dates. (p. 666)

sinking fund A fund established to ensure that sufficient funds are available to pay bondholders at maturity. (p. 666)

sinking-fund debentures Bonds that are retired by using the proceeds from a sinking fund. (p. 666)

straight-line amortization A method by which an equal amount of bond discount or premium is allocated to each interest period (p. 669).

times interest earned A ratio that measures a company's ability to cover and meet fixed interest charges. Computed as: Income before income taxes and interest ÷ interest expense. (p. 678)

CHAPTER QUIZ

The five questions that follow relate to several issues raised in the chapter. Test your knowledge of the issues by selecting the best answer. (The answers appear on p. 707.)

1. Bonds payable are sold at 98 when there is a difference between the:
   a. issue date and maturity date.
   b. contract interest rate and effective interest rate.
   c. carrying value and maturity value.
   d. face value and maturity value.

2. Bonds payable sold at 104 should be disclosed on the balance sheet at their face value:
   a. plus any unamortized discount.
   b. plus any unamortized premium.
   c. minus any unamortized discount.
   d. minus any unamortized premium.

3. Effective-interest amortization:
   a. always produces increasing bond carrying values.
   b. can be used with bond discounts but not with bond premiums.
   c. can be used by bond issuers and bond investors.
   d. is the result of multiplying a bond issue's face value by the effective interest rate.

4. On June 1, 19X7, Denver, Inc., issued $100,000 of 10%, 5-year debenture bonds at 105. The bonds were dated June 1, 19X7; the company uses the straight-line amortization method. If the bonds are called and retired at 105 on June 1, 19X9, the company would experience:
   a. a loss of $2,000.
   b. a gain of $2,000.
   c. a loss of $3,000.
   d. neither a gain nor a loss.

5. The equity method:
   a. requires that an investment's carrying value be adjusted to reflect fair market value.
   b. is a common way to account for bond investments.
   c. requires that an investment's carrying value be adjusted to reflect changes in the investee's retained earnings.
   d. would typically be used when an investor owns 5% or more of an investee corporation.

Summary Problem

On January 1, 19X1, Kristopher Corporation issued $100,000 of 8%, 10-year bonds for $87,538. The bonds were priced to generate an effective yield of 10% to investors, are dated January 1, 19X1, and pay semiannual interest on June 30 and December 31. Kristopher uses the straight-line method of amortization and rounds all computations to the nearest dollar.

Instructions

a. Prepare journal entries to record (1) the bond issuance on January 1, 19X1, and (2) the semiannual interest payment and discount amortization on June 30, 19X1, and December 31, 19X1. *Note:* Combine the interest payment and amortization into a single entry (see p. 670).
b. Compute total bond interest expense for 19X1.
c. Present the proper disclosure of the bond issue on Kristopher's December 31, 19X1, balance sheet.
d. Compute the discount amortization that would have been recorded on June 30, 19X1, and December 31, 19X1, if Kristopher had used the effective-interest method rather than the straight-line method.
e. Suppose that an investor purchased $15,000 of Kristopher's bonds. Would the investor report these bonds on the year-end balance sheet at fair market value if the bonds are considered held-to-maturity securities? Briefly explain.

Solution

a.

Jan. 1	Cash		87,538	
	Discount on Bonds Payable		12,462	
	Bonds Payable			100,000
	To record issuance of bonds.			
June 30	Bond Interest Expense		4,623	
	Discount on Bonds Payable			623
	Cash			4,000
	To record semiannual interest payment and amortization.			
Dec. 31	Bond Interest Expense		4,623	
	Discount on Bonds Payable			623
	Cash			4,000
	To record semiannual interest payment and amortization.			
	Calculations: See part (b)			

b.

Cash payment for interest each six months ($100,000 × 0.08 × 6/12)	$4,000
Straight-line discount amortization each six months [($12,462 ÷ 10 years) × 6/12]	623
Total bond interest expense	$4,623
Number of six-month periods	× 2
Bond interest expense for 19X1	$9,246

c. Long-term liabilities

Bonds payable	$100,000	
Less: Discount on bonds payable	11,216*	$88,784

*$12,462 − $623 − $623.

d.

Semiannual Interest Period	(A) Effective Semiannual Interest Expense (5% × Carrying Value)	(B) Semiannual Interest Payment (4% × Face Value)	(C) Discount Amortization (A – B)	(D) Bond Discount Balance	(E) End-of-Period Bond Carrying Value (Face Value – D)
Issue date				$12,462	$87,538
6/30/X1	$4,377	$4,000	$377	12,085	87,915
12/31/X1	4,396	4,000	396	11,689	88,311

e. No. Held-to-maturity bond investments are reported at amortized cost, not fair market value.

Assignment Material

Questions

Q18–1 Are bonds normally used to meet current obligations and pay operating expenses? Explain.

Q18–2 Differentiate between the rights of stockholders and those of bondholders.

Q18–3 What are junk bonds?

Q18–4 Jupiter Corporation is issuing bonds that have an individual face value of $500. If the bonds are sold at 104, will Jupiter receive $104 for each bond? Explain.

Q18–5 Bates, Inc., recently issued $400,000 of 10% bonds at 102.
a. Were the bonds sold at a discount or at a premium?
b. In all likelihood, was the prevailing rate of interest in the marketplace for similar bonds equal to, greater than, or less than 10%?
c. Is the effective interest rate equal to, greater than, or less than the contract interest rate?

Q18–6 What is meant by the term "bond carrying value"? Will carrying value increase or decrease over the life of a bond issue when bonds are issued at a discount?

Q18–7 Differentiate between a bond discount and a bond premium.

Q18–8 Differentiate between straight-line and effective-interest amortization. Which method is preferred? Why?

Q18–9 How does bond retirement differ from bond refunding?

Q18–10 Briefly differentiate between held-to-maturity securities and available-for-sale securities.

Q18–11 Discuss the rationale that underlies the equity method of accounting for long-term stock investments.

*Q18–12 What is meant by the term "future value"?

*Q18–13 Explain the concept of present value to someone with a limited business background.

* An asterisk preceding an item indicates that the material is covered in an appendix to this chapter.

*Q18–14 Explain the relationship between compound interest and present value.

*Q18–15 What is an annuity?

*Q18–16 Briefly explain how present value is used to determine bond issue prices.

Exercises

E18–1 Overview of bonds (L.O. 3, 4)

Evaluate the comments that follow as being True or False. If the comment is false, briefly explain why.

a. When bonds are issued at a discount, the proceeds received exceed the bonds' face value.
b. The effective interest rate is lower than the contract interest rate for bonds that are issued at a premium.
c. For bonds that are sold at a discount, carrying value is lower than face value.
d. Premium amortization results in a company's interest expense being less than interest paid.
e. The journal entry to amortize a discount involves a debit to Discount on Bonds Payable.

E18–2 Bond discount; straight-line amortization (L.O. 3, 4)

Triangle Company issued $800,000 of 12% bonds on January 1, 19X3, for $767,600. The bonds are due on December 31, 19X8, and pay interest semiannually on June 30 and December 31.

a. Prepare the required journal entry to record the bond issuance on January 1, 19X3.
b. Prepare entries to record the interest payment and discount amortization on June 30 and December 31, 19X3. Triangle uses the straight-line method of amortization.
c. Compute 19X3 bond interest expense.
d. Present the proper disclosure of the bond issue on Triangle's December 31, 19X3, balance sheet.

E18–3 Bond premium; straight-line amortization (L.O. 3, 4)

Castillo Company issued $200,000 of 10%, 4-year bonds on January 1, 19X1, for $216,000. The bonds pay interest semiannually on June 30 and December 31.

a. Prepare the required journal entry to record the bond issuance on January 1, 19X1.
b. Prepare entries to record the interest payment and premium amortization on June 30 and December 31, 19X1. Castillo uses the straight-line method of amortization.
c. Compute 19X1 bond interest expense.
d. Present the proper disclosure of the bond issue on Castillo's December 31, 19X1, balance sheet.

E18–4 Bond discount; effective-interest amortization (L.O. 3, 4)

The Eagle Corporation issued $400,000 of 8% bonds for $382,056 on January 1, 19X1. The bonds pay interest semiannually on June 30 and December 31 and were priced to yield an effective interest rate of 9%.

a. Prepare the required journal entry to record the bond issuance on January 1.
b. Prepare entries to record the interest payment and discount amortization on June 30 and December 31, 19X1. Eagle utilizes the effective-interest method of amortization; round to the nearest dollar.

c. Compute 19X1 bond interest expense.
d. Present the proper disclosure of the bond issue on Eagle's December 31, 19X1, balance sheet.

E18–5 Using an amortization table (L.O. 3, 4)
Several years ago Garza Corporation issued bonds having a maturity value of $100,000. A partial amortization table revealed the following:

Date	Interest Expense	Interest Paid	Amount Unamortized	Carrying Value
6/30/X8	$4,912	$4,500	$1,361	$98,639
12/31/X8	4,932	4,500	929	99,071

a. Prepare the balance sheet disclosure for the bonds as of December 31, 19X8.
b. Compute the amount of amortization for the six-month period ended December 31, 19X8.
c. What is the effective interest rate for these bonds?

E18–6 Bond premium; effective-interest amortization (L.O. 3, 4)
The Baltic Corporation issued the following bonds on January 1, 19X6:

Face value: $300,000   Maturity: 3 years
Proceeds: $315,228   Effective interest rate: 10%
Contract interest rate: 12%

Interest is paid semiannually on June 30 and December 31.

a. Prepare the required journal entry to record the bond issuance on January 1.
b. Prepare entries to record the interest payment and premium amortization on June 30 and December 31, 19X6. Baltic uses the effective-interest method of amortization; round to the nearest dollar.
c. Compute 19X6 bond interest expense.
d. Present the proper disclosure of the bond issue on Baltic's December 31, 19X6, balance sheet.

E18–7 Bonds issued between interest dates (L.O. 5)
Sage Corporation issued $500,000 of 12% bonds on May 1, 19X1, at 100 plus accrued interest. The bonds are dated January 1, 19X1, and pay interest each June 30 and December 31.

a. Prepare journal entries to record (1) the bond issuance on May 1, 19X1; (2) the first interest payment on June 30, 19X1; and (3) the second interest payment on December 31, 19X1.
b. Compute Sage's 19X1 bond interest expense.

E18–8 Bond retirement (L.O. 4, 5)
Hackberry Corporation issued $400,000 of 12% bonds at 97 on January 1, 19X2. Interest is paid semiannually on June 30 and December 31. The bonds have a 10-year life from the date of issuance; Hackberry uses the straight-line method of amortization. On July 1, 19X8, the bonds were called at 105 and retired.

a. Compute the amount of unamortized discount as of the call date.
b. Present the entry necessary on July 1, 19X8.
c. Discuss possible reasons why Hackberry exercised the call provision.

E18–9 Debt on the balance sheet (L.O. 6)

Highland Fashion, Inc., a leading marketer and manufacturer of basic family apparel, reported the data that follow.

> As of December 31, 19X7
>   Total assets: $4.7 billion
>   Total current liabilities: $250 million
>   Total noncurrent liabilities: $1.395 billion
> For the year ended December 31, 19X7
>   Interest expense: $74 million
>   Income before income taxes and interest: $555 million

The company has been in business for 40 years and reported steadily rising sales and earnings from 19X1–19X7.

a. Suggest several ratios that an analyst might use to evaluate the level of debt outstanding.
b. Do you believe that Highland's use of debt is excessive? Explain and show appropriate calculations.

E18–10 Bond investments; effective-interest amortization (L.O. 7)

Windsor Devices, Inc., purchased $500,000 of 8% bonds on January 1, 19XX, for $437,689. The bonds have a 10-year life, pay semiannual interest each June 30 and December 31, and were priced to generate a 10% effective interest rate.

a. Prepare Windsor's journal entry to record the bond purchase on January 1.
b. Prepare entries to record the interest receipt and discount amortization on June 30 and December 31, 19XX. Windsor uses the effective-interest method of amortization; round calculations to the nearest dollar.
c. Compute total interest revenue for 19XX.
d. Present the proper disclosure of the bond investment on Windsor's December 31, 19XX, balance sheet.

E18–11 Bond investments; discount and premium amortization (L.O. 7)

On January 1, 19X2, Hopkins Company purchased two different bond issues that are classified as held-to-maturity securities. The following information is available:

Bond Issue	Face Value	Contract Interest Rate (%)	Effective Interest Rate (%)	Purchase Price
1	$100,000	8%	10%	$ 87,538
2	100,000	7	6	107,439

All bonds pay interest on June 30 and December 31. Hopkins uses the effective-interest method of amortization.

a. Compute the total interest received during 19X2.
b. Compute amortization to be recorded during 19X2. Round calculations to the nearest dollar.
c. Determine the amount of bond interest revenue to be reported on the firm's 19X2 income statement.

E18–12 Available-for-sale stock investments (L.O. 8)

On January 1 of the current year, Tirado Company acquired a 5% ownership interest (5,000 shares) of Vail Oil's common stock at $15 per share. During the year, Vail had record net income of $130,000 and paid dividends of $20,000. The year-end market price of Vail's common stock is $12, and the shares are classified as an available-for-sale security.

a. Prepare all necessary journal entries to account for Tirado's investment in Vail Oil.
b. Compute the year-end carrying value of Tirado's investment.

E18–13 Basic accounting for stock investment (L.O. 8)

On January 1, 19X4, Emerson Services purchased 8,000 common shares of Affiliated Enterprises for $8 per share. Information pertaining to Affiliated follows.

Common stock outstanding ($1 par, 25,000 shares), Dec. 31, 19X4	$25,000
Net income, 19X4	80,000
Dividends paid, 19X4	10,000

Affiliated's year-end market price was $7 per share.

a. What method should Emerson use to account for its investment in Affiliated? Why?
b. Prepare the journal entries that Emerson would record in 19X4 pertaining to the investment.
c. Show how the investment would appear in the long-term investments section of the 19X4 year-end balance sheet.

E18–14 Overview of bond and stock investments (L.O. 7, 8)

Evaluate the comments that follow as being True or False. If the comment is false, briefly explain why.

a. Common stock investments are often classified as held-to-maturity securities.
b. The equity method of accounting for stock investments is used when an investee has significant influence over the investor.
c. Available-for-sale stock investments are accounted for at fair market value.
d. Available-for-sale securities and held-to-maturity securities are accounted for differently.
e. Dividends received are accounted for as revenue when an investor is using the equity method of accounting.

*E18–15 Understanding future and present value concepts (L.O. 9)

The appendix covered the following topics, among others:

1—Future value
2—Present value of a single sum
3—Present value of an annuity

Determine the concept(s) most appropriate to compute the following amounts:

____ a. The amount that must be invested today to purchase a $25,000 automobile 10 years from now.
____ b. The amount that a savings account will contain in six years because of additional interest that will be earned.
____ c. The amount that a company should be willing to pay for a machine that promises $10,000 cash savings in each of the next five years.
____ d. The issue price of bonds that have semiannual interest payments.

*E18–16 Time value of money and present value (L.O. 9)

Stephanie Rogers requires a 14% rate of return on all investments. She is considering an investment that will provide the following cash inflows:

At the End of Year	Cash Inflow	
1	$15,000	$30,000
2	15,000	
3	16,000	$30,000
4	14,000	
	$60,000	

a. Observe how the investment results in two cash inflows of $30,000, each of which is spread over two years. Which of the $30,000 inflows would be more attractive to Rogers? Explain your answer.
b. By using present value, compute the maximum amount that Rogers should be willing to pay for this investment. Round to the nearest dollar.

*E18–17 Present value computations (L.O. 9)

Otis Leonard is in the process of signing a contract with the San Diego Thunderbirds, a professional basketball team. Leonard has been offered the following choices for a cash-signing bonus: (1) $100,000 now, (2) $20,000 each year for the next six years, (3) $9,000 every six months for the next nine years, or (4) $180,000 at the end of ten years.

a. Assuming a 10% discount rate, determine the present value of the four alternatives. Round your calculations to the nearest dollar.
b. If you were Leonard's agent, which alternative would you recommend? Why?

*E18–18 Bond pricing (L.O. 3, 9)

Austin Manufacturing is considering the issuance of $600,000 of 8-year bonds that have a 10% contract interest rate. The bonds pay interest semiannually on June 30 and December 31. Assume a prevailing interest rate of 12% for similar bonds.

a. Determine whether the bonds will be issued at a premium or a discount. Explain your answer. *Hint:* No computations are necessary.
b. Determine the anticipated proceeds (i.e., present value) of the bond issue. Round your calculations to the nearest dollar.

PROBLEMS

Series A

P18–A1 Bonds: Balance sheet presentation and analysis (L.O. 2, 3, 4)

The following account balances were extracted from the general ledger of Richmond Corporation on January 1, 19X7:

12% secured bonds	$200,000
9% debenture bonds	100,000
Premium on secured bonds	1,000
Discount on debenture bonds	3,000

Monthly amortization of premium and discount amounts to $20 and $50, respectively.

Instructions

a. A study of the company's accounts reveals the presence of both secured bonds and debenture bonds. All other things being equal, would an investor prefer secured bonds or debenture bonds? Briefly explain.
b. Determine the company's net bond liability to investors on January 1, 19X7.
c. Prepare the proper balance sheet disclosure for the bond issues outstanding as of December 31, 19X7.
d. Explain the need for discount and premium amortization.
e. Which of the two bond issues (secured or debenture) has a contract interest rate that is less than the effective interest rate? Briefly explain.

P18–A2 Bond computations: Straight-line amortization (L.O. 3, 4)

Alliance Stores issued $900,000 of 8% bonds on January 1, 19X1. The bonds pay interest on June 30 and December 31 and mature in 10 years. Assume the independent cases that follow.

- Case A—The bonds are issued at 100.
- Case B—The bonds are issued at 96.
- Case C—The bonds are issued at 105.

Alliance uses the straight-line method of amortization.

Instructions

Complete the following table:

	CASE A	CASE B	CASE C
a. Cash inflow on the issuance date	_____	_____	_____
b. Total cash outflow through maturity	_____	_____	_____
c. Total borrowing cost over the life of the bond issue	_____	_____	_____
d. Interest expense for the year ended December 31, 19X1	_____	_____	_____
e. Amortization for the year ended December 31, 19X1	_____	_____	_____
f. Unamortized premium as of December 31, 19X1	_____	_____	_____
g. Unamortized discount as of December 31, 19X1	_____	_____	_____
h. Bond carrying value as of December 31, 19X1	_____	_____	_____

P18–A3 Bonds: Journal entries, issuance through retirement (L.O. 3, 4, 5)

The following information relates to a bond issue of Hickory Products, Inc.:

Date of bonds	January 1, 19X4
Issue date	January 1, 19X4
Maturity date	January 1, 19X7
Face amount	$800,000
Proceeds from issuance	$818,000
Interest payment dates	June 30, December 31
Contract (nominal) interest rate	12%
Amortization method	Straight-line

Instructions

a. Prepare journal entries to record (1) the bond issuance on January 1, 19X4; (2) the semiannual interest payment and premium amortization on June 30, 19X4; and (3) the semiannual interest payment and premium amortization on December 31, 19X4.
b. Compute total bond interest expense for 19X4.
c. What is the net carrying value of Hickory's bonds on December 31, 19X4? Show how this amount would be disclosed on the company's year-end balance sheet.
d. Assume that the entire bond issue was called at 103 at the start of business on July 1, 19X5. If the interest payment and premium amortization were handled correctly on June 30, prepare the necessary journal entry to record the bond retirement.

P18–A4 Amortization analysis and journal entries (L.O. 3, 4)

The schedule that follows reflects Burk Corporation's issuance of 3-year bonds on January 1, 19X1, and the subsequent interest amounts:

DATE	INTEREST EXPENSE	INTEREST PAID	AMOUNT UNAMORTIZED	CARRYING VALUE
1/1/X1			$6,000	$ 94,000
6/30/X1	$6,500	$5,500	5,000	95,000
12/31/X1	6,500	5,500	4,000	96,000
6/30/X2	6,500	5,500	3,000	97,000
12/31/X2	6,500	5,500	2,000	98,000
6/30/X3	6,500	5,500	1,000	99,000
12/31/X3	6,500	5,500	—	100,000

Instructions

a. Determine whether the bonds were issued at a premium or at a discount. Explain your answer.
b. Did Burk use the straight-line or effective-interest amortization method? Explain your answer.
c. What is the annual contract interest rate on the bonds?
d. Present the journal entry to record the bond issuance on January 1, 19X1. The bonds are dated January 1, 19X1.
e. Present the journal entries required on June 30, 19X1.

P18–A5 Bonds: Effective-interest discount amortization (L.O. 3, 4)

Bombay Imports issued bonds during 19X5 to finance a store modernization program, receiving proceeds of $468,950. Information about the bonds follows.

Face value	$500,000
Issuance date	July 1, 19X5
Maturity date	June 30, 19X9
Contract interest rate	10%
Effective interest rate	12%
Interest payment dates	June 30 and December 31

Instructions

a. Prepare the journal entry necessary to record issuance of the bonds.
b. Assuming that Bombay uses the effective-interest method of amortization, prepare the following:
   (1) A discount amortization table similar in format to Exhibit 18–4. Round calculations to the nearest dollar.

(2) Compound journal entries to record semiannual interest payments and discount amortization for the first full year the bonds are outstanding.

c. Present the proper disclosure of the company's bonds on the December 31, *19X7*, balance sheet.

P18–A6 Stock investments (L.O. 8)

Regal Ice Cream invested $70,000 at the beginning of 19X2 by purchasing common stock of Atlantic, Inc., and Pacific, Inc. Information about the two investments follows.

	ATLANTIC, INC.	PACIFIC, INC.
Regal's percentage of ownership	10%	35%
Number of shares acquired	3,500	35,000
Acquisition cost	$35,000	$49,000
19X2 year-end market price	$8 per share	$0.75 per share

Assume that 19X2 net income and total dividend payments of each investee amounted to $50,000 and $10,000, respectively.

Instructions

a. What method of accounting should Regal use to account for its investment in Pacific, Inc.? Why?
b. Focusing on the investment in Pacific, Inc., prepare any journal entries that Regal would record for:
   (1) Acquisition of the common shares.
   (2) Dividends received.
   (3) Net income earned by the investee.
   (4) Year-end market valuation.
c. Repeat part (b) for the investment in Atlantic, Inc.
d. Present the proper disclosure of the two investments on Regal's 19X2 year-end balance sheet.

Series B

P18–B1 Bonds: Balance sheet presentation and analysis (L.O. 2, 3, 4)

The following information relates to a $1,200,000 bond issue of American Media, Inc.:

Contract (nominal) interest rate	10%
Issue date	January 1, 19X3
Interest payment dates	June 30, December 31
Maturity date	January 1, 19X7
Amortization method	Straight-line

Instructions

a. If American Media were in marginal financial health, would it likely have more success in issuing these bonds if the obligations were secured bonds or debenture bonds? Briefly discuss, assuming the interest rates would not differ.
b. How much cash will American Media pay to bondholders on each interest date?
c. If the market rate of interest for similar obligations is more than 10% on January 1, 19X3, will the bonds be issued at, above, or below face value? Briefly explain.
d. Assume that the bonds were issued at 98. Calculate monthly amortization and show how the bonds would be presented on American Media's December 31, *19X4*, balance sheet.

P18–B2 Bond computations: Straight-line amortization (L.O. 3, 4)

Broadway Corporation issued $600,000 of bonds on January 1, 19X5, to finance a new musical comedy. The bonds pay 12% interest on June 30 and December 31 and mature in five years. Assume the following independent cases:

- *Case 1*—The bonds are issued at face value.
- *Case 2*—The bonds are issued at a 5% premium over face value.
- *Case 3*—The bonds are issued at a 3% discount under face value.

Broadway uses the straight-line method of amortization.

Instructions

a. Determine the following for Case 1:
   (1) Proceeds from bond issuance
   (2) Total cash outflow through maturity
   (3) Total borrowing cost over the life of the bond issue
   (4) Amortization for 19X5
   (5) Interest expense for 19X5
   (6) Unamortized premium or discount, if any, on December 31, 19X5
   (7) Bond carrying value on December 31, 19X5
b. Repeat part (a), using the data for Case 2.
c. Repeat part (a), using the data for Case 3.

P18–B3 Bonds: Journal entries, issuance through retirement (L.O. 3, 4, 5)

On January 1, 19X1, Taylor Corporation issued $300,000 of 10%, 5-year bonds for $294,000. The bonds are dated January 1, 19X1, and pay semiannual interest on June 30 and December 31. Taylor uses the straight-line method of amortization.

Instructions

a. Prepare journal entries to record (1) the bond issuance on January 1, 19X1; (2) the semiannual interest payment and discount amortization on June 30, 19X1; and (3) the semiannual interest payment and discount amortization on December 31, 19X1.
b. Compute total bond interest expense for 19X1.
c. Present the proper disclosure of the bond issue on Taylor's December 31, 19X1, balance sheet.
d. Assume that the entire bond issue was called at 101 at the start of business on January 1, *19X3*. If all entries in 19X2 were recorded correctly, prepare the journal entry needed for the bond retirement.

P18–B4 Amortization analysis and journal entries (L.O. 3, 4)

The following schedule reflects Zeta Corporation's issuance of 3-year bonds on January 1, 19X5, and the subsequent interest amounts:

Date	Interest Expense	Interest Paid	Amount Unamortized	Carrying Value
1/1/X5			$10,152	$210,152
6/30/X5	$10,508	$12,000	8,660	208,660
12/31/X5	10,433	12,000	7,093	207,093
6/30/X6	10,355	12,000	5,448	205,448
12/31/X6	10,272	12,000	3,720	203,720
6/30/X7	10,186	12,000	1,906	201,906
12/31/X7	10,094*	12,000	—	200,000

* Difference due to rounding.

Instructions

a. Did Zeta use the straight-line or effective-interest amortization method? Explain your answer.
b. Determine whether the bonds were issued at a premium or at a discount. Explain your answer.
c. What is the annual contract interest rate on the bonds?
d. Present the journal entry to record the bond issuance on January 1, 19X5. The bonds are dated January 1, 19X5.
e. Present the journal entries required on June 30, *19X6*.

P18–B5 Bonds: Effective-interest premium amortization (L.O. 3, 4)

Hilo Electronics issued $600,000 of 9%, 5-year bonds on January 1, 19X3. The bonds pay interest semiannually on June 30 and December 31 and were priced to generate an effective yield of 8% to investors. The bonds were sold for $624,330.

Instructions

a. Prepare the journal entry necessary on January 1 to record issuance of the bonds.
b. Assuming that Hilo uses the effective-interest method of amortization, prepare the following:
   (1) A premium amortization schedule similar in format to Exhibit 18–6. Round calculations to the nearest dollar.
   (2) Compound journal entries to record semiannual interest payments and premium amortization for the first year the bonds are outstanding.
c. Present the proper disclosure of the company's bonds on the December 31, 19X5, balance sheet.

P18–B6 Stock investments (L.O. 8)

Oak Harbor Corporation recently acquired a long-term investment in Ambrose, Inc. Ambrose has 40,000 shares of $2 par-value common stock outstanding. The following information is available:

Jan. 1   Purchased 3,000 shares of Ambrose common stock at $20 per share.
Dec. 31   Ambrose declared and paid a cash dividend of $0.60 per share.
      31   Received a copy of Ambrose's income statement that disclosed net income of $42,000.
      31   The market price of Ambrose's stock was $17 per share.

Instructions

a. Should Oak Harbor use the equity method to account for its long-term investment in Ambrose, Inc.? Why or why not?
b. Present Oak Harbor's required journal entries.
c. Present the proper disclosure of the Investment account on Oak Harbor's December 31 balance sheet.
d. Repeat requirements (a), (b), and (c), assuming that Oak Harbor had purchased 10,000 shares of Ambrose's stock at $20 per share.

EXPANDING YOUR HORIZONS

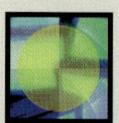

EYH18–1 Bond ratings (L.O. 3)

Bonds are rated by several organizations, including Moody's and Standard and Poor's. These ratings indicate the risk associated with the bonds with respect to payment of interest and repayment of principal at maturity. Such information is useful to investors.

Instructions

Using library resources or materials from a stockbroker, obtain the rating for specific bond issues of three corporations. (One of the companies selected should have marginal profit performance in recent years.) In a brief report, specify the name of the bond rating service, the bond issue and corporation involved, the rating, and what the rating means.

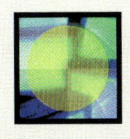

EYH18–2 Appropriateness of bond financing (L.O. 6)

Corporations have distinctly different needs for issuing bonds and environments from which to make periodic interest payments. For example, public utilities seem to have a continual need for funds to modernize, and operate as a virtual monopoly. Thus, if funds are insufficient to pay interest, a state public utility commission will often authorize a hike in commercial and residential rates. Alternatively, corporations that operate in a highly competitive market are dependent on their own skills to meet bond obligations. Given that the risk of default is higher in the latter case, such companies should have a lower level of bond financing.

Instructions

Using library resources, determine the extent of bond financing by (1) a public utility that services your area and (2) a corporation that operates in a much more competitive marketplace. Contrast your findings in a short report. *Note:* Be sure to calculate the debt to total assets ratio and times interest earned for the two most recent years of available data.

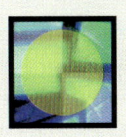

EYH18–3 Bond investments (L.O. 7)

Bonds represent a vehicle for entities that desire to earn a predetermined rate of interest for relatively long periods of time. Occasionally, bond investors will have some surprises—both pleasant and unpleasant.

Instructions

Form a group with two other students and prepare a short paper on any of the following topics:

- The use of junk bonds in the 1980s merger-mania.
- Why bond investments suffered a large market decline in 1994.
- Why bond investors generated huge returns in the early 1990s.

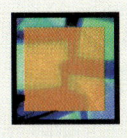

EYH18–4 An overview of debt disclosures: Reebok International and Procter & Gamble (L.O. 2, 7)

Reebok International creates consumer products for people with active lifestyles in sports, physical fitness, and recreation. Reebok, Rockport, and Avia are a few of the company's well-known brands. Procter & Gamble, on the other hand, markets various laundry, cleaning, health care, and food products (e.g., Tide, Crest toothpaste, and Crisco). The firm has operations in 56 countries and employs 96,500 people worldwide.

Instructions

By using the text's electronic data base, access the balance sheets and accompanying notes of both firms and answer the questions that follow. Unless otherwise indicated, responses should be based on data for the most recent year presented.

- **a.** Comment on the amount of detail presented on the balance sheet that relates to each company's long-term debt obligations.

b. Review the notes that accompany the financial statements, specifically, the long-term debt disclosure. Have either of the companies used debentures or subordinated debentures as a means of financing? If so,
   (1) What interest rate is being paid and when are the obligations due?
   (2) How significant are these obligations as a source of long-term funding?
c. Have either of the companies obtained financing from serial bonds? If "yes," briefly describe.
d. Which of the two firms improved its long-term debt position during the year? Explain.

EYH18–5 An overview of debt disclosures (L.O. 2, 7)
This problem is a duplication of Problem EYH18–4. It is based on two companies selected by your instructor.

Instructions

By using the text's electronic data base, access the specified companies' balance sheets and accompanying notes and focus on data for the most recent year reported. Answer requirements (a)–(d) of Problem EYH18–4.

EYH18–6 Bond financing versus stock financing (L.O. 2, 6)
Monet Fashion operates a chain of upscale clothing stores throughout the country. A recent balance sheet of the firm revealed $200,000 of 8% bonds payable and $400,000 of common stock. A proposed modernization program requires that the company raise $300,000 of new financing. Two alternatives are being considered: (1) issue 10% bonds or (2) issue 10,000 additional shares of common stock, increasing the total number of shares in the hands of stockholders to 30,000.

Monet has been marginally profitable over the last few years, generating income significantly below that of other firms in the same line of business. Fortunately, the company has been able to avoid operating at a loss. Inventories, receivables, and payables balances are at all-time highs; cash balances, on the other hand, are at dangerously low levels.

Instructions

a. Suppose you are a stockholder of Monet. Do you see any possible problems of financing the modernization program with bonds? Explain.
b. Suppose the current date is January 10, 19X2. The company can issue $300,000 of bonds that mature on January 10, 19X6, or a serial issue that is due at the beginning of 19X3, 19X4, 19X5, and 19X6 in $75,000 increments. If interest rates are the same for both issues, would Monet likely opt for the serial bonds? Why or why not?
c. Assume that Monet is subject to a 40% income tax rate. Calculate earnings-per-share figures for the two alternatives if management expects earnings of $50,000 before interest and taxes.
d. In general, what possible problems could arise from having too much debt outstanding?

COMMUNICATION OF ACCOUNTING INFORMATION

CAI18–1 Writing a recommendation report: AT&T (L.O. 5)
Communication Principle: One of the many types of reports in business is the recommendation report. The report's objective is to present an opinion that will lead to decisions or action. Like other types of formal communication, the recommendation report is divided into distinct sections that are set off by headings (see p. 505–506).

Given the nature of the report, the major conclusions are usually placed near the beginning. This practice allows the reader to quickly review the suggested alternatives, with perhaps only a quick scanning of the report's remaining sections. The recommendation report is geared to the requirements of busy executives who are pressed for time; it is direct and efficient.

After an introduction that contains a brief description of the problem or assignment, the report has a section entitled "Recommendations." This section should be no more than two paragraphs long and should contain the writer's major recommendations—often numbered and set off for easy reading. A follow-up section, typically the longest in the report, may have a heading such as "Presentation of Supporting Information." Here, the criteria for judgment and the reasons for the recommendations are presented. Graphic and tabular information (and related explanations) are introduced if appropriate.

Finally, the report ends with a conclusion. The recommendations are recapped in a brief paragraph that spells out what ought to be done. In a properly organized report, no new information is introduced at this point.

■ ■ ■ ■ ■ ■ ■ ■

AT&T's business is moving and managing information, domestically and globally. This includes providing long-distance telecommunications services along with systems and products that combine communications and computers. The corporation is huge; it has debenture bonds outstanding of approximately $3 billion. The interest rates, due dates, and maturities are as follows:

4 3/8% to 4 3/4%, due 1996–1999	$0.8 billion
5 1/8% to 7 1/8%, due 2000–2001	0.5 billion
8 1/8% to 9%, due 2022–2031	1.7 billion

Instructions

You are a member of AT&T's corporate staff and have been asked to write a report. The report should present a recommendation concerning the use of $400 million of cash on hand. Possible uses of the funds are the retirement of outstanding debt (be sure to specify which of the three bond issues should be selected), investment in various expansion and cost-saving programs that return 9%–11%, or the acquisition of government securities that yield approximately 7%. Assume that (1) the bonds were issued at face value and (2) indentures require that obligations be retired at face value (i.e., no gain or loss).

Answers to Chapter Quiz

1. b
2. b
3. c
4. a (Carrying value on June 1, 19X9, is $103,000: $100,000 + $3,000 unamortized premium; $105,000 payment − $103,000 carrying value = $2,000 loss)
5. c

Comprehensive Problem 3

Houston Consulting

Houston Consulting provides financial services to a variety of small businesses. Each business has its own accounting staff to record routine transactions, but relies on Houston's guidance in preparing selected complex journal entries and financial statements and in analyzing financing alternatives.

The company is in the process of completing engagements with five firms that are involved with computers and information-processing systems. A summary of the issues at hand and the tasks to be performed follows.

- *F&S Systems Design*—Management is considering a change from the partnership form to the corporate form of business organization. Gary Franklin, one of the partners, desires a checklist of the advantages and disadvantages of corporations. He also wants to know how a corporation is organized and what par value should be used.
- *Interstate Processing*—The January 1, 19X8, stockholders' equity section for Interstate Processing follows.

Common stock, $4 par value, 800,000 shares authorized, 50,000 shares issued and outstanding	$ 200,000
Paid-in capital in excess of par value	4,000,000
Retained earnings	3,800,000
Total	$8,000,000

Selected transactions and events for the year are:

Jan. 4	Declared a cash dividend of $0.25 per share on the common stock.
Feb. 4	Distributed the January 4 dividend.
Mar. 30	Authorized a 4-for-1 stock split to lower the price on the common stock.
Aug. 7	Declared a 5% stock dividend on all shares outstanding; the market price per share is $20.
Sept. 7	Distributed the August 7 stock dividend.

Interstate's accountant has just resigned from the firm. Management has requested that Houston prepare journal entries to record the preceding transactions and events. In addition, an end-of-year stockholders' equity section is needed. Net income for 19X8 amounted to $300,000.

- *Security Computers, Inc.*—In mid-August, Houston received the income statement of Security Computers, as prepared by Security's accountant. The income statement follows.

SECURITY COMPUTERS, INC.
Income Statement
For the Year Ended June 30, 19X8

Sales		$11,060,000
Cost of goods sold		6,000,000
Gross profit		$ 5,060,000
Less:		
Selling expenses	$2,000,000	
Administrative expenses	1,930,000	3,930,000
Income from operations		$ 1,130,000
Income taxes		452,000
Income from operations after taxes		$ 678,000
Other revenue (expense)		
Gain on sale of division		36,000
Net income		$ 714,000

Security disposed of its office furnishings division on June 29, 19X8. The division had generated 30% of the firm's sales and accounted for 20% of cost of goods sold and 30% of selling and administrative expenses. The division's assets and facilities were sold at a before-tax gain of $60,000. The company is subject to a 40% income tax rate.

Security's accountant did not separate the results of the office furnishings division from those of continuing operations because, as the accountant noted, "we helped that division become profitable and we want to receive credit on our income statement." Some additional information from Security indicates that:

- On January 15, Security experienced a $50,000 gain as the result of a flood. A building was destroyed in this extraordinary event, and insurance proceeds exceeded the book value by $50,000. Security's accountant recorded the gain as a credit to Sales.
- On May 4, one of the company's trucks was sold for $10,000 more than its book value. This gain was also placed in the Sales account.
- Traditionally, Security has used the double-declining balance depreciation method on all items of plant and equipment. At the beginning of the fiscal year, management agreed to change to the straight-line method and calculated that prior years' depreciation expense would have been $70,000 lower had the new method been used. To correct for the overstatement, Security's accountant recorded this amount as a reduction of the current year's depreciation (split equally between selling and administrative expenses).

The president of Security Computers is aware that several accounting errors have been made. She is in need of:

1. A corrected income statement (disregard earnings-per-share amounts). Hint: The percentages that relate to the office furnishings division should be applied to the corrected figures for sales and selling and administrative expenses.
2. An analysis of the business operations of the office furnishings division relative to the results of continuing corporate operations. Did the company err in selling the office furnishings division?

- *CompuTech, Inc.*—CompuTech is considering the issuance of bonds to raise some much needed long-term capital. The company has no experience in such matters and therefore desires a short report that details the general characteristics of bonds, along with the different types of bonds that could be issued.
- *Data Services*—On July 1, 19X8, Data Services issued $2 million of 12%, 5-year bonds for $1,859,530. The bonds pay interest semiannually on June 30 and December 31 and were priced to yield an effective rate of 14%. The firm has requested the following:
  1. The journal entry to record the bond issuance.
  2. The 19X8 entry to record interest expense and effective-interest amortization. Data Services has a December 31 year-end and rounds all computations to the nearest dollar.
  3. The proper disclosure of the bond issue on the December 31, 19X8, balance sheet.

Instructions

You are an employee of Houston Consulting. Respond to the specific requests of the five companies.

19 STATEMENT OF CASH FLOWS

LEARNING OBJECTIVES

After studying this chapter, you should be able to:

1. Explain the purpose of the statement of cash flows.
2. Classify and analyze operating, investing, and financing activities.
3. Discuss the proper accounting treatment for significant noncash investing/financing transactions.
4. Use both the direct and indirect methods of computing cash flows from operating activities.
5. Prepare a statement of cash flows.
6. Interpret a statement of cash flows.

George Faris of Banner Advertising recognizes the significance of the income statement when it comes to providing feedback about operations. Net cash flow, though, is perhaps more important to many business owners and managers. In plain and simple terms, a lack of cash will threaten an entity's survival. Bills go unpaid, creditors tighten terms, and suddenly a business finds itself without a steady source of goods and services. The result is all too predictable.

George is a firm believer in the income statement and also in the fourth key financial statement: the statement of cash flows. Yet he is a doubter. "I don't think that many people fully comprehend the information revealed by the statement of cash flows, and that's a shame. I'm sure that owners and managers still question how a company can be profitable and have very little cash on hand. They look at the differences between income and cash flow, but it's the details that truly mean something."

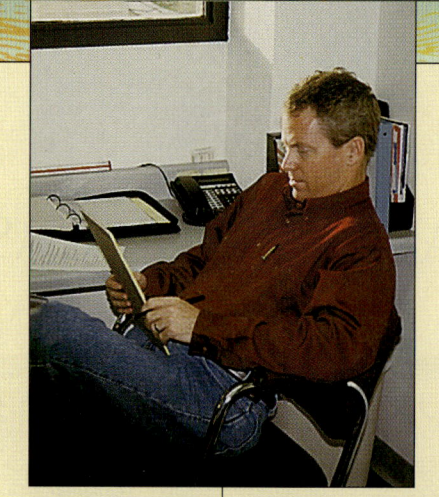

These observations are probably correct. In the case of Banner Advertising, net income differs from daily receipts and payments because of two major factors. First, billboard depreciation is an expense that reduces net income but doesn't consume any cash. Second, growing balances in accounts receivable represent revenues earned but not yet collected. George goes on to explain, "I always monitor cash flows and actually prepare a statement similar to the one in this chapter. The reason is more than just curiosity. I really need to know how much cash the company is producing so that we can pursue attractive investment opportunities and obtain cheap financing. A business must be proactive and not reactive to survive in this economy."

---

1 Explain the purpose of the statement of cash flows.

The cash flow statement is perfect for providing the information that George and many other business owners need. Why has the financial community clamored for yet another accounting report? Perhaps a look at the income statement and the balance sheet is the best way to answer this question.

Most accountants agree that the income statement and the balance sheet disclose valuable information. The income statement focuses on profitability and reveals an entity's revenues and expenses for a given period. The balance sheet, in contrast, discloses a company's economic resources, financial obligations, and owners' equity at a specific point in time.

One of the purposes of financial statements is to assist users in making predictions about an entity's future cash inflows and outflows. Users can predict the future only if they have a sufficient information base; unfortunately, the income statement and balance sheet alone are not capable of providing this base. The accounting profession therefore requires another report to improve financial disclosures of business enterprises. This report is the **statement of cash flows,** which reveals the cash flows generated or consumed by a firm's operating, investing, and financing activities. The information contained on the statement is helpful in answering questions such as the following:

- Did an entity fund its activities from operations? From bank loans? From stockholder investments?
- Were the funds obtained by an organization used to expand facilities? Reduce outstanding debt? Replace aging plant and equipment?
- Were the dividends paid greater than the funds provided by business operations?
- Why did net income differ from the firm's cash receipts and disbursements?

These and similar questions are routinely asked by creditors, stockholders, managers, and financial analysts. By collecting information on how funds are generated and used in an organization, the statement of cash flows provides insight that is not afforded by other financial disclosures and reports.

STATEMENT FORMAT AND CLASSIFICATIONS

2 Classify and analyze operating, investing, and financing activities.

The statement of cash flows has undergone considerable change in recent years. For a long time, companies revealed inflows and outflows of funds on a report known as the *statement of changes in financial position.* Businesses could employ differing definitions of funds and had few set rules to follow when presenting such information to external statement users. Because of this situation, analysts found it very difficult to compare the reports of different companies.

The Financial Accounting Standards Board studied the problem and decided that clearer definitional and presentation guidelines were needed.[1] The outcome of the Board's work is the statement shown in Exhibit 19–1. As you can

EXHIBIT 19–1
Example of a Statement of Cash Flows

MATRIX CORPORATION Statement of Cash Flows For the Year Ended December 31, 19XX	
Cash flows from operating activities	
Details	
Net cash provided (used) by operating activities	$ 70,000
Cash flows from investing activities	
Details	
Net cash provided (used) by investing activities	(15,000)
Cash flows from financing activities	
Details	
Net cash provided (used) by financing activities	4,000
Net increase (decrease) in cash	$ 59,000
Cash balance, January 1, 19XX	31,000
Cash balance, December 31, 19XX	$ 90,000
Schedule of noncash investing/financing activities	
Details	$ 12,000

[1] See "Statement of Cash Flows," *Statement of Financial Accounting Standards No. 95,* Financial Accounting Standards Board, Norwalk, Conn., 1987.

see, businesses must disclose the cash flows that arise from three broad categories: operating activities, investing activities, and financing activities. In addition, organizations are required to reveal significant *noncash* investing/financing transactions. Matrix Corporation was able to produce net cash inflows from operating activities and financing activities of $70,000 and $4,000, respectively. Investing transactions, on the other hand, were a cash drain, resulting in a $15,000 excess of disbursements over receipts. We will now discuss each of the statement's major sections in detail.

BUSINESS BRIEFING

The Statement of Cash Flows: A Banker's Perspective

Good collateral, a significant net worth, and a strong revenue stream—doesn't this sound like a winning combination for a company that desires to obtain a loan? The answer is "not necessarily," although it is a good start. The key missing element is cash flow.

Consider an individual who approached our institution with a loan request for his real estate development company. Earlier projects of the firm had been successful, having displayed consistent profitability. The company's rapid growth, however, had required some short-term borrowings. A review of the statement of cash flows indicated a serious cash deficiency problem caused by principal payments on existing bank notes. Because these payments do not directly affect profitability, a focus on the balance sheet and income statement alone would not have revealed the shortfall.

A clear understanding of a borrower's cash flow is one of the most important components of financial statement analysis in banking. This measure presents the lender with a moving picture of a company's financial health by focusing on receipts and disbursements. Stated simply, a business that cannot generate sufficient cash to cover its operating needs has a dismal future and does not represent a good credit risk.

LINDA WOODSIDE
Senior Vice-President
NationsBank

OPERATING ACTIVITIES

Generally speaking, **operating activities** give rise to transactions and events that enter into net income computations. Picture, for instance, the production and sale of goods and services—the major source of earnings for most large businesses. The cash flows related to these activities, such as receipts from customers, and payments for inventory, employee salaries and wages, taxes, interest, and other normal business expenses are classified as operating cash flows. Receipts of both loan interest and dividends also qualify for inclusion in this category. A review of *Statement No. 95* will find that the FASB defined operating activities in a "catchall" sense, namely, to include all cash transactions and events not otherwise classified as investing or financing items.

INVESTING ACTIVITIES

Investing activities, or those that involve investment of an entity's resources, constitute the next major type of activity for a business. Companies acquire the bonds and stocks of other firms and purchase long-term assets such as property, plant, and equipment. In addition, an entity (e.g., a financial institution) may make a loan to another organization. All of these transactions arise from a company's investing activities and result in a cash outflow during the period.

In a similar but opposite manner, these activities frequently generate cash inflows. The stock and bond investments and long-term resources may be sold, and outstanding loan principal may be collected. Needless to say, investing activities may take many different forms and consume and produce substantial amounts of cash.

FINANCING ACTIVITIES

Companies need funds for a variety of business purposes. These funds are often obtained from different sources, such as capital stock issuances, bonds, mortgage notes, and various types of loan agreements. Financing activities are those activities that supply a firm with funds from either the firm's owners or creditors. The items just cited (stock, bonds, and so forth) all provide an entity with cash inflows and normally commit the entity to specific cash outflows (e.g., dividends and the repayment of principal). These latter items are also considered to arise from financing activities, as do cash outflows for treasury stock acquisitions. Two exceptions to financing cash flows are trade payables and interest, both of which are related to the operating activities of the business.

Exhibit 19–2 summarizes an entity's various cash flow activities and presents examples of typical inflows and outflows for the operating, investing, and financing categories.

INVESTING AND FINANCING TRANSACTIONS THAT DO NOT AFFECT CASH

3 *Discuss the proper accounting treatment for significant noncash investing/financing transactions.*

Several significant investing and financing transactions affect the financial position of a business but do not affect cash. For example, a building may be acquired by securing a long-term loan such as a mortgage payable. Or land may be obtained in exchange for preferred stock. Neither transaction involves an immediate receipt or disbursement of cash; nonetheless, the financial position of the enterprise has changed through the increases in assets, liabilities, and stockholders' equity. Because a statement of cash flows would be incomplete if significant investing and financing transactions were omitted, the accounting profession requires that such transactions be reported even though no receipts and payments are involved.

Noncash transactions are disclosed on the statement as a separate noncash investing/financing activity. To illustrate, assume $10 million of common stock is exchanged for a building of the same value. The event would be separately reported as a $10 million noncash transaction, appropriately labeled as Common Stock Issued for Building. In essence, one could visualize that common stock is issued for cash (a financing inflow), and the cash is simultaneously disbursed to acquire the asset (an investing outflow). We emphasize that this scenario is mentioned merely to assist your understanding of the exchange. Keep in mind that no cash ever changed hands.

Exhibit 19–2
An Overview of Operating, Investing, and Financing Activities

OPERATING ACTIVITIES
- *General thrust*—Activities that are primarily related to the production and sale of goods and services and that enter into the determination of income for the firm.
- *Typical cash inflows*—Receipts from customers, loan interest, dividends.
- *Typical cash outflows*—Payments for inventory, employee salaries and wages, taxes, interest, and other normal business expenses.

INVESTING ACTIVITIES
- *General thrust*—Activities that involve investment of a company's resources.
- *Typical cash inflows*—Receipts from most sales of stocks and bonds of other firms and from the disposal of long-term resources such as land, buildings, and equipment; the receipt of loan principal from borrowers.
- *Typical cash outflows*—Payments made to acquire long-term assets or the securities of other firms; loans made by the entity to other businesses.

FINANCING ACTIVITIES
- *General thrust*—Activities that provide a business with resources from either its owners or creditors.
- *Typical cash inflows*—Receipts from stock and bond issuances, proceeds from mortgage notes and loans.
- *Typical cash outflows*—Payments of loan principal to creditors, acquisitions of treasury stock, and dividend distributions.

CASH AND CASH EQUIVALENTS

When preparing the statement of cash flows, companies broadly define "cash" to consist of both cash *and* cash equivalents. **Cash equivalents** are short-term, highly liquid investments that mature in 90 days or less. Examples include money market accounts, certain Treasury bills, and other financial instruments that firms may use to generate returns (e.g., interest) on excess funds.

A CLOSER LOOK AT OPERATING ACTIVITIES

Before we can illustrate the procedures needed to prepare the statement of cash flows, further study of operating activities is necessary. Recall that transactions and events related to operating activities affect a firm's net income. Also recall from earlier chapters that most large companies, to be in accord with generally accepted accounting principles, compute net income by using the accrual basis of accounting. Under the accrual basis, revenues are recognized when goods and services are sold or rendered, and expenses are recognized when incurred.

Because of the focus on amounts *earned* and *incurred*, the resulting net income figure likely includes revenues not yet collected from customers and expenses not yet paid to creditors. Sales, of course, may be made in one period and collected in another. In addition, expenses such as taxes, salaries, and interest are often accrued at the end of one period, with payment occurring in the future. As a consequence of these "timing" differences, the accrual-based net income figure must be adjusted in the statement-preparation process to achieve our objective: a focus on the entity's operating cash flows. The required adjustments basically involve a conversion to the cash basis of accounting, thereby

A FURTHER FOCUS

The statement of cash flows shows very clearly that there is no direct link between income and operating cash flows. Profitable businesses may consume more cash than they generate (i.e., have a negative operating cash flow), and vice versa. The statement also reveals that some companies rely heavily on outside funding. Consider the diversity in recent data reported by several well-known corporations.

	NET INCOME/ NET LOSS	OPERATING CASH FLOW	LARGEST PROVIDER OF CASH (ACTIVITY)	LARGEST USER OF CASH (ACTIVITY)
American Greetings	Net income	Positive	Operating	Financing
Sears, Roebuck	Net income	Positive	Operating	Investing
BF Goodrich	Net income	Negative	Financing	Investing
Best Buy Company	Net income	Negative	Financing	Operating
Hormel Foods	Net loss	Positive	Operating	Investing
Eastman Kodak	Net loss	Positive	Operating	Investing
USAir Group	Net loss	Negative	Financing	Investing
Zenith Electronics	Net loss	Negative	Financing	Operating

Source: Recent annual reports

---

allowing a business to report the revenues *received* and the expenses *paid*. This process is depicted pictorially in Exhibit 19–3.

The conversion may be accomplished by two different approaches: the direct method and the indirect method. Both approaches are acceptable for purposes of external financial reporting; however, use of the direct method is encouraged by the FASB. The Board feels that the detailed disclosures of the direct method provide more useful information for investors and other financial statement readers.

THE DIRECT METHOD

> **4** Use both the direct and indirect methods of computing cash flows from operating activities.

Under the **direct method,** individual items on the income statement are translated from the accrual basis to the cash basis of accounting. Sales, for example, is adjusted to reflect the actual cash inflows remitted by customers, while cost of goods sold and expenses are converted to show the amounts disbursed to suppliers, employees, and so forth. The result of this translation follows.

Cash received from customers		$XX,XXX
Less cash payments for:		
Purchases of merchandise	$XX,XXX	
Selling & administrative expenses	XX,XXX	
Interest	XX,XXX	
Income taxes	XX,XXX	XX,XXX
Net cash provided (used) by operating activities		$XX,XXX

EXHIBIT 19-3
The Relationship Between Income and Net Cash Provided (Used) by Operating Activities

```
┌─────────────────────┐                           ┌─────────────────────┐
│  Accrual-Basis      │                           │   Cash-Basis        │
│   Accounting        │                           │   Accounting        │
└──────────┬──────────┘                           └──────────┬──────────┘
           │                                                 │
           ▼                                                 ▼
┌─────────────────────┐                           ┌─────────────────────┐
│    A Focus on       │    Adjustments and        │    A Focus on       │
│  Revenues Earned,   │     Eliminations          │  Revenues Received, │
│  Expenses Incurred, │─────That Produce─────────▶│  Expenses Paid, and │
│   and Net Income    │                           │  Net Cash Provided  │
│                     │                           │  (Used) by Operating│
│                     │                           │     Activities      │
└──────────┬──────────┘                           └──────────┬──────────┘
           │                                                 │
           ▼                                                 ▼
┌─────────────────────┐                           ┌─────────────────────┐
│      Income         │                           │    Statement of     │
│     Statement       │                           │    Cash Flows*      │
└─────────────────────┘                           └─────────────────────┘
```

*Also discloses cash flows provided (used) by investing activities and financing activities.

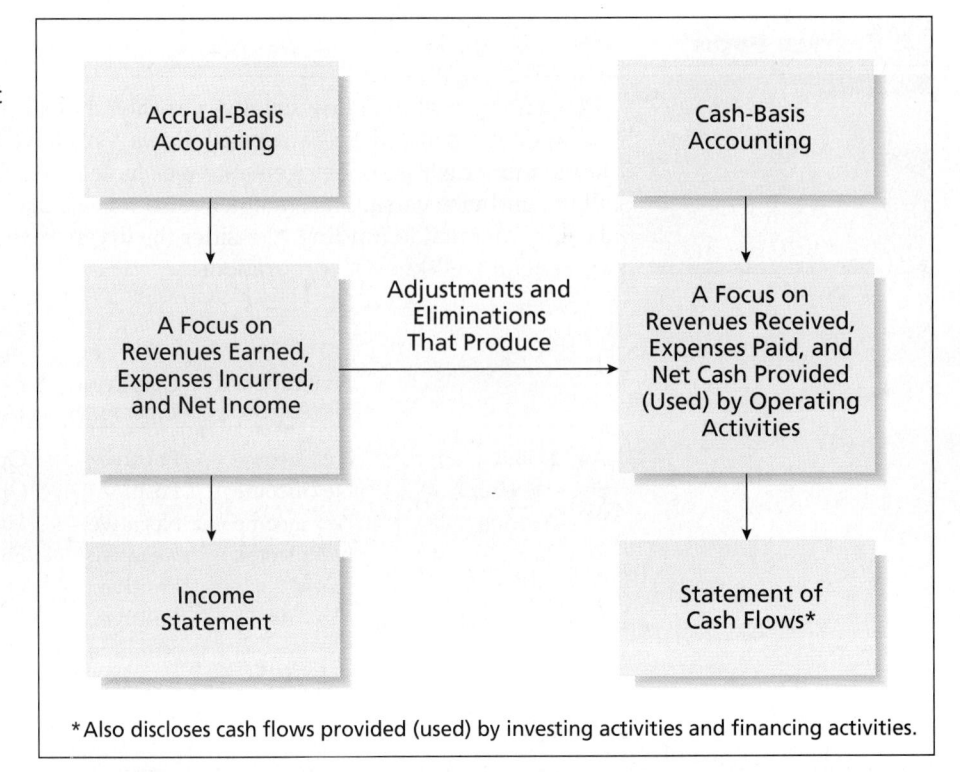

To illustrate the necessary procedures, we will use selected data of the Powell Corporation (see Exhibit 19–4).

Cash Received from Customers. Most companies extend credit to their customers. Because of both credit sales and the accompanying possibility of uncollectible accounts, accrual-based sales revenues generally do not coincide with cash collections. In Powell's case, for instance, Accounts Receivable rose by $23,000 during the year. This increase indicates that revenues have been earned; however, certain customers have yet to settle their balances with the firm.

The T-account shown on page 719 is based on figures in the preceding exhibit. To derive the ending balance of $398,000, it is apparent that Powell collected $2,977,000 ($3,375,000 – $398,000) from clientele. Accrual-based sales revenues may therefore be converted to cash collections via the following formula:

$$\text{Cash Received from Customers} = \text{Sales} \begin{cases} + \text{ Decrease in Accounts Receivable} \\ - \text{ Increase in Accounts Receivable} \end{cases}$$

$$\$2,977,000 = \$3,000,000 - \$23,000$$

Cash Payments for Merchandise. The computation of cash outlays for merchandise is slightly more complex than the calculation just illustrated. The starting point is the cost-of-goods-sold figure on the income statement. Complications

EXHIBIT 19–4
Powell Corporation Data

POWELL CORPORATION
Income Statement
For the Year Ended December 31, 19X2

Sales		$3,000,000
Cost of goods sold		1,200,000
Gross profit		$1,800,000
Expenses		
Selling & administrative	$1,462,000	
Building depreciation	18,000	
Equipment depreciation	70,000	1,550,000
		$ 250,000
Other revenue (expense)		
Interest expense	$ (200,000)	
Gain on sale of long-term stock investments	15,000	
Loss on sale of equipment	(5,000)	(190,000)
Income before income taxes		$ 60,000
Income taxes		20,000
Net income		$ 40,000

ACCOUNT	DEC. 31, 19X2	DEC. 31, 19X1	INCREASE (DECREASE)
Accounts receivable (net)	$398,000	$375,000	$ 23,000
Merchandise inventory	425,000	450,000	(25,000)
Prepaid selling expenses	7,000	4,000	3,000
Accounts payable	470,000	340,000	130,000
Income taxes payable	40,000	39,000	1,000

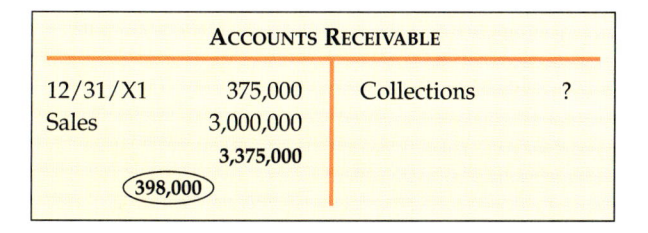

ACCOUNTS RECEIVABLE

12/31/X1	375,000	Collections	?
Sales	3,000,000		
	3,375,000		
(398,000)			

arise, however, since goods acquired during the period may still be in inventory or, conversely, goods purchased in previous periods may have been sold during 19X2. Furthermore, it is likely that cash payments to suppliers will differ from the total cost of merchandise acquired because of purchases made on credit. In view of this situation, changes in *both* the Merchandise Inventory and Accounts Payable accounts must be taken into consideration.

Data for Powell Corporation reveal a $25,000 decrease in inventory, meaning the company disposed of merchandise that was acquired prior to 19X2. The firm's cost of goods sold will therefore exceed the cost of goods purchased during the year. As the figures that follow indicate, 19X2 purchases amounted to $1,175,000.

MERCHANDISE INVENTORY			
12/31/X1	450,000	Cost of goods sold	1,200,000
Purchases	?		
	(425,000)		

Let X = purchases
$450,000 + X - $1,200,000 = $425,000
X = $1,175,000

The next issue is: Did Powell pay for all of these goods during the period? This question can be answered by examining the amounts owed to suppliers.[2]

ACCOUNTS PAYABLE			
Payments	?	12/31/X1	340,000
		Purchases	1,175,000
			1,515,000
		(470,000)	

The T-account shows that the $470,000 owed arises only if 19X2 payments totaled $1,045,000 ($1,515,000 − $470,000). Alternatively, we can arrive at the same conclusion by analyzing the change in Accounts Payable. For example, the $130,000 rise in the account ($470,000 − $340,000) means that some goods acquired in 19X2 were not paid for by year-end. Cash payments to suppliers were therefore less than the cost of merchandise purchased, with total disbursements amounting to $1,045,000 ($1,175,000 − $130,000). These computations are summarized in the formula that follows.

$$\text{Cash Payments for Merchandise} = \text{Cost of Goods Sold} \begin{cases} + \text{Increase in Inventory} \\ - \text{Decrease in Inventory} \end{cases} \begin{cases} + \text{Decrease in Accounts Payable} \\ - \text{Increase in Accounts Payable} \end{cases}$$

$1,045,000 = $1,200,000 − $25,000 − $130,000

[2] We are assuming that all accounts payable are related to purchases of merchandise.

Cash Payments for Selling and Administrative Expenses. There is a strong likelihood that selling and administrative expenses as reported on the income statement will not equal cash payments for services acquired. Several factors, including prepaid expenses, cause these two amounts to differ. Recall that companies often pay for items in advance (e.g., insurance, rent, and advertising), with the amounts spent being written off to expense upon consumption. As a result of this accounting treatment, a rising balance of prepaid expenses indicates that the cost of prepaid items acquired during the year exceeded the cost of those consumed. Thus, cash outflows would exceed the amounts expensed.

An examination of Powell's prepaid expenses revealed a $3,000 increase during 19X2. Given that the company reported $1,462,000 of selling and administrative expenses on its accrual-based income statement, cash payments must have amounted to $1,465,000 ($1,462,000 + $3,000). The following formula may be used in the conversion process:[3]

$$\text{Cash Payments for Selling \& Administrative Expenses} = \text{Selling \& Administrative Expenses} \begin{cases} + \text{Increases in Prepaid Expenses} \\ - \text{Decreases in Prepaid Expenses} \end{cases}$$

Cash Payments for Interest and Income Taxes. The final items to consider are interest and income taxes. For most businesses, the related cash outflows seldom coincide with the amount of expense incurred. Interest and taxes are often accrued at the end of one period, with payment taking place on some future date. For example, a review of Powell's data reveals a $1,000 increase in the Income Taxes Payable account, meaning that some reported expense has yet to be paid to taxing authorities. Cash payments for taxes will therefore be less than the accrual-based expense figure. An appropriate formula to use is:

$$\text{Cash Payments for Income Taxes} = \text{Income Tax Expense} \begin{cases} + \text{Decrease in Income Taxes Payable} \\ - \text{Increase in Income Taxes Payable} \end{cases}$$

The computation for Powell reveals that $19,000 was disbursed during the period:

$$\$19,000 = \$20,000 - \$1,000$$

A similar procedure is followed to derive interest payments. Because of the absence of an Interest Payable account, the company's expense as disclosed on the income statement ($200,000) equaled the funds remitted to lenders.

---

[3] This formula and the next one are sometimes modified. See the upcoming discussion entitled "The Need for Flexibility."

The Need for Flexibility. Our examples of prepaid expenses and accruals dealt with selling and administrative items and income taxes, respectively. Be aware that businesses often accrue amounts in the selling and administrative category (e.g., wages), and those same businesses may prepay income taxes and/or interest. The proper accounting treatment in such cases parallels that illustrated earlier. That is, the appropriate prepaid items would be handled with income tax and interest computations (increases being added and decreases subtracted). Also, relevant accruals such as Wages Payable would be merged with selling and administrative expenses, resulting in the following formula:

$$\text{Cash Payments for Selling \& Administrative Expenses} = \text{Selling \& Administrative Expenses} \begin{cases} + \text{Increases in Prepaid Expenses} \\ - \text{Decreases in Prepaid Expenses} \end{cases} \begin{cases} + \text{Decreases in Accrued Liabilities} \\ - \text{Increases in Accrued Liabilities} \end{cases}$$

An Overview. The calculations in the preceding sections can be summarized to show that operating activities generated a net cash inflow of $248,000:

Cash received from customers		$2,977,000
Less cash payments for:		
Purchases of merchandise	$1,045,000	
Selling & administrative expenses	1,465,000	
Interest	200,000	
Income taxes	19,000	2,729,000
Net cash provided by operating activities		$ 248,000

This information is eventually combined with the results of financing and investing activities to form the statement of cash flows.

Income Statement Items That Were Disregarded. A review of the data in Exhibit 19–4 will show that we disregarded several income statement items when computing net cash flows from operating activities. Depreciation, for instance, was ignored because it is a *noncash* expense. Picturing the year-end adjusting entry (i.e., a debit to Depreciation Expense and a credit to Accumulated Depreciation), it is apparent that cash is not affected. Amortization is a similar expense that also falls in this category.

We also ignored the gain from the sale of long-term stock investments and the loss on the sale of equipment. These items are examples of **nonoperating gains and losses,** or gains and losses that arise from investing and financing activities. Given the emphasis on *operating* transactions, such amounts are not used in the conversion process. (The related cash flow effects are reflected in a company's investing and financing disclosures, as we will show shortly.)

THE INDIRECT METHOD

A company's cash flow from operating activities may be computed by using an alternative approach to that just presented. Under the **indirect method,** operating cash flows are calculated by starting with accrual-basis net income as reported on the income statement. This figure is then converted to the cash basis by adding and subtracting certain amounts. Stated differently, rather than adjust the *individual* income statement items (sales, cost of goods sold, interest expense, and so forth) to reflect receipts and disbursements, the conversion is done indirectly through bottom-line income. The conversion process requires the accountant to address the issues of noncash expenses, gains and losses on nonoperating transactions, and changes in the balances of selected accounts (e.g., Accounts Receivable and Merchandise Inventory).

Noncash Expenses; Nonoperating Gains and Losses. Under the direct method, noncash expenses such as depreciation and amortization were ignored when deriving cash flows from operating activities. Keep in mind that with the *indirect* method, the starting point is net income. Depreciation and amortization, of course, are deducted from revenues when computing this figure. Because these expenses cause a decrease in profitability without an accompanying reduction in cash, they must be added back to net income to arrive at an entity's operating cash flows. In Powell's case, the $40,000 net income figure would be increased by the depreciation write-offs of $18,000 and $70,000 as the first step in computing the proper cash flow number.

Similar procedures are followed for gains and losses from nonoperating activities, which are also considered in the calculation of net income. The calculation of net cash flows from *operating* activities requires that such amounts be "backed out" of accrual income when performing the conversion process. To the extent that net income includes nonoperating gains, these gains must be subtracted to arrive at cash flows from operating activities. Conversely, losses must be added.

Current Assets and Current Liabilities. As a final step, changes in certain account balances must be studied to determine uncollected revenues, unpaid purchases, interest and income taxes incurred but not yet disbursed, and so forth. The accounts are the same as those utilized with the direct method: the current assets and current liabilities of Powell Corporation that appear in Exhibit 19–4.

When using the indirect method, the accountant is making additions to and subtractions from net income rather than adjusting individual income statement components. With one exception, the rules concerning the treatment of increases and decreases in account balances are identical to those shown on the preceding pages. Powell, for instance, subtracted its $23,000 increase in Accounts Receivable from sales when converting the accrual-based figure to cash received from customers (see p. 718). The same effect is achieved under the indirect method, but now the increase is subtracted from net income. Had there been a decrease in the accounts receivable balance, the decrease would have been added.

The exception just noted relates to components that are deducted from revenues in the determination of net income, namely, cost of goods sold, selling and administrative expenses, interest expense, and income tax expense. Rules for the addition and subtraction of current assets and current liabilities connected with these items are the opposite of those presented earlier. For example, Powell's $1,000 increase in the Income Taxes Payable account means reported expense exceeded disbursements to taxing authorities. A larger expense amount translates into less income than cash flow, calling for an *addition* to net income when converting to the cash basis. Generally stated, decreases in current assets and increases in current liabilities are added to accrual-based net income in the conversion process, whereas increases in current assets and decreases in current liabilities are subtracted.

These addition and subtraction rules apply only to current assets and current liabilities that are related to operations. Consider that certain short-term obligations (e.g., notes payable and notes receivable) are often created in borrowing transactions, which are *financing* activities. Placement of such items in the operating section of the cash flows statement is therefore not appropriate.

The procedures required by the indirect method are summarized in Exhibit 19–5. Application of these rules to the Powell Corporation data yields a net cash flow from operating activities of $248,000—the same as that achieved under the direct approach. The outcome is identical; only the methodology differs.

EXHIBIT 19–5
Computing the Cash Flow from Operating Activities: Indirect Approach

	ADJUSTMENT NEEDED TO ACCRUAL-BASIS INCOME
Net income, accrual basis	$XX,XXX
Add (deduct) items to convert net income to a cash basis	
Noncash expenses (e.g., depreciation, amortization)	Add
Gains/losses related to nonoperating activities	
Gains	Deduct
Losses	Add
Current assets related to operating activities	
Increase in account balance	Deduct
Decrease in account balance	Add
Current liabilities related to operating activities	
Increase in account balance	Add
Decrease in account balance	Deduct
Net cash provided (used) by operating activities	$XX,XXX

FOR POWELL CORPORATION

Cash flows from operating activities		
Net income		$ 40,000
Add (deduct) items to convert net income to a cash basis		
Building depreciation expense	$ 18,000	
Equipment depreciation expense	70,000	
Gain on sale of long-term stock investments	(15,000)	
Loss on sale of equipment	5,000	
Increase in accounts receivable (net)	(23,000)	
Decrease in merchandise inventory	25,000	
Increase in prepaid selling expenses	(3,000)	
Increase in accounts payable	130,000	
Increase in income taxes payable	1,000	208,000
Net cash provided by operating activities		$248,000

PREPARATION OF A STATEMENT OF CASH FLOWS

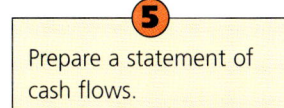

5 Prepare a statement of cash flows.

The information needed to construct the statement of cash flows comes from a variety of sources: the income statement, statement of retained earnings, comparative balance sheets, and ledger accounts. To illustrate the necessary procedures, we will continue the Powell Corporation example (see Exhibit 19–6 for additional data). As you study this material, proceed slowly and keep the previous discussion in mind.

STEP 1: ANALYZE THE CASH ACCOUNT

Because the statement will concentrate on the inflows and outflows of cash, the first step is to determine the change in Powell's Cash account. According to the comparative balance sheets, the company's cash increased by $43,000 during 19X2. The increase, which represents the bottom-line amount to be explained on the statement of cash flows, is caused by the firm's operating, investing, and financing activities.

STEP 2: DETERMINE NET CASH FLOW FROM OPERATING ACTIVITIES

Step 2, which is the focal point of the direct and indirect methods, has already been performed. Observe that the account balance changes introduced earlier for current assets and current liabilities (Accounts Receivable, Merchandise Inventory, Prepaid Selling Expenses, Accounts Payable, and Income Taxes Payable) are now reflected in the firm's comparative balance sheets.

A careful study of the balance sheets will find two current accounts—Cash and Notes Payable—that were ignored in the initial presentation (Exhibit 19–4). Cash was omitted because our objective was to show how changes in other current accounts affected the cash generated from operations. Similarly, Notes Payable was disregarded because the obligations arose from borrowing transactions (i.e., *financing* activities) conducted with First Pacific Trust. Remember, the current assets and current liabilities used with the direct and indirect conversion methods must pertain to operations.

STEP 3: ANALYZE REMAINING BALANCE SHEET ITEMS

The third step is to analyze the remaining balance sheet items to determine the effect, if any, of a company's investing and financing activities. We begin with an evaluation of the Long-Term Stock Investments account.

Long-Term Stock Investments. The comparative balance sheets indicate that Long-Term Stock Investments decreased from $1 million to $880,000 during the year. The ledger account appears as shown:

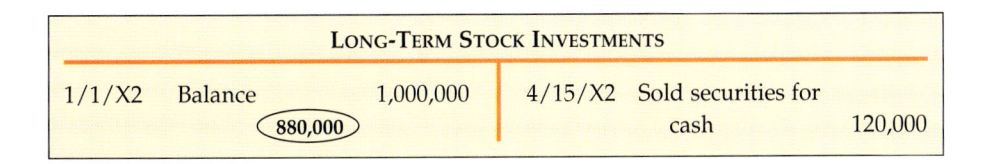

LONG-TERM STOCK INVESTMENTS				
1/1/X2 Balance	1,000,000	4/15/X2	Sold securities for cash	120,000
	880,000			

EXHIBIT 19–6
Powell Corporation Financial Information

POWELL CORPORATION
Comparative Balance Sheets
December 31, 19X2 and 19X1

	19X2	19X1	INCREASE (DECREASE)
ASSETS			
Current assets			
Cash	$ 93,000	$ 50,000	$ 43,000
Accounts receivable (net)	398,000	375,000	23,000
Merchandise inventory	425,000	450,000	(25,000)
Prepaid selling expenses	7,000	4,000	3,000
Total current assets	$ 923,000	$ 879,000	$ 44,000
Long-term stock investments	$ 880,000	$1,000,000	$(120,000)
Property, plant, & equipment			
Land	$ 200,000	$ 115,000	$ 85,000
Buildings	1,450,000	1,250,000	200,000
Accumulated depreciation: buildings	(43,000)	(25,000)	(18,000)
Equipment	725,000	800,000	(75,000)
Accumulated depreciation: equipment	(250,000)	(260,000)	10,000
Total property, plant, & equipment	$2,082,000	$1,880,000	$ 202,000
Total assets	$3,885,000	$3,759,000	$ 126,000
LIABILITIES & STOCKHOLDERS' EQUITY			
Current liabilities			
Accounts payable	$ 470,000	$ 340,000	$ 130,000
Notes payable*	—	300,000	(300,000)
Income taxes payable	40,000	39,000	1,000
Total current liabilities	$ 510,000	$ 679,000	$(169,000)
Long-term liabilities			
Bonds payable	$2,070,000	$2,000,000	$ 70,000
Stockholders' equity			
Common stock, par value $1	$ 195,000	$ 130,000	$ 65,000
Paid-in capital in excess of par	635,000	500,000	135,000
Retained earnings	475,000	450,000	25,000
Total stockholders' equity	$1,305,000	$1,080,000	$ 225,000
Total liabilities & stockholders' equity	$3,885,000	$3,759,000	$ 126,000

* Owed to First Pacific Trust for monies borrowed in late 19X1.

EXHIBIT 19–6
(continued)

POWELL CORPORATION
Statement of Retained Earnings
For the Year Ended December 31, 19X2

Retained earnings, 1/1/X2	$450,000
Add: Net income	40,000
	$490,000
Less: Cash dividend	15,000
Retained earnings, 12/31/X2	$475,000

Powell's management reports that the securities were sold for $135,000, thus generating the $15,000 gain that appears on the income statement in Exhibit 19–4. The gain was handled previously when computing the net cash flow from operating activities. The $135,000 inflow, on the other hand, would be disclosed in the investing activities section as follows:

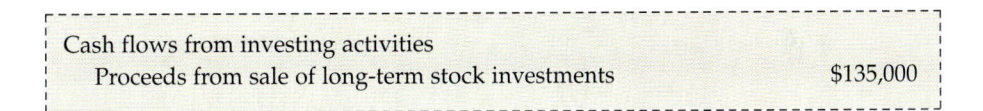

Cash flows from investing activities	
Proceeds from sale of long-term stock investments	$135,000

Land. The Land account increased by $85,000 during the year. An analysis of the ledger account revealed that land was purchased for cash on October 19.

LAND

1/1/X2	Balance	115,000
10/19/X2	Purchased land for cash	85,000
		200,000

The increase in this asset results from an $85,000 use of cash and would be reported in the statement of cash flows as an investing activity, as follows:

Cash flows from investing activities	
Purchase of land	$(85,000)

Buildings. Continuing down the balance sheet, the next account, Buildings, increased $200,000, from $1.25 million to $1.45 million. An examination of the ledger account revealed that a building was acquired on the last day of the year in exchange for 65,000 shares of the company's $1 par-value common stock.

	BUILDINGS	
1/1/X2 Balance	1,250,000	
12/31/X2 Acquired building; issued common stock	200,000	
	1,450,000	

Although the acquisition does not involve cash, the financial position of Powell Corporation has been significantly affected. Recall from our earlier discussion that such exchange transactions are reported on the statement of cash flows as a noncash investing/financing activity. Therefore, the building acquisition is disclosed in a separate schedule in the manner shown.

Schedule of noncash investing/financing activities
Common stock issued for building $200,000

Accumulated Depreciation: Buildings. The Accumulated Depreciation: Buildings account increased by $18,000 during 19X2 because of annual depreciation expense (see the income statement in Exhibit 19–4).

	ACCUMULATED DEPRECIATION: BUILDINGS	
	1/1/X2 Balance	25,000
	12/31/X2 Adjusting entry: annual depreciation	18,000
		43,000

The proper treatment of this expense was considered previously when computing net cash flows from operating activities and need not be addressed again.

Equipment and Accumulated Depreciation: Equipment. Powell's Equipment balance decreased by $75,000 during the year, perhaps because of a discard or a sale. A look at the general ledger revealed that two transactions actually occurred.

May 1   Sold $100,000 of equipment for cash.
Nov. 1 Purchased $25,000 of equipment for cash.

EQUIPMENT				
1/1/X2	Balance	800,000	5/1/X2 Disposal for cash	100,000
11/1/X2	Purchase for cash	25,000		
	(725,000)	825,000		

As you can see, overreliance on ending account balances could result in a failure to detect all changes in cash. In this case, for instance, Powell had a receipt and a disbursement of cash that require separate disclosure. Offsetting or netting is really inappropriate.

Continuing our examination of these two transactions, the Accumulated Depreciation: Equipment account reveals that (1) depreciation associated with the disposal totaled $80,000 and (2) 19X2 depreciation expense amounted to $70,000.

ACCUMULATED DEPRECIATION: EQUIPMENT				
5/1/X2	Disposal	80,000	1/1/X2 Balance	260,000
			12/31/X2 Adjusting entry: annual depreciation	70,000
			(250,000)	330,000

From an analysis of both ledger accounts, we can determine that the equipment sold on May 1 had a $20,000 book value (cost of $100,000 minus accumulated depreciation of $80,000). Furthermore, the income statement reported a $5,000 loss from equipment sales (see p. 719), meaning that Powell must have received cash proceeds of $15,000 on the disposal. The necessary calculations are:

Equipment cost	$100,000
Accumulated depreciation	80,000
Book value	$ 20,000
Proceeds from disposal	15,000
Loss	$ 5,000

The purchase and sale of equipment arose from investment-related activities and are disclosed on the statement of cash flows as follows:

Cash flows from investing activities	
Purchase of equipment	$(25,000)
Proceeds from disposal of equipment	15,000

Regardless of whether a loss (or gain) is produced, the proceeds received would be the amount reported on the statement. This procedure is logical because the statement is prepared to explain the change in a company's cash balance, and the proceeds would be the amount debited to the Cash account in the transaction's journal entry.

Notes Payable. The next balance sheet account to be considered is Notes Payable.

NOTES PAYABLE				
8/15/X2 Paid to First Pacific Trust 300,000		1/1/X2 Balance		300,000
				-0-

As stated in Exhibit 19–6, the balance in this account arose from a borrowing transaction with First Pacific Trust. The $300,000 debt reduction during 19X2 was caused by repayment of the note's principal and is therefore considered a financing activity of the firm. The proper presentation on the statement of cash flows follows.

```
Cash flows from financing activities
    Payment to settle short-term note                    $(300,000)
```

Bonds Payable. A review of the ledger showed that Powell had issued $70,000 of bonds on February 14.

BONDS PAYABLE	
	1/1/X2 Balance 2,000,000
	2/14/X2 Issued bonds at face value for cash 70,000
	2,070,000

The issuance is disclosed as a financing activity in the following manner:

```
Cash flows from investing activities
    Proceeds from bond issue                             $70,000
```

Common Stock and Paid-in Capital in Excess of Par. During 19X2, the Common Stock and Paid-in Capital in Excess of Par accounts increased by $65,000 and $135,000, respectively. These hikes were caused by the issuance of 65,000 shares of $1 par-value stock in exchange for a $200,000 building (see p. 727) and appear in the ledger as shown:

COMMON STOCK, PAR VALUE $1		
	1/1/X2 Balance	130,000
	12/31/X2 Issued 65,000 shares for building	65,000
		195,000

PAID-IN CAPITAL IN EXCESS OF PAR		
	1/1/X2 Balance	500,000
	12/31/X2 Issued 65,000 shares for building	135,000
		635,000

Proper disclosure of the December 31 issuance on the statement of cash flows was illustrated earlier when the Buildings account was discussed. Observe that *for statement presentation purposes,* it is not necessary to subdivide the $200,000 into the individual amounts that were credited to Common Stock and Paid-in Capital in Excess of Par.

Retained Earnings. The final account on Powell's comparative balance sheet is Retained Earnings, which increased by $25,000 during 19X2. As reported on the statement of retained earnings (see Exhibit 19–6), this increase was caused by $40,000 of net income and a $15,000 cash dividend. The Retained Earnings account therefore appears as follows:

RETAINED EARNINGS				
4/30/X2 Cash dividend	15,000	1/1/X2 Balance		450,000
		12/31/X2 Net income (via closing)		40,000
	475,000			490,000

Net income was previously considered when computing cash flow from operating activities. The dividend distribution, a financing transaction, is reported in the following manner:

> Cash flows from financing activities
>   Dividends paid $(15,000)

STEP 4: FINANCIAL STATEMENT PREPARATION

Once the changes in all balance sheet accounts have been determined and analyzed, the formal financial statement is prepared. The statement of cash flows for Powell Corporation appears in Exhibit 19–7 (direct method) and Exhibit 19–8 (indirect method). Observe that the statement is merely the summation of the operating activities discussion (direct, p. 722; indirect, Exhibit 19–5) and the

EXHIBIT 19–7
Statement of Cash Flows: Direct Approach

POWELL CORPORATION
Statement of Cash Flows—Direct Approach
For the Year Ended December 31, 19X2

Cash flows from operating activities		
Cash received from customers		$2,977,000
Less cash payments for:		
Purchases of merchandise	$1,045,000	
Selling & administrative expenses	1,465,000	
Interest	200,000	
Income taxes	19,000	2,729,000
Net cash provided by operating activities		$ 248,000
Cash flows from investing activities		
Proceeds from sale of long-term stock investments	$ 135,000	
Purchase of land	(85,000)	
Purchase of equipment	(25,000)	
Proceeds from disposal of equipment	15,000	
Net cash provided by investing activities		40,000
Cash flows from financing activities		
Payment to settle short-term note	$ (300,000)	
Proceeds from bond issue	70,000	
Dividend paid	(15,000)	
Net cash used by financing activities		(245,000)
Net increase (decrease) in cash		$ 43,000
Cash balance, January 1, 19X2		50,000
Cash balance, December 31, 19X2		$ 93,000
Schedule of noncash investing/financing activities		
Common stock issued for building		$ 200,000

> **ETHICS ISSUE**
>
> A statement of cash flows reveals a large cash increase because of one-time, unusual inflows. The company accountants want to add a special explanatory note for unsophisticated statement users, but management objects. What should happen?

individual investing, financing, and noncash investing/financing activities (noted in shaded blocks) from Step 3. The combined inflows and outflows under both methods produce a $43,000 increase in cash, which agrees with the company's comparative balance sheet presentation.

A review of Exhibits 19–7 and 19–8 will reveal identical investing and financing disclosures; only the operating sections differ. The direct approach is said to

EXHIBIT 19–8
Statement of Cash Flows: Indirect Approach

POWELL CORPORATION
Statement of Cash Flows—Indirect Approach
For the Year Ended December 31, 19X2

Cash flows from operating activities		
Net income		$ 40,000
Add (deduct) items to convert net income to a cash basis		
Building depreciation expense	$ 18,000	
Equipment depreciation expense	70,000	
Gain on sale of long-term stock investments	(15,000)	
Loss on sale of equipment	5,000	
Increase in accounts receivable (net)	(23,000)	
Decrease in merchandise inventory	25,000	
Increase in prepaid selling expenses	(3,000)	
Increase in accounts payable	130,000	
Increase in income taxes payable	1,000	208,000
Net cash provided by operating activities		$ 248,000
Cash flows from investing activities		
Proceeds from sale of long-term stock investments	$ 135,000	
Purchase of land	(85,000)	
Purchase of equipment	(25,000)	
Proceeds from disposal of equipment	15,000	
Net cash provided by investing activities		40,000
Cash flows from financing activities		
Payment to settle short-term note	$(300,000)	
Proceeds from bond issue	70,000	
Dividend paid	(15,000)	
Net cash used by financing activities		(245,000)
Net increase (decrease) in cash		$ 43,000
Cash balance, January 1, 19X2		50,000
Cash balance, December 31, 19X2		$ 93,000
Schedule of noncash investing/financing activities		
Common stock issued for building		$ 200,000

be more useful to lenders, who desire information on specific inflows and outflows when judging a company's ability to repay debt. However, many people find the indirect approach easier to understand because most businesses have used this means of disclosure in the past. In sum, neither method is clearly superior, and the method selected for reporting is a matter of personal preference.

SOME THOUGHTS ON INTERPRETATION

6 Interpret a statement of cash flows.

A large portion of our presentation has involved the procedures related to statement preparation. Although the procedures are important, knowledge of the information being conveyed by the numbers is equally if not more significant. Let us focus for a moment on the *relationship* among operating, investing, and financing cash flows, a useful indicator when evaluating managerial and business performance. Consider the following data of three different companies ($000 omitted):

	BROWN	GREEN	PURPLE
Net cash provided (used) by			
Operating activities	$ (500)	$ 900	$ 1,600
Investing activities	(2,600)	(1,500)	(1,100)
Financing activities	3,100	600	(500)
	$ —	$ —	$ —

Each of the firms has the same net cash flow ($0); however, the individual patterns differ.

Brown, for instance, is probably a young, growth-oriented firm. Initial cash flows from daily operating activities are negative, perhaps because of start-up losses. Additionally, the company may be experiencing sizable outlays to build inventories, and receivables may be growing as the customer base expands. During this same period, major investments are being made in various long-lived assets such as buildings and equipment. The net outflows from operating and investing activities dictate a need for external financing so that business endeavors may continue.

Green appears to be a more mature firm than Brown. Daily operations have grown to the point where a positive cash flow is being generated. The company is investing in needed plant and equipment, and though outside financing is necessary, operating activities are playing a major role in funding the acquisitions.

Finally, Purple seems to be a well-established entity in its field. Operating activities produce significant cash inflows that are more than enough to cover needed investment. In addition, the $500 excess cash flow ($1,600 − $1,100) is being used to reduce outstanding debt that arose during earlier life-cycle stages or perhaps for dividend distributions to stockholders.

These three scenarios illustrate cash flow relationships for different types of entities. Be cautioned that the three cases are generalized. Brown, for instance, may actually be a very mature company, one that has relied extensively on external financing to undertake a costly expansion. An example might be a regional airline that begins to offer service on a national and international level. Negative operating cash flows will be produced until passenger loads increase to a profitable level. In sum, these relationships often vary among industries and should be used only as a starting point when assessing performance.

BUSINESS FAILURE

The statement of cash flows also provides information that is useful in predicting business failure. As implied earlier, companies may produce a loss but still have an overall positive cash flow. This situation arises when an entity offsets negative flows from operating activities with outside borrowings and perhaps even the sale of key plant and equipment assets. Picture the long-term effects of rising debt levels and daily operations that consume more cash than they produce. The result is all too predictable: significant financial problems.

Sooner or later a business will become *insolvent,* with liabilities exceeding assets. Bills go unpaid, outside sources of funding become scarce, and the company is placed in a nonrecoverable position. The eventual outcome is *bankruptcy*—a filing with the U.S. courts that allows the affected firm to reorganize its financial affairs while continuing to operate. This process includes negotiated settlements with creditors, sometimes for pennies on the dollar, and even creditor control (through stock ownership) of the reorganized entity.

APPENDIX: WORK SHEET FOR PREPARING A STATEMENT OF CASH FLOWS—INDIRECT APPROACH

Some accountants use a work sheet when constructing the statement of cash flows. A work sheet provides structure and helps to ensure that no accounts are accidentally overlooked in the statement-preparation process. Whether or not a work sheet is used, the end result is the same: a financial report that reveals an entity's operating, investing, and financing activities.

To illustrate a work sheet for the indirect method of statement presentation, we will utilize data relating to Powell Corporation that were introduced earlier in the chapter. It is helpful to review Exhibits 19–4 and 19–6 at this time.

Construction of a work sheet requires performance of the five steps that follow.

- *Step 1*—Enter the beginning and ending account balances of all balance sheet items (see Exhibit 19–9). All accounts with debit balances are listed first, followed by those with credit balances. This procedure results in the accumulated depreciation accounts being listed together with liabilities and the components of stockholders' equity.
- *Step 2*—Obtain the total of the debits and credits, both at the beginning and end of the year, to assure that the required equality is maintained on the two dates.
- *Step 3*—Insert the headings "Operating Activities," "Investing Activities," "Financing Activities," and "Noncash Activities" on the work sheet where shown. Leave sufficient space so that a number of items may eventually be recorded.
- *Step 4*—Make entries in the Analysis columns of the work sheet to account for (1) changes in the noncash accounts during the reporting period *and* (2) the accompanying inflows and outflows of cash. These entries are used for work sheet preparation purposes only; they are never recorded in the general journal. The entries may be made in any order; our sequence will parallel Exhibit 19–5 and the discussion on pages 725–732.
    (a) *Generated net income of $40,000 during the year.* Profitable operations represent a source of cash for a firm. The analysis entry recognizes this fact by establishing a line entitled "Net Income" in the Operating Activities section. In addition, Retained Earnings is increased (credited) by

EXHIBIT 19-9
Cash Flow Work Sheet—Indirect Approach

POWELL CORPORATION
Work Sheet for Statement of Cash Flows—Indirect Approach
For the Year Ended December 31, 19X2

	Account Balances, 12/31/X1	Analysis of Transactions for 19X2 Debit		Analysis of Transactions for 19X2 Credit		Account Balances, 12/31/X2
DEBITS						
Cash	50,000	(x)	43,000			93,000
Accounts receivable (net)	375,000	(d)	23,000			398,000
Merchandise inventory	450,000			(e)	25,000	425,000
Prepaid selling expenses	4,000	(f)	3,000			7,000
Long-term stock investments	1,000,000			(i)	120,000	880,000
Land	115,000	(j)	85,000			200,000
Buildings	1,250,000	(k*)	200,000			1,450,000
Equipment	800,000	(l)	25,000	(m)	100,000	725,000
	4,044,000					4,178,000
CREDITS						
Accumulated depreciation: buildings	25,000			(b)	18,000	43,000
Accumulated depreciation: equipment	260,000	(m)	80,000	(c)	70,000	250,000
Accounts payable	340,000			(g)	130,000	470,000
Notes payable	300,000	(n)	300,000			—
Income taxes payable	39,000			(h)	1,000	40,000
Bonds payable	2,000,000			(o)	70,000	2,070,000
Common stock	130,000			(k)	65,000	195,000
Paid-in capital in excess of par	500,000			(k)	135,000	635,000
Retained earnings	450,000	(p)	15,000	(a)	40,000	475,000
	4,044,000					4,178,000

Operating activities					
Net income	(a)	40,000			
Building depreciation expense	(b)	18,000			
Equipment depreciation expense	(c)	70,000			
Increase in accounts receivable			(d)	23,000	
Decrease in merchandise inventory	(e)	25,000			
Increase in prepaid selling expenses			(f)	3,000	
Increase in accounts payable	(g)	130,000			
Increase in income taxes payable	(h)	1,000			
Gain on sale of long-term stock investments			(i)	15,000	
Loss on sale of equipment	(m)	5,000			
Investing activities					
Proceeds from sale of long-term stock investments	(i)	135,000			
Purchase of land			(j)	85,000	
Purchase of equipment			(l)	25,000	
Proceeds from disposal of equipment	(m)	15,000			
Financing activities					
Payment to settle short-term note			(n)	300,000	
Proceeds from bond issue	(o)	70,000			
Dividend paid			(p)	15,000	
Noncash activities					
Common stock issued for building	(k)	200,000	(k*)	200,000	
		1,483,000		1,440,000	
Increase in cash			(x)	43,000	
		1,483,000		1,483,000	

$40,000 to reflect that income is closed to this account at the end of the reporting period.

(b) *Building depreciation expense of $18,000.* Depreciation must be added back to net income to arrive at cash flows from operating activities. Recall that although depreciation is deducted from revenues to determine an entity's earnings, no cash is consumed. The required entry in the Analysis columns involves a credit to Accumulated Depreciation: Buildings and an offsetting debit to Building Depreciation Expense, immediately below Powell's net income figure.

(c) *Equipment depreciation expense of $70,000.* This amount is treated in similar fashion to the expense in item (b).

(d) *Increase in accounts receivable, $23,000.* As noted earlier in the chapter, changes in both current assets and current liabilities related to operations must be considered when deriving the cash flow from operating activities. Decreases in current assets and increases in current liabilities are added to net income to convert to a cash-basis figure, whereas increases in current assets and decreases in current liabilities are subtracted. The analysis entry reflects the rise in accounts receivable via a $23,000 debit to that account. Further, a credit appears in the Operating Activities section to produce a subtraction from net income, the net income amount having been entered earlier as a debit.

The following require similar entries on the work sheet to compute the net cash flow from operating activities:

(e) Decrease in merchandise inventory, $25,000.
(f) Increase in prepaid selling expenses, $3,000.
(g) Increase in accounts payable, $130,000.
(h) Increase in income taxes payable, $1,000.

As shown in Exhibit 19–5, two additional items were considered in the operating cash flow computation: a $15,000 gain from the sale of long-term stock investments and a $5,000 loss on the sale of equipment. These items will be discussed in a moment.

(i) *Sold $120,000 of long-term stock investments for $135,000; generated a $15,000 gain.* This transaction requires a decrease (credit) in the Long-Term Stock Investments account for $120,000 and recognition of a $135,000 receipt of cash in the Investing Activities section (via a debit). Also, because the $15,000 gain is (1) included in net income and (2) "investing" in nature, it must be subtracted when computing cash flows from *operating* activities. The gain is therefore set out (by means of a credit) in the Operating Activities section to produce the desired result.

(j) *Purchased land for $85,000 cash.* This transaction required the use of cash and resulted in an $85,000 increase to the Land account. The necessary entry is therefore a debit to Land, with an offsetting credit to establish a line for Purchase of Land in the Investing Activities section.

(k) *Acquired a $200,000 building in exchange for 65,000 shares of $1 par-value common stock.* This exchange transaction involves three accounts and is disclosed as a noncash activity. First, the Common Stock and Paid-in Capital in Excess of Par Value accounts are credited for $65,000 and $135,000, respectively, to reflect the issuance of additional shares, with a $200,000 debit then being made to the line "Common Stock Issued for Building." Next, the Buildings account is debited (see k*) to record the acquisition, and a credit is entered on the same line as that just noted: "Common Stock Issued for Building."

(l) *Purchased $25,000 of equipment for cash.* This acquisition resulted in a cash outflow and also a $25,000 increase in the Equipment account. The analysis entry requires a debit to Equipment. In addition, a corresponding credit is needed in the Investing Activities section to establish the Purchase of Equipment line item.

(m) *Disposed of $100,000 of equipment for cash; incurred a $5,000 loss.* The underlying details of this transaction are shown on page 729. The required work sheet entry involves recognition of $15,000 cash proceeds, along with reductions in Equipment ($100,000) and Accumulated Depreciation: Equipment ($80,000). The $5,000 loss is recorded by a debit and is added to net income to arrive at cash flows from operations.

(n) *Paid a short-term note payable, $300,000.* This financing activity resulted in a cash outflow during the period. The necessary entry involves a debit to the Notes Payable account and a credit to the line entitled "Payment to Settle Short-Term Note."

(o) *Issued $70,000 of bonds payable at face value.* The issuance increases cash via a financing activity. The work sheet entry recognizes this fact and also increases (credits) the Bonds Payable account.

(p) *Paid cash dividend, $15,000.* Powell paid $15,000 of dividends during 19X2. The analysis entry therefore requires a $15,000 debit to Retained Earnings to record the appropriate reduction. In addition, a $15,000 credit is made in the Financing Activities section to establish a line item for the payment.

- *Step 5*—Compute the difference between the beginning and ending cash balances, and place the difference (labeled x) on the Cash line in the Analysis columns. Increases are entered in the debit column and decreases in the credit column. Next, total the Analysis columns and place the difference, which should equal the increase or decrease, at the bottom of the work sheet for balancing purposes. The document is now complete and can be used to prepare the formal statement of cash flows. (Compare the bottom sections of the work sheet with the statement that appears in Exhibit 19–8.)

END-OF-CHAPTER REVIEW

LEARNING OBJECTIVES: THE KEY POINTS

1. **Explain the purpose of the statement of cash flows.** The statement of cash flows is designed to provide information about the nature and sources of an entity's cash inflows and outflows. These items are categorized into operating, investing, and financing classifications. Overall, this important report lends insight into a company's need for external financing and the firm's ability to generate future cash flows, meet obligations, and pay dividends.

2. **Classify and analyze operating, investing, and financing activities.** Operating activities give rise to transactions and events that enter into the determination of net income. The Financial Accounting Standards Board defines these activities to include all cash transactions and events that are not otherwise considered in the investing or financing categories. Examples include receipts from customers,

normal business expenses, and receipts of dividends and loan interest. In contrast, investing activities involve the investment of a firm's resources. Typical examples of such transactions are the acquisition and sale of both productive assets (e.g., property, plant, and equipment) and most securities of other firms. Finally, financing activities provide a business with resources from either its owners or its creditors. Common financing transactions include the issuance and retirement of stock and debt.

3. **Discuss the proper accounting treatment for significant noncash investing/financing transactions.** Noncash investing and financing transactions (e.g., the issuance of stock for land) are reported separately on the statement of cash flows. The purpose of this disclosure is to reveal the impact of such transactions on a company's financial position, even though no direct receipt or disbursement of cash has occurred.

4. **Use both the direct and indirect methods of computing cash flows from operating activities.** Under the direct method, individual income statement items are converted from the accrual basis of accounting to the cash basis of accounting. For instance, to translate sales revenues into the amount of cash received from customers, decreases in accounts receivable are added to sales, and increases are subtracted. To determine cash payments for merchandise, an entity's cost of goods sold is adjusted for changes in merchandise inventory (increases are added and decreases are subtracted) and accounts payable (decreases are added and increases are subtracted).

    The indirect method, on the other hand, begins with the net income figure, adds back noncash expenses (e.g., depreciation and amortization), and adjusts for gains and losses on nonoperating transactions. In addition, changes in current assets and current liabilities related to operations are added to or subtracted from net income. Decreases in current assets and increases in current liabilities are added to net income, whereas increases in current assets and decreases in current liabilities are subtracted.

5. **Prepare a statement of cash flows.** The statement of cash flows may be prepared by using either the direct method or the indirect method, although the former approach is encouraged by the FASB. The direct method begins with a presentation of cash receipts and disbursements for specific operating items (including interest and taxes) to arrive at cash flows from operating activities. Cash flows from investing and financing activities are reported next, followed by a schedule of noncash investing/financing transactions.

    The indirect method begins with a reconciliation of net income to cash flows from operations and then presents cash flows from investing and financing activities. The statement concludes with the same schedule of noncash investing/financing transactions.

6. **Interpret a statement of cash flows.** The relationship among cash flows from operating, investing, and financing activities varies from company to company and from industry to industry. New, emerging companies often have negative operating cash flows and need considerable external financing. In contrast, mature firms frequently produce enough cash flow from operating activities to both cover new investment and reduce outstanding debt. The statement of cash flows provides insights into these relationships. Also a key statement disclosure, cash flows from operating activities, is a useful predictor of forthcoming financial problems (especially if the figure is negative).

Key Terms and Concepts: A Quick Overview

bankruptcy A filing with the U.S. courts that allows a company to continue operating while it reorganizes its financial affairs. (p. 735)

cash equivalents Short-term, highly liquid investments that mature in 90 days or less. (p. 716)

direct method of statement construction An approach whereby individual income statement items are converted from the accrual basis to the cash basis of accounting. (p. 717)

financing activities Those activities that supply a company with funds from the company's owners or creditors. (p. 715)

indirect method of statement construction An approach whereby cash flow from operations is derived by making certain adjustments to accrual-basis net income. (p. 722)

insolvent A situation where a company's total liabilities exceed total assets. (p. 735)

investing activities Those activities that involve investment of an entity's resources. (p. 715)

nonoperating gains and losses Gains and losses that arise from investing and financing activities. (p. 722)

operating activities Company activities primarily related to the production and sale of goods and services, and that enter into the calculation of net income. (p. 714)

statement of cash flows A financial statement that reveals the operating, investing, and financing cash flows of a company. (p. 712)

Chapter Quiz

The five questions that follow relate to several issues raised in the chapter. Test your knowledge of the issues by selecting the best answer. (The answers appear on p. 760.)

1. Which of the following is a financing activity?
   a. Purchase of office equipment.
   b. Payment of dividends.
   c. Receipt of dividends.
   d. Sale of merchandise on account.

2. When preparing a statement of cash flows, the direct method is often used in calculating the cash flows from:
   a. operating, investing, and financing activities.
   b. investing and financing activities.
   c. operating and investing activities.
   d. operating activities only.

3. When converting accrual-based net income to the cash basis with the indirect method, which of the following items is added in the operating activities section of the cash flow statement?
   a. Dividends paid.
   b. Cash dividends received.
   c. Loss on the sale of land.
   d. Gain on the sale of land.

4. Blue Ocean Corporation's net cash flow provided by investing activities totaled $100,000 for the year. Dividends paid amounted to $5,000, payments to retire outstanding loans were $40,000, depreciation expense on buildings was $15,000, and new equipment acquired cost $30,000. If the company sold land for cash, the proceeds from the sale must have been:
   a. $10,000.
   b. $25,000.
   c. $100,000.
   d. $130,000.

5. The balance of Ebony's Machinery account increased by $50,000 during the year. Machinery that cost $80,000 was discarded at a local landfill; additional equipment of $130,000 was purchased via the issuance of common stock. In view of these transactions, an examination of the company's cash flows from investing activities will show:
   a. a $130,000 outflow for the machinery purchase.
   b. a $130,000 outflow for the machinery purchase and an $80,000 inflow from the disposal.
   c. a $130,000 outflow for the machinery purchase and an $80,00 loss.
   d. nothing.

SUMMARY PROBLEM

Colwell Corporation had the following balance sheet data:

	DEC. 31, 19X2	DEC. 31, 19X1
ASSETS		
Cash	$ 59,000	$ 87,000
Accounts receivable (net)	189,000	223,000
Inventory	65,000	45,000
Prepaid selling expenses	15,000	12,000
Land	150,000	120,000
Equipment	125,000	150,000
Accumulated depreciation: equipment	(85,000)	(75,000)
Buildings	280,000	200,000
Accumulated depreciation: buildings	(85,000)	(70,000)
Patents (net of amortization)	24,000	27,000
Total assets	$737,000	$719,000
LIABILITIES & STOCKHOLDERS' EQUITY		
Accounts payable	$ 88,000	$120,000
Notes payable	160,000	90,000
Income taxes payable	60,000	70,000
Bonds payable	100,000	150,000
Common stock, $10 par	210,000	180,000
Additional paid-in capital	50,000	50,000
Retained earnings	69,000	59,000
Total liabilities & stockholders' equity	$737,000	$719,000

The following additional information was extracted from the accounting records:

1. Three thousand shares of common stock were issued for land having a fair market value of $30,000.
2. Equipment having a book value of $13,000 (cost, $25,000; accumulated depreciation, $12,000) was sold for $20,000 cash, producing a $7,000 gain.
3. A building was constructed for $80,000 cash.
4. The notes payable relate to various borrowing agreements signed with Fairfax Savings Bank.
5. Long-term bonds of $50,000 were retired; no gain or loss was incurred.
6. Cash dividends of $10,000 were declared and paid during 19X2.
7. The 19X2 income statement revealed the data shown:

Sales	$1,450,000
Cost of goods sold	835,000

Selling & administrative expenses	$510,000
Equipment depreciation expense	22,000
Building depreciation expense	15,000
Patent amortization expense	3,000
Interest expense	32,000
Income tax expense	20,000
Net income	20,000

Instructions

a. Prepare a statement of cash flows for the year ended December 31, 19X2. Use the direct method.

b. Prepare a statement of cash flows for the year ended December 31, 19X2. Use the indirect method.

Solution

a.

COLWELL CORPORATION
Statement of Cash Flows
For the Year Ended December 31, 19X2

Cash flows from operating activities		
Cash received from customers		$1,484,000*
Less cash payments for:		
Purchases of merchandise	$887,000†	
Selling & administrative expenses	513,000‡	
Interest	32,000	
Income taxes	30,000‡	1,462,000
Net cash provided by operating activities		$ 22,000
Cash flows from investing activities		
Proceeds from sale of equipment	$ 20,000	
Payment for building construction	(80,000)	
Net cash used by investing activities		(60,000)
Cash flows from financing activities		
Proceeds from issuance of notes payable	$ 70,000	
Payment to retire bonds payable	(50,000)	
Payment of cash dividends	(10,000)	
Net cash provided by financing activities		10,000
Net increase (decrease) in cash		$ (28,000)
Cash balance, January 1, 19X2		87,000
Cash balance, December 31, 19X2		$ 59,000
Schedule of noncash investing/financing activities		
Common stock issued for land		$ 30,000

* Sales ($1,450,000) + decrease in accounts receivable ($34,000).
† Cost of goods sold ($835,000) + increase in inventory ($20,000) + decrease in accounts payable ($32,000).
‡ Selling and administrative expenses ($510,000) + increase in prepaid selling expenses ($3,000).
‡ Income tax expense ($20,000) + decrease in income taxes payable ($10,000).

b.

COLWELL CORPORATION
Statement of Cash Flows
For the Year Ended December 31, 19X2

Cash flows from operating activities		
Net income		$ 20,000
Add (deduct) items to convert net income to a cash basis		
Equipment depreciation expense	$ 22,000	
Building depreciation expense	15,000	
Patent amortization expense	3,000	
Gain on sale of equipment	(7,000)	
Decrease in accounts receivable (net)	34,000	
Increase in inventory	(20,000)	
Increase in prepaid selling expenses	(3,000)	
Decrease in accounts payable	(32,000)	
Decrease in income taxes payable	(10,000)	2,000
Net cash provided by operating activities		$ 22,000
Cash flows from investing activities		
Proceeds from sale of equipment	$ 20,000	
Payment for building construction	(80,000)	
Net cash used by investing activities		(60,000)
Cash flows from financing activities		
Proceeds from issuance of notes payable	$ 70,000	
Payment to retire bonds payable	(50,000)	
Payment of cash dividends	(10,000)	
Net cash provided by financing activities		10,000
Net increase (decrease) in cash		$(28,000)
Cash balance, January 1, 19X2		87,000
Cash balance, December 31, 19X2		$ 59,000
Schedule of noncash investing/financing activities		
Common stock issued for land		$ 30,000

ASSIGNMENT MATERIAL

QUESTIONS

Q19–1 What information does the statement of cash flows disclose? Give several examples.

Q19–2 Describe the nature of operating activities, including specific examples of operating cash inflows and outflows.

Q19–3 Define investing activities, citing several examples of typical investing inflows and outflows.

Q19–4 List five examples of financing activities. Which of these cause cash inflows and which cause cash outflows?

Q19–5 Why are noncash transactions, such as the exchange of common stock for a building, included on a statement of cash flows? How are these noncash transactions disclosed?

Q19–6 What is a cash equivalent?

Q19–7 Differentiate between the direct and indirect methods of preparing the statement of cash flows.

Q19–8 Both the direct and indirect methods of reporting are permitted when preparing the statement of cash flows. Which of the two approaches is encouraged by the Financial Accounting Standards Board?

Q19–9 Is net income normally equal to cash provided by operating activities? Why?

Q19–10 Items such as depreciation expense reduce net income without an accompanying decrease in cash. Under the indirect method, how are these and similar items treated when determining the cash provided from operating activities?

Q19–11 Meridian Corporation recently sold some equipment, generating a $6,000 loss on one transaction and a $5,000 gain on another. How are these items treated when computing the net cash flow from operating activities? Assume use of the indirect method.

Q19–12 Briefly discuss the relationship among operating, investing, and financing cash flows for many new, growing companies.

EXERCISES

E19–1 Classification of activities (L.O. 2)

Classify each of the following transactions as arising from an operating (O), investing (I), financing (F), or noncash investing/financing (N) activity.

____ a. Received $80,000 from the sale of land.
____ b. Received $3,200 from cash sales.
____ c. Paid a $5,000 dividend.
____ d. Purchased $8,800 of merchandise for cash.
____ e. Received $100,000 from the issuance of common stock.
____ f. Paid $1,200 of interest on a note payable.
____ g. Acquired a new laser printer by paying $650.
____ h. Acquired a $400,000 building by signing a $400,000 mortgage note.

E19–2 Direct calculation of operating cash flows (L.O. 4)

Selected balance sheet accounts of DDS Technology showed the following increases (decreases) during 19X5:

Accounts receivable	$ 12,000
Inventory	(46,000)
Accounts payable (to suppliers of merchandise)	30,000
Interest payable	(4,000)

DDS makes all sales and purchases on account and uses accrual accounting. The firm's 19X5 income statement revealed sales, cost of goods sold, and interest expense of $533,000, $407,000, and $37,000, respectively.

Assuming that DDS prepares a statement of cash flows by using the direct method, determine:

a. Cash collections from customers.
b. Merchandise purchases for the year.
c. Cash paid to suppliers of merchandise.
d. Interest paid during the year.

E19–3 Indirect calculation of operating cash flows (L.O. 4)

Video Corporation's balance sheet revealed the following account balance information:

Account	Dec. 31, 19X6	Dec. 31, 19X5
Accounts receivable	$52,000	$57,000
Merchandise inventory	75,000	68,000
Accounts payable	21,000	19,500

The accrual-basis net income, $107,000, reflected $12,600 of depreciation expense. There were no gains or losses from investing and financing activities.

On the basis of the preceding information, calculate Video's cash flows from operating activities by using the indirect method.

E19–4 Indirect calculation of operating cash flows (L.O. 4)

Bistro Centrale reported net income of $85,000 for the year just ended, after deducting a $22,000 loss on the sale of long-term investments. Comparative balance sheets revealed increases (decreases) in the following accounts during the year:

Accounts receivable	$ 34,000
Merchandise inventory	(48,000)
Accumulated depreciation: equipment	55,000
Accounts payable	11,000
Accrued liabilities	(23,000)

There were no purchases or disposals of equipment. The long-term investment had a carrying (book) value of $80,000 and was sold for cash.

Bistro Centrale uses the indirect method of statement presentation. On the basis of the preceding information, determine the cash provided by operating activities.

E19–5 Overview of direct and indirect methods (L.O. 4)

Evaluate the comments that follow as being True or False. If the comment is false, briefly explain why.

a. Both the direct and indirect methods will produce the same cash flow from operating activities.
b. Depreciation expense is added back to net income when the indirect method is used.
c. One of the advantages of using the direct method rather than the indirect method is that larger cash flows from financing activities will be reported.
d. The cash paid to suppliers is normally disclosed on the statement of cash flows when the indirect method of statement preparation is employed.
e. The dollar change in the Merchandise Inventory account appears on the statement of cash flows only when the direct method of statement preparation is used.

E19–6 Statement preparation from cash flow listing: Direct method (L.O. 5)

In response to a banker's request, Baxter Corporation's accountant has compiled the following cash flow information for the year ended December 31, 19X7:

Beginning cash balance		$ 173,000
Add: Cash receipts		
Receipts from customers	$945,000	
Proceeds from sale of land	30,000	
Proceeds from stock issuance	600,000	
Proceeds from long-term bank loan	83,000	1,658,000
		$1,831,000
Deduct: Cash disbursements		
Payments to suppliers*	$345,000	
Payments to employees	231,000	
Payments for interest	24,000	
Payments for dividends	50,000	
Repayment of mortgage note	100,000	
Purchase of building	700,000	1,450,000
Ending cash balance		$ 381,000

* For merchandise acquisitions.

A review of the company's accounting records revealed that Baxter had also purchased equipment in exchange for a $35,000 note payable.

Prepare a statement of cash flows by using the direct method.

E19–7 Statement preparation: Direct method (L.O. 5)

Comparative balance sheet data of Village Company follow.

	Dec. 31, 19X2	Dec. 31, 19X1
Cash	$ 5,000	$ 7,000
Accounts receivable (net)	12,000	18,000
Merchandise inventory	35,000	28,000
Property, plant, & equipment	40,000	30,000
Less: Accumulated depreciation	(17,000)	(10,000)
Total assets	$ 75,000	$ 73,000
Accounts payable*	$ 25,000	$ 21,000
Income taxes payable	4,000	1,000
Common stock	24,000	24,000
Retained earnings	22,000	27,000
Total liabilities & stockholders' equity	$ 75,000	$ 73,000

* Relate to purchases of merchandise.

The company's accrual-basis income statement revealed the following figures: sales, $120,000; cost of goods sold, $80,000; selling and administrative expenses, $25,000;

depreciation expense, $7,000; and income taxes, $3,000. (There was no interest expense.) Dividends declared and paid during 19X2 totaled $10,000. Finally, Village purchased $10,000 of equipment for cash on August 14.

a. Determine the increase or decrease in cash during 19X2.
b. Prepare a statement of cash flows by using the direct method.

E19–8 Statement preparation: Indirect method (L.O. 5)
Refer to the data of Village Company in Exercise 19–7.

a. Determine the increase or decrease in cash during 19X2.
b. Prepare a statement of cash flows by using the indirect method.

E19–9 Equipment transaction and cash flow reporting (L.O. 5)
The property, plant, and equipment section of ProComp, Inc.'s comparative balance sheet follows.

	Dec. 31, 19X4	Dec. 31, 19X3
Property, plant, & equipment		
Land	$ 94,000	$ 94,000
Equipment	652,000	527,000
Less: Accumulated depreciation	(316,000)	(341,000)

New equipment purchased during 19X4 totaled $280,000. The 19X4 income statement disclosed equipment depreciation expense of $41,000 and a $9,000 loss on the sale of equipment.

a. Determine the cost and accumulated depreciation of the equipment sold during 19X4.
b. Determine the selling price of the equipment sold.
c. Show how the sale of equipment would appear on a statement of cash flows prepared by using the indirect method.

E19–10 Evaluation of cash flows (L.O. 6)
Summaries of the cash flow statements issued by Halper, Porter, and Bryan follow.

	HALPER	PORTER	BRYAN
Cash flows provided by operating activities	$ 9,000	$63,000	$ 6,700
Cash flows provided by investing activities	2,200	4,900	56,200
Cash flows provided by financing activities	67,300	10,600	15,600
Total	$78,500	$78,500	$78,500

A review of the companies' statements found that Halper issued $70,000 of bonds during the period. Bryan, on the other hand, sold a parcel of land for $65,000.

Focusing solely on the facts presented, assume that Halper, Porter, and Bryan have approached you for a line of credit to buy merchandise from your store. Which of the three companies would you likely favor? Briefly explain.

E19–11 Evaluation of cash flows (L.O. 6)
The following information was excerpted from Rainbow Bay's statement of cash flows:

Cash flows from operating activities:
Net income (loss)	$(142,000)
Add: Depreciation expense	20,000
Net cash provided by operating activities	$(122,000)

Cash flows from investing activities:
Sale of equipment	$ 65,000
Sale of office furniture	5,000
Net cash provided by investing activities	$ 70,000

Cash flows from financing activities:
Issuance of common stock	$ 96,000

Management was very pleased with the year's performance, primarily because of a healthy increase in the company's year-end cash balance.

a. Calculate the increase in cash that occurred during the year.
b. Evaluate the nature of the increase in cash. Should management be pleased or does your analysis indicate some potential problems for Rainbow Bay? Explain.

E19–12 Bankruptcy, evaluation of operations (L.O. 6)

HJ Enterprises operates approximately 1,000 retail apparel stores throughout the country. The stores are divided into chains that focus on four highly diverse, specialized markets: children's, basic teen, trendy teen, and professional dress. Forty-five of the firm's stores are located in shopping malls where major tenants recently closed their doors because of ongoing losses.

After several years of deteriorating performance and increased borrowings "to keep afloat," HJ became insolvent and declared bankruptcy.

a. What does it mean when a company becomes insolvent?
b. In all likelihood, what caused HJ to become insolvent?
c. You are assisting in developing the company's reorganization plan. Recommend several possible changes in operations that might improve HJ's overall performance. What type of arrangement would you try to work out with HJ's current lenders and suppliers?

PROBLEMS

Series A

P19–A1 Transaction analysis: Operating, investing, and financing activities (L.O. 2, 3)

The management of Maui Corporation desires to know the nature of each of the following transactions and events:

1. Collected cash from customers for cash sales.
2. Purchased delivery truck for cash.
3. Obtained a mortgage note to finance the acquisition of a building.
4. Issued 10-year bonds for cash.
5. Paid a short-term nonoperating note.
6. Sold equipment having a book value of $30,000 for $30,000 cash.
7. Sold a parcel of land at cost; received a long-term note.
8. Received dividends on a short-term stock investment.
9. Paid income taxes.

10. Issued preferred stock in exchange for a valuable patent.
11. Reacquired treasury stock for cash.
12. Paid previously declared cash dividends.

Instructions

a. Briefly explain the difference between investing and financing activities and noncash investing/financing activities.
b. Design a table with the following columnar headings: operating activity, investing activity, financing activity, and noncash investing/financing activity. Classify the 12 transactions listed by using these headings. For all classifications except noncash investing/financing, indicate whether the transaction causes a cash inflow (+) or a cash outflow (−).

P19–A2 Operating activities: Direct and indirect methods (L.O. 4)

The following information appeared on the income statement of Caruso's Peppers, Inc., for the year ended December 31, 19X6:

Net sales	$420,000
Cost of goods sold	262,000
Selling & administrative expenses	66,500
Depreciation expense	44,000
Gain on sale of building	21,000
Income tax expense	18,400

Additional information was obtained from the general ledger:

1. Accounts payable related to the purchases of merchandise increased during the year by $23,800. The beginning inventory was $75,000; the ending inventory totaled $100,000.
2. Amounts due from customers increased by $63,700.
3. Prepaid selling expenses, wages payable, and income taxes payable decreased throughout 19X6 by $3,000, $5,600, and $900, respectively.

Instructions

a. Prepare the operating activities section of the statement of cash flows by using the direct method.
b. Prepare the operating activities section of the statement of cash flows by using the indirect method.

P19–A3 Statement of cash flows: Direct method (L.O. 5)

David Green, M.D., is disturbed that his practice, The Hair Transplant Center, has only $50 cash as of March 31, 19X5. He believes that the Center experienced a very profitable quarter of activity. In an effort to analyze what happened, you have determined the following account balance changes from January 1 through March 31:

	Increase (Decrease)
Cash	$(23,950)
Accounts receivable	91,000
Prepaid rent	1,580
Equipment	7,000
Accumulated depreciation: equipment	10,500
Patent	(1,000)

Accounts payable (for operating expenses)	$12,000	
Federal income taxes payable	(500)	
Long-term debt (advance payment)	(4,000)	
Common stock	7,000	
Retained earnings	49,630	

Other data are:

1. The accrual-basis income statement revealed net income of $60,000, composed of the following: service revenues, $172,000; operating expenses, $80,000; depreciation expense, $10,500; amortization expense, $1,000; income tax expense, $18,900; and interest expense, $1,600.
2. Cash dividends were declared and paid before the end of the quarter.
3. No disposals or sales of equipment took place. The Center purchased new equipment in March from a family friend, who accepted 200 shares of common stock for payment.

Instructions

a. Prepare a statement of cash flows for the quarter ended March 31, 19X5, by using the direct method.
b. Prepare a brief explanation for Dr. Green concerning his current cash dilemma. Suggest ways that he might be able to improve his cash flow.

P19–A4 Cash flow information: Direct and indirect methods (L.O. 5)

The comparative year-end balance sheets of Sign Graphics, Inc., revealed the following activity in the company's current accounts:

	19X5	19X4	INCREASE (DECREASE)
Current assets			
Cash	$ 55,400	$ 35,200	$ 20,200
Accounts receivable (net)	83,800	88,000	(4,200)
Inventory	243,400	233,800	9,600
Prepaid expenses	25,400	24,200	1,200
Current liabilities			
Accounts payable	$123,600	$140,600	$(17,000)
Taxes payable	43,600	49,200	(5,600)
Interest payable	9,000	6,400	2,600
Accrued liabilities	38,800	60,400	(21,600)
Note payable	44,000	—	44,000

Accounts payable arose from purchases of merchandise; prepaid expenses and accrued liabilities relate to the firm's selling and administrative activities. The company's condensed income statement is shown on the next page. Other data follow.

1. Long-term investments were purchased for cash at a cost of $74,600.
2. Cash proceeds from the sale of land totaled $76,200.
3. Store equipment of $44,000 was purchased by signing a short-term note payable. Also, a $150,000 telecommunications system was acquired by issuing 3,000 shares of preferred stock.
4. A long-term note of $49,400 was repaid.
5. Twenty thousand shares of common stock were issued at $5.19 per share.
6. The company paid cash dividends amounting to $128,600.

SIGN GRAPHICS, INC.
Income Statement
For the Year Ended December 31, 19X5

Sales		$713,800
Less: Cost of goods sold		323,000
Gross profit		$390,800
Less: Selling & administrative expenses	$186,000	
Depreciation expense	17,000	
Interest expense	27,000	230,000
		$160,800
Add: Gain on sale of land		21,800
Income before taxes		$182,600
Income taxes		36,800
Net income		$145,800

Instructions

a. Prepare the operating activities section of the company's statement of cash flows, assuming use of:
   (1) The direct method.
   (2) The indirect method.
b. Prepare the investing and financing activities sections of the statement of cash flows.

P19–A5 Statement of cash flows: Indirect method (L.O. 5)
Comparative balance sheet data of Goodrich Company follow.

	DEC. 31, 19X2	DEC. 31, 19X1
ASSETS		
Cash	$ 15,000	$ 45,000
Accounts receivable (net)	100,000	115,000
Inventory	485,000	400,000
Land	12,000	9,000
Machinery	90,000	70,000
Accumulated depreciation	(24,000)	(14,000)
Patents	3,000	4,000
	$681,000	$629,000
LIABILITIES & STOCKHOLDERS' EQUITY		
Accounts payable	$390,000	$370,000
Income taxes payable	10,000	8,000
Mortgage payable	6,000	7,000
Common stock	200,000	180,000
Retained earnings	75,000	64,000
	$681,000	$629,000

Additional information:

a. No dividends were declared or paid during 19X2.
b. The 19X2 accrual-basis income statement revealed net income of $11,000, along with the following: sales, $647,000; cost of goods sold, $579,000; selling and administrative expenses, $40,300; depreciation and amortization expense (total), $11,000; interest expense, $700; and income tax expense, $5,000.
c. Common stock of $20,000 was issued at par value to acquire machinery on February 4.
d. Land was purchased for cash on May 10.
e. Goodrich paid $1,000 on the mortgage note during the year.
f. Accounts payable arose from purchases of merchandise.

Instructions

Prepare a statement of cash flows by using the indirect method.

*P19–A6 Work sheet: Statement of cash flows (L.O. 5)

Refer to the data pertaining to Goodrich Company in Problem 19–A5.

Instructions

a. Prepare a work sheet similar in format to that shown in Exhibit 19–9.
b. Prepare a formal statement of cash flows by using the indirect method.

Series B

P19–B1 Transaction analysis: Operating, investing, and financing activities (L.O. 2, 3)

The management of St. Thomas Corporation desires to know the nature of each of the following transactions and events:

1. Issued common stock for cash.
2. Issued preferred stock in exchange for a parcel of land and a building.
3. Paid employee salaries.
4. Called and retired $200,000 of bonds.
5. Borrowed money by signing a note payable due in three years.
6. Purchased merchandise for cash.
7. Received interest on an outstanding loan.
8. Purchased new equipment for cash.
9. Reduced the balance of a long-term nonoperating note payable by issuing common stock.
10. Sold land for cash.
11. Paid dividends to stockholders.
12. Received cash from customers on account.

Instructions

a. Briefly distinguish among operating, investing, and financing activities.
b. Design a table with the following columnar headings: operating activity, investing activity, financing activity, and noncash investing/financing activity. Classify the 12 transactions listed by using these headings. For all classifications except noncash investing/financing, indicate whether the transaction causes a cash inflow (+) or a cash outflow (–).

* An asterisk preceding an item indicates that the material is covered in an appendix to this chapter.

P19–B2 Operating activities: Direct and indirect methods (L.O. 4)

The information that follows was taken from the financial statements of Fairfield General, Inc.:

	Dec. 31, 19X2	Dec. 31, 19X1
Balance sheet accounts		
Accounts receivable (net)	$ 49,700	$54,300
Inventory	88,500	68,600
Prepaid selling expenses	4,600	3,900
Accounts payable (relate to merchandise purchases)	61,800	59,700
Interest payable	6,200	7,300
19X2 income statement data		
Sales	$1,185,000	
Cost of goods sold	800,000	
Selling & administrative expenses	60,000	
Depreciation expense	40,000	
Interest expense	20,000	
Loss on sale of equipment	45,000	
Income tax expense	75,000	

Instructions

a. Prepare the operating activities section of the statement of cash flows by using the direct method.
b. Prepare the operating activities section of the statement of cash flows by using the indirect method.

P19–B3 Statement of cash flows: Direct method (L.O. 5)

The Tulsa Bulldogs, a minor league baseball team, is having great difficulty paying its bills. Management cannot understand how the firm can generate net income and continually be short of cash. The balance sheet accounts of the Bulldogs follow.

	Sept. 30, 19X2	Oct. 1, 19X1
Cash	$ —	$ 25,000
Receivable from major league affiliate	400,000	634,000
Concessions inventory	134,000	79,000
Prepaid selling expenses	25,700	19,000
Ballpark & other fixed assets	922,600	857,000
Accumulated depreciation	527,000	480,000
Accounts payable (for concessions)	29,000	50,800
Salaries & bonuses payable	97,200	230,500
Accrued taxes payable	16,000	14,000
Federal income taxes payable	—	129,000
Common stock	600,000	580,000
Retained earnings	213,100	129,700

Other data are as follows:

1. Net income was $100,000. Dividends declared and paid totaled $16,600.

2. Tulsa's accrual-basis income statement revealed revenues from admissions, concessions, and the major league affiliate that totaled $4,350,000. Other key figures are cost of concessions sold, $950,000; selling and administrative expenses, $3,179,000; depreciation expense, $47,000; income tax expense, $74,000; and interest expense, $0.
3. The Accrued Taxes Payable account is used for various taxes that are treated as selling and administrative expenses.
4. No disposals of fixed assets occurred during the year. In February, the Bulldogs acquired a new scoreboard for cash.
5. Additional common stock was sold on May 15 for $20,000 cash.

Instructions

a. Prepare a statement of cash flows for the year ended September 30, 19X2, by using the direct method.
b. Prepare a brief evaluation of the Bulldogs' existing cash problem.

P19–B4 Cash flow information: Direct and indirect methods (L.O. 5)

The following data were taken from the accounting records of Patel, Inc.:

- *Income statement data*
    1. Sales: $490,000
    2. Cost of goods sold, $210,000
    3. Selling and administrative expenses, $195,000
    4. Depreciation expense, $15,000
    5. Interest expense, $1,000
    6. Loss on sale of machinery, $3,000
    7. Income tax expense, $22,000
    8. Net income, $44,000
- *Comparative balance sheet data*
    1. Accounts receivable increased by $15,000.
    2. Inventory increased by $16,000.
    3. Accounts payable (related to purchases of merchandise) decreased by $37,000.
    4. Long-term notes payable decreased by $15,000.
- *Other data*
    1. The Machinery account (net) remained unchanged. A closer look revealed that machinery having a $13,000 book value was sold in May and machinery with a cost of $28,000 was purchased in August. Both transactions were settled with cash.
    2. Notes payable arose from borrowing transactions.
    3. The Common Stock and Paid-in Capital in Excess of Par accounts increased by a total of $5,000 from a stock issuance.
    4. Dividends totaling $6,000 were declared and paid.

Instructions

a. Prepare the operating activities section of the company's statement of cash flows, assuming use of:
    (1) The direct method.
    (2) The indirect method.
b. Prepare the investing activities and financing activities sections of the statement of cash flows.

P19–B5 Statement of cash flows: Indirect method (L.O. 5)

Comparative balance sheet data of Casa Linda, Inc., follow.

	Oct. 31, 19X5	Oct. 31, 19X4
ASSETS		
Cash	$ 427,000	$ 130,000
Accounts receivable (net)	195,000	377,000
Merchandise inventory	1,100,000	918,000
Long-term stock investments	105,000	205,000
Land	17,000	20,000
Equipment	500,000	300,000
Accumulated depreciation	(97,000)	(80,000)
Copyrights	7,000	8,000
	$2,254,000	$1,878,000
LIABILITIES & STOCKHOLDERS' EQUITY		
Accounts payable	$ 900,000	$ 732,000
Accrued liabilities	50,000	15,000
Income taxes payable	80,000	120,000
Bonds payable	650,000	900,000
Common stock	300,000	100,000
Retained earnings	274,000	11,000
	$2,254,000	$1,878,000

Additional information:

a. The company retired $250,000 of bonds during the year and sold $100,000 of long-term stock investments. No gain or loss was incurred on either transaction.
b. Common stock of $200,000 was issued at par value to acquire equipment.
c. The 19X5 accrual-basis income statement revealed net income of $263,000, along with the following: sales, $946,000; cost of goods sold, $419,700; selling and administrative expenses, $97,800; depreciation and amortization expense (total), $18,000; interest expense, $74,000; gain on the sale of land, $5,000; and income tax expense, $78,500.
d. No dividends were paid during the year.
e. Accounts payable arose from purchases of merchandise.

Instructions

Prepare a statement of cash flows by using the indirect method.

*P19–B6 Work sheet: Statement of cash flows (L.O. 5)

Refer to the data pertaining to Casa Linda, Inc., in Problem 19–B5.

Instructions

a. Prepare a work sheet similar in format to that shown in Exhibit 19–9.
b. Prepare a formal statement of cash flows by using the indirect method.

EXPANDING YOUR HORIZONS

EYH19–1 Importance of cash (L.O. 1)

Companies strive to operate in a profitable manner. Although the objective of the capitalist system is to achieve net income, "cash is still king" for many businesspeople.

Instructions

Interview two local retailers and determine whether the owners/managers are more concerned about net income or cash flows. Also inquire about any actions taken to (1) increase inflows from operating activities and (2) reduce or slow outflows from operating activities. Be prepared to report your findings to the class.

EYH19-2 Use of direct and indirect methods (L.O. 4)

When preparing the statement of cash flows, companies can use either the direct method or the indirect method to report cash flows from operating activities. This practice is permitted even though the Financial Accounting Standards Board (FASB) has voiced a preference for the former approach.

Instructions

a. Obtain a copy of *Statement of Financial Accounting Standards No. 95*, "Statement of Cash Flows," from your local library. Review this publication and determine why the FASB favors the direct method.
b. Review 20 corporate annual reports, selected at random, and calculate the percentage of companies that use (1) the direct method and (2) the indirect method.
c. Are your findings consistent or inconsistent with the FASB's preference? Briefly explain.

EYH19-3 Cash flows and bankruptcy (L.O. 6)

For many failed companies, significant decreases in both net income and cash flows from operating activities are the first warning signs of financial difficulties. If not corrected, this stage is often followed by net losses and net cash outflows. Eventually the company may be forced to seek protection under the U.S. Bankruptcy Code because of insufficient funds to pay creditors.

Instructions

Using the reference materials at your library, identify a public corporation that declared bankruptcy within the past three years. Create a graph that shows the firm's assets, liabilities, net income (loss), and cash flows from operating activities for a five-year period, including the year of bankruptcy. Prepare a short report of your findings, including an evaluation of whether the impending bankruptcy was apparent from the data.

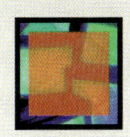

EYH19-4 A look at the statement of cash flows: NIKE, Inc., and General Mills (L.O. 6)

NIKE is involved with the design and production of athletic and casual footwear, apparel, and accessories. General Mills, in contrast, manufactures a variety of food products (including Wheaties and Betty Crocker cake mixes) and operates the Red Lobster and Olive Garden restaurant chains.

Instructions

By using the text's electronic data base, access the income statements and cash flow statements of both firms and answer the questions that follow. Unless otherwise indicated, responses should be based on data for the most recent year presented.

a. Do these companies use the direct or indirect methods of reporting cash flows from operating activities?
b. Did either of the firms experience an extremely significant change in cash flows from operating activities over the past two years? If "yes,"
   (1) Briefly explain the major cause(s) of the change.
   (2) Determine whether the change is expected, given the information reported on the income statement.
c. What are the four largest uses of cash for each company?

d. Study the *relationship* of the cash flows from operating, investing, and financing activities for the two corporations. Determine how each company is funding its investing activities.

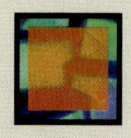

EYH19–5 A look at the statement of cash flows (L.O. 6)

This problem is a duplication of Problem EYH19–4. It is based on two companies selected by your instructor.

Instructions

By using the text's electronic data base, access the specified companies' income statements and statements of cash flow and focus on data for the most recent year reported. Answer requirements (a)–(d) of Problem EYH19–4.

EYH19–6 Analysis of a statement of cash flows (L.O. 6)

The statements of cash flow for Computer World, Inc., for 19X6 and 19X7 follow.

	19X7	19X6
Cash flows from operating activities		
Net income (loss)	$ 63,600	$ (29,800)
Add (deduct) items to convert net income to a cash basis		
Depreciation expense	61,300	56,000
Write-off of worthless patent	—	94,900
Gain on sale of equipment	(9,000)	(39,200)
Decrease in accounts receivable	11,700	200
Increase in inventories	(200)	(5,400)
Decrease in accounts payable	(17,300)	—
Increase in accrued liabilities	8,000	4,100
Decrease in income taxes payable	(22,100)	(27,300)
Net cash provided (used) by operating activities	$ 96,000	$ 53,500
Cash flows from investing activities		
Proceeds from sale of equipment	$ 50,300	$ 146,900
Acquisition of property, plant, & equipment	(52,000)	(64,500)
Purchase of long-term investments	(2,900)	(261,600)
Net cash provided (used) by investing activities	$ (4,600)	$(179,200)
Cash flows from financing activities		
Proceeds from short-term notes payable	$ 7,800	$ 1,800
Proceeds from long-term debt	67,500	316,900
Repayment of long-term debt	(148,700)	(181,700)
Purchase of treasury stock	—	(9,100)
Payment of cash dividends	(19,900)	(18,800)
Net cash provided (used) by financing activities	$ (93,300)	$ 109,100
Net increase (decrease) in cash	$ (1,900)	$ (16,600)

Instructions

As part of the training to become a stockbroker, you have been asked to analyze the preceding statements of cash flow. Answer the questions that follow.

a. Operating activities provided (as opposed to used) cash in 19X6. Briefly explain how this is possible when the company actually generated a net loss for the year.
b. Depreciation is treated as a "positive number" when computing net cash provided by operating activities. Does this treatment mean that depreciation is a source of cash for the company? Briefly discuss.
c. Briefly discuss the major differences in investing activities during the two years.
d. Study the relationship among operating, investing, and financing cash flows and activities for 19X6. Would the relationship parallel that of a young firm, a middle-aged firm, or a mature firm? Why?
e. Repeat part (d), using the data of 19X7.

COMMUNICATION OF ACCOUNTING INFORMATION

CAI19–1   Constructing a group report: The Coca-Cola Company (L.O. 4)

Communication Principle: Many reports are written by groups (teams) rather than individuals. Individuals are likely to be responsible for certain parts of the report, and then one or more team members will assemble the parts into a coherent whole. The greatest challenge in writing a group report often involves combining dissimilar segments to achieve a "common voice." In other words, the final product should sound and look as though it was written by one person. This is often an editing nightmare of the highest order—just ask the authors of your textbook! The first challenge, though, is for a writer to complete his or her assigned part so it can be merged with the others.

Let us consider what is involved. Each writer must directly answer the specific questions assigned in a clear and complete way. Look at the needed response in the context of the entire report. How important is the response to the whole? How long will it be? What will be the main headings and subheadings? What is needed in terms of illustrations, graphics, calculations, and tables?

Eventually the parts will be combined, and an introduction and conclusion will be added. To help make this process more efficient, each team member (when possible) should use the same style and format. For example, place a heading before the discussion of each main idea. Then begin each section with a brief statement that explains the subject. Use short, complete sentences and short paragraphs, with each paragraph addressing one question or concern at a time. Do anything that will help the compilation of the final product. A team effort and spirit of cooperation are needed. If every group member thinks only of him- or herself, the project will consume additional hours and generate considerable ill will.

■ ■ ■ ■ ■ ■ ■ ■

Coca-Cola is a global soft drink company, operating in over 195 different markets. The firm also has a sizable foods division that manufactures and distributes citrus products under the Minute Maid name.

Coca-Cola's statement of cash flows is prepared by using the indirect approach. A highly summarized presentation of the statement's operating activities section follows (amounts in millions):

Net income		$2,176
Adjustments		
Depreciation and amortization	$ 360	
Gains on asset sales	(84)	
Other items	2	
Increase in receivables	(151)	
Increase in inventories	(41)	
Increase in prepaid expenses	(76)	
Decrease in accounts payable	(44)	
Increase in other current liabilities	366	332
Net cash provided by operating activities		$2,508

Assume that Howard Goetz, Amy Lawson, and Larry Wong are enrolled in an introductory accounting course at State University. The professor has assigned a class project that involves a written overview of Coca-Cola's disclosure. In addition to a basic discussion of the nature of cash flows from operating activities, the students must address the following questions:

- Why is depreciation, a noncash expense, needed to compute the net cash provided by operating activities?
- How could the company release an erroneous statement, given that one increase (receivables) is deducted from net income, whereas another (other current liabilities) is added?
- What, if anything, constrains Coca-Cola from making its presentation more user friendly? (A clearer presentation would disclose cash received from customers, minus a detailed listing of individual cash payments for purchases and normal business expenses.) Also, how would such a presentation affect cash flows from investing and financing activities?

Instructions

a. Form a team with two other students in your class to assume the roles of Goetz, Lawson, and Wong. Divide the issues to be addressed among the team members and prepare written responses. Be sure that one team member is given the responsibility of combining and editing the individual responses into a coherent, polished product. The final report to the professor should include a brief introduction and conclusion.

b. Have the class member who performed the final edit briefly describe his or her experience. Are there any suggestions for improvement?

Answers to Chapter Quiz

1. b
2. d
3. c
4. d (Proceeds − $30,000 = $100,000; proceeds = $130,000)
5. d

20 Introduction to Managerial and Cost Accounting

Learning Objectives

After studying this chapter, you should be able to:

1. Distinguish between financial and managerial accounting.
2. Describe the planning, control, and decision-making components of managerial accounting.
3. Define cost accounting and identify several of its recent changes.
4. Explain the composition of the three basic manufacturing costs: direct materials, direct labor, and factory overhead.
5. Differentiate between product costs and period costs.
6. Identify the unique features of a manufacturer's balance sheet and income statement.
7. Explain variable and fixed cost behavior.

Banner Advertising constructs each of its billboards to unique specifications. Some of the signs are high and some are low. The board itself may be centered, left justified, or right justified at the top of a pole. The pole on which the board sits must be sunk into the ground, with the depth of the hole varying with area moisture levels and soil types. These variations give rise to differences in costs—costs that George Faris must determine to maintain adequate profit margins.

George knows exactly how much was spent on each structure when it comes to drilling, materials, construction labor, and painting. These costs are easily traced to specific projects and create few difficulties in the accounting records. But, how much does a billboard *really* cost? George notes, "I have a hard time dealing with certain 'nontraceable' costs. For example, picture a salesperson who assists in the sign construction process for an hour or so. How much cost should be charged to the project? What if that same salesperson called on other clients on the trip to the construction site? I know that I should consider all costs to make good decisions and better manage operations, but tracking and assigning these amounts becomes tricky."

Fortunately, as George knows, Banner Advertising is not a "true" manufacturer. George only touches on manufacturing concerns when the company builds new signs, so resolving the preceding issues is not overly critical to Banner's success or failure. It is a totally different story for companies that routinely produce goods for sale to others. These firms typically have many nontraceable costs and manufacture massive amounts of goods that must be inventoried on the balance sheet until the time of sale. Determining the proper cost is therefore of utmost importance.

As we move into Chapter 20, a look back at previous discussions reveals that many diverse topics have been presented. These topics have ranged in scope from earnings per share, to uncollectible accounts and depreciation, to the statement of cash flows. Although diversity appears to have been the theme, a substantial amount of this material does have some common ground. This common ground is known as financial accounting. A brief overview of financial accounting is helpful at this point because of the differences between it and the focus of the text's remaining chapters—managerial and cost accounting.

FINANCIAL ACCOUNTING

Financial accounting is concerned primarily with external reporting, that is, reporting the results of economic activities to parties outside the firm. Interested recipients of financial accounting information include present and potential owners, suppliers, bankers, and bondholders. Owners and investors use this information in determining whether to buy, hold, or sell ownership interests (i.e., shares of stock). Suppliers, bankers, and bondholders will conduct

> **1** Distinguish between financial and managerial accounting.

business with an entity if repayment will be forthcoming. As a result, these latter groups find financial accounting information useful in deciding whether or not to extend credit. In general, by communicating such information as earnings (income statement) and financial position (balance sheet), financial accounting strives to present a fair picture of the business in which the preceding parties have an interest.

A review of our earlier presentations will find several other distinguishing characteristics of financial accounting. For example, the financial statements that are constructed for external distribution tend to be highly aggregated, with a focus on disclosures for the company as a whole. Segmented reportings, although required in some instances, normally present minimal detail on "parts" of the firm.

Further, the financial statements serve to summarize transactions and events that have already occurred. In other words, the focus is on past, historical data. The data are summarized and reported in conformity with generally accepted accounting principles (GAAP), which facilitates the comparison of widely varying businesses by analysts. In addition, the use of GAAP assures outsiders that an entity's financial disclosures are based on a set of common rules that have been accepted by the accounting profession. Thus, users need not worry about unique measurement methods that may have been "created" by a company to inflate economic well-being.

Finally, much of financial accounting is mandatory, with a business having little or no say in the matter. The underlying reason is regulation—a fact of life in our society. Ranging in scope from the powerful Securities and Exchange Commission (SEC) to the departments that handle state sales tax collections, various agencies must determine whether a business has complied with the laws and mandates to which it is subject. Financial accounting and an historical record-keeping system are the information sources for satisfying the demands of these agencies (e.g., the issuance of financial statements to investors, the filing of a tax return with the Internal Revenue Service, and so forth).

MANAGERIAL ACCOUNTING

Exhibit 20-1 summarizes the key issues just raised and shows that financial accounting can be contrasted with managerial accounting. As its name implies, managerial accounting is oriented toward reporting the results of operations to managers and other interested parties within a business. Much of this information, unlike that produced via financial accounting, is often concerned with small segments of activity. For example, a company may construct a quarterly income statement for stockholders as part of its financial-reporting requirements. Managers, however, generally need more detail to properly perform their duties. Thus, for internal use, profitability reports are often generated on a monthly basis and subdivided by divisions, departments, and products.

Given that many managers are involved with planning activities (to be discussed shortly), reports that are issued to executives frequently have a strong future orientation. Historical data are accumulated and reported, but only to the extent that such figures help to assess (1) conformity with current plans or (2) what the future will bring. In view of this situation, it is not uncommon for managerial reports to focus on *forthcoming* costs, revenues, cash flows, and resource needs—items that are ignored in financial accounting because of the historical emphasis.

EXHIBIT 20–1
Differences Between Financial and Managerial Accounting

ISSUE	FINANCIAL ACCOUNTING	MANAGERIAL ACCOUNTING
Users of information	External parties: stockholders, creditors, analysts, regulatory agencies	Internal parties: managers of the firm
Scope of reports	Highly aggregated	Focus on a firm's segments (e.g., products and departments); often cover a short period of time
Information reported	Past transactions and events	Both past and future items (e.g., costs, cash flows, and so forth)
Reporting standards	Based on generally accepted accounting principles (GAAP)	No constraining factors
Nature of reporting	Mandatory: reports must be filed consistent with regulatory agency requirements	Highly discretionary; considerable diversity among businesses and managers

It is important to note that internal reports may be prepared by using an "anything goes" philosophy. GAAP, which apply to financial accounting only, need not be followed, thereby allowing a company to do whatever it pleases when reporting to in-house personnel (i.e., management). For instance, if a business wanted to ignore depreciation on internally distributed financial statements, it could do so. Or if a company desired to write up inventory to reflect market values in excess of cost, that, too, would be permissible.[1]

A Cost/Benefit Theme

Accounting systems produce a wide assortment of information so that executives can manage a business. As an example, see Exhibit 20–2. Given the absence of preestablished rules, much of the information generated for use within a firm is discretionary (optional). The information is produced because it is helpful to a manager when performing his or her duties. Varying responsibilities among managers, of course, create different information needs, and some of the needs are more important than others.

Because of limited resources, an organization normally cannot satisfy all the desires of its executives. A guideline must therefore be established for the generation of discretionary information. A suggested approach employs cost-benefit analysis, where a manager compares the cost of producing information against the benefits to be derived from the information's use. If the benefits exceed the costs, generation of the needed facts and figures is appropriate; if not, rejection is in order.

---

[1] Although diversity is the rule, most firms have not strayed too far from the norm.

EXHIBIT 20–2

Examples of Information Generated for Internal Use

COMPANY	INFORMATION REPORTED
Hyatt Hotels	Construction cost per room at a planned facility
Toys "R" Us	Profit per square foot of selling space
Time Warner	Subscriber renewal rates on *Time*, *People*, and *Money* magazines
MCI Communications	Uncollectible accounts experience with residential and commercial users
United Airlines	Percentage of seats filled and number of discounted tickets sold for specific flights

> **2**
> Describe the planning, control, and decision-making components of managerial accounting.

MANAGERIAL ACCOUNTING APPLICATIONS

Managerial accounting plays an important role in three basic functions of management: planning, control, and decision making.

Planning. Virtually every company is formed to achieve certain goals and objectives. The owners, for example, expect the firm to earn a profit and an adequate return on investment, while management strives to produce goods and services that are characterized by quality and dependability. Marketing and the sales force attempt to achieve a reasonable share of the market by attracting loyal customers.

An organization attains its objectives by planning. Planning involves the formulation of methods and strategies that implement a company's objectives in definite terms. As an example, consider the common business practice of establishing specified credit policies. These policies permit the generation of profitable sales volume without an abnormally high rate of uncollectible accounts, thereby providing a return to the owners. At the same time, if the entity's credit policies are consistent with the terms offered by competitors, an acceptable market share can be attained.[2]

Sometimes, the objectives of a business will conflict with one another. For instance, suppose a company decided to enlarge its market share. To attract new customers, the firm might loosen its credit policy. Conceivably, an excessive concentration on obtaining market share could result in high levels of uncollectible accounts, thus undermining the objective of profitability. A business must continually evaluate its objectives and the policies implemented for their attainment. Although eliminating all conflict is extremely difficult, harmony and consistency (achieved by intensive planning) help an organization improve overall results.

Planning takes place in all facets of an organization. Often, plans are expressed quantitatively in formal reports known as budgets, which are prepared for areas that management deems critical and in need of close monitoring and evaluation. Such areas include sales, production, capital expenditures, and cash flow. Even entire financial statements can be forecast. Although budgeting and forecasting are readily associated with managerial accounting, managerial accounting assists in other planning activities as well. These activities

---

[2] Many other factors influence market share, such as price, advertising policies, and product quality.

> **ETHICS ISSUE**
>
> The president of the company has asked you to prepare a performance report showing that John Wallace is an inept manager and a candidate for dismissal. What is your response, knowing the desired results are easily attained by a minor change in the accounting for operating costs?

are examined in higher-level courses and in the study of other business disciplines such as quantitative methods, marketing, and finance.

Control. The control function is an outgrowth of planning. No matter how extensively and effectively a business plans, unexpected events can occur. Furthermore, because plans merely reflect an organization's best guess about the future, prediction errors are common.

If management is to have insight regarding a company's progress toward its objectives, feedback is a necessity. Frequently, the feedback is in the form of a performance report (see Exhibit 20–3). The performance report pinpoints variances, or deviations from the budget. The individual in charge of Western Territory operations, for example, analyzes the variances, explains to management why August income was $6,700 less than budget, and takes corrective action. Such action may entail generating additional sales, cutting costs, or changing personnel.

Whatever the form, the common feature is control, which helps bring an organization back on target in terms of achieving the original plan. Control not only assists in eliminating deviations from budgets, but it also provides valuable perspectives for the next round of planning..By closely monitoring operations, managers generally obtain a better "feel" for the business, which, in turn, leads to more effective budgeting and policy formation. The relationship between planning and control is shown in Exhibit 20–4.

Decision Making. Managerial accounting also plays an important role in decision making. Decision making can be viewed as an integral part of planning and control rather than as a separate, independent management function. The implementation of a successful planning program, for example, requires that managers choose from among alternative objectives and policies. Similarly, the fine-tuning and control of operations dictate that appropriate corrective action be selected and implemented.

EXHIBIT 20–3
Performance Report

THORNDIKE ENTERPRISES
Western Territory Performance Report
For the Month Ended August 31, 19XX

	BUDGET	ACTUAL	VARIANCE	EXPLANATION
Sales	$68,000	$62,100	$5,900U	
Cost of goods sold	42,500	42,700	200U	
Gross profit	$25,500	$19,400	$6,100U	
Operating expenses				
Salaries	$ 6,400	$ 6,600	$ 200U	
Fuel	3,100	3,800	700U	
Advertising	4,500	4,200	300F	
Rent	2,000	2,000	—	
Total expenses	$16,000	$16,600	$ 600U	
Operating income*	$ 9,500	$ 2,800	$6,700U	

U = unfavorable; F = favorable.
* As used in this exhibit and throughout the remainder of the text, operating income is equivalent to income before taxes.

EXHIBIT 20–4
Planning and Control

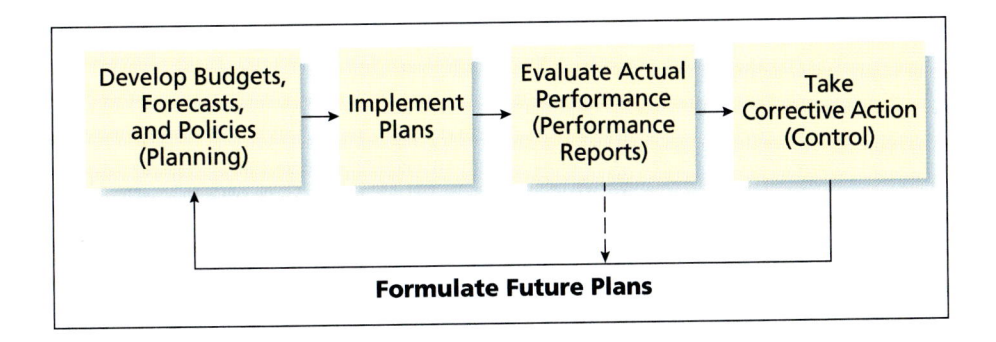

Develop Budgets, Forecasts, and Policies (Planning) → Implement Plans → Evaluate Actual Performance (Performance Reports) → Take Corrective Action (Control)

Formulate Future Plans

The decision process has far-reaching effects and normally involves much more than just "number crunching." Many managers, especially those involved with accounting and finance, place considerable emphasis on net income, cash flow, and other quantitative measures of performance. Often, important qualitative factors such as business ethics, corporate image, and employee morale are mistakenly disregarded.

To illustrate the importance of qualitative factors in decision making, assume that Lawrence Rosa is employed as a supervisor by the Nicholson Manufacturing Company. Management has decided to install some new machinery in Rosa's department. Although Rosa and his workers will be using the machines, they were not consulted in the selection process. Rosa has received minimal pay increases over the past few years, and with this latest

---

BUSINESS BRIEFING

MANUEL HERRERA III
Chief Financial Officer/Director of Administrative Services
San Joaquin (CA) Regional Transit District (SMART)

Let's Get Tough on Problems, Not People

Often, when faced with both financial constraints and the demand for more services, governmental/nonprofit organizations adopt policies that have a negative impact on people. Sometimes the organization's employees are affected; on other occasions it is the customers. Many potential problems can be avoided with a proactive management information system, one that facilitates short- and long-term planning, timely control, and effective decision making.

At SMART, a $12 million Central California transportation district, we strive for an end-of-month accounting that establishes a disciplined structure for performance reporting. We can evaluate, on a route-by-route and departmental basis, whether operations are cost effective or whether improved control is needed. Employees are empowered and brought into the decision-making process. They are a vital part of our efforts; without a cooperative spirit, our end product (transportation services) would be severely affected. The result may be fewer riders and reduced amounts of revenue—both undesirable outcomes.

Our reporting system strives to achieve high marks with the five Cs: continuity, cooperation, communication, competency, and customers. It is a relatively simple philosophy; it is also the SMART (and only) way to go if businesses are to succeed in the 1990s.

incident, he has an extremely negative attitude about the company. His "I don't give a darn," or "who cares," outlook is reflected in his work and possibly in the work of his subordinates. Because negativism at the top of an enterprise tends to permeate lower levels of the organizational structure, Rosa's workers may be disenchanted and could have low morale. Low morale often affects productivity, which, in turn, impacts profitability. In Nicholson's case it is apparent that employee morale and the involvement of users in the decision process (two qualitative considerations) are indeed important. Effective decision making requires an evaluation of qualitative factors in conjunction with the quantitative outcome.

COST ACCOUNTING

> **3**
> Define cost accounting and identify several of its recent changes.

All businesses need an intimate knowledge of their costs to help ensure successful performance. As we progress through the study of managerial accounting, you will find that cost analysis can be somewhat troublesome. Some costs vary as activity changes, while other costs remain constant. Certain costs are relevant when evaluating a decision alternative; others can be ignored. Because of management's dependence on cost information, a brief introduction to cost accounting is a logical starting point for understanding the planning, control, and decision-making processes.

Cost accounting deals with the collection, assignment, and interpretation of cost. Cost data are captured by an organization's information system and then assigned to various business segments and activities. Examples of such segments include territories, departments, and products. Activities, in contrast, may encompass the design of a new advertising campaign, the operation of a summer recreation program by a city, and the implementation of a new all-day ticket plan by an amusement park. The purpose of the assignment process is to answer the age-old question, "How much does it cost?" Once cost is determined, management can proceed with an analysis of the following:

- Anticipated cost for various planning needs.
- Budgeted versus actual cost for control and evaluation.
- Relevant costs of different alternatives for use in decision making.
- Costs of producing goods and services for use in pricing and inventory valuation.

A CHANGING FACE

For many years, the field of cost accounting could be characterized as rather stagnant. The methods and practices that were employed in the 1930s seemed appropriate for the 1960s and even the 1970s—at least in their users' eyes. Recently, though, companies have begun to modify their systems and thinking. These modifications are discussed in the next few sections.

Increased Focus on Managerial Accounting. Historically, cost accounting has had a heavy financial accounting orientation because of its use by manufacturers to determine production costs. The cost of goods produced influences inventory valuation on the balance sheet and cost of goods sold on the income statement. As we have just shown, cost accounting also provides information to management for planning, controlling, and decision making. Thus, cost accounting is now viewed as an integral part of both financial *and* managerial accounting. In many companies the managerial emphasis is growing because of business restructurings and mergers, expansion into international markets, and changing operating environments.

Expanded Use by Service Businesses. The service sector is probably the fastest growing segment of our economy. Firms that specialize in medical, legal, financial, transportation, and communication services all need some knowledge of their costs so that they can set and attain profit targets. As this sector explores new endeavors and continues to expand, its managers will undoubtedly have an increased demand for cost information.

Consideration of the Value Chain. Companies perform a number of activities when providing a good or service. These activities collectively comprise the firm's value chain—a set of business functions that work together in adding value to products and services. An airline's value chain would include the basic flight, along with scheduling, ticketing, aircraft maintenance, airport services, and customer service. A manufacturer's value chain is depicted in Exhibit 20–5.

As you can see, the focus is on an entire package of activities, not just on what is commonly envisioned as the company's end product (i.e., the flight and the manufactured good). These functions, when combined, create value and help to generate revenues for the firm.

Historically, companies have focused primarily on end products such as those just cited. It is only recently that increased attention has been given to the entire chain, mainly because many of the "front-end" and "back-end" activities are expensive. Omission of the related costs when evaluating a product or service may therefore result in erroneous decisions and ongoing losses. The newly-emerging practice of managing the activities and relationships in the entire value chain to improve profitability is known as strategic cost management.

EXHIBIT 20–5
The Value Chain of a Manufacturer

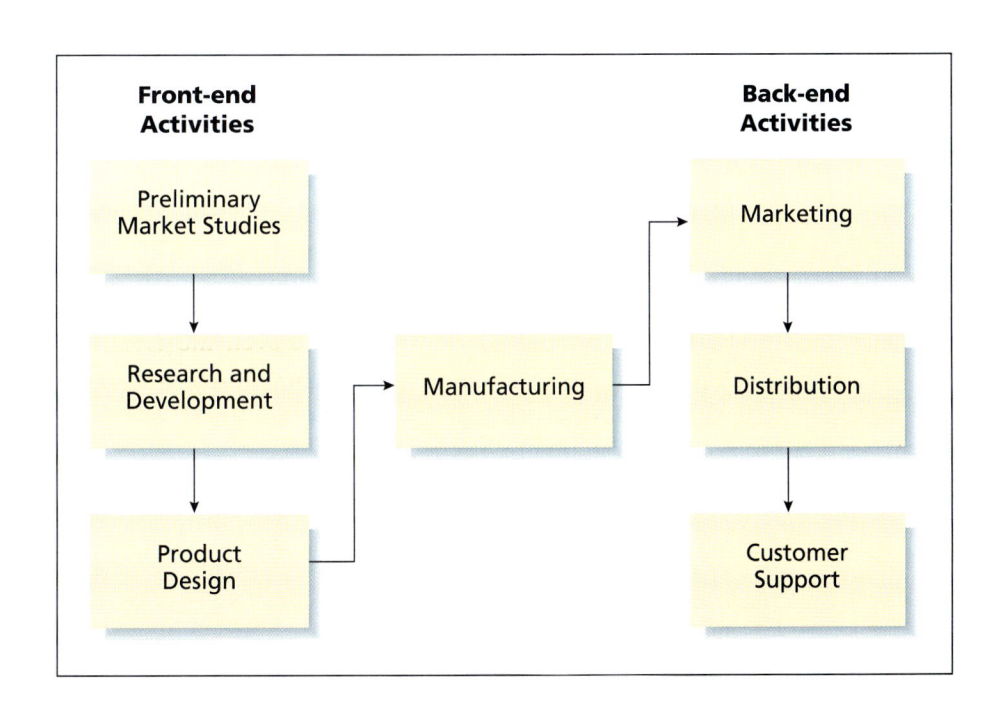

Front-end Activities
- Preliminary Market Studies
- Research and Development
- Product Design

Manufacturing

Back-end Activities
- Marketing
- Distribution
- Customer Support

Growing Emphasis on Product Quality and Globalization. In today's competitive business climate, companies are striving more than ever to turn out quality services and products. Many managers have learned the hard way that dissatisfied customers and flawed goods can spell financial disaster for an entity. Quality, though, costs money, requiring the accountant to measure the related outlays for inspections, defective units, rework, and warranties. Yet quality is necessary to compete in a global economy.

The world is changing. Products from Japan, Taiwan, Hong Kong, and China are creating havoc for many American manufacturers. Third World countries are emerging, and Russia and other countries in Eastern Europe are adapting to a free-market system. Stated simply, U.S. businesses need sound cost information so that proper decisions can be made. Antiquated costing procedures or a lack of adequate data will place a firm at a competitive disadvantage, allowing other companies to prosper at the deficient firm's expense.

Integration with New Manufacturing Technologies and Philosophies. Production processes in recent years have shifted away from labor-intensive methods in favor of automation. It is not uncommon today for state-of-the-art facilities to employ computer integrated manufacturing (CIM). With such a system, product engineering, design, testing, and production are electronically linked through the use of computers, computer-controlled machines, and robots. One aspect of CIM is a *flexible manufacturing system*—a group of machines that can make a family of goods (e.g., different models of engines, VCRs, and so forth). Upon completing a batch of one product, the machines and robots are quickly reprogrammed so that they can promptly begin manufacturing another.

Manufacturers have also implemented just-in-time (JIT) production techniques. These techniques require that inventories be reduced to bare minimum

---

A Further Focus

CIM and JIT allow a company to "do it cheaper and do it better." Sometimes, a simple design change will achieve the same outcome, permitting a firm to be more competitive. Consider Parker Hannifin, a Cleveland-based manufacturer of valves, hoses, filters, and pumps. The company recently reorganized a production line that is used to make aluminum cylinders (the type found in such applications as air tanks and fire extinguishers). The rearranged line reduced total manufacturing time from 19 days to under 5 minutes! As it turned out, for most of the 19 days, partially completed cylinders sat in bins to await further processing. In another application dealing with air conditioner parts, a rearranged production line gave rise to a 30% increase in the output per man-hour and a 40% reduction in scrap. The end result of engineers working on similar applications in six different Parker-Hannifin plants netted the company annual savings of $1.6 million.

Source: "A Process That Never Ends," *Forbes,* December 21, 1992, pp. 52, 54.

levels, in some cases close to zero, to eliminate waste and to save carrying costs. (The costs of insurance, storage, obsolescence, taxes, spoilage, and financing all fall into this category.) With JIT, materials ideally arrive at the plant just in time to enter manufacturing, and goods are produced just in time for delivery to the customer.

The impact on cost accounting of computer integrated manufacturing and just-in-time techniques is significant. As you will see in Chapters 21–23, these innovations change the types of and relationships among the various manufacturing costs incurred.

MANUFACTURING ORGANIZATIONS

4

Explain the composition of the three basic manufacturing costs: direct materials, direct labor, and factory overhead.

Given this introduction to cost accounting, we now turn our attention to the specifics of manufacturing organizations. Unlike the merchandising company, which purchases goods for resale, a manufacturer acquires raw materials and uses its plant, equipment, and employees to produce a finished product. Because of these additional activities, accounting for manufacturers is more complex than that for service businesses and merchandisers. Realize, however, that like the other two types of organizations, the manufacturer also has sales, administrative, and financial-reporting responsibilities. Thus, manufacturers face many of the same measurement problems and use many of the same accounting practices as service and merchandising concerns.

MANUFACTURING COSTS

In order to produce finished goods from raw materials, a manufacturer incurs three types of costs: direct materials, direct labor, and factory overhead.

Direct Materials. Direct materials include all materials that (1) form an integral part of the finished product and (2) are easily traced to the finished product. Several examples of direct materials are major subassemblies such as the seat, back, and frame of a chair; the wheels of a bicycle; the electronic components of a computer; and the sheet metal and glass in an automobile. Direct materials do not include minor items like glue, varnish, and nails. Although no one would dispute the importance of these latter items to a finished product, determining and tracing their cost to the units manufactured is troublesome (and expensive). Imagine, for example, the difficulty of calculating the cost of glue consumed in producing a single piece of wooden furniture. As a result of these problems and for purposes of expediency, minor materials are normally accounted for as indirect materials and treated as part of factory overhead.

Direct Labor. Direct labor represents the gross wages of personnel who work directly on the goods being produced. The wages of assembly-line workers and machine operators are included in this cost classification.

A manufacturer employs many other personnel who indirectly contribute to the production of finished goods. Examples include maintenance workers, supervisors, plant guards, and storeroom personnel. As with indirect materials, tracing the cost of these latter personnel to specific units manufactured can be difficult. Wages of the factory employees just mentioned are therefore treated as indirect labor and accounted for as part of factory overhead.

Factory Overhead. *Factory overhead,* sometimes called manufacturing burden, consists of all factory-related costs other than direct materials and direct labor. Included in this classification are indirect materials, indirect labor, factory and equipment depreciation, utilities, taxes, repairs, and maintenance. Observe that *factory overhead costs pertain solely to manufacturing activity.* For example, depreciation on machinery used in production is properly considered part of overhead, whereas depreciation on cars used by the sales staff is not. The latter cost is a selling expense. Similarly, insurance on the factory facilities is overhead. Insurance on the corporate offices, however, is treated as an administrative expense. Frequently, costs incurred by an entity as a whole (e.g., utilities and general maintenance) must be allocated among factory overhead, selling expense, and administrative expense to ensure proper accounting. This allocation is necessary because, as we will soon illustrate, the accounting treatment of selling and administrative expenses is considerably different from that for overhead.

Like indirect materials and indirect labor, the other elements of factory overhead are extremely difficult to trace to specific units of production. Thus, accountants normally estimate the overhead that goes into each product as opposed to determining the actual cost incurred. Overhead is discussed in more detail in Chapter 21.

FINANCIAL STATEMENTS OF A MANUFACTURER

Direct materials, direct labor, and factory overhead eventually find their way to the financial statements. This process is easily understood if we first review the accounting practices of a merchandising concern. As a merchandising business acquires goods for resale, the related costs are inventoried on the balance sheet as an asset. Later, when sales are made, the inventory is taken off the balance sheet and transferred to the income statement in the form of cost of goods sold. The reason for this procedure is to match the cost of the items sold against related sales revenues.

Essentially the same practice is performed by the manufacturer. Rather than pay significant sums of money to acquire merchandise for resale, the manufacturer purchases direct materials, hires and compensates a labor force, and incurs factory overhead. These costs are all put "in process" and eventually result in the manufacture of finished product. At the end of the accounting period, the finished goods still owned appear as inventory on the balance sheet, whereas the units sold are written off via cost of goods sold. This process is illustrated in Exhibit 20–6.

> **5**
> Differentiate between product costs and period costs.

Product and Period Costs. The costs that go into inventory—direct materials, direct labor, and factory overhead—are termed *product costs.* These costs are attached to the units they helped to produce and are inventoried until the time of sale. This accounting treatment can be contrasted with that of *period costs*—noninventoriable costs that are deducted as expenses of the current reporting period. Such treatment is justified because no future benefits are said to result from the expenditure. Period costs consist of selling and administrative expenses and include sales commissions, outlays for customer entertainment, advertising, and management salaries.

EXHIBIT 20-6
The Manufacturing Process

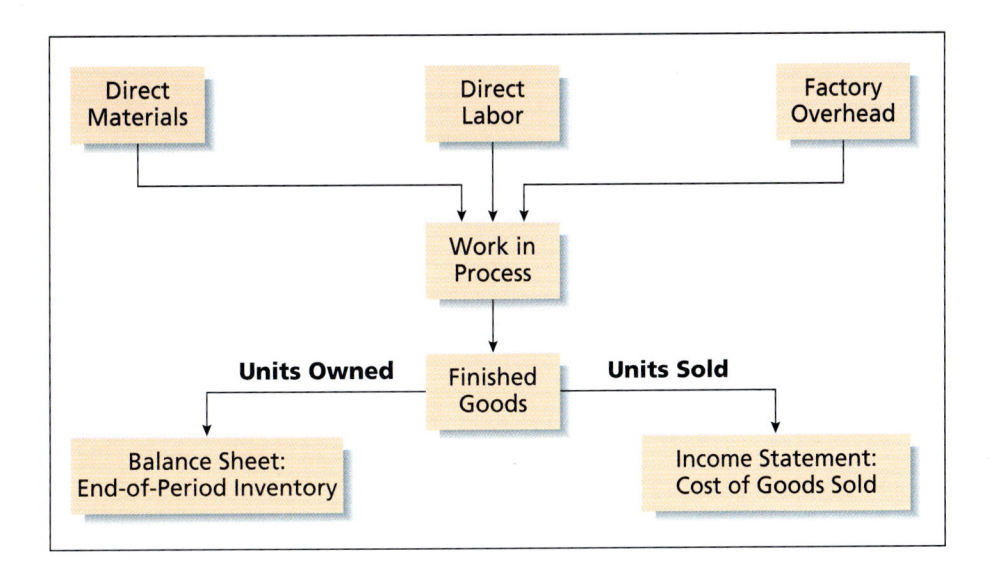

```
Direct Materials ──┐
Direct Labor ──────┼──▶ Work in Process ──▶ Finished Goods
Factory Overhead ──┘
                                                │
                    Units Owned ◀───────────────┼───────────────▶ Units Sold
                           │                                             │
                           ▼                                             ▼
                  Balance Sheet:                               Income Statement:
                  End-of-Period Inventory                      Cost of Goods Sold
```

To better illustrate these differences, assume that Conant Manufacturing Corporation began operations in 19X1. Building depreciation for the year amounted to $50,000, with 50% relating to sales and administrative facilities and 50% to the factory. Of the total units produced, 80% were sold in 19X1 and 20% in 19X2. Assuming no ending work in process, Exhibit 20-7 depicts the timing of the 19X1 building depreciation on the company's income statements.

To explain, the selling and administrative costs are expensed immediately when incurred. In contrast, the factory (product) cost is attached to inventory. Because only 80% of the production is sold in 19X1, $20,000 ($25,000 × 0.80) of depreciation is initially written off through cost of goods sold. The $5,000 balance is included in the cost of inventory. When these latter units are sold in 19X2, the remaining factory depreciation is released to the income statement. Overall, it is a matter of timing. Period costs are expensed upon incurrence; product costs are written off when the related inventory is sold.

The correct determination of product and period costs is important since errors will likely affect net income and the reported inventory valuation. Unfortunately, the distinction between these two costs is not always clear. Consider, for example, the salary of the manufacturing vice-president. This individual spends considerable time overseeing production policies and problems. Should the salary be treated as part of factory overhead or as an administrative operating expense? Perhaps the salary should be allocated between the two cost classifications on some equitable basis. If so, what basis should be used? Although most companies would treat the salary of the manufacturing vice-president as an administrative expense, issues like these are sometimes difficult to resolve.

6 *Identify the unique features of a manufacturer's balance sheet and income statement.*

Balance Sheet. Now that you have a better grasp of production cost flows, we can examine the manufacturer's financial statements. The balance sheet of a manufacturer is identical to that of a merchandising concern, with one exception (see Exhibit 20-8). A merchandiser normally discloses one inventory account: Inventory or Merchandise Inventory. In contrast, businesses engaged

EXHIBIT 20–7
Timing of Product Costs and Period Costs

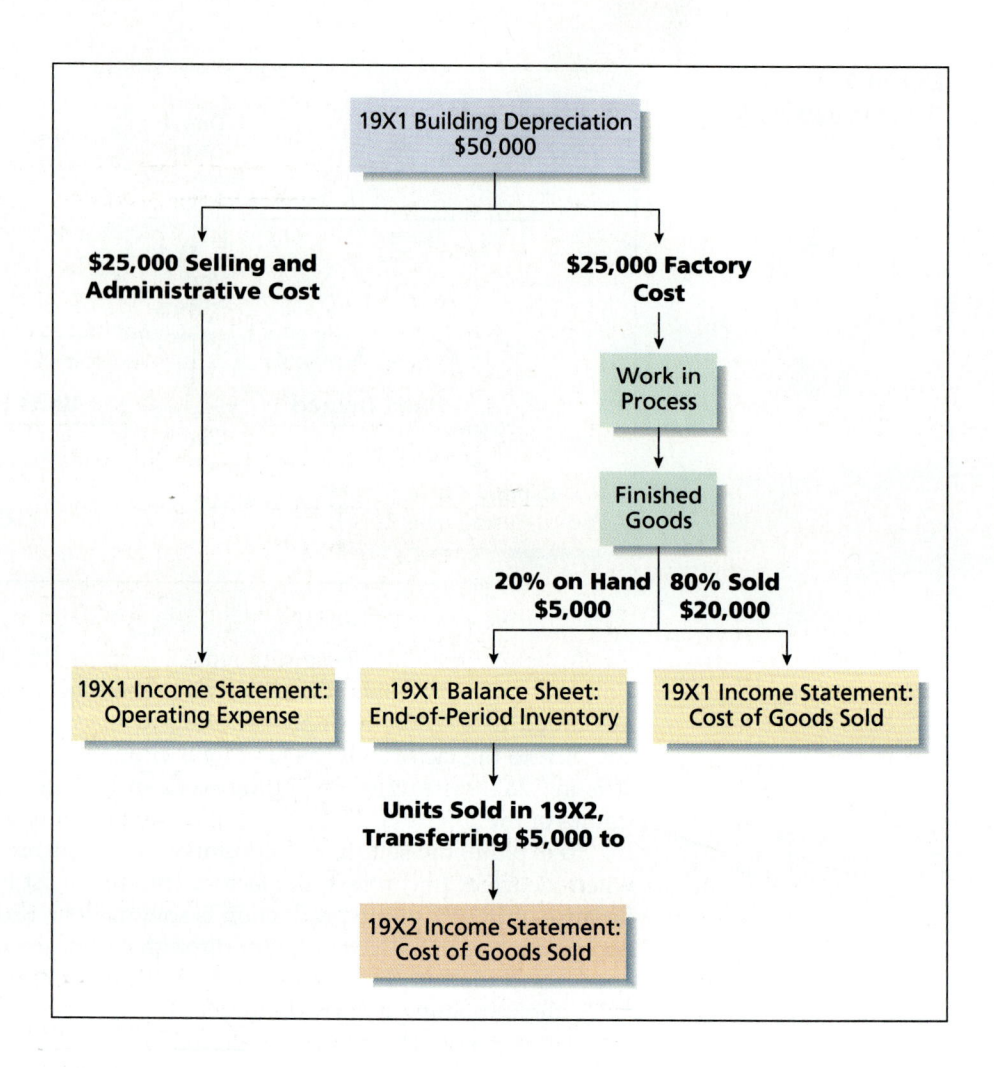

```
                    19X1 Building Depreciation
                            $50,000
                   ↙                    ↘
     $25,000 Selling and          $25,000 Factory
     Administrative Cost               Cost
              │                          ↓
              │                     Work in
              │                     Process
              │                          ↓
              │                     Finished
              │                      Goods
              │                   ↙         ↘
              │          20% on Hand     80% Sold
              │            $5,000         $20,000
              ↓                ↓              ↓
     19X1 Income Statement:  19X1 Balance Sheet:   19X1 Income Statement:
     Operating Expense       End-of-Period Inventory   Cost of Goods Sold
                                    ↓
                           Units Sold in 19X2,
                          Transferring $5,000 to
                                    ↓
                           19X2 Income Statement:
                             Cost of Goods Sold
```

EXHIBIT 20–8
Merchandising and Manufacturing Balance Sheets

MERCHANDISING FIRM			
Current assets			
Cash			$ 15,000
Accounts receivable		$64,000	
Less: Allowance for uncollectibles		4,000	60,000
Inventory			190,000
Prepaid expenses			6,000
Total current assets			$271,000

MANUFACTURER			
Current assets			
Cash			$ 10,000
Accounts receivable		$ 43,000	
Less: Allowance for uncollectibles		3,000	40,000
Inventories			
Finished goods		$115,000	
Work in process		51,000	
Raw materials		24,000	190,000
Prepaid expenses			11,000
Total current assets			$251,000

in production activities usually establish three such accounts: Raw Materials, Work in Process, and Finished Goods.

Raw Materials includes the items to be processed into salable goods. **Work in Process** represents the cost of goods started but not completed by the end of the reporting period. The balance in this account is computed by totaling the direct material, direct labor, and factory overhead charges that pertain to the production in progress. Finally, as its name implies, **Finished Goods** contains the cost of completed production that is owned by the firm.

These three accounts represent the traditional split of inventory, with variations frequently found in practice. Consider the disclosures in Exhibit 20–9, which appeared in recent corporate annual reports. These businesses have adapted the general model to meet their own unique needs. This practice is acceptable providing that it results in adequate disclosure and a fair measure of financial position.

Income Statement. To illustrate the computation of income for a manufacturer, assume that Golden, Inc., produces paint and various decorating supplies. Exhibit 20–10 contrasts Golden's income statement with that of Meadow Paint and Wallpaper, a retailer.

Notice that the two income statements are very similar. Meadow's cost of goods sold is calculated in the same manner as that shown earlier in the text. The procedure is somewhat different for Golden, Inc., which makes (rather than acquires) products for resale:

- Finished Goods, the inventory held for resale to customers, replaces Merchandise Inventory, and
- Cost of goods manufactured replaces net purchases.

Cost of goods manufactured (see the supporting schedule in Exhibit 20–10) is derived by examining the three cost elements of a manufactured product. Direct materials used, direct labor, and factory overhead are summed to arrive at the total production costs for the period. Next, the beginning and ending work in process inventories are respectively added and subtracted from

EXHIBIT 20–9
Inventory Disclosures

PACIFIC GAS AND ELECTRIC	CHIQUITA BRANDS INTERNATIONAL
Inventories	Inventories
Materials and supplies	Bananas and other fresh produce
Gas stored underground	Other food products
Fuel oil	Growing crops
Nuclear fuel	Materials and supplies
	Other
CHEVRON CORPORATION	**QUAKER OATS COMPANY**
Inventories	Inventories
Crude oil and petroleum products	Finished goods
Chemicals	Grains and raw materials
Materials and supplies	Packaging materials and supplies
Other merchandise	

MEADOW PAINT AND WALLPAPER
(Merchandiser)
Income Statement

Sales		$224,000
Cost of goods sold		
Beginning inventory	$ 36,000	
Net purchases	161,000	
Goods available for sale	$197,000	
Less: Ending inventory	55,000	
Cost of goods sold		142,000
Gross profit		$ 82,000
Operating expenses		
Selling	$ 46,000	
Administrative	24,000	70,000
Operating income		$ 12,000

GOLDEN, INC.
(Manufacturer)
Income Statement

Sales		$356,000
Cost of goods sold		
Beginning finished goods inventory	$ 45,000	
Cost of goods manufactured	277,000	
Goods available for sale	$322,000	
Less: Ending finished goods inventory	61,000	
Cost of goods sold		261,000
Gross profit		$ 95,000
Operating expenses		
Selling	$ 58,000	
Administrative	29,000	87,000
Operating income		$ 8,000

GOLDEN, INC.
Schedule of Cost of Goods Manufactured

Direct materials used		
Beginning raw materials inventory	$ 21,000	
Net purchases	109,000	
Direct materials available	$130,000	
Less: Ending raw materials inventory	28,000	
Direct materials used		$102,000
Direct labor		79,000
Factory overhead		
Indirect materials used	$ 6,000	
Indirect labor	36,000	
Utilities	15,000	
Depreciation: factory	23,000	
Taxes	17,000	
Insurance	4,000	101,000
Total manufacturing costs		$282,000
Add: Beginning work in process inventory		7,000
		$289,000
Less: Ending work in process inventory		12,000
Cost of goods manufactured		$277,000

Note: This example assumes that the Raw Materials account contains direct materials only, with indirect materials being housed in a separate Factory Supplies account. Under an alternative procedure that is shown in the next chapter, the cost of both material types may be entered in the same account.

EXHIBIT 20–10
Income Statements of a Merchandising Firm and a Manufacturer

this total. The underlying logic for these procedures can best be described as follows. At the beginning of the accounting period, Golden had $7,000 of goods in production. During the period $282,000 of manufacturing costs were incurred, yielding $289,000 ($7,000 + $282,000) of costs "in process." If $12,000 of production remains in progress at year-end, $277,000 ($289,000 − $12,000) of goods must have been completed. This amount represents the cost of goods manufactured and is later transferred to the income statement to compute cost of goods sold.

COST BEHAVIOR

7 Explain variable and fixed cost behavior.

The manufacturing, selling, and administrative costs of an organization are not always presented in the traditional financial statement formats for purposes of planning and control. Costs are frequently subdivided and studied in terms of their behavior. As noted earlier, some costs vary with changes in activity, whereas others remain constant. We will now overview variable and fixed cost behavior to help you better understand the subject matter that follows. An in-depth study of this topic appears in Chapter 23.

VARIABLE COSTS

Variable costs vary in direct proportion to a change in an activity base. The activity base may be sales, production, miles driven, students in a university, hours of machine operation, or any other measure of volume. To illustrate the concept of a variable cost, assume the Green Company is a manufacturer of ballpoint pens. The firm's top selling model, the Smoothwriter, requires $0.30 of direct materials. Green markets the Smoothwriter for $1.20 and pays its sales force a 5% commission. Two activity bases are involved in this example. The cost of direct materials used varies with production, and total commissions vary with the number of pens sold. This distinction is shown in the table that follows. Observe that a variable cost changes in total, but the cost per unit remains the same.

	DIRECT MATERIALS			SALES COMMISSIONS	
NUMBER OF PENS PRODUCED	MATERIAL COST PER PEN	TOTAL MATERIAL COST	NUMBER OF PENS SOLD	COMMISSION PER PEN*	SALES COMMISSIONS
50,000	$0.30	$15,000	45,000	$0.06	$2,700
60,000	0.30	18,000	55,000	0.06	3,300
70,000	0.30	21,000	65,000	0.06	3,900
80,000	0.30	24,000	75,000	0.06	4,500

* $1.20 × 0.05 = $0.06.

In addition to direct materials and sales commissions, other common examples of variable costs include direct labor, supplies, and fuel.

FIXED COSTS

Unlike variable costs, fixed costs remain constant in total when changes occur in the activity base. As a result of this behavior, the fixed cost *per unit* fluctuates. That is, an increase in activity will cause a given number of dollars to be spread over a greater volume level, thereby causing a decrease in the per-unit figure. Naturally, opposite results will occur if activity falls. Typical fixed costs include management salaries, advertising, straight-line depreciation, rent, property taxes, and insurance.

Continuing the Green Company example, assume that the firm uses an $85,000 machine in its manufacturing activities. The machine has a $5,000 residual value and a five-year service life, generating annual straight-line depreciation of $16,000 [($85,000 − $5,000) ÷ 5]. On the basis of different production levels, the depreciation per pen will be as follows:

Annual Depreciation	Number of Pens Produced	Depreciation Per Pen
$16,000	50,000	$0.32
16,000	60,000	0.267
16,000	70,000	0.229
16,000	80,000	0.20

From the preceding figures, it is apparent that the fixed cost per unit (i.e., depreciation per pen) is relevant at one and *only* one activity level. Multiplying a $0.20-per-pen depreciation rate, for example, by production levels other than 80,000 fails to yield the total depreciation charge of $16,000. When working with fixed costs, it is usually safer to deal in terms of total costs rather than unit costs.

END-OF-CHAPTER REVIEW

LEARNING OBJECTIVES: THE KEY POINTS

1. **Distinguish between financial and managerial accounting.** Financial accounting focuses on reporting financial position and the results of operations to external parties (i.e., those outside an organization). The information presented is highly aggregated and is really a summary of an entity's past transactions and events. Financial accounting disclosures are based on generally accepted accounting principles (GAAP) and, for the most part, are mandatory.

    In contrast, managerial accounting is concerned with reporting to managers within a business. Both past and future data items are reported, normally for selected "parts" of the firm (e.g., divisions, products, and so forth). There are no rules and regulations that must be followed for internal reporting, with the result being a wide variety of reports and disclosures among businesses and managers. The decision to produce internal information is usually made on a cost-benefit basis.

2. **Describe the planning, control, and decision-making components of managerial accounting.** Planning involves the study of an organization's objectives and the translation of those objectives into various methods, strategies, and programs. One form of planning is the creation of budgets. Control involves the monitoring of actual results in comparison with an entity's original plan. Feedback is provided by performance reports and variances, allowing a manager to focus on areas where corrective action may be needed. Finally, decision making requires the selection of a given alternative from a set of alternatives. If good decisions are to be made, a manager must consider both the quantitative outcome and the related qualitative factors.

3. **Define cost accounting and identify several of its recent changes.** Cost accounting involves the collection, assignment, and interpretation of cost to answer an age-old question, "How much does it cost?" Costs may be compiled for anything from a product, to a department, to a program run by a city. Several recent changes have occurred in this field. Cost accounting is assisting more in the planning, control, and decision-making (i.e., managerial) activities of companies. Further, with the growth of the service sector, it has seen an expanded use by service businesses. Firms now pay more attention to the entire value chain, a set of business activities that work together in adding value to goods and services. The growing emphasis on product quality and international trade has led to increased use of cost information to measure the costs of quality and to help secure global markets. Finally, the rising popularity of computer integrated manufacturing and just-in-time production methods has affected cost accounting in terms of the nature of and relationship among the various manufacturing costs incurred.

4. **Explain the composition of the three basic manufacturing costs: direct materials, direct labor, and factory overhead.** Direct materials, direct labor, and factory overhead are the three cost components of manufactured goods. Direct materials are those materials that form an integral part of the finished product and, at the same time, are easily traced to the product. Direct labor consists of the wages of those employees who work directly on the product (e.g., assembly-line workers). Finally, factory overhead comprises all other factory costs such as indirect materials, indirect labor, and equipment depreciation. Unlike direct materials and direct labor, factory overhead is not easily traced to a manufactured good.

5. **Differentiate between product costs and period costs.** Product costs are the costs incurred in manufacturing operations, namely, direct materials, direct labor, and factory overhead. These costs are inventoried until the manufactured good is sold, at which time the costs are transferred to cost of goods sold on the income statement. In contrast, period costs are unrelated to production operations. Such costs are expensed as incurred and include those that arise from selling and administrative activities.

6. **Identify the unique features of a manufacturer's balance sheet and income statement.** The balance sheet of a manufacturer typically reveals three inventory accounts: Raw Materials, Work in Process, and Finished Goods. The manufacturer's income statement is the same as that for a merchandising firm, with two exceptions: net purchases is replaced by an entity's cost of goods manufactured, and Finished Goods inventory is used in place of Merchandise Inventory. Cost of goods manufactured is computed by summing the costs of direct materials used, direct labor, and factory overhead, and then adding the beginning work in process balance and subtracting the ending work in process.

7. **Explain variable and fixed cost behavior.** Variable costs are those that change in direct proportion to a change in an activity base (sales, production, and so on). Fixed costs, on the other hand, remain constant. Because of these behavior patterns, variable costs per unit are constant and per-unit fixed costs fluctuate.

Key Terms and Concepts: A Quick Overview

budget A formal management plan that is expressed in quantitative terms. (p. 765)

computer integrated manufacturing A system that electronically links product design, testing, and production. (p. 770)

control An activity that helps bring an organization back on target in terms of achieving its original plans. (p. 766)

cost accounting An area of accounting that deals with the collection, assignment, control, and evaluation of costs. (p. 768)

cost-benefit analysis An approach to decision making in which an alternative's costs are compared against the accompanying benefits. (p. 764)

cost of goods manufactured The total of direct materials used, direct labor, and factory overhead, plus the beginning work in process inventory, minus the ending work in process inventory. (p. 775)

decision making An integral part of the planning and control process that requires managers to choose from among alternative courses of action. (p. 766)

direct labor The gross wages of personnel who work directly on the goods being produced. (p. 771)

direct materials All materials that form an integral part of and are easily traceable to the finished product. (p. 771)

factory overhead All factory-related costs other than direct materials used and direct labor. (p. 772)

financial accounting An area of accounting concerned primarily with external reporting. (p. 762)

finished goods The inventory of completed production that is owned by a firm. (p. 775)

fixed cost A cost that remains constant in total when changes occur in an activity base. (p. 777)

indirect labor The wages of factory employees who do not work directly on the product; treated as part of factory overhead. (p. 771)

indirect materials Minor materials (such as glue, varnish, and nails) used in manufacturing a product; treated as part of factory overhead. (p. 771)

just-in-time production A production method in which inventories are reduced to bare minimum levels, sometimes close to zero. (p. 770)

managerial accounting An area of accounting oriented toward reporting the results of operations to managers and other interested parties within an organization. (p. 763)

period cost A cost unrelated to the acquisition or manufacture of inventory. It is expensed when incurred. (p. 772)

planning The development of methods and strategies that implement a company's objectives in definite terms. (p. 765)

product cost A cost that goes into inventory—specifically, direct materials, direct labor, and factory overhead. (p. 772)

raw materials The items to be processed into salable goods (i.e., the direct and indirect materials owned). (p. 775)

strategic cost management The practice of managing the activities and relationships in the entire value chain to improve profitability. (p. 769)

value chain A set of business activities that work together in adding value to products and services. (p. 769)

variable cost A cost that varies directly with a change in an activity base. (p. 777)

variance Deviations from a budgeted amount. (p. 766)

work in process The inventory of goods started but not completed during the period. (p. 775)

Chapter Quiz

The five questions that follow relate to several issues raised in the chapter. Test your knowledge of the issues by selecting the best answer. (The answers appear on p. 795.)

1. Managerial accounting:
    a. focuses primarily on reporting to regulatory agencies.
    b. is governed by generally accepted accounting principles.
    c. is highly discretionary and varies greatly from business to business.
    d. should be considered as a substitute for financial accounting.

2. Which of the following items is properly classified as factory overhead?
    a. Wages of a carpenter who builds fine wooden furniture.
    b. The cost of sandpaper used in the production of furniture.
    c. The cost of the plastic keys on a personal computer's (PC's) keyboard.
    d. Depreciation on office equipment used at a company's corporate headquarters.

3. Which of the following statements is correct?
    a. Period costs are properly inventoried on the balance sheet.
    b. Direct labor is a typical example of a period cost.
    c. Product costs are expensed as incurred.
    d. Direct material is a typical product cost.

4. Cost of goods manufactured:
    a. is added to the cost of the beginning finished goods inventory on the income statement.
    b. includes selling and administrative expenses.
    c. ignores the beginning and ending balances of the Work in Process account.
    d. is normally disclosed on a company's balance sheet.

5. Which of the following is an example of a variable cost?
    a. Salary of a plant supervisor.
    b. Advertising costs.
    c. Direct materials.
    d. Straight-line depreciation on a factory machine.

Summary Problem

The following data were extracted from the accounting records of Bradley Plumbing Fixtures for the year ended December 31, 19X7:

Purchases of direct material	$235,700
Direct labor	458,900
Factory utilities	18,700
Work in process, Jan. 1	24,400
Advertising costs	6,000
Finished goods, Dec. 31	124,400
Factory depreciation*	11,600
Indirect labor	43,500
Raw materials inventory, Jan. 1	55,600
Finished goods, Jan. 1	112,000
Raw materials inventory, Dec. 31	45,000
Indirect materials used	11,300
Plant insurance	3,200
Work in process, Dec. 31	26,600

*Computed by the straight-line method.

Instructions

a. Calculate the company's cost of goods manufactured and cost of goods sold for the year ended December 31, 19X7.
b. Whose wages did Bradley likely classify as indirect labor?
c. Assume that Bradley has been experiencing steadily rising costs in recent years. Briefly describe a report that management probably receives in its efforts to control operations.
d. Three of Bradley's costs are plant insurance, indirect materials used, and factory depreciation. Classify these costs as being either variable or fixed in terms of behavior.

Solution

a. Cost of goods manufactured

Direct materials used		
Beginning raw materials inventory	$ 55,600	
Net purchases	235,700	
Direct materials available	$291,300	
Less: Ending raw materials inventory	45,000	
Direct materials used		$246,300
Direct labor		458,900
Factory overhead		
Factory utilities	$ 18,700	
Factory depreciation	11,600	
Indirect labor	43,500	
Indirect materials used	11,300	
Plant insurance	3,200	88,300
Total manufacturing costs		$793,500
Add: Beginning work in process inventory		24,400
		$817,900
Less: Ending work in process inventory		26,600
Cost of goods manufactured		$791,300

Cost of goods sold		
Beginning finished goods inventory		$112,000
Cost of goods manufactured		791,300
Goods available for sale		$903,300
Less: Ending finished goods inventory		124,400
Cost of goods sold		$778,900

Note: Advertising costs are selling expenses and are therefore excluded from these calculations.

b. Indirect labor includes wages of factory personnel who do not work directly on the product. Typical examples are factory supervisors, maintenance people, plant guards, and storeroom employees.

c. Management likely receives a performance report that details actual and budgeted amounts for all costs incurred. The differences, or variances, between the amounts are studied to see if any corrective action is necessary.

d. Plant insurance, fixed; indirect materials used, variable; factory depreciation, fixed.

Assignment Material

Questions

Q20–1 Briefly discuss several of the major features associated with financial accounting.

Q20–2 Is managerial accounting concerned solely with the reporting of past transactions and events? Why or why not?

Q20–3 What agency, if any, establishes the "ground rules" for managerial accounting practices?

Q20–4 The sales manager of Snyder Company desires to maximize the firm's market share and has proposed a loosening of credit terms. Discuss the conflict that might arise between the sales manager and the vice-president of finance.

Q20–5 What is the purpose of issuing performance reports?

Q20–6 Briefly define the terms "computer integrated manufacturing" and "flexible manufacturing system."

Q20–7 What types of cost information might interest a company that is greatly concerned about product quality?

Q20–8 Why are indirect materials and indirect labor treated as part of factory overhead?

Q20–9 Differentiate among direct materials, direct labor, and factory overhead in terms of cost traceability to the finished product.

Q20–10 Dave Malloy, an engineer at Lexton Manufacturing, has just spent an exhausting weekend analyzing utility costs. Management desired a percentage breakdown of electricity consumed by the company's (1) sales and administrative offices and (2) manufacturing plant. Dave mumbled under his breath, "Who cares? Utility cost is utility cost." Explain to Malloy why his analysis is needed.

Q20–11 When does a product cost appear on a balance sheet? On an income statement?

Q20–12 Discuss the balance sheet differences between a merchandiser and a manufacturer.

Q20–13 Blakely Manufacturing and Diaz Wholesalers both employ a sales manager. Discuss the differences, if any, in the accounting treatment of the salaries of the two sales managers.

Exercises

E20–1 Cost/benefit analysis (L.O. 1)

Benedetti Waste Management Co., handles waste removal for the city of Larkspur. To reduce demand on the city's landfill, citizens are asked to separate their recyclables (paper, aluminum, glass, and plastic), garden and lawn clippings, and remaining garbage into three different containers for weekly pick-up. In recent months and without any data to substantiate his hunch, Benedetti's president believes that more people than usual are disposing of recyclables in the garbage containers.

a. What could Benedetti's president ask the truck drivers to do in an effort to prove his point?
b. What economic guideline should be followed in part (a)? Briefly explain.
c. Is it possible that the president's curiosity might affect driver productivity? Briefly discuss.

E20–2 Value chain (L.O. 3)

Lucky-Goldstar, a large Korean electronics company, incurred the following costs for its line of consumer products:

1. Advertising costs in Central Europe.
2. Direct labor costs in a Malaysian assembly plant.
3. Redesign costs to accommodate new miniaturization technology.
4. Transportation costs to move finished goods from Asian manufacturing plants to U.S. warehouses.
5. Cost of toll-free telephone lines to handle customer complaints.
6. Cost of discussion sessions to determine features that the general public wants in the next generation of CD players.
7. Cost of plastic used in making product carrying cases.

a. Briefly explain the concept of the value chain.
b. Which of the costs are attributed to "front-end" activities? To "back-end" activities?
c. Which of the costs should be considered when evaluating the profitability of Lucky-Goldstar's consumer products?

E20–3 Product costs and period costs (L.O. 5)

The costs that follow were extracted from the accounting records of several different manufacturers:

1. Weekly wages of an equipment maintenance worker.
2. Marketing costs of a soft drink bottler.
3. Cost of sheet metal in a Honda automobile.
4. Cost of president's subscription to *Fortune* magazine.
5. Monthly operating costs of pollution control equipment used in a steel mill.
6. Weekly wages of a seamstress employed by a jeans maker.
7. Cost of compact discs (CDs) for newly recorded releases of Salt-N-Pepa, Billy Joel, and Garth Brooks.

a. Determine which of these costs are product costs and which are period costs.
b. For the product costs only, determine those that are easily traced to the finished product and those that are not.

E20–4 Overview of manufacturing costs (L.O. 4, 5, 6)

Evaluate the comments that follow as being True or False. If the comment is false, briefly explain why.

a. The cost of cement in a road-building project would typically be classified as direct material.
b. Normally, direct labor and factory overhead costs are easily traced to a finished product.
c. The Finished Goods inventory account contains the period costs of a manufacturer.
d. Direct materials used + direct labor charges + beginning work in process inventory − ending work in process inventory = cost of goods manufactured.
e. Product costs appear as inventory on a balance sheet until such time as the related units are sold.

E20–5 Definitions of manufacturing costs (L.O. 4, 5)

Allstate Manufacturing produces seat belts for automobile companies. During the year just ended, the company incurred the following costs (in millions):

Materials and supplies used
- Strapping — $240
- Metal clasps — 85
- Thread — 3
- Machine lubricants — 1

Wages and salaries
- Machine operators — 222
- Production supervisors — 67

Other factory costs
- Maintenance personnel — 14
- Janitorial personnel — 9
- Plant security — 7
- Insurance — 22

Administrative expenses — 110
Selling expenses — 99

Compute:

a. Total direct materials consumed
b. Total direct labor
c. Total factory overhead
d. Total product cost
e. Total period cost

E20–6 Understanding cost flows (L.O. 6)

Executive Wares, which began business on January 1, 19X4, sells high-priced office accessories to executives. One of the company's products, catalog item no. 12, consists of a leather appointment book and a matching pen and pencil set—all assembled and packaged in a gift box by Executive Wares.

During 19X4, the firm purchased 8,000 19X5 appointment books from its supplier at $14 each. The following data are available as of June 30:

Appointment books issued to the Packaging Department from the storeroom	6,500
Gift sets completed	5,400
Completed gift sets in the warehouse	2,200
Completed gift sets given to customers as samples	20

If no errors or theft occurred during the period, determine the cost of the appointment books that would appear:

a. In the company's (1) raw materials, (2) work in process, and (3) finished goods inventories as of June 30.
b. As cost of goods sold for the period ended June 30.
c. As an operating expense for the period ended June 30.

E20–7 Understanding financial statements (L.O. 5, 6)

Consider the following elements of financial statements:

A—Inventories on the balance sheet
B—Cost of goods sold on the income statement
C—Operating expenses on the income statement
D—Schedule of cost of goods manufactured

Identify where the following items would be found in the financial statements:

____ a. The newspaper advertising of the Buffalo Bills football team.
____ b. The wages of refinery personnel employed by Shell Oil.
____ c. The cost of Whoppers eaten by customers of Burger King (from Burger King's viewpoint).
____ d. The year-end incompleted production of Goodyear Tire.
____ e. Depreciation on a passenger jet owned by British Airways.
____ f. Utilities incurred by Whirlpool Corporation in assembling washers and dryers.
____ g. The products held for sale by Macy's department store.
____ h. The compensation paid to the president and vice-presidents of Dow Chemical.
____ i. The fabric acquired during the period by Levi Strauss for use in its Dockers product line.

E20–8 Basic manufacturing computations (L.O. 6)

Lyon Manufacturing reported total manufacturing costs (direct materials used, direct labor, and factory overhead) of $549,000 for 19X3. Sales and operating expenses were $759,200 and $142,500, respectively. The following information appeared on company balance sheets:

	FOR THE YEAR ENDED 12/31/X3	12/31/X2
Finished goods	$150,000	$153,700
Work in process	86,400	74,100

Compute cost of goods manufactured, cost of goods sold, and operating income for 19X3.

E20–9 Schedule of cost of goods manufactured, income statement (L.O. 6)

The following information was taken from the accounting records of Lakewood Industries, Inc.:

Direct material purchases	$ 440,000
Indirect materials used	87,000
Direct labor	720,000
Indirect labor	126,000
Other factory overhead	169,000
Selling expenses	254,000
Administrative expenses	364,000
Sales	2,100,000

INVENTORIES	JANUARY 1	DECEMBER 31
Raw (direct) materials	$124,000	$ 54,000
Work in process	75,000	62,000
Finished goods	200,000	300,000

Prepare the following:

a. A schedule of cost of goods manufactured for the year ended December 31.
b. An income statement for the year ended December 31.

E20–10 Understanding cost behavior (L.O. 7)

The planning department of Herzog Company has prepared budgets for three probable levels of operation for the upcoming year. Because of their significance, the following costs have been selected for study:

	LEVEL OF ACTIVITY (UNITS)					
	10,000		12,000		15,000	
	TOTAL	PER UNIT	TOTAL	PER UNIT	TOTAL	PER UNIT
Direct materials	$ 90,000	$ 9.00	$108,000	$ 9.00	$135,000	$ 9.00
Direct labor	120,000	12.00	144,000	12.00	180,000	12.00
Advertising	300,000	30.00	300,000	25.00	300,000	20.00
Management salaries	180,000	18.00	180,000	15.00	180,000	12.00
	$690,000	$69.00	$732,000	$61.00	$795,000	$53.00

Addressing his executive staff, Herzog's president commented: "It's imperative that we implement cost-cutting programs to reduce advertising and management salaries. As shown by the per-unit costs, these variable expenditures are destroying our profit margins. Our fixed outlays of direct materials and direct labor (constant at $9.00 and $12.00 per unit, respectively) also need some improvement. I know our competitors are paying approximately $19.25 for these same two items."

Comment on the president's remarks.

E20–11 Basic cost behavior patterns (L.O. 7)

Indianapolis Precision manufactures selected parts for jet skis. The accounting records revealed the following behavior for two component costs of factory overhead in May and August when production totaled 10,000 units and 12,500 units, respectively:

Cost A: $22,500   Cost B: $3.20 per unit

On the basis of this information, determine:

a. The fixed cost per unit in May and August.
b. The variable cost per unit in May and August.
c. The total cost of A and B incurred during August.
d. The total expected cost for A and B of producing 11,600 units, assuming that present cost behavior patterns continue.

PROBLEMS

Series A

P20–A1 Cost classification (L.O. 4, 5, 7)

E. Turner & Sons manufactures barbecue grills. For each of the following costs, determine cost behavior (variable or fixed) and whether the cost is a product or a period cost. If a product cost, identify the cost as direct materials (DM), direct labor (DL), or factory overhead (FOH). Item (a) is presented as an example.

COST	VARIABLE/FIXED	PRODUCT/PERIOD	DM/DL/FOH
a. Property taxes on the factory	Fixed	Product	FOH
b. Salary of the production supervisor			
c. Freight costs on shipments to out-of-state customers			

Cost	Variable/Fixed	Product/Period	DM/DL/FOH
d. Wages of assembly personnel	_____	_____	_____
e. Grill tops and frames	_____	_____	_____
f. Straight-line depreciation on factory equipment	_____	_____	_____
g. Paint used to touch up production scratches	_____	_____	_____
h. Customer rebate offered on grill no. 301	_____	_____	_____
i. Heating costs for manufacturing facilities	_____	_____	_____
j. Wheels attached to portable models	_____	_____	_____
k. Fees paid for plant security	_____	_____	_____
l. Advertising costs for new product line	_____	_____	_____

P20–A2 Straightforward manufacturing statements (L.O. 6)

The information that follows pertains to Hampton Manufacturing for the year ended December 31:

Direct material purchases	$ 297,000
Sales commissions	80,000
Direct labor	270,000
Indirect labor	162,000
Sales	1,050,000
Advertising expense	25,000
Indirect materials used	35,000
Insurance	20,000
Utilities	90,000
Taxes	30,000
Depreciation	50,000

Insurance, utilities, taxes, and depreciation are incurred by the company as a whole and must be allocated proportionately among manufacturing, selling, and administrative activities. The proper allocations are:

	Manufacturing	Selling	Administrative
Insurance, utilities, and taxes	60%	30%	10%
Depreciation	80	10	10

Inventory data follow.

	January 1	December 31
Raw materials	$ 35,000	$ 40,000
Work in process	115,000	160,000
Finished goods	421,000	400,000

Instructions

a. Prepare a schedule of cost of goods manufactured.
b. Prepare an income statement.

P20–A3 Manufacturing accounting computations (L.O. 6)

The following information was obtained from the 19X6 accounting records of the Ruiz Corporation:

Inventories

	RAW MATERIALS	WORK IN PROCESS	FINISHED GOODS
January 1	$30,000	$10,500	$12,600
December 31	41,500	14,400	5,000

Operating data

Purchases of direct materials	$56,000
Direct labor	40,500
Indirect labor	16,800
Administrative salaries	38,600
Sales salaries	63,200
Building depreciation (factory, 70%; sales, 20%; administrative, 10%)	90,000
Other factory costs	6,500
Other selling expenses	22,300
Other administrative expenses	18,800

Ruiz sold 12,200 units of product at an average price of $29.50 per unit. The beginning and ending finished goods inventories consisted of 900 units and 350 units, respectively.

Instructions

a. Calculate the cost of direct materials used.
b. Compute cost of goods manufactured.
c. Compute the company's cost of goods sold.
d. Determine operating income for 19X6.
e. Determine the number of completed units manufactured during the year.

P20–A4 Estimate of ending inventories (L.O. 6)

On May 23, the Oklahoma branch of Horizon Chemicals suffered extensive damage from a tornado. The building that housed the raw material and work in process inventories was totally destroyed. Management has gathered the following information in an attempt to estimate the company's loss:

Direct labor averages 40% of the company's total direct labor and factory overhead cost.
Gross profit averages 30% of sales.
Total manufacturing costs (direct materials used, direct labor, and factory overhead) through May 23 amounted to $726,000. Operating expenses were $187,000.
Sales, direct material purchased, and factory overhead incurred through May 23 totaled $1,200,000, $233,000, and $300,000, respectively.

Inventory data are:

	JANUARY 1	MAY 23
Raw materials	$142,000	$?
Work in process	310,000	?
Finished goods	408,000	370,000

Instructions

Estimate the raw materials and work in process inventories destroyed. *Hint:* Prepare a detailed schedule of cost of goods manufactured and an income statement for the period ended May 23.

P20–A5 Manufacturing statements and cost behavior (L.O. 6, 7)

Tampa Foundry began operations during the current year, manufacturing various products for industrial use. One such product is light-gauge aluminum, which the company sells for $36 per roll. Cost information for the year just ended follows.

	VARIABLE COST PER UNIT	FIXED COST
Direct materials	$4.50	$ —
Direct labor	6.50	—
Factory overhead	9.00	50,000
Selling	—	70,000
Administrative	—	135,000

Production and sales totaled 20,000 rolls and 17,000 rolls, respectively. There is no work in process. Tampa carries its finished goods inventory at the average unit cost of production.

Instructions

a. Determine the cost of the finished goods inventory of light-gauge aluminum.
b. Prepare an income statement for the current year ended December 31.
c. On the basis of the information presented:
   (1) Does it appear that the company pays commissions to its sales staff? Explain.
   (2) What is the likely effect on the $4.50 unit cost of direct materials if next year's production increases? Why?

Series B

P20–B1 Cost classification (L.O. 4, 5, 7)

Sassafras, Inc., produces various herbal teas that are sold in supermarkets throughout the country. The following costs were incurred during a recent accounting period:

a. Factory flood insurance
b. Machine lubricant
c. "Buy 10 boxes—Get a T-shirt" promotion
d. Salary of quality control supervisor
e. Herbs
f. Sales commissions
g. Tea boxes and liners

h. Air-conditioning of executive offices
i. Wages of packaging department employees
j. Units-of-output depreciation on production equipment
k. Freight charges on shipments to stores
l. Sweeteners and special spices

Instructions

For each of the preceding costs, determine whether the cost is a product cost or a period cost. If a product cost, classify the item as direct materials (DM), direct labor (DL), or factory overhead (FOH). Finally, evaluate whether the cost exhibits variable or fixed behavior. Item (a) is done as an example:

Factory flood insurance—Product, FOH, Fixed

P20–B2 Straightforward manufacturing statements (L.O. 6)

The following information was extracted from the accounting records of Olympic Company for the year just ended:

Sales	$628,000
Work in process, Jan. 1	56,700
Advertising expense	23,500
Direct material purchases	231,500
Finished goods, Dec. 31	67,800
Indirect materials used	12,300
Direct labor	85,600
Direct materials, Jan. 1	45,500
Finished goods, Jan. 1	55,900
Direct materials, Dec. 31	38,200
Sales staff salaries	33,300
Work in process, Dec. 31	47,400
Indirect labor	50,700

Utilities, taxes, insurance, and depreciation are incurred jointly by Olympic's manufacturing, sales, and administrative facilities. The costs were as follows:

Utilities	$40,000
Taxes	25,000
Insurance	10,000
Depreciation	36,000

The first three costs are allocated proportionately on the basis of square feet occupied by the three functional areas. A review of the company's facilities revealed the following percentages would be appropriate: manufacturing, 50%; sales, 30%; and administrative, 20%. Depreciation is allocated 70%, 20%, and 10%, respectively.

Instructions

a. Prepare a schedule of cost of goods manufactured.
b. Prepare an income statement.

P20–B3 Manufacturing accounting computations (L.O. 6)

The following information was obtained from the records of Post Corporation for the current year ended December 31:

Direct materials
    Beginning inventory   1,600 units @ $8.30
    Purchase no. 1   2,300 units @ $8.30
    Purchase no. 2   1,000 units @ $8.30

Payroll costs
Direct labor	$59,700
Indirect labor	30,000
Administrative salaries	24,600
Sales salaries	29,500

Other costs
Building depreciation (80% of the building is devoted to production activities, with the remainder split equally between sales and administration)	$35,000
Other factory costs	22,700
Other selling expenses	9,100
Other administrative expenses	15,800

Post's beginning work in process inventory totaled $8,900; the ending work in process was $10,100. During the accounting period, the finished goods inventory declined from 2,100 units (cost: $206,400) to 1,650 units (cost: $178,800). The company produced 750 completed units, sold 1,200 completed units at $320 each, and consumed 3,500 units of direct materials.

Instructions

a. Calculate the cost of the ending direct materials inventory.
b. Compute Post's cost of goods manufactured.
c. Compute the company's cost of goods sold.
d. Determine operating income for the year just ended.

P20–B4 Estimate of ending inventories (L.O. 6)

Hillside Products, a manufacturer of painting equipment, suffered extensive damage at its main manufacturing plant on March 31 as a result of a fire. Fortunately, all raw materials inventories were stored in an adjacent warehouse. The following information has been gathered in an attempt to estimate the cost of the work in process and finished goods inventories destroyed:

Goods available for sale on Mar. 31	$220,000
Direct labor	70,000
Sales through Mar. 31	280,000
Work in process, Jan. 1	13,000
Finished goods, Jan. 1	29,000
Operating income through Mar. 31	25,000

The company's accounting staff indicated that sales are usually made at a gross profit rate of 40%. Furthermore, the cost of direct materials consumed averages 30% of the costs easily traced to production (i.e., direct materials + direct labor), and factory overhead amounts to 50% of total manufacturing costs. Hillside expects full reimbursement from its insurance company for any losses suffered.

Instructions

Estimate the work in process and finished goods inventories destroyed. *Hint:* Prepare a detailed schedule of cost of goods manufactured and an income statement for the quarter ended March 31.

P20–B5 Manufacturing statements and cost behavior (L.O. 6, 7)

The Willow Creek Company, a manufacturer of specialized calculators, began operations on January 1 of the current year. Each calculator requires the following variable costs:

Direct materials	$12
Direct labor	5
Variable factory overhead	14
	$31

The fixed costs incurred during the year are shown below.

Factory overhead	$ 80,000
Selling	40,000
Administrative	120,000
	$240,000

Production totaled 40,000 calculators, of which 38,000 were sold at $40 each. Assume no work in process. Willow Creek carries its finished goods inventory at the average unit cost of production.

Instructions

a. Determine the cost of Willow Creek's ending finished goods inventory.
b. Prepare Willow Creek's income statement for the current year ended December 31.
c. Suppose Willow Creek reduced production to meet decreased demand. If the present cost behavior patterns continue, determine the effect of the new production policy on the manufactured cost per calculator. Explain the reasoning behind your answer.

Expanding Your Horizons

EYH20–1 Planning, control, and decision making (L.O. 2)

Managerial accounting provides information so that owners and managers can plan, control, and make decisions. Whether an entity is for- or not-for-profit in nature, managerial accounting assists in attaining the organization's goals and objectives.

Instructions

Form a team with two other class members and visit two distinctly different businesses in your area. The businesses should differ in both type and size. Determine how (and if) budgets are used and whether variances are reported. Also determine whether a business decision has recently been made with the assistance of accounting information. Be prepared to report your findings to the class.

EYH20–2 Cost incentives/differentials (L.O. 2, 4)

In economic terms, states and cities are at war—a war to attract conventions, events, industry expansions, and companies that desire to relocate. Conventions, events, expansions, and relocations bring money, jobs, and financial prosperity to the winner's geographic area.

Instructions

a. Locate two articles that discuss promotion and/or incentive plans used by states or cities to attract business activity. List the incentives offered. Indicate whether the incentives are likely to affect the attracted organization's material, labor, overhead, or selling/administrative costs.
b. Did the article acknowledge some dissenting opinion (i.e., a feeling that too much was being offered in view of the benefits to be received)? Briefly discuss.

EYH20–3 Manufacturing cost elements (L.O. 3, 4)

The text explains the basics of manufacturing activities and production costs. Work in process, factory overhead, computer integrated manufacturing, and just-in-time production are often "foreign" terms, especially if one has never set foot in a factory.

Instructions

Form a team of five or more students and visit a manufacturing company in your area. Tour the facility and then interview the firm's cost accountant (or another knowledgeable individual in the accounting department). Determine the following information for presentation to the class: products manufactured, types of direct materials used, average hourly direct labor rate, major elements of factory overhead, extent of automation, quality control procedures in use, and major changes in manufacturing methods during the past five years.

EYH20–4 Decisions and college athletics (L.O. 2)

Although having only 4,000 students on campus, the University of the Southwest (UOS) operates an extensive intercollegiate sports program. The program includes playing "big-time" college football, often scheduling several universities that have teams ranked in the top twenty in the country.

During the last decade, UOS has had only one winning season. Attendance has stagnated at about 12,000 fans per home game, and annual losses from football operations have approximated $700,000. Knowing that many other colleges and universities throughout the nation have abandoned such programs, UOS undertook an extensive study to see what should be done. Several committees were formed that consisted of students, faculty, alumni, and local residents and businesspeople. After receiving considerable input, university administrators decided to continue the program in its present form. The program would be reviewed again in three years to determine if any progress had been made.

Instructions

What quantitative and qualitative factors may have influenced the University of the Southwest to keep its football program?

COMMUNICATION OF ACCOUNTING INFORMATION

CAI20–1 The executive summary (L.O. 3)

Communication Principle: Daily business activities require that managers absorb large amounts of information quickly, often without the benefit of significant study time. Detailed written reports, prepared by key staff members, are an important element of this process. Such reports customarily include an executive summary (or cover letter) that:

- Identifies the critical issues requiring attention.
- Highlights potential solutions and their possible outcomes (and shortcomings).
- Includes a recommendation, if appropriate.
- Concludes by noting that staff members are waiting for a decision and specifies any deadlines that must be met.

The executive summary should always be brief and to the point and should be consistent with the content of the accompanying report. The summary's writer must assume that the executive lacks the time for an in-depth study of the key issues despite being held accountable for the eventual results.

■ ■ ■ ■ ■ ■ ■ ■

Zeos Machine Tools, Inc., is a large manufacturer located in Indianapolis. The company's profit has been deteriorating over the years because of inefficient facilities, antiquated production policies, and increased pressures from foreign competition. Joe Baker, an assistant to the manufacturing vice-president, has completed a detailed study that proposes several major changes for Zeos. These changes include the installation of a computer integrated manufacturing (CIM) system, just-in-time (JIT) production techniques, and the calculation and monitoring of quality costs.

Joe believes that once authorization is received, the first phase of CIM and JIT could be fully operational in 18 months at a cost of $5.8 million. Quality reports could be produced in 6 months, after necessary computer programs are developed. Related costs and data-gathering procedures are expected to total $85,000. Combined, these improvements will lead to overall, nonquantifiable increases in long-term profitability.

Instructions

Assume the role of Joe Baker and write the report's executive summary.

Answers to Chapter Quiz

1. c
2. b
3. d
4. a
5. c

21 JOB ORDER COSTING SYSTEMS

LEARNING OBJECTIVES

After studying this chapter, you should be able to:

1. Explain the nature and use of a job order costing system.
2. Compute an overhead application rate and apply overhead to production.
3. Account for over- or underapplied overhead at the end of the reporting period.
4. Recognize the impact of automation on overhead application rates.
5. Apply job costing systems to service organizations.

To many clients, outdoor advertising is a relatively expensive way to promote goods and services—even *without* complete knowledge of all the related costs by the sign company. Banner Advertising, for instance, has substantial outlays for the sign structure, land, taxes, and other fixed amounts. In addition, the company maintains a business office that creates a seemingly endless stream of administrative expenses. Each client's billboard also gives rise to design, painting, and illumination costs as well as occasional "cutouts" that are constructed and attached to the frame.

To control costs and determine pricing strategies, George Faris gathers detailed information for each client's advertising project. As George notes, "We keep a tracking card for each new client on which we collect material, labor, and other costs, all subdivided by job. Tracking this information is extremely important, especially in firms like ours where profit margins are slim. Without first-hand knowledge of client costs, it is easy to lose control and sell products and services at a loss."

In this chapter you will learn about job order costing, which is a tool that accumulates the costs of goods, services, and activities. Our initial discussion will focus on the use of job costing by manufacturers, to be followed by several applications in service businesses. Banner Outdoor Advertising is actually somewhat of a hybrid organization because its output can be viewed as both a product and a service. Nevertheless, the firm is highly dependent on job costing concepts for adequate managerial control and decision making.

JOB ORDER SYSTEMS

1 Explain the nature and use of a job order costing system.

With a job order system, costs are gathered by job or order. Such systems are commonly used when cost accumulation by job is a fairly easy task, a situation that often arises when goods are made (1) upon the receipt of a customer order, (2) according to customer specifications, or (3) in separate batches. Custom-home builders, for example, frequently employ job systems because of the ease in tracing costs to specific building sites. Similarly, print shops use job systems to cost individual customer orders.

The costs of each job are accumulated on a separate job cost sheet (see Exhibit 21–1). Direct materials used and direct labor are identified with and charged to the client job on which they were incurred. Since factory overhead is not easily traced to a manufactured product, individual jobs are charged with an estimated overhead cost. (Recall that factory depreciation, utilities, plant security, and other comparable production costs are incurred by manufacturing activities as a whole, and identification with specific goods is very troublesome.)

The operation of a job cost system follows the flow of costs illustrated in Chapter 20. The three cost elements of direct materials, direct labor, and factory overhead are combined and put "in process" to manufacture products.

Exhibit 21-1
Job Cost Sheet

JOB COST SHEET

Manufactured for:
　Stock _____
　Customer _____

Product _____

Job No. _____
Date:
　Needed _____
　Started _____
　Completed _____
No. of Units _____

Direct Materials			Direct Labor			Factory Overhead	
Date	Requisition No.	Amount	Date	Ticket No.	Hours	Amount	Date	Amount

Overhead Rate: _____

COST SUMMARY

Direct materials　　$ _____
Direct labor　　　　　_____
Factory overhead　　_____
Total cost　　　　$ _____

Eventually, the work in process is completed. The completed goods that are sold are reported as cost of goods sold on the income statement; the unsold units are carried in the Finished Goods inventory account on the balance sheet. This process is shown in the top half of Exhibit 21–2.

PERPETUAL INVENTORIES

To handle the necessary record keeping, a manufacturing firm establishes various accounts and procedures that parallel the general cost flow (see the specific cost flow in the bottom half of Exhibit 21–2). Many manufacturers employ computerized perpetual inventory systems in which the Raw Materials, Work in Process, and Finished Goods accounts are continually updated during the period. To illustrate the use of a perpetual inventory system in conjunction with job order costing, we will explore the August transactions of Valley Manufacturing Corporation.

Accounting for Materials. As noted in the previous chapter, the costs of direct and indirect materials owned may be housed together in a single Raw Materials inventory account. We will assume that this procedure is followed by Valley Manufacturing and all companies in our end-of-chapter exercises and problems. The following entry was therefore made when Valley purchased $80,000 of materials and factory supplies (i.e., indirect materials) on account:

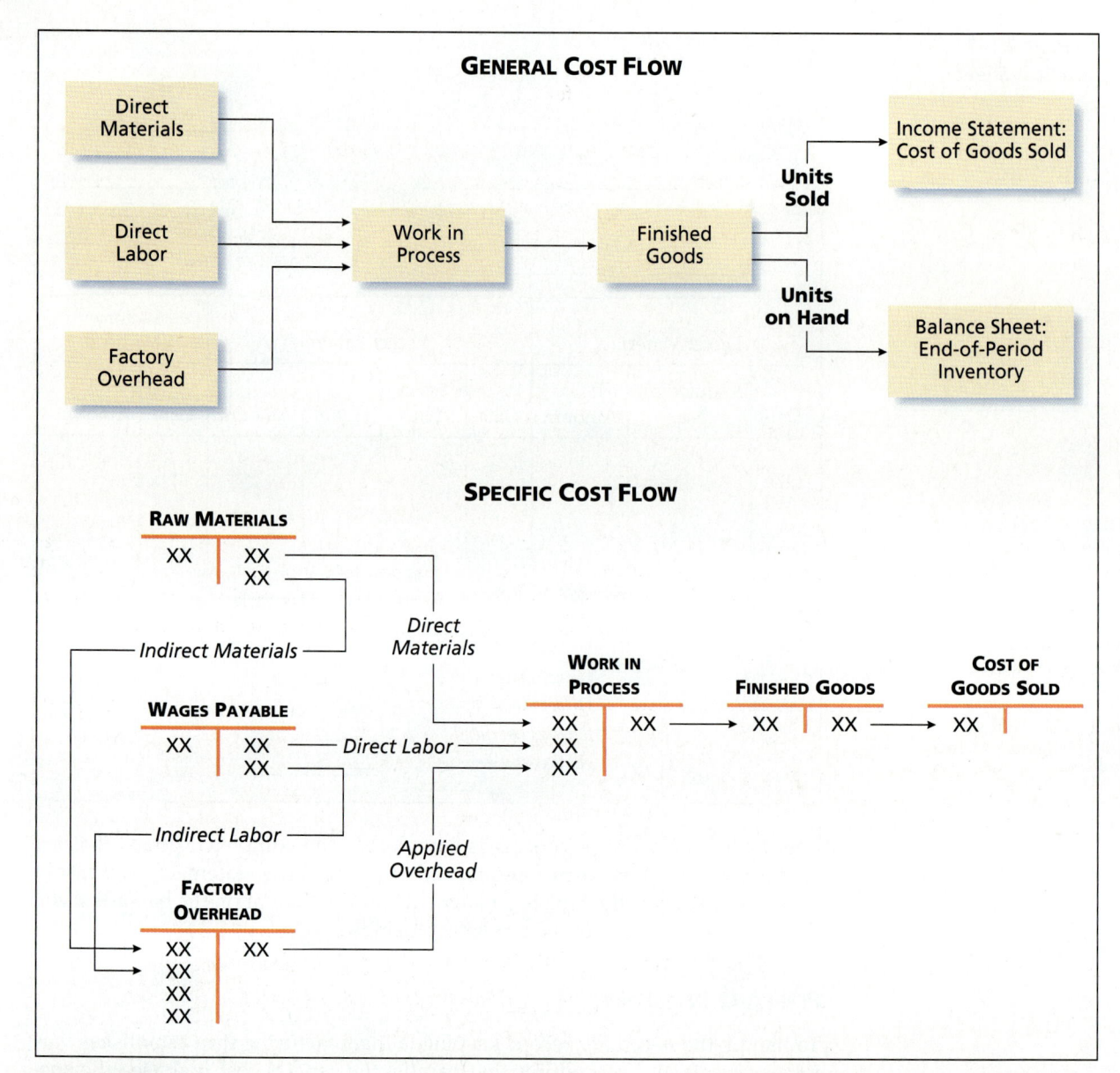

EXHIBIT 21–2
Manufacturing Cost Flows

| Raw Materials | 80,000 | |
| Accounts Payable | | 80,000 |

Purchased direct materials and factory supplies.

Materials are kept in a storeroom or warehouse and issued upon receipt of a **materials requisition.** As shown in Exhibit 21–3, $4,000 of materials have been issued for use on job no. 864, and the requisition has been posted to the related cost sheet. These materials are *direct materials* because they can be identified with a given job. The entry to record the issuance follows on page 801.

```
Work in Process                        4,000
     Raw Materials                            4,000
Issued direct materials for job no. 864.
```

Indirect materials (e.g., sandpaper, lubricants, and so on) are not easily (or economically) traced to individual jobs; thus, no attempt is made to charge specific cost sheets. Instead, indirect materials consumed are treated as part of factory overhead. During August, Valley used $2,800 of miscellaneous factory supplies in manufacturing operations. The following entry is needed:

```
Factory Overhead                       2,800
     Raw Materials                            2,800
Issued indirect materials.
```

The Factory Overhead account is debited to record *actual* overhead charges. The manner in which each job is charged with an *estimated (applied)* share of overhead will be illustrated shortly.

Accounting for Labor. The accounting treatment for labor is very similar to that of materials. Factory labor costs are classified as either direct or indirect. Recall that direct labor, like direct materials, is easily identified with given jobs. Indirect labor, on the other hand, is not and is considered part of factory overhead.

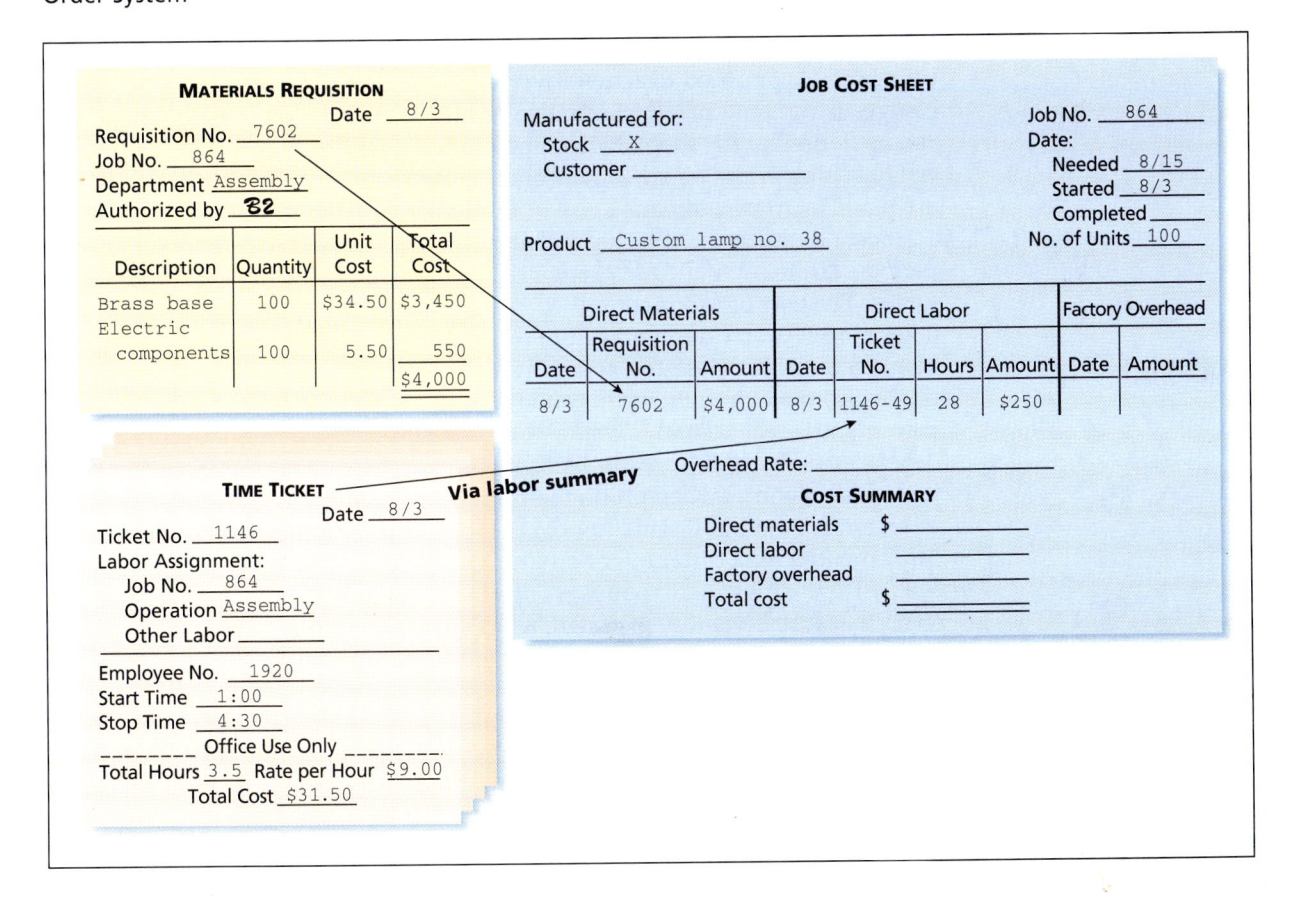

EXHIBIT 21–3
Document Interrelationships in a Job Order System

MATERIALS REQUISITION
Date 8/3
Requisition No. 7602
Job No. 864
Department Assembly
Authorized by 82

Description	Quantity	Unit Cost	Total Cost
Brass base	100	$34.50	$3,450
Electric components	100	5.50	550
			$4,000

JOB COST SHEET
Manufactured for:
Stock X
Customer _____
Product Custom lamp no. 38

Job No. 864
Date:
Needed 8/15
Started 8/3
Completed _____
No. of Units 100

Direct Materials

Date	Requisition No.	Amount
8/3	7602	$4,000

Direct Labor

Date	Ticket No.	Hours	Amount
8/3	1146-49	28	$250

Factory Overhead

Date	Amount

Overhead Rate: _____

COST SUMMARY
Direct materials $ _____
Direct labor   _____
Factory overhead   _____
Total cost $ _____

TIME TICKET
Date 8/3
Ticket No. 1146
Labor Assignment:
    Job No. 864
    Operation Assembly
    Other Labor _____
Employee No. 1920
Start Time 1:00
Stop Time 4:30
_____ Office Use Only _____
Total Hours 3.5 Rate per Hour $9.00
Total Cost $31.50

Via labor summary

> **ETHICS ISSUE**
>
> A factory accountant charges labor time against specific projects. Because the project that Joe is working on is over budget, the accountant has charged $800 of Joe's wages to another job. Management does not feel that this is a problem as long as "some job" absorbs the cost. Comment.

Labor costs are accumulated by means of time tickets and labor summaries. Each day, each factory employee completes a time ticket. As shown in Exhibit 21-3, the time ticket gathers daily information and shows the specific job to which the employee was assigned. If the employee was not working on a job, the type of indirect labor activity performed would be noted as "Other Labor." At the end of the day the time tickets are collected, sorted, and summarized in the form of a *labor summary*, which shows the total direct and indirect labor costs incurred. Direct labor costs are subdivided by job and then posted to job cost sheets.

The proper entry to record the direct labor on job no. 864 and the incurrence of $200 of indirect labor follows.[1]

Work in Process	250	
Factory Overhead	200	
Wages Payable		450
To record direct and indirect labor.		

Like the cost of direct materials, direct labor is charged to Work in Process to accumulate the cost of jobs in production. When the employees are paid, Wages Payable will be debited and Cash will be credited.

Accounting for Overhead. Up to this point the computation of job cost has not been difficult, primarily because direct materials and direct labor could easily be traced to individual jobs. We now turn our attention to the third and most complicated element of product cost: factory overhead.

Because of tracing and record-keeping problems, jobs are charged with an estimated (as opposed to actual) overhead cost. The use of estimated overhead charges is not only practical but also has two side benefits. First, total job cost can be figured at the time of job completion. Timely cost information is beneficial in setting prices for customers and in other routine operating decisions that are made by management.

Second, estimated overhead charges tend to smooth product costs over a period of time. Actual costs change each month, and in addition, volume fluctuates. The cost of production is therefore dependent on when manufacturing takes place. As an example, picture the highly seasonal business of a soft drink manufacturer. Suppose the company's *fixed* production costs each month are relatively stable. In light of this situation, when volume peaks in the hot summer months, the actual manufacturing cost per bottle will decrease. This decrease results from spreading constant dollar amounts over increased activity levels. In winter when production is lower, the cost per bottle will rise. Thus, in an effort to avoid fluctuating overhead charges, estimated rates are set and implemented for a certain period of time, often one year. This practice removes the cost "penalties" and "bonuses" of producing in December and July, respectively, because inventory is costed at the same amount no matter when manufacturing occurs.

> **2**
>
> Compute an overhead application rate and apply overhead to production.

Overhead Application Rates. The estimated overhead cost of a job or product is determined by using an overhead application rate. The rate relates overhead to a specific application base and is computed as follows:

---

[1] We are ignoring employee withholdings in this example.

$$\frac{\text{Estimated Factory Overhead}}{\text{Estimated Application Base}} = \text{Overhead Application Rate}$$

To explain, product costs must be calculated as accurately as possible. Therefore, at the beginning of a reporting period the accountant performs an in-depth study of factory overhead. The accountant is interested in learning how overhead behaves in relation to changes in various factors of production (e.g., direct labor hours, direct labor cost, or machine hours). If a strong correlation exists between factory overhead and, say, direct labor cost, overhead on a given job is best determined by selecting direct labor as the application base. In a heavily automated situation where much of the overhead is caused by the operation of machines, machine hours may be more appropriate.

In general, we select an application base that (1) is inexpensive to compute, (2) is easily traced to the job or product, and (3) has a strong cause and effect relationship with overhead. The last guideline means that the base should have a significant influence on the amount of overhead incurred, thereby helping to improve the accuracy of the costing process.

Use of the Overhead Application Rate. Once the application base is chosen, the overhead rate can be developed and used in product costing. The amount of overhead charged to an individual job is determined by multiplying the rate by the amount of application base associated with that job. This process is best understood by using a numerical example.

Assume that Valley Manufacturing has chosen direct labor hours as an application base because of the company's heavy emphasis on manual assembly work. After a review of operations, Valley's accountant anticipates 40,000 direct labor hours of activity for the year. In addition, the following factory overhead estimates have been derived:

Indirect materials used	$ 20,000
Indirect labor	140,000
Utilities	15,000
Taxes	30,000
Insurance	10,000
Building depreciation	40,000
Equipment depreciation	25,000
Total estimated overhead	$280,000

The firm's overhead application rate of $7 per direct labor hour is computed as follows:

$$\frac{\text{Estimated Factory Overhead}}{\text{Estimated Application Base}} = \text{Overhead Application Rate}$$

$$\frac{\$280,000}{40,000 \text{ direct labor hours}} = \$7 \text{ per direct labor hour}$$

The $7 rate can now be applied to individual jobs to determine the estimated overhead cost. Examine Exhibit 21–4, which contains the completed cost sheet for job no. 864. Compare this exhibit with Exhibit 21–3, and notice that additional material costs (requisition no. 7638) and additional labor costs (tickets no. 1187–89 and no. 2010–11) have been incurred. On the basis of 58 total direct labor hours, Valley has applied or determined an overhead cost of $406 (58 hours × $7).[2] The proper entry to record the applied overhead is:

Work in Process	406	
Factory Overhead		406
To record applied overhead.		

The Work in Process account is debited to add factory overhead to the other two costs of production: direct materials used and direct labor. As a result of the preceding entry, Work in Process now contains all the costs that pertain to job no. 864. The credit to the Factory Overhead account takes a small portion of Valley's total overhead and applies it to specific jobs—a process that will become clearer after the next two sections.

EXHIBIT 21–4
Completed Job Cost Sheet

JOB COST SHEET

Manufactured for:
Stock __X__
Customer _____

Product __Custom lamp no. 38__

Job No. __864__
Date:
Needed __8/15__
Started __8/3__
Completed __8/5__
No. of Units __100__

Direct Materials			Direct Labor				Factory Overhead	
Date	Requisition No.	Amount	Date	Ticket No.	Hours	Amount	Date	Amount
8/3	7602	$4,000	8/3	1146-49	28	$250	8/5	$406
8/5	7638	1,050	8/4	1187-89	20	185		
		$5,050	8/5	2010-11	10	89		
					58	$524		

Overhead Rate: __$7 per direct labor hour__

COST SUMMARY

Direct materials	$ 5,050
Direct labor	524
Factory overhead	406
Total cost	$ 5,980

[2] If desired, overhead could be applied daily as the number of direct labor hours becomes known. If a job is not completed by the end of the accounting period, overhead should be applied on the basis of the work performed to date to properly value the production in process.

A FURTHER FOCUS

Overhead application is practiced not only in manufacturing but in many other fields as well. One of the most "interesting" examples occurs in hospitals, where overhead can play a major role in transforming a $0.006 aspirin into a $7 charge on a patient's bill. An insurance company executive noted that it is common practice to add the overhead costs that follow to the cost of the tablet:

- A departmental record keeping charge, indicating that medication was prescribed, dispensed, and administered.
- A surcharge for a hospital's unreimbursed Medicare patients.

One could logically argue that the following costs are shifted to the tablet as well: the cost of care provided to impoverished patients who have no insurance and cannot pay for medical treatment; uncollectible accounts receivable; the cost of malpractice insurance; the cost of new high-tech equipment; and hospital administrative and operating costs. If this is not enough, the hospital will also add an amount for profit—it, of course, cannot sell its products at cost.

Source: "The Legacy of the $7 Aspirin," *Management Accounting*, April 1990, pp. 38–41.

Actual Overhead. The Factory Overhead account is used to accumulate both actual and applied overhead. As shown earlier, for example, Factory Overhead is debited to record indirect materials used and indirect labor. Other actual overhead items are entered in this account as well. To illustrate, assume that Valley Manufacturing experienced the following factory costs during August:

Utilities	$ 1,300
Taxes	2,500
Insurance	900
Building depreciation	3,500
Equipment depreciation	2,200
Total	$10,400

Further assume that payments for utilities and taxes are not due until September and that the insurance figure represents the expiration of a prepaid policy. Valley's required journal entry to record these overhead costs is:

Factory Overhead	10,400	
Accounts Payable		1,300
Taxes Payable		2,500
Prepaid Insurance		900
Accumulated Depreciation: Building		3,500
Accumulated Depreciation: Equipment		2,200
To record actual overhead costs.		

The entry's credits should be familiar: they are identical to those shown in the first part of the text. The expiration of a prepaid expense calls for a reduction in an asset account; recording depreciation generates a credit to Accumulated Depreciation; and so forth. The debit, however, is different. In earlier chapters all these costs were charged to expense accounts. Now, because of a change in business purpose, the costs are debited to Factory Overhead. Recall that these items are product costs, which must be attached to the units manufactured and carried as inventory on the balance sheet. This attachment takes place through the application of factory overhead discussed earlier.

Observe that only *factory* costs are recorded in the overhead account. Selling and administrative costs (e.g., advertising, managerial salaries, and sales commissions) continue to be written off as expenses. Remember, these costs are period costs and, as such, never inventoried.

Applied Overhead. The accumulation of actual charges throughout the period and the application of overhead to jobs force the Factory Overhead account to assume the following status:

FACTORY OVERHEAD			
Actual overhead costs are recorded by debits as incurred.	XXX XXX XXX	XXX XXX XXX	Overhead is applied to jobs during the period via credits.

It should now be apparent that the application process simply takes a "chunk" of overhead and attaches it to production. By the end of the reporting period, if all goes according to plan, overhead applied will equal total overhead incurred. This situation rarely occurs, however, and a later section of the chapter will show the proper accounting treatment for such cases.

Accounting for the Completion and Sale of Manufactured Products. By viewing Exhibit 21–5, you can see the interrelationships among the journal entries illustrated in the preceding sections, the job cost sheet, and Valley's Work in Process account. In practice, separate entries would be made on August 3, 4, and 5 to record the individual transactions.

Upon completion, jobs are transferred to the finished goods warehouse to await sale. Paralleling this physical transfer, Valley would record the following entry to recognize the completion of production:

Finished Goods	5,980	
Work in Process		5,980
Completed job no. 864.		

Eventually, the finished goods inventory will be sold. Suppose, for example, that 25 of the 100 lamps manufactured on job no. 864 are sold on account at $80 apiece. From information found on the job cost sheet, the cost per lamp is $59.80 ($5,980 ÷ 100 lamps). Thus, two entries are needed:

Cost of Goods Sold	1,495	
Finished Goods		1,495
To record the cost of lamps sold.		
Accounts Receivable	2,000	
Sales		2,000
To record sale on account.		

The first entry transfers the production cost of the 25 lamps sold ($59.80 × 25 = $1,495) from Finished Goods to the Cost of Goods Sold account. The second entry places the sales revenues generated ($80 × 25 = $2,000) in the accounting records. As noted at the beginning of this example, Valley Manufacturing uses a perpetual inventory system. Should you need a review of inventory systems, we refer you to Chapter 10.

A Recap. The sale of finished production completes the flow of manufacturing costs through the accounting system. Please reexamine the bottom half of Exhibit 21–2. Notice that material, labor, and overhead costs all begin in their own accounts. Indirect materials used and indirect labor are transferred to Factory Overhead to join other miscellaneous production costs. Direct materials used, direct labor, and overhead *applied* are then charged to Work in Process. As production is completed, manufacturing costs are debited to the Finished Goods account. Finally, the sale of inventory requires a transfer of cost from Finished Goods to Cost of Goods Sold. Although variations of this flow are found in practice because of manufacturing complexities (e.g., multiple processing departments), Exhibit 21–2 accurately depicts the movement of costs for both small manufacturing firms and industrial giants.

EXHIBIT 21–5
Interrelationships Among Manufacturing Journal Entries, the Job Cost Sheet, and the Work in Process Account

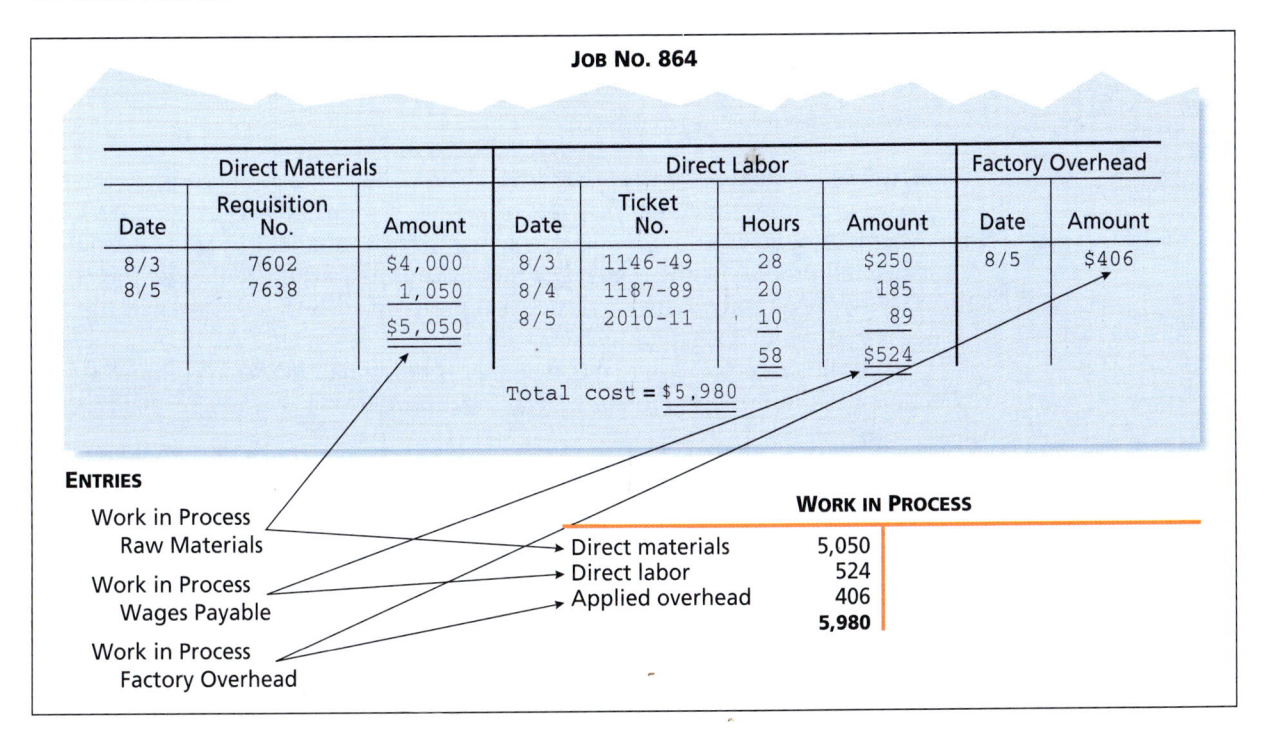

JOB NO. 864

Direct Materials			Direct Labor				Factory Overhead	
Date	Requisition No.	Amount	Date	Ticket No.	Hours	Amount	Date	Amount
8/3	7602	$4,000	8/3	1146-49	28	$250	8/5	$406
8/5	7638	1,050	8/4	1187-89	20	185		
		$5,050	8/5	2010-11	10	89		
					58	$524		

Total cost = $5,980

ENTRIES

Work in Process
    Raw Materials

Work in Process
    Wages Payable

Work in Process
    Factory Overhead

WORK IN PROCESS

Direct materials	5,050
Direct labor	524
Applied overhead	406
	5,980

Business Briefing

Sid Benouared
Manager
La Bistro
Italian Restaurant

Job Order Costing and Menu Pricing

Job order cost collection is a major element of our accounting system. In this case the job is a meal—and the cost of the meal is an important determinant of menu prices. Consider the costs of a very popular dish: chicken marsala.

Chicken	$ 1.50
Mushrooms	0.50
Wine	0.50
Spices	0.10
Pasta and tomato sauce	0.27
Table setting, bread, and water	1.50
Labor	3.60
Rent, utilities, and taxes	0.62
Subtotal	$ 8.59
Profit margin, 20%	1.72
Approximate menu price	$10.31

Although this approach to menu pricing looks relatively simple, there are many complications. Meat and vegetable costs can change every week; also, accurate ordering from suppliers is a must because excess goods will spoil (and increase operating costs). Sometimes we "turn" our tables only once a night; on other occasions each table is occupied three times before we close. Turnover will influence the number of customers we serve and the restaurant's target profit margin percentage.

In short, La Bistro's survival depends on cost control and our ability to offer quality meals at reasonable prices. Accounting and accurate job data play a key role in this process.

Work in Process: A Control Account. The Work in Process account in the previous example contained the costs of job no. 864 until the job was completed. Normally, a business manufactures many jobs simultaneously and is unable to finish all production by the end of the accounting period. To handle the necessary record keeping, Work in Process assumes the role of a control account and is supported by individual job cost sheets.

To illustrate, assume that Avanti Corporation had job no. 614 in process on January 1. Information relating to job no. 614 follows.

Direct materials used	$ 5,500
Direct labor	8,000
Factory overhead applied, 150% of direct labor	12,000
	$25,500

Manufacturing activity that took place during the year is shown in Exhibit 21–6.

EXHIBIT 21–6
Avanti Corporation
Manufacturing Activity

	JOB NO. 614	JOB NO. 615	JOB NO. 616	JOB NO. 617	TOTAL
Direct materials used	$ —	$ 9,000	$20,000	$ 4,000	$ 33,000
Direct labor	5,000	10,000	18,000	8,000	41,000
Factory overhead applied, 150% of direct labor	7,500	15,000	27,000	12,000	61,500
Total	$12,500	$34,000	$65,000	$24,000	$135,500
Job status, 12/31	Completed	Completed and sold	In process	In process	

Avanti's Work in Process account and summary journal entries appear in Exhibit 21–7. Observe that the cost of completed jobs (no. 614 and no. 615) has been removed from Work in Process and transferred to Finished Goods. Jobs no. 616 and no. 617 are still in production; thus, the $89,000 ending Work in Process balance coincides with the total of the related cost sheets ($65,000 + $24,000 = $89,000). The Work in Process and job cost sheet relationship is an example of the control account/subsidiary ledger arrangement discussed in Chapter 6. Recall that a control account (such as Work in Process) appears in the general ledger and

EXHIBIT 21–7
Work in Process Control Account of Avanti Corporation

WORK IN PROCESS

Beginning balance (no. 614)	25,500	Completed job (no. 614)	38,000*
Direct materials	33,000	Completed job (no. 615)	34,000
Direct labor	41,000		72,000
Overhead applied	61,500		
(89,000)	161,000		

* $25,500 + $12,500 = $38,000.

ENTRIES

Work in Process	33,000	
Raw Materials		33,000
Work in Process	41,000	
Wages Payable		41,000
Work in Process	61,500	
Factory Overhead		61,500

COST SHEET—JOB NO. 616

Direct materials	$20,000
Direct labor	18,000
Overhead applied	27,000
	$65,000

COST SHEET—JOB NO. 617

Direct materials	$ 4,000
Direct labor	8,000
Overhead applied	12,000
	$24,000

is composed of various lower-level accounts. The lower-level accounts (in this case, job cost sheets) are collectively known as a subsidiary ledger.

Computerized Job Costing Systems. As you may have concluded, the record keeping associated with a job costing system is burdensome, especially if manual accounting procedures are used. Thankfully, computerized systems are available that electronically capture the needed data and make the amount of bookkeeping bearable. For example, bar codes and scanners are often used to track the materials issued to production. Management may gather direct labor data by requiring employees to insert their magnetically encoded identification cards into a terminal. Also, machines may be linked on-line to computers, with software capturing the equipment's start and stop times. (Such information is important if machine hours are used as the overhead application base.) Indeed, without computerized systems, product costing (the prime objective) would likely take a back seat to paper shuffling and record keeping.

A CLOSER LOOK AT OVERHEAD

③ Account for over- or underapplied overhead at the end of the reporting period.

At the end of a reporting period, it is unlikely that the overhead applied to production will equal the actual overhead incurred. The application rate that is used to charge overhead to jobs is based on two estimates: estimated overhead and an estimated application base. Unexpected price changes from suppliers, variations in production levels, and increases and decreases in plant efficiency all cause actual experience to differ from amounts originally forecast.

Overhead can be either overapplied or underapplied. If, for example, a company applied $74,000 of overhead but actually incurred $68,000, overhead is said to be overapplied by $6,000. If the situation was reversed, overhead would be underapplied. To examine the implications of these situations, we will continue the Avanti Corporation example.

Avanti has been applying overhead to jobs at 150% of direct labor cost. The rate was computed by taking the year's forecasted factory overhead and direct labor costs, $60,000 and $40,000, respectively, and performing the following calculation:

$$\text{Application Rate} = \frac{\text{Estimated Factory Overhead}}{\text{Estimated Application Base}}$$

$$= \frac{\$60,000}{\$40,000}$$

$$= 150\%$$

The 150% rate says that for every $1.00 of direct labor expected to be incurred, the firm anticipates $1.50 of factory overhead.

Throughout the accounting period Avanti applied $61,500 of overhead to jobs no. 614–617 (see Exhibit 21–6). If we assume that actual overhead incurred amounted to $62,600, overhead would be underapplied by $1,100:

Actual overhead	$62,600
Applied overhead	
Direct labor cost × 150% ($41,000 × 150%)	61,500
Underapplied overhead	$ 1,100

Exhibit 21–8 depicts the entire process in pictorial form.

EFFECTS OF OVER- AND UNDERAPPLIED OVERHEAD

Avanti's underapplication means that insufficient overhead has been charged to the Work in Process account. Unfortunately, the problem does not stop here, because each job produced during the period has been costed incorrectly. From the job status that appears in Exhibit 21–6, jobs no. 616 and no. 617 are still in process (Work in Process), job no. 614 has been completed but is still on hand (Finished Goods), and job no. 615 has been sold (Cost of Goods Sold). Because of the understated application rate, the ending balances in these three accounts are understated as well. Thus, an adjusting entry is needed upon conclusion of the reporting period.

The adjusting entry first considers the status of the Factory Overhead account. In Avanti's case the account appears as follows:

FACTORY OVERHEAD	
Actual	Applied
62,600	61,500

The overhead account must be closed so the company can start anew, accumulating costs for the next period's production activities. Thus, Factory Overhead is credited for $1,100. The $1,100 debit can either be (1) allocated to Work in

EXHIBIT 21–8
Application of Factory Overhead for Avanti Corporation

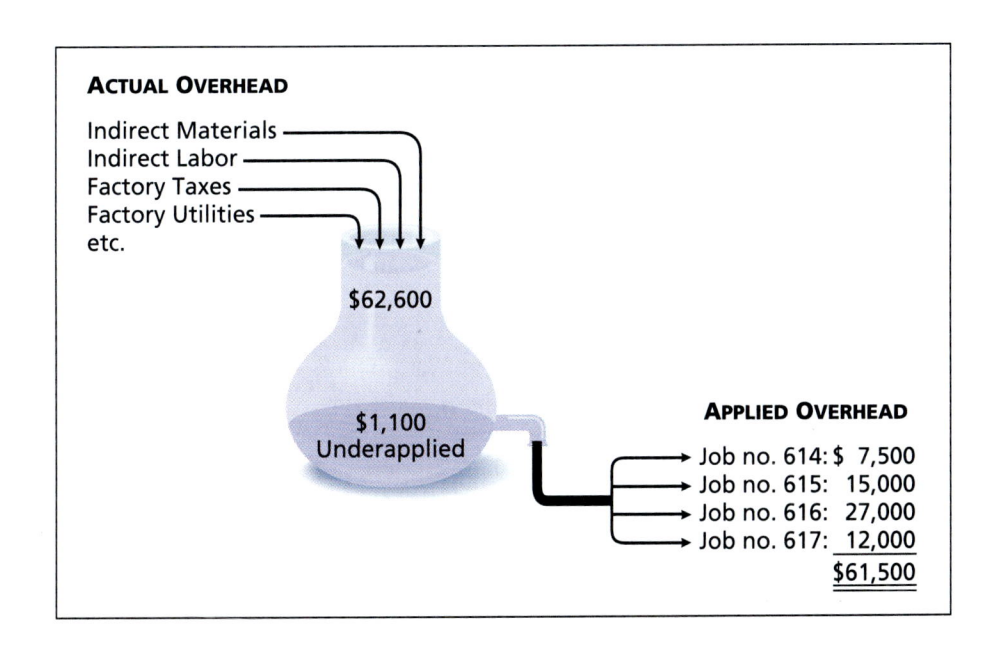

ACTUAL OVERHEAD
Indirect Materials
Indirect Labor
Factory Taxes
Factory Utilities
etc.

$62,600

$1,100 Underapplied

APPLIED OVERHEAD
Job no. 614: $ 7,500
Job no. 615:   15,000
Job no. 616:   27,000
Job no. 617:   12,000
$61,500

Process, Finished Goods, and Cost of Goods Sold on some equitable basis or (2) charged entirely to Cost of Goods Sold.

The first approach, which raises each account's balance to counteract the understatement, is theoretically correct. However, because the balances in the three accounts cited consist of the costs of individual jobs, each job cost sheet must be adjusted as well. Avanti had only four jobs; in a more realistic environment, the amount of bookkeeping could be troublesome. Consequently, the allocation approach is used only when the amount of over- or underapplied overhead is so great that a lack of proration will produce misleading financial statements.

The second method, charging the entire $1,100 to Cost of Goods Sold, is the more popular approach. The necessary journal entry follows.

Cost of Goods Sold	1,100	
Factory Overhead		1,100
To adjust cost of goods sold for underapplied overhead.		

The entry raises Cost of Goods Sold to $35,100 ($34,000 from job no. 615 + $1,100), and this amount is reported on Avanti's income statement.

The procedures illustrated are reversed for overapplied overhead.

TODAY'S MANUFACTURING ENVIRONMENT

> **4** Recognize the impact of automation on overhead application rates.

Earlier in the chapter we noted that the application base selected should have a strong cause and effect relationship with overhead. Labor hours or labor cost may be appropriate in a setting where considerable manual assembly work is required to complete a product; hospital beds occupied may explain a large portion of the overhead incurred at a health-care facility; a company's building maintenance costs may be tied to square footage; and so forth. These application bases are said to be **cost drivers**, or factors that cause specific costs to be incurred within an organization.

Companies naturally have a wide selection of application bases to choose from, with some bases being much better than others. If an improper base is selected—one that fails to cause (i.e., drive) overhead costs—the outcome will be questionable overhead application rates. Such rates typically result in distorted product costs, inventory valuations, and income measurements, perhaps leading to erroneous decisions on the part of management.

Surveys of manufacturers' accounting practices have found (and continue to find) that direct labor is one of the most popular, if not *the* most popular, application base for factory overhead. This finding is interesting, especially when one considers the dramatic change in cost drivers over the years. Factory workers are continually being replaced by robots and computer-controlled machines, as companies strive to trim costs and improve product quality. In heavily automated facilities, it is not uncommon for overhead (which includes equipment depreciation and operating costs) to account for more than half of all production costs. Direct labor, on the other hand, which may have comprised 40% of total manufacturing costs as recently as 30 years ago, frequently amounts to no more than 5% today. The declining labor component, coupled with increasing overhead charges, has led some businesses to experience application rates in excess of 1,000% of direct labor!

Robots Versus People. To present a very clear (and perhaps frightening) picture of the trade-off between factory overhead and direct labor, we cite two examples from Japan.[3] Matsushita Electric has a factory where Panasonic VCRs are produced. Here, 530 robots wind wire slightly thinner than a human hair 16 times through a pinhole in the video head. This operation goes on 24 hours a day. The outcome? The robots work five times faster and more reliably than the 3,000 part-time workers they replaced. (The employees did the work for Matsushita on a subcontract basis.) These computer-driven marvels also inspect their own output.

The Yokohama camcorder factory of The Victor Co. of Japan (JVC) is another interesting example. Automated vehicles deliver components to 64 robots that perform 150 assembly and inspection tasks for eight different models—all on a single production line. The entire process is controlled by 2 workers, down from 150 in pre-robot days.

Cases such as these are becoming more commonplace. Although direct labor may be an appropriate cost driver in some situations, it certainly is not in all. To conclude, many firms' cost accounting systems are obsolete and in need of change, especially in light of automation and modern manufacturing environments. Ask many professionals and they will say that accurate cost information is often the deciding factor in gaining the strongly pursued competitive advantage, foreign or otherwise.

JOB COSTING: SERVICE APPLICATIONS

Apply job costing systems to service organizations.

Thus far, most of our discussion has dealt with production-type settings, perhaps leaving you with the impression that job costing systems are used exclusively by manufacturing organizations. This is not the case, as cost accumulation by job is popular in the service sector of our economy as well. Such systems are used to determine the cost of:

- Servicing clients by accountants, financial planners, management consultants, architects, and lawyers.
- Providing patient care by hospitals.
- Implementing drug abuse programs by social service agencies.
- Beginning new flights to vacation resort areas by airlines.

In the preceding examples, the "job" becomes the client, patient, program, and flight segment, respectively.

Job cost information is used in several of these situations for setting prices, which, of course, affect profitability. Even for those organizations that operate without a profit motive (e.g., colleges and universities, charitable organizations, and so forth), job cost input assists managers when planning, controlling operations, and allocating resources.

[3] These illustrations are taken from "Why Japan Loves Robots and We Don't," *Forbes*, April 16, 1990, pp. 148, 150–53.

DIRECT AND INDIRECT COSTS

Job costing in service entities revolves around the proper handling of direct and indirect costs. **Direct costs,** or those easily traced to a job, are charged to the individual jobs that are worked on during the accounting period. In contrast, **indirect costs** (those not easily traced) are treated as general overhead and applied in the same manner as factory overhead for a manufacturer.[4]

A review of job costing systems and procedures over the years will find an increased attempt by businesses to have more of their costs fall in the direct category. This practice, which is now more easily accomplished because of available software, helps satisfy client inquiries concerning fee composition and leads to improved costing of services.

AN ILLUSTRATION

Given the distinction between direct and indirect costs, we now focus on the operations of InfoNet, a consulting firm that specializes in the design of management information systems. A portion of InfoNet's budget for 19X3 follows.

Revenue from billings		$10,500,000
Less direct costs		
Professional staff time	$4,000,000	
Computer charges	2,600,000	
Long-distance charges	350,000	
Overnight delivery	50,000	7,000,000
		$ 3,500,000
Less indirect costs (rent, utilities, other nontraceable items)		2,100,000
Operating income		$ 1,400,000

The company's accountants and management feel that total direct costs is the most appropriate base to charge overhead (i.e., indirect costs) to client jobs. Accordingly, a 30% application rate was developed:

$$\text{Application Rate} = \frac{\text{Estimated Overhead}}{\text{Estimated Application Base}}$$

$$= \frac{\$2,100,000}{\$7,000,000}$$

$$= 30\%$$

During March, InfoNet completed a consulting job for Oregon Department Stores. The job cost sheet for this project is shown in Exhibit 21–9. Directly traceable costs total $30,000 and are charged to the Oregon project. In addition,

[4] These definitions will be expanded somewhat in Chapter 26.

EXHIBIT 21–9
Job Cost Sheet for a Service Business

```
JOB COST SHEET

Client  Oregon Department Stores        Job No. 165
        Portland, Oregon
                                        Date:
Engagement  Design of marketing         Started    1/10/X3
            retrieval system            Completed  3/29/X3

Direct costs:
    Professional staff time                    $ 19,000
    Computer charges                             10,500
    Long-distance charges                           400
    Overnight delivery                              100
    Total                                      $ 30,000
General overhead ( 30 % of total direct costs)    9,000
Total cost of engagement                       $ 39,000
Target income (___% of total direct costs)     $
Client billing                                 $
```

$9,000 ($30,000 × 0.30) of overhead is applied to the job, bringing the total cost to $39,000.

CLIENT BILLINGS

Notice that the last two lines of the client's cost sheet are left blank. If desired, InfoNet could compute a target income amount to be earned on each job—a target so the company can proceed toward attaining its overall income goal of $1,400,000. The job's income and costs are eventually combined to yield the amount that InfoNet must bill the client.

For example, InfoNet's original budget reveals estimated operating income and direct costs of $1,400,000 and $7,000,000, respectively. If each job is anticipated to produce the same rate of profit for the firm, an income computation rate could be developed in a manner similar to that shown for an overhead application rate, namely:

$$\text{Income Computation Rate} = \frac{\text{Estimated Income}}{\text{Estimated Application Base}}$$

$$= \frac{\$1,400,000}{\$7,000,000}$$

$$= 20\%$$

InfoNet wants to earn $6,000 ($30,000 × 0.20) from the Oregon job, meaning that the amount billed must equal $45,000 ($39,000 + $6,000). Stated differently, if revenues from the job are $45,000 and costs amount to $39,000, the Oregon project will contribute $6,000 toward InfoNet's 19X3 total operating income.

END-OF-CHAPTER REVIEW

LEARNING OBJECTIVES: THE KEY POINTS

1. **Explain the nature and use of a job order costing system.** Job costing systems are used in environments where it is relatively easy to classify costs by job or order. This situation often arises when goods are manufactured upon receipt of a customer's order, according to customer specifications, or in separate batches. The costs of direct materials used, direct labor, and factory overhead applied are all accumulated on a job cost sheet. These costs are charged to the Work in Process account. Upon job completion the costs are transferred to Finished Goods inventory and, at the time of sale, to Cost of Goods Sold.

2. **Compute an overhead application rate and apply overhead to production.** Because of the difficulty and/or cost of tracing factory overhead to a manufactured product, it becomes necessary to apply (i.e., estimate) overhead for inventory costing purposes. An application rate is developed by dividing a company's estimated factory overhead by an estimated application base. The rate is then multiplied by the amount of the application base associated with the job in question. Overhead bases should be relatively inexpensive to compute, easily traced to the product, and have a strong bearing on the amount of overhead actually incurred.

3. **Account for over- or underapplied overhead at the end of the reporting period.** Overhead is applied in the manner just described under learning objective 2. The required journal entry involves a debit to the Work in Process account and a credit to Factory Overhead. The Factory Overhead account is also used to accumulate (on the debit side) the actual overhead incurred by the company. At the end of the reporting period, the amount of over- or underapplication is calculated as the difference between actual overhead and applied overhead. Over- or underapplied amounts are most commonly adjusted against the Cost of Goods Sold account or, if significant, allocated among Work in Process, Finished Goods, and Cost of Goods Sold.

4. **Recognize the impact of automation on overhead application rates.** Automation has resulted in people being replaced by robots and computer-controlled machines. Thus, for many companies, direct labor as a percentage of product cost is shrinking, while factory overhead is increasing. The rise in factory overhead is attributed to equipment operating costs, including lease payments and depreciation. The outcome for those firms that continue to use direct labor as an application base is an increase in overhead rates.

5. **Apply job costing systems to service organizations.** Job costing systems can be used by service enterprises to accumulate the costs of rendering a service. The "job" may consist of providing consulting services to a client, repair services to a customer, health-care services to a patient, and so forth. Direct costs (those easily traced to a client job) are charged to the job cost sheet. Indirect costs, or those not easily traced, are treated as overhead and applied in a manner similar to that used for factory overhead.

JOB ORDER COSTING SYSTEMS 817

KEY TERMS AND CONCEPTS: A QUICK OVERVIEW

cost driver A factor that causes given costs to be incurred within an organization. (p. 812)

direct cost A cost that is easily traced to a job. (p. 814)

indirect cost A cost that is not easily traced to a job; treated as overhead. (p. 814)

job cost sheet A document that is used to accumulate costs in a job order system. (p. 798)

job order system A system of cost accumulation that gathers costs by job or order. (p. 798)

materials requisition An order for materials to be issued from the storeroom. (p. 800)

overapplied overhead A situation arising when the factory overhead applied to production is greater than the amount of factory overhead actually incurred. (p. 810)

overhead application rate The rate used to apply factory overhead to jobs or products. Computed as estimated factory overhead divided by the estimated application base. (p. 802)

time ticket A ticket used to gather labor time. Shows the specific job or jobs to which an employee was assigned. (p. 802)

underapplied overhead A situation arising when the factory overhead applied to production is less than the amount of factory overhead actually incurred. (p. 810)

CHAPTER QUIZ

The five questions that follow relate to several issues raised in the chapter. Test your knowledge of the issues by selecting the best answer. (The answers appear on p. 835.)

1. Which of the following businesses would be least likely to use a job costing system?
   a. Automobile repair shop
   b. Custom-home builder
   c. Crude oil refinery
   d. Motion picture producer

2. The journal entry to record the use of indirect materials in production activities is:
   a. debit Work in Process; credit Raw Materials.
   b. debit Factory Overhead; credit Raw Materials.
   c. debit Raw Materials; credit Work in Process.
   d. debit Work in Process; credit Factory Overhead.

3. Direct materials, direct labor, and factory overhead applied are initially brought together in which of the following accounts?
   a. Work in Process
   b. Finished Goods
   c. Cost of Goods Sold
   d. Income Summary

4. SRT, Inc., applies factory overhead on the basis of direct labor cost. The company's accountant has forecast $180,000 of factory overhead and $200,000 of direct labor for 19X5. Actual factory overhead and direct labor for 19X5 amounted to $185,000 and $210,000, respectively. Overhead for 19X5 is:
   a. underapplied by $4,000.
   b. underapplied by $9,000.
   c. overapplied by $4,000.
   d. overapplied by $9,000.

5. In today's modern manufacturing environment, many companies:
   a. are experiencing a decrease in overhead application rates.
   b. are experiencing a decrease in factory overhead and an increase in direct labor cost.
   c. can ignore cost drivers because of a recent pronouncement from the Financial Accounting Standards Board.
   d. have a labor component that may be as low as 5% of total product cost.

SUMMARY PROBLEM

Riverdale Manufacturing Company uses a job order system to accumulate production costs. The firm, which applies overhead on the basis of direct labor hours, derived the following estimates for 19X3 manufacturing activity: direct labor hours: 45,000; factory overhead: $180,000. Selected data applicable to January 19X3 follow.

> January 1 balance of work in process: $19,000
> Direct materials used: $60,000
> Direct labor incurred (3,500 hours): $28,000
> Indirect materials used: $3,900
> Indirect labor incurred: $7,600
> Factory utilities: $1,000
> Equipment depreciation: $2,000
> Cost of goods completed: $94,500

Instructions

a. Determine Riverdale's overhead application rate.
b. Calculate the amount of overhead applied to production during January.
c. Present entries to record (1) direct materials used, (2) direct labor incurred, (3) factory overhead incurred, (4) factory overhead applied to production, and (5) cost of goods completed during the month.
d. Determine the cost of the company's work in process inventory on January 31.
e. Determine the amount of over- or underapplied overhead during January.

Solution

a. Overhead Application Rate $= \dfrac{\text{Estimated Factory Overhead}}{\text{Estimated Application Base}}$

$= \dfrac{\$180,000}{45,000 \text{ hours}}$

$= \$4$ per direct labor hour

b. Overhead applied: 3,500 hours × $4 = $14,000

c.
(1) Work in Process 60,000
    Raw Materials 60,000
    Issued direct materials to production.

(2) Work in Process 28,000
    Wages Payable 28,000
    To record direct labor incurred.

(3) Factory Overhead 14,500
    Raw Materials 3,900
    Wages Payable 7,600
    Accounts Payable 1,000
    Accumulated Depreciation: Equipment 2,000
    To record actual factory overhead costs.

(4) Work in Process 14,000
    Factory Overhead 14,000
    To record applied overhead [see part (b)].

(5) Finished Goods 94,500
    Work in Process 94,500
    To transfer completed units to finished goods.

d. Riverdale's ending work in process inventory is $26,500, as shown by the following T-account:

WORK IN PROCESS				
Balance	19,000	(5)		94,500
(1)	60,000			
(2)	28,000			
(4)	14,000			
	26,500 121,000			

e. Overhead is underapplied by $500.

Overhead incurred	$14,500
Overhead applied	14,000
Underapplied overhead	$ 500

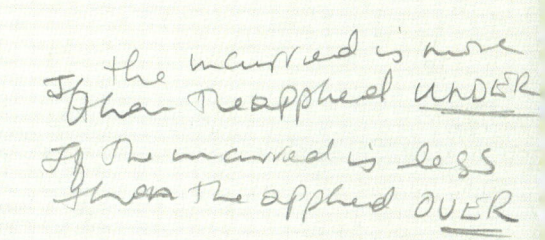

ASSIGNMENT MATERIAL

QUESTIONS

Q21–1 Discuss the general features associated with a job order costing system. In what types of applications are job order systems used?

Q21–2 Explain how the flow of costs through an accounting system parallels the flow of goods and materials through a manufacturing plant.

Q21–3 Contrast the proper accounting treatments of direct materials and indirect materials.

Q21–4 How does the use of a predetermined overhead rate smooth product costs over a period of time?

Q21–5 Explain how an overhead application rate is developed and used to apply overhead to specific jobs.

Q21–6 List the characteristics of a good overhead application base.

Q21–7 Ritten Company's factory depreciation for the year just ended totaled $40,000 and was recorded as follows:

Depreciation Expense	40,000	
Accumulated Depreciation: Factory		40,000

Comment on the appropriateness of Ritten's journal entry.

Q21–8 Discuss the relationship between the Work in Process account and individual job cost sheets.

Q21–9 If overhead is underapplied, will the Factory Overhead account contain a debit or credit balance? What is the probable effect of the underapplication on the Work in Process balance (before adjustment) at the end of the accounting period?

Q21-10 What is probably the most popular application base for overhead? Can this base be criticized in light of a modern manufacturing environment? Briefly explain.

Q21-11 List several possible applications of job costing systems by service enterprises.

Q21-12 Distinguish between a direct cost and an indirect cost.

EXERCISES

E21-1 Manufacturing journal entries (L.O. 1, 2)

The following selected transactions and events occurred at Pipeline Manufacturing during March:

Mar.	3	Purchased $10,000 of direct materials and $7,300 of indirect materials on account from Sunbelt Distributors.
	7	Issued $3,100 of direct materials and $700 of indirect materials from the storeroom.
	14	Incurred $5,600 of direct labor and $3,400 of indirect labor.
	17	Recorded $1,300 of overhead incurred on account.
	20	Applied $2,800 of overhead to production.
	23	Noted that $6,200 of production had been completed.
	26	Sold goods on account at a profit of 30% of cost. The goods cost $5,000.

Prepare journal entries to record the preceding transactions and events.

E21-2 Analysis of job cost sheet (L.O. 1, 2)

Sumpter Manufacturing began job no. 587 in December 19X6 and recorded material, labor, and overhead charges of $38,800 through year-end. The bottom portion of page 2 of the job's cost sheet is reproduced below.

```
Summary of January charges
    Direct materials used          $12,600
    Direct labor (580 hours)         4,350
    Factory overhead applied         6,728
       Total                       $23,678
```

Job no. 587 was completed on January 30, 19X7.

a. Determine Sumpter's overhead application rate, assuming the company uses direct labor hours for an application base.
b. What is the total cost of job no. 587?
c. Prepare the journal entries recorded in January that relate to job no. 587.

E21-3 Cost flows and overhead application (L.O. 1, 2)

Cleveland Metals uses a job cost system and applies factory overhead to production at a predetermined rate of 180% of direct labor cost. Data pertaining to recent operations follow.

- Job no. 636 was the only job in process on January 1 of the current year. The Work in Process account contained a $24,600 balance on this date.
- Job nos. 637, 638, and 639 were started during January.

- Direct material requisitions and direct labor incurred during January totaled $89,200 and $114,500, respectively.
- The only job that remained in process on January 31 was job no. 638, with costs of $15,000 for direct materials and $20,000 for direct labor.

a. Compute the total cost of the work in process inventory on January 31.
b. Compute the cost of jobs completed during January and present the proper journal entry to reflect job completion.

E21–4 Job costing and overhead application (L.O. 1, 2, 3)

Authentic Furniture, Inc., applies overhead on the basis of direct labor cost. At the beginning of 19X5, the company's cost accountant made the following predictions about the year's operations: direct labor cost, $4 million; factory overhead, $5 million.

The first two jobs manufactured in 19X5 were no. X5-01 and no. X5-02. Selected costs and the production status of these two jobs follow.

Job no. X5-01
  Direct materials: $22,000
  Direct labor: $40,000
  Status: In process

Job no. X5-02
  Direct materials: $48,000
  Direct labor: $75,000
  Status: Completed but not shipped

By the end of 19X5, actual direct labor costs amounted to $4,200,000 and factory overhead incurred totaled $5,180,000. There was no work in process on January 1, 19X5.

a. Compute the company's overhead application rate.
b. Determine the balance in the Work in Process account on January 31, 19X5.
c. Calculate the cost of production transferred to the finished goods warehouse during January.
d. Determine the amount of over- or underapplied overhead for 19X5. Be sure to indicate whether overhead was overapplied or underapplied.

E21–5 Job costing and overhead application (L.O. 1, 2)

Oxford Enterprises uses a job costing system to accumulate manufacturing costs. Overhead is applied to products on the basis of machine hours in the machining department and direct labor cost in the assembly department. The following estimates pertain to 19X4:

	MACHINING	ASSEMBLY
Machine hours	40,000	5,000
Direct labor cost	$270,000	$800,000
Factory overhead	810,000	960,000

Job no. 328 was the only job in process at the end of 19X4. Its cost sheet revealed the data that follow.

	MACHINING	ASSEMBLY
Machine hours	100	10
Direct labor cost	$1,100	$3,500
Direct materials cost	1,900	3,400

a. Compute Oxford's overhead application rates in the machining department and the assembly department.
b. Calculate the total amount of overhead applied to job no. 328.
c. Determine the total cost of job no. 328.

E21–6 Overview of job costing and overhead application (L.O. 1, 2, 3, 4)

Evaluate the comments that follow as being True or False. If the comment is false, briefly explain why.

a. A materials requisition forms the basis for the following journal entry: debit Work in Process; credit Raw Materials.
b. The Work in Process account normally contains the following costs for the jobs in production at year-end: direct materials used, direct labor, and actual factory overhead.
c. Direct labor cost is a good overhead application base to use if a company is highly automated.
d. The amount of over- or underapplied overhead at year-end is normally closed to the Work in Process account.
e. An overhead application rate is derived by the following computation: estimated factory overhead divided by an estimated application base.

E21–7 Overhead application: Working backward (L.O. 3)

The Towson Manufacturing Corporation applies overhead on the basis of machine hours. The following divisional information is presented for your review:

	DIVISION A	DIVISION B
Actual machine hours	22,500	?
Estimated machine hours	20,000	?
Overhead application rate	$4.50	$5.00
Actual overhead	$110,000	?
Estimated overhead	?	$90,000
Applied overhead	?	$86,000
Over- (under-) applied overhead	?	$6,500

Find the unknowns for each of the divisions.

E21–8 Selection of an overhead application base (L.O. 4)

Grand Corporation is in the process of choosing either direct labor cost or direct labor hours as an overhead application base. The company has several workers who have recently been hired at $9 per hour; more senior employees earn $16 per hour. All laborers are equally efficient, and fringe benefit costs are a relatively small part of total factory overhead.

Assume that Joe Robbins and Susan Hess are currently working on job no. 17 and job no. 21, respectively. Joe earns $9 per hour, Susan earns $16 per hour, and both jobs are similar in nature.

a. What is likely true about the amount of overhead *incurred* on job no. 17 versus that on job no. 21?
b. Compare the amount of overhead *applied* on the two jobs, assuming an application base of direct labor cost.
c. Repeat part (b), assuming an application base of direct labor hours.
d. Which of the two bases, labor cost or labor hours, appears more equitable in this situation? Why?

E21–9 Direct costs and indirect costs (L.O. 5)

Executive Airlines is studying whether to begin flight service from Chicago to St. Louis. Identify the following costs as a direct cost or an indirect cost of the Chicago/St. Louis flight segment, assuming the route would be serviced by aircraft that would continue to be flown throughout Executive's extensive route system:

a. Passenger beverage service
b. Airport landing fees
c. Monthly engine maintenance
d. Fuel consumed
e. Commissions paid to travel agents on tickets sold
f. Salary of Executive's director of route planning

E21–10 Job costing in a service business (L.O. 5)

Richard Mullen is a sports agent who represents several professional football players. To determine the cost of servicing each of his clients, Mullen uses a job order system. All traceable outlays are charged directly to clients; other costs are charged by using an overhead application rate. A 40% markup on all costs is then added when billing for services performed.

Mullen recently assisted Deon Jones in contract negotiations with the Memphis Thunderbolts. The job sheet for Jones indicates the following charges:

Professional negotiating:	
$300 per hour × 30 hours	$9,000
Airfare and travel costs	2,500
Telephone/telecommunications charges	250
Photocopying charges	100
Overnight delivery of papers	50

If the general overhead rate is 50% of direct costs, compute the amount that Mullen would bill Jones for contract negotiations.

E21–11 Cost drivers, service business (L.O. 5)

Don't Bug Me treats insect-infested homes and trees in Omaha, Nebraska. The company utilizes many liquid pesticides that are purchased in 55-gallon drums and later divided into 10-gallon containers for crew use. The pesticides are accounted for as indirect materials (i.e., supplies) in the firm's job cost system.

a. Why do you think the company treats pesticides as indirect materials (as opposed to direct costs) of servicing a client?
b. What is a cost driver?
c. Management insists that crews estimate square footage and tree height, respectively, for homes and trees serviced. Why is this procedure necessary?

PROBLEMS

Series A

P21–A1 Preparation of job cost sheet and journal entries (L.O. 1, 2)

Durable Goods manufactures items that are used in the plastics industry. The company, which uses a job costing system, has two departments: cutting and finishing. The cutting department applies overhead to products at the rate of $20 per machine hour. Finishing, in contrast, uses an application rate of 300% of direct labor cost.

On August 12, 19X4, Durable received an order from Arriva, Inc., for 450 wedge forms, model no. 19. Production began immediately, and the order (known as job no. 3434) was completed on August 31. Paperwork supporting the order revealed the following:

Document*	Date	Department	Hours	Amount
MR 2298	8/12	Cutting	—	$1,500
MR 2317	8/15	Cutting	—	6,400
MUR 59	8/17	Cutting	80	—
TT 1190–92	8/17	Cutting	30	300
MR 6680	8/19	Finishing	—	800
MUR 62	8/31	Cutting	140	—
TT 1235–38	8/31	Cutting	50	500
TT 6608–14	8/31	Finishing	200	1,800

* MR = materials requisition; TT = time ticket; MUR = machine usage report.

Instructions

a. Prepare a job cost sheet for the Arriva order as of August 31. Use the following column headings:

	Direct Materials		Direct Labor			Machine Usage		Factory Overhead
Date	Requisition	Amount	Ticket	Hours	Amount	Report	Hours	Amount

b. Prepare journal entries to record (1) the issuance of direct materials, (2) direct labor incurred on the order, and (3) the application of factory overhead. All materials requisitions should be combined in one entry, all time tickets in another, and so forth.

c. If company policy is to sell goods at a profit of 60% of total job cost, present the journal entries necessary to recognize completion and sale of the wedge forms.

P21–A2 Basic job costing with journal entries (L.O. 1, 2)

Santos Manufacturing, which uses a job cost system, applies overhead to production at the rate of $8 per labor hour. The company reported a work in process inventory of $86,900 on December 1 of the current year, consisting of job no. 362. The following activity took place during December:

1. Issued direct materials from the storeroom and incurred direct labor charges on various jobs as shown.

Job No.	Direct Materials	Direct Labor Cost	Direct Labor Hours
362	$10,500	$ 4,500	450
365	20,700	3,000	280
366	16,900	8,400	830
367	5,400	2,200	240
368	9,600	6,300	600
	$63,100	$24,400	2,400

2. Incurred miscellaneous factory charges: indirect materials used, $3,500; indirect labor, $5,900; and equipment depreciation, $4,000.
3. Completed jobs no. 362 and no. 366.
4. Sold job no. 366 on account for $43,100.

Instructions

a. Prepare journal entries for December to record the following. (*Note:* Use summary entries where appropriate by combining individual job data.)
   (1) The issuance of direct materials, the direct labor incurred, and the application of factory overhead to production.
   (2) The indirect materials used, the indirect labor charges, and equipment depreciation.
   (3) The completion of jobs no. 362 and no. 366.
   (4) The sale of job no. 366.
b. Establish a T-account for Work in Process and determine the account's ending balance on December 31.
c. Prepare a schedule of the jobs still in process (and the related costs) as of December 31.

P21–A3 Computations using a job order system (L.O. 1, 2)

General Corporation employs a job order cost system. On May 1, the following balances were extracted from the general ledger:

Work in process	$ 35,200
Finished goods	86,900
Cost of goods sold	128,700

Work in Process consisted of two jobs, no. 101 ($20,400) and no. 103 ($14,800). During May, direct materials requisitioned from the storeroom amounted to $96,500, and direct labor incurred totaled $114,500. These figures are subdivided as follows:

DIRECT MATERIALS		DIRECT LABOR	
JOB NO.	AMOUNT	JOB NO.	AMOUNT
101	$ 5,000	101	$ 7,800
115	19,500	103	20,800
116	36,200	115	42,000
Other	35,800	116	18,000
	$96,500	Other	25,900
			$114,500

Job no. 115 was the only job in process at the end of the month. Job no. 101 and three "other" jobs were sold during May at a profit of 20% of cost. The "other" jobs contained material and labor charges of $21,000 and $17,400, respectively.

General applies overhead daily at the rate of 150% of direct labor cost as labor summaries are posted to job orders. The firm's fiscal year ends on May 31.

Instructions

a. Compute the total overhead applied to production during May.
b. Compute the cost of the ending work in process inventory.
c. Compute the cost of jobs completed during May.
d. Compute the cost of goods sold for the year ended May 31.

P21–A4 Job order costing, overhead emphasis (L.O. 1, 2, 3)

Witte Corporation, a company that produces customized conveyors for food processing, uses a job order system. The following data are available:

Estimated costs for 19X6

Direct labor	$380,000
Factory overhead	247,000
	$627,000

Actual costs for 19X6

Direct materials used	$269,600
Direct labor	425,000
Indirect materials	32,800
Indirect labor	126,750
Factory depreciation	65,000
Factory taxes	22,650
Other factory costs	45,600
	$987,400

Work in process on January 1, 19X6, totaled $37,200 and consisted of job no. 764. This job and all others started during the year were completed and sold by December 31, with the exception of job no. 821. Job no. 821 was still in production and contained direct material costs of $11,200 and direct labor charges of $23,800.

Overhead is applied to goods on the basis of direct labor cost. Any under- or overapplied overhead at year-end is charged to Cost of Goods Sold.

Instructions

a. Determine the 19X6 overhead application rate.
b. Determine the amount of under- or overapplied overhead for the year. Be sure to indicate whether overhead was underapplied or overapplied.
c. Determine the total cost of the company's work in process inventory as of December 31, 19X6.
d. Compute the company's cost of goods sold. Witte had no finished goods inventory at the beginning of the year.

P21–A5 Flow of costs: Finding unknowns (L.O. 1, 2)

Selected ledger accounts for Ruffin Manufacturing for the year ended December 31, 19X4, follow.

RAW MATERIALS

Balance, 1/1	19,000		89,000
	?		

WAGES PAYABLE

		58,000

FACTORY OVERHEAD

Indirect materials	7,000		?
All other	97,000		

	WORK IN PROCESS	
Balance, 1/1	?	240,000
Direct materials	?	
Direct labor	51,000	
Applied overhead	?	

	FINISHED GOODS	
Balance, 1/1	114,000	?

	COST OF GOODS SOLD
	296,000

A year-end count revealed ending raw materials and work in process inventories of $25,000 and $14,000, respectively. Ruffin uses an overhead application rate of 200% of direct labor cost.

Instructions

a. Compute the amount of indirect labor incurred in operations.
b. Compute total direct materials used.
c. Determine Ruffin's purchases of raw materials during the year.
d. Calculate the amount of overhead that was applied to production.
e. Determine the cost of the ending finished goods inventory.
f. Compute the cost of the beginning work in process inventory.

P21–A6 Job costing in a service business (L.O. 5)

Hartwell and Associates provides consulting services to a number of medical practices. To determine the cost of each consulting engagement, Hartwell uses a job order system. All costs traceable to specific clients are charged to individual client jobs. Other costs incurred by the firm, but not identifiable with specific clients, are charged to jobs via a predetermined overhead application rate. Clients pay Hartwell for directly chargeable costs, overhead, and a markup—a markup that allows the firm to earn its budgeted operating income for the year.

On the basis of past experience, Hartwell has prepared the following budget for the upcoming year:

COST	TOTAL	DIRECTLY TRACEABLE TO SPECIFIC JOBS	NOT TRACEABLE TO SPECIFIC JOBS
Consulting staff	$200,000	$180,000	$20,000
Office staff	30,000	12,000	18,000
Travel	20,000	15,000	5,000
Other office costs	10,000	1,000	9,000
	$260,000	$208,000	$52,000

The budget also revealed expected revenues and operating income of $364,000 and $104,000, respectively.

Instructions

a. Determine the company's overhead application rate. The rate is based on total costs traceable to client jobs.
b. Compute Hartwell's estimated income for the year as a percentage of costs traceable to client jobs.
c. In January, Hartwell completed a project for the Ohio Medical Group (OMG). The following costs were directly chargeable to OMG:

Consulting staff	$4,500
Office staff	300
Travel	1,100
Other office costs	100

Compute the total billing to OMG.

d. Observe that part of the consulting staff's time is not directly traceable to specific jobs. List several possible underlying reasons.

Series B

P21–B1 Preparation of job cost sheet and journal entries (L.O. 1, 2)

Nycom, Inc., manufactures items that are used in the electronics industry. The company, which uses a job costing system, has two departments: machining and finishing. The machining department applies overhead to products at the rate of $15 per machine hour. Finishing, in contrast, uses an application rate of 250% of direct labor cost.

On March 19, 19X3, Nycom received an order from Sensormatic for 225 photons, model no. 116. Production began immediately, and the order (known as job no. 4155) was completed on March 31. Paperwork supporting the order revealed the following:

DOCUMENT*	DATE	DEPARTMENT	HOURS	AMOUNT
MR 1165	3/19	Machining	—	$5,600
MR 1169	3/21	Machining	—	3,500
TT 1450–52	3/23	Machining	45	400
MUR 46	3/23	Machining	105	—
MR 4330	3/27	Finishing	—	700
TT 1475–76	3/31	Machining	30	300
MUR 47	3/31	Machining	50	—
TT 6608–13	3/31	Finishing	200	2,000

* MR = materials requisition; TT = time ticket; MUR = machine usage report.

Instructions

a. Prepare a job cost sheet for the Sensormatic order as of March 31. Use the following column headings:

	DIRECT MATERIALS		DIRECT LABOR			MACHINE USAGE		FACTORY OVERHEAD
DATE	REQUISITION	AMOUNT	TICKET	HOURS	AMOUNT	REPORT	HOURS	AMOUNT

b. Prepare journal entries to record (1) the issuance of direct materials, (2) direct labor incurred on the order, and (3) the application of factory overhead. All materials requisitions should be combined in one entry, all time tickets in another, and so forth.
c. If company policy is to sell goods at a profit of 80% of total job cost, present the journal entries necessary to recognize completion and sale of the photons.

P21–B2 Basic job costing with journal entries (L.O. 1, 2)

Academy Entertainment makes music videos. The company had two productions in process at the start of 19X3: Barry James ($78,500) and Amy Murphy LIVE ($42,700). The following activity occurred during the first quarter:

1. Costs that are directly traceable to the videos produced amounted to $387,700, subdivided as shown.

Production	Film and Costumes	Actors and Directors	Costume and Set Designers
Barry James	$15,000	$ 35,600	$ 2,900
Amy Murphy LIVE	6,300	20,000	5,700
Malibu Troupe	32,000	75,000	57,300
A Kiss in Time	21,900	54,000	62,000
	$75,200	$184,600	$127,900

2. Overhead included charges for indirect materials used ($5,000), indirect labor ($42,000), and utilities ($14,000).
3. Video production times totaled 450 hours, allocated as follows: Barry James, 40 hours; Amy Murphy LIVE, 65 hours; Malibu Troupe, 150 hours; and A Kiss in Time, 195 hours. Overhead is applied to each production at the rate of $26 per hour.
4. Academy completed Barry James and Malibu Troupe. Barry James was sold on account to a distribution syndicate for $175,000.

A review of the firm's general ledger found accounts entitled Film, Props, and Supplies (i.e., Raw Materials); Videos in Process; Completed Videos; Cost of Videos Sold; and Studio Overhead.

Instructions

a. Prepare journal entries as of March 31 to record the following. (*Note:* Use summary entries where appropriate by combining individual video data.)
   (1) The issuance of film and costumes, and the direct labor incurred.
   (2) The studio overhead incurred during the quarter.
   (3) The application of studio overhead to video production.
   (4) The completion of Barry James and Malibu Troupe, and the sale of Barry James.
b. Determine the videos still in production as of March 31 and calculate the costs incurred to date on the individual projects.
c. Establish a T-account for Videos in Process and determine the account's balance on March 31.

P21–B3 Computations using a job order system (L.O. 1, 2)

Route 65, Inc., employs a job order system. On August 1, 19X3, the company had the following balances in the general ledger: Work in Process, $101,800; Finished Goods, $423,400; and Cost of Goods Sold, $1,237,000. Information about each job produced during the last five months of 19X3 (and related costs incurred during that time) is shown on page 830.

Job no. 425 was the only job in process at year-end. Job no. 422, no. 424, and one job completed earlier in the year (no. 411) were sold during the last quarter at a profit of 40% of cost. Job no. 411 cost $65,000 to manufacture.

Job No.	Work in Process, August 1	Direct Materials Used	Direct Labor Charges
421	$ 63,400	$20,100	$ 3,000
422	38,400	—	19,600
423	—	22,400	24,300
424	—	29,300	8,800
425	—	11,900	17,500
	$101,800	$83,700	$73,200

Route 65 applies overhead daily at the rate of 120% of direct labor cost as labor summaries are posted to job orders. The company uses the calendar year for accounting and reporting purposes.

Instructions

a. Compute the cost of the ending work in process inventory.
b. Compute the total overhead applied to production during the last five months of 19X3.
c. Compute the cost of jobs completed during the last five months of 19X3.
d. Compute 19X3 cost of goods sold.

P21–B4 Job order costing, overhead emphasis (L.O. 1, 2, 3)

Madison Brothers uses a job order system to accumulate manufacturing costs. On December 31, 19X4, the work in process inventory consisted of job no. 176, costed as follows:

Direct materials	$ 39,800
Direct labor	50,000
Applied overhead	60,000
	$149,800

Because of changing plant conditions and labor markets, the cost accounting department calculated a new overhead application rate for use throughout 19X5. Estimated totals for direct labor cost and factory overhead for 19X5 amounted to $700,000 and $910,000, respectively. Actual results follow.

Direct materials used	$ 822,500
Direct labor	710,000
Indirect materials	64,500
Indirect labor	461,900
Factory depreciation	122,700
Factory insurance	10,900
Factory utilities	238,600
	$2,431,100

All jobs were completed and sold by December 31, 19X5, except for job no. 229, which contained direct material costs of $31,400 and direct labor charges of $42,800. This job was still in production and was anticipated to be completed in early January. The company charges any under- or overapplied overhead to Cost of Goods Sold.

Instructions

a. Determine the 19X5 overhead application rate, using direct labor cost as the application base.
b. Determine the total cost of the company's work in process inventory as of December 31, 19X5.
c. Determine the amount of under- or overapplied overhead for the year. Be sure to indicate whether overhead was underapplied or overapplied.
d. Compute the company's cost of goods sold. Madison Brothers had no finished goods inventory on January 1, 19X5.

P21–B5 Flow of costs: Finding unknowns (L.O. 1, 2, 3)

Selected ledger accounts for Ormsby Manufacturing for the year ended December 31, 19X3, follow.

RAW MATERIALS

Balance, 1/1	17,000	84,000
	92,000	

WAGES PAYABLE

	104,000

FACTORY OVERHEAD

Indirect labor	16,000	132,000
Other	120,000	

WORK IN PROCESS

Balance, 1/1	26,000	?
Direct materials	72,000	
Direct labor	?	
Applied overhead	?	

FINISHED GOODS

Balance, 1/1	37,000	?
	286,000	

COST OF GOODS SOLD

?	

The year-end count of completed goods on hand revealed the following:

Item No.	Quantity (Units)	Unit Cost
118	4,500	$5.20
124	6,400	8.40
131	10,100	6.50

Ormsby applies overhead on the basis of direct labor cost.

Instructions

a. Compute the amount of indirect materials used in operations.
b. Compute total direct labor for the period.
c. Determine Ormsby's overhead application rate.
d. Compute the ending work in process balance.
e. Determine total credits to the Finished Goods account.
f. Compute the over- or underapplied overhead.

P21–B6 Job costing in a service business (L.O. 5)

Diego, Hyatt, and Stevens, a prestigious law firm located in San Antonio, uses a job order system to monitor the cost of servicing clientele. The office manager has prepared the following budget for 19X7:

Client billings		$11,520,000
Less: Professional staff costs (85%)	$6,000,000	
Administrative staff costs (75%)	2,000,000	
Computer time (80%)	500,000	
Photocopying (70%)	200,000	
Other office costs (20%)	300,000	9,000,000
Operating income		$ 2,520,000

The numbers in parentheses indicate the percentage of cost that is directly traceable to client jobs. The remaining, nontraceable portion is charged to clients by using a predetermined overhead application rate. The office manager feels that total direct cost is the most appropriate overhead application base.

In March, the firm completed work on a suit for Picante Foods. The following costs were directly chargeable to Picante:

Professional staff	$25,000
Administrative staff	6,400
Computer time	2,500
Photocopying	3,700
Other office costs	400

Instructions

a. Determine the firm's total budgeted traceable and nontraceable costs and the overhead application rate.
b. Calculate the firm's estimated income for the year as a percentage of traceable costs.
c. Compute the total cost of the Picante job and the amount that Diego, Hyatt, and Stevens would bill the client.
d. The office manager can acquire new software that would allow the firm to increase the percentage of direct (as opposed to indirect) costs. Briefly explain why Diego, Hyatt, and Stevens would be interested in this software.

EXPANDING YOUR HORIZONS

EYH21–1 Analysis of direct labor as an application base (L.O. 4)

Many surveys have shown that direct labor is the most widely used overhead application base. Even companies that are heavily automated continue to employ this base as a way to cost their products.

Instructions

Locate a recent article that focuses on the problems of using direct labor as an application base in an automated production environment. Prepare a one page summary of your findings.

EYH21–2 Junior college/university indirect cost allocation (L.O. 5)

Junior colleges and universities are nonprofit, service enterprises. Such enterprises incur many indirect (overhead) costs that are often allocated to specific academic schools, programs, and departments. These costs would include the monies expended for security, maintenance, the registrar's office, and the president's office.

Instructions

Form a group of five students and make an appointment to visit an administrator on your campus (dean, assistant dean, associate dean, department chair, or program director). Determine how indirect cost allocations are made and how much (or what percentage) is charged against the administrator's budget for these amounts. Does the administrator have any complaints about the current allocation system? Briefly describe, and be prepared to report your findings to the class.

EYH21–3 "Hidden" overhead and income (L.O. 5)

Repair shops charge their customers only for parts and labor. Having read this chapter, you can see that this procedure would result in a loss, as the shop would fail to cover its overhead costs. The charges to customers for parts and labor actually include "add-ons" that go to cover overhead and provide a profit.

Instructions

Form a team with three other students and visit two different types of repair shops (e.g., computer, appliance, automobile, and so forth). After explaining the purpose of your visit to the manager, determine the shop's hourly charge for direct labor versus the average hourly wage actually paid to mechanics. How much of the "add-on" is for overhead and how much is for profit? Also determine the shop's policy with respect to a markup on parts. Be prepared to report your findings to the class.

EYH21–4 Overhead application and cost drivers (L.O. 2, 4)

Cost Management Systems, Inc., provides consulting services to businesses throughout California, Washington, and Oregon. Victor Santos has applied for an entry-level position with the firm and, during the interview process, was given an aptitude test that dealt with overhead allocation (i.e., application). The test involved an analysis of overhead application bases in a variety of settings (products, departments, and divisions) by means of the five cases that follow.

- *Case A*—The Drury Manufacturing Company has extensive automated facilities, with many machines and robots controlled by computers. The firm applies factory overhead to products on the basis of direct labor cost.
- *Case B*—Amber Company's corporate headquarters is occupied by five divisions. The firm's building maintenance cost is allocated (charged) to the five divisions on the basis of the square footage occupied by each division.

- *Case C*—Rent All rents a wide variety of equipment, including bulldozers, servingware for parties, small garden and workshop tools, and so forth. The servingware and small tools divisions generate a large number of rentals for short periods of time (e.g., a few days and/or hours). In contrast, the construction equipment division has fewer rentals, but the rentals produce more revenue and cover a longer period of time. The divisions vary greatly in terms of profitability and operating problems. Rent All allocates company administrative cost on the basis of the number of rental invoices written in each division.
- *Case D*—Rent All (from Case C) has a maintenance and repair department that furnishes repair services to the company's divisions. Periodically, the department totals all maintenance costs, including major parts, and divides by the total service calls made. The result is the cost per service call. Each division is then charged on the basis of the number of service calls requested during the period.
- *Case E*—Crossroads Company operates a cafeteria for the convenience of its personnel. The cafeteria offers meals at extremely low prices and generates a loss. The loss is allocated to the firm's six departments on the basis of the number of employees in each department.

Instructions

Recall that in overhead allocation, the application base selected should have a strong bearing on the amount of overhead incurred. Consider the allocation bases and procedures used in the five cases presented. Assume the role of Victor Santos and briefly evaluate whether the allocation described is acceptable or could be improved.

COMMUNICATION OF ACCOUNTING INFORMATION

CAI21–1 The employee evaluation (L.O. 1)

Communication Principle: Many companies use written employee evaluations to provide feedback about on-the-job performance. These evaluations identify problem areas and clearly instruct the employee as to what is expected.

Depending on the circumstances, it is generally better to enhance (but not dilute or confuse) the communication with something positive. For example, managers may note an employee's strengths, point out the contribution of the employee's actions to the overall organization, and so forth before focusing on the problem areas.

Generally speaking, a manager's remarks should be carefully packaged, as the goal is to move the organization forward, not backward. Managers who are successful and well respected by their peers have learned that everyone responds differently to criticism. These managers also know that "it's not what you say but how you say it."

■ ■ ■ ■ ■ ■ ■ ■

Richard Weglin acquired a medium-size manufacturing business several years ago. The company produces a quality product but has never been very profitable. Weglin's goal in buying the business was to institute cost controls, which have always been lacking, and to guide the company toward becoming a leader in its field. Thus far, things are going according to plan, and a job cost system is working well.

Weglin's best employee is Randall Hughes, a machinist who makes a critical precision part used in the company's product. Hughes is a model employee in almost every way. His workmanship is unsurpassed, and other employees respect and treat him as their role model. Unfortunately, though, there is a problem. Hughes has been with the firm for many years, long before the present job cost system was implemented. Despite being reminded over the years, he continually forgets to record the time spent on each job. In discussing this problem, Hughes has said:

- "Did I do that again? I guess old habits are hard to break."
- "These procedures are for the young guys. I know exactly how long it should take me to make each part."
- "You know I stay busy—what are you worried about?"
- "Just write something down for me; it will all work out in the end."

Weglin, in complete frustration, has decided to approach Hughes about this problem through a written employee evaluation.

Instructions

Assume the role of Weglin and prepare the evaluation. Assume that Hughes does not understand the operation and importance of a sound job cost system.

Answers to Chapter Quiz

1. c
2. b
3. a
4. c [Application rate = 90% ($180,000 ÷ $200,000); applied overhead = $210,000 × 0.90 = $189,000; $189,000 − $185,000 = $4,000 overapplied]
5. d

22
Process Costing, Activity-Based Costing, and Just-in-Time Production

Learning Objectives

After studying this chapter, you should be able to:

1. Explain the basic features that are associated with a process cost accounting system.

2. Define and calculate equivalent units of production.

3. Identify the factors that affect the computation of equivalent units.

4. Allocate production costs between completed units and units still in process.

5. Distinguish between conventional and activity-based costing systems and use the latter to compute product costs.

6. Describe the basic features associated with a just-in-time production system.

7. (Appendix) Use the weighted-average process costing method to calculate the cost of goods completed and ending work in process inventory.

The subject matter content in this chapter is somewhat varied, as George Faris of Banner Advertising so correctly observed. During our initial planning session, George quickly focused on the pages that discuss activity-based costing (ABC). He had never heard of ABC; however, when we overviewed the concept, he indicated that much of the material could be used by Banner.

As George explained, "Every client is different, especially with respect to the activities that we perform in approving the final artwork to be painted on a billboard. Some clients need to see only one or two rounds of samples before settling on something they really like. With others you can make up to ten separate visits, and each visit requires travel time, not to mention the art development and redesign time for the individual presentations."

Banner's current accounting system does not allow George to identify the hours (and money) spent on the specific steps of the art approval process. But, as he observed, "I know we are spending more than it is worth to please certain clients. I guess we should consider improving our accounting system to allow cost accumulation by activity and the identification of unprofitable customers."

The activity-based concepts discussed in the last part of this chapter are designed to help companies deal with the issues that George has raised. ABC is a fairly recent accounting innovation and is one of several contemporary topics introduced over the next 15+ pages. Other such topics include just-in-time production and total quality management (TQM).

Our presentation begins by continuing and extending the topic of cost accumulation systems. As you saw in Chapter 21, many companies accumulate production costs (and service costs as well) by use of a job order system. These systems are often employed by businesses such as custom-home builders, furniture manufacturers, and print shops, all of which typically operate in an environment that is subdivided into specific jobs or orders.

There are, as you can well imagine, numerous applications that lack the job order "orientation." Picture the manufacture of paint, for example, where finished goods (e.g., one-gallon cans) continually roll off a production line. The manufacturing plant does not produce a batch of paint for the Decorating Den (say, job no. 376), then stop, and later resume operation to process the goods needed by Discount City (job no. 377). Manufacturing is ongoing and continuous; thus, product costing by job or order becomes difficult, if not impossible.

In these situations, accountants turn to a **process costing system** to accumulate costs. Process costing systems are often employed in steel, petroleum, soft drink, chemical, and flour production as well as in many assembly types of industries (e.g., appliances and bicycles).

PROCESS COSTING

> **1** Explain the basic features that are associated with a process cost accounting system.

To a great extent, process costing systems operate in much the same manner as job order systems. Both systems are established to accumulate costs for a business and both employ the same accounts. These accounts include Raw Materials, Work in Process, Finished Goods, Cost of Goods Sold, and Factory Overhead—all introduced earlier in the text. Furthermore, the flow of costs through these accounts is essentially the same no matter what system is used. The issuance of direct materials to production, for instance, would be recorded under process costing by a debit to Work in Process and a credit to Raw Materials; the cost of completed units is debited to Finished Goods and credited to Work in Process; and so forth. Should you need a refresher of production cost flows, we refer you to pages 799 through 807.

HOW PROCESS COSTING DIFFERS FROM JOB COSTING

There are three basic differences between job order and process cost accounting, all of which arise because of the nature of a continuous manufacturing environment. Such environments normally result in the manufacture of mass-produced, homogeneous goods. In other words, the units are virtually identical, all having received the same amounts of direct material, direct labor, and factory overhead through the process.

Since activities cannot be subdivided by job and there is really no need to do so, costs under a process system are accumulated by *process or department* for a *specified period of time* (e.g., one month). Often a process and department are synonymous—the blending process takes place in the blending department, the assembly process in the assembly department, and so on. Then, since all units are identical, equal costs are assigned to each unit produced during the period.

A second difference between the systems arises because in many manufacturing applications, several steps (i.e., processes) are required to complete a product. In our earlier paint illustration, for instance, various chemicals and colorings are combined in the mixing department. Next, the filling department pours the paint into cans, adds lids, and passes the cans along to a subsequent packaging operation. Here, labels are attached and the containers packed four to a case. As a final step, the cases are transferred to a finished goods warehouse.

This sequence of events is depicted in the middle of Exhibit 22–1, which shows the basic differences between job order costing and process cost accounting. Notice that the separate operation and departmental orientation requires a separate Work in Process account for each major manufacturing activity. Direct materials and direct labor, costs easily traced to production, are charged to the department where consumed or incurred. Factory overhead is then applied by using an overhead application rate.

The lack of cost accumulation by job or order does away with the use of job cost sheets. The sheets are replaced by *production cost reports*—the third basic difference between the two systems. These reports, which document the units and costs that flow through a manufacturing department, will be shown later in the chapter.

MEASURING PRODUCTION VOLUME

Earlier in the discussion we noted that process costing systems accumulate departmental costs *for a period of time*. Most businesses do not complete all production by the period's end; some units typically remain in process.

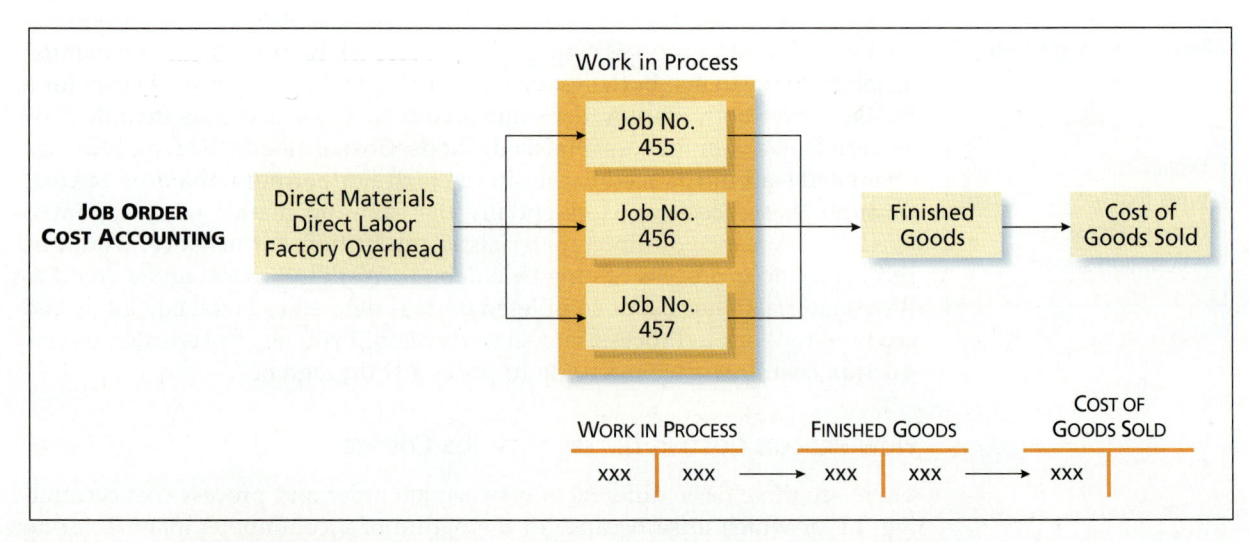

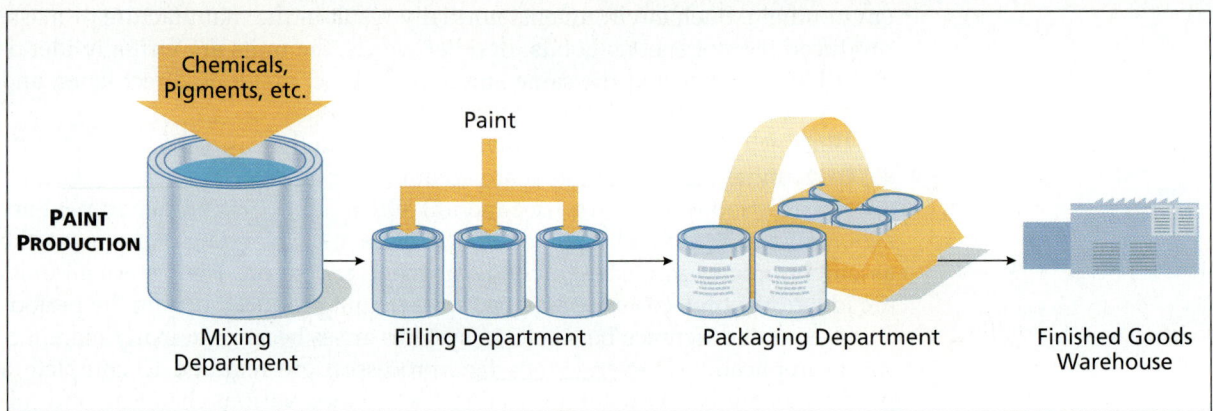

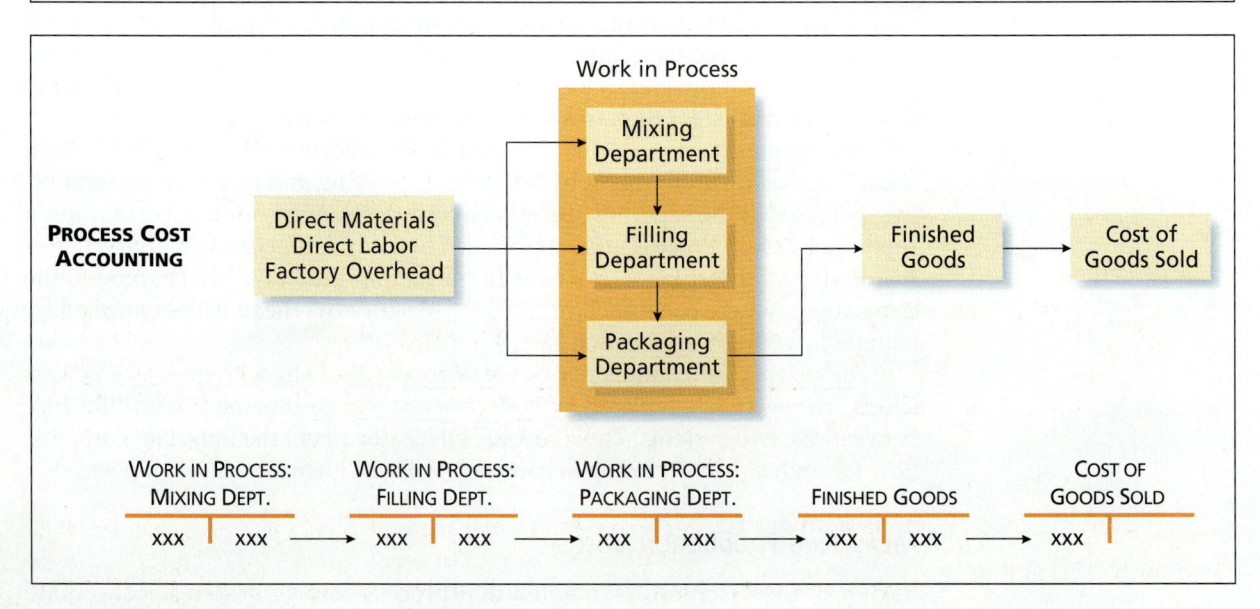

EXHIBIT 22–1
Job Order Costing Versus Process Cost Accounting

As the following example reveals, in-process inventories create a measurement problem when calculating the manufacturing costs assignable to a company's goods.

The Paige Corporation, which uses a process cost system, began operations on January 2 of the current year. The following information pertains to the first month of activity:

MANUFACTURING COSTS		PRODUCTION	
Direct materials used	$ 90,000	Units completed	80,000
Direct labor	50,000	Units in process,	
Applied factory overhead*	60,000	¼ complete	80,000
Total manufacturing costs	$200,000		

* 120% of direct labor cost.

Paige has a $200,000 cost pool that must be split between 80,000 completed units and 80,000 units in process, as shown by the accompanying diagram:

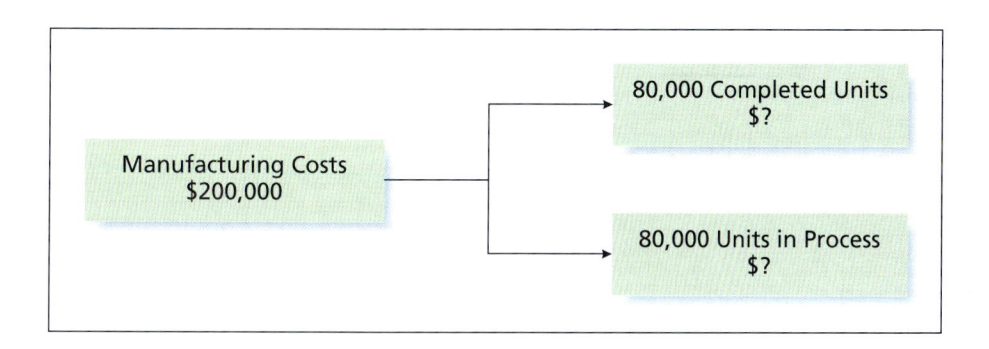

Manufacturing Costs $200,000 → 80,000 Completed Units $?

Manufacturing Costs $200,000 → 80,000 Units in Process $?

In more familiar terms, the cost pool is located in the Work in Process account at the end of January. To ensure that direct materials, direct labor, and factory overhead follow the flow of production, a portion of the $200,000 must be removed from this account and transferred to Finished Goods.

Some individuals would say that Work in Process should be credited for $100,000 (i.e., one-half of the cost pool) because 50% of Paige's total production is completed. Stated differently, since the average cost per unit is $1.25 ($200,000 ÷ 160,000 units), $100,000 (80,000 completed units × $1.25) should be transferred to the Finished Goods account. Although the preceding computation is straightforward, it is, at the same time, logically unsound. We cannot add 80,000 completed units to 80,000 units in process. It's like adding apples and oranges—a meaningless total is generated.

Equivalent Units. To arrive at a proper measure of performance, accountants use a base known as equivalent units. An *equivalent unit* is a physical unit stated in terms of a finished unit. For example, if a company started work on 9 physical units (e.g., cars, tons, gallons) and the units are 2/3 complete at the end of the period,[1] 6 equivalent units (9 × 2/3) have been produced. It is important

---
[1] The 2/3 figure refers to an average stage of completion in a continuous process.

> **2**
> Define and calculate equivalent units of production.

to note that *none* of these units are currently completed—all are still in process. The company has simply done the work *equivalent* to manufacturing six finished goods (see Exhibit 22–2).

Returning to the Paige Corporation example, 100,000 equivalent units of production took place in January:

	Physical Units		% of Work Completed During January		Equivalent Units
Units completed	80,000	×	100%	=	80,000
Units in process, 1/4 complete	80,000	×	25%	=	20,000
					100,000

Because operations commenced at the beginning of the year, the 80,000 units completed were all started in January. Consequently, 100% of the work on these goods occurred during the month.

Factors That Affect Equivalent Production

> **3** Identify the factors that affect the computation of equivalent units.

Having introduced the concept of equivalent units, we must now become a bit more detailed. Three factors must be considered in all equivalent-unit computations:

- The presence of a beginning work in process inventory
- The introduction of production costs at different points in the manufacturing process
- The method of process costing used

Beginning Work in Process Inventory. If a firm has a beginning work in process inventory, the goods must be studied to determine the work performed

Exhibit 22–2
The Concept of Equivalent Units

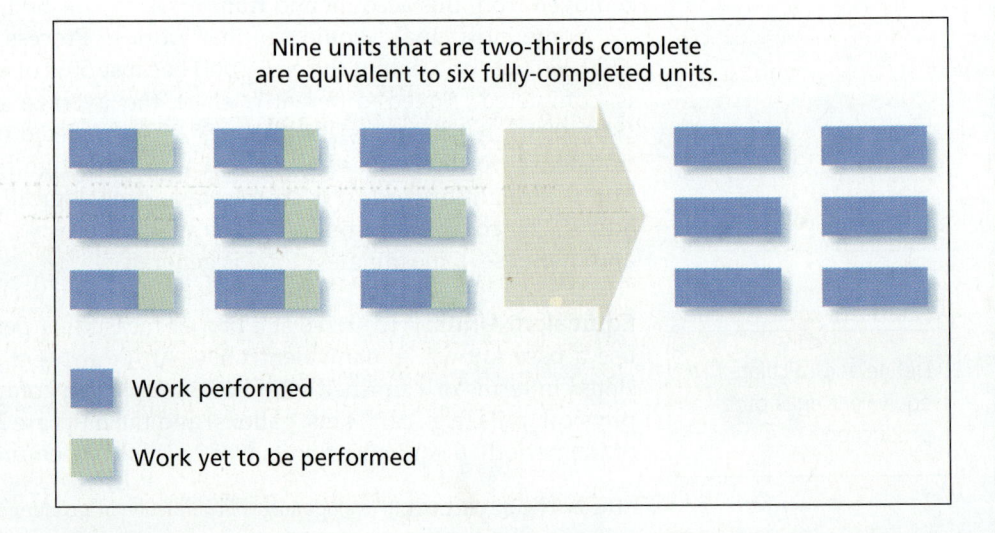

Nine units that are two-thirds complete are equivalent to six fully-completed units.

■ Work performed
■ Work yet to be performed

in prior periods. Assume, for instance, that at the start of May a company has 500 units in process that are three-fifths complete. To finish the goods during the current accounting period (i.e., May), 200 equivalent units of production are needed (500 × ⅖ = 200). *Equivalent-unit calculations focus on the work performed during the present period* because of the need to figure the current unit cost of manufacturing.

Cost Incurrence in the Manufacturing Process. A second point to consider is that the three factors of production (direct materials, direct labor, and factory overhead) are generally introduced in different ways throughout manufacturing. Labor and overhead, collectively known as conversion cost, are often incurred uniformly through the process.[2] Direct materials, however, can be introduced at different stages of production. In some products, for example, all materials enter manufacturing at the beginning. With other goods, materials are introduced at specific points after manufacturing has commenced (e.g., a part may be added at the 50% stage of completion, the product may be encased in protective packaging at the end of the process, and so forth).

The uniform introduction of conversion cost and the introduction of materials at specified points require the calculation of separate equivalent-unit figures. For example, assume that Sparks Company uses a process cost system. At the beginning of July, the firm had a work in process inventory of 3,000 units, 30% complete. During July, the beginning work in process was completed along with 7,500 other units that had entered production. Finally, on July 31 the factory supervisor determined that the ending work in process totaled 5,000 units, 20% complete. All materials are introduced at the start of manufacturing, and labor and overhead are incurred uniformly throughout the process. The equivalent units for July are calculated as follows:

	PHYSICAL UNITS	EQUIVALENT UNITS MATERIALS	CONVERSION
Completed			
Beginning work in process	3,000	—	2,100
Units started and completed	7,500	7,500	7,500
Ending work in process	5,000	5,000	1,000
	15,500	12,500	10,600

To explain, the beginning work in process inventory received no additional material. Remember, these units were begun last period, and all material is introduced at the start of production. To complete the beginning inventory, 70% of the work was performed in July, resulting in 2,100 (3,000 × 0.70) equivalent conversion units. Next, observe that 7,500 units were started and completed. Thus, all material for these units was introduced during the current month along with 100% of the processing, giving rise to 7,500 equivalent units of materials and conversion. Finally, we assume that the ending work in process was started in July, resulting in the introduction of 5,000 equivalent units of material. Because the ending inventory is only 20% complete, Sparks did 1,000 (5,000 × 0.20) equivalent units of conversion. These facts are depicted graphically in Exhibit 22–3.

---

[2] These two costs are needed to *convert* raw material into finished products.

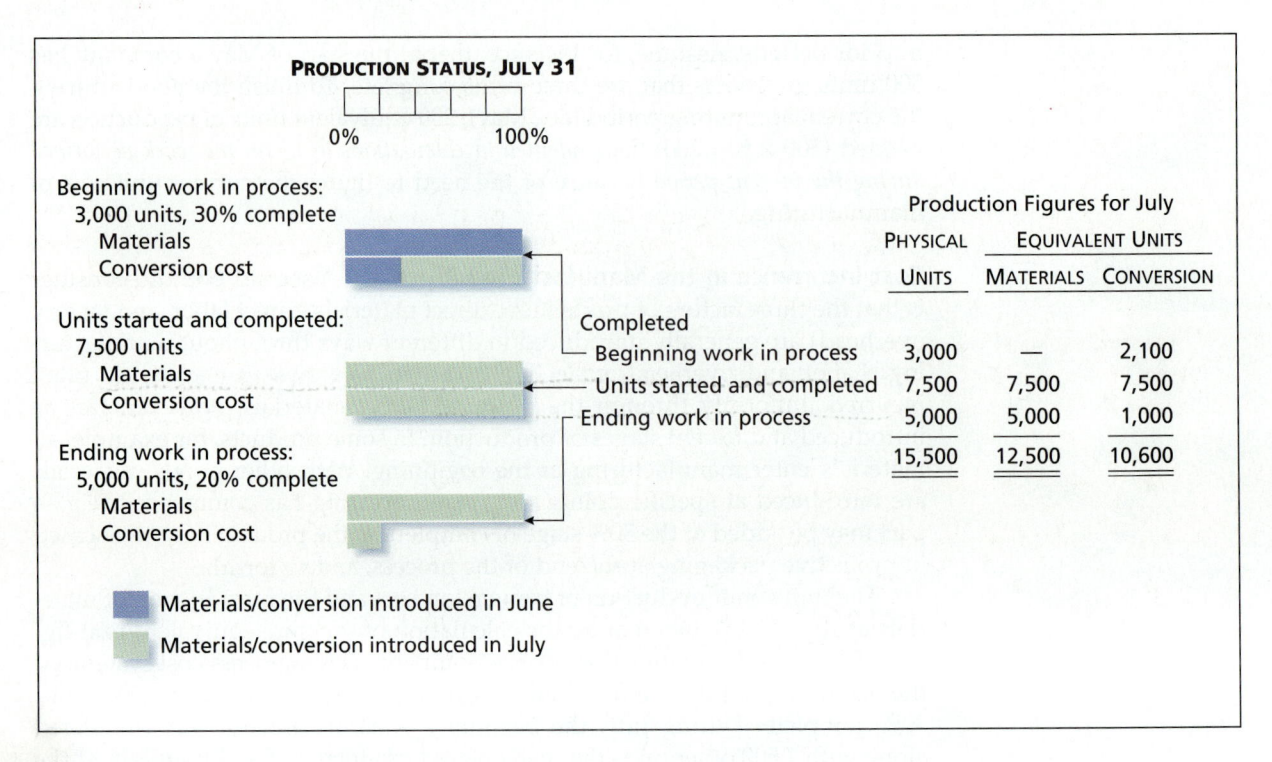

Exhibit 22–3
Computation of Equivalent Units

PRODUCTION STATUS, JULY 31

0% — 100%

Beginning work in process:
3,000 units, 30% complete
- Materials
- Conversion cost

Units started and completed:
7,500 units
- Materials
- Conversion cost

Ending work in process:
5,000 units, 20% complete
- Materials
- Conversion cost

■ Materials/conversion introduced in June
■ Materials/conversion introduced in July

Production Figures for July

	PHYSICAL UNITS	EQUIVALENT UNITS MATERIALS	CONVERSION
Completed			
Beginning work in process	3,000	—	2,100
Units started and completed	7,500	7,500	7,500
Ending work in process	5,000	5,000	1,000
	15,500	12,500	10,600

Process Costing Method. The third issue to address in the computation of equivalent units is the process costing method used by the firm. Two approaches are available: FIFO and weighted average.

Under the **FIFO method,** the beginning work in process inventory is assumed to be the first batch of goods completed (i.e., the first-in are the first-out). This batch is therefore treated as being separate and distinct from those units that are started and completed during the period. In addition, under the FIFO method, any work performed on the beginning work in process inventory in the previous accounting period must be considered when calculating the current period's equivalent units. These features are not new; they were both discussed and illustrated in the just-concluded Sparks Company example.

The remainder of our presentation will use the FIFO process costing approach. The weighted-average method, which typically results in different equivalent-unit figures, is shown in an appendix to this chapter.

COMPREHENSIVE EXAMPLE

❹ Allocate production costs between completed units and units still in process.

To bring together a number of the concepts discussed thus far, we will study the manufacturing operations of Berloff, Inc. The following information pertains to September:

- Beginning work in process inventory: 4,000 units, 75% complete; cost, $21,900
- Number of units started during September: 13,000

- Total units completed: 11,000
- Ending work in process inventory: 6,000 units, 40% complete
- September manufacturing costs: direct materials used, $32,500; conversion cost, $48,880

All materials are introduced at the start of the process, and conversion costs are incurred uniformly throughout manufacturing. The following approach is suggested to calculate the cost of goods completed during September and the cost of the ending work in process inventory.

Step 1: Analyze the Physical Flow. Berloff must trace the units through the manufacturing process. On the basis of the information presented, the proper physical flow is as follows:

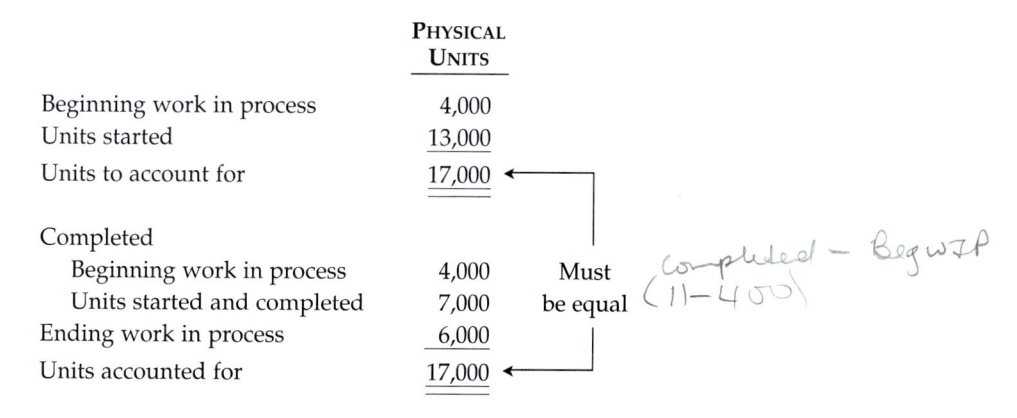

	PHYSICAL UNITS	
Beginning work in process	4,000	
Units started	13,000	
Units to account for	17,000	
Completed		
Beginning work in process	4,000	Must
Units started and completed	7,000	be equal
Ending work in process	6,000	
Units accounted for	17,000	

[handwritten annotation: Completed − Beg WIP (11−4000)]

The production manager has 17,000 units to account for during the month: the beginning work in process and the units started in September.

Assuming no spoilage, these units have either been completed by the company's manufacturing activities or are still in production at month-end. As you can see, the completed goods are really composed of two separate batches: the units in process on September 1 and an additional 7,000 units that were started and completed during the period. The latter batch is obtained by subtracting the beginning work in process from the total finished units manufactured (11,000 − 4,000 = 7,000).

Step 2: Compute Equivalent Units. Once the physical flow is determined, September (i.e., current) production is then translated into equivalent units. Because materials are introduced at the start of the process, and labor and overhead are incurred evenly, the figures presented in Exhibit 22–4 are obtained (see the numbers in color type).

Step 3: Compute Equivalent-Unit Costs. The cost per equivalent unit is calculated by dividing production costs by the equivalent units computed in Step 2. Just as the equivalent production figures are calculated for September activity, so, too, are the unit costs. The necessary procedures appear below the exhibit on page 846.

EXHIBIT 22–4
Equivalent Production Figures for Berloff, Inc.

	PHYSICAL UNITS		
Beginning work in process	4,000		
Units started	13,000		
Units to account for	17,000		

			EQUIVALENT UNITS	
			MATERIALS	CONVERSION
Completed				
Beginning work in process*	4,000		—	1,000
Units started and completed†	7,000		7,000	7,000
Ending work in process‡	6,000		6,000	2,400
Units accounted for	17,000		13,000	10,400

* All materials were added during August; 25% of the conversion was performed in September.
† All materials and conversion were introduced during September.
‡ Units were started in September; all materials were introduced plus 40% of the conversion.

COSTS	TOTAL	MATERIALS	CONVERSION
Beginning work in process	$ 21,900	$ —	$ —
Current	81,380	32,500	48,880
Total cost to account for	$103,280	$32,500	$48,880
Equivalent units*		÷13,000	÷10,400
Cost per equivalent unit		$2.50	$4.70

* From Step 2.

ETHICS ISSUE

The controller of Webcore, Inc., does not want to take the time to study the stage of completion of the ending work in process inventory. "It's a trivial exercise for our company because production is steady. Let's forget about equivalent-unit calculations; who cares if the work in process valuation is slightly in error? Just assume the goods are 50% complete." Comment.

Note that the cost of the beginning work in process inventory ($21,900) is disregarded in unit-cost computations—a logical procedure because this amount represents work performed in the previous period. The production manager, however, is still held accountable for the related expenditures, requiring that the $21,900 figure be reflected in the $103,280 total.

Step 4: Cost Assignment. Berloff's cost pool of $103,280 must now be assigned to the goods completed during the period and the ending work in process inventory. This assignment is accomplished by multiplying the cost per equivalent unit by the proper number of equivalent units. As shown in Exhibit 22–5, the cost of goods completed is $77,000, and the ending work in process is $26,280.

Because the prior period cost of $21,900 was not considered when computing equivalent-unit figures, it is attached entirely to the beginning work in process inventory. That is, no prior period cost is allocated to either the units started and completed or the partially completed production at the end of the period. Observe that the total cost accounted for ($103,280) agrees with the total cost to account for (as shown in Step 3).

Production Cost Report. Companies that use a process costing system document the period's manufacturing activity on a production cost report. The

EXHIBIT 22–5
Cost Assignment of Berloff, Inc.

	EQUIVALENT UNITS	
	MATERIALS	CONVERSION
Completed		
Beginning work in process	—	1,000
Units started and completed	7,000	7,000
Ending work in process	6,000	2,400
Units accounted for	13,000	10,400

Completed			
Beginning work in process			
Prior period cost		$21,900	
Conversion cost: 1,000 × $4.70		4,700	$ 26,600
Units started and completed			
Materials: 7,000 × $2.50		$17,500	
Conversion cost: 7,000 × $4.70		32,900	50,400
Total cost of completed goods			$ 77,000
Ending work in process			
Materials: 6,000 × $2.50		$15,000	
Conversion cost: 2,400 × $4.70		11,280	26,280
Total cost accounted for			$103,280

report is a summary of the units and costs that have passed through a department. In actuality, it is the combined result of Steps 1–4 just discussed. Briefly review these steps and then focus on Exhibit 22–6—the end product of the entire process.

The Work in Process Account. The production cost report is really a disclosure mechanism for various amounts contained in the general ledger. As evidence, we present Berloff's Work in Process account:

WORK IN PROCESS	
Beginning balance	21,900
Materials	32,500
Conversion	48,880
	103,280

The balance of $103,280 coincides with the costs that Berloff's production manager had to account for during the period. Because the cost of completed units totals $77,000, the following journal entry is needed on September 30:

Finished Goods	77,000	
Work in Process		77,000
To transfer the cost of completed units to finished goods.		

This entry, identical to that shown in Chapter 21 for a job order system, makes the Work in Process account consistent with the figures presented on the production cost report.

ACTIVITY-BASED COSTING

In recent years, several significant changes have occurred in the ways that companies determine the cost of their products. These changes are due, in part, to increased competition and a feeling that the costs derived by using conventional

BERLOFF, INC.
Production Cost Report
For the Month Ended September 30, 19XX

	PHYSICAL UNITS		EQUIVALENT UNITS	
			MATERIALS	CONVERSION
Beginning work in process	4,000			
Units started	13,000			
Units to account for	17,000			
Completed				
Beginning work in process	4,000		—	1,000
Units started and completed	7,000		7,000	7,000
Ending work in process	6,000		6,000	2,400
Units accounted for	17,000		13,000	10,400

COSTS		TOTAL		
Beginning work in process		$ 21,900	$ —	$ —
Current		81,380	32,500	48,880
Total cost to account for		$103,280	$32,500	$48,880
Equivalent units			÷13,000	÷10,400
Cost per equivalent unit			$2.50	$4.70

COST ASSIGNMENT

Completed			
Beginning work in process			
Prior period cost	$21,900		
Conversion cost: 1,000 × $4.70	4,700	$ 26,600	
Units started and completed			
Materials: 7,000 × $2.50	$17,500		
Conversion cost: 7,000 × $4.70	32,900	50,400	
Total cost of completed goods		$ 77,000	
Ending work in process			
Materials: 6,000 × $2.50	$15,000		
Conversion cost: 2,400 × $4.70	11,280	26,280	
Total cost accounted for		$103,280	

STEP 1, STEP 2, STEP 3, STEP 4

EXHIBIT 22–6
Production Cost Report: FIFO

procedures were highly inaccurate. Products that consumed few manufacturing resources were often charged with a high amount of cost, and vice versa. Unfortunately, incorrect costs may have significant ramifications for a firm when it comes to price setting and decision making. Because prices are often based on cost, product overcosting may result in a loss of sales since the affected

> **5**
> Distinguish between conventional and activity-based costing systems and use the latter to compute product costs.

firm cannot compete against companies that sell cheaper goods. Undercosting, in contrast, may mislead a business into boosting volume of what is actually an unprofitable product. The greater the activity, the bigger the negative impact on bottom-line income.

THE PROBLEM OF AVERAGING

The problem of over- and undercosted products often arises because of the averaging that occurs in many accounting procedures. To illustrate, let us focus on a straightforward nonmanufacturing example. Assume that the Gibsons, Hartleys, Mortons, and Weavers have developed close ties over the years through various social gatherings. On a weekly basis, each couple has paid $10 into a "pool" that will be used for a dream vacation in Hawaii. The total contributions now stand at $14,000. Suppose the couples take the vacation and their expenditures total exactly $14,000, subdivided as follows:

	GIBSONS	HARTLEYS	MORTONS	WEAVERS
Airfare	$1,400	$1,400	$1,400	$1,400
Condominium*	600	800	900	700
Rental car	100	200	150	100
Meals	300	500	600	400
Tours	200	400	500	300
Miscellaneous	300	400	550	400
Total	$2,900	$3,700	$4,100	$3,300

* Varies with the number of bedrooms and view.

Friendships aside, when the pool is used to pay the preceding outlays, the Gibsons and Weavers would no doubt object. Each of these couples put in $3,500 ($14,000 ÷ 4) and spent less than they contributed. If we assume the pool's funds are divided equally, the Gibsons and Weavers would have subsidized the "good times" of the Hartleys and Mortons. The end result of the averaging procedure follows.

	GIBSONS	HARTLEYS	MORTONS	WEAVERS
Actual cost (i.e., amount paid)	$3,500	$3,500	$3,500	$3,500
Trip expenditures	2,900	3,700	4,100	3,300
Over-/undercosted	Over	Under	Under	Over

As these figures indicate, the use of averages will over- or undercost each couple's trip. The Gibsons, for example, *actually paid* $3,500, but their expenditures totaled only $2,900. Their true cost will exceed their outlays in Hawaii by $600, resulting in an "overcosted" vacation. The situation is reversed for the Hartleys and Mortons, whose pool contributions (i.e., costs) were less than the total they paid for food, lodging, airfare, and other items.

Extending the Concept to a Business

This simplified example has shown the problems encountered when costs are averaged. These same problems occur in business organizations, particularly in entities that have widely varying departments and activities. Consider the graphic that appears in Exhibit 22–7. Here we depict a manufacturing company that is composed of four departments: painting, machining, assembly, and finishing. Each department, in turn, performs various activities. The machining department, for instance, is involved with production run setups, material handling, processing, inspection, and rework of defective units.

Suppose our focus is on factory overhead. To improve accuracy, overhead costs are accumulated in each department rather than tallied for the company as a whole and spread (i.e., averaged) among the four units. This procedure would be akin to the Gibsons, Hartleys, Mortons, and Weavers abandoning the pool concept and paying solely for their own expenditures. When the time comes to figure product costs, each department is now free to select an application base that best drives the department's overhead incurrence. Machining might use machine hours, assembly might use labor hours, and so forth.

Although this procedure seems logical, it may contain an inherent deficiency. Just as work performed and overhead incurrence vary widely among departments, activities may vary widely *within* a department. The use of machine hours by the machining operation appears reasonable at first glance. Consider, however, that some of the department's activities (e.g., setup and inspection) bear little relation to the number of hours processed. Also, some products may be manufactured in long production runs of many units and require few setups and inspections. Others may have the opposite attributes: small production runs and constant testing. The use of machine hours in this case (1) is an inappropriate cost driver and (2) fails to discriminate between the high-cost/low-cost good. To solve these problems, many companies are turning to a technique known as activity-based costing (ABC).

Exhibit 22–7
Organization of a Manufacturing Company

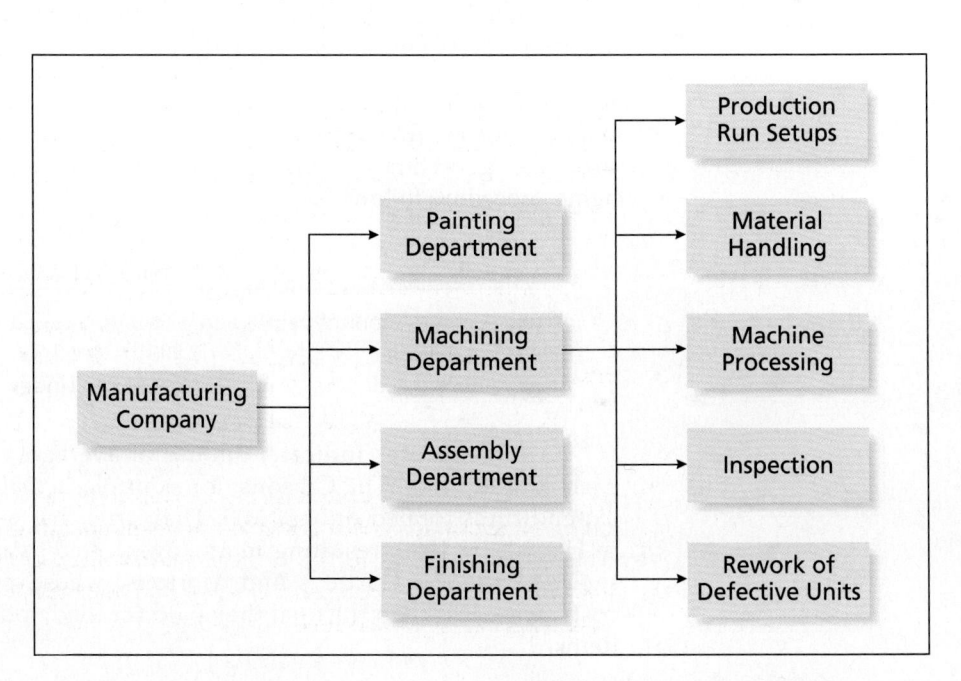

THE NATURE OF ABC

Activity-based costing (ABC) involves dividing a department into specific activities and then selecting an application base (cost driver) for each activity. To illustrate the related procedures, we will focus on the machining department of Superior Metal Works. The firm, which uses a conventional accounting system, applies overhead to its two products (Standard and Deluxe) on the basis of machine hours. The following data are available:

- Estimated departmental overhead for the period: $500,000
- Machine processing time per unit: 8 hours
- Expected production volume of each product: 625 units

Superior calculated an overhead application rate of $50 per machine hour in the manner shown.

$$\text{Overhead Application Rate} = \frac{\text{Estimated Machining Overhead}}{\text{Estimated Machine Hours}}$$

$$= \frac{\$500,000}{10,000 \text{ hours}^*}$$

$$= \$50 \text{ per machine hour}$$

* (625 units of Standard × 8 hours) + (625 units of Deluxe × 8 hours).

On the basis of the information presented, Superior would charge $400 of overhead ($50 per hour × 8 hours) to both Standard and Deluxe.

Suppose a closer look at the company's machining department found three different activities being performed: setup, machine processing, and inspection. In addition, we now learn that the Standard model is produced in several large runs and requires minimal inspection to achieve quality standards. With the Deluxe model, manufacturing runs are small and quality is assured through a series of detailed performance tests. If Superior decides to use ABC, the company would identify cost drivers for its activities and then develop individual activity application rates. The necessary procedures follow.

	SETUP	MACHINE PROCESSING	INSPECTION
Cost driver	Number of setups	Machine hours (MH)	Inspection hours (IH)
Activity cost	$150,000	$300,000	$50,000
Driver volume	10	10,000	2,000
Application rate	$15,000 per setup	$30 per MH	$25 per IH

The amounts used in these calculations are yearly estimates, with the result being an estimated cost divided by an estimated application base (cost driver). The volume figures for each base are obtained by summing the individual activity of both Standard and Deluxe. The accompanying table shows the costs computed for both products.

	STANDARD		DELUXE	
	DRIVER VOLUME	COST	DRIVER VOLUME	COST
Setups at $15,000	2	$ 30,000	8	$120,000
Machine processing at $30 per machine hour	5,000	150,000	5,000	150,000
Inspection at $25 per inspection hour	500	12,500	1,500	37,500
Total		$192,500		$307,500

When each of these figures is expressed on a per-unit basis, the results are rather startling when compared with those obtained by using conventional accounting:

	STANDARD	DELUXE
Conventional accounting	$400	$400
Activity-based costing*	308	492

* $192,500 ÷ 625 units = $308; $307,500 ÷ 625 units = $492.

You can see that by averaging all departmental activities together and using a base that failed to discriminate between the activities performed, the Standard model was penalized. That is, it was charged with $400 of cost when a better estimate would have been only $308. The situation is reversed for the Deluxe model.

As noted earlier in the discussion, incorrect cost figures can lead to incorrect decisions on the part of management. Suppose, for example, that direct material and direct labor costs on the Deluxe model were $200, raising total conventional product costs to $600 ($200 + $400). Assume further that the Deluxe selling price had been set at $660. ABC would reveal that instead of making $60 profit on every unit sold, Superior was really losing $32 [$660 − ($200 + $492)]. It is evident that any attempts to boost sales would actually have been detrimental to the firm.

THE PROBLEMS AND BENEFITS OF ABC

An overview of our illustration will show that the procedures related to ABC are definitely more involved than those followed with conventional systems. Rather than just one cost driver, the system requires use of multiple cost drivers. Multiple cost drivers give rise to additional computations and record-keeping chores. Fortunately, computer-controlled machines, scanning systems, and software accumulate much of the needed information automatically, thus eliminating potential drudgery for the accountant.

Turning to benefits, companies that implement ABC frequently experience a dramatic improvement in costing accuracy. In addition, subdividing a department and then studying the individual activities performed furnishes insight about an activity's efficiency and its overall contribution to the organization. Through this process, cost savings may be identified, and the activity may be restructured (or perhaps even eliminated). The purpose is to identify those activities that add value to the product and business, known as **value-adding activities,** and those that do not **(nonvalue-adding activities).** The actual time consumed in manufacturing a good or providing a service is an example of an activity that falls in the first category. In contrast, activities such as machine setup, movement of goods through a factory, quality control, rework of defective goods, and inventory receiving and storage add little or no value to a firm's output.[3]

ABC helps management better distinguish between these two activity classes. Generally speaking, companies strive to minimize the related time and cost of nonvalue-adding activities—a practice that allows lower prices without an accompanying decrease in product or service quality to the customer.

A Further Focus

General Electric Medical Systems, which manufactures and services equipment used in health care, quickly saw the benefits of focusing on nonvalue-adding activities. Field service technicians historically carried 200 pounds of manuals in the trunks of their cars, which often meant several trips between the equipment and parking lot when checking detailed repair procedures. Overall, technicians estimated that 15% of their time on service calls was spent going back and forth.

An analysis of this activity provided ammunition for a better, more efficient way to conduct business. The company equipped the 2,500 technicians with laptop computers that had up-to-date CD-ROM databases and were easily carried to the job site. Switching to laptops raised productivity by 9%—the equivalent of a $25 million sales increase with no added costs. There was a side benefit as well: an improvement in gas mileage because of reduced vehicle weight.

Source: "A New Tool for Managing Costs," *Fortune*, June 14, 1993, pp. 124–126, 128–129.

Just-in-Time Production

6 Describe the basic features associated with a just-in-time production system.

On several occasions throughout the text, we have noted that manufacturers have three types of inventories: raw materials, work in process, and finished goods. Until recently, you could walk into most any factory and warehouse facility and see stockpiles of goods awaiting, in, or through production. In the 1980s, many companies adopted procedures used by Japanese firms—procedures that strive for minimal (and sometimes zero) inventories on hand.

Let us stop and think about why companies, especially manufacturers, carry inventories. In the simplest case, finished goods are held to satisfy customer demand, and raw materials are stored to keep production running smoothly. Some writers have suggested that American manufacturers operate with a *just-in-case (JIC)* mind-set. In other words, finished goods are needed because the firm is unable to accurately predict product demand. Raw materials are held to offset any defects

---

[3] One could logically maintain that quality control and various inspections result in a better product and therefore add value. Most businesspeople take the opposite view, arguing that these activities could have been avoided if production processes had functioned properly when initially performed.

that may be discovered during manufacturing or just in case a supplier cannot meet agreed-on delivery dates. Thus, keeping extra units on hand is really a means of compensating for fluctuating customer demand, defective parts, and late shipments.

Unfortunately, this "insurance" is costly. Inventories must be stored and moved through the production facility. The goods are taxed by local governments and are subject to obsolescence and deterioration. Further, a considerable amount of money is tied up and gathering dust in warehouses and on plant floors. The company could likely use these funds elsewhere for more profitable endeavors or perhaps to reduce outstanding debt. Stated simply, in many situations the acquisition or manufacture of goods for inventory is viewed as wasteful. To help eliminate these problems and regain a competitive edge, many American businesses have begun to use just-in-time (JIT) production systems.

CHARACTERISTICS OF JIT PRODUCTION

Under a **just-in-time (JIT)** system, goods are manufactured just in time to fill customer orders. This philosophy extends backward through the system, with manufactured parts (such as subassemblies) being produced just prior to being used in making the finished good. In addition, raw materials are acquired only when they are ready to enter production. In theory, the goal is to cut inventory levels to zero. Normally, however, management is more than satisfied if inventories are reduced to bare minimum levels after JIT procedures are instituted. These bare minimum levels are often amounts that will satisfy demand or usage for only a few days and, in some cases, a few *hours*!

Just-in-time systems are characterized by a "demand-pull" philosophy. That is, the sale of a finished unit triggers the whole process. The sale dictates the need to produce a finished good and for various preceding workstations to perform the necessary manufacturing tasks. These workstations require raw materials and thus activate the request to a supplier for shipment. Under a JIT system, nothing is produced until the sales order is in hand. The "pull" system may be contrasted with a "push" system, which has been and is still used by many companies. Here, raw materials are put into production and pushed through various fabrication activities, perhaps accumulating on the shop floor in the form of work in progress. Eventually these goods will be completed, but the lack of a sales order contributes to stockpiling in warehouses. As noted earlier, inventory accumulation becomes a very expensive proposition.

A number of factors must be satisfied if a company is to be successful at JIT production. Two elements worthy of mention at this point are supplier reliability and a commitment to total quality management.

Supplier Reliability. Because a company has drastically reduced its raw material inventories, JIT production gives rise to changes in purchasing patterns. Where a firm would have acquired a month's supply of parts and stored them in a warehouse, JIT dictates that many small purchases be made. Several shipments per day from a given supplier are not uncommon. Suppliers must be willing to work under these conditions and, most importantly, must be reliable. Since materials basically enter production shortly after arrival, late deliveries and partially filled orders cannot be tolerated. To streamline the entire process, the manufacturer's and suppliers' computers often communicate with each other when it comes time to order and ship goods.

Further complicating matters, the materials received must be of top quality. The quality standards sought are often much higher than normal, given the lack of backup to cover defects. Many suppliers have been able to meet JIT manufacturers' rigid standards; however, some have not. This inability to upgrade quality, the reliability problem just discussed, and a desire for stronger buyer/seller relations have created an interesting trend: large manufacturing firms are slashing the number of suppliers used. The manufacturers are demanding higher levels of service and are willing to pay a price to get the job done. As an example, Xerox found that its cheapest suppliers were sometimes lax in pulling substandard goods out of the company's purchases. Partly in response to this situation, Xerox has reduced its suppliers from 5,000 to about 500 and cut the reject rates on parts by a factor of 13.[4]

Total Quality Management (TQM). Some spoilage and defective units are common in almost all manufacturing operations. Given the lack of inventories in a JIT system, spoilage and defects can bring an entire manufacturing plant to a grinding halt. Consistent with JIT is a commitment to total quality management (TQM), a concept that strives for perfection in both materials acquisition and the production process.

Manufacturing excellence is of such concern in today's business climate that many companies are now computing and monitoring so-called quality costs. These are costs related to dealing with or eliminating the acquisition or manufacture of marginal goods. Examples include amounts associated with:

Quality engineering	Production stoppages
Product design changes	Rework of bad units
Equipment maintenance	Lost sales and lost customers
Inspection	Warranties
Field testing	Product liability suits

Given the wide diversity of quality costs, TQM advocates feel it is cheaper in the long run to set tight standards and operate in a zero-defect environment. This fact is made very clear by the general manager of Hewlett-Packard's Computer Systems Division, who stated:

> The earlier you detect and prevent a defect, the more you can save. If you throw away a defective 2-cent resistor before you use it, you lose 2 cents. If you don't find it until it has been soldered into a computer component, it may cost $10 to repair the part. If you don't catch the component until it is in the user's hands, the repair will cost hundreds of dollars. Indeed, if a $5,000 computer has to be repaired in the field, the expense may exceed the manufacturing cost.[5]

This quotation summarizes a key facet of total quality management. Companies engaged in TQM practices strive for *prevention* rather than after-the-fact detection—detection through a series of quality inspections after the problem occurs. The end result of TQM is a shifting of quality costs, lower overall expenditures, and an improved profit picture (see Exhibit 22–8).[6]

---

[4] For an interesting discussion of suppliers and quality, see "Suppliers Struggle to Improve Quality As Big Firms Slash Their Vendor Rolls," *The Wall Street Journal*, August 16, 1991, pp. B1, B2.
[5] See "Product Quality: Profitable at Any Cost," *The New York Times*, March 3, 1985, Section 3, p. 3.
[6] J. Simpson and D. Muthler, "Quality Costs: Facilitating the Quality Initiative," *Journal of Cost Management,* Spring 1987, pp. 25–34.

Exhibit 22–8
Traditional Quality Control vs. Total Quality Management

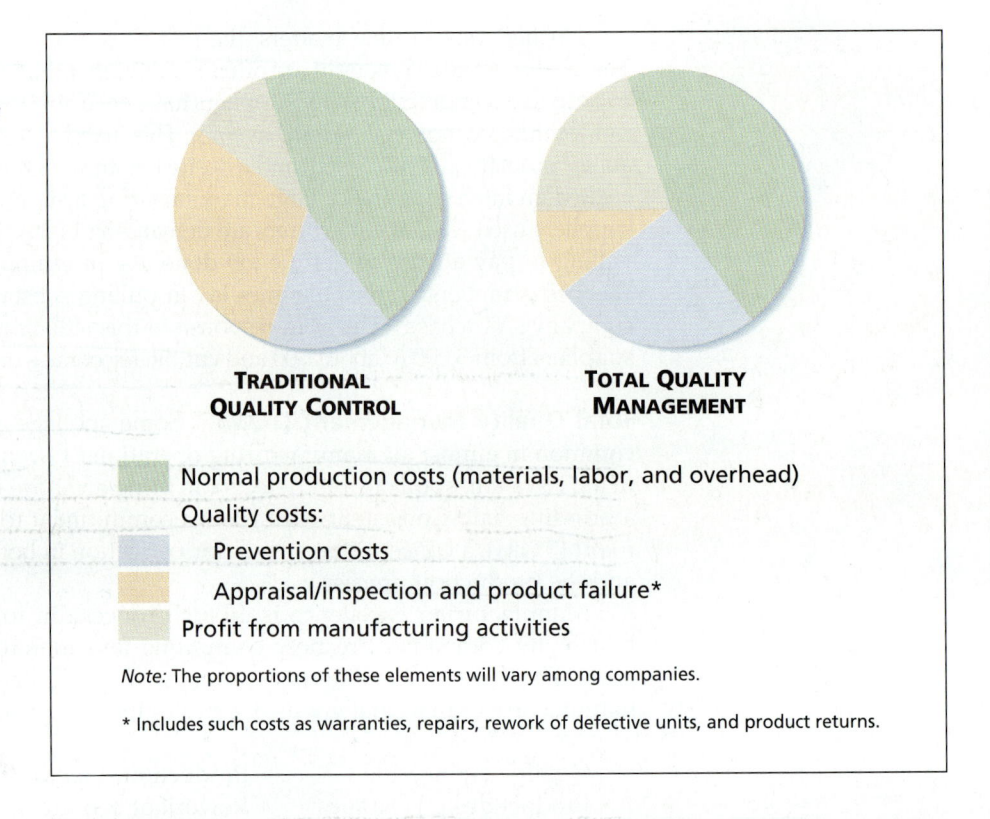

TRADITIONAL QUALITY CONTROL   TOTAL QUALITY MANAGEMENT

- Normal production costs (materials, labor, and overhead)
- Quality costs:
  - Prevention costs
  - Appraisal/inspection and product failure*
- Profit from manufacturing activities

Note: The proportions of these elements will vary among companies.

* Includes such costs as warranties, repairs, rework of defective units, and product returns.

Benchmarking. Companies that stress quality sometimes follow a practice known as *benchmarking,* comparing their own operating methods against those of other firms. The firms selected for the comparison are considered "world-class" in either the products or services they provide or the processes they perform. The idea of benchmarking is to learn from the experts—not to copy verbatim what these companies are doing, but to observe and then modify existing techniques. An abbreviated list of several so-called "world-class" American businesses and areas of expertise follows.[7]

AREA OF EXPERTISE	COMPANIES
Distribution and logistics	L.L. Bean, Wal-Mart
Equipment maintenance	Walt Disney
Health-care programs	Allied-Signal, Coors
Marketing	Procter & Gamble
Supplier management	Bose, Ford, Levi Strauss, 3M, Motorola, Xerox

A FOCUS ON SPEED

We conclude our presentation with a look at speed and its use by companies as a competitive weapon. With a just-in-time system, raw materials are delivered just prior to their need in production, and completed goods are shipped as soon as manufacturing operations conclude. Time is definitely of the essence.

[7] See "America's World-Class Champs," *Business Week,* November 30, 1992, pp. 74–75.

BUSINESS BRIEFING

DON WINE
Plant Manager
General Motors Corporation

Quality in a Competitive Marketplace

I went to work for General Motors as an assembly-line worker when I was 18 years old. Over the next 25 years with the company, not only did I achieve my formal educational goal of a master's degree, but I truly learned the "nuts and bolts" of car building. GM implemented numerous operating changes during this time, many of which were tied to global competition.

At the plant level, employees rarely have the opportunity to meet customers face-to-face, making it very easy for line-workers to forget that "real people" are going to buy each car produced. To overcome this problem, we constantly emphasize that the purchase of an automobile is a very significant investment; if we don't satisfy the customer, then another company will. Pleasing the customer in today's competitive business climate requires a *total*, undeniable commitment to quality—one that may require some trade-offs.

As a case in point, consider the following. When I detect a problem of quality, even if it is a relatively minor matter such as an ill-fitting glove-compartment door, I may stop the entire assembly line. As you can well imagine, this is an extremely expensive decision. Does this decision, to address a problem that can be measured in two or three millimeters, hinge on a detailed financial analysis? The answer quite frankly is no, as the costs would far outweigh the benefits. Rather, the decision is based on the knowledge that quality is the foundation on which our company's survival depends. I will therefore sacrifice the plant's short-run, bottom-line performance in order to achieve a more important goal, that of long-term customer satisfaction.

In many organizations today, speed is a general theme for anything from introducing new products to billing customers. A recent survey of 200 large corporations that were in the midst of re-engineering found a shortening of process times as the primary goal. Evidence of the popularity of this practice can be seen by studying the following examples:

- Bell Helicopter reduced the normal time to build helicopters from 24 months to 12 months, a factor that was important in winning a $113 million Army contract.
- Gillette is decreasing the time it takes to introduce new products on a global level from three years to two years.
- The Bank of Boston is striving to cut the decision time for a mortgage application from more than 25 days to 10 days.[8]
- Honda recently sliced new car development time from five years to three years.

---

[8] "The Latest Big Thing At Many Companies Is Speed, Speed, Speed," *The Wall Street Journal*, December 23, 1994, pp. A1, A5.

- Brunswick cut by two-thirds the lead time that normally arose between the receipt of a sales order for fishing reels, and completed production.[9]

Companies that focus on speed often experience decreases in cost and increases in quality, as processes are streamlined and waste is trimmed. These outcomes are linked to the concept of value-adding and nonvalue-adding activities that was discussed earlier in the chapter. The most obvious advantage associated with the drive to shorten process cycles is the ability to deliver a product or service faster than the competition. As the chairman of Avalon Software, a maker of software that is used to speed up manufacturing, so aptly observes, "It's not the big companies that eat the small; it's the fast that eat the slow."[10]

APPENDIX: PROCESS COSTING AND THE WEIGHTED-AVERAGE METHOD

> **7**
> Use the weighted-average process costing method to calculate the cost of goods completed and ending work in process inventory.

The physical flow of goods in many continuous manufacturing processes is on a first-in, first-out basis, with units in process at the beginning of a period being the first ones completed. As we explained in Chapter 10, the costing method used to account for inventory may be entirely different from the actual flow of goods through a warehouse (or in this case, a manufacturing facility). Accordingly, many companies have adopted weighted-average process costing.

FEATURES OF WEIGHTED-AVERAGE COSTING

The focus of **weighted-average costing** is that all goods completed during the period are carried at the same unit cost. This cost, a weighted average, is derived by combining costs that are present in the beginning work in process inventory with those that arise from current manufacturing activities. On a per-unit basis, such amounts could differ because of recent wage increases, changes in supplier prices for materials, and a variety of other factors. Nevertheless, any differences are downplayed in favor of the weighted-average method's primary advantages: simplicity and reduced record-keeping requirements.

Given the preceding cost treatment, there is no need to account for the units completed as two separate batches of goods: those from the beginning work in process and those actually begun during the period (see p. 844). These batches are lumped together in the weighted-average approach, and *it is assumed that all units completed are started and completed during the period*. As an outgrowth of this assumption, any work performed previously on the beginning work in process inventory is ignored when computing equivalent units.

AN EXAMPLE

To illustrate these features we will use data from Berloff, Inc., which appear in the body of the chapter. Key data from pages 844–845 are reproduced here for your convenience.

---

[9] "How Managers Can Succeed Through Speed," *Fortune*, February 13, 1989, pp. 54–59.
[10] "The Latest Big Thing At Many Companies Is Speed, Speed, Speed," p. A1.

- Beginning work in process inventory: 4,000 units, 75% complete; cost, $21,900 (materials, $8,470; conversion, $13,430)[11]
- Number of units started during September: 13,000
- Total units completed: 11,000
- Ending work in process inventory: 6,000 units, 40% complete
- September manufacturing costs: direct materials used, $32,500; conversion cost, $48,880

All materials are introduced at the start of the process, and conversion costs are incurred uniformly throughout manufacturing.

The four steps that follow are required to figure the cost of finished goods manufactured and the cost of ending work in process inventory.

Step 1: Analyze the Physical Flow. To ensure that all units are properly accounted for, the company must trace its goods through production activities. As shown by the following tabulation, the 17,000 units charged to the department (beginning work in process plus units started) have either been completed or are still in process:

	PHYSICAL UNITS
Beginning work in process	4,000
Units started	13,000
Units to account for	17,000
Completed	11,000
Ending work in process	6,000
Units accounted for	17,000

Must be equal

Step 2: Compute Equivalent Units. Next, the preceding figures are converted into equivalent units, as shown in Exhibit 22–9. Because the 11,000 finished

EXHIBIT 22–9
Equivalent Production Figures: Weighted-Average Method

	PHYSICAL UNITS	EQUIVALENT UNITS MATERIALS	EQUIVALENT UNITS CONVERSION
Beginning work in process	4,000		
Units started	13,000		
Units to account for	17,000		
Completed	11,000	11,000	11,000
Ending work in process	6,000	6,000	2,400
Units accounted for	17,000	17,000	13,400

[11] The material and conversion cost figures ($8,470 and $13,430, respectively) are new here. The weighted-average method requires these amounts for the calculation of average costs.

units are assumed to be *started and completed* during the month, these units have 100% of the materials and conversion introduced in September (and, thus, 11,000 equivalent units each). The fact that the beginning work in process inventory actually had the materials added and 75% of the conversion work performed in August is ignored under the weighted-average method. Finally, the ending work in process inventory was started in September and progressed through 40% of the manufacturing operation, giving rise to 6,000 and 2,400 equivalent units for materials and conversion cost, respectively.

Step 3: Compute Equivalent-Unit Costs. The computation of the cost per equivalent unit, shown below, is very straightforward: production costs are divided by equivalent-unit totals.

Costs	Total	Materials	Conversion
Beginning work in process	$ 21,900	$ 8,470	$13,430
Current	81,380	32,500	48,880
Total cost to account for	$103,280	$40,970	$62,310
Equivalent units*		÷17,000	÷13,400
Cost per equivalent unit		$2.41	$4.65

* From Step 2.

The combination of previous period and current costs and the related division procedure result in the calculation of *average* costs. These figures are now allocated to the month's manufacturing output.

Step 4: Cost Assignment. Berloff incurred $103,280 of production costs to complete 11,000 units and partially manufacture 6,000 units. The cost of these goods is determined by multiplying the amount of material consumed and work performed (i.e., the equivalent-unit figures) by the unit costs just computed. Step 4, the cost assignment process, appears at the bottom of the company's production cost report in Exhibit 22–10. These figures give rise to the journal entry that follows.

Finished Goods	77,660	
Work in Process		77,660
To transfer the cost of completed units to finished goods.		

BERLOFF, INC.
Production Cost Report
For the Month Ended September 30, 19XX

	PHYSICAL UNITS		
Beginning work in process	4,000		
Units started	13,000		
Units to account for	17,000		

[STEP 1]

		EQUIVALENT UNITS	
		MATERIALS	CONVERSION
Completed	11,000	11,000	11,000
Ending work in process	6,000	6,000	2,400
Units accounted for	17,000	17,000	13,400

[STEP 2]

COSTS	TOTAL		
Beginning work in process	$ 21,900	$ 8,470	$13,430
Current	81,380	32,500	48,880
Total cost to account for	$103,280	$40,970	$62,310
Equivalent units		÷17,000	÷13,400
Cost per equivalent unit		$2.41	$4.65

[STEP 3]

COST ASSIGNMENT

Completed		
Materials: 11,000 × $2.41	$26,510	
Conversion cost: 11,000 × $4.65	51,150	$ 77,660
Ending work in process		
Materials: 6,000 × $2.41	$14,460	
Conversion cost: 2,400 × $4.65	11,160	25,620
Total cost accounted for		$103,280

[STEP 4]

EXHIBIT 22–10
Production Cost Report:
Weighted-Average Method

END-OF-CHAPTER REVIEW

LEARNING OBJECTIVES:
THE KEY POINTS

1. **Explain the basic features that are associated with a process cost accounting system.** Process costing systems are used in continuous process and assembly-line types of industries. With such systems, the manufacturing costs incurred flow through the Raw Materials, Work in Process, Finished Goods, and Cost of Goods Sold accounts—the same as those established for a job order firm. In contrast, however, the cost accumulation method is significantly different, with costs being accumulated by department (or process) for a given time period. Furthermore, each

department maintains its own Work in Process account and reports manufacturing activity on a production cost report.

2. **Define and calculate equivalent units of production.** Equivalent units are the basis for assigning inventoriable costs under a process costing system. On conclusion of a typical accounting period, many units have been fully manufactured, whereas others are still in production. Because fully completed units cannot be combined with in-process units (i.e., the two batches are not the same), some common measurement base must be found. This base is equivalent units, or physical units that are stated in terms of finished units. If, for example, a company started 1,000 units into production and these goods are 70% complete at the end of the period, the firm has done the work equivalent to manufacturing 700 finished units. None of these goods are finished, however; they are all still in process.

3. **Identify the factors that affect the computation of equivalent units.** Three factors must be considered in the calculation of equivalent units: the presence of a beginning work in process inventory, the introduction of various production factors at different points in the manufacturing process, and the method of process costing used by the firm. If a company has a beginning work in process inventory, then some manufacturing work occurred on these units in the previous accounting period. Should the FIFO method of costing be in use, as illustrated in the body of the chapter, the work performed last period must be evaluated when determining equivalent-unit totals. In addition, because materials tend to be introduced at specific points in a manufacturing operation and conversion costs (i.e., the sum of direct labor and factory overhead) are incurred uniformly throughout a process, separate equivalent-unit figures must be computed for these elements.

   The final factor to consider is whether the firm is using FIFO or weighted-average costing. As just noted, previous period manufacturing activity affects equivalent-unit calculations under FIFO. With weighted average, however, as explained in the chapter appendix, such work is ignored.

4. **Allocate production costs between completed units and units still in process.** The allocation of manufacturing costs is a multi-step process that involves determining the physical flow of goods through a department and the calculation of equivalent units for work performed during the current period. The cost per equivalent unit is then calculated for direct materials and conversion cost. The final step is cost assignment, which involves multiplying the equivalent units for completed goods and production in process by the unit costs just described. All of these procedures are documented on a company's production cost report.

5. **Distinguish between conventional and activity-based costing systems and use the latter to compute product costs.** Under a conventional accounting system, the costs of various activities are merged together and averaged over the units produced. With activity-based costing (ABC), a cost driver is selected for each activity to compute an application rate, which is then used to apply cost to the product. The use of ABC normally results in improved costing and decision making. Further, companies gain a clearer understanding of their value-adding and nonvalue-adding activities.

6. **Describe the basic features associated with a just-in-time production system.** In a just-in-time (JIT) production system, inventories are reduced to bare minimum levels (ideally, zero). The system operates on a "demand-pull" basis, meaning that the manufacture of a finished good is triggered by the receipt of a sales order. JIT sys-

tems reduce inventory carrying costs and are highly dependent on supplier reliability and the user's commitment to total quality management (TQM).

7. **(Appendix) Use the weighted-average process costing method to calculate the cost of goods completed and ending work in process inventory.** The weighted-average method is employed by many businesses to simplify costing and reduce record keeping. Under this approach, all goods completed during a period are assumed to be started and completed during that period. Any previous manufacturing activity on the beginning work in process inventory is therefore ignored in the computation of equivalent units. This method is known as the weighted-average approach because the previous period costs in the beginning work in process are averaged together with current manufacturing costs, and all units produced during the period are carried at the same unit-cost figure.

Key Terms and Concepts: A Quick Overview

activity-based costing (ABC) A costing method under which departments are divided into activities, and the cost of individual activities is applied to manufactured products. (p. 851)

benchmarking Comparing a company's operating methods against those of other firms. (p. 856)

conversion cost The cost to convert raw material into finished products; more specifically, the sum of direct labor and factory overhead. (p. 843)

equivalent unit A physical unit stated in terms of a finished unit. (p. 841)

FIFO process costing A method whereby the beginning work in process inventory is assumed to be the first batch of goods completed. (p. 844)

just-in-time (JIT) production A production system in which inventories are deemed to be wasteful and the manufacturing process is "pulled" by the receipt of a sales order. (p. 854)

nonvalue-adding activity An activity that fails to add value to a product and business; for example, machine setup and inventory receiving and storage. (p. 853)

process costing system A system of cost accumulation that gathers costs by process or department. (p. 838)

production cost report A report that is used in a process costing system; shows costs and units, classified by department. (p. 846)

quality costs The costs of dealing with or eliminating the acquisition or manufacture of marginal goods. (p. 855)

total quality management (TQM) A concept that focuses on zero defects in both raw materials acquisitions and the manufacturing process; stresses prevention rather than after-the-fact detection. (p. 855)

value-adding activity An activity that increases the value of a product and business; for example, manufacturing a good and providing a service. (p. 853)

weighted-average process costing A process costing method under which all goods manufactured during a period are carried at the same unit cost. (p. 858)

Chapter Quiz

The five questions that follow relate to several issues raised in the chapter. Test your knowledge of the issues by selecting the best answer. (The answers appear on p. 879.)

1. Process cost accounting systems:

a. use distinctly different general ledger accounts than job order systems.
b. frequently accumulate costs by department. *(circled)*
c. are seldom found in assembly-line manufacturing plants.
d. may, in selected cases, use job order cost sheets.

2. Equivalent units:
a. are normally computed separately for direct materials and conversion cost. *(circled)*
b. are finished units stated in terms of physical units.
c. cannot be used to calculate the cost of the ending work in process inventory.
d. are generally equal (in total) for both completed goods and the ending work in process inventory.

3. Harris Company introduces direct material at the beginning of its manufacturing operation. The following data pertain to July:

> Beginning work in process: 4,000 units, 20% complete
> Units started and completed: 7,000
> Ending work in process: 3,000 units, 60% complete

Assuming the use of FIFO process costing, the total equivalent units for direct materials amounted to:

a. 8,800. c. 12,000.
b. 10,000. *(circled)* d. 14,000.

4. A production cost report:
a. documents manufacturing costs of companies that use process costing systems and job order systems.
b. discloses equivalent units but not the cost per equivalent unit.
c. discloses the cost of completed goods but not the cost of the ending work in process inventory.
d. summarizes equivalent-unit calculations, unit-cost calculations, and the assignment of manufacturing costs to goods completed and the ending work in process inventory. *(circled)*

5. A just-in-time production system:
a. relies on the use of activity-based costing.
b. can be brought to a halt by defective units acquired from suppliers. *(circled)*
c. normally has minimal impact on the inventory levels that are carried by a company.
d. is characterized as being "demand-push" in nature.

SUMMARY PROBLEM

Santa Fe Manufacturing uses a FIFO process costing system to accumulate production costs. Selected data applicable to January of the current year follow.

Beginning work in process inventory: 8,000 units, ¼ complete; cost, $17,500
Number of units started in January: 20,000
Total units completed: 22,000
Ending work in process inventory: 6,000 units, ⅔ complete
Direct materials used in January: $60,000
January conversion cost: $42,000

Instructions

a. Compute January's equivalent production figures for materials and conversion cost. Materials are added at the start of the process; conversion costs are incurred evenly throughout manufacturing.

b. Compute the equivalent-unit costs for materials and conversion costs.
c. Determine the cost of goods completed during January and the ending work in process inventory.
d. Present the journal entry to transfer completed production to finished goods.

Solution

a.

	PHYSICAL UNITS
Beginning work in process	8,000
Units started	20,000
Units to account for	28,000

		EQUIVALENT UNITS	
		MATERIALS	CONVERSION
Completed			
Beginning work in process*	8,000	—	6,000
Units started and completed†	14,000	14,000	14,000
Ending work in process‡	6,000	6,000	4,000
Units accounted for	28,000	20,000	24,000

*All materials added last period; three-fourths of the conversion performed in this period.
†All materials and conversion introduced in this period; 14,000 units derived by subtracting the beginning work in process inventory from the total units completed (22,000).
‡Units were started in this period; all materials were introduced plus two-thirds of the conversion.

b.

COSTS	TOTAL	MATERIALS	CONVERSION
Beginning work in process	$ 17,500	$ —	$ —
Current	102,000	60,000	42,000
Total cost to account for	$119,500	$60,000	$42,000
Equivalent units		÷20,000	÷24,000
Cost per equivalent unit		$3.00	$1.75

c. Completed
  Beginning work in process
    Prior period cost $17,500
    Conversion cost: 6,000 units × $1.75   10,500 $ 28,000

  Units started and completed
    Materials: 14,000 units × $3.00 $42,000
    Conversion cost: 14,000 units × $1.75   24,500   66,500
  Total cost of completed units $ 94,500

  Ending work in process
    Materials: 6,000 units × $3.00 $18,000
    Conversion cost: 4,000 units × $1.75   7,000   25,000

  Total cost accounted for $119,500

    d. Finished Goods   94,500
         Work in Process   94,500
         To transfer the cost of completed
         units to finished goods.

Assignment Material

Questions

Q22–1 In what type of production setting is a process cost accounting system often found?

Q22–2 How are job order systems and process costing systems similar?

Q22–3 Explain the concept of equivalent units to someone who has no background in cost accounting.

Q22–4 The Gateway Company uses a process costing system. An examination of goods in production at the end of the accounting period revealed 6,000 units, two-thirds complete. Would it be correct to say that 4,000 finished units were manufactured? Why?

Q22–5 Why is it usually necessary to compute separate equivalent-unit totals for direct materials and conversion cost?

Q22–6 Explain the basic features that are associated with a FIFO process costing system.

Q22–7 List the four steps that are required when preparing a production cost report.

Q22–8 Briefly explain why costing accuracy generally improves when a company adopts activity-based costing.

Q22–9 How might activity-based costing lead to the elimination of a company's non-value-adding activities?

Q22–10 What normally happens to inventories after a just-in-time production system is installed?

Q22–11 List several of the conditions that must exist for a company to use just-in-time production successfully.

Q22–12 Maxell Company is striving for significant improvements in product quality. List several of the quality costs the firm will likely incur in its quest for zero defects.

*Q22–13 What basic features are associated with weighted-average process costing?

*Q22–14 What benefits does the use of weighted-average process costing offer in comparison with FIFO?

Exercises

E22–1 Industry characteristics and costing systems (L.O. 1)
Consider the activities of the following businesses. Determine whether each business would be more likely to use a job order system or a process costing system.

---

* An asterisk preceding an item indicates that the material is covered in an appendix to this chapter.

a. Shipbuilder
b. Petroleum refiner
c. Candy manufacturer
d. Trophy shop
e. Brick manufacturer
f. Shopping mall developer
g. Book publisher
h. Manufacturer of nuts and bolts
i. Brewery
j. Motion picture studio
k. Frozen orange juice producer
l. Manufacturer of jet aircraft
m. Manufacturer of washers and dryers
n. Nuclear power plant

E22–2 Overview of process costing (L.O. 1, 2, 3, 4)

Evaluate the comments that follow as being True or False. If the comment is false, briefly explain why.

a. The basic objective of a process costing system is to determine the cost of goods completed during the period and the cost of the ending work in process inventory.
b. Under a FIFO process costing system, all goods completed during May are assumed to be started and completed in May.
c. Unit manufacturing costs are the result of dividing the period's costs by the number of physical units (e.g., tons, gallons, and so forth) produced.
d. Each manufacturing department that uses a process costing system will maintain its own Work in Process account.
e. Process costing systems are normally found in continuous manufacturing environments.

E22–3 Calculation of equivalent units (L.O. 2, 3)

Consider data from the following companies:

	GOLDEN	RETRIEVER
Beginning work in process:		
Units and stage of completion	1,500; ⅓	8,000; ¾
Units started and completed	5,000	
Total units completed		17,000
Ending work in process:		
Units and stage of completion	1,800; ¼	6,500; ⅖

All materials are added at the start of the process, and conversion costs are incurred uniformly throughout manufacturing. Assuming use of FIFO, compute equivalent units for materials and conversion costs for Golden and Retriever.

E22–4 Computation of physical and equivalent units (L.O. 2, 3)

Baylor Manufacturing produces industrial chemicals and uses a FIFO process costing system. The data that follow relate to September operations.

		PERCENTAGE COMPLETE	
	POUNDS	MATERIALS	CONVERSION
Work in process, 9/1	17,500	70%	60%
Work in process, 9/30	15,000	20%	10%

Sixty thousand pounds were started into production during the month.

a. Compute the number of pounds completed in September.
b. Calculate Baylor's equivalent units for materials and conversion cost.

E22–5 Understanding a process costing system (L.O. 2, 3, 4)

Entek Manufacturing uses a FIFO process costing system. The following figures pertain to June:

	PHYSICAL UNITS	EQUIVALENT UNITS MATERIALS	CONVERSION
Completed production			
Beginning work in process	1,100	—	715
Units started and completed	3,700	3,700	3,700
Ending work in process	1,900	1,900	380
	6,700	5,600	4,795

All materials are introduced at the start of the process; conversion cost is incurred uniformly throughout production. Current costs per equivalent unit are: materials, $4.40; conversion cost, $12.

a. No equivalent units are computed for materials with respect to the beginning work in process inventory. Why?
b. What percentage of the conversion work was performed on the beginning work in process during May?
c. What is the total cost of direct materials used during June?
d. How many units will be transferred to the finished goods warehouse in June?

E22–6 Cost of goods completed and ending work in process (L.O. 4)

Accutech Manufacturing's cost accounting department has calculated the following equivalent production figures for August:

	PHYSICAL UNITS	EQUIVALENT UNITS MATERIALS	CONVERSION
Completed production			
Beginning work in process	900	—	600
Units started and completed	2,600	2,600	2,600
Ending work in process	1,500	1,500	1,000
	5,000	4,100	4,200

Prior period costs pertaining to the August 1 work in process inventory amounted to $4,500. Current costs per equivalent unit are: materials, $3.50; conversion, $5.00.

a. Determine the cost of production completed in August.
b. Determine the cost of the ending work in process inventory.

E22–7 Cost of goods completed and ending work in process (L.O. 2, 3, 4)

Ozark Manufacturing uses a FIFO process costing system to accumulate production costs. The following information pertains to April:

- Beginning work in process: 4,000 units, ¼ complete; cost, $42,000
- Units started into production: 7,000
- Total units completed during the period: 8,000
- Ending work in process: 3,000 units, ⅔ complete

All materials are introduced in the initial processing stages, and conversion cost is incurred evenly throughout production. Materials used during April amounted to $70,000; conversion cost totaled $36,000.

a. Compute equivalent-unit figures for materials and conversion cost.
b. Compute the cost of production completed during April and the ending work in process inventory.

E22–8 Activity-based costing (L.O. 5)

Allied Fabricating uses machine hours to apply factory overhead to units that are processed in the machining department. The company's accountant has computed the following estimates for the current period: machine hours, 25,000; factory overhead, $350,000.

The firm is considering a switch to an activity-based costing system and has derived the data that follow for the machining department's various activities:

Activity	Cost Driver	Application Rate
Production setup	Number of setups	$700 per setup
Machine processing	Machine hours	$8 per machine hour
Inspection	Inspection hours	$3 per inspection hour

Allied recently manufactured 2,500 units of part no. A431 for use in auto transmissions. Each part took 15 minutes of machine time to produce. Four machine setups were involved, and inspection time totaled 85 hours.

a. Compute the amount of overhead that would be applied to the A431 production if Allied's existing accounting procedures are used.
b. Compute the cost of A431 production, assuming the use of activity-based costing.
c. Suppose the company is in a very competitive market, where cost is a big factor in determining a product's selling price. With part A431, would Allied's existing accounting procedures or activity-based costing seem more appropriate? Briefly explain.

E22–9 Value-adding and nonvalue-adding activities (L.O. 5)

Sunshine Motor Homes manufactures a 36-foot "starter" home for sale to retirees. Company personnel recently calculated a 25-day production-to-delivery cycle time, as shown on the following page.

a. Calculate the time spent by Sunshine in performing value-adding activities.
b. What percentage of the total production-to-delivery cycle time is spent on nonvalue-adding activities?
c. Generally speaking, what should Sunshine do with respect to its nonvalue-adding activities? What benefit might result from this action?

Activity	Elapsed Days
Unloading materials from suppliers	1
Storage of materials prior to use	5
Movement of materials to production area	1
Assembly of frame to chassis	1
Exterior assembly	2
Interior construction	4
Carpeting and painting	1
Inspection/tests of completed vehicle	1
Storage of vehicle prior to delivery	9
	25

E22–10 Just-in-time production (L.O. 6)

Del Mar Manufacturing is considering the installation of a just-in-time production system. The company expects the following items will change if the new system is implemented:

Warehousing costs	Number of suppliers used
Lost sales to customers	Inventory obsolescence costs
Quality of raw materials purchased	Funds available for investment

a. Briefly discuss the meaning of a just-in-time production system.
b. Evaluate the six items that are expected to change, and determine whether each item would likely increase or decrease. No explanations are needed.

E22–11 Benchmarking, speed (L.O. 6)

The Pet Set, a mail-order retailer of novelty, impulse products for pets, issues a colorful catalog each quarter that is sent to over one million homes. Even though the company's merchandise has high profit margins, recent years have seen income rise at a much slower rate than sales. Also, sales returns have skyrocketed because goods are received by customers weeks after orders are placed.

The company's president recently read an article about benchmarking and is considering applying the technique to four of the firm's activities: purchasing, order entry, shipping/handling, and customer relations.

a. Briefly explain the concept of benchmarking. What will be its probable impact on bottom-line profit performance?
b. Why would sales returns likely decrease with a speed-up of the company's shipping/handling procedures?

*E22–12 Equivalent units and unit cost computations (L.O. 7)

Fittings Unlimited uses a weighted-average process costing system. The data that follow pertain to May.

Units started into production	19,000
Units in process, May 31 (40% complete)	7,000
Units in process, May 1 (30% complete)	6,000
Units completed	18,000

The beginning work in process contained material and conversion costs of $10,000 and $22,000, respectively. The firm's current manufacturing costs amounted to: materials, $40,000; conversion, $264,000.

a. Determine the company's equivalent units for May.
b. Calculate the cost per equivalent unit for materials and conversion cost.

*E22–13 Cost of goods completed and ending work in process (L.O. 7)

Bowling Green Corporation has a two-stage production operation. Goods pass from cleaning to milling to finished goods. The following information pertains to the cleaning department for October:

Total goods completed	6,000 units
Ending work in process (40% complete)	1,200 units
Beginning work in process (30% complete)	1,500 units

All materials are added at the beginning of production; conversion costs are incurred uniformly throughout manufacturing. The weighted-average costs per equivalent unit are: materials, $3.20; conversion, $12.00.

a. Calculate the cost of goods completed in the cleaning department.
b. Calculate the cost of the ending work in process.

PROBLEMS

Series A

P22–A1 Straightforward process costing (L.O. 2, 3, 4)

Bozeman, Inc., uses a FIFO process costing system to accumulate production costs. All materials are introduced at the start of the process, and conversion costs are incurred uniformly throughout manufacturing. Units pass directly from Bozeman's sole production department to the finished goods warehouse. The following information relates to January operations:

1. The beginning work in process inventory consisted of 14,000 units, 70% complete. A review of the work in process on January 31 found 10,000 units, 20% complete.
2. The production supervisor noted that 36,000 units had entered manufacturing during the month. A total of 40,000 units were completed.
3. The beginning work in process was carried in the accounting records at a cost of $183,400. January's manufacturing costs were: direct materials used, $162,000; conversion cost, $394,450.

Instructions

a. Prepare a production cost report.
b. Prepare the necessary journal entry to record the completed production for January.

P22–A2 Production cost report; partial computations for second month (L.O. 2, 3, 4)

HRS Assembly, Inc., operates a FIFO process costing system. All materials enter production at the beginning of the process; conversion costs are incurred evenly throughout manufacturing. The data that follow pertain to November of the current year.

- Work in process, 11/1: 20,000 units, 70% complete; cost, $81,500
- Units started into production: 70,000

- Total units completed: 85,000
- Direct materials consumed: $140,000
- Conversion costs: $240,500
- Work in process, 11/30: 5,000 units, 60% complete

Instructions

a. Prepare a production cost report for November.
b. The following data relate to December: new production started, 78,000 units; total units completed, 76,000. If the ending work in process is 20% complete, calculate December's equivalent units for materials and conversion cost.

P22–A3 Production cost computations (L.O. 2, 3, 4)

Consumer Health Foods produces a variety of health food items that are available at retail stores throughout the country. One of the company's products is Fruit & Grain, a popular breakfast cereal. The cereal is a combination of grain, bananas, and raisins, all of which are introduced at the beginning of the blending process. During June, the company used the following: grain, $19,200; bananas, $20,000; and raisins, $16,900. Other data for June are:

- Conversion cost
    Direct labor: Five employees worked 160 hours each and were paid $12 per hour.
    Overhead: Overhead is applied at the rate of $29 per labor hour.
- Beginning work in process: 20,000 pounds, 30% complete; cost, $7,900
- Ending work in process: 25,000 pounds, 40% complete
- Total production completed during the month: 160,000 pounds

Conversion cost (i.e., direct labor and overhead) is incurred uniformly throughout manufacturing; a FIFO process costing system is used.

Instructions

Compute:

a. Total production costs for June.
b. Cost of goods completed during the month.
c. Cost of the work in process inventory on June 30.

P22–A4 Process costing and cost flow (L.O. 2, 3, 4)

Tallahassee Co., uses a FIFO process costing system. All materials are introduced at the start of the process, and conversion costs are incurred uniformly throughout manufacturing. Information on Tallahassee's Work in Process and Finished Goods accounts follows.

Work in Process:
　May 1 balance: 3,600 units, ⅓ complete; cost, $10,100
　Production started during May: 12,000 units
　May manufacturing costs: Materials, $27,000; conversion cost, $18,560
　May 31 balance: 4,000 units, 30% complete

Finished Goods:
　May 1 balance: 7,500 units; cost, $30,000
　Transferred from work in process: 11,600 units
　May 31 balance: 4,200 units; cost, $16,170

Instructions

Compute the following:

a. Total equivalent units and the cost per equivalent unit for both materials and conversion cost.
b. The cost of units started in previous months and completed in May.
c. The cost of units started and completed in May.
d. The cost of units transferred to finished goods.
e. The cost of the May 31 work in process inventory.
f. The number of units sold during May.
g. The cost transferred from Finished Goods to Cost of Goods Sold during May.

P22–A5 Activity-based costing (L.O. 5)

Pratt Manufacturing applies factory overhead to its products on the basis of machine hours. The rate in effect for the current accounting period is $100 per hour. The company's two products, Superior and Regular, require the same amount of direct labor ($65) but differing amounts of direct material ($75 and $40, respectively). Pratt anticipates that it will produce 5,000 units of Superior and 4,000 units of Regular.

Suzanne Batzer, the company's controller, is studying the use of activity-based costing for the firm. She has determined that overhead can be identified with three major activities and has gathered the following data:

Activity	Cost Driver	Cost
Production setups	Number of setups	$ 60,000
Machine processing	Number of machine hours	340,000
Packing and shipping	Number of shipments	100,000
		$500,000

Estimated cost-driver data for the two products and the company as a whole are:

	Total	Superior	Regular
Number of setups	40	11	29
Number of machine hours	5,000	3,000	2,000
Number of shipments	125	30	95

Instructions

a. Assuming use of the present $100-per-hour application rate, compute the total costs of Superior and Regular production if the expected manufacturing volume is attained.
b. Compute activity application rates for production setup, machine processing, and packing and shipping.
c. Assuming use of activity-based costing, compute the total costs of Superior and Regular if the expected manufacturing volume is attained.
d. The company currently sells a unit of Regular for $162. If Pratt's marketing manager suggested a campaign to promote sales of Regular, how would Batzer likely respond?

*P22–A6 Straightforward process costing: Weighted average (L.O. 7)

Red River, Inc., uses a weighted-average process costing system. The following information relates to operations for October:

- Work in process
    - October 1: 10,000 units, 40% complete; cost, $41,600 (materials, $18,000; conversion, $23,600)
    - October 31: 4,000 units, 75% complete
- October manufacturing costs
    - Direct materials used: $46,600
    - Conversion cost: $174,400
- Units started into production: 24,000
- Total units completed: 30,000

All materials are introduced at the start of manufacturing; conversion cost is incurred uniformly throughout the process. Units pass directly from Red River's sole production department to the finished goods warehouse.

Instructions

a. Prepare a production cost report for October.
b. Prepare the journal entry necessary to record the month's completed goods.

Series B

P22–B1 Straightforward process costing (L.O. 2, 3, 4)

Venice Company uses a FIFO process costing system to accumulate production costs. The following information pertains to July:

- Number of units started: 12,000
- Total units completed: 9,000
- Ending work in process inventory: 5,000 units, 40% complete
- Beginning work in process inventory: 2,000 units, 25% complete; cost, $8,600
- Costs incurred in July: direct materials used, $38,400; conversion cost, $47,250

All materials are introduced at the start of the process, and conversion costs are incurred uniformly throughout manufacturing. Completed units pass directly from the manufacturing plant to finished goods.

Instructions

a. Prepare a production cost report.
b. Prepare the necessary journal entry to record the completed production for July.

P22–B2 Production cost report; partial computations for second month (L.O. 2, 3, 4)

MicroMatic uses a FIFO process costing system. The following data pertain to July of the current year:

	Units	Cost
July 1 work in process, 30% complete	6,000	$ 42,750
July 31 work in process, 20% complete	3,000	?
Total units completed	18,000	?
Units started during July	15,000	
July manufacturing costs		
Direct materials used		69,000
Conversion cost		147,840

A review of the next month's accounting records found that 22,000 units were started into production during August. Completed units totaled 17,500, and the August 31 work in process was 40% complete.

All materials are introduced at the start of manufacturing; conversion costs are incurred uniformly throughout the process.

Instructions

a. Prepare a production cost report for July.
b. Compute the equivalent units for materials and conversion cost in August.

P22–B3 Production cost computations (L.O. 2, 3, 4)

Singapore Electronics assembles various components that are used in the aircraft industry. The company's major product, a pressure gauge, is the result of assembling three parts: DR532, HB4–786, and 429GY. All parts are introduced at the beginning of Singapore's manufacturing process; labor and overhead (i.e., conversion costs) are incurred uniformly throughout production. During March, the following costs were incurred:

- Direct materials used: DR532, $100,500; HB4–786, $207,300; 429GY, $32,400
- Direct labor: 2,500 hours at $8

The overhead application rate is 260% of direct labor cost.

The beginning work in process inventory (8,000 units, 80% complete) was carried in the accounting records at a cost of $85,000. The ending work in process amounted to 4,000 units, 60% complete. Singapore finished a total of 40,000 gauges during the period.

Instructions

Assuming use of a FIFO process costing system, determine:

a. Total production costs for March.
b. Cost of goods completed during the month.
c. Cost of the work in process inventory on March 31.

P22–B4 Process costing and cost flow (L.O. 2, 3, 4)

Spare Parts, Inc., uses a FIFO process costing system. All materials are introduced at the start of the process, and conversion costs are incurred uniformly throughout manufacturing. The following T-accounts were extracted from the company's records as of December 31:

WORK IN PROCESS			
12/1 Balance 4,000 units, ¾ complete	33,500	To finished goods: 4,000 units from 12/1 inventory	?
Started 9,000 units		6,000 units started and completed in December	?
Materials	32,400		
Conversion	43,450		

FINISHED GOODS			
12/1 Balance 7,000 units	63,000	To cost of goods sold: ? units	134,136
From work in process: 10,000 units			

The ending work in process inventory is 30% complete.

Instructions

a. Compute the following:
   (1) Total equivalent units and the cost per equivalent unit for both materials and conversion cost.
   (2) The cost of units started in November and completed in December.
   (3) The cost of units started and completed in December.
   (4) The cost of units transferred to finished goods.
   (5) The cost of the company's ending work in process inventory.
b. If 2,400 finished units were on hand on December 31, determine (1) the ending balance in the Finished Goods account and (2) the number of units sold during December.

P22–B5 Activity-based costing (L.O. 5)

Telecom Manufacturing applies factory overhead to its two products (L23 and L24) on the basis of direct labor hours. Estimated factory overhead and direct labor time for the current accounting period are $400,000 and 10,000 hours, respectively. Information about the products follows.

	L23	L24
Estimated production volume	1,000	1,400
Direct materials per unit	$30	$19
Direct labor per unit		
3 hours at $8	24	
5 hours at $8		40

The company, which installed a considerable amount of automated equipment several years ago, has seen a significant decline in profit. Management believes that incorrect and "outdated" calculations of product cost are a major contributor to the problem.

Telecom's overhead can be identified with three major activities. These activities and other relevant data are summarized as shown.

		COST DRIVER VOLUME*		
	COST	L23	L24	TOTAL
Purchase order processing	$ 40,000	300	100	400
Machine processing	220,000	4,500	3,500	8,000
Inspection	140,000	250	750	1,000
	$400,000			

* Number of purchase orders processed, machine hours worked, and inspection hours, respectively.

Instructions

a. Assuming use of direct labor hours to apply overhead to production, compute the total costs of L23 and L24 if the expected manufacturing volume is attained.
b. Compute activity application rates for purchase order processing, machine processing, and inspection.
c. Assuming use of activity-based costing, compute the total costs of L23 and L24 if the expected manufacturing volume is attained.
d. Telecom's selling prices are based heavily on cost. Use the data presented and the results from parts (a) and (c) to determine why the firm is experiencing a significant decline in profit.

*P22–B6 Straightforward process costing: Weighted average (L.O. 7)

Heritage Ski Poles uses a weighted-average process costing system. All materials are introduced at the start of manufacturing; conversion cost is incurred uniformly throughout the process. Units pass directly from the company's sole production department to the finished goods warehouse. The following information relates to November's activities:

1. Heritage started 17,000 units into production and completed a total of 14,500 units.
2. November manufacturing costs were: Direct materials used, $204,000; conversion cost, $227,610.
3. The work in process inventory on November 1 totaled 3,500 units, 70% complete. These units had related materials and conversion cost of $42,000 and $32,940, respectively.
4. Ending work in process on November 30 totaled 6,000 units, 80% complete.

Instructions

a. Prepare a production cost report for November.
b. Prepare the journal entry needed to record the month's completed production.

EXPANDING YOUR HORIZONS

EYH22–1 Contemporary manufacturing methods (L.O. 5, 6)

Much of the competitiveness of the American manufacturing sector is attributed to recent improvements made to streamline or speed up production processes.

Instructions

Form a team with three other students and contact a manufacturing company in your area. Inquire as to which contemporary manufacturing methods have been implemented (just-in-time production, benchmarking, activity-based costing, identification of nonvalue-adding activities, and so forth) and the impact of the methods on operations and profitability. Be prepared to report your findings to the class.

EYH22–2 A focus on quality (L.O. 6)

A number of American businesses have implemented total quality management (TQM) programs in recent years. In recognition of the importance of quality to our economic well being, the U.S. government created the Malcolm Baldrige National Quality Award. The award is given to selected companies that excel in their quality achievements.

Instructions

Using the resources of your library, locate several articles that report on the quality practices of three recent Baldrige award winners. The recipients should be engaged in different types of businesses (such as manufacturing, service, and so forth). Prepare a one-page report that summarizes the firms' accomplishments.

EYH22–3 International quality standards (L.O. 6)

As the text explained, supplier reliability is a key issue in just-in-time production systems. It is also very important for those companies that have implemented programs in total quality management (TQM). Not too long ago, the International Organization for Standardization created a set of procedures known as ISO 9000 that relate to certification of supplier quality. The program has been successful in Europe; it is a requirement of U.S. companies that do business there.

Instructions

Using the resources of your library, locate several articles that summarize the experiences of U.S. businesses that have applied for ISO 9000 certification. What benefits and problems have these firms encountered? Prepare a one-page summary of your findings.

EYH22–4 Activity-based costing, value-adding activities (L.O. 5)

Dalfort Corporation produces high-precision components for commercial aircraft manufacturers. The business is either "feast or famine." That is, Dalfort will operate at 100% of capacity when airlines are placing orders for new planes or at about 25% of capacity when the carriers are tightening their belts.

During a recent downturn, Dalfort considered diversifying its product line by manufacturing goods used in the drilling and extraction of oil. To its surprise, preliminary financial analyses showed that the company would be the highest cost producer of oil field equipment. Dalfort's costs were actually higher than the competitors' selling prices.

Dalfort had used its established plantwide overhead rate to determine the oil field equipment manufacturing costs. This rate included all indirect production costs, including those related to aviation research and development, Federal Aviation Agency compliance testing, wind tunnel testing, and precision machining. As a result of these findings, management decided not to diversify, and Dalfort continued to operate at 25% of capacity.

Instructions

a. Did Dalfort err in its financial analyses? Briefly explain.
b. What is the basic difference between value-adding and nonvalue-adding activities? Did the change in Dalfort's business focus perhaps change the nature of several of the company's activities? Briefly discuss.
c. Recommend an alternative accounting procedure that may have provided added insight about the company's true cost structure of diversifying. What benefits and problems are typically associated with this procedure?

COMMUNICATION OF ACCOUNTING INFORMATION

CAI22–1 Documentation of procedures (L.O. 2, 3, 4)

Communication Principle: Businesses spend considerable sums to design and install reporting systems and procedures. Generally, these efforts are successful, and the monies invested produce the intended results. Occasionally, though, things don't work out as planned. If key personnel leave and the details of system operations are sketchy, the company may be in for troubled times.

To avoid this situation, employees are often asked to document business procedures—accounting and otherwise. In drafting such documentation, the following goals and considerations should be kept in mind:

1. Although an employee may have a clear understanding today, memories frequently fail. Recalling the past is easier if extra effort is taken initially to develop good explanatory material.
2. Other employees are unaware of the "fine points" stored in current users' brains. Incomplete documentation can create as many problems for later users as the documentation is supposed to solve. Detailed, logically organized instructions are therefore a must.
3. Writing should be concise. Extraneous thoughts or comments are apt to confuse the reader.
4. Information should be filed in an accessible manner and updated as necessary. Lost or out-of-date supporting materials have marginal, if any, value.

5. The documentation should be reviewed by an employee who is unfamiliar with the system and/or procedure. What may seem clear to one individual may not be as clear to others.

■ ■ ■ ■ ■ ■ ■ ■

Tyson Manufacturing has recently installed a FIFO process costing system identical to that described in the text. Materials are introduced at the start of production; conversion cost is incurred uniformly throughout manufacturing.

Instructions

Document the procedures that underlie the preparation of a production cost report for Tyson's system. Your documentation should be sufficiently detailed and aimed at an employee who has a limited accounting background. After reviewing the documentation, the employee should be able to apply the appropriate calculations to various fact situations.

Answers to Chapter Quiz

1. b
2. a
3. b (Beginning work in process, 0; units started and completed, 7,000; ending work in process, 3,000)
4. d
5. b

COMPREHENSIVE PROBLEM 4

DURHAM MANUFACTURING

Durham Manufacturing produces furniture in North Carolina. The firm uses a job costing system to account for its Russell wooden furniture line, which is produced upon receipt of a customer's order. The company is also involved with the manufacture and assembly of Easton office partitions, a brand noted for its durability and economical price. Durham uses a FIFO process costing system to account for these goods.

A review of the accounting records found that five "Russell jobs" were in inventory on January 1, 19X7. Data on these jobs follow.

JOB NUMBER	WORK IN PROCESS	FINISHED GOODS
457		$36,700
459	$12,200	
461	21,500	
462		57,300
463	18,300	

The January 1 work in process for the Easton line cost $26,500 and consisted of 1,200 units, ¼ complete. In the manufacture of these goods, all materials are introduced at the start of the process, and conversion costs are incurred evenly throughout production.

The company must calculate an overhead application rate for use during the next 12 months. Durham employs direct labor hours as an application base, and the firm's accountant has derived the following estimates for 19X7:

Direct labor (52,000 hours)	$420,000	Utilities	$33,000
Indirect materials used	18,000	Taxes	40,000
Indirect labor	49,600	Insurance	11,000
Factory depreciation	30,400		

The following data relate to operations for January:

- All direct and indirect materials are charged to the Raw Materials account when acquired. January purchases on account amounted to: direct materials, $58,000; indirect materials, $3,700.
- Materials requisitioned for production during the month are shown in the accompanying chart.

	DIRECT MATERIALS	INDIRECT MATERIALS	TOTAL
Job no. 459	$ 4,100		$ 4,100
Job no. 463	5,800		5,800
Job no. 464	13,700		13,700
Job no. 465	17,500		17,500
Russell production		$ 800	800
Easton production	54,600	1,100	55,700

Easton production started during January totaled 2,600 physical units.

- January payroll was distributed in the following manner:

	HOURS	COST
Job no. 459	300	$ 2,350
Job no. 461	150	1,200
Job no. 463	550	4,500
Job no. 464	200	1,700
Job no. 465	750	5,900
Easton production	2,500	20,000
Indirect labor—Russell	210	2,000
Indirect labor—Easton	250	2,200
Selling & administrative	—	6,000

- Other factory costs related to January were: depreciation, $2,400; utilities, $2,800; taxes, $4,000; and insurance, $900. The amount for insurance represents the expiration of a prepaid policy. Other amounts, except for depreciation, were paid as incurred.
- Durham completed job nos. 459, 461, and 464 during the month, along with a total of 2,000 units related to the Easton product line. Easton work in process on January 31 amounted to 1,800 units, ⅓ complete.
- The company prices its job orders at 150% of cost; in contrast, Easton goods are priced to sell at 130% of cost. Job nos. 457 and 459 were shipped and invoiced to customers. In addition, the firm sold Easton products on account that had a total manufacturing cost of $17,300.

Instructions

You have just been hired as a managerial accountant by Durham Manufacturing. Prepare answers to the following:

a. What functions would you expect to perform for the firm as a newly hired managerial accountant?
b. Distinguish between product and period costs, and specify the proper accounting treatment for each.
c. Easton production is expected to become heavily automated by the beginning of next year. Would the use of labor hours as an overhead application base continue to be appropriate for these goods? Explain.
d. Determine the overhead application rate for 19X7.
e. Determine the amount of under- or overapplied overhead as of January 31, 19X7. Be sure to label your answer as underapplied or overapplied.
f. Compute the cost of jobs completed during January.
g. Prepare a production cost report for January for the Easton product line. The report should reveal equivalent units of production, cost per equivalent unit, the cost of goods completed during the period, and the cost of the ending work in process inventory. *Hint:* Conversion cost should reflect applied (as opposed to actual) overhead amounts.
h. Analyze all data presented along with your answers to requirements (d)–(g) and present the necessary journal entries for January. Durham charges under- or overapplied overhead to Cost of Goods Sold at the end of each month. (*Note*: Prepare summary entries by combining individual job data.)

23 COST-VOLUME-PROFIT ANALYSIS

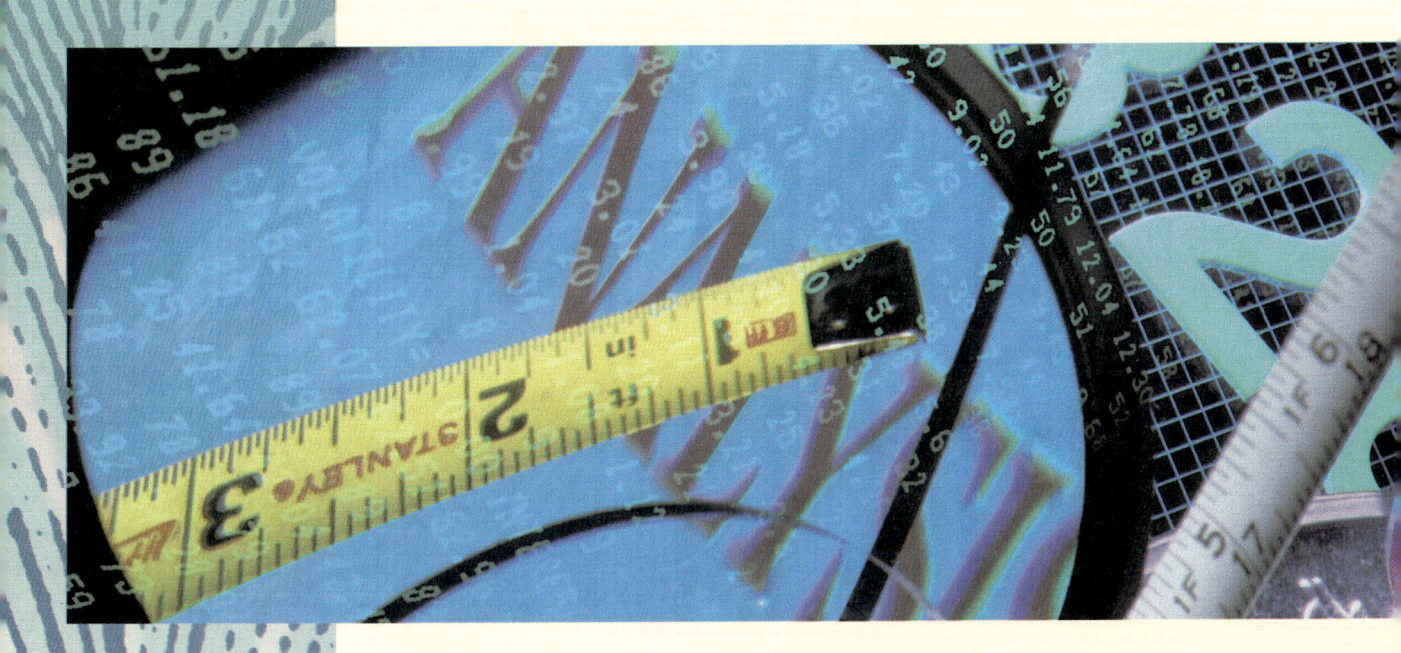

LEARNING OBJECTIVES

After studying this chapter, you should be able to:

1. Identify the characteristics of variable, step, fixed, and mixed (semivariable) cost functions.
2. Use the scattergraph and high-low method for examining cost behavior.
3. Compute and explain the meaning of a company's break-even point and contribution margin.
4. Calculate the sales needed to generate a particular target income figure.
5. Use sales price, cost, and volume data to determine the impact of various operating changes on profitability.
6. Apply cost-volume-profit analysis to multiproduct firms.
7. State the limiting assumptions on which cost-volume-profit analysis is based.

Understanding the nature and behavior of costs along with their impact on profit is critical for virtually all businesses. When your authors sat down with George Faris of Banner Advertising to plan this chapter's opening vignette, we could see excitement in his eyes. "If you want to talk about relevant material that I use everyday, then this is it," George observed, as he skimmed through the upcoming presentation.

He quickly started to list the following company decisions that are driven by a detailed analysis of costs: "Should we reduce rent to attract a new client or wait for higher revenues, even though the billboard's face may remain empty for several months? How many hours each night should a board be illuminated? Should we build a smaller sign in 'B-' and 'C-type' locations to reduce up-front fixed investment cost, and what will this do to the amount of revenue we can produce? Should the firm pay commissions or fixed salaries to sales agents? What minimal price can Banner charge and . . . ." We finally had to cut in as he continued to expand his list, "Okay, George, we get your point."

As you can see, understanding the impact of costs is important to Banner Advertising. The same can be said for many other firms that, during the past decade, have felt the effects of sharp competition. In an effort to maintain adequate earnings growth and cash flow generation, companies have been forced to alter existing business practices. Retailers have extended store hours and occasionally changed their image to appear more "lean and mean." Manufacturers have increased the use of "high-tech" production methods to improve efficiency and product quality. And, in an example that may be very close to home, consider something as basic as the menu of your favorite fast-food restaurant. No doubt that menu has undergone considerable expansion, with the addition of breakfasts, salad bars, specialty sandwiches, and desserts to the standard fare.

Operating changes such as those just cited can be implemented only after extensive analysis. Businesses must determine how increases and decreases in revenue, cost, and volume affect net income. As you learned in an earlier chapter, for example, certain costs fluctuate with changes in activity, while other costs remain constant. The study of interrelationships among the preceding factors is often termed cost-volume-profit (CVP) analysis, a powerful tool that many managers find useful in planning and decision making.

COST BEHAVIOR

Effective CVP analysis requires a thorough understanding of cost behavior and calls for an expansion of the material presented in Chapter 20. Before we do so, a word of caution is necessary. It is important to understand that costs often exhibit different behavior patterns under differing sets of circumstances. For instance, many costs do not change when small fluctuations in volume occur. Those same costs, however, may increase (or decrease) greatly when the activity change is more pronounced. Also, certain costs may follow a definite behavior pattern when closely monitored and controlled by management. Remove the controls and the predictable pattern may vary significantly from what was originally observed.

In sum, it is frequently difficult to generalize about the behavior of a given cost. An accounting educator once likened costs to people: they both have unique personalities and behave as individuals. Given this introduction, we will now explore four types of costs: variable, step, fixed, and mixed.

> **1** Identify the characteristics of variable, step, fixed, and mixed (semivariable) cost functions.

VARIABLE COSTS

Recall that a *variable cost* varies in direct proportion to a change in an activity base (e.g., sales, production, miles driven, and so forth). As a result, if an activity base triples, a true variable cost should triple; if the base is halved, the cost should decrease by 50%. Common examples of variable costs include direct materials, direct labor, supplies, sales commissions, and fuel.

Because variable costs change in direct proportion to fluctuations in an activity base, the variable cost *per unit* is constant. To illustrate, assume that Yellowstone Manufacturing normally produces 10,000 to 12,000 units each month. On the basis of the data in columns A and B, the accounting department has calculated labor cost at $8 per unit:

(A) UNITS PRODUCED	(B) TOTAL LABOR COST	(B) ÷ (A) COST PER UNIT
10,000	$80,000	$80,000 ÷ 10,000 = $8
10,500	84,000	$84,000 ÷ 10,500 = $8
11,000	88,000	$88,000 ÷ 11,000 = $8
11,500	92,000	$92,000 ÷ 11,500 = $8
12,000	96,000	$96,000 ÷ 12,000 = $8

Notice that the $8 figure holds true at all volume levels.

The Economist's View. Those readers who have taken an economics course may have noticed an apparent conflict between the economist's and accountant's views of variable cost behavior. Economic models generally assume that per-unit variable cost does not remain stable; rather, it changes with increases in activity. For example, picture a corporation that produces trucks by an assembly-line process. If the firm employed only two laborers, the number of trucks manufactured would surely be low. Furthermore, the process would be inefficient, because each employee would have to perform a multitude of tasks. As demand increases, the firm could raise its output by hiring more personnel. Instead of being a "jack of all trades," a worker could specialize, improve capital utilization, and become more efficient. The net result is a decreasing variable cost per unit. Naturally, a business can improve operations only so far. At some point production problems are encountered because of capacity constraints, lack of activity and departmental coordination, bottlenecks, and other factors. The culmination is a decrease in productivity and an accompanying rise in the variable cost per unit.

The accounting and economic views of variable cost behavior are graphed in Exhibit 23–1. The accountant's variable cost is graphed as a straight-line, linear

EXHIBIT 23–1
Differing Views of Variable Cost

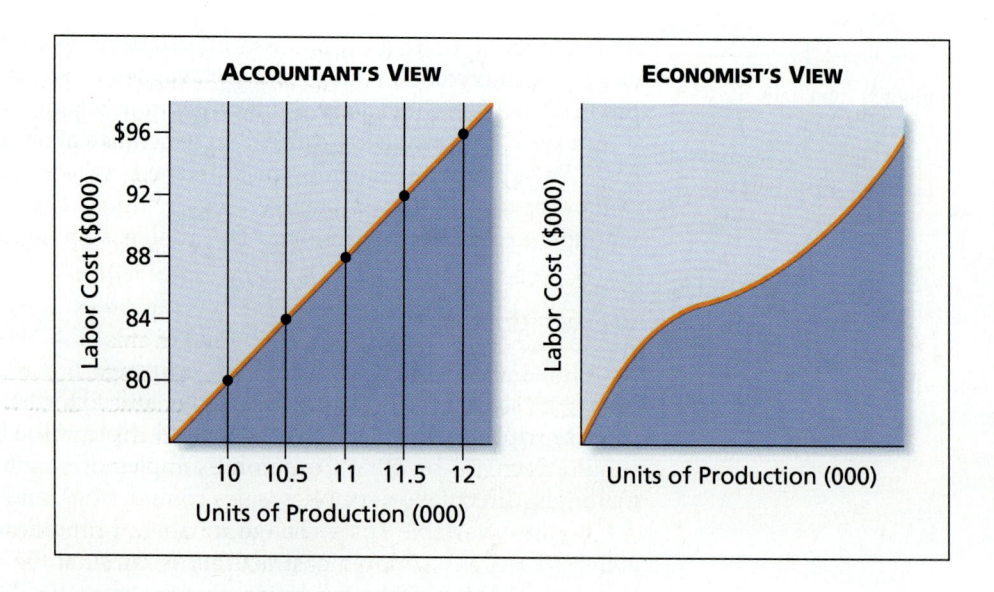

function. The economist's curve, in contrast, first depicts a decreasing cost per unit and later an increasing unit cost. The gradual upward slope to the right still indicates, however, that *total* variable cost increases with additional activity.

Both of the preceding views are correct. The accountant, however, normally studies costs over a smaller range of activity than does the economist. Examine Exhibit 23–2, which shows the behavior of a curvilinear cost function. Notice that within the narrow shaded band, linear behavior (i.e., a constant per-unit amount) is realistic. The band depicts the relevant range, or the area of activity where a specified cost relationship is expected to hold true. Normally, the relevant range is an area in which the entity has had some recent operating experience. Generally stated, the assumption of linearity within this narrow band is acceptable and not likely to result in substantial inaccuracies when analyzing costs.

Step Cost. A careful inspection of specific variable cost functions will often reveal different behavior patterns. Although direct materials and sales commissions change in response to small changes in production and sales, respectively,

EXHIBIT 23–2
Curvilinear Variable Cost and the Relevant Range

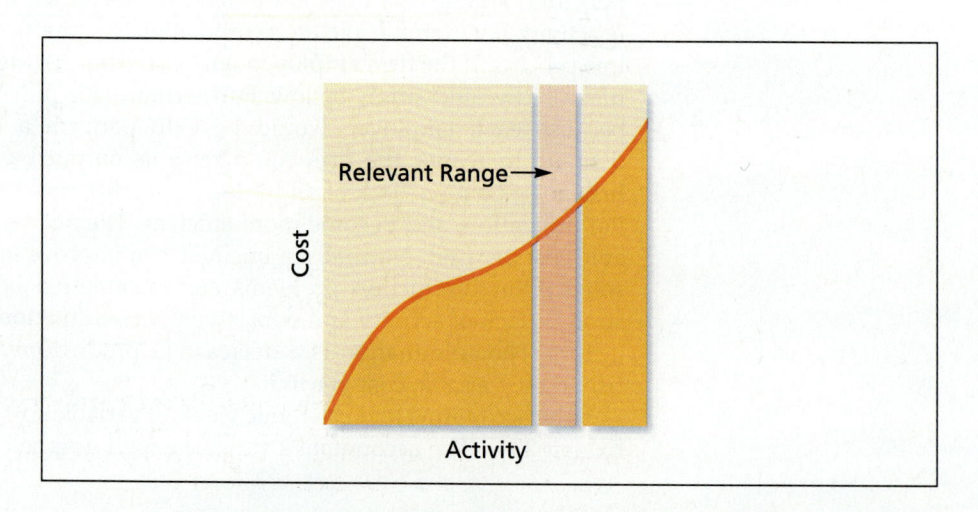

other variable costs vary only when substantial increases or decreases occur in the activity base. For example, consider the clerical staff needed to process customer orders in a mail-order firm. By working at different paces, employees can usually handle a wide range of orders. The number of orders processed will be low if the office staff is working at a relaxed pace or high if efforts intensify. Thus, when small fluctuations in volume occur, the total cost of office personnel remains constant. If activity dramatically increases, however, additional staff will be hired, and the total office costs will rise.

Because the personnel cost increases in proportion to the number of sales orders, the cost is classified as variable. In this case, though, the cost function changes only when sizable changes are experienced in the activity base. Specifically, the office cost will rise in "chunks" as new workers are added to the payroll. Cost functions that behave in this manner are frequently termed **step costs** and tend to approximate the behavior of a "true" variable cost (see Exhibit 23–3).[1]

A careful review of the step cost function provides the underlying explanation of a popular business practice: operating at the rightmost portion of a step. By so doing, an organization gets the most for its money, that is, maximum activity just prior to a cost increase.

FIXED COSTS

Fixed costs are costs that do not change when the activity base fluctuates. To illustrate a fixed cost, assume Yellowstone Manufacturing Co., leased machinery for $100,000 that is capable of producing from 40,000 to 60,000 units per year depending on utilization. Because the lease payment remains the same no matter how many units are produced, the graph shown in Exhibit 23–4 is appropriate.

Constant dollars combined with changing activity cause variations in the fixed cost *per unit*. If Yellowstone manufactures only 40,000 units, the lease cost is $2.50 per unit ($100,000 ÷ 40,000 units). On the other hand, if production

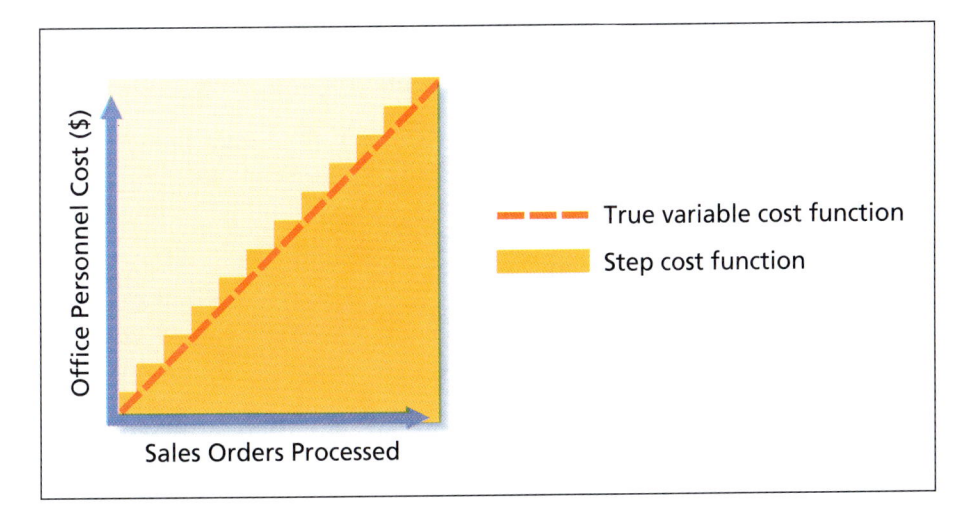

EXHIBIT 23–3
Step Cost Function

[1] Although our example has depicted a step cost as a type of variable cost, be aware that the step function may also resemble a fixed cost. This situation occurs when the steps become very wide or, in other words, when an extremely large activity change is needed to force an increase (or decrease) in cost. An explanation is provided on page 888.

EXHIBIT 23–4
Fixed Cost Behavior

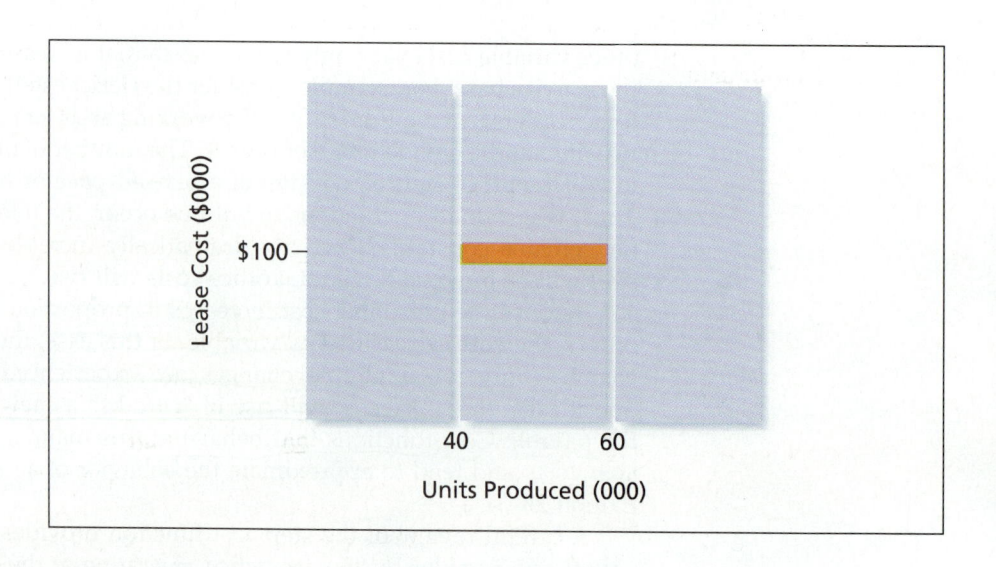

climbs to 60,000 units, the per-unit cost falls to $1.67 ($100,000 ÷ 60,000 units). In view of this behavior, we can summarize the movement of fixed and variable costs as shown in the accompanying chart.

TYPE OF COST	EFFECT OF CHANGES IN THE ACTIVITY BASE ON	
	TOTAL COST	COST PER UNIT
Variable	Increase or decrease	No effect
Fixed	No effect*	Increase or decrease

* This is a general rule, as further explained in the next section.

Total Fixed Costs Can Change. Although total fixed costs remain static, they can, in fact, vary. Both time and other ranges of activity will readily cause increases or decreases in this significant cost element. To explain, virtually all costs change over the years because of inflation and variations in business practices. In the previous illustration, for example, Yellowstone might have leased the same equipment in future years at an increased cost or perhaps have turned to another lessor to obtain advanced technology. Whether a cost is, indeed, fixed depends on the time period under study. In the long run, most costs change to match increases and decreases in manufacturing and sales activities.

Ranges of activity also affect fixed cost behavior. Notice that Yellowstone's equipment can manufacture up to 60,000 units per year. If production increases beyond this point, additional machinery must be leased, which forces fixed costs to rise. The additional machinery will allow the firm to handle a new range of activity, say, 60,001 to 80,000 units. If production increases once again, then even more machinery must be acquired. Costs that behave in this manner can be graphed as shown in Exhibit 23–5. The graph reveals that fixed costs will change with wide fluctuations in activity. The shaded band represents Yellowstone's most recent manufacturing experience—in essence, the relevant range. If the relevant range has been properly defined, normal operations should produce fixed costs that can be graphed as a single horizontal line.

EXHIBIT 23–5
Fixed Cost Behavior and Ranges of Activity

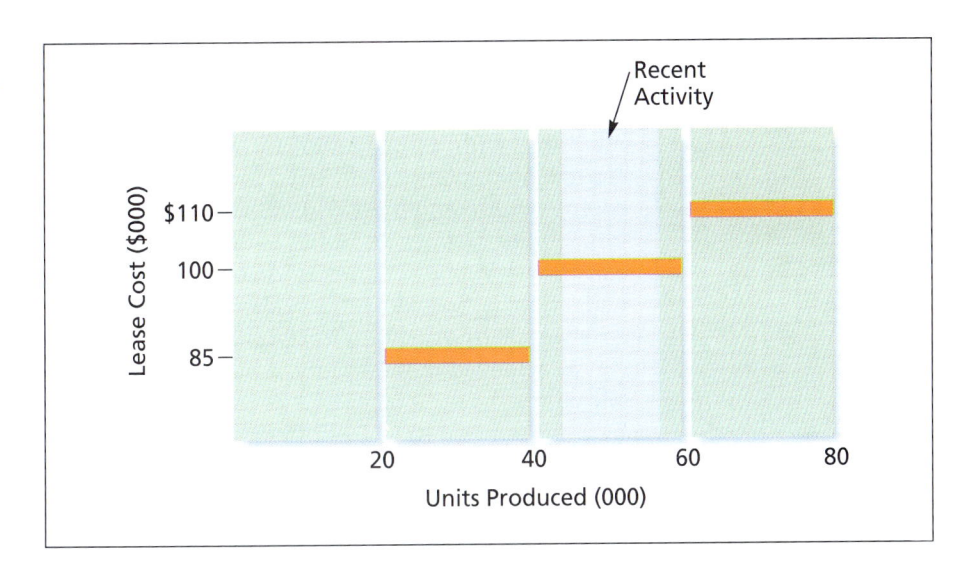

Committed and Discretionary Fixed Costs. Fixed costs are substantial for many companies, especially those engaged in manufacturing. Heavy capital equipment and inventory requirements generate sizable depreciation write-offs, lease costs, and various related outlays. For purposes of planning, fixed costs are often subdivided into two types: committed and discretionary.

Committed fixed costs arise from an organization's commitment to engage in operations. By opening its doors and commencing activities, a firm must secure a plant, equipment, and management team. Immediately, as a result, an obligation is made to incur such costs as depreciation, rent, insurance, property taxes, and executive salaries.

By their very nature, most committed costs are not easily changed by daily business activities and decisions. Even if activity slows because of a depressed economy, many of these costs will still be incurred. Obviously, executives can vote to take salary cuts, layoffs can be instituted, and certain operations may be sold or perhaps temporarily closed. However, significant cutbacks in committed costs normally prevent a company from achieving its long-run goals and objectives.

Discretionary fixed costs are those that originate from top management's yearly spending decisions. That is, in preparing the annual operating budget, management will decide the amount it wishes to allocate to certain forthcoming activities. Fixed costs typically determined in this fashion include advertising, research and development, employee training, and contributions.

The Underlying Differences. Aside from the manner in which they originate, committed and discretionary fixed costs differ in two important ways. First, when a business decides to engage in or expand operations, it conducts a careful study of both its current *and* future economic position. Buildings will not be built and equipment will not be acquired unless *long-run* profitability is anticipated. In view of their nature, it is apparent that committed costs are geared heavily to the future. Discretionary fixed costs, conversely, are short term in orientation and are based on management's expectations for the forthcoming accounting period.

The second distinction between committed and discretionary costs concerns cost elimination. As noted, committed costs are not easily changed. Once the decision to incur them is made, an organization becomes locked-in and must live with its obligation for a number of years. Because of this relative stranglehold, companies strive for effective facility utilization as a means of coping with committed costs. Such a strategy is very logical: the associated inflexibility dictates an uphill battle if cost reduction is attempted to improve earnings. While discretionary costs also lock in an organization, the period of obligation is normally much shorter. Frequently, for example, discretionary costs are set by yearly contracts. Should financial difficulties arise, cost cutbacks can be achieved more rapidly, possibly without significant damage to long-run objectives.

Increased Fixed Costs. Over the years there has been a shift by businesses toward higher levels of fixed cost incurrence (relative to variable cost). Consider that labor unions have fought long and hard for guaranteed annual wages and workweeks, both of which have transformed direct labor (a variable cost) into a cost that is not totally responsive to changes in production. Another factor is an increased use of automated facilities and robots, as discussed earlier in the text. Automation and its accompanying charges for depreciation, property taxes, leasing, and maintenance have added to a company's fixed costs while often, at the same time, reducing the labor force.

Although guaranteed wages and workweeks may be attractive from a social viewpoint, and automation may lead to improved efficiency and product quality, operating flexibility will frequently suffer. A manager will normally have additional decision-making alternatives available in a variable cost environment—one where costs are readily changed and/or eliminated should the need arise.

MIXED (SEMIVARIABLE) COSTS

Many cost functions contain both variable and fixed cost elements. Companies, for instance, often pay their salespeople a weekly salary plus a commission. The commission is generally a stipulated percentage of sales and varies with the revenues produced. As another example, electric utilities frequently bill their customers a fixed amount each month, plus a certain number of cents per kilowatt-hour used. Both of these cost functions are termed mixed, or semivariable, costs. Like a variable cost, a mixed cost changes in response to fluctuations in the activity base. Mixed cost movement, however, is not directly proportional because of the presence of a constant fixed charge. The elements of a mixed cost are shown graphically in Exhibit 23–6.

Observe that the variable and fixed cost elements are combined to generate the total mixed cost. To illustrate, assume that New England Products pays Howard Polk a $200 weekly salary plus a 10% sales commission. If Polk's sales for the week just ended total $2,450, New England's compensation cost of $445 would be computed as follows:

Fixed salary cost	$200
Variable cost: $2,450 × 0.10	245
Total (mixed) cost	$445

EXHIBIT 23–6
Mixed Cost

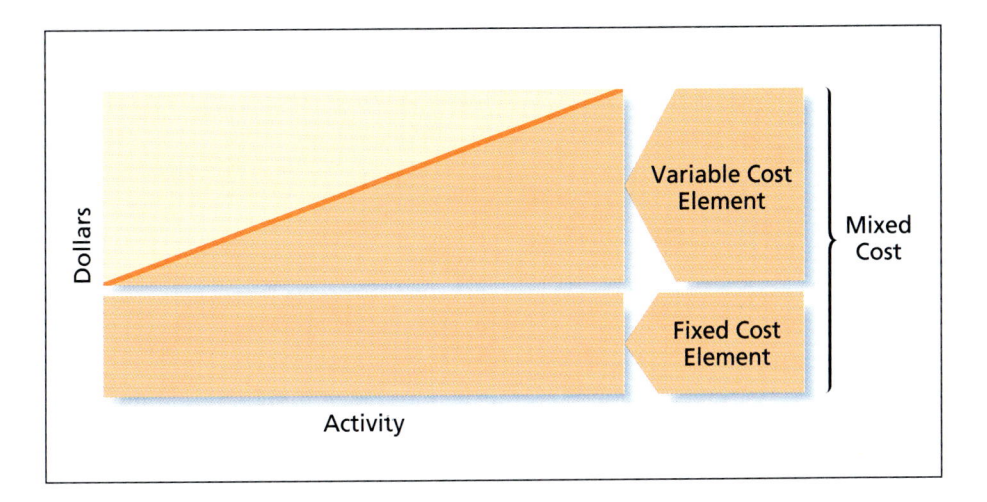

[Graph showing Dollars on the y-axis and Activity on the x-axis. An upward sloping line represents the Variable Cost Element, and a horizontal band represents the Fixed Cost Element. Together they form the Mixed Cost.]

COST ANALYSIS

Most accountants and cost analysts have little difficulty understanding the differences among variable, step, fixed, and mixed costs. The determination of how specific costs behave, however, is another matter. Recall our earlier warning—the same costs can behave differently in different situations. To further complicate the picture, many costs are influenced by more than one factor at a given time. Direct materials used, for example, is normally classified as a variable cost. Use varies with production but is also influenced by material quality and worker efficiency. Turning to another area, gasoline consumption increases with the number of miles driven. However, consumption is also affected by the vehicle involved, wind conditions, the type of driving (city or highway), and other factors.

You are probably beginning to realize that cost analysis is a difficult task. In practice, many companies assume that cost behavior can be sufficiently explained by concentrating on only one key factor rather than the many variables that may actually affect expenditure levels. Management must therefore exercise sound judgment when examining cost functions. Cost analysis in most organizations is heavily dependent on assumptions and estimates, with perfection being the exception rather than the rule.

Several techniques have been developed to study cost behavior. These techniques include the scattergraph, the method of least squares, and the high-low method.

SCATTERGRAPH

> **2** Use the scattergraph and high-low method for examining cost behavior.

A *scattergraph* is a graphical representation of observed relationships between costs and activity levels. Using operating data, one plots the costs incurred at various levels of activity. On the basis of the observed relationships, the costs are then identified as being fixed, variable, or mixed. To illustrate use of a scattergraph, assume that Zephyr Bus Lines wants to analyze the maintenance costs incurred to service its bus fleet. An examination of maintenance records for a recent six-month period revealed the following information:

Month	Maintenance Labor Hours	Maintenance Cost
January	1,400	$25,000
February	1,200	22,400
March	1,600	24,500
April	1,800	24,700
May	1,900	28,000
June	2,000	30,000

A casual inspection of the data reveals that some variable cost is present, since higher levels of activity (labor hours) generate higher costs. This observation is confirmed by examining the scattergraph in Exhibit 23–7. The line through the data points, drawn by visual approximation, intersects the cost axis at $10,000—the fixed cost of Zephyr's maintenance operation. The variable cost per hour can now be found by studying the total cost of any point that falls on the line.[2] The computations that follow show the proper approach.

Total cost at 2,000 hours	$30,000
Less fixed cost	10,000
Variable cost	$20,000

Variable cost per hour: $20,000 ÷ 2,000 hours = $10 per hour

The scattergraph is somewhat imprecise because of the manner in which the cost line is determined. Nevertheless it is a starting point for analyzing cost behavior.

METHOD OF LEAST SQUARES

The **method of least squares** is a statistical technique that overcomes the imprecision of the scattergraph. Rather than determine the cost line by approximation, the least-squares method relies on mathematical formulas to minimize the sum of the squares of the distances from the data points to the line. With

EXHIBIT 23–7
Scattergraph

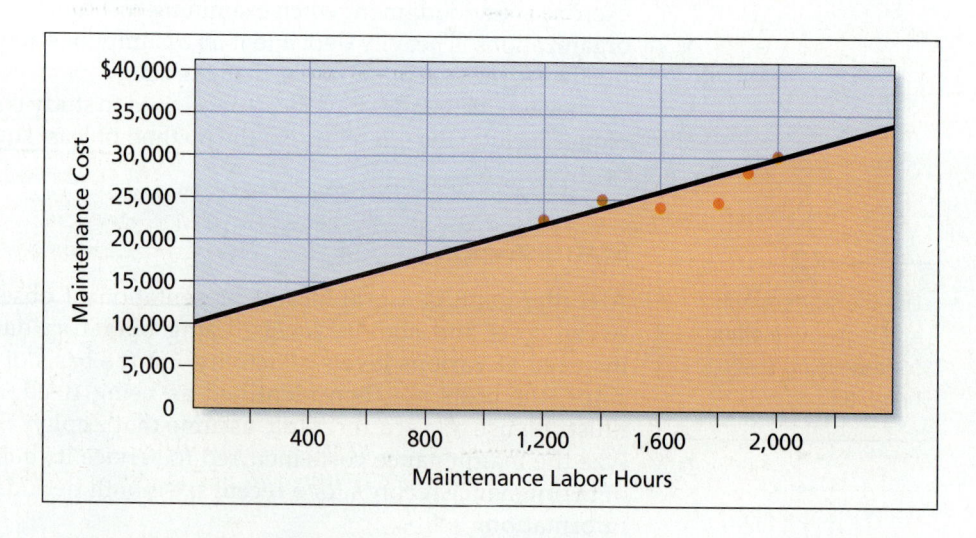

[2] The hourly variable cost is equal to the slope of the line.

this approach the best possible line fit is obtained, and higher accuracy is achieved. The details of the least-squares method are normally presented in most statistics courses and many advanced managerial accounting courses.

HIGH-LOW METHOD

Unlike the scattergraph and the method of least squares, the **high-low method** focuses on only two data points when analyzing costs: those at the highest and lowest levels of activity within the relevant range. From these two points a generalization about variable and fixed cost behavior is made.

To illustrate the related procedures, we will continue the Zephyr Bus Lines example. Observe that the highest and lowest activity occurred during June and February, respectively. By studying these two months, we see that an 800-hour increase in labor time caused maintenance cost to rise by $7,600. These figures are obtained from the following computations:

	MAINTENANCE LABOR HOURS	MAINTENANCE COST
Highest activity (June)	2,000	$30,000
Lowest activity (February)	1,200	22,400
Difference	800	$ 7,600

The increase in total cost represents variable cost. Thus, the variable maintenance cost per hour amounts to $9.50 ($7,600 ÷ 800 hours).

Once the variable portion is known, fixed cost can be determined by returning to either of the two months under study. Because total cost equals variable cost plus fixed cost, the latter amount is easily found by subtraction:

	HIGH POINT (2,000 HOURS)	LOW POINT (1,200 HOURS)
Total cost	$30,000	$22,400
Less variable cost @ $9.50 per hour	19,000*	11,400†
Fixed cost	$11,000	$11,000

* 2,000 hours × $9.50 = $19,000.
† 1,200 hours × $9.50 = $11,400.

As the calculations show, fixed costs are the same at both volume levels—an expected finding since we are working within one range of activity. Observe, though, that the fixed costs (and the variable costs as well) differ from the amounts obtained by using the scattergraph. This result is not unusual because the two techniques use different approaches when dealing with historical cost/activity relationships.

The high-low method is a straightforward approach to cost analysis; yet the method has been criticized because it relies on only two data observations and ignores all others. Given this situation, it is important that the points selected for evaluation be representative of normal behavior and not reflect unusual happenings. Selecting nonrepresentative points will taint the results obtained.[3]

> **ETHICS ISSUE**
>
> United, Inc., will be closing 2 of its 11 factories. A major deciding factor is a facility's variable and fixed cost structure. Your plant regularly uses the high-low method of analysis, but you know that the scattergraph will give a more accurate (and unfavorable) picture of the plant's actual cost behavior. Which method should be used? Why?

---

[3] A scattergraph is helpful in spotting such points. So-called *outliers* will fall far away from the other data.

COST-VOLUME-PROFIT ANALYSIS

3 Compute and explain the meaning of a company's break-even point and contribution margin.

Once variable and fixed costs are determined, cost-volume-profit analysis can begin. Managers utilize CVP analysis in many different ways. Various cost strategies can be explored, such as trade-offs between incurring fixed salary costs or variable sales commissions. CVP can also be used to examine pricing policies and their impact on market share; profit strategies such as purposely incurring a loss on a product to generate additional customer traffic in a retail store; and other similar issues.

An important and highly publicized facet of cost-volume-profit analysis is break-even analysis. This popular management tool concentrates on finding the **break-even point**—the level of activity where revenues and expenses are equal. Related income, as a result, is zero.

The break-even point can be calculated by employing either an equation or a contribution approach. To illustrate both methods, we will assume that the University Bookstore is studying whether to add a collection of mugs to its product line. Each mug costs $7 and will be sold for $10. The following additional monthly costs will be incurred:

Rental cost of display case	$300
Salary of part-time salesperson	600
	$900

EQUATION APPROACH

As its name implies, the equation approach relies on a mathematical equation to compute the break-even point. The equation is based on the calculation of operating income, that is:

Sales		$XXX
Less: Variable costs	$XXX	
Fixed costs	XXX	XXX
Operating income		$XXX

Because income equals zero at the break-even point, the following expression is constructed:

$$\text{Sales} - \text{Variable Costs} - \text{Fixed Costs} = 0$$

Transforming, we have

$$\text{Sales} = \text{Variable Costs} + \text{Fixed Costs}$$

The equation requires that variable costs be expressed as a percentage of sales. An examination of the University Bookstore data reveals that the $300 display case rental and the $600 salary are both fixed since neither amount changes with volume. The $7 mug cost, on the other hand, is variable, making variable cost in our example 70% of sales ($7 ÷ $10 selling price).

The break-even point can now be found in the following manner:

$$\text{Sales} = \text{Variable Costs} + \text{Fixed Costs}$$
$$S = VC + FC$$
$$S = 0.7S + \$900$$
$$0.3S = \$900$$
$$S = \$3,000$$

The calculations show that monthly sales must total $3,000 to break even. Stated differently, sales in excess of 300 mugs ($3,000 ÷ $10 selling price) will be profitable; in contrast, sales of less than 300 mugs will produce a loss.

CONTRIBUTION APPROACH

The contribution approach focuses on unit profitability. Because mugs are purchased for $7 and later sold for $10, the bookstore is better off by $3 for each mug sold. The $3 figure is termed the contribution margin, namely, selling price minus variable cost per unit. Stated simply, the contribution margin represents the amount that each mug contributes toward covering fixed costs and generating income.

To illustrate, examine the data in the following chart:

MUGS SOLD	REVENUE	TOTAL VARIABLE COST	FIXED COST	TOTAL COST	OPERATING INCOME
0	$ 0	$ 0	$900	$ 900	$(900)
1	10	7	900	907	(897)
2	20	14	900	914	(894)
⋮	⋮	⋮	⋮	⋮	⋮
300	3,000	2,100	900	3,000	0
301	3,010	2,107	900	3,007	3
302	3,020	2,114	900	3,014	6

The first line shows product-line profitability immediately after the decision to carry the mugs. Specifically, the salesperson has been hired and the display case has been rented; however, no merchandise has been sold. Each sale then contributes $3 toward covering the fixed costs and decreases the overall loss. Although the decision to stock the goods will eventually prove profitable, the bookstore must first generate sufficient volume to completely offset the fixed costs and break even. The break-even point is computed in the following manner:

$$\frac{\text{Fixed Costs}}{\text{Unit Contribution Margin}} = \text{Break-Even Point in Units}$$

$$\frac{\$900}{\$3} = 300 \text{ mugs}$$

After the 300th mug is sold, income will be produced at the rate of $3 per unit.

The contribution margin is a very powerful business tool and should not be dismissed lightly. In addition to its use in profit planning, the contribution margin also assists in performance evaluation and decision making. These applications are explored in Chapter 26.

A Further Focus

An interesting break-even application arose not too long ago with the opening of the Grand Wailea Resort, Hotel & Spa, a luxury facility on Maui, Hawaii. The complex cost $600 million to build, or approximately $800,000 per room, and came complete with a $2 million statue and 800 tons of imported granite from Japan. Financing costs alone ran close to $100,000 per day. Combining all the variable and fixed costs of operation, the Grand Resort had to charge an average room rate of $500 a day to break even—and that assumes a 100% occupancy rate.

These figures are obviously quite ambitious, especially considering that occupancy rates in the surrounding area were about 52%. Also, the average room rate was about $130. As a reporter from *Forbes* magazine noted, the project likely never made economic sense.

Source: "Banzai Loans," *Forbes,* November 11, 1991, p. 40.

A Graphical Representation. The break-even point and CVP relationships are frequently presented in a graphical format known as a **break-even chart.** The graph is useful because it allows managers to (1) review earnings over a wide range of activity and (2) examine the effects on profitability of changes in sales and costs.

The break-even chart for our mug example appears in Exhibit 23–8. With sales volume graphed on the horizontal axis and dollars on the vertical axis, the chart is constructed in the following manner:

1. Fixed costs are depicted by drawing a line parallel to the horizontal axis.
2. Total costs are represented by first computing the total cost of an arbitrarily selected volume level. The calculations for a volume of 500 mugs follow.

Variable cost (500 mugs × $7)	$3,500
Fixed cost	900
Total cost	$4,400

The total cost line is then extended from the intersection of the fixed cost line and the vertical axis to $4,400 (point A).

3. Sales revenues are plotted in a manner similar to that described in Step 2. A diagonal line is extended from the graph's origin through a point that represents the total revenues of an arbitrarily selected activity level. If we again choose 500 mugs, the line would be extended through point *B*, or $5,000 (500 mugs × $10).

Point *C* represents break-even operations: $3,000 of sales (300 mugs). The graph readily discloses that sales in excess of 300 mugs will be profitable because total revenues will exceed total costs. In contrast, should volume drop

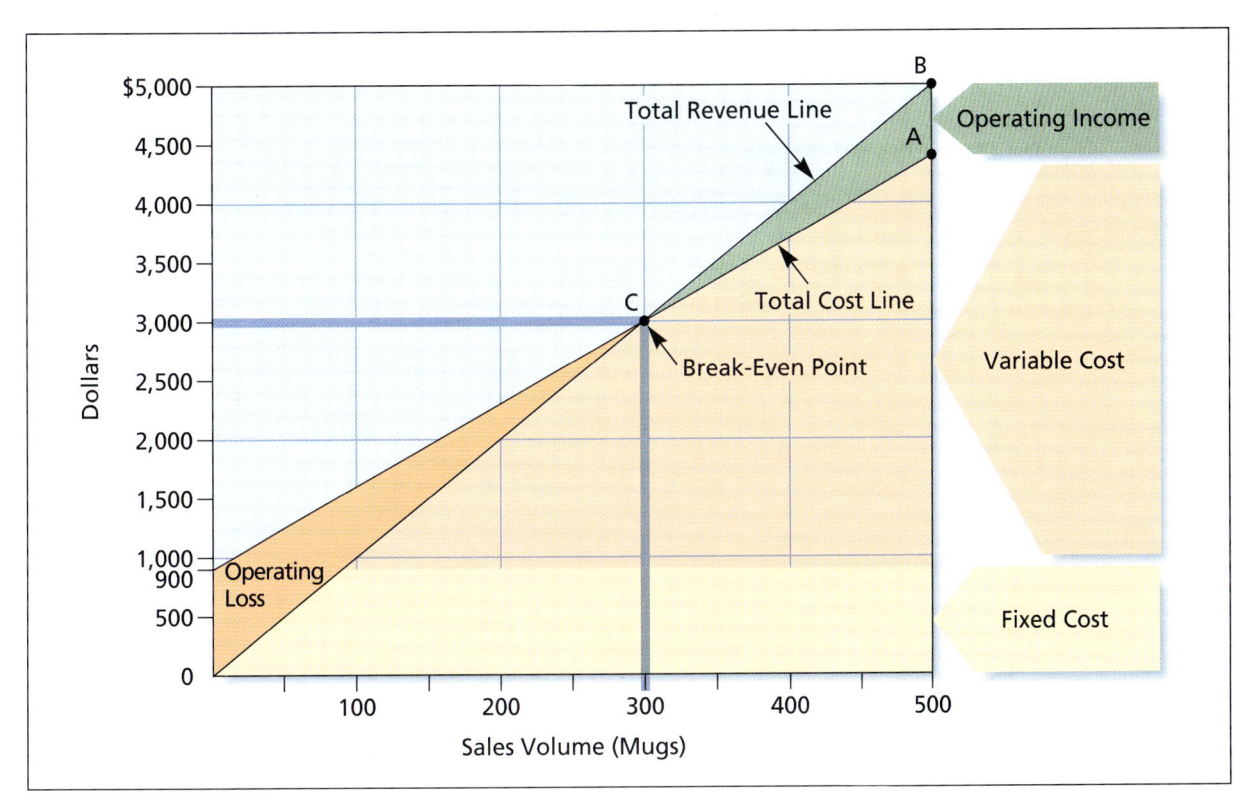

EXHIBIT 23–8
Break-Even Chart

BUSINESS BRIEFING

The Meaning of Cost-Volume-Profit Analysis to a Business

Several years ago, consumer research indicated that Wendy's was perceived as relatively high cost and, therefore, not as good a "value" as some of our quick-service restaurant competitors. We didn't feel this was true, since value is not just a low price, but "quality received for money spent." However, to a certain extent, perception is reality, so we developed a strategy to enhance our value image. The concept involved packaging a core of nine items, all priced at $0.99, which we call the Super Value Menu (SVM).

The products were primarily existing offerings; they were not modified in quantity or quality to offset the reduced $0.99 selling price and accompanying drop in per-unit profit (contribution) margin. The SVM proved to be popular, and *total* sales and contribution margin per store increased significantly. Since many restaurant operating costs are essentially fixed in nature, unlike food costs, which tend to vary directly with sales, the higher sales provided a greater overall profit. In addition, consumer perception of the "value" of Wendy's products has improved markedly since the Super Value Menu introduction.

R. DAVID THOMAS
Senior Chairman and Founder
Wendy's International, Inc.

below this figure, the University Bookstore will generate a loss from its new product line.

TARGET INCOME

> **4** Calculate the sales needed to generate a particular target income figure.

In addition to finding the break-even point, CVP analysis can be used to determine the sales necessary to produce a particular level of income (often called the *target income*). To illustrate the related procedures, we will continue the University Bookstore example. Assume that the mugs will be carried in stock only if they generate a monthly income of $150. The sales required to achieve this level of profitability can be calculated by modifying the equation and contribution approaches to break-even analysis.

Focusing on the first approach, we noted earlier that the following relationship is true at the break-even point:

$$\text{Sales} - \text{Variable Costs} - \text{Fixed Costs} = 0$$

Because we now desire to earn a given income figure, the equation becomes

$$\text{Sales} - \text{Variable Costs} - \text{Fixed Costs} = \text{Target Income}$$

or

$$\text{Sales} = \text{Variable Costs} + \text{Fixed Costs} + \text{Target Income}$$

Recall from the initial data that variable cost is 70% of sales and fixed costs total $900. The bookstore must therefore have sales of $3,500, as shown in the following computation:

$$S = VC + FC + TI$$
$$S = 0.7S + \$900 + \$150$$
$$0.3S = \$1,050$$
$$S = \$3,500$$

On the basis of the $10 selling price, volume must total 350 mugs ($3,500 ÷ $10).

Turning to the contribution method, the bookstore previously calculated that each mug contributes $3 ($10 selling price − $7 variable cost) toward covering fixed costs and producing a profit. As shown on page 895, 300 mugs must be sold just to break even. Now, to achieve the $150 target figure, volume must increase by 50 units per month ($150 ÷ $3). In view of this fact, the break-even formula is modified as follows:

$$\frac{\text{Fixed Costs} + \text{Target Income}}{\text{Unit Contribution Margin}} = \text{Required Sales in Units}$$

$$\frac{\$900 + \$150}{\$3} = 350 \text{ mugs}$$

> **5**
> Use sales price, cost, and volume data to determine the impact of various operating changes on profitability.

OPERATING CHANGES

New technology, shifts in management, and variations in efficiency are commonplace for most businesses. These events and others are usually accompanied by changes in costs and revenues and thus affect an organization's CVP relationships. Consider, for example, the following break-even load factors[4] for several of this country's airlines:

	1993	1992	1991	1990	1989
Delta Air Lines	65.5%	63.0%	62.6%	58.0%	56.1%
Northwest Airlines	67.2	69.8	69.0	69.8	64.9
USAir	61.7	63.2	62.7	64.5	60.6
United Airlines	65.6	70.4	69.5	66.5	63.0

Observe the variation over the years and among different carriers within the same year. Although there are a number of underlying causes, several of the more significant include fleet composition in terms of size, age, and fuel efficiency; route systems and structures (e.g., long haul versus short haul, business versus vacation); fleet financing methods; passenger fare composition (i.e., full-fare versus discount traffic); and labor and jet fuel contracts.

Airlines must respond to changes in these factors to stay in the black. Some have done so successfully, whereas others have not. Those in the latter category have incurred significant operating losses (occasionally leading to bankruptcy) or, in some cases, been absorbed by another carrier. Airlines are not alone—all businesses are faced with variations in their cost and revenue patterns.

Because management's ability to analyze operating changes often spells the difference between prosperity or failure, it is desirable to focus on the impact of changes in CVP relationships. To do so, we will continue the University Bookstore example. As a refresher, recall the following data:

Selling price per mug	$10	Fixed costs	
Variable cost per mug	7	Display case rental	$300
Contribution margin	$ 3	Salary of salesperson	600
			$900

Sales necessary to reach break-even point: 300 mugs
Sales necessary to generate a target income of $150: 350 mugs

Change in Fixed Costs. Assume the bookstore is considering hiring a more experienced salesperson who requires a $720 monthly salary. Management wants to know the effect on the break-even point of this $120 increase in fixed cost. The desired information can be obtained in several different ways. Employing the contribution approach, we see the new break-even volume is 340 mugs:

$$\frac{\text{Fixed Costs}}{\text{Unit Contribution Margin}} = \frac{\$1,020}{\$3} = 340 \text{ mugs}$$

---

[4] The break-even load factor is the percentage of seats that must be filled on scheduled flights to break even.

Or, since each mug contributes $3 toward fixed obligations, an additional 40 mugs must be sold to cover the $120 cost increase ($120 ÷ $3 = 40 mugs). Thus, the break-even point will jump from 300 to 340 units.

Changes in Fixed Costs and Variable Costs. Returning to the original data, assume the bookstore is exploring different compensation methods. Rather than a $600 monthly salary, a plan is being considered that calls for a base salary of $200 plus a $1-per-mug sales commission. Specifically, management wants to learn the sales volume required to yield the target monthly income of $150. In this case, total fixed costs fall to $500 ($200 + $300 display case rental). Furthermore, because variable costs rise by $1 from the commission, the mug's contribution margin decreases to $2 ($10 – $8). These two changes are combined to produce the following results:

$$\frac{\text{Fixed Costs} + \text{Target Income}}{\text{Unit Contribution Margin}} = \text{Required Sales in Units}$$

$$\frac{\$500 + \$150}{\$2} = 325 \text{ mugs}$$

The computation shows that with the change in salary structure, the bookstore can suffer a drop in monthly sales of 25 mugs (350 – 325) and still produce the target income figure. The plan is therefore advantageous and should be implemented. Not only do the numbers support the change, but an important qualitative consideration is present as well. The compensation plan under study—reward via commission—often increases employee motivation, which, in turn, leads to improved sales performance.

Changes in Fixed Costs and Sales Volume. Again returning to the original data, assume that operations have been quite profitable, with monthly sales averaging 400 mugs. Management is now considering a larger display case at an increased rental cost of $75 per month. The added space will allow the bookstore to carry a greater selection of merchandise, and sales are expected to total 440 units. Should the new display case be acquired?

Because both revenues and costs will change, management should compare the additional revenues that arise from the decision against the additional costs. If additional revenues exceed additional costs, the proposal should be accepted; if not, rejection is in order. The following evaluation reveals a net benefit in favor of the larger display case:

Additional revenues: 40 mugs × $10		$400
Less additional costs		
Variable: 40 mugs × $7	$280	
Increased rental	75	355
Net monthly benefit		$ 45

Observe that we have ignored the current volume of 400 mugs in our analysis. No matter which alternative is selected (i.e., maintain the present situation or acquire the larger case), these goods will continue to be sold. The analysis should concentrate on those items that change as a result of the decision, namely, the 40-unit increase in sales and the higher rental charge. Decisions of this nature are explored further in Chapter 26.

Changes in Sales Price and Sales Volume. Independent of the previous example that focused on a change in fixed costs and sales volume, assume that monthly sales have averaged 550 mugs. The bookstore is considering an increase in selling price from $10 to $12 despite a possible drop in the number of units sold. Before the final decision is made, management desires to know how much sales can decline before there is a detrimental effect on profitability.

Because current sales total 550 mugs, the present product-line income is $750 per month:

Sales (550 mugs × $10)	$5,500
Less variable cost (550 mugs × $7)	3,850
Contribution margin	$1,650
Less fixed cost	900
Operating income	$ 750

With a new selling price of $12, the unit contribution margin becomes $5 ($12 − $7). Using the following technique, which was illustrated earlier in the chapter, we find that 330 mugs must be sold to maintain current profit levels.

$$\frac{\text{Fixed Costs + Target Income}}{\text{Unit Contribution Margin}} = \text{Required Sales in Units}$$

$$\frac{\$900 + \$750}{\$5} = 330 \text{ mugs}$$

Thus, the bookstore can suffer a monthly sales loss of 220 units (550 − 330) without any impact on operating income.

A Word of Encouragement. The preceding illustrations have shown several different methods of examining and solving business problems. As you gain more experience in cost-volume-profit analysis, you will often find that the

---

A Further Focus

A careful analysis of CVP relationships recently allowed Sega of America to make considerable headway against Nintendo in the U.S. videogame market. In 1989, just prior to making several major operating changes, Nintendo had 30 million customers compared to Sega's 1 million. Sega took charge and cut the price of its more advanced machine by 25% to better compete with Nintendo's less expensive equipment. Sega also enlisted the help of various software houses to design new games, agreeing to take a lower royalty rate—sometimes 15% below that of Nintendo's—to encourage and motivate development. These changes, coupled with a more aggressive marketing campaign and promotional tie-ins with other firms (Coca-Cola and Lifesaver), have paid huge dividends. In three short years, sales of Sega's U.S. division increased approximately $720 million. Market share has increased from 7% to almost 50%, while that of Nintendo has slid from around 90% to an estimated 50%.

Source: "Games Companies Play," *Forbes*, October 25, 1993, pp. 68–69.

CVP Analysis for Multiproduct Firms

Most businesses engaged in retailing, wholesaling, and manufacturing activities sell more than one product, normally in differing volumes and at different markups. Although the University Bookstore example focused on the use of CVP analysis for a single item only, the procedures illustrated can, with minor modification, be employed when multiple goods are involved. As an example, assume that Stewart Distributors sells toasters, food processors, and mixers. The following data are anticipated for the upcoming year:

Product	Forecasted Sales (Units)	Selling Price	Variable Cost
Toaster	40,000	$20	$16
Food processor	100,000	44	37
Mixer	60,000	34	26
	200,000		

Fixed costs: $335,000

As before, the break-even point can be found by dividing fixed costs by the unit contribution margin. Rather than dealing with the contribution margin of one product, however, Stewart has three margins to consider. Adding a further complication, the margins are not expected to occur with the same frequency. For every toaster sold, for example, the firm anticipates selling 2½ food processors and 1½ mixers. In view of this situation, Stewart must weight the unit contribution margins by the **sales mix,** or the relative proportion of individual product sales to total sales. The computations that follow reveal a weighted "unit" contribution margin of $6.70:

Product	Forecasted Sales (Units)	Sales Mix*		Unit Contribution Margin†		Weighted Contribution Margin
Toaster	40,000	20%	×	$4	=	$0.80
Food processor	100,000	50%	×	7	=	3.50
Mixer	60,000	30%	×	8	=	2.40
	200,000					$6.70

* Forecasted individual product sales ÷ 200,000 units.
† Selling price minus variable cost for each product.

Stewart's break-even point is therefore 50,000 "units" ($335,000 ÷ $6.70). Because each "unit" is really a combination of the three products in the same proportions as the predicted mix, the following product-line sales are necessary:

Product	Sales Mix		Break-Even "Units"		Break-Even Sales by Product (Units)
Toaster	20%	×	50,000	=	10,000
Food processor	50%	×	50,000	=	25,000
Mixer	30%	×	50,000	=	15,000

A MARKETING CONSULTANT'S PERSPECTIVE

Sales Force Compensation: The compensation plan for a sales force is often more complicated than that for other employees. When a high level of aggressiveness is desired, the salary structure should be (and often is) heavily weighted with commissions. Determining the computational "base" for these commissions, however, is a problem area for many businesses.

Given the nature of salespeople to focus on revenue, commissions are typically calculated on dollar and/or unit volume. This procedure frequently results in employees "pushing" products that have high selling prices and/or products that are easier to sell. In both cases, the company may end up having a less-than-optimal sales mix. Keep in mind that contribution margins vary among goods, and it is possible that higher volumes sold of less profitable (i.e., the "wrong") products will actually reduce income below originally budgeted levels.

A possible solution to the problem is to reward employees by using a higher commission *rate*, but calculate the commission on the basis of contribution margins and not gross sales dollars. In this way the "right" products are pushed—those that produce a "richer" sales mix, a lower break-even point, and more income for the company.

On the basis of the calculations presented, it is evident that if the sales mix varies, the "unit" contribution margin will differ. Thus, the break-even volume will change.

LIMITING ASSUMPTIONS OF CVP ANALYSIS

State the limiting assumptions on which cost-volume-profit analysis is based.

The CVP model that we have presented is used to analyze the financial relationships within an organization. Businesses continually change their operating practices, and a number of the changes affect the relationships expressed in the model. CVP studies are therefore based on several limiting assumptions, a few of which have been touched upon in the preceding pages:

1. All costs can be classified as fixed or variable.
2. Fixed costs remain constant through the range of analysis (i.e., the relevant range).
3. The behavior of costs and revenues is linear through the range of analysis.
4. Technology, efficiency, costs, and selling prices remain as predicted.
5. The sales mix remains as predicted (i.e., constant).
6. Inventory levels remain fairly stable.

Management must be fully aware of the preceding assumptions if CVP analysis is to be used properly. Given the dynamic nature of business, a failure to recognize the model's restrictive features could lead to serious deficiencies in the planning and decision processes.

END-OF-CHAPTER REVIEW

LEARNING OBJECTIVES: THE KEY POINTS

1. **Identify the characteristics of variable, step, fixed, and mixed (semivariable) cost functions.** A variable cost is one that varies in direct proportion to a change in an activity base (e.g., sales, production, and so forth). As a result of this behavior, the total cost incurred increases or decreases, and the per-unit amount remains constant. Sometimes, a sizable movement is needed in the activity base for a cost to change. A function that behaves in this manner is known as a step cost because the cost fluctuations really occur in "chunks."

   Step functions are often viewed as a specialized type of variable cost. However, when an extremely large activity change is needed to force a change in the dollar amount incurred, the function's behavior tends to approximate that of a fixed cost. A fixed cost remains constant in total over a range of activity; however, the cost per unit fluctuates. Finally, a mixed (semivariable) cost shifts with a change in the activity base but does not move in direct proportion to the base. The mixed cost contains both variable and fixed elements.

2. **Use the scattergraph and high-low method for examining cost behavior.** The scattergraph is a graph of past observations between an activity base and the level of cost incurred. Points are plotted and a straight line is then fit through the points by visual approximation. The line's intersection with the cost axis is the amount of fixed cost; the line's slope is the unit variable cost.

   In contrast, the high-low method focuses only on the highest and lowest data observations. The variable cost per unit (or hour) is calculated by studying the cost change between the two points in question relative to the activity base change. Fixed cost is then determined by subtracting the variable cost incurred at the highest (or lowest) point from that point's total cost.

3. **Compute and explain the meaning of a company's break-even point and contribution margin.** The break-even point is the level of activity where total revenues and total costs are equal. Operating income is therefore zero. Break-even sales may be computed in both dollars and units, as follows:

   Dollars (equation method): Sales = Variable Costs + Fixed Costs
   Units (contribution approach): Fixed Costs ÷ Unit Contribution Margin

   The contribution margin is the mathematical difference between selling price and variable cost. This figure is the amount that each unit contributes toward covering fixed costs and generating income. That is, if the contribution margin is $8 per unit, overall income will rise by $8 for each unit that is sold by the firm.

4. **Calculate the sales needed to generate a particular target income figure.** The break-even model can be modified to find the sales required to produce a target income level. In both the equation approach and the contribution approach, the desired income is added to the fixed cost figure and treated as a "dollar obligation" that must be covered by sales.

5. **Use sales price, cost, and volume data to determine the impact of various operating changes on profitability.** The formulas to find the break-even point, whether modified for the target income figure or not, are helpful in studying the impact of various operating changes on the entity. Such changes include increases and decreases in sales prices, variable costs, and fixed costs; the addition of new prod-

Cost-Volume-Profit Analysis 905

uct lines; and so forth. All that a user need do is adjust the variable under study, perform the necessary computations, and analyze the results.

6. **Apply cost-volume-profit analysis to multiproduct firms.** CVP analysis can be used in single- or multiple-product settings. To compute the break-even point, fixed costs are once again divided by the contribution margin per unit. A "unit" in this case is really a combination of a company's various products in preset proportions known as a sales mix (i.e., the percentage of individual product sales to total unit sales). A weighted contribution margin is found by weighting (multiplying) individual product margins with the sales mix percentages, the result then being divided into total fixed costs.

7. **State the limiting assumptions on which cost-volume-profit analysis is based.** The CVP model assumes that all costs can be classified as variable or fixed, with costs falling in the latter category being constant through the range of analysis. Further, costs and revenues have linear, straight-line relationships. The components used in the model (e.g., costs, revenues, and sales mix) must remain as predicted, and inventory levels must remain fairly stable during the accounting period.

Key Terms and Concepts: A Quick Overview

break-even chart   A presentation of the break-even point and other CVP relationships in a graphic format. (p. 896)

break-even point   The level of activity where revenues and expenses are equal and income is zero. (p. 894)

committed fixed cost   A cost that arises from an organization's commitment to engage in operations—for example, property taxes, rent, and depreciation. (p. 889)

contribution margin   Selling price minus variable cost per unit. (p. 895)

cost-volume-profit analysis   The study of price, cost, volume, and profit interrelationships. (p. 884)

discretionary fixed cost   A fixed cost that originates from top management's yearly appropriation decisions—for example, advertising expense and research and development expense. (p. 889)

fixed cost   A cost that remains constant in total when changes occur in an activity base. (p. 887)

high-low method   A method of cost analysis that uses two data observations (the highest and lowest) to make generalizations about variable and fixed cost behavior. (p. 893)

method of least squares   A statistical technique for determining cost behavior. (p. 892)

mixed (semivariable) cost   A cost that contains both fixed and variable elements. (p. 890)

relevant range   The area of activity where a cost relationship is expected to hold true. (p. 886)

sales mix   The relative proportion of individual product sales to total sales. (p. 902)

scattergraph   A graphic representation of observed relationships between costs and activity levels. (p. 891)

step cost   A cost function that increases or decreases in "chunks," namely, when substantial changes occur in the activity base. (p. 887)

target income   A particular level of income that a company strives to attain. (p. 898)

variable cost   A cost that varies in direct proportion to a change in an activity base. (p. 885)

Chapter Quiz

The five questions that follow relate to several issues raised in the chapter. Test your knowledge of the issues by selecting the best answer. (The answers appear on p. 920.)

1. Variable costs (from the accountant's viewpoint):
   a. are graphed by means of a curvilinear line.
   b. remain constant in total through the relevant range.
   c. are constant on a per-unit basis through the relevant range.
   d. are commonly divided into committed and discretionary classifications.

2. The high-low method of analyzing cost behavior:
   a. can be used to determine the variable and fixed components of a mixed cost function.
   b. uses the same number of data observations as a scattergraph.
   c. relies on the following computation to figure the variable cost per unit (or hour): Change in activity between the high and low points ÷ change in cost between the high and low points.
   d. results in different amounts of fixed cost at the high and low data points.

3. Foster Company has sales of $800,000, variable costs that total 60% of sales, and fixed costs of $180,000. The firm's break-even point is:
   a. $140,000.
   b. $300,000.
   c. $450,000.
   d. $560,000.

4. The contribution margin:
   a. is the amount that each unit contributes toward covering variable costs and producing income.
   b. is the result of subtracting both the variable and fixed costs per unit from the selling price.
   c. may, in selected cases, be less than operating income.
   d. is the difference between a unit's selling price and variable cost and, when divided into fixed costs, will produce the unit sales required to break even.

5. The cost-volume-profit model:
   a. can be used only by single-product companies.
   b. assumes that the sales mix will remain as predicted.
   c. assumes that technology, efficiency, and costs can change.
   d. cannot be used to study operating changes of the firm.

Summary Problem

Kennett Company manufactures and sells a single product. Sales peak in March and generally bottom out in October. The following cost and volume information was extracted from the accounting records:

	MARCH	JULY*	OCTOBER
Production and sales (units)	25,000	19,000	14,000
Total cost incurred	$195,300	$176,200	$156,800

*An average month.

The company's product sells for $9 per unit.

Instructions

a. Using the high-low method, compute Kennett's variable cost per unit and total monthly fixed cost.

b. Compute the firm's contribution margin per unit.
c. Determine the break-even point in both units and dollar sales.
d. Determine the sales volume (in units) required to generate a target income of $29,150 per month.
e. Assume that Kennett wants to add a second product (known as product no. 2). Data related to this product follow.

Selling price per unit	$7.00
Variable cost per unit	$4.20
Additional fixed costs	$65,800

Management anticipates that product no. 2 will initially account for 20% of the company's total sales volume; the remaining 80% will be generated by the existing product (known as product no. 1). If Kennett adds the new product to its merchandise line, compute the new monthly break-even point (in units).

Solution

a.

	Units	Total Cost
Highest activity (March)	25,000	$195,300
Lowest activity (October)	14,000	156,800
Difference	11,000	$ 38,500

Variable cost per unit = $38,500 ÷ 11,000 units = $3.50

	High Point (25,000 Units)	Low Point (14,000 Units)
Total cost	$195,300	$156,800
Less variable cost @ $3.50 per unit	87,500*	49,000†
Fixed cost	$107,800	$107,800

* 25,000 units × $3.50 = $87,500.
† 14,000 units × $3.50 = $49,000.

b.
Selling price	$9.00
Less variable cost per unit	3.50
Contribution margin	$5.50

c.

$$\frac{\text{Fixed Costs}}{\text{Unit Contribution Margin}} = \text{Break-Even Point in Units}$$

$$\frac{\$107,800}{\$5.50} = 19,600 \text{ units}$$

A break-even point of 19,600 units produces a sales level of $176,400 (19,600 units × $9).

d.

$$\frac{\text{Fixed Costs} + \text{Target Income}}{\text{Unit Contribution Margin}} = \text{Required Sales in Units}$$

$$\frac{\$107,800 + \$29,150}{\$5.50} = 24,900 \text{ units}$$

e.

Product	Selling Price		Variable Cost		Contribution Margin		Sales Mix		Weighted Contribution Margin
1	$9.00	−	$3.50	=	$5.50	×	80%	=	$4.40
2	7.00	−	4.20	=	2.80	×	20%	=	0.56
									$4.96

Fixed costs now total $173,600 ($107,800 from product no. 1 + $65,800 from product no. 2). Therefore:

$$\frac{\text{Fixed Costs}}{\text{"Unit" Contribution Margin}} = \text{Break-Even Point in "Units"}$$

$$\frac{\$173,600}{\$4.96} = 35,000 \text{ "units"}$$

Each "unit" is a mixture of product no. 1 and product no. 2 in the 80:20 sales mix. The break-even point is thus computed as follows:

Product	Sales Mix		Break-Even "Units"		Break-Even Sales by Product (Units)
1	80%	×	35,000	=	28,000
2	20%	×	35,000	=	7,000

Assignment Material

Questions

Q23–1 In evaluating the cost of operating his automobile, a professor once commented: "Fuel is a fixed cost and insurance is a variable cost. I always pay the same amount per gallon and my mileage is fairly constant. On the other hand, the cost per mile for insurance varies with the distance that I drive." Comment on the professor's observations.

Q23–2 Differentiate between the accountant's and economist's views of variable cost behavior.

Q23–3 What is meant by the relevant range of activity?

Q23–4 Discuss the characteristics of a step cost function. In general, where is the best place to operate on a step?

Q23–5 An accounting professor once commented: "In the long run even fixed costs are variable." Evaluate the professor's comment.

Q23–6 Distinguish between committed and discretionary fixed costs. Which type can be cut back more easily without doing significant long-run harm to the organization? Explain.

Q23–7 Briefly comment on the trend toward increased fixed cost incurrence by businesses during the past decade. How does this trend affect operating flexibility?

Q23–8 Identify the inherent problems of the scattergraph and the high-low method.

Q23–9 Define the break-even point.

Q23–10 Define the contribution margin. What does the contribution margin represent, and how is it used in finding the break-even point?

Q23–11 Product A has a negative contribution margin. Explain how a negative contribution margin can arise, and determine whether product A should continue to be sold.

Q23–12 Discuss the benefits associated with using a break-even chart.

Q23–13 Determine the effect, if any, on the break-even point that each of the following events would have:
a. An increase in sales price
b. A decrease in fixed cost
c. An increase in the number of units sold

Q23–14 Will a change in a company's sales mix likely affect the break-even point? Briefly explain.

Q23–15 What are the limiting assumptions of CVP analysis?

EXERCISES

E23–1 Cost behavior (L.O. 1)
Determine whether the following costs are variable (V), committed fixed (CF), discretionary fixed (DF), or mixed (M):
a. Monthly rental of office space by a law firm.
b. Utility bill for a small business, which includes a $10 per month minimum use fee.
c. Cost of hot dogs for a concessionaire at a baseball game.
d. Annual business license fee that allows a florist to operate in the city limits.
e. Annual political contribution by a road construction company to the incumbent state governor's campaign fund.
f. Cost of attending a professional education seminar by a practicing dentist.
g. Cost of single hotel rooms for each member of a touring country and western band.
h. Cost of protective rubber gloves for operating room personnel of a hospital.

E23–2 Cost behavior patterns (L.O. 1)
Consider the graphs that follow, each of which represents a different cost or expense of Society Jewelers, an operator of 22 jewelry stores throughout Illinois.

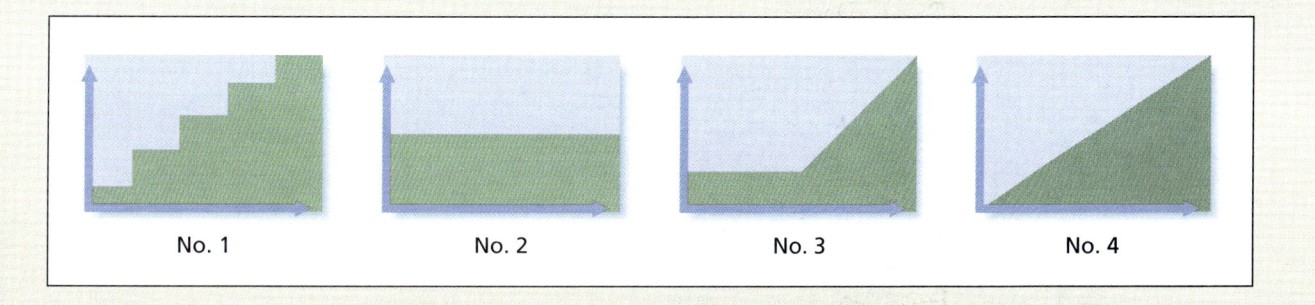

No. 1   No. 2   No. 3   No. 4

The vertical axis measures dollars and the horizontal axis represents an activity base (number of sales, clerks, and so forth). Select the graph that best describes the following items:
a. Straight-line depreciation on store equipment.
b. Store manager compensation. Each store manager is paid a monthly salary, plus a commission after a certain level of sales is reached.
c. Cost of jewelry sold during the period.

d. Weekly wages of store clerks who work a 40-hour week. One clerk is hired for every 100 sales made during the month.
e. Rental charges on the firm's warehouse and distribution center.

E23–3 High-low method (L.O. 2)
The following cost data pertain to 19X6 operations of Heritage Products:

	QUARTER 1	QUARTER 2	QUARTER 3	QUARTER 4
Shipping costs	$58,200	$58,620	$60,125	$59,400
Orders shipped	120	140	175	150

The company uses the high-low method to analyze costs.

a. Determine the variable cost per order shipped.
b. Determine the fixed shipping costs per quarter.
c. If present cost behavior patterns continue, determine total shipping costs for 19X7 if activity amounts to 570 orders.

E23–4 High-low method; cost determination (L.O. 2)
Dempsey and Associates experienced the following selected costs when manufacturing 800 and 900 units, respectively:

	800 UNITS	900 UNITS
Direct material	$ 9,200	$10,350
Property taxes	1,100	1,100
Maintenance	6,200	6,850
	$16,500	$18,300

Determine the anticipated outlays for direct material, property taxes, and maintenance cost if 880 units are produced. Dempsey uses the high-low method to analyze cost behavior.

E23–5 Cost behavior and cost analysis (L.O. 1, 2)
Richard Wolfe is a dentist located in Trenton, New Jersey. A major part of his practice involves simple dental hygiene services (cleaning, x-rays, and so forth), all provided by two recent hires who are paid a monthly salary. Rosa Gomez, Wolfe's office manager, determined not too long ago that the practice's hygiene costs typically increase with the number of patients seen.

a. More than likely, did the cost increase observed by Gomez directly parallel the increase in patients? Why?
b. What methods were available to Gomez to study the practice's costs?
c. Wolfe is considering a new branch office in a suburban location.
   (1) What will probably happen to the practice's level of fixed cost incurrence?
   (2) Is there any danger of signing a long-term lease if the demand for dental services suddenly becomes "soft" because of advances in oral hygiene? Explain your answer from a cost perspective.

E23–6 Break-even and other CVP relationships (L.O. 3, 4, 5)
Delta Gamma Upsilon sorority is in the process of planning its annual homecoming dinner and dance. The treasurer anticipates the following costs for the event, which will be held at the Regency Hotel:

Room rental	$300
Dinner cost (per person)	25
Chartered buses	500
Favors and souvenirs (per person)	5
Band	900

Each person would pay $40 to attend; 200 attendees are expected.

a. Will the event be profitable for the sorority? Show computations.
b. How many people must attend for the sorority to break even?
c. Suppose the sorority encouraged its members to drive to the hotel and did not charter the buses. Further, a planned menu change will reduce the cost per meal by $2. If each member will still be charged $40, compute the contribution margin per person.

E23–7 Break-even and other CVP relationships (L.O. 3, 4, 5)
Island Escape generates average revenues of $80 for each of its ecologically oriented tours of Oahu. Variable costs are $12 per tour, primarily for admissions to scenic attractions and a picnic lunch. Fixed costs total $340,000 per year.

a. How many tours must be conducted to break even?
b. What level of revenue is needed to earn a target income of $102,000?
c. If variable costs increase to $20 per tour, what decrease in annual fixed costs must be achieved to keep the same break-even point as calculated in part (a)?

E23–8 Break-even and other CVP relationships (L.O. 3, 4, 5)
In 19X4, Century Manufacturing produced and sold 70,000 pressure gauges at $32 each. This level of activity amounted to 70% of the firm's total productive capacity. The costs related to the pressure-gauge line were as follows:

	VARIABLE	FIXED
Manufacturing	$770,000	$240,000
Selling	210,000	180,000
Administrative	—	390,000
Total	$980,000	$810,000

a. Compute the income or loss generated from sales of pressure gauges in 19X4.
b. How many gauges must be sold to break even?
c. Considering your answer in part (b), at what percentage of total productive capacity must Century operate to achieve a break-even operation?
d. Suppose that management wants to lower the break-even point. Should it attempt to increase or decrease fixed administrative costs?

E23–9 CVP relationships: Working backward (L.O. 3, 4)
Determine the missing amounts in each of the independent cases that follow.

CASE	UNITS SOLD	SALES	VARIABLE COSTS	CONTRIBUTION MARGIN PER UNIT	FIXED COSTS	OPERATING INCOME
A	?	$70,000	$?	$6	$14,000	$10,000
B	7,000	?	42,000	5	?	8,000
C	4,000	53,000	?	?	21,000	(2,000)
D	8,000	92,000	40,000	?	24,000	?

E23–10 Overview of CVP relationships (L.O. 3, 4, 6)

Evaluate the comments that follow as being True or False. If the comment is false, briefly explain why.

a. The contribution margin is computed by subtracting the fixed cost per unit from the selling price.
b. The sales required to produce a certain target income figure will exceed a firm's break-even sales.
c. An automobile dealer has a negative contribution margin on each auto sold. The owner nonetheless claims that the dealership can be profitable by selling more cars than the competition. (*Note:* Ignore leasing, body shop, and service department considerations.)
d. An increase in selling price will decrease a company's break-even point.
e. The sales mix is an important consideration when figuring the break-even point in a multiproduct company.

E23–11 Break even with multiple products (L.O. 6)

Infant Products sells three different models of car seats: Economy, Standard, and Superior. Projected information on the three models follows.

	ECONOMY	STANDARD	SUPERIOR
Sales (units)	5,000	30,000	15,000
Selling price	$30	$40	$55
Variable cost	16	23	35

Total fixed costs are anticipated to be $739,200.

a. Determine the company's sales mix.
b. Calculate the number of Economy, Standard, and Superior models that must be sold to break even.
c. Analyze your calculations from parts (a) and (b). If Infant Products desires to improve overall profitability, should it attempt to increase or decrease sales of the Superior car seat relative to the other two models? Why?

PROBLEMS

Series A

P23–A1 Scattergraph and high-low method (L.O. 2)

Velez Manufacturing has a highly automated machine shop. The firm is studying utilities cost behavior and has gathered the following data for a recent six-month period:

MONTH	MACHINE HOURS	UTILITIES COST
January	22,000	$26,100
February	24,000	28,500
March	25,000	29,000
April	27,000	31,200
May	26,000	29,900
June	28,000	32,100

Instructions

a. Prepare a scattergraph by plotting machine hours on the horizontal axis and utilities cost on the vertical axis.

b. By fitting a line through the plotted points, determine Velez's monthly fixed cost and the variable cost per machine hour.
c. Determine the variable and fixed costs by using the high-low method.
d. In general, will the scattergraph and the high-low method yield identical results? Why?

P23–A2 Cost behavior and analysis (L.O. 1, 2)

Conway Zinc owns the rights to extract zinc ore from the bottom of Windy Gorge in northern California. Four of the company's costs are:

- Monthly straight-line depreciation of $19,000 on roads and mine buildings.
- Truck transportation to Eureka, the nearest deepwater port, where ore is sold to an Australian company for processing. Panella Trucking charges Conway $80,000 per month for hauling up to and including 800 tons, $100,000 for hauling between 801 and 1,000 tons, $120,000 for hauling between 1,001 and 1,200 tons, and so on.
- Direct labor and labor-related fringe benefits.
- Royalties paid to the State of California because Windy Gorge is located on state property. The royalty reflects a flat fee plus a per-ton charge.

Normal extraction often ranges between 800 tons and 1,200 tons per month. Data from Conway's accounting records revealed the following selected costs for February and October of last year, which were the "peak" and "valley" of ore extraction activity:

	FEBRUARY (1,150 TONS)	OCTOBER (820 TONS)
Direct labor and fringe benefits	$143,750	$102,500
Royalties	27,650	24,020

Instructions

a. On the basis of the information presented, is direct labor and fringe benefits a fixed, variable, or mixed cost? Explain your answer.
b. Calculate the total cost for an upcoming month when 850 tons are expected to be extracted. Conway uses the high-low method to analyze cost behavior.
c. Comment on the cost-effectiveness of extracting 850 tons with respect to the trucking agreement. If you feel this is an ineffective level of activity, describe how effectiveness could be improved.
d. There is a high probability that Conway's volume will triple in forthcoming months as buyers try to beat anticipated price increases for zinc ore. Can the data and methodology used in part (b) for predicting the cost of extracting 850 tons be employed to estimate total costs for, say, 2,700 tons? Why or why not?

P23–A3 Straightforward CVP analysis (L.O. 3, 4, 5)

The following information pertains to 19X6 operations of Downey Enterprises:

Sales (11,100 units at $50)	$555,000
Variable costs	
Cost of goods sold	233,100
Sales commissions	77,700
Fixed costs	
Salaries	180,000
Rent	60,000
Other	13,000

The company sells a single product through a series of retail outlets; no manufacturing activities are involved.

Instructions

a. Compute the 19X6 break-even point in both dollar and unit sales.
b. What sales level is needed to achieve a target income of $9,900?
c. Assume that management wants to cut salaries by $30,000 and increase sales commissions to $10 per unit. Determine the effect of these changes on the unit contribution margin, and explain the meaning of the contribution margin to Downey's president, who has a manufacturing background.
d. Returning to the original data, assume that management is willing to pay an extra $3 commission on all units sold in excess of the company's break-even point. If 19X7 sales are expected to be 11,850 units, calculate the year's operating income (or loss).

P23–A4 Break-even and other CVP analysis (L.O. 3, 4, 5)

Foggy Day Raincoats sells outerwear in factory-outlet stores at $80 per coat. The company is considering two countries for its worldwide manufacturing center: South Korea and the United States. A projected income calculation for the U.S. operation, assuming sales of 55,000 coats, follows.

Sales		$4,400,000
Less: Variable cost	$ 935,000	
Fixed cost	3,150,000	4,085,000
Operating income		$ 315,000

Locating the center in South Korea will give rise to variable costs of $18 per coat and fixed costs of $2,480,000.

Instructions

a. Calculate the number of raincoats that must be sold to break even if Foggy Day locates the manufacturing center in the United States.
b. If the center is located in South Korea, what level of dollar sales is needed to produce income of $527,000?
c. Assume that management desires to achieve the South Korean break-even point with the U.S. operation.
   (1) Compute the unit contribution margin needed to attain this goal.
   (2) Given the company's projections, is this contribution margin realistic? Explain your answer.
d. Determine the impact of the following operating changes by filling in the blanks that follow with "increase," "decrease," or "not affect."
   (1) A decrease in Korean shipping costs will _____ total variable costs, _____ the contribution margin, and _____ operating income.
   (2) A decrease in U.S. fixed manufacturing costs will _____ the contribution margin and _____ the break-even point.

P23–A5 CVP and analysis of operations (L.O. 3, 4, 5)

The Ditmar Company is exploring two possible manufacturing methods to produce a short-lived, fad product. The following unit-cost data have been generated by the firm's accounting department:

	PROCESS A	PROCESS B
Direct materials	$ 3.00	$ 4.50
Direct labor	4.00	5.00
Variable overhead	10.00	12.50

The fixed manufacturing costs associated with processes A and B total $760,000 and $541,000, respectively. Management anticipates that regardless of which process is selected, the fad product will require the following selling and administrative expenses: advertising, $80,000; sales commissions, 10%. The marketing department has tentatively set a selling price of $50. Ditmar will manufacture sufficient units to meet demand; no inventory will be carried.

Instructions

a. Compute the number of units that Ditmar must sell to break even if process A is selected.
b. Which of the two processes will be more profitable for the company if sales total 35,000 units?
c. Compute the dollar sales necessary to generate a target income of $69,000 if process B is selected.
d. At what volume level (in units) will management be indifferent between process A and process B?

Series B

P23–B1 Scattergraph and high-low method (L.O. 2)

P. Thurmond has a highly automated machine shop. The firm is studying maintenance cost behavior and has gathered the following data for a recent six-month period:

MONTH	MACHINE HOURS	MAINTENANCE COST
July	18,000	$36,000
August	20,000	39,600
September	18,500	37,000
October	19,000	38,200
November	22,000	36,400
December	17,000	35,400

Instructions

a. Prepare a scattergraph by plotting machine hours on the horizontal axis and maintenance cost on the vertical axis.
b. By fitting a line through the plotted points, determine Thurmond's monthly fixed cost and the variable cost per machine hour.
c. Determine the variable and fixed costs by using the high-low method.
d. In view of Thurmond's cost behavior, which of the two methods (scattergraph or high-low) appears more appropriate? Explain your answer.

P23–B2 Cost behavior and analysis (L.O. 1, 2)

Recent cost and activity data from the machining department of Eastbay Manufacturing follow.

Month	Machine Hours	Factory Overhead*
August	35,000	$484,000
September	42,000	547,000
October	46,000	616,000
November	38,000	529,500

* Excludes supervision costs.

Conversations with the company's accountant revealed that October's costs consisted of machine supplies ($138,000), plant insurance ($13,000), and maintenance ($465,000). These costs are characterized as being variable, fixed, and mixed, respectively. Eastbay's supervision costs displayed the following step behavior during the period under study:

Monthly Activity Range (Machine Hours)	Cost
Up to 20,000	$ 47,000
20,001–35,000	77,000
35,001–50,000	107,000

Instructions

a. Determine the amount of maintenance cost incurred in August.
b. Analyze the department's maintenance cost by using the high-low method. Determine the monthly fixed portion and the variable cost per machine hour.
c. If present cost behavior patterns continue, estimate the total amount of factory overhead the company can expect in December if 43,000 machine hours are worked.
d. Suppose that the department worked only 22,000 machine hours in July because new equipment was being installed. Would you have any reservations about using the July data in the high-low method? Briefly explain.

P23–B3 Straightforward CVP analysis (L.O. 3, 4, 5)

FRB, Inc., sells a single product for $40. The following costs and expenses were incurred at store no. 504:

Variable Costs Per Unit		Annual Fixed Costs	
Invoice cost	$24	Salaries	$60,000
Sales commission	4	Advertising	14,000
		Other	16,000

The company sold 8,200 units during 19X4.

Instructions

a. Compute the 19X4 break-even point in both dollar and unit sales.
b. By how much will sales have to increase in 19X5 over 19X4 levels if management desires to earn a target income of $14,400?
c. At present, how much does each unit provide toward covering FRB's fixed costs and generating income? Assume that management feels this amount is too low. What alternatives are available to FRB?
d. What would be the effect on the break-even point if management reduced salary costs by $11,600 and increased the $4 sales commission by 20%?

P23–B4 Break-even and other CVP analysis (L.O. 3, 4, 5)

Quebec, Inc., manufactures and sells a single product. The information that follows relates to the year just ended, when 230,000 units were sold:

Sales price per unit	$ 10
Variable cost per unit	4
Fixed costs	930,000

Instructions

a. Determine the number of units that Quebec sold in excess of its break-even point.
b. If current revenue and cost patterns continue, compute the dollar sales needed next year to produce a target income of $492,000.
c. Assume that a different compensation plan was in effect during the current year. Rather than pay six salespeople an average salary of $36,000 each, management has proposed that the salespeople receive a $10,000 base salary and a 6% commission based on gross sales.
  (1) Would the company have been better off financially if the new plan had been adopted for the year just ended? By how much?
  (2) What effect might paying a commission have on gross sales? Briefly explain.
d. In addition to the compensation plan described in part (c), Quebec is studying the impact of other operating changes as well. State whether you agree or disagree with the following findings of a newly hired staff accountant:
  (1) A rise in property taxes will increase the break-even point.
  (2) A decrease in raw material cost will increase the contribution margin and decrease total fixed costs.

P23–B5 CVP and analysis of operations (L.O. 3, 4, 5)

Oceanic, Inc., is performing some basic computations related to automating its Michigan plant. Two different proposals are under study: basic and extensive. The following manufacturing cost information is available:

	VARIABLE COST PER UNIT	ANNUAL FIXED COSTS
Basic	$8.00	$460,000
Extensive	6.40	612,000

Other data are:

Selling price per unit	$ 32
Fixed selling and administrative costs	60,000

The company pays a 10% sales commission on all units sold.

Instructions

a. If annual sales are expected to average 120,000 units, would Oceanic be better off with basic automation or extensive automation? Show computations.
b. How many units must the company sell to break even if the basic proposal is selected?
c. Suppose that the basic proposal requires that Oceanic purchase additional equipment that is not reflected in the preceding figures. The equipment will cost $83,200

and will be depreciated over a five-year life by the straight-line method. In light of this new information, what would you have done differently in part (b) when computing the break-even point?

d. Ignoring part (c), at what sales level (in units) will Oceanic be indifferent between the basic and extensive automation proposals?

EXPANDING YOUR HORIZONS

EYH23–1 Break-even analysis, cost behavior (L.O. 1, 3)

Cost-volume-profit analysis is one of the most basic tools of planning and decision making. You will find it very useful in both your professional and personal lives.

Assume that you belong to an organization that is planning a lavish year-end awards banquet. The organization has 250 members, and roughly 80% of the membership will likely attend. You have been placed in charge of deriving a break-even ticket price for the event.

Instructions

Form a team with two other students in your class to gather the necessary information. Call a hotel or banquet hall that is suitable for the function and determine room rental charges and the cost of food and refreshments. Other items that you would likely consider include party favors, flowers, plaques, awards, entertainment, speaker expenses, transportation to and from the facility for attendees and guests, and any non-paying guests. Prepare a one-page report of your findings.

EYH23–2 Changing patterns of cost behavior (L.O. 2, 5)

Many manufacturing firms have automated in recent years, adding massive fixed cost obligations in place of "people costs" (direct labor). Automation has its advantages, but at the same time, the associated fixed costs may limit operating flexibility.

Instructions

Form a team with three other students in your class and visit two local manufacturing firms. The firms should be different in size and manufacture different products. Interview each company's chief accountant to determine patterns of cost behavior (i.e., proportions of fixed and variable costs) over the years. Determine what, if anything, has happened to each firm's break-even point from operating changes such as automation and whether management is concerned about the amount of fixed cost incurred. Be prepared to report your findings to the class.

EYH23–3 Compensation plans, multiple products (L.O. 5, 6)

Salespeople earn compensation through a variety of different plans. Some plans call for a flat salary; others involve a salary plus commission. These commissions are often based on gross dollar sales, thus ignoring a product's profitability and overall importance to the company.

Instructions

Interview three people who are involved with sales in distinctly different types of businesses. Inquire about their compensation plans, including the related strengths and weaknesses. Determine if any of the individuals has ever been compensated by an "incongruent" plan, that is, one that truly rewards the salesperson but is marginal from the company's viewpoint, or vice versa. Have any of the salespeople deliberately generated dollar sales at the expense of company profitability? Prepare a one-page summary of your findings.

EYH23–4 Sales compensation plans, motivation (L.O. 5, 6)

Rhodes Corporation sells two products, Regular and Enhanced. Data pertaining to the two products follow.

	REGULAR	ENHANCED
Selling price	$80	$120
Variable cost	32	85
Contribution margin	$48	$ 35
Forecasted sales (units)	40,000	10,000

The company expects total fixed costs of $1,906,000, including $540,000 of sales salaries.

Assume that management recently restructured the sales force compensation, abandoning all fixed salaries in exchange for a 10% commission computed on gross sales dollars. As a result of the new plan, sales increased to 55,000 units, subdivided as follows: regular, 22,000 units; enhanced, 33,000 units.

Instructions

a. Prior to restructuring the compensation plan, what sales mix did the company expect?
b. From a gross sales dollar standpoint, did the new plan function as one would logically expect? Briefly explain.
c. Prepare a profitability analysis of the firm's performance both before and after the change. Discuss your findings.
d. Who came out ahead from the restructuring, the company or the sales force? Why?
e. Suppose a different compensation plan was installed, one that abandoned the fixed salary outlays in favor of a 25% commission calculated on product-line contribution margins. Sales totaled 55,000 units, now divided as follows: regular, 44,000 units; enhanced, 11,000 units. Is this result somewhat expected? Explain.
f. Prepare a profitability analysis of this new plan. Who is the ultimate winner, the company or the sales force? Why?

COMMUNICATION OF ACCOUNTING INFORMATION

CAI23–1 Presentation visuals (L.O. 3, 4)

Communication Principle: Accountants (and employees in general) must often communicate information to persons who have little or no understanding of the relevant subject matter. Given that "one picture is worth a thousand words," communication can frequently be enhanced by the use of graphs and pictures.

Fortunately, various computer software packages are available to aid in this process. Basic graphics can be prepared on most electronic spreadsheets. In addition, other packages are available that assist in the development of sophisticated artistic presentations.

You should plan to become familiar with these tools. Reading levels are declining, managers are busier than ever, and preparing graphics is as easy as pressing a few keys on a computer's keyboard. Effective communication in today's electronic age is not only written but is visual as well.

■ ■ ■ ■ ■ ■ ■ ■

Hiotech, Inc., manufactures an expensive piece of equipment that is inserted into blood vessels to remove blockages and other obstructions from the heart area. (The associated technology involves a laser beam that is attached to a very thin fiber optic cord.) The equipment has variable manufacturing and distribution costs of $2,460,000 and sells for $3,460,000. Related fixed manufacturing costs are $15,000,000 per year.

Because of such a high cost, the market for the product is very limited. Annual sales are expected to total only 12 units. Hiotech's directors, mostly doctors, are nevertheless very excited about the medical advances associated with the equipment. They are also delighted that each unit makes $1,000,000 for the company.

Instructions

a. Calculate the number of units that must be sold to break even.
b. Comment on the economic viability of this particular product.
c. Prepare one or more pie charts (i.e., circle graphs) that could be used in a presentation to the doctors. The charts should demonstrate the concept of break even and show that the product is not profitable for the company. (*Note:* If available, computer software should be used for this part of the solution.)

Answers to Chapter Quiz

1. c
2. a
3. c (S = VC + FC; S = 0.6S + $180,000; S = $450,000)
4. d
5. b

24 BUDGETING

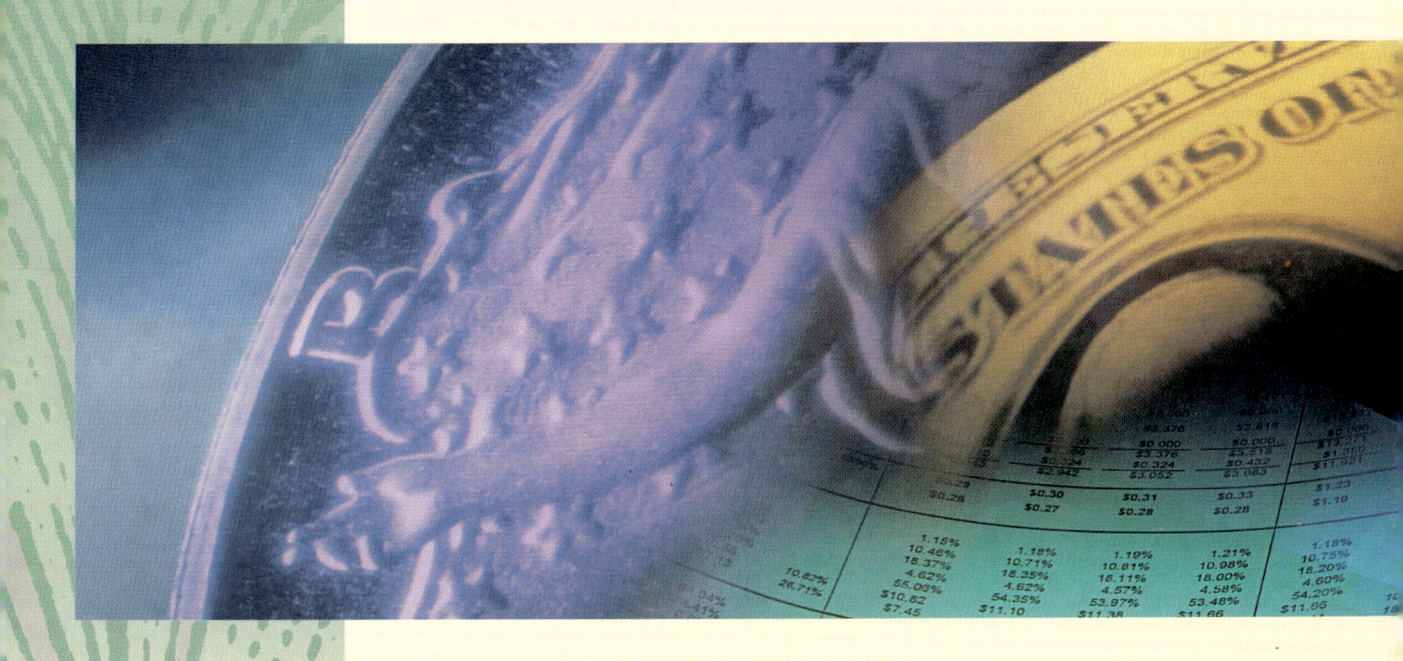

LEARNING OBJECTIVES

After studying this chapter, you should be able to:

1. Identify the benefits of budgeting.
2. Distinguish between top-down and bottom-up budgeting.
3. Explain the concept of slack as it relates to the estimation process.
4. Recognize the variations in budget periods.
5. Discuss the limitations of budgeting, especially in the human relations area.
6. Prepare a master budget.
7. Recognize the adaptability of budgets to computers.

When asked about the budgeting process, George Faris of Banner Advertising said that his involvement had somewhat of an evolutionary flavor. George observed that when the company first began, budgets provided few benefits because he could easily track, control, and plan most everything in his head.

Banner then undertook a growth spurt, with growth so rapid that unexpected transactions regularly affected economic projections. "Each day brought new business, and our projections were out-of-touch with reality only a week or two after being developed. This was obviously a pleasant but frustrating problem," he noted.

As Banner continued to mature and prosper, George's views changed. He found that even a simple budget is a very useful organizational tool. "The budget gives employees a clear indication of our goals and expectations—it is a document that allows us to think about and control future direction. Also, we find that budgets are helpful in trying to establish a sound financial relationship with our bankers."

George went on to say that "... the term 'budget' may conjure up the image of a sophisticated document, and that is probably the case for many large companies. But in a smaller firm like ours, the budget is only a spreadsheet in the computer. It is frequently adjusted and often reduced to charts and graphs that are pinned on the wall. Without a doubt, budgets certainly help to 'decorate' our otherwise drab office space!"

This chapter focuses on budgeting, an important aspect of the planning process. Businesses first formulate generalized goals and then set a series of strategies and policies to achieve those goals. As an example, suppose a manufacturer of household cleaning products desires to enter the car care market. Accordingly, the company could establish a strategy to acquire an existing manufacturer of car care products or perhaps engage in an extensive research program to develop new products internally. The eventual decision will likely be based on dollars and cents, amounts that are derived from various economic projections.

These projections involve **budgets,** or formal quantitative expressions of management expectations. Unlike strategies and policies, budgets contain considerable financial detail. In effect, a budget can be likened to a blueprint, that is, an intricate plan that serves as a framework for future action.

BENEFITS OF BUDGETING

1 Identify the benefits of budgeting.

If done correctly, budgeting is a time-consuming, arduous process. It goes without saying that an in-depth look at the future involves numerous assumptions, much uncertainty, and often considerable employee input. Furthermore, managers must frequently turn away from current, pressing problems to devote full attention to the budget effort. With all these unattractive features, the question arises, "Why budget?" Normally, as George Faris saw, the benefits outweigh the associated problems. Budgets formalize planning, serve as a basis for performance evaluation, and assist in communication and coordination within the entity.

FORMALIZE PLANNING

Budgets are an outgrowth of the planning process. Because budgets force managers to look ahead and study the future, a formal "plan of attack" can be prepared. To picture the related benefits, imagine building a home without the previously mentioned blueprint. The contractor might encase the walls in plasterboard, only to discover that electrical outlets and heating vents were forgotten. Or the foundation might be laid and then found to be over the property line. Indeed, the building process would be chaotic at best. Similarly, without a formal plan, management will have to spend considerable time "fighting fires" rather than concentrating on the attainment of long-run goals and objectives.

The implementation of a budget allows companies (and individuals) to pinpoint potential problems before the problems occur. Operating distractions are thus greatly reduced, since anticipation often leads to the introduction of preliminary corrective action. The eventual outcome of planning is a direction-oriented entity—one that knows where it wants to go and how it wants to get there.

SERVE AS A BASIS FOR PERFORMANCE EVALUATION

Although best known for its role in planning, a budget also assists management in the appraisal of performance and control of operations. As explained in Chapter 20, organizations often prepare reports that compare actual results against predetermined budgeted amounts. The budget therefore serves as a yardstick in judging whether performance has been up to par. Should deficiencies arise, corrective action can be taken to bring the organization back on target.

Some businesses attempt to evaluate performance by comparing current results against the *actual* results of previous accounting periods. Unfortunately, this type of evaluation has an inherent deficiency. To illustrate, assume that a company's total operating expenses last year amounted to $200,000. If the company was subjected to a 10% inflation rate and current expenses total only $210,000, the immediate conclusion might be that management has done a creditable job in controlling costs. However, if last year's expenses were excessive because of significant inefficiencies, the entire evaluative picture could change. For instance, suppose that last year's expenses would have been $180,000 under reasonably efficient operating conditions. Allowing for an $18,000 increase from inflation, current expenses would exceed the $198,000 target by $12,000 ($210,000 − $198,000).

Comparisons with past data simply do not reveal whether current performance is acceptable. Bear in mind that historical data bring all that was bad about the past into the evaluation. Furthermore, if a company's operating environment has changed significantly because of new technology, a new management team, or other factors, studies of past versus present very quickly approach the meaningless level. Current performance is best judged against a budget for the same period.

Assist in Communication and Coordination

Business operations require the performance of many diverse activities. These activities include the production and sale of goods and services, purchasing, credit extension and the collection of accounts, data processing, and the financing of operations. In very small enterprises these functions are often supervised by the same person. In larger organizations, however, operations are normally divided and are the responsibility of different managers.

To achieve company objectives, close coordination of activities is a necessity. Imagine the problems that could arise if coordination was lacking. The marketing department could undertake a large advertising campaign for a new product and then find that production was halted by a shortage of needed raw materials. Or at a time when marketing was attempting to expand the company's market share, the credit department might be tightening credit standards because of recent problems with uncollectible accounts. In both of these cases, embarrassment is sure to result.

Where do budgets fit in? When a budget for the overall organization is being prepared, individual managers must communicate their plans. The plans are then examined to determine whether they are feasible and consistent with the plans of other operating units. The budget process therefore serves as a gigantic blender that integrates and coordinates diverse activities to help attain company goals.

A Product-Line Manager's Perspective

Coordination and Integration: I oversee the development of new consumer products in a large corporation, a job that requires a highly integrative approach to planning and budgeting. We interact daily with marketing managers to assess market size, competition, buyer loyalty, market segmentation, pricing, and issues related to distribution and anticipated advertising and sales force efforts. Our engineers provide insights about technological change, product design, product quality, and manufacturing costs. Purchasing assists in furnishing information about suppliers and raw material availability. Finance massages the numbers to determine the required capital investment and whether specific new product introductions make sense from an economic perspective. And finally, with some ventures we also secure advice from our legal staff about governmental regulations that must be followed.

In sum, our planning efforts require that we work closely with other parts of the company—in effect, it is a "team mentality." New products do not just happen overnight; rather, they are the result of complicated interactions. It is these interactions that form the basis for our future revenues and financial projections. Should a faulty effort occur, the end result would likely be budget cutbacks, employee layoffs, and/or sizable operating losses.

BUDGET CONSTRUCTION

The construction of a budget varies dramatically from one business to the next. Many companies establish formal procedures that are followed to the letter. In contrast, other businesses employ "seat of the pants" management and merely scribble some hastily derived projections on the back of an envelope. Because of the wide variety of approaches found in practice, any attempt at a detailed discussion on how to budget or a list of "The Ten Easy Steps to Budgeting" is fruitless. There are, however, several general concepts with which you should be familiar. A short discussion of these concepts follows.

CONSTRUCTION FLOWS

Most medium- and large-size entities are composed of several management levels. See Exhibit 24–1, for example, which depicts a typical organizational hierarchy. The budget-building process generally follows the organizational structure, with construction proceeding from higher- to lower-management levels, or vice versa.

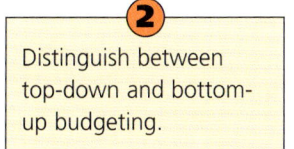

> **2** Distinguish between top-down and bottom-up budgeting.

Top-Down Approach. With the top-down approach, virtually all budget development takes place at the upper echelons of management. The budget is imposed on lower-level personnel, who rarely become involved in the construction process. On paper, the top-down approach offers the advantage of producing a document that reflects overall organizational goals. Preparation is carried out by those who have the best view of companywide operations, namely, top management. Upper-level executives can study the interactions of the lower units and determine the consistency of the units' plans and expectations.

In most cases this apparent advantage gives rise to a significant problem. When the budget is imposed from above, lower-level managers often feel that their opinions and operating perspectives are not important. Although lower-level employees will be evaluated against the budget, they have done little to assist in its development. Consequently, they often resent this "dictatorial" approach and adopt a "who cares" attitude, both of which result in a negative outlook toward budget achievement.

EXHIBIT 24–1
Organizational Hierarchy

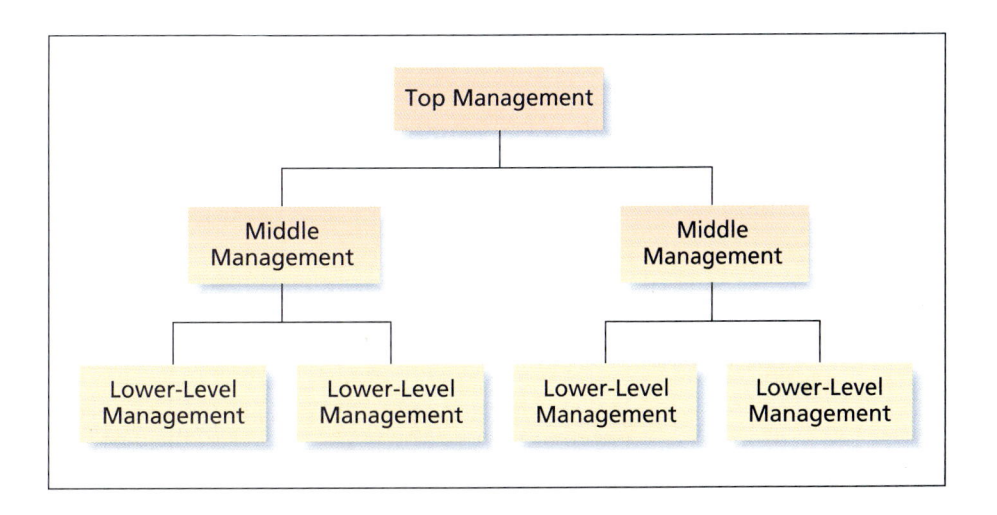

Bottom-Up Approach. Unlike the top-down approach, bottom-up budgeting stresses lower-level employee participation in the development process. The bottom-up approach usually begins with the issuance of general budget guidelines by top management or perhaps by a budget committee. The budget committee normally consists of company executives along with representatives from functional areas such as sales, production, and finance. The guidelines often include yearly goals, anticipated inflation rates, available resources, and other similar data.

Once this information is communicated, the employees responsible for achieving the desired results assemble appropriate budgets. The process begins at the lower levels of the organizational structure and works its way upward. Individual budgets are grouped by major operating units, such as divisions and territories, and eventually reach top management or the budget committee. The budgets are reviewed, and suggestions for improvement are offered. Lower-level managers then make the necessary revisions, and ultimately, a compromise is reached.

The bottom-up approach offers several distinct advantages over a budget that is handed down from top management:

1. Bottom-up (i.e., *participative*) budgets are really self-imposed. By consulting with and incorporating the goals of lower-level employees, greater strides are made toward budget achievement. That is, individuals throughout the organization know their views are valued and considered by top management. As a result, employee morale and job satisfaction generally increase, and employees make extensive efforts to meet the agreed-on targets.
2. The budget is constructed by employees who are close to the action and know the intricate details of daily activity. The same cannot be said for a budget that is prepared solely by top management with no lower-level input. Consequently, the bottom-up approach usually results in a more realistic performance target.

On the negative side, increased employee involvement makes the bottom-up method time-consuming and expensive to administer. Nevertheless, it is a popular tool among progressive companies. Because the broad perspectives of upper management are combined with the detailed operating knowledge of lower-level personnel, a very powerful budget document is created—one that encompasses the views of all ranges of the organizational hierarchy.

Budget Estimation

By its nature, a budget is a series of future estimates. These estimates should not be arrived at haphazardly; instead, significant care should be exercised in their determination.

Normally, budget estimates are based on both the past and the future. Although historical information is often a good starting point for prediction, modification of past trends may be necessary because of changing conditions. As an example, suppose that a company is attempting to budget sales for a particular product. The company currently has a 26% market share and has improved its position by 1% in each of the past five years. Should business conditions remain relatively stable, the firm would be correct in anticipating a 27%

share of total sales for the upcoming period. If, however, new competition or technological innovations are present, these factors must be considered if the sales estimate is to have much meaning.

Estimation and Slack. As noted earlier, budgets are frequently used in performance evaluation. Well aware of this fact, many managers build slack, or padding, into their budgets to avoid unfavorable appraisals. For instance, sales and operating capabilities may be underestimated and expenses may be overestimated. Thus, when the actual results are tabulated and sales are "down" and expenses are "up," the manager is still deemed to have met his or her budget (and company objectives). In essence, slack has given the manager some leeway in the performance of daily activities.

Slack permeates the entire budget process and sometimes tends to perpetuate itself. As an example, in many not-for-profit entities, operating units are given a maximum spending limit for specific types of expenditures. A governmental entity, for instance, may be authorized to spend $50,000 for new equipment acquisitions during the fiscal year. If the year-end is rapidly approaching and considerable funds have yet to be used, the unit may go on a buying spree. Why? If funds remain, administrators might take the position that the current equipment budget was apparently in excess of amounts really needed. Consequently, there could be a strong tendency for cutbacks in the next budget period. This "use it or lose it" philosophy often gives rise to status-quo or larger (i.e., slack-filled) budgets in future years and may result in questionable operating practices that conflict with an entity's goals.

Slack is a significant problem for many budget makers and is extremely difficult to eliminate. Although it is easier said than done, budget estimates should be realistic and should shy away from excessive optimism and pessimism. Unrealistic estimates defeat the entire purpose of the budgeting effort. The net result is aptly described by the acronym GIGO: garbage in, garbage out.

THE BUDGET PERIOD

Budgets normally cover differing periods of time. Those prepared for acquisitions of property, plant, and equipment (i.e., capital expenditures), often involve substantial dollar outlays and extend five to ten years into the future. Such a long time horizon is necessary so that costly mistakes can be avoided. To illustrate, a company would likely study long-term sales forecasts before deciding whether to undertake a multistore expansion into new retail markets. Although the coming year's forecast may appear favorable, long-run prospects may be bleak. By relying on too short a time period for evaluation, the firm could be making a bad investment from which it would be unable to recover.

In contrast, budgets that pertain to *operations* are generally prepared for a one-year time frame and usually coincide with the period employed for external financial reporting. For purposes of control and evaluation these budgets are often subdivided into quarters and months. The benefit of following this latter procedure is evident after studying Exhibit 24–2, which depicts a company's budgeted monthly cash balances. Notice that if the budget is viewed over a one-year period, we see a favorable cash position—the balance increases by $20,000 (from $80,000 in January to $100,000 in December). A breakdown by months, however, shows the need for short-term financing from the end of May

---

③ Explain the concept of slack as it relates to the estimation process.

ETHICS ISSUE

In your position as a department manager, you must submit a budget for next year. You know that other managers "pad" their budgets by at least 10%. Would you follow this same procedure?

④ Recognize the variations in budget periods.

EXHIBIT 24–2
Fluctuations in Monthly Cash Balances

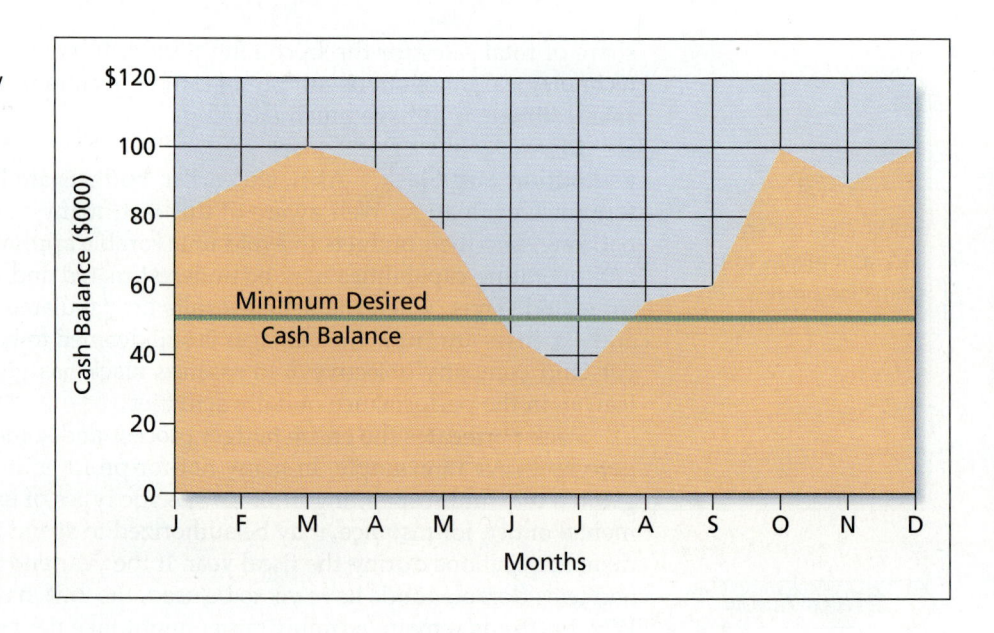

through July because of sporadic needs and a drop below the $50,000 minimum. Generally speaking, shorter budget periods usually allow a closer monitoring of operations.

In actuality, many businesses use a combination of monthly, yearly, and long-term budgets. In recent years a number of organizations have turned to continuous budgets. A **continuous budget** covers a one-year period, with a new month being added as the current month is completed. For example, assume that a budget for 19X1 operations is prepared. As soon as January 19X1 ends, a budget is added for January 19X2. Continuous budgets offer the advantage of forcing management to continually think about the future. The planning process is not confined to only a few months of each year but becomes an ongoing, stabilized activity.

BUDGET LIMITATIONS AND HUMAN RELATIONS

> **5**
> Discuss the limitations of budgeting, especially in the human relations area.

Critics contend that several limitations are associated with budgeting. First, a budget is only as good as the effort that goes into its preparation. Top management must thoroughly support the budget process, or the entire exercise will be a lesson in futility. Second, budgeting cannot replace effective day-to-day management. That is, the budget is a tool to be used by managers; it is not an end in itself and will not automatically improve a faltering operation. Although the critics' observations are correct, the preceding comments really apply to all tools of management.

Perhaps the most significant limitation of budgeting lies in the human relations and administration area. Many organizations overemphasize the use of budgets in control—and they often do so in an incorrect manner. To explain, employees are frequently disenchanted with the methods used to evaluate performance. Budgets disclose weaknesses and are often studied by upper management when finding who's to blame in unfavorable times. To avoid possible employee negativism, management should emphasize that budgeting is a positive tool that assists in achieving company goals, monitoring progress toward those goals, and setting standards of performance.

The administration of a budget program is a difficult task. Executives often become overly involved with the numerical aspects of budget construction and lose sight of the fact that employees are people. Employees have feelings and are sensitive to management looking over their shoulders to appraise performance. Unless the budget process considers human relations, even the best efforts will go for naught and be met with resistance.

A Further Focus

Budgets do not always work as intended. Consider, for instance, the federally mandated budgeting procedures that were followed by Oregon's million-acre Ochoco National Forest. Until recently, 70 separate budgets were prepared for relatively fundamental activities: one for fence maintenance in the north sector, one for brush burning in the south, and so forth. The budgets were divided into 556 management codes and 1,769 accounting lines, consuming roughly 45–60 days of the managers' time each year.

In 1993, President Clinton announced the National Performance Review, a six-month look at the federal government to identify problems and offer ideas for savings. In referring to the Ochoco National Forest's plight, an executive summary of the Review noted:

> The federal government does at least one thing well: It generates red tape. But not one inch of that red tape appears by accident. In fact, the government creates it with the best of intentions. It is time now to put aside our reverence for those good intentions and examine what they have created—a system that makes it hard for our civil servants to do what we pay for . . . .

Source: *Creating a Government That Works Better and Costs Less: Executive Summary*, Government Printing Office, Washington, D.C., 1993, p. 3.

Comprehensive Budgeting

6 Prepare a master budget.

Earlier in the chapter we noted that budget preparation often follows a company's organizational structure. Budgets for the company's individual operating units (e.g., departments, divisions, territories, and so forth) are generated and later combined. This process culminates in the **master budget**, a comprehensive set of integrated budgets that serves as the financial plan for the entire organization. Although variations are found in practice, the master budget generally consists of the following:

1. Sales budget
2. Production budget
3. Direct material purchases budget
4. Direct labor budget
5. Factory overhead budget

6. Selling and administrative expense budget
7. Capital expenditures budget
8. Cash budget
9. Budgeted income statement
10. Budgeted balance sheet
11. Budgeted statement of cash flows

These budgets cannot be prepared independently. Sales levels, for example, influence production plans. The number of units manufactured affects direct material, direct labor, and overhead costs, and all of these items have a bearing on an entity's cash budget and financial statements. The relationships within a master budget are shown in Exhibit 24–3. Observe (1) how the sales budget is

EXHIBIT 24–3
Relationships Within the Master Budget

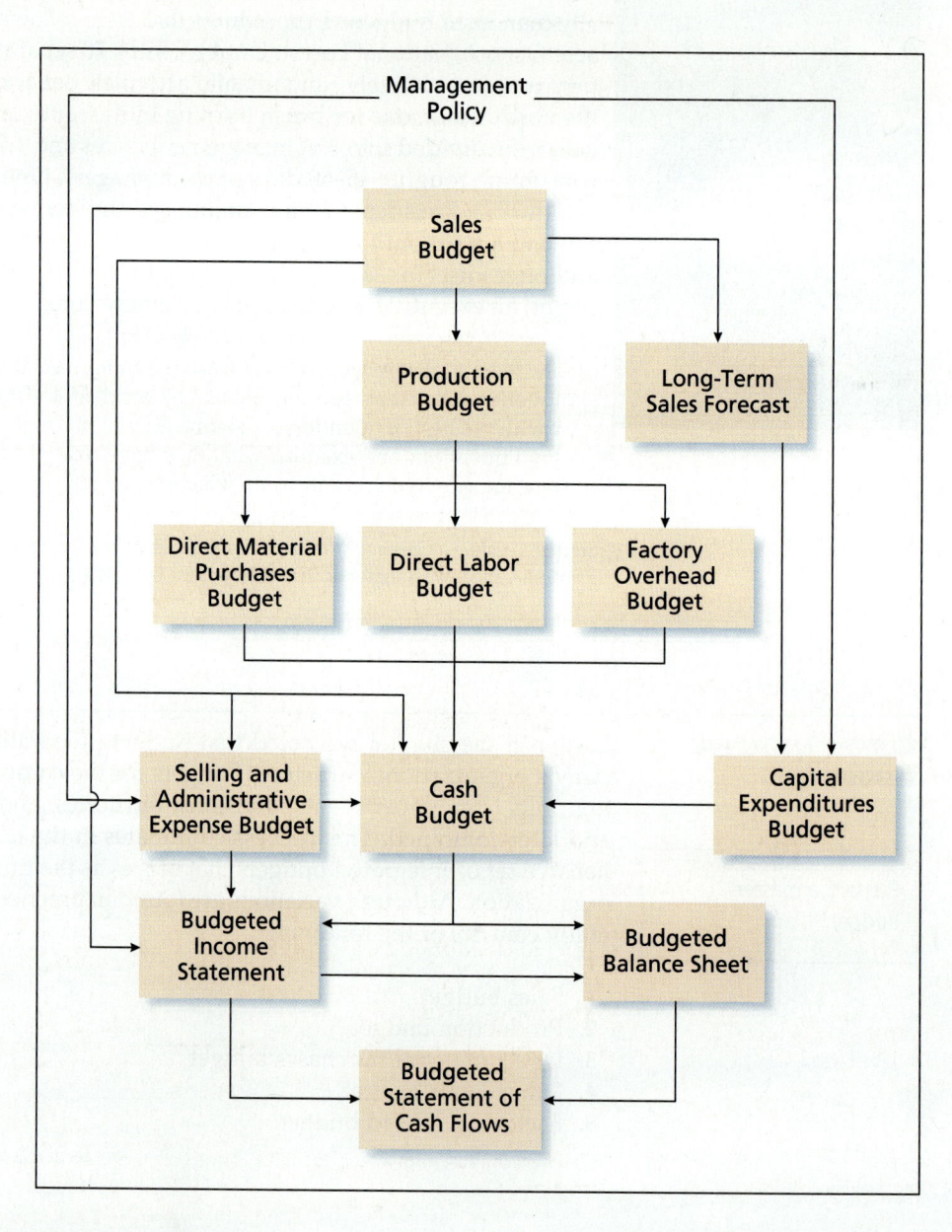

the starting point of the entire process and (2) how the cash budget and the financial statements tend to summarize the overall planning effort.

To illustrate preparation of a master budget, we will focus on Hillcroft Corporation. The company wants to study first-quarter activity for 19X2 by constructing a master budget similar to that just discussed.[1] The firm's December 31, 19X1, balance sheet appears in Exhibit 24–4.

SALES BUDGET

The sales budget is probably the most important element of the master budget. Production, cash flow, the financial statements, and a number of other items all depend on sales, in terms of both units sold and revenues generated. A grossly incorrect sales budget will thus create significant problems, as its effects are carried forward to other budget documents.

The sales budget is based on a forecast of sales volume. Forecasted volume is influenced by such factors as previous sales patterns, current and expected economic conditions, actions of competitors, and advertising and marketing strategies. Estimates of volume can be calculated by using several different techniques. For example, a company can study the relationship of sales to various economic indicators (such as interest rates and disposable income), use statistical forecasting methods, or quiz its sales staff.

EXHIBIT 24–4
Opening Balance Sheet of Hillcroft Corporation

HILLCROFT CORPORATION
Balance Sheet
December 31, 19X1

ASSETS

Current assets		
Cash	$ 8,000	
Accounts receivable	14,400	
Finished goods (1,500 units × $8.00)	12,000	
Direct materials (6,900 units × $1.50)	10,350	$ 44,750
Property, plant, & equipment		
Plant & equipment	$70,000	
Less: Accumulated depreciation	5,000	65,000
Total assets		$109,750

LIABILITIES & STOCKHOLDERS' EQUITY

Current liabilities		
Accounts payable		$ 8,000
Stockholders' equity		
Common stock	$40,000	
Retained earnings	61,750	101,750
Total liabilities & stockholders' equity		$109,750

[1] We will omit the capital expenditures budget and the statement of cash flows to simplify the presentation.

Exhibit 24–5
Sales Budget of Hillcroft Corporation

HILLCROFT CORPORATION
Sales Budget
For the Quarter Ended March 31, 19X2

	JANUARY	FEBRUARY	MARCH	TOTAL
Expected sales (units)	4,500	5,500	7,000	17,000
Selling price per unit	× $12	× $12	× $12	× $12
Budgeted sales revenues	$54,000	$66,000	$84,000	$204,000

Once the forecast is derived, the sales budget is prepared by multiplying the expected volume by the estimated selling price per unit. Hillcroft's sales budget is shown in Exhibit 24–5.

Schedule of Cash Collections. Although not part of the formal sales budget, a schedule of expected cash collections is easily generated at this time. The schedule provides information that will be needed when preparing the cash budget. To illustrate the necessary procedures, assume Hillcroft's sales are all on account. Seventy percent of the sales are collected in the month of sale; the remaining 30% are collected in the following month. The corporation's cash collection schedule appears in Exhibit 24–6.

PRODUCTION BUDGET

Once the sales budget is completed, a company's production requirements can be determined. Aside from sales, the number of units scheduled for manufacturing depends on raw material and facilities availability and desired finished goods inventory levels. Finished goods are often budgeted in advance so that adequate stock levels can be maintained. As explained in Chapter 22, businesses try to avoid carrying excessive goods because of associated storage, insurance, taxes, and interest costs, and the possibility of deterioration and

Exhibit 24–6
Schedule of Cash Collections for Hillcroft Corporation

HILLCROFT CORPORATION
Schedule of Cash Collections
For the Quarter Ended March 31, 19X2

	JANUARY	FEBRUARY	MARCH	TOTAL
Accounts receivable, 12/31/X1	$14,400*			$ 14,400
January sales ($54,000)	37,800	$16,200		54,000
February sales ($66,000)		46,200	$19,800	66,000
March sales ($84,000)			58,800	58,800
Total budgeted cash collections	$52,200	$62,400	$78,600	$193,200

*From Exhibit 24–4.

Note: Because only $58,800 of March sales are collected in March, the remaining $25,200 ($84,000 − $58,800) will appear on Hillcroft's end-of-quarter balance sheet as accounts receivable.

obsolescence. Further, these same entities resist precariously low inventories that could lead to stockouts, lost sales, and even lost customers.

The budgeted units of production in any given period can be calculated as follows:

Number of units to be produced	
Number of units sold	XXX
Add: Desired ending finished goods inventory (units)	XXX
Total finished units needed	XXX
Less: Beginning finished goods inventory (units)	XXX
Number of units to be produced	XXX

By adding budgeted sales to the units desired for the ending finished goods inventory, we obtain the total units needed during the period. Because some of these units are already on hand in the form of beginning finished goods inventory, only the remainder will have to be manufactured.

Hillcroft wants to maintain an ending finished goods inventory that covers 50% of the following month's sales. This inventory policy gives rise to the production budget shown in Exhibit 24–7.

DIRECT MATERIAL PURCHASES BUDGET

Now that production requirements are known, the direct material purchases budget can be prepared. Budgeted purchases are based on anticipated manufacturing schedules and a firm's desired ending raw material inventories. The latter amounts are sometimes influenced by supplier delivery schedules, the

EXHIBIT 24–7
Production Budget of Hillcroft Corporation

HILLCROFT CORPORATION
Production Budget
For the Quarter Ended March 31, 19X2

	JANUARY	FEBRUARY	MARCH	TOTAL
Number of units sold (Exhibit 24–5)	4,500	5,500	7,000	17,000
Add: Desired ending finished goods inventory (50% × following month's sales)	2,750	3,500	3,800[†]	3,800[‡]
Total finished units needed	7,250	9,000	10,800	20,800
Less: Beginning finished goods inventory*	1,500	2,750	3,500	1,500[‡]
Number of units to be produced	5,750	6,250	7,300	19,300

* The beginning finished goods inventory is the ending finished goods inventory from the preceding month. January's beginning inventory of 1,500 units appears on the balance sheet presented in Exhibit 24–4.

[†] April's sales are assumed to be 7,600 units. Thus, the desired ending finished goods inventory in March is 3,800 units (7,600 units × 50%).

[‡] The ending and beginning inventories are used here, not the *total* of the inventories. Insertion of totals will result in incorrect calculations.

availability of "specials" and quantity discounts, and management's purchasing strategy for heading off price increases.

The amount of materials to purchase can be computed in a manner similar to that for finding the budgeted units of production, namely:

Direct materials to be purchased
    Direct materials used in production (units)   XXX
    Add: Desired ending direct materials inventory (units)   XXX
    Total direct materials needed   XXX
    Less: Beginning direct materials inventory (units)   XXX
    Direct materials to be purchased (units)   XXX

Assume that Hillcroft uses two units of direct material in each completed product and that each direct material unit costs $1.50. Management desires to maintain an ending materials inventory equal to 60% of the materials needed in the following month's production. The company's purchases budget is shown in Exhibit 24–8.

Schedule of Cash Disbursements for Material Purchases. Given Hillcroft's purchasing program, we can now construct a schedule of the required cash disbursements. This schedule, like the schedule of cash collections, is useful when preparing the cash budget. To illustrate the necessary procedures, assume that Hillcroft expects to pay 60% of its purchases during the month of purchase and the remaining 40% in the following month. The schedule of cash disbursements for materials appears in Exhibit 24–9.

Direct Labor Budget

The direct labor budget is also based on the production schedule. Direct labor must be budgeted so that management can determine if sufficient personnel are available to manufacture the company's goods. Lack of proper planning could lead to labor shortages or overstaffing, both of which result in production inefficiencies. Furthermore, employee morale could suffer because of possible layoffs or extensive overtime to meet manufacturing schedules.

Direct labor requirements are determined first multiplying the number of direct labor hours per finished unit by the units to be produced. The result is then multiplied by the estimated hourly wage rate to generate total budgeted labor costs. Assume that Hillcroft Corporation pays its workers $8 per hour and each finished unit requires 0.5 hours of direct labor time. The necessary computations appear in Hillcroft's direct labor budget, which is shown in Exhibit 24–10.

Factory Overhead Budget

The factory overhead budget incorporates all production costs other than direct materials and direct labor. Such costs include indirect materials, indirect labor, depreciation, maintenance, and utilities. The first step in constructing a realistic overhead budget is to study the behavior of individual overhead costs.

EXHIBIT 24–8
Direct Material Purchases Budget of Hillcroft Corporation

HILLCROFT CORPORATION
Direct Material Purchases Budget
For the Quarter Ended March 31, 19X2

	JANUARY	FEBRUARY	MARCH	TOTAL
Planned production in units (Exhibit 24–7)	5,750	6,250	7,300	19,300
Units of direct material per finished unit	× 2	× 2	× 2	× 2
Direct materials used in production (units)	11,500	12,500	14,600	38,600
Add: Desired ending direct materials inventory (units)*	7,500	8,760	9,960	9,960
Total direct materials needed	19,000	21,260	24,560	48,560
Less: Beginning direct materials inventory (units)†	6,900	7,500	8,760	6,900
Direct materials to be purchased (units)	12,100	13,760	15,800	41,660
Cost per unit	× $1.50	× $1.50	× $1.50	× $1.50
Cost of direct material purchases	$18,150	$20,640	$23,700	$62,490

* The desired ending inventory equals 60% of the direct materials used in the following month's production. Ending inventories are computed as follows:

January: 60% × 12,500 = 7,500
February: 60% × 14,600 = 8,760
March: 60% × 16,600 (assumed) = 9,960

† The beginning direct materials inventory is the ending direct materials inventory from the preceding month. January's beginning inventory of 6,900 units appears on the balance sheet presented in Exhibit 24–4.

EXHIBIT 24–9
Schedule of Cash Disbursements for Material Purchases of Hillcroft Corporation

HILLCROFT CORPORATION
Schedule of Cash Disbursements for Material Purchases
For the Quarter Ended March 31, 19X2

	JANUARY	FEBRUARY	MARCH	TOTAL
Accounts payable, 12/31/X1	$ 8,000*			$ 8,000
January purchases ($18,150)	10,890	$ 7,260		18,150
February purchases ($20,640)		12,384	$ 8,256	20,640
March purchases ($23,700)			14,220	14,220
Total disbursements for purchases	$18,890	$19,644	$22,476	$61,010

* From Exhibit 24–4.

Note: Because only $14,220 of March purchases are paid in March, the remaining $9,480 ($23,700 − $14,220) will appear on Hillcroft's end-of-quarter balance sheet as accounts payable.

EXHIBIT 24–10
Direct Labor Budget of Hillcroft Corporation

HILLCROFT CORPORATION
Direct Labor Budget
For the Quarter Ended March 31, 19X2

	JANUARY	FEBRUARY	MARCH	TOTAL
Planned production in units (Exhibit 24–7)	5,750	6,250	7,300	19,300
Labor time per unit (hours)	× 0.5	× 0.5	× 0.5	× 0.5
Total labor hours needed	2,875	3,125	3,650	9,650
Direct labor cost per hour	× $8	× $8	× $8	× $8
Total budgeted direct labor cost	$23,000	$25,000	$29,200	$77,200

Observe, for example, that several of the preceding costs vary with changes in production volume, whereas others remain static. Once cost behavior is determined, we then compute overhead application rates similar to those described in Chapter 21.

Assume that Hillcroft's variable overhead application rate is $1.40 per direct labor hour. Fixed overhead charges are anticipated to be $1,930 per month, which includes $700 of straight-line depreciation. Exhibit 24–11 contains the company's factory overhead budget.

Notice there is a difference between total budgeted overhead and the firm's required cash disbursements for overhead. Depreciation, although a factory cost, does not entail a cash outlay and is therefore subtracted to calculate monthly cash payments. We are assuming that all other overhead is paid when incurred.

EXHIBIT 24–11
Factory Overhead Budget of Hillcroft Corporation

HILLCROFT CORPORATION
Factory Overhead Budget
For the Quarter Ended March 31, 19X2

	JANUARY	FEBRUARY	MARCH	TOTAL
Budgeted direct labor hours (Exhibit 24–10)	2,875	3,125	3,650	9,650
Variable overhead rate	× $1.40	× $1.40	× $1.40	× $1.40
Budgeted variable overhead	$4,025	$4,375	$5,110	$13,510
Budgeted fixed overhead	1,930	1,930	1,930	5,790
Budgeted total overhead	$5,955	$6,305	$7,040	$19,300
Less: Depreciation	700	700	700	2,100
Cash disbursements for factory overhead	$5,255	$5,605	$6,340	$17,200

Note: Fixed factory overhead is listed at the same amount each month. It is inappropriate to multiply a fixed application rate by the number of labor hours since these costs are constant and do not vary with activity.

SELLING AND ADMINISTRATIVE EXPENSE BUDGET

All manufacturing organizations incur costs unrelated to production activities, namely, selling and administrative (S&A) expenses. Like factory overhead, S&A expenses have variable and fixed components and require a review (in terms of cost behavior) prior to budget preparation.

Hillcroft's variable selling and administrative costs are freight-out and sales commissions, which total $0.80 per unit. Fixed costs include salaries, advertising, insurance, and other miscellaneous items. The firm's S&A expense budget appears in Exhibit 24–12. It is important to note that a new activity base is employed because these expenses vary with *sales*, not production.

CASH BUDGET

The cash budget, which is based on many of the budgets previously discussed, serves to summarize a considerable portion of the budgeting process. This important document provides management with assistance in assessing a company's future cash needs. The cash budget is typically composed of four major sections:

- Cash receipts
- Cash disbursements
- Analysis
- Financing

The *receipts section* discloses the total cash available during the period before considering any disbursements. Total cash available is computed by adding an entity's beginning cash balance to total cash receipts. For most businesses the major sources of receipts are cash sales and collections from customers on account.

EXHIBIT 24–12
Selling and Administrative Expense Budget for Hillcroft Corporation

HILLCROFT CORPORATION
Selling and Administrative Expense Budget
For the Quarter Ended March 31, 19X2

	JANUARY	FEBRUARY	MARCH	TOTAL
Expected sales, in units (Exhibit 24–5)	4,500	5,500	7,000	17,000
Variable S&A expense per unit	× $0.80	× $0.80	× $0.80	× $0.80
Budgeted variable expenses	$3,600	$4,400	$5,600	$13,600
Fixed S&A expenses				
Salaries	$2,000	$2,000	$2,000	$6,000
Advertising	600	2,600	1,500	4,700
Insurance	1,900	—	—	1,900
Miscellaneous	500	3,500	1,800	5,800
Total fixed expenses	$5,000	$8,100	$5,300	$18,400
Total budgeted S&A expenses	$8,600	$12,500	$10,900	$32,000

The cash *disbursements section* details expected cash payments during the budget period. Such payments include outlays for materials, labor, overhead, selling and administrative expenses, dividends, taxes, and capital improvements.

The *analysis section* combines the information presented in the previous two sections and discloses whether an organization has excess cash or a cash deficiency. Excessive cash balances should be used to retire outstanding loans or be invested in safe, liquid securities such as certificates of deposit and government notes. If the latter course of action is followed, a firm can generate a return on its investment and can reacquire the cash (if needed) in a short period of time. Should the analysis section reveal a deficiency, the need for additional cash is dictated. Because the deficiency is disclosed before it actually occurs, management can take corrective action to prevent possible loan defaults, past-due bills, and other undesirable outcomes.

Finally, the *financing section* provides a schedule of expected borrowings and repayments and also discloses the related interest on borrowed funds. Overall, this section allows companies to determine financing requirements and thereby give banks and other lending institutions advance notice of funding amounts.

Cash Budget Illustration. To illustrate the cash budget, we will continue the Hillcroft Corporation example. Assume that Hillcroft requires a minimum cash balance of $6,000, with bank loans available in $1,000 multiples at a 12% interest rate. For simplicity we assume that loans are obtained at the beginning of the month and are settled at the end of the month of repayment. Interest is disbursed at the time the principal is repaid. Finally, the company will distribute a $500 cash dividend in January and will have a $6,000 quarterly tax payment in March. Hillcroft's cash budget appears in Exhibit 24–13.

To explain the financing section, management requires a $6,000 minimum cash balance. Because borrowings are in $1,000 multiples, $7,000 of funding is needed in January ($7,000 − $545 = $6,455). All borrowings are assumed to be repaid as soon as possible, also in $1,000 increments. In view of this situation, $3,000 of debt can be retired in March without reducing the cash balance below the desired minimum. Interest is figured for three months, because the obligation was outstanding from January 1 through March 31 ($3,000 × 0.12 × 3/12 = $90).[2]

BUDGETED INCOME STATEMENT

The preparation of budgeted financial statements, often called **pro forma statements,** is the final step in budget construction. The first of these statements, the income statement, projects the forecasted results of operations and serves as a useful tool against which actual performance can be measured. Information needed for its construction is taken from the various budgets discussed in preceding sections of the chapter. Hillcroft's budgeted income statement is shown in Exhibit 24–14.

The most difficult part of the statement is the computation of cost of goods manufactured and the ending finished goods inventory. As noted in Hillcroft's production budget (see Exhibit 24–7), the firm produced 19,300 units during the quarter. The cost per unit of $8 is computed in the manner shown on page 939.

---

[2] This example assumes that the interest payment pertains solely to the amount of principal being repaid.

EXHIBIT 24–13
Cash Budget of Hillcroft Corporation

HILLCROFT CORPORATION
Cash Budget
For the Quarter Ended March 31, 19X2

	JANUARY	FEBRUARY	MARCH
Beginning cash balance*	$ 8,000	$ 6,455	$ 6,106
Add receipts: Customer collections (Exhibit 24–6)	52,200	62,400	78,600
Cash available before disbursements	$60,200	$68,855	$84,706
Less disbursements			
Material purchases (Exhibit 24–9)	$18,890	$19,644	$22,476
Direct labor (Exhibit 24–10)	23,000	25,000	29,200
Factory overhead (Exhibit 24–11)	5,255	5,605	6,340
S&A expenses (Exhibit 24–12)	8,600	12,500	10,900
Income taxes	—	—	6,000
Dividends	5,000	—	—
Total disbursements	$60,745	$62,749	$74,916
Cash excess (deficiency) before financing	$ (545)	$ 6,106	$ 9,790
Financing			
Borrowing to maintain $6,000 minimum balance (at beginning of period)	$ 7,000	$ —	$ —
Repayment (at end of period)	—	—	(3,000)
Interest at 12% per annum	—	—	(90)
Ending cash balance	$ 6,455	$ 6,106	$ 6,700

*January's beginning cash balance of $8,000 is obtained from Exhibit 24–4. Subsequent beginning balances are the ending cash balances of the preceding period.

Direct material (2 units of direct material at $1.50 per unit; see Exhibit 24–8)	$3.00
Direct labor (0.5 hours per unit at $8 per hour; see Exhibit 24–10)	4.00
Variable factory overhead (0.5 hours per unit at $1.40 per hour; see Exhibit 24–11)	0.70
Fixed factory overhead (see Exhibit 24–11 and the following discussion)	0.30
Manufactured cost per unit	$8.00

The fixed factory overhead is calculated on the basis of estimated direct labor hours. Because Hillcroft anticipates $5,790 of fixed overhead and 9,650 labor hours (both figures taken from Exhibit 24–11), the rate per hour is $0.60 ($5,790 ÷ 9,650 hours). As a result, each finished unit is charged with $0.30 (0.5 labor hours × $0.60) of fixed production cost.

Once the $8-per-unit manufacturing cost is computed, the ending finished goods inventory can be determined. From information that appears in Exhibit 24–7, the company has estimated its finished goods at 3,800 units as of March 31. The inventory is therefore costed at $30,400 (3,800 units × $8).

EXHIBIT 24–14
Budgeted Income Statement of Hillcroft Corporation

HILLCROFT CORPORATION
Budgeted Income Statement
For the Quarter Ended March 31, 19X2

Sales (Exhibit 24–5)		$204,000
Cost of goods sold		
Beginning finished goods inventory (Exhibit 24–4)	$ 12,000	
Cost of goods manufactured (19,300 units × $8)	154,400	
Goods available for sale	$166,400	
Less ending finished goods inventory		
(3,800 units × $8)	30,400	
Cost of goods sold		136,000
Gross profit		$ 68,000
Less S&A expenses (Exhibit 24–12)		32,000
Income before interest and taxes		$ 36,000
Less interest expense		210*
Income before taxes		$ 35,790
Income taxes (Exhibit 24–13)		6,000
Net income		$ 29,790

* Interest expense is calculated as follows:
  From Exhibit 24–13 $ 90
  Accrued interest on remaining loan balance ($4,000 × 0.12 × 3/12)   120
                                                                                   $210

BUDGETED BALANCE SHEET

The budgeted balance sheet as of March 31 is derived by combining the beginning balance sheet (see Exhibit 24–4) with the information presented in the other budgets. Hillcroft's end-of-quarter balance sheet is shown in Exhibit 24–15.

BUDGETING AND COMPUTERS

7 Recognize the adaptability of budgets to computers.

No doubt you have gotten the impression that budget preparation is extremely tedious and procedural. Furthermore, as discussed earlier in the chapter, the budget process usually consists of several rounds, with changes and refinements being added along the way. These characteristics make budgeting very adaptable to computers. Computers speed up the process and eliminate much of the drudgery for the accountant, thereby allowing more time for analysis and evaluation.

Computerized budgeting applications have expanded greatly in recent years, primarily because of the increased use of personal computers and the availability of software packages known as *electronic spreadsheets*. The spreadsheet (i.e., work sheet) configures the memory of a computer to resemble an accountant's columnar pad, actually, a pad that is much larger than could be printed on a piece of paper. This vast working area is employed to perform mathematical operations (e.g., the multiplication of data in cell D15 by that

EXHIBIT 24–15
Budgeted Balance Sheet of Hillcroft Corporation

HILLCROFT CORPORATION
Budgeted Balance Sheet
March 31, 19X2

ASSETS

Current assets
    Cash (Exhibit 24–13) $ 6,700
    Accounts receivable (Exhibit 24–6)   25,200
    Finished goods (Exhibit 24–14)   30,400
    Direct materials (Exhibit 24–8)   14,940* $ 77,240

Property, plant, & equipment
    Plant & equipment (Exhibit 24–4) $70,000
    Less: Accumulated depreciation   7,100†   62,900

    Total assets $140,140

LIABILITIES & STOCKHOLDERS' EQUITY

Current liabilities
    Accounts payable (Exhibit 24–9) $ 9,480
    Loan payable (Exhibit 24–13)   4,000‡
    Interest payable (Exhibit 24–14)   120 $ 13,600

Stockholders' equity
    Common stock (Exhibit 24–4) $40,000
    Retained earnings   86,540§   126,540

    Total liabilities & stockholders' equity $140,140

---

* 9,960 units × $1.50 per unit = $14,940.

† Accumulated depreciation, Jan. 1 (Exhibit 24–4) $ 5,000
  Straight-line depreciation, Jan.–Mar. (Exhibit 24–11)   2,100
  Accumulated depreciation, Mar. 31 $ 7,100

‡ Original loan – repayment ($7,000 – $3,000 = $4,000)

§ Retained earnings, Jan. 1 (Exhibit 24–4) $61,750
  Add: Net income (Exhibit 24–14) $29,790
  Deduct: Dividends (Exhibit 24–13)   5,000   24,790
  Retained earnings, Mar. 31 $86,540

---

contained in cell D19, with the result being stored in cell E24) and to format various schedules and reports.[3]

USE OF A SPREADSHEET

To prepare a budget with a spreadsheet, the user must enter mathematical formulas into the computer. The formulas express the financial relationships of the entity, for example, the fact that the ending cash balance is equal to the beginning cash balance + receipts – disbursements. Or that 70% of a firm's sales are on account, with the following collection pattern: 60% collected in the month

---

[3] A cell is a spreadsheet component that stores data. Each cell is referenced by its address, as determined by a column and row location. Cell G37, for instance, is found at the intersection of column G and row 37.

after sale, 38% collected in the second month after sale, and 2% uncollectible. The company's data (e.g., expected monthly sales) are then keyed into the computer, and the computer performs the necessary calculations as instructed by the formulas.

Once the formulas are developed, spreadsheets allow managers to perform "what if" testing. That is, a manager can study the financial impact of changes in specified budget variables. As an example, refer to Exhibit 24–16, which contains a simplified spreadsheet prepared by an executive of the Drake Company. The first half of the exhibit depicts quarterly sales, cost of goods sold, and gross profit—all computed by assuming an initial sales level of 90,000 units, a 4% growth rate, a selling price of $9, and a 55% cost of goods sold. The second half shows the resulting calculations if three of the underlying budget assumptions are changed.

If these variables were integrated in the company's master budget and had to be computed manually, the related mathematics would easily take hours to perform. And even then, Drake might not be satisfied with the results and might want to study a different set of assumptions. With a spreadsheet, the three variables can be changed by depressing a few keys on the keyboard; electronics does the rest. Newly generated reports and pro forma statements are produced in seconds, thereby giving the manager additional insights in a cost-effective and timely manner.

EXHIBIT 24–16
Spreadsheets and Financial Planning

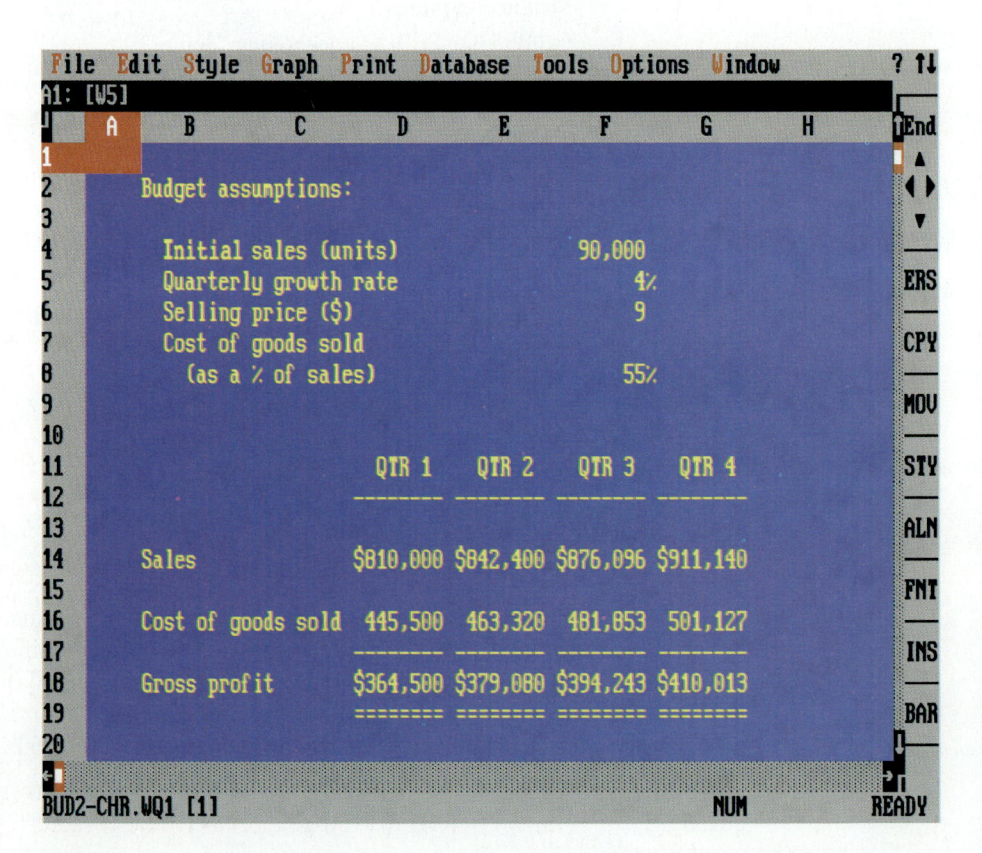

	QTR 1	QTR 2	QTR 3	QTR 4
Sales	$810,000	$842,400	$876,096	$911,140
Cost of goods sold	445,500	463,320	481,853	501,127
Gross profit	$364,500	$379,080	$394,243	$410,013

Budget assumptions:
- Initial sales (units): 90,000
- Quarterly growth rate: 4%
- Selling price ($): 9
- Cost of goods sold (as a % of sales): 55%

EXHIBIT 24–16
(continued)

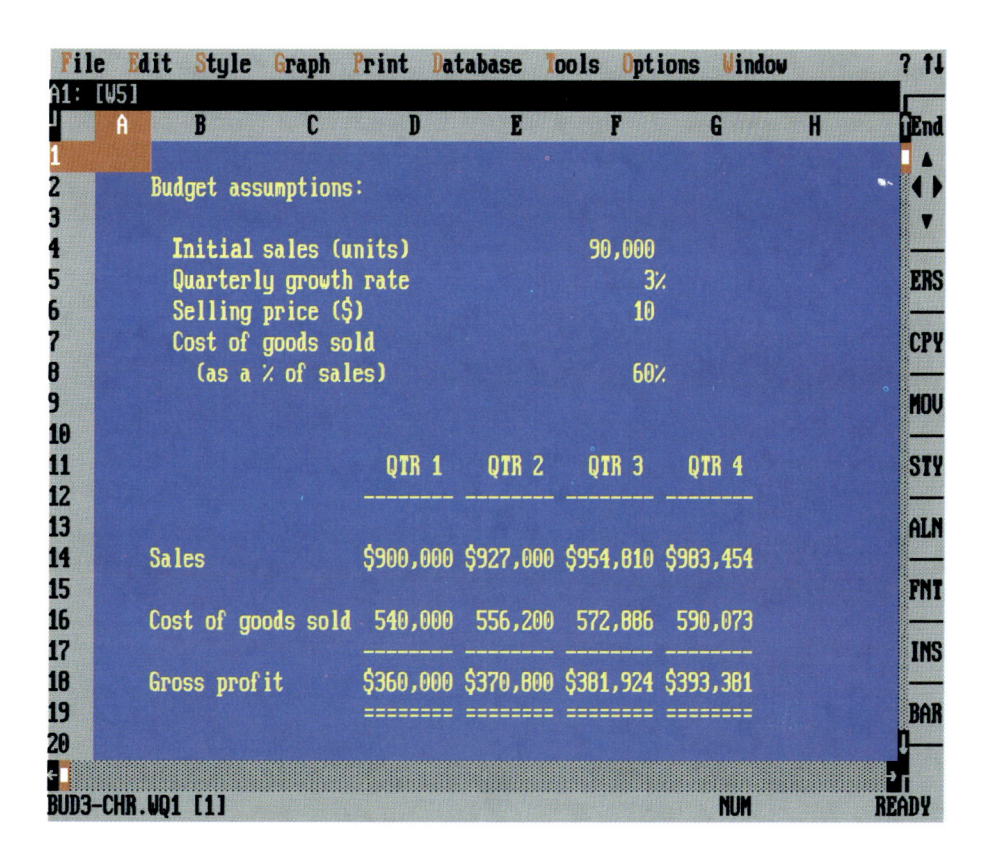

```
File  Edit  Style  Graph  Print  Database  Tools  Options  Window       ? ↑↓
A1: [W5]
      A        B           C         D         E         F         G         H      End
 1                                                                                    ▲
 2         Budget assumptions:                                                       ◄►
 3                                                                                    ▼
 4             Initial sales (units)              90,000
 5             Quarterly growth rate                  3%                             ERS
 6             Selling price ($)                     10
 7             Cost of goods sold                                                    CPY
 8               (as a % of sales)                   60%
 9                                                                                   MOV
10
11                                    QTR 1     QTR 2     QTR 3     QTR 4           STY
12                                   --------  --------  --------  --------
13                                                                                   ALN
14         Sales                     $900,000  $927,000  $954,810  $983,454
15                                                                                   FNT
16         Cost of goods sold         540,000   556,200   572,886   590,073
17                                   --------  --------  --------  --------          INS
18         Gross profit              $360,000  $370,800  $381,924  $393,381
19                                   ========  ========  ========  ========          BAR
20
BUD3-CHR.WQ1 [1]                                                    NUM       READY
```

END-OF-CHAPTER REVIEW

LEARNING OBJECTIVES: THE KEY POINTS

1. **Identify the benefits of budgeting.** Budgets provide three basic benefits for an organization. First, a formal plan of attack is created, allowing managers to pinpoint problems before the problems actually occur. Daily operating distractions are therefore reduced, because a look at the future often leads to adoption of corrective actions. A second benefit is that budgets serve as a basis for performance evaluation. Actual performance is compared against budgeted amounts, giving management insight into whether operations have been up to par. Finally, budgets assist in communicating and coordinating the goals of different operating units (e.g., divisions, departments, and so forth). The budgets of these units are examined and integrated when developing a plan for attaining overall company objectives.

2. **Distinguish between top-down and bottom-up budgeting.** With top-down budgeting, virtually all budget development takes place at the higher levels of the entity. This approach tends to reflect the goals of the entire firm as opposed to those of individual subunits (e.g., divisions). However, because of their lack of involvement, lower-level employees often resent the budget effort and do little toward budget achievement.

   In contrast, the bottom-up approach stresses active participation of lower-level employees in the budget construction process. Given their involvement, these employees usually make greater strides toward attaining budgetary goals. Further, budgets are more realistic because people who best know the operation are providing valuable input.

3. **Explain the concept of slack as it relates to the estimation process.** Slack refers to the use of padding in budget estimates to avoid unfavorable performance appraisals. As an example, a manager may underestimate sales and overestimate expenses when preparing a budget. Later, when actual sales are "down" and expenses are "up" and both amounts are compared against budgeted figures, the manager is deemed to have met his or her target for the period.

4. **Recognize the variations in budget periods.** Different types of budgets tend to cover differing time periods. Budgets for capital expenditures are long term in nature, often extending five to ten years into the future. Operations budgets are typically prepared for a one-year period. Finally, budgets used to assess actual performance are frequently subdivided into quarters and months.

5. **Discuss the limitations of budgeting, especially in the human relations area.** Several limitations are associated with budgets. Like other management tools, a budget is only as good as the effort that goes into its preparation. The degree of support by top management is a key factor in the success (or failure) of any budget program. In addition, budgets are not ends in themselves; they cannot replace effective day-to-day operating decisions.

    Because budgets are used in performance appraisals, employees often become disenchanted with the budgetary effort and its end product. Employees should be educated that budgets are helpful tools that assist in the attainment of company goals, not a means to fix blame when evaluating personnel.

6. **Prepare a master budget.** A master budget is a series of integrated budgets that serves as a financial plan for an organization. The starting point in the budget process is the sales budget, which logically flows into the production budget. Production levels, in turn, affect direct material purchases, direct labor, and the factory overhead budgets. Other elements of the master budget include the selling and administrative expense budget, a capital expenditures budget, a cash budget, and pro forma (i.e., forecasted) financial statements.

7. **Recognize the adaptability of budgets to computers.** Because of the heavy computational emphasis, budgets are extremely adaptable to computers. Computers eliminate much of the procedural drudgery for the accountant, thereby allowing more time for analysis and evaluation. An electronic spreadsheet is a helpful tool that allows different scenarios to be explored by changing only a few key input variables.

Key Terms and Concepts: A Quick Overview

bottom-up budgeting An approach that emphasizes lower-level employee participation in the development of a budget. (p. 926)

budget A formal quantitative expression of management expectations; generated for any area that management deems critical. (p. 922)

continuous budget A budget that covers a one-year period. A new month is added when the current month is completed. (p. 928)

master budget A comprehensive set of integrated budgets that serves as an entity's financial plan. (p. 929)

pro forma financial statements Forecasted financial statements that are prepared as the final step of the budgeting process. (p. 938)

slack The use of padding in budgets to avoid unfavorable appraisals. (p. 927)

top-down budgeting A budgeting approach in which a large portion of the development takes place at the upper echelons of management and the budget is imposed on lower-level personnel. (p. 925)

CHAPTER QUIZ

The five questions that follow relate to several issues raised in the chapter. Test your knowledge of the issues by selecting the best answer. (The answers appear on p. 962.)

1. Which of the following statements is false?
   a. Budgets are used in both the planning and control of daily operations.
   b. Budgets assist in coordinating the diverse goals of a company's different sub-units (e.g., divisions, departments, and so forth).
   c. Top-down budgeting is sometimes known as participative budgeting.
   d. Budgets help to formalize a company's planning process.

2. Bottom-up budgeting:
   a. generally results in increased efforts toward budget attainment by lower-level employees.
   b. often results in less realistic budgets than top-down budgeting.
   c. is used solely by manufacturing companies.
   d. is another name for top-down budgeting.

3. The first budget to be prepared is normally the:
   a. cash budget.
   b. production budget.
   c. pro forma balance sheet.
   d. sales budget.

4. Which of the following listings is the most logical sequence of budget preparation?
   a. Production budget, sales budget, cash budget, pro forma income statement.
   b. Sales budget, cash budget, production budget, pro forma balance sheet.
   c. Sales budget, production budget, direct labor budget, cash budget.
   d. Production budget, direct material purchases budget, pro forma balance sheet, cash budget.

5. The cash budget:
   a. assists management in predicting both cash shortages and cash deficiencies.
   b. is dependent on the figures that are generated in other, previously prepared budgets.
   c. discloses any borrowings and loan repayments that are expected to occur.
   d. possesses the characteristics noted in (a), (b), and (c) above.

SUMMARY PROBLEM

Rochester Manufacturing sells a single product. Last year's sales (19X7) totaled 60,000 units, but volume is expected to increase by 10% in 19X8 because of a strong economy. In view of this situation, Rochester will raise its selling price to $22.

Each unit produced requires four square feet of direct material at $1.75 per square foot. The following selected inventory information for 19X8 is available:

Finished goods inventory, Jan. 1	5,600 units
Desired finished goods inventory, Dec. 31	4,200 units
Direct materials inventory, Jan. 1	18,700 square feet
Desired direct materials inventory, Dec. 31	21,300 square feet

The January 1 accounts receivable balance is $63,000. All sales are on account and are spread evenly throughout the year. Rochester's collection pattern is: 35% collected in the month of sale and 65% collected in the month following sale.

Instructions

a. Determine the amount of cash the company would expect to collect in January and February.
b. Compute the number of units that Rochester expects to produce in 19X8.
c. Compute the cost of direct material purchases for 19X8.
d. Suppose that morale is low because of recent layoffs. If management wants to improve employee relations, would it likely use the top-down or the bottom-up approach to budget preparation? Briefly explain.
e. Rochester's management wants to examine the financial impact of several different selling prices and advertising programs. What should management consider doing to its budget preparation to avoid giving its office staff an overwhelming amount of procedure?

Solution

a. Sales in 19X8 will total 66,000 units (60,000 units × 1.10). Transactions are spread evenly through the year at the rate of 5,500 units per month (66,000 units ÷ 12 months). Collections are 35% in the month of sale and 65% in the month following sale.

	JANUARY	FEBRUARY
Accounts receivable, Jan. 1	$ 63,000	
January sales ($121,000)*	42,350	$ 78,650
February sales ($121,000)*		42,350
Total cash collections	$105,350	$121,000

* 5,500 units × $22 per unit.

b.
Number of units to be sold	66,000
Add: Desired ending finished goods inventory	4,200
Total finished units needed	70,200
Less: Beginning finished goods inventory	5,600
Number of units to be produced	64,600

c.
Planned production	64,600
Direct materials (square feet) per finished unit	× 4
Direct materials used in production	258,400
Add: Desired ending direct materials inventory	21,300
Total direct materials needed	279,700
Less: Beginning direct materials inventory	18,700
Direct materials to be purchased	261,000
Cost per square foot	× $1.75
Cost of direct material purchases	$456,750

d. The company should use bottom-up, or participative, budgeting. By becoming involved in the budget process, the employees will likely view their knowledge and insight as being important to top management. What the employees do not need at this point is a top-down ("dictatorial") approach.

e. Management should consider the use of electronic spreadsheets. "What if" analysis is simplified by pressing only a few keys on the computer as opposed to generating various rounds of time-consuming procedure.

Assignment Material

Questions

Q24–1   Briefly discuss the advantages of budgeting.

Q24–2   Is a budget a planning tool, a control tool, or both? Explain.

Q24–3   When evaluating performance, many organizations compare current results with the actual results of previous accounting periods. Is an organization that follows this approach likely to encounter any problems? Explain.

Q24–4   Explain how a budget assists in coordinating the plans of an organization's various subunits (divisions, departments, and so forth).

Q24–5   Define and fully explain the top-down approach to budgeting.

Q24–6   Briefly explain the bottom-up approach to budgeting.

Q24–7   Should budget data be based on the past, the future, or both? Explain.

Q24–8   Briefly discuss the concept of slack as it pertains to budgeting.

Q24–9   Calabro Corporation, a manufacturer with annual sales approaching $75 million, is beginning the budget process for the upcoming year. Should Calabro use long-term budgets, yearly budgets, or monthly budgets? Explain your answer.

Q24–10   What is a continuous budget?

Q24–11   Aside from the work involved in the preparation process, why do some employees resent budgets?

Q24–12   Why is an accurate sales forecast so important in the preparation of a master budget?

Q24–13   What factors influence a company's expected direct material purchases?

Q24–14   Why is it necessary to carefully budget direct labor requirements for an upcoming period?

Q24–15   Explain how a cash budget leads to effective management of an organization's cash balances.

Q24–16   Explain the concept of "what if" testing and how the computer can be of assistance.

Exercises

E24–1   Overview of the budgeting process (L.O. 1, 2, 4, 6)

Evaluate the comments that follow as being True or False. If the comment is false, briefly explain why.

a. When assessing current performance, a comparison of actual results against a predetermined budget is generally preferred over a comparison of the current period's actual results with those of the preceding period.
b. Lower-level managers are inclined to work harder to achieve budgeted targets if the top-down (rather than the bottom-up) budget approach is used.
c. Virtually all budgets are one year in duration.
d. Land & Sea plans to sell 36,700 units of its single product during the coming year. If the beginning and ending finished goods inventories are 15,900 and 17,700 units, respectively, the company's production budget will reveal that 38,500 units should be manufactured.
e. The last step in the construction of a master budget is the preparation of a cash budget.

E24–2 Coordination of activities (L.O. 1)

After long periods of testing, Bio-Vancouver recently received government approval to produce and market a new drug for the treatment of male baldness. Rita Hillis, the corporation's marketing manager, is jubilant, as she has waited three years to promote this revolutionary product. At a recent meeting of the firm's executive board, Rita requested permission from Bio-Vancouver's president to immediately place full-page ads in *The Wall Street Journal* and thirty major metropolitan newspapers.

To Rita's surprise the president was reluctant to act; he first wanted to contact other key company managers. Assuming that the drug is likely to be a blockbuster hit, develop a list of managers that the president would likely confer with before approving Rita's request.

E24–3 Participative budgeting; slack (L.O. 2, 3)

Mark Jacobs is the newly hired marketing manager of Electronics, Etc., a retail chain of 68 stores located in the northeast. The company recently adopted a participative approach to budgeting and uses performance reports to compare actual and budgeted results.

Mark has been asked to prepare the 19X8 advertising budget. Business has been relatively stable over the past few years, with annual advertising outlays averaging $6.5 million. Top management does not expect any new marketing programs during 19X8 nor are any hikes in media rates anticipated. Mark's budget called for outlays totaling $6.8 million.

a. Does Electronics, Etc., use a top-down or a bottom-up approach to budgeting? Briefly explain.

b. Did Mark appear to understand the concept of slack when he prepared the advertising budget? Briefly discuss, being sure to explain why the budget reflected a $300,000 increase in expenditures.

E24–4 Schedule of cash collections (L.O. 6)

Sugarland Company sells a single product and anticipates opening a new facility in Charlotte on May 1 of the current year. Expected sales during the first three months of activity are: May, $60,000; June, $80,000; and July, $85,000.

Thirty percent of all sales are for cash; the remaining 70% are on account. Credit sales have the following collection pattern:

Collected in the month of sale	60%
Collected in the month following sale	35
Uncollectible	5

a. Prepare a schedule of cash collections for May through July.

b. Compute the expected balance in Accounts Receivable as of July 31.

E24–5 Production budget (L.O. 6)

Pine Decorations anticipates January sales of 50,000 units and sales increases of 10% in each of the next three months. The company wants to maintain its finished goods inventory at 20% of the following month's sales.

Assuming there are 9,000 completed units on hand on January 1, prepare a production budget for January through March.

E24–6 Direct material purchases budget (L.O. 6)

Manchester United produces hand-sewn soccer balls that require 12 leather panels per ball. Manufacturing volume will increase throughout the year to meet rapidly rising demand and is expected to be as follows: first quarter, 8,000 balls; second quarter, 11,000 balls; third quarter, 15,000 balls; and fourth quarter, 20,000 balls.

The company wants to stock enough panels to meet 30% of the following quarter's production needs. Each panel costs $0.70, and there are 3,100 panels in stock on January 1. Prepare a direct material purchases budget for the first three quarters of the year.

E24–7 Production and cash-outlay computations (L.O. 6)

RPR, Inc., anticipates that 120,000 units of product K will be sold during May. Each unit of product K requires four units of raw material A. Actual inventories as of May 1 and budgeted inventories as of May 31 follow.

	May 1	May 31
Product K (units)	55,000	60,000
Raw material A (units)	40,000	37,000

Each unit of raw material A costs $8; RPR pays for all purchases in the month of acquisition. Invoices that account for 80% of the cost of materials acquired will be paid within 10 days of receipt, entitling the company to a 2% cash discount.

a. Determine the number of units of product K to be manufactured in May.
b. Compute the May cash outlay for purchases of raw material A.

E24–8 Analysis of operations: Cash emphasis (L.O. 6)

Lexington Wood Products manufactures and distributes wooden baseball bats. Business is seasonal, with a large portion of the sales occurring in late winter and early spring. Production is heavy during the last quarter of the year to meet demand, and Lexington experiences a temporary cash strain during this period. Payroll costs rise because considerable overtime is scheduled. Furthermore, customer collections are low because the fall season produces only modest sales. This year there are added problems because of high inflation rates and declining sales, the latter caused by the increased popularity of aluminum bats. Also, only 25% of the customers are paying their balances in the month of sale. The average collection period is approximately 62 days.

Fortunately, the cash strain arises only during the last quarter. The Cash account builds up during the first two quarters as sales exceed production. Excess cash is invested in U.S. Treasury bills and other trading securities.

Assume that Lexington regularly experiences the preceding cash strain. What actions could the firm take to "ease the squeeze" on cash? Consider possible changes in operations when preparing your answer.

E24–9 Abbreviated cash budget; financing emphasis (L.O. 6)

An abbreviated cash budget for Big Chuck Enterprises is shown on the following page. The company desires to maintain a $10,000 minimum cash balance at all times. Additional financing is available (and retired) in $1,000 multiples at a 12% interest rate. Assume that borrowings take place at the beginning of the month; retirements, in contrast, occur at the end of the month. Interest is paid at the time of repaying principal and computed on the portion of principal repaid.

a. Find the unknowns in Big Chuck's abbreviated cash budget.
b. Determine the outstanding loan balance as of September 30, after any repayments have been made.

	JULY	AUGUST	SEPTEMBER
Beginning cash balance	$ 10,000	$?	$?
Add: Cash receipts	50,000	63,000	71,000
Deduct: Cash payments	(64,000)	(58,000)	(64,000)
Cash excess (deficiency) before financing	$ (4,000)	$?	$?
Financing			
Borrowing to maintain minimum balance	?	?	?
Principal repayment	?	?	?
Interest payment	?	?	?
Ending cash balance	$?	$?	$?

E24-10 Cash budget (L.O. 6)

Tennessee Merchandising has had continual problems with cash flow. The following information has come to your attention:

a. The company has an opening cash balance of $10,000 on January 1. Management wishes to maintain a minimum cash balance of $8,000 at all times.
b. Budgeted sales for January total $200,000 and are expected to increase at the rate of 5% per month over the next six months. Sales from the preceding November and December amounted to $170,000 and $180,000, respectively.
c. All sales are on credit and subject to the following collection pattern:
   - Sixty percent collected in the month of sale.
   - Thirty percent collected in the month following sale.
   - Ten percent collected in the second month following sale.
d. All merchandise purchases are paid for in the month of purchase. The cost of acquisitions is expected to average 70% of the month's sales revenues.
e. Operating expenses are budgeted as follows:

	JANUARY	FEBRUARY	MARCH
Selling (excluding depreciation)	$16,000	$20,000	$25,000
Administrative (excluding depreciation)	12,000	12,000	12,000
Depreciation	6,000	6,000	7,000

f. The company will acquire $28,000 of new equipment in March for cash.
g. Additional financing is available (and retired) in $1,000 multiples at a 16% interest rate. Assume that all borrowings take place at the beginning of the month; retirements occur at the end of the month. Interest is paid at the time of repaying principal and computed on the portion of principal repaid.

Analyze Tennessee's cash position by preparing a cash budget for January through March. Has the company solved its cash flow problems or will additional financing be necessary?

E24-11 Master budget relationships (L.O. 6)

Jordan Enterprises sells a single product for $20. All sales are on account, with 60% collected in the month of sale and 40% collected in the following month. The company's schedule of cash collections for January through March of 19X5 revealed the following receipts for the period:

	JANUARY	FEBRUARY	MARCH
December receivables	$32,000		
January sales	54,000	$36,000	
February sales		66,000	$44,000
March sales			72,000

Determine:

a. The number of units sold in February.
b. December 19X4 sales revenues.
c. Total sales revenue to be reported on Jordan's pro forma income statement for the first quarter of 19X5.
d. Accounts receivable to be reported on the March 31 pro forma balance sheet.

PROBLEMS

Series A

P24–A1 Production and purchases budgets; purchasing policy (L.O. 6)

Mason, Inc., manufactures and distributes various parts for lawn mowers. The company's main product, a bilateral assembly, requires five units of direct material at a cost of $0.60 per unit. To keep production moving smoothly, the firm must maintain a direct materials inventory equal to 70% of the following month's production needs.

Sales projections in units for the last six months of 19X6 follow.

MONTH	ESTIMATED SALES
July	9,000
August	12,000
September	16,000
October	22,000
November	29,000
December	26,000

Management wants to carry a finished goods inventory equal to 40% of the following month's sales. On June 30, 19X6, the finished goods inventory totaled 3,200 assemblies. On the same date, 30,000 units of direct material were in the warehouse.

Instructions

a. Prepare a production budget for July through September.
b. Prepare a direct material purchases budget for July through September.
c. List several factors that could cause a change in the company's present direct material inventory policy.

P24–A2 Cash budget covering three months (L.O. 6)

Mapes Corporation is a distributor of athletic wear. Management is studying the company's cash needs for October through December and has assembled the following information:

- *Sales*—Projections reveal net sales of $30,000, $27,000, and $25,000 for October, November, and December, respectively. Sixty-five percent of all customer accounts are collected in the month of sale; 30% are collected in the following month; and 5%

are uncollectible. Management expects to collect $10,000 from the receivables outstanding on September 30.
- *Purchases*—Purchases of merchandise in October, November, and December are anticipated to be $13,000, $10,500, and $9,500, respectively. Forty percent of the merchandise purchases are paid for in the month of purchase to take advantage of a 2% discount. The remaining 60% are paid in the month following purchase. Accounts payable at the end of September total $9,000.
- *Depreciation*—Monthly depreciation expense is projected at $2,000.
- *Other expenditures*—The following additional cash outlays are expected:

	OCTOBER	NOVEMBER	DECEMBER
Operating costs	$15,000	$16,000	$21,000
Long-term investments	8,000	4,000	—

- *Stock issuance*—The company plans to issue $25,000 of common stock in early December.

The September 30 cash balance is $6,700. The company maintains a $6,000 minimum cash balance at all times. Should borrowing be necessary, financing is available (and retired) in $1,000 multiples at a 10% interest rate. Assume all borrowings take place at the beginning of the month; retirements occur at the end of the month. Interest is paid at the time of repaying principal and computed on the portion of principal repaid.

Instructions

a. Prepare a schedule of cash collections for October through December.
b. Prepare a schedule of cash disbursements for merchandise purchases for October through December.
c. Prepare a cash budget similar to that shown in Exhibit 24–13.

P24–A3 Cash budget for service enterprise; analysis of operations (L.O. 6)

Pat Mallory operates Green Up, a year-round lawn service and landscape business in Florida. The following information has been assembled to prepare a cash budget for 19X5:

1. Green Up has two types of clients (commercial and residential) and offers two types of services (regular and enhanced). The number of clients and weekly billing rates are:

	TOTAL NUMBER OF CLIENTS	WEEKLY BILLING RATE REGULAR	WEEKLY BILLING RATE ENHANCED
Commercial	60	$30	$50
Residential	40	25	35

Sixty-five percent of the clients use the regular service; the remaining 35% use the enhanced service.

2. The firm will provide 50 shrub planting jobs throughout the year. Each job averages six hours, and the billing rate is $25 per hour.
3. With the exception of $17,000 of uncollectibles, all amounts billed are expected to be received during 19X5.
4. Trees, shrubs, and supplies acquired from wholesalers will cost $28,000. Green Up adds 30% to cost for a profit and then bills clients.

5. Operating expenses incurred during 19X4 were: labor, $95,000; gasoline, $4,000; other, $5,000; and depreciation, $1,400. A 5% increase in labor, gasoline, and other is expected; depreciation will remain constant.
6. In 19X4, Green Up purchased an office refrigerator, fax machine, mobile telephone, microcomputer, new mowers, and a pickup truck. Total cost was $20,500, of which $4,300 will be paid during 19X5.
7. Green Up is organized as a sole proprietorship, and Mallory expects to withdraw $5,000 per month from the business.
8. The beginning cash balance on January 1, 19X5, is $4,500.

Instructions

a. Prepare the 19X5 cash budget for Green Up. Disregard the financing section.
b. Assume that the budget revealed an ending cash balance of $6,200. If Mallory wants to adopt a new policy of maintaining a $10,000 minimum balance throughout the year, what changes in operations would you recommend?

P24–A4 Pro forma statements (L.O. 6)

Kirkland, Inc., is preparing pro forma financial statements for January 19X6. The following information has been assembled:

- *Sales*—Budgeted sales total $45,000, 70% of which are made on account. Sixty percent of the firm's credit sales will be collected in the month of sale; the remainder will be collected in the following month.
- *Purchases*—Merchandise purchases are expected to be $37,000. Obligations to suppliers will be settled as follows: 40% in the month of purchase, subject to a 2% discount; 20% in the month of purchase after the discount period has lapsed; and 40% in the month following purchase. Management anticipates that $8,000 of inventory will be on hand as of January 31.
- *Operating expenses*—Monthly cash operating expenses are paid as incurred. Variable costs are 25% of sales; fixed costs, including $1,500 of depreciation, total $7,200.
- *Land acquisition*—The company plans to acquire $5,000 of land on January 15 by paying $1,000 down and signing a short-term note for the remaining balance.
- *19X5 Balance sheet data*—A review of the company's December 31, 19X5, balance sheet revealed the following figures:

Cash	$ 50,000	Accounts payable	$ 12,000
Accounts receivable	14,000	Common stock	80,000
Inventory	4,200	Retained earnings	28,200
Equipment	70,000		$120,200
Accumulated depreciation	(18,000)		
	$120,200		

Instructions

a. Determine the January 31 cash balance.
b. Prepare a pro forma income statement for January. Disregard income taxes.
c. Prepare a pro forma balance sheet as of January 31.

P24–A5 Comprehensive budgeting (L.O. 6)

The balance sheet of Mid-America Company as of December 31, 19X8, follows.

ASSETS

Cash		$ 14,800
Accounts receivable		26,000
Finished goods (1,200 units × $8.00)		9,600
Direct materials (6,000 units × $1.50)		9,000
Plant & equipment	$115,000	
Less: Accumulated depreciation	12,000	103,000
Total assets		$162,400

LIABILITIES & STOCKHOLDERS' EQUITY

Accounts payable to suppliers		$ 12,000
Common stock	$ 50,000	
Retained earnings	100,400	150,400
Total liabilities & stockholders' equity		$162,400

The following information has been extracted from the company's records:

1. All sales are made on account at $15 per unit. Forty percent of the sales are collected in the month of sale; the remaining 60% are collected in the following month. Forecasted sales for the first five months of 19X9 are: January, 2,600 units; February, 2,900 units; March, 3,100 units; April, 3,500 units; May, 3,200 units.
2. Management wants to maintain the finished goods inventory at 20% of the following month's sales.
3. Mid-America uses three units of direct material in each finished unit. The direct material price has been stable and is expected to remain so over the next six months. The ending direct materials inventory will be established at 70% of the following month's production needs.
4. Eighty percent of all purchases are paid in the month of purchase; the remaining 20% are paid in the subsequent month.
5. Mid-America's product requires 20 minutes of direct labor time. Each hour of direct labor costs $9.

Instructions

a. Rounding computations to the nearest dollar, prepare the following for January through March:
   (1) Sales budget
   (2) Schedule of cash collections
   (3) Production budget
   (4) Direct material purchases budget
   (5) Schedule of cash disbursements for material purchases
   (6) Direct labor budget
b. Determine the balances in the following accounts as of March 31:
   (1) Accounts Receivable
   (2) Direct Materials
   (3) Accounts Payable

P24–A6 Budgeting and spreadsheets (L.O. 6, 7)

Fashion Sense is in the process of preparing a budgeted income statement for the first quarter of 19X8. The information that follows is known.

January sales	$150,000
Cost of goods sold	60% of sales

Operating expenses
    Variable   20% of sales
    Fixed $10,000 per month
    Sales growth rate   2% per month

Management wants the budget to be established in the following format:

Budget assumptions	
Sales growth rate	1.02
Cost of goods sold	0.60
Variable expenses	0.20
Fixed expenses per month	10,000

	JANUARY	FEBRUARY	MARCH
Sales	150,000		
Cost of goods sold			
Gross profit			
Operating expenses			
Variable			
Fixed			
Total			
Operating income			

Instructions

a. Manually prepare the budgeted income statement as requested by management.
b. Prepare a spreadsheet model for the income statement and print the desired budget.
c. Repeat part (b), assuming January sales of $180,000 and a variable expense percentage of 15% rather than 20%.
d. On the basis of your answer to part (c), what benefits would a company experience by using a spreadsheet model in the budgeting process?

Series B

P24–B1 Production and purchases budgets; inventory policy (L.O. 6)

Pennsylvania, Inc., manufactures various products that are used in the home. The following information relates to the model no. 33 storage cabinet:

- *Sales*—Unit sales projections for the first six months of the year are: January, 20,000; February, 23,000; March, 21,000; April, 25,000; May, 26,000; and June, 28,000.
- *Finished goods*—Management wants to carry a finished goods inventory equal to 30% of the following month's sales. Six thousand storage cabinets were in stock at the end of 19X1.
- *Direct materials*—Each cabinet requires four units of direct material at a cost of $3 per unit. The company maintains a direct materials inventory equal to 40% of the following month's production needs; on December 31, 19X1, 35,000 units of direct materials were in the warehouse.

Instructions

a. Prepare the 19X2 production budget for January through March.
b. Prepare the 19X2 direct material purchases budget for January through March.
c. List several factors that could cause a change in the company's present finished goods inventory policy.

P24–B2 Cash budget covering three months (L.O. 6)

Atra Corporation is a distributor of recording equipment. Management is studying the company's cash needs for July through September and has assembled the following information:

	JULY	AUGUST	SEPTEMBER
Credit sales	$60,000	$70,000	$85,000
Purchases of merchandise	40,000	46,000	48,000
Cash operating costs	37,500	35,500	39,000
Depreciation expense	3,000	3,300	3,300
Equipment acquisitions	11,000	—	—
Sale of delivery trucks	—	—	20,000

The pro forma balance sheet on June 30 revealed the following account balances:

Cash	$23,000
Accounts receivable	22,800
Accounts payable	15,900

Sixty percent of all customer accounts are collected in the month of sale; 35% are collected in the following month. Because of a liberal credit policy, uncollectibles amounting to 5% of sales are anticipated. Management feels that only $19,000 of the accounts outstanding on June 30 will be received.

Sixty percent of the merchandise purchases are paid for in the month of purchase to take advantage of a 2% discount. The remaining 40% are paid in the month following acquisition.

Atra maintains a $5,000 minimum cash balance at all times. Should borrowing be necessary, financing is available (and retired) in $1,000 multiples at a 16% interest rate. Assume all borrowings take place at the beginning of the month; retirements occur at the end of the month. Interest is paid at the time of repaying principal and computed on the portion of principal repaid.

Instructions

a. Prepare a schedule of cash collections for July through September.
b. Prepare a schedule of cash disbursements for merchandise purchases for July through September.
c. Prepare a cash budget similar to that shown in Exhibit 24–13.

P24–B3 Cash budget for service enterprise; analysis of operations (L.O. 6)

The Eastside Tennis Club frequently experiences cash flow difficulties, with its checking account often below a desired minimum balance of $12,000. The following information pertains to club operations for the upcoming year (19X2):

1. The directors anticipate that 400 memberships will be sold. Family memberships ($150) will comprise 60% of this total; the remainder are individual memberships ($50).

2. Members are assessed hourly fees for court time; the rate depends on whether usage occurs during "prime" time or "regular" time. The following hours and rates are expected:

	PRIME TIME	REGULAR TIME
Rate per hour	$10	$7
Hours of use	4,300	6,500

3. With the exception of accounts that total $2,500, all billings for memberships and court fees are expected to be collected during the year.
4. John Connors, club pro, is paid a salary of $20,000 plus 20% of all court fee revenues. Connors gives private lessons and expects to earn an additional $3,500. Lesson fees are paid directly to Connors by the participating members.
5. Expenses incurred during 19X1 were: maintenance, $34,000; utilities, $13,500; and taxes, $6,200. Maintenance and utilities are expected to increase by 10% during 19X2; taxes should amount to $6,800. All expenses will be paid when incurred.
6. An examination of the club's records revealed outstanding accounts payable of $1,000 on January 1, 19X2. These amounts will be paid by the end of February.
7. The addition of one new court and improved lighting will cost $45,000. The club will pay $20,000 down, with the remaining balance financed by a short-term note. Interest and principal payments during 19X2 will amount to $3,600.
8. The cash balance on January 1, 19X2, is $5,000.

Instructions

a. Prepare a cash budget for 19X2 for the Eastside Tennis Club. Disregard financing [except for that noted in item (7)] to meet minimum balance requirements.
b. Assume that the budget revealed a $4,400 cash balance on December 31, 19X2. In light of the target minimum of $12,000, what actions could the directors take to improve the club's ending cash position?

P24–B4 Pro forma statements (L.O. 6)

Data from Aircon Company's balance sheet as of December 31, 19X6, follow.

ASSETS

Cash		$ 10,900
Accounts receivable		31,200
Merchandise inventory		64,500
Plant & equipment	$84,000	
Less: Accumulated depreciation	16,000	68,000
Total assets		$174,600

LIABILITIES & STOCKHOLDERS' EQUITY

Accounts payable		$ 56,000
Common stock, $1 par	$30,000	
Retained earnings	88,600	118,600
Total liabilities & stockholders' equity		$174,600

Management has gathered the following information relating to January 19X7:

1. Budgeted sales total $200,000. Historically, cash sales have averaged 10% of total sales. Seventy percent of the firm's credit sales are collected in the month generated; the remainder are collected in the following month.

2. Merchandise purchases are expected to total $120,000. Obligations to suppliers are settled as follows:

- Sixty percent are paid in the month of purchase, subject to a 1% discount.
- Five percent are paid in the month of purchase after the discount period has lapsed.
- Thirty-five percent are paid in the month following purchase.

Management has budgeted the January 31 inventory at $47,800.

3. Monthly operating expenses are paid as incurred and subdivided as follows:

Variable	7% of sales
Fixed (includes depreciation)	$17,900

4. The plant and equipment have a 20-year service life. Aircon uses the straight-line method of depreciation.
5. The company plans to acquire $16,000 of land on January 31 by paying $3,000 down and signing a short-term note for the remaining balance.
6. Aircon will declare a $0.15-per-share cash dividend on January 24. The dividend will be distributed on February 24.

Instructions

a. Determine Aircon's January 31 cash balance.
b. Prepare a pro forma income statement for January. Disregard income taxes and earnings-per-share computations.
c. Prepare a pro forma balance sheet as of January 31.

P24–B5 Comprehensive budgeting (L.O. 6)

The balance sheet of Watson Company as of December 31, 19X1, follows.

ASSETS

Cash		$ 4,595
Accounts receivable		10,000
Finished goods (575 units × $7.00)		4,025
Direct materials (2,760 units × $0.50)		1,380
Plant & equipment	$50,000	
Less: Accumulated depreciation	10,000	40,000
Total assets		$60,000

LIABILITIES & STOCKHOLDERS' EQUITY

Accounts payable to suppliers		$14,000
Common stock	$25,000	
Retained earnings	21,000	46,000
Total liabilities & stockholders' equity		$60,000

The following information has been extracted from the firm's accounting records:

1. All sales are made on account at $20 per unit. Sixty percent of the sales are collected in the month of sale; the remaining 40% are collected in the following month. Forecasted sales for the first five months of 19X2 are: January, 1,500 units; February, 1,600 units; March, 1,800 units; April, 2,000 units; May, 2,100 units.
2. Management wants to maintain the finished goods inventory at 30% of the following month's sales.

3. Watson uses four units of direct material in each finished unit. The direct material price has been stable and is expected to remain so over the next six months. The ending direct materials inventory will be established at 60% of the following month's production needs.
4. Seventy percent of all purchases are paid in the month of purchase; the remaining 30% are paid in the subsequent month.
5. Watson's product requires 30 minutes of direct labor time. Each hour of direct labor costs $7.

Instructions

a. Rounding computations to the nearest dollar, prepare the following for January through March:
   (1) Sales budget
   (2) Schedule of cash collections
   (3) Production budget
   (4) Direct material purchases budget
   (5) Schedule of cash disbursements for material purchases
   (6) Direct labor budget
b. Determine the balances in the following accounts as of March 31:
   (1) Accounts Receivable
   (2) Direct Materials
   (3) Accounts Payable

P24–B6 Budgeting and spreadsheets (L.O. 6, 7)

Harbor Wear is in the process of preparing its 19X4 budget. The following facts are known:

1. Sales for the last quarter of the year will be: October, $80,000; November, $95,000; and December, $120,000.
2. Twenty percent of the firm's sales are for cash; the remainder are on account. Sixty percent of the credit sales are collected in the month of sale; 36% are collected in the month following sale; and 4% are uncollectible.
3. October collections from September credit sales are expected to total $18,800.

Management has requested that the following budget report be prepared:

Budget assumptions			
Cash sales			0.20
Credit sales collected in the:			
Month of sale			0.60
Month following sale			0.36

	OCTOBER	NOVEMBER	DECEMBER
Total sales	80,000	95,000	120,000
Cash sales			
Credit collections:			
Previous sales			
Current sales			
Total			
Total collections			

Instructions

a. Manually prepare the budget report as requested by management.
b. Prepare a spreadsheet model for the cash collections and print the desired budget.
c. Repeat part (b), assuming October sales of $70,000 and a cash sales percentage of 25% rather than 20%.
d. On the basis of your answer to part (c), comment on the number of alternatives that a spreadsheet user can effectively explore when preparing a budget.

Expanding Your Horizons

EYH24–1 The "use it or lose it" philosophy (L.O. 3)

Many administrators in governmental and not-for-profit organizations believe they will be penalized if they fail to spend all budgeted amounts during an accounting period. The penalties come in several forms. First, the administrators may be viewed as poor budget estimators by superiors. Second, and perhaps more important, the administrators will typically be given fewer budget dollars in the future because it appears "they don't need the money."

Instructions

Form a team with three other students and interview two administrators who are employed in governmental and not-for-profit institutions. Inquire about whether the administrators have played a "use it or lose it" game to avoid future budget cuts and what types of expenditures have been made. What is their opinion of this policy from a spending effectiveness and ethical perspective? Prepare a brief summary of your findings.

EYH24–2 Sales forecasting (L.O. 6)

The most critical ingredient in preparing a master budget is the sales forecast, an estimate provided by top management, a budget committee, or the sales/marketing department. Determining sales for an ongoing product in a stable environment is relatively straightforward. Unfortunately, the same cannot be said for new products in a rapidly changing business climate.

Instructions

Form a group with three other students and assume that you have the responsibility to develop a national sales forecast for a new breakfast cereal. The multi-grain cereal is vitamin-enriched and fat-free and has no cholesterol. Consult various sources (trade journals, periodicals, annual reports of cereal producers, marketing textbooks) and determine first-year sales. Be prepared to tell the class the results of your calculations, how you arrived at your forecast, and any assumptions made.

EYH24–3 Budgeting and spreadsheets (L.O. 7)

Computers have affected virtually all aspects of business operations, including the budgeting process. The use of spreadsheets to assemble budgets is relatively commonplace.

Instructions

Form a team with three other students and interview managers employed by three distinctly different types of organizations. The organizations should also vary somewhat in size. Have the managers compare the budgeting process of, say, ten years ago versus that of today. How extensively have computers changed the process? What benefits have the managers encountered by computerizing? Have any problems been encountered? If the managers could change one thing about their current budget procedures (computer-related or not), what would it be? Prepare a short report of your findings.

EYH24–4 Budgeting in a small business (L.O. 1, 2, 3, 6, 7)

Manny's Automotive is a small company that specializes in the repair of foreign cars. The firm has been successful over the years as evidenced by growing sales, profitable operations, and expanded facilities. Manny's recently financed some sizable equipment purchases by securing a loan with Florida National Bank. A portion of this equipment included the firm's first computer, to be used in the office for billing and job costing.

Shortly after assuming the debt, the company began to experience cash flow problems. Manny's cash position deteriorated very rapidly, and employees actually had to wait an extra week for their paychecks not too long ago. Manny discussed the problem with his CPA, and the accountant recommended the installation of a formal budget program to help solve the problem.

Instructions

a. Budgets provide several basic benefits for an organization. Which of these benefits would be most applicable to Manny's Automotive? Why?
b. What benefits would Manny's likely derive by using a cash budget?
c. Is it likely that slack would be a problem in this situation? Briefly explain.
d. What could Manny do to eliminate many of the procedural headaches that are associated with budgeting?
e. Briefly distinguish between top-down and bottom-up budgeting. Which of the two approaches, if any, would Manny's likely use? Why?

COMMUNICATION OF ACCOUNTING INFORMATION

CAI24–1 The justification memo (L.O. 1, 2, 3)

Communication Principle: The business environment is often characterized as a world in which scarce resources must be allocated among alternative courses of action. Not only is this statement true for our entire economy, but it is also valid within a single organization.

In view of this situation, individuals (and departments) are frequently called upon to defend their resource requests—especially at budget time. Keep the following points in mind when developing a memorandum or verbal presentation for this purpose:

- *Be truthful.* Honesty with superiors is a fundamental obligation. Managers who exaggerate their budgetary needs in order to provide a "cushion" may soon find that their requests are subjected to arbitrary cuts, as superiors assume that padding is the rule rather than the exception.
- *Be consistent.* Provide clear descriptions of the consequences of alternative budgetary actions and show how prior projections have been fulfilled. Upper-level managers are more likely to take heed of budget requests if there is consistency between past forecasts and actual results.
- *Be concise.* Don't ramble on and on. Cases should be stated simply and precisely, leaving the ultimate decision to those responsible. If a manager's presentation is perceived as "whining," it will likely do more harm than good.
- *Focus on organizational goals.* Resource requests should show how the overall organization will benefit. Upper-level managers normally favor team players who take a corporate rather than an individual division or department perspective.

Mill Road Products recently adopted a zero-defect policy for its manufactured goods. In addition, management wants to reduce the firm's overall inventory investment and avoid hiring any new employees.

Frank Barnett heads Department 109, which produces an electrical component requiring minimal manufacturing time and lengthy, detailed inspections. Previously, inspectors randomly tested finished goods. In light of Mill Road's new policy, however, they must now check every unit produced. As a result, the inventory of completed but uninspected goods is rising rapidly.

Barnett's corrective options include occasional reassignment of production personnel to inspection. This action will reduce long-run output but will remedy the inventory buildup problem. Another possibility is to hire additional inspectors, increasing the annual payroll by $90,000.

Instructions

Draft a persuasive memo to upper management that defines Barnett's problem and requests that management provide additional funds to hire more inspectors. Barnett is well respected by his superiors but senses that they have minimal interest in eliminating the department's problem. You may assume that sufficient customer demand exists to absorb all the units that can be manufactured.

Answers to Chapter Quiz

1. c
2. a
3. d
4. c
5. d

25
Performance Evaluation via Flexible Budgets and Standard Costs

Learning Objectives

After studying this chapter, you should be able to:

1. Explain the purpose and structure of a responsibility accounting system.
2. Construct and use a flexible budget.
3. Explain what a standard cost is and how standards are developed.
4. Distinguish between ideal and attainable standards.
5. Calculate direct material, direct labor, and factory overhead variances.
6. Describe the problems encountered in the variance investigation process.
7. Discuss the use of standards in nonmanufacturing settings and the popularity of nonfinancial performance measures.

George Faris of Banner Advertising usually evaluates operations by studying both bottom-line profit on the income statement and the firm's ending cash balance. As long as income is reported and the cash balance is rising, George concludes that he must be doing something right. How the firm *should* be doing is another matter.

"Did you ever think about comparing actual performance against your budget?" we asked when we sat down to discuss the chapter's content. "It's a very common business practice. You can compare actual against budgeted figures, and determine where the company went right and where corrections are needed." George thought for a moment and then said, "Promise you won't laugh?" We promised and he then went on to tell the following story.

"I understand fully what you're talking about. While we don't follow the practice to a great extent, I guess our monitoring of utility costs somewhat fits the bill. As you know, our area is plagued throughout the year with pests known as fire ants—one of the fiercest insects for their size. For some reason, these ants are attracted to most anything that produces a low voltage electrical current. They really cause havoc with our billboard time clocks that turn the lights on and off during the day. Keep in mind that these lights use quite a bit of electricity, and we know roughly what the monthly utility bill should be for each board. Trouble is when the ants invade the clock system, the lights stay either totally on or totally off. In both cases the bill varies greatly from our estimate—and then it's time to send out the ant patrol to fix the problem. This is an admittedly unusual procedure, but it certainly beats driving around from sign to sign to look for the pests!"

While we couldn't argue with Banner's approach and George's conclusion, we nevertheless decided that the chapter should take a more conventional look at performance evaluation. Our underlying rationale is that performance analysis is widespread and affects virtually everyone. For example, economists continually examine unemployment rates and changes in the Consumer Price Index to assess our country's monetary and fiscal policies. Sales personnel are judged against budgeted sales quotas. Baseball players are ranked on batting averages, runs batted in, and fielding percentages. And finally, you are probably being evaluated in this course on the basis of examination scores. Although our list of evaluative measures is far from complete, suffice it to say that in one form or another, performance measurement is a way of life.

This chapter focuses on two popular tools that are used to study performance in a business organization: flexible budgets and standard costs. These tools allow a manager to monitor operations against a preset target and provide insight to the age-old question: "How am I doing?" Before we proceed with a discussion of flexible budgets and standard costs, it is helpful to first present the underlying foundation of performance measurement—responsibility accounting.

RESPONSIBILITY ACCOUNTING

> **1**
> Explain the purpose and structure of a responsibility accounting system.

Responsibility accounting is a reporting system that is based on the organizational structure of a firm. In essence, the firm is subdivided into various centers (i.e., segments) such as departments, plants, territories, or divisions. Managers are appointed to oversee individual center activities, held accountable for operating results, and evaluated accordingly. The thrust of responsibility accounting is that centers are charged only for costs and credited only for revenues that are subject to their control. By operating in this manner, top management can better assess performance and monitor progress toward the attainment of company objectives.

RESPONSIBILITY UNITS

As noted, responsibility centers may be organized in different ways: by territories, by departments, and so forth. Each center, in turn, may be established as a cost, profit, or investment center.

Cost Center. A responsibility unit in which a manager is held accountable for cost incurrence is termed a *cost center*. Generally, cost centers are operations or departments that are not directly involved in revenue-generating activities. Managers are thus evaluated on the level of cost incurred, not net income. Common examples of cost centers include billing, purchasing, payroll, and janitorial departments.

Contrary to what many people believe, a cost center manager should not necessarily strive for cost minimization. Such a goal is actually inconsistent with the center's purpose. To explain, most cost centers render services (as opposed to manufacture and/or sell a product). With increased activity comes increased cost, namely, variable cost. A minimization philosophy would therefore dictate that the center provide "bare bones" service to the remainder of the organization, that is, just enough to get by. A more appropriate philosophy holds that the center should furnish adequate assistance to other firm segments while keeping costs at reasonably low levels.

Profit Center. A responsibility unit in which a manager is held accountable for profit (i.e., revenues minus expenses) is called a *profit center*. Because revenues now enter the evaluation process, profit centers must be involved with the sale of goods or services. The sales in many cases are *intracompany*, or within the firm. For example, the filmmaking division of a large entertainment concern could produce and sell a "made-for-television" movie to the organization's broadcasting division. Although both divisions are part of the same overall company, one division is actually selling its output to the other. Further examples of profit centers include computer and repair centers, which charge other operating segments for data-processing services and maintenance work, respectively.

Investment Center. The most complex of the responsibility centers is the *investment center*, where a manager is evaluated not only on revenues and expenses but also on asset investment. More specifically, the head of an investment center is concerned with both profitable operations *and* the effective use of capital funds. Capital funds are normally disbursed for long-term projects such as the acquisition of new buildings and equipment; investment in other companies for purposes of control and affiliation; and entry into new product lines. In effect, the investment center structure allows a manager to run his or her own small business. The business, however, is part of a larger organization.

To determine the success (or failure) of an investment center manager, most companies employ a measure known as **return on assets.** Sometimes referred to as *return on investment (ROI)*, this measure shows the amount of income generated from a given level of assets. For example, if division A has operating income of $100,000 and an asset investment base of $500,000, the division is said to have an ROI of 20% ($100,000 ÷ $500,000).

Because the evaluation is done on a percentage basis, segments of different sizes can be compared more readily.[1] Comparative analysis might reveal, for example, that assets employed in a "low-return" division could be better used by another unit of the firm. Or perhaps certain assets should be sold, with the proceeds invested in new, more profitable endeavors. We stress that any comparative studies be done with caution because segments often have vastly different operating characteristics.

A Chief Information Officer's Perspective

The "Ideal" Form of Organization: The role of the information systems function within a company varies according to the function's strategic importance. When viewed as a very basic provider of service (like a purchasing department), information systems is likely to be treated as a cost center. With this structure, there is no incentive to keep up with technology, make substantial investments for the future, and design new products that could change the nature of business—actions that all produce short-term increases in operating costs.

The systems function is often organized as a profit center to encourage more aggressive entrepreneurial behavior. This way, there is great motivation to develop new "products" and market them so that revenues are generated. The most sophisticated form of accountability occurs when information systems is established as an investment center. This transforms systems activity into what is essentially a "business within a business," concerned not only with yearly profits but also effective hardware and software acquisitions, return on funds invested, and long-term strategic growth.

Reporting System

The responsibility accounting system established for cost, profit, and investment centers is typically tailored to the entity's organization chart. That is, performance reporting begins at lower levels of the firm and continues upward.

---

[1] Further discussion of this topic is found on page 268.

This design approach is used to reflect the pyramiding of responsibility that exists in a typical management hierarchy. The system's reports therefore show an executive's own performance plus the performance of lower-level employees in the chain of command.

To illustrate, we will focus on the organization chart of Sakowski Manufacturing Corporation (see Exhibit 25–1). Sakowski has divided its operations into divisions that are organized along territorial lines, with each division being composed of several plants. For purposes of simplicity, only the details of the Eastern Division are presented. In addition, smaller responsibility units that may be established at the plant level (such as departments and work stations) are omitted. Overall, our example will focus on three reporting levels: plant, division (vice-president), and president.

Performance Reports. Sakowski, like most other organizations, provides its responsibility center managers with a series of performance reports. These reports furnish management with feedback on operating results and are used for purposes of evaluation and control.

The exact format and detail level of a performance report are determined by the needs and preferences of the user as well as by the type of responsibility center being evaluated. For example, the management of a manufacturing firm may desire feedback about the number of units produced during a given period. A company involved with the production of Broadway musicals, on the other hand, may be concerned with attendance and sales of particular seat classifications, such as orchestra and mezzanine. Regardless of the specific content, most performance reports compare budgeted figures to actual figures. The differences, or *variances*, may be expressed in dollars or as percentages of budgeted amounts.

The series of reports used by Sakowski Manufacturing appears in Exhibit 25–2. Observe the bottom-up progression of operating information. The operating results at the plant level are compiled first and then included in the vice-president's report. The report of the vice-president summarizes all plants under his or her supervision and also reveals the cost of running the vice-president's

EXHIBIT 25–1
Sakowski Manufacturing Corporation Organization Chart

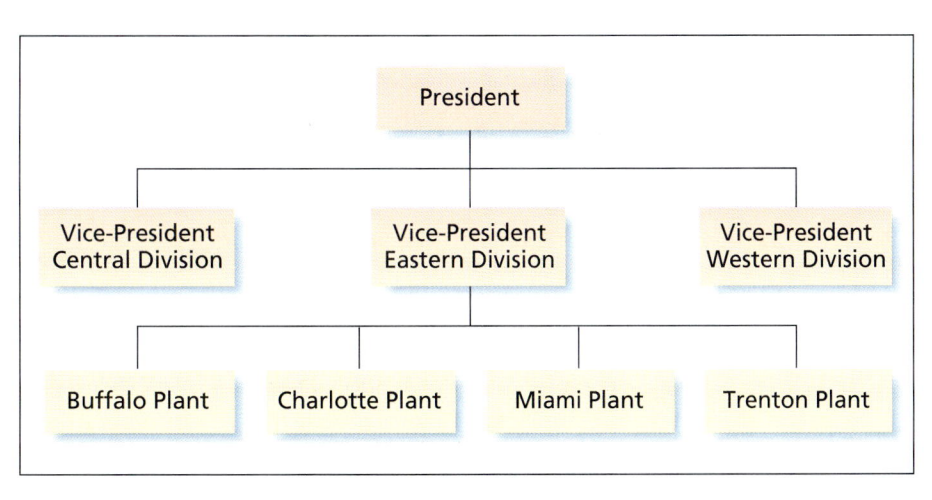

EXHIBIT 25–2
Responsibility Accounting at Various Organizational Levels ($000 omitted)

PRESIDENT'S OCTOBER PERFORMANCE REPORT

	BUDGET	ACTUAL	VARIANCE* DOLLARS	VARIANCE* PERCENTAGE OF BUDGET
President's office	$ (100)	$ (95)	$ 5	5%
Central division	490	485	(5)	(1)
▶Eastern division	400	416	16	4
Western division	350	360	10	3
Operating income	$1,140	$1,166	$26	2

* ( ) = unfavorable.

EASTERN VICE-PRESIDENT'S OCTOBER PERFORMANCE REPORT

	BUDGET	ACTUAL	VARIANCE* DOLLARS	VARIANCE* PERCENTAGE OF BUDGET
Vice-president's office	$ (28)	$ (30)	$ (2)	(7)%
Buffalo plant	66	70	4	6
▶Charlotte plant	75	85	10	13
Miami plant	55	61	6	11
Trenton plant	232	230	(2)	(1)
Operating income	$400	$416	$16	4

* ( ) = unfavorable.

CHARLOTTE PLANT'S OCTOBER PERFORMANCE REPORT

	BUDGET	ACTUAL	VARIANCE* DOLLARS	VARIANCE* PERCENTAGE OF BUDGET
Sales	$360	$365	$ 5	1%
Cost of goods sold	$240	$233	$ 7	3
Administrative expense	25	25	—	—
Selling expense	20	22	(2)	(10)
Total	$285	$280	$ 5	2
Operating income	$ 75	$ 85	$10	13

* ( ) = unfavorable.

office. The summarization process continues upward to the president. The president's report discloses the monthly operating performance of the three vice-presidents (i.e., divisions) as well as the costs associated with the top administrative function.

It is now apparent that the responsibility reporting system is both consistent with Sakowski's organizational structure and reflects the progression of authority that exists in most businesses. Also, note that as one goes higher and higher in the structure, the reports become more summarized. This summarization reflects upper-level management's unwillingness to sift through reams of detailed data on activities for which subordinates are responsible. Given the nature of top management positions and the type of work performed, summarized information is normally satisfactory. If for some reason more detail is needed, the reporting system is designed so the desired facts and figures are readily accessible.

CONTROLLABILITY: THE KEY TO RESPONSIBILITY ACCOUNTING

When evaluating performance under a responsibility accounting system, management should consider only those revenues, expenses, and investments that a segment can control. Holding a segment and its employees accountable for uncontrollable items and happenings clearly diminishes the usefulness of the responsibility system. The end result is often low morale and high employee turnover. If a responsibility system is to be effective, the reports should clearly distinguish between those performance factors that are controllable and those that are not.

Generally speaking, the ability to control means being able to influence or change. Consequently, if a responsibility center can significantly influence revenues, expenses, or investment funds through its own direct actions, the center's management should be held accountable for these items. Although this concept seems straightforward, it is sometimes difficult to apply in practice. Stated simply, revenue generation and cost incurrence are frequently affected by two or more managers.

For example, the total cost of raw materials used in production is influenced by both the purchasing manager and the production manager. The production manager bears primary responsibility for raw material usage since worker efficiency directly affects the materials consumed and the amount of waste incurred. The purchasing manager, on the other hand, is chiefly concerned with the prices paid to secure needed materials. Assume that in an effort to curb soaring costs in an inflationary economy, the head of purchasing has purposely acquired lower-quality goods. As a result, no matter how efficient the production workers are, overall consumption will be influenced by factors beyond their control.

Even though multiple influences are brought to bear, somebody is usually in the best position to explain the amount of revenues and costs and the reasons for variances from budgeted amounts. The goal is to trace revenues and costs to their source and thereby fix responsibility for their creation. An attempt is therefore made to associate control and accountability with the person or center that has the greatest potential influence over the item in question.

A FURTHER FOCUS

Pinpointing revenues and expenses and tracing them to an accountable individual was recently implemented at Georgia Tech to, in part, guarantee a future for the school's sports programs. Football and basketball have long generated the majority of Tech's athletic revenue, but they are only two of 14 varsity sports offered. A responsibility system was established that looked at the cost of each program, including expenditures for scholarships, recruiting, telephones, cheerleaders, and sports medicine. The individual coaches were designated as the accountable employees and were given decision-making authority with respect to operating their programs within budget. This approach to management requires that a school have multifaceted personnel who can successfully coach athletes on the field and later don a different hat as an administrator. The coach/entrepreneur must work with the athletic director, juggle operating costs, and even identify additional sources of revenue (e.g., advertising, development of a support group such as the "Grand Slam Club," and so forth).

Source: "Financial Management at Georgia Tech," *Management Accounting*, February 1993, pp. 59–63.

FLEXIBLE BUDGETS

2 Construct and use a flexible budget.

Given the framework of responsibility accounting, let us now become a bit more detailed. Suppose it is your first day on the job as assistant to the president of Coleman Industries. On the basis of figures provided by the accounting department, the president has prepared the performance report that appears in Exhibit 25-3 for the company's Oregon plant.

The budget was based on an initial production target of 50,000 units; however, 54,000 units were actually manufactured. The president has given you the report and wants to know whether Oregon's production manager should be praised for outstanding performance or called on the carpet for ineptness.

At first glance it appears that performance was not satisfactory, because actual costs were $35,400 in excess of budget. When we consider only the variable costs, unfavorable variances total 6.6% of budgeted amounts ($37,900 ÷ $575,000), an overrun that some managers would deem significant. Before proceeding to terminate the production manager's employment, though, we must consider one important fact. The performance report compares the actual costs of manufacturing 54,000 units against budgeted costs for only 50,000 units. By the nature of the comparison, a number of unfavorable variable cost variances are bound to arise because of the increase in activity.

Your conclusion about the production manager's performance? It's really impossible to judge from the report that has been prepared. What we have illustrated is one of the classic problems associated with using a static budget for evaluative purposes. A **static budget** is a budget developed for one level of activity. Should output vary from the level anticipated (50,000 units in Oregon's case), comparisons with actual costs become meaningless. In plain and simple terms, we cannot compare expected costs against actual costs at different activity levels. An adjustment is needed for the change in volume.

EXHIBIT 25–3
Coleman Industries
Performance Report

COLEMAN INDUSTRIES
Oregon Plant Performance Report
For the Quarter Ended March 31, 19X3

COST	BUDGET, 50,000 UNITS	ACTUAL, 54,000 UNITS	VARIANCE*
Variable production costs			
Direct materials used	$150,000	$159,300	$ 9,300U
Direct labor	350,000	367,200	17,200U
Variable factory overhead	75,000	86,400	11,400U
Total	$575,000	$612,900	$37,900U
Fixed factory overhead	$215,000	$212,500	$ 2,500F
Total production costs	$790,000	$825,400	$35,400U

* F = favorable; U = unfavorable.

CONSTRUCTING A FLEXIBLE BUDGET

In order to overcome the preceding problem, performance reports normally incorporate flexible budgets. A flexible budget covers a *range* of activity as opposed to a single level. Specifically, the relevant range of activity is determined for the forthcoming accounting period. Then, individual budgets are prepared for various levels within the anticipated range of operation.

To illustrate the concept of a flexible budget, we will continue the Coleman Industries example. The 50,000-unit budget that appears in Exhibit 25–3 was prepared after a thorough study of cost behavior, with the following costs judged to be realistic targets of performance:

Direct materials used	$3.00 per unit
Direct labor	$7.00 per unit
Variable factory overhead	$1.50 per unit
Fixed factory overhead	$215,000

A review of past accounting records disclosed that quarterly production volume usually varies between 50,000 and 54,000 units. A flexible budget that covers this range of activity is presented in Exhibit 25–4. The figures shown were obtained by multiplying the unit variable costs by the different activity levels and then adding the fixed factory overhead. We did not calculate a fixed cost per unit because the unit cost will fluctuate with the volume level used in the computation.

FLEXIBLE BUDGETS AND PERFORMANCE EVALUATION

Given the nature of flexible budgets, we can now appraise the performance of the Oregon plant's production manager. As shown in Exhibit 25–5, a properly prepared performance report allows management to compare the actual costs incurred in the manufacture of 54,000 units against budgeted costs for the same level of activity.

EXHIBIT 25–4
Flexible Budget

COLEMAN INDUSTRIES
Oregon Plant Flexible Budget
For the Quarter Ended March 31, 19X3

		Units of Activity		
Cost	Cost Per Unit	50,000	52,000	54,000
Variable production costs				
Direct materials used	$ 3.00	$150,000	$156,000	$162,000
Direct labor	7.00	350,000	364,000	378,000
Variable factory overhead	1.50	75,000	78,000	81,000
Total	$11.50	$575,000	$598,000	$621,000
Fixed factory overhead		$215,000	$215,000	$215,000
Total production costs		$790,000	$813,000	$836,000

Once the impact of the 4,000-unit variation between the original static budget and actual production is eliminated, the manager appears to have done an acceptable job. With the exception of variable factory overhead, all costs were less than budgeted, and a total favorable variance was generated. Overall, the flexible budget provides a useful tool for performance evaluations, because like volumes are compared. Activity level fluctuations no longer influence the appraisal process.

A COMMON MISUNDERSTANDING

Before leaving this example, we wish to clear up a common misconception about flexible budgets. Careful study of Exhibit 25–4 normally leaves the impression that many different budgets must be prepared when using the flex-

EXHIBIT 25–5
Performance Report Based on Flexible Budgets

COLEMAN INDUSTRIES
Oregon Plant Performance Report
For the Quarter Ended March 31, 19X3

Cost	Budget, 54,000 Units	Actual, 54,000 Units	Variance*
Variable production costs			
Direct materials used	$162,000	$159,300	$ 2,700F
Direct labor	378,000	367,200	10,800F
Variable factory overhead	81,000	86,400	5,400U
Total	$621,000	$612,900	$ 8,100F
Fixed factory overhead	$215,000	$212,500	$ 2,500F
Total production costs	$836,000	$825,400	$10,600F

* F = favorable; U = unfavorable.

ible approach. This is not the case. Even if this practice were followed, an organization could establish budgets for numerous operating volumes and still miss the actual level of activity. For most entities, the likelihood that a budget prepared in advance will coincide precisely with the actual volume level is extremely small.

The preceding discussion should not be taken to mean that flexible budgets have limited application. For instance, suppose the Oregon plant's output for the first quarter amounted to 53,000 units—an activity level that was not considered when establishing the budgets presented in Exhibit 25–4. Nonetheless, the manager's actual performance can still be compared against budgeted performance of $824,500, computed as follows:

Variable production costs per unit	
Direct materials used	$ 3.00
Direct labor	7.00
Variable factory overhead	1.50
Total	$11.50
Budget for 53,000 units	
Variable production costs	
(53,000 units × $11.50)	$609,500
Fixed production costs	215,000
Total	$824,500

It is apparent that flexible budgets can be prepared to coincide with any volume of operation. Companies determine the flexible budget characteristics (i.e., variable production costs of $11.50 per unit and fixed production costs of $215,000) in advance. The "proper" budget and accompanying performance report must then wait until after the fact, that is, after the actual activity level is known.

STANDARD COSTS

3 *Explain what a standard cost is and how standards are developed.*

Par on a golf course, a four-minute mile, and an eight-hour workday are well-recognized standards of performance. These measures and others are used to gauge accomplishments in a variety of diverse activities.

Standards are also popular among businesses as a means of measuring efficiency and monitoring cost incurrence. Defined as preset norms of what should occur under reasonably efficient operating conditions, standards normally refer to the expected quantity and cost of items needed to produce a good or service. Typical manufacturing standards include the cost per pound of direct materials, the wage rate for direct labor, and the number of hours needed to complete a task.

STANDARD COSTS AND BUDGETS

The concept of a standard cost is really nothing new. Although they were not described as such, you were introduced to standard costs earlier in the chapter. Standard costs are used in the construction of both static and flexible budgets. Specifically, standard costs are a per-unit concept; budgets, conversely, deal in totals.

To illustrate the difference between standards and budgets, assume Centre Enterprises manufactures a single product that requires five square feet of direct material at an anticipated cost of $4 per square foot. The standard direct material cost per unit of output is computed as follows:

Standard Quantity Per Finished Unit	×	Standard Price	=	Standard Cost Per Unit of Output
5 square feet		$4 per square foot		$20

Once the standard cost is known, a budget (flexible in this case) can be prepared, as the accompanying figures show.

Production Component	Standard Cost Per Unit of Output	Flexible Budget: Units of Activity		
		10,000	10,500	11,000
Direct materials	$20	$200,000	$210,000	$220,000

As our example illustrates, a standard cost is merely the budgeted cost for a single unit of activity.

Setting Standards

The setting of standards is a complex process, requiring skills that often surpass the expertise possessed by the average accountant. Generally, a team effort involving participation from many different areas within the organization is needed. In a manufacturing entity, for example, all persons who have responsibility for prices and quantities of finished product inputs should assist in the standard-setting process.

Recall from Chapter 20 that manufactured products contain three cost elements: direct materials, direct labor, and factory overhead. Standards for both price and quantity must be established for each of these items. Beginning with direct materials, engineering and production employees should participate in the calculation of standard inputs by both type and quantity of materials used. Given these calculations, the purchasing department can then determine the proper dollar amounts. Standard material prices should include transportation charges and be net of any expected cash discounts.

Direct labor standards are determined jointly by production, engineering, and human resources staffs. Standards for labor time are established, often by using *time and motion studies*. In such studies, individual manufacturing operations are monitored and clocked by industrial engineers. Once labor time is known, the cost standard can be computed from information furnished by the human resources department. Although wage rates will vary among employees because of differences in seniority, skill levels, and other factors, many companies use a single (average) rate to cost specific manufacturing procedures. The accountant's role in the area of labor is to formalize and coordinate the standard-setting process and to establish an effective system of performance reporting once the standards have been determined.

The development of an overhead standard parallels the calculation of an overhead application rate, a topic that was discussed in Chapter 21. Normally, however, separate standards are established for variable and fixed cost components. To explain the necessary procedures, we will again focus on Centre Enterprises, which applies factory overhead to products on the basis of direct labor hours. Management estimates that 10,000 units will be produced in the upcoming period, requiring 80,000 hours of labor time. Variable and fixed overhead at this level of activity are budgeted at $80,000 and $120,000, respectively. Centre must first compute the overhead standard per direct labor hour, as shown.

Variable:
$$\frac{\text{Estimated Variable Overhead}}{\text{Estimated Activity}} = \frac{\$80,000}{80,000 \text{ hours}} = \$1.00 \text{ per hour}$$

Fixed:
$$\frac{\text{Estimated Fixed Overhead}}{\text{Estimated Activity}} = \frac{\$120,000}{80,000 \text{ hours}} = \$1.50 \text{ per hour}$$

Since each unit requires 8 hours of production time (80,000 hours ÷ 10,000 units), the standard overhead cost per finished unit is derived in the following manner:

Variable overhead: 8 hours × $1.00 per hour	$ 8.00
Fixed overhead: 8 hours × $1.50 per hour	12.00
Standard overhead cost per finished unit	$20.00

The outcome of the standard-setting process is summarized in a *standard cost sheet* (see Exhibit 25–6).

EXHIBIT 25–6
Standard Cost Sheet

CENTRE ENTERPRISES
Standard Cost Sheet
Product No. 626

PRODUCTION COMPONENT	STANDARD QUANTITY PER FINISHED UNIT	×	STANDARD PRICE	=	STANDARD COST PER UNIT OF OUTPUT
Direct materials	5 square feet		$4.00		$ 20.00
Direct labor	8 hours		9.00*		72.00
Variable factory overhead	8 hours		1.00		8.00
Fixed factory overhead	8 hours		1.50		12.00
Total standard cost					$112.00

* Assumed.

LEVELS OF STANDARDS

> **4** Distinguish between ideal and attainable standards.

Should a standard be set high, low, or somewhere in-between? How much effort should workers put forth in attempting to achieve a standard? In many cases, these and related questions are difficult to answer. Production supervisors, engineers, laborers, and other veterans of manufacturing activities have grappled with the preceding issues for years. Although there is a diversity of opinion, companies must address the problem and somehow derive a "correct" standard for each facet of their production operations.

The starting point for the development of standards is a look at the past. The costs incurred in prior years can provide considerable insight about a company's experience at different levels of activity. The past should be interpreted with care, however. Changes in the form of new suppliers, state-of-the-art technology, and employee training programs can rapidly make historical data obsolete and not representative of the entity's current manufacturing environment. Further complicating matters is the fact that past inefficiencies are often built into the data under examination. Standards strive to reflect what *should be*, not what *has been*. Management must be aware of these deficiencies when analyzing earlier experiences and adjust its findings accordingly.

Ideal Standards. Despite the diversity that is encountered when setting standards, most standards can be classified as either ideal or attainable. An **ideal standard** is one that can be achieved under perfect operating conditions. By essentially assuming maximum efficiency at minimum cost, ideal standards make no allowances for spoilage, machine breakdowns, worker fatigue, inefficiency, human error, and other similar factors. In most applications, the perfection emphasis of these performance targets results in variances that have little meaning. Realize that nothing is perfect, and normal inefficiencies are a fact of life.

Managers who favor ideal standards feel that setting difficult goals will improve overall output and efficiency, as employees attempt to attain the target. This outcome is in contrast to the situation that arises when using a loose standard, or one that is easily attained with minimal effort. Behavioral scientists have observed that ideal standards do cause an increase in productivity when first introduced, as employees strive for the unreachable. Subsequently, however, performance tends to fall after numerous failures and a constant barrage of unfavorable variances. Workers soon become discouraged and adopt a "what the heck" attitude.

Attainable Standards. To overcome the problems associated with ideal standards, most companies turn to attainable standards. An **attainable standard** is one that can be achieved by efficient, not perfect, operations. In setting standards for direct materials, for example, allowances are provided for *normal* scrap, waste, and spoilage. Similarly, when establishing direct labor targets, provision is made for *normal* worker inefficiencies, machine breakdowns, and so forth.

The level of attainable standards varies from firm to firm. Most organizations use a high but reachable standard and thereby encourage employees to achieve above-average levels of operating efficiency. The standard is not unreasonable and therefore avoids worker frustration and other behavioral problems.

Attainable standards offer the further benefits of improved planning and decision making. Realistic budgets can be prepared, and as we will show in the next chapter, decisions are facilitated because they are based on reasonable estimates of cost.

VARIANCE ANALYSIS

5
Calculate direct material, direct labor, and factory overhead variances.

Standard costs provide management with information that is useful in the control of an enterprise's affairs. Much of this information comes in the form of **variances,** or deviations from standard. Actual costs are compared against standard costs to determine whether operations are running according to plan or whether significant deviations exist. Management is then alerted to potential problems and can take corrective action. By focusing on variances, managers can avoid spending countless hours in a review of what is going right. Their efforts instead can be devoted to areas that need attention, a process frequently known as **management by exception.**

To illustrate the fundamentals of variance analysis, we will begin by concentrating on direct materials and direct labor. Suppose that a manufacturer reported the following results on conclusion of a recent month's activity:

COST	ACTUAL	STANDARD	VARIANCE
Direct materials used	$36,500	$33,000	$3,500U
Direct labor	59,400	62,700	3,300F

ETHICS ISSUE

A company's accountant knows the production standards are set so as to continually reveal favorable variances (and increased rewards). The accountant is a "people person," and top management recognizes the benefits of high employee morale. Should the accountant propose to amend the standards?

Notice that both direct material consumption and direct labor incurrence failed to conform to the original plan. The company spent $3,500 more than anticipated for materials, giving rise to an *unfavorable variance*. In contrast, direct labor cost was $3,300 less than planned and created a *favorable variance*.

Management now wants to know why the variances arose. Material and labor costs will stray from standard because of deviations in the following factors:

1. Direct materials:
   a. The per-unit acquisition cost of materials
   b. The quantity of materials consumed
2. Direct labor:
   a. The hourly wage rate
   b. The number of hours worked

VARIANCE CALCULATION

The impact of these price and quantity factors on the total variances can be determined by several relatively simple calculations. The calculations are perhaps best illustrated by the model that appears in Exhibit 25–7.

Careful study of the model reveals that the price variance is really the difference between the actual and standard prices, multiplied by the actual quantity of material or labor put into production. For direct materials the variance is commonly known as the **materials price variance.** With labor, the name changes slightly to the **labor rate variance** to be more attuned to the area of study.

EXHIBIT 25–7
General Model for Variance Analysis of Direct Materials and Direct Labor

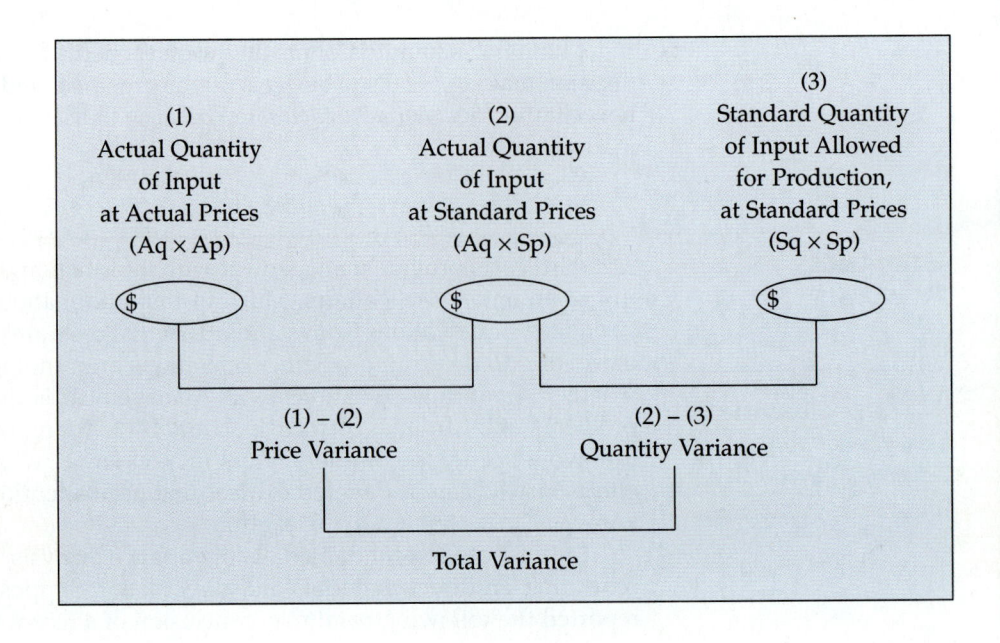

```
 (1)                      (2)                       (3)
Actual Quantity      Actual Quantity        Standard Quantity
   of Input             of Input            of Input Allowed
at Actual Prices    at Standard Prices        for Production,
  (Aq × Ap)            (Aq × Sp)            at Standard Prices
                                                (Sq × Sp)

          (1) − (2)                (2) − (3)
        Price Variance           Quantity Variance

                       Total Variance
```

The quantity variance is slightly more difficult to understand. Exhibit 25–7 shows the quantity variance is calculated by comparing (Aq × Sp) and (Sq × Sp). If we take the difference between these two expressions, the following formula is derived:

$$\text{Quantity Variance} = Sp\,(Aq - Sq)$$

The formula shows that by weighting the difference in quantities by the standard price, the quantity variance is actually measured in dollars.

Additionally, it is important to note that the standard quantity is subtracted from the actual quantity. The actual quantity represents the actual input (pounds, gallons, hours, and so on) placed in production. In contrast, *the standard quantity is the amount of input that should have been used in manufacturing activities during the period.* As an example, assume that a company manufactures a single product that requires three pounds of direct materials. Production totaled 4,000 completed units for the month just ended. If 11,800 pounds of materials were consumed, Aq would be 11,800 pounds and Sq would be 12,000 pounds (4,000 completed units × 3 pounds per unit).

The quantity variance is called the materials quantity variance when working with direct materials. For labor the name is changed to the labor efficiency variance to reflect the cause of the difference between actual and standard labor hours.

AN ILLUSTRATION OF DIRECT MATERIAL VARIANCES

To illustrate use of the preceding model, assume that Sanco, Inc., has developed a direct materials standard of 3 pounds per finished unit at $5.00 per pound. During a recent period the following activity took place:

- Direct materials purchased and used in production: 6,000 pounds at $5.10 per pound
- Production completed: 1,900 units

Exhibit 25–8 shows Sanco's price and quantity variances for direct materials, both of which are unfavorable. The unfavorable price variance occurred because Sanco paid $0.10 in excess of the $5.00 standard price to acquire needed materials. The unfavorable quantity variance resulted from the company's usage of 300 pounds more than planned (6,000 versus 5,700) in manufacturing activities.

AN ILLUSTRATION OF DIRECT LABOR VARIANCES

To explain the calculation of direct labor variances, we will continue the previous example. Assume that Sanco has established the following labor standards for each unit of completed product:

- Direct labor: 2 hours at $9.00 per hour

In producing the 1,900 finished units, direct labor incurred totaled 4,100 hours at $8.80 per hour, or $36,080. The company's direct labor variances are shown in Exhibit 25–9.

As you can see, the labor variance computations are similar to those for materials. Rather than employ pounds and the material purchase price, labor calculations require the respective use of hours worked and the firm's wage rate. Sanco's labor rate variance was favorable because the actual rate paid ($8.80) was $0.20 less than standard. Labor efficiency was unfavorable, however, since actual hours worked exceeded the standard time allowed by 300 hours (4,100 − 3,800 = 300).

EXHIBIT 25–8
Sanco, Inc., Direct Materials Variances

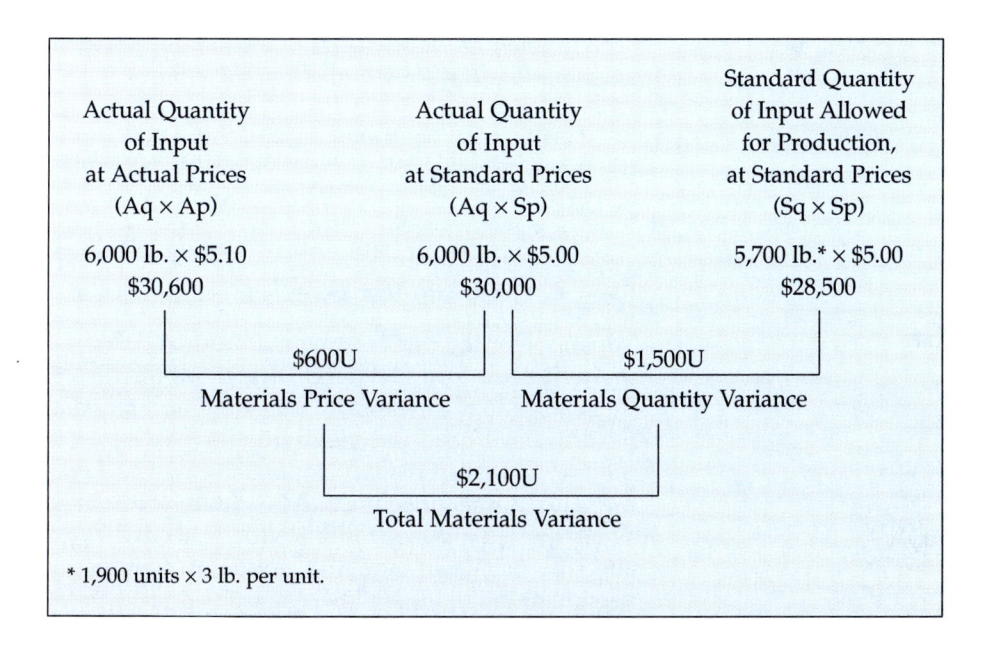

Actual Quantity of Input at Actual Prices (Aq × Ap)	Actual Quantity of Input at Standard Prices (Aq × Sp)	Standard Quantity of Input Allowed for Production, at Standard Prices (Sq × Sp)
6,000 lb. × $5.10	6,000 lb. × $5.00	5,700 lb.* × $5.00
$30,600	$30,000	$28,500

$600U Materials Price Variance

$1,500U Materials Quantity Variance

$2,100U Total Materials Variance

* 1,900 units × 3 lb. per unit.

EXHIBIT 25–9
Sanco, Inc., Direct Labor Variances

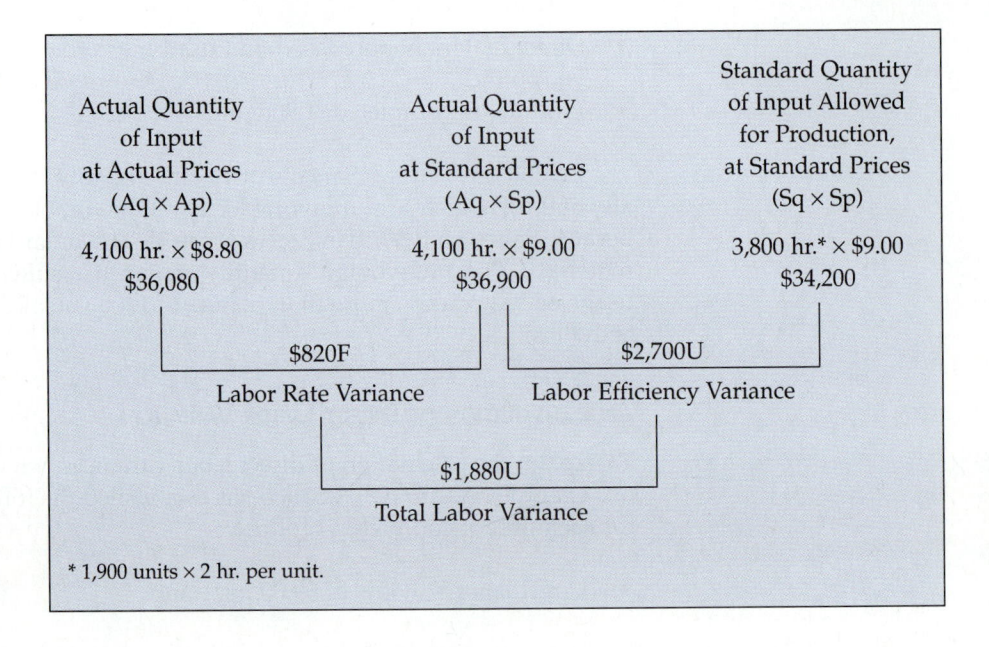

```
Actual Quantity              Actual Quantity              Standard Quantity
   of Input                     of Input                  of Input Allowed
at Actual Prices             at Standard Prices           for Production,
  (Aq × Ap)                    (Aq × Sp)                  at Standard Prices
                                                              (Sq × Sp)

4,100 hr. × $8.80            4,100 hr. × $9.00            3,800 hr.* × $9.00
   $36,080                      $36,900                      $34,200

           └────$820F────┘              └────$2,700U────┘
           Labor Rate Variance          Labor Efficiency Variance

                    └──────────$1,880U──────────┘
                         Total Labor Variance
```

*1,900 units × 2 hr. per unit.

A Further Focus

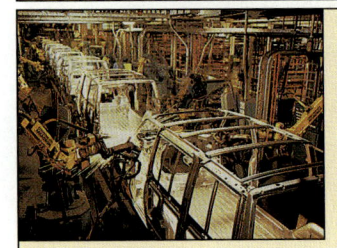

Efficiency is a concern for small companies like Sanco and corporate giants like General Motors. A study conducted not too long ago showed that GM would have to reduce its payroll by about 20,000 workers to become as efficient as Ford. General Motors is gaining on its competitor, though, because another study just two years earlier pegged the figure at 70,000. The gap between the two corporations is still significant and costs GM approximately $2.2 billion annually in excess labor costs. The following figures, compiled in cooperation with domestic and foreign manufacturers, show the number of workdays per vehicle assembled in North American plants: General Motors, 3.94; Chrysler, 3.52; Ford, 2.99; Toyota, 2.44; and Nissan, 2.29.

Source: "GM Would Have to Cut 20,000 Workers to Match Ford Efficiency, Report Says," *The Wall Street Journal*, June 24, 1994, p. A3.

FACTORY OVERHEAD VARIANCES

Variances for the third element of product cost, factory overhead, are generally more difficult to understand than those for direct materials and direct labor. Remember that for flexible budgeting and standard costing purposes, manufacturing overhead is divided into its fixed and variable components. In addition, recall that in the development of overhead standards, an activity level is estimated to calculate the overhead rate per hour (or unit).

Although a minor modification is needed, we can compute overhead variances by using the model illustrated in Exhibit 25–7. To explain, a simplified version of the model follows.

$$Aq \times Ap \qquad\qquad Aq \times Sp \qquad\qquad Sq \times Sp$$

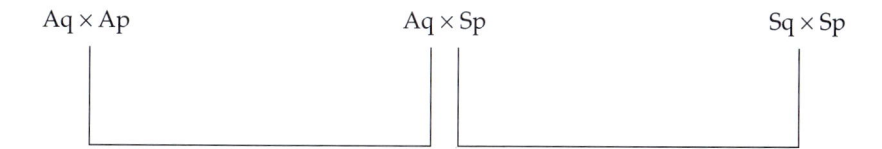

Study the nature of the middle term (Aq × Sp), which is the amount that the actual quantity of input should have cost. Observe that as activity increases or decreases, the Aq × Sp expression will fluctuate—a result that is easily seen by picturing the computations for direct materials and direct labor. As production increases, for example, the actual quantity of materials consumed and labor hours will rise because of the variable nature of the cost functions. With *fixed costs*, however, it is an entirely different story. No matter what the actual level of activity, the same amount of cost should be incurred. The Aq × Sp expression must therefore remain constant.

Given the foregoing, we can now proceed with the calculation of overhead variances for Sanco, Inc. Assume that Sanco applies overhead to products on the basis of direct labor hours. The following information is available:

- Actual factory overhead incurred (fixed plus variable): $73,000
- Standard variable overhead rate per direct labor hour: $7
- Standard fixed overhead rate per direct labor hour: $10
- Budgeted fixed factory overhead for the period: $40,000
- Estimated activity in labor hours during the period: 4,000 hours

The company's overhead variances are shown in Exhibit 25–10.

Spending Variance. The difference between actual overhead incurred (both variable and fixed combined) and the total overhead budgeted for 4,100 direct labor hours of production is measured by the spending variance. Because Aq × Ap must equal the company's *actual* overhead, we merely inserted the $73,000 figure on the left-hand side of the exhibit. The *planned* amount of variable overhead is computed in the same fashion as planned amounts for other variable cost elements (direct materials and direct labor), that is, Aq × Sp (4,100 hours × $7 = $28,700). Turning to fixed costs, Sanco has budgeted $40,000 of fixed factory overhead for the period. Given the nature of the expenditure, this figure should be incurred if direct labor input totals 4,100 hours, 4,200 hours, 4,000 hours, or any other level of activity within the relevant range. In sum, Sanco's spending variance is unfavorable because the actual overhead exceeded budgeted amounts by $4,300 [$73,000 − ($28,700 + $40,000)].

Variable Overhead Efficiency Variance. Sanco used 300 labor hours in excess of standard (4,100 hours − 3,800 hours), resulting in a $2,100 unfavorable variable overhead efficiency variance. This variance is somewhat misleading because it really has nothing to do with the use of overhead. Rather, the variance reflects inefficiencies experienced with the base used to apply the overhead—direct labor hours in this case. By reviewing the direct labor calculations in Exhibit 25–9, the relationship between the two efficiency variances becomes apparent.

EXHIBIT 25–10

Sanco, Inc., Factory Overhead Variances

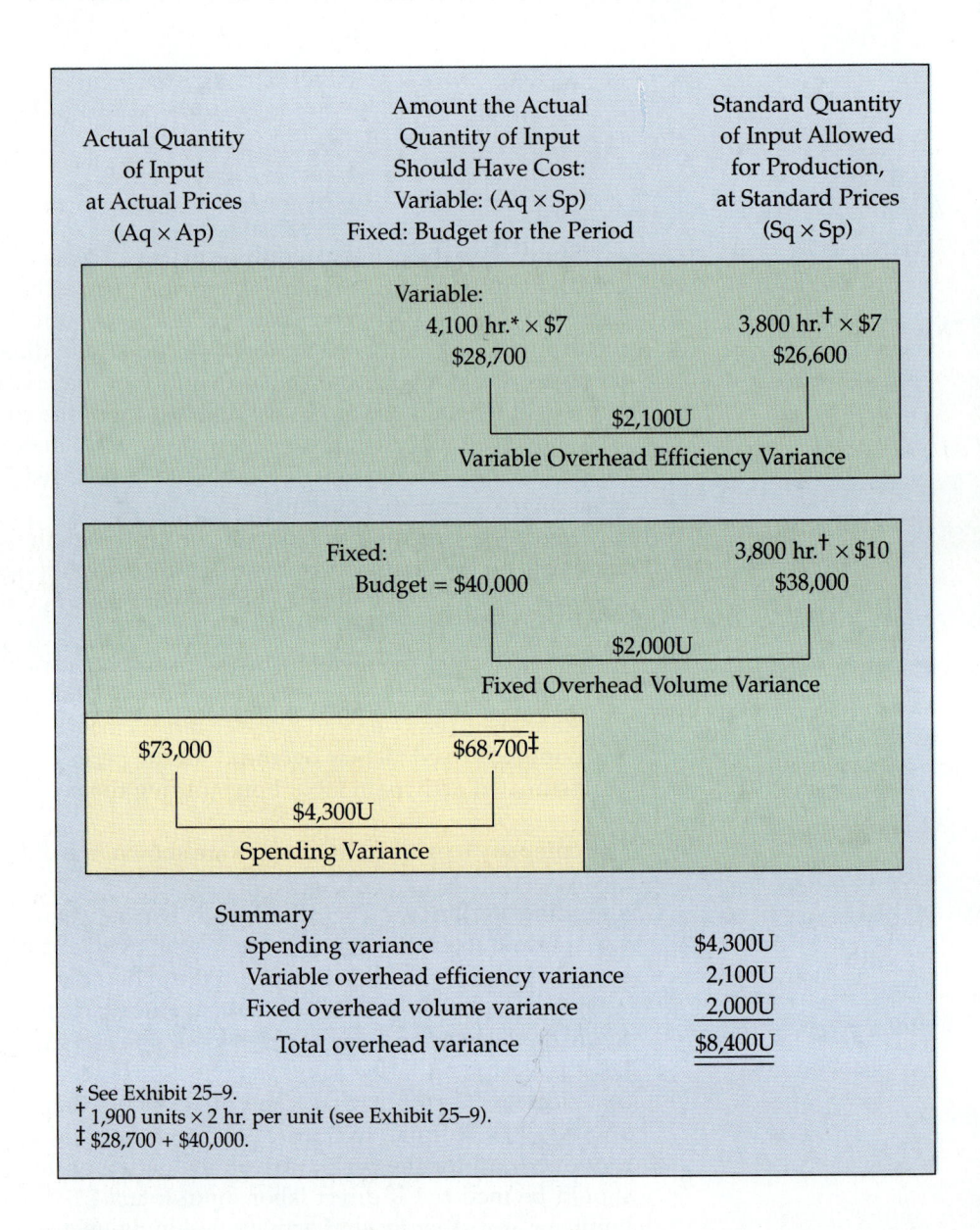

Actual Quantity of Input at Actual Prices (Aq × Ap)	Amount the Actual Quantity of Input Should Have Cost: Variable: (Aq × Sp) Fixed: Budget for the Period	Standard Quantity of Input Allowed for Production, at Standard Prices (Sq × Sp)
	Variable: 4,100 hr.* × $7 = $28,700	3,800 hr.† × $7 = $26,600
	$2,100U Variable Overhead Efficiency Variance	
	Fixed: Budget = $40,000	3,800 hr.† × $10 = $38,000
	$2,000U Fixed Overhead Volume Variance	
$73,000	$68,700‡	
$4,300U Spending Variance		

Summary
Spending variance	$4,300U
Variable overhead efficiency variance	2,100U
Fixed overhead volume variance	2,000U
Total overhead variance	$8,400U

* See Exhibit 25–9.
† 1,900 units × 2 hr. per unit (see Exhibit 25–9).
‡ $28,700 + $40,000.

Fixed Overhead Volume Variance. The fixed costs associated with an under- or overutilization of manufacturing facilities are represented by the **fixed overhead volume variance.** To explain, Sanco has budgeted fixed overhead for the period at $40,000. This level of expenditure provides the company with an estimated capacity of 4,000 direct labor hours (see p. 981). As a result, each hour has an associated fixed cost of $10 ($40,000 ÷ 4,000). Observe that this amount is Sp: the standard fixed overhead rate per direct labor hour.

For the period just ended, Sanco produced only 1,900 units. The standard hours allowed for these units total 3,800 (1,900 units × 2 hours per unit), leaving the company 200 hours shy of using its 4,000-hour capacity. Because each hour costs $10, the volume variance amounts to $2,000. In this particular case the volume variance is unfavorable since utilization was less than capacity. Had utilization been greater than capacity, the variance would have been favorable, thereby indicating a theoretical "savings" in fixed costs.

Volume variances are caused by a number of factors, including an abnormally high number of machine breakdowns, strikes, sloppy production scheduling, changes in inventory policies, raw material shortages, and a lack of (or unanticipated) sales orders. In many situations, volume variances are very difficult to control or eliminate. Management, though, should do some analysis to determine the cause of the variance and whether operational changes are needed.

VARIANCE INVESTIGATION

> **6** Describe the problems encountered in the variance investigation process.

The calculation of variances is only one step in the drive for effective cost control. Additional tasks, namely, variance investigation and the implementation of corrective action, are necessary to complete the process. Frequently, investigations are straightforward and relatively few problems are encountered. Sometimes, however, managers must assume the role of a detective to determine both the underlying cause and the correct party to hold accountable for a variance's creation.

In the simplest of cases, a variance arises because of problems directly identified with the production factor itself. For instance, a direct labor rate variance may be caused by a temporary change in the labor mix required for production. Because of illness or perhaps a rush order, workers who earn $12 per hour may be temporarily transferred to jobs that are normally performed by lower-paid employees. Turning to another example, a labor efficiency variance may arise from a lack of proper employee training or morale problems among the workers.

A variance investigation is often complicated by the strong interrelationships that exist among manufacturing activities. Difficulties with machine operation, for instance, can destroy labor efficiency and cause excessive use of raw materials. In a multidepartment setting, sloppy performance in a production department may lead to unfavorable efficiency and spending variances in subsequent assembly work. Furthermore, variance trade-offs may be a factor. A manager may purposely buy subpar materials and hope the accompanying favorable price variance will exceed the costs of any excess usage or additional labor time.

Our discussion thus far has taken the position that actual operations are to blame for the creation of variances. It is possible, of course, that the standard is the problem. Variance investigators should examine standards to determine whether the standards are set correctly and up-to-date. Standards should be reviewed periodically, usually once each year, and adjusted if necessary.

The Decision to Investigate. Realize that a variance is merely the mathematical difference between two numbers. Like ratios, which were discussed earlier in the text, these measures offer a hint that something is right or that something is wrong. Only in rare circumstances can they tell the complete story.

The decision to investigate normally depends on the size of the variance involved. Large variances are of obvious concern to management; small ones are not. Most firms establish a general guideline, such as, "Review all variances that differ from standard amounts by 10% or $1,000, whichever is lower."

Bear in mind that variance investigation costs money. The cost of determining the cause of a variance and taking the necessary corrective action may very well exceed the amount of the variance under study. Thus, variance review and correction should be based on the principle of cost-benefit analysis—making the evaluation and control of operations a profitable endeavor for the parties involved.

A Broader View of Standards and Performance Evaluation

> **7**
> Discuss the use of standards in nonmanufacturing settings and the popularity of nonfinancial performance measures.

A large portion of this chapter has dealt with standard costs and variance analysis, presented from a manufacturer's perspective. Quite frankly, our discussion would be incomplete if we ended it at this point. Service and merchandising businesses are free to use—and *do* use—these tools. In addition, service and merchandising entities (as well as manufacturers) evaluate performance by analyzing a number of *nondollar* measures. We therefore conclude the chapter by taking a look at two "nons": standards in nonmanufacturing settings and nonfinancial performance measures.

Standards in Nonmanufacturing Settings

The use of standards in nonmanufacturing settings is increasing. It is not uncommon to find standards in place at banks, automotive repair shops, hospitals, hotels, fast-food chains, and delivery services. Many of these standards focus on the time and efficiency required to perform straightforward, routine tasks. Examples include the time to complete a tune-up on a six-cylinder car, the number of hotel rooms to be cleaned per hour, the number of customer checks that should be processed per hour, and the number of meals to serve on a given day. Once established, these standards can be compared against actual results to calculate variances and determine where improvements are needed. (The related calculations are virtually identical to those shown earlier for direct labor costs.)

Consistency and competitiveness are two factors that are often cited to explain the growing popularity of standards in nonmanufacturing organizations. Focusing on consistency, picture something as basic as a McDonald's hamburger. The company wants customers in one location, say, Milwaukee, to avoid being "surprised" when they purchase the exact same product elsewhere (e.g., Seattle). To achieve this goal, McDonald's has developed standards for meat content, buns, toppings, cooking methods, and cooking time that are followed by all of its restaurants.

Another reason advanced for the use of standards by nonmanufacturers is the growing inability of many firms to compete on the basis of price. That is, in a very competitive marketplace, companies may have their prices established (dictated) by the actions of other businesses. Given that these companies have little control over the revenue side of the profit equation, cost becomes the key issue. Improvements in bottom-line performance are achieved by a focus on productivity. Standards are an important tool in evaluating the level of service provided from a given amount of input and assessing whether a task is being performed in an efficient manner.

A FURTHER FOCUS

United Parcel Service (UPS) is one company that has experienced this situation first-hand, having been locked in a battle with Roadway Package Service (RPS) and Federal Express. Price freezes are basically the industry rule rather than the exception. To help counter the problem, UPS has an army of over 3,000 industrial engineers, many of whom focus on driver productivity. In exchange for higher-than-normal wages, UPS drivers must adhere to a vast set of efficiency standards that include:

- How to step from their trucks, fold their money, and carry packages (with their right foot, face-up, and under their left arm, respectively),
- How fast to walk (three feet per second), and
- How many packages to pick up and deliver each day (an average of 400).

Drivers considered slow are accompanied by supervisors who are armed with stopwatches and clipboards.

Source: "As UPS Tries to Deliver More to Its Customers, Labor Problems Grow," *The Wall Street Journal*, May 23, 1994, pp. A1, A5.

NONFINANCIAL PERFORMANCE MEASURES

Traditional management control systems have focused on a variety of dollar measures to evaluate performance. Today's business environment, however, is more complex than just being able to generate adequate profitability and an attractive return on the stockholders' investment. Introducing a new product to the marketplace on a timely basis, adhering to stipulated personnel practices, keeping customers satisfied, and meeting safety and environmental regulations are key aspects of business that cannot be ignored. Accordingly, many companies now use a set of *nonfinancial* performance measures to evaluate their managers.

The number of nonfinancial performance measures available is constrained only by one's imagination. Typical measures include market share, number of customer complaints, customer time in check-out lines, number of repeat customers, manufacturing cycle time, percentage of defective goods produced, percentage of on-time deliveries, and percentages of minority and physically challenged employees on the payroll. Blockbuster Entertainment looks at active members as a percentage of total members along with customer transactions (i.e., rentals) per visit. Southwest Airlines, which recognizes that aircraft earn revenue only when in the air, studies turnaround time, or how rapidly a plane can be unloaded, fueled, cleaned, and boarded for the next flight segment. The complete list of measures cited certainly indicates the diverse nature of management responsibilities in today's business environment—responsibilities that go well beyond the fixation with dollar measures of years past.[2]

---

[2] Realize that many nonfinancial measures ultimately affect an organization's bottom-line income. Over time, for instance, the number of repeat customers and a company's percentage of on-time deliveries will likely impact sales revenues.

END-OF-CHAPTER REVIEW

LEARNING OBJECTIVES: THE KEY POINTS

1. **Explain the purpose and structure of a responsibility accounting system.** Responsibility accounting involves the division of a company into various segments (e.g., divisions, territories, and so forth), with a manager appointed to oversee each segment's activities. The manager is held accountable for the unit's operating results and is evaluated accordingly.

   The units in a responsibility accounting system may be organized as cost, profit, or investment centers. With a cost center, a manager is evaluated on the basis of costs incurred. Departmental heads strive to provide adequate service while keeping costs at a reasonably low level. In contrast, if the unit is organized as a profit center, the performance evaluation focuses on the level of profit generated. Finally, an investment center manager is concerned with the amount of income produced from a given level of asset investment, as measured by the segment's return on assets.

2. **Construct and use a flexible budget.** A flexible budget is a budget constructed for different levels of operation within the relevant range of activity. Costs are normally subdivided into variable and fixed categories, with amounts often integrated into performance reports once the actual level of activity is known. Flexible budgets are useful in performance evaluations because actual costs can be compared against budgeted amounts for the same volume level.

3. **Explain what a standard cost is and how standards are developed.** Standard costs are preset targets of performance—targets that are reachable under reasonably efficient operating conditions. These per-unit amounts are easily incorporated into budgets.

   Standards are normally established by using a team approach. Engineering and production personnel, for example, are often consulted when determining the amount of direct material that is consumed in a product. Once the proper quantities are known, the standard cost is calculated by using information obtained from the purchasing department. In a similar manner, engineering and production staffs work jointly to compute the direct labor time needed to perform a particular task. The figures are then converted to dollars on the basis of wage rate data furnished by the human resources department.

4. **Distinguish between ideal and attainable standards.** An ideal standard is one that can be achieved in a perfect operating environment (i.e., maximum efficiency at minimum cost). By setting standards at such high levels, companies hope to improve output as employees increase their efforts to hit the target. Often, however, workers become frustrated in their attempts and morale may suffer. Most companies use attainable standards, or those achievable under efficient, not perfect, operating conditions. The standard is set high enough to motivate employees, but is not so unreasonably high as to cause frustration.

5. **Calculate direct material, direct labor, and factory overhead variances.** The variances for direct materials and direct labor are easily computed by use of the general model:

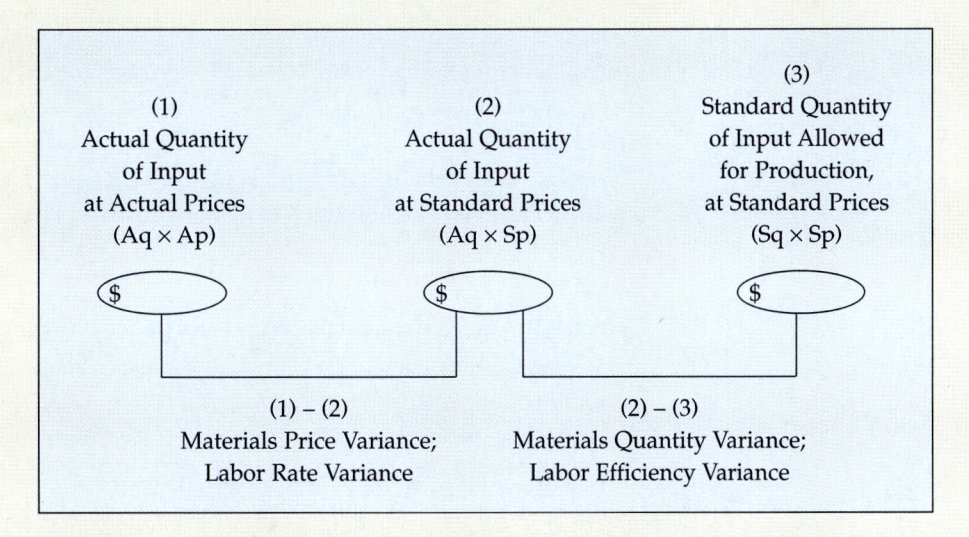

```
          (1)                           (2)                    (3)
     Actual Quantity              Actual Quantity        Standard Quantity
        of Input                     of Input            of Input Allowed
     at Actual Prices            at Standard Prices        for Production,
        (Aq × Ap)                    (Aq × Sp)          at Standard Prices
                                                            (Sq × Sp)
           $                             $                      $
           └─────────────┬───────────────┴──────────┬───────────┘
                    (1) − (2)                       (2) − (3)
              Materials Price Variance;      Materials Quantity Variance;
                 Labor Rate Variance           Labor Efficiency Variance
```

The calculations for factory overhead variances are slightly more complex and may be summarized as follows:

- *Spending variance*—The difference between the actual total overhead incurred (Aq × Ap) and the sum of the amounts budgeted for the actual hours worked (variable, Aq × Sp; fixed, budget for the period).
- *Variable overhead efficiency variance*—The difference between Aq × Sp and Sq × Sp for variable overhead.
- *Fixed overhead volume variance*—The difference between the fixed overhead budgeted for the period and the Sq × Sp computation.

6. **Describe the problems encountered in the variance investigation process.** A variance investigation involves a look at both actual and standard costs. Differences between these two amounts may arise from problems with the production factor itself (e.g., variable overhead) or interrelationships that exist among manufacturing activities. As an example of the latter, problems with labor efficiency may affect the amount of direct materials used during the period. Given that variance investigations are often time-consuming and costly, the decision to investigate is generally made on a cost-benefit basis.

7. **Discuss the use of standards in nonmanufacturing settings and the popularity of nonfinancial performance measures.** Service and merchandising businesses often use standards to evaluate performance, particularly with respect to time and efficiency. The growing popularity of standards in these settings is often explained by two factors: consistency and competitiveness. Companies (such as fast-food chains) seek to provide a consistent product among their various locations. Also, many businesses are forced to focus on productivity to generate meaningful changes in income—especially in highly competitive markets where prices are sometimes "set" by other dominant entities.

    In recognition of the growing complexities of business operation, numerous organizations now look at nonfinancial performance measures when evaluating their managers. Typical nonfinancial measures include market share, number of repeat customers, percentage of defective goods produced, and compliance with safety and environmental regulations.

Key Terms and Concepts: A Quick Overview

attainable standard   A standard that can be achieved by efficient, not perfect, operations; allows for normal scrap, waste, and spoilage. (p. 976)

cost center   A responsibility unit in which a manager is held accountable for cost incurrence. (p. 965)

fixed overhead volume variance   A variance that discloses the fixed costs associated with an under- or overutilization of manufacturing facilities. (p. 982)

flexible budget   A budget that covers a range of activity as opposed to a single level. (p. 971)

ideal standard   A standard that is achieved under perfect operating conditions. (p. 976)

investment center   A responsibility unit in which a manager is evaluated on profit and the effective use of asset investment. (p. 965)

labor efficiency variance   The difference between actual and standard labor hours, multiplied by the standard wage rate. (p. 978)

labor rate variance   The difference between actual and standard wage rates, multiplied by the actual hours of labor used in production. (p. 977)

management by exception   The practice of focusing a manager's attention on those aspects of operations that deviate from planned or expected results. (p. 977)

materials price variance   The difference between the actual and standard prices, multiplied by the actual quantity of materials purchased and put into production. (p. 977)

materials quantity variance   The difference between actual and standard quantities of materials used, multiplied by the standard price. (p. 978)

performance report   A report designed to provide the manager of a responsibility center with timely feedback of operating results. (p. 967)

profit center   A responsibility unit in which a manager is held accountable for profit. (p. 965)

responsibility accounting   A reporting system based on the organizational structure of a firm. Managers of each segment are held accountable for operating results and evaluated accordingly. (p. 965)

return on assets   A ratio that measures company profitability from a given level of asset investment. Also called return on investment (ROI). (p. 966)

spending variance   The difference between actual overhead incurred and the total amount of overhead budgeted for production. (p. 981)

standard   A norm used by businesses to measure what should occur under reasonably efficient operating conditions. (p. 973)

static budget   A budget developed for one level of activity. (p. 970)

variable overhead efficiency variance   A variance that reflects inefficiencies experienced with the base used to apply variable overhead cost to production. (p. 981)

variance   A deviation from standard. (p. 977)

Chapter Quiz

The five questions that follow relate to several issues raised in the chapter. Test your knowledge of the issues by selecting the best answer. (The answers appear on p. 1005.)

1. Which of the following statements about responsibility accounting is false?
    a. An investment center manager is usually evaluated on the basis of return on assets.

b. Managers should be held accountable for controllable costs.
   c. Performance reports tend to be summarized at lower levels of an organization and more detailed at higher levels.
   d. Normally, cost centers are not involved with revenue-generating activities.
2. Flexible budgets:
   a. tend to result in improved performance reporting.
   b. are the same as static budgets.
   c. are constructed for one level of activity.
   d. normally exclude fixed manufacturing costs.
3. Standard costs:
   a. are inconsistent with budgets.
   b. should be based on attainable levels of performance.
   c. are normally calculated by the accountant without any other departmental input.
   d. are calculated for direct materials and direct labor but not factory overhead.
4. Ace Corporation recently completed the manufacture of 4,000 computer tables. Each table's standard direct labor cost is $16 (2 hours at $8 per hour). If the actual payroll totaled $63,990 (8,100 hours at $7.90), the company's labor efficiency variance is:
   a. $800F.
   b. $800U.
   c. $810F.
   d. $810U.
5. The difference between the actual factory overhead incurred during the period and the overhead budgeted for the actual hours worked is known as the:
   a. overhead spending variance.
   b. variable overhead efficiency variance.
   c. fixed overhead volume variance.
   d. total overhead variance.

SUMMARY PROBLEM

Mahoney, Inc., manufactures a single product and uses a standard costing system. A conversation with the firm's accountant revealed that each unit of finished product has the following material and labor standards:

- Direct materials: 4 units @ $2.50
- Direct labor: 2 hours @ $8.50

Mahoney applies factory overhead on the basis of direct labor hours. Management estimates that budgeted production levels during the upcoming period will require a total of 50,000 direct labor hours. Variable and fixed overhead at this level of activity are estimated to be $150,000 and $275,000, respectively. Additional data follow.

1. Direct materials purchased and consumed during the period totaled 100,000 units at a cost of $2.65 per unit.
2. Direct labor incurred totaled 51,000 hours at a rate of $8.70 per hour.
3. Total overhead incurred amounted to $436,000.
4. Actual production totaled 26,000 units, all of which were completed.

Instructions

a. Compute the company's variable and fixed overhead rates per direct labor hour.
b. Compute the total standard cost of a finished unit.

c. Determine Mahoney's direct materials variances.
d. Determine Mahoney's direct labor variances.
e. Determine Mahoney's factory overhead variances.

Solution

a. $$\text{Variable Overhead Rate} = \frac{\text{Estimated Variable Overhead}}{\text{Estimated Activity}}$$

$$= \frac{\$150,000}{50,000 \text{ direct labor hours}}$$

$$= \$3 \text{ per direct labor hour}$$

$$\text{Fixed Overhead Rate} = \frac{\text{Estimated Fixed Overhead}}{\text{Estimated Activity}}$$

$$= \frac{\$275,000}{50,000 \text{ direct labor hours}}$$

$$= \$5.50 \text{ per direct labor hour}$$

b.
Direct materials: 4 units @ $2.50	$10.00
Direct labor: 2 hours @ $8.50	17.00
Variable overhead: 2 hours @ $3.00*	6.00
Fixed overhead: 2 hours @ $5.50*	11.00
Total standard cost per finished unit	$44.00

* From part (a).

c.

Actual Quantity of Input at Actual Prices (Aq × Ap)	Actual Quantity of Input at Standard Prices (Aq × Sp)	Standard Quantity of Input Allowed for Production, at Standard Prices (Sq × Sp)
100,000 units × $2.65	100,000 units × $2.50	104,000 units* × $2.50
$265,000	$250,000	$260,000

$15,000U — Materials Price Variance

$10,000F — Materials Quantity Variance

$5,000U — Total Materials Variance

* 26,000 finished units × 4 units of direct materials.

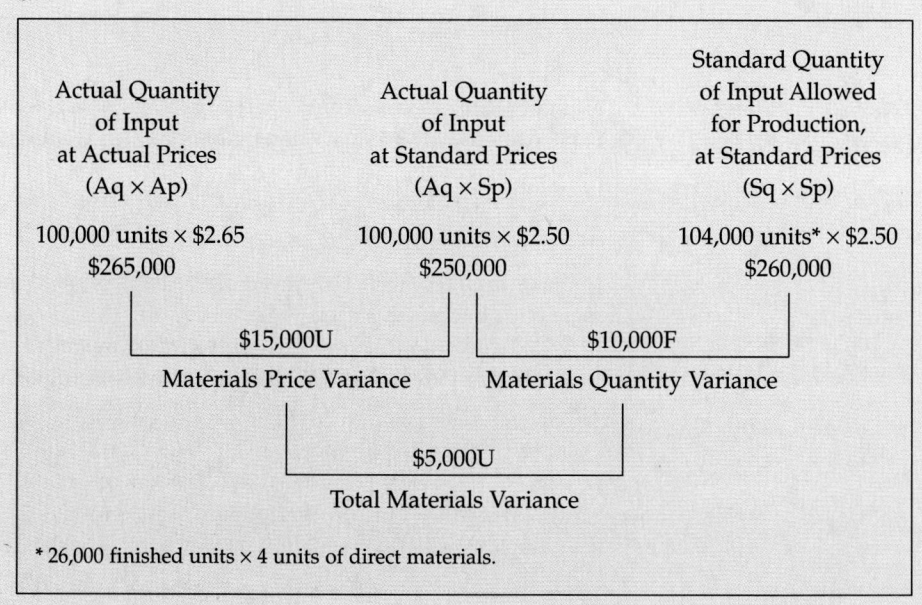

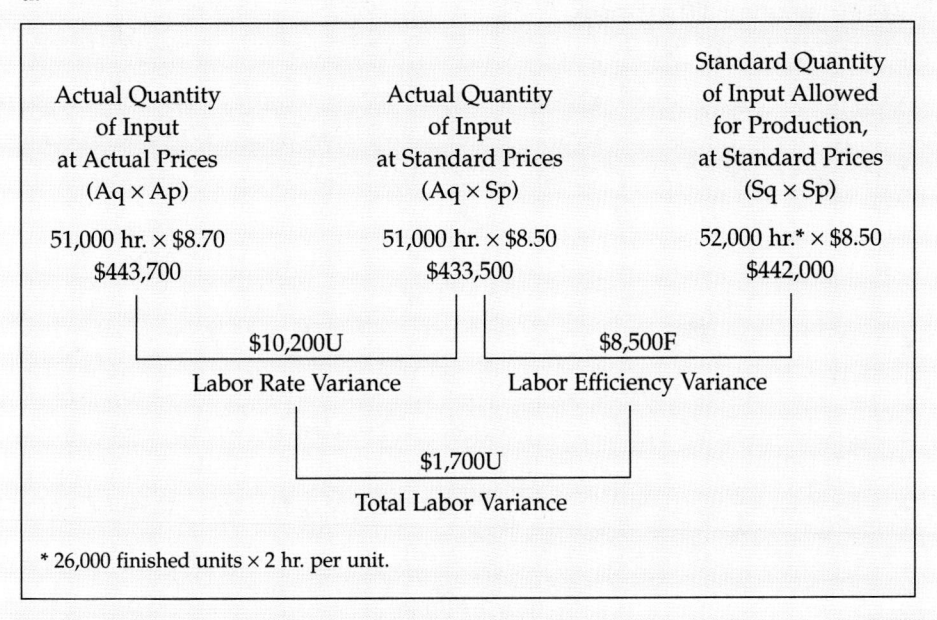

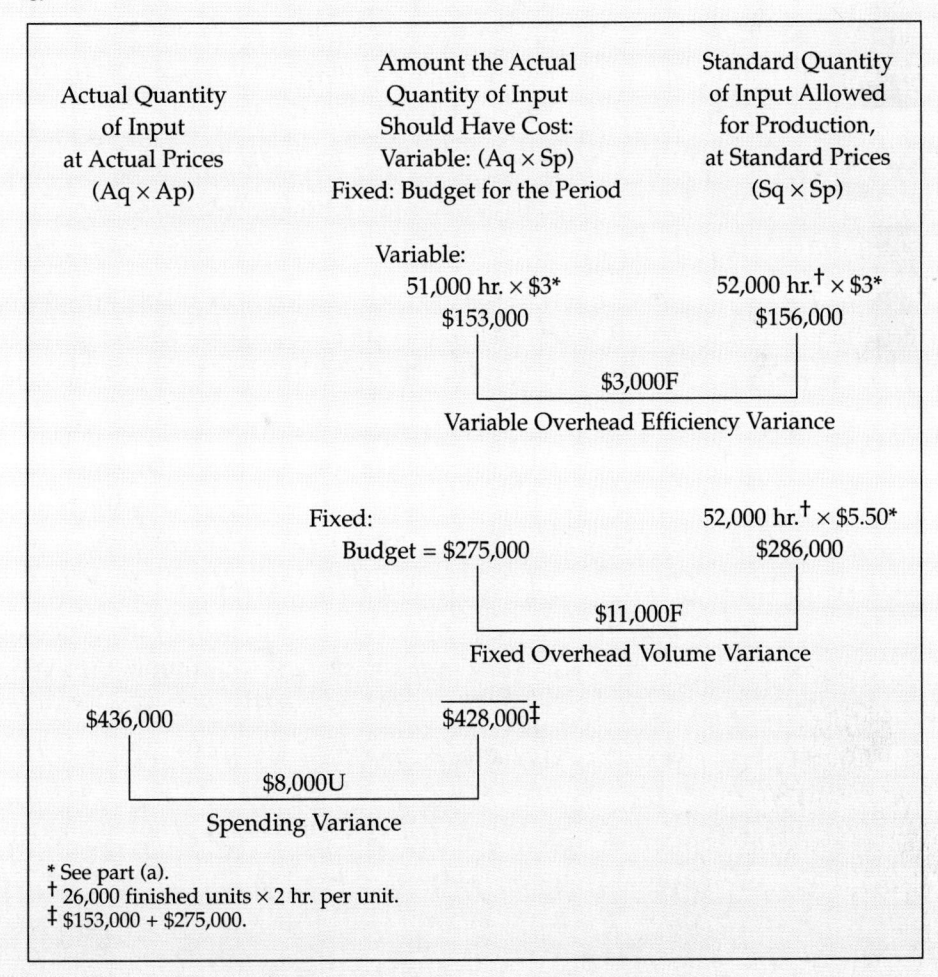

d.

Actual Quantity of Input at Actual Prices (Aq × Ap)	Actual Quantity of Input at Standard Prices (Aq × Sp)	Standard Quantity of Input Allowed for Production, at Standard Prices (Sq × Sp)
51,000 hr. × $8.70	51,000 hr. × $8.50	52,000 hr.* × $8.50
$443,700	$433,500	$442,000

$10,200U — Labor Rate Variance
$8,500F — Labor Efficiency Variance
$1,700U — Total Labor Variance

*26,000 finished units × 2 hr. per unit.

e.

Actual Quantity of Input at Actual Prices (Aq × Ap)	Amount the Actual Quantity of Input Should Have Cost: Variable: (Aq × Sp) Fixed: Budget for the Period	Standard Quantity of Input Allowed for Production, at Standard Prices (Sq × Sp)

Variable:
51,000 hr. × $3* $153,000
52,000 hr.† × $3* $156,000
$3,000F — Variable Overhead Efficiency Variance

Fixed:
Budget = $275,000
52,000 hr.† × $5.50* $286,000
$11,000F — Fixed Overhead Volume Variance

$436,000 $428,000‡
$8,000U — Spending Variance

*See part (a).
†26,000 finished units × 2 hr. per unit.
‡$153,000 + $275,000.

Assignment Material

Questions

Q25–1 Briefly discuss the features associated with a responsibility accounting system.

Q25–2 Should a cost center manager strive for cost minimization? Why?

Q25–3 Differentiate between a profit center and an investment center.

Q25–4 Describe the flow of information in a typical responsibility reporting system.

Q25–5 Generally speaking, are performance reports more summarized at lower or higher levels of an organization?

Q25–6 Differentiate between a static budget and a flexible budget.

Q25–7 Explain the relationship, if any, between a standard cost and a flexible budget.

Q25–8 Identify the parties normally involved in establishing the following:
a. Price standards for materials
b. Efficiency standards for direct labor

Q25–9 An engineer once commented: "Standards must be based on a perfect operating environment, as anything less assumes inefficient working conditions." Evaluate the engineer's comment.

Q25–10 Why do some companies use ideal standards? What often occurs shortly after the introduction of ideal standards?

Q25–11 What is meant by an attainable standard?

Q25–12 Explain the concept known as "management by exception." Is variance analysis consistent or inconsistent with management by exception? Why?

Q25–13 Should managers investigate all variances? Why or why not?

Q25–14 Briefly discuss two factors that, in part, account for the growing popularity of standards in nonmanufacturing organizations.

Exercises

E25–1 Cost centers and profit centers (L.O. 1)

Crest Manufacturing produces a single product at its Albany plant. Units are processed through departments A and B and then sent to finished goods. The firm has a maintenance department that performs repair jobs for the manufacturing departments.

The maintenance operation has always been evaluated as a cost center. Now with a change in management, a switch to a profit center setup is being considered. Prices charged for repair jobs would be based on the maintenance department's cost of operations.

a. Discuss the difference between a cost center and a profit center.
b. Mike Mizer, the head of maintenance, has always managed with a cost minimization philosophy. Will the change to a profit center likely alter the quality of service provided by the maintenance department? Explain your answer.
c. What will be the reaction of the manufacturing departments to the change to a profit center? Consider the probable effect on the number of service requests when structuring your answer.

E25–2 Responsibility accounting, flexible budgets (L.O. 1, 2)

Event Services, Inc., runs the concession operation at Metro University's home basketball games. Prior to the start of the season, the company signed a contract with Metro and agreed to contribute 10% of its game-day profits to the library for the purchase of computerized data bases.

At the season's end, Event Services reported a net loss from concession operations and stated that no contribution would be forthcoming. The company blamed the loss on two factors: lower-than-expected attendance due to the team's sub-par record and higher costs for labor. Labor costs increased dramatically because of both a hike in the minimum wage and ineffective supervision of concession personnel. Needless to say, the university is extremely upset.

a. Rebecca Greene, the company's vice-president, has requested a meeting with university personnel to explain the season's performance. From a responsibility and control perspective, what position will she likely take? Should Event Services be held accountable for the loss as currently reported? Why or why not?
b. Would flexible budgets have any applicability here in presenting a clearer picture of performance? Briefly explain.

E25–3 Basic flexible budgeting (L.O. 2)

The Stockton Ballet uses flexible budgeting for cost control and performance evaluations. Based on historical relationships, management has determined that variable costs amount to $2 per patron for a printed program, complimentary soft drinks, and an "I Support Ballet" bumper sticker. Budgeted fixed costs for the season total $35,000.

a. Calculate total expected costs for 4,000 patrons and 5,000 patrons.
b. Assume that 3,800 patrons attended performances during the season and that variable costs and fixed costs were $9,800 and $37,000, respectively. Prepare a report to evaluate the ballet's operations. Was the ballet's financial performance better or worse than expected?

E25–4 Flexible budgets and performance reports (L.O. 2)

Ventura Headgear has experienced various labor problems in recent months, including two work stoppages during May. Management was therefore pleased to learn that May's production costs resulted in a $66,000 favorable variance, as follows:

	BUDGET	ACTUAL	VARIANCE
Direct materials used	$120,000	$ 99,000	$21,000F
Direct labor	180,000	148,000	32,000F
Variable factory overhead	90,000	72,000	18,000F
Fixed factory overhead	100,000	105,000	5,000U
Total production costs	$490,000	$424,000	$66,000F

The budget was based on an anticipated production level of 15,000 units, but only 11,000 units were manufactured.

a. Prepare a performance report for Ventura by using the flexible budgeting approach.
b. Compare the report prepared in part (a) with that originally given to management. Comment on (1) a major cause of the $66,000 favorable variance and (2) whether management should be pleased with May's performance.

E25–5 Variances for direct materials and direct labor (L.O. 5)

Frank Wallace & Sons manufactures various products for industrial use. The following costs relate to the manufacture of the firm's leading product, a heavy-duty cleaner:

Direct materials
- Actual: 460,000 pounds purchased and consumed at a cost of $3.20 per pound
- Standard: 5 pounds per finished container at a cost of $3.25 per pound

Direct labor
- Actual: 17,800 hours at an average wage rate of $8.40 per hour
- Standard: 0.2 hours per finished container at an average wage rate of $8.50 per hour

Compute variances for direct materials and direct labor assuming that 90,000 finished containers were manufactured during the period.

E25–6 Variances for direct materials and direct labor (L.O. 5)

Banner Company manufactures flags of various countries. Each flag has a standard of eight square feet of fabric and three hours of direct labor time. Information about recent production activity follows.

Actual cost of fabric: $4.50 per square foot
Fabric consumed: 32,080 square feet
Standard price per square foot of fabric: $4.25
Standard direct labor rate: $10.00 per hour
Actual direct labor rate: $10.20 per hour
Actual labor hours worked: 11,940
Actual production completed: 4,000 flags

a. Compute the materials price variance and the materials quantity variance.
b. Compute the labor rate variance and the labor efficiency variance.

E25–7 Variance analysis: Working backward (L.O. 5)

Quick Lube performs oil changes and other minor maintenance services (e.g., tire pressure checks, fluid checks, and so forth). The company advertises that all services are completed in 15 minutes. Eighty cars were serviced on a recent Saturday, resulting in the following labor variances: rate, $8U; efficiency, $72U. If the labor rate standard is $6 per hour, determine the:

a. Standard hours allowed for Saturday's work.
b. Actual hours worked.
c. Actual wage rate.

E25–8 Computation and analysis of food variances (L.O. 5, 6)

Executive Chefs provides food service to various airlines at New York's LaGuardia Airport. The company uses a standard cost system and is very concerned about cost control.

During a recent two-day period, the firm prepared 1,600 seafood platters. Standards for the platter are 0.5 pounds of fresh fish at $4 per pound. A performance report for this period follows and showed nothing unusual.

	BUDGET	ACTUAL	VARIANCE
Fresh fish	$3,200	$3,264	$64U

The company's purchasing director resigned shortly after the report was distributed. A review of the accounting records showed that Executive Chefs bought and consumed 1,020 pounds of seafood.

a. Compute the company's price variance and quantity variance.

b. Evaluate the company's activity over the two-day period. Include in your answer a possible reason behind the purchasing director's resignation.

E25–9 Determining the effect on variances (L.O. 5, 6)
Consider the following events that relate to Consolidated Industries:

a. A machine malfunction caused higher-than-normal spoilage rates and required increased attention by the machine operator.
b. The company had to absorb unexpected air freight charges on a rush order of direct materials.
c. A slowdown occurred on the production line because of low morale among the workers.
d. The local power company raised its rates by 5%.
e. The firm hired 10 part-time workers to meet an increase in production activity. Consolidated had to pay premium wages because of a shortage of qualified help.

Picture the nature of the materials variances (price and quantity) and labor variances (rate and efficiency). Determine which variances, if any, are affected by each event and whether the variance will be favorable or unfavorable. *Note:* If a revision of standards is necessary, assume that no revision occurs until the next accounting period.

E25–10 Overview of standards and variances (L.O. 3, 4, 5)
Evaluate the comments that follow as being True or False. If the comment is false, briefly explain why.

a. The direct labor rate variance is computed as the difference between the actual and standard pay rates, multiplied by the actual hours worked.
b. By hiring employees who possess below-average skill levels, a company is likely to generate favorable labor rate variances and unfavorable labor efficiency variances.
c. In most cases, ideal standards are preferable to attainable standards.
d. Standard costs are generally integrated into a company's budgets.
e. An unfavorable volume variance indicates that fixed overhead incurred exceeded budgeted amounts.

E25–11 Overhead variances (L.O. 5)
Nova Manufacturing applies factory overhead to products on the basis of direct labor hours. At the beginning of the current year, the company's accountant made the following projections for the upcoming period:

- Estimated variable overhead: $500,000
- Estimated fixed overhead: $400,000
- Estimated direct labor hours: 40,000

It is now 12 months later. Actual total overhead incurred in the manufacture of 7,900 units amounted to $895,100. Actual labor hours totaled 39,800. Assuming a direct labor standard of five hours per finished unit, calculate the following:

a. Variable overhead efficiency variance
b. Fixed overhead volume variance
c. Overhead spending variance

E25–12 Overhead variances (L.O. 5)
The city of Rolling Hills employs a standard cost system for its park operations. The following standards have been established for the monthly maintenance of one acre of developed land:

Direct materials: 1 pound of chemicals	$ 10
Direct labor: 10 hours @ $10	100
Variable overhead: 10 hours @ $8	80
Fixed overhead: 10 hours @ $4	40
	$230

Budgeted annual fixed overhead of $42,000 is spread evenly throughout the year. Actual results for August were: total overhead incurred, $15,400; labor hours worked, 1,150; and land maintained, 100 acres.

Determine the city's spending variance, variable overhead efficiency variance, and fixed overhead volume variance. Be sure to label the variances as favorable or unfavorable.

E25–13 Variance investigation (L.O. 6)

Padilla Enterprises recently reported a sizable loss from operations even though most of its variances were favorable. Of particular concern were the labor rate variance ($92,000 favorable) and the amount spent on advertising ($124,500 less than budget).

a. As judged by the labor rate and advertising expense variances, what are some possible contributing factors to Padilla's loss?
b. Are actual operations always to blame when a variance arises? Briefly explain.
c. How should the company decide whether to undertake a detailed investigation of its variances?

E25–14 Nonfinancial performance measures (L.O. 7)

Consider the following positions:

- Admitting clerk in a hospital
- Manager of a restaurant
- Accounting instructor at your college or university

For each of the positions listed, cite three nonfinancial performance measures that could be used in a year-end personnel evaluation.

PROBLEMS

Series A

P25–A1 Basic flexible budgeting (L.O. 2)

Lone Star Electronics manufactures satellite navigation systems for automobiles. A recent monthly budget revealed that 5,000 units are produced at the following costs:

Direct materials used	$100,000
Direct labor	50,000
Variable factory overhead	125,000
Fixed factory overhead, including depreciation	250,000
	$525,000

Annual straight-line depreciation is expected to amount to $360,000.

During July, the company produced 7,200 systems at a total cost of $651,250, subdivided as follows:

Direct materials used	$130,750
Direct labor	72,500
Variable factory overhead	180,000
Fixed factory overhead, including depreciation	268,000
	$651,250

An accounting department staff member noted that there were no acquisitions or disposals of property, plant, and equipment since the original budget was prepared.

Richard Li, a production vice-president, is extremely upset with July's performance. Given recent operating losses at Lone Star, Richard feels that the $126,250 unfavorable variance ($651,250 − $525,000) could seriously affect his upcoming personnel evaluation.

Instructions

a. How useful is Richard's variance calculation in assessing performance? Briefly explain.
b. Prepare a flexible budget for 4,500, 6,000, and 7,500 units of activity.
c. Was Lone Star's experience in July better or worse than anticipated? Prepare an appropriate performance report and explain your answer.

P25–A2 Setting standards (L.O. 3, 4)

Big Country Manufacturing is considering the implementation of a standard costing system. The information that follows pertains to one of the company's products, HD–24.

Direct materials used*		$1,020,000
Blending labor†		406,000
Other traceable variable costs		
Blending department	$148,000	
Packaging materials	40,700	
Miscellaneous	74,000	262,700
Total variable costs		$1,688,700

* 240,000 gallons at $4.25 per gallon.
† 58,000 hours at $7.00 per hour.

These costs were incurred in the production of 185,000 gallons of HD–24, which were packaged four gallons to a case. Starr has been experiencing problems with the quality of materials used and plans to change suppliers in the forthcoming period. The price per gallon of direct materials is expected to rise to $4.40. The company anticipates that HD–24 output will total 80% of the direct materials used in production; the remainder is lost through evaporation during the blending operation.

Management estimates that abnormal production problems in the prior period led to the incurrence of an additional 2,500 labor hours. These problems have been corrected and are not expected to recur. Other variable costs are anticipated to remain stable, with the exception of packaging materials. Packaging cost is expected to increase by $0.04 per gallon.

Instructions

a. By analyzing the data presented, compute an attainable standard variable cost for a case of HD–24.

b. Compare and contrast ideal and attainable standards. What benefits normally result from the use of attainable standards?
c. Discuss several problems that may be encountered in the standard-setting process by relying too heavily on past experience.

P25–A3 Straightforward variance analysis (L.O. 5)

Arrow Enterprises uses a standard costing system. The standard cost sheet for product no. 549 follows.

Direct materials: 4 units @ $6.50	$ 26.00
Direct labor: 8 hours @ $8.50	68.00
Variable factory overhead: 8 hours @ $7.00	56.00
Fixed factory overhead: 8 hours @ $2.50	20.00
Total standard cost per unit	$170.00

The following information pertains to activity for December:

1. Direct materials acquired during the month amounted to 26,350 units at $6.40 per unit. All materials were consumed in production.
2. Arrow incurred an average wage rate of $8.75 for 51,400 hours of activity.
3. Total overhead incurred amounted to $508,400. Budgeted fixed overhead totals $1.8 million and is spread evenly throughout the year.
4. Actual production amounted to 6,500 completed units.

Instructions

a. Compute Arrow's direct material variances.
b. Compute Arrow's direct labor variances.
c. Compute Arrow's variances for factory overhead.

P25–A4 Variance analysis and interpretation (L.O. 1, 5, 6)

Imtex Manufacturing uses a standard costing system. The variable cost standards for product no. 628 follow.

Direct materials: 3.2 pounds @ $5	$16.00
Direct labor: 8.5 hours @ $8	68.00
Variable overhead: 8.5 hours @ $3	25.50

The company has been experiencing rough times of late, with constant complaints from customers about poor product quality. In addition, the production supervisor is very unhappy with the performance reports that he receives to monitor factory operations. A typical report appears as shown.

IMTEX MANUFACTURING
Performance Report
For the Month Ended June 30, 19X3

	ACTUAL	STANDARD	VARIANCE
Direct costs*	$XX,XXX	$XX,XXX	$XX,XXX
Factory overhead	XX,XXX	XX,XXX	XX,XXX
Total	$XX,XXX	$XX,XXX	$XX,XXX

* Direct materials + direct labor.

In an effort to improve product quality, the supervisor has campaigned for a change to a better supplier and the hiring of more competent employees. He has recently been given permission to pursue both of these alternatives. Actual data follow.

1. Direct materials purchased and consumed amounted to 6,000 pounds at $5.80 per pound.
2. Direct labor incurred in the manufacture of 2,000 completed units totaled 15,400 hours at $10.50 per hour.
3. Variable overhead incurred totaled $47,200.

Instructions

a. Suggest several ways that Imtex's performance report could be improved to provide better information for the supervisor.
b. Prepare a complete variance analysis for direct materials, direct labor, and variable overhead. *Note:* Compute the overhead spending variance with regard to variable overhead only.
c. Does the production supervisor's plan seem to be working? Discuss.

P25–A5 Variance analysis: Working backward (L.O. 5)

Marvel Company has a single manufacturing department that applies factory overhead on the basis of direct labor hours. Selected department information follows.

Cost of material purchased and consumed	?
Material standard per finished unit	3 pounds
Standard material cost per pound	$4
Materials price variance	$4,370U
Materials quantity variance	$8,600F
Actual labor hours worked	?
Labor standard per finished unit	5 hours
Standard labor rate per hour	$7
Labor rate variance	$22,800U
Labor efficiency variance	$14,000F
Total actual overhead incurred	?
Standard variable overhead rate	$2 per hour
Standard fixed overhead rate	$6 per hour
Budgeted fixed overhead	?
Variable overhead efficiency variance	?
Fixed overhead volume variance	$12,000U
Overhead spending variance	$4,800U
Number of units manufactured	8,000

Instructions

Determine each of the unknowns. *Hint:* It is helpful to solve separate models simultaneously for materials, labor, and overhead by filling in the given information.

Series B

P25–B1 Basic flexible budgeting (L.O. 2)

Paragon, Inc., normally manufactures between 36,000 and 42,000 units each month. A static budget based on 36,000 units and actual results for April follow.

	BUDGET	ACTUAL
Direct materials	$172,800	$175,900
Direct labor	270,000	258,000
Variable factory overhead	115,200	109,000
Supervision	105,000	82,600
Insurance & taxes	60,000	61,500
Depreciation	84,000	88,000
	$807,000	$775,000

Conversations with Paragon's accountant revealed the following information:

1. April's production totaled 35,000 units.
2. Supervision, insurance and taxes, and depreciation are fixed costs.
3. Should production fall below 36,000 units, supervision costs are expected to be reduced by $20,000 because of temporary layoffs.

Instructions

a. Prepare a flexible budget for 36,000, 39,000, and 42,000 units of activity.
b. Prepare a performance report for April that can be used to judge Paragon's success or failure in meeting budgeted targets. Comment on your findings.
c. Explain the flexibility that is associated with a flexible budget.

P25–B2 Setting standards (L.O. 3, 4)

Rencore, Inc., manufactures wooden bookends for office and home use. Wood is cut, shaped, and processed into the completed product. Just prior to completion and the attachment of felt pads that prevent scratches on furniture, the wood is inspected for defects. The following information is available:

- Normally, 104 bookends must be processed for every 100 good units completed.
- Each pair of bookends requires 2.5 board feet of lumber at $1.40 per board foot.
- Each bookend has four felt pads on its base. Last year, when 15,000 pair were manufactured, pad cost amounted to $3,600. Rencore's management was just informed of a $0.01-per-pad price hike by the felt supplier.
- All direct laborers are paid $12 per hour. Expected labor times for a pair of bookends are:

Cutting, shaping, and processing	15 minutes
Finishing (attaching felt pads, polishing)	1 minute

- Actual packaging costs recently totaled $0.32 per pair, which was $0.02 higher than standard. Because of a change to a sturdier, more attractive box, the standard should be increased by 10%.

Instructions

a. On the basis of the information presented, calculate an attainable standard cost for materials and labor for a pair of bookends.
b. What parties would typically participate in the development of material and labor standards? What roles would these parties play?
c. Assume that management is studying a decrease in labor time for the cutting, shaping, and processing operations to 14 minutes per pair even though the company's work force views 15 minutes as more realistic.
   (1) Would any benefits result from setting a tighter standard for Rencore's workers?
   (2) What problems might result from the change to a 14-minute standard?

P25–B3 Straightforward variance analysis (L.O. 5)

AV Corporation manufactures a single product and uses a standard cost system. The following information was taken from the company's accounting records:

	STANDARD	ACTUAL
Direct materials		
Cost per gallon	$6.50	$6.30
Gallons per finished unit	5	
Direct labor		
Cost per hour	$10.50	$10.70
Hours per finished unit	3.0	2.8
Factory overhead		
Total overhead incurred		$402,000
Variable overhead rate per hour	$3.00	
Fixed overhead rate per hour	$7.00	
Units produced		12,900

AV purchased and used 65,000 gallons of direct materials during the period. Budgeted fixed factory overhead was $280,000.

Instructions

a. Compute the company's variances for direct materials.
b. Compute the company's variances for direct labor.
c. Compute the company's variances for factory overhead. AV applies factory overhead to products on the basis of direct labor hours.

P25–B4 Variance analysis and interpretation (L.O. 1, 5, 6)

RX–54 Industries uses a standard costing system to assist in the control of operations. The company's May performance report for variable manufacturing costs follows.

RX–54 INDUSTRIES
Performance Report
For the Month Ended May 31, 19X7

Direct materials variance, favorable	$ 300
Direct labor variance, favorable	780
Variable overhead variance, favorable	100
Total variances, favorable	$1,180

The president is extremely satisfied with the figures. He notes: "It looks like we've finally gotten operations under control. Apparently the change to a new supplier did the trick, and I think the new supervisor is working out well. I've noticed a much happier and more efficient work force on my daily tours through the plant."

Assume that the following information has come to your attention:

1. Standard variable costs per unit of finished product:

Direct materials: 2.5 pounds @ $2.00		$ 5.00
Direct labor: 3.4 hours @ $9.00		30.60
Variable overhead: 3.4 hours @ $5.00		17.00
Total standard variable cost per unit		$52.60

2. Direct materials purchased and consumed amounted to 8,400 pounds at $1.75 per pound.
3. Direct labor incurred in the manufacture of 3,000 completed units totaled 11,100 hours at $8.20 per hour.
4. Variable factory overhead incurred amounted to $50,900.

Instructions

a. Criticize the format and content of the performance report as currently constructed.
b. Prepare a complete variance analysis for direct materials, direct labor, and variable overhead. *Note:* Compute the overhead spending variance with regard to variable overhead only.
c. Explain the results of your findings to the president. Are things going as smoothly as the president believes? Discuss.

P25–B5 Variance analysis: Working backward (L.O. 5)

Southern Air, Inc., has a single manufacturing department that applies factory overhead on the basis of direct labor hours. Selected departmental information follows.

Cost of materials purchased and consumed	$23,125
Materials standard per finished unit	4 pounds
Materials price variance	$2,775F
Materials quantity variance	$1,600U
Actual labor hours worked	3,000 hours
Labor standard per finished unit	1.1 hours
Standard labor rate per hour	$9
Labor rate variance	$2,550U
Total actual overhead incurred	$65,100
Standard fixed overhead rate	$10 per hour
Budgeted fixed overhead	$32,000
Variable overhead efficiency variance	$3,050U
Number of units manufactured	2,500

Instructions

Determine the following amounts:

- Standard material cost per pound
- Labor efficiency variance
- Standard variable overhead rate per hour
- Fixed overhead volume variance
- Overhead spending variance

Hint: It is helpful to solve separate models simultaneously for materials, labor, and overhead by filling in the given information.

EYH25–1 Cost centers and profit centers (L.O. 1)

For years, many governmental and not-for-profit organizations viewed their operations as cost centers. Center managers were asked to achieve certain objectives by spending monies that were budgeted for that purpose. Recently, a number of these organizations have changed their thinking and have begun to look at particular units as profit centers. Managers have been given the authority to collect user/service fees that exceed, or help cover, operating costs.

Instructions

Form a team with four other students in your class and contact the treasurers of three governmental and/or not-for-profit entities in your area. Determine if any of the operations have changed (or will change) so that managers act with a profit-center orientation. Describe the changes along with the underlying rationale for change. Be prepared to report your findings to the class.

EYH25–2 Development of standards (L.O. 4)

Because subjects and people differ, it is not surprising that instructor expectations differ from course to course. As judged by the material presented in this chapter, instructors should develop high but attainable standards—standards that are neither too tight (i.e., difficult) nor too lax.

Instructions

Develop a 10-point rating scale where "1"="too lax" and "10"="too difficult." Evaluate this course and one other course that you are taking (or have taken) with respect to (1) tests that have been given and (2) overall instructor expectations. How, if at all, would you change the standards in this course? Why do you feel these changes are needed? Submit your recommendations anonymously.

EYH25–3 Nonfinancial performance measures (L.O. 7)

Many managers are evaluated on the basis of bottom-line profit performance. In recent years, a number of companies have begun to study nondollar measures to produce a better, more well-rounded organization.

Instructions

Form a team with three other students and interview two managers of large companies. The companies may be as diverse as a large local manufacturing plant, a local franchise of a fast-food chain, or the local outlet of a massive discount merchandiser. Summarize answers to the following in a one-page report.

a. Determine what types of nonfinancial performance measures are used to (1) evaluate business operations and (2) individual personnel.
b. What major benefits do the managers see from the use of nonfinancial performance measures?
c. Which of the nonfinancial performance measures have been the most troublesome to achieve? Why?

EYH25–4 Responsibility accounting and variances (L.O. 1, 3)

Burdick Manufacturing is a small producer of decorative accessories used in the home. Various materials are carefully shaped and formed by skilled craftsmen, with the final product being sold in fine furniture stores and specialty shops. The company uses responsibility accounting and has recently installed a new computerized standard cost system. The system has been tested thoroughly and is operating correctly.

Six weeks ago, the firm's sales manager accepted a large rush order for a nonstock item from a valued customer. The sales manager forwarded the order to Joe Perry, the production supervisor. Perry, in turn, filed the necessary paperwork with the purchasing department so that needed raw materials could be acquired. Unfortunately, a purchasing clerk temporarily lost the paperwork, and by the time it was located, it was too late to order from the normal supplier. A new supplier was found, who quoted a very attractive price. When the materials arrived, production personnel found them to be of poor quality.

Perry has recently returned from vacation, only to be confronted by Burdick's manufacturing vice-president about "inept performance in the period just ended." A heated discussion took place, with Perry being told to shape up or ship out.

Instructions

a. Briefly explain the essence of a responsibility accounting system.
b. What variances for materials and labor would *ordinarily* be controllable by and appear on a production supervisor's performance report?
c. Briefly explain the probable reason behind the heated confrontation between Perry and the manufacturing vice-president. Does the manufacturing vice-president have a valid reason to be upset? Why?
d. Given that the company has a responsibility accounting system, what could be done to correct the situation? Briefly discuss.

COMMUNICATION OF ACCOUNTING INFORMATION

CAI25–1 The follow-up message (L.O. 5, 6)

Communication Principle: Business relationships are carefully built and nurtured. Customers must be solicited and satisfied, and a quality network of suppliers must be established and monitored. Although considerable energy is typically expended in building such associations, continued *support* of the relationship is often neglected. This situation is mostly human nature—we grow content with the status quo or take a good thing for granted.

To help further these alliances, lines of communication should be opened and maintained in much the same way as a company does routine maintenance on equipment. The ongoing communications should have a theme. For example, when dealing with a supplier, an occasional note or phone call is in order and may take the following forms:

- Just wanted to thank you for a dependable delivery schedule.
- Checking in to make sure that our payments are in a form and timing that are convenient for you.
- We have been experiencing some difficulties with your sales representative and thought you might want some feedback.

In each case you are accomplishing multiple goals: strengthening the association; providing positive feedback; furnishing an early indication of a problem that might grow if unchecked; and so forth. In the long run, such communication paves the way for continued good relations and establishes a pool of goodwill that affected parties can draw upon if major difficulties arise.

■ ■ ■ ■ ■ ■ ■ ■

Consider the three scenarios that follow.

- *Scenario A.* Adobe Company's material quantity variances reveal that excessive amounts of material are being used in production. The excess usage reflects a higher-than-normal defect rate associated with a part provided by Adobe's key supplier. The supplier should be notified and told that it is important for the situation to be corrected.
- *Scenario B.* The materials price variance of Heritage Corporation is favorable because of a supplier's special "customer appreciation" discount. The discount was totally unexpected.
- *Scenario C.* Fastrac Wholesale, a major supplier, has sent you a very nice personal gift. The gift must be returned because accepting it would violate your company's ethics policy.

Instructions

Draft an appropriate letter, note, or memo to the three suppliers. You may assume that prior dealings have put you on a "first-name" basis with a contact person in each of the firms.

Answers to Chapter Quiz

1. c
2. a
3. b
4. b [(Aq × Sp) − (Sq × Sp) = (8,100 hours × $8) − (8,000 hours × $8) = $800. The variance is unfavorable because actual hours exceeded standard hours.]
5. a

26 Decision Making and Contribution Reporting

Learning Objectives

After studying this chapter, you should be able to:

1. Explain the effect of relevant costs and sunk costs on decision making.
2. Evaluate different types of decision situations (e.g., make or buy).
3. Explain why the contribution margin must be analyzed in terms of capacity constraints.
4. Distinguish between direct costs and indirect costs.
5. Prepare and use a contribution income statement.
6. Identify the features of variable costing and absorption costing.

Not too long ago, George Faris was reflecting on the history and growth of Banner Outdoor Advertising. He noted, "Many factors have contributed to our success, but perhaps the most important has been our ability to evaluate alternatives and make decisions. The decisions have been short-term, long-term, one-time, and recurring in nature—a real hodgepodge if you stop to think about it."

Although sound decision making has been an important part of the firm, George confessed that he still has trouble with the related fundamentals. "They sometimes go against human nature," he said, elaborating with the following example. Several years ago, Banner constructed a billboard in a bad location. "We should have never done it. Not only was it hard to lease but the rents were poor—we were working like crazy just to break even. Then we got lucky. Along came a company that wanted to buy the sign. It was a miserable offer, one that was considerably less than what we had invested. But it *was* an offer and a way to bail out of a lousy situation."

George felt at first that Banner should "hang in there" and avoid taking a loss. But, when he put a pencil to the deal, he realized that Banner would be better off to recover its cash and pursue other alternatives. George had a tough time accepting the loss, but he actually did the right thing. "What's done is done," we said. "That investment is history and should be ignored in making the decision."

George was surprised that we agreed with his analysis, especially considering his lack of formal training in the area. "Right or wrong, most of my knowledge has been self taught, and I sometimes have to rely on gut feelings." We will not deny that gut feelings are an important part of decision making. You will soon see, however, that several well-defined principles are involved as well.

This chapter is the first of a two-chapter sequence that explores the fundamentals of decision making. Although much of our presentation will focus on the decision process from a business viewpoint, many of the concepts illustrated are also relevant to individuals. Students, employees, and family members are continually confronted with financial problems or issues that need attention. Knowing how to correctly evaluate alternatives can therefore be very valuable in attempts made to improve one's financial position and economic well-being.

General Approach to Decision Making

Over time, management faces a number of different decisions. Certain decisions, such as the selection of a supplier for raw materials, are fairly routine; others, in contrast, are more complex (e.g., the addition of a major product line). Exhibit 26–1 reveals recent decisions of several well-known corporations.

A review of the exhibit provides strong evidence of the breadth of issues that these entities must struggle with and resolve. Future events will determine

> **1**
>
> Explain the effect of relevant costs and sunk costs on decision making.

whether the companies' actions were wise or whether other alternatives would have been preferable. Cost, no doubt, is bound to be a major factor—both in the decision process itself and as a follow-up in assessing the success or failure of management's efforts.

Because of the variety inherent in the decision process, a general approach to decision making is extremely useful. The general approach first involves the identification of future costs, specifically, those associated with the alternatives under review. To illustrate, assume that management is studying whether to replace an existing machine with a newer, more efficient model. The expected future costs must be evaluated, because these amounts will be the only ones incurred as a result of making the decision. Past historical costs may serve as a basis for predicting what the future costs will be, but *old costs are just memories* and are not considered in the selection of alternatives.

The next step in the general approach is to focus on **relevant costs,** or future costs that differ among the various courses of action. In the replacement decision just cited, for example, any differences in maintenance costs between the old machine and the new machine are relevant and must be considered. Future costs that are identical for both pieces of equipment can be ignored, as such amounts have no impact on the ultimate selection.

FULL PROJECT OR INCREMENTAL APPROACH?

Relevant costs can be studied by using either a full project or an incremental approach. As an example, assume that Merchants Company must make a delivery 150 miles from its warehouse (300 miles for a round trip). Two trucks are available: A and B. Truck A gets 10 miles per gallon and consumes one quart of

EXHIBIT 26–1
Recent Business Decisions

CORPORATION	DECISION
Bristol-Myers Squibb	Sold the appliance division of Clairol to Remington Products.
Colgate-Palmolive	Initiated restructuring projects in Europe that are estimated to save $40 million.
Intel Corporation	Invested $970 million in research and development.
ITT Sheraton	Entered into an agreement for 50% ownership of four hotels to be constructed at Universal Studios Florida.
Sunbeam-Oster	Installed a new top management team.
Time Warner	Launched a Chinese version of *People* magazine.
Turner Broadcasting System	Entered the film business by acquiring Castle Rock Entertainment.

oil every 100 miles. Truck B gets 7.5 miles per gallon and uses one quart of oil every 150 miles. Other data are as follows:

Gasoline	$1 per gallon
Oil	$2 per quart
Driver's wage	$7 per hour
Trip time	8 hours
Road tolls	$10

The costs of operating the two trucks are as follows:

	TRUCK A	TRUCK B	DIFFERENCE
Gasoline*	$ 30	$ 40	$10
Oil†	6	4	(2)
Driver's wage (8 hours × $7)	56	56	—
Tolls	10	10	—
Total cost	$102	$110	$ 8

* Truck A: [(300 miles ÷ 10 miles per gallon) × $1] = $30.
Truck B: [(300 miles ÷ 7.5 miles per gallon) × $1] = $40.

† Truck A: [(300 miles ÷ 100 miles per quart) × $2] = $6.
Truck B: [(300 miles ÷ 150 miles per quart) × $2] = $4.

On the basis of the expected costs, the company should use truck A. Notice that the driver's wage and road tolls are the same for both vehicles, making these two items "nonfactors" in the selection process. Given this situation, the proper approach would have been to focus solely on the cost of gasoline and oil. These costs are relevant because they will be incurred in the future and will differ between the trucks.

If using the **full project approach,** management would compare $36 against $44 (gasoline + oil cost) to make the proper decision. Specifically, the total relevant costs associated with each alternative are evaluated. Conversely, with the **incremental approach,** only the net differences are considered. Management would therefore focus its attention on the $8 variation that appears in the right-hand column, which favors vehicle A.[1]

Although the incremental approach is often used in practice, it has two serious drawbacks. The method is cumbersome when more than two alternatives are being evaluated, and the act of netting often leads to mathematical errors. For these reasons we will stress the full project approach throughout the remainder of this chapter.

DECISION MAKING: AN EMPHASIS ON THE FUTURE

Keep in mind that the thrust of decision making is a focus on the future. Let us expand on this thought by concentrating on a problem faced by Malibu Construction, a builder of custom homes in southern California. Recently, the company agreed to build a spacious home for a valued customer. Work on the project began several months ago and is nearing completion. Most of the remaining work involves optional decorative accessories, landscaping, and the construction of a swimming pool and a tennis court. To date, Malibu has spent

---
[1] Costs that differ among alternatives are sometimes called **differential costs.**

$650,000 on the project in the form of materials, labor, and overhead. Much to the dismay of management, the customer has just declared bankruptcy and must back out of the contract.

Malibu has conducted a thorough study of available alternatives and identified two courses of action:

1. Sell the unfinished residence as is for $610,000.
2. Make several design changes at a cost of $80,000 and complete the project. The company has found a buyer who is willing to pay $700,000 for the home if the changes are made.

A conventional "income statement" analysis reveals the undesirability of both alternatives. As the following figures show, losses will be incurred regardless of the selected option:

	SELL AS IS		REDESIGN	
Revenue		$610,000		$700,000
Costs				
Existing	$650,000		$650,000	
Additional	—	650,000	80,000	730,000
Loss		$(40,000)		$(30,000)

Malibu's president, obviously displeased, was overheard complaining: "We've already got $650,000 in this venture. Incurring a loss on top of all this would be foolish."

The Concept of Sunk Cost. A careful inspection of the preceding figures will reveal an inconsistency with the general approach to decision making that was illustrated earlier. Notice that the existing cost of $650,000 is common to both alternatives and, therefore, should have no effect on the eventual selection. This amount is considered a sunk cost—a past cost that has already been incurred. Regardless of whether Malibu sells the residence as is or pursues the redesign option, the existing costs are like "water under the bridge" and cannot be changed by management's actions. As originally alluded to by our George Faris/Banner Advertising chapter opener, sunk costs are thus an irrelevant consideration in decision making.

How, then, should the evaluation be made? A more appropriate analysis would be as follows:

	SELL AS IS	REDESIGN
Revenue	$610,000	$700,000
Additional future costs	—	80,000
Net benefit from sale	$610,000	$620,000

With a focus on future revenues and costs that differ among the alternatives (i.e., those that are *relevant*), the analysis shows that Malibu should spend $80,000 for the redesign work and sell the property for $700,000. In comparison with the "as is" sale, the company will be better off by $10,000 ($620,000 − $610,000).

> **ETHICS ISSUE**
>
> Your boss has promised a $20,000 bonus if you prepare a report showing that Division A is unprofitable and should be sold. To do so you would have to include several irrelevant costs that will probably go unnoticed. What would you do?

QUALITATIVE FACTORS

In addition to quantitative considerations, various qualitative factors must be addressed in the decision-making process. Qualitative factors are those whose evaluation in terms of dollars is impossible or, at best, difficult to determine. As an example, the manager in the Merchants Company truck illustration may decide to send Truck B on the delivery because the vehicle is brand new and customer impressions are important. Or, in another situation, machine operators may rebel if they are not given a say in the proposed acquisition of new equipment. Ignoring employee input would be detrimental to the firm and could lead to low morale and decreased productivity.

The preceding factors, although not quantifiable, can be important and should not be disregarded. Quite honestly, however, most business decisions are based primarily on dollars. Qualitative issues are perhaps most significant when the mathematical difference between alternatives is small and management needs a "tie breaker."

A SUMMARY OF THE DECISION-MAKING PROCESS

The general approach to decision making can be summarized as follows:

1. Identify each alternative and examine the future costs (and revenues).
2. Disregard items that are the same among the alternatives.
3. Identify and consider the qualitative factors.
4. Make a decision after studying both the quantitative analysis and the qualitative concerns.

These steps can be applied to many different decision-making areas. The next few sections of the chapter will explore several of these areas, including make or buy decisions, special order pricing, and the addition or deletion of products or departments.

MAKE OR BUY DECISIONS

Evaluate different types of decision situations (e.g., make or buy).

Manufacturing firms often purchase needed parts for their operations from outside suppliers. As an example, the roughly six million components of a Boeing 747–400 come from 1,500+ different companies. (About the only items Boeing itself makes are the wings.)[2] Interestingly, many of the firms that rely on external sources of supply have the technical abilities to produce the needed parts and materials themselves. Apparently, an analysis has deemed the purchase alternative preferable.

The choice to manufacture internally or to rely on external suppliers is commonly known as a *make or buy* decision. The business press frequently refers to the term "outsourcing" in connection with this situation. Outsourcing means that a company has decided to acquire its goods and services from outside vendors rather than produce the same goods or services in-house.

To illustrate the proper approach to follow in this type of decision, assume that Crane Company, a manufacturer of mopeds, is now producing all of its own motors. As shown in the following analysis, the motors cost $75 each, based on an output of 10,000 units per year.

[2] See "No More Weekend Stands," *Forbes*, September 17, 1990, pp. 191–92.

	10,000 MOTORS	PER MOTOR
Direct materials	$180,000	$18
Direct labor	390,000	39
Variable factory overhead	100,000	10
Fixed factory overhead*	80,000	8
Total cost	$750,000	$75

*Allocated on the basis of capacity used.

Crane has solicited an offer from an external supplier to provide 10,000 motors at a set price of $72 each. To determine whether the motors should be manufactured internally or purchased externally, management must isolate the relevant costs. Future costs that differ between the make and buy alternatives must be studied. Sunk costs, in contrast, should be ignored.

In reviewing the previous information, we see that motor production was charged with $670,000 of variable costs, specifically, direct materials, direct labor, and variable factory overhead. Being variable, these costs will be eliminated if the motors are acquired from an outside supplier. The variable costs are thus relevant in an analysis of the make and buy alternatives. Turning to the fixed costs, Crane has allocated $80,000 of fixed factory overhead to motor production. In view of their fixed nature, these costs will be incurred even if the company decides in favor of an external purchase. As you already know, amounts that are the same among alternatives can be disregarded.

AVOIDABLE FIXED OVERHEAD

Frequently, when operations undergo a significant change, total fixed costs do not remain static. If manufacturing activities are discontinued, for example, it is conceivable that a production supervisor would be dismissed and some equipment leases terminated. Naturally, any future fixed costs that change should be included in the analysis.

In Crane's case, suppose that fixed factory overhead can be reduced by $20,000 if production is stopped. The following analysis indicates that management should reject the supplier's offer, because there is a $30,000 advantage in favor of manufacturing internally.

	10,000 MOTORS	
	MAKE	BUY
Purchase		$720,000
Direct materials	$180,000	
Direct labor	390,000	
Variable factory overhead	100,000	
Avoidable fixed factory overhead	20,000	
Total cost	$690,000	$720,000
	$30,000 difference	

The preceding evaluation is straightforward with the possible exception of the avoidable fixed overhead. Realize that Crane will incur $80,000 of fixed overhead if the motors are produced internally and $60,000 of fixed overhead if they are acquired from suppliers. Thus, $20,000 of fixed costs must be associated with the manufacturing option.

Looking at the analysis from a slightly different perspective, we observe a $20,000 savings in fixed costs if the purchase alternative is selected. Therefore, the net cost of dealing with an outside supplier is $700,000 ($720,000 − $20,000). Manufacturing costs would now consist solely of variable items and would total $670,000, which still maintains the $30,000 difference in favor of production ($700,000 − $670,000 = $30,000).

OPPORTUNITY COST

In performing a complete analysis of make versus buy, management must also evaluate alternative uses of manufacturing facilities. If, for example, a decision is made to acquire goods externally, the purchaser's factory and equipment may remain idle. On the other hand, such decisions frequently release facilities for use in other production applications. In the Crane Company illustration, suppose the resources committed to motor production could be redirected toward making a new line of golf carts. Naturally, any income from the golf cart line would be lost if the firm continues its motor operation.

The cost of a forgone alternative is termed *opportunity cost*. If the golf carts promise to generate a *contribution margin* (i.e., sales minus variable costs) of $75,000, the make or buy decision will assume the following form:

	MAKE	BUY
Cost of buying		$720,000
Cost of making	$690,000	
Forgone contribution on golf carts	75,000	
Total cost	$765,000	$720,000

$45,000 difference

The analysis now shows that the company would benefit by $45,000 if it acquired the motors from the outside supplier.[3,4]

QUALITATIVE CONSIDERATIONS

Given the quantitative outcome, we must also explore the related qualitative factors. In make or buy decisions, the decision to purchase externally means more dependence on suppliers and the accompanying worry about product quality, strikes against suppliers, transportation strikes and hazards, personnel changes at suppliers' offices, and product discontinuance. To some companies, the quality concern alone would dictate rejection of the purchase alternative.

---

[3] The same analysis in another format would show the net cost of buying to be $645,000 ($720,000 purchase cost − $75,000 contribution generated). The decision maker would then compare $645,000 against $690,000 and still note a $45,000 advantage in favor of the buy alternative.

[4] Be aware that opportunity costs are not restricted to make or buy decisions. Such costs arise in many different settings (e.g., the evaluation of competing job offers) and must be considered if the proper alternative is to be selected.

A Further Focus

Make-versus-buy decisions are not confined solely to the manufacture of products. In an effort to improve bottom-line profitability, many companies outsource services that were formerly performed in-house. Eastman Kodak, for instance, outsourced its data processing services not too long ago to IBM and Digital Equipment, allowing the firm to eliminate 1,000 jobs and avoid substantial investments in computer equipment. In another example, recent cost-cutting efforts of American Airlines included outsourcing the duties of airport agents in 30 cities. American also planned to hire outside contractors in its larger cities and hubs to provide baggage handling, priority parcel, and cargo services.

Sources: "Telecommunications: More Firms 'Outsource' Data Networks," *The Wall Street Journal*, March 11, 1992, pp. B1, B8 and "American Details Latest Cutback Plan," *The Dallas Morning News*, September 23, 1994, pp. 1D, 11D.

Special Order Pricing

The pricing of special orders is another decision faced by many firms. Although businesses prefer to sell their products at the highest prices possible, economic conditions sometimes dictate otherwise. Various situations may arise where special orders are considered at prices that are less than optimum. In an effort to reach the proper decision, management must again focus on the differential (or incremental) costs and revenues involved.

As an example, assume that the Smithfield Bicycle Company received an inquiry from a large national retailer to provide 20,000 R–18 racing bicycles at a price of $77 each. The bicycles will be marketed under the retailer's brand name. Although Smithfield has sufficient (idle) manufacturing capacity, management is reluctant to accept the order because the price is well below the company's normal selling price of $119. The costs that follow pertain to the R–18 bicycle.

Materials	$ 42.80
Labor	24.50
Factory overhead*	24.70
Variable selling costs	10.00
Total	$102.00

* Eighty percent of the factory overhead represents fixed cost.

At first glance it appears that the retailer's offer should be rejected because it fails to cover the $102 total cost. However, further investigation reveals that variable selling costs will not be incurred on the order. Furthermore, in view of the fact that Smithfield currently has idle facilities, total fixed costs are not expected to change. Eighty percent of the factory overhead ($24.70 × 0.80 = $19.76) will therefore be present even if the offer is refused and can be ignored. The following analysis shows that Smithfield would benefit by doing business with the retailer:

Special selling price		$77.00
Less variable costs		
Materials	$42.80	
Labor	24.50	
Variable factory overhead ($24.70 − $19.76)	4.94	72.24
Contribution margin per bicycle		$ 4.76

Recall from Chapter 23 that the contribution margin is the amount each unit generates toward covering fixed costs and producing net income. Given the preceding figures, acceptance of the special order will result in an overall profitability boost of $95,200 (20,000 bicycles × $4.76). Although each unit yields less than the normal R–18 sale, Smithfield has machines and other resources already in place that are not being used to the fullest extent possible. Thus, some extra business is really "icing on the cake."

Several qualitative issues must be addressed in this decision, including the following:

- Will there be a decrease in sales of Smithfield's own brand of R–18 bicycle?
- Are future orders from the retailer likely?
- Will factory capacity devoted to the special order soon be needed for Smithfield's regular production activity?

THE PRICING DECISION

The Smithfield Bicycle example simply touched the surface of a very troublesome area for many companies. The determination of the "proper" selling price

---

BUSINESS BRIEFING

NANCY ALTENBURG
Manager, Sports and Event Marketing
Federal Express Corporation

Orange Bowl Sponsorship: A Matter of Cost Versus Benefit

No matter what the form, companies make decisions by exploring the costs and benefits of decision alternatives. Consider, for instance, our firm's sponsorship of the Orange Bowl football game—a perfect example of reaping major benefit from the partnering of two highly compatible entities. The Orange Bowl has widespread appeal among the diverse groups in the FedEx customer base and reflects the high regard in which consumers generally hold the company.

Consequently, Federal Express realizes a far greater return than its investment in the big event. The return comes from the exposure it receives via commercials within the game and on-field graphics, as well as the incremental business the company gains by inviting key decision makers to attend a four-day seminar/sports entertainment gathering. While a little over $4 million per year is invested in sponsoring the event, the benefits in terms of exposure, additional revenues, and stronger relationships can be measured by at least a fivefold annual return over the initial outlay. This sponsorship, along with other events underwritten by FedEx, allow us to interact with a clientele of companies that spend millions of dollars in overnight shipping, the core of our business.

for goods and services can be quite perplexing. A company that sets its price too high will have a lack of customers and a deteriorating bottom-line profit performance. On the other hand, if the price is set too low, volume may be satisfactory but the firm may fail to cover costs. Again, the bottom line suffers. In general, when establishing a selling price, companies consider costs, competition, and what the customer is willing to pay.

An added complication arises when we look at **transfer prices,** or prices that are used for intracompany sales. Picture the data processing department of Baxter Industries. Say the department is organized as an investment center, providing (selling) services to other Baxter departments and divisions. The complication surfaces because both the seller and the buyer are part of the same company. The seller wants to make as much money as possible and advocates a high price; the buyer has the same profit objective and wants to pay very little. Again, considering that both units are part of the same organization, whose views are correct? The answer is debatable.

Transfer prices that are set incorrectly can actually hurt overall firm performance. Suppose, for example, that Baxter's data processing department has a $50-per-hour variable cost to provide a particular service and sets a $70 transfer price to earn a profit. Assume that another department, the billing department, needs this service but feels that the quoted price of $70 is too high. Looking around, the billing department finds that the exact same service can be obtained for $62 from Acme Data Corporation (an external supplier). The billing department wins because it saves $8 per hour ($70 – $62). However, Baxter loses because a service that it can provide for $50 suddenly costs $62. Arriving at a satisfactory transfer price that keeps all parties happy is a difficult issue to resolve but one that must be addressed. Such prices are often established through a negotiated settlement between the buyer and the seller and sometimes by the use of arbitration committees.

CONTRIBUTION MARGIN IN RELATION TO CAPACITY

> **3** Explain why the contribution margin must be analyzed in terms of capacity constraints.

In addition to the special order situation, managers frequently study contribution margins when faced with capacity constraints. Let us focus on a multiple-product company that is operating at capacity. The firm must evaluate which orders to accept and which to reject, and which products to promote and which to drop. The goal is to maximize contribution margin of the entire business, not just of one small facet. A common error in pursuing this goal is that given the resources available, items with the highest contribution margin per sales dollar are considered to be the most attractive.

To illustrate, assume that Beltline Manufacturing produces two models of computer furniture: Deluxe and Regular. The following information has been gathered:

	DELUXE	REGULAR
Selling price	$120	$80
Less variable cost	60	48
Contribution margin	$ 60	$32
Contribution margin ratio (contribution margin ÷ selling price)	50%	40%

DECISION MAKING AND CONTRIBUTION REPORTING   1017

It appears that the firm should concentrate its activity on the Deluxe model. Before we decide for certain, however, let us introduce some additional information. Suppose the furniture is extremely popular, with demand far exceeding the company's production capabilities. Further, it takes four hours to produce a Deluxe model and two hours to manufacture a Regular model. If only 30,000 labor hours are available during the period, Beltline would be better off to focus its efforts on the Regular model because of a higher payoff *per labor hour*.

	DELUXE	REGULAR
Contribution margin per labor hour		
Deluxe: $60 ÷ 4 hours	$15	
Regular: $32 ÷ 2 hours		$16
Available labor hours	30,000	30,000
Contribution margin per labor hour	× $15	× $16
Total contribution margin	$450,000	$480,000

The analysis shows that the Regular model provides the greatest total contribution given the firm's limited manufacturing resources. It should now be apparent that when a company is operating at capacity, management may be in error by emphasizing products or services that provide the greatest contribution per unit or per sales dollar. Stated simply, *contribution margin must be analyzed in terms of factors that limit its generation.*

Limiting factors assume many different forms, depending on the type of business. In heavily automated manufacturing companies, for example, the limiting factor is often the machine hours available for production. In entertainment situations it is the number of seats in a theater or an arena. Finally, in retail operations it is floor space.

ADDITION OR DELETION OF PRODUCTS OR DEPARTMENTS

Decisions to add or delete products, departments, and other major operating units (e.g., stores, plants, or divisions) are critical. Any errors that are made can normally be corrected only after suffering years of financial strife. In-depth analysis is therefore of utmost importance.

When a business unit is eliminated, the unit's sales are lost and there is a savings in variable costs. As a result, if a positive contribution margin is being generated and the unit is discontinued, overall profitability will suffer. One additional factor must be considered, however, and that is the behavior of fixed costs. As we noted earlier in the chapter, a significant change in operations will often influence the amount of fixed costs incurred by an enterprise. If a department or segment is eliminated, some fixed costs can normally be avoided. Those costs that can be avoided are really differential costs and, therefore, relevant to the decision.

To illustrate addition and deletion decisions, we will study the operations of Foodway, Inc., which owns a chain of supermarkets. Each Foodway store has four principal departments: groceries, meat, produce, and hardware. Earnings data for store no. 175 during the past year are shown in Exhibit 26–2. On the basis of the reported $1.1 million loss, management believes that total

	GROCERIES	MEAT	PRODUCE	HARDWARE	TOTAL
Sales	$42,000,000	$14,000,000	$7,000,000	$ 7,000,000	$70,000,000
Less variable costs	33,000,000	9,000,000	4,000,000	6,000,000	52,000,000
Contribution margin	$ 9,000,000	$ 5,000,000	$3,000,000	$ 1,000,000	$18,000,000
Less fixed costs					
Salaries	$ 2,000,000	$ 2,500,000	$1,900,000	$ 1,100,000	$ 7,500,000
Utilities	400,000	50,000	100,000	150,000	700,000
Depreciation	100,000	50,000	100,000	50,000	300,000
General & administrative	4,800,000	1,600,000	800,000	800,000	8,000,000
Total fixed costs	$ 7,300,000	$ 4,200,000	$2,900,000	$ 2,100,000	$16,500,000
Operating income (loss)	$ 1,700,000	$ 800,000	$ 100,000	$(1,100,000)	$ 1,500,000

EXHIBIT 26–2
Foodway, Inc., Store no. 175: Departmental Income Statements

profitability will increase if the hardware department is closed. A closer look at the figures and overall operation is needed, however, prior to any action being taken.

If customers remain loyal and sales in the other departments are not affected by the discontinuance of hardware, Foodway's profit will immediately decline by $1 million because of the loss in contribution margin. Notice, though, that the hardware department has four types of fixed costs: salaries, utilities, depreciation, and general and administrative. Specific information about these costs follows.

1. The salaries represent amounts paid to employees who work in the department. If hardware is dropped, employees who earn 40% of the salary amounts will be shifted to other areas. All other personnel in hardware will be discharged.
2. Utilities expense is allocated to each department on the basis of square feet. Total utilities cost is not expected to change if the hardware operation is closed.
3. Depreciation relates to the building and also to the fixtures used in each department. If hardware is eliminated, the department's display racks and equipment will be utilized by other segments of the firm. Again, total cost is not expected to change.
4. General and administrative charges represent the costs of functions common to all departments, including purchasing, accounting, and personnel. These costs, allocated to each department on the basis of sales, will be reduced by $120,000 because of employee terminations.

In view of this information, the following analysis can be made:

Contribution margin lost if hardware is dropped		$1,000,000
Less savings in fixed costs		
Salaries ($1,100,000 × 0.60)	$660,000	
General & administrative	120,000	780,000
Decrease in total company income		$ 220,000

Although hardware's present bottom line indicates a loss of $1.1 million, it is still beneficial to retain the department. The company will be better off by $220,000.

If desired, the same conclusion could have been reached by evaluating Foodway's earnings with and without the hardware department:

	WITH HARDWARE	WITHOUT HARDWARE
Sales	$70,000,000	$63,000,000
Less variable costs	52,000,000	46,000,000
Contribution margin	$18,000,000	$17,000,000
Less fixed costs		
Salaries	$ 7,500,000	$ 6,840,000
Utilities*	700,000	700,000
Depreciation*	300,000	300,000
General & administrative	8,000,000	7,880,000
Total fixed costs	$16,500,000	$15,720,000
Operating income (loss)	$ 1,500,000	$ 1,280,000

$220,000 difference

*These amounts are irrelevant to the decision and could have been omitted from the analysis.

A FURTHER FOCUS

The approach just shown to evaluate closure of the hardware department can be used in many other decision settings. As a case in point, Boston's Northeastern University recently faced a 28% drop in freshman enrollment. The loss of more than 1,000 students forced administrators into deciding whether to step up recruiting efforts, as so many other colleges and universities have done, or to emerge as a "leaner but meaner" institution. Northeastern chose the latter option by eliminating some majors (including physical education, recreation management, and community health) and combining colleges. Administrators were laid off and faculty size was reduced by 20% through attrition, buyouts, and early retirements. One of the most positive outcomes of this downsizing effort: the university ended its open admission policy and now accepts 71% of its applicants—steps that reduced the number of undergraduates from more than 15,000 to 11,000 and *raised* the average Scholastic Aptitude Test (SAT) scores from 930 to 995. The restructuring improved overall student quality and shows that benefits can result from a carefully executed downsizing plan.

Source: "A Big University Shapes Up by Downsizing," *The Wall Street Journal*, October 10, 1994, pp. B1, B8.

4
Distinguish between direct costs and indirect costs.

IMPROVEMENTS IN PERFORMANCE REPORTING

The departmental income statements prepared for Foodway, Inc., are fairly traditional in scope and format. By a minor rearrangement of the data, it is possible to improve the statements' usefulness in the evaluation of operations.

Before we explain the underlying procedures, it is necessary to revisit (and slightly modify) a cost classification scheme that was discussed in Chapter 21.

Many costs within an organization are easily traced to and associated with a business segment, whereas other costs are not. Amounts that fall in the first category are called **direct costs;** those in the latter classification are **indirect costs.** A business segment normally refers to a responsibility center of the firm, such as a territory, division, department, and so on.

Because a segment can be defined in different ways, a given cost may be direct with respect to certain segments and indirect with respect to others. In the Foodway example, for instance, utilities expense was easily traced to store no. 175. However, it was an entirely different story when the store tried to associate the expense with smaller segments—in this case, departments. Tracing was much more difficult, leading management to adopt cost allocation procedures. Total utilities expense was related to the total square feet in the store, yielding a cost per square foot. Each department was then charged an appropriate amount, based on the area occupied.

Cost Allocations. Companies have adopted a variety of allocation procedures that range from the simple to the complex. The reason normally advanced for such procedures is that indirect costs are incurred to benefit multiple responsibility centers (e.g., departments). As such, each center should absorb its "fair share" of the expenditures.

Although this argument is sound, most accountants recognize that cost allocations have two serious deficiencies. First, as you saw earlier in the text with depreciation, the same cost can be allocated several different ways. At best, then, allocations are arbitrary. A given allocation method is generally viewed as adequate or inadequate by a responsibility center, depending on the amount charged. Large cost allocations are branded as unfair; small cost allocations, in contrast, receive few complaints. Turning to the second deficiency, the total cost to be allocated normally results from the decisions of other managers in the organizational hierarchy. Thus, to a large degree, the amount of cost charged to a center is beyond the center's control.

Contribution Income Statement. It appears that when costs are allocated to business segments, the final income figure does not present a clear picture of the segment's operating results. In recognition of this fact, accountants have developed the **contribution income statement.** This statement provides top management with an understanding of how individual centers affect total firm profitability and serves as a useful tool in performance evaluation and decision making. Consistent with responsibility accounting, the statement incorporates the following features:

> **5** Prepare and use a contribution income statement.

1. The contribution margin is disclosed.
2. Fixed costs directly identifiable with a segment are divided into two classifications: controllable and uncontrollable.
3. Allocations of nontraceable costs are ignored.[5]

To illustrate the contribution income statement, we will study the EXOIL Corporation. EXOIL is divided into two divisions: Refining and Retailing.

---

[5] Although departmental contributions are disclosed, Exhibit 26–2 falls short of being a "true" contribution margin income statement. The upcoming discussion will clarify this point.

Retailing, in turn, has two major product lines: Parts and Fluids. Exhibit 26–3 contains the firm's contribution statements. The top half of the exhibit shows EXOIL's divisional operations; the bottom half displays Retailing's product lines.

The contribution statement begins with a segment's contribution margin, that is, sales minus variable costs. Variable costs are considered to be controllable by (and traceable to) responsibility centers because the costs vary with center activity. The calculation of the contribution margin is helpful not only for performance evaluation but also for cost-volume-profit (CVP) analysis, such as determination of the break-even point.

EXHIBIT 26–3
EXOIL Corporation Contribution Income Statements (in thousands)

	TOTAL COMPANY	DIVISIONS — REFINING	RETAILING
Net sales	$3,000	$2,080	$920
Less variable costs			
Cost of goods sold	$2,000	$1,390	$610
Variable selling & administrative expense	240	85	155
Total variable costs	$2,240	$1,475	$765
Contribution margin	$ 760	$ 605	$155
Less controllable fixed costs	290	225	65
Controllable contribution margin	$ 470	$ 380	$ 90
Less uncontrollable fixed costs	210	168	42
Segment margin	$ 260	$ 212	$ 48
Less nontraceable costs	115		
Operating income	$ 145		

	RETAILING DIVISION	PRODUCT LINES — PARTS	FLUIDS	NON-TRACEABLE COSTS
Net sales	$920	$645	$275	
Less variable costs				
Cost of goods sold	$610	$440	$170	
Variable selling & administrative expense	155	100	55	
Total variable costs	$765	$540	$225	
Contribution margin	$155	$105	$ 50	
Less controllable fixed costs	65	30	10	$ 25
Controllable contribution margin	$ 90	$ 75	$ 40	$(25)
Less uncontrollable fixed costs	42	13	7	22
Segment margin	$ 48	$ 62	$ 33	$(47)

Controllable Contribution Margin. Next, the **controllable contribution margin** is computed by subtracting fixed costs that are both controllable by the segment's management *and* directly traceable to the segment. Such costs are usually discretionary fixed costs (i.e., those that arise from management's decisions) and include certain supervisory salaries, local sales promotion costs, and outlays for research and development activities.

The controllable contribution margin is often considered the heart of the entire statement. This important measure represents the contribution to profit that is under the direction of the responsibility center manager and is probably the best overall indicator of a manager's performance.

Segment Margin. The controllable contribution margin minus uncontrollable fixed costs yields the **segment margin.** The uncontrollable costs used in this calculation are incurred for the benefit of a specific responsibility center but are only minimally affected by the center's management. Typical examples of such costs include committed costs (such as property taxes and depreciation on factory buildings) and costs that result from decisions made at higher levels in the organization (e.g., the salary of the center's manager).

The segment margin shows the contribution of each responsibility center to company income after considering all traceable costs. Many accountants feel the segment margin is a good indicator of ongoing profitability because a center's entire fixed cost obligation is considered in the computation.

Controllable Margin Versus Segment Margin. Students usually see minimal difference between the controllable contribution margin and the segment margin. Actually, these two performance measures serve distinctly different purposes. To explain, outstanding managers are frequently transferred to weak divisions to improve operations. Would you accept such an assignment if the company evaluated personnel and awarded bonuses on the basis of the "bottom line," namely, the segment margin? Probably not. No matter how hard you try, many uncontrollable factors would influence your performance appraisal. In addition, if the division was extremely weak, a heroic effort would be needed to show significant improvement in overall profitability. Thus, two performance measures are utilized. The controllable contribution margin is used for personnel decisions, such as raises and promotions. The segment margin, in contrast, is employed in exploring the long-run advisability of keeping a segment as an operating center of the business.

Nontraceable Costs. As we noted, the contribution approach ignores allocations of indirect costs. By studying the top half of Exhibit 26–3, you will notice that EXOIL incurred $115,000 of nontraceable costs. Also observe that not a single penny was charged against the segment margins of Refining and Retailing via allocations. These costs likely represent corporate administrative overhead incurred by the firm as a whole and not readily identifiable with either division.

In a similar manner, the bottom half of the exhibit reveals that Retailing's divisional manager had control over $65,000 of fixed costs. However, when the division was further segmented by product line, only $40,000 ($30,000 + $10,000) could be traced to Parts and Fluids. The remaining $25,000 related to a management consulting job that focused on a general reorganization of the

VARIABLE AND ABSORPTION COSTING

6 Identify the features of variable costing and absorption costing.

By viewing Exhibit 26–3, you will notice that (1) cost of goods sold is included under the variable cost caption and (2) fixed costs are written off entirely in the current reporting period. This accounting treatment appears to contradict the material introduced in Chapters 20 and 21. Specifically, both variable *and* fixed overhead were included in the cost of a manufactured product and thus reflected in the cost-of-goods-sold calculation.

Over the years, two product costing methods have evolved: absorption costing and variable costing. The more traditional approach (and that illustrated in earlier chapters) is full or absorption costing. Under absorption costing, all manufacturing costs are considered product costs and included in the valuation of inventory.

With an alternate approach known as variable costing, only variable manufacturing costs (direct materials, direct labor, and variable factory overhead) are assigned to products. Fixed manufacturing costs are regarded as period costs and charged against revenues when incurred.

FIXED MANUFACTURING OVERHEAD: THE KEY DIFFERENCE

Observe that the treatment of fixed manufacturing overhead is the basic difference between variable and absorption costing. Companies that employ absorption costing place fixed overhead in inventory on the balance sheet. At the time of sale, product cost (including fixed overhead) is transferred from the balance sheet to the income statement via cost of goods sold. Firms that use variable costing, on the other hand, write off fixed manufacturing overhead immediately. This difference in timing is depicted in Exhibit 26–4.

AN ILLUSTRATION

To illustrate the procedures that accompany these two methods, examine the following information, which was obtained from the records of Harris Corporation for the year ended December 31, 19X4:

Sales: 9,500 units at $9
Selling and administrative costs: fixed, $5,000; variable, $2.20 per unit
Variable production costs per unit:

Direct materials	$1.20
Direct labor	1.30
Variable factory overhead	0.50
Total	$3.00

Fixed factory overhead: $10,000
Production: 10,000 units

EXHIBIT 26-4
Comparison of Absorption Costing and Variable Costing

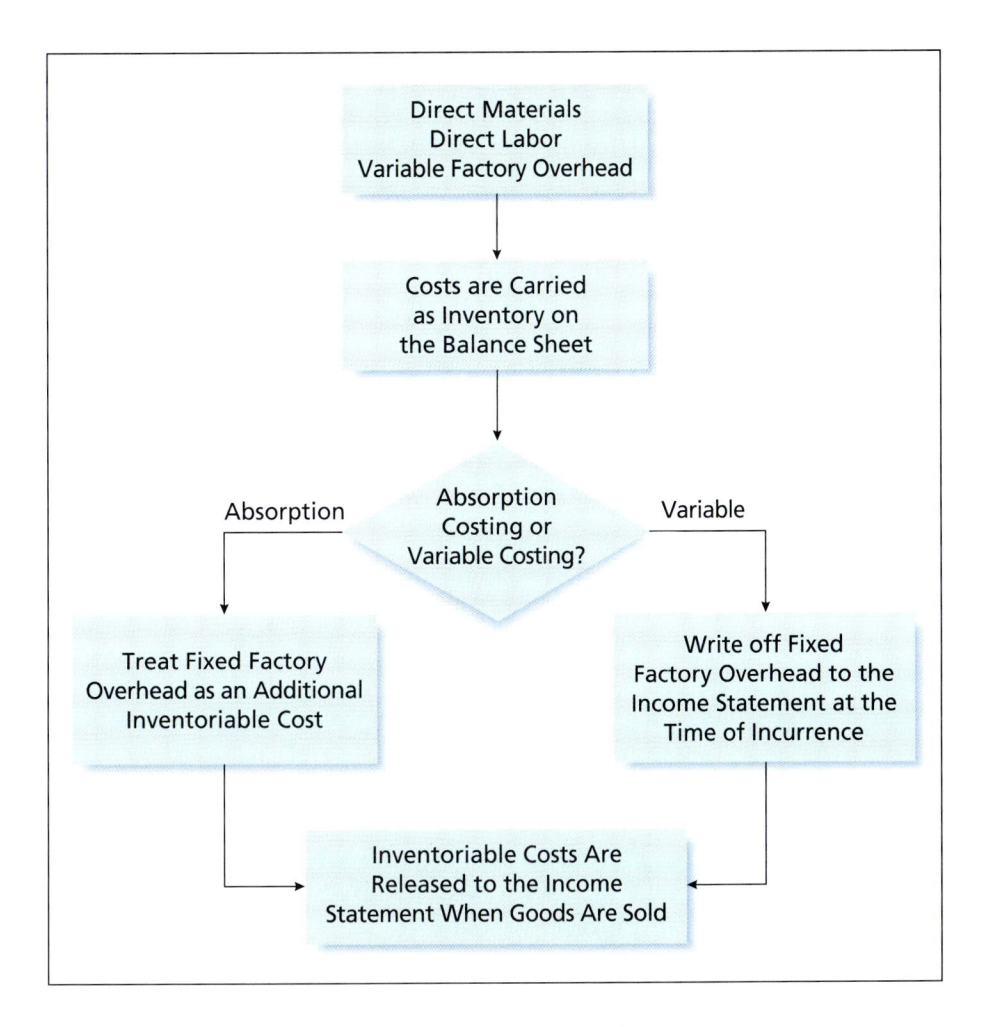

Under absorption costing the unit product cost is $4.00:

Variable production costs	$3.00
Fixed factory overhead ($10,000 ÷ 10,000 units produced)	1.00
Total	$4.00

With variable costing the product cost per unit drops to $3.00, because only variable production costs are inventoried. Remember from previous chapters that selling and administrative costs are never attached to manufactured units. These amounts are treated as expenses of the period.

Given the preceding calculations, the company's income statements under both costing methods appear as shown in Exhibit 26–5. Two important observations should be made. First, notice the similarity between the variable costing income statement and the contribution approach shown earlier in the chapter. Both presentations disclose the contribution margin, followed by the deduction of the period's fixed costs.

Second, observe that a $500 difference arises between the two operating income figures. Although both methods used the same data, keep the differing treatments of fixed manufacturing overhead in mind. Under variable costing, the entire pool of fixed production cost ($10,000) was deducted from current

EXHIBIT 26–5
Absorption Costing and Variable Costing Income Statements

HARRIS CORPORATION
Absorption Costing Income Statement
For the Year Ended December 31, 19X4

Sales (9,500 units × $9)		$85,500
Cost of goods sold (9,500 units × $4)		38,000
Gross profit		$47,500
Less selling & administrative costs		
Fixed	$ 5,000	
Variable (9,500 units × $2.20)	20,900	25,900
Operating income		$21,600

HARRIS CORPORATION
Variable Costing Income Statement
For the Year Ended December 31, 19X4

Sales (9,500 units × $9)		$85,500
Less variable costs		
Cost of goods sold (9,500 units × $3)	$28,500	
Selling & administrative (9,500 units × $2.20)	20,900	49,400
Contribution margin		$36,100
Less fixed costs		
Manufacturing	$10,000	
Selling & administrative	5,000	15,000
Operating income		$21,100

period revenues. With the absorption approach, however, $1 of fixed overhead ($10,000 ÷ 10,000 units manufactured) was attached to each unit produced. Because Harris completed 10,000 units but sold only 9,500, the fixed overhead charges were actually divided as follows:

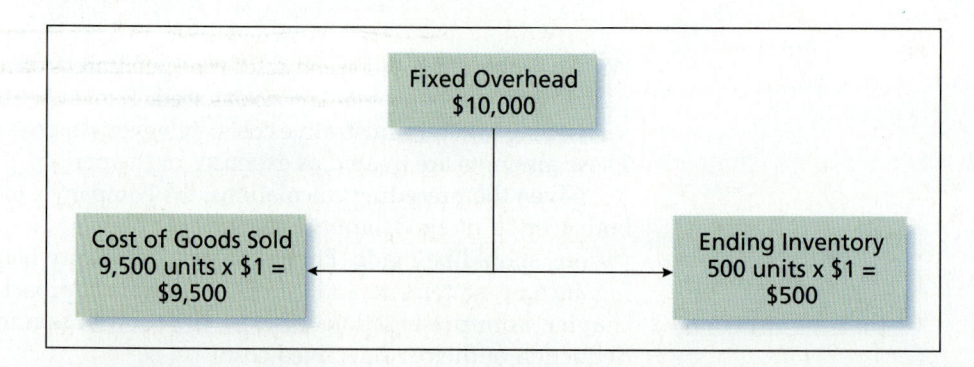

Fixed Overhead $10,000

Cost of Goods Sold
9,500 units × $1 = $9,500

Ending Inventory
500 units × $1 = $500

Cost of goods sold is written off in 19X4 and matched against sales. In contrast, the $500 of fixed overhead in ending inventory is carried as an asset on the balance sheet. The write-off of this latter amount is deferred until such time as the units are sold—probably 19X5. In sum, then, absorption costing would result in a higher income figure than variable costing because of the smaller charge against revenues ($9,500 versus $10,000). The opposite situation would occur in those periods where the number of units sold exceeds the number of units produced.

An Overview of the Two Methods

Companies are free to use either of the preceding methods for internal reporting to management. Variable costing is generally preferred, however, because of its consistency with contribution reporting and the fact that the contribution margin is employed in performance evaluation and decision making—two internal, management functions. Additionally, variable costing usually results in a "cleaner" measure of income than absorption costing, with the bottom line influenced by changes in sales and not by changes in inventory levels.

Despite these attributes, variable costing cannot be used for external financial reporting. The absorption method's approach of inventorying fixed manufacturing costs normally yields a better match on the income statement. At the time of sale, fixed costs are released to the income statement (via cost of goods sold) and matched against the sales revenues that have just been realized. In contrast, variable costing dictates that all fixed production costs be written off at the time of incurrence. This procedure thus ignores the fact that future revenues may result from the expenditure (and the units manufactured).

End-of-Chapter Review

Learning Objectives: The Key Points

1. **Explain the effect of relevant costs and sunk costs on decision making.** Decision making is concerned with the future, as the past is history and cannot be changed. The focus is on relevant costs, or those future costs that differ among alternatives. Sunk costs, which are past costs that have already been incurred, are therefore ignored when reviewing possible options.

2. **Evaluate different types of decision situations (e.g., make or buy).** The evaluation of decisions such as make or buy and the acceptance of special orders requires an identification of relevant costs and qualitative factors. Such costs would normally include variable costs, opportunity costs, and any avoidable fixed costs. Both special orders and addition and deletion decisions focus on the contribution margin, or the amount that a unit contributes toward covering fixed costs and generating income. The unit in this case is an order or perhaps a department.

3. **Explain why the contribution margin must be analyzed in terms of capacity constraints.** When a business is constrained in terms of performing its activities, management should down play the contribution margin per unit of product. Rather, the emphasis should be on those products or activities that generate the highest contribution margin per constraining factor (labor hour, machine hour, square foot, and so forth). By following this strategy, a company will make the most profitable use of its available resources.

4. **Distinguish between direct costs and indirect costs.** The direct and indirect classification scheme deals with traceability. Direct costs are easily traced to a business segment, whereas indirect costs are not. A business segment may be defined in several

different ways; for example, it may be a division, a department, or a product line. In an attempt to charge each segment with a fair share of the costs incurred, management often uses a chargeback procedure and allocates indirect costs to the units in question.

5. **Prepare and use a contribution income statement.** A contribution income statement discloses a segment's contribution toward the overall profit of the firm. All variable and direct fixed costs are charged to the segment where incurred, with the latter costs often categorized in terms of the degree of control exercised by the segment manager. Most important, the contribution statement contains no arbitrary allocations of indirect costs.

   The statement reveals three performance measures: the contribution margin (sales minus variable costs), the controllable contribution margin, and the segment margin. The second measure, calculated by subtracting controllable fixed costs from the contribution margin, focuses on the margin controllable by a manager and is often used in personnel decisions (raises, bonuses, and so forth). The segment margin, a good indicator of long-run profitability, is the result of subtracting a segment's uncontrollable fixed costs from the controllable contribution margin.

6. **Identify the features of variable costing and absorption costing.** These two methods of inventory costing differ in their treatment of fixed factory overhead. Under absorption costing, a specified amount of fixed overhead is attached to each unit produced. In contrast, with variable costing, fixed manufacturing charges are written off to the income statement when incurred. Variable costing is consistent with the contribution income statement and is therefore preferred for internal reporting. For external financial reporting, however, absorption costing must be used.

Key Terms and Concepts: A Quick Overview

absorption costing A method under which all manufacturing costs are assigned to products; used for external financial reporting purposes. (p. 1024)

contribution income statement An income statement that features disclosure of the contribution margin and fixed costs (both controllable and uncontrollable) directly identifiable with a segment. (p. 1021)

controllable contribution margin A performance measure computed by subtracting controllable fixed costs from a segment's contribution margin. (p. 1023)

differential cost A cost that differs among alternatives. (p. 1010)

direct cost Any cost that is easily traced to and associated with a business segment. (p. 1021)

full project approach An evaluation of the total relevant costs associated with decision alternatives. (p. 1010)

incremental approach An evaluation of the net difference in relevant costs associated with decision alternatives. (p. 1010)

indirect cost A cost that is not easily traced to a business segment. (p. 1021)

opportunity cost The cost of a forgone alternative. (p. 1014)

outsourcing The practice of a company to acquire goods and services from outside suppliers rather than produce the same goods and services internally. (p. 1012)

qualitative factors Decision factors that cannot be evaluated in terms of dollars. (p. 1012)

relevant cost A cost that must be considered in decision making because it differs among alternatives. (p. 1009)

segment margin The controllable contribution margin minus uncontrollable fixed costs. (p. 1023)

sunk cost A past cost that is irrelevant for decision making. (p. 1011)

transfer price The price that one division would charge another division on intracompany sales. (p. 1017)

variable costing A method that assigns only variable manufacturing costs (direct materials, direct labor, and variable manufacturing overhead) to products. (p. 1024)

Chapter Quiz

The five questions that follow relate to several issues raised in the chapter. Test your knowledge of the issues by selecting the best answer. (The answers appear on p. 1046.)

1. Which of the following statements is false?
   a. Decision making focuses on future costs.
   b. If a cost is identical for two alternatives under study, the cost can be ignored when making a decision.
   c. Sunk costs are the key to decision making.
   d. Fixed costs can be relevant when making a decision.

2. Martin Company has idle capacity and is studying whether to accept a special order for 1,000 units of its sole product. The product normally sells for $20 and has related variable and fixed manufacturing costs of $12 and $4, respectively. If the special order is accepted at a price of $15 per unit, Martin's overall profitability will:
   a. decrease by $1,000.
   b. increase by $3,000.
   c. increase by $11,000.
   d. increase by $15,000.

3. CEN Manufacturing has limited production time in its heavily automated factory. When determining which products to manufacture, management should study each product's:
   a. contribution margin.
   b. contribution margin ratio.
   c. total cost.
   d. contribution margin per machine hour.

4. Contribution income statements:
   a. disclose a segment's controllable contribution margin and the segment margin.
   b. contain allocations of nontraceable costs.
   c. make no distinction between direct costs and indirect costs.
   d. charge only controllable costs to the segment in question.

5. A company that uses absorption costing procedures:
   a. is in violation of generally accepted accounting principles.
   b. attaches fixed manufacturing overhead to each unit produced.
   c. normally generates the same amount of income as would be calculated by using variable costing.
   d. attaches a selected amount of the firm's total fixed costs (including selling and administrative) to each unit manufactured.

Summary Problem

Prestige of Ohio makes various parts for electric garage door openers. One of the subassemblies for the opener's gearbox has created a number of manufacturing problems, prompting management to obtain bids from an outside supplier. The following information is available:

Variable manufacturing cost per gearbox	$14
Fixed manufacturing overhead	90,000

Units produced are expected to total 20,000. The subassembly can be purchased from Stevenson Electrical for $1.65 per unit. If Prestige decides in favor of Stevenson, variable production costs of each gearbox will fall by 10% and fixed manufacturing overhead will decrease by $8,000.

Instructions

a. Should Prestige make or buy the subassemblies? *Note:* There is one subassembly in each gearbox.
b. Assume that Prestige will continue production of the subassemblies and the fixed manufacturing overhead of $90,000 can be subdivided as follows:

Costs traceable to the gearbox department and controllable by the department manager	$38,000
Costs traceable to the gearbox department and uncontrollable by the department manager	29,000
Costs allocated to the gearbox department	23,000

Determine the amount of fixed manufacturing overhead:
   (1) That would be included in the computation of the gearbox department's segment margin.
   (2) That should be used to evaluate the gearbox manager in a promotion decision.
   (3) That would appear on Prestige's contribution income statement.
c. Disregard part (b) and again assume that Prestige has decided to continue manufacture of the subassemblies. Further assume that in addition to the original data, the company has a $0.50-per-unit variable selling cost and fixed administrative costs that total $70,000. Calculate the inventoriable product cost for each gearbox under (1) variable costing and (2) absorption costing.

Solution

a. Prestige's costs will decrease if the company discontinues production of the subassembly. This decrease therefore represents the cost of manufacturing.

Manufacture		
	Variable: $14 × 0.10 × 20,000 units	$28,000
	Fixed	8,000
	Total	$36,000
Purchase		
	20,000 units × $1.65	$33,000

Prestige will save $3,000 ($36,000 − $33,000) if it buys the subassemblies from Stevenson Electrical.

b. (1) All traceable fixed costs would be included ($38,000 + $29,000 = $67,000).
   (2) Only controllable fixed costs would be used ($38,000).
   (3) The contribution income statement has no cost allocations ($38,000 + $29,000 = $67,000).
c. Selling and administrative costs are not inventoriable, as such amounts are written off as period expenses.
   (1) Variable: $14
   (2) Absorption: $14.00 + $4.50 ($90,000 ÷ 20,000 units) = $18.50

Assignment Material

Questions

Q26–1 Are all future costs relevant for decision-making purposes? Explain.

Q26–2 An educator once commented, "Not all future costs are relevant to decisions, but costs are not relevant unless they occur in the future." Evaluate the educator's comment.

Q26–3 What is meant by the term "sunk cost"?

Q26–4 Should decisions be made "solely on the numbers"? Briefly discuss.

Q26–5 The Crandall Corporation has been offered $34 per unit for a one-time special order. Variable cost and fixed cost per unit amount to $27 and $10, respectively. If Crandall has available facilities, should the order be accepted? Why or why not?

Q26–6 What is a transfer price?

Q26–7 If a retailer has limited square footage in its store, what guideline should be used in deciding which new products to carry?

Q26–8 Differentiate between a direct cost and an indirect cost. As segments become smaller and smaller, what generally happens to cost traceability?

Q26–9 Should a departmental manager be held accountable for allocations of corporate overhead? Briefly discuss.

Q26–10 What features are associated with a contribution margin income statement?

Q26–11 Discuss the computations and meaning associated with the controllable contribution margin and the segment margin.

Q26–12 Differentiate between variable costing and absorption costing.

Q26–13 Creekside, Inc., began business on January 1 of the current year. The company produced 42,000 units but sold only 35,000 by December 31. Would variable costing operating income be greater than absorption costing operating income? Why or why not?

Q26–14 Can variable costing be used for internal reporting? For external financial reporting?

Exercises

E26–1 Relevant decision factors (L.O. 1)

Consider the following:

a. The cost of special electrical wiring, in an equipment acquisition decision.
b. The sales revenues generated with an existing machine, which are not expected to change, in deciding whether to keep or replace the machine.
c. Avoidable fixed manufacturing overhead, in a make or buy decision.
d. The salary cost of a production supervisor who is already on the payroll, in a special order acceptance decision.
e. The direct materials cost, in a make or buy decision.
f. Product development costs incurred several months ago, in a product introduction decision.
g. Alternative uses of your time, in a job acceptance decision.
h. The cost of an old vehicle, in a keep-versus-disposal decision.
i. Fixed corporate overhead, in the acceptance or rejection of a special order.

Evaluate each of the factors listed as being relevant or irrelevant to the decision situation noted. If the factor is irrelevant, briefly explain why.

E26–2 Introductory decision making (L.O. 1)

A university's department of continuing education has agreed to hold a seminar on law office management, targeted to the 3,000 attorneys living within 100 miles of the campus. The department purchased mailing labels from the state bar association ($60 per 500 names), printed brochures ($0.07 each), and incurred postage and handling costs ($0.14 per brochure). One week prior to the course, 19 lawyers had enrolled and submitted their $129 registration fee.

If the seminar is held, the university would be responsible for the discussion leader's fee of $1,250, airfare of $350, hotel and meals of $150, and $50 of miscellaneous costs. There would also be a $100 outlay for coffee and soft drinks for seminar participants. The department's director is thinking about cancelling the course because enrollments are lower than expected. If the cancellation decision is made, the university would have no obligation to the instructor and the registration fees would be returned.

Should the seminar be held? Show calculations to support your answer.

E26–3 Outsourcing decision (L.O. 2)

Amador Hospital is considering a contract with Grossman Catering to handle food service operations. The hospital's current annual costs of providing this service follow.

Food costs	$215,000
Direct labor	70,000
Variable overhead	35,000
Fixed overhead (allocated)	90,000
	$410,000

Grossman plans to use its own facilities to prepare the meals and will charge Amador $6.10 per patient per day. Labor and variable overhead costs are expected to drop by 70%, since certain functions currently performed by hospital staff will be relinquished. Amador is a 200-bed facility that has an average occupancy level of 85%.

a. What is meant by the term "outsourcing"?
b. Should Amador outsource its food service? Why?
c. What qualitative factors should be considered in this decision?

E26–4 Opportunity cost (L.O. 2)

Greg Bishop, 53 years old, currently works as a high school history teacher and earns $40,000 per school year. Salaries for teachers have advanced at the rate of 3% annually.

Greg is thinking about leaving the teaching profession next year and going to graduate school to earn a Master's degree in Business Administration (MBA). He plans to attend a prestigious west coast university as a full-time student. The MBA would take two full years to complete, with annual tuition and living costs of $20,000 and $9,000, respectively. Greg's annual salary upon graduation is anticipated to be $55,000 and would likely rise at 8% per year.

a. What is an opportunity cost?
b. Does an opportunity cost arise during the two years that Greg attends graduate school? Briefly explain.
c. All items considered, what is the total cost of the degree? *Note:* Disregard any earnings after the degree is awarded.

d. What options might Greg consider to reduce the degree's cost?
e. How, if at all, should Greg's age affect his decision to attend graduate school?

E26–5 Special order (L.O. 2)

Hudson River Enterprises manufactures and sells various types of athletic equipment. The company's most recent product-line income statement revealed the following selected information for the Ball Division:

Sales		$1,278,000
Cost of goods sold		
Variable	$432,000	
Fixed	282,000	714,000
Selling & administrative expenses		
Variable	$174,000	
Fixed	210,000	384,000

The figures relate to the production and sale of 60,000 soccer balls.

The National Soccer League (NSL) recently approached Hudson River about purchasing 4,800 balls through a special order. The balls would be of slightly higher quality than Hudson River is currently manufacturing, requiring an increase in direct material cost of $1.20 per ball. No variable selling and administrative costs will be incurred on this order, and fixed costs will continue at current levels. NSL is willing to buy the balls at $14.50 each.

a. Will Hudson River's operating income increase or decrease if the special order is accepted? By how much?
b. Suppose you are given the additional information that the company's manufacturing capacity for soccer balls is 60,000 balls per year. If Hudson River's forecasts indicate a continuation of present sales trends, should the special order be accepted? Why or why not?

E26–6 Analysis of a special order (L.O. 2)

William Row builds custom homes that range in price from $125,000 to $300,000. The price of a home is determined by summing the estimated costs of materials, labor, and overhead, and then adding 15% for a profit margin. As an example, a home designed for Mr. and Mrs. David Presley was priced as follows:

Materials	$ 70,000
Labor	100,000
Overhead (20% of labor)	20,000
	$190,000
Profit—15%	28,500
Selling price	$218,500

Total overhead for the year has been estimated at $200,000, of which $120,000 is fixed and the remainder is variable in direct proportion to labor.

Business is currently very slow. The Presleys, feeling that the $218,500 price was too high, countered with an offer of $205,000.

a. Determine the contribution margin on the home if Row accepted the Presleys' offer of $205,000.
b. What is the minimum price that Row could have quoted without reducing or increasing his firm's operating income?

E26–7 Transfer pricing (L.O. 2)

You are the vice-president of a T-shirt manufacturer that sells its entire output to an affiliated company. The affiliated company applies heat-sensitive decals and then distributes the shirts worldwide. Currently, the goods are transferred at $6, which covers variable costs and fixed costs and produces a very small profit margin.

The affiliated company has stated repeatedly that quality is sub-standard and better shirts are available on the open market for $5.20. Management is thus arguing for a reduction in the current transfer price "to meet competition."

a. If we focus *solely* on the affiliated company's performance, should the shirts be transferred internally for $6 or purchased externally for $5.20? Briefly explain.
b. Is it possible that, collectively, the two firms would be better off if the transfers continue at $6? Why or why not?
c. How are transfer pricing disputes often resolved?

E26–8 Capacity constraint (L.O. 3)

Bayshore Enterprises manufactures three products known as X, Y, and Z. Pertinent data about the products follow.

	X	Y	Z
Selling price	$50	$48	$80
Less variable costs			
Direct materials	$ 2	$24	$30
Direct labor	24	9	30
Variable factory overhead	8	3	10
Total	$34	$36	$70
Contribution margin	$16	$12	$10

Direct laborers are paid $12 per hour. The demand for these products is very strong; unfortunately, Bayshore has experienced a severe shortage of qualified workers. As a result, the company's labor force is working close to capacity, and only 2,000 hours of labor time are available in the upcoming accounting period.

a. Determine the amount of labor time needed to manufacture a single unit of X, Y, and Z.
b. Does Bayshore face any constraints that limit the amount of contribution margin it can generate? If so, what strategy should the company follow when deciding which product to manufacture?
c. Determine which product should be selected for manufacture in the upcoming accounting period.

E26–9 Dropping an unprofitable store (L.O. 2)

Delmac, Inc., operates 35 pizza carry-outs in Ohio. The information at the top of the following page pertains to Akron's Bower Street carry-out for the year just ended. Management wants to close the operation because of the loss and would terminate all equipment and building leases. The manager (annual salary, $22,500) would be transferred to the nearby Fairlawn facility; other employees would be discharged.

Should the Bower Street carry-out be closed? Why or why not?

Sales		$165,000
Cost of food & beverages		59,000
Gross profit		$106,000
Less operating expenses		
Equipment & building leases	$26,700	
Wages	73,400	
Utilities	4,800	
Pizza boxes, cups, supplies	6,800	
Share of allocated corporate overhead (e.g., executive salaries, etc.)	8,700	120,400
Operating income (loss)		$ (14,400)

E26–10 Overview of decision making (L.O. 1, 2)

Evaluate the comments that follow as being True or False. If the comment is false, briefly explain why.

a. Decisions should be based solely on quantitative factors.
b. Unavoidable fixed costs can be ignored in decision making.
c. The cost of obsolete inventory can be disregarded when deciding whether to keep or dispose of the goods.
d. If Dixon Company stops the production of a particular item, it can lease currently-used factory space to another firm. The lease revenue is properly viewed as an opportunity cost should Dixon continue its manufacturing activities.
e. Special orders are frequently accepted even though an order's selling price may be less than the sum of direct material, direct labor, variable factory overhead, and fixed factory overhead charges.

E26–11 Controllable costs (L.O. 4, 5)

Yesterday, Inc., operates 33 stores that sell pre-owned, funky clothes, primarily to college students. Consider the following costs of the store located in Madison, Wisconsin:

1. Sales commissions paid to salespersons.
2. Salary of Madison's store manager.
3. Cost of goods sold.
4. Allocated corporate overhead.
5. Store rent (fixed); negotiated by the corporate office.

a. Which of these costs would be considered in computing Madison's controllable contribution margin? Madison's segment margin?
b. Which of these costs would be considered in computing Yesterday's operating income?

E26–12 Contribution margin income statement (L.O. 5)

The following information pertains to the Fairfax Division of Santa Monica Industries:

Net sales	$2,200,000
Controllable fixed costs traceable to the division	640,000
Allocated corporate overhead	150,000
Variable costs	
Cost of goods sold	510,000
Selling & administrative	440,000
Uncontrollable fixed costs traceable to the division	190,000

a. Compute the Fairfax Division's:
   (1) Contribution margin.
   (2) Controllable contribution margin.
   (3) Segment margin.
b. Which of the preceding measures (contribution margin, controllable contribution margin, or segment margin) should be used when making long-term decisions about divisional operations?
c. Which of the preceding measures should be used in pay-raise decisions for divisional managers?

E26–13 Variable and absorption inventory costing (L.O. 6)

Milsap Industries began business on January 1 of the current year, manufacturing and selling a single product. Consider the data that follow.

	UNITS	VARIABLE COST PER UNIT	FIXED COSTS
Production volume	80,000		
Sales volume	72,000		
Direct materials		$1.30	
Direct labor		2.80	
Factory overhead		4.40	$540,000
Selling expenses		0.20	180,000

a. Compute the cost of the company's ending inventory by using variable costing.
b. Compute the cost of the company's ending inventory by using absorption costing.
c. Suppose that Milsap's accountant had accidentally excluded straight-line depreciation on machinery from the data presented. Determine the effect of this error (overstate, understate, or no impact) on the company's:
   (1) Variable costing ending inventory.
   (2) Absorption costing ending inventory.

E26–14 Variable and absorption income computations (L.O. 6)

Diablo Systems manufactures a specialized video adapter that has a selling price of $79. During 19X6, the first year of sale, production and sales totaled 40,000 units and 37,000 units, respectively. The following information has been gathered from the accounting records:

Variable costs per unit
   Manufacturing: $18
   Selling & administrative: $22

Fixed costs
   Manufacturing: $1,200,000
   Selling & administrative: $207,200

a. Compute 19X6 operating income by using variable costing.
b. Compute 19X6 operating income by using absorption costing.

PROBLEMS

Series A

P26–A1 Make or buy (L.O. 2)

Anchor Manufacturing produces a full line of workshop tools. One of the company's products, a flat-head screwdriver, has a unit manufacturing cost of $6.85, computed as follows:

Direct materials	$2.40
Direct labor	0.90
Variable factory overhead	1.70
Fixed factory overhead	1.85*
Total	$6.85

* Consists of factory supervision ($0.60), equipment depreciation ($0.20), and "other" fixed charges ($1.05).

All fixed manufacturing costs are computed by using a projected volume of 120,000 units per year.

Anchor's management has been informed that a machine used in the production of screwdriver handles must soon be replaced—an expenditure that will increase annual straight-line depreciation by $50,400. To avoid the acquisition at this time, management has gathered the following information concerning an outside purchase of handles:

1. Injection Plastics will supply Anchor in lots of 30,000 units for $54,000. Anchor must pay freight, which should amount to $300 per shipment.
2. The current unit costs for direct materials, direct labor, and variable factory overhead will drop by 30%, 20%, and 20%, respectively.
3. Factory supervision and "other" fixed charges are not expected to change.
4. By dismantling handle production, Anchor will have added space and will be able to vacate rented storage facilities that cost $6,000 per year.

Instructions

a. Should Anchor make or buy the plastic handles? On an annual basis, how much will the company save with the preferred alternative?
b. The $6,000 rental charge could logically be called an opportunity cost. Explain the meaning of an opportunity cost and how the $6,000 charge qualifies.
c. List several reservations that Anchor might have about dealing with an outside supplier such as Injection Plastics.

P26–A2 Special order and pricing policy (L.O. 2)

Regal Company makes several products that are used in the home. Revenues and costs of the Portable Vacuum System follow.

Sales		$290,000
Less:		
Direct materials used	$88,000	
Direct labor	80,000	
Total factory overhead	56,000	
Sales commissions, 10%	29,000	
Allocated administrative expense	15,500	268,500
Operating income		$ 21,500

The figures shown are for the production and sale of 5,000 units. Factory overhead is applied on the basis of direct labor cost.

The Brower Corporation, which advertises heavily on television, has submitted an offer to purchase 2,200 vacuums at $51 each. Brower will market the product under its own brand name, and Regal's normal sales are not expected to suffer. Regal's president feels that the offer should be rejected because the price is below the current unit cost of $53.70 ($268,500 ÷ 5,000 units). An in-depth study revealed the following information:

1. Brower's units will require overtime at time and one-half the regular wage rate. *Note:* The overtime premium will be accounted for as direct labor.
2. Fixed factory overhead is applied by using a rate of 42% of direct labor cost.
3. No sales commissions will be paid on these units.
4. Administrative expenses are allocated to product lines on the basis of sales dollars. Because of the special order, an additional $13,600 will be charged to the vacuum line. Regal's total administrative costs will remain the same, however.

Instructions

Should Regal reject Brower's offer? Why or why not?

P26–A3 New product introduction (L.O. 1, 2)

The FHR Corporation is engaged in the manufacture of communications equipment. During the past 18 months, two new products have been developed: a voice module and a decoder unit.

FHR recently conducted market surveys for the voice module and the decoder at a cost of $42,000 each. Although the surveys indicate that both products could be introduced at this time, the firm has encountered difficulty in obtaining the required electronic components. Thus, only one product will be manufactured. FHR's accounting department has gathered the information that follows.

	VOICE MODULE	DECODER UNIT
Development costs over the past 18 months	$115,000	$135,000
Production costs per unit		
Direct materials	$22.50	$27.80
Direct labor	$15.00	$20.00
Variable overhead	$18.00	$24.00
Sales commissions (expressed as a percentage of sales)	10%	5%
Selling price	$85	$95
Projected sales (units)	35,000	41,000
Projected advertising	$25,000	$30,000

Instructions

a. List those costs that are irrelevant to the product introduction decision and explain why each is irrelevant.
b. Compute the contribution margin per unit for each product.
c. Which of the two products should be introduced at this time? Why?

P26–A4 Dropping an unprofitable program (L.O. 2)

Randolph College is noted for its prestigious faculty and small class sizes. Because of recent financial problems, the college is evaluating the classics program, which offers instruction in Latin and Ancient Greek. Randolph's office of business affairs has gathered the following information for the just-concluded academic year, figures that are typical of recent years' activities.

Tuition revenues earned		$280,000
Less costs of operation:		
Faculty salaries	$220,000	
Supplies	5,000	
Other fixed costs	145,000	370,000
Operating income (loss)		$(90,000)

Additional data follow.

1. If the program is dropped:
   - Overall college enrollment will decline, as students would transfer to other universities. Lost tuition revenue is estimated at $220,000.
   - Faculty members with combined salaries of $150,000 are untenured and would be terminated. The tenured faculty would retool and be transferred to the modern languages department.
   - Supplies cost will be reduced by $4,000.
   - Other fixed costs include $48,000 of salaries earned by office personnel. One of these employees (annual salary = $17,000) will be transferred to the pharmacy school; other employees would be laid off. The $145,000 total includes $97,000 of general college overhead costs that are allocated to the department.
   - Equipment will be removed and transferred to the school of music at a cost of $800.
   - The vacated space could be converted to a weight and physical conditioning facility for varsity athletes. This new facility would likely help attract better athletes and make the college's varsity programs more competitive.
2. The director of development reports that Hildagaard Olsen, an alumnus and supporter of the classics program and now sole owner of the highly successful Olsen Electronics Corporation, has designated the college as a major beneficiary of her estate.

Instructions

a. From a financial perspective, should the classics program be dropped? Show computations to support your answer.
b. What other factors should be considered if the program is dropped?
c. What options might be open to Randolph if the program is continued and the college's president mandates that "program losses must be eliminated within three years."
d. Other than allocated overhead charges, do tuition revenues cover the costs of the classics program?

P26–A5 Contribution income statement: Preparation and analysis (L.O. 4, 5)

Harold Brandt, president of Brandt Distributing, has just finished a review of the current year's operations. He noted, "These results look great. I was expecting overall performance to suffer, given the problems we've had with the Urbana Division. However, I believe we're now on sound footing and have few financial problems."

Harold's comments were based on the following figures, which were compiled by a new employee. The employee summarized data that relate to the firm's three divisions—Barrington, Springfield, and Urbana—for the year ended December 31, 19XX.

Net sales		$994,000
Less: Cost of goods sold	$632,000	
Sales commissions	49,700	
Salaries	130,000	
Advertising	80,000	
Other	75,000	966,700
Operating income		$ 27,300

Supplementary records revealed the following information:

1. Sales: Barrington, 29,000 units at $10; Springfield, 34,000 units at $8; and Urbana, 48,000 units at $9.
2. Each division purchases units from various manufacturers. The prices paid per unit were as follows: Barrington, $6; Springfield, $5; Urbana, $6.
3. Each division pays a 5% commission to its sales force. In addition, the Urbana Division employs a sales manager who earns $30,000 per year. The sales manager's salary is set by Urbana's divisional manager. Other salaries for executives are established by Brandt and subdivided as follows:

Barrington	$ 25,000
Springfield	40,000
Urbana	35,000
Total	$100,000

4. Advertising is handled by divisional managers. The following costs were incurred: Barrington, $10,000; Springfield, $20,000; and Urbana, $50,000.
5. Other costs of $75,000 consisted of the following:
   Uncontrollable costs traceable to the divisions: Barrington, $8,000; Springfield, $6,000; and Urbana, $27,000.
   General corporate overhead: $34,000.

Instructions

a. Give Brandt more insight about operations by preparing a contribution income statement for the three divisions. Are things going as well as he believes or could operations be improved? Explain.
b. If any of the divisions have a negative segment margin, present an analysis of the probable causes of poor performance.

P26–A6 Variable and absorption costing (L.O. 6)

The following information pertains to Turbo Enterprises for the year ended December 31, 19X8:

Variable cost per unit:	
Direct materials	$ 6
Direct labor	4
Factory overhead	9
Selling & administrative expense	3
Total	$22
Annual fixed costs:	
Factory overhead	$600,000
Selling & administrative expense	115,000
Total	$715,000
Other data (units):	
Sales	21,000
Production	25,000
Inventory, 12/31/X8	11,000

The unit selling price is $62. Assume that costs have been stable in recent years.

Instructions

a. Compute the number of units in the beginning inventory on January 1, 19X8.
b. Calculate the cost of the December 31 inventory assuming use of:
   (1) Variable costing.
   (2) Absorption costing.
c. Prepare an income statement for the year ended December 31, 19X8, by using variable costing.
d. Prepare an income statement for the year ended December 31, 19X8, by using absorption costing.

Series B

P26–B1   Make or buy (L.O. 2)

Westlake, Inc., manufactures a full line of small home appliances. The manufactured cost of one of the company's products, a toaster oven, follows.

Direct materials	$ 5.60
Direct labor	9.00
Total factory overhead	13.50
Total	$28.10

Fixed overhead generally averages 70% of the total overhead charge.

Westlake is currently producing all of the toaster oven's components. One of the components, part no. XY368, has created a number of manufacturing problems. The company is therefore considering an outside supplier. A supplier has agreed to provide XY368s in lots of 20,000 for $84,000. If Westlake accepts the supplier's offer, it is estimated that the oven's direct labor and variable overhead cost will decline by 20%. In addition, direct material cost should fall by approximately 10%.

Instructions

a. Should Westlake make or buy the component? Show computations to support your answer. *Note:* Each oven uses one of the XY368 components.
b. Assume that Westlake can manufacture and sell 60,000 toaster ovens per year. To eliminate the production problems, top management has proposed transferring Phil Hartley from the company's microwave division to oversee manufacturing. Hartley is currently earning an annual salary of $43,000. In addition, new equipment would be leased at a cost of $3,100 per month. If both of these actions take place, should Westlake make or buy the component? Show computations to support your answer.
c. List several qualitative factors that Westlake should consider in deciding whether to make or buy the component.

P26–B2   Special order and pricing policy (L.O. 2)

Hunter Corporation manufactures a variety of novelty items. Because of a weak economy, production and sales in the company's Leather Division are at an all-time low. The division's income statement revealed the following selected data:

Sales	$2,250,000
Fixed manufacturing & selling costs	420,000
Variable manufacturing & selling costs	70% of sales

Production and sales totaled 300,000 units.

An importer located in Sweden has approached Hunter about a special order arrangement. The importer would like to buy 25,000 leather key cases, the division's sole product, at $6.20 each. Although Hunter's normal 5% sales commission would not be paid on these units, several additional costs will be incurred:

1. Hunter must pay shipping charges and transfer taxes of $0.75 per case.
2. A special machine must be acquired to imprint the Swedish firm's logo. The machine will cost $6,000 and be of no use to Hunter once the order is completed. Materials, labor, and overhead costs will rise by $0.10 per case because of the related manufacturing operations.

Instructions

a. Management says that the order should be rejected because "it is a loser, especially when the current fixed cost per unit is considered." Show computations that support management's claim.
b. Should the order be accepted? Why or why not?

P26–B3 New product introduction (L.O. 1, 2)

BodyShapes, Inc., is planning to introduce a stomach flattening device to the marketplace. Detailed financial information on two different models follows.

	MODEL NO. 1	MODEL NO. 2
Selling price*	$81.00	$93.00
Costs		
Direct materials	$21.00	$27.00
Direct labor	10.00	12.00
Variable overhead	13.00	16.25
Fixed overhead	12.00	15.00
Variable handling costs	9.60	8.40

* Payable in three equal installments.

Both models have been under development during the past two years, with BodyShapes having invested $85,000 in model no. 1 and $106,000 in model no. 2. The company feels that an aggressive, $50,000 promotional campaign will allow it to capture a sizable share of the 24,000-unit market for this product. Anticipated market share percentages are: model no. 1, 55%; model no. 2, 45%. Unfortunately, limited resources allow BodyShapes to introduce only one new model at this time.

Instructions

a. List those costs that are irrelevant to the product introduction decision and explain why each is irrelevant.
b. Compute the contribution margin per unit for each model.
c. Which of the two models should be introduced at this time? Why?

P26–B4 Dropping an unprofitable segment (L.O. 2)

The Weekend Warrior sells running shoes, tennis shoes, and athletic apparel at a store on State Street. Product-line information for the year just ended follows.

	SALES	VARIABLE COSTS	FIXED COSTS	OPERATING INCOME (LOSS)
Running shoes	$120,000	$ 66,000	$28,000	$ 26,000
Tennis shoes	80,000	56,000	34,000	(10,000)
Athletic wear	250,000	150,000	64,000	36,000

Management is studying whether to drop tennis shoes because of the $10,000 loss. If the line is dropped, the following results are anticipated:

1. Fixed costs associated with tennis shoes will decrease by $7,000. All other fixed costs will continue to be incurred.
2. The space vacated by tennis shoes will be remodeled at a cost of $5,500. (This amount is considered immaterial and will be expensed when incurred.)
3. A vastly expanded line of running shoes will be offered for sale, especially lower-cost models. Sales of running shoes are expected to increase by $30,000, but the product line's contribution margin ratio (contribution margin ÷ sales) will fall by seven full percentage points.
4. Customers who shopped for tennis shoes often purchased athletic wear. Sales of athletic wear are anticipated to fall by 15%.

Instructions

a. Determine if tennis shoes should be dropped.
b. Suppose that management has decided to keep the tennis shoe line and run a promotional campaign. If the campaign will result in a fixed cost increase of $5,000, calculate:
   (1) The additional contribution margin that must be generated to achieve a break-even operation with the tennis shoe line.
   (2) The additional sales that must be generated to achieve a break-even operation with the tennis shoe line.

P26–B5 Contribution income statement: Preparation and analysis (L.O. 4, 5)
Marsha Warren, president of Warren Distributors, has just finished her review of the current year's operations. She noted, "We've been lucky. Given the state of the economy, I'm really pleased with these results. A 3% return on sales will probably beat the competition."

Marsha's comments were based on the following figures, which were compiled by a new employee. The employee summarized data that pertain to the company's three product lines—X, Y, and Z—for the year ended December 31, 19XX.

Net sales		$690,000
Less: Cost of goods sold	$444,000	
Sales commissions	63,300	
Local advertising	60,000	
Sales salaries	30,000	
Other	72,000	669,300
Operating income		$ 20,700

Supplementary records revealed the following information:

1. Sales: X, 60,000 units at $5.00; Y, 70,000 units at $3.00; and Z, 40,000 units at $4.50.
2. Warren purchases units from various manufacturers. The prices paid per unit were as follows: X, $3.00; Y, $2.20; Z, $2.75.
3. Sales personnel of X and Z are paid on a commission basis. Commissions total 10% and 15% of each product's respective gross sales. Sales of Y are handled by one salesperson who receives a 3% commission plus a $30,000 salary. The salary is set by Y's management.
4. Local advertising is handled by product-line managers. Advertising costs for the product lines were: X, $25,000; Y, $20,000; Z, $15,000.

5. Other costs of $72,000 are subdivided as follows:
    Uncontrollable costs traceable to product lines: X, $20,000; Y, $16,000; and Z, $12,000.
    Administrative overhead not traceable to product lines: $24,000.

Instructions

a. Give Warren more insight about operations by preparing a contribution income statement for the three product lines. Are things going as well as she believes or could operations be improved? Explain.
b. If any of the product lines have a negative segment margin, present an analysis of the probable causes of poor performance.

P26–B6 Variable and absorption costing (L.O. 6)

The information that follows pertains to Consumer Products for the year ended December 31, 19X6.

Inventory, 1/1/X6	24,000 units
Units manufactured	80,000
Units sold	82,000
Inventory, 12/31/X6	? units
Manufacturing costs	
Direct materials	$3 per unit
Direct labor	$5 per unit
Variable factory overhead	$9 per unit
Fixed factory overhead	$280,000
Selling & administrative expenses	
Variable	$2 per unit
Fixed	$136,000

The unit selling price is $26. Assume that costs have been stable in recent years.

Instructions

a. Compute the number of units in the ending inventory.
b. Calculate the cost of a unit assuming use of:
   (1) Variable costing.
   (2) Absorption costing.
c. Prepare an income statement for the year ended December 31, 19X6, by using variable costing.
d. Prepare an income statement for the year ended December 31, 19X6, by using absorption costing.

EXPANDING YOUR HORIZONS

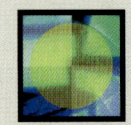

EYH26–1 Relevant costs (L.O. 1)

Having worked hard all semester or quarter, assume that you are more than ready for a lengthy vacation. Given the generosity of a wealthy relative, you have narrowed the choices to four-week stays in either Paris or Sydney. Your relative has requested a listing of the relevant costs associated with each city and prefers to select the least expensive destination.

Instructions

Prepare a schedule of all relevant costs for the trips to Paris and Sydney, including any appropriate opportunity costs. You may want to consult the Sunday travel section of a major metropolitan newspaper or a travel agent to get airfare and hotel room rates. Submit your findings in a one-page report.

EYH26–2 Lease or buy alternatives (L.O. 1, 2)

Recent years have seen an increased interest in leasing when it comes to new cars. Many customers, manufacturers, and dealers find the leasing alternative preferable to an outright purchase, especially when prices are high and demand is sluggish.

Instructions

Form a team with three other students in your class and visit a local automobile dealership. Talk to a salesperson about the benefits and costs of leasing. Obtain dollar amounts and then prepare a listing of the relevant costs of both buying and leasing a new automobile. Be sure to incorporate the nonfinancial (i.e., qualitative) aspects of the decision as well. Summarize your findings in a one-page report.

EYH26–3 Price determination (L.O. 2)

Determining the prices of goods and services is a very difficult process. Underlying factors to consider often include a company's costs, competition, and what the customer is willing to pay.

Instructions

Form a team with three other students in your class and visit the managers or sales managers of three distinctly different businesses. Ideally, the businesses should operate in different competitive environments. Determine how relevant the three preceding factors are in price-setting decisions for the company, along with each manager's favorite "war story." What approach does each manager use when the good or service is new or unique, and the manager has minimal knowledge/experience on which to base a decision? Be prepared to report your findings to the class.

EYH26–4 Analysis of costs; decision making* (L.O. 2)

Avalon, Inc., is a developer of hotels in Hawaii and other resort locations. The company is studying construction of a new facility on the island of El Reno, and two alternatives are under consideration:

- *Alternative A*—Build a "commercial class" hotel similar to Holiday Inn or Ramada, with an average room area of 550 square feet (including public spaces). There would be minimal meeting and banquet facilities.
- *Alternative B*—Build an "executive class" hotel similar to a Hyatt or a Hilton. The average room size would be 700 square feet; ample meeting and banquet facilities would be available for conventions, conferences, and so forth.

Avalon's accounting department has generated the following data:

> Land cost: $30 per square foot of floor area
> Construction cost: $105 per square foot
> Real estate taxes, interest, and other overhead during construction: 30% of land and construction costs

Per-room outlays for furnishings and equipment, supplies, and opening advertising and marketing costs are estimated as follows:

---

* This problem is adapted from "Room at the Top," *Forbes*, March 12, 1984, pp. 58, 59, 61.

	COMMERCIAL	EXECUTIVE
Furnishings and equipment	$8,000	$12,500
Supplies	1,000	2,000
Advertising and marketing	2,000	4,000

The accounting department recommends adding 10% to the total of all preceding costs to allow for contingencies and estimation errors. Construction is expected to take two years.

Avalon sets a room rental rate equal to $1 per $1,000 of cost. Upon completion, the going rates for similar rooms are anticipated to be: commercial, $109 per day; executive, $170.

Instructions

a. Compute the cost per room of building a commercial class hotel and an executive class hotel.
b. Consider all information presented and determine the type of hotel that Avalon should construct. What factors should be evaluated in reaching the proper decision?

COMMUNICATION OF ACCOUNTING INFORMATION

CAI26–1 The flowchart as a communication tool (L.O. 2)
Communication Principle: Businesses often use a variety of charts and graphs to convey information. A flowchart, for example, such as that shown in Exhibit 26–4, is frequently employed to simplify a sequential process. Various thoughts and/or processes are indicated by rectangular boxes, and decisions that must be made are depicted with diamonds. Finally, the arrows signify the sequence of events.

If you have ever studied computer programming or systems design, you probably know that flowcharts can display various degrees of sophistication. Some contain a vast assortment of symbols and connectors; others do not. The flowchart in Exhibit 26–4 is very basic in comparison with those encountered in practice. Nevertheless, it is still an effective tool—one that assists in the communication of a complex operation for better understanding of the task at hand.

■ ■ ■ ■ ■ ■ ■ ■ ■

The management team at Gopher Company routinely rejects special orders. Carolyn Tsay, a staff accountant, is very concerned that profitable opportunities are being lost and has communicated this fact to her supervisor. The supervisor has arranged a special meeting with top management for Carolyn to explain her observations.

Instructions

Assume the role of Carolyn Tsay. In contemplation of the meeting, prepare a flowchart of the financial logic that should be used in evaluating whether a special order should be accepted or rejected. Given the nature of the situation (i.e., a presentation to top management), the flowchart's final draft should be polished and impressive.

Answers to Chapter Quiz

1. c
2. b [Each unit has a $3 contribution margin ($15 − $12); thus, 1,000 units × $3 = $3,000]
3. d
4. a
5. b

27 CAPITAL BUDGETING

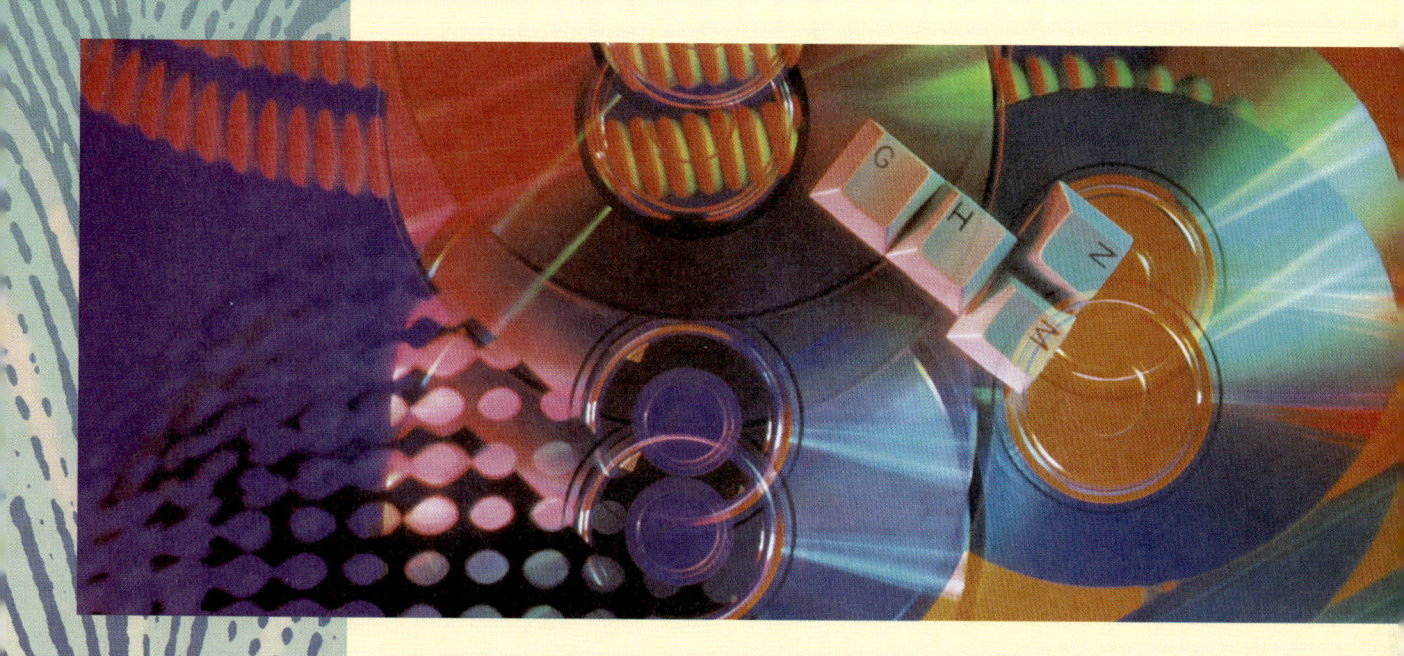

LEARNING OBJECTIVES

After studying this chapter, you should be able to:

1. Explain the nature of capital budgeting and identify the factors to consider in capital expenditure proposals.
2. Explain the concept of the time value of money.
3. Distinguish between compound interest and present value.
4. Use net present value, the internal rate of return, payback, and the accounting rate of return to evaluate long-term projects.
5. (Appendix) Demonstrate how income taxes affect cash flow calculations.

Ask most business owners and they will typically say that they're in it for the long haul. In other words, one does not begin a business by focusing totally on the near term. Most companies lose money or, at best, are marginally profitable during the first few years of operation. It takes time to establish a reputation and build a loyal customer base.

These observations struck a note with George Faris, founder of Banner Advertising. He commented, "We created Banner by making a long-term commitment of both time and resources. I therefore find this chapter's discussion very informative; it focuses on a variety of evaluation tools that we use before 'signing on the bottom line' and jumping blindly into business deals. Given the nature of our operation, the business ventures that we pursue must make economic sense—not only now but also for the foreseeable future."

George was referring to the firm's capital investment decisions, where Banner enters a land purchase or lease agreement and then proceeds through the various steps of constructing a billboard. To do this intelligently, George must consider (i.e., budget) all up-front capital costs and compare these amounts to the "value" of the expected future dollar returns. He went on to say, "Determining these future returns is tough enough, but valuing them is even more difficult. Receiving $12,000 immediately is obviously more advantageous to the company than receiving $12,000 three years down the road. Somehow we've got to take (and do take) these timing differences into account."

Banner Advertising is not alone; many businesses are actively involved in making long-term investments. As a typical example of corporate America's "building for the future," we present the following excerpt from a recent annual report of General Electric:

GE's total expenditures for new plant and equipment during [the year] were $1.6 billion.... Total expenditures for the past five years were $9.4 billion, of which 25% was to increase capacity; 24% was to increase productivity; 12% was to replace and renew older equipment; 12% was to support new business start-ups; and 27% was for such other purposes as to improve research and development facilities and to provide for safety and environmental protection.

Most executives will agree that a company's long-term investments often spell the difference between financial prosperity or lengthy periods of unprofitable performance. Investments such as those cited by General Electric are costly and require the commitment of resources for many years. As a result, poor decisions are usually very difficult to reverse.

This chapter looks at the evaluation of programs and projects that influence the financial performance of multiple accounting periods. Outlays for such undertakings are commonly called *capital expenditures;* the related planning and decision making is appropriately labeled **capital budgeting.**

A Further Focus

Capital budgeting techniques may be used with a variety of long-term investments. Although most textbook illustrations focus on machinery and equipment, the sky's the limit when it comes to these profitable undertakings. As examples, Kimberly-Clark, Johnson & Johnson, and PepsiCo have invested significant sums in wellness programs and centers that integrate exercise and education for employees. In contrast, an oilman named Jerry Jones risked $97 million of his own cash in 1989 to buy a stadium lease and the National Football League's Dallas Cowboys, a team that had lost $10 million in the previous year. He now owns a business that has more than doubled in value and whose financial performance has been characterized by another owner as being "far out of any realm of any other team." Finally, we cite the case of Barcelona, Spain, which invested close to $8 billion in getting the city ready to host the 25th Summer Olympics. Not only were sporting facilities built, but the city also constructed a new airport, freeways, apartments, and a communications infrastructure.

Sources: See "Fitness Programs: Hefty Expense or Wise Investment?" *Management Accounting*, January 1989, pp. 45–50; "A Gem of An Investment," *The Dallas Morning News*, January 30, 1994, pp. 1A, 20A–21A; and "Barcelona: The Gold Is Home," *Sky*, July 1992, pp. 34–36, 38, 40, 42.

Capital Budgeting Decisions

1 Explain the nature of capital budgeting and identify the factors to consider in capital expenditure proposals.

Most firms face the same problem when evaluating long-term investments: too many investment opportunities and not enough money. Management must therefore exercise extreme care in the analysis of alternative courses of action. This analysis process gives rise to two basic types of capital budgeting decisions. The first type involves *project screening* to determine whether an investment proposal meets certain preset criteria. Examples of such criteria include a specified rate of return or perhaps the recovery of invested funds within a certain number of years. If the screening tests are met, the proposal is considered for acceptance; if not, rejection is in order.

The second type of decision concerns *ranking*. Given that a number of projects will probably be acceptable, ranking must occur because of the limited availability of investment dollars. A distinction is necessary to determine the most attractive project, the second most attractive project, and so forth. Our presentation will concentrate on screening decisions, with ranking decisions being left for advanced accounting and finance courses.

Decision Factors to Consider

Assume that you recently inherited $10,000 from a wealthy relative and are now exploring various investment possibilities. Three opportunities appear particularly attractive:

1. Purchase a six-month, $10,000 certificate of deposit that carries an interest rate of 8%.

> **ETHICS ISSUE**
>
> X, Inc., requires that all capital projects in excess of $100,000 be approved by the board of directors. A remodeling project is estimated to cost roughly $120,000, subdivided as follows: building improvements, $80,000; new furniture, $25,000; and new computers, $15,000. To save time and avoid having to obtain board approval, you have been told to report the remodeling as three separate expenditures. How would you react?

2. Acquire $10,000 of stock in several so-called growth companies. The shares promise significant appreciation in market value but pay no dividends.
3. Purchase an $80,000 home by paying $9,000 down and securing a $71,000 mortgage loan. The loan will require payments over the next 30 years and carries a 10% interest rate.

Somehow you must decide which of the three investments to select. As a starting point, the following thoughts might be running through your mind:

- The first two investments require an immediate cash outlay of $10,000; the third requires only $9,000.
- The certificate of deposit yields a guaranteed interest rate of 8%.
- The stocks generate no dividends. However, the long-run income may be attractive if market prices increase substantially.
- The house requires monthly payments for mortgage principal and interest along with outlays for insurance, utilities, and property taxes. Furthermore, under the laws and regulations in effect at the time of this writing, interest and property taxes are deductible for federal income tax purposes. Homes have also appreciated in value over the years.

Although our list of decision factors is far from complete, these factors coincide with those studied by managers in the evaluation of capital expenditure proposals. Management is concerned with (1) the amount of an investment, (2) the periodic returns from an investment, and (3) the lowest rate of return acceptable to the company.

Initial Investment. The amount of an investment is measured by the cash outlays necessary for acquisition. These outlays usually coincide with the purchase cost of the acquired assets (e.g., buildings, machinery, and so forth). Be aware, however, that in addition to this type of investment, some projects may require a further commitment of funds to simply get "up and running." Consider a company that desires to expand its market area and customer base. In most cases, this type of business decision is accompanied by a rise in the level of cash needed to support daily operations, along with buildups in accounts receivable and inventory levels. This situation requires an *investment in working capital* by the firm, with related dollar amounts treated as part of the project's initial cost.

Most companies are able to partially recover invested funds when a project's life is over. For instance, equipment and other assets may be sold in secondhand markets. In addition, the working capital investment just mentioned may be recovered by the sale of inventory, the collection of receivables, and the return of cash for use in other business activities. Amounts received from these events are properly treated as cash inflows in the year of occurrence.

Periodic Returns. Investments are made to increase an organization's profitability. Added profitability results from projects that (1) produce income by generating revenues in excess of expenses or (2) decrease costs. Examples of income-producing investments include the addition of new product lines, an expansion of plant capacity, and the implementation of successful marketing programs. Cost reduction endeavors, on the other hand, often involve the installation of more efficient equipment and the acquisition of assets to perform services currently handled by outside entities. For instance, a company could acquire its own truck to eliminate dependence on outside delivery firms.

For both income-producing and cost-saving projects, managers desire a return. That is, managers seek to recover their initial outlays *and* to provide the company with a reward for the risk associated with the investment. Returns can be measured in terms of accounting profits or net cash flows (cash inflows minus cash outflows). *For long-term decisions cash flow is preferred.* Inflows and outflows can be evaluated in terms of their "present worth" to the company, a topic that was originally introduced in Chapter 18. We will expand on this idea shortly.

The Cost of Capital. The analysis of investment opportunities requires that a company set a cutoff rate for project acceptance or rejection. The cutoff rate (i.e., the minimum return acceptable to the firm) depends on the cost of obtaining investment funds. For example, if the cost of funds is 12%, a firm would ordinarily invest only in those projects that promise a return in excess of 12%.

As you are aware, funds for long-term investments are obtained from a variety of sources such as bonds, mortgages, stock issuances, and operations. The collective cost of these funds (which includes outlays for interest expense and dividends) is commonly referred to as the cost of capital.

Most managers will agree that proper determination of this measure is controversial and a topic related more to finance than to accounting. Although the underlying calculations are not considered here, realize that the minimum desired return for investments is typically set several percentage points higher than the cost of capital. Such a procedure helps to offset any errors that may occur in the cost of capital's accompanying assumptions and estimates.

THE TIME VALUE OF MONEY

2 Explain the concept of the time value of money.

Suppose that a manager has an option of receiving $1,000 today or $1,000 one year from now. Virtually every executive would prefer the first alternative for two basic reasons. Receipt of the money today offers the advantage of reduced risk. The future, of course, is full of uncertainty. As time passes, more and more events can occur that jeopardize the inflow of future dollars. Because the $1,000 is in hand, the executive is exposed to less risk and becomes less concerned about changing conditions in the forthcoming months.

The first alternative is also preferred because of the time value of money. As George Faris of Banner Advertising observed in the chapter's opening vignette, a cash receipt today is worth more than an inflow that occurs in the future. Money in hand can be reinvested to earn additional returns for an enterprise, whereas nothing can be done with future dollars until the amounts are received.

We caution that the preceding example is overly simplistic. When one compares equal sums of money (e.g., $1,000) at two different times, the preferred alternative is readily apparent. What happens, however, if we change the illustration? Assume that the second alternative now calls for an inflow of $1,050 or even $1,100 in one year. The decision becomes more difficult. Maybe the extra $50 or $100 is worth the wait; maybe not. An important consideration would surely be the investment opportunities available for the $1,000 just received.

Decisions such as those cited are facilitated if the time value of money is quantitatively incorporated into the evaluation process. This integration is accomplished by the use of present value, a derivation of compound interest.

COMPOUND INTEREST

> **3** Distinguish between compound interest and present value.

With **compound interest,** the interest is computed on principal plus previously accumulated interest. To illustrate, assume that you deposited $1,000 in a 6% savings account. If the interest is compounded annually, the deposit will grow to $1,191.02 by the end of three years, as the following figures show.

YEAR	BEGINNING BALANCE	+	INTEREST AT 6%	=	ENDING BALANCE
1	$1,000.00		$60.00		$1,060.00
2	1,060.00		63.60		1,123.60
3	1,123.60		67.42		1,191.02

Observe that the interest rate remains constant at 6%; however, the amount of interest earned each year has grown. This situation arises because the interest is based on principal and also on previously computed interest that is left on deposit.

PRESENT VALUE

An investment can also be evaluated from a different perspective. Reconsider the preceding example and assume an opportunity is available that promises a $1,060 cash inflow at the end of one year. If you are willing to accept a 6% return on your money, how much would you spend today to receive this cash flow? The answer is $1,000. Why? If $1,000 is invested immediately at a 6% interest rate, the outlay will grow to the $1,060 that you can receive.

In essence we found this amount by working backward. Rather than take a present amount and extend it out to the future, as we would with compound interest, we took a future amount and brought it back to today. This latter process is often called **discounting.** The $1,000 is termed the **present value** of the investment, or the amount an investor is willing to pay to secure a specified cash flow ($1,060) on a future date (one year from now) at a given rate of return (6%). Compound interest and present value can be contrasted as shown in Exhibit 27–1.

EXHIBIT 27–1
Compound Interest Versus Present Value

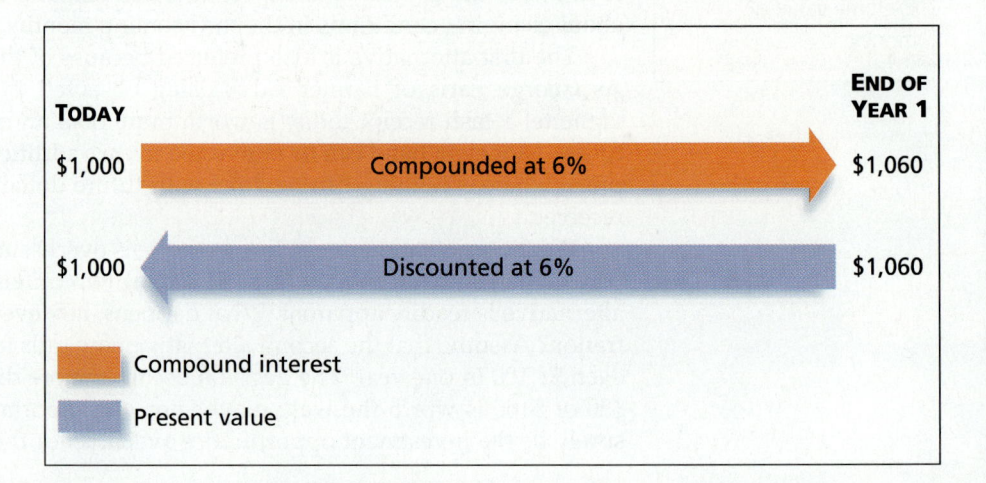

	TODAY		END OF YEAR 1
	$1,000	Compounded at 6% →	$1,060
	$1,000	← Discounted at 6%	$1,060

■ Compound interest
■ Present value

Present Value Tables. Several tables have been developed to assist in present value computations. Examine Table 1 in Appendix C at the end of the text. The table shows the present value factors of $1 at different rates of interest and for different time periods. Continuing our previous example, the factor for $1 to be received in one year given a 6% interest rate is 0.94340. Because we are trying to find the present value of $1,060, the calculation that follows is necessary.

Cash Flow		Present Value Factor		Present Value
$1,060	×	0.94340	=	$1,000

A quick review of the table reveals that as we go further into the future, the present value factors become smaller. Notice the impact of time on the receipt of $1,060.

If Received at the End of Year	The 6% Present Value Factor Would Be	Producing a Present Value of*
1	0.94340	$1,000
3	0.83962	890
5	0.74726	792
7	0.66506	705
9	0.59190	627

* $1,060 × present value factor.

These factors reflect the time value of money—the sooner cash inflows are received, the more valuable they are to the recipient. All other things being equal, companies are willing to pay greater sums of money for investments that promise quicker dollar returns.

Multiple Cash Flows and Annuities. Most long-term investments affect cash flows for more than a single year. To illustrate the necessary procedures, assume Target Industries acquired a machine that promised annual savings in cash operating costs of $2,000 over the next five years. Management requires a return on investment of 10%. For capital budgeting purposes, reductions in operating costs are viewed as cash inflows. Using the factors from Table 1, the present value of the machine's savings is $7,582:

Year	Cash Flow	×	Present Value Factor	=	Present Value
1	$2,000		0.90909		$1,818
2	2,000		0.82645		1,653
3	2,000		0.75132		1,503
4	2,000		0.68301		1,366
5	2,000		0.62092		1,242
Total present value					$7,582

These computations result in each of the individual cash flows being discounted back to the beginning of Year 1 (i.e., the "present"), as depicted in Exhibit 27–2.

A review of this process shows that in each year, a present value factor is multiplied by the $2,000 cash flow. The calculations would have required less work had the savings been multiplied by the summation of the individual factors (0.90909 + 0.82645 + 0.75132 + 0.68301 + 0.62092 = 3.79079). As the following figures show, the same result is achieved:

$$\$2,000 \times 3.79079 = \$7,582$$

Our example has focused on an **annuity**—a series of equal cash flows over a number of years. To further simplify procedures in this type of situation, accountants often use an annuity table (see Table 2 in Appendix C). The factor in Table 2 for a $1 annuity over the next five years, discounted at 10%, is 3.79079. As before, the factor is multiplied by the cash flow to derive the appropriate present value.

An Added Complexity. Sometimes, annuity calculations are needed to discount cash flows that *begin* several years into the future. Suppose, for instance, that the machine in our illustration promises annual operating savings of $2,000 for the first two years and $1,000 for each of the next three years. Target now has two separate annuities, and the present value is found as follows:

Years	Cash Flow	×	Present Value Factor	=	Present Value
1–2	$2,000		1.73554		$3,471
3–5	1,000		2.05525*		2,055
Total present value					$5,526

* 3.79079 – 1.73554.

Table 2 is once again the source of our data. The factor of 1.73554 is needed to discount the savings that occur during the first two years. The second factor,

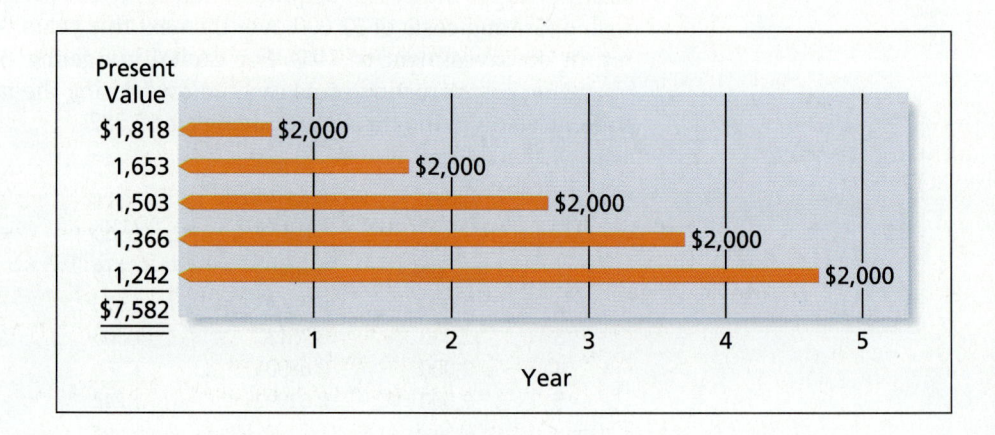

Exhibit 27–2
The Discounting of Multiple Cash Flows

computed as the difference between 3.79079 (the annuity factor that covers Years 1–5) and 1.73554, permits Target to discount the cash flows for Years 3–5.

CAPITAL BUDGETING EVALUATION METHODS

4 Use net present value, the internal rate of return, payback, and the accounting rate of return to evaluate long-term projects.

Four methods of evaluating capital budgeting proposals are frequently encountered in practice:

1. Net present value
2. Internal rate of return
3. Payback
4. Accounting rate of return

Several surveys have shown that these evaluation tools are normally used in conjunction with one another. This situation occurs because each of the techniques listed has strengths and weaknesses and provides different information to management.

The majority of our discussion will center on the discounted cash flow methods of net present value and the internal rate of return. Both of these approaches have conceptual advantages over the others cited and have seen increased use in recent years.

NET PRESENT VALUE

With the **net-present-value method,** the present value of an investment's cash inflows is netted against the present value of the cash outflows. The rate of return used for discounting corresponds to or is slightly in excess of the firm's cost of capital.

As an example of the necessary procedures, assume that Alpine Delivery is considering an expansion of service to the cities of High Point and Beeville. Two trucks must be acquired at a total cost of $95,000. The trucks have an eight-year life, will be depreciated by the straight-line method, and are expected to generate annual net cash inflows of $18,000 from new business. Alpine requires a 10% minimum return on all investments.

Some managers may be tempted to evaluate the truck acquisition as follows:

Initial investment	$ (95,000)
Annual net cash inflows ($18,000 × 8 years)	144,000
Difference in favor of acquisition	$ 49,000

This analysis is incorrect for two reasons. First, the computations imply that all of the cash inflows are equivalent when, in fact, they are not. (As discussed in previous sections of the chapter, inflows that occur in earlier years can be reinvested for longer periods of time.) Second, we cannot compare an immediate cash outflow with cash inflows that are spread over the next eight years. Since the timing differs, the result is a comparison of dollars of unequal values—basically a study of apples and oranges.

The proper approach is to discount the cash flows at 10%. The correct computations follow.

	Cash Flow	×	Present Value Factor	=	Present Value
Initial investment	$(95,000)		1.00000		$(95,000)
Annual net cash inflows	18,000		5.33493		96,029
Net present value					$ 1,029

A factor of 1.0 is used for the initial investment because the outlay takes place immediately. The other factor (5.33493) is obtained from the annuity table (Table 2) at the intersection of the 8-period row and 10% column.

The net present value of $1,029 indicates the present value of the inflows exceeds the present value of the outflows. The trucks are therefore an attractive investment and should be acquired if funds are available. Projects that produce a positive net present value are acceptable; those with a negative net present value should be rejected. A positive net present value means the returns from an investment exceed a company's minimum desired rate of return (10% in Alpine's case).

Before leaving this example, it is important to note the impact of the discounting process. Actual cash inflows exceed actual cash outflows by $49,000; yet when discounting is introduced, the present value of the inflows and outflows differs by only $1,029. The time value of money has greatly diminished the attractiveness of the investment.

Omission of Depreciation Expense. Although the trucks have an eight-year life, we disregarded depreciation expense in our evaluation. Depreciation is excluded from present value calculations because of the emphasis on cash flows and depreciation's noncash nature. The cost of the trucks took the form of a single, $95,000 cash outflow at the time of acquisition. An additional deduction for depreciation would therefore result in a double counting of the assets' cost.

Despite its noncash nature, depreciation expense does affect the amount of income taxes paid to federal and state governments. Income taxes, which were ignored in the Alpine example, are discussed in the Appendix to this chapter.

An Expanded Example Using Net Present Value. The illustration that follows shows how a business can integrate present value into a keep-versus-replace decision. As you progress through the presentation, observe how the relevancy concept (as introduced in Chapter 26) continues to play an important role in the evaluation of alternatives.

Assume the Delicious Baking Company is studying the replacement of some equipment acquired four years ago at a cost of $55,000. The equipment is expected to provide six more years of service if $4,000 of major repairs are performed two years from now. Annual cash operating costs total $13,000 and are not expected to change in future periods. Delicious can sell the equipment now for $24,000; the estimated residual value in six years is $5,000.

Management can acquire new equipment that costs $62,000. The new equipment has a service life of six years, is expected to reduce cash operating costs by $6,000 annually, and has an estimated residual value of $18,000. Annual company sales will total $240,000 regardless of the decision.

If Delicious has a minimum desired rate of return of 14%, what should the firm do? To determine the proper course of action, we must first identify all relevant cash flows, namely, those that occur in the future and differ among the alternatives. Such an analysis reveals that we can disregard the $55,000 cost of the old equipment (it is sunk) and the future sales revenues of $1,440,000 ($240,000 × 6 years), which are common to both the keep and the replace options. Once the relevant cash flows are decided, the amounts are discounted by using the 14% present value factors that appear in Tables 1 and 2. The appropriate computations are shown in Exhibit 27–3.

The analysis reveals a negative net present value for both the keep and the replace alternatives. At first glance it appears that both options should be rejected, but such action is not possible. Given that one alternative must be selected in this type of situation, Delicious Baking should keep the present equipment. On a discounted cash flow basis, the company stands to benefit by $5,667 [$(51,353) versus $(57,020)].[1]

INTERNAL RATE OF RETURN

The net-present-value method is only one of several tools that a company can employ to evaluate capital budgeting proposals. Another tool that incorporates discounted cash flows is the **internal rate of return (IRR).** Sometimes called the time-adjusted rate of return, the IRR represents the actual yield on a project. It is computed by finding the discount rate that equates the present value of a project's cash inflows with the present value of the cash outflows. As a result of this calculation, the net present value is zero.

EXHIBIT 27–3
Delicious Baking Company's Analysis of Keep and Replace Alternatives

	YEAR(S) OF OCCURRENCE	CASH FLOW	×	PRESENT VALUE FACTOR	=	PRESENT VALUE
KEEP THE PRESENT EQUIPMENT						
Cash operating costs	1–6	$(13,000)		3.88867		$(50,553)
Major repairs	2	(4,000)		0.76947		(3,078)
Disposal	6	5,000		0.45559		2,278
Net present value						$(51,353)
REPLACE THE PRESENT EQUIPMENT						
Initial investment	Immediate	$(62,000)		1.00000		$(62,000)
Sale of old equipment	Immediate	24,000		1.00000		24,000
Cash operating costs ($13,000 – $6,000)	1–6	(7,000)		3.88867		(27,221)
Disposal	6	18,000		0.45559		8,201
Net present value						$(57,020)
Net present value in favor of keeping the present equipment						$ 5,667

[1] The negative net present values arise because the company's sales revenues, a significant cash inflow, were omitted from the analysis.

To illustrate the related procedures, let us assume that Kim Enterprises is confronted with an investment opportunity that costs $12,009 and promises net cash inflows of $5,000 for each of the next three years. The following computation, where F is defined as the discount factor that equates the present value of the inflows and outflows, is needed:

$$\$5{,}000 \times F = \$12{,}009$$

$$F = \frac{\$12{,}009}{\$5{,}000}$$

$$F = 2.4018$$

The return on Kim's investment can now be found by determining the rate represented by a factor of 2.4018. Because the investment involves a three-year annuity, we must examine Table 2, part of which is reproduced below.

Periods	8%	10%	12%	14%	16%
⋮	⋮	⋮	⋮	⋮	⋮
3	2.57710	2.48685	2.40183	2.32163	2.24589
⋮	⋮	⋮	⋮	⋮	⋮

Except for an extremely small rounding error, the 2.4018 discount factor coincides with a 12% interest rate. Thus, Kim's investment yields a 12% rate of return. As noted earlier, this particular rate will produce a zero net present value:

Initial investment [$(12,009) × 1.00000]	$(12,009)
Annual net cash inflows discounted at 12% ($5,000 × 2.4018)	12,009
Net present value	$ —

Should the investment be pursued? Is a 12% return attractive to Kim? The answers to these questions depend on the company's cost of capital. If the internal rate of return is equal to or greater than the cost of capital, then the project should be considered for acceptance. If not, rejection is in order.

Two Complications. Two complications are normally encountered when figuring the internal rate of return. First, the factor that equates the present value of the inflows and outflows usually does not coincide with the factors that appear in the annuity table. Returning to the Kim example, suppose the investment called for an initial outlay of $11,775 rather than $12,009. The factor for the project would now be 2.355, calculated as follows:

$$\$5{,}000 \times F = \$11{,}775$$

$$F = \frac{\$11{,}775}{\$5{,}000}$$

$$F = 2.355$$

Scanning Table 2 for a three-period annuity, we find that the factor falls between a return of 12% and 14%. The actual return is found by using the mathematical process of *interpolation*, the details of which are omitted here.

The second complication relates to uneven cash flows. The Kim illustration had an immediate single outflow followed by three inflows of $5,000 each. Picture the difficulties that would arise if there were additional flows of, say, an extra payment in the second year and the receipt of a residual value in the third year. Finding the one factor that equates the present value of all inflows and outflows would be burdensome, to say the least, and would require numerous rounds of trial and error. Fortunately, calculators and computer programs are available that perform the necessary computations. Most spreadsheets, for example, contain built-in functions that readily handle the discounting of both single-sum cash flows and annuities. The user can therefore concentrate on the analysis of results instead of the drudgery of procedure.

A Computer Consultant's Perspective

Decision Support Systems: Computer support of decision making is the essence of management information systems. Unlike the automated transaction processing routines that were discussed earlier in your text, decision support systems are designed for middle and upper management to assist in the evaluation of alternatives. A hallmark of these systems is that they support "what if" queries from users.

For example, consider the introduction of a new product. There are many possible scenarios that deal with the degree of competition, sales prices, promotional expenditures, market size, and market share. Add to these variables a variety of inflation rates and discount rates, and a genuine computational headache is created when analyzing long-term projects.

A support system would likely contain a mathematical model, perhaps involving a spreadsheet, with numerous assumptions about the sales and financial environments. The system's "what if" capability allows the manager to vary these scenarios and study their impact on the new product decision. The system lets the manager simulate unique marketing strategies on the computer—a much safer environment than the "actual" business world, where a bad decision could financially strap a company for years to come.

The Payback Method

Few accountants question the superiority of discounted cash flow for investment analysis. Yet, as explained earlier in the chapter, methods other than net present value and the internal rate of return are in widespread use. One such method is **payback,** which measures the amount of time it takes to recover a project's initial cash investment.

To illustrate the necessary calculations, assume that Hill Corporation is examining the possibility of manufacturing a new product. Plant and equipment that cost $200,000 must be purchased and should result in net cash inflows of $60,000 for each of the next five years. When the cash flows are uniform, as they are in this example, the payback period is derived by use of the following formula:

$$\text{Payback Period} = \frac{\text{Initial Investment}}{\text{Annual Net Cash Inflow}}$$

$$= \frac{\$200,000}{\$60,000}$$

$$= 3.33 \text{ years}$$

Uneven Cash Flows. The formula just shown can only be used with uniform, or even, net cash inflows. In those situations where the annual inflows are unequal, the flows are summed until the amount of the original investment is reached. For instance, assume the inflows associated with Hill's $200,000 investment are now as follows: Year 1, $70,000; Year 2, $70,000; Year 3, $80,000; Year 4, $50,000; and Year 5, $30,000. The required computations are:

YEAR	ANNUAL NET CASH INFLOW	CUMULATIVE NET CASH INFLOW
1	$70,000	$ 70,000
2	70,000	140,000
3	80,000	220,000
4	50,000	270,000
5	30,000	300,000

The computations reveal that $140,000 is recovered by the end of Year 2 and $220,000 by the conclusion of Year 3. Thus, the 200,000th dollar arrives sometime during Year 3 as a result of the $80,000 net cash inflow. The payback method assumes that cash flows are spread evenly throughout a period. Consequently, the additional $60,000 that must be recovered to reach the payback ($200,000 − $140,000) is assumed to be received three quarters of the way through the year ($60,000 ÷ $80,000). The payback, then, is 2.75 years.

Use of Payback: Pros and Cons. The payback method provides its users with a very simple tool for evaluation purposes. By comparing a project's payback period against a preestablished standard, a manager can easily determine project acceptability. This type of comparison is especially useful for companies that have limited cash balances and wish to recover their investment dollars rapidly. Short paybacks allow cash-starved businesses to undertake additional opportunities: the sooner cash is received, the sooner reinvestment can occur.

Unfortunately, the use of payback is not problem-free. In addition to ignoring the time value of money, the payback method exhibits a serious weakness by disregarding project profitability. As an example, assume that a company can invest in one of the following projects:

PROJECT	INITIAL INVESTMENT	ANNUAL NET CASH INFLOW	PROJECT LIFE
A	$100,000	$50,000	3 years
B	100,000	40,000	6 years

If the decision is based solely on payback, project A would be selected, because the initial investment is recovered more quickly.

$$\text{Project A Payback} = \frac{\$100,000}{\$50,000} = 2.0 \text{ years}$$

$$\text{Project B Payback} = \frac{\$100,000}{\$40,000} = 2.5 \text{ years}$$

Is this the correct choice, however? Most entities make investments to generate profit, not to see how fast funds can be returned. Project B is really a better selection, because inflows *after* the payback period is reached will total $140,000 ($40,000 × 3.5 years) versus $50,000 ($50,000 × 1 year) for project A. Stated differently, the payback method considers net cash inflows up until the time the initial investment is recovered. Any receipts that occur after this point are disregarded in the computational process.

A FURTHER FOCUS

Payback periods will vary among projects. One of the latest entertainment concepts, for instance, is a simulated thrill ride that combines sound effects, motion, and big-screen film. *Forbes* reporters described the concept as "a kind of high-tech amusement park in a box." Charging $2.50 per person, Circus Circus Enterprises' Excalibur casino in Las Vegas was able to recover the $2 million cost of its thrill ride simulator in eight months.

In contrast, the city of Indianapolis and state of Indiana recently granted United Airlines $294.6 million of incentives (such as tax breaks) to attract a huge maintenance facility that was expected to create roughly 17,300 jobs. State officials estimated a 16-year payback for Indiana's investment, while the city anticipated a 12- to 15-year recovery period. In this particular case, it is somewhat obvious that long-term economic development was considered more important than the speed associated with the incentives' recovery.

Sources: "Hang on to Your Hats—and Wallets," *Forbes*, November 22, 1993, pp. 90–91, 93, 98; and "Ask and Your Company Shall Receive," *The Dallas Morning News*, February 4, 1992, pp. 1D, 6D.

ACCOUNTING RATE OF RETURN

A fourth evaluation tool, the **accounting rate of return,** focuses on the average income generated by a project in relation to the project's initial investment outlay. Unlike the methods discussed earlier, *this capital budgeting approach emphasizes income and not cash flows.* A proper measure of profit, of course, includes a deduction for depreciation expense.

The accounting rate of return is computed by the following formula:

$$\text{Accounting Rate of Return} = \frac{\text{Average Annual Increase in Income}}{\text{Initial Investment}}$$

To illustrate the related calculations, assume that a company is considering the acquisition of some new machinery that costs $80,000. The machinery has a service life of 10 years, has no residual value, and will be depreciated by using the straight-line method. Average annual net cash inflows from operations are expected to increase by $28,000. The accounting rate of return is 25%, derived as follows:

$$\text{Accounting Rate of Return} = \frac{\$28,000 - \$8,000}{\$80,000} = 25\%$$

The numerator is computed by subtracting depreciation expense of $8,000 ($80,000 ÷ 10 years) from the operating cash flows.

Because the machinery will be depreciated, some companies believe the accounting rate of return is more appropriately based on an average investment figure rather than on the initial outlay. The average investment can be calculated by adding the beginning and ending investment and dividing by 2, specifically, ($80,000 + $0) ÷ 2, or $40,000.

Evaluation of the Accounting Rate of Return. The accounting rate of return remains popular primarily because of its consistency with the techniques employed to evaluate companywide and divisional performance. Further, most users agree that the accounting rate of return is a simple tool that is easy to understand. The calculated return on an investment is merely compared against a cutoff that has been established by management to judge project attractiveness.

Like payback, however, this method has several serious drawbacks. The time value of money is ignored as is the timing of an investment's earnings. Two projects, for example, may produce identical rates of return over a period of, say, three years. One of these projects may generate uniform earnings through the three-year period; the other may actually produce negative returns in the first two years and a substantial payoff in Year 3. These problems require that management closely study the data that underlie the calculation and not rely totally on the rate of return itself.

CAPITAL INVESTMENT IN A COMPETITIVE BUSINESS CLIMATE

The four evaluation tools illustrated in this chapter are relatively straightforward when it comes to accepting or rejecting a project. Projects that have a negative net present value should be turned down; those that meet a company's target payback are viewed favorably; and so forth. Despite the relative ease of use, many firms in recent years have begun to "go against the numbers." That is, projects that fail a screening test are sometimes pursued so the company can remain competitive, and seemingly worthy projects are rejected. The problem is especially acute with respect to automation, which is very expensive and often produces cost savings far into the future. The overall attractiveness of these savings is greatly diminished, of course, when the dollar amounts are discounted.

Looking back at earlier presentations in the text, we noted that companies now review factors other than dollars and cost savings when assessing performance. Speed, customer satisfaction, and quality are three important considerations when it comes to operating in a competitive business climate—factors that are often influenced by a firm's capital investments. Unfortunately, these factors are difficult to quantify and are typically ignored by the traditional capital budgeting tools.

Managers who have a keen sense of awareness frequently think beyond the numbers and pay close attention to qualitative concerns in the decision making process. In sum, we advise that net present value, the internal rate of return, payback, and the accounting rate of return not be used in isolation but in conjunction with each other *and* with a listing of the other, more indirect benefits related to an investment. By following this approach, a business will maintain its competitive edge and help to ensure survival.

APPENDIX: CASH FLOWS AND INCOME TAXES

Businesses pay a substantial amount of their income to governmental authorities. In light of this fact, the revenues and expenses that accompany an investment must be examined to determine the effect on a company's taxes and related cash flows. In practice, the cash flows used with the evaluation methods discussed earlier are normally calculated on an aftertax basis.

5 Demonstrate how income taxes affect cash flow calculations.

THE AFTERTAX CONCEPT

The aftertax concept is probably best explained by means of a simplified illustration. Assume that San Juan Enterprises, a service business, is studying the impact of adding a new administrative assistant to the payroll. Yearly salary and fringe benefit costs are expected to average $40,000; the company is subject to a 40% income tax rate. A staff assistant has prepared the following analysis:

	PRESENT SITUATION	PROPOSED SITUATION
Revenues	$200,000	$200,000
Operating expenses		
Existing	$130,000	$130,000
Administrative assistant	—	40,000
Total	$130,000	$170,000
Income before taxes	$ 70,000	$ 30,000
Income taxes at 40%	28,000	12,000
Net income	$ 42,000	$ 18,000

Observe the effect of the hiring decision on the firm's income taxes. The increased salary and fringe benefit cost has reduced San Juan's taxes by $16,000 ($28,000 − $12,000). The true, *aftertax cost* of the administrative assistant, then, is $24,000 ($40,000 − $16,000).

In terms of cash flow, an analysis could have been made as follows:

Cash outflow for salaries and benefits	$(40,000)
Tax savings*	16,000
Net cash outflow	$(24,000)

* Recall that cost savings are treated as cash inflows.

The $24,000 net cash outflow would be employed in any type of capital budgeting analysis performed by the company (e.g., payback, net present value, and so forth).

Although our example has focused on an expense, the same concept could have been illustrated with an increase in revenue. Because revenues increase income (and related tax payments), we can say the following:

Cash inflow from added revenue	$ XX,XXX
Added taxes (a cash outflow)	(XX,XXX)
Net cash inflow	$ XX,XXX

The net cash flow computations just discussed can be simplified by use of the formula shown.

$$(\text{Cash Inflow or Outflow}) \times (1 - \text{Tax Rate}) = \text{Net Cash Flow}$$

In San Juan's case, the $24,000 figure could have been derived as:

$$\$40{,}000 \times (1 - 0.40) = \$24{,}000$$

Depreciation: Why Special Treatment Is Needed

On page 1056, we emphasized that depreciation is ignored in present value calculations because of its noncash nature. Bear in mind that depreciation is a deductible item when computing a company's tax obligation to the federal government. Such amounts therefore give rise to tax savings; however, special treatment is needed because depreciation itself is a noncash charge.

To illustrate this treatment, let us assume that San Juan's management is now considering an investment that will increase the firm's total depreciation expense by $40,000. (This figure was purposely selected to coincide with the cost of the administrative assistant for ease in understanding.) Like the company's outlay for salaries and fringe benefits, depreciation will produce a tax savings of $16,000. Unlike the earlier example, however, it would be improper to net the tax savings against the $40,000 depreciation figure. To do so would result in the offset of a cash flow against a noncash item—an illogical calculation. Keep in mind that the only cash flow related to depreciation is the tax savings.

We can conclude that depreciation has given San Juan a *tax shield* of $16,000. That is, the deduction has shielded ("protected") the company's revenues from taxation and has lowered the firm's tax payments to the government. If desired, this concept could be expressed in a formula, as follows:

$$\text{Depreciation Deduction} \times \text{Tax Rate} = \text{Cash Savings}$$

$$\$40{,}000 \times 0.40 = \$16{,}000$$

End-of-Chapter Review

LEARNING OBJECTIVES: THE KEY POINTS

1. **Explain the nature of capital budgeting and identify the factors to consider in capital expenditure proposals.** Capital budgeting is concerned with the planning and decision making related to long-term investments. Examples of long-term investments include equipment acquisitions, building construction, and the addition of new product lines. Such projects are evaluated by comparing various project characteristics (e.g., the rate of return) against guidelines that have been established by management. These evaluations are commonly known as screening decisions. Given that most companies have many acceptable projects but limited funds, management must determine the most attractive investment, the second most attractive investment, and so forth. This process is known as project ranking.

   Three factors are normally considered when analyzing an investment. First, there is the amount of the initial investment, which may include an investment in working capital (e.g., buildups in cash, accounts receivable, and inventory). Second, the returns from the investment must be studied. Project returns are usually measured in terms of net cash flows, or cash inflows minus cash outflows. Finally, companies must consider the minimum rate of return acceptable on a project. This rate is typically set equal to or slightly in excess of the firm's cost of capital.

2. **Explain the concept of the time value of money.** The time value of money recognizes that a dollar received today is worth more to an investor than a dollar received in the future. Earlier inflows can be reinvested to generate additional returns. This concept is integrated in the evaluation of capital projects by the use of present value, as described by the next learning objective.

3. **Distinguish between compound interest and present value.** Compound interest and present value are two different tools that are used to evaluate an investment. Compound interest is employed to figure the amount to which a given sum will grow by the end of a designated time period. The underlying procedures involve the calculation of interest on the original amount invested as well as on previously computed interest that is left "on deposit."

   Present value, on the other hand, discounts a future cash sum and figures the "current worth" to an investor. Stated differently, present value is the amount an investor is willing to pay today to receive specified future cash flows. The related computations recognize the time value of money by weighting the cash flows that occur in earlier years more heavily than those that occur in later years.

4. **Use net present value, the internal rate of return, payback, and the accounting rate of return to evaluate long-term projects.** As its name implies, the net-present-value method focuses on netting (i.e., offsetting) the present value of an investment's cash inflows against the present value of the cash outflows. If the result of this process is positive, the project should be considered for acceptance; if negative, rejection is in order. The internal rate of return is another present-value-based evaluation approach. This method finds the actual yield on an investment by equating the present value of an investment's cash inflows and cash outflows.

   Unlike the first two approaches, payback and the accounting rate of return do not consider the time value of money. Payback shows how rapidly an initial investment is recovered. This method of project evaluation, although simple, ignores all cash flows that occur after the payback point has been reached. The accounting rate of return, also considered very easy to use, focuses on a project's return in relation to the amount invested or perhaps an average investment amount. The return in this case is measured in terms of income and not cash flow.

In today's competitive business climate, managers should not rely totally on these evaluation tools when making long-term investments. The difficulty of quantifying such factors as quality, speed, and customer satisfaction requires that managers "look beyond the numbers" in their acceptance/rejection decisions.

5. **(Appendix) Demonstrate how income taxes affect cash flow calculations.** Capital budgeting models normally use aftertax amounts. Because many cash inflows and outflows (e.g., those from revenues and those for deductible expenses) affect a company's tax obligation, the tax implications for these items must be considered when analyzing a long-term investment. Deductible expenses result in a tax savings; conversely, revenues produce added tax for the firm. The tax effect is subtracted from the cash flow itself, with the net amount then used in the various capital budgeting evaluation tools. This netting procedure is not required for depreciation, which is a noncash expense.

KEY TERMS AND CONCEPTS: A QUICK OVERVIEW

accounting rate of return A method of evaluating long-term projects that focuses on the average income generated in relation to the amount of the investment. (p. 1061)

annuity A series of equal cash flows over a number of years. (p. 1054)

capital budgeting Planning and decision making for long-term programs and projects. (p. 1049)

compound interest Interest that is calculated on both principal and previously accumulated interest. (p. 1052)

cost of capital The cost of investment funds. (p. 1051)

discounting The process of taking a future amount and bringing it back to its value today. (p. 1052)

internal rate of return A discounted cash flow method of evaluating long-term projects that derives the actual return on an investment. (p. 1057)

net-present-value method A method used to evaluate long-term investments in which the present value of an investment's cash inflows and the present value of the cash outflows are netted against each other. (p. 1055)

payback A method of analysis that measures the amount of time necessary to recover a project's initial cash investment. (p. 1059)

present value The amount an investor is willing to pay to secure a specified cash flow on a future date at a given rate of return. (p. 1052)

time value of money The concept that a dollar received today is worth more than a dollar received in the future. (p. 1051)

CHAPTER QUIZ

The five questions that follow relate to several issues raised in the chapter. Test your knowledge of the issues by selecting the best answer. (The answers appear on p. 1079.)

1. Which of the following is rarely a consideration when analyzing a long-term project?
   a. The cost of the investment.
   b. The lowest rate of return acceptable to management.

c. The company's current ratio.
d. The investment's cash inflows and cash outflows.

2. The time value of money:
   a. is integrated in present value computations.
   b. weights cash flows that occur in five years more heavily than cash flows that occur in two years.
   c. is reflected by the accounting rate of return.
   d. should not be considered when analyzing an investment.

3. Hughes Corporation is considering a $200,000 machine that promises savings in cash operating costs of $40,000 over each of the next six years. The company requires a 10% return on its investments. Appropriate present value factors follow.

PRESENT VALUE OF $1	PRESENT VALUE OF A $1 ANNUITY
0.56447	4.35526

   Ignoring income taxes, the machine's net present value is:
   a. $(5,790).
   b. $(25,790).
   c. $(177,421).
   d. some amount other than those listed above.

4. The internal rate of return:
   a. ignores the time value of money.
   b. is another name for the accounting rate of return.
   c. results in a net present value of zero.
   d. cannot be used when the payback period is less than three years.

5. The payback method:
   a. normally incorporates the use of discount factors.
   b. cannot be used with uneven cash flows.
   c. evaluates the recovery of initial cash investments, with longer paybacks generally viewed more favorably than shorter paybacks.
   d. fails to consider all cash flows related to a project.

SUMMARY PROBLEM

The Ellison Corporation is studying the following investment opportunity:

Initial outlay required	$225,000
Net cash inflows, Years 1–5	75,000
Disposal value at the end of Year 5	5,000

Ellison desires a minimum return of 12% on all investments.

Instructions

a. Compute the investment's payback period.
b. Compute the net present value. Should the investment be considered for acceptance? Explain.
c. Approximate the internal rate of return. For simplicity, disregard the $5,000 disposal value.

Solution

a.

YEAR	ANNUAL NET CASH INFLOW	CUMULATIVE NET CASH INFLOW
1	$75,000	$ 75,000
2	75,000	150,000
3	75,000	225,000
etc.		

The payback period is three years.

b.

	CASH FLOW	×	PRESENT VALUE FACTOR AT 12%	=	PRESENT VALUE
Initial investment	$(225,000)		1.00000		$(225,000)
Annual net cash inflows	75,000		3.60478		270,359
Disposal value	5,000		0.56743		2,837
Net present value					$ 48,196

The net present value is positive, which means the investment should be considered for acceptance.

c. Let F = the discount factor that equates the present value of the investment's cash inflows and cash outflows

$$\$75,000 \times F = \$225,000$$
$$F = 3.0$$

Table 2 reveals that for a five-year annuity, a 3.0 factor lies between 18% and 20%.

ASSIGNMENT MATERIAL

QUESTIONS

Q27–1 Why must businesses exercise extreme care in the selection of long-term investments?

Q27–2 Describe the screening and ranking processes related to capital budgeting.

Q27–3 What three factors should be considered in the evaluation of an investment opportunity?

Q27–4 What is meant by an investment in working capital? Are such investments ever recovered? Briefly explain.

Q27–5 In general, are net cash flows or accounting profits preferred in the evaluation of long-term investment proposals?

Q27–6 What is the lowest rate of return acceptable to a company?

Q27–7 What is meant by the term "present value"?

Q27–8 What is an annuity?

Q27–9 Four methods are frequently used to evaluate capital budgeting proposals. Are these methods normally used by themselves or in conjunction with each other? Why?

Q27–10 Should depreciation be considered in a net-present-value computation if income taxes are ignored? Why or why not?

Q27–11 When examining a project's cash inflows and outflows, what present value relationship holds true at the internal rate of return?

Q27–12 Aside from ignoring the time value of money, what is another inherent problem associated with the payback method?

Q27–13 Does the accounting rate of return focus on income or cash flows?

Q27–14 What information should supplement the quantitative results provided by a capital budgeting tool (e.g., payback or net-present-value method) when evaluating a project?

*Q27–15 Should cash flows used in a capital budgeting evaluation be expressed on a beforetax or an aftertax basis?

*Q27–16 Briefly discuss the concept of a depreciation tax shield.

EXERCISES

E27–1 Time value of money (L.O. 2)

Kensington General Hospital is sponsoring a contest to raise money to refurbish all lounges in the east wing. The contest operates in the following manner. Contestants will purchase entry tickets for $50 each. If the contestant later catches a specially tagged fish from a nearby lake, he or she will receive money from an insurance policy purchased by Kensington to fund the event.

The winner has three options for receiving the money from the insurance company:

No. 1: Receive $10,000 at the end of each year for 10 years.
No. 2: Receive $70,000 immediately.
No. 3: Receive a lump sum of $500,000 in 22 years.

a. Briefly explain what is meant by the phrase "the time value of money."
b. Suppose that option no. 3 was revised, with the winner receiving $250,000 in 11 years and another $250,000 in 22 years. In all likelihood, would the winner prefer option no. 3 as originally stated or as revised? Why?
c. Ignoring part (b), do any of the three options involve an annuity? Explain.
d. What process should the winner perform to determine which of the payoffs is best? What does this process do?

E27–2 Basic present value calculations (L.O. 3)

Calculate the present value of the following cash flows, rounding to the nearest dollar:

a. A single cash inflow of $12,000 in five years, discounted at a 12% rate of return.
b. An annual receipt of $16,000 over the next 12 years, discounted at a 14% rate of return.
c. A single receipt of $15,000 at the end of Year 1 followed by a single receipt of $10,000 at the end of Year 3. The company has a 10% rate of return.
d. An annual receipt of $8,000 for three years followed by a single receipt of $10,000 at the end of Year 4. The company has a 16% rate of return.

* An asterisk preceding an item indicates that the material is covered in an appendix to this chapter.

E27–3 Present value analysis: Working backward (L.O. 3)

The following information pertains to four independent investments:

	A	B	C	D
Present value	?	$19,646	$34,625	$50,852
Interest rate	10%	?	14%	12%
Investment period	4 years	5 years	?	10 years
Annual cash inflows	$8,000	$6,000	$7,000	?

Determine the unknown for each of the investments. (*Note:* Amounts have been rounded to the nearest dollar; please consider this procedure in your calculations.)

E27–4 Straightforward net-present-value calculations (L.O. 2, 4)

El Taco, Inc., is considering remodeling its restaurants at a cost of $190,000 per location. The company believes that increased patronage will result over the next five years, creating the following additional net cash inflows:

Year 1	$70,000	Year 4	$30,000
Year 2	60,000	Year 5	10,000
Year 3	50,000		

El Taco uses the net-present-value method to analyze investments and desires a 12% minimum rate of return.

a. The company's bookkeeper summed the preceding cash flows and concluded that the remodeling should begin, noting that the net cash inflows of $220,000 exceeded the $190,000 construction cost. Did the bookkeeper err in his analysis of the project? Briefly discuss.

b. Compute the net present value of the proposed remodeling, ignoring income taxes and rounding to the nearest dollar. Does the remodeling appear to be a good investment? Explain.

E27–5 Cash flow calculations and net present value (L.O. 4)

On January 2, 19X1, Bruce Greene invested $10,000 in the stock market and purchased 500 shares of Heartland Development, Inc. Heartland paid cash dividends of $2.60 per share in 19X1 and 19X2; the dividend was raised to $3.10 per share in 19X3. On December 31, 19X3, Greene sold his holdings and generated proceeds of $13,000. Greene uses the net-present-value method and desires a 16% return on investments.

a. Prepare a chronological list of the investment's cash flows. *Note:* Greene is entitled to the 19X3 dividend.

b. Compute the investment's net present value, rounding calculations to the nearest dollar.

c. Given the results of part (b), should Greene have acquired the Heartland stock? Briefly explain.

E27–6 Straightforward net present value and internal rate of return (L.O. 4)

The City of Columbus is studying a 600-acre site on Route 356 for a new landfill. The startup cost has been calculated as follows:

Purchase cost: $450 per acre
Site preparation: $175,000

The site can be used for 20 years before it reaches capacity. Columbus, which shares a facility in Bath Township with other municipalities, estimates that the new location will save $40,000 in annual operating costs.

a. Should the landfill be acquired if Columbus desires an 8% return on its investment? Use the net-present-value method to determine your answer.
b. Approximate the internal rate of return on this project.

E27–7 Payback and cash flow analysis (L.O. 4)

Summer Recreation, Inc., uses the payback method to evaluate major new attractions for its amusement parks. Company policy is to accept projects that have a payback of three years or less.

The firm has been looking at a $1 million ride called The Whiplash for its Tennessee facility. The ride has a five-year service life and is expected to generate the following additional cash inflows:

YEAR	NET CASH INFLOWS
1	$400,000
2	300,000
3	250,000
4	200,000
5	100,000

a. Does The Whiplash produce a positive cash flow from operations over its five-year service life? Briefly explain.
b. Should the ride be acquired? Show appropriate calculations.
c. In general, are shorter or longer paybacks preferred by managers? Why?

E27–8 Payback and accounting rate of return (L.O. 4)

Instant Change offers 10-minute oil changes at numerous facilities in Kansas and Nebraska. The company wants to expand into Illinois and has picked a site that is expected to have the following annual results:

Sales revenue		$310,000
Less operating expenses		
Oil & supplies	$105,000	
Wages	90,000	
Insurance	10,000	
Utilities	5,000	
Depreciation	25,000	235,000
Operating income		$ 75,000

Land acquisition and building costs for the Illinois facility will require a $500,000 initial investment. Disregard income taxes.

a. If management desires a payback of less than six years, should the Illinois facility be opened? Why or why not?
b. Compute the accounting rate of return on the initial investment.
c. What do payback and the accounting rate of return have in common that the net-present-value method and the internal rate of return do not?

E27–9   Comprehensive capital budgeting (L.O. 4)

Usher Corporation is considering the purchase of a conveyor system that costs $92,133. The system has a 15-year life and will result in net cash inflows of $15,000 per year. Assume the use of straight-line depreciation, no residual value, and no income taxes, and round calculations to the nearest dollar.

a. Determine the system's net present value if Usher has a 12% rate of return.
b. Determine the system's internal rate of return.
c. Determine the payback period.
d. Determine the accounting rate of return on the company's initial investment.

E27–10   Capital budgeting methods (L.O. 4)

Consider the following capital budgeting evaluation tools:

1—Net present value
2—Internal rate of return
3—Payback method
4—Accounting rate of return

Match these tools with the comments that follow. In some cases more than one tool may apply.

__ a. Focuses on income, not cash flows.
__ b. Integrates the time value of money into the evaluation process.
__ c. Equates the present value of a project's cash inflows and cash outflows.
__ d. Stresses the recovery of the initial investment outlay.
__ e. Discounts cash flows by employing factors that relate to a company's minimum acceptable return.
__ f. A cash-flow-based approach that ignores selected cash flows on a project.

E27–11   Overview of capital budgeting (L.O. 1, 3, 4)

Evaluate the comments that follow as being True or False. If the comment is false, briefly explain why.

a. Generally speaking, cash flows are preferred over accounting income when evaluating long-term investments.
b. Present value is actually the "reverse" of compound interest.
c. Annuity factors can be derived by summing the present value factors for individual, yearly cash flows.
d. A project's internal rate of return will result in a zero net present value for the project.
e. If income taxes are ignored, depreciation expense amounts should be used when figuring an investment's net present value.

*E27–12   Aftertax cash flows and payback (L.O. 4, 5)

The Choate Company is considering the purchase of a new communication system for its sales offices. Details on the system follow.

> Cost: $160,000
> Service life: 8 years
> Annual beforetax increase in cash operating income: $50,000
> Depreciation method: straight-line
> Income tax rate: 40%

a. Determine the aftertax cash flows related to the new system. *Hint:* Be sure to include the tax savings from depreciation.
b. Compute the system's payback.

PROBLEMS

Series A

P27–A1 Straightforward net-present-value and payback computations (L.O. 4)
Outdoor Adventures is considering the purchase of eight new, state-of-the-art rafts for summer whitewater excursions. The rafts cost a total of $80,000; the service life and residual value are expected to be five years and $20,000, respectively.

Management believes that maximum additional revenues of $65,000 could be produced each season if the rafts are acquired. However, heavy discounting and new competition will likely reduce this figure by $10,000. Variable costs (food, wages, and supplies) are anticipated to be 10% of actual revenues. The company's fixed operating costs (permits, supervisory personnel, advertising, rent, insurance, and depreciation) will increase by $37,000 because of the acquisition. All amounts, except depreciation, are paid when incurred.

Instructions

a. Compute the payback period of the rafts.
b. Ignoring your answer in part (a), would you have any reservations about the acquisition if the payback period was six years? Briefly explain.
c. By using the net-present-value method, determine whether Outdoor Adventures should acquire the rafts. Assume a 12% desired return on all investments, round calculations to the nearest dollar, and ignore income taxes.

P27–A2 Make or buy; net present value; working capital investment (L.O. 4)
Nature's Finest, an environmental group, sends all new members an extensive promotional kit. The kits are currently purchased from an outside supplier for $0.68 each. At the suggestion of the board of directors, the group is considering producing the kits themselves. The following information is available:

- One million kits will be needed annually for the next four years.
- Variable production costs of $0.58 per kit are anticipated.
- The organization will hire a supervisor and assistant for $45,000 per year, plus 20% fringe benefits.
- Specialized equipment that costs $50,000 is needed. The equipment has a four-year service life and a $10,000 disposal value, and will be depreciated by the straight-line method.

Internal production would force the organization to make an immediate $20,000 investment in working capital to acquire needed inventories of paper and supplies. This investment will be recovered at the end of four years when production of the kits will cease because of a change to a different marketing approach. The equipment will be sold at this time as well.

Nature's Finest uses the net-present-value method to analyze investments, requiring a 16% rate of return. Ignore income taxes, and round calculations to the nearest dollar.

Instructions
Determine whether the organization should make or buy the kits.

P27–A3 Basketball player decision (L.O. 4)

The Phoenix Kings of the United Basketball League have a moody center by the name of Orlando Dawkins. Dawkins is under contract with the team and is scheduled to earn $650,000 in both 19X3 and 19X4. A $75,000 salary increase will take effect in 19X5.

Dawkins has not gotten along with several of his teammates and, as a result, management is exploring the possibility of a trade with the Philadelphia Rockets to acquire George Harper, a star player. The Kings would pay the Rockets $350,000 immediately for the trade to take place. Harper would be paid a $270,000 signing bonus at the beginning of 19X3 that management plans to expense over the next three years by using straight-line amortization. Harper's annual salary would be $950,000 from 19X3 through 19X5, highest on the team because of his ability to attract fans. The Kings expect that increased attendance will produce added annual net cash inflows of $525,000.

Phoenix officials feel that both players would play three more years for the Kings, at which time they would become free agents and move along to other clubs. The Kings would receive $380,000 compensation from the other club for Dawkins; for Harper the figure would increase to $500,000. Regardless of whether the trade takes place, the Kings are obligated to pay Dawkins $200,000 at the end of 19X4 under the terms of his original contract.

The Kings desire a rate of return of 14% and use the net-present-value method to analyze investments. Round all calculations to the nearest dollar and ignore income taxes.

Instructions

a. Determine whether the Kings should keep Dawkins or trade for Harper. Assume the trade would occur on January 1, 19X3.
b. Future cash flows are, in many cases, subject to change. List several events that could occur that might influence the cash flows in this situation.

P27–A4 Payback analysis; accounting rate of return (L.O. 4)

Tasty Treats is studying the acquisition of a new vehicle to expand its fleet of ice-cream trucks for service in suburban neighborhoods. The truck, which has an eight-year service life and $2,000 residual value, is expected to cost $20,000. The company's owner anticipates that annual sales will increase by $25,000 if the truck is acquired. Annual operating costs will be: gasoline, $2,000; license, $100; maintenance and repair, $1,200; driver's salary, $6,800; and insurance, $900. The cost of ice cream generally averages 40% of sales. Ignore income taxes.

Instructions

a. Compute the annual net cash inflow from operation of the additional truck.
b. Determine the payback period.
c. If Tasty Treats requires an accounting rate of return on initial investment of 12%, should the truck be acquired?

*P27–A5 Cash flow; taxes; net present value (L.O. 4, 5)

Central Plains Freight Company is studying the possibility of adding a new truck to its fleet. The vehicle will cost $80,000 and is expected to generate annual sales revenues of $70,000. Central depreciates all vehicles by the straight-line method over a six-year service life. An $8,000 residual value is anticipated.

Management expects that the vehicle will be driven approximately 25,000 miles each year. Cash operating costs will average $0.22 per mile in Years 1–3 and then jump to $0.26 in Years 4–6. A driver will be paid a $35,000 annual salary.

Central Plains is subject to a 40% tax rate on all items of revenue and expense and requires a 16% return on all investments. The company employs the net-present-value method to evaluate long-term projects.

Instructions

a. The following schedule has been designed to identify the net cash flows related to the truck. The first two items are done as examples.

ITEM	AMOUNT	TAX EFFECT, IF ANY*	AFTERTAX CASH FLOW
Truck cost	$(80,000)	None	$(80,000)
Revenues	70,000	$(28,000)	42,000

*Parentheses denote an increase in taxes.

Complete the schedule for the remaining items that result in an aftertax cash flow.

b. Use the aftertax cash flow amounts in a net-present-value analysis and determine whether Central Plains should acquire the truck. Round all computations to the nearest dollar.

Series B

P27–B1 Straightforward net-present-value and payback computations (L.O. 4)
The Calgary Eskimos play in the Canadian Hockey League. Although the Eskimos will soon be moving to a modern arena, management is studying the possibility of expanding the team's present facility to accommodate increased crowds. A $2.4 million expansion is planned that has a $200,000 residual value and will be depreciated by the straight-line method over four seasons. Information about the expansion follows.

	NUMBER OF SEATS	OCCUPANCY RATE	TICKET PRICE
Class 1 seats	2,500	80%	$6
Class 2 seats	2,000	60	4

The team will play 50 home games each season. Total added operating costs per game (ushers, cleanup, and depreciation) are expected to average $11,800. All such costs, except depreciation, require cash outlays.

Instructions

a. Compute the payback period of the expansion.
b. By using the net-present-value method and a 16% desired rate of return, determine whether the expansion should be undertaken.
c. In addition to the cash flows presented here, what other cash flows might change if the Eskimos expand the arena?

P27–B2 Make or buy; net present value; working capital investment (L.O. 4)
Equity Products manufactures electronic components used in the appliance industry. The company currently purchases a particular part for $1.75. Because of problems with product quality and supplier reliability, Equity is studying whether to manufacture the part internally.

To begin production, new machinery must be acquired that costs $380,000. The machinery, which has a six-year life and an estimated residual value of $50,000, will be depreciated by the straight-line method. Art Sanchez, a current Equity employee, will oversee manufacturing activities and will be given a $7,000 raise because of increased responsibilities. Sanchez's original position will remain unfilled.

The company's cost accountants and engineers have estimated the unit variable production costs that follow.

Direct materials	$0.22
Direct labor	0.40
Variable factory overhead	0.32

Equity must make an immediate $30,000 working capital investment to build needed direct materials inventories. Annual production should total 120,000 units over each of the next six years. Manufacturing activities will then be discontinued and the materials inventories depleted (i.e., working capital recovered) because of a planned change in Equity's product line. The machinery will be sold because of its specialized nature.

Management uses the net-present-value method to analyze investment opportunities, requiring a 10% minimum rate of return. Ignore income taxes, and round calculations to the nearest dollar.

Instructions

Determine whether Equity should make or buy the part.

P27–B3 Equipment replacement decision (L.O. 4)

Uncle Joe's Cheesecake Co., uses an old truck to deliver its products to area supermarkets. Information about the truck, which has a remaining service life of five years, follows.

Cost	$45,000
Engine overhaul cost in two years	5,000
Annual operating costs	22,000
Current market value	30,000
Estimated residual value in five years	10,000

Management is considering the acquisition of a new vehicle. The new truck costs $70,000 and is expected to have a five-year service life and a $15,000 residual value. Operating costs will total $14,000 per year.

Uncle Joe's has a minimum desired return of 12% and depreciates all equipment by using the straight-line method.

Instructions

a. By using the net-present-value method, determine whether Uncle Joe's should keep its present truck or acquire the new vehicle. Round all calculations to the nearest dollar, and ignore income taxes.
b. What other factors should be considered in this decision?

P27–B4 Payback analysis; accounting rate of return (L.O. 4)

Scenic Ventures is studying the acquisition of a helicopter for tours of the Caribbean islands. The helicopter will cost $5 million, is expected to have a $1.4 million residual value, and will be depreciated over a 12-year service life by the straight-line method. The following annual cash operating costs are anticipated:

Fuel	$60,000
Wages	85,000
Maintenance	45,000
Insurance	58,000
Licenses	2,000

Tours will be provided on a year-round basis, with five trips being made each day. Operations will be shut down for selected holidays (Thanksgiving and Christmas), bad weather (six days), and major maintenance procedures (seven days). Scenic charges $75 per passenger, and the average tour is expected to have eight passengers.

Instructions

a. Compute the annual net cash inflow from the new helicopter.
b. If Scenic requires a payback of five years, should the helicopter be acquired?
c. Calculate the helicopter's accounting rate of return.

*P27–B5 Cash flow; taxes; net present value (L.O. 4, 5)

The Medstar Family Clinic currently has limited lab facilities for its patients. As a result, the practicing physicians have obtained a proposal from SurgiTech to supply new, state-of-the-art equipment. The equipment will cost $650,000 and will be depreciated by the straight-line method down to a $50,000 residual value. The following information is known:

Service life of equipment	8 years
Annual number of lab tests performed	
Years 1–2	2,900
Years 3–8	3,300
Average patient billing per test	$52
Annual wage of part-time lab assistant	$17,000
Maintenance cost at end of Year 5	$3,000

Medstar requires a 12% rate of return on all investments and plans to use the net-present-value method to analyze the SurgiTech proposal. The clinic is subject to a 30% income tax rate on all items of revenue and expense.

Instructions

a. The following schedule has been designed to identify the net cash flows related to the equipment. The two items shown are done as examples.

ITEM	AMOUNT	TAX EFFECT, IF ANY*	AFTERTAX CASH FLOW
Equipment cost	$(650,000)	None	$(650,000)
Maintenance	(3,000)	$900	(2,100)

* Parentheses denote an increase in taxes.

Complete the schedule for the remaining items that result in an aftertax cash flow.

b. Use the aftertax cash flow amounts in a net-present-value analysis and determine whether Medstar should acquire the equipment. Round all computations to the nearest dollar.

Expanding Your Horizons

EYH27–1 The time value of money (L.O. 2)

The majority of states have a lottery. In many cases, if there is no winner for several weeks, the grand prize can accumulate to a multi-million dollar payoff. Most contestants fail to realize that the payoff is typically not made in a single, lump-sum amount; instead, it is disbursed in installments over several years.

Instructions

Form a team with three other students in your class and identify three states that have a lottery. Determine the payment method(s) of these lotteries by contacting the appropriate state officials. (It would be interesting to also learn how the states picked their distribution methods, but this information may be difficult to uncover.) Then, using a 10% interest rate, determine the present value of a $5 million payout under each of the approaches. Summarize your findings in a one-page report.

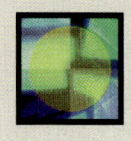

EYH27–2 Capital budgeting in practice (L.O. 4)

Although present value techniques have been around for decades, there are still many organizations that ignore discounted cash flows to evaluate their projects. These firms focus on payback and the accounting rate of return.

Instructions

Working in a group of five students, contact the chief financial officer (CFO) or controller of three large corporations in your area. Determine the methods employed by these firms when assessing capital projects. Ask about why these approaches are used and why other methods are not. Be prepared to report your findings to the class.

EYH27–3 Capital budgeting in practice, international (L.O. 4)

The use of capital budgeting methods will sometimes vary from one country to another. Periodic surveys are often taken that identify significant differences in usage.

Instructions

Locate three research studies in your library that focus on the popularity of net present value, the internal rate of return, payback, and the accounting rate of return in different countries. If disclosed, summarize any reasons that underlie differences in the methods' usage. Prepare a short report of your findings.

EYH27–4 Net present value; algebra; analysis (L.O. 1, 2, 4)

Nancy Petersen is considering various investment opportunities for her employer. One such opportunity involves obtaining a five-year franchise from Cookies, Inc., to operate a store at Pepperwood Mall. Cookies, Inc., requires a $40,000 immediate up-front payment. In addition, each store must be furnished with $200,000 of equipment that has a five-year life and a $20,000 disposal value. Additional information follows.

Anticipated annual sales	16,000 dozen
Annual franchise fee	5% of sales revenue
Variable cost per dozen	$2.25
Annual mall rent	
Years 1–2	$12,000
Years 3–5	$13,500

Cookies, Inc., will allow each franchise to set its own selling price on the basis of regional factors, local competition, and so forth. The price can range from $6.75 to $7.50 per dozen. In an effort to maximize sales, Petersen's employer would charge $6.75.

Assume a 10% rate of return is required on all investments. Ignore income taxes.

Instructions

a. Compute the net present value of the cookie franchise, rounding calculations to the nearest dollar. Should the store be opened? Why or why not?
b. At what selling price would the franchise produce a zero net present value? What has a strong possibility of changing if this selling price is charged?
c. How did Petersen's employer likely arrive at the 10% target return figure that is required for project acceptance?
d. What actions must Petersen's employer undertake to further improve the attractiveness of this endeavor?

COMMUNICATION OF ACCOUNTING INFORMATION

CAI27–1 An overview of communication techniques (L.O. 1)

Communication Principle: Effective communication is a key to business success. Memos, reports, charts, graphs, and oral presentations collectively convey information for a variety of purposes. Often, the ability to structure concise, understandable presentations has a significant impact on the situation at hand. Sloppy resumés, for example, are sure to eliminate a potential employee from consideration in a tight job market. A manager's report, to be reviewed by the board of directors, may be the major factor that underlies board acceptance or rejection of a given decision alternative.

In sum, the ability to communicate often makes the difference and should not be taken lightly. As you pursue a career in accounting, marketing, systems, or whatever your chosen profession may be, you no doubt will have many opportunities to experience the importance of effective delivery of information.

■ ■ ■ ■ ■ ■ ■ ■

In the next four weeks, Diane Horan must prepare a written and oral presentation for Fairfax Corporation's board of directors. The presentation focuses on the need for a new mainframe computer system, estimated to cost $2.7 million. Both the net-present-value and payback methods have found the computer to be an extremely attractive investment.

Because of other pressing obligations, Diane has enlisted the help of David Clark, a fellow employee. David is extremely bright and also very knowledgeable about the computer system. However, his communication skills are somewhat weak. Diane has therefore decided to prepare a list of "significant communication principles" for David's use.

Instructions

Assume the role of Diane Horan and prepare the list just mentioned. The principles should be taken from appropriate Communication of Accounting Information (CAI) problems in earlier chapters of this text.

Answers to Chapter Quiz

1. c
2. a
3. b $(200,000) × 1.00000 = $(200,000)
          40,000 × 4.35526 =   174,210
                              $ (25,790)
4. c
5. d

Appendix A: Special Journal Systems

As explained in Chapter 6, companies may choose from a variety of systems to process transactions and produce financial information. For those businesses that have rejected computerized systems in favor of manual accounting procedures, the use of special journals is a possible option. **Special journals** handle specialized (specific) types of high-frequency transactions. Careful study of Appendix A will show a distinct parallel between this form of manual processing and the computerized modular systems that now abound in practice.

Types and Benefits of Special Journals

A review of many companies' business operations will often find that roughly 90% of the accompanying transactions fall into one of four categories. The special journal system is based on this finding, with the following four types of journals normally used to record business activity.

Journal	Transactions Contained
Sales journal	Sales of merchandise on account
Purchases journal	Purchases of merchandise on account
Cash receipts journal	Receipts of cash
Cash payments journal	Payments of cash

Naturally, not all transactions and events will fit neatly into these classifications. Consider, for example, the need to record sales returns and allowances, purchases returns and allowances, adjusting entries, and closing entries. These and other similar items are therefore recorded in the general journal, which assumes a new role. Rather than being used to handle all business activity, as shown in Chapters 2–5, the general journal is now employed *solely* for miscellaneous transactions and events (namely, those not accommodated in special journals).

Companies that use special journals tend to receive two basic benefits. First, firms are able to spread their work load, since each journal can be maintained by a different employee. All credit sales can be accounted for by one person, all cash receipts by another, and so on. Second, special journals significantly reduce the amount of posting necessary to process transactions.[1]

SALES JOURNAL

The sales journal is employed to record sales of merchandise on account. We will illustrate the journal's use by examining various transactions of Stereo Unlimited, a wholesale distributor of stereo equipment, tapes, and compact discs. The firm had the following credit sales during January:

Jan. 4 Sold $1,350 of stereo equipment on account (invoice no. 101) to House of Music.
12 Secured a new customer (The Sound Center) and sold $400 of tapes on account (invoice no. 102).
18 Sold $150 of compact discs on account (invoice no. 103) to Treetops Lounge.
25 Sold $1,200 of stereo equipment and $200 of compact discs on account (invoice no. 104) to Walton's Music Store.

Stereo Unlimited's sales journal is shown in Exhibit A–1. The entries are taken from the data that appear on each sales invoice. Notice that only one line is necessary to record an individual transaction and the usual debit/credit format is absent. Also, journal entry explanations are not used because all transactions are of the same type: a sale of merchandise on account.

To understand the journal's operation, let us keep our objectives in mind. The customer accounts in the subsidiary ledger must be updated to reflect the added amounts due the firm. Furthermore, the Accounts Receivable and Sales accounts must both be increased, the former to achieve the required control account/subsidiary ledger equality and the latter because the company has generated revenues from each of the four transactions. The preceding objectives are carried out through the posting process, which is illustrated in the exhibit.

Posting the Sales Journal. Exhibit A–1 reveals that individual sales are posted daily to the appropriate customer's account in the subsidiary ledger. Daily posting is necessary to keep up-to-date balances, which are helpful in both credit decisions and in responding to customer queries. To signify completion of this process and to provide an *audit trail* (i.e., a means to trace and access accounting information), one enters the notation S1 (sales journal, page 1) as a reference in the customer's account. Finally, a check mark is placed in the sales journal to indicate that the transaction was transferred to the subsidiary ledger.[2] These procedures are repeated until all transactions are posted.

Next, the control account is updated to maintain the necessary equality. Because the only type of transaction recorded in the sales journal is a sale of merchandise on account, the total of the amount column is posted periodically (e.g., monthly) as a debit to Accounts Receivable control and a credit to Sales.

---

[1] If you have not already done so, please read the section in Chapter 6 entitled "Subsidiary Ledgers and Control Accounts" (pp. 220–221).
[2] Check marks are used because of the absence of account numbers in the subsidiary ledger. Companies that follow this practice arrange customer and creditor accounts alphabetically, thereby allowing for growth (or contraction) without having to modify numbering schemes.

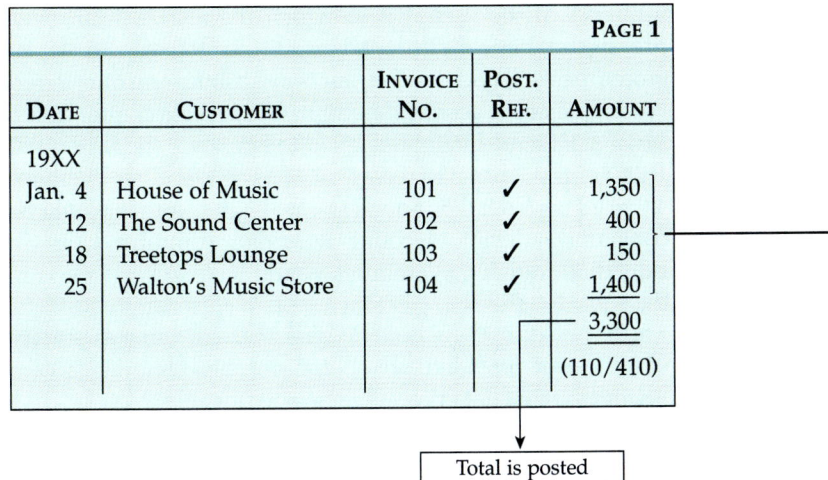

SALES JOURNAL

PAGE 1

DATE	CUSTOMER	INVOICE NO.	POST. REF.	AMOUNT
19XX				
Jan. 4	House of Music	101	✓	1,350
12	The Sound Center	102	✓	400
18	Treetops Lounge	103	✓	150
25	Walton's Music Store	104	✓	1,400
				3,300
				(110/410)

Total is posted monthly to general ledger accounts.

Individual amounts are posted daily to customer accounts in the subsidiary ledger.

GENERAL LEDGER

ACCOUNTS RECEIVABLE — ACCOUNT NO. 110

DATE	REF.	DEBIT	CREDIT	BALANCE
19XX				
Jan. 31	S1	3,300		3,300

SALES — ACCOUNT NO. 410

DATE	REF.	DEBIT	CREDIT	BALANCE
19XX				
Jan. 31	S1		3,300	3,300

ACCOUNTS RECEIVABLE SUBSIDIARY LEDGER

HOUSE OF MUSIC

DATE	REF.	DEBIT	CREDIT	BALANCE
19XX				
Jan. 4	S1	1,350		1,350

THE SOUND CENTER

DATE	REF.	DEBIT	CREDIT	BALANCE
19XX				
Jan. 12	S1	400		400

TREETOPS LOUNGE

DATE	REF.	DEBIT	CREDIT	BALANCE
19XX				
Jan. 18	S1	150		150

WALTON'S MUSIC STORE

DATE	REF.	DEBIT	CREDIT	BALANCE
19XX				
Jan. 25	S1	1,400		1,400

EXHIBIT A–1
Sales Journal and Related Postings

The notation S1 is then entered in these accounts in the general ledger. To finish the process, the numbers of the accounts to which the $3,300 figure was posted, 110 and 410, are written beneath the total.

A review of these procedures will find that the four transactions were transferred to the proper accounts by a total of six postings: Accounts Receivable control, Sales, and four subsidiary accounts. If Stereo Unlimited failed to employ a special journal system and instead used a general journal to record all of its transactions, the number of postings would increase considerably. Four separate journal entries would be constructed, each one containing a debit to Accounts Receivable control and a credit to Sales. Further, the individual transaction amounts would have to be charged to customer accounts in the subsidiary ledger, creating a total of 12 separate postings. As you can well imagine, the bookkeeping would become overwhelming as activity increases. Thankfully, the efficiency provided by a special journal accounting system is dramatic, thereby allowing manual data processing at a reasonable cost.

Journal Variations. The journals illustrated in this appendix are general models that can be altered to meet the needs of individual businesses. For example, if a company were charging its customers for sales taxes, an additional column could be added in the sales journal to record the taxes payable to the government. Or if management desired to report sales by product line, a minor design change would allow a firm to produce the necessary information. An expanded journal for Stereo Unlimited, for instance, might contain the following amount columns: Accounts Receivable debit, Stereo Equipment Sales credit, Tape Sales credit, and Compact Disc Sales credit.

A number of variations in journal design are possible. Generally speaking, separate amount columns are established when (1) more detailed accounting information is desired, as in the preceding case, or (2) transactions occur on a highly repetitive basis. These design "rules" will become more apparent in later sections of the appendix.

PURCHASES JOURNAL

The procedures associated with the sales journal very closely parallel those employed with the purchases journal. The **purchases journal** is used to record only one type of transaction: purchases of merchandise on account. Other types of acquisitions are recorded elsewhere. For example, an acquisition of merchandise for cash would be entered in the cash payments journal, whereas a purchase of equipment on account would be placed in the general journal.

Every purchase of merchandise on account requires a debit to Purchases and a credit to Accounts Payable. In addition, because a business needs detailed information regarding the amounts owed to each supplier, a separate subsidiary ledger must be established. The sum of the individual creditor accounts in the subsidiary ledger must again equal the balance in the general ledger control account—Accounts Payable in this case.

Stereo Unlimited's purchases journal and related postings appear in Exhibit A–2. Individual amounts for purchases are credited daily to suppliers' accounts in the subsidiary ledger, because the balances owed have increased. Once again, completion of posting is denoted by placing a check mark in the journal. The journal's total is then posted at month-end as a debit to Purchases and a credit to Accounts Payable control. The P1 references in the ledger accounts indicate that the entries were transferred from page 1 of the purchases journal.

PURCHASES JOURNAL

PAGE 1

DATE	SUPPLIER	INVOICE INFORMATION DATE	NO.	TERMS	POST. REF.	AMOUNT
19XX						
Jan. 3	Able Electronics	Jan. 3	1721	—	✓	2,100
8	Columbia Tapes & CDs	7	1777	2/10, n/30	✓	750
16	Pioneer Associates	16	AF471	—	✓	420
26	Sony Corp.	26	9576	3/10, n/30	✓	2,060
						5,330
						(501/201)

Total is posted monthly to general ledger accounts.

Individual amounts are posted daily to creditor accounts in the subsidiary ledger.

GENERAL LEDGER

ACCOUNTS PAYABLE — ACCOUNT NO. 201

DATE	REF.	DEBIT	CREDIT	BALANCE
19XX				
Jan. 31	P1		5,330	5,330

PURCHASES — ACCOUNT NO. 501

DATE	REF.	DEBIT	CREDIT	BALANCE
19XX				
Jan. 31	P1	5,330		5,330

ACCOUNTS PAYABLE SUBSIDIARY LEDGER

ABLE ELECTRONICS

DATE	REF.	DEBIT	CREDIT	BALANCE
19XX				
Jan. 3	P1		2,100	2,100

COLUMBIA TAPES & CDs

DATE	REF.	DEBIT	CREDIT	BALANCE
19XX				
Jan. 8	P1		750	750

PIONEER ASSOCIATES

DATE	REF.	DEBIT	CREDIT	BALANCE
19XX				
Jan. 16	P1		420	420

SONY CORP.

DATE	REF.	DEBIT	CREDIT	BALANCE
19XX				
Jan. 26	P1		2,060	2,060

EXHIBIT A–2
Purchases Journal and Related Postings

Overall, you should observe two similarities in the operation of the sales and purchases journals, namely:

- Individual transaction amounts that affect subsidiary ledgers are posted daily to the appropriate subsidiary ledger accounts.
- Totals that affect control accounts are posted monthly to the general ledger.

CASH RECEIPTS JOURNAL

A company receives cash from many different sources, including cash sales, customer payments on account, the sale of old equipment, and bank loans. The possibilities are numerous. The **cash receipts journal** must therefore have multiple amount columns since all cash receipts are recorded here. Normally, separate columns are established for transactions that occur on a frequent basis.

Stereo Unlimited had the following cash receipts during January:

Jan. 2 Received $2,000 from Patricia Monroe, owner of Stereo Unlimited, as an investment in the business.
    9 Sold $650 of stereo equipment and $150 of tapes for cash to Central Stereo.
  13 Received a check on account from House of Music for the sale on January 4, minus the correct discount.
  17 Received loan proceeds of $4,800 from California Trust Company to acquire several new display cases.
  22 Sold $200 of compact discs to Burrows Music Company for cash.
  28 Received a $280 check on account from The Sound Center in partial payment of the sale made on January 12.

Proper recording of these transactions is shown in Exhibit A–3. Assume that all credit sales were subject to terms of 2/10, n/30.

Operation of the Cash Receipts Journal. Transactions are entered in the cash receipts journal in accordance with accounting's normal debit/credit rules. To illustrate, examine the receipt on account from The Sound Center on January 28. An entry for $280 is placed in both the Cash debit column and the Accounts Receivable credit column. The Sound Center appears in the Account space because the firm's subsidiary ledger account must be updated.

Transactions that do not arise often are recorded in the Sundry or miscellaneous column. On January 2, for example, Stereo Unlimited received $2,000 from Patricia Monroe as an investment in the business. The receipt requires a debit to Cash. Because owner investments are infrequent, the company has not established a separate capital column. Instead, $2,000 is placed in Sundry and Patricia Monroe, Capital, is entered in the Account space.

Note that the Account space is left blank for cash sales. Stereo Unlimited, like many other businesses, makes no attempt to gather the names of its cash customers. An explanation of the transaction may be entered if desired (e.g., Daily Cash Sales).

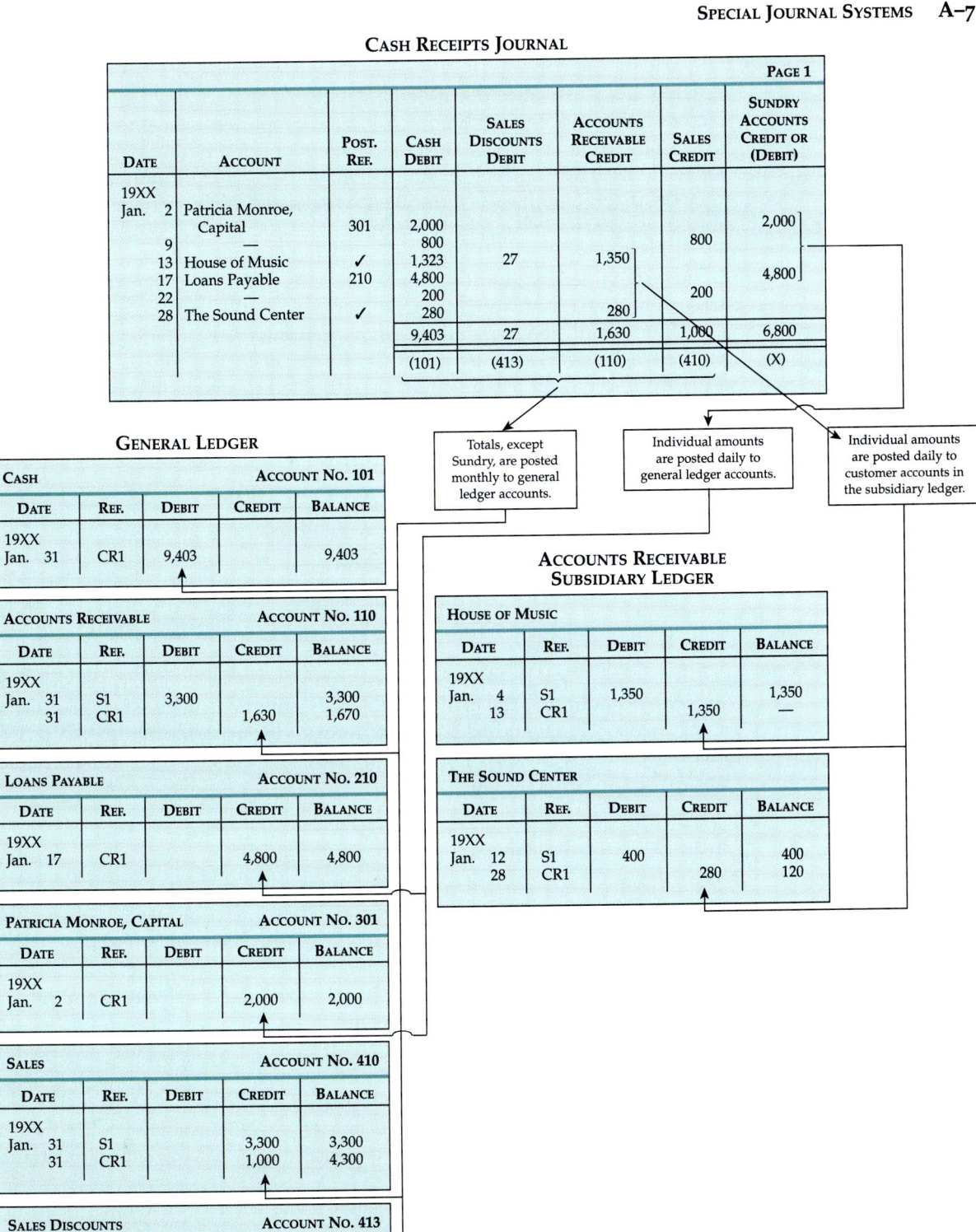

CASH RECEIPTS JOURNAL

PAGE 1

DATE	ACCOUNT	POST. REF.	CASH DEBIT	SALES DISCOUNTS DEBIT	ACCOUNTS RECEIVABLE CREDIT	SALES CREDIT	SUNDRY ACCOUNTS CREDIT OR (DEBIT)
19XX							
Jan. 2	Patricia Monroe, Capital	301	2,000				2,000
9	—		800			800	
13	House of Music	✓	1,323	27	1,350		
17	Loans Payable	210	4,800				4,800
22	—		200			200	
28	The Sound Center	✓	280		280		
			9,403	27	1,630	1,000	6,800
			(101)	(413)	(110)	(410)	(X)

Totals, except Sundry, are posted monthly to general ledger accounts.

Individual amounts are posted daily to general ledger accounts.

Individual amounts are posted daily to customer accounts in the subsidiary ledger.

GENERAL LEDGER

CASH — ACCOUNT NO. 101

DATE	REF.	DEBIT	CREDIT	BALANCE
19XX				
Jan. 31	CR1	9,403		9,403

ACCOUNTS RECEIVABLE — ACCOUNT NO. 110

DATE	REF.	DEBIT	CREDIT	BALANCE
19XX				
Jan. 31	S1	3,300		3,300
31	CR1		1,630	1,670

LOANS PAYABLE — ACCOUNT NO. 210

DATE	REF.	DEBIT	CREDIT	BALANCE
19XX				
Jan. 17	CR1		4,800	4,800

PATRICIA MONROE, CAPITAL — ACCOUNT NO. 301

DATE	REF.	DEBIT	CREDIT	BALANCE
19XX				
Jan. 2	CR1		2,000	2,000

SALES — ACCOUNT NO. 410

DATE	REF.	DEBIT	CREDIT	BALANCE
19XX				
Jan. 31	S1		3,300	3,300
31	CR1		1,000	4,300

SALES DISCOUNTS — ACCOUNT NO. 413

DATE	REF.	DEBIT	CREDIT	BALANCE
19XX				
Jan. 31	CR1	27		27

ACCOUNTS RECEIVABLE SUBSIDIARY LEDGER

HOUSE OF MUSIC

DATE	REF.	DEBIT	CREDIT	BALANCE
19XX				
Jan. 4	S1	1,350		1,350
13	CR1		1,350	—

THE SOUND CENTER

DATE	REF.	DEBIT	CREDIT	BALANCE
19XX				
Jan. 12	S1	400		400
28	CR1		280	120

EXHIBIT A–3
Cash Receipts Journal and Related Postings

Posting the Cash Receipts Journal. Individual amounts that appear in the Accounts Receivable and Sundry columns are posted throughout the month. Collections from credit customers are generally posted daily to the subsidiary ledger to maintain current account balances; Sundry entries are transferred as they occur to minimize work during the hectic end of the period. As a result of this latter procedure, respective credits of $2,000 and $4,800 were posted to Patricia Monroe, Capital (account no. 301) and Loans Payable (account no. 210) in the general ledger. Entries in these accounts and others show a reference of CR1, indicating the amounts originated on page 1 of the cash receipts journal.

Upon conclusion of monthly activity, column totals are transferred to their respective ledger accounts. Before this process is performed, however, the equality of debits and credits must be evaluated to ensure that the accounting records are in balance. In the case of Stereo Unlimited, the required equality is maintained:

DEBITS		CREDITS	
Cash	$9,403	Accounts receivable	$1,630
Sales discounts	27	Sales	1,000
	$9,430	Sundry accounts	6,800
			$9,430

All column totals are posted, with one exception: Sundry. As the X in Exhibit A–3 indicates, the total of the Sundry column is not posted, because its components ($2,000 and $4,800) have already been transferred to the proper accounts. The $6,800 total is generated only for use in determining whether total debits are equal to total credits.

CASH PAYMENTS JOURNAL

The **cash payments journal** is used to record virtually all cash disbursements that are made by a business.[3] This journal, too, is multicolumn in format, with separate columns established for high-frequency transactions or when more detailed accounting information is desired.

Stereo Unlimited's cash disbursements during January were as follows:

Jan. 4   Paid January rent of $750 to Kraft Management by issuing check no. 101.
    11   Issued check no. 102 for $100 to Central Stereo for the return of stereo equipment sold for cash on January 9.
    14   Paid invoice no. 1777, dated January 7, of Columbia Tapes & CDs by issuing check no. 103. The invoice totaled $750 and was subject to terms of 2/10, n/30.
    19   Paid $650 of sales commissions to John Harrison by issuing check no. 104.
    27   Issued check no. 105 to Able Electronics for $2,100, in payment of the purchase made on January 3.

These transactions are recorded in the cash payments journal that appears in Exhibit A–4.

---

[3] A minor exception occurs with small miscellaneous payments that are made from a petty cash system. The operation of a petty cash system is discussed in Chapter 8.

CASH PAYMENTS JOURNAL

PAGE 1

Date	Check No.	Payee	Account	Post. Ref.	Cash Credit	Purchases Discounts Credit	Accounts Payable Debit	Sundry Accounts Debit or (Credit)
19XX Jan. 4	101	Kraft Management	Rent Expense	530	750			750
11	102	Central Stereo	Sales Returns & Allowances	414	100			100
14	103	Columbia Tapes & CDs		✓	735	15	750	
19	104	John Harrison	Sales Commissions	540	650			650
27	105	Able Electronics		✓	2,100		2,100	
					4,335	15	2,850	1,500
					(101)	(504)	(201)	(X)

GENERAL LEDGER

CASH — ACCOUNT NO. 101

Date	Ref.	Debit	Credit	Balance
19XX Jan. 31	CR1	9,403		9,403
31	CP1		4,335	5,068

ACCOUNTS PAYABLE — ACCOUNT NO. 201

Date	Ref.	Debit	Credit	Balance
19XX Jan. 31	P1		5,330	5,330
31	CP1	2,850		2,480

SALES RETURNS & ALLOWANCES — ACCOUNT NO. 414

Date	Ref.	Debit	Credit	Balance
19XX Jan. 11	CP1	100		100

PURCHASES DISCOUNTS — ACCOUNT NO. 504

Date	Ref.	Debit	Credit	Balance
19XX Jan. 31	CP1		15	15

RENT EXPENSE — ACCOUNT NO. 530

Date	Ref.	Debit	Credit	Balance
19XX Jan. 4	CP1	750		750

SALES COMMISSIONS — ACCOUNT NO. 540

Date	Ref.	Debit	Credit	Balance
19XX Jan. 19	CP1	650		650

Totals, except Sundry, are posted monthly to general ledger accounts.

Individual amounts are posted daily to general ledger accounts.

Individual amounts are posted daily to creditor accounts in the subsidiary ledger.

ACCOUNTS PAYABLE SUBSIDIARY LEDGER

ABLE ELECTRONICS

Date	Ref.	Debit	Credit	Balance
19XX Jan. 3	P1		2,100	2,100
27	CP1	2,100		—

COLUMBIA TAPES & CDs

Date	Ref.	Debit	Credit	Balance
19XX Jan. 8	P1		750	750
14	CP1	750		—

EXHIBIT A–4
Cash Payments Journal and Related Postings

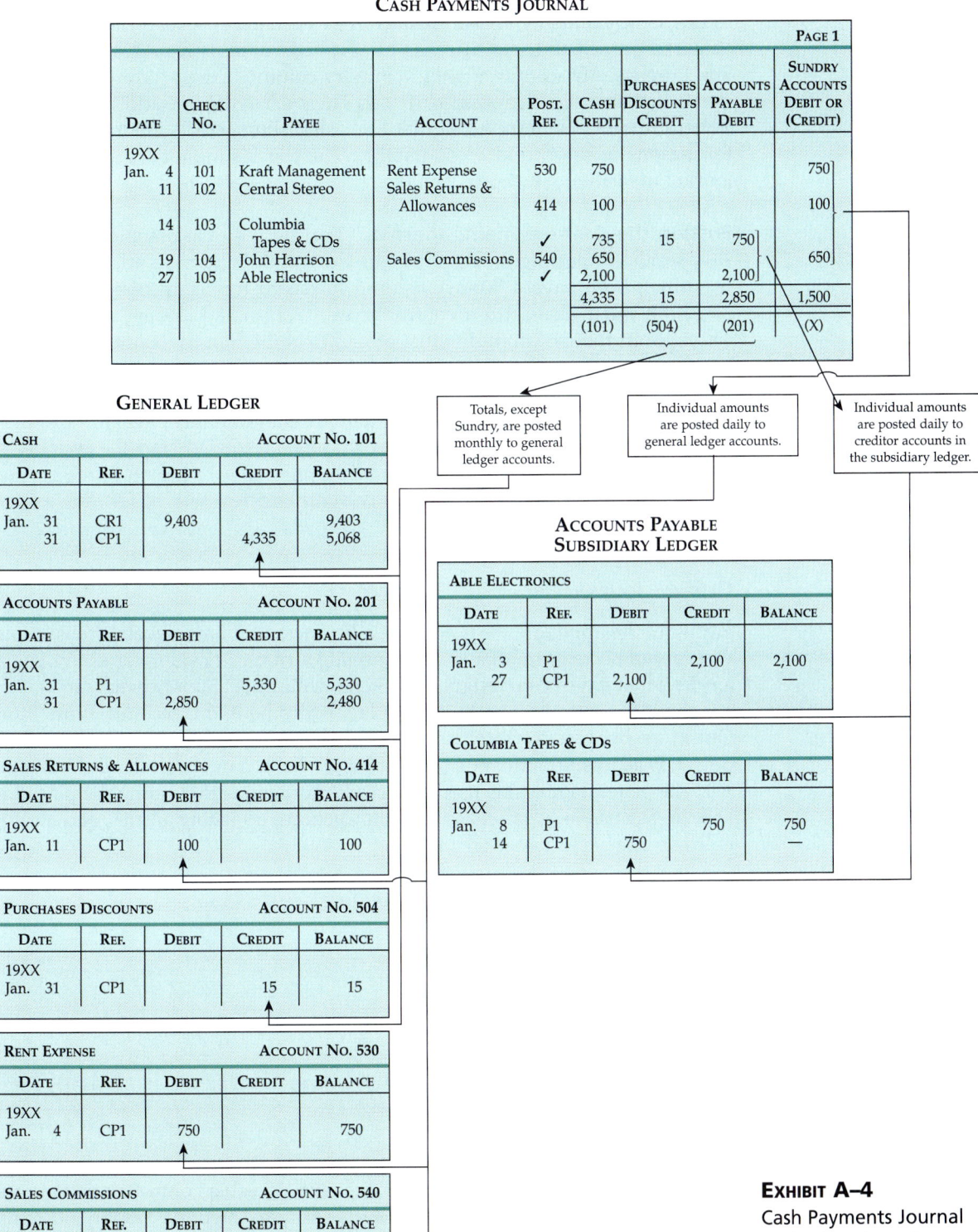

Observe that the journal has a Cash credit column since each payment reduces the company's cash balance. Furthermore, because merchandise is acquired on account, the firm has established columns for Accounts Payable and Purchases Discounts. Finally, a Sundry column is used to record disbursements that are made for other purposes. The journal has one additional feature: a check number column. All significant cash disbursements are made by check for reasons of safety and accountability. The check's number is entered in the journal to facilitate the audit trail (i.e., tracing) process.

Posting the Cash Payments Journal. Posting the cash payments journal is very similar to posting the cash receipts journal. Both journals are multicolumn in format, both have a Sundry column to record miscellaneous transactions, and both must deal with a control account/subsidiary ledger arrangement. Throughout the month, individual amounts in the Sundry column are posted to the proper accounts in the general ledger (e.g., Rent Expense, Sales Returns & Allowances, and Sales Commissions). Similarly, entries in the Accounts Payable debit column are transferred daily to the Accounts Payable subsidiary ledger. At the end of the month, the columns are totaled, and the equality of debits and credits is checked. Then all column totals are posted to the general ledger, with the exception of Sundry. The entries referenced by CP1 have come from the cash payments journal, page 1.

GENERAL JOURNAL

Earlier in the appendix we noted that a business will have several transactions that cannot be accommodated in its special journals. Consider, for example, the journals that have been designed for Stereo Unlimited. Suppose that on January 19, the firm bought $2,600 of display equipment on account from Store Outfitters. Because the purchases journal contains only purchases of merchandise, this acquisition must be recorded elsewhere, namely, in the general journal. The general journal is used to record transactions that cannot be placed in special journals (e.g., miscellaneous transactions, adjusting entries, and closing entries). The necessary entry follows.

GENERAL JOURNAL

PAGE 1

19XX				
Jan. 19	Display Equipment	130	2,600	
	Accounts Payable: Store Outfitters	201/✓		2,600
	Purchased equipment on account.			

As the posting references indicate, the transaction was transferred to the Display Equipment account and the Accounts Payable control account in the general ledger. In addition, Store Outfitters was credited in the Accounts Payable subsidiary ledger. The effect of the latter two postings can be seen by viewing the accounts depicted on page A–11.

Exhibit A–5
Accounts Payable Relationships for Stereo Unlimited

ACCOUNTS PAYABLE SUBSIDIARY LEDGER

PIONEER ASSOCIATES

DATE	REF.	DEBIT	CREDIT	BALANCE
19XX Jan. 16	P1		420	420

SONY CORP.

DATE	REF.	DEBIT	CREDIT	BALANCE
19XX Jan. 26	P1		2,060	2,060

STORE OUTFITTERS

DATE	REF.	DEBIT	CREDIT	BALANCE
19XX Jan. 19	J1		2,600	2,600

STEREO UNLIMITED
Schedule of Accounts Payable
January 31, 19XX

Pioneer Associates	$ 420
Sony Corp.	2,060
Store Outfitters	2,600
	$5,080

CONTROL ACCOUNT

ACCOUNTS PAYABLE — ACCOUNT NO. 201

DATE	REF.	DEBIT	CREDIT	BALANCE
19XX Jan. 19	J1		2,600	2,600
31	P1		5,330	7,930
31	CP1	2,850		5,080

Note: The January 19th purchase is shown in the Accounts Payable control account here but not in those depicted in Exhibits A–2 and A–4. The reason is that the transaction had not yet been presented, making inclusion in the earlier exhibits inappropriate.

SEVERAL FINAL COMMENTS

Once all postings are completed, a general ledger trial balance is constructed as the first step in summarizing the period's activity. The necessary procedures are identical to those discussed in Chapter 2 and are not repeated here. In addition to preparing a trial balance, the subsidiary ledger/control account equality must be checked. This technique was introduced in Exhibit 6–1; it is shown for Stereo Unlimited's Accounts Payable account in Exhibit A–5.

To conclude, be aware that the transaction-recording and posting processes illustrated in the previous pages are performed by bookkeepers, not accountants. The accountant, however, is often requested to audit the output of information systems, review internal controls, and design new systems for clients. He or she must therefore understand how transactions are processed into the dollar amounts that appear on the financial statements.

End-of-Appendix Review

KEY TERMS AND CONCEPTS: A QUICK OVERVIEW

cash payments journal A special journal used to record virtually all cash disbursements made by a business. (p. A–8)

cash receipts journal A special journal used to record all cash received by a business. (p. A–6)

purchases journal A special journal used to record purchases of merchandise on account. (p. A–4)

sales journal A special journal used to record sales of merchandise on account. (p. A–2)

special journals Journals that handle specific types of transactions (cash receipts, sales, and so forth). (p. A–1)

SUMMARY PROBLEM

Your friend is a candidate for an office position at Unique Creations. To qualify for the job, each candidate must successfully pass an examination that covers basic accounting and bookkeeping procedures. To prepare for the upcoming exam, all candidates were given a copy of last year's questions. Several of these questions follow.

1. Unique Creations uses a set of journals (sales, purchases, cash receipts, cash payments, and general) to record daily activity. In which journal would the following transactions and events be found?
    a. Received $600 from the sale of old equipment used in the business.
    b. Purchased a $75 calculator (to be used in the office) for cash.
    c. Recorded the adjusting entry for supplies consumed during the month.
    d. Recorded daily cash sales of $900.
    e. Acquired $400 of merchandise on account from BMI, Inc.

2. Unique Creations normally posts the total of its sales journal on a weekly basis. To what accounts would this total be posted?

3. Assume that a firm began operations on January 1 of the current year. Purchases of merchandise for the year totaled $50,000, of which 30% were for cash. The company paid 80% of the amounts owed to suppliers.
    a. Compute the balance in the Accounts Payable control account at the end of the period.
    b. Compute the end-of-period total of all balances in the Accounts Payable subsidiary ledger, assuming that all procedures had been performed correctly.
    c. Suppose that on December 29, the bookkeeper failed to record a $500 purchase of merchandise on account from Reliable Wholesale. Will the Accounts Payable control account still be in agreement with the subsidiary ledger? Briefly explain.

Instructions

In an effort to be well prepared for the examination, your friend has requested help in answering last year's questions. Draft a response to each of the questions listed.

Solution

1. a. Cash receipts
    b. Cash payments
    c. General
    d. Cash receipts
    e. Purchases

2. The total would be posted as a debit to Accounts Receivable and a credit to Sales.
3. a.
Beginning balance, Jan. 1	$ —
Add: Purchases on account ($50,000 × 0.70)	35,000
	$35,000
Deduct: Payments on account ($35,000 × 0.80)	28,000
Ending balance, Dec. 31	$ 7,000

b. The balances should total $7,000.
c. Yes. A failure to record the purchase means that the total posted to the Accounts Payable control account was understated by $500. Further, the bookkeeper failed to update Reliable Wholesale's account in the subsidiary ledger. Although both the control account and subsidiary ledger are understated, their balances will still be in agreement.

ASSIGNMENT MATERIAL

EXERCISES

EA–1 Special journal selection and use

Bancroft Wholesale sells electrical equipment and supplies to the construction trade. The following selected transactions and events took place during a recent month:

a. Sold merchandise on account to Reynolds Construction.
b. Recorded the adjusting entry for depreciation.
c. Purchased office supplies on account.
d. Collected 40% of the balance due from a customer.
e. Acquired a new delivery truck by paying $6,000 down and securing a bank loan payable for the remaining balance.
f. Processed checks for employee wages.
g. Acquired circuit breakers and cable on account from Hill Corporation, a supplier.
h. Returned $100 of the goods acquired from Hill Corporation. Hill has agreed to reduce Bancroft's account.

Bancroft uses sales, purchases, cash receipts, cash payments, and general journals similar to those illustrated in this appendix. Indicate in which journal each of the preceding transactions and events would be recorded.

EA–2 Operation of a special journal system

Yum Yum Yogurt operates 10 frozen yogurt stores in Florida. The company uses special journals for sales, purchases, cash receipts, and cash payments and a general journal. All are similar in format to those illustrated in this appendix. You have been requested to answer the following questions for an office clerk:

a. In which journal would a store's daily cash sales be recorded?
b. To which subsidiary ledger are the individual amounts in the purchases journal posted? How frequently should these amounts be posted?
c. To which account is the total of the sales journal debited at the end of the month? To which account is the total credited?
d. Where is the total of the Sundry column in the cash receipts journal posted at month-end?
e. By month-end, which of the company's journals would probably contain the fewest transactions and events? Why?

EA-3 Introduction to special journals

Peartree Computing had the following credit sales during March 19X6:

Mar. 6   Sold $1,800 of computer equipment on account to Burger City.
    16   Sold $2,900 of computer equipment on account to Dave's Automotive.
    24   Sold $550 of computer equipment on account to Dallas Wallpaper.

The March 1 balance in Accounts Receivable was $300, which arose from a sale to Dave's Automotive on February 22. There were no receipts on account from customers during February or March.

a. Record Peartree's March transactions in a journal similar to that shown in Exhibit A-1.
b. Open T-accounts for Accounts Receivable (no. 110), Sales (no. 400), and the firm's customers. Post the sales journal and show how the accounts would appear as of March 31. Assume that credit sales transactions were posted from page 6 of the journal in February and page 7 in March.
c. Prepare a schedule of accounts receivable as of March 31.
d. What is the balance in the Accounts Receivable control account on March 31?

EA-4 Understanding a purchases and cash payments journal

On May 1 of the current year, the accounting records of Optical City revealed the following information:

    Balance in Accounts Payable control account: $15,700
    Balances in Accounts Payable subsidiary ledger: A-1 Labs, $3,700; NY Eye, $6,100; and Optica, $5,900

The following purchases and cash payments took place during the month:

PURCHASES ON ACCOUNT			PAYMENTS ON ACCOUNT		
DATE	SUPPLIER	AMOUNT	DATE	SUPPLIER	AMOUNT
May 7	NY Eye	$4,700	May 3	A-1 Labs	$ 3,700
15	Optica	3,500	9	Optica	5,782*
17	NY Eye	5,000	30	NY Eye	10,800
28	A-1 Labs	2,200			

* Payment of the company's May 1 balance minus a 2% discount.

a. Determine the month-end total that would appear in Optical City's purchases journal. Where is this total posted?
b. Determine the total of the Accounts Payable column in Optical City's cash payments journal. Is this total posted to the company's control account or the subsidiary ledger?
c. Establish T-accounts for A-1 Labs, NY Eye, and Optica. Determine the amounts owed to each supplier at month-end.
d. Compute the month-end balance in the firm's Accounts Payable control account. Compare this balance with the total of the various supplier accounts from part (c) and comment on your findings.

EA-5 Special journal/control account operation

Summit Supply uses special journals similar to those illustrated in this appendix, along with a general journal to record miscellaneous transactions. On January 1 of the current year, the firm's Accounts Receivable and Accounts Payable control accounts revealed balances of $83,500 and $65,700, respectively.

The following information was obtained from a review of the journals on January 31:

Journal	Information
Sales	Total transactions, $24,300
Purchases	Total transactions, $19,900
Cash receipts	Collections from customers on account, $23,100
	Discounts taken by customers for prompt payment, $900
Cash payments	Payments to suppliers on account, $30,200
	Discounts taken on supplier invoices, $500
General	Purchases of machinery on account, $5,700
	Customer returns on account, $400

a. Compute the balance in the Accounts Receivable control account on January 31 after all postings are made.
b. Compute the balance in the Accounts Payable control account on January 31 after all postings are made. Assume that Summit uses the gross method of recording purchases.

PROBLEMS

PA-1 Detection of processing errors

The Hartman Company uses special journals to record sales, purchases, cash receipts, and cash payments. Hartman also employs a general journal to record miscellaneous transactions and adjusting and closing entries. During August the following errors were made:

a. The correct total of the sales journal, $7,510, was posted to the Sales account in the general ledger as $5,710. The debit to Accounts Receivable was posted correctly.
b. The total of the sales journal was accidentally overadded by $10.
c. A cash receipt on account from Norman Dresser was entered in the general journal.
d. A sale on account to Bob Smith was accidentally posted to Bill Smith's account in the Accounts Receivable subsidiary ledger.
e. A purchase of merchandise on account from Modern Equipment Sales was not entered in the accounting records.
f. A cash payment on account to Hardware Wholesalers was properly recorded in the cash payments journal. The bookkeeper neglected to post the disbursement to Hardware Wholesalers' account in the Accounts Payable subsidiary ledger.

Instructions

State how each error is likely to be discovered. If discovery is unlikely, tell why.

PA-2 Special journals, transaction processing, and schedules

Casual Wear began business on July 1. Selected accounts (and account numbers) follow.

Cash	100	Sales returns	401
Accounts receivable	110	Purchases	510
Merchandise inventory	120	Purchases returns	511
Prepaid advertising	130	Purchases discounts	512
Office equipment	140	Rent expense	610
Accounts payable	200	Salaries expense	620
Loan payable	210	Utilities expense	630
Tina Sharp, capital	300	Interest expense	640
Sales	400		

The company uses special journals for sales, purchases, cash receipts, and cash payments, and a general journal to record miscellaneous transactions and events. The journals are similar in format to those illustrated in this appendix.

All merchandise is purchased on account, subject to terms of 2/10, n/30. Casual Wear uses a periodic inventory system. The transactions of July follow.

July 1 Secured $30,000 of financing from a $20,000 investment by the owner and a $10,000 bank loan.

1 Paid the first month's rent to Vantage Management; issued check no. 100 for $1,600.

2 Purchased $13,000 of merchandise on account from Jeans, Inc. (invoice no. 4421, dated July 2).

3 Purchased $3,000 of office equipment on account from Bronco Office Supply.

3 Paid $800 for five months of advertising in *Clothing Weekly*; issued check no. 101.

5 Sold $7,000 of goods on account to Denver Woman (invoice no. 2000).

7 Purchased $9,500 of merchandise on account from New York Fashions (invoice no. 2487, dated July 7).

10 Paid the balance owed to Jeans, Inc.; issued check no. 102.

11 Returned $900 of the merchandise purchased on July 7 from New York Fashions.

13 Sold $3,700 of goods on account to Nan's (invoice no. 2001).

14 Cash sales for the week ended July 14 amounted to $1,250.

15 Paid the amount owed to Bronco Office Supply; issued check no. 103.

16 Paid the proper amount owed to New York Fashions from the transactions of July 7 and July 11; issued check no. 104.

19 Purchased $6,600 of goods on account from Seaside Creations (invoice no. 1824, dated July 19).

21 Cash sales for the week ended July 21 amounted to $2,300.

24 Paid $520 to Colorado Light & Power for July utilities; issued check no. 105.

26 Sold $5,800 of goods on account to Wild One (invoice no. 2002).

27 Received the amount due from Denver Woman.

28 Cash sales for the week ended July 28 amounted to $1,300.

29 Accepted a $600 return of goods on account from Wild One. The goods were shipped in error on July 26.

29 Paid salaries of $3,300; issued check no. 106.

30 Obtained a $500 cash refund from Bronco Office Supply for the return of unneeded office equipment that was acquired on July 3.

31 Paid the first installment on the July 1 loan. Issued check no. 107 to Mountain Trust for $700, of which $150 is interest.

Instructions

a. Record the transactions in the correct journals. Post the proper individual amounts and general journal entries daily; at the end of the month, post the appropriate totals.
b. Prepare a trial balance of the general ledger accounts, a schedule of accounts receivable, and a schedule of accounts payable.

PA–3 Special journals, transaction processing, and schedules

Midtown Camera Distributors is a small proprietorship located in South Carolina. A recent review of the accounting records disclosed that Evertson Photo owes the firm $2,600 from a purchase of merchandise on November 28. Further, Midtown owes $3,700 to Tokyo Camera Works (a supplier) for a transaction on November 29. All credit sales and merchandise acquisitions are subject to terms of 2/10, n/30. The following transactions took place during December:

Dec. 2 Received a $5,000 cash investment from the owner, Diane Pettit.
  3 Sold $500 of merchandise on account to Duke's Camera Shop (invoice no. 642).
  5 Purchased $2,900 of merchandise on account from Polaroid Corporation (invoice no. 6847, dated December 5).
  6 Paid the proper amount due Tokyo Camera Works for the purchase on November 29; issued check no. 4305.
  7 Cash sales for the week amounted to $2,330.
  9 Issued check no. 4306 for $520 to Smith and Son Printers for brochures to be used in January's advertising program.
  12 Duke's Camera Shop paid the proper amount due in settlement of its account balance.
  14 Cash sales for the week totaled $3,230.
  14 Issued check no. 4307 to Polaroid Corporation in payment of the purchase on December 5.
  15 Issued check no. 4308 to Susan Woodard in payment of her $1,800 salary.
  17 Sold $2,200 of cameras and $650 of accessories on account to Dave's Studio (invoice no. 643).
  19 Received $225 for consulting services provided to a suburban newspaper's photography staff.
  21 Cash sales for the week amounted to $1,120.
  22 Sold a $580 camera on account to Hawthorne Photo Supply (invoice no. 644).
  23 Purchased $1,950 of merchandise on account from Tokyo Camera Works (invoice no. 8041, dated December 23).
  24 Hawthorne Photo Supply returned the camera purchased on December 22, and its account was adjusted.
  24 Paid $85 for utilities to South Carolina Power and Light; issued check no. 4309.
  26 Received a $50 check from Smith and Son Printers. An accompanying note stated that Midtown's bill for the printing job on December 9 had been computed incorrectly.
  28 Sold a $620 camera on account to Hay Photography (invoice no. 645).
  29 Cash sales for the week totaled $910.
  30 Purchased a used delivery van from Savings National for $6,000; paid $2,000 down and secured a short-term loan for the remaining balance. Issued check no. 4310.

Midtown employs single-column sales and purchases journals and multicolumn cash receipts and payments journals similar to those illustrated in this appendix. In addition, a general journal is used for miscellaneous transactions. The general ledger revealed the following balances on November 30 (account numbers appear in parentheses):

Cash (110)	$ 14,700	Sales discounts (420)	$ 2,200
Accounts receivable (120)	2,600	Sales returns (430)	3,700
Inventory (130)	56,700	Miscellaneous revenue (450)	—
Prepaid advertising (140)	1,600	Purchases (510)	98,500
Delivery van (150)	—	Purchases discounts (520)	1,600
Accounts payable (210)	3,700	Wage expense (530)	24,400
Loan payable (220)	—	Travel expense (540)	3,200
Diane Pettit, capital (310)	85,300	Rent expense (550)	11,500
Diane Pettit, drawing (320)	15,000	Utilities expense (560)	3,100
Sales (410)	146,600		

Instructions

a. Open Midtown's accounts in the general ledger and the Accounts Receivable and Accounts Payable subsidiary ledgers.
b. Record the December transactions in the correct journals. Post the proper individual amounts and general journal entries daily; at the end of the month, post the appropriate totals. All terms of sale are strictly followed.
c. Prepare a trial balance of the general ledger accounts, a schedule of accounts receivable, and a schedule of accounts payable as of December 31.

Appendix B: Assessing a Company's Financial Health

In Chapter 7 and elsewhere, the text describes the importance of accounting and financial reporting. Accounting seeks to provide business owners, potential owners, creditors, and others with information that is useful in investment and credit decisions. Investors and creditors typically have a limited amount of capital, and they desire to make decisions that achieve the best possible returns.

In order to attain this goal, the groups just noted must study a company's financial disclosures with reasonable diligence. In addition, they must evaluate the information in light of prevailing economic conditions and in comparison with the disclosures of other firms. This appendix overviews two tools that are available to conduct such an evaluation: financial ratios and analysts' reports.

Financial Ratios

The vast bulk of our ratio presentation is actually placed throughout the text. Inventory ratios appear with other discussions that relate to inventory; debt ratios appear with other discussions that relate to debt; and so forth. We have taken such an approach to provide a unified, holistic presentation of the subject matter. This appendix, in contrast, summarizes—and we truly mean, summarizes—much of this material in one centralized location.

Ratios are often categorized according to their purpose, namely, to study liquidity, activity, profitability, and coverage relationships. These relationships focus on the following:

- *Liquidity*—the ability of a business to meet current debts as the obligations come due.
- *Activity*—a company's effectiveness in using specific resources.
- *Profitability*—an organization's ability to operate in a profitable (or unprofitable) manner.
- *Coverage*—the ability of an entity to remain solvent and settle its long-term obligations.

Exhibit B–1 contains thirteen ratios that are used regularly in the analysis of financial statements. The numbers that appear in parentheses indicate the text page where a detailed discussion of the ratio can be found.

ANALYSTS' REPORTS

Analysts' reports generally present an in-depth examination of a company's operations and financial condition. These reports take different forms and are prepared by various types of analysts. Some reports are merely factual, historical summaries of a firm's activities and financial health. In contrast, many promote the stock of the subject company, attempting to make a case that the stock is an attractive investment. A number of these latter reports are drafted by independent parties; however, some are prepared by analysts who are hired by the company itself. As noted in Chapter 7, reports are also written by brokerage houses, which earn commissions when the subject's stock is bought or sold.

Despite some possible shortcomings, analysts' reports *do* provide detailed information that is helpful when formulating investment strategies. Some truly outstanding companies have been identified in their infancy by people who make a livelihood of seeking out and reporting on new, emerging businesses. Exhibit B–2 contains a typical analysts' report, one that was prepared for a very well-known company by an actual financial analyst. At the request of the preparer, we have changed many of the names and facts to disguise the true identity of the firm. This procedure was mandated because of our ever-changing world, a world that could be very cruel to the analyst's carefully developed financial predictions and recommendations.[1]

There is a lesson to be learned from our experience: As you go forward in the business world, recognize that even the analysts themselves do not view their reports as infallible truths. Put simply, today's thoughts are likely to become dated very quickly due to tomorrow's developments. The reports are but one tool to use in the evaluation of alternatives; a number of other information sources are available and should be studied before a final credit or investment decision is reached.

---

[1] In view of the "static" nature of a textbook, most of the analysts that we spoke with refused to grant permission to publish their work (whether disguised or not).

Exhibit B-1
Summary of Financial Ratios

Ratio	Method of Computation	Significance
(1) Liquidity ratios		
(a) Current ratio (p. 146)	$\dfrac{\text{Current Assets}}{\text{Current Liabilities}}$	Measures the ability to meet short-term debts.
(b) Quick ratio (p. 147)	$\dfrac{\text{Cash + Short-Term Investments + Accounts Receivable}}{\text{Current Liabilities}}$	Measures very short-term debt-paying ability.
(2) Activity ratios		
(a) Accounts receivable turnover (p. 333)	$\dfrac{\text{Net Credit Sales}}{\text{Average Accounts Receivable}}$	Provides insight into credit and collection policies.
(b) Inventory turnover (p. 376)	$\dfrac{\text{Cost of Goods Sold}}{\text{Average Inventory}}$	Provides insight into inventory management policies.
(3) Profitability ratios		
(a) Operating income on sales (p. 268)	$\dfrac{\text{Operating Income}}{\text{Net Sales}}$	Shows the operating income produced from each sales dollar.
(b) Return on assets (p. 600)	$\dfrac{\text{Net Income + Interest Expense}}{\text{Average Assets}}$	Indicates the effectiveness of resources used in generating income.
(c) Return on common stockholders' equity (p. 599)	$\dfrac{\text{Net Income − Preferred Dividends}}{\text{Average Common Stockholders' Equity}}$	Reveals the earnings rate on capital provided by common shareholders.
(d) Earnings per share (p. 637)	$\dfrac{\text{Net Income − Preferred Dividends}}{\text{Weighted-Average Common Shares}}$	Measures the earnings applicable to a share of common stock.
(e) Price-earnings ratio (p. 638)	$\dfrac{\text{Market Price Per Share}}{\text{Earnings Per Share}}$	Shows the amount investors are willing to pay for each dollar of corporate earnings.
(f) Dividend payout ratio (p. 628)	$\dfrac{\text{Cash Dividend Per Share}}{\text{Earnings Per Share}}$	Reveals corporate policy regarding retention or distribution of earnings.
(g) Dividend yield (p. 628)	$\dfrac{\text{Cash Dividend Per Share}}{\text{Market Price Per Share}}$	Indicates an investor's short-term rate of return from dividends.
(4) Coverage ratios		
(a) Debt to total assets (p. 677)	$\dfrac{\text{Total Debt}}{\text{Total Assets}}$	Shows the percentage of assets financed by long- and short-term borrowings.
(b) Times interest earned (p. 678)	$\dfrac{\text{Income Before Income Taxes and Interest}}{\text{Interest Expense}}$	Measures a firm's ability to cover fixed interest charges.

* An alternative calculation used by many analysts, Operating Income ÷ Identifiable Assets, is shown on page 268.

EXHIBIT B–2
Sample Analyst's Report

Montgomery, Fitch, & Javier, Inc.
SECURITIES RESEARCH

UPDATE

Electronics Warehouse

January 18, 1995
DJIA 3928.98
S&P Indus. 558.02

Dennis Thomas, CFA, Associate Analyst

Symbol/Exchange	ELEC/NASDAQ		*Fiscal Year Ends January 31*	
			1994	1995E*
Recent Price	29 ⅝	EPS	$1.63	$1.98
52-Week Price Range	39—29 ⅛	P/E	—	15.0
Dividend	Nil	ROE	16.0%	16.4%
		E = Estimated.		

Description
World's largest electronics retailer with 618 domestic stores and 293 international stores.

Fundamental Data
1989–1994 EPS CAGR*	12.4%
Trailing 12 Months' Sales (mil.)	$8,737
Long-Term Debt to Total Cap.—10/94	21%
Current Ratio—10/94	1.0
Cash Flow Per Share—1995E	$2.54
Book Value Per Share—10/94	$10.35
Price/Book Value	2.9
Market Value (mil.)	$8,221
Market Value to Sales	0.94
Financial Strength Ranking	B+

* CAGR—Compound Annual Growth Rate

Trading Data
Shares Outstanding (mil.)	277.5
Estimated Float (mil.)	233.0
Insider Holdings	16%
Institutional Holdings	65%
Average Daily Volume—Oct.–Dec. 1994	764,000
Listed Options	None

Headquarters	Little Rock, Arkansas
Chairman	Bill Goble
CEO & Vice Chairman	Marilyn Howser

Segment Contributions in 1994
	Sales	Operating Profits
Domestic	79%	88%
International	21	12

Rating: Buy
Suitability: Aggressive

Investment Appraisal

We continue to recommend that investors take advantage of recent weakness to **purchase** the shares of Electronics Warehouse in long-term portfolios. Despite slightly disappointing Christmas results, we continue to view ELEC as one of the more attractive and consistent growth stories in the retail sector. With the stock now selling at the lowest valuation in more than a decade, we believe this pullback represents an excellent buying opportunity for long-term investors.

While we argue against the idea that Electronics Warehouse is strictly a "Christmas Story," we expect the market to demand tangible evidence of improvement in the company's fortunes before giving the shares a more traditional valuation, a process that may take several months. We expect this to occur as sales trends strengthen in ELEC's international division, building upon the positive signs in evidence this Christmas in Japan, Spain, and France.

A more immediate boost, however, could come from actions we believe the company may take in the next several weeks to support the stock price. While ELEC has approximately $500 million remaining on the $1 billion share repurchase authorization announced in January 1994, we expect the board of directors to approve an even more aggressive buyback program, reflecting both the current share price and the company's extremely strong financial condition.

Bottom line, we believe that shares of Electronics Warehouse represent tremendous value at current levels for long-term investors. Though several months may be needed to repair the damage, both technical and psychological, inflicted in recent weeks, the growth story that originally attracted us to the stock remains very much intact. As key elements of this story become increasingly visible in coming months—displacing the market's current focus on short-term sales results—we expect the stock to provide significant appreciation potential over the next 12 to 18 months.

Investment Features

- **International results, disappointing to date, approaching a breakout point.** Is ELEC's much-hyped international growth story for real or will it prove to be a continuing source of unfulfilled promise? Though benefits have accrued at a slower-than-expected pace, we are very confident that operating profits are nearing a "breakout point." While fiscal 1995 operating profits will come in below the company's original target of $150 million, revised expectations of $135 million to $145 million still represent more than a 30% improvement over 1994 levels despite difficult economic conditions in Japan and Europe. The improved results are primarily a reflection of greater expense leverage as a growing number of ELEC's international markets begin to achieve "critical mass," allowing more efficient use of existing infrastructure. With signs of a quickening economic pulse in many of ELEC's key international markets and further momentum expected over the next several quarters, we believe international operating profits could approach $180 million in fiscal 1996.

Fiscal 1996 results should reflect continued expense leverage, along with the additional benefits of economically driven improvement in same-store sales trends and a reduced drag on earnings from new store openings. ELEC opened 67 international stores in fiscal 1994 on an existing base of 167 stores and 59 stores on the 234 store base in fiscal 1995. Current plans for fiscal 1996 call for 50 to 60 new stores on top of the 293 in operation. Given that new store openings tend to negatively impact earnings until the fourth quarter of the year *after* the stores are opened, the more modest expansion schedule should take some of the pressure off of the international bottom line during 1996 and 1997. In fact, we believe that the modest expansion schedule in fiscal 1996 is due in part to the company's desire to post strong international operating results for the year, helping rebuild investor enthusiasm for ELEC's international prospects.

Thus, despite the disappointing pace of profit growth to date, our outlook remains extremely positive for ELEC's international division. As the overall number of international stores increases and a growing percentage of these stores reach sales maturity, we look for the interrelated benefits of strong sales growth, increased market share and expanding operating margins. We are confident that fiscal 1996 will mark the second consecutive year of strong operating profit growth for Electronics Warehouse International, restoring investor enthusiasm to this exciting story.

- **Domestic stores provide modest growth, significant cash generation.** We continue to view the domestic division as an attractive growth vehicle despite the fact that the pace of store base expansion continues to moderate. Our outlook calls for the domestic store base to grow at a 6% to 7% pace over the next few years. Along with our expectation of low-to-mid-single digit annual same-store sales growth, buoyed going forward by the likely rollout of the company's specialty shop concepts, we expect domestic sales to grow at an annual rate of 8% to 11%. With flat to slightly improved margins, operating profits should grow at a similar pace.

In addition, the division continues to generate significant amounts of cash flow. This has allowed the company to undertake the rapid, and costly, international expansion program without leveraging the balance sheet or impairing liquidity. As capital expenditures begin to trend downward in the next couple of years, ELEC's growing free cash flow will allow for possible acquisitions and even more aggressive share repurchase activity.

- **Share buyback program adds further attraction to very cheap stock.** ELEC has aggressively repurchased stock in recent months, having completed nearly 50% of the January 1994 $1 billion share repurchase authorization. The buyback activity gained momentum over the course of the year, with 8.1 million shares repurchased during the third quarter alone. Buyback activity has been limited during the fourth quarter, as ELEC does not repurchase stock during the Christmas season "quiet period" (November 14 through January 3). We expect ELEC to announce future additional steps intended to boost the share price, likely in the form of an even more aggressive share repurchase plan. Management has previously stated its intention to continue buying back shares regardless of price, although past actions indicate the company finds the low-to-mid-30s price range to be especially attractive. Given a current share price below that range, ELEC's strong financial condition, and our outlook for increasing free cash flow (see Figure No. 1), we look for management to send a rather bold message on the share buyback front.

Christmas Sales Recap

Sales for the eight weeks ended December 24 rose 8.7%, with domestic sales up 1% on a same-store basis. Both of these numbers were somewhat below expectations. For the first 11 months of the fiscal year, sales are up 10.6% overall and 3% on a same-store basis. The company indicated on its conference call that results were actually on plan through Thanksgiving and into early December but fell off domestically in the last couple of weeks before Christmas.

International sales increased 3% on a same-store basis in U.S. dollars for the Christmas period. In local currencies, on a same-store basis, ELEC reported strong sales gains in Japan, Spain, and France and small declines in the United Kingdom and Canada. Germany, on the other hand, continues to struggle badly. This appears to be solely an economic issue at this point, with other major retailers reporting even more significant sales declines. As stores in Germany (and bordering countries serviced out of Germany) currently represent more than 20% of ELEC's international store base, improving sales comparisons in Germany during 1996 would provide an additional boost to operating profits.

We find the strength in Japan to be especially encouraging in that it has been one of ELEC's weakest international markets in recent quarters. Strong Christmas results, along with strength in Spain and France, provide the first solid evidence of recovery in the company's international business. While economic vital signs improved recently in many of these markets, ELEC's business has lagged the overall economic rebound. The same lag effect was in effect two years ago, as ELEC's business resisted the economic downturn when many of these countries slipped into recession.

Figure No. 1
Financial Overview

	1995E	**1994**	**1993**	**1992**	**1991**	**1990**
Long-Term Debt/Total Capital	17%	19%	19%	14%	9%	9%
EBITDA/Interest Expense	15X	14X	13X	12X	9X	14X
Net Income (millions)	$531	$483	$438	$ 340	$326	$321
Depreciation and Amortization	151	133	119	101	79	66
Net Cash Flow	$682	$616	$557	$ 440	$405	$387
Capital Expenditures	500	555	422	549	485	375
Free Cash Flow	$182	$ 61	$135	$ (108)	$ (80)	$ 12

As evidence of further improvement in the international operating environment becomes more evident over the next several months, increasing the possibility of a breakout in international operating profits, the stock should regain its footing and investor confidence in the company should be restored.

Earnings Outlook

For fiscal 1995, we now project earnings of $1.98 per share, a 21% increase over fiscal 1994. On a quarterly basis, we would anticipate some sluggishness in the first half of fiscal 1995 to give way to more attractive comparisons in late 1995 and into 1996, as video demand rebounds and international operating margins expand.

Valuation

At the current price of 29 5/8, ELEC shares sell at just 15 times our fiscal 1995 earnings estimate of $1.98 per share. This represents the most attractive valuation level in almost a decade with respect to several traditional valuation parameters, including price-to-earnings, sales, cash flow, EBITDA and book value. In addition, the stock currently sells at a price level first reached in 1990. Over the course of this period, ELEC has nearly doubled sales from $4.8 billion to almost $9 billion while growing its domestic store base from 404 stores to the current 618 and the key international division to 293 stores from 74 stores. ELEC has also captured additional domestic market share, aided by the demise of two major look-alike superstore competitors. In addition, there have been significant improvements in store format, marketing and promotion, and working capital management. Even allowing for rather significant multiple contraction, we find the current valuation extremely attractive in light of the positive developments in recent years and what we believe is a very favorable outlook going forward.

Summary

We remain very optimistic about the prospects for Electronics Warehouse over the next several years despite our disappointment in the performance of ELEC shares over the past 12 months. While the market is likely to adopt a wait-and-see attitude on the shares, we expect an announcement regarding a more aggressive stock buyback authorization, followed by growing evidence of improving business trends at the company's international division, to return the stock to more traditional levels. As a result, we strongly encourage long-term investors to buy the shares of Electronics Warehouse at current levels, suggesting especially aggressive purchases in the low 30s and below.

SECURITIES RESEARCH

Selected Financial Data

(Figures in Millions, Except Per Share Data)

Fiscal Year Ends Jan. 31	1989	1990	1991	1992	1993	1994	1995E
Net Sales	$4,000	$4,788	$5,510	$6,124	$7,169	$7,946	$9,000
Pretax Income	429	514	523	539	689	773	829
Taxes	161	193	97	199	252	290	298
Net Income	$268	$321	$326	$340	$437	$483	$531
Average Shares Outstanding	296	294	295	296	298	298	268
Shareholders' Equity	$1,424	$1,705	$2,046	$2,426	$2,889	$3,148	$3,318
Pretax Margin (%)	10.7	10.7	9.5	8.8	9.6	9.7	9.2
Tax Rate (%)	37.5	37.5	37.7	37.0	36.5	37.5	36.0
Net Margin (%)	6.7	6.7	5.9	5.5	6.1	6.1	5.9
Return on Equity (%)	20.9	20.5	17.4	15.2	16.5	16.0	16.4
Share Data							
Earnings	$0.91	$1.09	$1.10	$1.15	$1.47	$1.63	$1.98
Equity	$4.94	$5.95	$7.11	$8.39	$9.95	$10.87	$12.22
Price Range	18-13¼	26⅞-16	35-19⅞	36-22	41-30⅜	42⅞-32⅞	—
P/E Ratio Range	20-15	25–15	32–18	31–19	28–21	26-20	—
Relative P/E Range (%)	158-136	157-121	175-125	107-89	105-85	106-88	—

Selected Balance Sheet Data
October 29, 1994
(Figures in Millions)

Cash and Equivalents	$ 103.5
Receivables	131.7
Inventories	3,207.5
Prepaid and Other	73.4
Total Current Assets	$3,516.1
Short-Term Borrowings	1,217.2
Accounts Payable	1,938.2
Other	433.1
Total Current Liabilities	$3,588.5
Working Capital	(72.4)
Property and Equipment & Other Assets	3,987.3
Total	$3,914.9
Less:	
Long-Term Debt	780.8
Deferred Items/Other	260.0
Shareholders' Equity	$2,874.1

ELEC   ELECTRONICS WAREHOUSE

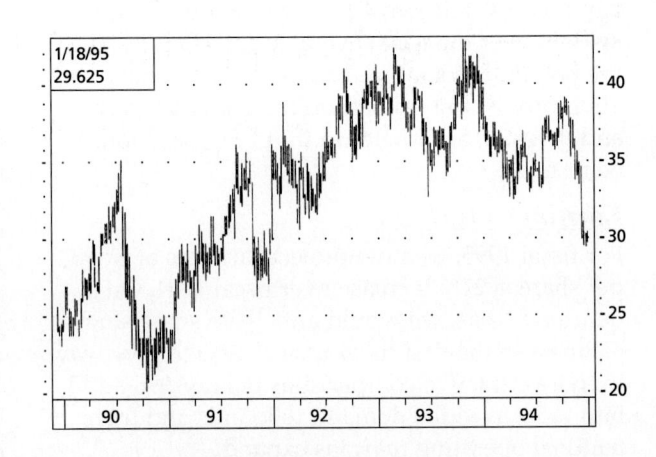

1/18/95
29.625

Source: Tracker Data Systems

Additional Information Available Upon Request
Montgomery, Fitch, & Javier, Inc.

This information is obtained from internal and external research sources considered to be reliable, but is not necessarily complete and its accuracy is not guaranteed by Montgomery, Fitch, & Javier, Inc. Any opinions expressed are subject to change without notice. Neither the information nor any opinion expressed constitutes a solicitation for the purchase or sale of any security referred to herein.

Appendix C: Present Value Tables

TABLE 1
Present Value of $1

Periods	2%	4%	5%	6%	8%	9%	10%	12%	14%	16%	18%	20%
1	.98039	.96154	.95238	.94340	.92593	.91743	.90909	.89286	.87719	.86207	.84746	.83333
2	.96117	.92456	.90703	.89000	.85734	.84168	.82645	.79719	.76947	.74316	.71818	.69444
3	.94232	.88900	.86384	.83962	.79383	.77218	.75132	.71178	.67497	.64066	.60863	.57870
4	.92385	.85480	.82270	.79209	.73503	.70843	.68301	.63552	.59208	.55229	.51579	.48225
5	.90573	.82193	.78353	.74726	.68058	.64993	.62092	.56743	.51937	.47611	.43711	.40188
6	.88797	.79031	.74622	.70496	.63017	.59627	.56447	.50663	.45559	.41044	.37043	.33490
7	.87056	.75992	.71068	.66506	.58349	.54703	.51316	.45235	.39964	.35383	.31393	.27908
8	.85349	.73069	.67684	.62741	.54027	.50187	.46651	.40388	.35056	.30503	.26604	.23257
9	.83676	.70259	.64461	.59190	.50025	.46043	.42410	.36061	.30751	.26295	.22546	.19381
10	.82035	.67556	.61391	.55839	.46319	.42241	.38554	.32197	.26974	.22668	.19106	.16151
11	.80426	.64958	.58468	.52679	.42888	.38753	.35049	.28748	.23662	.19542	.16192	.13459
12	.78849	.62460	.55684	.49697	.39711	.35554	.31863	.25668	.20756	.16846	.13722	.11216
13	.77303	.60057	.53032	.46884	.36770	.32618	.28966	.22917	.18207	.14523	.11629	.09346
14	.75788	.57748	.50507	.44230	.34046	.29925	.26333	.20462	.15971	.12520	.09855	.07789
15	.74301	.55526	.48102	.41727	.31524	.27454	.23939	.18270	.14010	.10793	.08352	.06491
16	.72845	.53391	.45811	.39365	.29189	.25187	.21763	.16312	.12289	.09304	.07078	.05409
17	.71416	.51337	.43630	.37136	.27027	.23107	.19785	.14564	.10780	.08021	.05998	.04507
18	.70016	.49363	.41552	.35034	.25025	.21199	.17986	.13004	.09456	.06914	.05083	.03756
19	.68643	.47464	.39573	.33051	.23171	.19449	.16351	.11611	.08295	.05961	.04308	.03130
20	.67297	.45639	.37689	.31180	.21455	.17843	.14864	.10367	.07276	.05139	.03651	.02608
21	.65978	.43883	.35894	.29416	.19866	.16370	.13513	.09256	.06383	.04430	.03094	.02174
22	.64684	.42196	.34185	.27751	.18394	.15018	.12285	.08264	.05599	.03819	.02622	.01811
23	.63416	.40573	.32557	.26180	.17032	.13778	.11168	.07379	.04911	.03292	.02222	.01509
24	.62172	.39012	.31007	.24698	.15770	.12641	.10153	.06588	.04308	.02838	.01883	.01258
25	.60953	.37512	.29530	.23300	.14602	.11597	.09230	.05882	.03779	.02447	.01596	.01048

TABLE 2
Present Value of Ordinary Annuity of $1

PERIODS	2%	4%	5%	6%	8%	9%	10%	12%	14%	16%	18%	20%
1	.98039	.96154	.95238	.94340	.92593	.91743	.90909	.89286	.87719	.86207	.84746	.83333
2	1.94156	1.88609	1.85941	1.83339	1.78326	1.75911	1.73554	1.69005	1.64666	1.60523	1.56564	1.52778
3	2.88388	2.77509	2.72325	2.67301	2.57710	2.53130	2.48685	2.40183	2.32163	2.24589	2.17427	2.10648
4	3.80773	3.62990	3.54595	3.46511	3.31213	3.23972	3.16986	3.03735	2.91371	2.79818	2.69006	2.58873
5	4.71346	4.45182	4.32948	4.21236	3.99271	3.88965	3.79079	3.60478	3.43308	3.27429	3.12717	2.99061
6	5.60143	5.24214	5.07569	4.91732	4.62288	4.48592	4.35526	4.11141	3.88867	3.68474	3.49760	3.32551
7	6.47199	6.00205	5.78637	5.58238	5.20637	5.03295	4.86842	4.56376	4.28830	4.03857	3.81153	3.60459
8	7.32548	6.73274	6.46321	6.20979	5.74664	5.53482	5.33493	4.96764	4.63886	4.34359	4.07757	3.83716
9	8.16224	7.43533	7.10782	6.80169	6.24689	5.99525	5.75902	5.32825	4.94637	4.60654	4.30302	4.03097
10	8.98259	8.11090	7.72173	7.36009	6.71008	6.41766	6.14457	5.65022	5.21612	4.83323	4.49409	4.19247
11	9.78685	8.76048	8.30641	7.88687	7.13896	6.80519	6.49506	5.93770	5.45273	5.02864	4.65601	4.32706
12	10.57534	9.38507	8.86325	8.38384	7.53608	7.16073	6.81369	6.19437	5.66029	5.19711	4.79322	4.43922
13	11.34837	9.98565	9.39357	8.85268	7.90378	7.48690	7.10336	6.42355	5.84236	5.34233	4.90951	4.53268
14	12.01625	10.56312	9.89864	9.29498	8.24424	7.78615	7.36669	6.62817	6.00207	5.46753	5.00806	4.61057
15	12.84926	11.11839	10.37966	9.71225	8.55948	8.06069	7.60608	6.81086	6.14217	5.57546	5.09158	4.67547
16	13.57771	11.65230	10.83777	10.10590	8.85137	8.31256	7.82371	6.97399	6.26506	5.66850	5.16235	4.72956
17	14.29187	12.16567	11.27407	10.47726	9.12164	8.54363	8.02155	7.11963	6.37286	5.74870	5.22233	4.77463
18	14.99203	12.65930	11.68959	10.82760	9.37189	8.75563	8.20141	7.24967	6.46742	5.81785	5.27316	4.81219
19	15.67846	13.13394	12.08532	11.15812	9.60360	8.95012	8.36492	7.36578	6.55037	5.87746	5.31624	4.84350
20	16.35143	13.59033	12.46221	11.46992	9.81815	9.12855	8.51356	7.46944	6.62313	5.92884	5.35275	4.86958
21	17.01121	14.02916	12.82115	11.76408	10.01680	9.29224	8.64869	7.56200	6.68696	5.97314	5.38368	4.89132
22	17.65805	14.45112	13.16300	12.04158	10.20074	9.44243	8.77154	7.64465	6.74294	6.01133	5.40990	4.90943
23	18.29220	14.85684	13.48857	12.30338	10.37106	9.58021	8.88322	7.71843	6.79206	6.04425	5.43212	4.92453
24	18.91393	15.24696	13.79864	12.55036	10.52876	9.70661	8.98474	7.78432	6.83514	6.07263	5.45095	4.93710
25	19.52346	15.62208	14.09394	12.78336	10.67478	9.82258	9.07704	7.84314	6.87293	6.09709	5.46691	4.94759

Index

A

ABC, nature of, 851
ABC, problems and benefits of, 852
absorption costing,
    and variable costing, comparison of, illus., 1025
    and variable costing income statements, illus., 1026
    def., 1024
accelerated cost recovery system (ACRS), def., 414
accelerated depreciation methods, def., 409
accessing the modules, 223
account,
    control, def., 220
    drawing, def., 65
    generation of revenue on, 18
    previously written off, collection of, 330
    recognition of expense on, 19
    running balance form of, def., 53
    statement, 225
    T, def., 53
accountability procedures, def., 231
accountant,
    a glorified bookkeeper, 7
    certified management (CMA), 9
    day in the life of, illus., 8
    ethical challenges for the, 27
accountants,
    certified public (CPAs), 7
    institute of management (IMA), 514
accounting,
    accrual-basis, 95
    additional problems with cash basis, 97
    cash-basis, 96
    concept of modular, 223
    def., 3
    differences between financial and managerial, illus., 764
    ethics and, 25
    financial, 5
        def., 762
    foundation of, 512
    governmental/not-for-profit, 10
    international, 523
    introduction to, 1
    introduction to managerial and cost, 761
    job order costing versus process cost, illus., 840
    managerial, 5
        def., 763
    partnership, 553
    private, def., 9
    profession of, 7
    public, def., 7
    responsibility, def., 965
    what is, 3
accounting and the communication process, illus., 4
accounting applications, managerial, 765
Accounting Association, American (AAA), 514
accounting choice, why allow, 256
accounting cycle,
    def., 139
    illus., 140
accounting entity, 551
accounting equation,
    an extended illustration, 17
    def., 13
    relationship of normal balances and the, illus., 55
accounting information,
    limitations of, 6
    processing, 49
    users and uses of, 3
accounting information system (AIS), 218
    def., 219
accounting period, 93
accounting policies, summary of significant and, 263
accounting principle, changes in, def., 634
accounting principles board (APB), def., 513
accounting principles, generally accepted (GAAP), def., 512
accounting process, basic sequence in the, illus., 69
accounting profession, 7
accounting rate of return,
    def., 1061
    evaluation of, 1062
accounting standards,
    development of financial, illus., 515
    statements of financial, 6, 514
    uniformity of international, 524
accounting standards board, financial, (FASB), def., 514
accounting standards committee, international (IASC), 524
accounting systems, 51
    and internal control, 217
    computerized, 221
accounts, 52
    chart of, def., 58
    def., 53
    direct write-off of uncollectible, 325
    real, def., 134
    specialized business, illus., 59
    temporary or nominal, def., 134
accounts payable, def., 14
    payment of, 19
accounts receivable,
    aging of, def., 328
    collection of, 19
    def., 14, 324
accounts receivable: balance sheet approach, relationship to, 327
accounts receivable subsidiary ledger, relationship between customer account statement and, illus., 227
accounts receivable turnover, def., 331
accrual basis, def., 95
accrual-basis accounting, 95
accruals,
    an overview of, 105
    def., 103

I–1

unrecorded expenses and revenues—, 103
year-end interest, 675
accrued expenses, 104
def., 103
accrued liabilities, def., 474
accrued revenues, 105
def., 103
accrued salaries, 104
activities,
financing, def., 715
investing, def., 715
nonvalue-adding, def., 853
operating, def., 714
overview of operating, investing, and financing, illus., 716
statement of, def., 270
value-adding, def., 853, 854
activity-based costing (ABC), def., 847, 851
addition or deletion of products or departments, 1018
additions, def., 437
adjusted trial balance, def., 105
adjusted trial balance, preparation of, illus., 106
adjusting entries, 98, 133, 196
income measurement and, 91
adjusting process, def., 98
adjustment errors, 107
adjustments, end-of-period, 527
adjustments, prior period, def., 629
administrative expenses, selling and, 188
admission of a new partner, 559
advantages, corporate form of organization, 585
aftertax concept, 1063
aftertax cost, 1063
aging of accounts receivable, def., 328
aging schedule, illus., 329
allocation,
intraperiod tax, def., 635
of inventory cost between the income statement and the balance sheet, illus., 361
allocations, cost, 1021
allowance, 176
trade-in, def., 441
allowance method, def., 325
of uncollectible accounts, def., 325
allowances,
interest, def., 557
purchases returns and, 181
salary, def., 556
sales returns and, 176
withholding, def., 483
American Accounting Association (AAA), 514
American Institute of Certified Public Accountants (AICPA), def., 513

amortization,
def., 450
discount, 477, 669, 679
def., 478
effective interest method of, def., 670
of intangibles, 450
premium, 680
procedures, 450
straight-line, def, 669
analysis,
cost-benefit, def., 764
costs, 891
cost-volume-profit (CVP), 883, 894
def., 884
for multiproduct firms, CVP, 902
of financial information, 266
of outstanding debt, 677
limiting assumptions of CVP, 903
management's discussion and, (MD&A), def., 263
variance, 977
annual report, 257
def., 254
annual report disclosures, additional, 263
annuities,
multiple cash flows and, 1053
present value and, 686
annuity, def., 686, 1054
applications, managerial accounting, 765
applied overhead, 806
arrears, dividends in, 590
articles of partnership, def., 551
asset, contra, def., 101
asset acquisition, plant and equipment costs after, 436
asset disposals, summary of accounting rules for, illus., 443
asset impairment, related issue, def., 442
asset preference upon liquidation, 590
assets, 99, 141
current, 141
debt to total, 677
def., 13
exchanges and trade-ins of similar, 441
intangible, def., 144, 446
limited access to, 230
other, 144
return on, def., 268, 600, 966
sale of depreciable, 440
sale of noncash at a gain, 566
sale of noncash at a loss, 563
assets other than cash, issuing stock for, 595
assignment, cost (step 4), 846, 860
assumption,
entity, def., 11, 515
going-concern, def., 515
monetary unit, def., 6, 517
periodicity, def., 93, 516

assumptions, cost flow, def., 363
assumptions of CVP analysis, 903
attainable standards, def., 976
audit report,
def., 265
of Microsoft Corporation, illus., 265
auditing,
def., 8
internal, 10
auditor, certified internal (CIA), 10
auditors, internal, def., 10
authorized stock, def., 588
available-for-sale securities, 681
def., 679
averaging, problem of, 849
avoidable fixed overhead, 1013

B

bad credit, cost to the customer:, 323
bad debts, 325
balance, normal, def., 55
balance sheet, 139, 188, 258, 773
budgeted, 940
classified, illus., 143
def., 22
of a merchandising firm, illus., 189
limitations of, 141
balance sheet approach,
def., 327
relationship to accounts receivable:, 327
balance sheet disclosure, 481
balance sheet presentation, 289, 475, 594
balance sheet reporting, 301
balance sheets,
of Microsoft Corporation (in millions), illus., 259
merchandising and manufacturing, illus., 774
balances,
compensating, def., 289
bank card sales versus nonbank card sales, 332
bank reconciliation, 293
def., 294
illus., 296
bank statement,
def., 294
illus., 295
bank statements versus cash accounts, 294
bankruptcy, def., 735
benchmarking, def., 856
benefits,
cost and, 232
fringe, 489

of budgeting, 922
postretirement health-care, 488
betterments, def., 437
billings, client, 815
board of directors, 587
bond, carrying value of a, def., 669
bond classifications, other, 666
bond discount,
    def., 668
    meaning of a, 669
bond indenture, def., 664
bond issues, 664
    and timing considerations, 675
    the basics, accounting for, 666
bond premium,
    def., 668
    meaning of, 673
bond prices, factors that affect, 667
bond prices, present value and, 687
bond refunding, def., 676
bond retirement, def., 676
bondholders and stockholders,
    differences between, illus., 665
bonds, 301
    callable, def., 666
    convertible, def., 666
    coupon, def., 665
    debenture, def., 665
    def., 664
    investments in, 6, 79
    junk, def., 666
    registered, def., 665
    secured, def., 665
    serial, def., 666
    types of, 665
bonds issued at a discount, 668
bonds issued at a premium, 672
bonds payable, 730
bonus to existing partners, 560
bonus to new partner, 561
book value, def., 102, 408
    meaning of, 599
    per share, def., 597
bookkeeping, def., 7
bottom-up budgeting, def., 926
break-even chart,
    def., 896
    illus., 897
break-even point, def., 894
budget
    cash, 937
        def., 290
    continuous, def., 928
    def., 922
    direct labor, 934
    direct material purchases, 933
    factory overhead, 934
    flexible, def., 971
        illus., 972
    master, def., 929
    production, 932

    sales, 931
    static, def., 970
budget construction, 925
budget estimation, 926
budget illustration, cash, 938
budget limitations and human relations, 928
budget period, 927
budgeted balance sheet, 940
budgeted income statement, 938
budgeting and computers, 940
budgeting, 921
    benefits of, 922
    bottom-up, def., 926
    capital, 1047
        def., 1049
    comprehensive, 929
    top-down, def., 925
budgets,
    def., 765
    flexible, 970
    standard costs and, 973
buildings, 727
    accumulated depreciation:, 728
business failure, 735
business organization, comparison of alternative forms of, illus., 584
business venture, financing, 662
businesses, expanded use by service, 769

C

calendar year, def., 93
callable bonds, def., 666
callable preferred stock, def., 591
capacity, contribution margin in relation to, 1017
capital,
    cost of, def., 1051
    def., 15
    ease of raising, 586
    investment in working, 1050
    legal, def., 591
    paid-in, def., 594
    recognition of invested, 557
    working, def., 146
capital budgeting, 1047
    decisions, 1049
    def., 1049
    evaluation methods, 1055
capital deficiency,
    creation of a, 564
    def., 564
    removal of a, 564
capital expenditures, 1049
    def., 436
capital investment in a competitive business climate, 1062

capital leases,
    accounting for, 416
    def., 416
capital stock, shares of, def., 145
carrying value of a bond, def., 669
cash,
    and accrual methods in practice, 97
    and cash equivalents, 716
    and liquid investments, 287
    def., 289
    investing and financing transactions that do not affect, 715
cash accounts, bank statements versus, 294
cash balances, fluctuations in monthly, illus., 928
cash basis,
    accounting, 96
    accounting, additional problems with, 97
    def., 96
    modified, def., 97
cash budget, 937
    def., 290
    illustration, 938
cash collections, schedule of, 932
cash control, 292
cash disbursements, 293
    for material purchases, schedule of, 934
cash discounts, def., 178
cash dividends, 624
cash equivalents,
    cash and, 716
    def., 716
cash flow statements of Microsoft Corporation (in millions), illus., 261
cash flow work sheet—indirect approach, illus., 736, 737
cash flows,
    and income taxes, 1063
    direct approach, statement of, illus., 732
    indirect approach, statement of, illus., 733
    preparation of a statement, 725
    statement of, 260, 711
        def., 22, 712
        illus., 713
cash inflows, acceleration of, 290
cash management, 289
    and control in a high-tech environment, 300
cash outflows, postponement/ elimination of, 290
cash payments,
    module, def., 225
    processing of purchases and, 225
        illus., 228
cash receipts,
    module, def., 225
    processing of sales and, 225, 226

cash received from customers, 718
cash sales, receipts from, 292
cause and effect, 95
center,
  cost, def., 965
  investment, def., 965
  profit, def., 965
certified internal auditor (CIA), 10
certified management accountant (CMA), 9
certified public accountants (CPAs), 7
Certified Public Accountants, American Institute of, (AICPA), def., 513
changes in, accounting principle, def., 634
changes, operating, 899
charges, freight, 184
chart, break-even,
  def., 896
  illus., 897
chart of accounts,
  def., 58
  general journal module and, illus., 224
charter, def., 586
checks,
  nonsufficient funds, (NSF) def., 295
  outstanding, def., 295
classifications, statement format and, 713
classified balance sheet, illus., 143
client billings, 815
closely held corporations, def., 585
closing,
  entries, 197
  entry method, def., 195
  expense accounts, 136
    illus., 137
  revenue accounts, 135
    illus., 136
  the drawing account, 136
    illus., 138
  the income summary account, 136
    illus., 138
closing process,
  def., 133
  overview, illus., 138
  purpose of, 133
  technique of, 135
co-ownership of property and income, 551
collection of accounts receivable, 19
collection of an account previously written off, 330
collections for third parties, 473
collusion, 231
committed and discretionary fixed costs, 889
committed fixed costs, def., 889
common stock, 639
  and paid-in capital in excess of par, 731
  def., 588

common stockholders,
  earnings available to, 639
  rights of, 588
common stockholders' equity, return on, def., 599
common-size financial statements, def., 267
comparability, def., 510
comparative standards, 266
compensating balances, def., 289
compensation, employee, 481
competitive business climate, capital investment in, 1062
completion and sale of manufactured products, accounting for, 806
compound interest,
  and present value, 684
  and present value, relationship between, 685
  def., 684, 1052
  versus present value, illus., 1052
comprehensive budgeting, 929
computer,
  consultant's perspective, decision support systems:, 1059
  fraud and misuse, 234
  fraud, def., 234
computer integrated manufacturing (CIM), def., 770
computerized,
  accounting systems, 221
  job costing systems, 810
  record keeping, 61
computers, budgeting and, 940
computers, inventory and, 194
computing the cash flow from operating activities: indirect approach, illus., 724
conservatism, def., 523
consignment, def., 358
consignment, goods on, 358
consistency in method application, 369
consistency principle, def., 521
consolidated financial statement,
  an introduction to, 270
  def., 270
construction, budget, 925
contingencies, accounting rules for, 479
contingent liabilities, 478
  def., 479
continuous budget, def., 928
contra asset, def., 101
contra liability, def., 477
contra revenue, def., 177
contract interest rate, def., 667
contractors, independent, def., 481
contribution approach, 895
contribution income statements, def., 1021
contribution margin, 1014
  controllable, def., 1023

  def., 895
  in relation to capacity, 1017
contribution reporting, decision making and, 1007
control,
  cash, 292
  def., 766
  internal, 227
    def., 229
  planning and, illus., 767
control account,
  def., 220
  work in process, 808
control accounts, subsidiary ledgers and, 220
controllability: the key to responsibility accounting, 969
controllable contribution margin, def., 1023
controllable margin versus segment margin, 1023
controller, def., 587
conversion cost, def., 843
convertible bonds, def., 666
convertible preferred stock, def. 591
copyrights, def., 447
corporate equity,
  a comprehensive illustration, 596
  illus., 597
  stock dividends and, 627
corporate form of organization,
  advantages, 585
  disadvantages, 586
corporate income reporting, 631
  intraperiod tax allocation, illus., 636
corporate organizational structure, illus., 588
corporation,
  def., 11, 145, 585
  organization of a, 586
corporations,
  additional equity issues and income reporting, 619
  closely held, def., 585
  introduction to, 583
  nature of, 585
  publicly held, def., 586
cost,
  accounting, def., 10, 768
  aftertax, 1063
  allocations, 1021
  analysis, 891
  and benefits, 232
  behavior, 777, 884
  center, def., 965
  conversion, def., 843
  drivers, def., 812
  flow of, 363
  incurrence in the manufacturing process, 843

step, 886
  to the customer: bad credit, 323
  variable, def., 885
cost-benefit analysis, def., 764
cost/benefit and materiality, 404
cost flow assumptions, def., 363
cost flows, manufacturing, illus., 800
cost management, strategic, def., 769
cost of capital, def., 1051
cost of goods manufactured, def., 775
cost of goods sold,
  def., 179
  determining, illus., 180
cost reports,
  production, 839
  def., 846
costing,
  absorption, def., 1024
  activity-based (ABC), 847
    def., 851
  how process costing differs from job, 839
  process, 839
  variable and absorption, 1024
  variable, def., 1024
  weighted-average, def., 858
costs,
  and revenues, multiperiod, 98
  committed and discretionary fixed, 889
  committed fixed, def., 889
  determination, 361
  differential, def., 1010
  direct and indirect, 814
  direct, def., 814, 1021
  discretionary fixed, def., 889
  fixed, 981
    def., 777, 887
  indirect, def., 814, 1021
  manufacturing, 771
  mixed (semivariable), def., 890
    illus., 891
  nontraceable, 1023
  opportunity, def., 1014
  organization, def., 587
  period, def., 772
  product, def., 772
  quality, def., 855
  relevant, def., 1009
  standard, 973
  step, def., 887
  timing of product costs and period, illus., 774
  variable, def., 777
  warranty, 480
cost-volume-profit (CVP) analysis, 883, 894
  def., 884
counterbalancing errors, 359
coupon bonds,
  def., 665
  registered and, 665

credit, 53
  card sales, 332
  memorandum, def., 176
  sales and receivables, 322
creditors, 5
credits,
  debits and, 54
  def., 54
  misconceptions about debits and, 56
cumulative effect, def., 634
cumulative preferred stock, def., 590
currency exchange rates, 525
current assets,
  and current liabilities, 723
  def., 141
current liabilities,
  and employee compensation, 471
  current assets and, 723
  def., 144, 473
current portion of long-term debt, 474
current ratio, def., 146
current worth, 517
curvilinear variable cost and the relevant range, illus., 886
CVP analysis,
  for multiproduct firms, 902
  limiting assumptions, 903

D

date of declaration, def., 624
date of payment, def., 624
date of record, def., 624
day in the life of an accountant, illus., 8
death of a partner, 562
debenture bonds, def., 665
debentures, sinking-fund, def., 666
debit, 53
  memorandum, def., 181
debit/credit rules, illus., 54
debits,
  and credits, 54
  and credits, misconceptions about, 56
  def., 54
debt to total assets, 677
debt to total assets ratio, def., 677
debt,
  analysis of outstanding, 677
  current portion of long-term, 474
decision
  factors to consider, 1049
  pricing, 1016
  support systems: a computer consultant's perspective, 1059
decision making,
  an emphasis on the future, 1010
  and contribution reporting, 1007
  def., 766
  general approach to, 1008

decisions,
  capital budgeting, 1049
declines in market value, 303
declining balance method, def., 410
deductions,
  from employee earnings, 483
  other, 484
deficiency,
  capital, def., 564
  creation of a capital, 564
  earnings, def., 558
  removal of a capital, 564
deficit, def., 624
depletion, def., 444
deposits in transit, def., 294
depreciable asset related to natural resources, 445
depreciable base, 407
depreciation, 95, 404
  and the tax laws, 414
  declining balance method, def., 410
  def., 100, 405
  double-declining balance method, def., 410
  methods of, 406
  revisions of, 412
  straight-line method, def., 407
  sum-of-the-years'-digits method, def., 410
  units-of-output-method, def., 408
depreciation methods,
  accelerated, def., 409
  graphical overview of, illus., 413
  selection of, 412
depreciation policies, comparison of, illus., 414
derivatives, 664
differential costs, def., 1010
direct and indirect costs, 814
direct approach, statement of cash flows:, illus., 732
direct costs, def., 814, 1021
direct labor,
  budget, 934
  def., 771
  variances, illustration of, 979
direct materials,
  def., 771
  purchases budget, 933
  variances, Sanco, Inc., illus., 979
direct method,
  def., 717
  of statement construction, def., 717
direct write-off method,
  def., 325
  of uncollectible accounts, def., 325
directors, board of, 587
disadvantages, corporate form of, 586
disclosure,
  balance sheet, 481
  EPS, 640
  of discontinued operations, illus., 633

of earnings-per-share data, illus., 640
of extraordinary items, 634
of international financial affairs, 529
disclosures,
- additional annual report, 263
- inventory, illus., 775

discontinued operations,
- def., 632
- disclosure of, illus., 633

discount amortization, 477, 669, 679
- def., 478
- effective-interest method, 670
- schedule, illus., 672
- straight-line method, 669

discount, bond,
- def., 668
- bonds issued at a, 668
- meaning of a bond, 669
- on notes payable, def., 477
- sales, def., 178
- trade, 177

discounts,
- cash, def., 178
- purchases, def., 182

discretionary fixed costs, def., 889
dishonoring a note, def., 336
disposals of property, plant, and equipment, 439
dissolution, def., 551
dividend,
- payout ratio, def., 629
- policy and evaluation, 628
- preference, 589
- yield, def., 629

dividends,
- accounting for stock, 626
- def., 145, 624
- in arrears, 590
- reasons for issuing stock, 626
- stock, def., 625

document interrelationships in a job order system, illus., 801
double taxation, 586
double-declining balance method, def., 410
drawing account,
- closing, 136
  - illus., 138
- def., 65

duties, separation of, def., 230
duty authorization, 231

E

earnings,
- available to common stockholders, 639
- deductions from employee, 483
- deficiency, def., 558
- employee, 482
- gross, def., 482
- nature and distribution, partnership, 555
- other items that affect retained, 629
- quality of, def., 256
- reporting changes in retained, 630
- restrictions on retained, def., 630
- retained, 731
  - def., 145, 594, 624
- statement of retained, def., 630
  - illus., 630

earnings per share, (EPS),
- data, disclosure of, illus., 640
- def., 637
- fully diluted, def., 639
- primary, def., 639
- primary versus fully diluted, 639

effect, cumulative, def., 634
effective-interest discount amortization: a graphic overview, illus., 671
effective interest method,
- discount amortization, 670
- of amortization, def., 670
- premium amortization, 674

effective-interest premium amortization: a graphic overview, illus., 674
effective interest rate, def., 667
electronic data interchange (EDI), def., 185
electronic debit card, def., 294
electronic spreadsheets, 940
elimination entries, def., 272
employee,
- compensation, 481
- compensation, current liabilities and, 471
- earnings, 482
- earnings, deductions from, 483
- leasing, 489
- records, 485

employer, payroll taxes of the, 485
end-of-period adjustments, 527
ending inventory, 180
enterprises, not-for-profit, 269
entity,
- accounting, 551
- assumption, def., 11, 515
- def., 515
- legal, 551

entries,
- adjusting, 98, 133, 196
- closing, 197
- elimination, def., 272
- reversing, def., 148

EPS disclosure, 640
equation,
- accounting, def., 13
- approach, 894

equity,
- a comprehensive illustration, corporate, 596
- corporate, illus., 597
- evaluations based on stockholders', 597
- return on common stockholders', def., 599
- statement of partner's, illus, 556
- statement of stockholders' def., 630
  - illus., 631
- stockholders', def., 594
- trading on the, def., 601

equity method,
- def., 682
- rationale for, 683

equivalent production,
- factors that affect, 842

equivalent units,
- computation of, illus., 844
- concept of, illus., 842
- def., 841

errors,
- adjustment, 107
- counterbalancing, 359
- in the petty cash fund, 300

estimation,
- and slack, 927
- budget, 926

ethical challenges for the accountant, 27
ethics,
- and accounting, 25
- def., 25

evaluation methods, capital budgeting, 1055
evaluations based on stockholders' equity, 597
excess of par, common stock and paid-in capital in, 731
exchanges and trade-ins of similar assets, 441
expenditures,
- capital, 1049
  - def., 436
- revenue, def., 437
- summary of capital and revenue, illus., 438

expense,
- income tax, 191
- omission of depreciation, 1056
- on account, recognition of, 19
- recognition—the matching principle, 94
- uncollectible accounts, 323

expense accounts, closing, 136
- illus., 137

expenses,
- accrued, 104
  - def., 103
- cash payment for selling and administrative, 720
- def., 17
- incurred, 98, 103

INDEX I–7

operating, def., 186
other revenues and, 189
payment of, 20
prepaid, def., 99
selling and administrative, 188
explanatory information, 263
extracted, unsold resources, 445
extraordinary gains and losses, 633
   def., 632
extraordinary items,
   def., 632
   disclosure of, 634

F

F.O.B.,
   def., 184
   destination, def., 184
   shipping point, def., 184
factory overhead,
   budget, 934
   def., 772
   variances, 980
failure, business, 735
fair market value, def., 441
favorable variance, 977
federal insurance contributions act (FICA), def., 483
federal, state, and city income taxes, 483
federal unemployment tax (FUTA), def., 486
FIFO method, def., 844
FIFO method of process costing,
   step 1: analyze the physical flow, 845
   step 2: compute equivalent units, 845
   step 3: compute equivalent-unit costs, 845
   step 4: cost assignment, 846
FIFO process costing, def., 844
FIFO, production cost report, illus., 848
financial accounting, 5
   and reporting: U. S. and global perspectives, 507
   def., 762
financial accounting standards board (FASB), def., 6, 514
financial accounting standards, statements of, 6
financial analysts, 5
financial and managerial accounting, differences between, illus., 764
financial information, 253
   analysis, 266
   characteristics of, 509
   understanding and using, 251
financial instruments,
   def., 663
   investing in, 678

financial planning, spreadsheets and, illus., 942, 943
financial position,
   and the entity, 13
   def., 13
   illus., 14
   statement of changes, 713
financial reporting,
   objectives, 509
   sampling of differences in, illus., 525
financial statement,
   preparation (step 4), 732
   presentation, 369
   totals, 132
financial statements, 133, 257
   common-size, def., 267
   consolidated, def., 270
   def., 21
   effects of inventory errors on, 358
   notes to, def., 145, 262
      illus., 264
   of a manufacturer, 772
   of a merchandising concern, 185
   pro forma, def., 938
financing a business venture, 662
financing activities, def., 715
financing, sources of, illus., 663
finished goods, 357
   def., 775
first-in, first-out calculations, 365
first-in, first-out (FIFO), def., 364
fiscal year, def., 93
fixed cost behavior and ranges of activity, illus., 889
fixed cost behavior, illus., 888
fixed costs, 981
   committed and discretionary, 889
   committed, def., 889
   def., 777, 887
   discretionary, def., 889
   increased, 890
fixed overhead volume variance, def., 982
flexibility, need for, 721
flexible budget,
   constructing, 971
   def., 971
   illus., 972
flexible budgets, 970
   and performance evaluation, 971
   and standard costs, performance evaluation via, 963
   performance report based on, illus., 972
flexible manufacturing system, 770
flow of cost, 363
foreign currency transactions, accounting for, 525
formalize planning, 923
foundation of accounting, 512
franchises, def., 447

fraud and misuse, computer, 234
fraud in corporate America, 233
freight charges, 184
freight-in and freight-out, 184
fringe benefits: the employer's perspective, 489
full disclosure, principle of, def., 145, 522
full project approach, def., 1010
full project or incremental approach, 1009
fully diluted earnings per share, def., 639
funds,
   def., 269
   sinking, 289
      def., 666
future value, def., 685

G

GAAP, development of, 513
gain, sale of noncash assets at a, 566
gains and losses, 189
   extraordinary, 633
      def., 632
   nonoperating, def., 722
general journal,
   module and chart of accounts, illus., 224
   module, def., 224
      illus., 224
   two-column, 57
general ledger,
   def., 53
   updating, 377
general model for variance analysis of direct materials and direct labor, illus., 978
generally accepted accounting principles (GAAP), def., 512
globalization, growing emphasis on product quality and, 771
going concern, 515
   assumption, def., 515
goods,
   available for sale, def., 179, 180
   finished, def., 775
   in transit, def., 357
   manufactured, cost of, def., 775
   on consignment, 358
   physical flow of, 363
goodwill, 448
   accounting for, 449
   def., 449
   guidelines for determining, 449
government agencies, 5
governmental/not-for-profit accounting, 10
governmental units, 269
gross earnings, def., 482
gross method, def., 182

gross profit,
  and operating expenses as a percentage of net sales revenues, illus., 192
  def., 186
gross profit method, def., 372

H

held-to-maturity securities, def., 679
high-low method, def., 893
historical-cost principle, 12
  def., 517
human relations, budget limitations and, 928

I

icons, 223
ideal standards, def., 976
improvements in performance reporting, 1020
inadequacy, def., 405
income,
  co-ownership of property and, 551
  how precise is, 255
  information and the focus on, 255
  measuring merchandising, 174
  net, 17
  target, def., 898
  the meaning of, 92
income measurement and adjusting entries, 91
income measurement, inventory valuation and, 360
income reporting, a closer look at, 188
income reporting, corporate, 631
income statement, 186, 257, 775
  approach, def., 326
  approach, relationship to sales:, 326
  budgeted, 938
  data, evaluation of, 191
  def., 22
  multiple-step, def., 188
    illus., 190
  of a merchandising firm, illus., 187
    simplified, illus., 175
  single-step, def., 191
    illus., 192
income statements,
  absorption costing and variable costing, illus., 1026
  contribution, def., 1021
  of a merchandising firm and a manufacturer, illus., 776
  of Microsoft Corporation (in millions, except earnings per share), illus., 258
income summary account, closing, 136
  illus., 138
income summary, def., 135
income tax, 9
  expense, 191
  services, def., 9
  withholdings, def., 483
incremental approach,
  def., 1010
  full project or, 1009
independent contractors, def., 481
independent review, def., 232
indirect approach,
  cash flow work sheet—, illus., 736, 737
  statement of cash flows:, illus., 733
  work sheet for preparing a statement of cash flows—, 735
indirect costs,
  def., 814, 1021
  direct and, 814
indirect labor, def., 771
indirect materials, def., 771
indirect method,
  def., 722
  of statement construction, def., 722
industry norms, def., 267
information,
  explanatory, 263
  sources, other, 266
  supplementary, 263
insolvent, def., 735
installment method, def., 520
institute of management accountants (IMA), 514
instruments, financial, def., 663
insurance, prepaid, 99
intangible assets, def., 144, 446
intangibles, amortization of, 450
intangibles, def., 144
intercompany transaction, def., 271
interest,
  accounting for notes and, 335
  allowances, def., 557
  compound, def., 684, 1052
  def., 334
  nature of, 334
  period, def., 687
interest rate,
  contract, def., 667
  effective, def., 667
interim financial data, def., 263
internal auditing, 10
internal auditors, def., 10
internal control, 227
  accounting systems and, 217
  def., 229
  structure, 229
internal rate of return (IRR), def., 1057
internal revenue service (IRS), 514
international accounting, 523
international accounting standards committee (IASC), def., 524
international financial affairs, disclosure of, 529
interpolation, 1059
intraperiod tax allocation and corporate income reporting, illus., 636
intraperiod tax allocation, def., 635
inventories, 264
inventories, perpetual, 799
inventory, 355
  and computers, 194
  cost between the income statement and the balance sheet, allocation of, illus., 361
  def., 357
  disclosures, illus., 775
  estimates, 372
  merchandise, def., 174
  taking a physical, def., 194
  turnover, 374
  turnover ratio, def., 374
  what is, 357
inventory systems, 193
  periodic, def., 193
  perpetual, def., 194
inventory valuation and income measurement, 360
inventory valuation, perpetual inventory systems and, 375
invested capital, recognition of, 557
investee, def., 680
investigation, variance, 983
investing activities, def., 715
investing and financing transactions that do not affect cash, 715
investment,
  by the owner, 17
  center, def., 965
  in working capital, 1050
  return on (ROI), 600
    def., 966
investments,
  by the owner, 16
  cash and liquid, 287
  in bonds, 679
  long-term, def., 142
  long-term stock, 725
  partnership formation and owner, 553
  stock, 680
invoice, illus., 178
invoice price, def., 177
issue price, 591

J

JIT production, characteristics of, 854
job cost sheet,
    and work in process account, interrelationships among manufacturing journal entries, illus., 807
    completed, illus., 804
    def., 798
    for a service business, illus., 815
    illus., 799
job costing,
    how process costing differs from, 839
    service applications, 813
    systems, computerized, 810
job order costing systems, 797
job order costing versus process cost accounting, illus., 840
job order systems,
    def., 798
    document interrelationships in, illus., 801
journal, def., 57
journal module,
    general, def., 224
        illus., 224
    purchases, def., 225
    sales, def., 225
        illus., 225
journal modules, 224
journal, two-column general, 57
journalizing, def., 57
journals, 56
journals, special, def., 221
junk bonds, def., 666
just-in-time (JIT) production, def., 770, 853, 854

L

labor,
    accounting for, 801
    direct, def., 771
    indirect, def., 771
labor efficiency variance, def., 978
labor rate variance, def., 977
land, 727
land improvements, def., 403
last-in, first-out calculations, 366
last-in, first-out (LIFO), def., 364
lease, def., 415
lease, operating, def., 415
leases, 415
    accounting for capital, 416
    capital, def., 416
    operating leases versus capital, 415
    employee, 489

least squares, method of, def., 892
ledger, general, def., 53
ledger, subsidiary, def., 220
ledgers and control accounts, subsidiary, 220
legal capital, def., 591
legal entity, 551
lessee, 415
lessor, 415
letter to stockholders, def., 264
levels of standards, 976
leverage, 601
liabilities, 144
    accrued, def., 474
    contingent, 478
        def., 479
    current, def., 144, 473
    def., 14, 472
    long-term, def., 144
liability,
    contra, def., 477
    limited, 586
    problems associated with unlimited, 551
    unlimited, def., 551
LIFO, 378
    and average costing under a perpetual inventory system, 377
    perpetual inventory system, illus., 378
limitations of accounting information, 6
limitations of the balance sheet, 141
limited access to assets, 230
limited liability, 586
    of stockholders, 586
    partnership (LLP), 552
limited life, 551
limiting assumptions of CVP analysis, 903
liquidation,
    asset preference upon, 590
    def., 563
    of a partnership, 563
liquidity, a closer look at, 146
liquidity, def., 142
list price, def., 177
lockbox system, def., 290
long-term debt, current portion, 474
long-term investments, def., 142
long-term liabilities, def., 144
long-term stock investments, 725
losses,
    extraordinary gains and, 633
        def., 632
    gains and, 189
    net, 17
    nonoperating gains and, def., 722
lower of cost or market, 370
lower-of-cost-or-market-rule,
    application of, 370
    def., 370
lump-sum purchase, def., 403

M

make or buy decisions, 1012
maker, def., 334
management,
    advisory services (MAS), def., 9
    by exception, def., 977
    cash, 289
    receivables insights and, 330
    reports, 263
    strategic cost, def., 769
    total quality (TQM), def., 855
management's discussion and analysis (MD&A), def., 263
managerial accounting, 5
    applications, 765
    def., 763
    increased focus on, 768
manual system, processing reduction in, 221
manufactured, cost of goods, def., 775
manufactured products, accounting for the completion and sale of, 806
manufacturer, financial statements of, 772
manufacturer, value chain of, illus., 769
manufacturing,
    company, organization of, illus., 850
    computer integrated (CIM), def., 770
    cost flows, illus., 800
    costs, 771
    environment, today's, 812
    journal entries, job cost sheet, and work in process account, interrelationships among, illus., 807
    organizations, 771
    process, cost incurrence in, 843
    process, illus., 773
manufacturing system, flexible, 770
margin,
    contribution, 1014
        def., 895
    controllable contribution, def., 1023
    segment, def., 1023
market price, 592
market value, 370
master budget, def., 929
master budget, relationships within the, illus., 930
matching principle, def., 94, 521
matching: the key objective, 361
material purchases, schedule of cash disbursements for, 934
materiality, cost/benefit and, 404
materiality, def., 404, 522
materials,
    accounting for, 799
    direct, def., 771
    indirect, def., 771
    price variance, def., 977

quantity variance, def., 978
raw, def., 775
requisition, def., 800
maturity date, def., 334, 335
memorandum,
debit, def., 181
credit, def., 176
menu, def., 223
merchandise acquisitions, accounting for, 181
merchandise inventory, def., 174
merchandising firm,
and a manufacturer, income statements of, illus., 776
work sheet, illus., 196
merchandising operations, accounting/reporting for, 173
merchandising work sheet, 195
Microsoft Corporation's statements of stockholders' equity (in millions), illus., 262
misconceptions about debits and credits, 56
mixed (semivariable) costs, def., 890
illus., 891
modified accelerated cost recovery system (MACRS), def., 414
modified cash-basis, def., 97
modular accounting, concept of, 223
module,
cash payments, def., 225
cash receipts, def., 225
general journal, def., 224
illus., 224
purchases journal, def., 225
sales journal, def., 225
illus., 225
modules, accessing the, 223
modules, journal, 224
monetary unit, 517
monetary unit assumption, def., 6, 517
money, time value of, def., 1051
mortgage notes, def., 474
moving average, 379
moving average method, def., 379
multiperiod costs and revenues, 98
multiple cash flows and annuities, 1053
multiple, discounting of, illus., 1054
multiple-step income statements, def., 188
illus., 190
multiproduct firms, CVP analysis, 902
mutual agency, def., 551

N

natural business year, def., 93
natural resources, 444

depreciable asset related to, 445
intangibles, property, plant, and equipment, 435
net assets, def., 15
net income/net loss, 17
net method, def., 183
net present value, 1055
net present value method, 1055
net realizable value, def., 326
net-of-tax reporting, 635
no-par stock, def., 594
nominal or temporary accounts, def., 134
noncash expenses: nonoperating gains and losses, 723
nonfinancial performance measures, 985
nonmanufacturing settings, standards in, 984
nonoperating gains and losses,
def., 722
noncash expenses:, 723
nonsufficient funds (NSF) checks, def., 295
nontraceable costs, 1023
nontrade receivables, def., 324
nonvalue-adding activities, def., 853
normal balance, def., 55
not-for-profit enterprises, 269
note,
dishonored, def., 336
dishonoring, def., 336
notes,
and interest, accounting for, 335
mortgage, def., 474
to the financial statements, def., 262
illus., 264
to the financial statements/full disclosure, 145
notes payable, 730
illus., 477
with interest included in the face value, illus., 478
accounting for, 476
def., 475
discount, def., 477
notes receivable, def., 334

O

objectives of financial reporting, 509
objectivity principle, 12
def., 518
obsolescence, def., 405
operating activities,
def., 714
determine net cash flow from, (step 2), 725
relationship between income and net cash provided (used) by, illus., 718

indirect approach, computing the cash flow from, illus., 724
operating changes, 899
operating cycle, 375
def., 141
illus., 142
operating expenses, def., 186
operating income on sales ratio, def., 268
operating lease, def., 415
operating leases versus capital leases, 415
operations, discontinued, def., 632
opinions, 513, 514, 515
unqualified and qualified, 266
opportunity cost, def., 1014
organization,
advantages:, corporate form of, 585
disadvantages, corporate form of, 586
manufacturing, 771
of a corporation, 586
organization costs, def., 587
organizational hierarchy, illus., 925
organizational structure, corporate, illus., 588
other revenues and expenses, 189
outsourcing, def., 1012
outstanding checks, def., 295
outstanding debt, analysis of, 677
outstanding shares, def., 594
overapplied overhead, def., 810
overhead,
accounting for, 802
actual, 805
application rate, def., 802
use of, 803
applied, 806
avoidable fixed, 1013
effects of over- and underapplied, 811
factory, def., 772
overapplied, def., 810
underapplied, def., 810
owner investments, partnership formation and, 553
owner's equity, 15, 144
a closer look at, 15
or capital, def., 15
statement of, 187
def., 22
ownership problems, 357
ownership, transferability of, 585

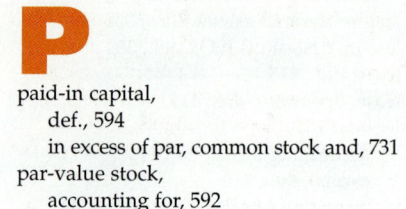

P

paid-in capital,
def., 594
in excess of par, common stock and, 731
par-value stock,
accounting for, 592

def., 591
issuing, 591
parent and subsidiary relationships, 271
parent, def., 271
partner,
    admission of a new, 559
    bonus to existing, 560
    bonus to new, 561
    death of a, 562
    withdrawal of a, 561
partner's equity, statement of, illus., 556
partner's interest, purchase of a, illus., 560
partnership,
    accounting, 553
    articles of, def., 551
    characteristics of, 550
    def., 11, 144, 550
    ease of formation, 550
    limited liability (LLP), 552
    liquidation of a, 563
partnership earnings: nature and distribution, 555
partnership formation and owner investments, 553
patents, def., 446
pay,
    calculation of take-home, 484
    take-home (net), def., 483
    vacation, 487
payable,
    bonds, 730
    notes, 730
        def., 475
    payment of accounts, 19
payback method, def., 1059
payback: pros and cons, use of, 1060
payee, def., 334
payroll,
    recording and record keeping, 485
    register, 485
    related costs of the employer, other, 487
    taxes of the employer, 485
PC-based system software, features of, 222
pension plans, def., 488
percentage, of completion method, (POC), def., 519
performance evaluation,
    flexible budgets and, 971
    via flexible budgets and standard costs, 963
performance measures, nonfinancial, 985
performance report,
    based on flexible budgets, illus., 972
    def., 967
    illus., 766
performance reporting, improvements in, 1020

period,
    budget, 927
    interest, def., 687
period costs,
    def., 772
    product and, 772
    timing of product costs and, illus., 774
periodic inventory system, def., 193
periodic system, problems with, 193
periodicity assumption, def., 93, 516
perpetual existence, 585
perpetual inventories, 799
perpetual inventory record: FIFO, illus., 376
perpetual inventory system, def., 194, 375
perpetual inventory system, LIFO and averages costing under, 377
perpetual inventory systems and inventory valuation, 375
perpetual systems, 194
    illustration of, 375
petty cash, 299
petty cash fund,
    errors, 300
    making disbursements, 299
    replenishing, 299
petty cash voucher, 299
physical deterioration, 405
physical flow of goods, 363
physical inventory, taking, def., 194
planning,
    and control, illus., 767
    def., 765
    departments, 10
plant and equipment costs after asset acquisition, 436
play the float, def., 290
post-closing trial balance, 138
    def., 139
posting,
    def., 59
    transactions from the journal to the ledger, illus., 60
postretirement health-care benefits, 488
preemptive right, def., 588
preferred stock,
    callable, def., 591
    convertible, def., 591
    cumulative, def., 590
    def., 589
    nature and characteristics, 589
premium amortization, 680
    effective-interest method, 674
    schedule, illus., 676
    straight-line method, 673
premium, bond, def., 668
premium, bonds issued at a, 672
prenumbered documents, 231
prepaid expenses,
    accounting for, 108
    illus., 100

adjustment errors, illus., 107
alternative accounting methods for, illus., 109
def., 99
prepaid insurance, 99
prepayments (advances) by customers, def., 473
present value, 683
    and annuities, 686
    and bond prices, 687
    compound interest and, 684
    compound interest versus, illus., 1052
    def., 685, 668, 1052
    relationship between compound interest and, 685
    tables, 1053
price,
    invoice, def., 177
    issue, 591
    list, def., 177
    market, 592
    transfer, def., 1017
price-earnings (P/E) ratio, def., 638
pricing decision, 1016
pricing, special order, 1015
primary earnings per share, def., 639
primary versus fully diluted earnings per share, 639
principal, def., 334
principle,
    consistency, def., 521
    matching, def., 521
    objectivity, def., 12, 518
    of full disclosure, def., 145, 522
    of historical cost, def., 12, 517
    revenue realization, def., 518
prior period adjustments, def., 629
private accounting, def., 9
pro forma financial statements, def., 938
process cost accounting, job order costing versus, illus., 840
process costing, 839
    and the weighted-average method, 858
    FIFO method, def., 844
    method, 844
    system, def., 838
processing accounting information, 49
processing reduction in a manual system, 221
product
    and period costs, 772
    costs and period costs, timing of, illus., 774
    costs, def., 772
    quality and globalization, growing emphasis on, 771
production,
    just-in-time (JIT), def., 770, 853, 854

revenue recognized during, 518
revenue recognized upon completion, 519
production budget, 932
production cost report, 839
   def., 846
   FIFO, illus., 848
   weighted average method, illus., 861
production volume, measuring, 839
products or departments, addition or deletion of, 1018
profession of accounting, 7
professional employer organization (PEO), 489
profit center, def., 965
profit, gross, def., 186
project screening, 1049
promissory note, illus., 334,
property, plant, and equipment, 264
   acquisition and depreciation, 399
   def., 142, 401
   determining the cost of, 401
   disposals, 439
   nature of, 401
   small items of, 404
   natural resources/intangibles, 435
prospectus, def., 591
public accounting, def., 7
publicly held corporations, def., 586
purchases discounts, def., 182
purchases journal module, def., 225
purchases returns and allowances, 181
purchasing activity in a high-tech era, 185

Q

qualitative factors, def., 1012
quality costs, def., 855
quality of earnings, def., 256
quick ratio, def., 147

R

range, relevant, def., 886
ranges of activity, fixed cost behavior and, illus., 889
rate,
   currency exchange, 525
   contract interest, def., 667
   effective interest, def., 667
   overhead application, def., 802
   spot, def., 525
   use of the overhead application, 803
rate of return, accounting, def., 1061
rate of return, internal (IRR), def., 1057

ratio,
   current, def., 146
   debt to total assets, def., 677
   dividend payout, def., 629
   inventory turnover, def., 374
   price-earnings (P/E), def., 638
   quick, def., 147
ratio analysis, several cautions about, 147
raw materials, 357
   def., 775
real accounts, def., 134
realization, 102
receipt, revenue recognized at the time of, 520
receipts from cash sales, 292
receipts from customers on account, 293
receivable,
   accounts, def., 324
   collection of accounts, 19
   def., 323
   notes, def., 334
receivables, 321
   credit sales and, 322
   insights and management, 330
   nontrade, def., 324
   trade and nontrade, 323
   trade, def., 324
recent business decisions, illus., 1009
reconciliation process, 296
record keeping,
   computerized, 61
   payroll recording and, 485
recording process, 57
records,
   employee, 485
   verification of, 232
redemption or liquidating value, 598
registered and coupon bonds, 665
registered bonds, def., 665
regulation, heavy, 586
reissuance below cost, 623
reissuance of treasury stock, 622
related issue: asset impairment, 442
relevancy, def., 253, 510
relevant costs, def., 1009
relevant range,
   curvilinear variable cost and, illus., 886
   def., 886
reliability, def., 253, 510
remittance advice, 226
removal of a capital deficiency, 564
removal of assets from the accounts, 439
repairs, def., 437
replenishing the petty cash fund, 299
report,
   annual, 257
   def., 254
   audit, def., 265
   production cost, def., 846

reporting changes in retained earnings, 630
reporting for specialized entities, 268
reporting, improvements in performance, 1020
reporting system, 966
reports,
   management, 263
   performance, def., 967
representation, graphical, 896
requisition, materials, def., 800
research and development, 264
residual value, def., 407
resources,
   extracted, unsold, 445
   natural, 444
responsibility accounting,
   at various organizational levels ($000 omitted), illus., 968
   controllability: the key to, 969
   def., 965
responsibility units, 965
restrictions on retained earnings, def., 630
retail method, def., 373
retained earnings, 731
   def., 145, 594, 624
   other items that affect, 629
   reporting changes in, 630
   restrictions on, def., 630
   statement of, def., 630
   illus., 630
return on assets, def., 268, 600, 966
return on common stockholders' equity, def., 599
return on investment (ROI), 600
   def., 966
returns and allowances, purchases, 181
returns and allowances, sales, 176
revenue,
   contra, def., 177
   sales, 175
   and expenses, other, 189
revenue accounts, closing, illus., 136
revenue expenditures, def., 437
revenue realization principle, def., 518
revenue recognition, 264
   def., 94
   time line, illus., 518
revenue recognized
   at the time of receipt, 520
   during production, 518
   upon completion of production, 519
revenues,
   accounting for unearned, 109
   accrued, 105
   def., 103
   alternative accounting methods for unearned, illus., 110
   def., 16
   earned, 98, 103

multiperiod costs and, 98
  unearned, def., 102
reversing entries, def., 148
revisions of depreciation, 412
rights of common stockholders, 588
rights, no voting, 589
robots versus people, 813
running balance form of account, def., 53

S

salaries, accrued, 104
salary allowances, def., 556
sale,
  goods available for, def., 179, 180
  of an asset, 20
  of depreciable assets, 440
  of manufactured products, accounting for the completion and, 806
  of noncash assets at a gain, 566
  of noncash assets at a loss, 563
sales,
  and cash receipts, processing of, 225, 226
  bank card versus nonbank card, 332
  budget, 931
  credit card, 332
  discount, def., 178
  journal module, def., 225
    illus., 225
sales mix, def., 902
sales ratio, operating income on, def., 268
sales returns and allowances, 176
sales revenue, 175
scattergraph, def., 891
  illus., 892
schedule of cash collections, 932
schedule of cash disbursements for material purchases, 934
secured bonds, def., 665
securities,
  available-for-sale, 681
    def., 679
  held-to-maturity, def., 679
  trading, 678
Securities and Exchange Commission, (SEC), def., 513
security, senior, 639
segment,
  def., 632
  reporting, def., 267
segment margin,
  controllable margin versus, 1023
  def., 1023
selling and administrative expense budget, 937
selling and administrative expenses, 188
separation of duties, def., 230

serial bonds, def., 666
service applications, job costing:, 813
service business, job cost sheet for, illus., 815
service life,
  def., 405
  determining, 405
  relative significance of the three factors, 406
setting standards, 974
share, book value per, def., 597
share, earnings per (EPS) def., 637
shares,
  of capital stock, def., 145
  of stock, def., 585
  outstanding, def., 594
single-step income statements, def., 191
  illus., 192
sinking fund, 289
sinking funds, def., 666
sinking-fund debentures, def., 666
slack,
  def., 927
  estimation and, 927
small items of property, plant, and equipment, 404
Social Security/Medicare taxes (FICA), 483, 485
sole proprietorship, def., 11, 144
source documents, def., 56
special journals, def., 221
special order pricing, 1015
specialized entities, reporting for, 268
specific identification, 362
  method, def., 362
speed, focus on, 856
spending variance, def., 981
spot rate, def., 525
spreadsheets,
  and financial planning, illus., 942, 943
  electronic, 940
  use of, 941
standard cost sheet, illus., 975
standard costs, 973
  and budgets, 973
  performance evaluation via flexible budgets and, 963
standards,
  and performance evaluation, broader view, 984
  attainable, def., 976
  comparative, 266
  def., 973
  ideal, def., 976
  in nonmanufacturing settings, 984
  levels of, 976
  setting, 974
  uniformity of international accounting, 524

Standards Committee, International Accounting (IASC), 524
state unemployment taxes, def., 486
stated-value stock, def., 595
statement,
  bank, def., 294
    illus., 295
  classification, 141
  format and classifications, 713
  income, 186, 257, 775
    def., 22
  interrelationships, 24
  of activities, def., 270
  of changes in financial position, 713
statement of cash flows, 260, 711
  def., 22, 712
  direct approach, illus., 732
  illus., 713
  indirect approach, illus., 733
  indirect approach, work sheet for preparing, 735
  preparation of, 725
  single-step income, def., 191
    illus., 192
statement of owner's equity, 187
  def., 22
statement of partner's equity, illus., 556
statement of retained earnings
  def., 630
  illus., 630
statement of stockholders' equity, 261
  def., 630
  illus., 631
  (in millions), Microsoft Corporation, illus., 262
statements, 514, 515
  consolidated financial, def., 270
  financial, 133, 257
    def., 21
  of a manufacturer, financial, 772
  of financial accounting standards, 6, 514
  pro forma, def., 938
static budget, def., 970
step costs, 886
  def., 887
  function, illus., 887
stock,
  accounting for par-value, 592
  acquisitions of treasury, 621
  authorized, def., 588
  callable preferred, def., 591
  common, 639
    def., 588
  convertible preferred, def., 591
  cumulative preferred, def., 590
  example with two classes of, 598
  for assets other than cash, issuing, 595
  investments in, 680

issuing par-value, 591
no-par, def., 594
par-value, def., 591
preferred, def., 589
reissuance of treasury, 622
shares of, def., 585
stated-value, def., 595
treasury, def., 621
nature and characteristics, preferred, 589
stock dividends,
    accounting for, 626
    and corporate equity, 627
    def., 625
    reasons for issuing, 626
stock investments, long-term, 725
stock pages, reading the, 592
stock splits, 627
    def., 628
stock subscriptions, def., 596
stockholders, 145
    def., 586
    differences between bondholders and, illus., 665
    earnings available to common, 639
    letter to, def., 264
    limited liability of, 586
    rights of common, 588
stockholders', equity,
    def., 594
    evaluations based on, 597
    return on common, def., 599
    statement of, 261
        def., 630
        illus., 631
stocks, shares of capital, def., 145
straight-line amortization, def., 669
straight-line method, 101
    def., 407
    discount amortization, 669
    premium amortization, 673
strategic cost management, def., 769
subsidiaries, def., 271
subsidiary ledgers,
    and control accounts, 220
    def., 220
    control account relationships, illus., 221
sum-of-the-years'-digits method, def., 410
summary of significant accounting policies, 263
sunk cost, concept of, 1011
    def., 1011
supplementary information, 263
supplier reliability, 854
supplies, 100
system,
    Accelerated Cost Recovery, (ACRS), def., 414
    accounting information (AIS), def., 219
    flexible manufacturing, 770
    lockbox, def., 290

Modified Accelerated Cost Recovery, (MACRS), def., 414
petty cash, def., 299
process costing, def., 838
refinements, 220
systems,
    accounting information, 218
    computerized job costing, 810
    departments, 10
    inventory, 193
    job order costing, 797
    job order, def., 798
    perpetual, 194

T

T-account, def., 53
tables, present value, 1053
take-home (net) pay,
    def., 483
    calculation of, 484
taking a physical inventory, def., 194
target income, def., 898
tax allocation, intraperiod, def., 635
tax departments, 10
tax laws, depreciation and, 414
taxation, double, 586
taxes,
    federal, state, and city income, 483
    federal unemployment (FUTA), def., 486
    recording the employer's, 486
    Social Security/Medicare (FICA), 483, 485
    state unemployment, def., 486
temporary or nominal accounts, def., 134
third parties, collections for, 473
time tickets, def., 802
time value, 684
    of money, def., 1051
times interest earned, def., 678
timing of product costs and period costs, illus., 774
top-down approach, def., 925
top-down budgeting, def., 925
total quality management (TQM),
    def., 855
    traditional quality control vs, illus., 856
totals, unequal, 69
trade,
    and nontrade receivables, 323
    discounts, def., 177
    receivables, def., 324
trade-in allowance, def., 441
trademarks, def., 447
trading on the equity, def., 601
trading securities, 678
    def., 301

traditional quality control vs. total quality management, illus., 856
transactions,
    and events, 93
    approach, def., 93
    intercompany, def., 271
    purchase, 525
    sale, 526
    that do not affect cash, investing and financing, 715
transfer prices, def., 1017
transferability of ownership, 585
transit, goods in, def., 357
transposition, def., 69
treasury bills, 301
treasury stock,
    acquisitions of, 621
    def., 621
    holdings, illus., 621
    reissuance of, 622
trial balance, def., 68
trustee, 664
turnover, accounts receivable, def., 331
two-column general journal, 57

U

uncollectible accounts,
    allowance method, 325
    direct write-off method, 325
    expense, 323
    writing off, 328
underapplied overhead, def., 810
understandability, def., 511
understanding and using financial information, 251
underwriter, 591
unearned revenues,
    accounting for, 109
        illus., 103
    alternative accounting methods for, illus., 110
    def., 102
unequal totals, 69
unfavorable variance, 977
unit, equivalent, def., 841
units, responsibility, 965
units-of-output method, def., 408
unlimited liability,
    def., 551
    problems associated with, 551
unqualified and qualified opinions, 266
unrecorded expenses and revenues—accruals, 103
usefulness, complications to, 253
user as a customer, 270
users and uses of accounting information, 3

V

vacation pay, 487
value,
  accounting for changes in, 302
  book, def., 102, 408
  carrying, 669
  declines in market, 303
  face, 666
  fair market, def., 441
  future, def., 685
  increases in market, 304
  market, 370
  maturity, def., 335
  meaning of book, 599
  measuring the decline, 370
  net-realizable, def., 326
  present, 683
    def., 668, 685, 1052
  redemption or liquidating value, 598
  residual, def., 407
  time, 684
value-adding activities, def. 853, 854
value chain,
  def., 769
  of a manufacturer, illus., 769
value per share, book, def., 597
variable cost, differing views of, illus., 886
variable costing,
  comparison of absorption costing and, illus., 1025
  def., 1024
  income statements, absorption costing and, illus., 1026
variable costs, def., 777, 885
variable overhead efficiency variance, def., 981
variance,
  favorable, 977
  fixed overhead volume, def., 982
  labor efficiency, def., 978
  labor rate, def., 977
  materials price, def., 977
  materials quantity, def., 978
  spending, def., 981
  unfavorable, 977
  variable overhead efficiency def., 981
variance analysis, 977
  of direct materials and direct labor, general model for, illus., 978
variance investigation, 983
verification of records, 232
voucher, petty cash, 299

W

W-2 form, illus., 486
wage and tax statement (W-2), def., 485
warranty,
  costs, 480
  def., 480
weighted average, 366
weighted-average costing,
  def., 858
  features of, 858
weighted average method,
  def., 366
  equivalent production figures:, illus., 859
  process costing and, 858
  production cost report, illus., 861
weighted-average shares outstanding, 638
window dressing, def., 147
withdrawal by the owner, 16, 21
withdrawal of a partner, 561
withholding allowances, def., 483
withholdings, income tax, def., 483
work in process, 357
  a control account, 808
  def., 775
work sheet,
  def., 130
  for preparing a statement of cash flows—indirect approach, 735
  merchandising, 195
  of a merchandising firm, illus., 196
  uses of the, 132
working capital,
  def., 146
  investment in, 1050
writing off uncollectible accounts, 328

Y

year-end interest accruals, 675
yield, dividend, def., 629

Photo Credits

Page 1	©1995 Ralph Mercer	Page 357	©1994 Ralph Mercer
Page 8a	©1992 Comstock	Page 366	©Camerique/H. Armstrong Roberts
Page 8b	©The Gladstone Studio Ltd.	Page 401	©W. Calabrese/Photonica
Page 8c	©David Wagenaar/WAK Pictures Inc.	Page 409	©Robert Bennett/FPG International
Page 8e	©Courtesy of Herman Miller, Inc.	Page 437	©David Muir/Masterfile
Page 13	©A. Gurmankin/Unicorn Stock	Page 446	©Martha McBride/Unicorn Stock Photos
Page 15	©James McLoughlin/FPG International	Page 450	©Art Shay/Tony Stone Images
Page 17	©Ralph Mercer/Tony Stone Images	Page 452	©Howard Spivak/FPG International Corp.
Page 24	©R. Rathe/FPG International		
Page 49	©1995 Ralph Mercer/Tony Stone Images	Page 471	©1992 Ralph Mercer/FPG International
Page 52	©Peter Gridley/FPG International	Page 480	©Tony Freeman/PhotoEdit
Page 55	©Betts Anderson/Unicorn Stock Photos	Page 482	©Teri Gilman/Tony Stone Images
Page 91	©1995 Ralph Mercer	Page 507	©Ralph Mercer/Tony Stone Images
Page 94	©H. Armstrong Roberts	Page 512	©The Bettman Archive
Page 98	©MacNeal Hospital/Tony Stone Images	Page 516	©Peter Gridley/FPG International Corp.
Page 101	©Gary Buss 1994/FPG International	Page 549	©1992 Ralph Mercer
Page 129	©FPG International	Page 552	©Comstock
Page 147	©Courtesy Chevron, Inc.	Page 554	©Howard Grey/Tony Stone Images
Page 173	©1993 Ralph Mercer	Page 557	©Photography by Alan Brown
Page 176	©Ken Kaminsky/Photri	Page 583	©1993 Ralph Mercer
Page 193	©Sylvain Coffie/Tony Stone Images	Page 593	©Cameramann International, Ltd.
Page 217	©1994 Ralph Mercer	Page 619	©1995 John Wilkes/Photonica
Page 220	©Art Montes de Oca/FPG International	Page 629	©Telegraph Colour Library/FPG International Corp.
Page 229	©Kessler Photography		
Page 232	©Cameramann International, Ltd.	Page 635	©Robert W. Ginn/Unicorn Stock Photos
Page 251	©1992 Ralph Mercer	Page 661	©1995 John Wilkes/Photonica
Page 254	©David Young-Wolff/PhotoEdit	Page 711	©Ralph Mercer
Page 287	©Jim Krantz/Tony Stone Images	Page 717	©Mark Gottlieb/FPG International
Page 291	©Fay Photo/FPG International	Page 761	©Lonnie Duka/Tony Stone Images
Page 294	©Gerald Lim/Unicorn Stock Photos	Page 770	©John Madere
Page 302	©Nick Koon/Orange County Register	Page 797	©1992 Ralph Mercer
Page 323	©1992 John Wilkes/Photonica	Page 805	©Jeff Kaufman/FPG International
Page 325	©Robert E. Daemmrich/Tony Stone Images	Page 837	©1992 Ralph Mercer
Page 326	©Amy Etra/PhotoEdit	Page 853	©Gary Buss/FPG International
Page 334	©Charles Thatcher/Tony Stone Images	Page 883	©1992 Ralph Mercer
		Page 896	©G. L. French/H. Armstrong Roberts

P–1

Photo Credits

Page 901 © Courtesy of Sega America
Page 903 © Ron Chapple/FPG International
Page 921 © 1995 Ralph Mercer
Page 924 © David Hanover/Tony Stone Images
Page 929 © Roger and Donna Aitkenhead/Ochoco National Forest
Page 963 © 1994 Ralph Mercer
Page 966 © Mike Malyszko/FPG International Corp.
Page 970 © Bettman Newsphotos
Page 980 © J. Pickerell/FPG International Corp.
Page 985 © Dick Young/Unicorn Stock Photos
Page 1007 © Jim Krantz/Tony Stone Images
Page 1015 © Tony Freeman/PhotoEdit
Page 1020 © J. D. Levine/Northeastern University
Page 1047 © Ken Davies/Masterfile
Page 1049 © Robert Frerck/Odyssey/Frerck/Chicago
Page 1059 © Arthur Tilley/FPG International
Page 1061 © James Blank/FPG International